Advanced Educational Psychology

for Educators, Researchers, and Policymakers

Michael Pressley
University at Albany,
State University of New York

with **Christine B. McCormick**
University of South Carolina

HarperCollins*CollegePublishers*

Executive Editor: Christopher Jennison
Project Coordination: Ruttle, Shaw & Wetherill, Inc.
Design Manager and Text Designer: Mary Archondes
Cover Designer: Kay Petronio
Art Studio: Fine Line
Electronic Production Manager: Valerie A. Sawyer
Desktop Administrator: Sarah Johnson
Manufacturing Manager: Helene G. Landers
Electronic Page Makeup: RR Donnelley Barbados
Printer and Binder: RR Donnelley & Sons Company
Cover Printer: The Lehigh Press, Inc.

Advanced Educational Psychology for Educators, Researchers, and Policymakers

Copyright © 1995 by Michael Pressley and Christine B. McCormick

Library of Congress Cataloging-in-Publication Data

Pressley, Michael.
   Advanced educational psychology for educators, researchers,
and policymakers / Michael Pressley, Christine B. McCormick.
      p.   cm.
   Includes bibliographical references and index.
   ISBN 0-673-46914-X
   1. Educational psychology. 2. Cognition. 3. Learning,
Psychology of. 4. Educational texts and measurements.
I. McCormick, Christine. II. Title.
LB1051.P68   1995
370.15–dc20   94-26476
                                                        CIP

Dedicated to educators, researchers, and policymakers who are working to improve education in the United States, Canada, and throughout the world

Contents

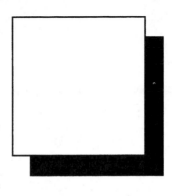

Preface

For some time I have had a vision of an advanced educational psychology and educational research text that focuses on the field as it is right now, as it is defined by the educational research community. This book is the fulfillment of that vision. It is organized around the theme of promoting good information processing: the construction and constructive use of strategic knowledge, metacognitive abilities, important world and cultural knowledge, and motivation. The good information processing framework is informed by traditional and contemporary literature in educational psychology, a variety of theoretical perspectives, current thinking in curriculum and instruction, and both conventional and reform-minded thinking about assessment and individual differences. Good information processing requires coverage of all of these topics. Throughout this book, the case is made that through modeling, explaining, and dialoguing, educators can stimulate the development of good information processing in their students.

My intent in *Advanced Educational Psychology for Educators, Researchers, and Policymakers* is to inform advanced graduate students, practicing educational researchers, and policymakers who have a need for state-of-the-science information about educational psychology and educational research. Because of the broad coverage of research in this text, it is appropriate for any course devoted to presentation of education in the 1990s as defined by psychologically oriented theories and research. It is especially appropriate for courses emphasizing the development of student understanding of promising directions in educational research that might be pursued either as part of thesis research or as a program of advanced scholarship. Throughout the book, what needs to be researched in the next decade is emphasized in the context of in-depth coverage of current research and theory.

Readers will find discussion of a variety of strategies-oriented interventions, from basic strategies to enhance memory, to reciprocal teaching to improve reading comprehension, to the most up-to-date strategic approaches to mathematics. Readers are also exposed to the full range of ways that knowledge is represented in the mind, with detailed coverage of the effects of knowledge on teaching, learning, and problem-solving. The social foundations of education also receive extensive coverage, including detailed discussions of contemporary perspectives on motivation; sociocultural approaches to cognitive development, such as Vygotsky's theory; and the social-dialogical foundations of thoughtfulness in classrooms. Traditional positions on social development in educational settings, such as social learning theory, are considered prominently as well, with clear relating of the traditional and more recent theories. There is ample coverage of both the laboratory problems that educational psychologists and researchers have addressed (e.g., distributed learning effects, mnemonics) and the applied issues (e.g., the nature of effective schools). The most up-to-date research-based practices in mathematics, science, reading, and writing education are covered in the context of the theories and research inspiring them. Assessment is presented as it has traditionally been conceived, with detailed coverage of the most important psychometric concepts, and as it is being reconceived, with coverage of all the most important emergent approaches in assessment, including dynamic assessment, performance assessment, and portfolios. The book concludes with analysis of the important categories of individual differences in education—retardation, learning disabilities, and giftedness—but also differences across the life span (i.e., cognitive changes between early and later adulthood). The final chapter, on human differences, complements presentations throughout the book about potential gender and cultural differences in thinking and learning.

Throughout the writing and development of this book, it was tried out on students in my courses at the University of Maryland and University at Albany, State University of New York. The complete book in prepublication form has been used for more than a year and a half by my students. The consistent feedback I have received is that reading this text transforms students from having only a vague notion of the nature of educational research to informed readers of the literature. When students complete this text, they understand how articles in basic research journals, such as *Journal of Educational Psychology* and *American Educational Research Journal*, as well as practitioner journals, such as *Educational Leadership* and *Phi Delta Kappan*, fit into the overall context of educational research and educational reform. At least a half dozen students have reported to me that they found direction in these pages to problems that they are pursuing as part of their graduate research. A number of senior colleagues who read particular chapters have also told me that my packaging of ideas provided them with new insights and, in a few cases, new directions for their research. Such feedback is my reason for confidence that *Advanced Educational Psychology for Educators, Researchers, and Policymakers* fulfills my vision of a sophisticated text that can inform advanced scholars about contemporary educational research and even inspire some of its readership to conduct new research.

Advanced Educational Psychology for Educators, Researchers, and Policymakers is part of a series of textbooks in educational psychology and research.

Cognition, Teaching, and Assessment is an abridgement of the *Advanced* book. The main difference between this *Advanced* text and *Cognition, Teaching, and Assessment* is that the *Advanced* text does more to orient its readers to where the field is moving. For students completing *Cognition, Teaching, and Learning*, who are looking for additional guidance with respect to potential research directions for their thesis work and beyond, the *Advanced* volume can take them there. For students taking an educational psychology course at the undergraduate level or as a short introduction at the graduate level, an entirely different volume has been prepared and will be available in the fall of 1995. The third book in the series, *Educational Psychology: Learning, Instruction, and Assessment* is an entirely new way to introduce students to educational psychology and research. It showcases the best of recent theory and research as it covers classic theory and empirical contributions. *Educational Psychology: Learning, Instruction, and Assessment* specifically develops the case that both new and traditional theories are relevant to the modern teacher. Thus, the most important ideas in this text are available in an advanced, an intermediate, and an introductory form. This volume is the advanced text. *Cognition, Teaching, and Learning* is the intermediate text, and *Educational Psychology: Learning, Instruction, and Assessment* is an introduction to the field as a theoretical and scientific discipline.

I could never have put together this trio of books alone. The project began with my drafting of the *Advanced* text. At that point I asked Chris McCormick, my friend and colleague of 20 years, to react to it and consider becoming the lead author for the undergraduate text. Chris provided many insights about the advanced book, and as the introductory volume was born and developed, the content of the advanced and introductory books affected one another. So many of the ideas in this *Advanced* text and the intermediate book were influenced by Chris that the authorships to *Advanced Educational Psychology for Educators, Researchers, and Policymakers* and *Cognition, Teaching, and Assessment* properly reflect her contributions as coauthor. Chris McCormick's brilliant reformulation of the ideas in the *Advanced* text, and her addition of important topics covered at the undergraduate level but not in graduate courses, became *Educational Psychology: Learning, Instruction, and Assessment*, so that the introductory book will appear with McCormick and

Pressley as authors in that order. Chris and I believe that the instructor who has read either the *Advanced* volume or *Cognition, Teaching, and Assessment* will be especially well prepared to use *Educational Psychology: Learning, Instruction, and Assessment*, although the introductory book is also accessible as a stand-alone resource. One motivation for developing the trio of books came from our awareness that many graduate students are asked to teach introductory courses in educational psychology. If they have read either the advanced or intermediate text in their graduate education, they will be ready to teach with *Educational Psychology: Learning, Instruction, and Assessment.*

There are so many people to thank. Joel Levin was a fine senior colleague to both Chris and me in the early years of our careers; he instilled in us the commitment to always be moving the field forward by learning its past and thinking hard about its future, a commitment reflected in the pages of this volume. I am especially grateful to Alan Wigfield, Jim Byrnes, Cathy Wentzel, Bill Halliday, and Vicky Kouba, who read preliminary drafts of parts of the manuscript. The reviewers for HarperCollins were terrific: Alice Corkill, University of Nevada, Las Vegas; Victoria Chou Hare, The University of Illinois at Chicago; Mary Lundeberg, University of Wisconsin, River Falls; Debra Mathinos, Bucknell University; Paul van den Broek, University of Minnesota; and Brent Wilson, University of Colorado, Denver. Many graduate students in my classes, who experienced drafts of the book as a course text, convinced me that the book worked and provided input that helped to make it work better. Chris Jennison, and his colleague Shadla Grooms, made it a pleasure to work with HarperCollins, as did everyone in the New York office who contributed to the three-book project. Tom Conville and his associates at Ruttle, Shaw & Wetherill, Inc. did a professional job of getting the text

ready for production. My wife, Donna, was a good sport about all those nights when I was wordprocessing at 3 A.M. Tim Pressley provided a constant reminder to Dad about how important it is to educate well the next generation of educators and educational researchers. When the book began, he was discovering the worlds of letters and numbers with his friends on *Sesame Street;* as the book goes to press, he is becoming an avid reader, promising that someday he will read one of Dad's books.

My own students, especially former undergraduate and graduate students who have worked with me (many of whom are now tenured professors), did much to shape my thinking about many of the issues covered in this text. Their impact on me is partially reflected by citations in the text to articles they have published on these issues. Thanks especially to Janice Almasi, Margaret Brigham, Rachel Brown, Susan Bryant, Jacqueline Burkell, Teresa Cariglia-Bull, Thommie DePinto, Patricia DeVolder (now deceased), Pamela El-Dinary, Darlene Elliott-Faust, Linda Lysynchuk, Marilyn Marks, Jacqueline A. McGoldrick, Jennifer Mistretta, Margaret Oatout, Robyn Russow, Julia O'Sullivan, Brynah Schneider, Barbara L. Snyder, Sonya Symons, Peggy Van Meter, Ruth Wharton-McDonald, Teena Willoughby, Vera E. Woloshyn, Eileen Wood, and Linda Yokoi. I hope that our interactions have been as good for your heads as they were for mine.

I expect that this book will be revised eventually, to reflect educational psychology as it evolves. If you have reactions to *Advanced Educational Psychology for Educators Researchers, and Policymakers* that might inform the next edition, I now hang my professional hat at the Department of Educational Psychology and Statistics, University at Albany, SUNY, Albany, NY 12222. I would love to hear from you.

Michael Pressley

Introduction: Good Thinking, Good Teaching, and Alternative Ways of Studying Good Thinking and Good Teaching

It would be easy to write a pessimistic book about education. Every week publications such as *Education Week* and *The Chronicle of Higher Education* carry articles documenting that test scores are down, increasing proportions of high school–age students are functionally illiterate, and even college students are not able to do simple problem solving. There is a real sense of crisis, with many arguing (e.g., Hudson Institute, 1987) that American schools are not producing people who will be able to survive in an ever more technological world, a world requiring higher levels of literacy and numeracy than ever before. Given this context, it may be surprising to some that this book is an optimistic book about education. A main message that will be presented here is that a great deal is now known about how to create better readers, thinkers, and citizens. An important purpose of this book is to develop an understanding in the next generation of teachers, educational researchers, and policymakers that psychological theory and research have succeeded in identifying ways to improve student learning. Such knowledge will make it into classrooms only if the next generation is educated about contemporary educational psychology.

A text in educational psychology that reflects the field in the 1990s must be rich in theory. Most research conducted by educational psychologists is motivated by particular theoretical conceptions about mind, the development of children, or the nature of effective educational environments. Thus,

this book is largely about theoretically inspired research. Particular emphasis is on the psychological research that is most relevant to complex human learning, curriculum, and instruction. One criterion for inclusion in this book was whether knowing the research in question would empower future teachers and educators, with content carefully selected so as to provide the reader with a great deal of information about potent educational treatments. This is not a book of "tricks of the trade," however. Rather, it is a scholarly introduction to educational psychology. Educational professionals will be most empowered if they understand why particular methods work and if they understand the types of evidence that have convinced educational psychologists that particular interventions are worthwhile.

As optimistic as this book is about the state of current knowledge, however, another important theme is that there is much more to find out. Thus, perhaps some readers will be sufficiently intrigued by educational psychology as a field of scholarly inquiry to consider careers in educational research. The case will be made throughout this book that the academic study of educational problems can be intellectually rigorous and fulfilling. Learning what is presented in this book can be an important first step in becoming an educational researcher.

The reader might not be convinced, wondering how anyone could find it fulfilling to contemplate why Scholastic Aptitude Test (SAT) scores keep falling! One reason is that many educational psychologists recognize that low academic achievement is not inevitable, that good thinking is possible— that education can do much to ensure that the next generation is much smarter than current students. Much of that optimism comes from a conception of intellectual prowess that reflects the profound impact of high-quality educational experiences on thinking and achievement. Understanding the nature of high intelligence and how education can promote skillful thinking can go a long way in motivating readers to take the discipline of educational psychology seriously. Thus, this book begins with a description of good thinking (e.g., Pressley, Borkowski, & Schneider, 1989), a description that will be encountered often in the book because much of educational research is aimed at promoting good thinking.

WHAT IS GOOD THINKING LIKE?

When we were young, we loved reading detective books. One reason was that the best thinkers we knew were inhabitants of such novels. We particularly devoured *Hardy Boys* books. A few years ago, now well armed with background in educational psychology, we revisited some of the detective books of childhood, interested in whether the Hardy boys were really as intellectually capable as we thought they were during our youth. When the Hardy boys' **cognition** (i.e., their thinking) is analyzed in light of what is now known about good thinking (Pressley, Snyder, & Cariglia-Bull, 1987), it is clear that the Hardy boys were really smart (see especially Dixon, 1972).

First, the Hardy boys had an incredibly rich repertoire of **strategies** for solving crimes. Thus, sometimes the boys would try to put themselves in the place of the criminal as they analyzed a crime. The boys had a host of specific tactics for lifting fingerprints from difficult places and for making certain that all of the physical evidence at the scene of a crime was collected. The boys recognized the importance of remembering important details, with the books including specific instances of them using cognitive strategies such as rehearsal and imagery to encode important information about a crime. One of our favorite strategies was their approach to remembering a physical description of a person, always beginning at the top of the head and working down to the shoes. The boys also knew that their memories were fallible—that there are memory errors reflecting prior knowledge and biases rather than what really happened—and thus the boys used photography to record crime scenes, made drawings when a camera was not available, and were extensive note takers. They knew when not to trust their memories.

The Hardy boys also possessed extensive **metacognition,** which is knowledge about and awareness of one's thinking (e.g., Flavell, 1985). In particular, they knew when and where to use the strategies they had acquired (i.e., they possessed extensive **metacognitive knowledge about strategies**). Thus, when first arriving at a crime, the boys knew it appropriate to use particular strategies to preserve the crime scene (e.g., cordoning it off). They also knew when to execute systematic search strategies and recording of information. Metacognitive knowledge about strategies is sometimes verbalizable (i.e., the person can say exactly when it is appropriate to use a particular strategy) and sometimes tacit (e.g., a person carries out the strategy on appropriate occasions, but cannot tell another person when and where the strategy works). Metacognitive knowledge is absolutely critical to the regulation of strategies, with knowledge of when and where particular strategies are appropriate guiding their application in the future (e.g., O'Sullivan & Pressley, 1984).

Often understanding of when and where strategies are useful occurs as a function of the learner **monitoring** that performance is better with a strategy that is currently being deployed compared with when comparable learning tasks have been attempted without the strategy in question (Ghatala, 1986; Pressley, Borkowski, & O'Sullivan, 1984, 1985; Pressley, Levin, & Ghatala, 1984). The Hardy boys often justified use of a strategy by recalling successful use of the strategy in a previous case involving a similar situation.

Strategies are used in conjunction with **nonstrategic knowledge** (e.g., Alexander & Judy, 1988). Because a criminal investigator knows that glass is a particularly good source of fingerprints, the boys took special care to make certain that glass at a crime scene was undisturbed until it could be examined systematically. The strategies possessed by the Hardy boys were used in particular ways because of their knowledge of the law, criminals' behaviors, criminals' language, physical evidence, drugs, and virtually every aspect of life. Good thinkers are rich in such nonstrategic knowledge—which is diverse, extensive, complex, and connected to one's experiences—and can flexibly use what they know.

No one could read the Hardy boys' mysteries without being struck by the boys' **motivation.** The boys were **motivated** to acquire more sleuthing strategies and knowledge needed by a detective. They were also motivated to figure out how to adapt what they already knew to new challenges they confronted. These fellows were always looking for crimes to solve and were determined to go about their investigations in a systematic way.

Good information processing requires a generally **healthy, normally functioning brain.** For instance, a tremendous amount of knowledge must be stored in long-term memory structures. Loss of long-term structures because of disease or injury results in loss of knowledge and a reduction in the competencies dependent on long-term knowledge.

Much of thinking also depends on **short-term memory,** variously referred to as consciousness, working memory, or short-term storage (see Baddeley, 1986). Short-term memory depends on an intact brain, with some regions of the brain more active in consciousness than other areas. When someone holds a telephone number in memory while searching for a scratch pad, thinking goes on in short-term memory. Short-term memory is active as an author juggles bits and pieces of meaning he or she is trying to combine into sentences and paragraphs. Close your eyes and try to keep in "view" the room you are sitting in; your image is in consciousness. Short-term storage is exactly what the name implies, however—short term. If a person does not continue to rehearse a phone number, the number will fade from consciousness. If a person is distracted while writing, he or she will lose some of the meaning in the elements being juggled. An image of a room remains vivid only because of conscious effort to maintain the vision in the mind's eye.

Moreover, short-term storage is limited with respect to the amount of information that can be attended to consciously at any one moment. Only so many numbers can be rehearsed at once. Only so many bits of information can be considered before new pieces of information literally seem to push out some of the information already in short-term memory. People usually cannot envision the room they are sitting in and another room at the same time; they manage to hold two such complex images in mind at the same time only by shifting attention back and forth from one image to the other.

When brain structures responsible for short-term memory are damaged, good thinking is difficult at best. Disruptions due to loss of short-term memory capacity are ever more apparent the more demanding the task—that is, the more a task requires simultaneous consideration or coordination of a great deal of information (McCarthy & Warrington, 1990, especially Chapter 13), the more likely it is that the individual with impaired short-term memory will falter on the task.

An important individual difference between people is their short-term capacity (Baddeley, 1986). That is, even among people with healthy brains, some can hold more things in memory and operate on more bits of information simultaneously than can others (Dempster, 1985). Suffice to advance here the conclusion that good thinkers have sufficient short-term capacity to carry out relatively complex tasks—a capacity that is at least partially due to an intact central nervous system.

In short, the Hardy boys possessed many characteristics of good thinking—strategies, metacognition, other knowledge, and motivation as well as healthy nervous systems—with these characteristics interacting to promote highly intelligent behavior and thinking. A view presented in this book is that developing thinking like that of the Hardy boys is a high ideal: Good schools teach important strategies, make certain students acquire metacognitive understandings about when and where to use strategies, convey a great deal of important knowledge about the world in general, stimulate academic motivation, and encourage lifestyles that will protect an all-too-vulnerable central nervous system. The case will be made throughout the book that good thinking—it will be called good information processing in this book—can be developed in contemporary school settings.

Understanding good information processing is so central to educational psychology in our view that Chapters 2 to 6 are concerned with the main components of good information processing just overviewed: Chapter 2 will provide detailed coverage of strategies and metacognition; Chapters 3 and 4 take up the role of nonstrategic knowledge in thinking; Chapter 5 is concerned with motivation; and Chapter 6 reviews the biological foundations of good information processing.

OTHER CHARACTERISTICS OF GOOD INFORMATION PROCESSING

In this section, some additional characteristics of good information processors are reviewed.

Good Information Processors Live in Richly Stimulating Environments

If an intact brain were raised in a closet, good thinking would not follow. A great deal is learned by the healthy brain as a function of experience. Even acquisitions, such as language, that human biology virtually guarantees, provided that there is some exposure to language (e.g., Anastasiow, 1990; Gleitman, 1986), are sensitive to environmental stimulation. Thus, when children are raised in isolation, language does not develop normally (e.g., see Puckering & Rutter, 1987, for a review). When raised by animals, such as the Wild Boy of Aveyron (Itard, 1801), human language does not develop at all. Other conditions that are associated with less severe deprivation have less severe effects on language development, although there are nonetheless detectable, pejorative effects. For instance, language acquisition is affected negatively by being reared in socially disadvantaged homes, as a twin, or in a large family—that is, whenever there are environmental pressures that reduce the amount that parents can play and verbally interact with their children (Puckering & Rutter, 1987).

Good Information Processors Have Well-Developed Language

Flexible, **well-developed language** unambiguously supports sophisticated thinking. There is a strong association between language delays and disabilities and learning disorders, especially difficulties with reading (Howlin & Rutter, 1987). The criticality of language as supportive of thinking has been especially apparent with the renaissance of Soviet models of thinking (Bakhtin, e.g., Morson & Emerson, 1990, and Todorov, 1984; Vygotsky, 1962; see Chapter 8, this volume), which emphasize the development of inner speech as an important determinant of skill in thinking (see Rogoff, 1990; Wertsch, 1991).

Good Information Processors' Attitudes and Emotions Support Their Cognition

Good thinkers are **appropriately confident.** They welcome challenges that are well matched to the skills and knowledge they possess. They recognize when they are equal to tasks as well as when academic tasks might be beyond them or when they need assistance to complete a task.

The Hardy boys had **well-controlled emotions.** For instance, anxiety did not overwhelm their thinking, even when they were confronted with great danger. They did not get so excited or agitated at a crime scene that their thinking was clouded, something that is all too common in less effective thinkers even in less objectively dangerous situations, such as during an examination (Hembree, 1988; Tobias, 1979, 1985).

Good Information Processors Are Appropriately Attentive and Reflective

Good thinkers have **attentional focus**—they are able to maintain attention even in the face of distraction (e.g., Aks & Coren, 1990). The German psychologist Julius Kuhl (e.g., 1985) refers to this ability to insulate goal-directed cognition from distraction as "action control."

Good information processors **inhibit inappropriate responses** (Bjorklund & Harnishfeger, 1990; Dempster, 1992) and are appropriately **reflective**—thinking through problems rather than reacting impulsively. Even so, they are not reflective to the point that reflection is paralyzing (e.g., Duemler & Mayer, 1988), always reconsidering rather than acting (Baron, 1985, 1988, 1990a).

Good Information Processors Do Much to Create Their Own Enriching Environments

Thinkers **contribute to their own education and development.** Good thinkers acquire many strategies and a great deal of nonstrategic knowledge because they place themselves in situations that present such information (see Bandura, 1986; Ford, 1987; Lerner & Busch-Rossnagel, 1981; Scarr, 1992; Scarr & McCartney, 1983). How did the 15-year-old down the block come to know so much more about the inner workings of her microcomputer than her parents do? That girl has spent hours with her computer, invested most of her allowance for the past 5 years on computer magazines, reads the magazines from cover to cover, figures out how to apply some of what is presented in magazine articles to her own computing, and spends time with other kids at school who are also interested in computing. She is knowledgeable about other topics, however, because she reads the *Washington Post* daily, listens to both popular stations and classical music while working on her computer, and engages in rich conversations with her family. Her friends are no slouches either. Her dialogues with them span a whole host of topics, from discussions about whether *Julius Caesar*, now being read in English class, is really history to reflections concerning effective ways of reducing drug and alcohol abuse in classmates. Good thinkers elect to do things that are enriching, and they seek out company that is intellectually engaging.

Just as important, other intellectually engaging people seek out the good thinker because the good information processor is stimulating for them to be with. The 15-year-old computer whiz received a call the other night from a classmate who was trying to persuade her to sneak into the free microcomputer seminars offered by the computer center at a local college! Good thinkers find one another, often with the explicit goal of engaging in activities that will further increase the competence of all involved in the interaction.

Summary

No one characteristic makes a person a good information processor, but rather good thinking is the product of a number of factors in interaction feeding on one another. For instance, by using efficient comprehension and learning strategies, more nonstrategic knowledge is acquired, which in turn can reduce the need to engage in strategic processing in the future. With greater knowledge, confidence increases so that what one knows can be applied with less concern for correctness. Thus, the young law student who systematically organized his cases on contract law and applies many specific learning strategies to acquire the fundamentals of contract law eventually will recognize automatically features of a typical contract that would make it nonbinding. He would correct the contract with little effort and no conscious strategies invoked to do so. Knowledge of the traditional contract law would also assist the young lawyer in recognizing features of an atypical contract, one not like contracts encountered previously. Recognizing the inadequacy of the knowledge base, the lawyer might engage in some strategies for coming to terms with the new type of

agreement (e.g., going to the law library, asking a senior attorney for guidance).

This introduction to the complexities of good information processing sets the stage for the rest of the book, which is concerned largely with encouraging the competencies that interactively sum to effective cognition. As most readers have probably inferred, much student thinking is not exceptionally skilled thinking, however.

NOT-SO-GOOD THINKING

There was a cottage industry during the last two decades in documenting the many deficiencies of poor learners. The same categories used to describe good thinking can also be applied to poor thinking. We encourage readers to compare the descriptions that follow with the thinking of the Hardy boys. The contrast is striking and should increase respect for good thinking when it does occur.

Consider first children who are having academic difficulties in school. These children are a diverse lot. Some do not have normally functioning brains, although the specific disorder is often difficult or impossible to pinpoint. Brain abnormalities can be reflected in a variety of ways, including language deficiencies, limited short-term capacity, lack of attentional focus, or impulsivity (Gaddes, 1985)—although, of course, language, short-term memory, attentional, and impulsivity problems can occur even in otherwise normal, healthy children, with these tendencies alone enough to undermine effective thinking and problem solving. Weaker students use fewer strategies than normal students, and they know less about when and where it is appropriate to use the strategies they do know (e.g., Forrest-Pressley & Waller, 1984; Schneider & Pressley, 1989, Chapters 4 & 5). Anxiety about academics is common in poor learners (Kasik, Sabatino, & Spoentgen, 1987; Perlmutter, 1987). Poor learners often hold beliefs that undermine their motivation to try (e.g., thinking that their learning problems are due to immutable ability factors; e.g., Pearl, 1982). Because poor learners acquire less from each lesson than classmates, often many aspects of their knowledge base are deficient relative to peers. Some poor learners have more difficulty than other children in applying what they know to academic work. In short, there are many children who lack one or more elements of good thinking, with interaction between components compounding difficulties (e.g., failing to use strategies decreases how much is learned, which decreases nonstrategic knowledge).

Many more mature students who are relatively successful (e.g., they are attending college) are not good thinkers all of the time. Pressley, El-Dinary, and Brown (1992) reviewed studies documenting that university students are often poor learners. For instance, they often study and restudy ineffi-ciently—that is they process what they are to learn inefficiently: For example, they read and reread rather than identifying more and less important in-formation and focusing on the important content. They frequently believe they are ready for tests when they are not. University students can com-pletely miss the main point of a reading and nonetheless believe they understand the text com-pletely. When searching for material, they often search ineffectively and fail to find what they are seeking. Often they possess prior knowledge that could be related to new content but is not (Pressley, Wood, Woloshyn, Martin, King, & Menke, 1992)—what would be required would be explicit use of as-sociation processes, which most people do not use unless the association is so salient that activating one element automatically activates other elements (e.g., thinking of "red" when someone talks about a "cardinal").

Even university students who, relative to peers, process academic content thoroughly are not all that thorough. For instance, Wade, Trathen, and Schraw (1990) observed college students attempting to learn factual text. Only about 10 percent of them used a diverse repertoire of strategies in attempting to un-derstand text. About a third of their sample relied on rote learning strategies—that is, they simply tried to "pound it in." Even the most strategic stu-dents in the Wade et al. (1990) study failed to learn much of what they studied.

It is not possible to know whether these ineffi-ciencies of thinking (i.e., processing inefficiencies) have always been present in college students. That is, there is no way to know whether the declining test scores and other indicators of poor academic performance indicate a decrease in the efficient, mo-tivated use of strategies and appropriate activation and use of nonstrategic knowledge. Whether they do or not, it seems likely that many indicators of academic performance would increase if students possessed repertoires of efficient strategies and ex-tensive nonstrategic knowledge, especially if they were highly motivated to apply what they knew to important academic tasks.

SUMMARY

Good information processing involves coordination of strategies and nonstrategic knowledge. Good thinkers are more aware of what they know and do not know than are weaker thinkers, and they are more likely to be aware of strategies that can im-prove their learning and performances (e.g., Leal, 1987). In addition, good information processors are highly motivated to use their intellectual resources to tackle important academic challenges. Although it is possible to identify instances of good thinking, it is anything but universal. How magnificent an ac-complishment good thinking is will become ever clearer as you proceed through this book.

One frequent reaction of students new to cogni-tion or educational psychology is that the conclu-sion just offered—that good thinking is an interac-tion of a number of factors—is so obvious that it is surprising that it could be offered as a scholarly in-sight. In fact, many cognitive psychologists have fo-cused (and, in some cases, still do) on one or a few of the factors that constitute good information pro-cessing. Thus, there have been (are) those who argue for the primacy of strategy use over other aspects of cognition. Other psychologists emphasize the non-strategic knowledge base. We frequently encounter the argument, both from the general public and some scholars, that being a good student is largely a matter of motivation. That many believe that good thinking reflects the operation of single factors makes our claim nontrivial: Good thinking depends on a number of factors in interaction.

DEVELOPMENT OF GOOD THINKING THROUGH INSTRUCTION

As complex as good thinking is, it can be developed through instruction. The perspectives on instruction offered in this book are decidedly catholic ones, em-phasizing a variety of approaches to teaching. School involves learning many different types of informa-tion, and no one or two instructional approaches are appropriate for all contents. One approach finds a great deal of favor throughout this book, however, largely because of the many research studies documenting its efficacy and because it works well with many other educational interventions (e.g., in homogeneous and heterogeneous classrooms, with cooperative learning, and in all of the content areas). Thus, direct explanation teaching is given special attention in this section on instruction.

Direct Explanation

When teachers provide explicit, detailed information about academic processes or concepts, they are engaging in **direct explanation** (e.g., Roehler & Duffy, 1984). Consider the teacher who directly explains to students how to write short essays using a plan-translate-revise strategy. The teacher explains and models alternative ways of planning an essay, including searching one's own mind for information that might be included, brainstorming with others, and seeking information from library resources. The teacher might also cover ways of organizing the many ideas that are generated, perhaps teaching methods of outlining an essay before writing it. Translation of the outline into a draft consists of taking the rough outline and putting it into phrases and sentences. Once a good first draft is achieved via planning and translation, it is time for revision, which in turn may require more planning and seeking of additional information to put into the essay, followed by construction of new phrases and sentences that mesh with what is already in the draft. Much of this information is conveyed during direct explanation teaching by the teacher talking through examples of good writing. That is, the teacher shows how these examples were constructed using planning, translating, and revising.

In addition to teaching the steps of the strategy, the direct explanation teacher also provides substantial information about when and where to use the strategy as well as how to coordinate the steps of the strategy with one another. Providing such information is intended to increase transfer of the writing strategy to new situations where it could be employed gainfully (O'Sullivan & Pressley, 1984). The direct explanation teacher in particular emphasizes the utility of the strategy being taught, focusing on how the student's writing can be improved through use of the strategy. The idea is to get students to attribute their successes and failures to whether they are making use of the knowledge they possess (e.g., Clifford, 1984; see Chapter 5, this volume).

How the direct explanation teacher combines explanation, modeling, and provision of metacognitive information (i.e., when and where to apply the strategy, the utility of the strategy) is illustrated well by a lesson taught by one of the teachers studied by Roehler and Duffy (1984):

> Consider a main idea lesson taught by Teacher B. The content of Teacher B's talk patterns reflected an explanation of what one needs to do to find the main idea of a paragraph. Information was initially presented about (1) what the mental process was, (2) how to use salient features of the skill, and (3) why the mental process is useful in connected text. After this direct explanation of what was to be learned, why it was important, and how to do it, Teacher B moved to a turn-taking model where he checked the students' restructuring of the skill and modified or reinforced that restructuring. Finally, when the students demonstrated that they understood, practice was provided. (pp. 268–269)

The most critical feature of direct explanation is up-front presentation of well-structured descriptions and demonstrations of the academic competencies being taught. The assumption is that children are quite capable of learning many academic competencies rapidly, although it is also recognized that general use of the competencies requires more extensive discussion and practice. A critical part of all this is the teacher actually modeling use of the strategies explained—and doing so in an authentic way, which includes struggling some with the task and having to work at it in order to use new strategies effectively. Exposure to such coping models deepens student understanding that constructive effort is required to respond to instructional explanations; that is, struggling with tasks is what academically talented people do, at least at first (e.g., Schunk, Hanson, & Cox, 1987).

We emphasize that direct explanation is a decidedly constructivist approach (e.g., Pressley, Harris, & Marks, 1992): Students do not passively learn from explanations but rather actively learn from them. They do not completely understand what the teacher is saying or doing, but the teacher's explanation and modeling are a starting point for the student. As the student struggles with the process the teacher modeled, he or she adapts it to the particular tasks at hand and modifies it in ways that are sensible to him or her. If a classroom of children hears and watches a demonstration (e.g., of multiplication of fractions) and then practices what was taught in the lesson, there will be much struggling, adaptation, and reflection on the part of the students, with the result that at the end of the instructional day, all will have somewhat different understandings of multiplication of fractions. If you do not believe it, go to the local school, listen to a lesson, and then interview a half dozen children at recess about what was taught. You will find that the students do not passively memorize but rather construct a personalized understanding. One of the reasons that teachers do not spend one day on a lesson is that many days of reexplanations and remodeling are often required before students begin to construct understandings that are conventional enough to allow them to meet the demands of the curriculum (e.g., actually be able to multiply fractions successfully and consistently, with an understanding of both the procedures and why the procedures work). Our view is that direct explanation is anything but in the service of passive learning but rather the start of an active exploration (Pressley, Harris, & Marks, 1992).

Other Approaches to Instruction

Every one of the alternative methods to instruction that are discussed in this section can be coordinated with direct explanation and the constructive learning that is stimulated by such explanations. In fact, some of the alternatives discussed here, such as observational learning and scaffolding, are components of direct explanation. Even so, each of the models reviewed here is sometimes regarded as a unique approach to teaching. After briefly reviewing some of these alternatives, this section concludes with some commentary about how a teacher who is committed to direct explanation might exploit all of the approaches to teaching considered here. Our view is that good teachers interconnect the various types of teaching, combining direct explanation with the methods that follow in this section and with other approaches presented at various points in this text.

Guided Participation   Guided participation involves extensive, explicit teacher direction of student processing. Teachers cue students step-by-step about how they should accomplish a task (e.g., solving a problem, writing a letter). The assumption of **guided participation teaching** is that students will eventually internalize the steps they are cued to use if they go through them enough times. Anyone who

has taken golf lessons knows about this approach to teaching, with the pro carefully directing every millimeter of the beginner's swing (or at least trying to).

An interesting example was provided by Hansen and Pearson (1983), who taught a set of reading strategies to grade-4 students. One process Hansen and Pearson wanted students to learn was to compare what is in text with one's own life. Thus, students were cued to do this before each new text was read. The students were also questioned about the text they were reading, questions that required relating personal knowledge to the content of the text and making predictions based on personal knowledge about what might happen next in text. This type of instruction went on for 10 weeks with some evidence, in the form of improved comprehension, that the processes cued during guided participation did come to be owned by the students. In contrast to guided participation, the approach discussed next emphasizes student decision making.

Discovery Teaching and Guided Discovery   Proponents of discovery and guided discovery approaches to teaching sometimes contrast their teaching with direct explanation instruction. Discovery learning deemphasizes instruction (Ausubel, 1961; Gagné, 1965; Wittrock, 1966), with Piaget's theory of intellectual development largely stimulating discovery-based approaches to instruction (see Brainerd, 1978a). Discovery is facilitated by presenting tasks to students that offer rich opportunities for discovery. Teacher input is often limited to answering student-generated questions about the task (see Suchman, 1960). Discovery learning is believed by its supporters to promote academic motivation by cultivating natural curiosity, producing more complete understanding of discovered strategies than would teacher explanation of the same strategies, and thus increasing the likelihood that students will know when and where to apply the processes they are learning and will be motivated to do so. Indeed, Piaget frequently claimed that nondiscovery approaches were harmful to the child: "Remember also that each time one prematurely teaches a child something he could have discovered for himself, that child is kept from inventing it and consequently from understanding it completely" (Piaget, 1970, p. 715).

Even though there are impressive demonstrations of children's invention of strategies (e.g., Groen & Resnick, 1977; Svenson & Hedonborg, 1979; Woods, Resnick, & Groen, 1975), there are also difficulties with discovery learning. Not all children discover the many strategies that they need to know to negotiate the academic demands of school. For many students, discovery is inefficient at best, requiring far longer than it would to teach the same strategies to children using direct explanation. Perhaps the "glitch" with discovery that has commanded the greatest attention, however, is that learners often discover errant strategies. One of the most impressive studies of this problem with discovery learning was reported by van Lehn (1990). van Lehn documented more than 100 subtraction strategies discovered by learners that are in fact incorrect. For instance, sometimes students "borrow" from columns when it is not necessary, do not write zeroes in their answers (e.g., generating an answer of 2 9 instead of 209), or subtract only from some of the columns.

That pure discovery sometimes produces less learning, less efficient learning, or less "correct" learning than educators might desire (Shulman & Keislar, 1966; Wittrock, 1966) stimulated some educators and theorists who favor discovery to modify the approach. Guided discovery teaching is more explicit than pure discovery teaching, typically involving the teacher posing questions to students, questions intended to lead students to understand ways that a problem could be solved. The questions lead the students to "discover" strategies. Not surprisingly, guided discovery does produce more certain and more efficient learning of strategies and ideas than does simple discovery (Gagné & Brown, 1961; Kersh, 1958).

An example of guided discovery is Collins and Stevens' (1982) **inquiry teaching.** Their approach to teaching is to present students a series of questions. Some of the questions focus on features of the concept that make it unique (e.g., is there a difference in the way plants and animals "obtain" food?). Others focus on dimensions that do not differentiate the concepts (e.g., do plants and animals both need to metabolize food?). "Trick" questions can be included to highlight misconceptions students might have (e.g., how long does it take a plant to move food out of the soil into its leaves?). After a series of such questions, the teacher asks the class to state rules that define the concepts under discussion (e.g., plants manufacture their own food whereas animals do not). The teacher may provide additional questions as necessary to clarify and refine the rules. Collins and Stevens (1982) believe their approach

encourages scientific thinking by encouraging students to internalize the idea that it is good to question and that by posing questions and constructing answers to probing questions, it is possible to come to understand important concepts and processes. By thinking about new concepts in different ways and coming to terms with misconceptions, Collins and Stevens believe students gain a deeper understanding of what they are learning. Similar to other discovery approaches, however, inquiry teaching is not particularly efficient: More material can be covered by reading or lecture than can be covered in the same amount of time devoted to inquiry teaching. Moreover, the method requires a teacher who can really think "on the run," who can pose telling questions and come up with pertinent examples (Collins & Stevens, 1982).

Despite the criticisms of discovery learning, learning how to discover is a critical ability—and if inquiry teaching promotes that, it is an important form of pedagogy. Life offers many more discovery learning opportunities than lectures! Indeed, if the lectures offered as part of direct explanation are successful, they get the student started on the road to discovering how to use and adapt the procedure that was explained and modeled. There will be plenty of discovery along the way, with effective education developing students who can systematically explore the world and reach important insights.

Scaffolding Of course, there are intermediate positions between discovery learning and guided participation. One considered already is guided discovery. Another is scaffolding, which involves provision of help to students on an as-needed basis.

A number of theorists take as their main tenet that mature thought in children is developed in adult-child interactions (e.g., Bakhtin, see especially Todorov, 1984; Feurstein, 1980; Vygotsky, 1962, 1978; see Chapter 8 of this book). Adults both model good thinking and provide subtle hints and prompts to children when they (their offspring or students) cannot manage on their own. Thus, adults direct children's attention to important dimensions of problems they are attempting to solve when the children do not attend to those dimensions in the absence of direction. Sometimes the adult suggests a strategy to the child. The theory is that eventually children adopt as their own the thinking processes and patterns adults have modeled and assisted children in using.

The children are said to **internalize** the processes that previously were **scaffolded** (Wood, Bruner, & Ross, 1976) for them by adults. The metaphor of scaffolding is appropriate because scaffolding is an external structure that supports another structure under construction; as the new structure is completed and capable of standing on its own, the scaffolding is removed. So it is with scaffolded adult-child academic interactions, with the scaffolding adult providing only enough support for the child to acccomplish an academic task—not too much or too little. The adult monitors carefully when enough instructional input has been provided to permit the child to make progress toward an academic goal. If a child catches on quickly, the adult's responsive instruction will be less detailed than if the child experiences difficulties applying the strategy and internalizing it.

One way to understand scaffolding is to compare it with direct explanation: (1) Direct explanations flow more from the teacher to the students, whereas scaffolded instruction is a result of continuous and mutually responsive interactions between students and teachers. (2) Direct explanations of entire processes are often presented early in instruction, with direct reexplanations provided by the adult on an as-needed basis as the child and adult attempt the academic task collaboratively. In contrast, more is left for the child to infer during scaffolding, although the scaffolding teacher attempts to lead the child to important understandings about the task being attempted and how the task might be accomplished.

Much more will be presented about both scaffolding and direct explanations later in this book, particularly in Chapter 8, with it then possible to relate both scaffolding and direct explanation to larger theoretical frameworks than can be presented in this introductory chapter. Suffice to point out here that scaffolding, direct explanation teaching that includes scaffolding, and other approaches that support student exploration, such as inquiry teaching, permit many more students to discover ideas that they must somehow learn in the accountability system that is school than would a pure discovery approach. Such supportive instruction will be encountered often in this volume.

Modeling and Observational Learning Humans learn a great deal from watching others—that is, the behaviors **modeled** by others are often learned by those observing the models. This is the main claim of **observation learning theory,** one that can hardly be disputed in the 1990s (see Bandura, 1977b, 1986). Particularly relevant here, there have been many demonstrations by educational psychologists that students can learn intellectual content and processes from observing others (Rosenthal & Zimmerman, 1978). Much observational learning research documented that people learn from **symbolic models,** especially characters on television. For example, both aggressive and altruistic behaviors can be learned from watching aggressive and altruistic television characters (see Bandura, 1969, 1977b; also Chapter 7 of this book).

Our perspective on such observational learning is that it is constructivist, not passive (see Moshman, 1982). What is learned from watching is not passive copying but an interpretation. The young boy who learns how to "bat" by seeing it on television "plays" with that perception—for example, tapping the plate in different ways with the bat when he steps into the batter's box, trying alternative stances, and experimenting with holding the bat far back versus nearer the shoulder. Even with no one around, the youngster who has intently observed batters on television for three or four innings will "play" at batting, with the play stimulated by the batting that was observed. The batting that is ultimately learned, however, is a construction of the child—often resembling very little the stance or actions of a major leaguer.

Textbooks That Teach The characters in books and stories can also serve as symbolic models to students, and a variety of materials are being created that are explicitly intended to teach particular content through such symbolic modeling. A well-known example is a series of novels by Matt Lipman, his *Philosophy for Children* (1985) program. Each novel is about fictional children who live in a classroom community. The children in these novels do a lot of thinking aloud about important philosophical problems. As these characters discuss concepts such as truth, fairness, and freedom, they provide models of sound, thorough thinking. The characters in these books specify concepts well, make appropriate generalizations from data, infer cause-and-effect relations, monitor the reasonableness of their arguments, and shun ambiguities and vague thinking. Because the novels are used in conjunction with classroom discussion, additional observational learning opportunities occur as classmates attempt to reason about some of the philosophical problems posed in the novels. This and other materials intended to stimulate critical thinking skills will be taken up in Chapter 11.

Classrooms are filled with all sorts of textbooks. Increasingly, these are designed by psychologists and those informed by psychological theory and research. Thus, there are now a number of basal reader series that are much more than a collection of stories but rather are set up to encourage student learning and practice of many different reading strategies. There are also elementary mathematics textbook series that have benefited from psychological research, with them designed to highlight sophisticated approaches to problem solving. Although published materials have played a role in instruction for a long time, it seems likely that, if anything, their role in teaching is going to increase. At least that is the hope of publishers, who are investing many millions of dollars to redesign their materials so the texts reflect the state of the art with respect to facilitation of learning and development of academic competencies (see, in particular, Chapter 14).

Educational Technology In addition to printed materials, there is also an explosion of other media and educational technology designed to teach various types of information in classrooms. Particularly notable are interactive videodiscs and microcomputer programs, both of which have the capacity to "explain" many types of information to learners, to elicit participation of students, and to provide feedback concerning the adequacy of student responses (e.g., see Chapters 12 and 13). These open up new worlds that, at their best, are not only richly informative, but also can stimulate student construction of understanding by patiently providing hints and clues (i.e., scaffolding the student).

Concluding Comment on the Nature of Instruction that Encourages Good Thinking

These various ways of teaching will be encountered again in later chapters. In some cases, strong claims will be presented about the potential efficacy of particular forms of instruction for particular purposes (e.g., many contemporary mathematics educators are enamored with variations on guided discovery). What must be emphasized, however, is that al-though these approaches to teaching can be placed in categories and operationalized separately—that is, instruction that involves a great deal more of guided discovery than any other component can be created for research purposes and evaluated in experiments—the various teaching methods typically are combined by skilled teachers rather than used exclusively.

For example, after the teacher explains a procedure, often through modeling, students are encouraged to try it on their own, with the teacher offering guidance and support as needed. Instructional books and other media sometimes are used during direct explanations or to supplement them. There are occasions when a direct explainer sets up classroom situations to promote discovery, with the effective teacher gently nudging students who might not be making good progress in the discovery process. Exceptionally capable teachers combine a variety of types of teaching to encourage the learning of strategies, nonstrategic knowledge, and metacognition that composes good thinking, with all of this occurring in an environment that encourages academic motivation. In presenting this claim about exceptionally good teaching, however, we also recognize that most teachers do not teach the many strategies that can improve academic performance and learning (e.g., Moely, Hart, Leal, Santulli, Rao, Johnson, & Hamilton, 1992), let alone do all that could be done to improve students' motivation to be cognitively active (e.g., Brophy, 1987).

That such teaching is not now common is one of the reasons we wrote this book. Instruction promoting effective thinking can become more common, however. A first step is for the next generation of educators to understand the various teaching and thinking models summarized in this book. Future teachers who learn the modern theories and understand the contemporary research that is discussed here will know much more about the nature of effective teaching than have previous generations of teachers who experienced the educational psychology courses of yesteryear. The explosion of theory and research on effective teaching and learning permits a much more realistic portrait of effective classroom instruction than was possible only a few years ago.

How various types of effective instruction can be combined can be illustrated by considering the Hardy boys again. The prime mover in their education with respect to detective work was Fenton

Hardy, famous detective. There can be little doubt that a good deal of direct explanation occurred in the father-sons triad as well as substantial scaffolding. The boys were also extremely well read, and there are plenty of instances of discovery learning in the books. In short, the Hardy boys' education was accomplished through diverse mechanisms. Fenton Hardy provided good instruction, but the boys also did much to create their own instruction, consistently placing themselves in settings where new detective skills could be acquired and practiced. Throughout this book, the argument will be made that learning and instruction require many different types of inputs. More positively, if high-quality instruction is provided, there is plenty of reason to expect academic success.

Just as the Hardy boys cultivated methods for investigating crimes, so too have researchers cultivated methods for investigating education. The results of many different types of studies are presented in this book. It is essential that readers understand, at least at a general level, the nature of the scholarly detective work that is research, with the next section presenting a brief overview of some of the most important paradigms and distinctions in educational scholarship.

METHODS OF EDUCATIONAL RESEARCH

Diverse methods are used in educational research, for different types of questions require different methods, and some situations permit some methods but not others. Thus, although experimental methods permit powerful conclusions with respect to causes and effects, true experiments require random assignment of participants to conditions. If an investigator is interested in the effects of social class, race, or gender on educational achievement, it is impossible to assign students randomly to socioeconomic or biologically determined categories. Nonmanipulative designs are essential when the investigator is interested in such variables.

Personal preferences and beliefs of investigators also affect the methods used in an investigation. For example, some educational scientists have much greater faith in observations that can be quantified and statistically analyzed, whereas other educational researchers are suspicious that with quantification comes reductions in data that distort conclusions. Many concerned about distortions produced by quantitative methods are now opting to conduct qualitative investigations, which rely more on the human investigator to use his or her interpretive skills to bring order to data that are collected. Others, including ourselves, are convinced that research programs are most likely to be fully revealing about important educational phenomena if both qualitative and quantitative approaches are combined. Both quantitative and qualitative methods have weaknesses, with use of complementary methods a powerful way of presenting a balanced picture that combines the advantages of the different approaches.

Presented in this section are brief summaries and commentaries about research methods that are encountered frequently in the educational research literature. Because quantitative studies are far more frequent in educational research literature than qualitative investigations, the discussion begins with the quantitative approach. Following summaries of quantitative and qualitative alternatives, a brief discussion about integrating results across studies will be presented. Throughout this coverage of methods, the emphasis will be on the conclusions permitted by particular designs.

Quantitative Methods in Educational Research

There are three main classes of quantitative studies: (1) manipulative investigations involving researcher control of variation (e.g., assignment to one educational treatment or another), (2) nonmanipulative studies involving the systematic analysis of naturally occurring variation between people (e.g., aptitudes) or settings (e.g., type of school), and (3) studies involving interactions between naturally occurring variables and manipulated variables (e.g., aptitude by treatment interactions).

Manipulative Investigations   One of the most typical designs in educational research is the comparison of a new or preferred educational intervention with conventional instruction or some other alternative (Campbell & Stanley, 1966). Thus, this book includes summaries of investigations comparing metacognitively enriched mathematics instruction with typical mathematics instruction, process-oriented writing instruction with less structured teaching of writing, and social problem-solving instruction based on stimulation of cognitive conflict with instruction covering social content alone. There are also many studies of basic processing that are true experiments. In subsequent chapters, there will be reports of comparisons between students taught to rehearse during list learning versus those learning lists using their own devices. The memories of students taught to use imagery to mediate their learning have been contrasted in true experiments with the memories of students not instructed to use imagery. A number of investigations involving teaching of reading strategies will be reported, with the typical contrast in these studies between reading performances by students taught a strategy and those not instructed to use the strategy.

What all experiments have in common is that participants are assigned randomly to treatments. That is, before the experiment begins, each subject has an equal chance of being assigned to the experimental or control condition. Such random assignment is the most likely approach to produce nonbiased groups at the start of the study (i.e., on average, at the start of the study, the participants assigned to the treatment and control conditions will not differ significantly). Because random assignment does not always produce equivalent groups, it is good to evaluate the performance of the treated and control groups before the experiment begins. If the treated and control groups do differ at the outset, the experimenter can choose to rerandomize or use the preexperiment data to control the postexperiment data statistically for prestudy differences between the groups.

For each cell in an experiment—and there are two cells when a single experimental condition is contrasted with a single control condition—two statistics are particularly important. One is the mean for the cell, which is the arithmetic average of all scores. The second is the standard deviation, which is an index of how much each individual score in the cell differs from the mean for the cell on average. If every person in the cell had the same score, each would have a score equal to the mean, and the standard deviation would be zero.

The means and standard deviations for the experimental and control conditions are used to construct tests that produce estimates of the likelihood that the experimental and control means differ at greater than a chance level. If, after a treatment has been implemented in the experimental condition, there is a statistically significant difference between the treated and the control performances with respect to variables expected to be affected by the treatment, the conclusion can be drawn that the experimental treatment *caused* the difference in performance. (A statistically significant difference is one that would be unlikely by chance, with it possible to determine the likelihood that the difference reflects chance. In general, unless there is a 95 percent chance that the difference is not random [i.e., $p < 0.05$], social scientists are reluctant to conclude the difference is real. Often, researchers require an even more stringent standard, such as 99 percent [$p < 0.01$] certainty or even 99.5 percent [$p < 0.005$] or even 99.9 percent [$p < 0.001$].)

Beyond statistical significance, it is often desirable to gauge the size of an effect—whether the difference between experimental and control conditions is small, medium, or large relative to the differences that naturally occur between people's performance on the task measured in the study. The way to do that is to compare the size of the difference between the experimental and control means on the task with the size of the standard deviation for the control condition (or the average size of the standard deviations in all of the cells of the study, depending on researcher preference). If the ratio of the mean difference to the size of the standard deviation exceeds 0.9, the difference between the means is usually considered to be large; if the ratio is between 0.4 and 0.9, the difference is often described as moderate in size; and if the ratio is less than 0.4, the effect is considered small (e.g., Cohen, 1988). Thus, if the experimental students average 65 percent on a posttest, with a standard deviation of 15, and the controls averaged 50 percent, with a standard deviation of 20, the effect size would be 0.75 or moderate, if the ratio is based on the standard deviation in the control condition alone (i.e., 15/20). It would be 0.85 and still be considered moderate if the ratio is calculated with the average of the standard deviations in the experimental and control conditions (i.e., 15/17.5). If there are a large number of participants in a study, it is possible for even small effects to be statistically significant. Thus, it is important to calculate the effect size to determine if the effect is striking and practically important, with the effect size not affected by the number of participants in the experiment. Calculation of effect sizes flags which treatments have large payoffs and which ones have small impact.

One persistent criticism of drawing cause-and-effect conclusions from instructional experiments is that the introduction of new instruction is inevitably confounded with other factors. Perhaps the improvements are simply a reaction to novel teaching, perhaps as a result of the concomitant increases in student arousal, motivation, or interest that accompany changes in instruction (e.g., Smith & Glass, 1987). Sometimes there are concerns that teachers' expectations change when new instruction is introduced, with shifts in expectations potentially affecting student motivation (i.e., the "Pygmalion" effect; Rosenthal & Jacobson, 1968; see Chapter 11 of this book). When students are aware that the goal of the study is to evaluate the effectiveness of the new instruction, they may want to do all possible to make obvious the efficacy of the treatment (i.e., the "Hawthorne" effect; Campbell & Stanley, 1966). (As the discussion about Hawthorne effects continues in what follows, readers should recognize that many attempts to produce Hawthorne effects have come up empty, suggesting such effects are perhaps not as much of a worry as researchers once feared they were; see Adair, Sharpe, & Huynh, 1989.)

There is a powerful way to evaluate the likelihood that the effects produced by an instructional innovation are due to general motivational factors, including Pygmalion and Hawthorne motivations. Motivation should have broad effects on learning. In contrast, educational treatments are expected to have more specific effects. For example, Russow and Pressley (1993) have been studying the effects of graphing calculators on student learning of mathematics. They hypothesized that students' conceptual understanding of how graphs relate to functions should improve with the calculators, but they could conceive of no reason that simple calculation skills should be affected by use of the calculator, unless the calculators were simply motivating or arousing. In fact, use of the calculators improved only conceptual understanding. When an intervention produces **discriminated effects** in a predictable fashion, as it did in Russow and Pressley's study of graphing calculators, there is powerful evidence that the specific intervention is producing the effects—that the benefits are not due to general shifts in motivation that might accompany instructional innovations.

In most studies, individuals are randomly assigned to conditions. Sometimes, however, in instructional experiments, classrooms are assigned to conditions (e.g., 10 classrooms are in the study, with 5 randomly assigned to the experimental and 5 to the control condition). When that is the case, statisticians believe that each classroom mean should be treated as an individual score, with the classroom means analyzed rather than the scores of individual students. We mention this "units of analysis" issue because in selecting studies for coverage in this book, we weighed in whether the appropriate unit of analysis was used in the analyses of the study. If individual student scores were analyzed in situations when classroom means should have been used, the statistical analyses in general are too liberal, resulting in the possibility that statistical significance might be reported when in fact such a claim was not justified. In selecting studies to discuss in this book, we included only studies that seemed to have defensible conclusions—conclusions that hold up when the analyses are reviewed critically by individuals well informed about the appropriate use of various methods of analysis.

Up until this point, only two-cell studies, in which an experimental condition is contrasted with a control, have been considered. Experiments are not limited to only two conditions, however. For example, if there are three possible instructional innovations, it sometimes make sense to run a study that is a horse race, comparing directly the three innovations to each other and comparing each of the three innovations to a control condition. Sometimes an investigator is interested in studying several different variables, each of which can be manipulated. For example, perhaps the investigator believes that both nutritional supplements and preschool-instructional enrichment promote the learning and thinking of young children. A factorial study can be conducted in that case—for example, one involving cells with and without nutritional supplement as well as cells with and without preschool enrichment. Such a study can be set up as a two (levels of nutrition) by two (levels of instruction) factorial design: In one cell, children receive nutritional and instructional enrichment; in a second, children receive only the nutritional supplement; in a third, participants are given instructional enrichment; and in the fourth (control) condition, children receive neither the nutritional nor the instructional enrichment. Such a design permits evaluation of whether nutrition, instruction, or nutrition and instruction combined produces differences in children's performances.

In principle, any number of factors can be manipulated in an experimental study (e.g., $2 \times 2 \times 2 \times 2$ designs are common, as are $3 \times 2 \times 2$ setups). Practically, however, large multifactorial studies are unwieldy, with the number of subjects required in a

16-cell (i.e., such as a $2 \times 2 \times 2 \times 2$) or larger design often so great as to make the study too expensive in terms of experimenter time and other resources. With respect to experimentation, studies involving a few conditions often are telling. Investigations that are limited in scope often permit greater quality control than much larger efforts, and when that is so, it is better to opt for quality than for scope.

One rule of thumb among quantitatively oriented researchers is that when it is possible to evaluate an intervention in a true experiment, do a true experiment. True experiments produce data that are more clearly interpretable with respect to issues of causality than any alternative approach. Still, there are many occasions when manipulation is not possible, but it is important to understand the intervention or variable in question. Carefully conducted nonmanipulative studies often can provide information in such situations.

Nonmanipulative Studies This section considers some of the fundamental types of nonmanipulative studies.

Diagnoses of Differences in a Population. The discovery of ways to categorize people is essential for science, with new categories increasingly apparent with increases in understanding about human life and functioning in general. In the late 19th and early 20th century, psychologists devised tests to classify people as more and less intelligent, an outgrowth of increasing understanding that human differences are heritable. In this generation, the medical profession has discovered it important to categorize people in terms of cholesterol number, dietary habits, and blood pressure status, largely because of new understandings of heart disease and its relation to diet and lifestyle. New methods of brain imaging are revealing differences in brain activity between people, permitting classifications based on neurophysiological structures and functions not possible previously.

Sometimes studies are conducted to determine the nature of cognitive processing differences in a population. Thus, some psychologists have been interested in the ways people differ with respect to memorization strategies, comprehension processes, and problem-solving tactics. The result has been studies demonstrating that people presented list-learning tasks (i.e., presented a long list of items

with the requirement that the items be remembered later) can be classified as rehearsers, elaborative rehearsers, and imagery users. There are active and passive readers. Some problem solvers are planful and others impulsive. There will be many classifications based on processing covered in this book.

Relating Differences Between People to Differences in Performance. Researchers are typically interested in how differences in people are predictive of important outcomes. Intelligence testing was important only because it promised to predict life success—and indeed, it at least predicts success in school. Cardiovascular and blood chemistry differences are important because they are predictive of long-term health.

Contemporary neurophysiologists expect to be able to link brain activity differences to many performance differences. Information-processing differences have consistently predicted performance: List learners who rehearse do not remember lists as well as people who integrate list items into memorable mental images. Active readers comprehend better than passive processors. Planfulness in problem solving predicts success at problem solving. (Of course, it is because processing differences are so predictive of performance that much of the emphasis in this book is on promoting processing that facilitates learning, thinking, and performance!)

Individual differences in cognitive processing can often be exploited in the service of theory testing. For example, suppose that a psychologist holds the position that construction of mental images during reading should improve understanding of the relations in text (i.e., imagery construction causes text comprehension in part). If that is true, people who naturally construct mental images while they read should comprehend what they read better. In fact, they do (Sadoski, 1983, 1985; see Chapters 3 and 14, this volume). Such a **correlation** between natural use of imagery and performance provides initial evidence relevant to the causal theory—if there had been no correlation between natural use of imagery and performance, the theory that imagery produces comprehension would be in big trouble. That is, causality implies correlation. Nonetheless, that there is a correlation does not cinch the case for the causal theory, because there can be correlation without causation. That is, correlation does not imply causation. For example, perhaps it is the case that people who naturally use imagery are more intelligent or in general deeper thinkers. If so, their greater comprehension could be due to greater intelligence or deeper thinking rather than their use of imagery.

In short, studies examining potential correlations between individual differences with performance can be used to separate unlikely from plausible causal hypotheses (Underwood, 1975). Because nonmanipulative studies are often cheaper and easier to conduct than manipulative investigations, it often makes good sense to use nonmanipulative studies to decide which hypotheses deserve the precious resources required to conduct manipulative evaluations.

There is also a larger reason to conduct correlational studies: They capture nature as expressed through natural variation better than do manipulations. If we only knew that instructing people to construct images improves their comprehension and memory of stories (which is all that we would know if imagery were manipulated only in experiments involving text processing), that would be knowledge removed from nature: What would not be known is whether anyone ever elects to use imagery to comprehend text on their own. Although some researchers choose to identify themselves as experimenters *or* differential psychologists (i.e., psychologists interested in naturally occurring differences), the best thinkers about social science methodology recognize that top-drawer research programs include complementary nonmanipulative and manipulative studies (e.g., Cronbach, 1957; Underwood, 1975). Such programs are revealing about what people are and do as well as about what people could be and do.

There are some individual difference characteristics that are evaluated frequently by researchers. Consider two examples: (1) Age: Developmental psychology thrives on potential age differences, with these sometimes examined at one point in time between different people at different age levels (e.g., 5-year-olds, 10-year-olds, and 15-year-olds in 1994). This is the **cross-sectional** approach. Less frequently, *changes* with age are examined, which can occur only in **longitudinal** studies—research that involves following the same people for some time (e.g., identifying 5-year-olds in 1994 who will be assessed as 10-year-olds in 1999 and 15-year-olds in 2004). Many age differences will be considered in this book. (2) Gender: There are salient differences

between males and females with respect to some important educational variables, with these taken up in the chapters that follow.

Diagnoses of Differences in Educational Settings. A great deal of effort has been expended in examining schooling environments for differences that can affect student processing, with some success. For example, some classrooms encourage competition and others cooperative learning. Some involve substantial questioning and others less questioning. Some include real conversations about subject matter, whereas others appear more like teacher drilling, with many teacher questions requiring student responses that the teacher evaluates (e.g., Mehan, 1979).

Relating Differences Between Settings to Differences in Performance. Sometimes researchers want to evaluate interventions but cannot randomly assign people to conditions. Often in education, such treatment differences boil down to differences in settings. For example, it is impossible to assign students randomly to public and private schools. Often it is difficult to assign students to classrooms emphasizing some particular form of instruction compared with another form (e.g., the whole language approach to beginning reading versus a more conventional approach; competition versus cooperation). What researchers typically do is to make comparisons between these different settings or interventions (i.e., they conduct a **quasiexperiment;** Cook & Campbell, 1979). Often the researcher will go to a great deal of effort to ensure that the subjects in the settings compared are as equal as possible at the beginning of the study except for the setting difference (e.g., studying public and private schools serving the same neighborhoods; checking the reading or intelligence scores at the beginning of the year of students enrolled in whole language and the more conventional comparison classrooms). The more certain it is that the participants in the cells of a quasiexperiment are equivalent except for the difference in the treatment (setting) in question, the more willing researchers are to interpret post-treatment differences produced in quasiexperimental studies as informative about causality. In general, our perspective is that if a true experiment is possible, it is much preferable to a quasiexperimental evaluation. Still, if a quasiexperiment is the best that is possible, and the issue is important, a quasiexperimental evaluation should be conducted. The cause-and-effect conclusion is not airtight in a quasiexperiment if a difference is found as a function of setting, but if other factors that might cause the difference can be ruled out because they were known to be equivalent in the two conditions, the case in favor of a causal relationship strengthens. A number of quasiexperiments informed the conclusions presented in this book.

One important approach in psychology to evaluating setting effects is the **cross-cultural study:** Sometimes cultures vary systematically with respect to critical educational variables (e.g., cultures that do not formally school their children differ from Western cultures that do). Cross-cultural researchers interested in education attempt to link such cultural differences to differences in performances between the cultures in question. There are a few exceptionally important cross-cultural efforts in educational psychology that are covered in the chapters that follow.

Concluding Comment. People differ in various ways, some reflecting biological differences (e.g., sex, age) and others reflecting differences in the settings they experience (e.g., culture, educational treatments adopted by the schools they attend). Whether there is systematic variation in various educational outcomes as a function of biological and socially mediated differences is often studied by educational researchers. When nontrivial relationships between human differences and performance are detected, there is said to be a **correlation** between the difference and the outcome. Often the statistic used to summarize relationships between individual differences and outcomes is a **correlation coefficient,** which can range from −1.00 to +1.00. The greater the absolute value of the correlation coefficient, the more certain it is that the individual difference dimension is predictive of the outcome in question (i.e., a 0 implies no relationship between the dimension of difference and the outcome, whereas either a −1.00 or a +1.00 implies perfect covariation between the dimension of difference and the outcome). When the correlation is positive, it means that high values on the individual differences dimension are associated with high values on the outcome dimensions. When the correlation is negative, it means that high values on the differences dimension are associated with low values on the outcomes dimension, and low values on the differences dimension are associated with high values on the outcomes dimension. There is no reason for making

much of the sign of a correlation, however, for the sign can be reversed simply by reversing the ends of either the individual differences scale or the outcome scale. Thus, the positive correlation between a person's height from the floor and their basketball ability can be transformed into a negative correlation by construing height as distance of the head from the ceiling!

Sometimes data in nonmanipulative studies are analyzed and summarized using statistics other than correlational coefficients. For example, a *t* test, which is a statistic often used to evaluate differences between means in experiments, can be used in a nonmanipulative study (e.g., male performances can be contrasted with female performances using a *t* test; recall by 5-year-olds can be contrasted with recall by 10-year-olds using *t*). The inference that can be made from such analyses does not change, however. Because it is not possible to assign people to the values contrasted (i.e., to male or female status, to 5- or 10-year-old levels), no causality between the individual differences dimension and the outcome can be inferred, even though a statistic that is often used in studies establishing causality is used to analyze the data in the nonmanipulative study. How data are collected determines whether inferences about causality can be made, not how the data are analyzed.

Combining Manipulative and Nonmanipulative Approaches in the Same Study: The Case of Aptitude by Treatment Designs Sly and the Family Stone made famous the line, "Different strokes for different folks." That is in fact the hypothesis inspiring studies of aptitude by treatment interactions (ATIs): Some types of individuals might benefit from one form of treatment, and others benefit from another type of treatment (Cronbach & Snow, 1977). It is easy to generate aptitude by treatment hypotheses. For example, it seems eminently sensible that people who are good at verbal processing should benefit from strategies requiring verbal fluency, and those who are more competent at spatial processing should benefit more from imagery strategies. The way to find out is first to identify students who are verbally facile and others who are spatially adept. Assign both types of students to perform a common task, with half of all students (of both types) using a verbally loaded approach and half using an imagery-loaded approach. The expectation is that performance with the verbally loaded approach would be greater than with the imagery approach for verbally facile students, with the outcome reversed for the spatially talented students. Such hypotheses are easier to advance than to support with data, with Cronbach and Snow (1977) filled with examples of ATI hypotheses that have not been confirmed or replicated (i.e., even though observed in one study, not obtained in follow-up research). The nonconfirmed ATIs include ones about differential susceptibility to treatment effects based on verbal-processing and spatial-processing competencies.

Studies of Potential Generalization of Findings from One Population to Another
Often a researcher will conduct an experiment and establish an effect. For example, researchers in the 1970s established that students at the end of the grade-school years could construct mental images that would improve basic forms of associative learning (e.g., if given paired items with an instruction to imagine the paired items doing something together, students in grades 5 through 7 remember more pairings than students left to their own devices to learn the pairings). What followed were investigations to determine whether the same instructional effects could be obtained with learning-disabled and retarded students (see Pressley, Heisel, McCormick, & Nakamura, 1982). In general, positive effects were obtained with these populations, although greater support and assistance were sometimes required for special populations to benefit from imagery instructions than were required with normal students.

One important issue is whether special education status "causes" the differences in learning observed between populations. We suspect that most readers recognize that what was obtained in these studies were correlations between outcome patterns and student status, for student status (i.e., normal, learning-disabled, retarded) cannot be manipulated. Often, separate studies will be conducted with different populations to study the generality of an outcome obtained in one population. The hypothesis often is one that could be construed as an aptitude by treatment interaction (i.e., a belief that an instructional treatment might affect different populations differently), but rather than studying students with differing aptitudes in the same study as occurs in ATI investigations, separate evaluations are made for each population.

Summary and Commentary on the Quality of Quantitative Investigations
There are many different types of nonmanipulative studies. Their common denominator is that there is some dimension of difference that cannot be manipulated. Quantitative, nonmanipulative studies were discussed in this subsection because the preponderance of nonmanipulative studies in educational psychology has involved formal quantitative analyses.

There are good and bad quantitative studies, good and bad manipulative investigations, and good and bad nonmanipulative research efforts. What are the criteria for determining whether a quantitative study is good or bad? One is whether the study has **internal validity**—whether there are design problems (such as a confounding in an experiment) that make interpretations ambiguous (Campbell & Stanley, 1966). Often quantitative researchers emphasize internal validity more than other factors when deciding, for example, whether a study is good enough to publish. A second important criterion is **external validity**, which is the extent to which the operations of the study are consistent with the processes and concepts the study is intended to illuminate (Bracht & Glass, 1968). Thus, someone attempting to study reading in college students has designed an externally valid study to the extent that real college students are reading real texts in a setting that is like the ones where college students typically read. The study would lack external validity to the extent that the sample was misrepresentative of college students (e.g., using perhaps a convenience sample of students enrolled in remedial English), the readings were contrived (e.g., passages from the Graduate Record Examination rather than from textbooks), and the place where reading occurred unnatural (e.g., at a computer screen). A third important criterion is **reliability**, which is high when the same results are obtained regularly and low when results differ from occasion to occasion. Fourth, quantitative researchers value **objectivity**, which is the use of measures that are publicly observable and clearly measurable. The number of times a teacher assists students is objective data; if the researcher asks the teacher why she intervened, the data are more subjective. Fifth, **triangulation** (e.g., Mathison, 1988), which is multiple indication of a phenomenon, is valued by quantitative researchers. Thus, if observations of overt behavior, differences in analyses of teacher verbalizations, and student performance all suggest differences in helpfulness between teachers, the quantitative researcher is more confident that there are differences in teacher helpfulness than if only one of the three measures were available.

The best quantitative studies are simultaneously high on internal and external validities, report outcomes proven to be reliable (e.g., there are replications of the phenomenon reported in the paper), and use a variety of objective measures so triangulation is possible. Readers should recognize, however, that far less is required for a study to be good enough to be published, with many studies reported in the literature that have nothing more going for them than that they are internally valid—there are no blatant confoundings, and there is one objective measurement. In this book, the better the study, the more likely it is to be featured in the discussion.

Qualitative Methods in the Social Sciences

Many discussions comparing quantitative and qualitative approaches are offered by methodologists who view themselves as representing one side of a debate, with their task to attack the other side. The rhetoric in the quantitative-qualitative discussion that has been in progress since the late 1970s and early 1980s is anything but collegial. We do not identify with that combative tradition but rather see strengths in both approaches. Even so, it sometimes helps students new to the quantitative-qualitative distinction to be presented a summary of the differences between the approaches. Thus, the qualitative approach is introduced by contrasting it to the quantitative approach (e.g., Hitchcock & Hughes, 1989, Chapter 2).

Differences Between Quantitative and Qualitative Approaches   There are entire volumes presenting and debating the differences between quantitative and qualitative approaches (e.g., Guba, 1990). A common theme in this literature is that the qualitative and quantitative approaches are incompatible, with incompatibility often argued based on philosophical underpinnings of the two approaches (see Howe, 1988): Quantitative approaches take as their ideal the classical scientific method, whereas qualitative researchers are more interested in interpretations, with the perceptions of participants in a setting valued as data. Although quantitative researchers do all possible to obtain objectivity, qualitative researchers are more comfortable with subjectivity. An especially important characteristic of quantitative researchers is that they are often in-

terested in testing theories using experiments, statistical correlations, and other quantitative analyses. In contrast, qualitative researchers are frequently interested in constructing theories based on observations and interviews (i.e., qualitative researchers are attempting to develop a **grounded theory;** e.g., Glaser & Strauss, 1967).

Howe (1988) summarized the differences between quantitative and qualitative researchers in the designs of their studies as follows:

> . . . [T]he qualitative researcher's design consists of some provisional questions to investigate, some data collection sites, and a schedule allocating time for data collection, analysis (typically ongoing), and writing up results. The quantitative researcher's design also has these elements, but the questions are more precisely and exhaustively stated and the schedule sharply distinguishes the data collection, analysis, and write-up phases of the research. Furthermore, the quantitative researcher will have clearly specified the research design (in a more strict sense) and the statistical analysis procedures to be employed.
>
> . . . The qualitative researcher (rightly or wrongly) is willing to assume relatively little, to keep the investigation open-ended and sensitive to the particulars of the context, especially the descriptions and explanations of events supplied by actors involved. In contrast, the quantitative researcher (rightly or wrongly) is willing to assume much . . . that all confounding variables have been identified, and that the variables of interest can be validly measured; quantitative researchers are also much less interested in actors' points of view. (Howe, 1988, p. 12)

Readers should keep the contrasts just outlined in mind as they read through the next section on the development of a grounded theory.

Development of a Grounded Theory   Strauss and Corbin (1990) particularly effectively summarized how grounded theories can be constructed. We describe here some highlights of their perspective, although in doing so import some ideas and emphases of others (in particular, Lincoln & Guba, 1985).

Construction of a grounded theory begins with collection of data. Thus, the researcher may spend a great deal of time observing behaviors in a setting of interest (e.g., many visits to first-grade reading groups for a researcher interested in constructing a theory of the grade-1 reading group). Alternatively the researcher may engage in many unstructured interviews (e.g., interviewing many grade-1 teachers about what goes on in their reading groups). In some cases, the observations may be made by the participants themselves, perhaps in the form of diaries (e.g., grade-1 teachers keeping daily journals about reading groups). Of course, there is also the possibility of combining methods of data collection, with many qualitative studies combining observational and interview data.

The task then is to induce regularities from the database. Thus, the researcher goes through the data systematically looking for meaningful clusters and patterns—behaviors that seem to go together logically. For example, if the teacher has students sometimes pair and read to each other, encourages students to ask one another about difficult words, and often encourages several students to read the same library book and engage in discussion, a meaningful cluster would be suggested. It is then necessary to name the cluster, to provide a category name for the behaviors included in the cluster. In this case, perhaps "cooperative reading" would be a reasonable name.

Such an analysis of extensive observations and interviews is likely to result in a number of categories. The next objective is to attempt to identify evidentiary support for the categories. The investigator, however, is always open to—and actually looking for—data inconsistent with an emerging category. This can be done by reviewing previous data. We note that qualitative researchers often begin their data analyses early in the data collection, so as tentative categories emerge, there is opportunity to look for support or nonsupport of categories with every new data collection opportunity. Analyses and data collection are seen as interwoven enterprises by the qualitative researcher.

One especially important check is to take the emerging categories back to those being observed and interviewed for them to indicate whether they find the categories that are emerging to be credible. (This is referred to by Lincoln and Guba, 1985, as **member checking.**) Often the subjects of the investigation can provide important elaboration of the categories at that point, citing potential refinements and extensions of the categories. As a result of member checking, the researcher may change categories or their names, consistent with the general qualitative emphasis on fluid interaction between data collection, data analyses, and construction of conclusions.

Eventually, there is a stable set of categories based on data collected to date. The task now is to begin to organize these categories in relation to one another. For example, the category of "teacher modeling" seems to subsume some of the other categories of behaviors that might have been observed during grade-1 reading groups, such as "thinking aloud about how to decode a word," "behaviorally acting out reading processes," and "behaviorally acting out deciding to read leisure material (e.g., 'I think during recess I will read the newspaper,' and 'Tonight I'm going to visit the library')." Thus, the category "teacher modeling" is higher in an organizational chart than the three categories it subsumes. Each of the categories that are placed in the hierarchical arrangement of concepts is then defined in terms of its properties and dimensions. For example, for the category "teacher modeling," one property of it is "abstractness," with this property measured on a dimension of "concrete to abstract." Other properties of teacher modeling might be "authenticity," "duration," and "timing in the lesson." Can you suggest potential dimensions for these properties?

Once the categories have been identified, placed in hierarchical arrangement, and dimensionalized, with these categorizations, arrangements, and dimensionalizations challenged by checking against the data, the researcher can begin to think that the data on hand are understood about as well as they are going to be understood.

It is now time to collect new data. For the grade-1 reading group example, it would be time to observe more groups, adjusting the categories and their arrangements in light of new observations, interviews, and so on. It would make sense to continue collecting data until no new categories are emerging from new observations, no new properties of categories are being identified, and no additional adjustments are being made to the hierarchical arrangement of the categories. This may take a while.

Once in possession of a great deal of data, it is possible to begin hypothesizing causal relationships between the categories of information that have been arranged as related to one another. There is a desire to know what causes each category as well as how categories affect one another. Thus, some reflection on the teacher interviews may make clear that teacher modeling is caused by contemporary teacher education practices (e.g., some teachers indicated they were running reading groups as they had learned to run them in college) or tradition (e.g., some teachers claimed they were running reading groups consistent with what they had experienced as children), or in-service resources (e.g., some teachers reported that there had been many in-services on teacher modeling of cognitive processes, especially during reading). Teacher modeling is not only caused, but also in turn causes reactions. Thus, perhaps students are observed modeling reading processes to one another or the processes modeled by a teacher seem to be prominent in student responses on the day they are modeled. The various causal possibilities, actions and reactions, are evaluated against all of the available data as completely as possible. Those that are supported by the data are retained; those that are not are deleted.

Often, there will be extensive **conditional information** placed in the model. For example, teacher modeling may be indicated as occurring more often when the teacher thinks that students do not understand the processing they are being asked to learn and may be indicated as less frequent once the teacher observes students using the processes under instruction. Strauss and Corbin (1990, Chapter 10) argue that such conditional information can be quite extensive and complex, so that what goes on in grade-1 reading might be affected by conditions in the classroom, the school, the community in which the school is located, the nation, or the world. For example, teachers might be more likely to emphasize modern cognitive processing views of reading, which specify that teachers should model effective reading for students, when the school is located in a community supporting education at the cutting edge. The pressure to teach in this fashion may also reflect the pressure of statewide assessments requiring students to demonstrate the cognitive processes that teachers can model as exemplary reading. Of course, we could go on suggesting a number of external factors. Such factors would emerge in the grounded theory only if the data suggested them. Thus, our example of state assessment pressure was mentioned because in our own work on process models of instruction, teachers frequently mention that their teaching is adjusting because of pressures from the state level; it is realistic to expect that data may provide insights into causality that operate at a number of levels, and that there will be evidence in the data that forces far removed from classrooms being observed are affecting what goes on in those classrooms.

As relations and conditional information emerge, it is important to check them against the data, always seeking support and making changes in light of discrepancies with data. More member checking should occur as well. This activity continues until no new categories or relations between categories emerge, until the point of **theoretical saturation.** Strauss and Corbin (1990) are emphatic that researchers must continue to analyze the data until this point is reached, for to do otherwise results in an incomplete grounded theory.

Eventually the data must be reported in a way that they are consumable by the public, or at least by other researchers. What is required is for the researcher to identify a key category or categories and to tell the story, in sufficient analytical detail to reflect the richness of the analysis done but in a fashion that makes the findings comprehensible. This emerging story should be member checked as well, until there is eventually a tale that seems reasonable to researchers and participants.

Quality of Qualitative Investigations   Just as it is possible to evaluate the quality of quantitative studies, it is also possible to evaluate qualitative studies—on about the same dimensions. The language is different, however (Guba & Lincoln, 1982; Lincoln & Guba, 1985). Thus, rather than worrying about internal validity, qualitative researchers are concerned with **credibility.** To the extent that the case is strong that the grounded theory captures the reality of the situation studied, the greater the credibility of the study. Rather than external validity, the qualitative analyst values **transferability**—whether the analysis was conducted in a setting representative of the universe to which the researcher wants to generalize. Evaluating transferability involves deciding whether the analysis would apply somewhere else, which may require analyzing somewhere else before a decision about transferability is possible. **Dependability** is the qualitative analysts' term for reliability. The qualitative analyst must convince that most people would come to the conclusions that are drawn based on the sample of data analyzed. **Confirmability** is the term used instead of objectivity, with confirmability generally high when something like triangulation occurs in the study—when multiple indicators are used to buttress conclusions. The best qualitative studies are high on all of these characteristics.

Why Do Qualitative Analyses?   Our view is that analyses of many issues have been substantially enriched by qualitative analyses. How students and teachers interpret educational interventions probably often affects how those interventions impact on students and teachers. When interpretations make a difference, it is important to know what those interpretations are. Students and teachers often have extensive knowledge about why the classroom day is organized as it is, so analyses tapping those understandings are going to be more complete than analyses that ignore teacher rationales for their behaviors (which was the predominant approach of quantitative, observational studies of teaching that predominated in teaching research in the 1960s, 1970s, and 1980s).

One exceptionally important value of qualitative analyses is that they can provide a theory worth testing. Thus in recent years, we have spent time constructing a theory of how reading comprehension instruction is carried out when it is done well, a grounded theory based on observations and interviews in schools providing effective comprehension instruction to their students (see Pressley, El-Dinary, Gaskins, et al., 1992; Chapter 14 of this volume). What that work provided to us is a theory of comprehension instruction that is being evaluated in much more quantitative studies. Those quantitative studies never could have been designed without the knowledge gained in the qualitative investigations.

Arguments against doing qualitative analyses are increasingly rejected by the researcher community, especially as researchers have come to realize that much of quantitative research involves qualitative decisions (Howe, 1988; Huberman, 1987). Every quantitative study involves deciding which variables to include and how to measure them, which are matters of interpretation. There are decisions about which statistical tests and criteria to apply, which again involves substantial subjectivity, especially because a number of assumptions are made about the data and the situation studied in order to make analysis judgments. The way the questions are framed in the introduction of the study, the hypotheses that are tested, and the story told in the discussion section of a quantitative article are also researcher interpretations.

Sometimes it is possible to quantify "qualitative" data. For example, there is nothing wrong with reporting proportions of participants who provide a particular rationale—supplementing observations and informal interviews with more formal and more quantifiable measurement (e.g., Pressley, Schuder, SAIL Faculty and Administration, Bergman, & El-

Dinary, 1992). We are decidedly pragmatic, believing researchers should do whatever they can to inform important issues, consistent with the thinking of others who have wrestled the qualitative-quantitative debate to a stalemate (e.g., Howe, 1988). We do not make a big deal in this book about when the focus is on quantitative versus qualitative data, comfortable with the value of both types of research in thorough analyses of educational phenomena, consistent with the perspective of other leading researchers whom we respect greatly (e.g., Rizzo, Corsaro, & Bates, 1992; Stanovich, 1990).

We both noticed years ago that the Hardy boys sometimes took precise measurements and made decisions based on objective evidence and other times spent time trying to make sense of a situation (i.e., organize it into related categories), with the personal interpretations of witnesses often helpful in the boys' theory construction processes. The Hardy boys' problems were much easier than most educational research problems—they always cracked the case in a few hundred pages, whereas years and thousands of pages can go by before there even begins to be a resolution of a mystery tackled by educational researchers. The Hardy boys would not have solved their cases if they had slept in a methodological Procrustean bed, however, either one emphasizing objectivity or another interpretation; neither should 21st century educational researchers, if they want to have a chance of solving the exceptionally challenging problems confronting education today.

Summarizing Across Studies

Every important topic in education results in many studies being conducted. How do researchers make sense of so much data? One method is to be decidedly qualitative. Read everything and try to sort the work and results into categories, figuring out how the categories are related to one another. Then write a review article summarizing what has been found. Historically, this has been the most common approach, with the journal *Review of Educational Research* and the annual volume *Review of Research in Education* both publishing many examples of this approach.

There are also quantitative options for summarizing across studies. All quantitative options also require some qualitative sifting, for example, deciding just what questions were asked in the literature and which studies asked which questions. The difference in the quantitative analyses, however, is that the reviewer attempts to provide exact numbers. One approach, known as the box-score (vote-counting) method, involves counting up the number of studies of an issue reporting a significant effect and the number reporting a null effect. For the most part, this approach is now rejected, largely because it ignores so much of the quantitative information reported in studies. Thus, what if a difference just misses statistical significance? It is a vote against the hypothesis, when in fact, it was almost a vote in favor. What if investigators in the various studies differ in the levels of statistical significance they are willing to interpret as significant or use analyses procedures that differ in sensitivity? For the most part, such distinctions are lost on the box scorer, who simply counts up the declared winners (i.e., those declared statistically significant) and the losers (i.e., those declared not significant).

The most important alternative to the box score is **meta-analysis** (e.g., Glass, McGaw, & Smith, 1981). With this approach, for each test of an issue, an **effect size** (defined earlier) is calculated. Then the average effect size is calculated based on all of the comparisons reported in the literature. If the issue is whether a treatment of interest is successful relative to control condition (e.g., conventional instruction), it is possible based on the average effect size to classify the effect as small (i.e., less than 0.4 ratio for the mean difference to the size of the standard deviation in the control group—or the average standard deviation depending on the preferences of the reviewer), moderate (i.e., a ratio of 0.4 to 0.9), or large (i.e., a ratio larger than 0.9) (Cohen, 1988). Educational researchers are increasingly relying on meta-analyses to summarize data on important issues, with this facilitated by the increasing availability of statistical software for calculating effect sizes (e.g., Mullen & Rosenthal, 1985). There are many examples of meta-analyses in *Review of Educational Research* and *Psychological Bulletin*.

Meta-analyses are now a fact of life in educational research, and students must understand at least that the unit of analysis in such summaries is the individual study effect size, and the goal of meta-analyses is the generation of average effect sizes. The logic is that the mean effect size is a more reliable indicator of the actual effect size than would be the effect size generated in any particular investigation. Meta-analysis is a quantitative approach for taking advantage of the efforts of many researchers. Some exceptionally important meta-analyses in education will be reported in the chapters that follow.

Meta-analyses must be interpreted with care, however. What is especially critical is that the individuals doing the meta-analyses are able to organize the data meaningfully. Often they cannot do so. As an example, consider a meta-analysis that crossed our desks a few years ago on vocabulary learning, an arena in which we both have published extensively. Some researchers doing vocabulary research have designed exceptionally analytical studies, studying variables expected to be affected by particular manipulations and other variables expected not to be affected by the same manipulation. (See the earlier discussion in this chapter on designs including both types of variables, designs that can help to eliminate potential alternative interpretations of differences produced in studies.) What was amazing was that the individual constructing the meta-analysis assumed that the experimenters had expected positive effects on all variables. Thus, the meta-analyzer interpreted the failures to obtain effects on variables that the researchers expected would not be affected by intervention as evidence that the researcher's theories were wrong. To construct an intelligent meta-analysis, it is essential to understand the issues being studied in the research reviewed and the logic of the methodological decisions made by the scientists conducting the original research. Unfortunately, there are a growing number of meta-analyzers who become proficient with the statistical machinery that is meta-analysis and then go looking for problems to plug into the machinery. The frequent result is an insensitive, misinformative review of the literature in question; another result is that different reviewers can review the literature on the same problem and come to different conclusions (Abrami, Cohen, & d'Apollinia, 1988).

One assignment we typically give students is for them to read one or two meta-analyses and compare the structure and style of such reviews to more prosaic reviews in the same journal. Such an exercise makes clear why so many believe that meta-analyses simplify review writing and comprehension of reviews; such an exercise also makes clear why many believe that meta-analysis is much more reductionistic than conventional review writing, which was already reductionistic. When students are able to locate meta-analyses related to problem areas they know in depth, they are often able to detect assumptions made by the meta-analytic reviewer that are questionable—sometimes they also detect assumptions that are unquestionably wrong. We encourage all readers of this book to examine some meta-analyses, if they have not done so before, especially ones that pertain to research problems with which they are familiar.

WHAT'S AHEAD?

What follows is a summary of what we perceive to be the best theory and research on the development of good thinking and good instruction. Much of this work has been generated under the general rubric of cognitive psychology or cognitive psychology pertaining to education (e.g., as research in cognition and instruction), although certainly not all of it has. Indeed, some of the best and most interesting research has been produced by those who identify more strongly with particular fields of curriculum and instruction than with cognitive or educational psychology. This book does not necessarily respect intellectual boundaries but rather picks and chooses research and theory from a variety of disciplines and subdisciplines that make contact with education and scholarship relevant to education.

There is definitely a mix of theory and research in what follows. In general, theories that enjoy some support in research are favored over those that are not tested or have failed to be supported when tested. There is also a mix of basic and applied research. We firmly believe that basic research can inform education, with many connections made between basic research and applications in this book. The more obvious the connection of a piece of basic research to educational practice, the more likely it is that the work appears here. Thus, there are some classic findings from cognitive psychology that do not appear here or are touched on only briefly because they are only tangential to educational issues. In some of these cases, the technical presentation required to understand the basic research would have gotten the presentation off track, with us electing to stay on track. The bottom line, however, is that we included the most visible psychological theory and research informing education today.

One of the most important criteria in deciding what to include was to rely on hearsay. We attend many education conferences, visit many schools, and talk with many educators and professionals concerned with education. Much of what appears here is what these professionals are talking about. Many of the issues taken up are ones of urgent importance to educators and to researchers concerned with education. We attempt to confront head-on many of the problems that are pestering educators and educational researchers the most.

If the chapters that follow stimulate discussion and arguments in readers about what is important in education and educational research, that will be one indicator that this book is a success. We also hope this book inspires at least a few young scholars to develop new solutions and new research directions, to go beyond what is in this book in pursuit of a new psychology of education that will render what is here obsolete. Any work our readers conduct that renders this book outdated will be exceptionally gratifying to us.

Writing this book has made us dramatically aware of how rare good thinking is. For instance, we were sure as youths that there were many famous detectives who knew a great deal about sleuthing. This surmise came from our awareness not only of the Hardy boys, but also of Nancy Drew, Dorothy Dale, Jack Ranger, the Dana girls, and the Bobsey Twins. Of course, these characters did not exist, but at least there were a lot of people who knew enough to write books reflecting the good thinking that is sophisticated detective work. Wrong! All of these characters were the creation of one writer, Edward Stratenmeyer (Watson, 1991). Outstanding detective-like thinking is extremely rare! (Have you ever met anyone like Sherlock Holmes?) As will become apparent in what follows, good thinking in general is a commodity that is anything but commonplace, the product of years of high-quality education and experiences. Thus, although we are optimistic throughout the book that education could be improved based on research insights, we are also realistic that there are no quick fixes, only fixes that are tantamount to years of effective education, education that can be informed profitably by the work summarized in this book. The next four chapters elaborate the theory of good thinking summarized in this chapter—the good information processor model, relying greatly on basic research to do so.

Part
1

Good Information Processing

Strategies and Metacognitive Regulation of Strategies: Basic Theory and Research

In Chapter 1, we established the broad outlines of the argument that sophisticated thinking involves complex interactions and interdependencies among strategies, metacognition, nonstrategic knowledge, motivation, a normally functioning brain, and other factors. This chapter is the first of five that specifically will elucidate these various components and provide detailed discussion about how the components interrelate to produce sophisticated thinking.

This first chapter is about strategies and their metacognitive regulation, including how a strategies-based approach to cognition relates to other models of cognition and learning. Basic research is featured, much of it conducted with respect to memory tasks—for example, list learning (e.g., giving a learner 10 objects to remember with recall of the list required at a later time) and associative learning (e.g., giving learners pairs of items such as "turkey and key" and requiring them to remember one given the other item). Admittedly, these tasks are not as **ecologically valid** (Bracht & Glass, 1968) as other tasks that will be considered in later chapters (i.e., they are not as representative of actual school-based learning problems). Use of such tasks in research, however, permits experimental control that is not always possible with more complicated tasks. Many important insights about learning and thinking emerged from this body of work. Because all serious students in educational psychology must have an understanding of such basic research to understand many of the main assumptions of the field,

this work is presented in some detail here. Even so, it is stressed that knowing this basic work alone cannot suffice for the educational psychologists of the 1990s because this basic work has been complemented with, and somewhat superseded by, research that is more ecologically valid, research about overviewed later in this book. The well-rounded educational psychologist must be aware of both the issues investigated in basic research and, applied cognitive psychological research, such as research about how students can learn science, mathematics, reading, and composing.

WHAT IS A STRATEGY?

Consider first a formal definition of strategies:

> [Strategies] . . . are composed of cognitive operations over and above the processes that are a natural consequence of carrying out [a] task, ranging from one such operation to a sequence of interdependent operations. Strategies achieve cognitive purposes (e.g., memorizing) and are potentially conscious and controllable activities. (Pressley, Forrest-Pressley, Elliott-Faust, & Miller, 1985, p. 4)

This stilted definition can be understood with an example. Suppose you must read an article for a class. What are the cognitive operations and processes that you must carry out—that are a natural consequence of reading the article? You must decode the words. In general, you do so by reading the article from front to back. These are not strategic activities according to the definition presented here because decoding of the words in order is pretty much obligatory in order to "read" the article front-to-back. Are there things that you could do that would be over and above front-to-back reading? In fact, there are many strategies that could be used to understand and remember the text better. Before reading, you could skim the title, pictures, and headings to get a sense of the topical coverage. This might lead you to make predictions about the content of the article. Once front-to-back reading began, you might monitor carefully whether the meanings you anticipated actually occurred in the text. As reading progressed, you might also attend to whether what is being read makes sense. If it fails to make sense, you might reread. Finally, after concluding one pass through the text, you might self-test your recall of what was presented in the article. Then you might look through the article and construct a summary, noting which parts of the article were not remembered during the self-test.

In short, there are a host of processes that you could execute that are over and above simple reading from front to back. These are strategies. Often these strategies are executed consciously and intentionally. Sometimes, however, good readers probably carry out at least some of these processes without conscious attention to whether they are doing so. An important point, however, is that even those readers who carry out such processes automatically could control them if they chose to do so. Strategies must be controllable. Strategies are different from processes that are so automatic that they are not controllable. For instance, when reading a passage about Queen Elizabeth, many readers would automatically infer the passage was about the queen of England. Such automatic inferential activity is not strategic because it is generally not controllable—you just cannot help but think of England when you think of Queen Elizabeth.

Finally, the reading comprehension strategies just mentioned are aimed at achieving important purposes. They facilitate understanding and memory of text. There are an infinite number of cognitive operations that can be performed on any text that would not facilitate important cognitive goals (e.g., the reader could begin at the end and read backwards; the reader could count the number of words including the letter "d"). Only operations that en-

hance important cognitive purposes earn the label "strategy."

We use reading comprehension as an example because it is such a familiar and obviously valid task for students. Progress has been rapid in strategies research with ecologically valid content because of the large body of well-conducted basic research that preceded it. There will be several occasions in this book when the discussion will return to reading comprehension, but for now the concern will be with more basic tasks and basic research. This basic work is important because it has been exceptionally analytical, with insights arising from it affecting instruction of many other strategies, including complex academic strategies, such as those that can mediate reading comprehension, writing, and problem solving. The lessons produced in basic research on memory strategies are exceptionally important for educators.

MEMORY STRATEGIES

A number of issues pertinent to educational psychology were at the heart of the research on memory strategies that was conducted in the last 30 years. This section is organized around some of the most important of these.

Development of Strategy Use in Children

A strategy investigated in many of the most prominent studies of children's memory was **rehearsal** of lists of items. Consider a typical **serial recall task.** A number of items are presented to learners in a particular order, perhaps in the form of picture cards, one picture to a card. A child might be presented a straight row of such cards, with the faces turned down. The researcher informs the child that the task is to remember the objects pictured on the cards in the order of presentation. Proceeding left to right, each card then is turned over by the researcher for a few seconds, so the child could see the object on it (e.g., Flavell, Beach, & Chinsky, 1966).

A good strategy that can be applied to this task is **cumulative rehearsal–fast finish** (Barclay, 1979; Butterfield & Belmont, 1977). This involves saying the early-list and middle-list items over and over in order as they are revealed. Suppose the order of the pictures is *chair, dog, cup, car, radio, book,* and *tree.* After seeing the picture of the chair, the learner would say "chair" several times. Then, when *chair* was turned face down and *dog* revealed, the learner would say, "Chair, dog," several times. By the time radio was presented, the rehearsal would include, "*Chair, dog, cup, car,* and *radio,*" as many times as time would permit. This adding-on of rehearsed elements would continue until the entire list was presented and thus the cumulative rehearsal part of the cumulative rehearsal–fast finish strategy. The "fast finish" is a test-taking strategy: When asked to recall the items on the list, the learner using fast finish immediately "dumps out" the last item or two that was presented (i.e., *radio* and *car* for the example list) and then recalls the earlier items in order. That is, the learner recognizes that the last two items still are in some type of shorter-term memory and can be recalled effortlessly if recalled first at the time of testing.

Use of the cumulative rehearsal–fast finish strategy develops slowly (see Schneider & Pressley, 1989, for a detailed review of the relevant literature). Preschoolers and early elementary-age students do not use it. Their most typical strategy is simply to say the name of the picture that is currently being displayed. This is a labeling strategy (Flavell et al., 1966). Cumulative rehearsal alone (without fast finishing) is commonly observed by the end of the grade-school years in western cultures, however (e.g., Flavell et al., 1966; Ornstein, Naus, & Liberty, 1975). The fast-finish component is not observed until late adolescence (Barclay, 1979).

An important question in research on rehearsal strategies was whether their increased use was because of organic factors that are indexed by age (i.e., brain maturation that is roughly indicated by age) or due to experience. The work that was conducted in western and industrialized nations was not revealing on this point because biological development and number of years of schooling experience are inevitably confounded in the West (i.e., most 7-year-olds have had between 2 and 3 years of formal schooling; most 10-year-olds have had between 5 and 6 years of school). Researchers were able to disentangle the contributions of development and formal schooling to improvements in strategy use, however, because the confounding between age and number of years in school is not nearly as certain in some other cultures as it is in North America. Western-schooled students in such cultures (i.e., those attending Western-type schools in their home countries) were compared with other members of

the culture who had not received Western schooling. Schooling made a difference. Use of strategies (and hence performance) on basic memory tasks was related to school experience in these cultures. Students who had experienced several years of Western-style schooling memorized much like students in the West with comparable education; students in the culture who had not attended Western-type schools did not resemble Western students nearly as much in the ways they used to try to remember information (Sharp, Cole, & Lave, 1979; Stevenson, Parker, Wilkinson, Bonnevaux, & Gonzalez, 1978; Wagner, 1974, 1978). The same basic research strategy has also been used to establish that nonmemory reasoning abilities that are common in the West are due largely to Western-style schooling (Artman & Cahan, 1993).

Work on the effects of education on use of basic strategies is more analytical. Not all Western countries are alike. Specifically pertinent here, parents in different Western cultures seem to provide different amounts of support for use of memory strategies. Carr, Kurtz, Schneider, Turner, and Borkowski (1989) performed an especially important study, demonstrating differences in parental encouragement of memory strategies, differences that were reflected in different approaches to memory by children as a function of culture. German parents in their study reported more instruction at home of memory strategies than did American parents. When German children are tested on recall tasks, there are differences in how they go about these tasks relative to Americans. In particular, when German students are presented lists of items to learn, with the items selected from several different categories (e.g., furniture, animals, foods), they are more likely to make use of the categories in the list during study than are same-age American children (see also Schneider, Borkowski, Kurtz, & Kerwin, 1986). When these results are combined with the cross-cultural research summarized previously, the case builds that use of strategies by children is determined by experiential factors.

More recent work reinforces the conclusion that culturally related experiences affect memory processing: For example, children in Morocco who are experiencing Quranic primary schooling are exposed to a great deal of practice doing rote learning. That is, they memorize passages from the Quran. The most obvious way that the memory capacities of these children differ from same-age Moroccan children receiving modern schooling is in the superiority of their serial learning, which is memory for information in order (Wagner & Spratt, 1987). The Quranic students have developed strategies for doing the memory task demanded of them most.

Many readers are probably already feeling somewhat dissatisfied with the research reviewed in this section. After all, rehearsal during list learning is artificial, even though people sometimes do rehearse text content that they need to remember, with learning gains produced by such rehearsal (e.g., Muth, Glynn, Britton, & Graves, 1988). Researchers also experienced such dissatisfaction, believing that much more interesting strategies might be observed if more naturalistic memory tasks were studied in more naturalistic settings. What resulted from this movement away from the study of basic strategies such as rehearsal to more ecologically valid strategies were demonstrations that even preschoolers are sometimes strategic, at least when simple strategies are considered or the children are tested in familiar surroundings or using methods that are sensitive to the strategies they use.

Strategy Use by Preschoolers

One important study establishing the strategic competence of preschoolers was conducted by DeLoache, Cassidy, and Brown (1985). They placed an object in a living room (e.g., under a pillow on the couch) as a child watched; the child was aware that he or she would have to retrieve the hidden object later. In this situation, even 2-year-olds are strategic. Although they will play in the living room during the retention interval (i.e., between when the object is hidden under the pillow and when they must retrieve it), preschoolers frequently look at the place where the object was placed, sometimes even pointing to the location and saying the name of the hidden object.

The research conducted by DeLoache and colleagues was sufficiently analytical to permit a strong conclusion that these "checking back" and simple rehearsal strategies were in fact memory strategies. One manipulation that was revealing on this point was the following: Sometimes the object was hidden in the room (e.g., under a pillow); other times it was placed in about the same position, but not hidden (e.g., on top of the same pillow). Only when the object was hidden from view did preschoolers look

back at the spot or say the object's name during the retention interval. That is, the strategies occurred only when there was a memory demand.

Preschoolers' use of memory strategies can be detected even with list-learning tasks if the measures are sensitive to the strategies preschoolers might use. Baker-Ward, Ornstein, and Holden (1984) presented preschool children with sets of toys. In both conditions of the study, children were permitted to play with the toys. In one of the conditions, only playing with the toys was mentioned during the directions given to the students. In the other condition, a memory demand was made. The children were asked to remember a subset of the toys. The addition of this memory demand changed the processing of preschoolers dramatically. The children given the memory instruction played with the toys less. Rather, they tended to look intensely at the to-be-remembered toys more and to name them. Even though the 4-year-olds in the memory condition engaged in strategic behavior more than did the children in the "play" condition, there was no difference in recall of the lists on a subsequent test. Baker-Ward et al. (1984) concluded that 4-year-olds have some memory strategies that are not yet useful to them.

The lack of a strong relationship between the strategies preschoolers use during list learning and their subsequent recall was confirmed by Lange, MacKinnon, and Nida (1989). They presented 3- and 4-year-old children with lists of items to learn and observed the strategies used by the children to learn them. In general, the correlations between use of strategies and recall were low. For instance, the highest was for visual inspection of the to-be-learned items, and it was only $r = 0.27$, a modest relationship at best. Even when data were aggregated over strategies so that children were coded for any use of strategies compared with no use of them, the correlation between being a strategy user and recall was modest, $r = 0.41$. More positively, at least all of these correlations were in the right direction, with strategy use associated with at least slightly increased memory performance. It isn't always so!

Some have reported that preschoolers can elect strategies that actually impair their performances relative to how much they would remember if they were not intentionally trying to remember the material. Newman (1990) used a task and design similar to the one in Baker-Ward et al.'s (1984) study. Moreover, the 4-year-olds in Newman's study evidenced the same strategies when asked to remember that Baker-Ward et al.'s (1984) subjects had. The difference was that the preschoolers in Newman's study in the memory condition remembered less on the subsequent test than preschoolers in the play condition. What was going on in the play condition? The children were creating verbal stories and constructing interactions between the toys. Taking unrelated objects and placing them in a meaningful context, such as a story that sensibly relates them or a picture that integrates them, facilitates memory (e.g., such stories and pictures are **elaborations;** Levin, 1976; Rohwer, 1973). Children who were asked to remember the items applied **rote** procedures, such as rehearsing the items and repeatedly looking at them, procedures that are known to be less efficient in learning lists than elaboration procedures (Levin, 1976; Rohwer, 1973). Sometimes preschoolers elect to use strategies that actually impair their performance.

All of the preschool strategies considered up to this point have been **encoding** strategies, strategies intended to create durable memory traces. What can be concluded from the studies reviewed is that preschoolers sometimes are strategic, although their efforts to create durable memory traces are not always successful. We close this section on preschoolers' use of memory strategies with an example that illustrates that even if preschoolers have a memory trace, that does not mean they will **retrieve** that trace later.

All of the preschool participants in Pressley and MacFadyen (1983) were presented paired associates to learn. Children in the control condition were presented each pair at study as separate pictures (e.g., for the pair rock-turkey, a picture of a rock and a separate picture of a turkey). At testing, the control children were given one of the pictures for each pair and were asked to recall the pairmate. In a second condition, the **elaborated** presentation condition, the pairs were presented in interactive pictures at study (e.g., a picture of a turkey sitting on a rock)— that is, the participants were presented elaborated pictures in which the paired items were embedded in a meaningful context. At testing, a single picture was presented as in the control condition and the preschoolers were asked to remember the pairmate—that is, exactly as it occurred in the control condition. Despite the presentation of the elaborated pictures during study, there was no difference in memory between this second condition and the control condition. This failure to find a performance dif-

ference was striking because presentation of elaborated pictures to slightly older children (i.e., grade 1 and older; Pressley, 1982) reliably improves learning of associations relative to control procedures similar to the ones used by Pressley and MacFadyen (1983). Performance in a third condition, however, made obvious that the elaboration had been encoded and was available in the children's memory to mediate test performance, but that the children in the simple elaborated presentation condition did not think to make use of the image they had encoded when presented the interactive picture. The elaborated presentation plus retrieval cue condition was identical to the elaborated presentation condition except for a change in the directions at testing. Elaborated presentation plus retrieval cue participants were told at testing to "think back to the pictures you saw at study to remember what goes with _____." Performance in this condition was considerably higher than in the simple elaborated presentation condition.

The **retrieval deficiency** detected at the preschool level by Pressley and MacFadyen (1983) is overcome with development. Pressley and MacFadyen (1983) ran the same study with kindergarten children and obtained strikingly different results. At the kindergarten level, simple presentation of elaborated pictures at study was sufficient to boost performance over that obtained in the control condition. Adding the retrieval cue at testing did not enhance performance further with kindergarten children. Using other paradigms, other researchers also noted retrieval difficulties in preschoolers that are not observed in slightly older children (e.g., Ritter, 1978; Sodian & Schneider, 1990).

Prolonged Development of Strategic Competence as the Norm

The clear increases in rehearsal during the elementary years that have been documented in Western cultures are not paralleled by equally dramatic shifts in use of other strategies between 5 and 11 years of age. Consider, for example, how elementary school–age children tackle paired-associate learning. The most efficient strategies for learning paired associates involve **elaborations,** either a verbal elaboration in the form of a meaningful sentence containing both pair members (e.g., *turkeys* have *rocks* in their gizzards) or a meaningful interactive image (e.g., a *turkey* scratching at *rocks* in the barnyard).

The evidence is quite unambiguous that elementary-age children do not use such elaboration strategies on their own (e.g., Pressley & Levin, 1977a, 1977b); even many adults fail to do so (e.g., Bower, 1972; Kliegl, Smith, & Baltes, 1990; Rohwer, 1980a; Rohwer & Litrownik, 1983; Rohwer, Raines, Eoff, & Wagner, 1977).

More positively, by the end of the grade-school years, children elaborate somewhat with some materials and tasks, for example, when reading material that can be related to prior knowledge. For example, Chan, Burtis, Scardamalia, and Bereiter (1992) asked children to think aloud as they processed texts about dinosaurs and germs. With increasing age during the elementary years, students were less likely to rely on rote, surface level processing and make irrelevant associations to text (e.g., associate to a single word in the text) and more likely to relate ideas in the text to one another and to their own prior knowledge in ways that made the ideas more sensible. Even so, there was still room for much more integration and elaboration even among the oldest students, who were in grade 6.

Indeed, there is a recurring theme in the literature on higher education: University students often do not study effectively (e.g., Mathews, 1966, Chapter 7), with failure to use effective memory strategies usually cited prominently in this literature, alongside failures to use effective reading comprehension, writing, and problem-solving procedures. University students' lack of strategic sophistication is recognized by colleges and universities, with most campuses now having study skills courses available. A main focus of such courses is strategies. For example, Devine's (1987) text is one of the most sophisticated of the studies skills textbooks. There is a chapter in Devine's book devoted exclusively to memory strategies, with instruction about imagery elaboration strategies and verbal elaboration procedures among others.

There are many strategies that many adults do not use routinely. Those offering studies skills courses assume that strategies can be taught so that student academic performances increase. Some of the foundational literature supporting this assumption is taken up in the next section. First, a recap follows of what is known about the development of memory strategy competence.

Summary

Whether children use a memory strategy or not varies from strategy to strategy. Some simple strategies, such as looking at a spot where a to-be-remembered item has been hidden, are used routinely by preschool-age children. The familiar setting of their own living room, the familiar materials (e.g., a Bugs Bunny or Big Bird doll usually is the hidden object), and the familiar task (i.e., finding something in the living room) probably combine to permit greater strategic competence by preschoolers in this situation than in other situations (e.g., list learning in a laboratory). Many more complex strategies are not always common even among university-age students. Of course, there are strategies that fall in between in that they are not common with preschoolers nor during the early elementary grades but rather emerge during the later grade-school and high school years (e.g., associative elaboration of paired associates is one of these; Pressley, 1982). Even within Western culture, there is variety in the patterns of strategy development, diversity that cannot be captured by simple summaries.

Rehearsal and elaboration were featured in this section so the reader could consider the main points being made without having to learn about a large number of memory strategies. There are, of course, many other memory strategies. For example, it often pays to study more important information first and more intensely than less important information (e.g., Brown & Smiley, 1978). Also, expending more effort on material not yet learned rather than rehashing material already mastered makes sense (Brown & Smiley, 1978). Other strategies promoting memory will be considered at various point in this book.

Things get more complex when memory strategy data from other cultures are considered. Some cultures encourage use of some strategies more than do other cultures. What strategies a person uses is determined largely by their personal sociocultural history (Kurtz, 1990). Whether parents and educators encourage strategy use in children is an important determinant of whether or not children use strategies. In the next section, we expand on the theme that children often can learn strategies and how to use them.

TEACHING OF STRATEGIES

Early in the last section, it was established that young children often fail to use cumulative rehearsal strategies when they are asked to learn lists. Only brief instruction is required, however, to teach 6- and 7-year-olds how to rehearse lists so they remember them later (e.g., Keeney, Cannizzo, &

Flavell, 1967). Children in kindergarten and grade 3 often fail to make use of organizational properties of lists that can aid memory. Thus, if given a list of items that could be sorted into different categories, which would facilitate memory, kindergarten to grade-3 children often fail to make use of the categories during learning. As was the case with rehearsal, however, it is fairly easy to teach children to sort list items into categories (Moely, Olson, Halwes, & Flavell, 1969). Outcomes such as these motivated the hypothesis that when children fail to use efficient memory strategies, they can be taught to use them. This stimulated many attempts to teach memory strategies to children. By the middle 1970s, there was a massive literature demonstrating that children could be taught to use memory strategies that they did not evidence without instruction (see Pressley, Heisel, McCormick, & Nakamura, 1982, for an overview). Nonetheless, it was also clear that instruction in strategy use was not always sufficient to convert nonstrategic students into strategy users.

Age Differences in Susceptibility to Some Forms of Strategy Instruction

Not all strategies can be taught to all children. This point was established clearly in a number of studies concerned with pair-associate learning, learning of vocabulary-definition associations, and simple prose learning. In a number of studies, children were presented picture paired associates (i.e., pairs of separate pictures with the task of remembering the pairings—a picture of a *turkey* and a *rock*). When preschoolers were asked to construct an interactive image for each pair, there was little facilitation of performance relative to a control condition in which children were given the paired pictures and simply asked to remember the pairings without instruction as to how to do so. This outcome was replicated a number of times by Joel Levin and associates in the 1970s (e.g., Levin, McCabe, & Bender, 1975), with a great deal of evidence converging to suggest that the problem really was in the generation of an image rather than any other factor. Thus, if preschoolers are asked to generate a sentence linking paired items, they can do so easily and it facilitates memory (Levin et al., 1975), making obvious that the failure to benefit from imagery instructions is not due to inability to think of linking relationships.

The ability to generate images that facilitate associative learning develops during the grade-school years. Some of the clearest evidence of this development was produced in research on the **keyword method** of foreign language vocabulary learning. If given a Spanish word (e.g., *carta* meaning *letter*), English-speaking adults can remember the vocabulary-definition linkage by identifying a part of the foreign word that sounds like an English word they already know, a keyword, (e.g., *cart* for *carta*) and generating a linking image between the keyword and the definition referents (e.g., a postal letter in a shopping cart). Grade-6 children have no difficulty applying the keyword method given a foreign word and its meaning. Grade-2 children, however, cannot do so, with the research analytical enough to establish that the difficulty for younger children was in the generation of a linking image (Pressley & Levin, 1978). (Because a number of the main points made in this chapter can be illustrated using research involving this simple strategy, readers should make certain they understand the keyword method before proceeding in this chapter.)

A number of investigations also established that children up to 8 years of age experience difficulties when they are asked to generate images representing the content of prose (e.g., Guttmann, Levin, & Pressley, 1977; Shimron, 1975). More positively, slightly older children benefit from instructions to construct images of prose content (Gambrell & Bales, 1986; Pressley, 1976).

In summary, some strategies that are helpful for older children and adults are not helpful at all for younger children, with the reasons for these developmental differences explored in greater depth later in this chapter. Generating images is one such strategy that has been explored in exceptional detail by researchers. Why susceptibility to imagery instructions increases with development will be taken up later in this chapter.

Continued Use of Strategies Following Instruction

Teaching students how to execute a strategy does not guarantee they will use the strategy on occasions when it would be appropriate to do so. Students sometimes fail to continue using strategies in situations almost identical to the instructional setting. That is, there are failures to **maintain** strategies. **Transfer** failures (sometimes referred to as **generalization** failures) occur when students do not apply strategies they have learned to new situations and tasks, in which the strategies could be applied profitably.

Why are there maintenance and transfer failures? (1) Sometimes students simply do not recognize that a strategy they have learned could be used in a new situation, but they are able to apply the strategy if given gentle hints to do so (Gick & Holyoak, 1980, 1983; Ross, 1984). (2) On other occasions, students recognize that a strategy they know is applicable, but their use of it in the particular situation is so jumbled that the strategy is neither recognizable nor effective (see Harris, 1988). Thus, we remember a student attempting to learn *carta* using the keyword method by identifying *carrot* as a keyword because it contained cart—car_ _t. The student thought of carrots being sent in a large postal letter. The problem later was that when given *carta*, the keyword *carrot* was not remembered, and thus it was impossible to retrieve the linking image between *carrot* and *letter* and impossible to remember the meaning of *carta*, despite the fact that the student had attempted to apply the keyword method during study. (3) Sometimes students do not use a strategy because they do not enjoy carrying it out or do not think that the gains produced by the strategy are worth the effort (e.g., Rabinowitz, Freeman, & Cohen, 1992).

Although it is now recognized that there can be many reasons for maintenance and transfer failures, that was not always the case. A great deal of research was conducted in the last 20 years aimed at identifying the "cause" of maintenance and transfer failures. A popular hypothesis was that the failures represented a **metacognitive** problem and, in particular, were due to a failure of students to understand the utility of the strategies they were learning (e.g., Borkowski, 1985; Brown, Bransford, Ferrara, & Campione, 1983). This possibility will be explored in detail in the sections that follow. Suffice for now to make the point that simply instructing a student about how to carry out a strategy in no way ensures maintenance or generalization of the strategy.

The failure of strategies to transfer beyond training situations is a specific instance of a phenomenon that will be encountered several times in this book. Learning tends to be tied to the context in which it occurs. This is something that has been recognized by researchers from many different perspectives, from Gestalt problem-solving theorists (e.g., Duncker, 1945) to behaviorists (e.g., Stokes & Baer, 1977) to modern cognitive developmentalists (e.g., Brown et al., 1983). One challenge for instruction is to produce learning that is not bound to specific contexts, with examples of how to do that scattered throughout this book.

Is Instruction Necessary? Are There Conditions That Might Facilitate Discovery of Strategies?

Best and Ornstein (Best, 1993; Best & Ornstein, 1986; also see Bjorklund, 1988) have studied whether children might continue to use categorization strategies during list learning if they are induced to use such strategies by practicing list learning with lists that have saliently related items (i.e., items that are easily and obviously categorizable—such as "tiger, bus, carrot, giraffe, celery, van, beans, car, camel...," which is obviously composed of zoo animals, vehicles, and vegetables). In fact, it seems that even children as young as third graders can do so, later using categorization strategies to learn lists containing not easily categorizable items. How is it certain that the learning of the highly related list caused the later strategy use? Because in other conditions of their studies, subjects first practiced learning with lists that did not have easily categorizable elements, with little evidence of use of categorization on subsequent lists. "Spontaneous" use of categorization on later lists was observed only when the third graders first studied lists containing highly relatable items.

Our view is that this is exceptionally important basic research, suggesting that students can discover strategies if they have experiences that support such discoveries. A real challenge is to explore in detail situations that might support the discovery of other strategies. Only through such investigations will it become clear whether it is realistic to expect that students can be encouraged to discover a number of different strategies through environmental manipulations that lead students to carry out the strategies because the materials so strongly suggest the strategic processing.

Summary

When given a memory task, students often fail to use a memory strategy that they could use if given a small amount of instruction about how to apply the strategy to the task in question. That such instruction is often successful was established in many experiments in which one group of children was taught to use a strategy and another group was left to their own devices as they attempted to learn some material. When learning in the instructed condition exceeded learning in the uninstructed condition, researchers concluded that the strategy could be learned and applied profitably to the task at hand by the types of students in the study. More negatively, not all strategies proved to be teachable to all students, with the example of mental imagery discussed explicitly here. Even when students can carry out strategic processes given instruction to do so, there is no guarantee that they will continue to use the strategies so learned. Indeed, there have been many demonstrations of failures to maintain and transfer strategies. Although these failures are probably caused by multiple factors, there was a great deal of research in the last decade examining whether such failures could be linked to metacognitive deficiencies—failures to understand when and where to apply strategies and failures to understand the gains produced by strategies when they are used. These possibilities are considered in detail in the next section.

METACOGNITIVE REGULATION OF STRATEGY USE

An important metacognitive hypothesis about strategy use was that simply teaching a student how to carry out a strategy in no way ensures that the student understands how the strategy benefits performance. Such understanding is critical for a student to continue to use a strategy following instruction. The theory is that such knowledge motivates use of the strategy being taught. This theoretical position stimulated a large number of experiments of the following form (e.g., Borkowski, Levers, & Gruenenfelder, 1976; Cavanaugh & Borkowski, 1979; Kennedy & Miller, 1976; Lawson & Fuelop, 1980; Rao & Moely, 1989; Ringel & Springer, 1980): One group of students was taught a strategy for some task. A second group was taught the same strategy for the same task but also was provided information about the effects of using the strategy on the task (i.e., that use of the strategy would increase learning). The outcome in such experiments was always the same. Students who were informed about the utility of the strategy were more likely to maintain the strategy than students who were not provided the utility information (see Pressley, Borkowski, & O'Sullivan, 1984, 1985, for a review).

Although it was sensible that understanding utility might increase persistent use of a strategy in a

situation extremely similar to the strategy instructional situation, it seemed likely that more would be needed to produce transfer of instructed strategies. For instance, O'Sullivan and Pressley (1984) hypothesized that embellishing strategy instruction with information about when and where the trained strategy might apply (sometimes referred to as **conditional knowledge** about a strategy; e.g., Paris, Lipson, & Wixson, 1983) would increase transfer of the strategy. In their study, children in grades 5 and 6 were taught to use the keyword method to learn associations between cities and the products produced in those cities. For example, that *submarines* are manufactured in *Long Beach* can be remembered by imagining a submarine running ashore on a long beach. The conditions of the study varied with respect to the amount of information that was provided to students about when and where to use the keyword strategy. Thus, children in the most complete instructional condition were taught that the strategy could be applied whenever there were pairings to learn and when it was possible to locate something that could be used as a keyword for the less familiar of the paired items (i.e., the city name for the Long Beach example).

The transfer task in O'Sullivan and Pressley (1984) involved Latin words and their meanings. It is important to emphasize that none of the participants were taught how to apply the keyword method to this task. Use of the keyword strategy to learn Latin words by students who had been taught to use keyword on the city-product task would have indicated transfer of the strategy. In contrast, transfer occurred only when students had been provided information about when and where to apply the keyword strategy as they were being taught its use for learning cities and their products. This was an exceptionally clean test of the hypothesis that strategy-specific/task-specific metamemory affects transfer, a conclusion supported in subsequent research (e.g., Weed, Ryan, & Day, 1990).

An important hypothesis advanced in the late 1970s and early 1980s was that durable use of strategies might be especially likely if strategies were taught using what Brown et al. (1983) referred to as self-controlled training. Such instruction involves teaching a strategy, encouraging the student to evaluate the gains produced by the strategy (i.e., attend to information about the utility of the strategy), and instructing students to remind themselves to use the strategy using self-verbalizations. Asarnow and

Meichenbaum (1979) trained a memory strategy using such a approach.

Asarnow and Meichenbaum selected kindergarten students who did not rehearse when given serial recall memory tasks (determined during observations taken before the experiment began). In the self-controlled training condition, students were taught to rehearse cumulatively when presented a serial recall task. The experimenter first modeled cumulative rehearsal for the students, followed by the child attempting the strategy with the experimenter offering support and additional instruction as needed. The students were taught explicitly to use a question-and-answer regimen to support their application of the cumulative rehearsal strategy to the serial recall task. Here is what the experimenter modeled for the children to convey to them how to self-instruct cumulative rehearsal:

> Now what is it I have to do? I have to find a way to remember the order in which the pictures are pointed to. How can I do that? Hmm. I know I can keep saying the names of the pictures over and over again until it is time to point to the pictures. Let me try it now. I have to remember three pictures . . . That's right. . . . I just keep saying the names of the pictures in the right order. I won't forget the order of the pictures if I keep saying their names in the right order. [The model covered the pictures and continued to repeat the names of the pictures, saying good after each complete series.] Good. I knew I could do it. All you have to do is keep saying the names of the pictures— remembering which picture came first, second, etc. (Meichenbaum & Asarnow, 1979, pp. 21–22)

Notice how much is in this instruction. The operations involved in rehearsal are reiterated several times. The utility of the rehearsal procedure is also emphasized. Moreover, because students were taught to instruct themselves in this way whenever they were presented a serial memory task, the rehearsal strategy was put in a larger framework for the subject. The kindergarten children were not only taught the strategy, but also were taught explicitly to evaluate whether the task they were presented was a serial recall task, and if it was, they were taught to use cumulative rehearsal procedures, including self-testing (i.e., covering up the pictures and checking to see if they could remember them). In short, there were multiple components in this instruction. Students were not only taught the strategy, but also how to use it—how to regulate it.

Did all of this self-control training make a difference? Self-controlled instruction of cumulative rehearsal was compared with more conventional cumulative rehearsal instruction, such as used by Keeney et al. (1967). This more conventional instruction consisted only of teaching the children to say the to-be-remembered pictures over and over. Memory performances in both the self-control training condition and the conventional instructional condition were compared with a control condition as well. Immediately following training, both self-control–trained students and conventionally instructed students outperformed controls. The really interesting data came a week later on a test of strategy maintenance. Only the self-control–trained students used the cumulative rehearsal strategy on this delayed assessment. This is the first of a number of outcomes that will be discussed in this book that suggest that long-term use of cognitive strategies requires instruction that involves a number of components. Effective instruction makes clear when and where to use cognitive strategies and makes obvious how useful cognitive strategies are for the learner. It is essential to do this because students often do not discover such utility information on their own, with this point made clear in the next section, which is concerned with whether and when students discover that cognitive procedures they are using are effective and how such knowledge regulates their use of strategies they know.

Monitoring Strategy Effectiveness: When Do Students Become Aware That a Strategy Is Affecting Their Performance Positively and What Difference Does Such Awareness Make?

Suppose that you are taught a new strategy for a familiar task and try it out. How can you know whether the strategy has worked for you, whether it has improved your performance relative to an old approach with the task? If you do recognize the value of the strategy, does it affect your decision to use the strategy in the future? These questions motivated a number of studies on **monitoring** of strategy effectiveness that were conducted in the 1980s, studies that yielded some surprising but consistent results.

In Pressley, Levin, and Ghatala (1984), adults and children in grades 5 and 6 were asked to learn some foreign vocabulary words. All participants were taught the keyword method and were asked to use it for half of the words that were presented on the first vocabulary list that they studied. For the remaining words on this first study list, they were required to rehearse the word and its meaning over and over (i.e., use rehearsal). As expected, items studied using the keyword method were learned better than those studied using rehearsal. More important, however, was that when the participants were asked to estimate how much vocabulary had been learned with keyword versus rehearsal immediately after the words were studied, *but before a memory test on the items,* neither the adults nor the children recognized that the keyword-studied items had been learned better. The students were not monitoring the effectiveness of the two strategies as they used them. Once given a test over the vocabulary items that had been studied with the two different procedures, there was clear perception by the adults that the items studied using the keyword method had been learned better than the ones studied using rehearsal. Following testing, children in the study also recognized there was a difference in learning favoring the keyword-studied items, although they were not as aware of how great an advantage the keyword method had produced.

That learners often fail to monitor how a strategy is affecting them as they use it has been demonstrated on a number of occasions. That learners can come to realize that a strategy is effective in promoting learning by being tested on what they learned with one strategy versus another also has been demonstrated on a number of occasions (Ghatala, 1986; Hunter-Blanks, Ghatala, Pressley, & Levin, 1988; Pressley & Ghatala, 1990).

What difference did awareness of differential strategy effectiveness have on decisions to use the more effective keyword strategy for future learning? After the test, when required to choose one of the two strategies to use to learn a new vocabulary list, both the adults and the children overwhelmingly chose the keyword method, specifying that they were doing so because it was more effective than rehearsal. There was some evidence that the adults were much more convinced of the effectiveness of the keyword method based on their perceptions of their test performance than the children were, however. There were several conditions in the experiment in which the experimenter tried to convince the participants that the rehearsal method was the better method. After taking the test, the adults would not believe this experimenter argument, although they believed it before the test. That is, once having seen for themselves on the test that they had learned more with the keyword method, the adults

adamantly resisted the suggestion that rehearsal was better. With children, it was a different story. The experimenter was able to talk the children into using the rehearsal strategy instead of the keyword strategy, even after the children had figured out on the test that they had done better with the keyword method. A fairly complicated follow-up study was conducted to determine whether experimenter intimidation was playing a role here or whether the children were persuaded by the experimenter because their perceptions of differential effectiveness were not that certain. Intimidation could not explain the results in the follow-up study. Unless provided detailed feedback about how they did on keyworded versus rehearsed items, children were uncertain of their perception that the keyworded items were learned better. When children and adults in Pressley, Levin, and Ghatala (1984) knew for certain that one strategy helped relative to another strategy (and with the children, this required explicit feedback), knowledge of strategy utility determined future use of the strategy, consistent with the point made earlier in this chapter that knowing the utility of a strategy affects maintenance of it.

In Pressley, Levin, and Ghatala (1984), all of the participants had an opportunity to compare how they did with the keyword strategy versus rehearsal. Often when students are taught a new strategy, however, they are not given an explicit opportunity to compare it with other strategies. Rather, they are taught the strategy and asked to use it exclusively. Pressley, Levin, and Ghatala (1988) conducted a study to determine whether maintenance of the keyword strategy would be likely when students were taught the strategy and practiced it alone. The evidence was clear. Simply practicing the keyword method and taking a test on keyword-learned items without an opportunity to compare this performance with learning using other methods resulted in little maintenance of the keyword method 2 weeks later. When participants in the study were given a chance to compare how they did with the keyword method relative to more familiar methods, they recognized better the relative effectiveness of the keyword method and were more likely to use the keyword method 2 weeks after their initial learning and practice of it. This finding is important because instruction in new ways (i.e., new strategies) of doing things so often involves simply teaching the new procedure and having the student practice it. The Pressley, Levin, and Ghatala (1988) data would suggest that maintenance of the newly taught strategy would be unlikely given such instruction, and indeed failures of maintenance following such instruction are common (for a review, see Pressley, Borkowski, & O'Sullivan, 1984, 1985). "Try it" to see whether it works is not pedagogically sound advisement; "try it" and then "compare how you did with the new approach versus your old approach" is much sounder.

In concluding that strategy comparison opportunities can lead to better understanding of the utility of a strategy, which in turn leads to continued use of a newly learned, effective procedure, it is important to emphasize that this finding holds with young adults. The clear effects of strategy comparison opportunities are not as certain with either children (recall Pressley, Levin, & Ghatala's, 1984, data) or older adults, as detailed in what follows.

Children   In Pressley, Ross, Levin, and Ghatala (1984), 10- to 13-year-old students practiced learning vocabulary definitions with two strategies, the keyword method and a more familiar method, although one that does not promote learning of vocabulary definitions well (see Pressley, Levin, & McDaniel, 1987, for a review): composing sentences in which new vocabulary are used correctly. After studying lists of vocabulary using the two methods, all of the children took a test over the vocabulary that had been studied with the two procedures. As expected, the keyword method produced reliably better learning than the make-a-sentence method.

The critical data involved choice of a strategy when the children were asked to learn another list of vocabulary. After practicing the two strategies, taking a test and recalling better the vocabulary that was learned with the keyword method than with the sentence method, only 42% of the children selected the keyword method for learning another list of definitions. This was despite the fact that three out of four of the students knew they had recalled more keyworded items on the test than sentence-studied items.

Pressley, Ross, Levin, and Ghatala (1984) had anticipated this result based on other work they had done. They believed that in making a strategy choice, children would not make use of utility knowledge they possessed about the two strategies (knowledge derived from the previous practice list and test over words learned with the two strategies). If that was the case, the authors reasoned that cuing the students to make use of what they knew about

the relative utility of the two strategies might make a difference in their strategy selections. Thus, Pressley, Ross, et al. (1984) included a condition in which subjects were told just before they made their strategy selection to consider how they had performed on the practice list and test in making a strategy selection:

> I want you to think back to the words you just remembered. Did you remember more of the words when you used [the keyword method], or did you remember more words when you made up a sentence using the word correctly. Which type of word did you remember more of, the ones you [used the keyword method for] or the words that you made a sentence using the word correctly. (p. 497)

When the children were provided this prompt before strategy selection, they selected the keyword strategy 89 percent of the time. What this study demonstrated was that children could possess metacognitive knowledge (i.e., in this case that the keyword method is more effective than the make-a-sentence method), knowledge that could be used in selecting a more effective strategy, but fail to use it in making a strategy selection. If children in the middle-elementary grades are to use their knowledge of strategy utility in making strategy selections, this study suggested it might be necessary to prompt them to use the utility knowledge they possess.

With younger children, it is clear, given a series of studies that were supervised principally by Ghatala (Ghatala, Levin, Pressley, & Goodwin,1986; see Ghatala, 1986, for an overview), that even more is required. As in most of the other research described in this subsection, children in the early grade-school years practiced two strategies, one of which was much more effective than the other in mediating a learning task. Then the children were required to choose one or the other strategy on a maintenance test. Grade-2 children did not select the more effective strategy on a maintenance trial, unless they were specifically instructed while they practiced the two procedures and took tests over the content learned with the two procedures to (1) assess how they were doing with the two strategies, (2) attribute performance differences as due to use of different strategies, and (3) use the knowledge they had gained about the utility of strategies in making their future strategy selections. When (but only when) the grade-2 children were instructed to assess, make attributions, and use strategy utility knowledge, they selected the more effective strategy 90 percent of the time. There was abundant evidence in this study that when grade-2 children simply practice two differentially effective strategies and take a test over practice items, little usable metacognitive knowledge about strategies (i.e., understanding that one is more effective than the other) is produced. For children to come to understand that the more effective strategy is more effective and that its effects on performance should be taken into account in making future strategy selections, primary-grades children must be given explicit instruction to attend to their performance differences, interpret these differences as indicators of relative strategy effectiveness, and use this information in future decision making.

In drawing these conclusions, we also recognize that there is evidence in list-learning situations that 5- to 8-year-olds become more aware of how many items they are likely to recall on a list-learning trial as a function of learning similarly demanding practice lists and being tested on the practice lists (e.g., Cunningham & Weaver, 1989), sometimes adjust their use of rehearsal as a function of whether the rehearsal strategy they just used was successful (McGilly & Siegler, 1989), and can in some situations coordinate use of rehearsal and other strategies (e.g., categorization of list items) to learn content (Cox, Ornstein, Naus, Maxfield, & Zimler, 1989). Unfortunately, none of this work was analytical enough to provide detailed knowledge of children's perceptions of their performances and how those perceptions affect future strategies selections. We are confident, however, based on the Pressley, Levin, and Ghatala data, that reflective strategy shifting does not occur much of the time with children in the primary-grades years and that it is not habitually efficient in the later grade-school years either. For complementary data using different tasks that corroborate our conclusion that there is development during the grade-school years in the coordination of performance awareness and decisions about academic processing, see Nelson-Le Gall, Kratzer, Jones, and DeCooke (1990).

Older Adults Brigham and Pressley (1988) used a setup similar to all of the other experiments discussed in this subsection. As in Pressley, Levin, and Ghatala (1984), participants practiced learning vocabulary with two strategies; one was the keyword method and the other was a less powerful alternative, making up sentences in which the new vocabulary were used correctly. The subjects in this study were younger (24 to 39 years of age) and older (60 to 88 years of age) adults.

The younger adults behaved just as the younger adults in Pressley, Levin, and Ghatala (1984) had behaved: They recognized during the test that they had learned many more words using the keyword method than using the sentence method. When they were presented another list of vocabulary to learn, the younger adults selected the keyword method. They based their decision on the greater utility of the keyword method relative to the sentence method.

The older participants' behaviors were different. Although they recognized during testing that they had learned more using the keyword method than the sentence method, they were not as aware as the younger subjects just how great an edge the keyword method provided. More interesting, however, was that the greater utility of the keyword method was much less of a determinant of subsequent strategy selections for the older compared with the younger participants. Although 93 percent of the younger participants made their subsequent strategy choice based on relative utility of the two strategies, only 47 percent of the older adults did so. The older adults were much more likely than the younger adults to select the less effective strategy, basing their selection on factors other than effectiveness. Often they chose the make-a-sentence method because they perceived it to be easier to carry out than the keyword method or because it was more familiar, being a strategy that they had used for many years. Selecting a strategy because it increases learning is much more an approach taken by younger than older adults, consistent with observations in other domains that older adults are much more likely to take a variety of factors into consideration when approaching a problem than are younger adults (Labouvie-Vief, 1985).

Summary When trying a new strategy, people typically are not aware of the effect the strategy is having on their performance unless there is an opportunity to compare performance when the new strategy is used versus alternative procedures. Understanding the differential effectiveness of strategies also requires a test over content studied using the different strategies—people do not seem to monitor well how much they are learning while they are actually studying (a point taken up again later in this chapter). Compared both with children and older adults, young adults more accurately monitor how great an advantage an effective strategy provides relative to a less effective strategy. Moreover, compared with children and older adults, young adults more certainly use their perceptions of differential strategy utility in making decisions about subsequent strategy use. When children monitor differences in test performance and understand that the differences are due to the differential effectiveness of strategies used during study, they seem not to understand that such information should be used in making subsequent strategy decisions. Other times they seem not to monitor the occurrence of differential performance effects or interpret such differences as reflecting differences in strategy effectiveness unless they are explicitly instructed to do so.

With older adults, their perceptions of differential strategy effectiveness may not be as accurate as those of young adults. There is more to their lower reliance on utility information in making strategy decisions, however. Although younger adults used knowledge of differential strategy utility to the exclusion of other considerations in making strategy selections, older adults were more likely to base their strategy selections on a variety of factors.

A good deal was learned about metacognitive regulation of strategies in the studies summarized in this section. A strong case could be constructed from this body of work that knowing when and where a strategy is useful can often be a determinant of strategy use. It also must be emphasized, however, that this is not a strict rule. People sometimes know a strategy is useful and appropriate, and they still elect not to use it. This suggests that factors other than metacognition often determine how humans go about their learning, a theme advanced in most sections of this book.

We emphasize in closing this section that students who do not naturally discover strategies can come to use them—all of those university study skills centers are not efforts in vain! Detailed evaluations of university-level study skills courses complement well the themes covered in this chapter. Learning the strategies is not enough; improving achievement also depends on learning how to choose strategies and doing so (e.g., Nist, Simpson, Olejnik, & Mealey, 1991).

PRODUCTION SYSTEMS AND OTHER COGNITIVE-THEORETICAL CONSIDERATIONS RELATED TO USE AND INSTRUCTION OF STRATEGIES

A frequent claim that has been presented to us when we give talks about strategies and their metacognitive regulation is that strategies seem to be specific instances of **productions,** particularly as they are specified in a model of thinking known as **ACT* theory** (e.g., Anderson, 1983). There are important similarities between strategies already considered in this chapter and the productions of ACT*.

Discussion of productions at this point as conceived in ACT* theory permits introduction of some important theoretical distinctions regarding forms of knowledge and the relationship of knowledge to structures of the mind. Strategies are different from productions, however, and thus this section concludes with an overview of some of the more striking differences between the two constructs.

At its most basic level, a production specifies some action and when the action should occur. Typically, productions are represented in "if-then" form, with the "if" portion establishing when the production should occur, and the "then" portion establishing the action that will occur when the conditions specified by the "if" portion of the production are met.

One function of productions is to permit recognition and classification of stimuli encountered in the environment, such as the following:

> If an animal has four legs,
> and the animal has an elliptical head,
> and the animal is longer than tall,
> and the animal is less than a foot and a half high,
> and the animal has claws,
> Then classify the animal as a cat.

> If an equation has the form $y = ax^2 + bx + c$,
> then classify the equation as a quadratic.

These **pattern recognition** productions are important because a situation must be recognized before it is possible to determine whether the conditions are met for other actions. Thus, in the following example, cat and sofa must be recognized by the system before it could be evaluated whether the conditions for the production are met:

> If a cat is on the sofa,
> then shoo the cat.

In the following, a quadratic must be recognized before there could be evaluation of whether the production applied:

If an equation is quadratic,
and the goal is to know the value of x,
then apply the formula of
$x = (-b \pm \sqrt{b^2 - 4ac})/2a$.

What patterns must be recognized before this production could operate?

If it is Monday,
and it is 2 P.M.,
then I go to my educational psychology course.

(Answer = Monday and 2 P.M.).

All of the if information in these examples could be thought of as conditional knowledge, metacognitive information about when and where the action in question applies. In general, the if information in action-sequence productions must be recognized via pattern-recognition productions before it can be determined whether or not the conditions for the action sequence are met. With productions, whenever the if conditions are met, the action associated with the if information occurs. If this sounds mechanical, it should, for production system models were developed and tested in artificial intelligence (i.e., computer) environments.

What is coded into the action portion of productions is **procedural** knowledge—knowledge of how to do things (e.g., strategic actions are procedures in this sense). The if portions of the productions specify when the actions (procedures) should be carried out. Human beings and computers know much more than how to do things, however. They also possess a great deal of factual information, **declarative knowledge.** Procedural knowledge is knowing *how*; declarative knowledge is knowing *that*, a distinction that has been recognized for some time by philosophers (e.g., Ryle, 1949) and cognitive theorists (e.g., Kolers, 1975; Scheffler, 1965).

The amount of declarative information possessed by any human being is enormous. Here are some examples from my own [MP] knowledge base:

I live outside Albany, New York.
My son is Tim.

The New York Yankees dominated the American League in the 1950s.
A square has four sides and four right angles.
Dostoyevsky wrote *The Brothers Karamazov*.
Richard Nixon was the only U.S. president to resign from office.
The department secretary, Stacy, bought a lot of paper for this school year.

Of course, this declarative knowledge is not disconnected, but rather there are many interconnections to other knowledge. Thus, a Yankee fan's understanding that the Yankees dominated the American League in the 1950s is linked rather strongly to knowledge of Mickey Mantle, Roger Maris, and Casey Stengel, all of whom were with the Yankees in the 1950s. It is also associated with knowledge that the Yankees' uniforms had bold pinstripes on them. Moreover, some of the knowledge about the Yankees links to other knowledge about the American League. So, when baseball fans think of the 1950s Yankees, they think of DiMaggio, which leads to thoughts of Ted Williams, who played for Boston. Memories of the 1950s Yankees link the book, *The Year the Yankees Lost the Pennant,* which is associated with the play based on the book, *Damn Yankees,* which might prompt some "golden oldies" in the mind's ear, such as Buddy Holly songs or early Elvis Presley hits.

There are many distinctions between procedural and declarative knowledge (Tulving, 1983, pp. 8–9): For example, procedural knowledge can be demonstrated only by performing the procedure. Evidence of declarative knowledge can come in a variety of forms (e.g., recall, recognition, application, association to other knowledge). Procedural knowledge is neither true nor false, whereas the truth value of much of declarative knowledge can be determined. Procedural knowledge is often acquired only after extensive practice. Much declarative knowledge is acquired with a single exposure.

Both procedural and declarative knowledge are stored in **long-term memory** stores. For all practical purposes, human long-term stores are unlimited, or at least there are no apparent limits. (Those who have run out of space on their computer hard drives know, however, that the same is not true of computers, although long-term storage on computers can be increased infinitely by adding "memory.")

When people or computers are using what they know—that is, when procedures are operating on declarative information, it happens in **working memory. Working** memory is often thought of as active consciousness or active memory. (Although there are some conceptual differences between working memory and **short-term memory,** these distinctions are more subtle than is required to understand the ideas used in this text, so working memory and short-term memory will be used somewhat interchangeably in this book and occasionally will be referred to as "attentional capacity.") The capacity of human short-term memory is extremely limited, with Miller (1956) presenting data that humans can hold only seven plus or minus two pieces of information in active consciousness at any one time.

A short thought experiment will make apparent the capacity limitations of short-term memory. Read the following list of digits one time, attempting to remember them, and then turn away from the page and try to recall them in order:

1, 8, 1, 2, 9, 8, 5, 8, 3

How did you do? A good bet is that you did not remember all nine digits despite the fact they had just been processed. You were certainly conscious of the numbers as you processed them (i.e., they were in short-term memory), but memory of each one faded quickly. That is what working memory is like—it is extremely short-term, lasting only as long as there is active working on its content. All of human thinking has to deal with the short-term memory "bottleneck" (i.e., it is not very big and it is fragile), and there will be several occasions in this book when specific recommendations will be made as to how to work around short-term memory limitations. (Again, computers are not nearly as limited, with many machines having the capacity to hold many pieces of information in active memory as they make a large number of complex computations on them.)

For the time being, do not worry much about declarative knowledge, which is the focus of Chapter 3, or short-term memory, which will be encountered often in this book. We introduced declarative knowledge at this point (1) simply to stress that procedural and declarative knowledge work together in cognition—consistent with the claim introduced in Chapter 1 that strategies and nonstrategic knowledge work together and (2) because in the next subsection, the case will be made that procedural knowledge starts as declarative knowledge. What follows in the remainder of this subsection is mostly about

procedural knowledge and mostly about when it is activated—that is, in working memory.

Many have espoused the view that development of procedural knowledge is an especially important mission of school. Tulving (1983, p. 52) provided an especially elegant statement of this point:

> . . . [p]rocedures learned in school—reading, writing, and arithmetic, and their higher-level equivalents—are better retained and more useful to people in life than is most [declarative] knowledge. A person who has learned how to learn and study in school, how to use sources of information, how to solve problems, and other similar skills, is much better equipped for what awaits him or her after school than is a hypothetical individual who has perfectly memorized everything in the curriculum.

Many of the chapters in this book specify educational programs that are intended to increase procedural knowledge. The steps of these strategies could be put in production form. Consider this strategy for estimating the solution to a multicolumn addition problem (based on Reys, 1984):

> If it is a problem with two multicolumn numbers and a plus sign between them, then it is a multicolumn addition problem.
> If it is a multicolumn addition problem and the goal is to estimate, then use the front end digits in the problem, rounding these based on the digits in the second-to-front column (e.g., for 8,294 + 3,885, use 8 and 4).

Many writing strategies can be reduced to plan-translate-revise cycles (see Chapter 15, this volume). Here is a set of production-type statements specifying one cycle through these three phases:

> If the goal is to write an essay on a content area, then search prior knowledge for information about the content and search external sources for information about the content.
> If information about the content has been identified, organize that information in a fashion consistent with the message one wants to convey and make an outline.
> If an outline has been constructed, then translate the outline into sentences and paragraphs until a first draft is accomplished.
> If a first draft is completed, then reread the draft and revise.

In each case, the product produced by a previous step in the overall strategy serves as part of the condition specifying the firing of the subsequent production.

Acquisition of Procedural Knowledge

According to Anderson's theory (e.g., Neves & Anderson, 1981), all procedural knowledge starts out as declarative knowledge. That is, how to do something starts out as a verbal characterization of the procedure. Thus, to continue with the keyword method example used earlier, when the learner first learns the method, they may have it represented something like the following:

> First, look to see if you have to remember two things go together. If that is what is required, then look to see if the less familiar term has some part that is familiar. Take that familiar part and make an image between it and the to-be-associated information.

When learners are first using the keyword method, they are conscious of each of the steps, perhaps even saying them aloud or at least verbalizing some of the steps (e.g., *carlin* sounds like car . . . an old lady could drive a car). In addition, it is not at all unusual for there to be errors during this stage (e.g., old lady has lad in it . . . I'll imagine a lad drinking a Carling's Black Label). With practice, errors become less frequent. There is less need to verbalize overtly. Execution of the entire sequence becomes smoother until the strategy is no longer a sequence of declarative directions but now one fluent procedure. The movement from declarative representation of a sequence of actions to a single procedure is known as **proceduralization.**

When a sequence of cognitive actions is represented declaratively, it is carried out slowly and with a high cost with respect to cognitive capacity (i.e., working or short-term memory). Most critically, more of this limited short-term capacity must be expended when executing a declarative sequence than an integrated procedure. For instance, when first learning an action sequence, the student will have to interpret each step as they do it (e.g., can I find something in this foreign word that sounds or looks like a word in my native language? . . . I wonder how close it has to be? . . . What if it sounds like an English word but looks a little different?. . .). Such interpretation and step-by-step consideration requires cognitive capacity (i.e., short-term or working memory). With practice, the sequence can be executed automatically and without the need to interpret the steps in the sequence.

A nonstrategic example can illustrate proceduralization well. Last year, my [MP] university acquired a new phone system with a phone mail sys-

tem. The first time I used it, I read each line of the direction from the card provided by the phone company and spent a lot of time making certain I understood each line. A few trials later, I was saying to myself, "Dial in 5-5-1-0-0 and wait until it answers, then punch in the extension. . . ." That did not work because I forgot to hit the pound sign after keying in the extension number! One more trial later, I was still verbally directing myself step-by-step but hitting the pound signs appropriately. Gradually, there was less and less verbal self-cuing. In fact, I can now do the entire key sequence without thinking about it, with my fingers moving automatically as I do so. The proof that not much short-term capacity is being used when I access the answering device is that I can easily do other things as my fingers run through the sequence (e.g., talk to a graduate student or think about what to put in one of the chapters of this book). For a good example of how proceduralization of a skill frees up cognitive processing and thus permits a person to be able to be more strategic, see Wierda and Brookhuis' (1991) analysis of how skilled bicyclists can perform another task while bicycling much better than can unskilled bicyclists.

Short-Term Memory Capacity: A Critical Individual Differences Variable

One value of a well worked out, detailed theory such as the ACT* conception of how cognitive procedures are executed is that it illuminates many different factors that might affect procedural competence: Whether a procedure is executed in a situation in which it would benefit performance depends on a number of factors. One, of course, is whether the learner has the procedure in long-term memory (i.e., knows the strategy). The learner also requires conditional knowledge about procedures (the ifs) to use them appropriately. Another determining factor is whether the learner possesses declarative knowledge that can be used in conjunction with the procedure. In addition to all of these components, all of which were considered earlier in the discussion of strategies, another determinant of whether and how well a strategy will be executed is that the learner has sufficient working memory capacity to execute the strategy in question. Strategies, similar to all procedures, are always executed in short-term memory.

So how do procedural and declarative knowledges work together? Consider the following example. Suppose an English-speaking student who has been taught the keyword method is presented a list of new Spanish vocabulary to learn. Consider the first word on the list, *carlin* meaning *elderly lady.* *Carlin–elderly lady* would be in active, short-term memory. Because the task is to learn the association between two elements and one of the elements is relatively unfamiliar (in this case, a foreign word) and the unfamiliar element contains a portion of it that sounds like an English word that is already well-known by the student (i.e., *car*), the keyword method procedure is activated into consciousness (i.e., short-term memory). That is, the three conditions (i.e., the three *if*s) required for use of the keyword method hold in this instance, and thus the keyword method procedure (i.e., the *then*) is carried out.

Long-term declarative memory also plays a role here, however. Application of the keyword procedure involves noting the keyword for an item and then searching long-term declarative memory for images of keyword and definition referents and for a relationship linking the keyword and definition. The learner's long-term memory includes images of cars and elderly ladies. One of each is activated. In addition, declarative knowledge includes a specification of how cars and elderly ladies can be related. For example, elderly ladies can drive cars. Application of the keyword method procedure results in the learner creating an image of an elderly lady driving a car. In summary, external input, long-term procedural knowledge, and long-term declarative knowledge are activated into working memory whenever a procedure operates. A lot of information must be activated and juggled simultaneously.

An hypothesis that follows from the fact that strategy execution is short-term memory capacity demanding is that those who have relatively larger short-term memory capacities will be more likely to be able to execute capacity-demanding strategies. Recall the earlier discussion about developmental differences in children's imagery-generation abilities. Pressley, Cariglia-Bull, Deane, and Schneider (1987) and Cariglia-Bull and Pressley (1990) investigated whether the ability to carry out imagery instructions is linked to differences in working-memory/short-term–memory capacity. The researchers anticipated a wide range of differences in the short-term capacities of the 6- to 12-year-olds who participated in their studies. Thus, tests were administered to participants to determine which students had rel-

atively greater and which had relatively smaller short-term memory capacities.

One of these tests involved learning lists of words varying from 3 items in length to 12 items in length. People with greater short-term capacity perform better on such tasks than people with lesser capacity, with those with greater capacity having less difficulty with the longer lists than those with less capacity. A second individual difference measure tapped in the study was general verbal competence of the participants (e.g., a measure of standardized reading achievement was used for this purpose in Cariglia-Bull & Pressley, 1990). After the short-term memory and verbal competence individual differences measures were collected in both the Pressley et al. (1987) and Cariglia-Bull and Pressley (1990) studies, the grade-school students who served as subjects in the studies were presented sentences to learn such as the following:

> The angry bird shouted at the white dog.
> The toothless man sat on the orange couch.
> The fat boy ran with the grey balloon. (Cariglia-Bull & Pressley, p. 396).

There were two conditions in both studies. In one condition, the children were instructed to attempt to to visualize the meaning of each sentence in their head. Control subjects were left to their own devices to learn the sentences, instructed to try really hard to learn them. After presentation of 10 sentences, the experimenter cued recall of each sentence by presenting the sentence subject (e.g., tell me about the boy sentence; tell me about the bird sentence).

The results were clear. As expected, general verbal competence did predict performance on this task. More critically, however, in the imagery-instructional condition, short-term memory capacity predicted performance even after verbal competence and age of the learner were taken into account. Short-term capacity had no predictive value in the control condition. That is, when students were asked to use a capacity-demanding imagery strategy, the benefits of the instruction were greater for students with relatively great short-term capacity compared with students with less capacity, with this claim holding even when general ability was taken into account. The ability to execute a short-term capacity-demanding strategy, such as imagery generation, depends on the amount of capacity one has.

Capacity differences may affect use of strategies in other ways, however. Consider another digit-span task. Like the one presented earlier, you will be given a row of digits for each trial and should try to remember them in order. Once the list has been read once, turn away from the book and try to recall it. There are four lists that follow, so you will be reading four times and turning away to attempt recall four times. Here are the lists:

5,4,8,5,7,3,8,5,7,0,3,5,1,7,6,7
4,8,7,3,5,6,7,3,4,5,2,9,3,5,9,8,6,8,5,6,8,5,0
9,2,4,7,5,9,2,3,8,7,4,2,9,8,4,1,3,0,9,4,8,4,1,3,8,4,5,7,1
4,6,4,3,8,7,9,4,5,7,8,5,4,3,3,5,6,7,8,6,8,9,3,2,6,5,7

Was it fun having heavy demand put on your capacity? Would you want to continue with more lists? If you are like many students we have taught, the answers are no and no: It is not fun doing a capacity-demanding task, and no thanks, most students pass on the opportunity to do more such lists! Guttentag (1984; also Guttentag, Ornstein, & Siemens, 1987) proposed that one of the reasons children may not use more strategies than they do is because many strategies are capacity demanding for them and thus somewhat unpleasant to carry out. Consistent with this hypothesis, as children's knowledge increases with development and is increasingly accessible (i.e., accessible with less effort), strategies that depend on knowledge for their operation (e.g., categorization during learning of categorizable lists, elaboration of paired associates) are easier to carry out and hence less capacity demanding. Moreover, the less capacity demanding a strategy is with development, the more certain the strategy is to be used (e.g., Bjorklund & Harnishfeger, 1987; Kee, in press).

Low capacity has the potential to undermine strategic competence in several ways. Some strategies require more capacity than some students possess. For students who have sufficient capacity to carry out particular capacity-demanding strategies, the strain associated with doing so may be so great that they simply will not use the strategy when in a free-choice situation.

In summary, ACT* theory emphasizes the criticality of short-term capacity as a bottleneck in cognition, consistent with a long history of cognitive theory and research extending back to Miller (1956). Once ACT* theory was available, no discussion of procedural competence (e.g., strategic competence) has been considered complete without discussion of potential short-term capacity constraints. Thus, the discussion of ACT* theory led us to a brief reconsideration of strategy instruction and strategy use in light of short-term memory demands and limitations. At several points in the book, there will be explicit discussion about how educational psychologists deal with short-term capacity demands and constraints so as to design instruction that does not overwhelm the short-term capacities of students.

Summary: How Strategies and Productions Are Similar and Different

Strategies are similar to the productions of ACT* theory in that both strategies and productions specify cognitive actions, are stored in long-term memory, and are regulated by conditional knowledge. Both operate on external input and nonstrategic declarative knowledge, which is also stored in long-term memory, only transferred into a working, shorter-term store when needed as part of conscious thought involving procedures. According to ACT* theory, if the conditions associated with a procedure are met (i.e., if the *ifs* occur), the procedure is transferred from long-term memory to short-term memory and executed, with the nonstrategic knowledge required to carry out the procedure also activated into short-term memory as the procedure needs the knowledge to operate.

For strategies, things are not nearly so certain. Strategies often fail to be used even when all the ifs are met, even on occasions when efforts have been made to ensure that students know when and where a strategy applies. Whether a strategy is executed depends on other factors, not the least of which is student motivation. Motivation does not play a role in ACT* theory. In short, the theory of good thinking in this book is sensitive to more factors than is ACT* theory, although ACT* theory is a powerful theory as far as it goes. ACT* theory will come up again in the next chapter on knowledge and its representation.

CONCLUDING COMMENTS

The theory and data considered in this chapter suggest a number of conclusions that in fact will prove to be extremely general, consistent with a great deal of theory and data presented in later chapters. Here are the most important of them:

1. Very young children are now viewed as more competent than they were 20 years ago, when psychology was dominated by models such as Piaget's theory (e.g., 1983; see Chapter 7 in this volume), in which preschoolers were portrayed in negative terms, in terms of what they could not do. Consistent with the theme of preschooler competence, which pervades the developmental and educational psychology literature of the 1990s, this chapter reviewed impressive strategic competencies during the preschool years. Even 2-year-olds evidence some simple strategies on some occasions.

2. More negatively, young adults seem less competent in the 1990s than they did in the 1960s and 1970s. Again, this reflects a shift in models in the last three decades. The preferred theories of the 1960s, such as Piaget's perspectives on formal operations, portrayed late adolescence as a period of enormous intellectual power (see Chapter 7, this volume). In contrast, the analyses inspired by information-processing theories, such as the study of strategies and ACT* theory, have revealed important gaps in the knowledge of young adults. The conclusion that young adults are not as competent as they could be will be reiterated in a number of places in this book, even though we are generally optimistic about cognitive development.

3. One reason to be upbeat about the development of students' minds is that there is voluminous evidence that when people do not carry out a procedure when left unprompted, they can carry it out if instructed to do so. Moreover, although transfer failures are common, much is being learned about how to encourage greater transfer of procedural knowledge learned through instruction, including transfer of strategies taught in actual classrooms (e.g., see Chapter 14, this volume). In short, instruction counts and human intellectual competencies are plastic (e.g., Lerner, 1986; Scarr & Kidd, 1983). A child in a rich instructional environment is more likely to be a good thinker than a child who endures schooling that does not convey important procedural and declarative knowledge.

4. There are age-related increases in use of strategies during the schooling years. Such increases often do not reflect biologically mediated advantages for older compared with younger students, however, but rather reflect greater schooling (and other cultural) experiences for older compared with younger students.

5. Conditional knowledge (i.e., metacognitive knowledge about where and when a procedure applies and the gains conveyed by a procedure) is a critical determinant of whether maintenance and transfer of procedural knowledge occur. Such knowledge is not always derived by students on their own (i.e., not all students monitor well performance gains as a result of a new strategy), with younger students at greater risk than older students for failing to discover critical metacognitive information as new procedures are practiced. Moreover, knowing when and where a procedure applies and that it benefits performance in particular ways does not guarantee that the procedure will be used appropriately. Some people sometimes use other factors (e.g., motivation to perform the task) to decide whether and when to use the strategic procedures they know.

6. Good thinking does not always work as mechanically as the thinking specified by models such as ACT*. Good thinking involves more components than models such as ACT*, with the failure of models such as ACT* to include motivational considerations especially striking. Student motivation often plays a critical factor in whether and when strategies are used (see Chapter 5).

7. Acquisition of procedural knowledge often takes a while. At first, execution is slow and often guided and supported by verbal representations of the sequence of actions composing the procedure. With experience, strategies are executed faster, with less explicit verbal mediation and with less demand on short-term capacity.

8. Educational interventions must be designed so the procedures can be carried out given the short-term capacities of targeted students. Strategies that require more capacity than students possess will not facilitate performance because the students will not be able to execute them; strategies that are within a student's capacity but are stressful to carry out because they require much of the available capacity may not be elected by students. It is aversive to carry out procedures that stretch one's capacity to its limits.

The basic research on strategies featured in this chapter is extremely important, for the insights produced in it have affected greatly the instruction of much more complex, academically important strategies—for reading, writing, and problem solving. A variety of strategies will be covered in this book with many associations documented between use of strategies matched to academic demands, developmental level, and academic achievement. In general, it will become clear that older students know more strategies for accomplishing tasks than do younger students. For example, Berg (1989) interviewed students in grades 5, 8, and 11 about how they would solve everyday problems encountered in school and outside of school. With increasing age, students endorsed strategies considered to be effective by adults.

Good students definitely know and use more strategies (as well as more effective strategies) to accomplish school tasks than do weaker students: Good students take notes, they plan essays, they prepare strategically for tests, and they schedule their time so schoolwork and everything else in their lives can occur (e.g., Zimmerman, 1990a, 1990b; Zimmerman & Martinez-Pons, 1986, 1988). Although sophisticated task analyses of academic tasks contributed much to the development of academic strategies, so did the developmental and metacognitive basic research reviewed in this chapter. Work on the development of memory strategies sensitized educational researchers to the possible differences in strategy functioning at different developmental levels; work on metacognitive regulation of memory strategies has been more analytical than most other metacognitive research, with the insights about metacognition obtained in basic studies consistently informing the development of instruction of more complex strategies.

Knowledge

This chapter is concerned with how knowledge can be represented and organized in long-term memory. Long-term memory includes representations of everything from the 26 letters of the alphabet and the numbers, to the concept "mother" and knowledge that some animals are more closely related to one another than other animals as well as images of dogs chasing cats, the rules of etiquette for eating at McDonald's, and so on. Given the diverse types of knowledge that people possess, it is not surprising that cognitive psychologists have explored diverse ways for representing the various types of things that people can know. Many alternative conceptions of knowledge that have been explored will be discussed in this chapter.

Much of the research on knowledge and representation of knowledge involved evaluation of memory and hypotheses about factors affecting memory. Other research was concerned with comprehension and, in particular, identifying how particular forms of knowledge can affect the understanding of new information. Sometimes both memory and comprehension were implicated in the research—for example, the forms of knowledge mediating comprehension were sometimes inferred from qualitative characteristics of memory. Various types of problem-solving research also have played a role in research on knowledge and its representation, from studies about how people decide that two geometric objects are identical except for their angle of rotation, to research on how students know

which algebra algorithm to apply in a particular situation. Because this chapter is more about representation than memory, comprehension, or problem solving, however, no explicit attempt will be made to separate the contributions to representational theory that come from memory, comprehension, and problem-solving research. We begin by describing some simpler forms of representation.

NEURAL NETWORKS

A number of cognitive psychologists are interested in the most fundamental ways that knowledge can be represented. Although these scientists are ultimately interested in the brain, some of them also are interested in the implications of fundamental neural representations for education (Schneider & Graham, 1992). A good deal of the research on neural networks is done with computer simulations—that is, with programs that can encode information in **neural networks.** Although these networks resemble biological neural networks and are intended as analogues of them, there are some differences between the neural networks now being developed in computer environments and the neural networks that exist in human heads.

There are three basic components in the neural networks being studied on computers (Bechtel & Abrahamsen, 1991; Martindale, 1991): (1) Units or nodes are similar to neurons except they have only one property, whereas neurons have many: Nodes can be activated at various levels. If nodes are activated at a high level, we often are conscious of what is activated. It is part of what we "have in mind" at the moment. Nodes, however, can be activated and affecting behavior and be outside of "consciousness" as well. That is, they can be activated at a low level of strength. (2) There are connections between nodes. Two nodes are connected either by simultaneous excitation of the nodes (i.e., if one is excited, the other is) or inhibitions precluding joint excitement (i.e., if one node is excited, the other node cannot be). These connections between nodes are the stuff of long-term memory according to neural network theory. (3) Learning (i.e., development of long-term memories) is the creation of connections and changing the strength of connections. One of the most basic ways that connections are strengthened is by simultaneous activation of nodes in a fashion analogous to strengthening of connections between neurons (Hebb, 1949).

Consider a sample network dealing with some knowledge that literate adults possess, knowledge of the letters of the alphabet (Selfridge, 1959). The nodes in this case correspond to features that letters can possess, such as a horizontal bar, a vertical bar, an acute angle, a curve bulging to the right, and a diagonal bar. Suppose a letter is presented to the system, in this case a letter activating the vertical bar and rightward bulge features. Each of these features is strongly connected to the capital letters P, R, and Q because adults have seen many Ps, Rs, and Qs in their lifetime, with each exposure strengthening the connection between these two features and these capital letters. Thus, when a P is presented, the two activated features connect to the P, R, and Q, activating the nodes representing those letters. The decision that this is a P is reached, however, because a clear signal that the letter is an R requires another feature be activated—a diagonal bar in the lower half of the letter. A clear signal that the letter is a Q requires activation of the lower-half diagonal bar feature as well as activation of a left-bulging curve feature. When the features add up to a P, inhibitory signals are sent out from the P node to the R and Q nodes as well as to all other letter nodes.

The child learning letters is building up connections between features and letters. Like many children, Michael Pressley's son Tim knew the names of the letters before he ever had any idea what the letters looked like (Adams, 1990)—he had been exposed to the "alphabet song" since infancy. Thus,

when Tim was later shown a P and was told it was a P, there was a strengthening of connections between the letter name P and the P features. Between *Sesame Street,* the refrigerator letters, and many sessions reading alphabet books on Daddy and Mommy's knees, Tim had many trials of exposure to the name P and the visual representation of a P. With each of these trials, the connections between the features of the letter P and the letter name strengthened. Eventually whenever the feature complex defining P was encountered, there was automatic activation of the letter name. Thus, what letter name is activated for English-speaking adults when the following features are encountered: top horizontal bar, bottom horizontal bar, top left vertical bar, bottom left vertical bar, and leftmost center horizontal bar (Rumelhart & Siple, 1974)? Most adults recognize an E when these features are coactivated.

The same type of strengthening of connections can be used to explain one-word recognition (e.g., McClelland & Rumelhart, 1981). Consider what happens when the word EACH is presented. Connections are activated between the individual features defining each letter and between the letters. Connections between E and the first position in a word also are activated, as are connections between A and the second position, C and the third position, and H and the fourth position. That is, activating the E also partially activates connections with words beginning with E. Activating the A also partially activates connections with words having A in the second position. (This is why letters encountered in words are recognized faster than single letters.) For adults who have experienced the set of connections between first-E, second-A, third-C, and fourth-H many times before, there is activation of the word EACH and inhibition of other words (e.g., words sharing letters with EACH). For readers who might want a state-of-the-science, detailed discussion of how connectionist models explain word learning, see Seidenberg and McClelland (1989).

Support for such a position includes the finding (Nagy, Anderson, Schommer, Scott, & Stallman, 1989) that words composed of common inflections and morphologically related to a number of other words (e.g., has the same stem word as many other words) are recognized more quickly than words composed of less common inflections and stems not contained in many other words (e.g., *slowly* is composed of a more common inflection and stem than *feeder*). The more common the word part, the quicker the activation according to neural network theory.

Each set of nodes encodes particular information, and thus the human brain is like a large number of little machines, each of which is dedicated to learning a particular type of information. Of course, these little machines are interconnected and operate simultaneously, with the term **parallel distributed processing** (McClelland & Rumelhart, 1986; Rumelhart & McClelland, 1986) capturing this property. This parallel operation can be appreciated with respect to the letter and word examples just presented.

When presented the word EACH, there is not a linear analysis beginning with the first letter, proceeding to the second, and so on. Rather the connections between the letters and their positions occur simultaneously. A number of constraints are considered simultaneously, and the decision that the word is EACH is deferred until all of the relevant constraints have been considered. A lot is happening at once—a lot is happening in parallel. Thus, there are features that define letters (Gibson, 1969). Activation of a particular subset of all features (and hence the connections between features) defines a letter. A particular set of letters activated in particular positions of a syllable (and the resultant pattern of connections) defines a particular syllable. A particular set of syllables activated and connected to particular positions in a multisyllable word permits recognition of a multisyllable word. All of this just to recognize the word EACH!

What does it take to connect the word to its conceptual meaning? According to theories of parallel distributed processing, activation of any concept (e.g., batter) depends on activation of lower-order units and patterns. Knowledge of anything of which we can be conscious (e.g., a word, an image, a concept) boils down to more basic representations in neural network models—in patterns of connections. Although the connectionists have proposed models that map out potential connections between perceptual input, pronunciation, and meaning (e.g., Seidenberg, 1989), the links to meaning are much less well worked out than the links from perceptual input to pronunciation, and we make no attempt here to work through the complex network of connections that might be required to go from perceptual features to meaning, suspecting that most readers have the main idea here, that knowledge is in a hierarchy of connections! (In the next subsection,

however, there is a brief explanation of a concept in connectionist terms.)

There is an extremely important message in connectionist analyses and the data supporting them. For efficient performance, lower-order knowledge must be mastered before higher-order knowledge. Thus, knowledge of particular letters—that is, associations between patterns of feature activations and their corresponding letter names and sounds—must be well established before it is possible to learn to recognize words. Because knowledge begins with low-level features that are progressively associated with one another to define higher-order units, this is decidedly a **bottom-up** approach to cognitive processing. This contrasts with **top-down** approaches to cognition in which thinkers begin with hypotheses about higher-order units and then process lower-order units as part of evaluating the hypothesis.

Many other theorists thinking about the mind have focused on higher-order information, such as concepts, without worrying much, if at all, about patterns of node, neural, or feature activation underlying the symbols in their representational system. Other theorists believe that connectionist models cannot represent some types of critical information that are at the heart of human knowledge. For example, such models do not capture the syntactical relations that are represented in propositions (Fodor & Pylyshen, 1988), which are taken up later in this chapter.

We do not take a position on whether all knowledge is reducible to neural networks, although we do believe, given the state of neural network theory and research at present, that other models of knowledge explain many patterns of data better than does connectionism. In fact, there are a number of important theories of knowledge representation that account for many exceptionally important phenomena. What follows is a sampler of highlights from this literature, featuring the models of knowledge having the greatest impact on education.

CONCEPTS

A person's **concept** of something is their understanding of it, which often corresponds to a larger societal conception (Klausmeier, 1990, whose historically rich coverage informed much of the discussion presented in this subsection). A concept is a decision rule for deciding whether an item is a member of a particular category. Thus, what a person thinks a dog is like is his or her concept of a dog; the labrador retriever next door, Lassie, and Big Red are members of the category "dog" (Bower & Clapper, 1989).

Many concepts are clear-cut, so independent observers readily agree on whether an item is an example of the "it" or not. Thus, given a triangle, most North American adults recognize it as such. Most Americans recognize a presidential inauguration when they see it as well. Other concepts are not as clear-cut and thus are referred to as **"fuzzy"** (Neisser, 1967; Oden, 1987). For example, it is not at all clear when a person stops being a juvenile and becomes an adult or when a small business becomes a large business. There is a great deal of conceptual fuzziness in the world.

Representation of Concepts

That people often can classify items into conceptual categories is more certain than exactly how they do it. Two approaches have received more research attention than others, and each approach accounts for some data better than the other one does, making it impossible to choose one or the other as the more adequate model.

Classical Theory According to this theory, concepts can be defined with respect to the necessary and sufficient features necessary for an item to qualify as a representative of the concept (e.g., Stillings, et al., 1987, Chapter 3). Thus, *grandmothers* are all females who had one or more children, one of whom has had one or more children. A *triangle* is a closed, planar figure with three straight sides and three interior angles. Learning a concept is largely a matter of learning its defining features according to classical theory. An item is regarded as a member of a conceptual category to the extent that its features match the defining features for the concept.

Both **simple concepts** and **complex concepts** have been proposed. It has been long held that there are simple concepts that reflect innate sensory processes (e.g., James, 1983, edition of the text originally appearing in 1890, Chapter 12). Thus, we have separate categories for red, orange, yellow, green, blue, indigo, and violet because of innate mechanisms for recognizing differences in color (e.g., Bornstein, Kessen, & Weiskopf, 1976). According to the classical view, complex concepts are learned and the result of combining properties of simple concepts. Thus, a triangle is defined by a conjunction of

the simple concepts *closed, planar, figure, three-sided, straight-sided,* and *three-angled*. These features are sufficient and necessary to define the complex concept of a triangle.

This classical conception of concepts is easily comprehended in terms of neural networks. Thus, when the set of neural nodes associated with plane figures, closed figures, three-sided figures, and three-angled figures are simultaneously activated, the decision is made that the item in question is a triangle because of a long history of association between these coactivated features and the concept of a triangle.

Classical theory, and hence neural network theory, can accommodate quite complex concepts. For example, a profession would require many features, and thus many nodes, to define it (Bechtel & Abrahamsen, 1991). Suppose the number is 50. Although a specific set of activations would be associated with the concept of an architect, the activation pattern would share many similarities with the activation pattern for landscape architect. That the activation pattern for architect and landscape architect would be more similar than the activation pattern of features for architect and physician would result in architect and landscape architect being perceived as more similar than architect and physician. For the same reason, civil engineer and architect might be perceived as similar, as might physician and dentist.

A complication to all of this is that we often possess understanding of many more attributes of a concept than are activated by presentation of an exemplar of it. Thus, if given an example of a *roof*, it is not likely that all of its features will be activated (e.g., it can be walked on). Even so, they can be activated if provided a relevant context that **primes** their activation (e.g., some comments about a television antenna being installed; Barsalou, 1982). There is a substantial amount of evidence that people have many features for many concepts stored in long-term memory, including many features that are activated only in particular contexts (e.g., Underwood, 1969).

Prototype Theory Classical theory is unsatisfactory for several reasons. For one, it is often difficult to define many concepts in terms of simple concepts (i.e., perceptual features). Second, the evidence is fairly strong that many concepts are defined by their functional characteristics rather than their perceptual characteristics (e.g., Nelson, 1974). Thus, balls are coded as things that roll, bounce, and can be thrown, even by young children. Third, fuzzy concepts also pose a problem in that they are not obviously reducible to a set of particular features that uniquely define instances of the concept. Fourth, the harder we look at many clear-cut concepts, the fuzzier they get. Thus, most of us would classify a woman who adopted one child, who in turn had a child, as a grandmother. Fifth, many noncritical features seem to be applied to our conceptual decisions, so that women over 40 and having gray hair are more likely to be classified as grandmothers than women under 40 with youthful hair color (Stillings et al., 1987). Sixth, it is possible based on the number of features presumably defining a concept to make predictions about how long it will take to process the concept relative either to concepts with fewer or more defining features. Such predictions, however, often do not transpire. For example, the sentence, "If practically all of the men in the room are *bachelors,* then few of the men in the room have wives," is processed faster than, "If practically all of the men in the room are *not married,* then few of the men in the room have wives." If *bachelors* was decomposed into its constituent features (i.e., *not married*), it would be expected that the two sentences would be comprehended at the same rate. That they are not suggests that understanding the concept *bachelor* depends on some other process than decomposition in terms of features (Fodor, Fodor, & Garrett, 1975).

Rosch (1975, 1978) and her colleagues (Rosch & Mervis, 1975) noted that people often classify based on resemblance rather than with respect to necessary, defining features. Thus, there are *typical* grandmothers who, in fact, are over 40 and gray-haired. *Atypical* grandmothers (e.g., a 35-year-old, whose child was born when she was 17 and who has in turn had a child at 17) are less readily classified as grandmothers. Because of its typicality, a robin is readily and quickly classified as a bird, whereas a penguin is less quickly classified as a bird. Rosch's theory is often referred to as **family resemblance theory.**

Family resemblance theory is a **prototype** theory because it is usually possible to construct a typical member of the category. Although this typical bird would be a concatenation of features that would never occur simultaneously in a real bird, the more an animal resembles this typical bird, the more certainly and quickly the animal would be classified

as a bird. When given a robin and asked whether it is a bird, the response is faster than to the same question posed with respect to a chicken (Rips, Shoben, & Smith, 1973; Rosch, 1973; Rosch and Mervis, 1975). In addition, typical category members are first learned by children as being members of the category. Also, when people are given lists of category members and asked to recall them later, the more typical members are recalled before the atypical members. (See Smith & Medin, 1981, for a review of the relevant literature.)

How are such prototypes formed? They are a sort of mental average of the many instances of the concept that have been encountered in the world, with both adults (Posner & Keele, 1968, 1970; Reed, 1972) and children (e.g., Lasky, 1974) capable of constructing such mental averages. In the Lasky (1974) study, for example, 8-year-olds and adults were presented patterns of geometric forms and later were asked to select patterns they had seen before on a recognition task. On this test, a prototypical pattern was rated as having been seen previously even though it had never been actually presented before, receiving even higher ratings than patterns that were actually presented. Such an outcome is consistent with the conclusion that a prototypical concept had been formed and was being used to guide decision making on the recognition test.

If you want some convincing that there are more or less typical members of categories, try the following exercise based on Rosch (1973). Ask a friend to rank order the following list of fruits from most representative of fruits to least representative of fruits and you do the same: strawberry, apple, pineapple, olive, plum, fig. Then, both of you rank order the following list from most representative to least representative crimes: stealing, blackmail, murder, vagrancy, assault, embezzling. Do the same ranking exercise for these diseases: measles, cancer, rheumatism, muscular dystrophy, cold.

With respect to fruit, there is a good chance that both you and your friend listed apple as the most representative fruit and olive as the least representative. Plum, pineapple, and strawberry were probably all considered to be representative of fruit and more so than fig. For crimes, it is a good bet that murder was the most representative crime for both of you and vagrancy the least representative. For diseases, the most representative was probably cancer and the least representative was cold. Rheumatism probably ranked low on the list for representative diseases, whereas malaria and muscular dystrophy were considered good representatives of diseases.

Features of stimuli are critical to classification in both classical and prototype theories. Prototype theories have been favored in recent years, however—although, to be sure, the debate between the classical and prototype theories rages on (e.g., see Ward, Vela, & Hass, 1990, favoring a feature-theory approach; also, a reply from Nelson, 1990, on the side of a prototype model of concept learning and categorization). How nondefinitive features contribute to classification (e.g., such as "over 40" for grandmothers) is more obvious with prototype theory; how people classify instances of fuzzy concepts is also more obvious using prototype theory. Really knowing a concept implies much more than being able to classify instances of it, however, with different degrees of conceptual understanding the focus of the next subsection.

Knowing Versus Really Knowing a Concept

Thus far, the focus has been on whether a person can classify an item as an instance of a category or not. What this entails is realizing that members of the category that vary on conceptually irrelevant dimensions are indeed equivalent—for example, recognizing that red pencils and blue pencils are indeed both pencils and that bananas and oranges are both fruits. Proficiency in such categorization involves rejecting category nonmembers as members of the category—for example, not accepting a blue pen as a member of the category pencil and not accepting potato as a member of the category fruit.

Of course, much more can be known about a concept. For instance, many people eventually can state the attributes that define many of the concepts they possess. Moreover, they can precisely specify why nonexamples are nonexamples in terms of deviation from defining attributes. For concepts to be understood completely, however, it is essential that knowledge of the concept go beyond labels and definitions, that the concept can be applied to understand new content (Klausmeier, 1990) and solve new problems. This theme will be reiterated at several points in this book.

For instance, many science concepts are understood incompletely by students after they encounter them in science classes. Many students can define

concepts on a test but cannot apply them in the everyday world. A well-worked example in the science education literature is that many students who can state precisely the processes involved in photosynthesis fail to realize that the tree in their front yard is manufacturing food in its leaves rather than getting food from the soil (e.g., Roth, 1990; see Chapter 12, this volume).

Consider a demonstration of a concept introduced to most readers in elementary school. Place five hockey pucks in a stack. What will happen if the bottom puck in the stack is struck hard with a hammer? When we have asked students this question, they often predict the stack will fall. Wrong. The bottom puck goes flying out, and the remaining pucks simply drop the width of one puck, leaving a stack of four pucks. Do you know what inertia is? If you are like our students, you know that it is the tendency of objects that are in motion to stay in motion and the tendency of objects at rest to remain at rest. If you really understood the concept, you would have predicted that only one puck would fall out of the stack, for you would have recognized that the four hockey pucks that were not struck were not in motion and thus should stay "at rest." Concepts can be known well enough so they can be defined and instances separated from noninstances, and still a person may not be able to use the concept when confronted with a problem requiring the concept. Whitehead (1929) referred to such knowledge as **inert knowledge** and accused school of creating too much of such useless knowledge and too little deep understanding of concepts.

Relations Between Concepts

There are many conceptual hierarchies, with each node in the hierarchy a whole that can be subdivided into parts. Thus, all living things can be subdivided into animals and plants. Animals can be further subdivided into reptiles, mammals, birds, insects, and spiders, each with associated features (e.g., hair, vertebrate, warm-blooded for mammals). Mammals can be divided by *genus* (e.g., bears, elephants, giraffes, moles), each with associated features. Each *genus* is further divisible into species (e.g., bears can be polar, black, brown, speckled). Each species has its associated features.

There are large networks of associations linked to each of these nodes, with many associations personal and others shared with most other adults.

Thus, for one of us, polar bears are connected to memories of the Antarctic exhibit at the Munich Zoo as well as to memories of specific trips to the National Zoo in Washington. Polar bears also bring to mind Klondike Bars, which have a polar bear on the wrapper. Some memories of Canada are also connected to polar bears, including a famous train that goes to the far north of Ontario, the Polar Bear Express. Knowledge of polar bears also is connected to knowledge of penguins, seals, and walruses, with knowledge of all of these animals tied to general knowledge of the arctic and antarctic regions of the earth.

Many complex connections between concepts are stored in long-term memory. Two important properties of these connections are that information is stored in hierarchies, and these connections permit concepts to stimulate the activation of other concepts: (1) Conceptual information is organized in **hierarchical semantic networks.** The most frequently cited evidence for this is that questions requiring consideration of information at different places in the hierarchy are answered more slowly than questions requiring consideration of information coded in nearby nodes (Collins & Quillian, 1969). Thus, the question, "Do birds have skin?" requires consideration of a feature (i.e., skin) coded with "animals" rather than directly with "birds." This question takes longer to answer than does, "Do robins have red breasts?" because "red breasts" is a feature stored directly with robins. Such an analysis is not above criticism, however, for it could be that "skin" is stored with robins but is a weak associate to robin, whereas "red breast" is a stronger associate (Conrad, 1972; Glass, Holyoak, & O'Dell, 1974).

(2) Collins and Loftus (1975) proposed an updated model to attempt to account for this difficulty and other outcomes that could not be accounted for with the original model—for example, that people readily make acoustic associations to words (i.e., red breast and nest are acoustically linked) and that the decision speed for false facts (e.g., rocks can meow, dogs can meow) often cannot be predicted by the original model (Anderson, 1984). Collins and Loftus referred to their updated model as a **spreading activation** theory of semantic processing to emphasize that activation of any particular part of the network results in spread of activation with parts of the hierarchy that are "closer" and more highly associated with the activated concept. Only a little thought is required to make obvious that the interconnections

in such a model are complex, and the patterns of activation logically could be extensive.

The idea that concepts are linked associatively, with the links varying in strength, is an old one (e.g., Deese, 1961, 1962, 1965; see Paivio & Begg, 1981, Chapter 5, for an overview). What is particularly striking about much of this work is how easy it is to demonstrate "clusters" of associations using various methods. Thus, "wings," "birds," and "fly" are strong associates. So are "yellow," "flower," "color," "sunshine," and "garden." One of the reasons that such association models are not studied as prominently today as they once were is that more powerful theories of knowledge representation have emerged that capture both the associations and specify more precisely the relations between associated elements (see the discussion of schemata later in this chapter). Even so, there are some tasks and some occasions when conceptual relations are perhaps best understood in terms of associations.

Consider the television game show *Family Feud*. Before each program, a panel of 100 people is given category labels (e.g., snack fruits) and is asked to generate associations (e.g., apple, banana, fig). Individual contestants on the show score points by "guessing" what the audience said. That individuals can do so reflects shared knowledge between members of the culture (for relevant analyses, see Garskof & Houston, 1963; Laffal, 1965). That individual contestants offer bizarre responses compared with the most frequent responses in the audience survey reflects that some knowledge is more personal.

An important consequence of spreading activation via hierarchical and associative networks is that activating some particular content can make it easier to understand related material. Thus, if the word "stone" is read by a person, followed by the word "rock," "rock" is recognized more quickly than if "stone" had not been presented (Meyer, Schvaneveldt, & Ruddy, 1975; Neely, 1976, 1977). The sentence, "The lawyer is in the bank," is understood more quickly if the sentence is preceded by a sentence containing words associated with *lawyer* and *bank* (Anderson, 1984; McKoon & Ratcliff, 1979).

There will be a number of times in this book when interventions will involve encouraging students to activate background knowledge about to-be-presented material. In part, this is to encourage spreading activation through a hierarchical network that encodes many associations between concepts, activation that should make it easier to understand content related to the activated knowledge.

One caveat is that there is at least some evidence that the spread through semantic nets may not be as extensive as Collins and Loftus (1975) proposed. De Groot (1983) developed word triads in which the first and second terms were strongly related as were the second and third terms (e.g., *bull-cow-milk*). If spread is extensive, it might be expected that *bull* would serve as a prime for both *cow* and *milk*. It did not, only priming *cow*. It may well be that the spread of activation is only to near concepts and associations.

Development of Hierarchical Concepts in Children

Do children have hierarchical conceptual networks that resemble adult networks? Classical Piagetian theory included the claim that preschool (preoperational) children experience great difficulties doing tasks that involved classification. Particularly relevant here, they were assumed to be unable to accomplish **class inclusion** problems. Thus, according to Piagetian theory, if a preschooler were given a set of 10 pictures of 7 elephants and 3 bears, he or she would have difficulty with questions such as, "Are there more elephants or animals?" Piagetians assumed that preschooler difficulties with such tasks reflect a lack of understanding of the hierarchical relationship between animals and specific animals (Inhelder & Piaget, 1964).

Many researchers have generated data substantiating that the Piagetians underestimated the competence of young children (Brainerd, 1978b; see Chapter 7, this book), and so it has been the case with class inclusion. When children are carefully instructed about what is required in such tasks—that is, the instructions are simplified somewhat over those used in the original Piagetian studies—there is considerable evidence that children can do class inclusion problems and have hierarchical representations (Winer, 1980), at least for familiar classes (e.g., Markman & Siebert, 1976; Smith, 1979; Steinberg & Anderson, 1975). One modification that makes a hierarchical classification task easier is to enumerate the objects presented in the problem for the preschooler. Thus, rather than presenting objects as "dogs and cats," with the task of deciding whether there are more "dogs" or "animals," present them as "six dogs and two cats," with the task of deciding

whether there are more dogs or animals (Winer, 1974). Another modification is to make certain that the relationship of the concrete objects to both the subordinate and the superordinate categories is apparent. Thus, wooden blocks that are half painted red are more likely to be seen as both "red" blocks and "wooden" blocks than blocks fully painted red, which presumably obscures their woodenness (Tatarsky, 1974). Class inclusion problems also are solved better when typical category items are used in the problems than when the problems are posed with atypical items (e.g., Carson & Abrahamson, 1976; Lane & Hodkin, 1985).

In general, there is substantial evidence that even preschool children possess knowledge about the semantic hierarchical relations between some of the concepts they know. They also know a lot of categories, for the ability to abstract categories from presentation of a number of examples of category members is present at least from infancy (e.g., Anglin, 1977; Bomba & Siqueland, 1983; Strauss, 1979)—and with sensitive measurement procedures that include familiar objects, even 2- to 3-year-olds can sort objects into appropriate categories (for data and reviews, see Carey, 1985; Gelman & Baillargeon, 1983; Horton, 1982; Markman & Callanan, 1983; Sugarman, 1983).

Children's categorization and processing of categories is anything but adultlike: (1) There are many reports in the literature of children failing class inclusion problems when unfamiliar concepts are presented. (2) Preschoolers also have difficulties when instructions do not make task requirements obvious. (3) Children's preferred way of representing categorizable content often is not along category lines, but with respect to thematic relations, they can detect between objects. Thus, when given a group of objects that can be sorted along categorizable lines (e.g., tiger, elephant, monkey, giraffe, banana, orange, grapes, apple), preschoolers often sort along thematic lines (e.g., monkeys eat bananas, elephants and giraffes live in the same house at the zoo, a tiger could eat an apple, mommy puts oranges and grapes in her fruit salad; e.g., Bruner, Olver, & Greenfield, 1966; Kagan, Moss, & Sigel, 1963). Such sortings suggest that schematic representations play a large role in children's early knowledge. (See the discussion of schemata later in this chapter.) (4) It is also evident that children's categories do not always correspond to those of adults from their underextensions of concepts—using *duck* to refer only to one's pet duck—and their overextensions—using *duck* to refer to any bird larger than a robin (Bloom, 1973; Clark, 1973). (5) Children often sort into many more categories than adults do (Saltz, Soller, & Sigel, 1972). Finally, (6) sophisticated studies of children's concepts have revealed striking qualitative differences between the concepts of preschoolers and those of older children and adults. For example, Carey (1985), in an investigation of children's biological knowledge, demonstrated that 10-year-olds' understanding of *animal* included relations between the processes of eating, breathing, growing, dying, and reproducing, whereas 4-year-olds did not understand the criticality of these functions in animals, although they could distinguish animals from nonanimals.

Although some of children's knowledge probably is in categorical hierarchies similar to those of adults, many concepts that children hold differ from those of adults. Moreover, children are less likely to rely on hierarchical categorical knowledge than are adults when they are performing tasks that could be mediated by hierarchical knowledge. How development of hierarchical categorical knowledge and its use occurs is not completely understood and the target of current research (e.g., Markman, 1989). These developments probably are due in part to experience, however. Data from cross-cultural psychology are informative on this point.

For instance, Sharp, Cole, and Lave (1979) established that rural Mexicans without formal schooling tended to classify objects based on functional properties (e.g., chicken and eggs would be seen as the two related objects in a triad composed of chicken, horse, and egg), whereas rural Mexicans with some formal schooling tended to use categories comparable to Western-educated adults (i.e., chicken and horse being selected as members of the same category—animals). Attendance in Western-style schools increases use of hierarchical categorical knowledge, just as it affects use of Western-style strategies (see Chapter 2, this book).

Summary

In closing this subsection, we emphasize that what was represented here was a mix of modern and classical thinking about concepts. We hope the simplicity of these models comes through, however, because we want to emphasize that neither neural nor concept models capture well many relationships that exist between ideas stored in long-term memory (i.e., there are more than hierarchical and associative relations). Other types of representations do a better job of this, and these more complex approaches will be covered in subsections that follow.

In admitting the limitations of neural network and concept models, that is not to denigrate them. Both connectionist and concept models account for some types of data well. Our guess is that the mind is big enough for a variety of different types of representations, and indeed the many functions performed by the mind may require such diversity, a theme that will be reiterated as this chapter proceeds.

SEMANTIC VERSUS EPISODIC MEMORY

Tulving (1972) introduced the distinction between **semantic memory** and **episodic memory** as two ways to classify what is referred to in this book as declarative knowledge. Semantic memory is knowledge of the world that is now independent of specific experiences. Episodic memory is memory of personally experienced events. Thus, your semantic memory contains an image of a cat. You also have episodic memories of specific cats, perhaps including a pet or one that you have seen hanging around your neighborhood. Baseball fans have semantic knowledge of baseball games and episodic knowledge of specific games.

Tulving (1983, Chapter 3) provided a number of distinctions between semantic and episodic memory. A few are especially telling: (1) The point of reference for semantic knowledge is the world: Is this knowledge true about the world? The point of reference for episodic knowledge is the self: Did this event happen to me? Is this what really happened on that occasion? (2) Semantic memory is not coded with respect to *when* the information was acquired. Episodic information often is. (3) Semantic knowledge is less susceptible to context effects than episodic knowledge (e.g., Kintsch, 1980). That is, often episodic information is more likely to be remembered in situations in which it had originally been encoded than in other situations. Recall of semantic information is not nearly so context bound. (4) Semantic information is unlikely to be forgotten; episodic information is easily forgotten. (5) Semantic knowledge is *known*; episodic knowledge is *remembered*. Baseball fans *know* that umpires sometimes miss close calls at first base. Some fans might *remem-*

ber that a first-base umpire blew a call at first in the eighth inning of the sixth game of the World Series between the Royals and the Cardinals. (6) Education is more concerned with the development of high-quality semantic knowledge than development of episodic knowledge. Even so, there are often many episodic memories. For instance, I [MP] remember the day that Timmy. . . . Then there was the time that an old friend Bob confused the metabolism of bacteria and the metabolism of humans in biology class . . . and the time Brent and I painted "The Rock" at Northwestern! Fortunately, however, a good deal of semantic information was acquired during and between these happy episodes.

Both semantic and episodic knowledge function in cognition. Although people make a general association to *cat* when they read *dog*, they also sometimes think of particular cats and dogs they have known. Although professors have general schemata for university campuses, administrations, and policies, they also have episodic knowledge of particular campuses, administrations, and policies, with both used during thinking and problem solving on committees involving college business. Just last week, as author CB wrote a proposal for changing a policy at South Carolina, she thought about how the situation had been handled at her previous institution, Illinois State. Indeed, the case is made later in this chapter that much of our most important knowledge is tied to the situations in which it was acquired, that much of thinking may be tied to the specific experiences giving rise to it, that abstract semantic knowledge may be much less prevalent in thinking than suggested by many cognitive models advanced in the past, that much of thinking is case based.

PROPOSITIONS AND MACROPROPOSITIONS

Beginning with this section, we discuss ways of representing knowledge that can capture properties other than simple hierarchical categorizability and associative relatedness.

Propositions are descriptions specifying relationships between things and their properties (Clark & Clark, 1977; Kintsch, 1974). Every proposition specifies at least one such relationship. Each proposition contains a verb or preposition and specifies one or several semantic roles that are related by the verb or preposition. Thus, a proposition contains in-

formation about the agents performing actions specified by verbs, the objects of actions, goals accomplished by an action, the recipient of the action (referred to as a patient in this system), time of the action, and so on. Propositions are equivalent to sentences in logic and are represented using a standard format that emphasizes the relationship specified by the verb or preposition. Thus, the proposition UNDER (DOG, HOUSE) specifies a relationship between a dog and a house, that the *dog is under a house*. TYPES (MICHAEL) conveys that *Michael types*. LOVE (MICHAEL, DONNA) is an expression of *Michael loves Donna*. Each of the propositional representations in this paragraph can be thought of as conveying one idea, one unit of meaning. What must be emphasized is that the representation of propositions on paper is as logical sentences; their representation in our heads is much more abstract. What is in the head is the abstract idea represented by the logical sentence, not necessarily the sentence itself.

Substantially more complex ideas that are composed of several idea units in interaction can also be expressed in multiple propositional units. Consider the sentence, "John carefully nailed down the loose shingles on the roof" (Kintsch, 1982). There are four units of meaning (**semantic units**) in this sentence: *Nailing is being done carefully, John nails shingles, shingles are on the roof,* and *shingles are loose* are the ideas that compose this sentence. These can be summarized in four propositions with NAIL as the main verb. JOHN is the agent performing the relation specified by this verb. The object of the relation is (LOOSE, SHINGLES). The location of the shingles is specified as (ON, SHINGLES, ROOF). The relation NAIL is modified by CAREFUL. Consider one more example: *John hit the big red ball.* Three propositions capture the meaning of this sentence: *Hit (John, ball), big (ball),* and *red (ball),* corresponding to *John hit the ball, ball is big,* and *ball is red* (Weaver & Kintsch, 1991). Each of these three propositions is a **microproposition** because it was directly derived from the text, as were all of the propositions considered in the examples presented until this point.

Many types of content can be specified propositionally (e.g., pictorial representations can be written as propositions, with how this can be done and the implications of this possibility taken up in the section on imagery later in this chapter). Even so, a great deal of research on propositional representations, and the most prominent work pertaining to propositions that is relevant to educational psychology, has been conducted with text, with the research and theoretical analyses provided by Kintsch and colleagues the most visible of these efforts.

In a nutshell, when a reader reads a text, Kintsch (e.g., 1983; van Dijk & Kintsch, 1983) believes the text is parsed implicitly by the reader into its micropropositions. These meaning units combine to capture the full meaning of the text. Of course, no one remembers everything about a text—no one can ever remember a text word for word unless they have gone to a great deal of difficulty to memorize the text verbatim. What people remember is the gist, which are the main ideas of the text, which are encoded into **macropropositions,** which are not derived directly from the text—they are derived from the micropropositions. Thus, a macroproposition for the passage containing the sentence about John nailing shingles might be *John repaired the house.*

With respect to long discourse, such as a book, there are layers of macropropositions. Thus, at the top level, there is an overall summary of the book. Each chapter in the book can be captured by macropropositions, as can each paragraph in each chapter. The lower-level macropropositions collapse into one another to create the higher-level macropropositions (van Dijk & Kintsch, 1983, e.g., Chapter 2). In general, what ends up in our long-term memory are macropropositions, summaries of more detailed information we have experienced. Macropropositions preserve the meaning of what has been processed, not the actual surface form of it. The nature of these macropropositions will be clearer after a brief discussion of how macropropositional representations are created.

Suppose that you are beginning a paragraph-long text. The first sentence is parsed into micropropositions, and a macropropositional representation is generated that captures the main meaning of the sentence, which is held in short-term memory as the second sentence is parsed and processed. Attempts are made to link the macroproposition from the first sentence to the micropropositions of the second sentence, with a new set of macropropositions emerging from this analysis. Sometimes there will be a need for the generation of **bridging inferences** that reconcile the meaning of the previous macroproposition with the new micropropositions—that is, that produce coherence between the previous text and new text. These bridging inferences are derived largely from world knowledge the

reader possesses. For instance, if a text about a worker pounding nails never mentions a hammer, the reader may infer "hammer" when the sentence, "The head slipped off," is encountered. Perhaps the resulting macroproposition would be, "The hammer broke while being used." By the end of the paragraph, a macrostructure capturing the gist of the entire paragraph would be generated.

Later, if the reader has to recall the paragraph, the most important ideas are recalled first (e.g., Kintsch & Keenan, 1973). The longer the retention interval between reading and recall, the fewer lower-level propositions are remembered (e.g., Kintsch & van Dijk, 1978). The recall data reflect bridging inferences made during the original presentation of text as well some inferences made during recall, inferences again based on what the reader already knows (more about this phenomenon, reflecting **reconstructive memory,** in subsequent sections of this chapter). After a while, only the most important information in the text is recalled.

Although it has been recognized for decades (at least since Bartlett, 1932) that gist is encoded during reading and that subsequent recall reflects memory for gist and reconstructions from world knowledge, Kintsch and his associates have provided a sophisticated model of how macropropositional models of text are constructed. The differences between an original text and the meaning constructed by the reader are apparent in an example provided by Kintsch and van Dijk (1978, p. 384). Consider the following passage (from an article by F. K. Heussenstam in a 1971 issue of *Transaction*):

> A series of violent, bloody encounters between police and Black Panther party members punctuated the early summer days of 1969. Soon after, a group of black students I teach at California State College, Los Angeles, who were members of the Panther party, began to complain of continuous harrassment by law enforcement officials. Among their many grievances, they complained about receiving so many traffic citations that some were in danger of losing their driving privileges. During one lengthy discussion, we realized that all of them drove automobiles with Panther Party signs glued to their bumpers. This is a report of a study that I undertook to assess the seriousness of their charges and to determine whether we were hearing the voice of paranoia or reality.

Here is a possible recall of that passage, one in which macropropositions are remembered. Some embellishment with bridging inferences is also apparent:

In the sixties, there was a series of riots between police and the Black Panthers. The police did not like the Black Panthers. After that, students who enrolled at the California State College complained that the police were harrassing them. They were stopped and had to show their driver's license. The police gave them trouble because they had Black Panther signs on their bumpers. The police discriminated against these students and violated their civil rights. They did an experiment for this purpose.

There is actually an impressive array of evidence that some information is acquired and represented as Kintsch and his collaborators claim (see van Dijk & Kintsch, 1983, Chapter 2, for a review of the evidence). For instance, if you are asked to recall the information in a sentence that is presented for study, you are more likely to recall portions that are from the same idea unit than from other portions of the sentence (Lesgold, 1972; Wanner, 1975). For the sentence, *The mausoleum that enshrined the czar overlooked the square,* presentation of *overlooked* as a recall cue is more likely to elicit *mausoleum* than *czar,* even though czar was physically more proximal to *overlooked* in the sentence: Both *mausoleum* and *overlooked* are part of the idea unit OVERLOOK (MAUSOLEUM, SQUARE). In addition, there is evidence that when any part of a proposition is recalled, the whole of it tends to be recalled (Buschke & Schaier, 1979; Goetz, Anderson, & Schallert, 1981; Graesser, 1981; Kintsch, 1974). Text that contains more propositions requires more processing time even if the number of words in the text is constant (e.g., Graesser, Hoffman, & Clark, 1980; Kintsch & Keenan, 1973; Kintsch, Kozminsky, Streby, McKoon, & Keenan, 1975). An especially important property is that once a macrostructure is formed, subsequent exposure to some part of the macrostructure activates other parts of the macrostructure (see van Dijk & Kintsch, 1983, Chapter 6; also Kintsch, 1988). That is, there is **spreading activation,** similar to that described with respect to semantic networks linking concepts. Spreading activation between propositions can also occur because propositions are linked via **propositional networks.** Any two propositions that share common elements are directly linked in such networks (e.g., Hayes-Roth & Thorndyke, 1979). For example, the propositions representing, "Jane caught the ball," and "Jane bought a dress," are linked through *Jane.* The propositions, "I moved the furniture from my home to the office," are linked to, "I helped Hal to move his family when I

was in graduate school," via *moved.* Similar to other linkages, the strength of the connection between propositions can be increased by simultaneous activation of the propositions. Thus, when a person tells a story about Jane catching the ball that is the last out at a baseball game and then rushing off to buy a dress, the linkage between Jane catching the ball and her buying a dress increases.

General knowledge of the world, in contrast to memory of a specific text, also can be built up from text as Kintsch describes. Macropropositional representations of what has been read are integrated with prior knowledge to create new knowledge, some part of which is propositional in form. (Indeed, there are some propositional theorists who believe that all knowledge ultimately is represented in this form; e.g., Anderson & Bower, 1973). Thus, if you read a *Time* magazine article about overcoming infertility, you construct a macropropositional representation of that text. At a party tomorrow, you could rely on this macroproposition to guide partial retelling of the article to a friend who might be interested in infertility. In addition, and this is critical, your long-term knowledge of infertility in general might be changed by reading the article. Thus, 6 months from now, when someone makes a claim about infertility that conflicts with what was in the article, you can respond, "But I thought. . . ," going on to relate a general point from the article, perhaps no longer aware of where the information was acquired. What has been changed, to use Kintsch's term, is your **situation model** of infertility. Such a situation model is **schematic,** capturing and organizing a number of propositions about infertility. **Schemata** are more complex than any representations considered up until this point and are taken up in the next subsection.

FRAMES, SCRIPTS, AND SCHEMATA

Every adult knows what goes on at a birthday party. Description of that knowledge in terms of neural networks, concept models, or propositions is clumsy and long-winded at best. (Imagine the incredibly complex set of propositions required to represent everything that occurs at a birthday party!) Dissatisfaction with the inability of the theories of knowledge reviewed thus far to represent such common but complex events economically was part of the motivation for theories of knowledge considered in this section.

These new theories have been given different names by their creators, and each is particularly well matched to some situations better than others. Their common thread is that a number of concepts that commonly co-occur in particular situations are related to one another in orderly systems of procedures and expectations. Events and situations are presumed to have skeleton structures that are pretty much constant, although the particular ways the skeleton ends up taking on flesh vary from instance to instance.

The first example of such a complex representation is Minsky's (1975) notion of a **frame:**

> A *frame* is a data structure for representing a stereotyped situation, like being in a certain living room, or going to a child's birthday party. Attached to each frame are several kinds of information. Some of this information is about how to use the frame. Some is about what one can expect to happen next. Some is about what to do if these expectations are not confirmed. We can think of a frame as a network of nodes and relations. The "top levels" of a frame are fixed, and represent things that are always true about the supposed situation. The lower levels have many *terminals*—"slots" that must be filled by specific instances or data. Each terminal can specify conditions its assignment must meet.... Simple conditions are specified by markers that might require a terminal assignment to be a person, an object of sufficient value.... More complex conditions can specify relations among the things assigned to several terminals. (p. 212)

A few examples will make more obvious what is implied here. Consider knowledge of birthday parties as Minsky (1975) did. There are certain objects that are always present and actions that always occur: (1) The attendees wear clothes. (2) They bring presents. (3) Games are played. (4) There are decorations. (5) There is a meal. (6) There is a cake. (7) There is ice cream. Items (1) through (7) specify the top level (i.e., the fixed level) of the birthday party frame. Associated with each of the parts of the fixed frame are constraints on how the frame can be filled out: (1) The clothes are usually Sunday best, although simply good clothes sometimes are acceptable. (2) The present must be something that the birthday child would like to receive. It is bought and wrapped in birthday gift wrap. (3) There are a set of acceptable games, such as hide-and-seek or pin-the-tail-on-the-donkey. (4) The decorations often include balloons, streamers, and banners. Attendees are sometimes given party hats and noisemakers. (5)

The "main dish" at the meal is kids' fare—hot dogs, hamburgers, or fried chicken. This is followed by cake and ice cream. (6) The cake is decorated and has candles, usually equal in number to the age of the birthday child. The cake is not cut until all party attendees have sung happy birthday and the birthday child has blown out the candles. (7) Ice cream is chocolate, vanilla, or strawberry.

Frames can be embedded in frames and thus can capture much more than a 2-hour birthday party. Consider a frame for a middle-school day (again, after Minsky, 1975): Get up. Dress. Breakfast. Go to school. Be in school. Home room. A class. A different class. A third class. Lunch. Another class. A second afternoon class. Recess. Last class of the day. Go home. Play. Do homework. Go to bed. Wasn't that just like middle-school (junior high school) for you? If it is not exactly like it, the frame is close. The power of this frame is that it does capture the image of the junior high day for so many Americans. In doing so, this middle-school day frame organizes a whole series of frames, from the one describing getting up to the one describing going to bed.

Schank and Abelson (1977) also sought to explain the common knowledge that people in a culture possess about recurring complex situations. They proposed that much of knowledge is represented in **scripts.** Although frames can be used to describe sequences of events, for a number of reasons that need not concern us here, scripts more completely capture sequences of events. Scriptlike representation of a sequence is an important human ability because there are many recurring sequences of events in life. For example, there is a *sequence* of events every time you go to a movie theater, including traveling to the theater, buying the ticket, buying some food or beverage, giving the ticket to an usher, finding a seat, watching the film, leaving the seat and heading for the exit, dropping the food wrappers or paper cups in the trash can near the exit, and leaving the building housing the theater.

Consider another script: going to a restaurant. First, because there are many different types of restaurants from cafeterias and fast food establishments to fancy restaurants, the sequence will vary somewhat depending on the the type of restaurant—in Schank and Abelson's terminology, depending on the restaurant track selected.

Let us suppose that you go to a fancy restaurant. You arrive at the restaurant. The maitre d' greets you and checks the reservation. You are either taken to a table or asked to wait a few minutes. Once led to the table, one or more waiting persons are introduced. Menus are delivered and drink orders taken. The drinks are served and a waiting person takes the order from each person. . . . After receiving the credit card and receipt from the waiter, all rise from the table. As you leave the restaurant, the waiting person(s) says farewell as does the maitre d'.

Each part of the fancy restaurant script can be filled out with numerous possibilities, although there are constraints, as there always are in schematic representations. The maitre'd can be male or female but is always somewhat dignified and well dressed. The drinks ordered can range from alcohols to waters to soft drinks to fruit juices but, except for children, cannot be milk. Continuing through the script, the entrée ordered can be anything from a variety of meat dishes to pasta dishes to vegetarian dishes. In short, there are many possibilities for every step of the script.

That such scripts are deeply engrained in all of us is apparent when a script is violated. Consider something that happened to us a few years ago. We were heading to dinner with a friend who wanted to show off their favorite fancy restaurant. After parking the car, we entered double glass doors that seemed to be part of a barber shop. We were confused to say the least. Our friend walked over to the barber's closet and pulled it open. We followed him into a restaurant in the motif of a speakeasy, with the barber shop front part of the camouflage. Until we were provided some explanation by our friend of this speakeasy motif, we were really lost about what was going on! The rest of the evening was a combination of familiar events, ones represented in the fancy restaurant and speakeasy scripts stored in our long-term memories. With both of these scripts activated, we were able to get through the evening without any more surprises. See Levy and Fivush (1993) for review of the script knowledge that underlies gender roles, a discussion that makes clear the profound impact of scripts on behavior.

Although both frame and script theories have been important in cognitive psychology, their close relative, **schema theory** as developed by Richard Anderson and his colleagues at the Illinois Center for the Study of Reading (e.g., Anderson & Pearson, 1984), had much more impact in education. The similarity of a schema to frames and scripts will be apparent with the consideration of an example, one originally provided by Anderson and Pearson (1984, pp. 259–265). (The similarities between frame, script, and schema theories are such that from this point on, we will simply refer to any theory of this type as schema theory.)

The schema for a ship christening includes its purpose—to bless the ship. It includes information about where it is done (i.e., in dry dock), by whom (i.e., a celebrity), and when it occurs (i.e., just before launching of a new ship). The christening action is also represented (i.e., breaking a bottle of champagne that is suspended from a rope). These parts of a schema are referred to as **nodes, variables,** or **slots.** At any particular christening, these slots are **instantiated** with particular instances (e.g., New Haven, with the President breaking a bottle of California-produced champagne on a particular new submarine). There are clear constraints on the instances that can occur in these slots. The celebrity would never be a person of ill-repute (e.g., a smut publisher, a famous criminal). The champagne might be a bottle of Rothchild's, but a bottle of $7.00 champagne would be unlikely. Once instantiated, the schema can be represented as a series of propositions capturing that it was the President who christened the ship, the ship was in the New Haven yards, the champagne was produced in California, and so forth.

Once some small part of the ship christening schema is encountered, for example, by the first image in a news clip showing a bottle of champagne breaking on the bow of a ship, the entire schema is activated. Once activated, comprehension and processing of the ship christening event will be different. (Schematic processing is decidedly **top-down** processing in that activation of the higher-order idea occurs first and constrains thinking about the details of the situation.) The activated schema will permit reasonable inferences to be made about details of the event (e.g., as the bottle is seen breaking on the bough, the viewer might infer that there was a platform beside the ship with one or more persons on it, one of them a celebrity) and affect the allocation of attention (e.g., to the celebrity, to the name of the ship, and memory of the event).

Much of the research on schema theory was generated with respect to comprehension of texts. Schema activation can dramatically affect comprehension, inferences, attention allocation, and memory of what is read. (See Anderson and Pearson, 1984, for a review of the relevant data.) Sometimes readers activate a schema near the beginning of their processing of text, with the schema then affecting subsequent inferences that are made about the text. Read the following text, which was used by Anderson, Reynolds, Schallert, and Goetz (1977):

> Every Saturday night, four good friends get together. When Jerry, Mike, and Pat arrived, Karen was sitting in her living room writing some notes. She quickly gathered the cards and stood up to greet her friends at the door. They followed her into the living room but as usual they couldn't agree on exactly what to play. Jerry eventually took a stand and set things up. Finally, they began to play. Karen's recorder filled the room with soft and pleasant music. Early in the evening, Mike noticed Pat's hand and the many diamonds. As the night progressed the tempo of play increased. Finally, a lull in the activities occurred. Taking advantage of this, Jerry pondered the arrangement in front of him. Mike interrupted Jerry's reverie and said, "Let's hear the score." They listened carefully and commented on their performance. When the comments were all heard, exhausted but happy; Karen's friends went home. (p. 372)

Did you infer that the story was about cards or music? Either fits. If early in your reading you inferred that it was about cards, a number of inferences consistent with card playing were made as the rest of the passage was read. For instance, participants in Anderson et al. (1977) who thought the passage was about cards also made inferences such as, "She is playing with a deck of cards," and "Mike sees that Pat's hand has a lot of diamonds." Those who concluded the passage was about music made inferences such as, "Mike brought out the stand and began to set things up," and, "As usual they couldn't decide on the piece of music to play." Once a schema is activated, it affects the inferences made about a situation, in this case, a text being read.

An activated schema also affects attention to information that would not be attended to if some other schema were activated. For instance, read the following passage (part of a passage used in Pichert & Anderson, 1977, and Goetz, Schallert, Reynolds, & Radin, 1983) as if you were a burglar making plans to rob the house described in the passage:

> The two boys ran until they came to the driveway. "See I told you today was good for skipping school," said Mark. "Mom is never home on Thursday," he added. Tall hedges hid the house from the road so the pair strolled across the finely landscaped yard. "I never knew your place was so big," said Pete. "Yeah, but its nicer now than it used to be since Dad had the new stone siding put on and added the fireplace."
>
> There were front and back doors and a side door which led to the garage which was empty except for three parked 10-speed bikes. They went in the side door, Mark explaining that it was always open in case his younger sister got home earlier than their mother.
>
> Pete wanted to see the house so Mark started with the living room. It, like the rest of the downstairs, was newly painted. Mark turned on the stereo, the noise of which worried Pete. "Don't worry, the nearest house is a quarter of a mile away," Mark shouted. Pete felt more comfortable observing than no houses could be seen in any direction beyond the huge yard.

Now reread the passage as if you were a potential homebuyer. What should be apparent during this second reading is that you attend to different parts of the passage when a burglar schema is activated versus when a homebuyer schema is activated. This was exactly the point of studies such as Goetz et al. (1983) and Pichert and Anderson (1977)—that schemata can guide attention.

The schemata that are activated when attempting to remember also can have a powerful impact on what is recalled. Thus, Anderson and Pichert (1978) had adults read the passage about boys playing hooky, again either reading from the perspective of a potential homebuyer or a burglar, followed by a memory test requiring recall of the passage. Then came the manipulation that is pertinent to the point being made here. Those participants who originally read and recalled from the perspective of a burglar were now asked to recall from the perspective of a homebuyer. Those who had read and recalled originally from the perspective of a homebuyer now attempted to recall from the perspective of a burglar. More information was recalled following this direction to switch perspectives, information consistent with the new perspective. An activated schema guides reconstruction of a previously encountered event (see also Kardash, Royer, & Greene, 1988). It can be used to guide retrieval, as it was in the case of this subject (cited by Anderson & Pearson, 1984) while attempting to recall the "hooky" passage from a burglar's perspective:

> I just thought of myself as a burglar walking through the house. So I had a different point of view, a different objective point of view for different details, you know. I noticed the door was open, and where would I go here, go there, take this, take that, what rooms would I go to and what rooms wouldn't I go to. Like,

you know, who cares about the outside and stuff? You can't steal a wall or nothing . . . I remember [the color TV] in the second one, but not in the first one. I was thinking about things to steal, things you could take and steal. In the den was the money. China, jewelry, other stuff in other places. [Q: Why do you think you remembered the color TV the second time and not the first time?] Because I was thinking of things to steal, I guess. (p. 283)

The research produced by Richard Anderson and colleagues substantiates that people have schematic knowledge and that it is used in processing new and recalling old information. Not surprisingly, this evidence has inspired a great deal of other work about the nature of human knowledge, with research conducted by Nelson, Hudson, Fivush, and their colleagues particularly important to educators. These investigators have asked whether children (e.g., preschoolers) store knowledge in schemata and, if they do, how such storage affects their processing of new material. In fact, children do use schematic representations much as adults do.

Not surprisingly, the schemata that children possess are determined by recurring events in their lives. Thus, children have schemata representing events such as dinner (e.g., at home and at McDonald's), bedtime, making cookies, birthday parties, and going to a museum (Hudson & Nelson, 1983; Hudson & Shapiro, 1991; McCarthy & Nelson, 1981; Nelson, 1978; Nelson & Gruendel, 1981). For instance, if children are presented a brief story pertaining to one of their schemata, they can answer inferential questions about the story—that is, questions that require knowledge about the situation described in the text that is beyond the information specified in the text.

As an example, consider what happens when a child is questioned about the following short story:

Johnny and his mom and dad were going to McDonald's. Johnny's father told him he could have dessert if he ate all his dinner. They waited in line. They ate their hamburgers. And they had ice cream. (Hudson & Slackman, 1990, p. 378)

When presented the question, "Why did they stand in line?," the 4- to 7-year-olds in the Hudson and Slackman study had no difficulty responding, despite the fact that there was no mention in the story of why they had stood in line. The McDonald's

schema contains this information, a schema understood by many preschoolers in the United States.

It is evident that schemata can have a powerful effect on children's comprehension and memory when children are presented stories that are not quite right in that they include information inconsistent with schemata stored by most children. Consider this less than perfect story that Hudson and Nelson (1983) presented to 4- to 7-year-olds:

One day it was Sally's birthday and Sally had a birthday party.
Sally's friends all came to her house.
Sally opened her presents and found lots of new toys.
Everybody played pin the tail on the donkey.
Then Sally and her friends ate the cake.
They had some chocolate and vanilla ice cream.
Everybody had peppermint candy, too.
Sally blew out all the candles on the cake.
Sally's friends brought presents with them.
Then it was time for Sally's friends to go home.

Most readers recognize that presents were opened before it was specified that the friends had brought the presents. In addition, the cake was eaten before the candles were blown out. These happenings are noted because they are inconsistent with the birthday party schema.

The use of the birthday party schema to comprehend and remember this story was apparent when the children in Hudson and Nelson (1983) attempted to recall the story. Sometimes the story was repaired during recall by not mentioning either one or both of the misordered elements. When the misordered acts were reported, they tended to be placed in schematically correct order rather than as specified in the story. In short, recall of the story was consistent with the schema for birthday party even though the original presentation of the story was not consistent with this schema.

Although the children in Hudson and Nelson (1983) tended not to recall many inferences, the ones that were made were consistent with what usually happens at birthday parties. Hudson (1988) presented data that demonstrated especially well that children are often willing to accept that some schema-relevant event occurred in a story even though it did not. The 4- to 7-year-olds in the 1988 study heard stories about going to McDonald's and grocery shopping. They were then given a recognition test and were asked to discriminate sentences they had heard before from those they had not heard. The most important finding was that the children were quite willing to accept script-relevant sentences that had not been presented in the story as if they had been presented.

In short, the evidence is quite compelling that adults and children have schemata for familiar events that determine how new information is processed, interpreted, and retrieved. What we emphasize in closing discussion of this point is just how early in development schematic-based knowledge occurs and affects thinking (for a review, see Hudson, Fivush, & Kuebli, 1992). A study reported in Fivush (1987) is revealing on this point.

Fivush presented 14- and 20-month-old children an array of objects, some of which were consistent with a kitchen schema (i.e., *pan, plate, cup, spoon*) and some of which were consistent with a bathroom schema (i.e., *comb, toothbrush, toothpaste, soap*). The children were instructed to play with the objects. The order of touching them was the main dependent variable, which was definitely not random. The majority of the children played with objects associated with only one of the two schemata. About 20% of the sample played with the items for one schema first and then played with the items associated with the other schema.

Bauer and Mandler (1989) presented simple sequences of events to children (e.g., taking a toy bear's shirt off, placing the bear in the tub, and washing the bear), with children required to re-enact the events both immediately after they were presented and 2 weeks later. Schematically familiar events were better recalled than events not related to schemata possessed by the children. Bauer and Thal (1990) observed that when 2-year-olds recalled naturally orderable sequences that had been presented to them out of sequence, they tended to "correct" the ordering of the information. Data such as these and those reported by Fivush (1987) suggest that children's representations of the world are organized along schematic lines from an early age and that these schematic relations are similar to the schematic relations of older children and adults (Bauer & Fivush, 1992). For data confirming that even 11.5- to 13.5-month-old children mediate their memory using familiar schemata, see Bauer and Mandler (1992).

Not surprisingly, students develop schemata for recurring intellectual tasks, with students' schematic understanding of academic tasks an arena of great interest to educational psychologists. Both students' knowledge of the schematic structure of texts and their understanding of the schematic structure of common mathematics problems have received attention from educational psychologists, with these two topics taken up in the next two subsections.

Text Structure Schema

Texts have conventional structures that are familiar to readers (Kintsch & Greene, 1978). Both **narrative** text structures (i.e., the structures of fictional stories) and **expository** text structures (i.e., the structures of factual texts) have been studied. Although slightly different systems have been proposed by different researchers, there are great similarities in the various **story grammars** that have been proposed as capturing the structures of fiction and great similarities in the various schematic systems proposed as representing the structures of exposition. Thus, rather than worry about subtle differences between alternative story grammars and expository structures, we present well-known examples that convey the general sense of these schemata.

Story Grammar   Jean Mandler (e.g., 1978, 1987) has been particularly active in analyzing the structure of stories. According to her theory, a story consists of a setting and an event structure composed of episodes. Each episode has a beginning, which is an event initiating a complex reaction; a complex reaction, which is composed of an emotional or cognitive response and a state the protagonist wishes to achieve; a goal path, which involves a plan of action by the character and the consequences of setting the plan of action in motion; and an ending, which is a reaction (for summary, see Pressley, 1983).

Here is a simple two-episode story adapted from Mandler (1978, p. 22):

> Once there were twins, Tom and Jennifer, who had so much trouble their parents called them the unlucky twins (*setting*). One day, Jennifer's parents gave her a dollar bill to buy a turtle she wanted, but on the way to the pet store she lost it (*beginning* of first episode). Jennifer was worried that her parents would be angry with her so she decided to search every bit of the sidewalk where she had walked (*reaction*). She looked in all the cracks and in the grass along the way (*plan of action* part of the *goal path*). She finally found the dollar bill in the grass (*consequence* part of the *goal path*). But when Jennifer got to the store, the pet store man told her that someone else had just bought the last

turtle, and he didn't have any more (*ending*). The same day, Tom fell off a swing and broke his leg (*beginning* of second episode). He wanted to run and play with the other kids (*reaction*). So he got the kids to pull him around in his wagon (*plan of action*). While they were playing, Tom fell out of his wagon and broke his arm (*consequence*). Tom's parents said he was even unluckier than Jennifer and made him sit in bed until he got well (second *ending*).

The most visible competing system to Mandler's was proposed by Nancy Stein and her colleagues (e.g., Stein & Nezworski, 1978; Stein & Glenn, 1979). The categories and their order of occurrence in a simple story are almost identical in the two systems. Thus, Stein and Nezworski (1978) proposed that stories start with a *setting,* which includes introduction of the protagonist as well as information about the physical, social, or historical context; an *initiating event,* which initiates a response by the protagonist; an *internal response,* which is an emotion, thought, or goal of the protagonist; an *attempt,* composed of overt actions to achieve the protagonist's goal; a *consequence,* marking the attainment or nonattainment of the goal; and a *reaction* in the form of an emotion, cognition, or end state.

There are at least four types of evidence that substantiate the existence and psychological importance of story grammar knowledge. (1) Stories that do not conform to the story grammar structure are difficult to remember (and are processed more slowly) compared with stories that do conform, with this finding holding for both children and adults (e.g., Kintsch, Mandel, & Kozminsky, 1977; Mandler, 1978; Mandler & Johnson, 1977; Stein & Nezworski, 1978). This conclusion holds not only for text that is heard but also for stories presented on television (e.g., Collins, Wellman, Keniston, & Westby, 1978). (2) Reminiscent of Hudson and Nelson's (1983) finding (discussed earlier), when story information is presented in an order other than one consistent with conventional story grammar, both children and adults tend to fix the story up at recall, remembering the elements of the story in an order consistent with the story grammar (Mandler, 1978; Mandler & DeForest, 1979; Stein & Glenn, 1979). (3) The probability that an element will be recalled from a story varies with the role it plays in the story as defined by story grammar. Thus, major setting, initiating event, and consequence elements are more likely to be recalled than attempts, which are more likely to be recalled than

internal responses and reactions (Mandler, 1984; Mandler & DeForest, 1979; Mandler & Johnson, 1977; Stein & Glenn, 1979). (4) Reading times at the beginning of episodes are greater than for material in the middle of episodes. Content at the end of episodes is processed especially quickly (Haberlandt, 1980; Mandler & Goodman, 1982). Although each of these findings can be explained by competing theories, when considered together, there is much reason to believe that people have schemata that specify the structure of fiction.

Expository Text Structures   Anyone who has studied rhetoric knows that there is ample guidance in the classical rhetoric literature about how writers should process text. Kintsch (1982) specified the recommendations from this literature from the perspective of a cognitive psychologist. Kintsch argued that there are texts (and parts of expository texts) that simply identify things, specifying what they are. There also are definitional texts. Classification texts provide information about how to decide something is this or that. Some texts provide illustrations of general principles. There are compare-and-contrast texts and analysis texts, which break events down into their component parts, functions, or causes.

Whether or not people possess schemata for these various types of expositions has not been evaluated extensively, although the information that is available suggests that expository text schemata do function in adult learning and thinking. Kintsch and Yarbrough (1982) provided the most visible empirical validation of the psychological importance of expository text structures to date. University students read classification, illustration, compare-and-contrast, and procedural description texts in this study. The most critical manipulation in the study involved presentation of the text in either a good expository form or a poorly organized one. Thus, for the well-organized passage concerned with classification of primate locomotor patterns, the topic was introduced in the first paragraph. Then the classifications were presented in the next four paragraphs in their evolutionary order. In the poorly organized passage, the paragraphs were presented in a random order.

The results in the study were clear. Readers were much better able to state the main idea and recall ideas from well-organized compared with poorly organized passages. Even though the issue of whether or not adults possess schemata for expository text is hardly resolved by a single study, it is heartening that the outcomes in Kintsch and Yarbrough (1982) were so clear-cut, for important reading comprehension interventions that are aimed at increasing reader knowledge of expository text forms are being proposed and disseminated. Some of these will be covered in subsequent chapters.

Mathematics Problem Schemata

Most of the mathematics problems presented in elementary and high school textbooks have typical structures. For instance, Mayer (1981) analyzed high school algebra texts and identified about 100 common problem types. Working through those problems has an effect on long-term knowledge of problems. Schematic representations of typical high school mathematics problem types reside in the long-term memories of people who have completed high school mathematics.

Any algebra 1 textbook will contain a problem like this one: If a car travels 10 hours at 30 miles per hour, how far will it go? For many algebra 1 graduates, this problem activates their schemata for "distance = rate × time" problems. Here are some additional examples from high school algebra and science and the problem-solving schemata associated with them (all from Mayer, Larkin, & Kadane, 1984, pp. 246–247):

> If a machine can produce 10 units per hour, how many units can be produced in an 8-hour day? (output = rate × time)
>
> If pencils cost 5 cents apiece, how much will a dozen pencils cost? (total cost = unit cost × number of units)
>
> How much will be earned if $1000 is invested at 8% interest for 1 year? (interest = interest rate × principal)
>
> If a TV set costs the seller $300 and the markup is 20%, how much profit will be made? (profit = markup rate × cost)
>
> John's living room is 9 feet long and 12 feet wide. How many square feet of carpet is required to cover the floor? (area = length × width)
>
> If the voltage of a dry cell is 1.5 volts, find the current that cell will produce in a single cell flashlight bulb having a resistance of 10 ohms. (current = voltage/resistance)

That students who have completed high school mathematics and science courses have developed schemata for the problem types in these courses has been confirmed in several studies. Students can clas-sify problems into types (e.g., identifying problems as representing one of the example schemata presented in the last paragraph; e.g., Hinsley, Hayes, & Simon, 1977). In addition, students use their problem-solving schemata as they identify which information in problems is critical to process and which is not (e.g., Hayes, Waterman, & Robinson, 1977; Mayer, 1982; Robinson & Hayes, 1978). This may be one reason that students who possess greater knowledge of problem schemata—and hence are more proficient at problem classification—also are better able to solve problems (e.g., Silver, 1987). Expert problem solvers in an area have well-developed schemata. For example, Chi, Feltovich, and Glaser (1981) demonstrated that physics experts sort physics problems consistent with higher-order principles of physics (e.g., problems that are examples of the law that objects in motion stay in motion and those at rest stay at rest), whereas novices sort problems consistent with surface features of the problems (e.g., all the problems concerned with rotating objects grouped together).

Mayer (1982) provided some striking data in support of the position that algebra problem types are represented schematically. Mayer (1981) had determined that some problem types are much more common than others, with Mayer's (1982) study including problem types that were common and others that were not common at all. The university students who participated in the investigation were asked to read these problems and to rewrite them (with the specific rewriting instructions varying in ways not relevant to this discussion). After participants had read and rewritten the eight problems presented to them, they were asked to recall each problem. Specifically, they were provided a one-word recall cue based on the content of the problem. For example, "age" was the recall cue for, "Laura is 3 times as old as Maria was when Laura was as old as Maria is now. In 2 years Laura will be twice as old as Maria was 2 years ago. Find their present ages" (p. 202). "Pipes" was the recall cue for, "One pipe can fill a tank in 6 hours while another can empty it in 2 hours. How long will it take to empty the full tank if both pipes are open at once" (p. 203). The data were quite striking—the more common the problem type, the more that was remembered from the problem. This would suggest that the participants had schemata in long-term memory for the more frequent problems that aided recall of the problems.

Other data in the study also supported the schemata hypothesis. Mayer (1982) reasoned that if participants were using schemata to aid recall, there should be an orderliness to their errors. In particular, they might be expected to convert low-frequency problem types into higher-frequency problem types. In fact, 80 percent of the time problems were recalled in converted form. The participants tended to distort their recall of atypical problems to be consistent with schemata associated with common problems.

All of the data presented in this subsection are consistent with the hypothesis that people who have experienced formal math and science instruction develop schemata representing the problem types encountered in such courses. In fact, an important hypothesis is that the development of such schemata is critical to the development of problem-solving competence (e.g., Riley, Greeno, & Heller, 1983), a possibility taken up in Chapter 13.

Summary

People have schematic representations about familiar activities and recurring events. These schemata abstract the relationships between different parts of these activities and events. That these types of representations seem to be available as young as it is possible to measure their presence suggests that schematic representation is a fundamental human competency. That it is possible to specify many different types of schemata, from those that code scenes (e.g., frames; Minsky, 1975), sequences in an evening (i.e., scripts; Schank & Abelson, 1977), elements of text (e.g., story grammar; Stein & Glenn, 1979), and mathematical relationships (e.g., Hinsley et al., 1977) provides another angle on their power. Schematic representations are used by everyone and in many different situations.

CASES

Before there can be a schema, there must be individual cases that include information about concepts, procedures, and how the components of the case are related. Even after a schema is formed, representations of individual cases will remain. Thus, even though a person may have a schema for fancy restaurants in general, he or she will have memory of the specifics of a fancy restaurant in their neighborhood. Case knowledge is important, for decisions often are based on a single case encountered in the past. The "case" method used in many law schools and some business and education colleges is based on the premise that humans often come to powerful general understandings in light of one case. Given this assumption, it is not surprising that great care is used in selecting examples for inclusion in sources like law school case books.

Research examining the case versus schematic knowledge of young children has succeeded in documenting some important differences between memory for specific episodes and what is encoded in schemata. For example, Fivush, Hudson, and Nelson (1984) studied kindergarten children's memories for a specific trip to a particular museum, one distinguished because it was a museum of archeology, and their general memories of what happens on trips to museums. Memories of the specific museum trip were tapped immediately after the trip occurred, 6 weeks following the trip, and 1 year later. One striking result was that memory of the specific museum trip did not include intrusions from the more general "museum-trip" script, nor did events that occurred on the specific trip receive mention when the kindergarten students told about museum trips in general. We agree with Fivush et al.'s (1984) conclusion that the clear separation of the memory for the specific trip and the general event schema suggests that memory for specific cases and schematic memory are two different types of encodings of information. (This is consistent with the more general theory of memory advanced by Tulving, summarized earlier in this chapter, that there are episodic memories and more general, semantic memories.) The potential for case knowledge to have long-term impact on thinking is also supported by these data in that memory of the specific case (especially the ability to recognize specific parts of the museum in a picture recognition task) was still quite good 1 year after the trip to the museum. Indeed, some specifics of the museum trip were remembered even 6 years after the trip occurred (Hudson & Fivush, 1991a; see Wagenaar, 1986, for additional evidence that single events are remembered for at least a half dozen years). Hamond and Fivush (1991) also provided data that slightly younger children (i.e., 3- to 4-year-olds) remember important events in their lives (e.g., a visit to Disneyworld) at least a year and a half later. Rich preschool experiences create rich memories that endure.

Hudson (1990) provided another interesting study contrasting memory for a specific event, attendance at one session of a creative movement workshop, with more general memory of repeated sessions at the workshop. The participants in the study were nursery school and kindergarten children. Memory of details was better for the workshop immediately preceding the test trial if only one workshop had been attended rather than four workshops. When four workshops had been attended, the children tended to recall the sequence of events during the workshop better than when only one workshop had been attended. That is, with repeated encounters of the workshop, some general knowledge of relationship between activities during the workshop had been built up, information critical to a schematic representation of such workshops. One cost of this improved memory for sequence with repeated visits to the workshop was that details from workshops 1, 2, and 3 were misremembered as having occurred during workshop 4. Once a schema is formed, memory of specific details declines, with an increase in the possibility of interference owing to memory of specific happenings on occasions during sessions other than the one that is to be remembered in detail. Once a schema forms, however, it is more than memorable. It can be useful in many ways. For example, Hudson and Fivush (1991b) demonstrated that preschoolers use their knowledge of grocery stores to plan trips to the store. Just as what adults know helps them to navigate the world, so it is with children.

In several studies, it has been established that a generalized event representation emerges from repeated experiences in a setting more quickly for older as compared with younger children. Farrar and Goodman (1992) demonstrated that 7-year-olds had a more stable generalized representation of an event experienced three times than did 4-year-olds. Fivush, Kuebli, and Clubb (1992) reported developmental improvements in generalized event representations between 3 and 5 years of age; Price and Goodman (1990) reported similar improvements between 2.5 and 5.5 years of age.

Even though there are differences between memories for single events and generalized memories of events experienced repeatedly, an important direction in research on case-based reasoning is whether a generalizable approach to problem solving can be developed from experiencing a single example (see Chapter 13 for additional information on case-based reasoning during problem solving). The answer is "probably yes," although general use of a procedure learned from an example is more likely if presentation of the example is embellished with explanations that increase learner understanding of the procedure and knowledge about when the procedure applies (i.e., metacognition about the procedure; e.g., Chen & Daehler, 1989, 1992).

It was apparent in studies reported by Gick and Holyoak (1980, 1983), that much generalizable knowledge can be gained from an example, although these same studies made clear that people often do not use the procedural knowledge they acquire from an example, as have other more recent investigations (e.g., Reed, 1989). In the Gick and Holyoak studies, subjects—always at least in high school—read a sample problem and its solution, such as the following:

> A small country was ruled from a strong fortress by a dictator. The fortress was situated in the middle of the country, surrounded by farms and villages. Many roads led to the fortress through the countryside. A rebel general vowed to capture the fortress. The general knew that an attack by his entire army would capture the fortress. He gathered his army at the head of one of the roads, ready to launch a full-scale direct attack. However, the general then learned that the dictator had planted mines on each of the roads. The mines were set so that small bodies of men could pass over them safely, since the dictator needed to move his troops and workers to and from the fortress. However, any large force would detonate the mines. Not only would this blow up the road, but it would also capture many neighboring villages. It therefore seemed impossible to capture the fortress.
>
> However, the general devised a simple plan. He divided his army into small groups and dispatched each group to the head of a different road. When all was ready he gave the signal and each group marched down a different road. Each group continued down its road to the fortress so that the entire army arrived together at the fortress at the same time. In this way, the general captured the fortress and overthrew the dictator. (Gick & Holyoak, 1983, pp. 35–36)

Following presentation of this example, the participants were given another problem to solve. See if you can come up with a solution to this problem:

> Suppose you are a doctor faced with a patient who has a malignant tumor in his stomach. It is impossible to operate on the patient, but unless the tumor is destroyed, the patient will die. There is a kind of ray

that can destroy the tumor. If the rays reach the tumor all at once at a sufficiently high intensity, the tumor will be destroyed. Unfortunately, at this intensity the healthy tissue that the rays pass through on the way to the tumor will also be destroyed. At lower intensities the rays are harmless to healthy tissue, but they will not affect the tumor either. What type of procedure might be used to destroy the tumor with the rays, and at the same time avoid destroying the healthy tissue? (Gick & Holyoak, 1983, p. 3)

Gick and Holyoak's (1980, 1983) participants often did not generate reasonable answers to the "radiation" problem, even though it is a situation analogous to the situation in the "general" problem. The answer is to use a number of lower intensity rays coming in at different angles so that they meet at the point of the tumor—and thus, the intensity of the radiation at the tumor would be equal to the sum of the intensities of the individual rays, although no healthy tissue would be exposed to rays of such intensity.

Even though adults often fail to recognize the analogous relationship between the radiation and general problems and hence fail to generate a correct solution when first presented the radiation problem, Gick and Holyoak provided substantial evidence that much was learned from the sample problem. In particular, if, when the radiation problem was presented, adults were presented a vague hint to use the previous story to solve the new problem, the probability of solving the radiation problem was actually quite high. It was not that the subjects had not learned the dispersion solution presented with the general problem or could not apply it to a new problem with an analogous structure. The problem was that they did not recognize the relevance of the previous problem and its solution unless they were prompted to notice its relevance with the hint. Quite a bit was learned from the single worked-out example—just not enough to ensure recognition of new problems similar in structure to the sample problem. This, of course, is a metacognitive failure—not knowing when and where to apply a problem-solving procedure that one has learned.

Others have also been exploring the potential of single examples to produce generalizable knowledge. Ahn (e.g., 1987) and colleagues (Ahn & Brewer, 1988; Ahn, Mooney, Brewer, & DeJong, 1987) presented adults with anecdotes about how a particular problem was solved, such as the following:

Tom, Sue, Jane, and Joe were all friends and each wanted to make a large purchase as soon as possible. Tom wanted a VCR, Sue wanted a microwave, Joe wanted a car stereo, and Jane wanted a compact disk player. However, they each only had $50 left at the end of each month after paying their expenses. Tom, Sue, Jane, and Joe all got together to solve the problem. They made four slips of paper with the numbers 1, 2, 3, and 4 written on them. They put them in a hat and each drew out one slip. Jane got the slip with the four written on it, and said, "Oh darn, I have to wait to get my CD player." Joe got the slip with the 1 written on it and said, "Great, I can get my car stereo right away!" Sue got the number 2, and Tom got number 3. In January, they each contributed the $50 they had left. Joe took the whole $200 and bought a Pioneer car stereo. In February, they each contributed their $50 again. This time, Sue used the $200 to buy a Sharp 600 watt 1.5 cubic foot microwave at Service Merchandise. In March, all four again contributed $50. Tom took the money and bought a Sanyo Beta VCR with wired remote at Service Merchandise. In April, Jane got the $200 and bought a Technics CD player at Service Merchandise. (Mooney, 1990, p. 502)

Depending on the experiment, subjects in Ahn's research produced an abstract summary of the problem-solving rule illustrated by the story, wrote another anecdote demonstrating the application of the approach to problem-solving illustrated in the story, or answered questions about the problem-solving tactic. In general, adults could perform these tasks after exposure to a single example—doing as well as subjects who had been presented a formal abstract summary of the problem-solving tactic. That is, they could induce a general principle based on a single example.

Weaver and Kintsch (1992) also demonstrated that failure to transfer because of failure to attend to the underlying structure of a problem can be remedied easily in some instances. With 20 to 30 minutes of brief instruction in analyzing algebra word problems with respect to their underlying structure, university students were able to recognize structurally similar problems that differed greatly with respect to surface features. By teaching students to analyze new problems with respect to their structure, Weaver and Kintsch (1992) were able to increase problem-solving competence.

Many who have reviewed evidence such as this as well as related outcomes have concluded that people often can and do reason about new situations based on analogies with previous situations (e.g.,

Hammond, 1990; Riesbeck & Schank, 1989)—that people often engage in case-based reasoning. Some detail in today's problem often reminds a person of a situation encountered previously, with the dimension of similarity prompting creation of a solution for today's problem that has some similarity to the solution used to solve the previous problem. When some low-level superficial similarity cues transfer of a strategy from one situation to another, it is known as "low-road" transfer (Salomon & Perkins, 1989). Low-road transfer is fairly common. For example, in Ross (1984), if a sample word problem illustrating a probability principle was based on the happenings in an IBM car pool, performance on a test item covering the principle was better if the test item story was about the happenings in an IBM car pool rather than the happenings among golfers or some other group of people. See Macario, Shipley, and Billman (1990) for evidence that children as young as 4 years of age can experience low-road, case-based learning of a generalizable rule.

The problem with low-road transfer, of course, is that often more than recognition of superficial similarity is required to solve a problem. Recognition of structural similarity between the current situation and a previously encountered situation is required. Salomon and Perkins (1989) refer to transfer based on recognition of structural similarity as "high-road" transfer. When taking the high road is required, people often act like Gick and Holyoak's (1980, 1983) subjects, failing to recognize analogies between new situations and situations they have dealt with in the past. Other times, people ignore the deep structural cues and are reminded instead of something that is only superficially related to the present case, resulting in a poor solution being generated—as in the example of a person applying the solution used to solve a previous problem mentioning an IBM carpool when the current problem mentioning an IBM carpool required an altogether different approach (see Gentner, 1989, for an analysis).

Are there any general principles about the likelihood of solving new problems with solutions similar to ones used in analogous problems? Brewer (1989) proposed that there are two important ones, and we add two more: The first is that people often can make analogies between a new situation and an old one if they are given a prompt to do so (Gick & Holyoak, 1980, 1983), or something about the new situation reminds the learner about the old situation (e.g., Ross, 1984, 1987, 1989). Second, it will be easier to notice analogies between items in domains in which one has greater expertise—the learner is more likely spontaneously to detect an analogy for problems in a domain of expertise, and the learner is more likely to be able to determine how to apply old knowledge gained from examples to new problems when cued to do so. Prior knowledge is important, a theme that will be expanded on in the next chapter. Third, we add that, in general, low-road transfer is more certain than high-road transfer. Fourth, we add that transfer of a problem solution to a new situation is more likely to the extent that people are taught when and where to apply a problem solution, why the solution works, and what outcomes the solution produces. For example, Chen and Daehler (1992) demonstrated that even children in the primary grades will transfer a problem solution from one situation to an analogous one if the initial presentation of the problem solution is metacognitively rich, specifying in particular the goals a problem solution facilitates and the outcomes it produces.

As we present this research on learning from one example, we feel some anxiety, for the conventional wisdom is that learning from examples is usually more certain when several examples are presented rather than one. Much of the work establishing the importance of multiple exemplars has been generated in studies aimed at determining how people learn how to identify new categories. Because much of this work was done with artificial materials, we do not want to emphasize it over some of the more ecologically valid research already presented in this section but believe that the prominence of the work with artificial materials demands some mention of it.

For example, one paradigm establishing the role of multiple examples in acquiring categorical knowledge involved presentation to subjects of two five-dot patterns, each of which was presented as a prototype for a concept—A and B (for one such study, see Peterson, Meagher, Chait, & Gillie, 1973). Then a number of five-dot examples were presented to subjects, with their task to decide whether each example was representative of concept A or B, often with feedback provided as to the correctness of attempted classifications. A criterion in such studies is whether subjects can identify whether a dot pattern presented several days (weeks, months) later is representative of A or B.

Collapsing across studies of this genre (see Druckman & Bjork, 1991, for a brief review; also

Smith & Medin, 1981), the following conclusions emerge: Acquisition of concepts is more certain as the number of examples presented increases. Training is more likely to permit identification of the full range of examples of the concept if the full range of examples is presented during training. One hassle involved in presenting the full range of examples during training is that it increases errors during training. In short, there is substantial evidence in the concept acquisition literature that multiple and varied examples can have an extremely positive impact on acquisition of conceptual knowledge.

Is there really a dilemma here with respect to making practical recommendations? No. People sometimes generalize based on one case. Often that is all they have to go on, and the situation is such that new cases cannot be created. (For example, an enormous amount of evidence in support of the claim that useful generalizations can emerge from single examples was generated by social learning researchers during the 1960s and 1970s; see Chapter 7.) In contrast, many of the concepts that must be discovered anew in school by each generation of students can be presented conveniently via multiple examples rather than just one. Although students may come to powerful understandings about the structure of a concept, procedure, or principle based on their first encounter with it or learn enough of its details to permit some low-road transfer, presentation of additional examples can permit practice working with the concept, procedure, or principle as well as exposure to various ways the concept, procedure, or principle can be packaged. Many and varied examples seems like a good idea when it is possible, and it is often possible in school. Such variety is essential if there is to be a schematic, generalized representation of the concept, procedure, or principle. When exposure to a variety of examples is not possible, the mind can store single cases that permit, at least some of the time, both low-road and high-road transfer.

VERBAL AND NONVERBAL REPRESENTATIONS: IMAGERY AND DUAL CODING

Paivio (e.g., 1971, 1986; especially Clark & Paivio, 1991, which provided the basis for much of what is presented in this subsection) posited that knowledge is composed of complex associative networks of verbal and imaginal representations. The verbal system contains word like codes for objects and events and abstract ideas, codes that are only arbitrarily related to what they represent (e.g., the word "book" has no physical resemblance to an actual book). The imagery system contains nonverbal representations that retain some resemblance to the perceptions giving rise to them (e.g., an image of a book shares features with the perception of an actual book). These include visual images (e.g., of a bell), auditory images (e.g., the sound of a bell), actions (e.g., ringing motion), skeletal sensations related to emotion (e.g., racing heart), and other nonlinguistic representations. Thus, the imagery representation for a book has visual and tactual qualities associated with books. Verbal representations tend to be sequential, whereas the imagery system can encode a number of features simultaneously. A single complex image (e.g., of a classroom) can encode a great deal about the classroom simultaneously, whereas a verbal representation of a classroom can only be made sequentially one bit of information at a time (e.g., the room has desks, aisles, and windows, until a sequence has been generated exhausting the details of the classroom). Images can be dynamically transformed, as when you mentally walk around an image of the classroom in which your educational psychology course meets.

Elements in the imagery representational system are linked to elements in the verbal representational system. Thus, there is a connection between most people's image of a book and their verbal representation of a book, with such **referential connections** permitting construction of mental images given words as stimuli and generation of names when objects are seen in pictures. (There is some evidence, in fact, that inefficiency in making such referential connections is implicated in learning disabilities, with that database interpretive as supportive of the hypothesis that dual-coding is an important dimension of effective and efficient thinking; Swanson [1989].) The richness of verbal-imaginal referential connections can be understood by considering the nonverbal associations to a word such as "surgery." These can include vivid images of excruciating pain and memories of feelings of both "coming apart" and tightness along suture lines. When someone mentions "Canada," some people envision a map outline of the country and the first bar of, "O Canada." There are also **associative connections** within both the verbal and the nonverbal systems. In the verbal system, words are associated with other words, so some students relate the word "school" with "hate," "boring," and "afraid." Categories and their instances are tied associatively within the verbal system, so "tree" is associated with "maple," "oak," and "pine." Within the nonverbal system, there are associative connections between images within sensory or across sensory modalities. Thus, author CB's image of an elephant is associated with an image of big logs, since she has often seen elephants carrying big logs with their trunks. She also associates the visual image of elephants with her memory of the smell of elephants.

A series of images can be linked, for instance, to create a nonverbal representation of the contents of a story. The ability to create linking images meaningfully integrating a number of concepts is an important human capacity that has been exploited in a number of methods for improving comprehension and memory (see Chapters 2 and 14, this volume). Humans are more adept at creating images for concrete verbal concepts than abstract ones, however, so it is easier to imagine a book than "liberty" or "freedom."

Activation of one concept results in activation of associated verbal and nonverbal representations. Thus, when author CB imagines an elephant at Columbia SC's Riverbanks Zoo, she is also likely to imagine the giraffes at the same zoo. Spreading activation can be increased by instructions to make associations. Thus, instructions to construct images when reading a text result in increased activation of the imagery system. Instructions that stimulate spreading activation can operate in a fine-grained fashion—consider the verbal concepts activated by an instruction to think of synonyms versus an instruction simply to make associations. Other contextual factors besides instruction can also affect spreading activation. For example, presentations of pictures can stimulate associations that might not be made in the absence of pictures. Presenting materials organized by categories can stimulate different patterns of activation than presenting materials in a random order. Different patterns of associations can be activated by small differences in context. For instance, $2 + 6$ activates "8," whereas 2×6 activates "12," at least for people who have sufficient experience with addition and multiplication facts to build up associations between two-digit addition equations and two-digit multiplication equations (see

Siegler & Shrager, 1984; also, Chapter 13 of this book).

A person's verbal and nonverbal associations are built up through experiences, with uniqueness in experiences resulting in somewhat unique representations for individuals. Even so, there is enough commonness to experience that there are associations shared by many people within a culture. Because the elements in the nonverbal representational system share features with the perceptions that arise from the referents of the representations, there are commonalities between the nonverbal representations people possess. CB's image of an elephant is very similar to your image of an elephant!

Paivio's dual-coding theory is supported by an enormous amount of evidence. For example, Paivio (1986) generated a list of 60 phenomena that can be explained by dual-coding theory. These include, among others, that concrete materials are more memorable than abstract materials, there are more synonym intrusions for concrete than abstract materials (consistent with greater spreading activation for the concrete materials), the amount of time taken to "generate" an image in response to an instruction to do so increases with the abstractness of the material, pictures are learned better than words, and words can be read faster than pictures can be named (suggesting the verbal code is accessed directly for words and only through the second, image, code in reaction to pictures). A variety of evidence exists that activation of visual imagery interferes with visual perception and vice versa (Craver-Lemley & Reeves, 1992). There is neuropsychological evidence supporting dual-coding theory. For instance, left hemisphere lesions disrupt verbal processing more than nonverbal processing, whereas right hemisphere lesions have the opposite effect. See Farah (1988) and Tippett (1992) for compelling summaries of neurophysiological evidence supporting the conclusion that visual imagery and visual perception involve similar representations and are the products of the same regions of the brain.

Roger Shepard and his colleagues (e.g., Shepard & Metzler, 1971) conducted a particularly telling series of experiments that documented one role of imagery in thinking. They presented their adult subjects with a complex geometric figure and a second figure, which was either the same figure (but rotated 0 to 180 degrees) or a mirror image (also rotated some number of degrees). The task was to decide whether the original figure and the rotation were the "same" figure or "different." The most critical outcome was that the amount of time to recognize the same figure as same was a linear function of the number of degrees of rotation required to make the figure parallel to the original figure. This result suggested that the participants were "flipping" the geometric figures in their heads, using some kind of spatial code. Even 4-year-olds can do this. Thus, it takes longer for a 4-year-old to decide that a capital R and an upside down R are the same letter than it takes for the 4-year-old to decide that the R and an R on its side (i.e., flipped 90 degrees) are the same letter (e.g., Marmor, 1975). In general, older children and adults are faster and more adept at mental imagery rotation than preschoolers (e.g., Kosslyn, Margolis, Barrett, Goldknopf, & Daly, 1990).

A variety of subjective reports support dual-coding theory. People report flipping objects in their head in the Shepard and Metzler (1971) task. Images are more likely to be reported when learning concrete materials than when learning abstract materials. Subjects report relying on their images during recall of concrete materials.

The greatest challenge to Paivio's position came from his colleague at Western Ontario, Zenon Pylyshen (1973), who argued that imagery effects could be explained in propositional terms (Anderson & Bower, 1973)—that in fact abstract propositional representations underpin images. It is true that any image can be defined by a propositional list—for instance, UNDER (DOG, TABLE); (RED, TABLE); (BROWN, DOG) is a list of propositions specifying an image of a brown dog under a red table. It takes little imagination, however, to recognize that even a moderately complex image can require many propositions to specify it. The real question, however, is whether the logical possibility of propositional encoding of images renders the idea of images as scientifically useless. That is, could it be that anything a propositional theory would predict and explain would be identical with what an imagery (dual-code) theory would predict and explain, a possibility raised by some (e.g., Anderson, 1978)?

Although the argument for the propositional position was complex, an important part of it was that imagery increased memory by activating the propositions defining the image. If that is so and the image itself is simply an uninteresting byproduct of

the propositional code, the size of the image "in the mind's eye" should not matter, or so reasoned Kosslyn (1975), for the relationships specified by propositions would be identical in big and little images. Thus, Kosslyn asked adults to imagine an animal, such as a rabbit, either next to a fly or next to an elephant. The subjects were then given the names of rabbit parts (e.g., eye, nose, ear) and were asked whether the part could be found on their image of the animal. The participants in fact "zoomed in" faster on features and made quicker decisions when the rabbit was next to a fly than when it was next to an elephant—that is, when the image of the rabbit should have been large compared with when the image of the rabbit was small. Kosslyn included a variety of controls to dismiss objections that might be raised by proponents of propositional theories. For instance, when subjects in Kosslyn (1976) were asked to verify in an animal image the existence of animal parts highly associated with the animal but perceptually small (e.g., whether an imagined cat had *claws*), their reaction times were slower than when they verified parts perceptually larger but less highly associated with the particular animal (e.g., whether an imagined cat had a *head*). When subjects did the same tasks without being instructed to consult an image (i.e., decide whether cats have *claws* and whether cats have *heads*), they reacted more quickly for parts highly associated with the animal compared with parts less highly associated with the animal. Findings such as this (see Finke, 1989, for a stimulating summary of such evidence), when combined with the vast amount of research evidence produced by Paivio and his co-workers at Western Ontario (see Paivio, 1971, 1986), make credible the claim that mental images can and often do function in human cognition—that part of our knowledge is composed of nonverbal images.

One of the most interesting chapters in the propositional representation versus imagery debate has been contributed by Kintsch (1983, 1989), the leading propositional theorist of the 1980s. As discussed earlier, Kintsch believes that ideas presented in text are coded propositionally. In addition, however, Kintsch argues that situation models are constructed from texts depicting spatial relationships, and these situation models involve imagery, with this coding permitting performances not possible (or at least not easy) with propositional coding (e.g., making of spatial inferences; see the discussion of

Perrig & Kintsch, 1985, in the section of this chapter on mental models).

Nonverbal coding, and imagery coding in particular, is specified by other major theories of learning and representation as well. For instance, many schema theorists (e.g., Schank & Abelson, 1977) explicitly specify that memory of complex schemata involves an imagery component. Such an imaginal conception of schemata is consistent with classical thinking in information processing theories. For instance, Miller, Galanter, and Pribram (1960, Chapter 2) explicitly tied the two constructs:

> A human being . . . builds up an internal representation, a model of the universe, a schema, a simulacrum, a cognitive map, an Image. (p. 7)

Miller et al. (1960) were informed by a much earlier theoretical analysis, however, for one line later, they quote Bartlett (1932), who made unambiguous the nonverbal component in schemata:

> "Schema" refers to an active organization of past reactions, or of past experiences. . . . All incoming impulses . . . go together to build up an active, organized setting: visual, auditory, various types of cutaneous impulses and the like . . . all experiences connected by a common interest. . . . (Miller et al., 1960, p. 7, quoting Bartlett, 1932, p. 201).

Interestingly, dual-coding theorists have emphasized that many effects explained by schema theory are equally well or better explained by dual coding (Sadoski, Goetz, & Fritz, 1993a; Sadoski, Paivio, & Goetz, 1991). In addition, Mandler (1992a, 1992b) has proposed that a fundamental type of representation available from infancy is the image schema. There are many eyes that see conceptual similarity between schematic and imaginal theories of representation, with a melding of these theoretical approaches in progress.

Many famous scientists (e.g., Albert Einstein, Neils Bohr) and mathematicians (e.g., Poincaré) reported vivid images as part of their thinking processes while working on cutting-edge problems (see Miller, 1984, for many examples; also, John-Steiner, 1985, included an entire chapter on visualization in the thinking of creative people, including scientists). Mozart reported auditory images of as-yet unwritten works in which the piece was not imagined as separate parts but as a whole (Ghiselin, 1952). Arnheim (1971) in a book entitled *Visual Thinking* provided an especially complete argument that visualization plays a prominent role in creative and effective thinking.

Much of Miller et al.'s (1960) *Plans and the Structure of Behavior* is concerned with how schematic images play an important role in guiding behaviors, a point not missed by other important social and cognitive theorists. One of the more notable of these was Albert Bandura (e.g., 1977b), who contended that a main mechanism of observational learning of behavior involves imagery coding (see Chapter 7). The connections between nonverbal sensation and nonverbal representations specified by Paivio (1971, 1986) as well as the referential connections between nonverbal representations and verbal representations were echoed by Bandura, although Bandura (1977b) did not reference Paivio's model or work.

Bandura described mechanisms mediating the retention of observed experiences as follows:

> Observational learning relies mainly on two representational systems—imaginal and verbal. Some behavior is retained in imagery. Sensory stimulation activates sensations that give rise to perceptions of the external events. As a result of repeated exposure, modeling stimuli [observations] eventually produce enduring, retrievable images of modeled performances. On later occasions, images (centrally aroused perceptions) can be summoned up of events that are physically absent. Indeed, when things are high correlated, as when a name is consistently associated with a given person, it is virtually impossible to hear the name without experiencing an image of that person. Similarly, mere reference to an activity that has been repeatedly observed (e.g., driving an automobile) usually arouses its imaginal counterpart. Visual imagery plays an especially important role in observational learning during early periods of development when verbal skills are lacking, as well as in learning behavior patterns that do not lend themselves readily to verbal coding.
>
> The second representational system, which probably accounts for the notable speed of observational learning and retention in humans, involves verbal coding of modeled events. . . . Details of the route traveled by a model, for example, can be acquired, retained, and later reproduced more accurately by converting the visual information into a verbal code describing a series of right and left turns (e.g., RLRRL). . . . Observational learning and retention are facilitated by such symbolic codes because they carry a great deal of information in an easily stored form. (Bandura, 1977b, pp. 25–26)

Bandura (1977) went on to make the case that these imagery and verbal codes served to guide subsequent behavior, a case he elaborated in his 1986 book.

By the 1986 book, Bandura had studied Paivio's theory and the debate concerning propositional versus imagery models. Although acknowledging the debate (e.g., pp. 56–57, 455–456), Bandura did not back down from his previous position (p. 57) asserting the functional significance of imagery and reiterating themes consistent with dual-coding theory: "... [T]he imagery system evolved because it aids effective transactions with the environment. The processes by which imagery functions as an internal model for the production and correction of response patterns command major interest in studies of psychological modeling. . . . After representational imagery has been developed, images (i.e., centrally aroused perceptions) can be readily summoned up of events that are physically absent" (p. 57).

A number of educational interventions based on imagery have been proposed, studied, and disseminated, with some of these taken up in later chapters. All of these interventions make the sensible assumption that people can create mental images that permit unique encodings relative to verbal encodings and that stimulate associations in a nonverbal representational system. For millennia, those interested in promoting learning have recognized the power of images to do so (Yates, 1966). The contemporary student of educational psychology must be cognizant of the potency of imagery in promoting thinking, understanding, and acquisition of new information.

PRODUCTIONS

In several important cognitive psychological theories, cognitive rules are represented as productions, which were introduced in Chapter 2 as procedural knowledge stored in "if-then" form—*if* these conditions hold, *then* execute this action. The argument was presented there that cognitive strategies resemble productions in many ways. How productions operate in thinking more generally can be illustrated by two models of thinking.

ACT*

ACT* also was introduced in Chapter 2. ACT* is a knowledge system that includes procedural knowledge encoded into productions as well as declarative knowledge, the factual knowledge in the system. Although ACT* is an artificial intelligence system (i.e., a computer program), ACT* attempts to mirror human cognition and has been an influential model with educational psychologists. Consideration of the dynamics of ACT* can provide insights into how productions might function in human cognition. In particular, it is possible to see how procedural and declarative knowledge can interact during thinking.

There are three types of declarative memory codes (Anderson, 1983, Chapter 2) in ACT*: (1) *Temporal strings* code the order of a set of items—which of a set of items occurs first, which second, third, and so on. A whole event that is composed of a sequence of steps can be captured by such a representation. (This is the ACT* version of a script, as discussed in the early section on schema theories.) (2) *Spatial images* code the spatial configuration of elements in an array (i.e., which items are above others, below others, to the left of others, and to the right of others). (This is the ACT* version of images.) (3) *Propositional representations* operate as they do in the Kintsch model discussed earlier—they encode meaningful relationships between elements.

In addition, declarative memory contains information about the category membership and attributes of the elements involved in each of these three types of representations. Consider two examples: (1) A square spatial array with a red triangle in the upper right corner, a blue circle in the upper left, a green rectangle in the lower right, and a black diamond in the lower right is encoded as a spatial image with four elements in the four corners of a square. The upper right element is categorized as a triangle, with its redness encoded as an attribute. The upper left element is categorized as a circle, with blueness being one of its features. (2) The sentence, "The tall lawyer believed the man came from Mars," is encoded BELIEVE (AGENT, OBJECT) with the object encoded as FROM (SUBJECT, MARS). The subject encodes that the category of the agent is lawyer, who has the attribute of being tall. The SUBJECT of the OBJECT is categorized as a man. The relation BELIEVE has the attribute of past tense.

Complex events can be represented in this system by combining the different types of declarative codes. Examples offered by John Anderson (1983) included a baseball game encoded as a string of propositions, each proposition encoding some meaningful event in the game, with the events occurring earlier in the game coded earlier in the string (i.e., *strings* and *propositions* were coordinated). Anderson (1983) also provided an example of how ACT* would handle a restaurant script such as the one studied by Schank and Abelson (1977). The central string (enter, order, eat, exit) has other strings branching from it. Thus, for an informal restaurant, the *enter* element on the main string branches to a string specifying how to enter an informal restaurant (walk in, look for table, decide, go to table, sit down). This hierarchy of strings has both propositional and imagery elements embedded in it. Thus, the *walk in* element in the informal restaurant string is the proposition WALKS INTO (SUBJECT, RESTAURANT) with the subject categorized as a customer with two attributes—he or she is hungry and has money. The *go to table* proposition in the informal restaurant string includes an image of a table.

As just outlined, the declarative memory of the ACT* system includes many of the types of representations included in models of human representation that have been discussed in this chapter, from categories to images to propositional relations to schemas. This declarative knowledge is used in conjunction with procedural knowledge. For instance, during pattern recognition, some declarative knowledge will be activated, as when the pattern recognition productions identify an example of a category member. Thus, when encountering a four-legged animal with a longish elliptical head, sharp claws, and a meow, the pattern recognition productions identify a cat. This information is used to determine which action procedures to activate. If your goal is to make the animal happy, and if the animal is a cat (two conditionals), you give it some milk (an action).

A point of emphasis in Anderson (1983) is that procedural and declarative knowledge are stored in different parts of long-term memory. That is, procedural and declarative knowledge work together only when coactivated in short-term memory structures—there is no communication between them while they remain in long-term storage. When the set of conditionals for a production, which is stored in long-term memory, are met, the production is activated into short-term memory. It fires, sometimes activating declarative knowledge in the process, declarative knowledge required to carry out the proposition.

Thus, for the plan-translate-revise writing strategy (see Chapter 15), executing the productions involved in planning an essay on a topic results in the activation of long-term declarative knowledge about the topic of the essay. The execution of the planning production creates products (e.g., an outline of the essay) that can satisfy the conditional requirements for the activation of other productions (e.g., the translate part of the plan-translate-revise strategy fires only if there is an outline plan already in place). The act of translation results in more declarative knowledge being activated in the creation of a rough draft. This product of the translation operation (i.e., the rough draft) serves as a conditional for the revise productions to fire (i.e., revise productions operate only if a rough draft is in existence). It is possible for a long chain of productions to be executed in sequence using such mechanisms: The conditions for a first production are met. When the first production fires, it creates products that fulfill the conditional requirements for another production to fire and so on through a number of conditionals met–productions fire–products produced cycles.

An important activity for scholars working on artificial intelligence systems is to demonstrate that these systems can perform the cognitive tasks that humans can perform and in doing so produce performances that resemble human performances. When a program can do so, the case builds that research on the program is relevant to human cognition. Some of the things ACT* can do are impressive. For example, using a set of productions and spatial images, it is possible to "flip" Shepard and Metzler's (e.g., 1971) geometric figures over in the computer, with performances much like those of people flipping the figures over in their heads. For example, it takes the computer longer to flip a cube to an upright position when it is 150 degrees from upright than when it is 90 degrees from upright. ACT* also exhibits spreading activation, with the likelihood of an element in short-term memory activating an element in long-term declarative memory determined by the strength of association between the element in short-term memory and the element in long-term memory. ACT* can also generate elaborations to material in the short-term store, again with the mechanisms for doing this a set of productions (all examples, Anderson, 1983).

ACT* provides a possible model for the knowledge that underlies some educationally important cognitive competencies—most emphatically the type of metacognitively guided strategy use coordinated with other knowledge that is discussed so prominently throughout this book! Young educational psychologists should be aware that some scientists interested in artificial intelligence are studying problems directly related to educational issues. For instance, ACT* can model how students approach geometry proofs and learn language (Anderson, 1983). Just and Carpenter (1987) have designed an artificial intelligence model of reading broadly conceived (CAPS)— attempting to simulate a variety of human reading performances from eye fixations to understanding of extended texts. The procedural knowledge in their model includes productions for word encoding, accessing the meanings of words, syntactic analysis, semantic analysis, and text-schema processing. The declarative knowledge base includes representations of words, the concepts referred to by words, world knowledge, and text schemata (e.g., story grammar). It is impressive just how many different types of knowledge about reading and other complex academic competencies can be included in an artificial intelligence model. We do not go into more detail about ACT*, CAPS, or other artificial intelligence systems, however, because this is a book about human abilities and performances rather than machine competencies.

One important characteristic of systems such as ACT* and CAPS is that many different types of representations are coordinated with one another—just as the many types of representations discussed in this chapter are coordinated in human minds. The production system discussed in the next subsection also displays this important property.

Mental Models

A number of researchers have been interested in **mental models** (Gentner & Stevens, 1983; Holland, Holyoak, Nisbett, and Thagard, 1986; Johnson-Laird, 1983). Their belief is that as people process the world, they construct a mental model (i.e., an internal representation) of what they are encountering. Holland et al. (1986) most explicitly spell out the role of productions in this process. Their theory is that as contact is made with the world, a number of productions are fired that contribute to a mental model of the situation.

Some of the productions that are activated by contact with the world permit categorization of elements in the world. Here are some examples (Holland et al., p. 42):

> If an object is a dog, then it is an animal. [specifies superordinate categorization when dog is encountered]

> If an object is a dog, then it can bark. [specifies feature defining category when dog is encountered]

In addition, there are productions that specify associations to elements encountered in the world. Consider the following productions that specify spreading activation from "dog":

> If an object is a dog, then activate the "cat" concept.
> If an object is a dog, then activate the "bone" concept.

The two types of productions considered thus far activate information in semantic nets—much as specified in the Collins and Loftus (1975) model.

Other productions that can be activated specify how change will take place—if particular conditions are met. Some of these are the basis for construction of expectations. Examples include the following:

> If a person annoys a dog, then the dog will growl.
> If a person whistles to the dog, then the dog will come to the person.

Others result in action on the environment, when particular conditions are met:

> If a dog chases you, then run away.
> If a dog approaches you with its tail wagging, then pet it.

Mental models also include productions that create new productions and modify old productions. These creation and modification productions evaluate whether the productions that are being fired are working as anticipated. When they are not, new ones are created or the old ones are revised. In addition— and this is a critical function—these creation and modification productions generate associations between and clustering among productions to create larger knowledge structures, ones involving the articulation of various productions, each of which permits some progress toward a common goal.

There are important differences between mental models and the simpler ACT* production system. For one, more than one production can operate at a time in the creation of mental models, whereas productions fire in sequence, one at a time in ACT*. That is, there is **parallel processing** in mental models as productions in a mental model interact, sometimes cooperating. Successful productions in a mental model are strengthened and more likely to be used in the future. If progress is made when two productions are simultaneously active, the association between the productions is strengthened, and they are more likely to be used conjunctively in the future. Sometimes productions in a mental model compete, *bidding* to be the ones activated. The "winners" in this competition better match the current situation than the "losers," are stronger because they have been more successful in the past in this situation than the losers, generate a better description of the situation than the losers, and are more compatible with other information activated in the system than the losers. Simultaneous activation of productions (as well as newly encountered information) is an important mechanism in the construction of higher-order knowledge. For example, simultaneous activation of the following productions eventually results in the construction of the category *zoo animal:*

> If an object is an elephant, then it is a zoo animal.
> If an object is a giraffe, then it is a zoo animal.
> If an object is a monkey, then it is a zoo animal.
> If an object is a zebra , then it is a zoo animal.

The mental modeling position is that representations of the world can be constructed using productions. Some of these productions have few and simple conditions, and others have many and complex conditions for them to fire. Some specify simple actions if conditions are met; others specify complex reactions. All of the different types of productions in the system work together to generate inferences and expectations about the world and solutions to problems. In doing so, higher-order knowledge is constructed. Thus, coactivation of the following propositions on several occasions might lead to an integrated sequence that becomes a unified piece of knowledge:

> If a person is saying an important telephone number, listen carefully.
> If a person is saying an important telephone number, repeat it.
> If a person is saying an important telephone number, write it down.

Success following simultaneous activation of this set of propositions should increase the likelihood of the listening-repeating-writing important number down sequence in the future.

If all of this seems vague at this point, keep reading in this subsection. What a mental model is—how it starts as prior knowledge that is transformed through encounters with new information and simultaneous activation with other prior knowledge and represents something never encountered before—should become clearer with additional discussion and examples.

An Example of Induction Holland et al. (1986, pp. 97–101) were particularly concerned with inductive processes during the creation of mental models. This was because they believe that prior knowledge could not possibly already hold all of the knowledge required to represent new situations. That is, as new circumstances are encountered in the world, new mental models must be constructed rapidly by processing of the new information in light of prior knowledge.

One of Holland et al.'s (1986) examples of induction during mental modeling involved a little girl who wanted to pet a cat: Jennifer sees a cat. Productions fire that activate the concept *cat* and its associated characteristics (e.g., animal, small, round head, longer than it is tall, four legs, sharp claws). Jennifer has a goal of getting closer to the cat in order to pet it. So far, nothing in her representation of cat includes information about how to approach a cat. Fortunately, as she searches for a solution to her problem, there is additional spreading activation. Productions fire activating associations to *cat*, such as *dog*. This provides useful information because *dog* has associated with it information about how to approach a dog: If person whistles, *dog* comes. Because both *cats* and *dogs* are *pets,* productions for creating new knowledge fire—in this case, productions for making analogies. The result is a new production: "If your goal is to summon X, and X is a certain kind of pet, then whistle." The result for Jennifer is a hypothesis: "The cat might come if I whistle." She does so, expecting the cat to come. The cat does not. This failure triggers the creation of new productions that compete with the active production. These might include, "If X is a pet and a cat, it will not come when you whistle"; "If X is a cat, it won't come when you whistle"; and "If X is a cat, then it ignores whistling children." The creation of these competing productions reduces the likelihood that Jennifer will whistle again. Perchance she does, the competing productions will strengthen when the cat does not come. If the competing productions are more powerful than the production governing "whistling," Jennifer will cease attempting to summon the cat with a whistle. The new productions created during this episode are encoded into long-term memory and can affect future performance.

Nature of Factual Knowledge Mental models clearly make use of the conceptual and associative information in the semantic networks of long-term memory. They also include mechanisms for generating images, with images being one type of mental model (Johnson-Laird, 1983, especially Chapter 7; 1989). The particular strength of an image is that it contains information more directly corresponding to the structure of situations that it represents. Thus, Mani and Johnson-Laird (1982) presented subjects with sets of descriptions such as the following (Johnson-Laird, 1989, p. 472):

> The spoon is to the left of the knife.
> The plate is to the right of the knife.
> The fork is in front of the spoon.
> The cup is in front of the knife.

Their data generated in the study strongly supported the conclusion that such a set of relations was stored in a spatial array such as the following:

> spoon   knife   plate
>   fork   cup

That is, the verbal input stimulated the construction of a mental model in the form of an image. As Johnson-Laird (e.g., 1983, Chapter 7) might express it: The description of the place setting is initially represented in propositions capturing the meaning of the individual descriptive statements with these linguistic expressions then translated into mental models via production rules, with the end product a mental image.

Images do not have to occur as a function of processing text specifying spatially representable information. For example, Perrig and Kintsch (1985, Experiment 1) provided data demonstrating that spatial information in text sometimes is coded propositionally without the creation of an image. Their subjects read texts describing the layout of a town: For example, "Going left on Main, after a few blocks you see the Lutheran church on your right. Returning on Main Street to the other end, you come to the general store. . . . The church is north of the inn. . . . The inn is on the highway" (Kintsch, 1989, pp. 38–39). Even though the subjects could recall between 25 and 35 percent of the propositions in the text, they performed at chance value when tested on the validity of spatial inferences (e.g., yes or no—the highway is south of the church). Such an outcome suggests that they had not constructed an image of the town. In a follow-up study in which the description of the town was simplified, the subjects recalled a higher proportion of the text and were able to verify spatial inferences at well above a chance level. Overall the pattern of results suggested that creation of a spatial mental model might occur only once most of a text was represented propositionally.

A development in mental model theory is the possibility that mental models are not entirely mental but rather often involve interactions between a partially complete internal representation and an environment that fills in the gaps in the mental model. For example, we use a word processing program (MacWrite), which requires users to access and select from menus specifying various word processing functions. If we were asked to recall the order of the menu cards or the actual items on the cards, we would have a tough time doing so. Our mental model contains information about the menu cards in general, their functions in general, and their location but does not include specifics. When we select functions with the program, some of the thinking goes on solely in our heads, and some depends on the presence of the screen—that is, thinking is distributed between the head and the computer screen (O'Malley & Draper, 1992). We will see in Chapter 8 that a number of scientists are beginning to think of thinking as more than an "in-the-head" thing and more of a "head-and-environment" thing, with cognition sometimes distributed across mind and the physical environment (as in the case of word processing) and sometimes distributed across minds (e.g., as with group problem solving) and sometimes distributed across minds and the physical environment (e.g., when two people work at a MacWrite screen and try to figure out how to accomplish a novel word processing task).

Holland et al. (1986, p. 12) and Johnson-Laird (1983) insist that mental models are not schemata. A schema is a chunk of information stored in long-term memory, specifying how a number of concepts relate to one another. In contrast, mental models are relationships that are constructed as input is encountered and processed. Mental models can involve schemata and use them in combination with new input and other knowledge. Thus, a restaurant script might be activated from long-term memory when a person enters a restaurant. If a goat walks into the restaurant, however, there is nothing in most people's restaurant schema to deal with the goat. Another piece of knowledge—a production in long-term memory such as, "If a threatening or obnoxious creature intrudes, then eject it or escape from it"—can be combined with the restaurant script using the productions that permit construction of new knowledge (i.e., productions that generate inferences from old knowledge) to create a solution to this never-before-encountered problem. Mental models are about creating new knowledge and understandings from old knowledge and understandings.

In constructing mental models, all of the forms of knowledge discussed in this chapter can come into play, a feature of many models of thinking that are being constructed around productions. Of course, what this really says is that production system–type mental models capture the procedural and declarative knowledge that interacts continuously as part of thinking and learning, a theme that will be reiterated in this book. One final point is that the exact form of a mental model depends somewhat on the media in which information is presented to students. For example, mental models can be developed based on pictures alone or through consideration of both picture and verbal content. In addition, if the picture or the text content relates to prior knowledge possessed by the learner, the mental model will be different than if the picture or text is from an unfamiliar domain. Mental models are the result of complex interactions between new information, the way the new information is presented, and prior knowledge, with the mental model shifting as new information is encountered and the information already experienced is related to prior knowledge in various ways (Kozma, 1991). The goal of some new types of interactive educational environments (e.g., interactive video) is to stimulate the development of rich mental models (see Chapter 13) by encouraging students to recombine various types of knowledge they now possess, creatively juggling it to find solutions to new problems.

Summary

The most comprehensive models of thinking developed to date include productions as part of their model of knowledge. Exactly how the productions

function and the extent of their role in cognition varies within models. Models such as the one proposed by Holland et al. (1986) and others (e.g., SOAR; Newell, 1990) posit that most of cognition is productions. In part, this probably reflects that production systems run well on computers. Alternatively, this may reflect how critical it is to know how to do things—that much of thinking is knowing how (i.e., procedural knowledge) and using such knowledge appropriately (i.e., possessing conditional knowledge as part of procedural knowledge).

SITUATED KNOWLEDGE

Brown, Collins, and Duguid (1989) believe that knowledge is not separable from the actions that give rise to it nor from the culture in which those actions occur, consistent with many ideas in Soviet psychological analyses of activity and thinking (see Chapter 8). (Note that this position is similar to the position introduced at the end of the mental models discussion–that thinking is not just an "in-the-head" thing.) Consider author MP's understanding of the concept "intelligence." His view of intelligence reflects a mix of respect and distrust for psychometric intelligence (see Chapter 16) as well as some disturbing suspicions about multiple intelligences (e.g., Gardner, 1983, 1993; see Chapter 6, this book). There is also distrust of Piagetian conceptual views on intelligence (see Chapter 7). Much of his knowledge was developed during interactions with other psychologists. Other insights were derived as MP attempted to work with the term intelligence, during either writing or teaching. MP's understanding of intelligence will continue to change as he grapples with the concept in future work and interactions. Because his use of the term is somewhat constrained by the beliefs of the intellectual communities in which MP resides and interacts, his understanding of intelligence will reflect the beliefs held within these intellectual communities.

What is critical to emphasize here is that *actions* undertaken in a *cultural milieu* largely determine the meaning of a concept rather than some abstract features. Consider the "knowledge" of intelligence and its measurement possessed by a young psychologist who has never had an internship. It was developed in the culture of school through the actions required to pass examinations and includes a lot of knowledge in the abstract, such as the types of items on IQ tests, the professional party lines on appropriate environmental settings for giving such tests, and the professional standards for reporting and interpreting test data. We have yet to meet a graduate of such a class, however, who was ready to give an intelligence test on the first day of an internship or even understood how such tests are used by mental health professionals. During many interactions with senior psychologists during the internship, however, the intern acquires many of the understandings held by senior psychologists about intelligence and testing for it. The intern picks up a lot from watching the experienced assessors give and interpret such tests. Interns quickly get a sense of what are acceptable departures from manual-specified practices and which steps in the manual must be followed rigidly. They develop an understanding of the test that is consistent with the understandings of senior psychologists. This occurs through observation of authentic testing, followed by opportunities to do authentic testing.

Much of knowledge is implicit according to this framework, and it is obtained by acting in authentic situations—such as the intern giving an intelligence test to a real client in a real clinical setting. Much of the knowledge is built up through real problem solving and real dilemmas (e.g., how noncommunicative must a child be to decide to administer a nonverbal intelligence assessment). It is constructed rather than given—that is, the senior practitioner does not offer precise rules but rather brainstorms with the intern about the options. There is reflection on the decision about what test to use, both during administration and after the session. The understanding of when to use nonverbal assessments is constructed through reflection on action. Moreover, after 10 years of practice, the former intern (now senior psychologist) will still be learning. Perhaps she constructs novel adaptations of nonverbal assessments to challenge children who have almost enough language to take a verbal assessment, or perhaps she does on-line revisions of verbal assessments to adapt items to nonverbal children, with this learning occurring in the culture in which she works.

The most intriguing part of Brown et al.'s (1989) proposal is that knowledge is intertwined with the activities and environments in which it develops, that knowledge is better thought of not as residing in the mind but spread across the mind and the environment. One proof of this is that there are some tasks that people can do only given environmental supports. For instance, a beekeeper can give a long lecture on beekeeping. The lecture improves, however, if the beekeeper has a beehive with a glass wall. A beekeeper's understanding of bees definitely involves an interaction between knowledge he can retrieve from his mind and information in the environment. This knowledge was built up largely by working with bees, with whatever "book learning" that occurred definitely expanded through interactions with beekeepers and bees. For example, any beekeeper's manual explains that swarming bees ordinarily will not sting while the swarm is being moved from a tree to a box hive (using a saw to cut off a branch). Real knowledge of the subtleties pertaining to this situation is gained only by removing a few swarms. Much of the knowledge gained is implicit (i.e., difficult to state). For instance, beekeepers often cannot convey in words how they know when some bees are about to attack out of a swarm, but they recognize the situation in an instant when holding in their hands a branch containing a swarm—knowledge about aggression by a swarm of bees is distributed across mind and situation.

Because of cognitive psychologists' growing awareness about the situated nature of much of cognition, there is a real effort in the 1990s to make education more authentic—for math problem solving and science teaching to involve more hands-on experiences and for readers to learn how to decode by processing authentic texts, with prominent examples of situation approaches to real-school learning featured in Chapters 12 through 15 of this book. If thinking is to develop from the perspective of situated cognition, it must be practiced with authentic tasks.

CONCLUDING COMMENTS

There is evidence that a variety of different types of representations function in thinking. Much of the research on mental representations has been concerned with identifying some knowledge structure that is more basic than others (e.g., research attempting to demonstrate that propositions underlie mental images). In the 1990s, research on connectionist models continues this tradition. Most researchers would concede that it is likely that there is some orderly neurological representational systems underlying higher-order representations, such as images, schemas, and propositions. Whether or not connectionist research will be successful in explaining how representation occurs at the neurological level and then be successful at explaining how neurological level representations translate into higher-order representations is an open question. We are skeptical, however, that a neurologically based representational theory will emerge in the near future that has the power to explain the many outcomes that are accounted for by models of higher-order representations, such as dual coding, schema, and propositional theories. What should be noted is that attempts to explain the representations discussed in this chapter in terms of more basic mechanisms have not been compelling. A striking example is the failure to generate evidence that imagery effects actually reflect the operation of propositional representations, despite substantial amounts of theoretical energy and research effort devoted to this problem.

At a phenomenological level, the analysis presented in this chapter is sensible. When we think about our own cognition, it is easy to generate examples of occasions when we depend on images and schemata. We also have a sense of thinking in terms of connected ideas. For example, we know that somewhere in our minds is stored the information that "dogs chase cats," and this is connected to the idea that "dogs chase postmen." There really is something to the idea of propositional representations that are connected in networks based on overlapping meanings. The idea of a semantic network is appealing for the same reason. We can easily think in categorical terms and know where many categories fit relative to other categories. We also have a vast network of associations between the concepts we know. Most people would concur that something like images, schemata, and abstract relationships between concepts (such as those represented by propositions) operate in their thinking, with the organization of these representations an important determinant of thinking.

The distinction between procedural and declarative knowledge also is a sensible one. Although we can state the steps involved in starting a car (i.e., generate a declarative representation of it), starting the car does not seem like a sequence of steps anymore but rather like one action—a compilation of steps that could be described declaratively because when first learned, it was represented declaratively. It is now represented in another form as well, one that cannot be talked about, a procedural representation that is evident only in its performance (i.e., in this case, in starting the car in one seamless motion).

By adulthood, adults have complex networks of procedural and declarative knowledge built up through experience. Experience has been repeatedly emphasized here. Procedures develop from declarative representations through repeated practice. Connections between procedures are strengthened when a sequence of procedures is executed with success. This process, which was taken up with respect to mental models here, is probably part of compilation, which is the integration of several procedures into a single procedure. Patterns of connections in neural networks are strengthened through repeated activation of the patterns, especially if activation of a pattern meets with some success in performing a task. Experience makes knowledge.

One question we are frequently asked by students is how the brain holds all that information. The brain not only holds information, but also is continuously constructing new information, as described briefly here with respect to mental models and inferences constructed when schemata are activated. With 100 billion neurons in the cortex, each of which has hundreds to thousands of synapses associated with it, with each synapse potentially making thousands of connections (e.g., Gardner, 1975), the capacity of the brain is great. There may be a quadrillion connections among neurons (Lerner, 1986). That capacity permits storage of a great deal of information and development of complex connections between different parts of the knowledge base. For example, it permits articulation between many pieces of procedural and declarative knowledge as part of carrying out a complex plan.

Even so, all of knowledge is not in the brain. Much of our knowing is situated, the result of mind and environment interaction at the moment. Moreover, new knowledge is constructed not simply in the mind but as the mind operates in the environment and as minds work together on problems. Increasingly, cognitive psychologists are realizing that thinking is not just an "in-the-head" thing and that the development of knowledge depends heavily on social interactions, themes that will be reiter-

Table 3.1

Types of Representations from Less Complex to More Complex

Connections, as part of neural networks

Episodic memory: Memory of specific concepts and relations between concepts

Semantic memory: Concepts and networks connecting concepts, both hierarchically and associatively, largely representing abstractions from many specific episodic memories. Includes images of concepts, feature complexes, prototypes, and the following types of more complex representations that include relational information

Procedural knowledge (knowledge of how to do things) encoded in productionlike structures, with this procedural knowledge used in conjunction with factual knowledge specified in schematic temporal, spatial-imagery, and propositional codes

Relations specified by propositions: Micropropositions and macropropositions incorporated into propositional networks, including schematic situation models.

Schemata, including frames and scripts. Includes nodes, variables, and slots that are meaningfully interrelated. May be based on complex images.

Mental models: Real world stimulates activation of a number of productions simultaneously, which are combined and adapted as productions that create new representation of current situation—i.e., the mental model of the current situation, which is a unique combination of procedural and declarative knowledge adapted in reaction to current stimulation

Situated and distributed representations: Knowledge distributed across different people and between people and the environment

---

ated in later chapters (especially Chapter 8 and Chapters 12 through 15).

To provide readers with a ready reference for the many approaches to representation covered in this chapter, Table 3.1 lists the many types of potential representations, from less complex to more complex. In general, the more complex representations subsume the less complex ones (e.g., schemata include concepts, which ultimately are represented by a system of connections).

The Role of Knowledge in Cognition

This chapter asks the questions: (1) What difference does a large knowledge base make? (2) What results from having extensive knowledge that is well organized? (3) What can such a person do that cannot be done by a person lacking that knowledge base? The short answer to all of these questions is, "quite a bit." The impact of extensive knowledge on cognitive performances is so great as to mandate a full chapter on the topic.

KNOWLEDGE AS A DETERMINANT OF PERFORMANCE

Several of the studies in the first subsection that follows are classics in educational psychology, ones cited frequently as powerful evidence in support of the hypothesis that prior knowledge and the extent of prior knowledge are powerful determinants of performance.

Demonstrations of the Potency of Knowledge as a Determinant of Performance

Suppose you know that 10-year-olds and adults are about to perform a memory task. The task involves memory for chess boards (i.e., chess pieces in particular, meaningful positions). Who would you bet on to perform better on this memory task? Make a prediction before reading on.

Now, consider this. The 10-year-olds are chess masters, and the adults are chess novices. Would you want to change your prediction? If you predicted that the 10-year-old chess experts would outperform the adult novices on this task, you made the right prediction (Chi, 1978).

Now, what if these two groups of subjects were given another memory task, perhaps a digit span task—a test in which a list of digits is presented one at a time with subsequent recall of the list required? Who would do better? In this case, the adults outperform the children.

What is going on? The children are experts in a particular domain of knowledge—chess. When they are presented arrays of chess pieces, their knowledge of the game permits them to categorize the arrangement of pieces (e.g., this is a checkmate), so they end up having to remember only a few chunks of information for each board. The adult novices see only chess pieces, with their relative positions meaningless, so they are learning the board on a piece-by-piece basis with little if any chunking. **Domain-specific knowledge** often permits those who possess it to process to-be-learned domain content differently than domain novices would process it. For a detailed analysis of what child chess experts know and how they think when operating in a chess-board environment, see Horgan and Morgan (1990).

Consider a second example. Suppose that university students are asked to learn some content pertaining to baseball and some content pertaining to music—in particular, lists of sentences such that given part of the sentence later on a test, they must recall the rest of the sentence. Suppose further that some of the students know a good deal about baseball and music already, some know only about baseball, some know only about music, and some have little familiarity with either baseball or music. Who remembers the most?

In Kuhara-Kojima and Hatano (1991), the students with prior knowledge in both areas outperformed students with prior knowledge in only one area. The students with prior knowledge in one of the two domains (either baseball or music) learned the content from their high-knowledge domain better than the content from their low-knowledge domain. Students lacking prior knowledge in either of the domains fared poorly in both domains.

Prior knowledge clearly mattered in this task. Consider what might have happened when a subject was presented the fact, "Kadota of the Hawks hit home runs in two consecutive at bats." For someone knowledgeable about Japanese professional baseball, this is a sensible statement—Kadota is a slugger who plays for the Hawks. Those who know a lot about Japanese baseball might know particular episodes that could be related to this fact. Later when given the matching test, requiring matching of baseball players with their accomplishments, the baseball experts would have a rich network of associations linking Kadota and the hitting of multiple home runs, a network of associations stimulated as they studied the fact as originally presented. This network of associations would assist in making matches. (The series of studies conducted by Kuhara-Kojima and Hatano included controls in which this matching test was administered without presentation of the facts for learning, with low performance in this case. High performance was possible only if there was an opportunity for learning.) Knowing about baseball was worthless in trying to learn the music facts. The knowledge of baseball experts who were music novices just could not be related to the music information. Baseball experts who were music novices performed poorly on the music task, much more poorly than music experts.

More than learning of single sentences is improved by prior knowledge. The classic work on learning of text as a function of prior knowledge was conducted by Voss and his colleagues (Chiesi, Spilich, & Voss, 1979; Spilich, Vesonder, Chiesi, & Voss, 1979; Voss, Vesonder, & Spilich, 1980). The adults participating in this research varied from knowing a great deal about the game to knowing very little. During the study, the participants read texts about baseball games, although the texts also contained content not related to baseball. Those with high knowledge of baseball remembered more of the text content pertaining to the baseball game and had better organized memory of the game described in the text than did baseball novices (e.g., the experts remembered critical information rather than unimportant details). Recall of the nonbaseball content was equivalent for the baseball experts and novices, however. That is, the baseball experts did not have better memories across the board—only better memory for baseball content. The errors in recall were also telling. That the experts had substantial schematic knowledge of baseball, and the novices did not, was apparent in the patterns of errors. When baseball experts misrecalled, they misrecalled details. When novices misrecalled, they often reported illegal plays and impossible situations.

It has been known for some time that children also tend to learn more from text pertaining to their knowledge-rich domains (e.g., Pearson, Hansen, & Gordon, 1979). For example, Means and Voss (1985) analyzed the learning of *Star Wars* text by students in grades 2, 3, 5, 7, 9, and college. It was possible to identify both *Star Wars* experts and novices at each of these grade levels. Once again, learning was better for experts than novices at every grade level. An interesting twist in this study was that expert performance increased with age, possibly owing to qualitative differences in the sophistication of *Star Wars* knowledge in older compared with younger students. Younger children saw *Star Wars* as being about good guys and bad guys, whereas older experts constructed layers of meaning, including themes of morality and the appropriateness of militarism.

Knowledge Versus Intelligence

The experts and novices were not randomly assigned to their statuses in the studies just summarized. A troubling possibility is that somehow only really smart people become experts at anything. Such speculation, especially when combined with the theoretical possibility that high intelligence might be reflected by high knowledge across a number of domains (e.g., Garcia, 1981; Sternberg &

Wagner, 1985), motivated the investigation of the relative potency of domain-specific knowledge and general intellectual aptitude as predictors of various performances.

Schneider, Körkel, Weinert, and their colleagues (e.g., Schneider, Körkel, & Weinert, 1990) have provided some of the most impressive research to date on the power of domain-specific knowledge, especially relative to another intellectual factor often considered to be a potent determinant of performance: general intelligence (see Chapter 16).

Their initial studies (Körkel, 1987; Weinert, Knopf, Körkel, Schneider, Voegel, & Wetzel, 1984; Weinert, Schneider, & Knopf, 1988) involved 8-, 10-, and 12-year-old children who read passages about soccer, which is a popular sport in Germany, where the work was conducted. Even so, just as in the United States, sports are not for everyone, so it is easy to locate children who know a great deal about soccer and those who know little. An important characteristic of the text that the children in this study were asked to read was that it contained some contradictions. Moreover, there were several points when inferences needed to be made to make sense of the content. Across the studies, there were measures of memory, construction of appropriate inferences, and detection of contradictions.

The outcomes, collapsing across studies, were generally as follows: Performances improved with age. More critically, soccer experts outperformed soccer novices. In addition, these data contained interactions reminiscent of Chi's (1978) outcomes. For example, in Körkel's (1987) study, the grade-3 experts recalled more than the grade-5 and grade-7 novices.

Schneider, Körkel, and Weinert (1989) and Schneider and Körkel (1989) measured both the soccer expertise and the general intelligence of their participants, in what were studies that otherwise resembled the earlier work. The data were absolutely striking. Again, performances (i.e., generation of appropriate inferences, detection of contradictions) improved with age from age 8 to 12. At every age level and on every measure, soccer expertise was associated with high performance compared with the performance of soccer novices. Most critically, general intellectual aptitude was not a strong determinant of performance (i.e., overall, there was a slight tendency for high general aptitude subjects to do better than low-aptitude subjects, although this was a small effect—especially compared with the huge effect of

soccer expertise). For example, 8-year-olds high in soccer expertise detected about 10 times more contradictions than 8-year-olds low in knowledge of soccer. In contrast, there was minimal difference between the levels of contradiction detection for high-ability and low-ability domain experts. The corresponding difference for novices was also minimal.

The German results with children processing prose are complemented in the adult literature by Walker (1987), who demonstrated that low general aptitude baseball experts can learn more from a baseball passage than high-aptitude baseball novices. Recht and Leslie (1988) also reported that junior high students high in prior knowledge about baseball learned more from reading a passage about baseball than students low in prior knowledge of baseball. In their study, weaker readers with high prior knowledge learned more than otherwise stronger readers who were low in prior knowledge. Hall and Edmondson (1992) found that immediate comprehension and memory of a passage about basketball was affected by prior knowledge about basketball on both a posttest immediately following reading of the passage and a posttest delayed by several weeks. Comprehension was also predicted by general ability in the Hall and Edmondson study, however, suggesting that additional investigations are required before it will be possible to make strong claims about the generality of the prior knowledge effects that Schneider and associates obtained with German children. Even when general ability effects were greatest in Hall and Edmondson (1992), which was at delayed testing, there was still a striking effect of prior knowledge on performance. We note as well that Schneider and colleagues never dismissed general aptitude as an important determinant of performance much of the time. For example, Schneider and Bjorklund (1992) reported that in list-learning situations, both general intelligence and prior knowledge have effects on recall: Soccer expertise predicted recall of lists composed of soccer terms but not recall of nonsoccer lists; intelligence predicted recall of both soccer and nonsoccer lists.

A memorable demonstration of the potency of domain-relevant knowledge in predicting performance compared to IQ was provided by Ceci and Liker (1986). They went to a racetrack and found patrons who knew a lot about horse racing and who had participated in betting on the sport for at least 8 years. Within this sample, however, were those who were extremely knowledgeable about how to handicap a horse race and those who were less knowledgeable. Thus, the 14 expert handicappers in Ceci and Liker's (1986) study were able, based on a large array of statistics pertaining to the horses and jockeys in races, to pick the horse most likely to be named "top horse" at race time for 9 out of 10 races. They were able to pick the top three horses for at least 5 of 10 races. In contrast, the 16 nonexperts picked the top horses much less often.

Ceci and Liker (1986) went to a good deal of trouble to make certain that the expert and nonexpert handicappers were otherwise comparable: The two groups had similar amounts of schooling (10 years on average), were similar in occupational prestige (full range, but with the mean in the craftsman range), and had comparable number of years of track experience (15 for the experts and 17 for the nonexperts). They also had comparable levels of general intelligence, with the mean equal to approximately 100 for both samples (i.e., equal to the average intelligence for the general population) and the range from approximately 80 to 130 for both samples.

The task given to these experts and nonexperts was to handicap 50 two-horse races. Fifty horses that were unnamed but were described by extensive statistics (14 different statistics typically available to handicappers before a race) were pitted against a standard horse in each race. The standard horse was an average horse on a number of measures pertinent to handicapping, such as speed, lifetime earnings, and record of the jockey. The subjects were asked to compute the odds for each of the 50 races involving this standard and the 50 unnamed horses.

The handicapping of the experts reflected extremely complex reasoning about potential interactions between the variables described by the handicapping statistics, with the reasoning of experts approaching the complexity of the reasoning of a professional handicapper who was also included in the study. That IQ did not determine expertise was evident in that the complexity of reasoning for low-IQ experts was greater than the complexity of reasoning for high-IQ nonexperts. That the reasoning of experts was complex can be appreciated by considering the reasoning offered by a 62-year-old crane operator with an 8th-grade education and an IQ of 92 (slightly below average for the overall population) as he analyzed a field of horses:

SUBJECT: The 4-horse should win easy; he should go off 3 to 5 or shorter or there's something wrong.

RESEARCHER: What exactly is it about the 4-horse that makes him your odds-on favorite?

S: He's the fastest, plain and simple.

R: But it looks to me that other horses are even faster. For instance, both the 2-horse and the 6-horse have recorded faster times than the 4-horse, haven't they?

S: Yeah, but you can't go by that. The 2-horse didn't win that outing. He just sucked-up.

R: Sucked-up?

S: You gotta read between the lines if you want to be good at this. The 2-horse just sat on the rail and didn't fight a lick. He just kept on the rail and sucked-up lengths when horses in front of him came off the rail to fight with front-runners (i.e., attempt to pass them on the outside).

R: Why does that make his speed any slower? I don't get it.

S: Now listen. If he came out and fought with other horses, do you think for one minute he'd have run that fast? Let me explain something to you that will help you understand. See the race on June 6 (point to the relevant line of the program)?

R: Yes.

S: Well, if the 2-horse had to do all of this fighting (pointing to indications in the program of attempts to pass other horses), he'd run 3 seconds slower. It's that simple. There ain't no comparison between the 2-horse and the 4-horse. The 4 is tons better!

R: I think I see what you're saying. But how about the 6-horse, didn't he do some fighting and still run faster than the 4-horse (pointing to indications of attempts to pass front-runners)?

S: Yeah, I like the 6-horse a little, but you can't bet him against this field because he's untried . . . he's been running in cheap company (pointing to the 6-horse's past purse sizes).

R: Why is purse size that crucial? He's still running faster than the 4-horse and fighting front-runners while he's doing it. What difference does the purse make?

S: (Sarcastically) It only makes all the difference in the world, that's all. Do you think for one minute he can pull those stunts with good horses (pointing to an indication of the 6-horse going around a "wall" of three horses)? Hell, if he tries to go three-wide in $15,000 company, they'll eat 'im up!

R: What do you mean?

S: You can't do these cheap tricks with horses of this caliber. They'll sit back and wait for him to get even with them on the outside, then they'll speed up and make him stay on the outside. You see, horses of this caliber ($15,000 claimers) can generate the speed to keep you parked outside the whole race. $10,000 claimers don't have the stamina, as a rule, to do that. . . . Now, with the $10,000 claimers, the 6-horse is a different story. He can have it all his way. But there's another horse in this race you have to watch. Do you know who I mean?

R: The 5-horse?

S: No! He'll still be running this time tomorrow! No I'm talking about the 8-horse. He don't mind the outside post because he lays back early. Christ, he ran a monster of a race on June 20th! He worries me because if he repeats here, he's unbeatable.

R: Do you like him better than the 4-horse?

S: Not for the price. He'll go off even money. He isn't that steady to be even money (i.e., 1 to 1). If he's geared up, there's no stopping him, but you can't bet on him being geared up. If he were 3 to 1, I'd bet him in a minute because he'll return a profit over the long run. But not at even money. (Ceci & Liker, 1986, p. 266)

This expert considered many variables in making decisions, simultaneously considering how these variables interacted (e.g., the meaning of the information that a horse fought for the front considered in the context of the quality of the field in the race as indicated by the purse). That experts such as these were so successful at picking winning horses validates the effectiveness of their thinking, and few would doubt that it is sophisticated, intelligent thinking. On the other hand, it is also situated cognition (see Chapter 3). The experts did not manifest highly intelligent thinking across a variety of situations but only in selected domains. With a racing form in his hand and talking about handicapping, this 62-year-old expert is a genius. Strip him of that piece of paper or ask him to do another task, and he performs slightly below the average level of the general population.

In short, the evidence is accumulating that knowledge relevant to the domain of a task is a much more important determinant of performance on many tasks than general intellect. When experts in a domain perform a task in their domain of competence, they invariably outstrip novices. Cognitive psychologists have devoted considerable resources to locating (and sometimes developing) domain ex-

perts who are capable of fantastic cognitive feats. What has emerged from this work is a sophisticated understanding of how the knowledge of domain experts differs from that of domain novices. What will be apparent in the next section is that having extensive networks of concepts, schemata, and associations permits extremely sophisticated thinking—the type of good thinking that was introduced in Chapter 1 during the discussion of the *Hardy Boys*.

THE NATURE OF EXPERT THINKING

Expert performances in a number of domains have been studied, including research on chess, typewriting, memorizing restaurant orders, mental calculation, computer programming, judicial decision making, solving of poorly structured problems, and medical diagnosis (for examples, see Chi, Glaser, & Farr, 1988). The methods used in these studies have been diverse, although one of the most prevalent methods has been analysis of **verbal protocols** generated by subjects as they do tasks. That is, subjects are asked to tell what they are doing while they work on a problem or do a task, or alternatively, they are asked to describe what they did do on a task just completed. A number of generalities have emerged from research in this tradition, despite the fact that many domains of expertise have been studied.

Glaser and Chi (1988) provided an overview of the main findings from research on expert performance. Each of their main points captured an important characteristic of expert thinking:

1. *Experts excel mainly in their own domains.* When an expert political scientist solves a problem in political science, the result is a sophisticated analysis. When an expert chemist tries the same problem, the solution is simplistic (Voss, Blais, Means, Greene, & Ahwesh, 1989). When you get into a cab with a driver who has extensive experience in a city, your chances of getting out of a traffic jam through some back alley route are better than if you are riding with a rookie cabbie (Chase & Ericsson, 1982). Such domain-specific expertise does not transfer far, however.

2. *Experts perceive large meaningful patterns in their domains.* A chess expert sees chunks of information on a chess board (e.g., Charness, 1989). In general, people who are good at games see patterns not discernible to novices (e.g., Reitman, 1976). Radiologists see organized patterns in x-

ray films that are patches of white and gray to the rest of us (e.g., Lesgold, Glaser, Rubinson, Klopfer, Feltovich, & Wang, 1988), and skilled lawyers and judges detect overarching principles in legal documents that cannot be seen by the novice (Lundeberg, 1987).

3. *Experts are fast. They are faster than novices at performing skills of their domain, and they quickly solve problems with little error.* One reason this is so is because experts have many skills in a domain practiced to the point of automatization. Another reason is that many problems for them are no longer problems that require searching for a solution—rather a solution has been stored. Thus, there was a time in our lives when we pondered how to analyze studies in which classrooms were randomly assigned to experimental conditions. We ponder no longer but automatically apply a solution that is stored as a whole in long-term procedural knowledge. What is striking is that experts are not only fast at identifying a schema (or constructing a mental model) that depicts the elements of the task and a potential solution, but also often the solution they devise is a good one, at least permitting a good start on solving the problem (e.g., Chase & Simon, 1973; Lesgold, 1984).

4. *Experts have superior short-term memory.* The biological capacity underlying short-term memory is no greater for experts than novices. What is different is that the experts have many skills and strategies automatized to the point that their execution requires use of little short-term capacity. Their vast knowledge of patterns and relationships in their domain of expertise also reduces the need for short-term capacity—demanding processing. Thus, chess novices may be consumed trying to anticipate the consequences of potential moves—literally playing out in their heads in a step-by-step fashion how their opponents might react to any move they would make. Chess experts need not play out such scenarios because they know the consequences of moving in particular ways in particular situations from years of experiencing the consequences of various moves. Think back to how effortlessly Ceci and Liker's (1986) expert handicapper considered the data in the racing program compared with the effort expended by the researcher in keeping up with the thinking of the handicapper.

5. *Experts see and represent problems in their domain at a deeper (more principled) level than novices; novices tend to represent problems at a superficial level.* Think back to the example in Chapter 3 (Chi et al., 1981) involving categorization of physics problems. Physics experts grouped the problems conceptually, grouping together problems that represented particular physics principles. Physics novices focused on surface features and thus grouped based on low-level features (e.g., problems involving rotating objects were grouped together). Yekovich, Thompson, and Walker (1991) observed that when expert credit analysts sized up the fiscal stability of a bank based on information provided to them, they were much more likely than less experienced analysts to make telling inferences about the bank. Both expert and less experienced analysts could encode the facts of a bank's status; the experts were able to do more with those facts and draw conclusions that eluded the less experienced analysts.

6. *Experts spend proportionately more time analyzing problems qualitatively than do novices.* Experts size up problems and attempt to identify patterns before attempting solutions. In general, experts attempt to construct mental models of the problem situation. What must be emphasized is that it is proportional time in planning that is greater for experts than novices. Experts often spend less total time on a problem or task than do novices and less total time planning than do novices. Of the time they spend on a problem or task, however, experts devote a higher proportion of it to planning rather than to the grunt-and-groan part of solving the problem or doing the task. This is because experts often identify efficient plans that once begun permit efficient solution of a problem or completion of a task.

In addition, experts are more efficient at each step of the problem solution, having honed many of the subskills to the point of automaticity and having quicker access to knowledge that might be used along the way in performing the task. For example, an expert might take 5 minutes to do a task that a novice would do in 10 minutes. For the expert, 60 percent of the solution time (3 minutes) might be devoted to planning and 40 percent to task execution. In contrast, the novice might spend a lesser time (e.g., 40 percent) planning, although still spending more total time planning (e.g., 4 minutes) than the expert. See Lesgold et al. (1988) for an example of how experts and novices apportion their time.

7. *Experts have strong self-monitoring skills.* Failures to monitor are epidemic (see Chapter 2). Students often do not know how a strategy they are using is affecting their performance. They do not know if they are ready for a test or have comprehended the main idea of a passage (see Chapter 14). A recurring theme in this book will be that monitoring is often flawed. With experts in their areas of expertise, however, it is a different story. They are well aware of how they are doing as they work on tasks in their domain of competence. Moreover, experts test their approaches to determine whether their solution plan is really permitting progress, with fine-tuning of solutions often observed as experts detect difficulties with approximate solutions (Voss, Greene, Post, & Penner, 1983).

The power of these conclusions is obvious when some examples of extremely expert behaviors in professions are considered. As we present these examples, we emphasize, however, that whenever high-level professional activities have been analyzed, there has been evidence of thinking consistent with the general model of expert thinking sketched in this section.

Expertise in Medical Diagnosis

Lesgold and his colleagues (e.g., Lesgold et al., 1988) have been studying how expert and novice radiologists read x-rays and thus provided an example of one of the most prevalent types of investigations in the study of knowledge: **expert-novice comparisons.** Lesgold et al. (1988) began their research by spending a lot of time watching expert radiologists work. They eventually devised a standardized situation involving reading of x-rays. This standard permitted them to do some analytical work that could not have been done by simply watching physicians at work. For instance, here were the procedures that were used in one of their more telling studies:

Subject examines [x-ray] film for as long as desired, thinking out loud.

Subject dictates formal diagnostic report as he would in his office.

Subject substantiates his diagnosis by drawing relevant anatomy and film features on the x-ray.

Subject draws all anatomy within a specified region of the film (previously known to be critical in diagnostic success). If it does not happen spontaneously, subject is asked to trace anatomical contours predetermined by the experimenters to be crucial.

Subject renders another diagnostic report. (p. 315)

The subjects in the study were highly experienced radiologists and residents in radiology. A number of interesting differences were noted between highly experienced and inexperienced radiologists as they performed this task. For the experts, they fairly quickly get a general idea of what might be going on in the x-ray. Which of the possible general schemata are activated depends on the characteristics of the x-ray, with the expert selecting a general schema for additional consideration that is consistent with certain general features of the x-ray (schema invocation phase). Once a general schema is invoked, a series of additional tests are conducted to reach a diagnosis and confirm it (fine-tuning). The young radiologists were less likely to come to an appropriate general schema. Once they arrived at a general schema, they were less likely to apply additional tests that could confirm or refute the initial diagnosis. Often the details of these tests were less complete than the details of the tests of the experts. Experts were much more flexible in their thinking and took advantage of whatever clues could be found in the x-rays.

Here is how one expert responded to a film. He took a 2-second look and began searching for a general schema that might fit the situation: "We may be dealing with a chronic process here. . . ." "I'm trying to work out why the mediastinum and the heart are displaced into the right chest." The expert considered the possibility that the subject had not been facing the plate directly: "There is not enough rotation to account for this. I don't see displacement of fissures [lung lobe boundaries]." After doing some mental tests of this possibility, it was dismissed because there was little in the x-ray to confirm this possibility. Then the expert generated a "collapsed lung" schema and tested it: "There may be a collapse of the right lower lobe but the diaphragm on the right side is well visualized and that's a feature against it. . . ." He continues to test this possibility, with it increasingly apparent that the collapsed lung schema would have to be tuned quite a bit if it were to explain the pattern in the x-ray. In testing the collapsed lung schema, he noticed clues that there had been a previous surgery: "I come back to the right chest. The ribs are crowded together. . . . The crowding of the rib cage can, on some occasions, be due to previous surgery. In fact . . . the third and fourth ribs are narrow and irregular so he's probably had previous surgery. . . ." The expert changes schemata and solves the problem: "He's probably had one of his lobes resected. It wouldn't be the middle lobe. It may be the upper lobe. It may not necessarily be a lobectomy. It could be a small segment of the lung with pleural thickening at the back." He keeps testing, however, especially the possibility that perhaps what is needed is an explanation involving both a collapsed lung and a lobectomy (i.e., he attempts to combine two schemata to build a unique mental model of the situation): "I don't see the right hilum . . . [this] may, in fact, be due to the postsurgery state I'm postulating. . . . Loss of visualization of the right hilum is . . . seen with collapse . . ." (Lesgold et al., 1988, pp. 319–320).

What was apparent was that the expert radiologist was building a mental model of the patient's anatomy while examining the x-ray, with the activation of schemata and attempts to tune and test these schemata as part of the mental model construction process. An interesting difference between experts and novices was that the experts applied their knowledge of normal anatomy to the x-rays but did not try to force-fit pathological features into their normal schemata. Novices were much more likely to explain away pathological features as normal.

In building the mental model, the experts quickly generated a candidate schema that might explain the data in the x-rays. The experts seemed to know where to look on the film to obtain information that would permit a rough guess as to what was depicted in the x-ray. Once activated, the schema guided the processing of the experts, with experts much more likely to search for information consistent with their candidate general schema than novices, who were more likely to be distracted by features of the x-ray irrelevant to the hypothesized explanatory schema. This difference showed up in the diagnostic reports, with the reports of experts concerned directly with the disorder depicted in the x-ray and the reports of novices more likely to be cluttered with mention of irrelevant x-ray features.

The fine-tuning of the experts was substantial compared with novices, who often were willing to accept a general schema as the correct diagnosis

without attempts to check further. Thus, when an x-ray was presented that superficially suggested a lung tumor, the novices concluded lung tumor. Half of the experts in the study, however, detected features in the film suggesting a less obvious—but as it turns out, correct—diagnosis. One possibility suggested by Lesgold is that the radiological novices may have had their short-term capacities full, using most of their capacity to discern just the gross features and come to an interpretation. If so, little capacity would be left over for consideration of nuances. Experts require less capacity to note gross features—years of experience make salient the telling features of the x-ray, with little investment of mental effort now required for experts to discern the informative parts of the picture.

Alternatively, the novices might not yet know the possible follow-up tests that could be applied or may not be as sensitive to subtle features in the films. This latter possibility was suggested by the results of the tracing exercise in Lesgold et al.'s study, with the tracings of novices often failing to depict subtleties that were apparent in the tracings of the experts. There were multiple indicators that the experts understood better than novices the technical process of obtaining x-rays and the types of subtle features that can be in an x-ray, with these understandings combined in testing general schemata that are generated as potential explanations for the pattern in the x-ray.

The expert radiologists possessed substantial knowledge not possessed by residents. Their perceptual analysis skills were especially keen, there were strong linkages between particular perceptual patterns and explanatory schemata, and the schemata had associated with them knowledge about how to test to determine the fine-grained fit of the schemata to situations. A great deal of procedural and declarative knowledge was available, much of it schematically organized, although a schema would be revised in light of data. That is, there was real construction of mental models here and not simply retrieval of a schema and interpretation of the situation in terms of the static schema.

Others studying medical diagnosis have provided additional evidence of flexible mental modeling. For example, Feltovich, Johnson, Moller, and Swanson (1984) studied decision making in pediatric cardiologists. A variety of input (e.g., patient histories, x-rays, electrocardiograms, other examination data) were given to specialists, residents, and students. The less experienced subjects focused in on one classical category of heart disease. The specialists were much more likely to work with several classical categories of disease to produce a diagnosis that uniquely combined characteristics from several types of disease. Pauker, Gorry, Kassirer, and Schwartz (1976) also observed that experienced physicians made an initial diagnosis and then adjusted it to take into account possible explanations of symptoms not consistent with the classical disease type. Extensive knowledge can be a powerful determinant of professional competence. This possibility is considered additionally for the case of classroom teachers in the next subsection.

Expertise in Teaching

David Berliner and his associates (Berliner, 1986, 1988; Carter, Cushing, Sabers, Stein, & Berliner, 1988; Carter, Sabers, Cushing, Pinnegar, & Berliner, 1987) have studied teachers early in their careers (novices) and teachers nominated by their schools (and then screened by outside observers) as expert teachers. The perceptions of these teachers about classroom events were analyzed in several studies. Although the novices were broken down in these studies by their degree of experience, from none to advanced beginner, the distinctions within the less experienced group are not critical here, and thus we use the term *novice* to refer to any member of this less experienced group.

Sabers, Cushing, and Berliner (1991) had teachers watch a videotaped lesson. Using a complex setup involving three screens, the videotape depicted the simultaneous events occurring in all parts of the room (left, center, right). During part of the session, the participants were required to talk aloud about what was happening in the classroom. They were also asked questions about classrooms events, including the routines in the lessons, the content covered, motivation in the classroom, students' attitudes, the teacher's expectations and roles, and the interactions between students and teacher. A number of findings emerged from the analyses of the data produced in this study. In general, the expert teachers had different understandings of the teaching they were watching than did the inexperienced teachers.

Sabers et al. (1991) concluded specifically that experts and novices differ in their abilities to monitor and interpret the complex set of events occurring

in a classroom. Expert teachers made proportionately more interpretations and evaluations of what they saw and made more coherent interpretations and evaluations. The following sample of interpretations and evaluations from the experts make obvious that these teachers were able to make sense of what was going on in the videotaped classroom:

EXPERT 6: On the left monitor, the students' note taking indicates that they have seen sheets like this and have had presentations like this before; it's fairly efficient at this point because they're used to the format they are using.

EXPERT 7: I don't understand why the students can't be finding out this information on their own rather than listening to someone tell them because if you watch the faces of most of them, they start out for about the first 2 or 3 minutes sort of paying attention to what's going on and then just drift off.

EXPERT 2: . . . I haven't heard a bell, but the students are already at their desks and seem to be doing purposeful activity, and this is about the time that I decide they must be an accelerated group because they came into the room and started something rather than just sitting down and socializing.

EXPERT 4: . . . I think there is an indication here of the type of structure of this classroom. It's pretty loose. The kids come in and go out without checking with the teacher. (Sabers et al., 1991, pp. 72–73)

In contrast, the less experienced teachers did not see as much and did not seem to perceive the overall structure of the classroom and the events taking place in it. A high proportion of the novice teachers' comments were simply descriptions of what was happening without interpretation or evaluations. When they attempted interpretations, they were less successful as evident in these comments:

NOVICE 1: . . . I can't tell what they're doing. They're getting ready for class, but I can't tell what they're doing.

NOVICE 3: She's trying to communicate with them here about something, but I sure couldn't tell what it was.

ANOTHER NOVICE: It's a lot to watch.

The experts were more able to classify the type of instruction they were watching as activity oriented, Socratic, or process oriented. Such higher-order classifications did not occur in the reports of the novice teachers. The experts also took in more of the room, distributing their attention between the left, middle, and right portions of the room more evenly than the novice teachers did. An especially interesting difference was that the novices tended to be captured by the visual information, whereas the experts processed both the visual and auditory input, using the language cues they picked up to aid in their interpretations of the classroom events. The result was that experts had a much better understanding of the managerial style of the classroom, the commitments of the teacher on the film, and the content being covered.

That the experts were attending to the verbalizations in the classroom was apparent in these rich descriptions:

EXPERT 3: In the middle . . . they're discussing notes that were taken on the reproductive system. On the right . . . she's asking specific individuals what the different parts of the digestive system are . . . she was very broad in just talking about the digestive system, rather than being specific and talking about parts or functions, and it seems like those are two separate objectives.

EXPERT 6: In the middle . . . she's talking about how the energy is released in the cell. Unless I missed it, she seemed to skip the lower digestive system, the two intestines, and how sugar and glucose get from the digestive system to the cells.

The novices did not understand as well the content being covered, with these comments about the verbalizations typical:

NOVICE 14: The teacher is talking a lot.

NOVICE 15: . . . she seems to be good at asking questions and getting the students to talk to her.

NOVICE 5: . . . it seems that the teacher is going over something; there doesn't seem to be much interest from the students . . . the teacher is still trying to get instructions across, and it's hard to believe that everyone is comprehending what she's saying or even hearing what she's saying. (p. 78)

Novices noticed student misbehavior and were critical of it but did not make inferences about the underlying causes. The experts' perceptions of misbehavior were less evaluative and included explanations for the disruptions. For example, one expert explained inappropriate behavior at the end of a class period in the following way:

EXPERT 1: She [the teacher] seems like she's finished now, and she's not really going around to help

students and to monitor how they're doing. There's time left in the class, and she's just kind of finished her work. She's not going around to check how students are doing. (p. 80)

Other experts had suggestions for improving the conduct in the class. In general, the experts were much more oriented to explaining the classroom behaviors than simply describing them or disapproving of the students.

Just as the expert radiologists were able to discern patterns in x-rays not apparent to novices, so it was with the expert teachers in Sabers et al. (1991). Just as the expert radiologists were able quickly to generate a possible general schema to explain the x-ray, expert teachers can size up a classroom quickly. Berliner (1988) described the differences between experts and novices in the descriptions of a classroom following a 1-second exposure to a slide of a classroom: The novices commented on superficial features of the class (p. 12): "A blond-haired boy at the table, looking at papers. Girl to his left reaching in front of him for something." ". . . a classroom. Student with back to camera working at a table." "A room full of students sitting at tables." In contrast, the experts perceived structure and organization and focused on instructionally important characteristics of the scene: "It's a hands-on activity of some type. Group work with a male and female of maybe late junior high school age." "It's a group of students maybe doing small group discussion on a project as the seats are not in rows." One second of viewing was all that was needed for experts to perceive structure, whether it was a blackboard activity that was seen for a second, independent seatwork, or a laboratory exercise.

Berliner is not the only one to have considered the nature of expert teaching from the viewpoint of cognitive psychology. When others have looked at expert teaching (e.g., Swanson, O'Connor, & Cooney, 1990), they too have produced data consistent with the expert literature in general. Peterson and Comeaux (1987) is one of the most cited studies illustrating this point. They studied how experienced and inexperienced high school teachers represented and remembered problem events that occur in classrooms. Their participants watched 4-minute videotapes of three such events, all involving misbehaviors common in classrooms. After watching each tape, the teachers were asked to describe what occurred in the incident, with the focus being exact recall of the behaviors and interactions depicted on the tape. Then the participants watched the same tape again, this time to identify places in the sequence where the teacher could have made a different decision than the one that was made. The participants were asked to generate alternative actions the taped teacher could have taken and to specify the action they themselves would have taken.

By a wide margin, the experienced teachers recalled more of the behaviors depicted on the tapes than did the novice teachers. A particular strength of the study was that another measure of memory was taken (i.e., digit span), with digit span not differentiating the two groups of subjects. This would suggest that there is not an across-the-board difference in memory ability between experienced and inexperienced teachers, making more certain the conceptual significance of the greater recall of classroom events by the experienced high school teachers.

In addition, the alternative courses of action recommended by the two groups differed, with the more experienced teachers more likely to offer principled suggestions than the novices, such as the following:

> You can use the test as a learning experience rather than just to hand back.
>
> I think he could have done well to have thought of other ways of involving other students in what was going on.
>
> . . . [He] . . . didn't really have classroom management.
>
> . . . [He] can stimulate a little interest without always leaning on the test . . . it's just not motivational enough . . . isn't decisive enough . . . isn't well organized enough. (p. 324)

In contrast, the comments of the novices focused on particular alternative behaviors that could have been encouraged, rather than a conceptual analysis of the situation, as is evident in the following examples:

> He probably should have told them to get their notebooks out and take notes or ask for general attention before he started going into what he was going to talk about.
>
> I'd have handed out the test after they had cleared their desks of all other materials.
>
> [The teacher should have said] "If you have any questions . . . come up and see me" and then put himself in a position where he can scan the room. (p. 324)

Peterson and Comeaux (1987) concluded that the experienced teachers had more sophisticated schemata

for encoding classroom events, with these schemata permitting more complete encoding and recall of the events and more principled interpretation of the classroom situation.

How do differences in knowledge about teaching translate into differences in teaching? Although there has been little research done linking knowledge as we have been conceiving it here to teaching at a fine-grained level, the work that is available suggests that the extensive knowledge of expert teachers affects their teaching continuously and in many ways. An analysis that particularly highlighted the flexible use of schemata by expert compared with novice teachers was reported by Borko and Livingston (1989). They studied three experienced mathematics teachers and the student teachers who were assigned to these more experienced teachers. Teaching was observed, with an interview preceding each day of observation. This interview focused on planning for the lesson. The interviews following observed lessons tapped reflections on the teaching that had been watched.

The experienced teachers did much more planning for the long term than did the novices. Although both experienced and novice teachers made daily plans that were detailed, the novice teachers' planning was exclusively focused on the lesson for just that day, whereas the more experienced teachers continuously thought about coming sections in the text and the overall organization of the chapter. An even more striking difference was that much of the planning of the experienced teachers was done in the context of teaching. For example, experienced teachers did not concern themselves with which examples would be covered. They were always able to come up with apt examples, either ones they knew from experience or ones that they could locate quickly in the text. The novices agonized over which examples to present and how to present them. The novices were not good at improvising, as Jane, one of the novices, noted:

> This is all so new to me that thinking up, I have to do a lot of thinking ahead of time. I really do. I have to think out what kind of questions to ask. I have to think out the answers to the questions . . . so that my answers are theoretically correct and yet simple enough to make sense. And I have to really think in math. I love it. But I have to really think carefully about it. I can't ad-lib it too well. (p. 487).

The schism between planning and what actually occurred in the classroom was great for the novices compared with the more experienced teachers. In particular, the novices had difficulties with student questions and had difficulty adjusting to student misunderstandings. Student questions in particular often got the presentation off track, with the novice teachers having difficulting getting it back on track. In contrast, the experienced teachers were expert in using student errors and questions to guide and shape instruction in meaningful ways.

What accounted for the teaching differences between the experienced and the inexperienced teachers? Undoubtedly, one difference was content knowledge. One of the more experienced teachers described the difference in content knowledge between the first and second year of doing a course:

> "When I begin teaching a course, I do a thorough outline on each chapter . . . I take out all the important words and define them . . . vocabulary words, examples, diagrams. If there's like a lot of information that I feel is important, I'll even copy that down right from the book . . . and emphasize certain things I want to emphasize. And then I do all the problems I assign." After the first year, her notebook is merely fine tuned. "It's a matter of rearranging it mentally and becoming more comfortable with it, have it become part of my knowledge, rather than just, you know, notes." (p. 490)

This teacher also recognized that the difference in her knowledge of the content translated into quality of instruction:

> Last year I was much too rigid because I didn't see some of the relationships I'm seeing now . . . and I've shared a lot of this with the students, which I think has helped them because their viewpoint is the narrow viewpoint I had last year. (p. 490)

Part of her increasing knowledge base comes from interaction with students as they attempt problems. In particular, there is an increase in understanding which parts of the content will pose difficulties for the students, with this increased understanding permitting preventive action by the teacher:

> As you see different types of mistakes the students make—they usually stay the same from year to year—you can pinpoint that out for the students ahead of time . . . but that kind of comes automatically. The more you teach in the class, the more you realize where the pitfalls are. (p. 490)

Over the years, good teachers accumulate cogent explanations and examples and develop understanding of when extensive explanations and demonstra-

tions are in order and when more rapid coverage is possible.

There were multiple indicators in the study that the teaching schemata of novices were not as extensive as the teaching schemata of experts and that the schemata novices did possess were not as well connected as the schemata of experts nor as accessible as the schemata of experts: Planning took much more time for novices. The novices failed to see connections between questions asked by students and the lesson, connections that could have helped to keep lessons on track. In the postlesson reflections, the expert teachers selectively focused on classroom events that affected achievement, offering coherent and interpretive summaries of the day. In contrast, the postlesson reflections of the novices touched on many more aspects of the day, many of which were not relevant to student achievement.

Expert teachers have extensive and connected teaching schemata. These are not applied rigidly. Rather the teacher constructs a mental model (see Chapter 3) of a teaching situation and flexibly combines and adjusts prior knowledge to fit the current situation. A strength of Borko and Livingston's (1989) analysis is their emphasis on the ability of expert teachers to improvise. The ability to improvise, to adjust what ones knows to new situations, is a mark of high competence.

As year-in, year-out classroom teachers at the university level, we really resonate to the Borko and Livingston analysis. During our early years of college teaching, we spent hours preparing. Sometimes we could answer student questions and sometimes we could not. There were more than a few occasions when student questions managed to sidetrack classes completely. Now we do relatively little preparation for classes we have taught many times before, often skimming the reading for the day and jotting down some key terms as our only notes for a 3-hour lecture. We know what most of the questions are going to be before the students ask them. Our problem now in responding to those questions is not to be too long-winded, for we could often talk on and on, making connection to connection. In contrast, with new courses, such as special topics graduate seminars, we feel like a novice because we often know little more about the particular content than many of the graduate students in the course. Our "seminar-teaching" schemata are well developed, however, so we can now keep a seminar discussion ongoing and lively (at least our teaching evaluations say so) for several hours, which was much more difficult to do earlier in our teaching careers.

In recent years, the nature of expert teaching and the knowledge base undergirding it have been the focus of intense study in some research centers. For instance, Leinhardt and her colleagues (e.g., Leinhardt & Greeno, 1986) have established that expert teachers have definite routines that they use when teaching lessons, routines that are embedded in schemata about classrooms, teaching, and behavior/performance relationships in classrooms. Teachers have extensive hierarchical classification schemes for student abilities and characteristics (Calderhead, 1983). With experience, teachers increase in their understanding about how to be flexible in their thinking and how teaching behaviors interrelate—thinking about teaching is more complex in experienced compared with inexperienced teachers (e.g., Strahan, 1989).

When the literature on teacher knowledge is read, it is clear that much of the knowledge of expert teachers is situated—they have built up coherent theories about and representations of good teaching through personal experiences. Experienced teachers claim they have "images" of good teaching that have developed as a result of their experiences in teaching. Here is how Elbaz (1983, p. 134) summarizes the practical knowledge of teachers:

> The teacher's feeling, values, needs, and beliefs combine as she forms images of how teaching should be, and marshals experience, theoretical knowledge, and school folklore to give substance to these images.

Teachers' knowledge is often described in terms of metaphoric images, with a broad range of practices captured in this way, from the "classroom as home" (Clandenin, 1986; Connelly & Clandenin, 1985) to the curriculum as a "conduit" through which the teacher leads the students (Russell & Johnston, 1988). Morine-Dershimer (1979) suggested that teachers have images of what ideal lessons look like. Eraut (1985) described the images teachers possess of everyday situations in classrooms. Many teachers claim that such images guide their practice (e.g., Calderhead & Robson, 1991). These images seem much like the images that Miller et al. (1960) described (see Chapter 3). For example, compare Miller et al.'s description of the "Image" with Elbaz's (1983) description (cited earlier in the paragraph) of images held by teachers:

> The Image is all the accumulated, organized knowledge that the organism has about itself and its world.

The Image consists of a great deal more than imagery, of course. What we have in mind when we use this term is esentially the same kind of private representation that other cognitive theorists have demanded. It includes everything the organism has learned—his values as well as his facts—organized by whatever concepts, images, or relations he has been able to master.

When all of the different types of evidence are combined, it is clear that experienced teachers have well-organized schemata for teaching, many of which are encoded as images. Experienced teachers are able to use what they know flexibly, so it is possible for them quickly to understand events in classrooms that are new to them.

One of the most interesting hypotheses emerging in the literature on teacher expertise and competence is that capable educators are reflective (i.e., reflective practitioners; Schön, 1983, 1988) and constantly creating new mental models. Thus, they do not attempt to transfer schemata unmodified from one situation to another but instead use their schemata and images as starting points, which are transformed to produce new educational experiences and environments.

Marlowe and Culler (1987) reported a case involving Uri Treisman, a Berkeley mathematics professor. Treisman observed a number of ethnic groups at the university, with a particular interest in how they studied mathematics and how their study patterns might affect their achievement. He noted that Asian students, who as a group excelled at math, studied together. They provided support for one another. If one student in the group could not work a problem, another would provide tutorial input. In contrast, other minorities fared much more poorly in math. Treisman observed that their study pattern was different. They engaged in solitary study, going to class alone and hitting the books alone. Treisman's solution was to create honors study groups for minorities that were similar in structure to the groups that Asians had formed on their own. (See Chapter 8 for a discussion of the power of shared cognition—that is, problem solving in groups compared with individual problem solving.) Although Treisman's approach has never been subjected to a true experimental evaluation (our own view is that an experimental evaluation of it should be a high priority for the math educator community), the improvements in achievement for the students participating in such groups are striking. Grades of *B* and better were common for participants who had been expected to perform much more poorly in their math course. Treisman saw an educational practice, reflected on it, and came up with an intervention.

But the tale of Treisman's intervention is not over. A number of others came to observe the program. Some attempted to copy it, and others attempted to take it and transform it, working it into their own setting in ways that made sense. Again, there are no evaluation data, but the sense of Marlowe and Culler (1987), who were well informed about the instructional practices of the various emulators, was that the transformers experienced much more success than the copiers. A reasonable hypothesis that follows from an anecdote such as this one (see Schön, 1988) is that expert teachers have sufficient knowledge to form sophisticated mental models of educational environments, models that draw on knowledge based on past experience. This knowledge is then modified to take new constraints in the environment into account, with the result a mental model that is unique and translates into a unique plan of action rather than simply a replication of a plan of action that worked in a different setting.

Teachers, similar to other professionals, have vast knowledge that permits them to make rapid and powerful inferences about teaching and learning. Understanding this expertise is a relatively new direction for educational psychologists but one that deserves substantial attention in future research (see Shulman, 1986). All indications to date, however, are that good teachers have substantial procedural and declarative knowledge about classrooms and teaching. Such pedagogical knowledge will be considered often in this text, as will teachers' knowledge of subject matter and the overall curricula (see Shulman, 1986, for one conceptualization of the various types of knowledges teachers can possess; also Carter, 1990; for an entire volume on the topic of the knowledge required for teaching, see Reynolds, 1989). We are optimistic that studying teacher knowledge in greater detail will pay off.

One reason to be sanguine about additional research on the knowledge of expert teachers is that cognitive psychologists are getting good at devising ways of understanding high competence. The next section illustrates how great such competence can be when procedural and declarative knowledge are combined. The accomplishments presented in this next section also make the point emphatically that expertise is often extremely specific!

DEVELOPMENT OF HIGH COMPETENCE

What does it take to become an expert? What is required to acquire the many procedures involved in expert performance as well as detailed metacognitive understandings about those procedures (i.e., knowing when and where to use them)? How long does it take to acquire an expert vocabulary, with accompanying understanding of how the various categories in a domain interrelate? How long to be able to coordinate one's extensive procedural and declarative knowledge to solve new problems?

In many instances, the answer is that it requires many years of experience. Consider that expert chess players spend thousands of hours playing chess and studying the game; grandmasters invariably have played for 10 or more years (DeGroot, 1965, 1966; Simon & Chase, 1973). Many of Lesgold et al.'s (1988) expert radiologists had read 200,000 x-rays in their careers. The expert teachers in Berliner's research had more than 5 years of teaching experience. In this section, we consider some analyses that have made cognitive psychologists aware that the brilliant performances of experts are the end product of years of training and practice (see especially Ericsson, Krampe, & Tesch-Römer, 1993).

Lives of Great Composers and Artists

Hayes (1985) analyzed the careers of the great musical composers and painters. He reasoned that if it takes a long time to become an expert, the early works of great composers and artists might not be as good as their later works. In the case of the composers, Hayes made the additional assumption that their better compositions would be recorded more often. As readers who are classical record buffs know, *Schwann's Guide* is a publication that provides listings of the recordings available for each composer. By graphing the number of recordings for each piece against the year when the piece was composed, it is possible to summarize the relative popularity of compositions as a function of the composer's years of experience in composing.

Consider the case of Mozart. His productivity increased during the first decade of his career (from ages 4 to 14) from 0 to about 2 compositions per year. For the remaining years of his career, he published between 1 and 4 pieces a year, with little consistency in total year-to-year productivity. That his early works were no great accomplishments, however, is reflected by the number of times these pieces have been recorded. Although 12 percent of Mozart's compositions were generated between 4 and 14 years of age, they represent only 5 percent of the total number of Mozart recordings. The early compositions were generally recorded for the sake of completeness, such as in anthologies. The first time that Mozart composed a piece that is preserved in as many as 5 recordings was when he was 16–12 years after he began to compose. All subsequent years resulted in pieces that are more popular than anything composed during Mozart's first decade.

Hayes analyzed an additional 75 composers. Their popularity curves were much like Mozart's. The number of pieces during the first decade was small compared with later periods in life. The pieces produced during the first 10 to 12 years are much less popular than pieces produced later in the career. There was a steep increase in the amount of work produced between years 12 and 24. In short, it took a while for a composer to become good and produce at a high, steady rate. More positively, once a composer achieved excellence, he maintained it for 30 years on average, with decline in distinguished works only apparent by the 50th year of a career on average! These data suggested that late blooming is the norm for great composers.

Hayes and colleagues did the same type of analysis for painters. The results were remarkably similar to those obtained for the composers. There was low productivity during the first 6 years for artists, with a steep increase in productivity between years 6 and 12 and steady productivity for many years after that.

Talented Young People

Benjamin S. Bloom (1985) and his colleagues sought out top-flight concert pianists, sculptors, research mathematicians, research neurologists, Olympic swimmers, and tennis players. Most of the subjects were under age 35 at the time of the study. The purpose of the investigation was to determine the role of parents, teachers, and other factors in the development of extraordinary talent. The talented individuals were interviewed about how they became interested in their vocation and how they learned it. They were asked to pinpoint factors that contributed to their extraordinary attainments. Parents and influential teachers also were interviewed.

The 500+-page report is fascinating reading and strongly recommended for all who want detailed insights into development of great talent. Although

there was some variability from talent area to talent area, there was also a great similarity across the talent areas. In every case, there were years of study and practice. These people had child-oriented parents who dedicated great resources to the development of their children. High achievement and striving for success were stressed in these homes. The work ethic was prominently in place: "To *excel*, to *do one's best*, to *work hard*, and to *spend one's time constructively* were emphasized over and over again" (p. 10). Good teaching in the area of expertise was available early in life. The children liked the domain of expertise from first exposure. Initial success led to selection into even better educational environments—opportunities to be coached by more expert coaches, attend special classes, and so on. With success, students invested more effort into their talent, although more expert teachers played an ever greater role in the actual instruction and monitoring of practice. Student commitment grew ever stronger, with many hours per week devoted to the emerging vocation. Eventually the young talent was ready for the master teacher, with virtually all of the student's time then spent mastering the field. Most critical here, the typical time course for the complete education was 15 to 25 years.

A main message in Bloom's (1985) book is that great accomplishment is the product of years of high-quality education. There were no real child prodigies identified. Even at age 11 to 12, there was little suspicion by parents or teachers that the student would become one of the top 25 people in the world in their field of expertise, which was true for many of Bloom's subjects.

The view in Bloom contrasts with some stereotypes of genius, which portray geniuses as doing poorly in school. For instance, many know of Einstein's difficulties in the *gymnasium* in Munich. According to this stereotype, it is not long periods of immersion in a discipline that permits the expertise that is genius but some type of innate talent. Simonton (1988), as part of a book-length treatment of the psychology of creative genius, countered this point: Many geniuses earn doctorates fairly early in life, suggesting great focus and immersion early in life. Moreover, many of the best scientists went to the best schools. Finally, there are many scientific geniuses, including Marie Curie, Sigmund Freud, and Max Planck, who earned glowing marks throughout their educations, which extended over many years. Geniuses tend to do well in school, despite stereotypic impressions to the contrary. (See Chapter 18, this volume, for more on the development of gifted students.)

Summary

Great accomplishment does not just happen. It is the result of years of preparation. In many fields, it takes one to two decades to become an expert. It takes one to two decades to accumulate vast procedural, declarative, and metacognitive knowledge, which can be used flexibly to great effect. Unfortunately, it is not possible to gauge how long it takes to become expert in the field most central to this book, which is teaching. Studies of expert teachers usually employ teachers with more than 5 years experience. Whether really high expertise in teaching can develop in 5 years should be studied. A good bet based on a growing body of evidence is that the answer is probably no. Retrospective interviews of superb teachers about their careers and the development of their expertise, something like the interviews conducted by Bloom (1985), might be an efficient method to begin study of this problem.

Experts in an area possess a great deal of procedural and declarative knowledge relevant to an area. They often manifest strategies that novices would not evidence. They make many automatic associations, classifications, and analogies that could not be made by novices. Short of expertise, there are, of course, increases in knowledge with development and education, so a grade-6 student is much more knowledgeable than a grade-1 student. A question that has been of great concern in the theoretical and basic research literature is whether improvements in performance associated with development and education are due to an increasing knowledge base or an increasing propensity to make use of the knowledge one possesses via strategies. Thus, the next section turns to extremely basic research conducted in typical laboratory situations rather than at racetracks or in x-ray departments. By turning to this work, we explicitly bring the reader back to the theoretical position introduced in Chapter 1, that good performance follows from components in interaction rather than the operation of single components—that capable performance could never be explained simply in terms of an expanding knowledge base that is applied automatically whether a person is attempting to apply the knowledge base to a task or not. Expertise reflects coordinated application of strategies and other knowledge, consistent with the perspective developed in the next section, which is devoted to basic research elucidating how knowledge and strategies determine intellectual competence.

PERFORMANCE INCREASES WITH DEVELOPMENT: INCREASES IN KNOWLEDGE OR STRATEGIES

Consider the following: Suppose children are given a list-learning task. Perhaps the list has 30 items on it. One-third of the list items are names of pieces of furniture (e.g., table, chair, piano), one-third names of fruit (e.g., cherry, orange, melon), and one-third names of zoo animals (e.g., lion, elephant, monkey). The items are presented in random order. If grade-1, grade-6, and grade-11 children are asked to learn such a list, memory performance increases. If asked simply to recall the items, with increasing age, students are increasingly likely to recall the pieces of furniture together, the fruit together, and the animals together—with increasing age, their recall is more **clustered** or **organized.**

One interpretation (e.g., Moely, 1977) of increasingly organized recall with development is that older students are more likely to use strategies intentionally, either to reorganize the input at study, and hence make to-be-learned content more memorable, or to use the category labels at testing to organize their recall. An alternative interpretation (Lange, 1973, 1978) is that the performance and organization increases represent nothing more than an expanding and more interconnected knowledge base. With increasing size and connectedness, the knowledge base is more accessible (see especially Rabinowitz & McAuley, 1990), so much so that presentation of a categorizable list results in automatic associations to category labels and interassociations between list items in the same category.

Bjorklund (e.g., 1985, 1987b), more than anyone else, has explored this problem, conducting many studies in which students at different developmental levels learn word lists. No complete discussion of the problem could exclude Bjorklund's research and the work of those who have emulated him. Even so, our view is that Bjorklund's research has not been (and could not be) definitive in determining whether increases in memory are due to increasing use of strategies or an expanding knowledge base: There is no pattern of outcomes that would definitely implicate either strategies or automatic use of knowledge-mediated associations and reorganizations, a point Bjorklund acknowledges (Bjorklund & Buchanen, 1989, p. 453).

There are some patterns, however, that Bjorklund believes are more telling than others. For instance, Bjorklund believes that if during recall, the latencies are short between same-category members (i.e., when people recall monkey, they also quickly recall elephant, zebra, or another zoo animal) and considerably longer between noncategory members (i.e., a much longer pause between recall of elephant and piano than between elephant and monkey), this is evidence that the categorical structure of the list is being used strategically.

Our interpretation of this situation, however, is that the same pattern of recall latencies would be produced by automatic reorganization at study stimulated by interassociations between the same-category items. We have never seen an outcome involving recall of categorizable lists that could not be interpreted with respect to either strategies or knowledge base perspectives. When recall is low, it is always possible that the poor performance reflects failure to use strategies or lack of a knowledge base. When recall is high, it could be due to intentional use of categorization as a strategy, automatic mediation by the knowledge base, or a combination of strategy and knowledge-base mediation. This third possibility may be closest to the truth in the case of list learning: With increasing knowledge, it may be easier to apply a categorization strategy—the associations between list items and the category label would be stronger, and the associations between list members would be stronger and more diverse—and thus use of the categorization strategy might be more likely (Guttentag, 1984; Guttentag, Ornstein, & Siemens, 1987). People are often more likely to use procedures that are easier to apply rather than more difficult-to-use procedures! That is, the increasing knowledge base increases motivation to use categorization strategies by reducing the amount of effort required to apply them to lists.

Bjorklund's main conclusion is quite different, however. His reading of the data is that performance increases in categorizable list learning with development reflect expansion of an ever more accessible knowledge base. If strategic use of categorization occurs at all according to Bjorkland, it does not develop until adolescence, long after striking performance improvements in categorizable list learning have been observed during development.

Unfortunately, the 15 years of research on knowledge and strategy tradeoffs have been less conclusive than research on other problems. To some extent, this is because of overreliance on the categorizable list-learning task by researchers interested in this problem. Moreover, researchers working in this paradigm have relied much less on sensitive research methods such as protocol analysis (thinking aloud; Ericsson & Simon, 1984) than other researchers interested in prior knowledge effects in cognition.

That is not to say there has been no progress in understanding relationships between strategies and knowledge. In fact, it is possible to cite clear instances in which (1) possession of prior knowledge reduces dependencies on strategies, (2) possession of prior knowledge enables use of strategies that require prior knowledge for their execution, and (3) both strategies and automatic prior knowledge mediation have been demonstrated to make separable improvements in performance. (4) There have also been demonstrations that strategic use of errant prior knowledge can undermine effective performance. Examples of each of these possibilities provide windows on the complicated articulations between knowledge and strategies that occur as part of effective cognition.

Effects of Prior Knowledge on Learning and Performance

Knowledge-Base Mediation Can Replace Use of Strategies   Sometimes children use strategies because they do not yet possess a knowledge base. For example, experienced readers have knowledge of thousands of words. Young readers, who do not, must rely much more on decoding strategies involving sounding out of words than do more experienced readers (see Chapter 14). Lesgold et al.'s (1988) experienced radiologists could recognize immediately many patterns in x-rays that less experienced radiologists could identify only by using inductive and deductive strategies.

The most complete analysis of tradeoffs between strategies and knowledge has been made with respect to development of children's knowledge of simple addition facts. Siegler and Shrager (1984) studied children's responses to simple addition problems such as $6 + 5 = 11$, $3 + 4 = 7$, and $2 + 5 = 7$. Their younger participants (5- to 7-year-olds) could solve such problems, relying on strategies to do so: They used their fingers or other manipulatives to represent the problem and generate a solution (e.g., four fingers up and then three more put up for 4 + 3). Sometimes they used counting up strategies (e.g., saying four, five, six, seven in response to 4 + 3). In contrast, older children (7- to 9-year-olds) rarely manifested these strategies. Rather, they simply retrieved the answers to problems from long-term memory. A telling sign of such retrieval was rapid responding compared with the responding of younger children. Moreover, there was no evidence of fingers or anything else being manipulated by most 8-year-olds, nor was there overt counting up. Siegler's interpretation of this pattern of data was that the younger children possessed some strategies for solving simple arithmetic problems but did not know their addition "facts" yet. Knowledge of arithmetic facts is built up during the first 3 years of school—school provides many trials of practice on such problems! After a number of presentations of an addition problem followed by correct solution of the problem, an association is established between the problem and its correct answer. Eventually, presentation of the addition problem results in automatic activation of the answer. (Expanded discussion of Siegler's work and findings related to it are presented in Chapter 13, this volume.)

It is proving easy to demonstrate that people high in prior knowledge relevant to learning tasks and problems process differently than do people who lack relevant prior knowledge. **Think-alouds** are often helpful in demonstrating such differences, especially with adults. For example, Pritchard (1990) studied reading in grade-11 students, some of whom were students living on a South Pacific island (Palua) and others of whom were U.S. residents. These high school students read two types of texts, ones containing cultural schemata pertaining to the United States and others based on schemata related to Palaun culture. As these students read text, they thought aloud about what they were doing to understand the text. There were some key differences in reported strategies as a function of whether the text was matched to the background knowledge of the reader. Rereading and paraphrasing strategies were more common with culturally unfamiliar texts than with familiar ones. When reading culturally familiar texts, readers were more likely to relate what they were reading to previous text and previous experiences and more likely to extrapolate beyond the

information presented in the text. In short, with culturally familiar text, processing largely involved relating to the knowledge base; with unfamiliar content, more general strategies such as rereading were common. Of course, this pattern is consistent with the pattern observed in all of the other studies addressed in this subsection.

Prior Knowledge Can Enable Use of Strategies
Some strategies simply cannot be carried out profitably in the absence of particular forms of prior knowledge. An obvious example is prior knowledge activation (Chapters 3 and 14). If a person is about to read a text on a particular content that is completely foreign to him or her, there should be little gain from asking the reader to think about related knowledge before reading the content or by instructing the reader to attempt to relate what one knows to the text.

Pressley and Brewster (1990) provided a telling demonstration that some strategies can only be executed if other knowledge has already been acquired. They asked Canadian middle-school students to learn some facts about Canadian provinces (e.g., Canada's first museum was in Ontario). The strategy that was studied in this investigation was an imagery strategy. Some students were instructed to construct an image depicting the fact occurring in a uniquely Ontario setting. Similarly, when presented facts about Nova Scotia, Saskatchewan, or British Columbia, students were instructed to construct images of the fact occurring in uniquely Nova Scotian, Saskatchewan, or British Columbian settings. The prior knowledge that was required, of course, were unique images for each province.

Pressley and Brewster (1990) determined in a pilot investigation, however, that many students lack unique images of the Canadian provinces in their long-term knowledge. Thus, the study included a condition in which students acquired a vivid image for each province before attempting to learn the facts (e.g., the picture for Saskatchewan was of a wheatfield, which is typical of the countryside in that province). These subjects were presented the 12 pictures corresponding to the 12 provinces until they could name perfectly the province shown in each picture. Those subjects who had acquired images of provincial settings in this fashion and who were instructed subsequently to remember each fact by imagining it occurring in the scene for the province in question learned the facts much better than students who were instructed to use imagery to learn the facts but who had not previously acquired an image corresponding to each province. Imagery participants who had learned the provincial scenes also outperformed control subjects. The imagery strategy of relating new facts about provinces to images of the provinces was potent but only if the student already possessed an image corresponding to the province in question.

Knowledge-Base Mediation and Strategy Use Can Make Unique Contributions to Learning   Even if students make some automatic associations to prior knowledge as they do a task, that does not mean that learning might not be improved additionally using strategies. For instance, there may be far more prior knowledge in long-term memory that could be related to a task than is related automatically by the learners. In some cases, the demands of the task are such that more is required than simple associations to prior knowledge for the task to be accomplished.

Woloshyn, Pressley, and Schneider (1992) asked Canadian and German university students to learn some new facts about Canadian provinces and German states. Even in the absence of strategy instruction, learning of new facts pertaining to jurisdictions in one's own country was far superior to learning new facts about the other country. That is, prior knowledge was automatically applied to this learning task when it was available. Even so, the automatic use of prior knowledge did not maximize learning. When subjects were taught a strategy that prompted extensive search of fact-related prior knowledge (i.e., they were taught to attempt to learn each fact by figuring out why the fact made sense for the province in question), their learning improved over what was learned via automatic association to prior knowledge. That is, German students learning German facts in the absence of strategy instruction did not learn as many German facts as German students using the elaborative interrogation strategy. The same held for Canadian students learning Canadian facts. Strategies that increase attention to prior knowledge can produce greater learning than occurs through automatic association to what one already knows (see Martin & Pressley, 1991, for a telling analysis) because automatic activation of prior knowledge does not guarantee that all of the prior knowledge that is relevant will be used by a student.

Some tasks require more than the learning that is engendered by automatic activation of prior knowledge. For instance, a common writing strategy among young children is to rely heavily on prior knowledge, essentially to write down associations that occur given the topic of the writing assignment (Scardamalia & Bereiter, 1986). This automatic activation results in an incoherent and incomplete written product. As will be covered more extensively in Chapter 15, writing involves such activation embedded in a larger strategy composed of planning activities, translation of plans into rough draft, and revisions of rough draft. Automatic prior knowledge association is not sufficient to accomplish this task completely because the task demands more—processes specified in plan-translate-revise writing strategies.

Knowledge-Base Activation Strategies Can Interfere with New Learning   Not all prior knowledge possessed by students is accurate or consistent with new knowledge presented in school. Scientific misconceptions are a case in point. For example, students often believe that plants get food from soil and water. This misconception persists even after students learn about photosynthesis (e.g., Roth, 1990), which is a bad outcome. Even so, it can be worse. Activation of errant prior knowledge can substantially interfere with acquiring new information at all.

Alvermann, Smith, and Readence (1985) provided telling data on the impact of errant prior knowledge. Grade-6 children in their study either activated or did not activate knowledge relevant to a passage they were about to read. Those who activated prior knowledge were asked before they read the passage to write down everything they knew about "light and heat," the topic of the passage. There were plenty of misconceptions activated during this exercise! The passage that was read subsequently was on the topic of light and heat and contained information that clashed with these misconceptions. After reading the passage, memory of its content was tested in several ways. Participants wrote down what they could remember from the passage and then responded to multiple-choice items over the passage content, including ones that had wrong answers based on misconceptions about light and heat.

The results were striking. Free recall of the text was better when participants had not activated prior knowledge. Specifically, when prior knowledge had been activated, there was less recall of new information in the passage that was incompatible with students' prior knowledge about light and heat. In addition, multiple-choice items containing misconception foils were less likely to be responded to correctly in the prior knowledge activation condition. Activation of prior knowledge can undermine learning of content incompatible with it.

Joanna Williams (1991) produced data additionally substantiating the power of prior knowledge to disrupt learning of new content. She studied learning-disabled students who heard stories in a situation that encouraged them to make personal interpretations. What distinguished the interpretations offered by learning-disabled students compared with normally achieving readers was that their interpretations were bizarre. (For complementary data, see Purcell-Gates, 1991.) Moreover, these bizarre relationships persisted when the prose was recalled. Although encouraging students to activate prior knowledge related to the content of to-be-read material has become common in reading instructional programs, data such as Williams (1991) and Alvermann et al. (1985) make clear that prior knowledge activation can be a double-edged sword, affecting learning of new content pejoratively in some cases.

Summary   The effects of prior knowledge are diverse. For the most part, researchers have focused on how rich prior knowledge can empower learners, permitting them to complete some tasks more quickly and certainly than strategy use would, permitting them to carry out some strategies that can only be carried out when prior knowledge is high, and permitting additional learning over what is permitted by strategy use alone. Increases in prior knowledge enable diverse cognitive actions that have powerful positive effects on performance. Nonetheless, not all knowledge that students acquire is correct. Students often have great faith in and commitment to misconceptions. Such misconceptions can impede performance, with data reviewed in this section suggesting that such disruption may be especially likely if the misconceptions are activated. (In Chapter 12, there will be explicit discussion about how activation of misconceptions can be engineered so as to increase the likelihood that students will come to understand the inconsistency of new information with misconceptions and restructure their knowledge so the new, more accurate concepts replace misconceptions.)

Large-*n* studies have provided a great deal of information about relationships between procedural knowledge and declarative knowledge, about how

some procedures are replaced by knowledge-base mediation and how other procedures are enabled by knowledge-base mediation. Other types of research, involving few subjects, have also enriched our understanding of strategy and knowledge-base relationships, however. One especially prominent line of study contributing to this understanding has been studies of individuals with extraordinary intellectual abilities.

How Do They Do It?

Some people can perform extraordinary memory or computation feats. The ability to remember long lists of digits or perform abstruse computations such as calculating square roots often is an isolated ability—the only extraordinary aspect of cognition in an otherwise average thinker. Cognitive psychologists have studied some people who demonstrate extraordinary but isolated competencies. The result is a growing body of data documenting that splinter competencies are often the result of application of sophisticated, specialized strategies to extensive, particularized prior knowledge. Even extraordinary competence can be understood in terms of good information processing.

Memory for Digits   A group at Carnegie-Mellon University has worked with two people who have developed exceptional ability to recall long lists of digits in order. One, SF, was studied by Chase and Ericsson (1982). SF increased his digit span to more than 80 digits. This feat required about 2 years of practice, which was monitored and analyzed in detail by the researchers.

How did SF do it (Ericsson & Staszewski, 1989)? It helped that he had extensive prior knowledge of track and field records, especially running times. What SF did was to chunk short groups of digits and then recode them as running times, dates, and ages:

> For instance, he would encode the sequence 3492 as "3 minutes, 49.2 seconds—a near world record for the 1-mile run . . . " 798 would be coded as a, "79.8-year-old man" and dates (e.g., 1860, 1963) to accommodate digit sequences not easily encoded as running times. (Ericsson & Staszewski, 1989, p. 239)

In addition, SF devised mechanisms for keeping track of the order of these chunks. He would code several of the mnemonically encoded groups of digits into a supergroup. This supergroup would be embedded into a hierarchical network. With practice, SF's facility and speed in coding digit strings using prior knowledge that was elaborated into hierarchical networks increased dramatically. The increasing speed in chunking short strings of information dramatically increased SF's functional short-term capacity, permitting the holding of a large number of these smaller chunks, which in turn facilitates coding into the hierarchical memory structures. In terms used in this book, SF used complex mnemonic strategies that were possible because of extensive prior knowledge of track times, ages, and dates.

Staszewski (e.g., 1990) studied another subject, DD, who also had extensive knowledge of running times, dates, and ages. For 4.5 years, DD practiced the methods devised by SF and eventually was able to code 106 digits. These excerpts from a coding of 75 digits provide a sampler of how prior knowledge was used strategically to construct long-term encodings:

0204 OK, first group was a half mile, oh, two, oh, four. I said oh, two, oh, four, half mile.
4927 And then, ah, I had back-to-back fours, that's forty-nine twenty-seven, a ten mile, and I said that two and seven add up to that nine and had that forty-nine.
5832 Then, ah, five, eight, three, two was a ten mile and I just said I got back-to-back ten miles and then the three and two add up to that five. I said OK, five's the first digit and these add up to it.
1800 And um, then the eighteen hundred I just said was a date. (Staszewski, 1990, p. 258)

In this way, approximately 20 clusters of three to four digits were constructed by DD. These were clustered into groups of two or four to form supergroups. The seven or so supergroups were arranged into a set of four or so groups. This structure included coding of the order in which the original 20 groups had occurred, although we must admit that after much study of this research, we are still not entirely clear about how order was encoded.

Consistent with other studies of expertise, SF and DD did not demonstrate better memory for tasks other than digit span. Exceptional memory for digits in order did not even generalize to learning of other order materials (e.g., lists of consonants; Chase & Ericsson, 1981, 1982).

Memory for Restaurant Orders   A waiter in Boulder, Colorado, can remember the orders for 20 customers at once, an ability that pays off handsomely in large tips. Ericsson and Polson (1988) studied how this fellow carried out this exceptional feat. They particularly examined how JC remembered material in a laboratory version of restaurant ordering, comparing the performance of JC with others who are not exceptionally proficient at remembering such lists. The participants in the study learned dinner orders consisting of an entrée (one of seven possibilities) prepared at a particular temperature (one of five choices). Each order included a salad complete with one of five dressings and fries, baked potato, or rice.

JC was definitely strategic. First, he dealt with orders in groups of four. He studied and rehearsed a group of four orders at the table, developing a memory structure that could be retrieved later. For each person in the group, he constructed a mnemonic image of the person's face in interaction with the entrée item. As part of this, he "sized up" the customer and included information in the image about the fit between the entrée and the type of person (e.g., Steak Oscar doesn't seem to fit that guy). Each salad dressing had a mnemonic letter associated with it: B for blue cheese, O for oil and vinegar, T for thousand island, and so on. If the four salad dressings ordered at a table were blue cheese, oil and vinegar, oil and vinegar, and thousand island, they would be encoded into the word BOOT. For temperature, an internal graph would be formed in JC's mind. The ordinate would encode the temperature, with the lowest point representing rare, moving higher to medium-rare, higher still to medium, up to well-done. For the first order, the leftmost point on the graph would be plotted. The rightmost point on the graph corresponded to the fourth person in the order. Thus, if the first person wanted rare, the second well-done, the third rare, and the fourth medium-rare, the internal image of a graph started low, spiked up, dipped low, and then ended up halfway up the ordinate. Because there were only three different starches, these were always rehearsed as a serial order—for example, "rice, rice, fries, baked."

Not surprisingly, JC recalled much more in the formal studies of his memory than did control subjects. The naive subjects performed few transformations of the incoming data, instead attempting to memorize the information exactly as inputted. There were some other interesting outcomes in the study, which lasted for a year. Over the year, JC improved, getting more accurate and faster. Of course, this is consistent with SF and DD's data. JC clearly had knowledge of the four categories of information that would occur in restaurant orders and used this knowledge in devising a memory plan (e.g., mnemonic letter codes for salad dressing, an image of a graph for temperatures, serial rehearsal for the starches). He also had extensive prior knowledge about different people and their characteristics, information that was used to construct interactive images and elaborations with information about the entrée. This waiter used strategies that were enabled by prior knowledge.

There was only one major difference in the general conclusions that followed from study of JC and studies of DD and SF. JC was able to transfer his skill to other types of items, learning other materials that could be placed into categories, whereas DD's and JF's digit-learning abilities did not transfer.

Mental Calculation   Ericsson and Staszewski (1989) and Staszewski (1988) reported on their work with an expert mental calculator, one who had been at it for 15 years and had achieved world acclaim (Smith, 1983). This subject, AB, was an expert in multiplication and in calculation of squares of numbers. Two other subjects, GG and JA, received training in mental calculation (instruction in computation strategies used by AB combined with a lot of practice) as part of the research and eventually achieved great proficiency, able to do problems as complicated as two-digit by five-digit multiplications with the same speed and accuracy as AB. Consistent with other work on expertise, however, GG's and JA's improvements showed limited transfer, with AB maintaining a great advantage for problems involving more digits, such as four-digit by four-digit problems—that is, types of problems not covered during GG's and JA's training.

How did these subjects perform complicated mental calculations? For one, following training, their knowledge of basic arithmetic facts was extensive, something that is almost always true of great mental calculators. Learning math facts (e.g., two-digit by two-digit products—24×17 is 408; 39×61 is 2379; and so on) seems to be an incidental product of practicing mental computation. Both of the trained subjects reported that with practice, they recognized many multiplication problems and immediately knew their answers (e.g., a two-digit by two-digit problem embedded in a larger problem). Once recognized, familiar problems embedded in larger problems were used in calculation of an overall product. Thus, the overall product was calculated

using an articulation of strategies, one of which was to break the problem into subproblems and solve these. The exact sequence that was elected depended on the nature of the problem, with the expert calculator selecting a sequence aimed at maximizing efficiency. Key in all of this was that subproblems that were known as math facts were simply retrieved and used rather than calculated.

Here is a sample protocol that illustrates how calculation proceeded, this one generated by GG in solving 266×97 (Staszewski, 1988, p. 100):

2 times 9, 18
66 times 9
54
9 times 6 is 54
and 54, 594
18 and 594
18 and 5, 23
retrieve 94
23 94
expand 23 940
23,940   23,940   (Up until this point, solving subproblem 90×266, which is decomposed into 90×200 and 90×66, which is decomposed into 90×60 and 90×6—that is, decomposition and calculation is done in a hierarchical fashion that permits keeping track of the magnitude of the component multiplications.)

OK, 266 times 7
OK, 7 times 2, 14
7 times 6, 42
and 42, its gonna be 462
so 14 and 462
14 and 4 is 18
retrieve 62
18 62   (Solution of 266×7 subproblem in hierarchical fashion so it is possible to keep track of the magnitude of the answer.)

retrieve . . . uh, 29 . . . 240 was it?
23 940
23 940 and 18 62
that to . . . 18 62 1 862
umm . . . 940 and 862, carry
uh. . . , 23, 1, and carry, 25
retrieve 940 and 862
40 and 62 will be a carry, so . . .
umm, gonna be 9, 980
carry will be 18
strip the 1 . . . 8
40 and 62 is 102, strip the 1
8 and 02
802

As was true with expert memory performances, both GG and JA increased their speed with practice.

Staszewski's discussion of AB, GG, and JA emphasized the similarities in mental calculation and in skilled memory. We agree. Both involve use of particular strategies that are executed most efficiently with high knowledge of content—in the case of calculation, extensive knowledge of math facts.

Summary

This section began with discussion of a program of research concerned with developmental changes in memory of categorizable lists. We argued that the paradigm in question made it difficult to separate out whether the development of accessible knowledge or the use of strategies accounted for developmental increases in memory of categorizable lists. Much of the other work in this section suggests that that may have been the wrong question.

Memory experts and expert calculators do not rely on strategies *or* prior knowledge, but rather they use strategies and nonstrategic knowledge in coordination, resulting in efficient performance on demanding tasks. Even research suggesting that knowledge-based mediation can come to replace less efficient strategic functioning, such as Siegler's work with primary-grade children solving addition problems, also includes descriptions of functioning that is more complicated than use of either knowledge or strategies. For example, Siegler (1988) reported that some children who had the single-digit addition facts down nonetheless calculated the solution to problems such as 4 + 3. They did so, apparently just to make certain they had reported the correct answer.

Finally the strategy versus knowledge base debate is strained as a legitimate question because part of any domain of knowledge is the strategies that can be used to learn new content in the domain. Students who are high with respect to declarative knowledge in a domain are also often high with respect to procedural knowledge for the domain, so a "strategic" younger student is not really the same as a "strategic" older student. Thus a grade-2 child who solves 3×13 using an addition strategy is strategic but not in as advanced a way as an older, more knowledgeable child who recognized $3 \times 13 = (3 \times 10) + (3 \times 3)$ and applied such an approach to the problem effortlessly, since the multiplication facts $3 \times 10 = 30$, $3 \times 3 = 9$, and $30 + 9 = 39$

had been mastered long ago. The point of view adopted in this text is that with education and development, both strategic competence and other knowledge increase in completeness and complexity with ever better articulation between strategies and other knowledge. That is, performance increases with education or development are due to increases in strategies, increases in other knowledge, and increased efficiency in the articulation of strategies and other knowledge.

EDUCATIONAL IMPLICATIONS

The data in this chapter have important implications for educational policy decisions. The data reported in this chapter are extremely consistent and in ways that suggest that some instructional practices make more sense than others. We begin with some of the societal issues first and then take up some more precise recommendations for instruction.

Inequality of Educational Opportunity

High-quality performance in many arenas requires long-term, high-quality education. Sometimes the education that is required is available in the culture (e.g., in the case of baseball expertise) or in nonschool settings (e.g., in the case of horse betting). For some of the most valued forms of expertise in our culture, however, years of formal schooling, including highly specialized training, are required (e.g., the talented youth in a variety of fields studied by Bloom and his associates).

Analyses such as those reviewed in this chapter cast a special light on the many studies of inequality of educational opportunity in the United States. Because schools in the United States are financed largely with property taxes, students who live in high-income communities have many more dollars spent on their education than students living in less economically advantaged communities. As this book was being written, Jonathon Kozol's (1991) *Savage Inequalities* was attracting the attention of the nation. The book documents many such inequalities, both in cold terms (e.g., Chicago city high schools spend about $5200 a year per pupil whereas some Chicago suburban high schools spent $9300 per pupil) and in vivid, human terms. The rich enjoy small classes in beautiful, well-furnished buildings, with lots of course diversity and enrichment. Their teachers are often exceptionally well-qualified for their positions.

In contrast, the poor reside in large classes in settings where even basic equipment is missing or broken. Although there are some exceptionally dedicated teachers, there are many ill-qualified teachers in these schools. We know of no analysis of inequality of schooling in the United States that does not conclude that the poor have much less access to knowledge and the instruction of knowledge than do the rich. For extremely scholarly analyses of the same points made by Kozol (1991), see Goodlad and Keating (1990). If knowledge is intellectual power, as suggested by the many analyses reviewed in this chapter, schooling in the United States is designed to be more empowering for the well to do than for the disadvantaged. Some have recognized that schooling is not producing certain increases in knowledge for many students and have offered potential solutions, with one of the most prominent of these in the early 1990s being the "cultural literacy" movement.

Cultural Knowledge

Hirsch, Kett, and Trefil (1988) and their supporters believe that to participate meaningfully in American society, it is necessary to have command of a certain core of knowledge that is essential to understand American life and thinking. Such a person is said to be in possession of **cultural literacy.** Important policymakers (e.g., Finn, 1991; Ravitch, 1989), who were close to the Bush administration, embraced this perspective. The most recent accomplishment of Hirsch has been the editing of a series of books that specify what cultural literacy should be taught at each grade level. Thus, *What Your 2nd Grader Needs To Know* (Hirsch, 1991) covers the language arts, social studies, fine arts, mathematics, and natural sciences that grade 2 should cover.

What are the difficulties with this approach? Hirsch et al.'s (1988) original presentation of what they regarded as important cultural knowledge was in the form of a dictionary, with the result being pages and pages of fragmented information, thousands of short definitions of concepts. The scattered approach is not as extreme in the grade-school series of books, but the content is still fragmented. The lack of coherence in the grade-school series can be appreciated by considering what a 2nd grader should know, for instance, in geography:

World Geography: The third-largest ocean, the Mediterranean and Aegean Seas, a review of the continents.

United States Geography: The U.S. map of states, including coverage of why some states have strange shapes; the first states.

Geography of Mexico, Central America, and South America: A smorgasbord of facts including that Spanish is the main language, a few explorers, Spanish ownership at one time except for Brazil, independence movements in Latin America.

In short, there are smatterings of information in the grade-2 curriculum (as well as the curricula specified for the other grade levels). The superficiality and lack of coherence so apparent in these volumes contrast with everything that is now known about knowledge that permits powerful thinking: Knowledge that effectively mediates important performances is well organized and connected. Learning disconnected facts is a certain way to create what Whitehead (1929) referred to as inert knowledge, knowledge that can be remembered for a test but not applied elsewhere.

Another striking shortcoming of the *Cultural Knowledge* approach is a complete lack of a theory of learning—although the dictionary includes an introductory chapter attempting to make the case that the cultural literacy perspective is consistent with schema theory. Moreover, there are enormous individual differences in students, so much so that it is hard to imagine any set of knowledge that would be appropriately matched to the needs of all students.

Although we do not want to imply that it is not important to build general knowledge in students, it is clear that general knowledge alone is not what is needed for high achievement in many fields. The contemporary world needs expertise in many domains, and analyses such as Bloom (1985) suggest that the development of many forms of expertise should begin in the grade-school years. Bloom's work, and other research on focused talent (see Chapters 6 and 18), suggests that specialized talent will not develop as a function of development of general cultural knowledge. We worry a great deal that an overemphasis on a common curriculum, which is what the cultural literacy approach advocates, would overshadow the importance of individualizing instruction to encourage the exceptional strengths and interests of students.

Finally, cultural ethnocentrism aside—and there is no doubt that white, mainstream thinking is more salient in the cultural literacy movement than other ways of thinking—a great deal of what is in Hirsch's books is pretty dated and corny, less enticing than alternative content that is arguably as defensible. Organizations such as the International Reading Association (see annual issue of *The Reading Teacher* devoted to outstanding children's literature) and the National Council of Teachers of Mathematics (e.g., 1989) also prepare opinions about what should and could be in the curriculum. These organizations generally represent a broader view than do the cultural literacy lists and in doing so seem to be aware of more interesting materials than the cultural literacy advocates. The materials and content cited by well-informed professional groups seem more likely to us to be the emerging American knowledge base (if there is such a thing), whereas cultural literacy listings seem to be nostalgic, reflecting knowledge favored by earlier generations of Americans, and even then, reflecting only some ingredients in the melting pot.

Even so, as this book is being written, we are aware of attempts to evaluate the impact of cultural literacy–inspired curricula in schools. Our view is that these evaluations should be studied carefully and with an open mind, for it may be that in the hands of experienced educators, the cultural literacy volumes will take on life not apparent from our reading of them.

One Way the Smart Get Smarter: Experts Become Their Own Teachers

All the experts reviewed in this chapter exhibited **self-regulated** learning and problem solving. No one was leading them by the hand through the tasks they were doing or even providing hints. They kept themselves on task and guided their own thinking. That good thinkers invariably are self-regulated has provided great impetus for educational interventions that promote self-regulation, especially self-regulated use of complex sequences of procedures that are combined and coordinated with prior knowledge. What must be emphasized is that much of the self-regulation that goes on feeds back on the system, making the person an even more powerful thinker. Good thinkers can rapidly size up a situation in terms of their prior knowledge. To the extent that prior knowledge does not fit the current situation, the self-regulated expert makes adjustments and inferences, with the result being new knowledge that will be available in the future. Self-regulated thinking builds on itself, with the self-regulated thinker always becoming a better thinker.

Years ago author MP was very ill. He had to have a particular type of surgery. Unfortunately, after the surgery, he suffered an unforeseen side effect: He could not keep food down at all. His physicians, several of whom were top people in the world in their surgical specialty, felt the difficulty was X. Treating X did nothing but make MP worse, however. Then one of them formed an hypothesis and tested it with some laboratory analyses not typically performed. This physician concluded that because of the surgery, Y had occurred and that X had nothing to do with the post-surgical inability to eat. The doctors treated Y successfully, which if not diagnosed would have killed MP. A couple of years ago, MP had reason to talk with one of his doctors from that era. The physician brought up spontaneously, "I'll never forget you. That's when we figured out that when doing the type of surgery we did on you, look out for Y. Checking for Y is now standard practice everywhere following the type of operation you had." Experts have powerful knowledge that sometimes does not solve a current problem. Being self-regulated thinkers, they search for new solutions when old solutions do not work, with the result that their knowledge grows. Experts make themselves more expert as they practice in their domain of expertise (Simon, 1980). People who have suffered postsurgical Y since MP's experience in part owe their lives to physicians whose understanding of their domain increased by persisting until they figured out what was wrong when MP could not eat for weeks after an operation. There is little doubt that life all over the planet could be improved by increasing the number of fully self-regulated thinkers in our midst—the number of good information processors.

CONCLUDING COMMENTS

This chapter opened with the question: "What difference does a large knowledge base make?" Knowledge is intellectual power. A domain-knowledgeable 10-year-old often is more than equal to an adult lacking knowledge of the domain in question. For many tasks, the knowledgeable person with a 90 IQ has it all over the unknowledgeable person with a 130 IQ. The person high in knowledge about horses wins at the betting window; the soccer expert processes information about soccer more completely than a soccer novice, no matter how many IQ points the novice has.

Although expertise can be detected using a variety of measures, no method of investigation has been more helpful in understanding the nature of expertise than verbal protocol analysis—having experts and novices talk aloud as they do tasks. Regardless of area of expertise or task, many similarities in expert performance have emerged from such analyses: Expertise is domain specific. Experts can identify large and meaningful patterns in their domain of expertise that novices cannot identify. Experts process material in the domain of expertise efficiently. They understand problems in the area of expertise at a more principled level than do novices. Their problem solving in the area of expertise is planful. Experts monitor well their performances in the area of expertise, attempting to account for discrepancies between their expectancies and events as they unfold.

The knowledge of experts is rich in every way that knowledge can be rich. All of the forms of representation reviewed in Chapter 3 function in the mind of the expert. Highly organized, tightly connected, yet flexible knowledge empowers. Although experts have rich networks of concepts and associations, the schemata they possess have been singled out for scrutiny. Experts have many schematic images corresponding to situations common to the domain. Moreover, their images and other schemata are flexible, with experts modifying them as necessary to deal with new situations. Because experts are ever modifying their schemata, their education never really stops.

That experts have a long education has been documented using a number of analyses. One to two decades of preparation is typical, with much of the second decade a period of immersion in the discipline. Chess masters have seen hundreds of thousands of chess boards, and expert radiologists have analyzed hundreds of thousands of x-rays.

One of the most important questions in the developmental literature during the 1970s and 1980s was whether performance increases with development reflected increases in use of strategies or increases in automatic mediation by the knowledge base (i.e., the ever expanding and ever more accessible knowledge base permits more and more certain associations to prior knowledge when new content is processed). That proved to be the wrong question, with performance proving to depend both on strategies and on other automatic knowledge-based mediation. Detailed analyses of exceptional memory (enormous digit spans) and problem solving (exceptional mental calculation) have provided important windows on how experts coordinate strategies and other knowledge. Research on more mundane performances, such as addition of single-digit numbers by children and learning of facts about home and foreign countries, has made obvious that there are elegant articulations of strategies and other knowledge in the thinking of more typical children and adults than those who earn big tips by remembering many restaurant orders and who earn a place in histories of the great arithmeticians (e.g., Smith, 1983).

Chapters 3 and 4 have provided an intellectual foundation for many of the interventions that will be presented in this book, and there will be frequent reference back to these chapters. Many of the interventions reviewed in this book can be thought of with respect to the representational systems reviewed in Chapter 3; the development of many academic competencies that will be covered here have been affected by the insights produced by analyses of expert performance—for example, many of the interventions reviewed in this book are long-term treatments, consistent with the perspective emerging from study of experts that skilled performance can only be developed in the long term. It is important that you connect what was presented in Chapters 3 and 4 with what follows, and we will provide cues at appropriate points along the way for readers to do so.

One way to remember some of the points covered in Chapters 3 and 4 is to think of the *Hardy Boys* again. The boys' knowledge of the criminal world was extremely well connected and could be applied in many different settings. They were capable of many complex sequences of behavior, sequences that seemed compiled (e.g., the entire sequence of events involved in lifting fingerprints and analyzing them might be thought of as a compilation). Many of their strategies (e.g., notetaking at the scene of a crime) were automatically carried out as part of an overall plan that was carefully controlled by each of the boys. They were constantly aware of what they wanted to accomplish, and they kept themselves on task. For teenage boys to have achieved such expertise must have meant old Fenton Hardy had been at the boys since birth, for experts are educated over a long period of time and not born . . . although by the point in their development when they are introduced to readers of the *Hardy Boys* series, the boys are really educating themselves, just by doing their trade. Practicing expertise is one way that the smart get smarter (Rohwer, 1980b).

5

Enhancing Student Motivation

Students are not always motivated to learn more or to use what they know already. Good information processing and effective thinking require more than know-how; students must be motivated to put their know-how to use. Thus, this chapter is specifically devoted to insights about how to motivate students to learn and do well academically, although important principles of motivation are covered throughout the book.

For example, in Chapter 2, the case was made that whether students used strategies they have learned depends on whether they understand their value. This is a specific instance of a general principle that will be presented more completely in this chapter and in Chapter 7, that the likelihood of a behavior that a person possesses occurring is a function of the expectancy of reward for performing the behavior and the value of the reward. Thus, when students know that a strategy improves performance on tasks that they wish to accomplish, the expectancy for reinforcement increases contingent on execution of the strategy. The probability of the strategy being executed is high not only because this expectation is high, but also because the reward for strategy execution is something the student wants—completion of some task that is perceived as desirable to complete.

A second example of motivation covered elsewhere in this book is the recurring theme that pre-

sentation of information just a bit beyond the current competence of the learner is motivating. Although the precise mechanisms mediating the motivational effectiveness of new content slightly beyond current knowledge vary from theory to theory, there is little disagreement that such content is engaging. The Piagetians emphasize that the learner's conceptual understanding is most likely to advance through assimilation followed by accommodation when presented information slightly in advance of current understandings (Chapter 7). The Vygotskians see such content as within the zone of proximal development and thus manageable, at least if there is some support from a more knowledgeable adult or peer (Chapter 8). The behaviorists emphasize that the learner is likely to make correct responses and receive reinforcements if new demands are slightly greater than old demands (Chapter 7).

Many volumes on motivational theory and the role of motivation in education have been compiled. Special issues of education journals on academic motivation are now common. The goal in this chapter is to present what seems to be the most influential contemporary perspectives on the role of motivation in education. The most logical place to begin such a discussion is with evaluation of the need to understand student motivation in order to enhance it.

NEED TO UNDERSTAND ACADEMIC MOTIVATION MORE FULLY: HOW MOTIVATION AND ACHIEVEMENT CAN BE UNDERMINED

In this section, we review three types of evidence that make very clear that academic motivation can be undermined easily. Such evidence makes obvious that there is an urgent need to understand academic motivation better and to consider new ways of arranging schooling so that academic motivation is enhanced rather than destroyed by classroom experiences.

Expectations and Their Impact on Long-Term Motivations and Educational Outcomes

Most children entering elementary school have great expectations for success. Present them with a task—almost any academic task that could possibly be within their competence—and ask them how they will do. A high proportion of kindergarten, grade-1, and grade-2 children assume that they will do extremely well, something that has been confirmed in many investigations (e.g., Clifford, 1975, 1978; Entwisle & Hayduk, 1978; Flavell, Friedrichs, & Hoyt, 1970; Goss, 1968; Levin, Yussen, DeRose, & Pressley, 1977; Parsons & Ruble, 1977; Stipek & Hoffman, 1980). For example, Pressley and Ghatala (1989) presented a vocabulary test to children in grades 1 and 2, a test that included 30 four-choice, multiple-choice items. The youngsters were asked to predict how many they would get right. Fourteen of the 16 grade-1 and grade-2 participants predicted that they would identify either 29 or 30 of the correct answers. Even more striking is the robustness of young children's optimism. Most children in the early grade-school years continue to believe they will do well even after they experience less than great success with a task (Clifford, 1975, 1978; Parsons & Ruble, 1977; Phillips, 1963; Stipek & Hoffman, 1980). For example, even though none of the grade-1 and grade-2 participants in Pressley and Ghatala (1989) scored anywhere near 29 or 30 out of 30 on their first try, 9 of the 16 children believed if given another chance at a comparably difficult vocabulary test, they would score 29 or 30.

Such optimism is generally not seen in older children (for a review, see Stipek & MacIver, 1989). (Many studies cited in the last paragraph provided striking data on this point.) Middle-grade and upper-grade elementary students are more aware of

their academic failures than their academic successes (Kloosterman, 1988). Often students perceive they are doing much worse than their teachers believe they are doing (Juvonen, 1988). The academic self-perceptions of lower-achieving students especially suffer (e.g., Renick & Harter, 1989). Not surprisingly, students' expectations about themselves as academic achievers decline during the elementary years, and once children decide that they cannot do well in school, their beliefs tend to persist, undermining future academic achievement (e.g., Fincham, Hokoda, & Sanders, 1989).

There is an interesting little twist, however. Boys' expectations about their academic performances tend to be higher than girls' expectations. For example, in the Pressley and Ghatala (1989) study, whenever there were significant sex differences between boys and girls with respect to confidence in their academic abilities, the boys were more confident, an outcome consistent with many other reports in the literature (e.g., Crandall, 1969; Entwisle & Hayduk, 1978; Frey & Ruble, 1987; Parsons & Ruble, 1977; Pressley, Levin, Ghatala, & Ahmad, 1987; Stipek & Hoffman, 1980; Whitley, McHugh, & Frieze, 1986).

The potential importance of the lack of optimism in older children compared with younger children is appreciated when it is remembered that motivation is largely a function of the expectation of reinforcement, with reinforcement in academic settings often boiling down to task success. As would be expected given declining expectations with advancing grades in school, there are clear declines with advancing grades in interest in school and what can be learned there (e.g., Harter, 1981; Wigfield, Eccles, MacIver, Reuman, & Midgley, 1991). The gender differences in expectations about academic achievement, in particular, have been hypothesized to have enormous impact on girls' willingness to pursue some challenging academic arenas compared with boys' willingness to do so, an area of intense concern to researcher Carol Dweck and colleagues.

Dweck (e.g., 1986) and associates have been intrigued by the fact that during the early elementary years, girls exceed boys in mathematics achievement, with this pattern reversing at junior high and continuing reversed for the remainder of schooling (see also Chapter 13). They have offered an explanation in terms of sex differences in expectations that translate into sex differences in motivation to tackle mathematics. This complex tale is among one of the more compelling in the contemporary literature on academic motivation.

Dweck (1986) reported a study in which otherwise high-achieving boys and girls reacted differently to a failure experience on a concept formation task. The high-ability girls tended to be devastated by the failure much more than the high-ability boys, with this affecting subsequent performances—the high-ability boys going on to outperform the high-ability girls on subsequent trials of the same task. High-ability girls seemed to be especially disadvantaged, with initial failures and difficulties disrupting their subsequent performances more than the performances of less able girls (Licht & Dweck, 1984). In this same program of research, Dweck (1986) determined that girls are more likely than boys to prefer tasks with which they are successful. In contrast, boys prefer tasks that present some challenge for mastery. Girls are more likely than boys to attribute difficulties they have to unchanging abilities (i.e., rather than to low effort, high task difficulty, or bad luck).

How girls think about task performances and task difficulties makes likely that they will reduce their motivation to continue a task when it proves difficult. That is, when they experience frustration, girls tend to believe it is because of low ability. Given a choice, they elect tasks that are not so frustrating, ones that are already familiar to them. Boys shrug off initial failures more certainly, attributing them to something other than their own ability. Because they prefer some challenge and novelty anyway, they are more likely to forge onward.

Dweck (1986) reasoned that secondary-school mathematics is more likely than other secondary content to present difficulties to students when they encounter it. Moreover, it is likely to look different from elementary-school arithmetic, with algebra, geometry, and calculus full of new terms, symbols, and concepts. Thus, for girls who are more disrupted by frustration and more likely to avoid the unfamiliar, deciding not to pursue mathematics could be a motivating option for them in secondary school. Because, if anything, bright girls seem to be more disrupted by initial difficulties than less able girls, the girls most likely to gain from advanced mathematics instruction are also at special risk to flee from it when difficulties with it are experienced. These girls are much more likely to think of themselves as having difficulties in mathematics than are much less mathematically able boys (see Fennema, 1974), who are not daunted by initial difficulties.

Believing that one is able can be extremely motivating even when it is not true! Believing one is not able can undermine motivation to try new and challenging tasks even when objective ability is high. That boys have more confidence in themselves in general relative to girls probably has a profound impact on their willingness to take on domains such as mathematics. When girls' tendencies to underrate their mathematical abilities are combined with powerful cues from teachers and counselors that math is not a "girl thing" (Stallings, 1985) and from societal stereotypes discouraging women from pursuing mathematics (Armstrong, 1985), it perhaps is not surprising that girls are not motivated to do well in mathematics.

This example makes clear that some thinking needs to be done about how mathematics instruction might be re-engineered so as to increase the motivation of mathematically talented girls to continue plugging away at it. This analysis also makes clear that the problem must be addressed at several different levels. There is a need to change the way girls think about their own mathematical competencies, especially when they are evaluating themselves in light of recent difficulties in an academic arena. There is also a need to change the way that teachers and others communicate to girls about mathematics, perhaps by increasing the awareness of educators and parents that if there are objective differences in the mathematical abilities of boys and girls, they are very small at best (Hyde, Fennema, & Lamon, 1990). On a positive note, a great deal of progress has been made in increasing the awareness of educators about the need to encourage girls with talents in mathematics to develop their abilities. Evidence suggests that this is translating into greater expectations by both female students and their teachers concerning mathematics achievement by girls, with these changes in attitudes and expectations perhaps mediating a reduction in the mathematics achievement gap between girls and boys (Eccles, 1989). We will return to the topic of gender differences in mathematics achievement in Chapter 13.

Rewards and Their Impact on Intrinsic Motivations

The intuitively reasonable claim will be made in Chapter 7 that reinforcements (rewards) can increase the probabilities of behaviors that occurred just before the reward is administered (e.g., Skinner's perspective). Even so, rewards also have the potential for undermining performance, especially those behaviors that we might do in the absence of reward because they are intrinsically interesting to us. The researcher most frequently associated with this effect is Mark Lepper, although as Lepper and Hodell (1989) made clear in their review of how intrinsic motivation can be undermined, this effect has been observed in diverse settings and with diverse tasks.

Lepper and Hodell (1989) cited three studies in particular as classic demonstrations of this effect:

- Deci (1971) demonstrated that when college students were paid money to work on a puzzle they would have worked on in the absence of payment (i.e., because it was intrinsically interesting to them), their willingness to play with the puzzle in a subsequent session when no reward was offered was lower than the willingness of college students who had played with the puzzle previously without receiving payment for their efforts.
- Kruglanski, Friedman, and Zeevi (1971) asked high school students to perform a series of laboratory tasks. Some of the students were promised a reward for their participation in the form of the personal tour of the university, whereas others received no such promise. Those promised the reward were less happy about performing the tasks than were those doing the tasks without the anticipation of a reward.
- Lepper, Greene, and Nisbett (1973) asked preschoolers to do an art activity, one that was interesting to preschoolers when they did it as part of class activities. Some children were rewarded for completing the activity and others received no reward. When given an opportunity to do the art activity in class later, the nonrewarded children were more interested in the activity than the rewarded children.

A great deal of follow-up research was devoted to determining when and why rewards undermine performance. They do so when initial interest in the rewarded activity is high and when the reward to perform the behavior is so salient that it could be construed as a bribe (Lepper & Hodell, 1989). When subjects can justify their willingness to do something in terms of an extrinsic reward, it is harder in the long term to justify doing the same activity in the absence of reward—an outcome that Lepper et al. (1973) dubbed the **overjustification effect.**

Rewards can be effective even when intrinsic motivation is high, however, if the situation is arranged so the rewards come after the fact of performance—that is, as a bonus (Lepper, 1983; Lepper & Hodell, 1989).

Given this pattern of outcomes, why would anyone ever use rewards to motivate performance? One reason is that people often are not intrinsically motivated to perform tasks that are good for them! When initial interest in a task is low, rewards can increase the likelihood of academic engagement and performance of important academic tasks (Bandura & Schunk, 1981; Lepper & Hodell, 1989; Loveland & Olley, 1979; McLoyd, 1979), something that has been understood for many years by behavior modification theorists concerned with education (e.g., see Pitts, 1971). A second reason is that when all of the evidence is considered, rather than just the often-cited evidence that favors the overjustification effect, it is clear that the overjustification effect is not always obtained. Tang and Hall (1993) meta-analyzed (see Chapter 1) all of the available comparisons and concluded that the overjustification effect is not consistently observed. What remains, of course, is to determine when the overjustification effect occurs and when it does not.

In closing this section, we cannot resist pointing out that variations of the overjustification effect are regular fare in sports sections. Anyone who is now a professional athlete spent years doing their sport without receiving payment for it (i.e., they played because doing so was intrinsically motivating). Yet, once successful in the majors, some players actually stop playing when they do not get umpteen dollars over the next 5 years rather than just millions of dollars. Imagine that someone would stop doing something they love to do because they were only getting $5000 a game rather than $10,000 a game. Once a baseball player starts playing ball for the money—and has a history of steadily increasing rewards for playing baseball—even what would be a staggering reward for most people can seem insufficient for the player to continue doing something he loves.

Ego Involvement in Classrooms

Nicholls (e.g., 1989) has noted that most classroom reward (goal) structures foster ego involvement, with success in the classroom (especially relative to peers) implying high capacity (i.e., that one is smart) and failure implying low capacity. Such a system has high potential for undermining effort when success is not certain (e.g., with new task demands), because trying and failing leads to feelings of low ability. Attributing a failure to low ability does nothing to motivate additional effort: What good is it to try, since the student believes he or she lacks the ability to do the task.

Nicholls (1989, pp. 153–154) points to a variety of classroom practices that stimulate ego involvement and the conclusion for many students that they are not as able as their peers:

- Grading on the curve. (Only a few students can be on the top of any curve. Most students must experience failure relative to others in such a grading system.)
- Emphasis on student percentile ranks on standardized achievement tests. (Only in Lake Woebegon can everyone be above average, let alone be above the 90th percentile.)
- Making grades salient and public. (Oh, how many classes do we remember in elementary and secondary school where students "called in" their test grade when the teacher reached their name on the role!)
- Comments on the achievement of students, comments that tie achievement to worth, something originally reported by Weinstein (1976). (Author MP remember vividly the first day in grade 7 when the principal introduced the 7-1 section as the students, "We really expect great things from." Section 7-6 was introduced as the students, "We know are going to have a lot of difficulty with grade-7 work.")

Nicholls goes on to make the case that the tendency of the school to rank order students and make evaluative judgments that can affect a person's conception of his or her ability is complementary to other societal forces that do the same:

- Parents forcing their sons and daughters to make unfavorable ability evaluations relative to other children. (How many parents respond to their children's report card by asking how "So-and-so" did, followed by remarks about how it would be nice if their son or daughter were like "So-and-so"?)
- Local papers carrying news about the academic achievements in the school. (That we felt great reading in the local paper about our presence on the honor role probably came at a cost in terms

of academic self-esteem for those students never listed in the local paper.)

What is the result of this obsession with identifying publicly who is smart? Nicholls argues that such a practice probably undermines academic motivation for many children in the system. Students will often go to great lengths to avoid having to try something academic, rather than risk failure, public humiliation, and additional confirmation of low ability relative to other chidren.

There is plenty of evidence to support Nicholls' beliefs, with substantial research on classroom structures that foster ego involvement (sometimes called by other names, such as competitive classrooms; e.g., Ames, 1984). In such classrooms, how a student does compared with others is an important determinant of whether he or she feels successful (e.g., Ames & Ames, 1981). Indeed, doing better than other students in the class is far more important in determining whether one feels successful in competitive classrooms than is doing well in an absolute sense—that is, actually performing the educational task competently (Ames & Felker, 1979; Barnett & Andrews, 1977; Johnson & Johnson, 1974; Levine, 1983): Because most students will not end up doing "best" in the class, feelings of failure, self-criticism, and negative self-esteem often occur (Ames, 1984).

One likely reason that there is a clear decline in perceptions of academic self-efficacy from kindergarten to the middle grades is that comparative evaluations are less frequent and salient in the early primary years compared with the later primary and middle grade years (Harter, Whitesell, & Kowalski, 1992; Stipek & Daniels, 1988). With increasing age, children are more aware of the competitiveness in their classrooms (see Harter et al., 1992; also Schmidt, Ollendick, & Stanowicz, 1988) and of the implications of not succeeding. What is certain based on both the classroom research already cited and basic research (e.g., Wigfield, 1988) is that by the middle-elementary years and continuing into the high school years, paying attention to how one does compared with others affects perceptions of one's own competency, with these perceptions having the potential to affect school performance. Thus, a student may have more positive perceptions about his or her own academic ability and better school performance (measured in some absolute way) if enrolled in a low-ability class rather than a high-ability class because what one thinks about one's own ability is determined with reference to class standing;

such social comparisons with others can motivate additional effort (i.e., when one is at the top of a low-ability class) or undermine effort (i.e., when one is near the bottom of a high-ability class; e.g., Marsh, 1987).

More positively, there is another approach to schooling than the competitive classroom that is typical in the United States, one completely consistent with the reason society sends children to school: to improve themselves. Rather than rewarding students for being better than one another, it is possible to reward students for doing better than they did previously, to reward personal improvement on academic tasks. Nicholls refers to such classrooms as fostering task involvement, an apropos name in light of research findings by Nicholls and Thorkildsen (e.g., 1987): When these investigators rated and studied 30 grade-5 classrooms ranging in ego and task involvement, what they found was that work avoidance was much more commonly reported in ego-involved classrooms than in task-involved classrooms. That is, students in ego-involved classrooms were much more likely than students in task-involved classrooms to endorse claims such as the following: "I don't have to do any homework, I don't have to work hard, all the work is easy, I don't have any tough tests, and the teacher doesn't ask hard questions." The students in the task-oriented classrooms believed that success in school depended on interest, effort, and attempting to learn, whereas the students in the ego-involved classrooms believed that success depended on being smarter than other kids and trying to beat out other students.

When we read Nicholls and Thorkildsen's (1987) work, we get angry. We want students to be interested in school and to believe they can succeed if they try hard, and Nicholls and Thorkildsen (1987) found that students in the task-oriented classrooms were much more satisfied with school and learning in school than students in ego-oriented classrooms (see also Duda & Nicholls, 1992, for additional evidence that focusing on academic improvement is more satisfying than competing with other students). Nicholls (1989) summarized much additional evidence that task-oriented classrooms are much more likely to keep students interested in and committed to school than are ego-oriented classrooms. The problem is that many more classrooms are ego-involved than task-involved; many more classrooms are committed to motivational orientations that defeat student interest and effort rather than promote it; in far too many classrooms, the goal is to get better grades than the ones earned by peers rather than to learn (e.g., Ames, 1992; Blumenfeld, 1992).

A study by one of Nicholls' former students illuminates the relevance of work on classroom motivational orientation for the good information processing model. Nolen (1988) assessed whether grade-8 students were task-oriented or ego-oriented. In addition, Nolan asked the students to indicate whether they would use particular strategies for reading and understanding textbook material, with their reported strategy use then compared with actual strategy use when the same students were observed while they studied some passages. What is important here is that although both task-oriented and ego-oriented students endorsed and used surface-level strategies for processing text (e.g., read the whole thing over and over), the task-oriented students were much more likely than the ego-oriented students to endorse and use strategies that involved deeper processing of text (e.g., try to see how this fits with what I've learned in class). What Nolen's (1988) study suggested is that task orientation and use of sophisticated strategies may be linked. A result like this makes it clear that good strategy instruction should include explicit efforts to encourage task orientation in students—to encourage students to recognize that the goal of education is to improve and that such improvement is possible in part through acquisition of powerful strategies.

We close this section on classroom motivational orientation by noting that there is one exceptionally nasty side to competitive classrooms in the United States. How one does in such a classroom with respect to grades is determined by more than what one learns and can do. Farkas, Sheehan, and Grobe (1990) analyzed the grades given in grades 7 and 8 of one urban school district, taking into account whether the students knew the material as reflected on course mastery tests and their rate of absenteeism. With mastery and absenteeism controlled, some students still earned better grades than others: Girls received higher grades than boys, Asians receives higher grades than whites, and nonpoverty children received higher grades than children in poverty. Farkas et al. (1990) speculated that either the behaviors of girls, Asians, and nonpoverty children suggest they are working harder or their behaviors are somehow more pleasing to teachers. Regardless, if grades are important as long-term motivators, and they are in competitive classrooms, girls, Asians, and nonpoverty children have an advantage over other students. Such biases in grading that have nothing to do with real academic competence do little to inspire confidence in traditional competitive classroom motivational systems.

Summary

There are three important messages in this section. The first is that conventional wisdom about motivation often is wrong. Consider these examples:

- Explanations of male superiority in mathematics in terms of differences in innate abilities are problematic when it is considered that girls often exceed boys at mathematics in the elementary years. Sophisticated researchers interested in mathematics achievement have made a plausible case that much of the problem is that girls are much more likely to attend to initial difficulties and to react to initial difficulties by avoiding the task situation than are boys. Additional environmental determinants of sex differences in mathematics and science achievement will be presented in the next section.
- The belief that reinforcements strengthen the behaviors that precede them was sacrosanct to many Skinnerian-inspired behaviorists. This principle of reinforcement seems to fall apart, at least on some occasions, when intrinsically reinforcing behaviors are considered. Start paying a person to do something they like to do, and there is a risk that they will stop doing it if you stop paying them. When people receive reinforcements for doing something, they might come to believe they are performing the action to obtain the tangible reward. Once the tangible reward disappears, so does the motivation for performing the action.
- Many American educators believe strongly in classroom competition as a way to motivate academic behaviors. That there is little reason for many students even to think about attaining rewards in such classrooms—because the best students are already so far ahead of them—has gone unnoticed. That the vast majority of students will feel deprived and unappreciated in such a system has not been apparent to generations of educators. When examined in light of contemporary theories of motivation and new understandings about how classrooms and learning might be restructured, the old system

seems much less defensible. Additional indictments of competitive classroom environments will be offered as the chapter proceeds.

Sometimes conventional wisdom has been wrong about motivation and achievement.

The second message of this section is that there is a lot wrong with student motivation in traditional classrooms. High expectations are transformed into low expectations as schooling continues. Many students view school as a place where inherent ability is more of a determinant of success than effort. Many students feel as if they are failing. Feelings of success are obtained by outperforming others, even if that does not require excellent performance in any absolute sense. Mathematically competent girls who could do well in advanced math get discouraged and stop taking it. In short, society is spending billions of dollars on an educational enterprise that more certainly undermines academic motivation than promotes it. Far too many students are not academically motivated (Doyle, 1983; Harter, 1981; Lepper, 1983). How schools can both undermine and promote achievement will be themes that recur throughout this chapter.

The third message is much more positive. Researchers and theorists are more interested in student motivation now than at any previous point in history. There is increasing recognition that low student motivation often is the result of structural failures of schools rather than some inherent deficiency in students. We do not know how many times we have heard teachers over the years claim that a student's problem is that he or she is not motivated. In many cases, what they should have been claiming is that the schooling environment they had created was not motivating! We expect a great deal of research in the coming decade about how classroom goal structures affect motivation to learn (see especially, Blumenfeld, 1992) and about how school can be re-engineered to increase the interest, involvement, and achievement of most students, rather than just the top students.

WHAT CAN BE DONE TO MAKE SCHOOL MORE MOTIVATING AND TO CREATE MORE MOTIVATED STUDENTS?

This section comprises some theory, some data, and many hypotheses. To date, researchers have been better at figuring out the motivational properties of existing schools (e.g., Nicholls, 1989, analyses) than they have been at testing hypotheses that emerge from this work, hypotheses about how to increase interest in and engagement during schooling. We present some of the best hypotheses we have encountered related to increasing motivational properties of schools for three reasons: (1) It permits presentation of many ideas that motivational scholars have about specific mechanisms that influence student motivation. (2) This section provides a smorgasbord of ideas for readers who are future educational researchers. (3) We hope that those readers who are about to become teachers reflect carefully on the vast array of ways they could affect student motivation for the better. Even though many of these ideas are not fully tested at the time of this writing, there is theoretical support for much of what is presented in this section. If the next generation of teachers were to design their classroom environments consistent with these suggestions, it is likely that future generations of students would be much more motivated than the current generation. The need to improve student motivation is great, enough so that waiting for all of the evidence to be in before proceeding cannot be defended.

We start this section with a discussion of one of the best validated approaches to increasing classroom motivation and learning. This work on cooperative learning should make clear that strong research on motivational interventions is possible, research that is readily translatable into real school interventions.

Cooperative Learning Rather Than Competitive Learning

Cooperative learning interventions are now common in U.S. schools. All sophisticated students of educational psychology must understand the rationale and implementation of cooperative learning approaches to instruction.

Johnson and Johnson David W. and Roger T. Johnson have been studying various ways of structuring classroom interactions since the 1970s (e.g., Johnson & Johnson, 1975, 1979). They argue that whether social interactions in classrooms are positive, negative, or neutral will have dramatic effects on long-term motivational achievement. Three types of social structures are considered in detail by the Johnsons (e.g., 1985):

> A *cooperative* social situation exists when the goals of the separate individuals are so linked together that

there is a positive correlation among their goal attainments. An individual can obtain his or her goal only if the other participants can achieve their goals. Thus, a person seeks an outcome that is beneficial to all those with whom he or she is cooperatively linked. A *competitive* social situation exists when the goals of the separate individuals are so linked that there is a negative correlation among their goal attainments. An individual can obtain his or her goal only if the other participants cannot obtain their goals. Thus, the person seeks an outcome that is personally beneficial but is detrimental to the others with whom he or she is competitively linked. Finally, an *individualistic* social situation exists when there is no correlation among the goal attainments of the participants. Whether an individual accomplished his or her goal has no influence on whether other individuals achieve their goals. Thus, a person seeks an outcome that is personally beneficial, ignoring as irrelevant the goal achievement efforts of other participants in the situation. (Johnson & Johnson, 1985, p. 251)

Johnson and Johnson's analysis, consistent with all of the others presented in this book, is that school is much too competitive and individualistic in orientation and too little cooperative, with the Johnsons estimating that cooperative learning occurs only 7 to 20% of the time in American education (Johnson & Johnson, 1985). How should learning occur according to the Johnson's? Four characteristics are essential (Johnson & Johnson, 1985, pp. 252–253):

- Learning should be *interdependent*. Tasks should be large enough that more than one student is needed to get it all done. Rewards need to be structured so everyone has incentive to pitch in and help.
- There should be *face-to-face interactions among students within small learning groups*. The likelihood that all students will participate is greater with small groups than with large groups.
- *Individual accountability* is essential. Students can assist one another effectively only if there is sufficient awareness among students about who knows what and who needs help.
- Students need to be taught *interpersonal and small group skills*. Students who do not interact well in groups naturally can be provided the social skills that permit more productive interactions.

Great things happen when children learn in such small groups according to the Johnsons, with their conclusions supported by data from many different types of studies conducted at many different sites.

Getting kids together in small groups to work on academic tasks has the following striking advantages:

- It increases **intrinsic motivation.** Learning is more fun. Learning seems more personally meaningful.
- There are **high expectations** for success among cooperative learning participants.
- The mutual benefits of cooperation increase **incentives** to learn.
- There is high **epistemic motivation,** that is, high interest in the topic being studied, interest that extends beyond the small group. This is largely due to the motivational advantages provided by **cognitive conflict** in cooperative groups. (See the discussion of cognitive conflict later in this subsection.) This can increase willingness to read more on a topic or watch films and television programs related to academic content being covered in the small groups. Johnson and Johnson (1985) presented an analysis suggesting that cooperative learning might promote the long-term commitment to learning required to keep students in school, largely by improving students' attitudes about school.
- There is high task persistence.

It almost goes without saying that the Johnsons conclude that competitive and individualistic orientations do not have these advantages. They particularly point out, consistent with Nicholls's, Ames's, and Dweck's analyses presented earlier in this chapter that although the most able students may be motivated in competitive and individualistically oriented classrooms, these classrooms are likely to reduce the academic motivation of most students compared with what is possible in cooperative environments.

The research and integrative writing of the Johnsons have made a tremendous impact on education, with their approach to educational scholarship admiringly broad—from books aimed at practitioners to basic research studies to the most elegant of integrative reviews. For young students who want instruction in how to have an impact on educational practice, theory, and research, study of the work of Johnson and Johnson (e.g., 1985) is certainly worthwhile.

One of their papers is notable to author MP personally because it convinced him that there really was something to cooperative learning. Johnson, Maruyama, Johnson, Nelson, & Skon (1981) re-

viewed 122 studies that evaluated the effectiveness of cooperative learning, competitive learning, and individualistic learning. Cooperative environments produced better learning than the alternatives, with the overall effect sizes consistently in the "moderate" range—a 0.3 to 0.8 standard deviation advantage for cooperative groups. Since that 1981 paper, we have seen plenty of evidence that confirms the conclusions of their 1981 analyses, including ones offered by Slavin, the other "most prominent" contributor to the cooperative learning literature, whose perspective is considered next.

Before moving on, we offer one interesting biographical note about the Johnsons. Their commitment to cooperative learning is probably fueled by their first-hand experiences with cooperative learning. They attended the Burris Laboratory School at Ball State University, which was (and is) a cooperative learning environment.

Slavin   Robert Slavin and his colleagues at The Johns Hopkins University generally offer recommendations consistent with those made by the Johnsons, although they emphasize one aspect of cooperative learning more than others. Cooperative learning is most likely to be effective if there are both group rewards and individual accountability (e.g., Slavin, 1985a, 1985b). This works as follows: A cooperative group's score is calculated by summing over the scores of the individuals in the group on some individual assessment (i.e., perhaps at the end of a week or unit), with the group having the high score receiving a reward. This effectively eliminates the freeloader problem, for students who are capable cannot sit by and allow teammates to learn nothing; if they did, the team score would suffer, because one or more of the individual assessment scores would be low (i.e., those of the freeloaders).

An example of one of Slavin's programs, team assisted instruction (TAI; e.g., Slavin, 1985b) for mathematics, illustrates the Hopkins' approach to cooperative learning. A class is divided into four- to five-member teams, with each including both males and females, a racial mix, and a distribution of abilities. Students remain in their teams for 8 weeks or so at a time, changing teams at the end of this period.

Instructional sessions are divided into periods of individualized study and team study. During the individualized portion, each student works on self-instructional materials. Each such assignment includes an instruction sheet, detailing the skill to be mastered, including step-by-step instructions about how to do assigned problems. There are 20 problem work sheets followed by two practice tests and a final test.

During the team study period, students work with group mates in pairs or in triads. The students do the work sheets, assisting one another with the instructions or with specific problems. Students work on problems and then check group mates' answers against the answer key. If a student gets all four problems correct, he or she can go on to the next skill sheet. Otherwise, the student works another block of four problems from the same skill sheet, which is followed by checking. After working through all skill sheets, a student takes the first practice test, which is then checked by a group mate. If a student works 8 of the 10 practice test examples correctly, the student is certified by the team to proceed to the final examination. If the practice test score is less than 8, the adult teacher is called in to provide guidance, which usually means assigning the student to work on the skill sheets some more, leading up to a second practice test. Students monitor carefully whether group mates make the required score of 8 on the practice test before they are permitted to proceed to the final test.

At the end of each week, a group score is calculated based on the total number of units completed per group member, with additional points given for exceptionally high performances on final tests. The teams that do exceptionally well receive certificates denoting their accomplishments. The teacher does not disappear completely in this process but rather provides tutorials to small groups of students daily, ones who are at about the same point in the various units, bringing students together to form tutoring groups of three to four students.

Slavin is a great respecter of data, and his endorsement of the TAI approach is based on a number of studies conducted by him and his associates with children in grades 3 through 6. In general, math achievement has proven superior in classrooms experiencing TAI compared with conventionally instructed classrooms. In addition, there is substantial evidence across the studies that students' attitudes toward mathematics improve following participation in TAI. See Slavin (1985b) for a review.

In recent years, Slavin has been especially interested in reading achievement, designing and studying the cooperative integrated reading and composition program (CIRC; Stevens, Madden, Slavin, & Farnish, 1987). The group arrangements are similar to TAI. Basal stories are read; reading and composition strategies are taught by the teacher to the class as a whole. Students read trade books at home.

Activities in small groups follow reading of a basal selection. These exercises include reading, analysis of narrative structures of stories, writing, word mastery and learning of definitions, story retelling, and spelling. All of this work is done with partners, who also monitor each other's progress, as occurs in TAI, in preparation for formal tests over stories and story-related activities.

In evaluations with grade-3 and grade-4 students to date, CIRC has fared well, improving standardized comprehension relative to control classes reading similar basal stories. Writing and oral reading effects have been positive as well.

Commentary Johnson and Johnson are exemplary integrative scholars, complementing their research with fine overviews of the entire cooperative learning literature. Slavin is one of the most prolific educational psychologists in the United States. He has generated impressive programmatic research documenting the effectiveness of cooperative learning in improving what were already high-quality elementary arithmetic and reading programs. There is much to admire in both the research and the conceptions of both the Johnsons and Slavin, although there has been a disturbing tendency by cooperative learning researchers to ask only whether cooperative learning works, rather than to focus on more analytical questions (e.g., are some components more essential than others? Perhaps only the entire mix of components promotes performance, rather than a subset of them?)

Fantuzzo and associates are conducting exceptionally analytical research on cooperative learning, with their initial efforts yielding extremely interesting outcomes, especially given the challenging environments in which they have conducted their studies. Fantuzzo and his colleagues (Fantuzzo, King, & Heller, 1992) went to one of Philadelphia's most economically disadvantaged schools. Their concern was the mathematics achievement of grade-4 and grade-5 students, individuals at great risk for school failure based on demographic predictors (e.g., socioeconomic status). The experiment included four conditions and permitted evaluation of the contributions of two cooperative learning components on achievement: the effects of group reward and paired learning. In the condition with both paired learning and group reward, two or more students worked together on math problems, alternating between teacher and student roles in a structured format: Students monitored each other's problem solving and prompted each other when one of the group experienced difficulties. They taught and encouraged one another. The rewards earned by the group were determined by combining the performances of all students so there was incentive for pair mates (or for all group members, depending on the size of the particular group) to make certain that one's partner learned the material. In two other conditions of the study, students were taught to use the cooperative structure only, *or* they were administered group rewards so the effects of the individual components could be evaluated. In the control condition, students were teamed up to learn mathematics but were not required to use the student-teacher cooperative structure, nor were they provided group rewards.

The most critical variable in the study was a mathematics computation test that measured achievement in grade-4 and grade-5 mathematics, although the test covered the entire range of mathematics from grade-2 level to advanced grade-5 level. The test was a timed test, with the goal to complete as many of 48 problems in 20 minutes as possible. The results confirmed the importance of combining the cooperative learning components, with the performance of students in the cooperative pairing structure plus group reward condition clearly superior to performance in the other three conditions of the study. Neither providing the paired cooperative structure alone nor providing the group rewards alone produced performance better than in the control condition.

The Fantuzzo et al. (1992) outcome supports cooperative learning: Gains did not follow from rewards alone or simply working together but from working together in the context of cooperative structures and incentives that promote the learning of all students in a group. Cooperative learning works because of the mix of components, rather than because of any one of the components constituting the intervention. In instructional research, there is a dialectical tension between designing and evaluating packages of components and evaluating the impact of individual components. The most informative way to resolve that tension is to conduct research permitting insights about both the packages as wholes and the individual components in the packages. That is what Fantuzzo et al. (1992) did.

In closing this section on cooperative learning, we emphasize how flexible the approach is. Cooperative learning can be combined with other prosocial interventions (e.g., activities promoting social understanding, instruction highlighting social values through literature and content-area learning), and when it is for the long term, the effect can be a friendlier, more supportive, and kinder classroom world than is typical in American classrooms (Solomon, Watson, Delucchi, Schaps, & Battistich, 1988). Cooperative learning can be used with a variety of curricular content, as exemplified by the reading and math examples presented in this subsection. Additional examples of cooperative learning will occur in the chapters that follow—be on the lookout for them. We warn you, however, that sometimes the interventions will be more subtle than the examples discussed here. Thus, in Chapter 14, we will discuss reading groups that involve a lot of cooperation. In that case, the "group reward" is a more interesting story for all, produced by all students participating in the development of story interpretations. Great teachers often exploit natural rewards of group participation and cooperation.

One paradox of cooperative learning is that if it is done well, the participating students will be involved in a great deal of conflict with one another. They will mix it up intellectually, one student pushing for one perspective on the problem of the moment and someone else pushing for another perspective. Such cognitive conflict is healthy and stimulates students, with the theory and data supporting this assertion presented next.

Stimulating Cognitive Conflict

We think about issues more deeply when challenged by others; we sometimes think about things in new ways and sometimes change our minds when interacting with folks who see the world differently than we do. We suspect that most readers have had spirited discussions with friends over controversial issues, resulting in the airing of many viewpoints and much rethinking of perspectives.

When there is conflict between one's current knowledge or beliefs and new knowledge, the discrepancy motivates efforts to understand the new perspective, with it likely that knowledge will change as the new perspective is understood. Piagetians (see Chapter 7) view such conflict as critically important to cognitive growth—much more important than other mechanisms. Cognitive conflict can be a powerful motivator for engaging in intellectual activity.

Kohlberg (e.g., 1969; see Chapter 9, this book) and his student Blatt (e.g., Blatt & Kohlberg, 1975; see Chapter 9, this book) were particularly instrumental in translating Piaget's ideas about cognitive conflict into educational methods. One of Kohlberg's greatest interests was in developing sophisticated moral reasoning in students. The principal pedagogical approach was to present groups of students with moral dilemmas—problems with alternative perspectives, problems that elicit spirited discussion and conflict. Cognitive growth was hypothesized to occur because ideas that come up that are different from one's own result in reflection on one's assumptions, the viewpoints of others, and the differences between one's own views and other perspectives.

There were many evaluations of the cognitive conflict hypothesis with respect to increases in the sophistication of moral judgment (see Enright, Lapsley, & Levy, 1983, for a definitive review). The evidence was orderly and generally positive:

> Despite the variety of techniques . . . teacher variations . . . and treatment lengths [reviewed by us], one pattern is clear: [Cognitive conflict] . . . works. Only 4 of the 28 studies . . . [reviewed] show no effect. . . . It also appears, however, that this strategy is ineffective in the elementary-school years and only begins to be consistently effective in junior high. All three studies accepting the null hypothesis were done with elementary school children. (Enright et al., 1983, p. 59)

Although the evidence of effectiveness was not obtained with elementary students, we observed moral dilemma discussions in many elementary classrooms in the late 1970s and early 1980s (e.g., Galbraith & Jones, 1976). Students responded to tales about principals censuring school papers when students printed a controversial story, whether it is just to send escaped prisoners back to prison even if they have lived honorably on the outside for a long period of time, and whether a husband should steal a curative drug he cannot afford to purchase if his wife's life depends on it. What we remember best is how "into it" the students were as they tackled these dilemmas. Students loved these discussions. We recall several teachers who used moral dilemma discussions as a reward: If work was completed efficiently, students were presented a moral dilemma for discussion. Students were definitely motivated

to participate in this type of instruction—even elementary students. Sometimes when we think about the failures to observe benefits from cognitive conflict at the elementary levels, we wonder how completely the cognitive conflict intervention was implemented in these studies. Our view is that the impact of moral discussions and the cognitive conflict in such discussion deserve additional study at the elementary level.

The use of cognitive conflict to motivate academic engagement is not restricted to moral issues. Indeed, stimulating cognitive conflict is at the heart of some of the most important of science education interventions. Although these approaches will be taken up in much more detail in Chapter 12, the method is based on students' inaccurate scientific beliefs. For example, the following are common misconceptions about blood and circulation (e.g., Arnaudin & Mintzes, 1985; Barrass, 1984): All organisms have blood. Blood is made up only of red cells. Under the microscope, blood looks like a bunch of red cells clustered closely together. The heart cleans, filters, makes, and stores blood. There are air tubes from the lungs to the heart. Blood is not responsible for transporting nutrients throughout the body. The heart is one pump, pumping blood from itself to the body. The heart pumps only oxygenated blood.

According to Nussbaum and Novick (e.g., 1982) and other science educators, inaccurate beliefs should be brought out early during instruction. As more accurate conceptions are presented, the conceptual conflicts between the inaccurate prior knowledge and the new information should be stimulated—through demonstrations, but also through discussions. This is complemented by additional input to elaborate the new scientific understandings and beliefs. Debate about the adequacy of old views in light of new understandings is critical to the development of deep understanding of the new information according to Nussbaum and Novick.

Such debate is also possible in mathematics. Contemporary mathematics educators also foster comparisons of errant prior knowledge with more adequate mathematical understandings (see Chapter 13). In particular, many contemporary mathematics educators believe that students should discuss and debate problems, generating alternative solutions (e.g., see Charles & Silver, 1989). Anyone who has watched these discussions knows that there is real energy as students debate the merits of various ways of doing problems like 13 + 19 most efficiently (e.g., reconstrue as $10 + 3 + 10 + 9$ or as $10 + 3 + 20 - 1$ or as $20 - 7 + 20 - 1$).

Although Piagetian thinking did much to inspire the cognitive conflict approach to learning, the idea that people are motivated to become more competent is an old one (see White, 1959). Being exposed to information that is discrepant with current knowledge or beliefs makes clear that one's knowledge may be off a bit, which motivates efforts to understand the new and somewhat different positions now in the air. Cognitive conflict is bound to receive more attention in the coming years because discussion between students and between students and teachers that involve alternative interpretations is emerging as a favored approach to teaching and learning from a number of perspectives in science and mathematics education. Discussion of student dialogues is common in this book.

Encourage Moderate Risk Taking

Many students are afraid to try for fear of failing. This is counterproductive, for learning inevitably involves some mistakes. Moreover, there is growing evidence that risk taking is motivating, with greater academic effort expended by risk takers than by non–risk takers and greater achievement by risk takers compared with non–risk takers (Clifford, 1991). Perhaps it is not surprising that many of the curriculum interventions covered in Chapters 12 through 15 include encouraging students to take academic risks.

Praising Students

Brophy (1981) summarized the available literature on praise and offered a set of prescriptions about how praise should be delivered in classrooms to have maximally positive effects. Some of the most critical attributes of effective praise are the following:

- Effective praise is delivered contingent on desirable student behaviors (i.e., following desirable behaviors; see Chapter 7).
- In delivering the praise, the teacher makes clear what the student did that was praiseworthy, focusing attention on the student behaviors leading to the praise. Students are told they are competent and why what they have done is valuable.
- Effective praise is sincere, reflecting that the teacher is attentive to the student's accomplishments.

- There is an implication that the student can be similarly successful in the future if he or she exerts appropriate effort.
- There is a message that the student expended the effort that led to praise because he or she enjoyed the task or wanted to develop the competencies that have been praised.

What a simple message, consistent with reinforcement theory (e.g., Bandura, 1986; Skinner, 1953; see Chapter 7, this book): Provide lots of positive reinforcement, with Brophy considering positive reinforcement as richly informative about what behaviors can lead to reinforcement and hence extremely motivating. (Contingent praise in particular should increase students' perceptions that they are capable of performing an academic task—that is, increase their self-efficacy [e.g., Bandura, 1977a, 1986] regarding the task—see the discussion of self-efficacy later in this section.) What a simple message consistent with metacognitive theory (e.g., Borkowski, Carr, Rellinger, & Pressley, 1990): Provide lots of information about what it is that the student is doing right and why the student should engage in the desirable behaviors in the future. What a simple message designed to circumvent Lepper et al.'s (1973) overjustification effect: Efforts are made to convince students they are carrying out the desirable behaviors because they want to do them, not simply to receive praise.

Effective praise as described by Brophy (1981) is difficult to give, however, and thus rarely occurs in classrooms. Rather, there is a lot of noncontingent praise in most classrooms, praise that does not make clear what the student did well, and praise for behaviors that really are not praiseworthy (e.g., praise for participation alone, rather than participation consistent with the processes being taught—"I'm so glad you are taking part"). When we review Brophy's (1981) discussion of praise, we always find ourselves wishing that some student would come along and run the study that needs to be done, comparing teachers who have learned how to praise effectively with those who have not. This is potentially a great program of research that would be informative about a cheap but too rarely exploited approach to classroom motivation.

Making Academic Tasks More Interesting

People pay more attention to content that is interesting (e.g., Hidi, 1990; Renninger, 1990; Renninger &

Wozniak, 1985; Shiefele, 1991), prompting many materials developers to create academic materials that "grab" students. Of course, there is good reason to do this because many students in school, especially ones at risk for school dropout, find what they are asked to learn to be boring (e.g., Farrell, Peguero, Lindsey, & White, 1988).

There is a terrible paradox in attempting to increase the interestingness of school learning, however. Sometimes motivational embellishments result in attention to and processing of something other than what the materials were intended to teach. Prominent theoretical positions on the role of interest in text learning and during learning from computers are reviewed here, because these are the areas of instruction that have been considered most completely by interest theorists.

Learning from Text Richard Anderson and colleagues at the University of Illinois Center for the Study of Reading (e.g., Anderson, Mason, & Shirey, 1984) largely reawakened interest in the study of interest as a mediator of learning from text. In the studies conducted at Illinois, children read sentences that had been rated either as interesting or uninteresting. Interesting sentences were much more certain to be remembered later than were uninteresting sentences, with the interestingness manipulation producing a large effect relative to the size of effects produced by other manipulations (e.g., readability of sentences).

Anderson's group (e.g., Anderson, Shirey, Wilson, and Fielding, 1987) also conducted some extremely analytical studies to determine the mechanisms underlying the interest effect, hypothesizing that more interesting materials were more likely to be attended. In fact, that seemed to be the case, with students spending more time reading interesting compared with less interesting texts; in addition, interesting texts were so absorbing that readers failed to respond to an external signal (e.g., pressing a button in response to a sound heard while one is reading) as quickly as they did when reading uninteresting texts. Even so, greater attention alone did not account for the greater learning of the interesting materials because when differences in attention and effort are factored out of learning data (i.e., amount of time spent reading sentences was controlled statistically), there are still large differences owing to interest (e.g., Shirey & Reynolds, 1988). Thus, interest can affect directly both attention and learning,

with only some of the increases in learning owing to interest because of the effects of interest on attention to academic content.

Anderson et al. (1987, pp. 293–295) offered some hypotheses about how to make texts more interesting:

- Include in them characters with whom readers can readily identify, such as characters similar in sex, age, race, religion, and occupation to readers, an hypothesis supported by subsequent research (e.g., Bleakley, Westerberg, & Hopkins, 1988).
- Ordinary occurrences bore; thus, place novel and extraordinary relations in text to the extent that it is possible to do so.
- Base the texts on life themes important to the readers.
- Construct texts that depict intense action and feeling rather than passive states.

Anderson et al. (1987) acknowledged that the textbooks presented to children in school, especially social studies and science texts, are often dull. They also reviewed the ideas of others about how to make stories more interesting. These included Brewer and Liechtenstein's (1982) claim that good stories arouse emotions, Jose and Brewer's (1984) concern with suspense, and Bruce's (1983) analyses suggesting that complex stories with multiple interpretations are to be preferred over simpler, more literal stories.

Anderson et al. (1987) indicted the practice of adding interesting anecdotes to text as a motivational device, however. Texts filled with anecdotes often lack coherence. In addition, often the anecdotes are remembered, but the point of the text is either missed or forgotten—personally stimulating information is recalled, but memory of the abstract and general points is unaffected (e.g., Hidi & Baird, 1988). Garner's work particularly is telling on this point.

Garner and colleagues (e.g., 1992; Garner, Gillingham, & White, 1989; Garner, Alexander, Gillingham, Kulikowich, & Brown, 1991) documented that readers often pay so much attention to interesting details and anecdotes in text—referred to as **seductive details** by Garner—they neglect the main ideas (see also Wade, Schraw, Buxton, & Hayes, 1993). For example, adults in Garner et al. (1989) read texts such as the following:

Some insects live alone, and some live in large families. Wasps that live alone are called solitary wasps. A

Mud Dauber Wasp is a solitary wasp. Click beetles live alone. *When a click beetle is on its back, it flips itself into the air and lands right up while it makes a clicking noise.* Ants live in large families. There are many kinds of ants. Some ants live in trees. Black ants live in the ground. (p. 46; seductive detail highlighted here, but not in original text)

The most critical finding in the study was that recall of the main ideas was approximately half as likely when the text contained a seductive detail than when readers processed texts with the tantalizing details deleted. The effect has proven robust over texts and positioning of seductive details in text (Garner et al., 1991; for a complementary outcome, see Wade & Adams, 1990).

Since Dewey (1913), educational theorists have argued for increasing the interestingness of to-be-learned materials. Work like that of Garner makes clear that extensive thinking and research are required before Dewey's (1913) seemingly simple-minded recommendation can be carried out. Much work remains to be done to determine the most effective ways of simultaneously increasing the interestingness of expository text and its learnability.

Learning from Educational Software Many classrooms now contain microcomputers, and there are growing lists of educational software. Some programs are dressed-up drill-and-practice routines, which involve little more than presentation of electronic flashcards, whereas others incorporate all the bells and whistles of the most elaborate arcade games.

Lepper and his colleagues at Stanford (e.g., Lepper & Malone, 1987; Malone & Lepper, 1987) have taken the lead in analyzing the motivational properties of computer software. In general, they have had little difficulty demonstrating the motivational appeal of gamelike versions of computer programs compared with drill-and-practice programs that cover the same content (see also Rieber, 1991): Children are willing to spend much more time with the games than the drills. Unfortunately, it is difficult to make the case that the gamelike programs produce greater academic achievement.

Lepper and Malone offered analyses of the motivational characteristics of these programs that would make them intrinsically appealing and motivating to students: They are appropriately *challenging*—not too easy but not so difficult that they cannot be played competently with some effort. They

also *provoke curiosity*—how will the lights and sounds change *this?* They *provide a sense of control* to players, feelings that their actions determine what happens in the miniature world of the computer program, which is critical because controlling events is a powerful intrinsic motivator. The games involve *fantasy.* In addition, some of the games offer opportunities to cooperate with others, which can be interpersonally motivating; other games increase motivation by providing opportunities to compete. Some games provide explicit opportunity for recognition—for example, the program includes a "Hall of Fame" for players who have played exceptionally good games on the program.

Lepper and Malone also believe that computer games and software could be programed so they would be instructionally effective: They could be programmed to enhance attention to to-be-learned content, provide appropriate feedback about learning and performance, increase the meaningful processing of the content being taught by the program, and result in multiple representations of content (e.g., imagine all the ways that number concepts can be portrayed in computer environments—the numbers themselves, various sequential and simultaneous picture displays). The problem with the current generation of computer programs is that they were designed to be intrinsically motivating with less attention to whether the games would increase attention to and processing of the educationally relevant content. An anecdote provided by Lepper and Malone (1987) makes the point:

> . . . [W]e have been watching young children learn to program in a Logo environment. Although most of the hard data are not yet in, it was difficult not to have the feeling that for every child lost in thought on some complex, planful, and potentially mind-expanding program, there was another in hot pursuit of what one might call a behavioristic "minimax" strategy—looking for the maximum payoff from a minimum investment of effort—leading to a plethora of programs exploring, for example, the results of sending the turtle forward 12,000 or 27,000 steps at a time and watching the screen successively fill with seemingly random lines. The path of least mental effort produced a big motivational "bang for the buck" but may have limited instructional value. (p. 281)

It is all too easy to have a lot of fun with many of the programs without learning much. In fact, during a visit to a school, we learned from a grade-5 student all the ways to trick a math program so as to extend one's turn and thus remain at the microcomputer (which was much preferred to working at one's seat). The "trick" was simply to make certain *not* to perform at mastery, for to do that meant the program would produce a fireworks display in celebration of the student's success, a display that ended the student's day at the computer!

Another motivational problem with computers and computer programs is that for some students, they are so motivating that these students would do nothing else except computing if given a free choice. From time to time in our careers, we have labored in university computer centers analyzing data. Thus, when we encountered this description by Weizenbaum (1976), we recognized immediately the type of student described:

> . . . [B]right young men of disheveled appearance, often with sunken glowing eyes, can be seen sitting at computer consoles, their arms tensed and waiting to fire their fingers, already poised to strike, at the buttons and keys on which their attention seems so riveted as a gambler's on the rolling dice. When not so transfixed, they often sit at tables strewn with computer printouts over which they pore like possessed students of a cabalistic text. They work until they nearly drop, twenty, thirty hours at a time. Their food, if they arrange it, is brought to them: coffee, Cokes, sandwiches. If possible, they sleep on cots near the computer. But only for a few hours—than back to the console or the printouts. Their rumpled clothes, their unwashed and unshaven faces, and their uncombed hair all testify that they are oblivious to their bodies and to the world in which they move. They exist, at least when so engaged, only through and for computers. These are computer bums, compulsive programmers. (p. 116)

In recent years, we have begun to meet such students far beyond the university gates. With the proliferation of microcomputers, there are children and adolescents growing up who are thoroughly dedicated to PCs and Macintoshes, with much of their youth spent in the world of programs and computing machines. From the perspective of the development of expertise, perhaps these students should be viewed as a blessing: Many years of computer experience are required to be an expert in computing, and there is no shortage of need for such expertise now and in the future. From the perspective of educational well-roundedness, however, we do worry. Even without the developers of computers and com-

puter programs trying, these devices and the potential worlds they open up are appealing to some youth, so motivating that some students sacrifice exposure to many other things to have more time with their machines.

In short, producing motivating computer environments is not a problem. Ensuring that students learn well in these environments is an important issue; so is guaranteeing that some students who really get hooked on computers also spend sufficient time in other educational pursuits. Computers are going to be in classrooms and in homes from now on. A great deal of research will be required to determine how to make the most of these extremely motivating tools.

Attributional Alternatives for School Successes and Failures

When a person succeeds or fails, they can explain their success or failure to themselves in various ways. Weiner (e.g., 1979) specified four types of explanatory attributions, with each of these having different motivational consequences. Students can explain outcomes by referring to their (1) efforts—success was due to hard work; failure was due to lack of effort; (2) abilities—success was due to inherently high ability; failure was due to low ability; (3) task factors—success occurred because the task was easy; failure was caused by unreasonable demands of the task; or (4) luck—success reflects good luck; failure reflects bad luck.

Only the first of these attributions, however, is likely to promote adaptive motivational tendencies. Believing that successes and failures are due to effort is believing that one's fate is personally controllable. One can decide to try hard and be successful or to loaf and experience failure. The other explanatory possibilities—ability, task difficulty, and luck—are all out of one's control, due to genes, teacher task selection, or the whimsical nature of supernatural forces. Knowing that one's fate is under personal control has been referred to by motivational theorists as self-efficacy (e.g., Bandura, 1982; more about this later in the chapter), personal causation (e.g., deCharms, 1968), and self-agency (e.g., Martin & Martin, 1983). All theorists who have considered this type of knowledge recognize that those who believe they can control their destinies are likely to be more motivated to exert great effort in pursuit of goals than are those who believe their achievements are out of their control—for example, students with high mathematics self-efficacy have more positive attitudes about mathematics, which translates into higher mathematics achievement (Randhawa, Beamer, & Lundberg, 1993).

The role of attributions in motivating academic efforts has been studied especially with respect to the motivations of students who have experienced difficulties in school. For example, Jacobsen, Lowery, and DuCette (1986) interviewed learning-disabled and normally achieving students. Consistent with the results of other studies (e.g., Pearl, 1982), Jacobsen et al. (1986) determined that learning-disabled children were much more likely than their normally achieving classmates to believe that their achievements reflected low ability. Normally achieving children were more likely to believe that with effort they would be able to succeed in school. This belief in effort is telling even within low-achieving populations: Low achievers who believe they can control their academic progress through effort, in fact, do achieve at higher levels than low achievers who believe their low achievement reflects low ability (Kistner, Osborne, & LeVerrier, 1988).

Some anecdotal evidence drives home the point here. Often we speak to groups of special educators. At the point of the talk when we are about to discuss attributions and how attributions can affect effort, we ask the audience the following question: What if you talk with a grade-5 or grade-6 learning-disabled student about how they are doing in school and ask the student to explain why he or she is having problems in school? What do such children say? Every audience provides the same answer: The kid says, "It's because I'm stupid." Years of school failure have led these students to conclude that their academic achievement is not controllable. What is going on here? Failure following great effort leads to negative affect (Covington & Omelich, 1979a) and decreasing expectancies for future success (Covington & Omelich, 1979b). That other students are experiencing success following their efforts does not help and, in fact, probably intensifies feelings of personal incapacity (Covington, 1987). Learned helplessness—that is, the belief that nothing one can do could lead to success—develops in such a situation (Dweck, 1987). Doing nothing can actually be therapeutic for these children, because at least failure following lack of effort does not lead to the conclusion that one is stupid (Covington & Omelich, 1981,

1984). Is it any surprise that learning-disabled children often seem passive in school? Trying gets them nowhere; not trying permits an explanation of failure that is not as damaging to the ego as failure following effort.

That the attributions of many low-achieving children are dysfunctional (i.e., the students attribute their failures to uncontrollable ability factors and hence are not motivated to exert academic effort; e.g., Carr, Borkowski, & Maxwell, 1991) has inspired some to attempt to retrain attributional tendencies as part of larger educational programs aimed at children experiencing problems with school work, work that seems especially worthwhile given that academic progress in low-achieving children is related to the attributions they make: Borkowski and colleagues at Notre Dame (e.g., Borkowski, Weyhing, & Carr, 1988; Reid & Borkowski, 1987) have provided the most compelling analyses and data about interventions aimed at shifting the attributions of low achievers to promote their academic performances.

Borkowski recognized that only getting students to attribute success to effort would probably do little for low-functioning students, consistent with the perspective offered since Chapter 1 of this book that sophisticated academic performances depend on a variety of factors. (Recall that Borkowski is one of the prime movers of the good information processor perspective; e.g., Pressley, Borkowski, & Schneider, 1987, 1989.) Thus, Borkowski's group has been training students to use strategies to accomplish intellectual tasks at the same time that they persuade students that their successes and failures on academic tasks are due to their efforts using appropriate strategies (Clifford, 1984; see the Chapter 2 discussion of the criticality of students understanding the value of academic strategies they are learning). That is, Borkowski and his colleagues persuade students that as they learn strategies, they are acquiring tools that will permit them to improve their academic performances, which is a powerful motivation to use the strategies students are learning (Chapman, Skinner, & Baltes, 1990).

For example, in one study (Carr & Borkowski, 1989), underachieving elementary students were assigned to one of three conditions: (1) In the strategies plus attribution training condition, children were taught comprehension strategies. They were instructed to read paragraphs and to self-test whether they understood the content. The students were also taught summarization, topic sentence, and questioning strategies as means of understanding text (see Chapter 14). The attributional part of the training consisted of emphasizing to students that they could understand text by applying the comprehension strategies, that their comprehension of text was a function of how they approached text rather than any inherent comprehension abilities. (2) Strategies-only subjects were taught the strategies, without the benefit of attributional training. (3) Control subjects were provided neither strategies instruction nor attributional training.

Children in all conditions participated in six half-hour sessions. In the strategies plus attribution and strategies conditions, these sessions were devoted to receiving the instruction appropriate to the condition and to practicing the strategies with actual text. In the control condition, students practiced reading with the same tasks and passages processed by students in the instructional condition, although no information was provided about comprehension strategies.

What a difference in the strategies plus attributional training condition! When tested 3 weeks after the conclusion of the training sessions, the strategies plus attribution participants were more likely to be using the strategies than other participants in the study, with recall of text higher in this condition than in the other conditions of the study. In addition, the strategies plus attribution subjects seemed to be using the training strategies in the classroom much more than the students in the other conditions of the study.

Although much more work analyzing the effects of attributional retraining needs to be conducted to understand completely its potential for modifying views of oneself as a learner, many who work with learning-disabled students in particular are already including attributional retraining with their students. For example, a key ingredient in the University of Kansas strategies instructional model (e.g., Deshler & Schumaker, 1988) is promoting the understanding in students that they can do better if they master strategies well matched to the demands of school. As students are taught comprehension, writing, and memory strategies, there is consistent emphasis on the role of controllable factors, such as use of strategies, as a determinant of performance. That is, the Kansas group recognizes that the attributions made by learning-disabled students (e.g., I am stupid) are dysfunctional. Such attributions, if permitted to persist, have high potential for defeat-

ing other instruction: Believing that one is stupid is also believing that there is nothing that can be done about it. Both applied efforts and basic research (e.g., Stipek & Kowalski, 1989) have documented that attribution retraining can make a substantial difference in the motivations of students who otherwise tend to attribute their poor performances to factors other than effort.

Before closing this section, we should also emphasize that ability attributions have potential for undermining the efforts of others besides learning-disabled students. Occasionally as university professors, we are confronted by students who are extremely bright but doing poorly in school. Perhaps our understanding of motivational psychology has sensitized us, but we have been struck by how often such students indicate that they have not been working that hard because they perceive themselves to be smart enough to succeed in college without expending much effort. If as a university student, you have not yet come to the understanding that much of academic success involves exceptional effort, think again. For example, review the Chapter 4 discussion of the development of high expertise. Is high expertise the product of high ability alone? Not at all. Although high ability may be necessary to become a great physician, pianist, or chess player, hours, months, and years of effort go into the development of expertise in these domains. See Perry and Penner (1990) for some preliminary evidence that inducing college students to make effort attributions to explain their performance successes and failures rather than ability attributions can improve the performance of at least some university students.

Incremental Development of Intelligence: Encouraging Students to Understand That Intelligence Is Not a Fixed Entity But an Incrementally Improving Function

Dweck and Leggett (1988; also Henderson & Dweck, 1990) have proposed that a critical determinant of achievement motivation is whether a person believes that intelligence is fixed biologically and hence not affected by environmental variables or malleable. People who believe intelligence is fixed are said to possess an **entity theory** of intelligence—that is, intelligence is a thing that one either has in great quantity or does not. Those who believe intelligence is modifiable subscribe to an **incremental theory** of intelligence.

The particular view of intelligence held by an individual has a powerful impact on his or her achievement behaviors. First, consider academic goals as a function of the theory held: Entity theorists are oriented to seek positive evaluations of their abilities and to avoid negative evaluations. Such a perspective can be damaging when negative feedback occurs, as it inevitably does in school. Such students are likely to interpret failures as indications of low intelligence and hence be discouraged by failures. In contrast, incremental theorists are much more oriented to increasing abilities, believing that daily efforts lead to small gains, all of which can sum up to substantially higher intelligence when effort is persistent and long term. Such students persist when obstacles occur because they see obstacles as a natural part of the learning process.

In short, entity theorists are more likely to experience negative emotion when confronted with failure, believing that failure signals low ability, with that belief undermining future attempts at the academic task in question. Indeed, the entity theorist may be motivated not to engage in the task in the future to avoid additional evidence of low ability. Incremental theorists experience much less negative affect in response to failure, interpreting the failure as part of the improvement process, which motivates high persistence. As long as there is success, there is little difference in the behaviors of entity and incremental theorists. It is when failure occurs that the differences in their outlooks become apparent, with the entity theorists much more at risk for believing they are helpless when they experience difficulties during challenging tasks, with low persistence and task avoidance the likely outcomes. Incremental theorists just keep plugging away following a failure.

Dweck and her colleagues have produced quite a bit of evidence for this perspective (see Dweck & Leggett, 1988; Elliott & Dweck, 1988; Henderson & Dweck, 1990), as have others (e.g., Meece, Blumenfeld, & Hoyle, 1988; Wood & Bandura, 1989). Some of the most prominent research has been generated by Ames and associates. For example, Ames and Archer (1988) studied students in grades 8 through 11, all of whom were attending a high school for academically gifted students. The students in this study answered a number of questions. Some of the questions were designed to determine whether students were incremental or entity theorists with respect to a particular class in which they were enrolled, with Ames and Archer (1988) believing that one's theory of achievement would vary depending on the reward structure in the class. Ames and Archer (1988) referred to incremental beliefs as **mastery-oriented** beliefs, reflecting that the incremental theorists are concerned with mastering material presented in class. They referred to entity beliefs as **performance-oriented** because such students are concerned with performing well. Items likely to be endorsed by students believing they are in a class promoting increments in ability (i.e., in mastery-oriented classrooms) included the following:

- The teacher makes sure I understand the work.
- The teacher pays attention to whether I am improving.
- Students are given a chance to correct mistakes.
- The teacher wants us to try new things.
- Making mistakes is part of learning.
- I work hard to learn. (Ames & Archer, 1988, p. 262)

Items likely to be endorsed by students believing they are in classrooms driven by an entity theory of intelligence (i.e., performance-oriented) included the following:

- Students want to know how others score on assignments.
- I really do not like to make mistakes.
- Only a few students can get top marks.
- I work hard to get a high grade.
- Students feel bad when they do not do as well as others. (Ames & Archer, 1988, p. 262)

Other questions that were posed in the study were designed to get at the learning strategies used by students, their choice of academic tasks, their academic attitudes, and the causal attributions they make about school.

Students who perceived themselves in classrooms that encouraged incremental improvements reported using more strategies and more effective strategies, seemed more open to challenging tasks, were more positive about their classes, and were more likely to believe that improvements follow effort. Those perceiving their classes to be driven by an entity model were more likely to have a negative view of their own ability and believe that classroom difficulties reflect low ability.

Ames (1990) believes that analyses such as Dweck's and her own have profound implications for education. She believes in particular that to the extent that classrooms foster performance goals rather than mastery goals—that is, are ego-oriented, to use Nicholls' (1989) term, or foster entity views of mind, to use Dweck's vernacular, classroom goal structures discourage students from trying hard, using potentially effective learning procedures, or being optimistic in the face of academic difficulties. Our own reading of Ames, Nicholls, Dweck, and like-minded motivational theorists is that there is already substantial evidence in support of their perspective, which is one of the most important contemporary hypotheses motivating additional analyses of classroom processes that can foster student motivation and achievement. For now, we feel safe in concluding that students are better off in classrooms in which the mentally healthy messages associated with mastery-oriented classrooms are prominent: (1) Trying hard fosters achievement and intelligence. (2) Failure is a natural part of learning. (3) Being best is not what school is about; getting better is.

Possible Selves: Encouraging Students to Believe It Is Possible for Them to Learn and Do Well in School and in Life

Ask yourself the following question: What am I going to be in 10 years from now? What this question is tapping is your conception of "possible selves" that you might become, a concept developed most fully by Markus and colleagues (Cantor, Markus, Niedenthal, & Nurius, 1986; Markus & Nurius, 1986). We suspect that many readers of this book will provide answers to this question that reflect the expectation of upward mobility. Thus, undergraduates reading it may anticipate that they will be teachers or other professionals; teachers in master degree programs may envision that they will be principals, reading specialists, or curriculum developers; and graduate students in educational psychology may aspire to be professors, government officials, or product developers in business. What is critical to note here is that these possible selves are not frivolous fantasies but rather realistic goals, envisionments that provide a great deal of motivation to continue reading this book and completing the educational psychology course, to enroll in more courses next term, and to look for advancement opportunities (with the expectation of landing one) once school is through. As Markus and Nurius (1986, p. 960) put it, a possible self can provide

". . . direction and impetus for action, change, and development." It can provide energy for behaviors that reduce the distance between the current true self and the possible self that one aspires to become.

Unfortunately, there is plenty of reason to suspect that many students do not have desirable or realistic possible selves. Last evening on the Washington, D.C., news, we listened in horror to a conversation involving some 10-year-olds enrolled in schools in the District. One little boy related that he expected to become a drug dealer and maybe a pimp. A little girl reported that she suspected she would never have a job. These are terrible possible selves!!

Almost as tragic are more positive but unrealistic possible selves because they can motivate enormous efforts during youth in directions that are unlikely to pay off for youth. A prime example is that many minority youth in the United States believe that they have a high probability of becoming a professional athlete, when in fact the odds against any particular youth attaining such a possible self are thousands to one (e.g., Edwards, 1973). Such unrealistic possible selves can motivate much effort directed toward athletic accomplishment, effort that could have been expended in pursuit of a self that is realistically possible. Gooden (1989), for example, presented analyses of how attainable "dreams"—to use Levinson et al.'s (1978) term for possible selves—could motivate young black men. For example, Gooden reported a dishwasher whose dream was to become a chef, a dream that motivated him to make it through cooking school. Gooden also presented cases of young black men with unrealistic horizons, such as becoming a famous scientist or physician. In these cases, however, the dreams kept the young men on track academically, so they did become professionals (teachers, for the group analyzed in Gooden, 1989). A young person's possible self (or dream) can be a powerful motivator.

Given the potential of possible selves for motivating interest in and commitment to academic attainment, and given that many students have dysfunctional possible selves, an obvious intervention possibility is to attempt to shift students' possible selves from unrealistic dreams to dreams that are more likely to keep the students on track. Day, Borkowski, Dietmeyer, Howsepian, and Saenz (1994) have begun to study such a possibility. They have particularly been concerned with improving the academic performances of Mexican-American students, enough so that these students will complete high school. Their studies to date have been with Mexican-American students in grades 3 through 7.

Most of the students come from neighborhoods with few, if any, professionals. Thus, there is little opportunity to see models of Mexican-Americans working in high status occupations, models that could inspire these children to believe they could become professionals. Even so, these children have ambitious possible selves: 92 percent expect to graduate from high school, 75 percent from college, and 17 percent from graduate or professional school. They highly value success in school (5.2 on a 6-point scale). They also fear, however, that these dreams may not come true. Half of the children Day et al. (1994) have studied fear that they will end up in jobs that require less than a high school education.

Day et al. (1994) reasoned that even though Mexican-American children may have dreams, they may not know how to maintain those dreams through the many steps of the educational process, including frustrations that might be experienced along the way. The training package Day et al. developed is aimed at increasing awareness of the many types of jobs these students might attain in their lives and to make obvious that completion of middle school and high school is essential for obtaining multiple vocational opportunities. In addition, the training package focused on coping with negative feedback and failure, including unjustified reactions of others. Consistent with attribution theory, the training was designed to increase student understanding that their successes were under their control—that academic effort pays off.

The instruction involved a metaphorical piece of art, "The Possible-Me Tree." Two important leaves on the tree represent student hopes (e.g., a good job) and fears (e.g., dropping out of high school). These leaves are used in exercises designed to inspire students to work toward their goals and to avoid the feared outcomes. The give-and-take discussion, which is the intervention, emphasizes that there are various definitions of success, what people enjoy doing can become their life work, education is essential for obtaining desirable jobs, and obstacles are encountered in obtaining dreams.

The preliminary data regarding this intervention are promising, although not definitive at this point. Relative to control students not receiving the intervention, those participating in the Possible-Me Tree exercises have greater expectations of success in the future. Possible-Me–Tree students were more likely to believe they might attain especially high status occupations, such as judge or physician. There are modest improvements in grades (Estrada, 1990). Since the initial evaluations, Day, Borkowski, and their colleagues have recognized that possible-selves interventions are most likely to have effects if they are part of a larger intervention, and thus they have been developing training programs with parents. These programs provide information about what parents can do to increase their children's academic successes (e.g., enforce a study time in the evening; ask children about what is going on in school). Day and Borkowski's current hypothesis is that larger effects will be obtained by intervening with both students and parents, emphasizing the importance of school for attaining occupational goals, and informing students and parents about what they can do to increase student academic and vocational successes.

We believe that it is important to foster realistically ambitious possible selves and provide support to students so they maintain their motivation to pursue positive possible selves. Day and Borkowski's work is a first venture in this domain, an area that should be explored in great detail in future research. Such work is going to be expensive, for what counts is achievement in the very long term, and thus longitudinal research is needed. Such work seems essential, however, because the social and economic welfare of the United States demands that many more students (especially minority students) are prepared to participate in an economy that demands ever more sophisticated competencies (Johnson, Packer, et al., 1987). The country's future depends on every child entertaining possible selves that would contribute productively to the society if attained and maintaining the motivation required to make the long trip from the elementary-school classroom to vocational dreams. The dreams of minority children in the elementary grades (Day et al., in press) are decidedly American dreams of betterment through hard work; if these children continue to fail in the proportions that many are now failing, their personal failures will translate into nightmares for all of us in terms of severe constraints in the economy and increasing social malaise associated with unemployment, underemployment, and long-term frustration. We must restructure schools so that few high school students believe that their only possible successes could be through participation in gang cultures and trading in criminal economies. Such possible selves are disastrous for all of us.

Increasing Student Self-Efficacy

Social learning researchers (see Chapter 7) have increasingly offered perspectives that are consistent with views of good information processing that have been emphasized throughout this book. The concern of social learning theorists with motivation comes through in the definition of self-regulated learning provided by Barry Zimmerman:

> [Self-regulated learners] approach educational tasks with confidence, diligence, and resourcefulness. Perhaps, most importantly, self-regulated learners are aware when they know a fact or possess a skill and when they do not. Unlike their passive classmates, self-regulated learners proactively seek out information when needed and take the necessary steps to master it. When they encounter obstacles such as poor study conditions, confusing teachers, or abstruse textbooks, they find a way to succeed. Self-regulated learners view acquisition as a systematic and controllable process, and they accept greater responsibility for their achievement outcomes.... [T]hese learners report high self-efficacy, self-attributions, and intrinsic task interest.... [T]hey are self-starters who display extraordinary effort and persistence during learning.... They seek out advice, information, and places where they are most likely to learn; they ... self-reinforce during performance enactments.... (Zimmerman, 1989b, pp. 4–5)

A particularly critical part of this definition of self-regulated learning is the idea that self-regulated learners have high **perceived self-efficacy** (Bandura, 1977a, 1986; Schunk, 1990, 1991; Zimmerman, 1989a, 1989b, 1990a, 1990b)—that is, they believe they are capable of doing well on academic tasks. High self-efficacy in a domain is important because it motivates attempting tasks in the same domain in the future and thus is a causal factor in future academic achievement (e.g., Marsh, 1990a; Zimmerman, Bandura, & Martinez-Pons, 1992). For example, one motivation for a first-year university student to enroll in introductory calculus is previous success in mathematics. That is, the decision to pursue the goal of earning credit in first-year calculus is determined in part by previous success in prerequisite courses. Suppose that the calculus course goes well, with concepts learned easily and grades high on quizzes and tests. Self-efficacy with respect to

mathematics is increased even more, which in turn can motivate future election of mathematics courses. What if things went badly in the calculus course? Self-efficacy with respect to mathematics should decline, with this reducing the likelihood of seeking mathematics credit in the future. Self-efficacy is determined in part by present attempts at learning and performance; it then affects future attempts at learning and performance.

What are the other determinants of self-efficacy besides previous success in the domain? For one, there are social models: When people who are similar to us can do something, we are more likely to believe that we could do it and should attempt to do so (Schunk, 1991). Other people also attempt to persuade us concerning our competencies. How many times did we hear from our gym teachers in junior and senior high school to try the parallel bars because they were sure we could do it! That motivated our attempts to learn how to perform on the parallel bars, as did watching classmates who did well on the parallel bars. Even so, we consistently received negative feedback for our efforts (i.e., we fell off the bar, executed maneuvers clumsily), with this feedback overriding the effects of modeling and teacher persuasion. Although modeling and the opinions of others have an impact on self-efficacy, feedback from one's own efforts has a greater impact (Schunk, 1990, 1991).

Self-efficacy is highly domain specific; thus there are students who have high self-efficacy with respect to math and low self-efficacy with respect to composition, and this self-knowledge is generally accurate (i.e., people know their academic strengths and weaknesses: Marsh, 1990b, 1992a—even middle-elementary grades students: Marsh & Craven, 1991—even children as young as 5 years of age: Marsh, Craven & Debus, 1991, although there certainly is greater differentiation with respect to academic self-concept with increasing age during the grade-school years; Stipek & MacIver, 1989). There are those with high self-efficacy with respect to most academic areas and low self-efficacy with respect to athletics. Within specific domains, there are differences in self-efficacy. As an illustration of the specificity, consider that as a senior in high school author MP had high self-efficacy with respect to tumbling and low self-efficacy with respect to the parallel bars. He had high self-efficacy with respect to the 440-yard dash and low self-efficacy with respect to the 220-yard race. He had high self-efficacy with respect to playing first base and low self-efficacy with respect to playing third base. All of us possess detailed knowledge about what we can do well (e.g., university students are aware of their proficiencies in reading and writing; Shell, Murphy, & Bruning, 1989), with the detailed perceptions of self-efficacy playing a large role in determining future efforts. For example, as a middle-aged adult who now plays only slow-pitch softball, author MP would never think of playing third base but would have no trepidation about playing first base.

There has been substantial investigation of self-efficacy and its role in goal selection and persistence in efforts to attain goals (see Wigfield & Karpathian, 1991). For example, Bandura and Cervone (1983, 1986) studied college students as they worked an exercise-type machine. Subjects' self-efficacy during this task was determined by the feedback they received about the amount of improvement that occurred. The amount of effort subjects were willing to expend attempting to improve on the task on a future trial was related to the subjects' perceptions of successful improvement on previous trials. (The feedback in this study was false feedback, so feedback could be manipulated—and hence perceptions of improvement—independent of objective efforts and improvements made on the initial trials.) See Schunk (1989, 1990, 1991) for additional research documenting that perceptions of effectiveness on a task in the present increase task efforts in the future.

The self-efficacy perspective makes clear why it is important to provide students with tasks that are just a bit beyond them. If subjects attempt an easy goal, they make progress rapidly, but the rub is that they do not acquire information about their abilities to tackle more ambitious tasks. If students attempt too difficult a task, there is little success in meeting the goal or making success toward meeting it, with the result diminished self-efficacy and motivation to continue with the task. Only tasks that are challenging for the learner, but not so challenging as to prevent progress, are capable of providing information to students that increases self-efficacy in ways that are likely to promote future attempts at challenging tasks. To the extent that teachers provide goals in school, it is incumbent on them to recognize this principle, because failure to do so will do little good for the motivation of students when they are not under strong instructional control (i.e., when the teacher is not watching over them and requiring them to attempt the task in question). To the extent

that students select their goals in school, much thinking needs to be done about how to encourage them to select goals that are appropriate—for example, to select courses that do not cover content identical to information in their previous courses but not so far beyond present competence and knowledge that students will be discouraged. Thus, students entering university with A's in algebra, geometry, trigonometry, and introduction to analysis should be taught to select the "next" course in the math sequence rather than a remedial course that would be very easy. At the same time, they need to learn of the complete inappropriateness of electing mathematics courses intended for students who have mastered the calculus.

Although self-efficacy theory can be related to a variety of theoretical perspectives pertaining to motivation (see Pintrich & de Groot, 1990; Schunk, 1991; Skinner, Wellborn, & Connell, 1990), one that seems particularly appropriate to consider is its relationship to **expectancy × value theory,** an important theory specifying when people will perform behaviors that they are capable of performing (see Chapter 7 for more extensive coverage of this theory). If self-efficacy is high in domain A, the expectancy of reinforcement contingent on performing in domain A is also high, and hence if the potential reinforcements for performing in domain A are also valued, the likelihood of domain A behaviors would also be high (i.e., high expectancy of reinforcement × high valuation of a reinforcement = high probability of performing the behavior producing the reinforcement in question). If domain A behaviors occur and there is success, expectancy of reinforcement remains high contingent on domain A behaviors. In contrast, if domain A behaviors occur and there is failure, expectancy of reinforcement for domain A behaviors should decline, as should the likelihood of performing domain A behaviors in the future. Shifts in self-efficacy probably produce changes in expectations, which alter the likelihood of performing behaviors in a domain (Schunk, 1991).

A critical assumption of expectancy × value theories is that successful students both expect and value academic success. In a study analytical enough to determine whether there are strong relationships between expectations of academic success, valuation of success, and academic achievement, Berndt and Miller (1990) observed that the success of grade-7 students in English and math was linked strongly both to expectations of success in these domains and to valuation of potential rewards for success in math and English (i.e., successful students expected and valued academic success).

So far we have made it sound as if every attempt at doing something has great consequences for self-efficacy. In particular, this is not correct when a person already has a strong sense of self-efficacy built up over years. Consider the following: A major league batting star strikes out four times in one day. Is there an effect on the batting star's self-efficacy with respect to hitting? Probably not, or if it is, it is likely a specific shift, such as, "I have a lot of trouble against Lefty Smith (i.e., today's pitcher)." When attempting some new goal, the feedback on one occasion can have a dramatic impact on self-efficacy and long-term motivation; performing below par on some one occasion in an arena where one enjoys a long record of accomplishment has less impact on self-efficacy with respect to that goal (see Bandura, 1986, for other examples; also, Schunk, 1991).

Now that readers are well armed with an understanding of self-efficacy theory and its relationship to expectancy × value theory, it is time to return to a problem of motivation cited earlier in this chapter. Can self-efficacy theory help explain why girls are unlikely to take mathematics? An analysis by Eccles (1989) suggests that it can. Young women are less confident in their mathematics abilities than young men (Eccles, 1985), translating to lower expectations with respect to success in mathematics. In addition, women are less likely than men to value careers involving mathematics and physical sciences (Eccles, 1985). With lower expectancies of reward for taking math and lower interest in the potential rewards associated with mathematics achievement, both components of the expectancy × value product are lower for females than for males, and hence the probability of taking mathematics is lower for girls than for boys.

Eccles's (1989) analysis went further, probing the origins of the lower expectations and valuations by girls for mathematics. Parents tend to have gender-stereotypic expectations about math achievement and valuation (Eccles & Jacob, 1986; Eccles-Parson, Adler, & Kaczala, 1982), with their lower expectations and valuation of mathematics with respect to daughters communicated to girls. How teachers undermine female confidence in mathematical abilities is harder to peg except there are some

consistencies across classrooms in which female confidence is lower than male confidence (Eccles, MacIver, & Lange, 1986; Eccles-Parson, Kaczala, & Meece, 1982):

> Classrooms in which there were no sex differences were more orderly, had less of both extreme praise and criticism, and were more business-like. The teacher also maintained tighter control over student-teacher interactions, ensuring equal participation by calling on everyone, rather than focusing on the small subset of students who regularly raised their hands. In contrast, classrooms marked by sex differences in the students' attitudes were characterized by student-teacher interactions dominated by a few students. Essentially, these teachers were more reactive, focusing their attention primarily on those students who raised their hand or insisted on attention in other ways. Consequently, a running dialogue emerged between the teacher and two or three other students . . . more often than not . . . white males.
>
> . . . [C]lassrooms in which males and females had similar views of their abilities were less public and more private . . . more dyadic interactions between the teacher and the student and less public drills involving the whole class. . . . This teaching style appears to have a beneficial effect on females, perhaps because it induces a less competitive classroom environment. (p. 50)

Eccles, MacIver, and Lange (1986; Eccles, 1989; see also Casserly, 1980) intensively studied classrooms in which girls had favorable views of their mathematics abilities, boys had more favorable views, and boys and girls had equal conceptions of their abilities. Girls fared better in classrooms that were not competitive, ones in which ability comparisons were played down. Girls fared better when the teacher emphasized the value of mathematics. Girls also fared better with warmer teachers, ones who were fairer in their distribution of attention to students. Part of the classroom formula for high math self-efficacy in girls is (1) low classroom competition, (2) private and personal contact with the teacher, and (3) little public drill and practice. Much of the rest involves sending the message that math is important for boys and girls alike, regardless of race or socioeconomic status (e.g., Kahle, 1984). Classrooms that foster high self-efficacy with respect to math and science achievement also tend to involve a great deal of hands-on, cooperative activity between students over math and science problems (see Eccles, 1989, review; also Kahle, 1984;

Wilkinson & Marrett, 1985). Teachers that foster high self-efficacy in girls do not give into attention-demanding tactics from boys (and boys are naturally more likely to engage in such tactics), but rather they make certain that all students are involved in class discussion, interacting productively with one another and with the teacher. Lest anyone feel that encouraging such classrooms would encourage a sort of reverse discrimination, girl-friendly classrooms (Kahle, 1984) are supportive of minorities and lower-achieving boys as well (Malcolm, 1984). Our view is that Eccles (1989) and others have succeeded in identifying classroom environmental variables that foster high self-efficacy for many more students than occurs in competitive classrooms in which interactions with a few students predominate, an all-too-frequent phenomenon in American classrooms.

In closing this discussion of self-efficacy, it is essential to emphasize as well that self-efficacy is only one determinant of motivation and selection of goals. One way to emphasize this is to reiterate that the probability of a behavior is a function of the expectation of reinforcement and the value of the expected reinforcement. If the expected reinforcement is of no value to the student, behavior is unlikely no matter how high the student's self-efficacy may be. Our perceptions of whether we can perform a task are important determinants of our selection of goals but not the only determinant.

Encourage Volition

Since the earliest formulation of the good information processing model (Pressley et al., 1987), there was recognition that good information processors "stick with" important tasks and are not easily distracted from them. The work of German psychologist Julius Kuhl (e.g., 1985) influenced that early conception, with Kuhl claiming that people differ in the extent to which they can shield themselves from distractions, an individual difference that is an important determinant of performance on many tasks. Others (e.g., Corno, 1989) have also been impressed by Kuhl's analyses, with Corno arguing that Kuhl's work has special significance for understanding student **volition,** which contrasts with motivation in that motivation involves a decision to initiate action toward a goal and volition involves continuing to pursue the goal once begun:

Kuhl (1985) conceptualizes volition after Ach (1910) as a series of "action control processes," that is, "post-decisional, self-regulatory processes that energize the maintenance and enactment of intended actions" (p. 90). Although Kuhl's theory is general, the specific intended actions of concern here are concentrating and working toward the completion of academic tasks. That volitional processes are "postdecisional" is the distinguishing point between volition and motivation: Volitional processes come into play *after* the decision is made to learn or complete an academic task. Most motivational processes underlie or precede the decision to learn or complete a task—these include the weighing of success and outcome expectancies, the assessment of value, and so on. They *promote* the intent to learn. . . . A student brings in volition once there is a commitment to learn, and volition *protects* that commitment to learn and concentrate from competing action tendencies and other potential distractions. (Corno, 1989, p. 114)

Corno (1989) also analyzed what students would need to be taught to increase their volitional capabilities: They need to learn to control their attention to the task at hand and especially to shield that attention from distractions in the environment, since schools are filled with distractions, from the antics of the class clown to the sounds of bell signals pertaining to other classrooms. How can this be accomplished? One way is by teaching children to generate verbal self-instructions to attend to a task. See the many examples reviewed by Pressley (1979); that review featured many interventions involving children simply learning to tell themselves to ignore distractions at the first notice of the distraction (Meichenbaum, 1977, covered many of the same interventions; see Chapter 7 for extensive discussion of Meichenbaum's work and other self-instructional research). Students need to learn how to manage their study—for instance, knowing when to take much-needed breaks versus when to push on. Often, difficulty with an academic task is accompanied by emotional responses. Such responses need to be suppressed, because anxiety and distress can disrupt information processing. Often this also can be accomplished by teaching students to instruct themselves to remain calm and task focused (e.g., "I can't worry about this, I can't get irrational"; Corno, 1989, p. 120). Students need to learn how to motivate themselves if they begin to become discouraged. This can be accomplished by teaching students to review the dire consequences of failures and the rewards of successful task completion. Students can also be taught to self-verbalize encouragements (Corno, 1989), such as, "I know this material, and I'll succeed next time," or to think of new strategies for reviewing the material on a next round (e.g., "This time I'm going to reread closely and take notes"). In addition to controlling themselves, good students learn to control their environments. Thus, if there are environmental distractions, one can move to a less distracting environment. If "bothered" by the poor lighting in a room, students can learn to take action to overcome the problem, such as fetching a lamp from another room or moving over to the window and taking advantage of sunlight. In short, students can learn strategies that will keep them focused on their ongoing work (see Corno & Kanfer, 1993, for an extensive discussion).

Much of the research on cognitive self-instruction during academic tasks is aimed specifically at volition, with a number of examples of self-instruction in chapters to follow. Classroom teachers' modeling of strategies for maintaining task persistence is an important starting point; for students who are especially distractible, explicit instruction to cue themselves in particular ways when they are at risk for distraction (e.g., in a noisy environment) can be extremely helpful. Much more work on the encouragement of volition is required, however. The research to date by Corno, Manning, and others suggests there is great potential for increasing volition of students—the well-documented distractibility of many students (e.g., Messer, 1976) makes clear that there is also a need!

Informing Teachers About How to Motivate Students

This entire section has been about what can be done to enhance academic motivation in classrooms. One question that probably occurred to most readers is why teachers do not use these approaches already. An hypothesis offered by Brophy (1986, 1987) is that many teachers do not understand all that they could do and need to do to maximize motivation in their classrooms (for an example of a group of teachers who did not, see Newby, 1991). Thus, Brophy hypothesized that a profitable way to improve motivation in school would be to teach teachers the many tactics for increasing motivation that have been validated in various types of basic research. Brophy

then proposed his own "greatest hits" list of motivational interventions, ones most defensible from classical conceptions of motivation. To motivate students, teachers should do the following according to Brophy:

- Model interest in learning. Teachers should let students know they like learning (reading, writing, problem-solving) and find academic activities rewarding and generally satisfying. They should let students know about especially interesting aspects of upcoming content and why people value the knowledge covered in school. Consistent with the direct explanation models (see Chapters 1 and 8), teachers should model thinking and problem-solving as they occur. This can be a powerful way of conveying both how to approach tasks and that academic tasks are engaging and meaningful.
- Communicate to students that there is plenty of reason to be enthusiastic about what is going on in school. When new content is presented, send the message that the students will find the material interesting. Never send the message that there is drudgery in what is being covered.
- Classrooms should be low-anxiety places. What goes on in school should be presented as learning experiences, rather than tests. The more classrooms are task-oriented rather than ego-oriented, to use Nicholls's (1989) terms, the better.
- Send the message that what is occurring in school deserves intense attention. Teachers need to stage their presentations so their words, tone, and manner send the message that, "This stuff is important." Of course, this approach is used selectively and is especially reserved for truly important material.
- Induce curiosity and suspense. This can be done, for example, by encouraging students to make predictions about what might be in an upcoming text or lesson, stimulating students to want to determine whether their prediction holds. Sometimes this can be accomplished by demonstrating to students that their current knowledge is inadequate. One effective mechanism is to induce cognitive conflict, pointing out apparent contradictions in materials, stimulating students to come up with ways to resolve the contradictions (e.g., see Chapter 12 for discussion of scientific misconceptions).

- Make abstract material more personal, concrete, and familiar. Remember from Chapter 3 that relating material to prior knowledge is a good way to understand it. Recall from Chapter 3 as well that concrete material is easier to understand and remember than abstract material. Recall also the coverage of case-based reasoning in that chapter: People often understand specific cases much better than the abstract principles the cases can be used to illustrate. For many reasons, people are more motivated to learn and better able to work with familiar and concrete content than with abstract and remote materials and ideas.
- Let students know the learning objectives—provide them with advance information about upcoming content.
- Provide informative feedback to students (e.g., feedback in the form of praise, as discussed in the last subsection). As much as possible, give students tasks that provide automatic feedback. For example, not being able to complete a writing assignment on a story provides feedback that understanding of the story may be incomplete.
- Adapt tasks to student interests as much as possible.
- Offer students choices between alternative tasks or alternative ways of learning content.
- Provide novel input as much as possible.
- Design instructional tasks to allow as much student autonomy as possible.
- Design tasks so there is opportunity for activity. Projects, discussions, role playing, and simulations all induce student activity. (See, for example, Chapter 8 for information about the potential impacts of educational interventions that encourage interaction rather than passivity.) Providing higher-order questions for class consideration is one way to encourage activity that has high potential for increasing the meaningfulness and memorability of material (e.g., see the work on elaborative interrogation in Chapter 10). Opportunities to interact with peers can be reinforcing for students and are a natural part of doing a project or working on higher-order questions.
- Design learning tasks that produce a product. (The many "books" we have seen "published" by classes provide great reinforcement for students attempting to write, followed by revision until the piece is "publishable.")
- Include games as part of learning. (We still remember how motivated it was to learn spelling words for class spelling bees.)

Brophy (1986, 1987) emphasized that simply attempting to add these components to instruction would do little good in the absence of other considerations, including some already encountered in this book:

- In general, classrooms should be orderly and well-managed.
- Content should be at an appropriate level, not too easy but not so difficult that most students will not be able to meet task demands with reasonable effort.
- What is being taught should be worth learning.
- A teacher's repertoire of motivational devices is extensive enough so that none must be used so frequently that it becomes "old hat."

In short, Brophy recognizes that effective instruction is not informed simply by one or even a few perspectives but by many traditions, including in this case motivational theories and research, research on classroom management, and understanding of age-appropriate and grade-appropriate curricula. If you have not done so already, go through the Brophy lists and compare the recommendations made there with the recommendations presented elsewhere in this chapter. What you will find is that Brophy's perspective is congruent with most of the thinking in this chapter, with his particular contribution an emphasis on the many things that can be done, whereas other theorists and researchers have usually been more narrow in their focus, either interested in or believing in one or a few motivational mechanisms more than others.

Brophy (1987) discussed a preliminary study in which grade-7 and grade-8 social studies teachers were provided brief training in the various ways for making instruction more motivating. The teachers in the study used the motivational tactics they learned with one of their classes and continued to teach another section in their customary fashion. Although the positive effects of the intervention were not great, and the effects were obscured somewhat by teachers carrying over what they had learned about motivation into their "control" classes, the outcomes were in the right direction. We did not find the outcome reported by Brophy (1986) to compel the conclusion that teachers could translate a few hours of training in how to motivate students into dramatic achievement gains for students. The possibility that teachers can be stimulated to develop more motivating classrooms by providing them much more information about motivation is one that deserves much additional study. A broad range of dependent variables should be tapped in such investigations, from objective shifts in traditional academic gains (e.g., as measured by standardized test scores) to more subjective, but nonetheless important effects about how students feel about school, including their willingness to expend effort to learn what is being taught. Some young scholar's career could get off to a great start by tackling this problem and providing telling data about the short-term (e.g., observed in the classroom today) and long-term (e.g., willingness to stay in school) effects of teaching teachers how to be more motivating.

Summary

When discussing motivation, it is tempting to parse up the discussion into environmental versus cognitive influences on motivation. The message encountered again and again in this chapter, however, is that such parsing misses an important point: Classroom environments can have powerful effects on cognitive processes affecting motivation. Thus, we offer a sample set of relationships between educational environments and cognitive-motivational processes:

- Providing positive reinforcement can decrease long-term motivation if the reinforcement is presented in such a way that students infer they are working for rewards per se. If students believe they are working for tangible rewards, their efforts are likely to diminish if they no longer receive the rewards.
- Classrooms filled with praise and other rewards can motivate students in the long term, if the reinforcement is presented so as to be informative (e.g., flagging what the child did that was praiseworthy). Some forms of praise, such as claims that, "You are so smart," have the potential for undermining effort, if the recipient begins to attribute his or her success to ability rather than effort (e.g., Barker & Graham, 1987; Meyer et al., 1979).
- Task-oriented (or cooperative or mastery-oriented) classrooms produce high self-esteem for

a much higher proportion of children than do ego-oriented (or competitive or performance-oriented) classrooms, which in turn accounts in part for the greater motivation in task-oriented classrooms. Such classroom environments increase student expectancies of success if appropriate effort is exerted. Such classrooms also signal that intelligence is incremental rather than an entity that is fixed.

- The ego (competitive, performance) orientation of many classrooms probably does much to undermine intrinsic motivation to learn and naturally high expectations that one can do well and hence the declines in academic motivation and expectations with additional years of schooling.
- Attempts to make tasks more interesting must be engineered so that attention and other cognitive processes are not diverted to the high interest part of the presentation at the expense of the intended content.
- Classroom environments that encourage the attribution that high performance follows from effort expended on appropriate academic strategies increase student awareness of the utility of the strategic knowledge acquired in school and hence student motivation to use what they have learned.
- Classroom instruction that highlights when and where new knowledge is useful has the potential to increase metacognitive awareness about knowledge (including knowledge of strategies) and hence increase motivation to use knowledge on occasions when it would be useful.
- Teachers can encourage students to believe that they can do well in school and in life and hence affect the possible selves the children imagine.
- When teachers consistently require students to work on tasks that are just beyond their competence, there is high potential for students to develop the understanding that effort pays off—to develop high self-efficacy with respect to academic tasks. Presentation of appropriately matched tasks increases cognitive conflict and engagement, with the resolution of such conflict following cognitive effort likely to increase self-efficacy and long-term academic efforts.
- Students who are especially distractible can be taught to self-instruct themselves to initiate academic efforts and to stay on task (see Chapter 7)—that is, instruction can be designed so that even the most difficult students can regulate

their cognitive efforts, so they can be motivated learners with high volition.

We could go on for a long time proposing additional relationships between educational environments, cognition, and motivation. The point is that educational environments are designed explicitly to develop the mind, and there are some types of input to the mind that can result in great long-term motivation to maximize one's mental resources and other inputs that can undermine long-term cognitive efforts. The trick is to design instruction to take advantage of as many motivational mechanisms as possible.

Theorists who are interested in good information processing (Chapter 1) and instruction that encourages good information processing have been especially intrigued by the instructional implications of contemporary research on motivation. Borkowski and colleagues (e.g., Borkowski et al., 1990) have been at the forefront of these efforts, with their attention to the motivation literature apparent in Borkowski and Muthukrishna's (1992) list of essential elements in good information processing. The good information processor:

- Knows a large number of learning strategies.
- Understands when, where, and why these strategies are important.
- Selects and monitors strategies wisely and is extremely reflective and planful.
- Adheres to an incremental view regarding the growth of mind.
- Believes in carefully deployed effort.
- Is intrinsically motivated and task-oriented and has mastery goals.
- Does not fear failure and, in fact, realizes that failure is essential for success, and hence is not anxious about tests but sees them as learning opportunities.
- Has concrete, multiple images of "possible selves"—hoped-for selves in the near and distant future.
- Knows a great deal about many topics and has rapid access to that knowledge.
- Has a history of being supported in all of these characteristics by parents, school, and society at large. (p. 483, adapted slightly)

Thus, this version of the model introduced in Chapter 1 maintains the importance of strategies, metacognition, knowledge, and motivation but highlights motivation. In doing so, it makes clear that without high academic motivation, many students will not develop extensive repertoires of strategies, the metacognition required to regulate the strategies they do have, or other knowledge.

Much of the attention to motivation in recent years has been due to widespread perceptions that many students are not motivated by school. Worse still was the realization that the low motivation may not be due to inherent deficiencies in children (or particular children), but rather that schools as they now exist shape up **learned helplessness** (e.g., Dweck & Licht, 1980): That is, many students come to believe there is nothing they can do to achieve at a high level in school, and thus they do nothing. This realization at the end of the 1970s that many students were extremely discouraged in American schools did much to stimulate thinking about how schools might be reshaped so the intrinsic academic motivations of 5-year-olds and their great expectations might be maintained rather than destroyed.

The work on motivation is as important as anything covered in this book. If the new knowledge about motivating students is used well, there is high potential for increasing the achievement of the nation's schoolchildren. Not to use this knowledge would be deplorable, for there is nothing more tragic than a learned helpless 10-year-old. Unfortunately, we have many personal memories of 10-year-olds who are academically discouraged and despondent. There seems to exist the potential to change this situation; we have to try.

CONCLUDING COMMENTS

There really is a new look to academic motivation research. Bernard Weiner (1990) made this point by reviewing the content of chapters on motivation in the editions of the *Encyclopedia of Educational Research* published since 1941. Physiological mechanisms underlying motivation dominated in the 1940s and 1950s, with a little bit of Freud (e.g., defense mechanisms) and behaviorism mixed in. Drives and grand theories (e.g., psychoanalytic) dominated the 1960s, with motivation in relation to the cognitive processes of learning, perception, and memory showing up by 1969. By 1982, about one-third of the chapters were concerned with issues covered in this chapter, with contributions on attribution theory, self-esteem, and reinforcement theory. The 1990 volume featured chapters on cognition, including causal attributions, self-efficacy, and learned helplessness. There were also chapters on environmental determinants of motivation, including cooperative and competitive structures, intrinsic and extrinsic rewards, and praise. Our reading of the 1990 volume makes us confident that what is presented here captures well much of the contemporary thinking on academic motivation.

When educational implications were suggested in this chapter, they were with respect to individual classrooms. If there is to be real reform of motivation in education, however, there needs to be restructuring at higher levels. Fortunately, there is now some thought as to how to restructure entire schools so as to improve academic motivation, with one model being proposed by policy researchers who have been influenced by Carol Ames's work on mastery-oriented versus performance-oriented classrooms. Maehr and Midgley (1991) have analyzed how a school could be restructured to promote task orientation, to use Nicholls's (1989) term. Their proposal is much too extensive to take up here, except to say that many of the suggestions in this chapter are ones promoted across the school in their model. Those readers who believe that all of what was covered here is pie-in-the-sky should study Maehr and Midgley's (1991) proposal.

We emphasize in closing that it is no accident that this chapter ended by referring readers to a paper on school-level policies regarding reward structures in schools and classrooms. As we reflected on the data that informed this chapter, the case in favor of the perspective common to Dweck, Nicholls, Borkowski, and Ames's writing is strong. A great deal of evidence exists that one of the biggest problems with respect to reforming school so it is more motivating is that Americans are caught up with rank-ordering themselves and others. Whenever we talk with educators about restructuring their classrooms to enhance motivation, there is a terrible specter that always enters the conversation: Report cards. The idea that everyone could make an A if every student was making progress just does not fit well with the evaluation system that is in place in American schools. Somehow it is seen as un-American or unethical or un-something not to rank order students. If Nicholls, Borkowski, Dweck, and Ames are right—and we think they are—then we have a perspective on education (one that seems to pervade the nation) that is not only damaging to large numbers of individual children, but also to the nation as a whole. If it were possible to kill the obsession that classrooms always have a few A students, a few more B students, mostly C students, and a few who trail the pack, a lot of new life might be breathed into American students and schools. Powerful and revolutionary ideas are emerging from the careful scientific work conducted by the likes of Borkowski, Dweck, Nicholls, and Ames. We hope some readers of this book choose to join the revolution, either as researchers extending these ideas or as educators translating them into practice.

6

Biological Foundations

Although this chapter is concerned explicitly with biological factors that affect learning and cognition, what will become evident as it unfolds is that biology and environment are completely intertwined in determining learning. Biological potential can never be realized without relevant environmental input. The chapter begins with an overview of methods used by researchers to understand biology and its effects on learning and cognition. Sections detailing biological development and biological biases as determinants of intellectual functioning and biological factors affecting specific academic competencies (e.g., reading) follow. The chapter concludes with three sections on extremely important problems in biological psychology related to education: the effects of disease on cognitive functioning, potential gender differences in intellect, and potential biologically determined modules of mind.

METHODS IN BIOLOGICALLY ORIENTED RESEARCH ON INTELLECT

Some biological methods have been used for a long time and are common in psychological studies. Others represent the cutting edge in the assessment of the mind. Although such state-of-the-science measures are contributing to contemporary psychological research, they are not yet used extensively by psychologists studying thinking and learning. The 21st century educational psychologist requires some knowledge of all of these measures, however, for all

of them will be used commonly in work in the coming decades.

Psychophysiological Indicators of Intellectual Functioning

Typically, biologically oriented research psychologists rely on a variety of psychophysiological measurements that are revealing about basic neurological functioning. Such measurements can permit sensitive tests of biologically oriented theories of intellectual functioning and individual differences in intelligence.

The first one to be described here is simple: Jensen and colleagues have been studying a simple form of **choice reaction time.** The subject sits in front of a panel with a 180-degree arc of lights (one, two, four, or eight lights, depending on the particular study). Below each light is a button. The subject's finger rests on a "home" button at the bottom and center of the arc. The task is to move as quickly as possible from the home button to the button next to a light on the arc as soon as the arc light comes on. Thus, the subject is touching the home button as one light of the arc comes on; the subject leaves the home button and quickly pushes the button adjacent to the lit arc light. Although a number of dependent variables can be extracted from such reactions, an important one is the subject's mean reaction time (i.e., time taken on average to depress the correct button once a light comes on). Jensen (e.g., 1982) and his colleagues have consistently obtained correlations between IQ (see Chapter 16) and mean choice reaction time (i.e., *r* often in the 0.3 to 0.4 range), documenting that more intelligent people react more quickly. Another important parameter is variability in reaction time, with greater variability associated with lower intelligence.

One variation of the paradigm that is more complex involves three lights coming on, with two closer together than the third "odd-man-out" light. The subject's task is to hit the button adjacent to the odd-man-out light. This more complex variation produces correlations with intelligence measures in the 0.6 range (Frearson & Eysenck, 1986).

How could being quicker influence intelligence? Jensen's answer (see also Vernon, 1987) is **neural efficiency theory.** Recall that all conscious processing occurs in limited-capacity, short-term memory. Slow processes consume more capacity than do fast processes (e.g., see Chapter 14 for review of data substantiating that one of the ways to make the most of one's capacity during reading is to read quickly). Thus, those who process more quickly have greater functional capacity because they can perform more processes given the limited capacity they have. An important prediction from neural efficiency theory is that any capacity-demanding task should seem less demanding for intelligent compared with less intelligent people (e.g., note the positron-emission tomography (PET) scan correlations with intelligence that will be reported in a subsequent subsection of this chapter).

Other psychophysiological reaction time data support the conclusion that there are correlations between speed of information processing and psychometric intelligence and thus corroborate neural efficiency theory. For example, (1) Vernon (see 1991) is studying individual differences in **nerve conduction velocity,** with differences in conduction speed taken using electrodes attached to the arm. His initial studies are reporting correlations of 0.4 and better between this measure of the speed of information processing and psychometric intelligence. (2) In the Sternberg (1966, 1969) task, subjects are presented between one and seven digits to hold in short-term memory followed by a single digit, with the subject asked to decide whether the single digit is one of the numbers in short-term storage. More intelligent subjects perform this **short-term memory scanning** task more rapidly than less intelligent subjects (e.g., Keating & Bobbitt, 1978; see Vernon,

1990a, 1990b for reviews). (3) In Posner's (1969) task, subjects are presented pairs of letters that are physically identical (AA, BB, aa, bb), semantically identical (Aa, bB), or different (AB, ab, Ab, aB). They must decide whether the letters presented are the same or different. Letters differing physically and semantically can be judged using recognition processes, whereas semantically identical letters require some retrieval of semantic information from long-term memory. The difference in reaction time for semantically identical pairs and semantically/physically different pairs is a measure of **speed of retrieval from long-term memory.** Again, more intelligent people retrieve information more quickly from long-term memory than less intelligent participants. Some of the more complex variations on this paradigm can produce reaction time–intelligence correlations over 0.6 (Vernon, 1990a, reviews this issue).

There is also psychophysiological evidence supporting Jensen's hypothesis that there is an inverse correlation between effort that a person needs to expend on a task (i.e., with less effort presumably reflecting greater functional capacity) and intelligence. For example, when people are experiencing a greater processing load, the pupils of their eyes dilate. Ahern and Beatty (1979, 1981) reported that pupil dilation was less when highly intelligent people performed intellectual tasks than when average intelligent people did so. Their interpretation was that the same tasks were less demanding for the more intelligent students.

Some of the best-known work supporting neural efficiency theory involves one of the best-known psychophysical measures, the **electroencephalogram (EEG).** An EEG is an assessment of the electrical activity of the brain as detected by electrodes attached to the scalp (e.g., Marshall-Goodell, Tassinary, & Cacioppo, 1990) as a person performs various tasks. Correlations between such electrical activity and psychometric intelligence have been reported a number of times, although these tend not to be simple relationships (see Eysenck, 1987; Carlson & Widaman, 1987). For instance, relationships have been demonstrated between intelligence and what Jensen, Schafer, and Crinella (1981) referred to as "neural adaptability," which is producing greater electrical activity in reaction to an unexpected than to an expected stimulus, which represents efficient processing in that more processing should occur to comprehend a new compared with an old stimulus. Hendrickson and

Hendrickson (e.g., 1980) have used EEG data to measure differences in ability to transmit error-free electrical impulses in reaction to stimuli, which they consider an indicator of the efficiency of the nervous system. They have reported correlations greater than 0.8 between their measures of brain efficiency and psychometric intelligence.

One criticism of the EEG has always been that the data produced using this method are very gross—that the EEG provides information that is about as revealing as hearing the cheers outside a football stadium. With detailed acoustic analyses of those sounds, good guesses can be made about where something on the field is happening; attention to the tone and affect of the crowd can reveal a lot about which team is playing well; and temporal patterns can be revealing about the specific plays on the field (one huge cheer with postscoring celebration for a minute or two suggests field goal by the home team, whereas one huge cheer followed by a little celebratory noise and another large cheer followed by celebration indicates touchdown with successful extra point). Many believe that those relying on EEG data are about as informed about brain processes as a hot dog vendor outside the stadium is informed about the game.

At the same time, it must be emphasized that new analysis procedures with EEG data are producing more information. For example, Kutas and Van Petten (1988) have identified an EEG pattern indicative of the detection of semantic incongruity, such as occurs when encountering the last word in, "The pizza was too hot to *cry*." As readers may recall from Chapter 2, the detection of incongruities has been used to measure whether people monitor their understanding of material; Kutas and Van Patten's (1988) work suggests that sensitive physiological analysis of processes such as monitoring is possible and that it may be possible to index individual differences in theoretically interesting information processes (such as monitoring) using psychophysiological approaches. (For fascinating evidence that the Soviets have been aware for some time about how to measure processes such as monitoring using psychophysiological indicators, see Tikhomerov and Klochko, 1981.)

In short, there are multiple psychophysiological indicators (i.e., reaction time, nerve conduction rate, EEG, pupil dilation) pointing to individual differences in the efficiency of basic information processing in humans, differences in processing that, in turn, are related to global intelligence. Studies as-

sessing the heritability of speed of processing differences that are related to differences in intelligence (Baker, Vernon, & Ho, 1991; Ho, Baker, & Decker, 1988) have produced data consistent with the conclusion that speed of processing differences are highly heritable and that the association between speed of processing and intelligence is probably due to inherited common factors underlying both processing speed and intelligence. (A discussion about how psychologists study the heritability of intelligence and other characteristics is presented later in this chapter.)

Cognitivists working in traditions other than classical psychometric intelligence theory also are offering data consistent with the perspective that biologically mediated processing efficiency is related to intellectual growth. Kail's (e.g., 1992) research is especially notable in this regard. Kail studied 9-year-olds and adults. He measured their speed of processing as well as their performance on memory tasks, tasks that could be mediated by verbal rehearsal (e.g., digit span, letter span, free recall; see Chapter 2, this volume). The hypothesis was that speed of processing would predict memory performance, such that those who process faster would remember more. The assumption was that those who can process more quickly would be able to rehearse more, and this would improve memory. In general, the data supported this perspective. Moreover, consistent with Kail's (1991) previous research, there was a great increase in processing speed with development. One of the reasons that young adults are smarter than children is that they process more quickly (see also Kail, 1986), which results in more processing of to-be-learned content given the same amount of time, which results in greater total learning.

We expect much more such work as psychologists continue to probe potential linkages between biological competence, developmental changes in biology, and intelligence. We also expect more research on the biological determinants of individual differences in memory, language, and other complex competencies, including propensity to monitor one's processing. For the moment, we remind readers that from the outset of this book, we have emphasized the need for a healthy nervous system if a person is to be a good information processor, including relatively large functional short-term capacity, which is largely determined by the efficiency of information processing. Work like that conducted by Jensen and his colleagues as well as the research produced by neuroscientists investigating structure and function using neuroimaging supports these basic tenets of good information processing theory. These approaches are producing insights about academic competencies that are of focal concern to educational psychology. These traditional approaches are increasingly being superseded by methods yielding more direct evidence of physiological involvement in learning and thinking.

New Directions in Neurological Assessment

For many years, the best that physicians could do in producing brain images was x-rays (see Martin, Brust, & Hilal, 1991, for a review of conventional x-ray methods and the new developments covered in this subsection). A major limitation of x-rays is that they are two-dimensional images of three-dimensional objects. In addition, x-rays are useful for detecting only a limited range of disorders. More positively, **angiography** is a method of x-radiation that permits detailed study of the vascular system. This is accomplished by injecting the patient with material that is opaque to x-rays. The usefulness of this procedure is obvious when a suspected stroke victim comes to the emergency room. Angiography can be performed quickly to confirm or disconfirm the presence and location of cerebral bleeding and thus provides invaluable information about the probable immediate cause of the strokelike symptoms. The technique remains useful to the researcher community because it produces clearer images than some of the newer techniques.

Computed tomography (CT) scanning is a technology that involves x-ray beams projected through the head from different angles, with the beams received by x-ray detectors on the opposite side of the head from where the x-ray is currently being projected. The x-ray detectors feed the input into computer programs, with the end result being x-ray images of sections of the brain (i.e., cross-sections). These sections permit distinction between gray and white matter, with many structures within the brain distinguishable. CT scanning was a great advance over conventional x-rays in providing information about the structure of the brain.

Positron-emission tomography (PET) is an exceptionally important tool in studies of cognitive processing. As with CT scanning, x-rays are taken by rotating the camera around the head, producing images from a number of different angles. With

PET scanning, however, the subject has either been injected with or inhaled a substance that emits radiation. When neurons are active, they metabolize glucose. Some substances that emit radiation, such as radioactive fluorine, can bind with one of the products of metabolized glucose that accumulate in the active brain cells. The PET scan then detects the radiation being emitted from the active sites. The result is an image that literally glows. Because the PET scan is able to produce a number of cross-sections of the head, it is possible to map out in some detail the location of conscious processing. That is, x-rays and CT scans can provide only information about brain **structures;** with PET scans, there is the possibility of generating information about brain **functions.**

As a research tool, PET scanning is being used to determine the parts of the brain that are active in reaction to particular types of sensory and psychological stimulation. For example, studies have been conducted determining that different regions of the brain are activated by simple compared with complex visual stimulation. Other studies have established the parts of the brain affected by listening to complex auditory input, such as a story, as well as the parts of the brain affected by various types of dementia (e.g., Phelps, Mazziotta, and Huang, 1982; Risberg, 1986; Vernon, 1991). The potential of such technology is illustrated well by findings relating brain activity to performance on intelligence assessment subtests (see Chapter 16).

For example, in Haier et al. (1988), PET scans were made as subjects worked problems that appear on intelligence assessments. In Parks et al. (1988), PET scans were made as subjects performed verbal fluency items. There were clear correlations in these studies between brain activity as measured in the PET scans and performance on both the problems and verbal fluency items. The really interesting finding was that less glucose was metabolized by the subjects who solved more problems and answered more verbal items. That is, more intelligent subjects exerted less intellectual effort to do the test items. As Vernon (1991) concluded: "Persons of higher intelligence can solve . . . more complex . . . problems . . . than can persons of lower intelligence, and expend less energy in the process" (p. 391).

Magnetic resonance imaging (MRI) is a further advance in CT, one permitting exploration of neurological structures with higher resolution than permitted by PET scans. In fact, the resolution on these images approaches the resolution possible with light microscopic examinations of brain tissue obtained postmortem. This method involves placing the brain in strong magnetic fields (i.e., a person lies in the machine for about 15 minutes). Changes in the orientations of atomic nuclei in the molecules of the brain are induced and measured (Churchland & Sejnowski, 1992, Chapter 7). The precise measurement provided by MRI is permitting psychologists to resolve some old debates about intelligence. For example, does brain size correlate with psychometric intelligence (see Chapter 16)? The difficulty in resolving this debate before MRI was that brain size could only be determined through primitive means (e.g., measuring the girth of the head), and these primitive measurements often correlated little with differences in intelligence. MRI may change the verdict on the relationship of brain size to intelligence: Willerman, Schultz, Rutledge, and Bigler (1991) obtained a correlation of 0.41 between brain size as measured by MRI and psychometric intelligence, with other factors appropriately controlled in the calculation of this correlation. If Willerman et al.'s (1991) correlation is replicated, it would establish clearly the power of MRI as a tool for resolving debates that have not been resolvable using less sophisticated technologies (see Gould, 1981).

Since the middle of the 19th century, there have been students of brain who have postulated that particular functions are localized in particular parts of the brain—for example, Paul Broca's 1864 claim after discovering left hemisphere lesions during autopsies of the brains of people with verbal difficulties, *"Nous parlons avec l'hemisphere gauche!"* (Kandel, 1991, p. 10; translation: "We speak with the left hemisphere!"). Technology now exists to study in detail the anatomical regions involved in thinking by both healthy and injured brains, technology that can document the complex patterns of activation that undoubtedly underlie many functions. There is every reason to believe based on initial data that these methods are not simply going to confirm what is already known. For example, PET studies have failed to find any evidence of brain activity in the inferior parietal lobe when subjects are performing language tasks (e.g., Peterson, Fox, Posner, Mintun, & Raichle, 1988; Posner, Peterson, Fox, & Raichle, 1988), despite the fact that many biologically oriented models of language posit this region as critical to language (Caplan, 1992, Chapter 10). The betting is that a great deal about brain and how it functions is going to be learned as imaging research becomes more common.

The possibilities for scientific exploration of the brain and its relationship to intelligence and other psychological functions have expanded enormously with the development of new imaging techniques. Although neural scientists have hypothesized for more than a century (e.g., J. Hughlings Jackson who worked in the mid-19th century; Golden et al., 1992; Kosslyn & Koenig, 1992; McCarthy & Warrington, 1990) that complex cognitive functions involved interconnections between many parts of the brain, it is only as we approach the 21st century that the technological (e.g., imaging techniques) and conceptual (e.g., connectionist theories; see Chapter 3) machinery has existed to study how the brain does complex things. Some of the wonders that we have known about for some time, such as the ability of a young brain to find a new way to carry out a function when some important structure involved in its old way of functioning is damaged (discussed in detail in a subsequent section in this chapter), will undoubtedly be understood better in the decades ahead. That is not to say that we understand nothing about such functions at present, with much of the remainder of this chapter a testimony to the impressive understandings about relations between biology, cognition, and behavior that we have in the 1990s.

NEUROLOGICAL FOUNDATIONS OF COGNITION, LEARNING, AND BEHAVIOR

Although it is not possible in the 1990s to specify in detail how the brain permits learning, there has been enormous progress in understanding connections between neurological development, thinking, and performance. Much of the most impressive work has been conducted in the last decade. We summarize in this section some of the most important relationships between neurology and learning. Command of this small amount of knowledge can go a long way in understanding neurological ideas relevant to education. For those readers, however, who desire more detailed coverage, we strongly recommend Brown, Hopkins, and Keynes (1991); Goldman-Rakic, Isseroff, Schwartz, and Bugbee (1983); Johnson (1993); Martinez and Kesner (1991); and Parmelee and Sigman (1983), all of which informed the discussion presented here.

Human neurology begins as a single layer of cells lining the neural tube (Goldman-Rakic et al., 1983). These cells proliferate through normal cell division at an extremely rapid rate: At some points during development, approximately 48,000 new nerve cells are formed every second (Diamond, 1992). Through processes not completely understood, neural cells migrate to destinations corresponding to the beginnings of various parts of the nervous system. Most neurons will be formed and will have moved to their destinations by birth (Konner, 1991), with many of them making the migration long before birth. Once this period of **neurogenesis** is concluded, there will be no new neurons. Any that are lost owing to disease, injury, or normal death will not be replaced.

Axons and dendrites appear once neurons have migrated to their designated locations. Each nerve cell normally has one **axon,** which conducts impulses away from the cell body. **Dendrites** are branch like extensions of the cell body that transmit impulses toward the cell body from other cells. Eventually, **synaptic connections** between neurons are established. These connections involve an axon meeting a dendrite, a cell body, or another axon. Once the physical connections are formed, physical and chemical characteristics that permit transmission of impulses can develop (Gibson & Petersen, 1991). If that occurs, transmissions from a nerve cell to other cells can be sent via the synapses involving the axon for the cell (Gardner, 1975, Chapter 3).

The basic neuroanatomical structures that compose the human nervous system are in place by about 8 weeks following fertilization (Gardner, 1975, Chapter 9). The first reactive behaviors can be detected at this time as well, in the form of some basic reflexes. Even so, compared with other mammals, human newborns are neurologically immature (Gibson, 1991a, 1991b). There is substantial development of human neurological competence following birth. In particular, the cerebral cortex, the part of the brain responsible for many of the complex thought processes carried out during human thinking, expands greatly after birth.

Neurological Development Following Birth

Three-fourths of brain development occurs following birth, even though all of the neurons a person will ever have have been formed (Prechtl, 1986). Neurons take a long time to mature (Gibson & Petersen, 1991). With maturity, there are changes in the dendrites and the axons. Dendrites start out as short, tubular, and unbranched. With development,

they become longer and have many branches. The longer and more numerous the branches, the more sources that potentially can stimulate the dendrites and thus result in transmissions to the nerve cell (e.g., Diamond, 1992). Neuronal cell functioning is increasingly more adaptive and flexible with increasing dendritic arborization. As the dendrites are branching, the axons acquire a layer of axon sheathing. This permits more rapid firing of the axons and much greater specificity of firing. It then takes less stimulation for a myelinized axon to fire, and the recovery period between firings decreases.

Other structures that support the functioning of the nervous system are maturing at the same time (e.g., blood vessels). One type of cell that becomes more evident during this period, **glial cells,** is particularly interesting. Glial cells provide nourishment to neurons and thus are critical to the functioning of the central nervous system. An anecdote that is often cited as correlational evidence that glial cells may play an important role in determining individual differences in mental functioning is that Einstein's brain had a much larger proportion of glial cells than average brains (Diamond, Scheibel, Murphy, & Harvey, 1985).

There are some forms of experience that the brain is genetically programmed to expect. Some areas of specialization in the brain correspond to perceptual systems (visual, haptic, gustatory, olfactory); others to affective systems, cognitive capacities, or linguistic competencies (Anastasiow, 1990; Fodor, 1983; Panksepp, 1986). One mechanism of genetic preparedness is the generation of **experience-expectant synapses** (Greenough & Juraska, 1986), with a proliferation of these 2 to 3 months following birth. Experience-expectant synapses for the visual system are sensitive to light; those corresponding to hearing are sensitive to auditory input. When relevant stimulation is encountered, neurons are activated, and their functioning results in the establishment of permanent synaptic connections with other neurons. Experience-expectant synapses that do not stabilize die off—they are pruned (see Anastasiow, 1990, for a review of evidence pertaining to these conclusions; Black & Greenough, 1991; Crutcher, 1991). The existence of experience-expectant synapses makes clear that there can be simultaneous biological predetermination of learning and environmental determination of learning: Each member of a species is programmed to be sensitive to particular types of input, but learning occurs only if that input is experienced.

In general, experience-expectant synapses either stabilize or die off during **critical periods.** For the sensory systems, these critical periods tend to be early in life (Greenough, Black, & Wallace, 1987). For example, if particular visual experiences do not occur early in development, visual perception is impaired for life regardless of subsequent remediation efforts. Thus, Hubel and Wiesel's (1970) kittens, who were deprived of light for the first 8 weeks of their lives, seemed as if they were blind once they were exposed to light. What happened is that experience-expectant synapses did not function during their critical period and hence failed to stabilize—they died off before the expected input was experienced (Black & Greenough, 1991).

For humans, the critical period for some visual capabilities is considerably longer than 8 weeks. For example, Aslin (1981) demonstrated that strabismus (a disorder involving poor muscular control of the eyes) treated before age 5 produced no long-term impairment; left untreated for more than 4 years, strabismus has a marked dysfunctional impact on the organization of the visual system (Anastasiow, 1990). That is, the stimulation provided to neurons via strabismus-disordered sensory organs and encoded via experience-expectant synapses is the wrong information, resulting in stabilization of the experience-expectant synapses in dysfunctional ways.

Other synapses, **experience-dependent synapses** (Greenough & Juraska, 1986), are not genetically predetermined. Instead, they stabilize in reaction to unique environmental stimulation that an individual encounters. The environment provides "unexpected" input to the organism that can be learned because of the possibility of stabilizing experience-dependent synapses. These types of synapses can be stabilized at any time during life (Anastasiow, 1990).

That synaptic connections are stabilized by repeated firing of one neuron near another was originally proposed by Hebb (1949) in *The Organization of Behavior:* "[When] . . . an axon of cell A is near enough to excite cell B or repeatedly or persistently takes part in firing it, some growth process or metabolic change takes place in one or both cells such that A's efficiency, as one of the cells firing B, increased" (p. 62). In simpler terms, the more often excitation of cell A results in the firing of cell B, the stronger the connection between the two and the more certain that B is fired whenever A is fired. If neuron A is never stimulated by the environment, it cannot fire and form a connection at its synapses

with B. Of course, more than two neurons are involved in most learning, with Hebb proposing that what are formed are **cell assemblies** or closed paths including a number of neurons synaptically connected to one another (see the related discussion of connectionism in Chapter 3, this book, a modern theory that borrows this idea from Hebb's perspective). Thus, humans can process visual information the way they do because they have formed cell assemblies organizing neurons that are sensitive to visual input. These cell assemblies were formed when visual information was experienced during the critical period, when the cells sensitive to visual input were particularly rich with open experience-expectant synapses. If visual stimulation does not occur within a particular period after the formation of the open experience-expectant synapses, the synapses will be pruned.

In addition to pruning of synapses (Gibson, 1991b; Gibson & Petersen, 1991), there also is substantial death of neurons during this early period of life. In fact, half of the neurons a person generates before birth have already died by the time birth occurs. Up to half of the remaining neurons in some sites of the brain die within a few years after birth (Crutcher, 1991; Diamond, 1992; Oppenheim, 1981; Shonkoff & Marshall, 1990). Such death is genetically preprogrammed for the most part, with the cells that are eliminated not critical to later functioning (e.g., Gardner, 1975, p. 183). In fact, it is likely that elimination of excess synapses and nerve cells is necessary for cognitive development to proceed to maturity (Goldman-Rakic, 1987).

The remainder of this section is concerned with three additional ways that the central nervous system matures (i.e., besides physical growth of neurons, formation of synapses, and pruning of excess synapses and neurons). Two of these additional mechanisms are global, physical growth and myelination; the third involves development of a particular region of the brain that is the contemporary focus of intensive investigations because of its probable contributions to self-regulation, with discussion of this region important in this book because good information processing is self-regulated cognition if it is anything.

Physical Growth

There are striking changes in brain structure and function in the two years following birth (Konner, 1991). For instance, between birth and age 1, the brain doubles in volume. By age 1, it is a little more than half the size of an adult brain. The growth rate continues to be high during year 2.

Is the physical growth of the brain simply a preprogrammed unfolding, or is its development tied to experience? The work of Marian Diamond (e.g., 1991) and her colleagues with rats suggests that experience can play a large role in the physical development of the brain. They have conducted a number of experiments in which rats (from pups to "elderly" rats) have either received environmental enrichment (e.g., objects to explore, climb, and sniff) or they have not. In general, environmental enrichment has increased the size of the brain, in particular cortical thickness. Enrichment also increases dendritic branching and the number of the dendritic spines. It promotes proliferation of capillaries, increasing blood flow in the brain. The growth of glial-type cells also is stimulated by appropriate environmental stimulation (Diamond, 1992; Greenough, 1993). In contrast, isolating animals can retard neurological growth as well as development of tissue that supports central nervous system functioning, such as blood vessels and glial cells. See M. Diamond (1988, 1991) and Greenough, Black, and Wallace (1987; also Greenough, 1993) for reviews of the evidence pertaining to physical growth of the brain as a function of environmental stimulation.

Does enrichment as M. Diamond has defined it make a difference in learning? M. Diamond (1991, p. 117) concluded: "At every age at which they have been tested, enriched rats have run a maze better than the nonenriched animals." This, of course, parallels the finding that the physical size of the brain can be affected by experience across the rat's life span. In summary, M. Diamond and other researchers have amassed considerable evidence that the brain is plastic, that its fundamental physical properties, including size and number of synaptic connections, vary with environmental stimulation. Although extrapolations from rats to humans must be made with caution, the extrapolation is tempting and M. Diamond makes it:

> . . . [E]nriched rats . . . become smarter than average rats with larger than average brains. We expect the same is true of humans. Environmental enrichment will produce smarter than average humans. (M. Diamond, 1991, p. 120)

Myelination

The speed and specificity of neurological functioning are determined by myelination (i.e., the development of a myelin sheath that envelops neurons), which in turn is determined by genetic programming (Gibson, 1991a, 1991b). Myelin is a fatty sheath that insulates both peripheral and central nerve fibers in mammals (Konner, 1991). This sheath permits rapid conduction of impulses. Myelination begins before birth in humans. By 8 to 12 months of age, those parts of the nervous system responsible for sensorimotor functioning are myelinated at a density consistent with adult myelination. Myelination continues for many years in humans, however. In general, myelination occurs first in the inner areas of the cortex and later in the outer cortical areas. For example, some outer layers of the cortex involved in learning of associations—areas critical in learning of complex behaviors and ideas—do not myelinate until 4 to 8 years of age. The cortical areas of humans continue to acquire myelin at least until adolescence and may do so until 30 years of age.

The importance of myelination is obvious when it is lost owing to either disease or an intentional experimental manipulation (Konner, 1991): Impulse speed is slowed. It takes longer for a nerve cell to recover after firing (i.e., the latency between firings is greater). Conduction failures are more frequent. There is an increased likelihood of inadvertent electrical effects from neighboring axons. There is greater risk of dysfunction owing to mechanical and thermal factors as well as other stimulation. When myelin is reacquired, cell functioning returns to normal. In short, the evidence that myelination affects neural cell functioning is strong.

The evidence is also strongly suggestive (i.e., it cannot be definitive because other changes are correlated with myelination) that myelination makes a difference at grosser levels than the cell level (Konner, 1991). For example, just before birth, major neurons affecting vision are myelinated; there is rapid development of visual capability during this same period. Parts of the cerebral cortex concerned with hearing achieve myelination during the first 2 years of life, with myelination in these centers paralleling the development of language. See Konner (1991) for an extended discussion of the correspondences between neurological myelination and behavioral development.

Development of Frontal Lobes

The frontal lobes are especially critical with respect to self-regulation and self-control—which are key as part of the development of good information processing. There are massive developments in these lobes during the first 2 years of life, accompanied by shifts in behavior.

Shifts in frontal lobe structure are apparent in that the layers of the frontal cortex are not as thick in newborns as in 1- to 2-year-olds (Larroche, 1966). Synaptic branching and connections are not extensive in the frontal lobes of infants in the first few months of life (Schade & van Groennigen, 1961) but are more apparent and more complex by 1 year of age (Huttenlocher, 1979). Myelin sheathing is lacking in the frontal lobes during the early months of life but develops over the course of the first year (Yakovlev & Lecours, 1967). In addition, the density of neurons in infancy is greater than during the preschool years because some of the neurons die as a function of normal development.

There also are dramatic changes in behavioral functioning with the development of the frontal cortex during the first year of life. The work of Adele Diamond (e.g., 1990a, 1990c, 1991) and her colleagues has been especially illuminating with respect to relationships between frontal lobe development and cognitive functioning. They have studied human infants' ability to find an object hidden at one of two locations (A or B) as an indicator of frontal lobe development, based on a paradigm developed by Piaget (1954 [1937]). An object is hidden in full view of a baby with a delay imposed between the hiding and when the child can retrieve the object. The object is consistently hidden on one side (either A or B) until the child is correct and then the object is hidden on the other side.

A classic error in young infants (i.e., under 6 months) is that they make what is known as the "A, not B" error, which involves reaching to the place where the object was hidden and retrieved on the last trial rather than reaching to the place where the object was hidden on this trial. This error is more likely the longer the delay. A. Diamond (1985) identified a developmental progression such that the "A, not B" error could be induced with delays of 2 to 5 seconds in $7\frac{1}{2}$- to 9-month-old infants. By 12 months of age, the "A, not B" error did not occur even with delays of 10 seconds. The point is that this improvement in performance occurs during the period when the frontal lobe is developing.

Some of the most striking evidence in support of this position has been produced by Fox and Bell (1990) at the University of Maryland. They have documented changes during the second semester of life in frontal lobe functioning using electrophysiological methods. They have also found clear associations between these changes and performance on tasks such as "A, not B."

Other tasks involving retrieval following a delay are solved more capably by the end of the second semester of life than they were at the beginning of the second semester. The "delayed response" task is identical to the "A, not B" task except that where the object is hidden is randomly varied. Successful retrieval by 7-month-olds is more likely with a 2- or 3-second delay than with a 10-second delay. Twelve-month-olds perform the delayed response task well at a 10-second delay interval. The "object delay" task involves retrieving an object from a box with an open side that faces away from the baby. Infants aged $6\frac{1}{2}$ to 8 months cannot retrieve the object if the side of the box facing them is opaque. With increasing age, there are improvements in performance so that by 11 to 12 months there were no babies in A. Diamond's sample who could not retrieve the object from the box—even in the most demanding situation, which was with an opaque side of the box facing the baby.

What these three tasks ("A, not B," delayed response, and object retrieval) have in common is that infants must relate information over space or time in order to solve them. In addition, all involve inhibiting a predominant response—the last response in the case of the first two tasks and the tendency to reach straight for an object as seen in the object retrieval task (especially apparent when a transparent closed side of the box faced the child, with the child required to reach around the box to retrieve the object). By considering the data described thus far as well as the performance of adults with frontal lobe damage on similar tasks, A. Diamond (e.g., Diamond & Gilbert, 1989) reached the conclusions that frontal lobe development during the first year of life mediated the performance gains by permitting greater integration over space and time and by permitting inhibition of dominant responses (i.e., by permitting organization and regulation of behavior, which is another way of saying that frontal lobe development improved self-regulative abilities). Impressive correlations between changes in electrophysiological indices and performance on these tasks (Fox & Bell, 1990, who studied both "A, not B" and object retrieval) go far in increasing confidence in A. Diamond's conclusions.

We expect that many intricate linkages between development of the frontal lobes and development of thinking and learning skills will be mapped out as researchers continue to study development of the frontal lobes in the early days of life. Dempster (1992) provided an extremely expansive essay of the importance of inhibition in cognition across the life span, linking life-span developmental shifts in inhibition and self-regulation to developmental changes in the frontal lobes (see also Bjorklund & Harnishfeger, 1990, for development of similar themes).

Concluding Comments

With changes in neurological capacity, ones owing to either experience or normal development, there are changes in cognitive capabilities. All of the data discussed here suggest close linkages between neurological and psychological development during infancy. The importance of biology as a determinant of thinking, learning, and performance is apparent, especially when something goes wrong, which is taken up later in this chapter.

One of the values of the type of research reviewed in this section is that it has helped in understanding some interventions that can prevent development from going terribly wrong. One famous example makes this point dramatically.

Some children are born with the inability to metabolize the amino acid phenylalanine. (Children with this deficiency have come to be known as PKU [phenylketonuria] babies.) This is a problem because greater than normal amounts of phenylalanine can cause severe neurological damage. There is at least a partial cure, however. First, determine at birth whether a child lacks the capacity to break down phenylalanine, which can be done with a simple urine test. The diets of PKU children are then strictly controlled so that they ingest only a small amount of phenylalanine. If PKU is not detected until 3 years of age, intervention does little good, however, with profound retardation the outcome (see Zigler & Hodapp, 1986, Chapter 9 for a review). When dietary control commences shortly after birth, general intelligence seems to be impaired little, although there is evidence of subtle impairments in executive functioning (i.e., self-regulation of cognition; Welsh, Pennington, Ozonoff, Rouse, & McCabe, 1990), presumably because of subtle dysfunctions in the frontal lobes (see the discussion of the role of the frontal lobes in cognition presented earlier in this section). With increasing age, less strict dietary control is necessary (Scarr & Kidd, 1983); nonetheless, with increasing evidence that high levels of phenylalanine can produce damage even in later childhood, dietary controls are only relaxed and not eliminated (Stern, 1985).

Why so much damage if the disorder is not identified early in life and less need to control the diet later in life? The myelinated nervous system is much more resistant to the biological assault from high levels of phenylalanine than is the nervous system that is not yet myelinated. Moreover, the first several years of life are characterized by enormous growth in the central nervous system. During periods of growth, biological systems are much more vulnerable than at other times.

There is at least one important danger for adults with PKU. A PKU woman who is not on a low-phenylalanine diet who becomes pregnant runs a great risk of giving birth to a retarded baby whose developing nervous system has been largely destroyed by high levels of phenylalanine in the mother's blood (Scarr & Kidd, 1983; Stern, 1985). By understanding biology, it is possible not only to reduce the impact of PKU on affected individuals, but also protect the children that PKU women conceive.

Although PKU is the most well-known of birth disorders that can be treated through diet interventions, there are a number of biological-dietary disorders that if left untreated result in mental retardation (e.g., Fernandez & Samuels, 1986). With treatment, usually the addition of a dietary supplement, the risks of retardation generally are reduced or eliminated. Unfortunately, not all biological risks are so easily handled, apparent from the work reviewed later in this chapter.

BIOLOGICALLY DETERMINED BIASES AND CONSTRAINTS IN COGNITION, LEARNING, AND BEHAVIOR

There are many similarities in the knowledge that all people acquire and the things that people can do. The most likely explanation of human universals is that biology prepares humans to attend to some information more than other information and to be able to do some things and not others. Of course, this is an idea consistent with the earlier argument that there are experience-expectant synapses and with an argument that will be advanced later in this chapter, that there are modules of competencies sensitive to particular modes of input. Another possibility is that biological competencies constrain what can be learned. The credibility of both of these perspectives is taken up in this section.

Sensation Preferences

Even young babies prefer some forms of visual stimulation over others, although preferences change with development. Thus, 1-month-olds prefer stripes over a bull's-eye pattern, whereas slightly older children prefer the bull's-eye (Fantz & Nevis, 1967). With increasing age, there is increasing preference for more complex visual stimulation (Brennan, Ames, & Moore, 1966; Hershenson, Munsinger, & Kessen, 1965; Munsinger & Weir, 1967). From birth onward, there is a bias toward looking at contours of shapes, which is adaptive because the contour defines the shape (for a review, see Banks & Salapatek, 1983). There are clear biases in visual perception that result in humans processing some types of information more than others.

Biological Preparedness for Particular Acquisitions

Seligman and Hager (1972) and others (e.g., Foree & LoLordo, 1973) advanced the theory that organisms are biologically prepared to emit some responses and learn some associations more easily than others. For instance, some complex responses are innate. Thus, many species of animals have characteristic defensive and avoidance actions. For instance, mice do not learn to run and flee from owls—they run and flee the first time they see an owl (Bolles, 1970). Running and fleeing is biologically hardwired for mice as a defensive reaction, which makes it easy to "teach" as a behavior that can be carried out in situations other than in the presence of an owl. A few electrical shocks in a particular situation and a mouse will learn to run and flee when the situation is encountered in the future (Bolles, 1970). An example of biologically mediated associative learning is that taste aversions to poisonous foods seem to be acquired easily by many animals (Garcia & Koelling, 1966; Garcia & Garcia y Robertson, 1985). In humans, this form of classical conditioning is the famous "sauce bernaise" effect (Seligman & Hager, 1972): Nausea shortly after eating a preferred food (e.g., sauce bernaise) can produce aversion to that food for a long time. Author MP once experienced

severe nausea and vomiting shortly after eating fruit gelatin. For a number of years after this episode, MP never had room for Jello! If he was going through a cafeteria line that included Jello, he had to turn away when he came to that portion of the line or risk conditioned nausea. Humans have evolved to avoid foods that make them sick because it often is dangerous to eat sickening food, and doing so reduces the likelihood that one will survive long enough to parent offspring who will carry one's genes into the future.

There is little doubt that from early in life (probably from birth), humans can learn some associations via classical conditioning readily (Lipsitt, 1990). Thus, if a puff of air to the eyelid, which elicits an unconditioned eyelid blinking response, is preceded consistently by a tone, which by itself has no capacity to elicit eye blinking, the tone alone eventually will come to elicit eye blinking. This ability to acquire conditioned blinking is inherited as part of the genetic blueprint for humanness; humans have evolved to be so readily conditioned to blink eyes because blinking before something hits the eye prevents injury of a critical sensory organ and thus increases the likelihood that the blinker will survive long enough to reproduce.

A good case can also be made that long-lasting fearful reactions to stimuli associated with pain are easily learned by humans via classical conditioning (Bandura, 1986, Chapter 5; Hoffman, 1969). Again, a personal example comes to mind immediately. During his hospitalization a number of years ago, MP had a nasogastric tube in him for some time, an extremely uncomfortable situation. To this day when he visits a hospital, there is a rush of anxiety when he sees a nasogastric apparatus in a hallway.

One possibility is that at least some biological preparedness may decrease with advancing age. This is because with advancing age, some forms of classical conditioning (e.g., eyelid conditioning) are much less certain than they were earlier in life (Woodruff-Pak, Logan, & Thompson, 1990). Neurological decline with advancing age reduces conditionability (e.g., loss of Purkinje cells in the cerebellum probably accounts for age-related reductions in susceptibility to eyelid conditioning). From a biological perspective, this is an understandable development because what counts is preserving the young organism; once an organism is past the age of reproduction, there is less biological need to equip the organism for survival because survival of the postreproductive organism does not have as certain consequences for the survival of the organism's genes.

Biological Preparedness for Language

Biological preparedness is not limited to acquisition of simple associations or basic perceptual processing. Indeed, the evidence is strong that humans are unique in being biologically prepared to learn the exceptionally complex systems of representation that compose language (e.g., Chomsky, 1965, 1980a, 1980b). For example, Chomsky claims that humans all have the competence to acquire language, that there is a genetically determined "language acquisition device" in the human mind.

To be certain, many of the particulars of the biological claims made by Chomsky and his associates are debated (e.g., Lieberman, 1984, 1989): For example, Chomsky's claims about universal and invariant grammatical capabilities that are uniquely human flies in the face of the principle that genetically determined behaviors manifest genetic variability. Any language acquisition device would have to be transmitted by multiple genes, with the potential for variability enormous given the many potential combinations of genetic parameters. That there are enormous variabilities in human language competencies is, in fact, more consistent with the conclusion that language ability varies similar to other genetically determined characteristics than it is consistent with Chomsky's position that human language capabilities are generally invariant. At the very least, multigenic determination of individual differences in language capabilities is a reasonable hypothesis (Hardy-Brown, 1983; Hardy-Brown & Plomin, 1985; Hardy-Brown, Plomin, & DeFries, 1981).

The "uniquely human" claim made by Chomsky also flies in the face of what is known about genetics. Chomsky's position on this point is so extreme as to elicit ridicule from biologically oriented scholars in language, for example, by references to Chomsky as "the creationists' grammarian" (Greenfield & Savage-Rumbaugh, 1990). Evolution is gradual, and differences between species with respect to communications and symbolic skills tend to reflect this gradualness (Parker & Gibson, 1990). It is not credible to claim, based on what is now known about comparative communication and cognition, that humans have a language capacity that is completely different from the capacities of the great

apes. A diverse number of characteristics have evolved in humans that support language and the learning of language (Lieberman, 1984, 1989). For instance, Lieberman argues that human speech and neural speech perception mechanisms have evolved. Great apes other than humans have some understanding of number (Boysen & Berntson, 1990), use categories to some extent (Matsuzawa, 1990), can learn to use sign language with some sophistication (e.g., Miles, 1990), and, perhaps most interesting, given Chomsky's particular emphasis on the grammatical competence of humans relative to other species, may be able to invent grammatical rules (Greenfield & Savage-Rumbaugh, 1990).

Theories linking biology and language comprehension and learning have been supported by a variety of data (Maratsos, 1989): For example, left hemisphere damage results in language disabilities, with particular sites in the left hemisphere associated with particular language difficulties (McCarthy & Warrington, 1990). Children acquire languages in many different settings and in many different cultures. Despite such biological determinism, however, language learning is also diverse. Maratsos (1989) specified many ways that languages vary across cultures. For example, different parts of sentences receive focus in different languages. Also, the constituents of sentences (e.g., agents and patients [objects]) are typically ordered in one way in some languages such as English and are not marked for order in other languages. Some variation in what humans can acquire makes clear that humans have the capacity to learn a range of language rules, a capacity that is certainly biologically determined.

One recurring issue in the language literature is whether there is biological constraint with respect to the age at which a second language can be acquired: Is there a critical period for second-language learning? Lenneberg (1967), in particular, proposed that language learning would be much more difficult after puberty than before puberty, arguing that biological biases facilitating incidental learning of language decrease with increasing age during childhood and into adolescence. As it turns out, the issue is complicated. When the early stages of learning are considered, adults clearly learn both syntax and pronunciation more rapidly than children. As far as eventual attainment is concerned, however, the earlier one begins learning a second language, the more certainty that there will be eventual facility in the foreign language with respect both to syntax and pronunciation, with those who begin a second language in early childhood decidedly advantaged over those who begin later (Johnson & Newport, 1989).

For example, when the English of native Korean and Chinese adults who immigrated to the United States is examined, there is a strong correlation between the age at which they immigrated and syntactical competence (Johnson & Newport, 1989): Those who arrived between 3 and 7 years of age are more competent than those who arrived between 8 and 10, who are more competent than those arriving between 11 and 15, who are more competent than those arriving at an older age. In general, data such as these are consistent with Lenneberg's position that language proficiency is more certain if acquisition of a language begins before puberty, although Lenneberg suggested more precipitous decline in language-learning abilities with the onset of puberty, whereas Johnson and Newport (1989) observed a gradual developmental decline.

Biologically Determined Constraints in Cognitive Capacity

A final biologically determined constraint is due to short-term capacity limitations (see the discussions of short-term memory in all previous chapters). In particular, it has been known since Baldwin (Hollander, 1920) that how much children can attend at any one time increases with development. Baldwin assumed that the increases in **attention span** were somehow tied to maturation of the nervous system and that the attention span constrained a child's cognitive development. Variations on this theme have recurred in the developmental psychology literatures, with the most recent versions offered by Pascual-Leone (1970) and Case (1985).

Case's version of attention span is called **executive processing space** and refers to the number of pieces of information a child can have active at any one time while working toward some cognitive goal. Much of this executive processing space is **short-term storage space,** which is specifically dedicated to maintaining the activated information in consciousness rather than other executive activities (i.e., manipulations of the information aimed at accomplishing some cognitive goal). Much of Case's (1985) book is concerned with demonstrating that children can only do tasks that do not require more executive processing space than the children have. Some of the educational prescriptions that follow

from Case's (1985) viewpoint are that (1) tasks should be analyzed for the capacity demands they put on students relative to the capacities possessed by students; (2) many complex tasks should be simplified; (3) teacher assistance, in the form of coaching and prompting, is often required to complete many complex tasks; and (4) materials and the learning environment should sometimes be engineered to reduce short-term capacity demands, with concomitant increases in performance with decreases in short-term demands (e.g., see Miller, Woody-Ramsey, & Aloise, 1991, for a demonstration of performance improvements as capacity demands decrease). Indeed, at several points in this book, there will be reference to interventions that are hypothesized to improve student performance by reducing short-term capacity demands. In particular, there will be expansion of Case's views on the role of short-term memory in cognition.

Biological Constraints on Intelligence and Academic Achievement

Beginning with Galton's 19th century insight that distinguished people tend to be closely related to one another, psychologists have entertained the hypothesis that talents of various sorts—including high psychometric intelligence—are inherited. Such hypotheses have not been accepted uncritically, however. When two bright people marry and have children, they would be expected to create a different environment for their offspring than would a husband and wife of average intelligence. That intellectually superior people and talented people provide environmental opportunities to their children not available to other children logically could be the critical factor in stimulating the intelligence or talents of the offspring rather than biological advantages.

A subfield of both psychology and genetics has emerged to address questions of nature or nurture through analyses of behavioral similarities as a function of biological relatedness. **Behavior geneticists** use several different approaches to unravel the relative contributions of heredity and environment to individual differences in human characteristics. We review the two most common methodological approaches used by behavior geneticists and the conclusions about biological determination of intelligence emanating from these studies.

Twin Studies   In humans, there is only one way to have two people with absolutely identical genes:

Identical twins have the same genes because the two children were produced by a division of the same fertilized egg. When identical twins are reared together (i.e., in the same family), their environments are also similar, perhaps as similar as any two person's environments could be. Thus, the high correlations in intelligence between identical twins (i.e., usually 0.80 to 0.90 or higher) reared together cannot alone be revealing about genetic versus environmental determinants of intelligence.

Sometimes, however, identical twins are reared apart. In that case, their genes are identical but their environments differ. If genes determine intelligence, the correlation in intelligence between identical twins reared apart should remain high; to the degree that environment determines differences in intelligence, the correlation in intelligence should be lower for identical twins reared apart than the correlation for identical twins reared together. Another comparison possibility is to look at fraternal twins reared together. Fraternal twins share one-half of their genes (i.e., they are the product of two different fertilized eggs). When they are reared in the same family, they should have roughly comparable environments. If the correlations in their IQs are lower than the IQ correlations for identical twins reared together, the case would be bolstered for genetic determination of environment. If the IQs of fraternal twins raised together approximated the IQs of identical twins reared together, the environmental hypothesis would be supported.

Summarizing over 19 studies involving more than 5000 pairs of twins, Loehlin and Nichols (1976) concluded that the average IQ of identical twins is 0.86, which is higher than the 0.62 IQ correlation for fraternal twins. Bouchard and McGue (1981) reviewed the world twin literature, which includes data on more than 10,000 twin pairs, and concluded that the average IQ correlation for identical twins is 0.86 and for fraternal twins is 0.60. Bouchard and McGue (1981) identified three IQ correlations involving identical twins reared apart, with the average correlation being 0.72.

Behavior geneticists use data such as these to calculate the **heritability** of intelligence, or the fraction of observed variation in intelligence that is due to genetic variability (Plomin et al., 1990, Chapter 9). In general, they have concluded that roughly half of the variability in intelligence is due to genes. That genes matter is obvious from the higher correlations for identical than for fraternal twins. That environ-

ment matters also is obvious as well: The IQs of identical twins reared together are more similar than the IQs of identical twins reared apart.

Family and Adoption Studies In family and adoption studies, family members are thought of as sharing either heredity only (i.e., parents and their biological children living in other families), family environment only (i.e., parents and adopted children), or both heredity and family environment (i.e., parents and biological children living in the same household). In general, if genes determine individual differences in intelligence, correlations should be higher when there is shared heredity. If family environment determines individual differences in intelligence, there should be higher correlations when correlated pairs live in the same family environment. If both genes and environment matter, the highest correlations in intelligence between family members should occur when there is both shared heredity and family environment. Thus, if intelligence is inherited, the IQs of adopted children should correlate with the IQs of their biological parents more than with the IQs of their adoptive parents. If environment matters more than genes, the IQs of adopted children should correlate more highly with the IQs of the adoptive than the biological parents. If intelligence is determined by genes, there should be a higher correlation for the intelligence of children who are biological siblings (i.e., because they have 50 percent of their genes in common) than for the intelligence of siblings by adoption (i.e., because they have no genetic relationship to one another).

Bouchard and McGue's (1981) review provided a comprehensive analysis of the available data up until 1981. In support of the role of heredity as a determinent of individual differences in IQ are comparisons such as the following: (1) The IQ correlation for parents and their offspring when reared in the home of their biological parents is 0.42. This contrasts to a .19 correlation between adopting parents and adoptees. (2) The IQ correlation for biological siblings reared together is 0.47. This contrasts with the IQ correlation for biological half-siblings (who share one-quarter of their genes) reared together of 0.31 and the IQ correlation for nonbiological siblings of 0.32. (3) Parents share half their genes with their offspring; biological siblings share half their genes. It is striking that the biological parent-offspring correlation of 0.42 is close in magnitude to the biological sibling correlation of 0.47.

The role of the environment in the determination of differences in IQ is supported by the following comparisons in Bouchard and McGue (1981): (1) The IQ correlation for biological siblings reared together is 0.47 compared with an IQ correlation for biological siblings reared apart of 0.24. (2) The IQ correlation between biological parents and their children when they live together is 0.42 versus 0.22 when they do not live together. (3) Half-siblings and cousins both share one-quarter of their genes; the IQ correlation for half-siblings is 0.31 compared with a 0.15 correlation for cousins. (4) That the IQ correlation of 0.47 for biological siblings raised in the same family is the highest correlation in the nontwin family data is consistent with the overall conclusion that emerges from considering the differences just summarized: Both genes and family environment are important in determining individual differences in IQ. Using some extremely sophisticated statistical methods, Chipeur, Rovine, and Plomin (1990) estimated from the twin and family/adoption data that 45 percent of the variance in IQ scores is determined by heredity.

Three aspects of the adoption data provide especially striking support for the effects of environment in determining individual differences in intelligence. (1) The correlation in intelligence between adopted siblings increases as they live together longer, from 0.00 to 0.25 over the first 4 years of life in Plomin, DeFries, and Fulker's (1988) study; the correlation in intelligences of adopted children and their adopting parents increases from 0 to 4 years of age as well, from about 0.1 to 0.2 in the Plomin et al. (1988) study. The longer adoptive families are together, the greater the correlations in intelligence.

(2) As children grow up, the family accounts for less of their environment as friends become more important and children make progressively greater inroads into the world. Perhaps not surprisingly, the intelligence level of the adopting family is progressively less of a determinant of individual differences in intelligence of adoptees as adoptees move through childhood into adolescence and adulthood (Loehlin, Horn, & Willerman, 1989).

(3) In a number of adoption studies, children have been raised in families in which the family level of intelligence was higher than the biological-family intelligence of the adoptee. The intelligence of the adoptees tends to be higher on average than the average intelligence expected based on biological-group/socioeconomic-group of the biological parents, often closer to the average of the biological-

group/socioeconomic-group means for the adopting family. This is one of the most frequently cited pieces of evidence favoring the hypothesis that environment makes a profound difference with respect to level of intellectual functioning. These effects are especially likely when the adoption occurs at an early age for the child (e.g., Scarr & Weinberg, 1976, 1983; Weinberg, Scarr, & Waldman, 1992; see Storfer, 1990, Chapter 4, for a review of the adoption data supportive of strong environmental effects of rearing environment). Even those critical of adoption studies, and who tend to favor environmental interpretations over genetic explanations of intelligence differences, admit, based on the adoption data, that there is probably a 10- to 12-point IQ advantage associated with rearing in a more favorable environment (see Locurto's, 1990, review of the adoption study data).

Before leaving adoption studies, it is also important to point out that there is evidence in the adoption studies that long-term exposure to an environment lower in quality than the environment of one's biological parents decreases IQ. A particularly relevant study was conducted by Capron (1987) and Duyme (1987) in France (also, Capron & Duyme, 1989). The design was a two × two setup: Biological parents were either of upper-middle-class socioeconomic status (SES) or lower-class status; rearing parents were either of upper-middle-class SES or lower-class status. That is, some children born into upper-middle-class families were adopted into similar families, and some were adopted into poorer families; some children born of poor parents were adopted into upper-middle-class families, and some were adopted into other poor families. The results were clear:

High SES birth family, high SES rearing family:
　　IQ = 120
High SES birth family, low SES rearing family:
　　IQ = 108
Low SES birth family, high SES rearing family:
　　IQ = 104
Low SES birth family, low SES rearing family:
　　IQ = 92

There was about a 12-point decrement when a child born into a high-SES family experienced a low SES environment; there was a 12-point advantage when a child born in a low-SES family was adopted by a high-SES family. What should be apparent from this example is that both the birth family (i.e., genes) and the rearing family (i.e., environment) affect psychometric intelligence.

Academic Achievement For those who might want more direct evidence about the potential role of heredity in determining academic success than can be gleaned from IQ studies, there is evidence that academic success is substantially heritable (Plomin et al.,1990): The school grades of identical twins correlate more highly than do the school grades of fraternal twins (Husén, 1959). Correlations on standardized academic achievement tests are higher for identical than fraternal twins (Loehlin & Nichols, 1976). If one twin is reading-disabled, an identical twin mate is more likely to be reading-disabled than a fraternal twin mate (Bakwin, 1973; Decker & Vandenberg, 1985; DeFries, Fulker, & LaBuda, 1987). Analyses of adoption data also suggest that reading ability is largely, but not completely, inherited (Cardon, DiLalla, Plomin, DeFries, & Fulker, 1990), although the adoption data also substantiate that success in school is determined in part by the quality of the adopting environment (e.g., Duyme, 1988).

More Evidence of Both Biological and Environmental Determinism There are three additional pieces of evidence that support the position that environment plays an important role in determining individual differences in intelligence: (1) The degree of heritability of a trait such as intelligence varies with environment. (2) One's genes (i.e., **genotype**) specify a potential range of outcomes (i.e., a **reaction range** of **phenotypes**); where one ends up in that range depends on environment. (3) Intelligence can be increased by environmental manipulations.

These points are important to make because there are many misunderstandings about the roles and potential roles of biology and environment in shaping intelligence. For example, over the years we have heard some legislators argue against additional funding for schooling of disadvantaged children because they believe that intelligence is biologically determined (based on their "reading" of behavior genetics evidence), and thus environmental interventions should make little difference. Alternatively, we have been audience to many claims by extreme environmentalists who point to environmentally induced increases in cognitive functioning as evidence that environment is really what matters and that biologists' claims of genetic determination of intelligence are overblown or untrue. Neither of these camps has a well-informed

opinion about the relative contributions of genes and environment to the development of intelligence or individual differences in intelligence, which will become more obvious as we discuss three points about heredity and environment:

1. Heritability varies with environment: Even if the heritability of intelligence for white populations is about 0.50 based on studies to date, it is entirely possible that with a shift in environment, the heritability of intelligence would change dramatically:

> Heritability describes a situation involving a particular phenotype with a certain array of genetic and environmental factors at a given time. Heritability does not indicate an eternal truth concerning the phenotype, for it can vary from population to population and from time to time. (Plomin et al., 1990, p. 232)

In particular, if the range of environments experienced by different members of a population increases, heritability will decrease. Heritability is increased to the degree that there are few environmental options for a population. Most emphatically, heritability indices generated under one set of environmental conditions do not generalize to other environmental conditions (see Scarr & Kidd, 1983, for discussion of all of these points). In short, no measure of heritability generated given today's environmental options is predictive of heritability in the future if subtantial efforts are made to improve the educational and social environments experienced by children.

2. Genotypes specify a range of possible phenotypes: Any given set of genes specifies a variety of outcomes depending on the environment. For example, recall the case of PKU discussed earlier in this chapter. If a child with the genetically determined inability to metabolize phenylalanine experiences a nutritional environment rich in phenylalanine, the result is severe retardation. If the child experiences a nutritional environment in which phenylalanine has been eliminated, normal intelligence is the outcome. Consider a second example. Heart disease has a reasonably high heritability. Suppose one has the misfortune to be born of parents who both suffer from heart disease. Whether such an offspring develops coronary problems depends largely on environmental factors, however, such as diet, exercise, and lifestyle. That is, genes and environment interact to determine outcomes: There is a **reaction range** of **phenotypes** associated with each **genotype** (Gottesman, 1963; Lewontin, 1974; Scarr & Kidd, 1983).

Reaction range seems to be a concept that extreme biological determinists do not understand. If behavior genetic theories of intelligence are correct, intelligence should vary with quality of environments. If it were somehow provable that intelligence did not vary with environments, the concept of reaction range would bite the dust and with it much of modern genetics theory. Reaction range is also a concept that extreme environmental determinists do not understand either. Demonstrating that intelligence is affected by environment in no way falsifies genetic theory because modern genetic theory predicts exactly that outcome.

The concept of reaction range is an important one for interventionists. The goal of the interventionist should be to do all possible to ensure that their students, patients, or clients end up on the favorable end of the reaction range. Thus, with respect to IQ, educators should be doing all possible to make certain that their students are as close as possible to the top of their reaction range for intelligence. There has been substantial progress in understanding how to accomplish this goal.

3. Psychometric intelligence is increased by exposure to high-quality educational environments (Ceci, 1991; see Chapter 11): Extreme biological determinists have launched vigorous attacks on the hypothesis that intelligence can be improved through environmental manipulations, with Spitz (e.g., 1986a, 1986b, 1991a, 1991b, 1992), Jensen (e.g., 1969, 1972, 1973, 1980, 1992), and Locurto (e.g., 1988, 1991a, 1991b, 1991c) persistently critical of claims that educational interventions can increase psychometric intelligence or other meaningful indications of educational achievement. These criticisms come despite many replications of the basic finding that high quality environmental manipulations at home and preschool produce increases in measured intelligence (for an especially complete review, see Storfer, 1990, Chapter 10; also Chapter 11).

The skeptics point out that IQ advantages following educational interventions are most likely to be observed at the immediate conclusion of the treatment, with the IQs of treated children often indiscrimate from the IQs of nontreated children several years after the special intervention has ceased. The critics believe that if intelligence really had been modified, there should be enduring gains.

The interventionists have several retorts, however, with Storfer (1990, Chapter 10) providing a nice overview of them. The most important included that even though IQ measures may not reflect preschool intervention effects in the long-term,

educational achievement and societal adaptation more broadly conceived and measured in the long term are affected consistently by preschool interventions—including less school failure, reduced behavior problems, and less need for special education services (e.g., Lazar et al., 1982), advantages that even critics such as Locurto (1991a) admit. Moreover, it is unreasonable to expect maintenance of intelligence advantages following an intervention if children return to an unstimulating environment. One of Storfer's (1990, Chapter 10) important insights from his review of the literature was that preschool enrichment–induced increases in intelligence are more likely to be sustained for middle-class populations than lower-class populations: Storfer hypothesized that middle-class environments are more likely to stimulate expansion of the cognitive skills developed in preschool stimulation programs.

We find compelling the consistent effects of high-quality interventions during the preschool years, including increases in intelligence at least in the short term and other measures of academic and social competence in the long term. See Chapter 11 of this book for expansion of the theme that education can positively affect psychometic intelligence and intelligent adaptation to the world.

Concluding Comments About Biological Determination of Intelligence Explanations of individual differences in intelligence in terms of either genetics or environment are off the mark: We conclude as do others (e.g., Fletcher, 1991) that there is no reason to continue such debates because they do not map on to the theories advanced either by sophisticated geneticists or sophisticated environmentalists. Genes provide potential; whether a person's intelligence is at the high or low end of that range of potential depends on the environments encountered during development. Rather than accept low levels of achievement, it makes good sense to provide educational environments that encourage students to function nearer the upper boundary of their reaction range than they would in conventional environments.

Based on current behavior genetics methodologies, given current environments, individual differences in intelligence and academic ability are determined in part by genetic factors, with estimates of heritability typically in the 50 percent range. Readers should bear in mind in interpreting this figure that there have been important methodological criticisms of both twin studies and adoption studies (e.g., see Lewontin, Rose, & Kamin, 1984; Locurto, 1990; Plomin et al., 1990). For example, two key assumptions in twin studies are that identical twins reared apart experience different environments, whereas fraternal twins reared together experience similar environments (Goldberger, 1977; Grayson, 1989; Wilson, 1982). The former assumption is strained by analyses of twin studies revealing that the adopting families of separated identical twins often are similar in socioeconomic status to the biological families; the latter assumption is strained by fraternal twins that all of us know who seem to lead extremely different lives—even during childhood. In adoption studies, there is an assumption that a reasonable estimate can be made of what IQ would have been for an adopted child if the child had been reared in the birth environment. Such estimations are often difficult to make, however, because of incomplete knowledge of the psychometric intelligence of biological parents. Despite the methodological limitations of particular studies, there are, nonetheless, enough replications of twin studies and adoption studies with similar results—and the conclusions emerging from twin and adoption data converge—that confidence is growing in the conclusions emanating from behavior genetics analyses, including the major conclusion from such studies that both genetics and environment contribute to the determination of individual differences in intelligence.

Concluding Comments About Biologically Determined Biases and Constraints

Human biology biases humans to attend to certain types of information over others, makes some learning more likely than others, determines that some learning (e.g., acquisition of language) will almost certainly occur given exposure to any part of the human family, and constrains other learning and performance demands to those not exceeding short-term capacity. Not every hypothesis advanced about biological constraint has proven telling, however.

For instance, there is substantial evidence that the hippocampus plays an important role in human memory (e.g., lesions to it result in memory impairments; Bachevalier, 1990). A strong biological constraint hypothesis was that development of most important forms of human memory would lag be-

hind the development of the hippocampus. The strong version of that hypothesis has fallen, however, for impressive recognition memory capacities develop well before the hippocampus is fully mature (Diamond, 1990b; Rovee-Collier, 1990). Recognition memory competence probably cannot be accounted for by considering only one biological mechanism, but more likely is determined by multiple biological mechanisms (Diamond, 1990b)—a situation certain to frustrate many simple hypotheses about biological determination of recognition memory and constraints on recognition memory owing to developing biological functions. In a subsequent section of this chapter, gender differences in cognition will be discussed, with the case made that some important biological hypotheses about the determination of behavior have fallen.

In drawing the conclusion that intelligence in general is a function of both biology and environment, we do not ignore that there are some intellectual characteristics that seem immune to environmental influences. That is, some people seem to lack the innate ability to perform particular academic functions, or at least, they cannot do them given the range of educational environments currently available. For example, dyslexia (a form of inability to read) and dyscalculia (a form of inability to do math), both of which seem impervious to current educational interventions, are taken up later in this chapter as conditions that are difficult to treat given current remediation efforts. In addition, there are some biological assaults that are devastating with respect to intellect, with those taken up in the next section of this chapter.

HOW CONTEMPORARY METHODS ARE INCREASING UNDERSTANDING OF THE BIOLOGICAL FOUNDATIONS OF ACADEMIC COMPETENCE

Biological studies offer a tremendous opportunity to expand understanding of important academic competencies. Without a doubt, the greatest progress in analyzing the biological foundations of academic achievement has been with respect to reading.

Biological Studies of Reading

Reading researchers are using psychophysiological and radiological imaging in combination with artificial intelligence analyses to provide windows on reading processes that cannot be understood using more conventional research tactics. Some of the most pertinent brain imaging studies of reading have been conducted by Posner, Petersen, and their colleagues (e.g., Petersen, Fox, Posner, Mintun, & Raichle, 1988; Petersen, Fox, Snyder, & Raichle, 1990; Posner, Petersen, Fox, & Raichle, 1988). These investigators have made brain images under a number of different conditions, such as when their subjects were looking at a dot, passively and silently reading a word (or pseudoword), reading a word aloud, repeating a word that was read, generating an associate to a word (e.g., given *hammer*, responding with *pound*), or determining whether a word referred to a member of a particular class (i.e., is this a dangerous animal?). By "subtracting" the activations caused by tasks requiring less complete processing from the activations caused by slightly more complex tasks (e.g., subtracting activation associated with looking at a dot from activation due to silent, passive reading), it is possible to determine the parts of the brain implicated in various types of word processing tasks.

Posner and colleagues have observed that passive reading of familiar words stimulates processing in the back part of the brain, more in the right hemisphere than the left, in an area of the brain known to be implicated in pattern recognition. This is a sensible result because passive reading involves recognition of visual patterns. Passive reading of real words also activates the left frontal lobe (known to be implicated in associative memory), although reading of pseudowords does not. This is also sensible because there is a meaning to associate to a real word but not a pseudoword, with meaningful verbal processes conceptualized more as left-brain activities by neuroscientists than as right-brain activities. Consistent with this interpretation, the left frontal lobe activation is also prominent when subjects are generating associations to real words or attempting to determine whether a word refers to a dangerous animal. (See Kosslyn and Koenig, 1992, for a nontechnical summary of the subtractive method and its use in reading research as well as additional discussion of the results produced by Posner, Petersen, and their co-workers.)

Cognitive neuroscientists are combining their talents with those of workers in artificial intelligence to produce biologically plausible models of reading, approaches that can be simulated in neural net-

works that can be created on computers. Great progress is being made in understanding how connections are built up between features of letters and between letters to create long-term memories of words, memories that can be fired given only part of the word. These models are permitting increased understanding of how word recognition can occur, both normally and under atypical conditions. Thus, when a reader sees a dim neon M _ _ _ L (blanks standing for letters that are obscured), the connections between initial M and final L stimulate activation of all the words that the reader knows that start with M and end in L. The system also looks for other cues that would be consistent with one possibility or another. Is the second letter fat or thin? If it is thin, connections to words like *MICHAEL* and *MINERAL* are activated additionally; if it is fat, there is additional activation of words like *METAL*, *MOTEL*, *MANTEL*, and *MATERIAL*. It's fat. Perhaps the brain looks for length cues, concluding that there are at most three letters between the M and L: Activation of *METAL* and *MOTEL* grows stronger. The brain scrutinizes the middle three positions. When the eye makes out that the letter just to the left of the L is more squarish than triangular, there is additional activation of *MOTEL* than of *METAL*. Eventually, there are enough cues that the brain concludes that the word is *MOTEL*. In general, artificial intelligence theorists are making progress in developing computer programs that can perform tasks such as the one just described (e.g., McClelland & Rumelhart, 1988). (See Chapter 3, this book, for additional discussion of how neural networks recognize words; also Kosslyn & Koenig, 1992, Chapter 5.)

The new neuroscience is permitting analyses of brain function that potentially may validate models such as neural network approaches to word recognition as well as identify their deficiencies as explanations of reading. For example, the neuroscience analyses to date (such as those provided by Posner and Petersen) suggest that familiar word recognition involves parts of the brain specialized for pattern recognition, spatial relatedness, and association, going beyond artificial intelligence neural network models that emphasize association to the relative neglect of sorting out pattern recognition from spatial position determination processes (Kosslyn & Koenig, 1992, p. 179). Suffice to conclude here that cognitive neuroscience and artificial intelligence will both play a role in evaluation of both some new and some old theories of reading.

Biological Determination of Academic Dysfunctions

Some students experience extreme difficulties in acquiring particular academic competencies that others acquire given normal schooling. Sometimes these difficulties reflect biological differences between these students and other people.

Dyslexia **Dyslexia** is the failure to learn to read despite substantial instructional attempts to teach reading (e.g., Farnham-Diggory, 1992, Chapter 2). There has been progress in identifying different types of dyslexia (see Caplan, 1992, Chapter 5; also Rayner & Pollatsek, 1989, Chapter 11). One important distinction is between **acquired dyslexia** resulting from some type of brain injury and **developmental dyslexia,** which involves otherwise normal children experiencing difficulties in reading that cannot be explained easily (e.g., they are not due to obvious brain injury, such as the acquired dyslexias). Within the acquired and developmental categories, there are subcategorizations. For example, acquired phonological dyslexics cannot sound out nonsense words but can read actual words they learned before they suffered brain injury; in contrast, acquired surface dyslexics can sound out pseudowords but cannot read words they knew before their injury; and acquired deep dyslexics sometimes misread a word by producing a semantically related item (e.g., saying *table* when presented the word *chair*).

Developmental dyslexia is much more important for most educators than is acquired dyslexia. There are a variety of potential symptoms of developmental dyslexia: eye-scan patterns that appear erratic or at least do not match the normal pattern of fixations and predominantly forward saccades, difficulties with spatial orientation including confusing left and right elements in arrays, and better reading of upside-down text than right-side-up text. The particular symptoms manifested by developmental dyslexics differ from student to student, however. The most important one, however, is poor word recognition and decoding during childhood, persisting throughout life in most cases (Bruck, 1990).

Scarborough (1990) reported that as early as 2 years of age, dyslexic children are evidencing language difficulties not observed in children who will become normal readers. At 2 and 3 years of age, children who will become dyslexic produce relatively short utterances, ones not as syntactically complex as other children. Their pronunciations tend to be less accurate. Their receptive vocabularies are not as well developed, and they have more difficulties providing labels for common objects than do normal children. In short, Scarborough's data suggest that dyslexia is part of a more general language-processing deficiency, consistent with the best-supported theory of the cause of developmental dyslexia (Vellutino, 1979).

Many possibilities were considered before a research-defensible conception of the causes of dyslexia was uncovered. Some of the historically prominent explanations of developmental dyslexia that have been discounted (see Gaddes, 1985, Chapter 8; also Rayner & Pollatsek, 1989, Chapter 11, for reviews) include the following: Dysfunctional eye movements do not cause dyslexia (i.e., they are symptoms rather than causes); general perceptual deficiencies do not cause developmental dyslexia (Vellutino, 1979); the hypothesis that dyslexia reflects a "maturational lag" has failed; and the evidence favoring claims of an underdeveloped left hemisphere (claims beginning with Orton, 1925, 1926, 1937) are not well supported. Other studies using sophisticated methodological advances in neuropsychology (e.g., PET scans) as well as studies using old methods, such as autopsies, have provided evidence of physiological differences between developmental dyslexics and normal readers: Left-hemisphere activity (as reflected in brain imagery studies) is not as predictable in dyslexics as in normals. Abnormal tissue growth in the brain, especially in the left hemisphere, has been documented (see Galaburda, 1983). Taken as a whole, the best available evidence suggests that the probable cause of developmental dyslexia in many cases is a physiological difference or differences in the left hemisphere, ones translating into generalized verbal deficiencies (Scarborough, 1990; Vellutino, 1979). Among the various verbal abilities, the phonological processes implicated in decoding print to sound seem to be especially problematic for dyslexics (Rack, Snowling, & Olson, 1992). This conception of dyslexia is in turn stimulating research to identify the genetic underpinnings of such brain differences (e.g., claims that differences between dyslexics and normals on chromosome 15 might be responsible for the physiological differences; Smith, Kimberling, Pennington, & Lubs, 1983).

Dyslexia affects a fairly small proportion of readers (i.e., 5 percent collapsing across all categories of dyslexia). We know many reading clinicians who simply work with students until they find something that works, trying many different techniques that are part of reading teachers' bags of tricks. Sometimes this approach works; other times it does not.

Researchers continue to design and evaluate novel ways of teaching reading-disabled students how to recognize words, with some successes. For example, Lovett, Warren-Chaplin, Ransby, and Borden (1990) succeeded in increasing the word recognition abilities of 7- to 13-year-olds who had previously failed to learn word recognition. Both a whole-word method and a technique involving explicit instruction of letter-sound relationships worked. Others have improved the word recognition skills of weak readers by teaching them to make extensive use of semantic context cues and clues (see Farnham-Diggory, 1992, Chapter 7 for an example). Much work is ahead before there will be systematic understanding of how to treat developmental dyslexic students, however.

Disorders in Mathematics Competency Neuroscientists are increasingly interested in mathematical thinking skills. Some physiological psychologists have studied patients who have lost their capacity to calculate because of head injury or disease, who manifest **acquired dyscalculia.** McCloskey (1992) in particular has been attempting to validate a model of calculation consistent with the good information processor perspective favored in this book. McCloskey posits that calculation involves both knowledge of arithmetic facts and calculation procedures. To calculate, people must be able both to comprehend numbers and to produce them. Comprehension mechanisms translate numbers into internal representations, which can be operated on by mathematical procedures. The results of these procedures can be communicated to the outside world only if the person also has intact numerical production capabilities. The model specifies a number of complexities with respect to both comprehension and production. Thus, one patient is described who can understand that a number such as 70 involves "tens" quantities but who cannot decide which of the tens quantities it is, with the result that the patient perceives sometimes that the number is 40, 50, 60, 80, and so forth. Some comprehension functions are intact; others are not.

In addition to studies of brain-damaged people, neuropsychologists are also busy evaluating people who never acquire calculating competence, with the hypothesis that **developmental dyscalculia** (analogous to developmental dyslexia) is due to brain differences between those with dyscalculia and normal calculators. As with acquired dyscalculia, there are huge individual differences in the specifically impaired processes, including students whose problems are mainly verbal (e.g., they cannot name numbers, symbols, or mathematical relationships; they cannot read math; or they cannot write mathematical symbols) and others that involve calculation and calculating subprocesses (Keller & Sutton, 1991).

When all of the physiological and psychological evidence on both acquired and developmental dyscalculia is considered, there is considerable regularity with respect to pinpointing specific brain sites implicated in mathematical disabilities (Keller & Sutton, 1991): Difficulties in reading and understanding word problems as well as difficulties in understanding mathematical concepts and procedures involve the higher association areas of the individual's dominant hemisphere. Quick mental calculation ability is linked to the functioning of the frontal lobes, as is abstract conceptualizing and some problem-solving skills. Sequencing abilities depend on the left parietal lobe; visual processing of mathematical symbols involves the occipital lobes; and auditory perception of numbers requires intact temporal lobes. Progress is being made in understanding the contributions of brain structures to mathematical cognition, and we expect it to continue. Such work has high potential for informing the good information processing perspective developed throughout this book.

BIOLOGICALLY DETERMINED DISRUPTIONS OF NORMAL DEVELOPMENT

Disease and injury are potential dangers from the moment of conception until old age. Tremendous progress has been made in understanding the effects of many neurological diseases and injuries, with important insights about the treatment and education of people following from this work.

Teratogens

A critical determinant of the effects of neurological disease or environmental insult to the nervous system is the timing of the sickness or trauma. A particularly bad period for adverse neurological events is during **neurogenesis,** when many new nerve cells are forming (i.e., during the first 2 to 3 months of life), and thus there is much greater concern about the impact of many **teratogens** (i.e., agents that can damage a developing brain and thus have effects on behavior) during the first trimester of a pregnancy than during the second and third trimesters. A large number of disease (e.g., cytomegalovirus, rubella, toxoplasmosis) and chemical (e.g., methylmercury, alcohol, lead) teratogens have been identified. In many cases, prenatal exposure to a disease or a chemical will do so much damage to the developing nervous system that normal learning and development can never occur. For example, rubella during pregnancy can produce extreme retardation as well as a host of other symptoms, such as growth retardation and heart disease (Shonkoff & Marshall, 1990). Maternal alcoholism can produce the retardation associated with fetal alcohol syndrome. Prenatal exposure to PCBs (polychlorinated biphenyls) translates into visual information processing and short-term memory functioning deficits that are detectable during the preschool years (Jacobson, Jacobson, Padgett, Brumitt, & Billings, 1992). By educating expectant mothers about teratogens and by providing them with prenatal care, many birth disorders could be avoided.

Malnutrition

Prenatal and postnatal malnutrition also can reduce mental competency (Chase, 1973). The timing of malnutrition is an especially important determinant of outcomes (Morgan & Gibson, 1991). There is greater damage as a result of malnutrition when it occurs at periods corresponding to rapid development of the nervous system. Thus, from neurogenesis through the second year of life, when neural cell growth via arborization and proliferation of dendritic synapses is rapid, is an especially vulnerable period (Dobbing, 1974). Because substantial myelination occurs during the middle preschool years (3 to 4 years of age), this is also a period of great sensitivity to the effects of malnutrition. That the children who are most likely to suffer malnutrition are children from lower SES homes does not improve the

situation. One of the many good reasons to feed the poor in the United States is that the long-term mental competency of the children who are now living in poverty will be improved. In developing countries where long-term malnutrition is common, the effects translate into lower cognitive development and reduced attentional capacity for many children (e.g., Sigman, Neumann, Jansen, & Bwibo, 1989).

Neurological Injury/Trauma Early in Life

Injury (e.g., during childbirth) can also reduce mental competency. A common form of injury is asphyxiation during birthing, as is intracranial hemorrhage, with the latter especially probable among premature infants. Fortunately the incidence of these types of disorders is on the decline because of better fetal monitoring procedures and widespread dissemination of improved methods of delivery (Rosen, 1985).

On delivery day, physicians can determine by using ultrasound procedures when a baby is presenting feet first. Once the medical team knows that the baby is in a breech position (i.e., any position except head first and engaged in the birth canal), a plan for caesarean delivery often is constructed, one that includes permitting the labor to progress to the point at which a caesarean birth is easiest and safest for both child and mother. Not so long ago, discovery of breech presentation occurred only after the baby came into view of the delivery team. Such deliveries sometimes took hours, with great risk of anoxia and hemorrhage owing to injury involved in pulling the baby from the womb. New technology is improving the mental health of many children. Even so, high-quality prenatal care and birthing resources are not as available to lower SES groups in American society. Providing such care to the poor would do much to increase the mental competency of the children of the poor.

There is a happy ending of sorts to this section, one that emphasizes the role of environment in learning, development, and cognitive competency. In many cases, children who are at biological risk at birth (e.g., low birth weight, birthing injury) manifest few if any long-term problems. For example, Sostek, Smith, Katz, and Grant (1987) found little difference at age 2 between children who had been preterms with intracranial hemorrhage and former preterms who experienced no hemorrhage. Children who are at risk at birth are more certain to thrive if they experience diverse and stimulating environments during their first few years of life, environments with caregivers who are attentive and responsive to them (Anastasiow, 1990; Beckwirth & Parmelee, 1986; Goldberg & DeVitto, 1983; Gottfried, 1984; Morgan & Gibson, 1991; Sameroff & Chandler, 1975; Sameroff & Fiese, 1990; Werner, 1990; Werner, Bierman, & French, 1971; Werner & Smith, 1982).

One of the most compelling demonstrations that a rich environment can do much to make up for initial biological disadvantage was provided by an experiment conducted by the Infant Health and Development Project (1990; for complementary data, see Wasik, Ramey, Bryant, & Sparling, 1990). The target children were low-birth-weight infants, a group at substantial risk for later academic difficulties (Scott, 1987). The study was conducted at eight sites distributed across the United States, with this the largest multiple-site, randomized experiment of long-term early childhood intervention ever published. Approximately one-third of the children in the study were randomly assigned to the treatment condition and two-thirds to the control condition.

The treatment consisted of home visits during the child's first year of life. The visitor provided health and developmental information to the family as well as other forms of support as needed. Two curricula were introduced into the home during this first year. One was a cognitive, linguistic, and social development curricula consisting of games and activities that encouraged parent-child interaction. The second curricula provided child management information to parents, aimed specifically at problems parents often encounter with infants. At 1 year of age and continuing until 3 years of age, the treated children attended a child development center 5 days a week. The learning curriculum initiated at home was continued and extended at the center, with adjustments made as the child developed to keep the curriculum consistent with the child's level and progress. There was an excellent adult-to-child ratio in these centers, with one adult for each three 1-year-olds and one adult for each four 2-year-olds. The parents of the children at the center met twice a month in groups to receive information about child rearing, safety, and health.

The effects produced by this treatment were dramatic. By age 3, the IQs of treated children were substantially higher than the IQs of controls. For those children who had weighed between 5 and 6 pounds at birth, there was a 13.2 IQ point advantage owing to the treatment (i.e., treated condition mean = 98.0; control mean = 84.8); the corresponding gain for infants who had weighed less than 5 pounds at birth was 6.6 points (i.e., treated condition mean = 91.0; control mean = 84.4), with the gains for both the heavier-birth-weight and lighter-birth-weight infants statistically significant. The gain for the heavier children is especially striking in that all of these children were functioning almost at the mean of the normal distribution of intelligence. Their cognitive functioning could not possibly be construed as impaired.

Many questions arise in light of such a dramatic demonstration of the effects of early environment on the intellectual development of at-risk children. One is whether such services could be provided on a large scale. On the positive side, U.S. Public Law 99-457 provides for no-cost services to all infants who are at risk for developmental delay if left untreated. More negatively, this public law is not being enforced in many jurisdictions. Another issue is whether the gains produced by the Infant Health and Development (1990) treatment will persist (see Lazar, Darlington, Murray, Royce, & Sipper, 1982) and whether normal intelligence will translate into normal academic achievement when these children reach school age. One possibility is that even if the expenses of multiple-year interventions cannot be covered, briefer programs might be fiscally possible. Notably, there is some evidence of success even for fairly brief programs that are aimed at teaching parents how to stimulate the cognitive development of their at-risk infants (Rauh, Achenbach, Nurcombe, Howell, & Teti, 1988).

Fortunately, longitudinal data now are being collected by the Infant Health and Development Project, so long-term evaluations of their program will be possible. This is essential because long-term disadvantages for at-risk infants are common even for those experiencing the most fortunate of early childhood environments. For instance, very-low-birth-weight infants are more likely than peers to have perceptual problems and learning disabilities during the schooling years (see Bennett, 1987, for a review; Meisels and Plunkett, 1988). Those children who experience especially severe prenatal malnutrition are less likely to function normally than those experiencing less severe prenatal or postnatal malnutrition (Morgan & Gibson, 1991).

What might explain the benefits provided to at-risk children by high-quality early childhood environments? (In addition to the data cited in this subsection, think back to the discussion of early education interventions discussed earlier in this chapter; see also Chapter 11). There is an overabundance of experience-expectant synapses during this interval. This abundance during the early preschool years permits greater plasticity than compared with later in development (Anastasiow, 1990). In addition, there seems to be a correlation between plasticity and myelination, which is sensible because myelination is an index of nervous tissue maturity. Once myelination occurs, the nervous system is less open to change than before myelination. Regardless of the specific mechanisms mediating the effects of interventions, it is clear that there are advantages to providing treatment to at-risk children early in life. Waiting until the grade-school years often means opportunity lost: Sensitive periods for stimulation will have passed.

We note in closing this subsection that although our concern here was with environmental effects on at-risk children, many of the same investigators doing such work are also providing striking demonstrations that intellectual outcome of all children—not just those biologically at risk—is determined in large part by the quality of the home environment during the first 3 years of life. For dramatic evidence in support of this claim from six different sites in the United States, see Bradley et al. (1989).

Children with Medical Conditions

Some children who attend school are seriously ill, and as a general rule of thumb, chronic physical illness is associated with increased risk for academic difficulties (e.g., Sexson & Madan-Swain, 1993). For some of these victims of disease and trauma, their illness will be terminal; for others, there will be complete recovery; some will live with lifelong handicaps caused by the childhood sickness. Some diseases and injuries cause mental impairment; some treatments produce side effects that affect participation and progress in school. We review in this subsection a few of the more prominent disease categories encountered in contemporary schooling, noting that other sicknesses also can cause disruption of education, including cystic fibrosis and hemophilia among others (Bartel & Thurman, 1992).

AIDS Somewhere between 15,000 and 30,000 babies were born in 1992 with human immunodeficiency virus (HIV) infection (Stevens & Price, 1992). A critically important effect of acquired immunodeficiency syndrome (AIDS) early in life is that it causes central nervous system damage, including in many instances mental retardation. There is progressively greater brain damage as life proceeds from birth because HIV produces powerful neurotoxins (Seidel, 1992).

There is no disease-transmission possibility that precludes HIV-infected children from attending school, however. AIDS is not contracted through the types of contacts that occur in school. It is both legal and appropriate to keep a child's HIV status confidential. For children who contract the disease long after childbirth, the neurological assault is much less complete. Often the only obvious difference between such children and other children is the presence of the AIDS virus in their bodies. That is, the severe retardation that follows from AIDS during infancy does not occur when older children contract the AIDS virus.

Although there are not a large number of studies assessing the impact of cognitive interventions on young children who are HIV infected, the available data support the use of cognitive stimulation programs for children with AIDS. For example, Seidel (1992) reported that a year of cognitive stimulation intervention resulted in cognitive and motor gains for a sample of preschool children with AIDS. More than 80 percent of the sample was at least holding steady. Given the neurological assault these children are experiencing, holding steady is a good sign. Another optimistic sign is that the use of drugs such as AZT to treat AIDS reduces brain infection and thus has a positive impact on cognitive performance (Armstrong, Seidel, & Swales, 1993).

Cancer The most common childhood cancer is leukemia (Bartel & Thurman, 1992, for this point and what follows). Because of great advances in treatment, most childhood leukemia victims survive, however, so there is reason for optimism about leukemic children. Brain tumors are the next most common form of childhood cancer, and although the survival probabilities are not as great as for leukemia, the chances of survival are increasing steadily with new understandings about effective treatments. In a school district with 1000 elementary-school children, it would be likely that there would be at least one childhood cancer survivor, so even though childhood cancer victims are not common, many educators encounter them.

At a minimum, these children are at risk for getting behind in school at the time they are treated. The illness and treatment dramatically disrupt normal life and school attendance. Often the treatment produces side effects that preclude normal academic engagement, such as fatigue. The period of treatment is difficult for the child. The treatments also can affect long-term cognitive development negatively, with radiation because of a brain tumor especially likely to impair cognitive functioning in the long term (Brown & Madan-Swain, 1993). How much impairment depends on a number of factors, including the age of the child when the cancer occurs, whether there is postsurgical infection of the nervous system, and how much radiation therapy is administered. For example, brain tumors during the preschool years, when the brain is developing rapidly, seem to produce more impairment than brain tumors later in childhood. Even in the more favorable situation afforded by leukemia, many more postleukemic students require special educational interventions to keep them at grade level than do children who are free of disease. More positively, with a reduction in the use of radiation therapy to the head to treat leukemia, there seems to be less impairment.

Medically Fragile Children   Some children have diseases or disabilities that require continuous life support, such as ventilation because of tracheotomy (Bartel & Thurman, 1992). The educational needs of these children are often increased because parental resources (e.g., financial and psychic) are completely expended in coping with the medical condition. Many of these children have limited energy; others experience chronic pain; it is often a struggle for these children to be in school at all, with little fight left to put into academic challenges. Many such children are absent frequently, sometimes because of prolonged hospital stays. In general, such children have less total academic engaged time than other children. At a minimum, there is a need for great flexibility in dealing with children with fragile medical conditions. Many more adjustments are required to meet these children's needs than those of other children.

Chemical Assaults   Perhaps the saddest cases of mental impairment are the ones due to chemical assaults on developing nervous systems, for in virtually all such cases the assault did not have to happen: Parents who abuse chemical substances, especially mothers who drink or use drugs during pregnancy, create great risks for their children. Even if a child is in an environment filled with lead paint, that paint would do no harm with proper supervision of the child and management of the environment to prevent the child from ingesting paint chips.

More people are retarded because of prenatal exposure to *alcohol* than for any other reason (Burgess & Streissguth, 1992, for this point and the remainder of the commentary on alcohol effects). The child experiencing the full effects of **fetal alcohol syndrome** is born small and with low birth weight (itself a risk factor), has facial disfigurations, and experiences central nervous system damage that can translate into a small head and behavioral disorders ranging from retardation at the low end to learning disabilities and hyperactivity at the more favorable end of the spectrum of possibilities (e.g., the mean IQ is about 65 or 70, with a range of 30 to a little more than 100—that is, the distribution of IQ scores is significantly lower than the distribution of IQ scores in the normal population; see Chapters 16 and 18, this book). Often children with fetal alcohol syndrome will be so impulsive and out of control that the school will refer the child for evaluation and treatment. Although not every mother who drinks heavily gives birth to such a disordered child, there is a 30 percent to 40 percent probability of fetal alcohol effects in heavy drinkers. Streissguth, Barr, Sampson, Darby, and Martin (1989) reported that on average, 4-year-olds whose mothers had consumed more than three drinks a day during pregnancy had an IQ 5 points lower than children of nondrinking mothers, with this effect obtained when many other potential factors that might have influenced IQ were controlled statistically. In a school with 1000 children in it, approximately 3 of the students might be expected to have experienced serious fetal alcohol effects, with all of the available evidence making clear that heavy drinking during pregnancy increases dramatically the likelihood of cognitive impairment in offspring.

Many physicians advise complete abstinence from alcohol during pregnancy, recognizing that even light-to-moderate levels of alcohol consumption increase the odds for birth defects in offspring. For example, even small and moderate alcohol consumption during pregnancy can result in detectable motor deficiencies in the preschool years (Barr, Streissguth, Darby, & Sampson, 1990).

A common problem for fetal alcohol syndrome children throughout their schooling years is inappropriate behavior, with lying, stealing, and acting out common. One interpretation of the lying is that it reflects limited communication abilities, so the child is inadequately communicating what happened rather than intentionally telling mistruths. Of course, such poor communications skills also negatively impact social relations. If anything, the social problems worsen with advancing grade in school, with these dysfunctions producing an isolated and depressed adolescent in many cases.

At present, there is little knowledge about how to intervene with fetal alcohol syndrome children except there is general consensus that early intervention is better. In addition, there is a recognition of especially great need to improve the social and communications skills of fetal alcohol syndrome children.

Firm conclusions about the effects of other chemical addictions produced through prenatal exposure, including *cocaine* addiction, are difficult to put forward. One reason is that drug users rarely rely on one drug exclusively. Thus, the discussion now turns to "cocaine/polydrug-exposed" children (Griffith, 1992, for this point and the remainder of this subsection).

The effects of prenatal drug exposure are apparent early in life, effects owing to both the neurotoxicity of the drugs directly and indirect effects of drugs, such as retarded growth during the intrauterine period and abnormal, dysfunctional parent-infant interactions because of drug-induced characteristics of the infant (e.g., Lester et al., 1991; Lester & Dreher, 1989). A salient effect of prenatal exposure to drugs is poor self-regulation, with affected infants not displaying the "quiet alert" state that permits information from the environment to be processed. Much more swaddling, rocking, and pacification is required to induce quiet alertness in these children than in normal babies. Even so, these children can be overstimulated easily, with disorganized crying and extended sleeping ways of reacting to overstimulation. (That is, the flailing, crying infants commonly displayed on television as "crack" babies represent one type of reaction to overstimulation.) Great care must be taken to avoid overstimulation if drug-exposed babies are to be able to attend to their environments for prolonged periods of time, which is absolutely essential for cognitive growth.

At the time of this writing, little is known about the long-term effects of crack-cocaine exposure during the prenatal period on mental functioning. One possibility suggested by early studies is that at least for some children whose mothers opted into treatment during pregnancy and who experience postnatal environments that provide appropriate levels of stimulation, the long-term effects may be much less than suggested by the sensationalistic accounts in the mass media. Still, 3-year-olds who were drug-exposed prenatally have smaller heads on average than normal children, a symptom usually not associated with normal mental development. Also, a nontrivial proportion of those receiving the best treatments manifest communications and attentional problems at age 3. They are less likely to be able to control themselves and are easily overwhelmed by the environment, resulting in them withdrawing when challenged or going out of control. When working with such children, therapists attempt to determine variables that can overstimulate the youngster, setting him or her off, and adjust the environment as much as possible to eliminate potential overstimulation. We expect that there will be substantial research with such populations to determine if the approaches to increasing self-regulation that work with other populations (e.g., teaching children to self-instruct; see Chapter 7) can improve the adaptive functioning of drug-exposed children.

Unfortunately, chemical poisoning of a child can occur even if the parent is drug free. For example, we live in a world of lead-based paint that chips, with many poor children especially at risk for unwittingly eating and breathing *lead*. The most visible American scientist studying the effects of lead on intelligence is Needleman (1992; Needleman & Bellinger, 1991). Although his views are controversial, we know of no compelling evidence that is contrary to his main conclusion that even low levels of lead exposure pose a long-term risk to neurological functioning. Needleman argues that 16 percent of American children have blood lead levels that are reason for concern, with poor children much more likely to be exposed to dangerous levels of lead in their environment. Lead exposure can reduce IQ, impair language, and decrease self-regulation and attention.

In one of Needleman's studies, teachers described students who had high blood lead levels as ". . . more distractible, less persistent, more dependent, less well-organized, less able to follow directions, and general lower in overall functioning. . . " (Needleman, 1992, p. 36) than students with low blood lead levels. Low levels of lead exposure in early childhood are associated with long-term risks as well, including reading disability and increased likelihood of failing to graduate from high school.

Needleman and his colleagues argue that the costs of repairing homes with lead paint are quite small relative to the long-term savings in medical and special education costs if the repairs are not made. Unfortunately, however, policy decisions are often made with short-term budgetary considerations in mind, such as the cost of the cleanup, which can seem enormous if absorbed in a single year or two. When the harm is to powerless constituents, such as poor children, politicians are unlikely to vote the dollars needed to prevent paint chips that end up being nibbled or to clear the air of lead-filled dust. More positively, the political community acted to remove what was once a major source of environmental lead when they mandated lead-free gasoline.

Concluding Comment

After seeing a crack baby, it is difficult even to contemplate supporting the legalization of now illicit drugs. After witnessing the effects of fetal alcohol syndrome, it becomes clear that funds for treatment of alcohol addiction in young women are well spent. When the costs of lead-induced retardation are factored into the costs of allowing American housing of the poor to continue to decay, there is additional impetus to support funding of new and repaired housing for those living in poverty.

Educational psychologists must play an increasing role with respect to children who live with biological disadvantage. The laws are changing to assure that such children receive normal schooling—we as a society have decided that noncontagious-diseased children cannot be excluded from public school (a stance the authors strongly endorse). The evidence is also becoming overwhelming that there is a great deal of neurological plasticity, especially with young children. Given what we now know about how much difference a stimulating environment can make for biologically at-risk infants who become toddlers who become preschoolers, it is high time for educational psychologists to get serious about the creation of environments and interventions that get the most out of the young at-risk child's intellectual capacity. Although there is less plasticity in older children and adults, environmental support and psychological intervention often make a difference. It is the business of educational psychology to do all possible to find ways to make a maximum positive difference in the lives of students, with our moral obligation to do so especially great for those who have experienced biological misfortunes through no fault of their own.

The disorders covered in this section are in many ways the tip of the iceberg, with important programs of research now under way aimed at determining the effects of a number of disease/injury factors on school learning and achievement. Such research is paying off, even though only tentative conclusions can be advanced for many diseases because only a limited amount of research has been completed at this time. For example, although childhood *diabetes* is not associated with large deficits in cognitive functioning, there are subtle problems for diabetic children with respect to visuospatial and visuomotor processing (e.g., Rovet, Ehrlich, & Hoppe, 1988), verbal abilities (Kovacs, Goldston, & Ivengar, 1992), and memory and attention, which translate into increased risk for difficulties in academic achievement—that is, in reading, spelling, and arithmetic (Kovacs et al., 1992; Rovet, Ehrlich, Czuchta, & Akler, 1993). Particularly important given the themes emphasized in this book, diabetic children seem less likely to use strategies to mediate their learning than non-diabetic children (Hagen et al., 1990). Sickle cell anemia, an inherited disorder found in people of African descent, also produces some subtle cognitive impairments that affect school achievement negatively (Brown, Armstrong, & Eckman, 1993). Children who survive cardiac arrest perform at below-average levels on a number of intellectual measures (e.g., averaging almost a full standard deviation below the mean for overall intelligence; Morris, Krawiecki, Wright, & Walter, 1993). On the positive side, difficulties with school achievement seem less likely for children with asthma (Celano & Geller, 1993), a common childhood disorder, and for children who receive kidney or liver transplants (Hobbs & Sexson, 1993). Just as medical advances are permitting many more children to survive and function well after serious illnesses, we expect that psychologists will come to understand the psychological effects of many illnesses well enough to be able to engineer interventions that will increase the educational achievements of children disadvantaged by medical conditions.

GENDER DIFFERENCES IN COGNITION

The first question that must be addressed in any discussion of potential gender differences in cognition is whether there are any believable differences between males and females in their abilities to perform cognitive tasks. Are there differences in their fundamental cognitive processes? Are there biological differences in the central nervous systems of males and females that produce differences in their abilities to perform particular intellectual tasks? This section provides some answers to these questions, with what is presented here informed by the work of Diane F. Halpern (e.g., 1992), who is now the most visible integrative scholar in the area of gender differences in thinking. For anyone seriously interested in gender differences in cognition, her *Sex Differences in Cognitive Abilities* (2nd edition) is a must read, elaborating much of the following.

Although interpreting null effects can be dangerous, there are voluminous data supporting the conclusion of no overall difference in the intelligence of males and females as measured by psychometric tests of intelligence (i.e., the mean IQ scores for males and females are both about 100; intelligence is normally distributed for both males and females, with the standard deviation for IQs equal to 15 for both sexes; see Chapter 16). When processing and abilities are examined more closely, however, there are differences. Females are favored with respect to one extremely important ability:

- **Verbal ability,** including word fluency, grammatical competence, spelling skills, reading, vocabulary, and oral comprehension, is greater in females than in males. A particularly important point is that dysfunctions in verbal abilities are much more male problems than female problems, with most stutterers and dyslexics being male. Verbal impairment following stroke is more likely for males than females. Verbal differences favoring females are apparent from early childhood, with females talking first and more proficient in language earlier than boys. Differences are apparent throughout the schooling years as well, although not as pronounced as during preschool nor as pronounced as they will be in adulthood. It must be emphasized that gender differences in verbal abilities are small on average (see also Hyde & Linn, 1988), however, consistent with the effect size for most gender differences. It is certainly not inconsequential, however, that clinically significant verbal impairments are much more likely in males than in females. (For example, walk into any reading treatment clinic. Most of the students in the clinic will be boys.)

Males are superior to females for the following processes and tasks:

- **Visual-spatial** tasks, which involve the ability to imagine figures, including moving them around "in the head," are easier for males. Differences in visual-spatial ability can be detected during childhood. Although the effect size varies with task, it is not at all unusual for gender differences on visual-spatial tasks to be large. Although practicing spatial tasks improves the performance of both boys and girls, gender differences persist after such practice (Ben-Chaim, Lappan, & Houang, 1988). What such a pattern of results suggests is that spatial skills are affected by both biology and experience but that biologically determined individual differences persist if males and females receive comparable experiences. Notably, experienced girls in Ben-Chaim et al. (1988) outperformed inexperienced boys, making clear that females are not biologically destined to remain lower than males with respect to their performances on spatial tasks.
- **Field independence** is more common in males than females. What this means is that males are less influenced by context effects in perceptual tasks. For example, if presented a printed figure embedded in a more complex form, males locate the figure more quickly than females. A reasonable hypothesis supported by some research is that field independence only reflects male superiority on visual-spatial tasks, with all tests that produce male-female differences in field independence having a large spatial component.
- **Quantitative skills** as measured by standardized tests typically favor males over females when gender differences are detected, and often they are detected. Particularly striking is that males are much more likely to score high on tests like the SAT mathematics sections than are females, as reflected by scores in excess of 700 (i.e., there is a 17:1 ratio favoring males among 700 + test takers; Stanley & Benbow, 1986). In general, gender differences in mathematics abilities tend to be medium in size (see Chapter 1), although again the more important effect is the disproportionate representation of males at the upper end of the talent scale. At least some of the gender difference in mathematical test performances seems to be due to gender differences

in visual-spatial skills. There are clear developmental effects with respect to mathematical ability differences between the sexes: Females actually outperform males on math tasks in the elementary-school and middle-school years, with male superiority appearing for the first time in high school; the difference favoring males seems to increase into the adult years (Hyde, Fennema, & Lamon, 1990). Even so, the female advantage during the elementary years is with respect to computation skills; elementary-level males do better on measures of problem solving than do their female classmates.

One important characteristic of the differences favoring males is that males tend to be more variable than females for the characteristic in question (Feingold, 1992). A higher mean with much higher variability often implies that much of the mean difference is due to a relatively few outstanding performers and that otherwise there is great overlap in the distribution of scores. That conclusion does, in fact, hold for the few differences favoring males over females with respect to cognitive ability (Feingold, 1992).

There are several striking aspects to the entire list of differences. For one, it is so short! There are many aspects of performance that produce no gender differences, with the shortness of the list even more impressive when it is realized that most of the male differences can be accounted for by visual-spatial factors in measurements of field independence and mathematics abilities. We concur with Halpern's (1992, p. 97) conclusion, ". . . that cognitive similarities between the sexes are greater than the differences."

A question probably occurring to many of our readers is whether there are gender differences in use of cognitive strategies, metacognition about strategies, and other knowledge. The only gender difference in these areas consistently suggested in the literature is in computational versus problem-solving skills (strategies) at the elementary level favoring males. We note especially emphatically, however, that we know of no evidence that would suggest differences in the abilities of males and females to learn most problem-solving strategies (i.e., all except those involving visuospatial manipulation of mathematical representations).

Some motivational differences between males and females were considered in Chapter 5, espe-

cially with respect to mathematics. There have been claims by Benbow and Lubinski (see Raymond, 1992; also Benbow, 1992) that female motivations undermine the mathematics achievements of even the most highly mathematically talented of females. Benbow and Lubinski have been studying males and females who turn in the best performances on the math SAT to understand better why so few women choose careers in math and physics. They have found that even females who are strong in mathematics are less likely to aspire to scientific careers. Females want more social contact than they perceive is permitted by work in mathematics and physical sciences. As we consider gender differences in both children and adults, it is essential to keep in mind that motivations to do mathematics are more supportive of math efforts by males than females. Indeed, if Benbow and her colleagues are correct, motivation may be one of the greatest determinants in the development of some abilities versus others.

Are Gender Differences in Cognitive Abilities Due to Biological Differences Between Males and Females?

As with every other area of individual differences, there are two broad types of explanatory theories with respect to gender differences in cognition. Some theorists argue that gender differences can be explained via biological differences between males and females. Others argue that gender differences represent differences in the experiences of males and females. Halpern (1992) again provides the most definitive review available of this evidence, with us relying on her review to formulate the conclusions that follow.

Biological Theories Some theories about how biology affects gender differences in cognition have received at least some support; others have failed to prove telling. The supportable ones include the following:

• Sex hormones may operate in various ways. **Prenatal sex hormones** are critical to the determination of sex, with testosterone particularly important (i.e., it stimulates the development of male external genitalia, with its absence resulting in female sex organs). Testosterone also affects development of gender differences in the brain as do hormones secreted by the fetal ovaries. Studies of rats have manipulated the presence of such hormones at various points in development, producing changes in brain structures such as the corpus callosum, which is the bundle of fibers linking the two hemispheres of the brain. Although true experiments manipulating prenatal hormones are not possible with humans, there are medical conditions that result in abnormal levels of sex hormones during the fetal period. There is evidence that exceptionally high levels of androgen (a male hormone) increase spatial abilities in females. Some biological males do not respond to androgen and thus develop female characteristics, including a pattern of higher verbal than spatial ability. Women with Turner's syndrome have low levels of both male and female hormones, with strikingly reduced spatial skills relative to other females. In short, there are correlational differences favoring the hypothesis that prenatal hormones influence development of cognitive skills, but, of course, there are a host of other abnormal influences on individuals with abnormal sex hormone patterns and the differences associated with them. An especially prominent hormonal theory has been proposed by Geschwind and Galaburda (1987), who believe that high levels of prenatal testosterone slow development of the left hemisphere and reduce the size of the thymus gland, producing more left-handers in males, more immune disorders in males including allergies, and more pronounced superiority in males of "right" hemisphere functions, such as spatial abilities. There is some support for this position, although much more research is needed.

- A related argument about gender differences being caused by differential brain lateralization in males and females is linked to the hypothesis that testosterone affects the development of the right and left hemispheres. Males have more clearly lateralized brains than do females, with verbal skills more a left-hemisphere function for males than for females (e.g., Kee, Gottfried, Bathurst, & Brown, 1987). For females, verbal skills are carried out more by both hemispheres, with spatial abilities confined to the right hemisphere. The result is that there is less right hemisphere capacity in females dedicated to spatial abilities than in males and more overall capacity in females dedicated to verbal skills. Thus, Levy (e.g., 1976) proposed that spatial skills get "squeezed out" of the right hemisphere in females to provide more verbal capacity. Support for this hypothesis comes in the form of sex by handedness interactions: Consistent with the theory, left-handed males perform more poorly on spatial tasks than right-handed males (i.e., in males, clearer differentiation of the hemispheric functioning is in right-handers, with the result better spatial performance for males who are not "squeezing" spatial abilities out of the right hemisphere). Also, consistent with the theory, left-handed females perform better on spatial tasks than right-handed females (i.e., in females, clearer differentiation of hemispheric functioning is in left-handers, with the result better spatial performance for females who are not "squeezing" spatial abilities out of the right hemisphere; e.g., Harshman, Hampson, & Barenboim, 1983).

- For females, cognitive abilities vary somewhat with **hormonal differences during the menstrual cycle.** The work of Hampson and Kimura at Western Ontario (e.g., Hampson, 1990a, 1990b; Hampson & Kimura, 1988) has been especially telling, with demonstrations of better performance by women at menstruation on tasks typically performed better by males, such as map problems, mazes, and visual-spatial problems. This was as predicted because female hormones are at the low ebb at this point in the monthly cycle. When female hormones are at the peak of their cycle (i.e., at midcycle), females do better on tasks that are typically performed better by females than by males, such as speech articulation, verbal fluency, and manual dexterity. It does seem that cognitive abilities in women vary with the point in their menstrual cycle.

- There are within-hemisphere differences in the organization of males and females. Kimura's (e.g., 1987) work on this problem has been conducted with patients having various types of brain injury. For example, although females' language areas in the left hemisphere are focused in some regions more than others, males' processing tends to be more diffuse.

- Some portions of the *corpus callosum*—the bundle of fibers connecting the two hemispheres—are larger in females than in males, supporting the possibility that greater verbal facility in females is due in part to greater interhemispheric communication in females than in males.

There are three brain-based possibilities about gender differences in cognitive functioning. One is that they are due to gender differences in lateralization; the second is that they are due to intrahemispheric differences in organization; and the third is that differences in the size of the corpus callosum account for such differences. Of course, there is also the possibility that any two or all three of these brain differences are related in intricate ways to gender differences in cognition. Before there can be functional and structural differences, however, there are prenatal hormonal differences between males and females, differences that seem to affect development of the brain. In short, there is no simple biological explanation for the different patterns of male and female thinking but at best a developmentally complex explanation.

This seems to be a good point to offer clarification of a confusion that has sometimes occurred in the courses we teach. Based on an historically prominent conception of lateralization (e.g., Lenneberg, 1967, who argued that clear lateralization was not present until adolescence), students have objected to the argument that gender differences in cognition could be due to lateralization because gender differences are apparent even in early childhood. The response to this objection is that substantial research in the 1970s and 1980s elucidated the development of lateralization, with evidence of lateralization from infancy (see Kinsbourne & Hiscock, 1983; Molfese & Segalowitz, 1988) or even before birth (Previc, 1991), so that gender differences in thinking abilities observed in childhood could be due to lateralization differences between the sexes.

In finding favor with the biological perspective, we also note that some biological theories have *not* received support as potential explanations of gender differences. These include the following:

- Genetic theories that gender differences in cognition are **X-chromosome linked** have failed on examination. The argument is that females have two X chromosomes, whereas males have only one. Thus, if high spatial ability was a recessive trait carried on the X chromosome, females would require two recessives if they were to enjoy the advantages provided by such a gene, whereas any male with the gene on his single X chromosome would be advantaged.
- Differences in **pubertal hormones** and maturation rate at puberty have not produced reliable differences in the cognitive abilities that differentiate male and female thinking. The exceptions are that at least some testosterone at puberty seems necessary for normal spatial skills and that spatial abilities may vary with the level of the hormone estradiol.
- There are no differences in the size, weight, and complexity of male and female brains, although there has been frequent speculation of differences.

In concluding that there are probably biological foundations to gender differences in cognition, we recognize we are treading on an explosive topic, with many people opposed to such a conclusion (Halpern, 1992, Chapter 5). Such critics rightly point out that biologically oriented theorists and researchers usually have ignored environmental and social factors that might affect gender differences in cognition. (We are definitely in sympathy with this concern; on more than a few occasions, we have reacted with alarm when differences in SAT math performances of 16- and 17-year-olds are attributed to biological differences, acutely aware of the many social factors that possibly contribute to such differences.) The failure to consider socialization factors is striking in light of findings such as Benbow and Lubinski's report that even highly mathematically talented females do not wish to pursue careers in math and science, reporting preferences for careers that they believe will permit more social contact and interactions.

We close this subsection on biology noting the tendency of many to come to too strong conclusions about the inevitability of differences based on the findings reported here. Thus, the small verbal advantage is often exploded in the minds and rhetoric of some into an easily detected advantage for females over males on verbal tasks. That small advantage on average for females is swamped by the huge differences in verbal abilities within both sexes, so there are many males who are more verbally facile than many other females. Even the larger spatial abilities difference does not predict to individuals, with large numbers of females doing well on spatial tasks and in areas such as mathematics. Strong conclusions about how individuals will fare on cognitive tasks cannot be predicted from their sex.

Most emphatically, this work on gender differences is not evaluative with respect to whether the thinking patterns exhibited by one sex or the other are better or not. Halpern's (1992) sophistication in appreciating gender differences comes through in many parts of her book, but we found her statement on the issue of the value of some patterns of thinking over others to be especially compelling:

> We know that there are gender differences in cognitive abilities, sex hormone concentrations, and probably patterns of cerebral organization. There are also undisputable gender differences in the reproductive organs or genitals. No one would argue that either sex has better reproductive organs or genitals. They are clearly different, but neither sex would be considered deficient in these biological organs. However, when cognitive differences are considered there is sometimes an implicit notion that one sex will be found that is better than the other. Is it better to be high in verbal skills or spatial skills? This is a moot question. The answer depends on the type of task that needs to be performed, the quantification of how much better, and individual predilection. To argue that female hormones are better than male hormones or that male brains are better than female brains is as silly as arguing which sex has the better genitals. It seems almost embarrassing and obvious to state that neither sex has the better biology for intellectual ability and that differences should not be confused with deficits. (pp. 169–170)

As we continue consideration of potential causes of gender differences in cognition, we urge readers to keep Halpern's comments about differences in mind. We embrace the position that different people may have different intellectual strengths, which contribute to the richness of life, and that all of these strengths deserve positive recognition and resources. Even if there were no biological differences underpinning different abilities, there is certainly systematic societal encouragement of different abilities in males and females, with it decidedly sexist to denigrate the abilities encouraged in females more than males.

Psychosocial Theories of Gender Differences in Cognitive Abilities

Males and females are treated differently from the moment the delivery room nurse reaches for a blue blanket for a boy or a pink one for a girl. That differences in treatment exist is not the problem. The problem is that the behaviors encouraged in females are often less positively regarded and rewarded than the behaviors encouraged in males. Moreover, societal stereotypes often ascribe less valued roles for females compared with males (e.g., physicians are males and nurses are females; lawyers are males and paralegals are females; well-paid athletes are males and their admirers are females). The pervasiveness of such sexism can affect behavior if internalized, so that much of the reason girls might have less interest in math and careers requiring mathematics is that they internalized stereotypical beliefs such as "math is for boys," "engineers and scientists are men," and "science requires cold objectivity—a male stereotypic trait—rather than interpersonal warmth and human contact—female stereotypic traits." Parents, television, teachers, and community members all contribute to the stereotyping (see Halpern, 1992, for a review).

If being surrounded by sex-role stereotypes is not enough, more obvious and tangible rewards are given to boys when they do well in math and science than to girls who do so (e.g., Stage & Karplus, 1981). Indeed, math and science classes foster boys more than girls in a number of ways. Boys ask more questions in these classes, and they get more answers, with males generally dominating science and math discussions in school (e.g., Morse & Handley, 1985; see Chapters 12 and 13, this book). When volunteering is a main mechanism for determining who participates, when competitive grading is the norm, and when public recitation is a large part of the culture of the math and science classroom, and it often is, male interactional patterns of aggression and competitiveness are favored more than female patterns of cooperation (e.g., Eccles & Blumenfeld, 1985), with males getting more experience in operating in competitive and publicly interactive activities from the preschool years on (Huston & Carpenter, 1985). When boys and girls work on problems together, boys dominate the interactions and the decisions that are reached (see Lockheed, 1985). After several years of such gender differences in interaction, males are better able to pose questions to other group members that produce assistance and are more likely to seek assistance when they need it (see Webb & Kenderski, 1985). This is despite the fact that females are generally better communicators than males in that they are more sensitive to the feelings and needs of others and able to speak with greater fluency (i.e., fewer speech errors and pauses) than males (see Hall, 1984). When males and females are in situations requiring negotiation, however, males dominate (see Tannen, 1990, for book-length coverage of the differences between males and females with respect to communication styles; also Chapter 13, this volume, for additional commentary on the consequences of gender differences in communicative style for cooperative learning in mathematics).

Halpern (1992, Chapter 7) considered some of the particular social-cognitive experiences that might contribute to the gender differences in cognition that have been observed, making the case that there is at least correlational evidence (and in some cases, experimental evidence) for each of the following possibilities: Gender differences in spatial abilities might be accounted for by greater male experience with games that require such skills (e.g., video games, billiards). Boys' toys and play activities in general may encourage development of spatial skills more than do girls' toys. Boys may be more curious about the environment than girls, a difference reinforced by adults who are more willing to allow boys to roam the world in search of new possibilities than they are willing to allow girls to do so (e.g., Lindow, Marrett, & Wilkinson, 1985). Greater exploration would be expected to foster visual-spatial skills. One dramatic piece of data consistent with the possibility that differences in experience cause gender-related differences in thinking abilities is that grade-school girls who are more interested in male activities than female activities become adolescent girls who have spatial abilities that exceed the spatial abilities of girls in general (Newcombe & Dubas, 1992).

With respect to gender differences in mathematics, the socialization differences are less subtle; there are many reports that boys are encouraged more in mathematics than are girls (see Chapter 9; Halpern, 1992, Chapter 7): Girls take fewer mathematics courses, with much greater tolerance of high-ability girls dropping out of mathematics sequences than high-ability boys doing so. The majority of math teachers expect more from boys than girls and are more responsive to male achievements in mathematics than female achievements. Many adults who interact with children believe that math is harder for girls than boys, with such a bias expected to affect the messages sent to students about the possibility of mathematics achievement by girls. If we were attempting to design a world that would turn girls off to math and science, it seems unlikely we could be more successful than is the case now.

As far as verbal abilities are concerned, there is much less evidence favoring the differential social-ization hypothesis. The lack of research on causes of verbal gender differences is striking, with little attention to this problem relative to the gender differences in visual-spatialization and associated mathematical abilities—perhaps reflecting the greater societal valuation of male-stereotypical characteristics, such as quantitative abilities.

Because how people respond to new material is largely a function of their prior knowledge, an important hypothesis about verbal differences between males and females, one critically important to educators, has been offered by feminists. They contend that many forces combine to offer different verbal knowledge to girls than to boys. Here is how Elizabeth Segel (1986) said it:

> One of the most obvious ways that gender influences our experiences as readers is when it determines what books are made available to us or are designated as appropriate or inappropriate for our reading. Nowhere is this fact so apparent or its implications so disturbing as in childhood reading. This is partly because the child does not have direct access to books, by and large, but receives them from adult hands. Adults decide what books are written, published, offered for sale, and, for the most part, purchased for children. And over the last century and a half, most adults have firmly believed that literary sauce for the goose is not at all sauce for the gander. The publisher commissioning paperback romances for girls and marketing science fiction for boys, as well as Aunt Lou selecting a fairy tale selection for Susie and a dinosaur book for Sam, are part of a powerful system that operates to channel books to or away from children according to their gender. (p. 165)

Parents and teachers can powerfully affect the prior knowledge developed in children by their selection of books for them. In a world where knowledge of science (e.g., as reflected in books about dinosaurs and science fiction) is more valued than a romantic outlook, there is a good possibility that well-intending parents and teachers help to shape prior knowledge in boys that is more valued than the knowledge shaped by reading the books intended for little girls.

Concluding Comments

There are multiple forces that might affect gender differences in cognition. Contrary to many societal stereotypes, most differences in thinking that exist between men and women are small. Although some of the gender differences in cognition that do exist are probably due to biology, there are massive socialization differences between boys and girls that undoubtedly are important in determining how males and females construe the world and the academic content they encounter in it.

Differences in cognitive socialization become a problem to the extent that the knowledge and behaviors encouraged in one sex are more valued by the culture than the knowledge and behaviors encouraged in the other sex. Unfortunately, female-stereotypic behaviors do not have the payoff in our society that male-stereotypic behaviors do, nor do female ways of thinking pay off as well as male ways of thinking. Extensive thinking about how to create more equitable experiences for males and females is in order, a theme that is revisited in Chapters 12 and 13. It is impossible to make a case based on biology that males' ways of knowing, rationalizing, and problem solving are better than females' ways of dealing with the world.

GENETICALLY DETERMINED MODULES IN THE MIND AND MULTIPLE INTELLIGENCES

The idea that the mind includes particular faculties that are specialized to deal with particular types of information has been around for a long time. It can be traced to Descartes's doctrine of innate ideas. Thinly disguised versions of the Descartes perspective appear periodically. These vary from the incredible (e.g., Gall's belief that the bumps on the head could provide insights about individual differences in capacities; Hollander, 1920) to very credible, if not always well-supported, positions.

One piece of highly credible evidence supporting the hypothesis of separate mental faculties is that there are different sensitive periods for some acquisitions compared with others. Thus, as suggested earlier in this chapter, the sensitive period for organization of visual processing in humans appears to be the first 4 or 5 years of life. The sensitive period for acquisition of language may be longer, perhaps the entire prepubertal period (Goodman, 1987). Many believe that the critical period for the establishment of a first intense attachment with another human being is in the first year of life (e.g., Bowlby, 1969).

Such observations fuel the argument that there are distinct human capacities that are inherited and that the mind involves an interaction of faculties. The

renaissance of faculty psychology was heralded in the first paragraph of Fodor's (1983) book *The Modularity of Mind:*

> Faculty psychology is getting to be respectable again after centuries of hanging around with phrenologists and other dubious types. By faculty psychology I mean, roughly, the view that many fundamentally different types of psychological mechanisms must be postulated in order to explain the facts of mental life. Faculty psychology takes seriously the apparent heterogeneity of the mental and is impressed by such prima facie differences as between, say, sensation and perception, volition and cognition, learning and remembering, or language and thought. Since, according to faculty psychologists, the mental causation of behavior typically involves the simultaneous activity of a variety of distinct psychological mechanisms, the best research strategy would seem to be to divide and conquer: first study the intrinsic characteristics of each of the presumed faculties, then study the ways in which they interact. Viewed from the faculty psychologist's perspective, overt, observable behavior is an interaction effect par excellent. (Fodor, 1983, p. 1)

Fodor goes on to argue throughout the book that humans inherit **cognitive modules;** these are "cognitive systems that are domain specific, innately specified, hardwired, autonomous. . . " (p. 37). An important point is that these modules are only independent, in Fodor's (p. 37) words, "to some interesting extent." That is, the modules interact and there is some overlap in the architecture of the mind—there are many connections between the modules. (Minsky, 1986, pp. 314–317, provided a credible discussion of how there could be modules that interconnect.)

There are modules for each sensory/perceptual mode: hearing, sight, touch, taste, and smell. There are also modules for language (MIT-based Chomsky and Fodor are closely colleagual on this point!). It must be emphasized that there are a number of specific modules within each mode:

> [These] . . . might include, in the case of vision, mechanisms for color perception, for the analysis of shape, and for the analysis of three-dimensional spatial relations. They might also include quite narrowly task-specific "higher-level" systems concerned with the visual guidance of bodily motions or with the recognition of faces of conspecifics. Candidates in audition might include . . . systems that assign grammatical descriptions to token utterances; or ones that detect the melodic or rhythmic structure of acoustic

arrays; or, for that matter, ones that mediate the recognition of *voices* of conspecifics. (p. 47)

How many modules there are could be debated at length, although Fodor suggests there are many, that we inherit diverse capacities that are at least partially separable and separated from one another. It must be stressed that Fodor's view is not really a particularly extreme one either, with many cognitive scientists voicing similar sentiments. For example, Marvin Minsky (1986) offered *The Society of Mind*:

I'll call "Society of Mind" this scheme in which each mind is made of many smaller processes. These we'll call agents. Each mental agent by itself can only do some simple things that needs no mind or thought at all. Yet when we join these agents in societies—in certain very special ways—this leads to true intelligence. (p. 17)

The specificity of the agents in this system is obvious from this analysis of the agents required to pick up a cup of tea:

Your GRASPING agents want to keep hold of the cup.
Your BALANCING agents want to keep the tea from spilling out.
Your THIRST agents want you to drink the tea.
Your MOVING agents want to get the cup to your lips. (p. 20)
. . . If each [agent] does its little job, the really big job will get done by all of them together: drinking tea. (p. 20)

According to Minsky, learning is genetically predestined. What is inherited are agencies with particular structures that are sensitive to particular types of information and process such information in particular ways. The agencies and processes that are inherited by humans constrain what humans can learn as does the physical world that humans inhabit (including our own bodies). Thus, how does Minsky (1986) answer a question such as, "Is the child's conception of space acquired or inherited?" (p. 115):

We acquire our conceptions of space by using agencies that learn in accord with processes determined by inheritance. These agencies proceed to learn from experience—but the outcomes of their learning processes are virtually predestined by the spatial geometry of our body parts. (p. 115)

Inherited capacities and processes operating in a real world with particular characteristics (including the constraints associated with human body structure) determine learning.

A conception that is related to that of modularity, and one that was informed directly by Fodor's views, is Howard Gardner's (1983) **theory of multiple intelligences.** Gardner believes that people have a set of specific intelligences that are biologically determined—they are **biopsychological potentials** (Gardner, 1993). These include linguistic, musical, logic-mathematical, spatial, body-kinesthetic, interpersonal (i.e., ability to notice and make distinctions among other individuals), and intrapersonal (i.e., access to one's own feelings) intelligences. These seven abilities exist in the context of other abilities or knowledge that may be more general, such as common sense, originality, metaphorical abilities, and wisdom. One of the most critical features of Gardner's theory is that people vary in the strength of their particular faculties. From this perspective, it makes no sense to think of someone as smart or not-so-smart in general, as is implied in traditional psychometric theory (Chapter 16, this book; see the discussion of the heritability of intelligence presented earlier in this chapter). Rather people with musical intelligence would be expected to excel in music given appropriate stimulation; those who have superior capacity with respect to mathematics would be expected to do well given appropriate exposure to mathematics.

Gardner believes that a major problem with contemporary schooling is that linguistic, logical-mathematical, and intrapersonal intelligences are emphasized in school to the exclusion of others. There is little attempt to gauge the strengths and weaknesses of students with respect to the various intelligences.

Even if relative strengths and weaknesses were known, however, it would be difficult to know what to do. Should strengths be emphasized or weaknesses bolstered? What is known, based on the work of Bloom (1985), which was presented in Chapter 4, is that even when a person is favored biologically with respect to ability, enormous educational resources must be expended to produce someone who is expert with respect to the intelligence in question. Bloom's data make clear that if people inherit multiple intelligences, what they inherit are potentials, potentials that will be fully realized only given extremely favorable educational and environmental circumstances.

Of course, we hope it is obvious, in light of this lengthy discussion of biological determination of learning and cognition, that biological potential remains exactly that until it plays out in an environment that permits that potential to function. This is a fundamental understanding that is true no matter how fine or coarse the level of analysis: Environment-expectant synapses that organize visual competence do not stabilize unless there is appropriate visual stimulation; people high in body-kinesthetic intelligence do not become great athletes without years of coaching and practice.

As we close this subsection, we warn that Fodor, Minsky, and Gardner have yet to offer detailed research to support their positions, although there are lines of research that can support some of the assumptions of the theories they have proposed (e.g., Gardner, 1993). There are rich possibilities in these conceptions of mind for young educational researchers looking for good problems to study. For the budding educator, we are certain that Gardner's multiple intelligences theory is going to have an important impact on education, for it is often referred to in outlets designed for practitioners. The theory is viewed as strongly supportive of individualized instruction and, at least for some children, deemphasizes language and mathematics instruction in favor of other faculties. It is a theory consistent with a long history of recognition of special abilities by psychologists. Gardner's and Foder's new versions of faculty psychology, however, are substantially more refined and defensible than many of their predecessors and deserve more serious consideration than much of the faculty psychology of the past.

CONCLUDING COMMENTS

A great deal of research and theory generated during the last several decades support the case that how learning occurs and what is learned is determined by biology. Humans are prepared better to learn some information than others. They are prepared to learn better some information at particular points in development compared with other points. Some humans are capable of learning contents that are much more difficult for others to acquire, possibly because of biologically based differences in faculty strengths.

Biology and Experience

In the past, there have been many naive arguments about whether human intelligence is a product of heredity or environment. The answer based on all of the biological perspectives reviewed here is that human intelligence and competence depend both on biology and on environment. What biology provides is genetically determined potential. Whether that potential is realized depends critically on experiencing particular types of stimulation. The existence of critical periods with respect to neuronal plasticity makes obvious that it is often not possible to put off providing stimulation to a child until some later point in development. Throughout this book, we will present evidence that what is acquired during the early childhood years has great impact on later development. The critical period perspective reviewed here suggests that at least some of the reason that is true is tied to biological preparedness for learning from certain types of experiences during particular periods in life.

The data in this chapter also make clear that from the time of conception, there is reason to be concerned about the environment the child encounters. There is an old story about a mother listening incessantly to classical music during her pregnancy in an attempt to foster a love of classical music in the child growing in her womb. Nothing quite like that is being proposed here. What is being proposed is that maternal malnutrition, chemical dependency, or disease during a pregnancy can affect the biological development of an embryo or fetus. The result can range from mild mental handicap to severe retardation. There are good reasons to direct educational resources at children who have had adverse prenatal experiences because the severity of disability at maturity can often be reduced or eliminated by responsive stimulation during infancy and the preschool years.

That individual differences in mental functioning might be based in part at least on biological differences between people has been a hypothesis entertained by psychologists throughout the 20th century, with a number of specific biological routes to individual differences proposed: Thus, prenatal exposure to testosterone may affect a person's pattern of cognitive strengths. Subtle individual differences in neurological structure (e.g., number of dendrites) might make a difference in general intelligence achieved by adulthood. Differences in the extent of support tissues, such as capillaries and glial cells, could be implicated in the determination of individual differences in overall intellect. Perhaps the encapsulated modules inherited by different people differ in their relative strengths, a position consistent with Gardner's theory of multiple intelligences. In short, there is real progress in understanding the potential biological mechanisms that underlie human differences.

A Warning

In urging attention to biological evidence pertaining to and explanations about human commonalities and differences, we also urge some caution. All too often we have heard biologically oriented psychologists make exaggerated claims about the inevitability of function and inevitability of differences based on biology. Thus, a few years ago, we listened to a prominent physiological psychologist make the case that math and engineering were not subject areas for girls, with this claim made in light of some then current work on male-female differences in physiological mechanisms related to spatial representation. What our physiologist friend did not indicate (and perhaps did not understand) is that there are great overlaps in the distributions of males and females for most intellectual characteristics, including basic skills related to mathematics and science abilities (e.g., spatial thinking). The really troubling part of the anecdote about our friend who is a physiological psychologist is that sometimes girls have been denied opportunities for math experiences or have been discouraged from pursuing math because of presumptions about biological differences between males and females. Because biology is only potential that requires experience for it to be realized, denying relevant experiences goes far in guaranteeing that the competencies in question will never blossom. Even a girl with many biological dispositions that would support acquisition of mathematics could not be expected to fulfill her potential without instruction and environmental supports for learning of mathematics. Sweeping generalizations about ability based on gender, race, or health are not warranted.

Unfortunately, some biologically oriented types have advanced extremely bad ideas that have been translated into interventions that are disseminated. The Doman-Delacato "patterning" technique for the treatment of mental retardation and brain damage is an example (e.g., Doman, Spitz, Zucman, Delacato, & Doman, 1960). Consider the case of a brain-damaged child. The first step is to determine the developmental point at which the injury occurred. What follows is an attempt to "train" functioning from

that point onward. The theory is that if the body can be exercised in particular ways that are associated with normal development, neurological organization will be achieved that will compensate for the neurological organization that cannot develop naturally because of the injury. The treatment consists of several adults manipulating the limbs and body of the child to mirror the movements that would have occurred in the absence of neurological injury. The assumption is that if the body is put in motion enough times, noninjured brain cells, ones ordinarily unused, will become programmed to perform the functions usually carried out by the injured region of the brain (compare the discussion of how synaptic connections and neurological organization occur as a function of experience).

The one study providing the most compelling evidence in favor of the Doman-Delacato procedure (Doman et al., 1960) contained a number of methodological errors (see Zigler & Hodapp, 1986, pp. 184–191, for a more extensive discussion of these points and of what follows). Follow-up research was not much better, suffering from a variety of shortcomings, including teaching-to-the-test artifacts. Better studies, for example, Neman, Roos, McCann, Menolascino, and Heal (1974), reported few and inconsistent effects of the therapy. Notably the effects that have been obtained in the better investigations have been questioned as potentially reflecting methodological biases favoring the treatment groups (see Zigler & Seitz, 1975, as well as Zigler & Hodapp's, 1986, commentary). There is no miracle cure here, despite persistent claims by Doman-Delacato enthusiasts that the treatment produces miracles.

Another intervention rationalized in biological terms was vitamin therapy as a treatment for mental retardation. Harrell, Capp, Davis, Peerless, and Ravitz (1981) reported large IQ gains in retarded children who were treated with large doses of vitamins. The explanation of the effect was that mental retardation was a genetotrophic disease—a disease that can be brought about by particular nutritional patterns in people possessing certain genetic makeups. Unfortunately, this was a study plagued by methodological difficulties, including loss of subjects. Researchers who did the intellectual testing were not blind to the treatment assignment of the subjects or the purpose of the study (see Zigler & Hodapp, 1986, pp. 191–197). A number of better controlled replication studies failed to produce significant effects in favor of vitamin therapy (Zigler & Hodapp, 1988, provided a review).

For example, in an elegantly controlled study, Smith, Spiker, Peterson, Cicchetti, and Justice (1984) matched pairs of retarded children on a number of variables before the study began. One member of each pair was assigned to a vitamin-treatment group, the other to a placebo-treatment condition. The situation was arranged so that both those delivering the dosages to the subjects and those doing the testing were blind to the treatment condition of the subjects. After 8 months of treatment, vitamin subjects went from an IQ of 45 on average to an IQ of 43.9; placebo control subjects went from 46.2 to 45.0. In short, there was no evidence of intellectual gain owing to vitamin therapy.

A third example of ineffective interventions based on biological conceptions of intellect are treatments inspired by hemispheric specialization research. There can be little doubt that the left and right hemispheres are specialized to perform different functions, with much of this evidence produced by studying the processing of stimuli presented to the right and left hemispheres of people who have had the interconnection between the hemispheres surgically severed. (So that no readers infer that researchers are cutting anyone's *corpus callosum* just to see what happens, we point out that such surgery is a treatment for severe epilepsy.) In recent years, other methods have also been of value in studying functioning in the two halves of the brain, for example, brain imaging and other methods of measuring relative cerebral blood flow.

Perhaps the most important result emerging from this literature is that the left hemisphere is specialized for processing of verbal material and the right for nonverbal, visuospatial content. This now uncontroversial finding can be elaborated somewhat into a set of more controversial, although defensible claims. These include that the left hemisphere is specialized for processing of sequential and temporal content and that the left hemisphere is more logical, analytical, and rational than the right hemisphere. The right hemisphere is better than the left in processing simultaneous, spatial, and analogical information. The right hemisphere's functioning is described by many as synthetic and intuitive. Springer and Deutsch (1989) have produced the most complete summary of hemispheric

specialization research that is accessible to nonspecialists, and we strongly recommend their text as an exceptionally clear presentation of an extremely technical literature.

Some have examined this division in hemispheric function in light of what goes on in school and have concluded that Western schooling is only concerned with one side of the brain, the left hemisphere (e.g., Bogen, 1975; Ornstein, 1977, 1978). In response to this perceived crisis in education, there have been many "right-brain" proposals. Most that we have seen over the years are concerned with encouraging more teaching of art, music, and intuitive interpretation in school. Such proposals do not bother us because we believe that such activities are underrepresented in the curriculum, and many students would benefit enormously from additional opportunities to develop in these domains. Other proposals, however, can only be characterized as bizarre (e.g., teaching people to dance and attempt to read ideas from patterns of smoke to suppress verbal and logical thinking and promote more intuitive thought; see Prince, 1978, and Springer & Deutsch, 1989, Chapter 11, for more). Doman and Delacato, in particular, include methods in their treatment that are intended as a "left-hemisphere curriculum" because their clients are in need of stimulation that will make them more responsive to the left hemisphere–dominant curriculum of Western schooling. That some children are subjected to the following as part of Doman-Delacato therapy on the grounds that it stimulates the development of one hemisphere over another makes clear that biological analyses can go far in affecting the educational resources made available to children:

> A team of therapists, parents, and volunteers take turns manipulating the head and limbs of a child who is unable to make the necessary movements alone. Other techniques used in particular children include restricting the use of one arm, occluding one eye, and prohibiting singing and listening to music. The rationale is to develop total cortical dominance extending not only to language but to a dominant eye, hand, and foot. (Springer & Deutsch, 1989, p. 300)

The short of it, with respect to interventions that are aimed at developing one hemisphere over another, is that there is little evidence that they are effective. Conceptually, it is hard to believe they could be. Most people have an intact corpus callosum, which guarantees that even if someone were to be successful in devising input that would directly stimulate only one half of the brain—and that would be difficult to do—the two halves of the brain are in constant communication. What stimulates one half of the brain is going to stimulate the other half in most people. See Lauren Harris' (1988) chapter on right-brain training for an elaboration of the conclusions in this subsection and a well-informed, scathing indictment of the right-brain movement in education.

Final Comments

We emphasize in closing that far more good than harm seems to be coming out of biological analyses of learning, thinking, acquisition of knowledge, and development. The more we learn about human potential from biological research, the more it should be possible to ensure that every child has a chance to maximize their potential. Biological differences should be used as a tool for deciding how to create more effective educational opportunities, not a tool for attempting to decide what people cannot do before they are given a chance to try to do it! In some cases, understanding of biology has already permitted the creation of interventions that completely transform the quality of some lives (e.g., dietary modifications to prevent PKU retardation). In other cases, the potential of biology is not yet fulfilled, such as with Fodor and Gardner's ideas about innate differences in particular capacities being used to determine how to allocate scarce and valuable educational opportunities. Thus, if some have clear biologically determined capacities that permit much higher achievements in art than would ever be possible for most of us, it might make sense to use knowledge of their biological endowment in redesigning their education from early in life. The wisdom of this is supported by studies such as Bloom (1985; see Chapters 4 and 16, this book) in which extremely high achievement in a domain was often supported by supplemental instruction for that domain from early in life.

Although we criticized the hemispheric specialization types in the last subsection, there is increasing evidence of differences in hemispheric functioning associated with particular talents. Thus, English majors have more blood flow to the left hemisphere than do architecture majors, who have more blood flow to the right hemisphere than typical people (Dabbs, 1980). Eye movements consistent with left hemispheric dominance are more common in English majors than in engineering majors, who display eye movements more indicative of right hemispheric dominance (Bakan, 1969). It may be that such differences have been shaped by years of processing more of one type of information over the other. Alternatively, if such differences are predictive of success in some endeavors more than others, they could be useful in making decisions about curricular emphasis for some students from an early age. Before such a speculation would ever be defensible as a basis for making curriculum reform decisions, a great deal of additional research on hemispheric functioning patterns would be necessary, including longitudinal work on the stability of individual differences in hemispheric functioning. We are far from that point now.

And that is an appropriate way to end this chapter: A great deal of additional research will be necessary before most of the concepts in this chapter could or should be translated into educational applications. Anticipate that such work will occur, for the many exciting findings in neuropsychology and biologically oriented approaches to psychology in the recent past are stimulating much additional thinking and analyses of cognitive functioning. Our bet is that with every revision of this textbook, we will be adding information about new advances in understanding of biology, advances that will have increasing impact on educational practice as this edition of this text is relegated to antiquarian bookstores.

Part

2

Other Grand Theoretical Perspectives

7

Classical Theories of Learning and Development

In addition to information processing models of cognition, there are other theoretical perspectives that are important for an educational psychologist to understand. This chapter is a summary of a diverse array of traditional theories that are of enduring importance. Then Chapter 8 is dedicated to the many social collaborative approaches to education proposed in recent years, covering both teacher-student interactions and student-student interactions that can contribute to long-term cognitive development. Chapter 9 continues the themes began in Chapter 8, focusing on the development of moral judgment and creation of thoughtful educational communities.

This chapter features traditional theories of learning and development, theories that would appear in most courses and texts in educational psychology. For many experienced readers of the educational psychology literature, however, it might seem strange to encounter discussions of Eleanor Gibson, Jean Piaget, B. F. Skinner, Donald Meichenbaum, and Albert Bandura in the same chapter. We put all of these theorists together because we believe that none of them offers a conception that can stand alone, but that all of them offer perspectives that complement one another. Each theorist proposes mechanisms of knowledge acquisition that must be understood to have a complete understanding of the development of knowledge. Many of the mechanisms identified in this chapter probably play a role in knowledge acquisition. An

important challenge is to understand how and when particular mechanisms are likely to be operative and to engineer educational opportunities so the various mechanisms in concert can have maximally positive effects.

The theories considered in this chapter are decidedly more psychological than the biologically oriented conceptions of knowledge acquisition considered in Chapter 6. Nonetheless, each theorist considered in this chapter has conceptions about how biology influences the development of knowledge and how biology interacts with experience. A recurrent theme in this chapter is that humans have evolved to be sensitive to particular forms of stimulation, stimulation that can be informative about the nature of the world. Thus, the case will be developed here that humans are hardwired to be sensitive to the types of sensory input that are in the world. We are also biologically prepared to process feedback offered by the world and have more obvious capacities to imitate what we experience than do other species. Each of the theories presented here includes claims that learning and development of knowledge are determined in part by biology.

Biology provides potential. For the potential to be realized, however, there must be appropriate experiences. The theories in this chapter specify how particular biological proclivities translate into knowledge and behavior as a function of the natural environment.

PERCEPTUAL LEARNING

Perceptual learning theory highlights interactions between biologically determined potential and environment. A baby enters this world inherently active from this point of view. From the beginning, babies want to do things; they have goals—to touch things, to see things, to begin to understand the world. What is critical according to Gibson's (e.g., 1969) theory is that the stimulation in the world is inherently filled with information. Thus, at about 4 months of age, author MP's son, Tim, received his first set of rubber alphabet letters, ones that floated in the bathtub. These letters were composed of features that differentiate letters (e.g., curves, straight lines, diagonals) plus color. Although Tim could tell that two letters were the same or different from an early age, he did not notice the features that differentiated one letter from another until quite a bit later. By age $2^1/_2$, Tim was able to spot Mommy's letter (i.e., M), Daddy's letter (D), and Timmy's letter (T) reliably, not only when playing with the bathtub letters but whenever large, block letters were encountered. At age 4, he could reliably spot all of the letters of the alphabet and name them, although there were occasional slipups, almost always involving letters that share features (e.g., "h" being mistaken for "n").

The features defining letters (and other things) are always out there in the world; with experience, people discover the critical features differentiating a set of items. Thus, for many preschoolers, every airplane is the same. After years of experience with aircraft, including many explicit attempts to figure out how particular aircraft and models differ from one another, people can differentiate easily a 737 from a 747 and even a 737-100 from a 737-200. Many experienced air travelers can tell at a glance whether they are looking at a 747-200 or a 747-400. With experience, frequent flyers increase their knowledge of the **distinctive features** of different types of aircraft, sometimes as a function of incidental learning and sometimes by intentionally trying to distinguish the various aircraft at airports. (See Eleanor Gibson [1969, p. 83] for a fascinating discussion about how Robert Gagné and James J. Gibson taught World War II fighter pilots to distinguish aircraft by getting them to focus on distinctive features in relation to one another.)

The distinctive features diffentiating members of a class are not isolated pieces of information but instead are in relation to one another. One manufacturer sells a customized car kit that is a small-scale front end of a Rolls Royce. This front end can be attached to the body of a Volkswagen. We have seen several such customized vehicles but have never once mistaken one of these cars for a Rolls Royce. A Rolls has more than a particularly shaped hood! There are many features in relation to one another that define a Rolls: The hood is proportional to the projected length of the car in particular ways. The ratio of the car body to the body in the driver's seat is much larger for the Rolls than for the kit car. The reflection off a Rolls is more striking because the paint is deeper in color and the surface smoother. Somehow the trim on a Rolls projects a sturdiness that is not projected by the trim on the kit car. So it is for any object, be it a letter of the alphabet, a person's face, or the leaves on trees. Thus, in the autumn, at one glance people fear red, three-leafed arrays that are near to the ground (i.e., poison ivy) but have no thoughts of danger when confronted with red leaves in general, other leaves near to the ground, or three-leaf clusters. Distinctive features are distinctive only in relation to one another.

Gibson's theory is that the processes underlying perceptual learning are the same in adults and children, although adults are sometimes quicker at any given perceptual learning task because their previous experiences have produced understanding of what to look for, what types of information define distinctive features. Thus, it takes most children several years to learn to differentiate the letters of the alphabet. In contrast, however, English-speaking adults who begin to study Russian acquire the distinctive features of the Cyrillic alphabet in a matter of days, largely because of a great deal of prior knowledge about the types of features that can differentiate letters of an alphabet.

What is required for perceptual learning to occur? Repeated exposure to a set of objects differing in particular ways is essential. In general, if the ways that the objects differ are essential to obtaining some goal, it is more likely the features will be noticed. Thus, for Tim to figure out which letter was the one Mommy kept referring to as her letter, it was necessary to discern how Mommy's letter differed from other letters. With increasing practice, there was an **increase in specificity** of the objects that were classified as Mommy's letter. At first, any letter with verticals would do (e.g., H, M, N, P, R, D), then two verticals were required (e.g., H, M, N), then two verticals and at least one diagonal (e.g., M, N), and finally only Ms—although many variations on M would do, from *M* to **M** to M to ᴍ to *M,* and so on. When Tim classified any M as an M and never confused it with another letter, it was clear he had acquired the distinctive features associated with M.

With increasing age and experience, children's attention to and processing of perceptual information become more efficient. Younger children's attention is often captured by salient environmental stimuli (see Turnure, 1970), whereas older children can more often ignore salient, distractible properties of stimulation that are not relevant to a task (e.g., Druker & Hagen, 1969). With increasing age, children are also much more likely to examine stimuli more systematically and completely. Thus, when Vurpillot (e.g., 1968) asked young children to examine visual patterns, preschoolers examined far fewer features and did so unsystematically compared with children 3 to 4 years older, who systematically and exhaustively scanned features that were potentially relevant in the task given to the children (i.e., to decide if two similar, complex patterns differed or were the same). In general, with development, children focus in on more information that is relevant to the task they are asked to perform; they are more flexible in attending to object features, sometimes systematically examining in one way and sometimes in another depending on the task; they learn to know what to expect and thus are better at knowing what to look for; and their attention becomes more economical in that task-relevant features come to dominate attention, with these increasingly perceived simultaneously or in quick succession. Thus, adult frequent flyers can quickly abstract many features of an airplane, whereas a preschooler covers features slowly (e.g., Dad, it's got a door in the back, and there's two engines on the plane and one more on top, and this is a blue, red, and white plane—except up front, which is black on the nose. And so it goes, slowly processing a feature at a time, ones a frequent-flyer Daddy picks up with a glance or two.)

Perceptual information is important because it often provides important information about how to use the objects in the world. James J. Gibson (e.g., 1979) proposed the concept of **affordances:**

> The *affordances* of the environment are what it *offers* the animal, what it *provides* or *furnishes,* either for good or ill. The verb *to afford* is found in the dictionary, but the noun *affordance* is not. I have made it up. I mean by it something that refers to both the environment and the animal in a way that no existing term does. It implies the complementarity of the animal and the environment. The antecedents of the term and the history of the concept will be treated later; for the present, let us consider examples of an affordance.
>
> If a terrestrial surface is nearly horizontal (instead of slanted), nearly flat (instead of convex or concave), and sufficiently extended (relative to the size of the animal), and if its substance is rigid (relative to the weight of the animal), then the surface *affords support*. It is a surface of support, and we call it a substratum, ground, or floor. It is stand-on-able, permitting an upright posture for quadrupeds and bipeds. It is therefore walk-on-able and run-over-able. It is not sink-into-able like a surface or a swamp, that is, for heavy terrestial animals. Support for water bugs is different. (J. J. Gibson, 1979, p. 127).

Once again, human biology determines cognition. According to Gibson, there is something in our biology that makes us see a supporting structure when we perceive a terrestrial, horizontal, flat, extended, and rigid surface. Once again, the environment determines cognition as well, for "Affordances are not invented or read into events by the perceiver. They are there to be perceived" (E. J. Gibson, 1982, p. 57).

There are a few basic mechanisms of perceptual learning according to Eleanor Gibson. **Abstraction** is the finding of distinctive features or invariant relationships (i.e., relations that remain constant for a class of events). After experiencing many of Mommy's letter, Tim abstracted the distinctive features for M. Middle-aged softball players who played baseball in their youth have abstracted the invariant relationships in baseballs and softballs (e.g., white leather, stitched all around, smooth) as well as the features distinguishing them from one another (i.e., size, perceived "hardness"). **Filtering** involves ignoring the irrelevant dimensions. Thus, children learn to classify maple and oak leaves, coming to rely on shape, which differentiates these leaves, and filtering out color and size, which do not reliably differentiate maple and oak leaves. A third mechanism is **peripheral attention.** Processing of information that is out of central attention is critical to determining where next to focus attention. Thus, it is well known that peripheral visual mechanisms "look ahead" and guide the movement of the eyeball from fixation at one point A to a next point B, which is anything but randomly selected (e.g., Just & Carpenter, 1987). For example, if there is a noun and a function word (a, the) to the right of the current focus of attention during reading of a sentence, the eyeball is much more likely to land on the noun than on the function word. The eye moves to highly informative parts of text, not to uninformative parts of text owing to guidance provided by peripheral attention.

The Gibsons' view is that people are inherently motivated to learn from a world that is filled with what can be known. People are biologically prepared to abstract particular types of information from the environment. Learning is gradual and covaries with experience. Diverse perceptual experiences and many opportunities to interact with the world in meaningful ways is a Gibsonian prescription for high-quality perceptual learning. Humans have evolved to fit their environment: Human evolution has been shaped by the environment, and, in turn, each generation of humans comes to understand the environment in particular ways because of that evolutionary shaping. Our perception has evolved to guide our functioning in the world. We do not walk off cliffs because our perceptual apparatuses have evolved so the perceptual array that defines the edge of a cliff affords falling to us (see Walk & Gibson, 1961):

> ... [W]e are animals living in an environment we evolved in. We behave in it more or less adaptively to survive. We occupy a niche, like other animals. (E. J. Gibson, 1991, p. 607).

There is much of importance for the educational psychologist in Gibson's theory. The need for experiences that require processing of important distinctive features is critical. Being forced to decide whether similar situations, patterns, or events are the same or different and how they are the same or different can have great impact on coming to understand which features are critical and distinctive. Many different types of educational contents require such discriminations, from learning of letter forms to recognition of particular plays in football or baseball. Perceptual learning continues well past childhood. Fighter pilots must learn to discriminate "our" planes from "their" planes; physicians must be able to differentiate a benign mole from a probable malignant skin growth; and baseball players must be able to see the difference between a slider and a curve ball. All involve learning distinctive features.

One of the most important parts of this theory is one that was emphasized in Chapter 5 on motivation. Children seek information, actively searching

for new input that permits them to function more capably in the world. As children learn to read, there is the active pursuit of perceptual learning opportunities every day. They self-initiate reading of books, construction of letter puzzles, playing with games that require discrimination of letters, sounds, and words. Moms and Dads play, too, but often long after they have tired of a letter or reading activity, their children still want to play. Fortunately for the parents, the intrinsic motivation in the perceptual learning system is often more than enough to keep the children going at a task on their own. Children learn more than just letters and words; they get ideas from those books and new knowledge. The final two thoughts in Eleanor Gibson's (1991) most recent book sum it up: "... we perceive to learn, as well as learn to perceive."

PIAGETIAN THEORY OF COGNITIVE DEVELOPMENT: EQUILIBRATION AND COGNITIVE CONFLICT AS MECHANISMS FOR LEARNING AND DEVELOPMENT

No single individual has had as much impact on the study of children's mind and mental capacities as Jean Piaget. Although many of the specific descriptions and explanations of development offered by Piaget are no longer accepted, Piaget and his collaborators defined many of the problems that continue to occupy researchers interested in children's minds and the development of mental capacities. Moreover, his theory inspired a philosophy that continues to affect education, especially the education of young children. No serious student of educational psychology would not know about Piaget's theory, nor would any serious student of educational psychology not know about the many reasons for caution in accepting it.

Brief Outline of Cognitive Development According to Piaget

Four Stages According to Piaget (e.g., 1983), there are four stages of cognitive development that occur in an invariant sequence. Although Piaget frequently warned against applying age norms to the stages, the **sensorimotor stage** was generally considered as the first two years of life. Intelligence during this period of time is not yet in the mind but rather is in the actions of the child on the environment. Piaget and Piagetians devoted substantial resources to understanding the development of motor actions and the coordination of motor actions (schemes, in Piagetian terms). A particularly important acquisition during this period is the development of the **object concept,** the understanding that objects continue to exist independent of one's self. Before this acquisition, children act as if objects that are out of their sight no longer exist; once the object concept is acquired, children understand that objects have an existence independent of their perception of the objects. By the end of the sensorimotor period, **symbolic functioning** has begun, especially the use of language. An organism that can use language and understands that there is a world independent of itself can no longer be considered to be functioning only on sensory and motor planes.

The **preoperational stage** roughly corresponds to the preschool years. There are significant advances in language and other competencies during this period. What is emphasized about the preoperational stage, however, are the child's incompetencies rather than competencies. The incompetency that has received the most attention from researchers is the preschool child's failure on **conservation tasks.** On a conservation problem, a substance is transformed in a way that does not alter its amount but changes its appearance (e.g., liquid is poured from a tall beaker to a stout beaker). The preschooler will claim that the amount changed despite the fact that nothing was added or subtracted. Thus, for the example of liquids in different-shaped beakers, the preschooler might argue that there is more liquid after pouring because the water is wider or that there is less liquid because it is not as tall in the glass. The child is attending to and interpreting perceptual cues that are misleading with respect to the constancy of the amount of liquid.

Several years later, when the child can conserve, he or she can give explanations about how height and width offset one another and about how amount cannot change when nothing is added or subtracted. That is not to say that there is no logic during the preschool years. Thus, if asked whether it is the same water when water is transferred from beaker A to beaker B, preschoolers understand that it is. Understanding that the **identity** of the water survives a perceptual transformation does not permit children to make logical claims about the relative amounts of water in the tall versus the wide beaker, however—the same child who will respond

that it is the same water before and after pouring will also claim that there is now more or less water than there was before the pouring. Whatever logic is present is limited, however, with illogical responding produced easily by even small increases in difficulty of problems (e.g., asking whether it is the same amount of water versus the same water).

The preschool years are characterized, according to Piaget, by **egocentrism,** the inability to take the perspective of others. Thus, studies were offered by Piagetians in which preschoolers claimed that others, who viewed a set of objects from an angle different than their own angle of view, saw the set of objects from exactly the same perspective as they saw them. The Piagetians also contended that egocentric speech predominated in the language of preschoolers so that a high proportion of utterances offered by preschoolers were not intelligible to others or social in the sense that they communicated information to other people well. In short, preschoolers generally were depicted as incompetent in Piagetian theory, despite a great deal of rhetoric by Piagetians about their focus on the competence of children.

The reason preschoolers' thought is so deficient according to Piaget is that they lack the logical **operations** that underlie mature thought. Basically these are cognitive rules. One is the **identity** function already described. A second is **negation,** that an operation can be undone by returning to the point of departure (i.e., by reversing it, such as pouring the water back in the tall beaker—or doing so mentally). **Reciprocity** is recognition that change on one dimension can be compensated for by changes on another dimension (e.g., the same amount of water will be higher in a narrow than in a broad beaker).

Having such rules permits conservation according to Piagetians: The child with **operational intelligence** can reason that the amount of water in the wider beaker is the same as it was in the taller beaker because he or she can mentally undo the pouring (i.e., can reverse it). The child can also point out the reciprocal relationship between height and width of the liquid. The child who is in one of the two stages of operational intelligence is a much more powerful thinker than the preoperational preschooler.

During the **concrete operational stage,** which corresponds roughly to the elementary-grade years, the child can apply the cognitive operations, so long as the problem involves concrete objects (i.e., does not involve abstract manipulation or hypotheticals). Thus, if shown two rows of seven buttons lined up evenly, the child continues to believe the two rows contain the same number of buttons even when one of the rows is "stretched" so that there is greater space between individual buttons (i.e., the child can do number conservation problems). If two balls of clay are the same weight as evidenced by them exactly balancing a pan scale, the conserving child will predict that the scale will stay in balance even if one of the two balls is reshaped, perhaps flattened like a pancake or rolled into a snake (i.e., the child can do conservation of weight problems).

Concrete operations permit the performance of other tasks as well, such as **class inclusion** problems. These involve presenting children with sets of objects, some of which are subsets of each other. The child's task is to answer questions about the subset relationships. Thus, if given a set of five robins and four bluebirds, the conserving child understands there are more birds than robins, whereas the preoperational child is more likely to respond that there are more robins because there are more robins than bluebirds apparent in the perceptual array that the child is viewing. According to Piagetian theory, concrete operations also permit children to seriate items (i.e., ordering them on some dimension, such as shortest to tallest or lightest to heaviest).

Children who have acquired **formal operations** are capable of more still. First, they can handle problems that involve more factors. Thus, although the concrete operational child can seriate with respect to one dimension, the formal operational child can do so with respect to several dimensions simultaneously. Formal operational thinkers can also generate all combinations of possibilities for a given situation. Formal operational thinkers can infer "invisible forces" and thus can solve problems involving such forces (e.g., determining how hydraulic presses work given some weights and several presses).

In our classes, we frequently use one of the Piagetian tasks designed to tap formal operations to demonstrate the nature of formal operational thought to university students. For the pendulum problem, we provide three lengths of string and three different weights that can be attached to the string. The question posed to students is to determine what factors determine the rate at which a pendulum swings. In most classes, the first student volunteer will propose the following: (1) Use one of the strings and try each weight in succession, and (2) use

one of the weights and try each string in succession. What becomes apparent is that the speed of swinging varies with the length of the string but not the weight. Really good students also vary systematically how much force they use to set the pendulum in motion, determining that this is not a critical factor in the speed of the pendulum swing. In summary, some students act like fully rational scientists in this situation, varying one factor at a time while holding other factors constant. Such thinking is possible only with the onset of the formal operational stage according to Piagetian conceptions of intelligence.

There are "stronger" and "weaker" versions of Piagetian theory, corresponding roughly to earlier and later versions of the framework. The strong version of the theory is that once in a stage, all behavior and thinking reflect the stage because it is determined by the underlying competencies characteristic of the stage. Thus, a child who is concrete operational for one task should be concrete operational for all tasks. The stages build on one another, with each one a prerequisite for the next one. This requires that progress through the stages be an invariant sequence. By training and by conviction, Piaget was a biologist (see Brainerd, 1978b, Chapter 1; Piaget, 1967) and thus believed there was a biological inevitability to the stages and hence a universality to them. Thus, sensorimotor intelligence was part of being a human. The acquisition of object permanence and the beginnings of language permit the competencies that characterize the preoperational stage. The mistakes of the preoperational period are necessary and play an integral role in the development of the concrete operations, which must develop before the formal operations (which logically depend on the concrete operations). If there is individuality in the acquisition of the stages, it is in that some individuals move through the stages more rapidly than do others, and some do not make it all the way to formal operations.

A weaker version of the theory permits "stage mixture" (see Brainerd, 1978b, 1978c; Flavell, 1971, 1972), so that a child might be preoperational for some tasks and concrete operational for others. Some children may be able to attack some problems in a formal operational fashion while still requiring concrete manipulatives for other problems. This stage mixture notion was developed after it became obvious that not all problems requiring the same logical operations are mastered at the same time (i.e., there is **horizontal décalage**). Thus, conservation of length (i.e., recognizing that the length of a string does not vary if the string is shaped one way or another) is acquired before conservation of continuous quantity (i.e., liquid), which is acquired well before conservation of volume (i.e., the understanding that volume of a piece of matter does not vary with its shape, so that a ball of clay has the same volume as a flattened pancake made from the same clay).

Development according to this perspective is biologically determined, following an inevitable sequence. Not surprisingly, the most important mechanisms underlying the movement through the stages are also biologically determined according to Piagetian theory.

Mechanisms of Cognitive Change   Piaget (e.g., 1983) recognized that there were multiple determinants of developmental change. The first, **maturation,** is biological. Piaget's view was that as the organism matured physically, new possibilities for development were opened. Although biological development is necessary for cognitive growth, it is not sufficient for such growth to occur. **Experience** plays a role as well: New cognitive acquisitions are exercised (i.e., practiced). Experience with the physical world permits the abstractions of important regularities (e.g., that as the amount of something increases, its weight increases; color and weight do not always covary). There are also opportunities for what Piaget refers to as **logicomathematical experiences,** which involve learning about the effects of actions on objects:

> . . . For example, if a child, when he is counting pebbles, happens to put them in a row and . . . make[s] the astonishing discovery that when he counts them from right to the left he finds the same number as when he counts from the left to the right, and again the same when he puts them in a circle, etc., he has discovered experimentally that the sum is independent of order. But this is a logicomathematical experiment and not a physical one, because neither the order nor even the sum was in the pebbles before he arranged them in a certain manner (i.e., ordered them) and joined them together as a whole. What he has discovered is a relation, new to him, between the action of putting in order and the action of joining together . . . and not . . . a property belonging to pebbles. (Piaget, 1983, p. 119).

The **social environment** also plays a role in development, with Piaget believing that the speed of movement through the stages could be affected by the quality of the child's social environment at home and school, with environments that permitted practice of new skills and logicomathematical experiences increasing the speed of movement from one stage to the next.

An especially critical mechanism affecting cognitive growth according to Piaget is **equilibration.** At any given point of development, children understand the world in terms of the cognitive operations they have developed (i.e., they **assimilate** new information). Thus, consider how a preoperational child, who does not have cognitive structures that permit understanding of compensation, responds to a conservation of weight problem. A ball of clay is presented. When rolled out into a sausage shape, the child indicates there is less clay now than when the clay was in a ball, because the sausage is "thinner." The cognitive structures possessed by a preoperational child foster attention to only one dimension in making conservation judgments. If the experimenter continues to roll the sausage out, it gets longer and longer so the length dimension becomes more salient and more difficult to overlook. Some of the time the child responds based on this increase in length, reporting that there is more clay when the clay is in the shape of a sausage than in the shape of a ball. The child eventually becomes aware of the oscillation between responding one way based on length and another way based on width, with the result being **cognitive conflict—** there is increasingly obvious difficulty in making a conservation judgment based on only one dimension. There is disequilibrium in that the cognitive structures that had been perceived by the child to work well on conservation tasks are no longer perceived to be adequate. This motivates reflection that results in the construction of new cognitive structures permitting compensation. This occurs through a process known as **accommodation:**

> . . . [A]ccommodation [is] any modification of [an] assimilatory scheme or structure by the elements it assimilates. (Piaget, 1983, p. 107)

Once this accommodation occurs, there is a return to equilibrium: The structures that permit compensation produce solutions to conservation problems, responses that are perceived to be adequate.

We know from years of teaching these ideas that they are confusing, so here is another run through the notion of equilibration, this time with respect to conservation of liquid in Flavell's (1985) words:

... [T]he nonconserver usually focuses his attention only on the greater height of the liquid column in the taller, thinner glass, and therefore concludes that it has more liquid than the standard [in a shorter, wider glass]. His thinking about this problem is said to be in equilibrium, albeit at an immature, nonconservation level.

Suppose, however, that at some point he notices that the new column is thinner, a fact that by itself would incline him to conclude that the new glass contains less liquid than the standard. If he finds both of these opposing conclusions plausible at the same psychological moment, his cognitive system has moved from a state of equilibrium to one of disequilibrium or cognitive conflict with respect to this problem. According to Piaget, states of cognitive conflict and disequilibrium impel the child to make cognitive progress. In this case, the child achieves a new more intellectually advanced equilibrium state by conceptualizing both the height increase and the width decrease as predictable, mutually compensatory changes in a process of physical transformation that leaves liquid quantity unchanged. (Flavell, 1985, p. 289)

Natural development of conservation occurs when the child discovers the inadequacy of his or her belief in nonconservation (a belief long held without question and thus considered to be an **equilibrated** belief in Piagetian terms). A disconfirmation of such an expectation leads to destabilization of the belief that amount varies with appearance (such destabilization is **disequilibration**). Disequilibration motivates efforts to understand the principle that amount does not vary with appearance. Resolution of the cognitive conflict between a long-held belief and a new, more adequate conception of a situation produces a new **equilibrium.**

Equilibration involves both assimilation and accommodation, with assimilation the tendency to interpret new situations in terms of existing cognitive structures and accommodation the tendency to adapt cognitive structures so that they produce expectations more in accord with what actually occurs in the world. The most important mechanism of cognitive change acknowledged by the Piagetians is equilibration, with the assumption that cognitive development was many cycles of equilibrium, disequilibrium, followed by equilibrium at a higher level of competence (see Piaget, 1983, for one of the most accessible discussions of this concept by Piaget). Although the Genevans resisted the idea that concepts such as conservation could be developed through instruction, they eventually conceded

that instruction could affect conceptual development (e.g., Inhelder, Sinclair, & Bovet, 1974). Their concession was limited, however, to instruction that stimulated disequilibration, which led to accommodation and the achievement of a new equilibrium. That is, conservation could be achieved through natural equilibration or through equilibration stimulated by a teacher making obvious the inadequacy of one's nonconservation expectations. This perspective contrasts dramatically with alternative views of conceptual learning, including acquisition of conservation, that will be taken up in the section on social learning presented later in this chapter.

Equilibration involves discovery of new structures. Self-regulated change and development are emphasized in Piaget's model. The organism is inherently motivated to reduce cognitive conflict, resulting in accommodations that produce new, more powerful cognitive structures. A good educational environment is one that provides a great deal of exercise in developing skills as well as challenges that are well matched to the child's level. That is, only a small amount of cognitive growth is required for the organism to solve challenging problems. Thus, the conservation problem involving the clay required the child be able to relate changes in two dimensions, a competency not yet acquired by the preoperational child but one within reach of a child who can effortlessly monitor changes in one dimension because of years of practice doing so. The likelihood of the preoperational child detecting the inadequacy of his or her current unidimensional approach to the conservation problem varies with the ways of presenting the problem. Thus, repeated presentation of the problem as the ball is rolled into a thinner and thinner sausage is a situation likely to induce notice of the width dimension some of the time and the length dimension other times, which in turn leads to cognitive conflict, which in turn motivates the accommodations necessary to construct the understandings about compensation necessary to accomplish the conservation of weight task. Good educational environments include many well-structured tasks designed to permit discovery of the effects of actions on objects (i.e., logicomathematical experiences), experiences that sometimes produce cognitive conflict and eventual accommodations.

Educational Environments Inspired by Piaget's Theory   One of the frustrations for educational psychologists who read Piaget is that he made few explicit recommendations for education. This was because of Piaget's conviction that cognitive development was largely a biological unfolding of cognitive stages. In 1974, the Genevans (Inhelder et al., 1974) produced a volume on *Learning and the Development of Cognition.* The strong belief in biological inevitability came through clearly in this volume. Piaget was an extreme "readiness" theorist! The view developed in Inhelder et al. (1974) was that instruction of a concept would be profitable only when children were on the verge of acquiring the concept naturally (i.e., acquisition of a concept might be speeded up but within the constraints of natural development—only for those concepts that are just a bit beyond where the child is already). Inhelder et al. expressed this conclusion in biological terms:

> . . . [M]odification of acquisition speeds because of training and absence of modification of the main course of development—brings to mind a parallel in embryogenesis: the internal regulatory mechanisms called "homeorhesis" (the regulatory process compensating for disturbances resulting from interaction with the environment) in the epigenetic development of the embryo. (p. 268)

Such a conclusion is hardly surprising. After all, Piaget's culminating work was entitled *Biology and Knowledge* (1967), and he was trained as a biologist, with concepts such as assimilation and accommodation derived from 19th century biological theories of stability and change in organisms (see Brainerd, 1978b, Chapter 1).

Piaget's distaste for research on educational acceleration is well known, with Piaget and his Genevan colleagues derogating work on instruction as the "American question" (see Brainerd, 1978a). In conceding that acceleration was possible, Inhelder et al. (1974) made clear the Genevan view that the only educational mechanisms that could produce legitimate conceptual change were ones that would mirror naturalistic development via equilibration (cognitive conflict):

> The interpretation given of the acquisition processes as observed in the learning experiments [reported in Inhelder et al., 1974] thus converges with Piaget's equilibration model. . . . In Piaget's words: "The subject does not intentionally seek incoherence and so always aims at certain forms of equilibrium. . . . " The problem is therefore to determine which psychological mechanism is responsible for the progressive im-

provements in the successive forms of equilibrium, improvements, and perfections that Piaget refers to as . . . "heightening equilibration." The source of the progress is to be sought in the disequilibrium which incites the subject to go beyond his present state in search of new solutions. (p. 264)

The mechanisms bring about improvements and progress in the various forms of equilibrium consist, first, in an application of existing schemes to an increasing variety of situations. Sooner or later, this generalization encounters resistance, mainly from the simultaneous application of another scheme; this results in two different answers to one problem and stimulates the subject seeking a certain coherence to adjust both schemes or to limit each to a particular application, thereby establishing their differences and likenesses. The situations most likely to elicit progress are those where the subject is encouraged to compare modes of reasoning which vary considerably both in nature and complexity, but which all are already familiar to him. Training procedures in which one type of reasoning is artificially isolated and exercised, as is often the case in certain programmed learning projects, are not, in our opinion, very useful, since they eliminate the element we consider necessary for progress, i.e., the dynamics of the conflict between schemes. (p. 265)

A number of educators attempted to design environments so discovery via equilibration would be likely, believing that such discovery would lead to deeper understanding than would other forms of learning, consistent with the general Piagetian theoretical position (see Brainerd, 1978a). The tasks given to children in such environments are ones that are developmentally appropriate, so it is essential to diagnose the child's current developmental stage and match instruction to it (Brainerd, 1978a; 1978b, Chapter 7). Children are active participants in their own learning, with instruction largely aimed at increasing children's awareness of conflicts between their approaches to problems and features of the problems (e.g., that in considering the width of a clay sausage, they are neglecting its length).

Kamii (1985, Chapter 8 written with Georgia DeClark) summarized Piagetian principles of education (adapted slightly here): (1) Adult power should be reduced as much as possible, with instruction encouraging the exchange of points of view between teachers and children and between children and children. (2) Children should be encouraged to think in their own ways rather than to produce the right answers in the right way as defined by a teacher. (3) Instruction should be intrinsically motivating. For example, much of arithmetic instruction can occur in the context of games. (4) Teachers should not correct wrong answers but rather should provide hints and nudges about information the child might not be taking into account or may want to reconsider.

Kamii (1985), who was principally concerned with instruction of mathematics via Piagetian principles, urged teachers to tie instruction to problems of daily living (e.g., construct math lessons about potential outcomes in class votes; develop graphs and representations of attendance patterns in the class as well as demographics of the class). She encouraged teachers to provide students with challenging problems and to take the time necessary to solve the problems in ways that encourage deep student understandings of the problems and alternative solutions. Teaching of math should occur throughout the school day (e.g., graphing information generated during a class science experiment). Consistent with Piagetian principles, such teaching is concrete and tied to personal understandings that permit ready assimilation of much of the information. Piagetian views on education will be reiterated later, especially in the chapters on math and science instruction (Chapters 12 and 13). In these two arenas, Piagetian-inspired thinking about education is enjoying a renaissance. Some additional comments about instruction according to the Piagetian perspective will be offered later in this chapter as well, as part of an evaluation of the social learning instructional alternative to the more discovery-based approach favored by Genevans.

Evaluation of Piaget's Theory

From the mid-1960s to the mid-1970s, Piaget's theory was the preeminent theory of cognitive development. Much of the interest and enthusiasm followed publication of Flavell's (1963) book-length summary of the theory. Voluminous research on various aspects of Piaget's theory was generated during these two decades. Partially as a result of this work, however, much of the interest and enthusiasm for the theory died.

Many research outcomes were not consistent with Piaget's theory. Brainerd's (1978b) book was a culminating blow to the Piagetian perspective. Brainerd summarized evidence making obvious that some abilities were acquired earlier than Piaget had supposed (e.g., making simple inferences; some abstract logical processes). Other acquisitions came in later than specified by the theory (e.g., conservation of volume). Some behaviors reported by Piaget never were manifested anything like Piaget proposed (e.g., Piaget's depiction of preschooler speech as extremely egocentric was not consistent with the many communicative competencies possessed by preschoolers).

Some of the most important constructs and mechanisms specified in the theory proved challenging to study. For example, equilibration was almost impossible to operationalize. Measures of the various concrete and formal operations were difficult to devise. These difficulties resulted in great logical circularity in many tests of Piagetian ideas because there was no way to assess stage attainment independent of performing tasks presumably mediated by the cognitive structures characterizing a stage (Brainerd, 1978c). For example, arguments were made that if a child was concrete operational, the child should be able to do the concrete conservation tasks. How would one know if a given child possessed the concrete operations? He or she could do the concrete conservations!

At the same time that Piaget's theory was being challenged by disconfirming data, an alternative conception of thinking and the development of intellectual competence was doing better. Many information processing models and interventions based on information processing analyses of thinking and learning (i.e., models compatible with the models covered in Chapters 1 through 5) were being tested and faring well. Moreover, information processing models could be applied more flexibly to analyses of many more school-valid tasks than could Piagetian perspectives. Thus, this book is filled with information processing analyses of writing, problem solving, reading, and science learning. The alternative was not only a better predictor of research outcomes, but also it was capable of producing predictions about and interventions relevant to more domains.

Two other limitations to the Piagetian approach became obvious as familiarity with the theory increased: (1) The theory is minimally informative about determinants of individual differences in mental functioning. Although information processing theories provided insights about intellectually disabled children as well as understandings about how to educate such populations (see Chapter 18), no such insights or guidance followed from Piagetian analyses. (2) Piaget's developmental theory accounts only for a fraction of life span development. Once formal operations are obtained, Piaget's theory is in general silent about additional developments. Rarely did Piaget ever even discuss adult development. When he did (e.g., Piaget, 1972), development across the life span was seen as extending the operational competence developed during childhood and adolescence to new arenas and tasks. There have been only a few attempts to evaluate Piaget's thinking about adulthood, although studies to date in this tradition have generally confirmed Piagetian expectations. Thus, Kuhn, Kohlberg, Langer, and Haan (1977) demonstrated that formal operational competence does extend into new domains with increasing age and experience during adulthood. In contrast, the information processing frameworks have proved to be extremely helpful in understanding many more aspects of aging, from the mechanisms that underlie diseases of aging, such as Alzheimer's (see Poon, 1986) to explanations of exceptional competence during old age despite biological decline (e.g., Labouvie-Vief, 1985; Poon, 1985; see Chapter 18). Information processing models have stimulated many more studies of intellectual development across the life span than have Piagetian conceptions.

Interest in Piaget's theory waned owing to weaknesses in its predictive validity as well as limits in its scope (i.e., it was concerned mostly with development of normally functioning children). Piaget's thinking declined in prominence as well because of the success of other theories, such as the information processing conceptions of thinking and learning that are covered throughout this book. Even so, Piagetian-inspired analyses continue to have powerful impacts in mathematics and science education today, and thus this is not the last mention of Piaget in this book. In addition, Piagetian thinking is inspiring new theoretical analyses of education that take into account information processing, with the most prominent of these approaches developed by Case and co-workers.

We close this coverage of Piaget's theory with brief discussion of Case's framework, a point of view that is not yet fully developed but is important because it is a thoughtful attempt to reconcile two important traditions in cognitive development, one in which stages of development are considered critical and the other in which processing mechanisms are the main concern. Case explains stages in terms of information processing mechanisms.

Case's Neo-Piagetian Theory of Development

Similar to Piaget, Case (e.g., 1991) argues for four distinct stages of cognitive development, which occur in an invariant sequence. The sequencing is invariant because each stage reflects differentiation, coordination, and consolidation of schemes present in the immediately previous stage. Smaller schemes that were once separate combine to form larger, more powerful schemes. These larger schemes are increasingly coordinated with one another. More powerful schemes that are coordinated better permit more adequate performances.

Thus, a 4-year-old can draw a human figure that has many of the global features of human beings. A slightly older child can draw a more differentiated figure and do so in relation to a larger scene. Case's explanation is that the drawings of the older child represent a differentiation not present in the younger children, with the parts of a drawing differentiated into figure (the human) and ground (the larger scene). The 6-year-old's systems for drawing figures and for drawing the larger scene also represent integrations of skills that are not integrated for 4-year-olds. The 6-year-old coordinates these two systems to produce the more complete picture, a complex coordination relative to the coordinations possible for 4-year-olds.

How and why is there an improvement in drawing ability according to Case's theory? Part of the explanation is practice. Only schemes that are highly practiced can be differentiated into new schemes and then integrated with other schemes. Thus, a great deal of practice in drawing global figures is required before there is differentiation of drawing schemes. This practice must occur until the child can perform automatically the behaviors that once were done only with considerable effort and attention. Thus, although a young 4-year-old might have to expend all available mental energy to draw a stick figure, a slightly older child who has drawn many such stick figures can do so automatically, and thus less working memory is consumed during drawing of global human figures. This frees up some working memory for attention to other things, including acquisition of new understandings of how figure and ground can be separated. That is, with increasing automaticity in execution of skills, a child has more functional short-term capacity. The more functional short-term capacity, the better thinking in general.

Increasing functional short-term memory with development is the critical determinant of increases in cognitive competence according to Case's theory, with multiple factors accounting for developmental increases in working memory capacity: (1) As just explained, practicing a procedure increases its automatic functioning, with available capacity then used more efficiently, allowing more processes to be coordinated simultaneously and integrated in consciousness. (2) Children improve in their ability to shift their attention rapidly, getting better and better at moving between different sources of information and deploying attention (i.e., devoting capacity) to task-relevant information and ignoring task-irrelevant input (e.g., Bjorklund & Harnishfeger, 1990; Pearson & Lane, 1991; Tipper, Bourque, Anderson, & Brehaut, 1989). (3) In addition, as long-term memory develops and is better organized, information chunks are larger, so the preschooler's "chunks" when attending to verbal material are single letters; the chunks held in memory by teenagers are whole words and phrases.

In addition to increases in functional capacity owing to increases in automaticity, ability to shift attention, and extent and organization of knowledge, the actual working memory available to a child probably increases as a function of neurological maturation. Because both functional increases and maturational increases in short-term capacity are indexed by age, it is difficult to determine how much of the increase in apparent short-term abilities with development is due to functional increases in capacity and how much is due to biological increases in capacity.

In short, with development there are two sources of capacity-mediated increases in performance: There are both increases in functional capacity because of greater efficiency in executing skills and increases in actual capacity. Note that Case focuses on developmental increases in functional capacity, although classical neo-Piagetian theory based on Pascual-Leone's (1970) model focused much more on presumed actual increases in biological capacity. According to Case, the greater a child's functional short-term capacity, the more complex a task the child can undertake, so a child whose entire

attention once was required to draw a stick figure can eventually draw a much more sophisticated human figure in a much more complex scene—for as drawing skills are automatized, attention is more readily shifted between various component pieces in the scene, and larger, more complex parts of the scene can be juggled in the mind's eye (i.e., although once only a circle containing three dots and a smile, representative of a head, could be held in memory at one instance, an older child can hold a fully featured head in mind because the older child's knowledge of head features is much more complete). Case and his colleagues are testing their latest version of neo-Piagetian thinking (previous versions were provided by Pascual-Leone, 1970, and Case, 1985), with this work particularly important to educational psychologists because of Case's interest in developing instruction that is appropriate to the developmental level of the child.

In broad terms, Case (1991) argues for beginning instruction with a task the child can understand and perform. The child should be made aware of how they are performing tasks, with tasks practiced until the child can carry them out automatically. Gradually task demands are increased, although care is taken to make certain that the working memory demands placed on the child by more demanding versions of a task do not exceed the child's capacity. Guidance is provided at first as the child attempts the task, with this guidance and support faded as the child is able to execute the new task independently. The amount of working memory required to execute this new task decreases with practice, as execution of it becomes more automatic. Case and his colleagues have been investigating such an instructional approach with respect to a variety of tasks, including learning of mathematics and everyday quantitative skills, such as telling time and working with money (see Case, 1991).

That Case's analyses may be on target is suggested by the similarity of his approach to instruction of other theorists and researchers considered in this book. By the end of this book, readers will be familiar with the instructional prescription of starting with a task within the child's competence, gradually increasing the demands, with supports provided as needed. Concerns with the limits of short-term capacity also recur in this book. Case's approach is an important bridge between Piaget's historically important theory and contemporary theories of learning and instruction based on information processing analyses. Thus, Piaget's notion of stage development is translated into neo-Piagetian terms as reflective of development of capacity: Rather than explaining the superiority of the 8-year-old relative to the 4-year-old on conservation as a function of acquiring concrete operations—as Piagetians would, neo-Piagetians explain it as reflecting development of capacity, with the 8-year-old having the capacity to meet demands of conservation tasks (e.g., paying attention to several dimensions, such as the height and width of a column of liquid, and keeping track of their covariations) and 4-year-olds lacking the required capacity (e.g., Chapman & Lindenberger, 1989).

To understand contemporary approaches to instruction fully, more than Piaget and information processing is required, however. The behaviorists' long concern with problems of learning and instruction has produced an indelible mark on contemporary instruction, with the introduction to these approaches composing the remainder of this chapter. Following in this chapter are essential theoretical ideas that must be understood to comprehend the significance of many contemporary instructional practices.

THREE CLASSICAL MECHANISMS OF LEARNING: CLASSICAL CONDITIONING, REINFORCEMENT, AND PUNISHMENT

One of the best summaries of classical learning theory as it applies to education is more than 30 years old, an article in *Harvard Educational Review* by Michael and Meyerson (1962). Any discussion of behavioral approaches to education must touch on the categories covered in Michael and Meyerson (1962). Almost a quarter century later, Jack Michael (1985) offered another summary of behavioral theory, this time as a master lecturer at a meeting of the American Psychological Association. Any contemporary discussion of the theoretical implications of B. F. Skinner's work must cover the categories in Michael (1985). We relied heavily on Michael's overviews of behavioral theory in constructing what follows.

The behaviorists had a different orientation than any of the other theorists and researchers considered in this book thus far. They focused on directly observable behavior rather than internal, unobservable explanatory variables. There are no schemata in behavioral theory, no cognitive strategies, and no metacognition. Thus, a behaviorist interested in reading would focus on observable reading behaviors, from orienting in the direction of and attending to a book to turning pages to completing whole books. If studying decoding, a behaviorist would be willing to accept attempted decodings of words (so long as such attempts were verbalized aloud and thus were observable) or eye movement data. A behaviorist would not make inferences about the representations of words or letter-sound associations that might account for decoding errors. A behaviorist would not make inferences about morphological knowledge that might account for eye movements while processing a word. Because of the emphasis on observable behaviors, many interested in education have considered behavioristic analyses to be superficial, believing that if education is anything, it is reshaping minds that cannot be observed directly. Many educators accept that inferences about potential mental structures can be made from observable data and that to stop at the level of the observation is not to do justice to the complexity of human learning. For the most part, we agree.

Even so, the contributions of the Skinnerians to education cannot be questioned, and the importance of their perspective to students of educational psychology is undeniable. The teacher who understands behavioral principles better understands behavior. Those who are critical of the behaviorists are critical largely because of the behaviorists' conviction that behavioristic conceptions are sufficient to understand human psychology. The view presented throughout this book is that many perspectives are necessary to understand human behavior and thinking, with Skinnerian principles important in human conduct but not exhaustively comprehensive as explanations of learning.

Basic Principles

The three most critical mechanisms in learning according to classical behaviorism are **classical conditioning** (sometimes known as respondent conditioning), **operant conditioning,** and **punishment.** **Classical conditioning** has been understood since the late 19th century, when the phenomenon was first explained by Ivan Pavlov (Bower & Hilgard, 1981). Pavlov observed that when meat powder is placed in a dog's mouth, the dog salivates. The food is an **unconditioned stimulus** that elicits an **unconditioned response,** salivation. As a boy, author MP knew that he could get the family's pet Irish Setter, Red, to salivate anytime, simply by approaching Red's dog house with a pan of food. The food pan was a **conditioned stimulus** that had acquired the power to elicit a **conditioned response,** salivation. That is, the approach of MP with the food pan had occurred so many times that classical conditioning had occurred. (The conditioned response of salivation is usually not exactly like the unconditioned response, and thus two different terms to refer to salivation. In the present case, Red definitely salivated more intensely when food entered her mouth than she did in response to the sight of the food pan. That is, the unconditioned response of salivating was more intense than the conditioned response.) A great deal of research (see Bower & Hilgard, 1981), beginning with Pavlov, has established that initially neutral stimuli that accompany (usually precede) unconditioned stimuli often become conditioned stimuli.

Although behaviorists such as Skinner and Michael acknowledge that classical conditioning occurs—and evidence suggests that some forms of classical conditioning can occur even before the human is born (e.g., Thoman & Ingersoll, 1993), behavioral theorists also emphasize that such conditioning is not a prominent part of human learning, especially human learning in school. Thus, Michael and Meyerson (1962) and Michael (1985) dedicated little space to it. The one prominent place in human affairs that seems to be affected frequently by classical conditioning is emotional responding. Readers might recall from Chapter 5 the emotional responses to Jello following a classical conditioning experience.

Classically conditioned emotional responses often are not maintained. They are **extinguished** when there is subsequent experience with the conditioned stimulus that is not followed by the unconditioned response. Thus, if after eating gelatin, one experiences conditioned nausea, what is needed to extinguish the conditioned nausea are several occasions when fruit gelatin is eaten without negative consequences.

Far more important than classical conditioning in human learning, however, is **operant conditioning.** Although the focus of learning with classical conditioning was with respect to the stimulus, the focus in operant learning is on an emitted response. Note that the operantly conditioned response is not elicited but emitted, reflecting that such responses are not reflexive behaviors but ones the organism can control. **The likelihood of an operant response being emitted is increased when it is followed by a reinforcer.** This is the most fundamental principle in Skinner's psychology, a principle that is derived directly from Thorndike's **law of effect.**

Let us consider an example. Suppose you are thirsty. Put 75¢ in a Coke machine and receive a Coke. Receipt of the Coke is reinforcement for depositing the 75¢. When you are thirsty in the future, you should be more likely to put 75¢ in a Coke machine as a function of this experience. The operant response of feeding a Coke machine money can extinguish, however. Thus, if you deposit 75¢ in a Coke machine and receive no Coke, you will not be as likely to feed money into a Coke machine in the future or at least not that particular Coke machine.

Receiving a Coke is an **unconditioned reinforcer** in that it satisfies a biological deprivation. Other unconditioned reinforcers include food, sex, and exposure to aesthetically pleasing stimuli. For example, many hard days of climbing have been reinforced by magnificent views from mountaintops. Effort and money expended to go to the theater are reinforced by an aesthetically magnificent performance. Most reinforcers that people receive are not unconditioned reinforcers, however, but **conditioned reinforcers.** Thus, for coming to work daily, teaching class, supervising students, and doing research, the university gives your professor a check. No biological needs are satiated by the check directly. What the check permits is the purchase of goods and services that fulfill basic needs, such as for food, beverage, and stimulation. As the label conditioned reinforcer implies, conditioned reinforcers have acquired their reinforcement properties by being paired with unconditional reinforcers (i.e., money was not always valuable to us but came to be so because its presence permitted acquisition of unconditioned reinforcers). Conditioned reinforcers can lose their power through extinction as well. Consider the fate of companies that hand their employees bad checks, as when the company is in serious financial trouble. If the checks come on Friday, many employees will not show up on Monday, even if there are promises that the company will make good on the checks in the future. The conditioned reinforcement value of the company's checks has extinguished.

For many schoolchildren, positive attention is an unconditioned reinforcer. Teachers also pass out conditioned reinforcers in the forms of grades and stickers, concrete rewards that often lead to unconditioned reinforcement, such as direct teacher praise and parental approval. For graduate students, however, often there is absolutely no praise or positive attention for good grades. Consequently, graduate students often stop putting effort into making good grades in classes because the grades have little conditioned reinforcement value. All of the consequences associated with research activity come to have conditioned reinforcement value for the graduate student, however, for there is high praise and extremely positive faculty attention when graduate students do research. Thus, coming up with a design for a study can be a conditioned reinforcer for study design behavior by a graduate student; completing running of subjects is often a conditioned reinforcer for running of experimental subjects; and finishing a first draft of an article can be a conditioned reinforcer for composing a draft. All of these conditioned reinforcers eventually lead to another conditioned reinforcer, acceptance of studies in journals. Once that happens, faculty congratulate the graduate student as they would peers. Moreover, attention comes from outside the home institution, with faculty at other universities noticing graduate student work and providing direct praise. Indeed, our writing of this book is accompanied by conditioned reinforcers—completion of each chapter is reinforced by movement of a chapter from the "in-progress" disk to the "draft completed" disk. Eventually, we will receive a conditioned reinforcer in the form of a bound book. Praise might follow from colleagues and some students. So will additional conditioned reinforcers in the form of royalty payments, which will permit the purchase of food, drink, and entertainment!

Could most of the student readers of this book write an entire article and thus receive the conditioned and unconditioned reinforcements just outlined? Many could not at this point in their careers, but that does not mean that operant learning theory is irrelevant to development of the scholarly abilities of these students. Responses can be **shaped** gradually. Thus, when a graduate student cannot design an entire experiment independently, we reinforce them for whatever they can do and keep at them to attempt to design more studies. Each time the demands go up. Thus, a student in the first week of a course in research design receives reinforcement for a simple design containing some fundamental errors. By the end of the course, reinforcement occurs only when the student produces a complex design that is free of obvious problems. Such shaping occurs all of the time. When a child first learns how to bat a ball, even gross approximations to a good swing are reinforced by the coach. After years of playing baseball and softball, only swings that result in well-hit balls from demanding pitchers are reinforcing. Although such hits are reinforcing for their own sake, a good hitter also receives reinforcements from teammates and the team captain in the form of praise and attention. Another example of shaping is seen down in the university's computer laboratories. During a first lesson, the student is reinforced for figuring out how to turn on the machine and boot up a program. For the experienced student, reinforcement occurs only when the student succeeds in solving a complex computing problem with the desired output generated.

Reinforcement occurs only under particular conditions. If the conditions in the future are similar to the conditions that were in place when the reinforcement occurred, the response that was reinforced is more likely than if the conditions are different. This is known as **stimulus control of behavior.** The particular conditions that were in place when a response was reinforced come to be a **discriminant stimulus** for emitting the response, signaling that a reinforcement is likely if the response in question is emitted in this situation.

For example, author MP has been reinforced in the past for wearing a particular red bow tie to student lectures, one that includes small images of the University of Nebraska mascot, Herbie Cornhusker. The students think it is a "fun" piece of apparel and provide lots of positive attention for wearing it. The one time MP wore this tie to a meeting with the Provost, the Provost spent some time in the meeting looking disconcerted, trying to figure out what figure was on this tie. When MP explained, he replied, "Oh," in a tone that implied, "How strange!" MP now wears the tie on some class days but never on days when meeting with the Provost, so that class meeting days have become discriminative stimuli for emitting Herbie-tie wearing. Meeting days with the Provost have become discriminative stimuli for not wearing the same tie.

Reinforcements do not occur every time a person emits a response. Rather they tend to occur intermittently. Such **intermittent reinforcement** has an interesting and important property. Learning that occurs via intermittent reinforcement is more resistant to extinction than learning that occurs under continuous reinforcement. Thus, perhaps one in three football games that football fans watch are really exciting. They come back for more, however. Suppose a person's first exposure to football involved five exciting games in a row. If the sixth game were dull, that might tend to decrease the likelihood he or she would go to a seventh game than if only the first and fourth games seen previously had been exciting. Although Skinner did not use the term **expectation,** we do (and will develop the concept more fully later in this chapter), since continuous reinforcement produces expectations about reinforcement every time a response is emitted, which increases vulnerability to extinction whenever a reinforcement fails to occur. In contrast, intermittent reinforcement creates an expectation that reinforcement is a sometimes occurrence and that if a person persists, reinforcement eventually occurs.

There are two ways that reinforcement can be intermittent. One is that it can follow a given number of responses (i.e., a **ratio reinforcement schedule**). Thus, a child who receives a sticker for completing 10 work sheets is on a ratio schedule of reinforcement. Alternatively, reinforcement can be delivered at particular time intervals. Some teachers reinforce a class on Fridays with extra afternoon recess if the class has been able to get weekly work in on time. This is an **interval reinforcement schedule.** The two types of schedules have dramatically different impacts on responding. The ratio schedule tends to produce high rates of responding that do not vary much except perhaps for a small reduction in responding immediately after payoff. The intermittent schedule tends to produce a rapid decline in performance immediately after payoff that only gradually increases until it reaches a maximum just before payoff. Thus, a teacher with a reinforcements-on-Friday schedule should expect fewer assignments coming in on Monday, Tuesday, and Wednesday, compared with Thursday and Friday.

Students might be able to understand intermittent reinforcement by considering their own situation. The opportunities for reinforcement in university courses come at the examinations. Learning a great deal about educational psychology should result in reinforcement for studying. When does the most studying in this course occur, right before a test or after it? Is there an increase in studying as the time for an opportunity for reward (i.e., a test) draws nearer? Over the years, this example has convinced many students in our classes that their be-haviors are often under the control of reinforcement contingencies.

There are two important classes of reinforcers, **positive reinforcers** and **negative reinforcers.** The occurrence of either of these types of reinforcers following a behavior increases the probability for future performance of the behavior preceding the reinforcement. Thus, many people are positively reinforced for turning on the radio and hearing classical music that they like. If many of these same people turn off a radio that is playing loud "heavy metal" music, negative reinforcement occurs. Positive reinforcement involves the presentation of a stimulus following a response; negative reinforcement involves the cessation of aversive stimulation following a response. Thus, if heavy metal music is aversive, any action leading to its cessation (e.g., turning off the radio) is negatively reinforcing. If listening to classical music is reinforcing, any action that results in classical music (e.g., tuning the radio to a classical station) is positively reinforced.

Negative reinforcement is often confused with punishment. **Punishment** involves presentation of aversive stimulation following a response. Thus, if a child sticks a finger in an electrical outlet, the jolt of electricity serves as a punisher. The response was sticking in the finger, which was followed by presentation of the aversive stimulation of electrical shock. The difference between negative reinforcement and punishment is that negative reinforcement involves the cessation of ongoing aversive stimulation as a result of an action taken by the responding organism, whereas punishment involves presentation of an aversive stimulus following a response, aversive stimulation that was not present before the response was emitted.

Students often experience great difficulty distinguishing these two terms, with the situation not helped much by many textbook authors who mistakenly present negative reinforcement and punishment as synonymous. Check your understanding with these examples. Classify each of the following as an example of negative reinforcement or punishment:

- Jumping up after sitting on a tack. Jumping up is . . .
- Being spanked after swiping some money. Swiping money is . . .
- Receiving a ticket after speeding. Speeding is . . .

- Entering an air-conditioned building after near heat exhaustion outside. Entering the building is . . .
- Lifting one's hand from a hot stove. Lifting the hand is . . .

The answers respectively were negatively reinforced, punished, punished, negatively reinforced, and negatively reinforced.

All teachers are expected to understand the basics of behavioral psychology outlined in this subsection. Although applications of behaviorism in school are not as popular or prevalent as they once were, behaviorism is still having some impact as outlined in the next subsection.

State of the Practice

In the 1960s, there was a great deal of thinking about how to use principles of operant psychology in school. Although the first example discussed in this section, programmed instruction, is no longer being used widely as originally designed, it was the forerunner of much of the current generation of educational software and deserves mention for that reason alone. The second example, behavior modification and token economies in classrooms and other educational settings, is faring a little better, although it tends to be used in settings serving special populations more than in settings serving normally achieving students. The third application, classroom management, is more than alive and kicking. Modern principles of classroom management are essential knowledge for any teacher.

Programmed Instruction and Teaching Machines

In the late 1950s, many supermarkets sold teaching machines and teaching machine units, much as supermarkets today offer 20 volumes of *Sesame Street* or some encyclopedia. The summer between grade 8 and grade 9, author MP spent a fair amount of time working through an algebra II program provided by his school district as a way of accelerating mathematics instruction for seemingly able math students. During the summer of MP's junior year, he was fortunate enough to be able to attend a summer session at Western Michigan University, sponsored by the National Science Foundation, that was dedicated to behavioral psychology. (Jack Michael, the author of the articles cited at the beginning of this section on

behaviorism, was the most inspiring teacher in that summer institute.) As part of that experience, MP went through the Holland and Skinner (1961) programmed instructional text on behavioral psychology. All of the terms introduced in the last subsection were covered in detail in that text, with many opportunities to generate correct responses about behavioral psychology. That programmed instruction is not entirely dead is apparent from the fact that the Holland and Skinner text is still in use at many universities.

Conceptions of teaching machines appeared well before B. F. Skinner's views were well known (e.g., Pressey, 1926), although Skinner's (e.g., 1961) writing would do more to spur the movement than previous contributions had done. The idea of programmed instruction was that if learning could be parsed up into small enough segments, with segments presented in sequence, exercises could be devised in which students would learn a little bit at a time with few misconceptions or misunderstandings. For each little bit of knowledge, students would be given an opportunity to respond. A correct response would be reinforced by showing the student that he or she was correct. Because learning was one little bit at a time, most responses would be correct and reinforced.

As an example, consider this sequence of frames from the Holland and Skinner (1961, pp. 52–56) program (an example that fortuitously permits review of the difficult concept of negative reinforcement):

> Reinforcement which consists of *presenting* stimuli (e.g., food) is called *positive* reinforcement. In contrast, reinforcement which consists of *terminating* stimuli (e.g., painful stimuli) is called ____ reinforcement. [Answer: negative]
>
> Turning off a television commercial is reinforced by the *termination* of a(n) (1) ____ reinforcer; turning on a very funny program is reinforced by the *presentation* of a(n) (2) ____ reinforcer. [Answers: (1) negative, (2) positive]
>
> A stimulus is called a negative reinforcer if its ____-tion reinforces behavior. [Answers: termination or elimination]
>
> Elimination of a television commercial may be a negative reinforcement. If so, the television commercial is a(n) ____ reinforce-____. [Answers: negative, reinforcer]

Immediately after producing a response, there would be an opportunity to check the response, for example by opening an answer window on a teaching machine or turning the page in a printed program. Determining that one's response matches the response provided by the program is reinforcing. Such reinforcement keeps motivation high so that the student stays with the course and answers many such questions.

Author MP's high school required a senior-year term paper. MP's was on teaching machines and programmed learning. By the time he wrote that senior paper in 1969, many doubts about teaching machines were being expressed, doubts MP understood firsthand from his experiences with programmed learning. There was no way MP really knew much about algebra II from going through the set of programmed materials, although the materials were masterfully constructed so that almost every response MP made was a correct one and thus reinforced. The operant psychologists had great confidence that by structuring material so that correct responding was likely, and thus making reinforcement for correct responding frequent, student learning of higher-order content could be fostered. MP had his doubts based on the algebra experience. Although he learned more from the Holland and Skinner materials, MP's understanding of the principles of behavioral psychology was superficial following the programmed instruction, compared to his understanding after many interactions with professors and fellow students as part of the classes at Western Michigan.

Sidney Pressey did much to start the programmed learning revolution, but he also did much to point out its limitations. As part of offering a number of criticisms of programmed instruction, Pressey (1963) elegantly summarized what was wrong with programmed mathematics:

> But did not Socrates so teach the slave boy? The boy could not read. What about the often-cited skilled tutor? He assumed that the student had done some reading. However, both Socrates and the tutor did further learning by asking questions. The writer would contend that neither simply presented an idea and then reinforced it. Brownell's (1928) early research regarding primary school children's learning of arithmetic here seems relevant. Simply telling them that $2 \times 3 = 6$ did *not* bring about real learning of that number combination. These sturdy little empiricists had not merely to be *told*; they had to be *shown*,

as by putting out two sets each of three pennies and demonstrating that they did indeed count to six. They had similarly to verify, and to differentiate, that $2 + 3$ was 5 and $3 - 2$ was only 1. As Piaget (1954) and others have described, children gradually develop a number system, also cognitive schema as of space, causality; and they do this not by so crude a rote process as the accretion of bits of learning stuck on by reinforcements, but by progressive processes of cognitive integration and clarification. (p. 2)

The wisdom of Pressey's final comment in that quote will become obvious in Chapter 13, since this type of thinking is at the heart of contemporary conceptions of good mathematics instruction.

Although behaviorally oriented educators in the 1960s produced programmed materials for everything from beginning reading to mathematics to foreign language learning to science and religion (see de Grazia & Sohn, 1964, for a sampler of the range of possibilities), the movement died for the most part. Its appeal was theoretical: The prediction that high levels of learning could be produced by shaping through reinforcement of one small performance at a time was a straightforward extension of Skinner's theory. Programmed instruction was also taken seriously because it seemed to be a potentially economical way of teaching large bodies of knowledge. After all, programmed instruction was eliminating the need for teachers and tutors, with teachers and tutors often the greatest expense in any instructional system.

Although this sounds like an epitaph for programmed instruction, much of contemporary educational computing is constructed on similar principles. Many children today are becoming *Reader Rabbit* addicts. This popular program involves four different games (each with a number of variations) appropriate for children first learning to read words. Thus, there is a game involving an array of 12 "cards," each of which can be illuminated one at a time to reveal a word or a picture. The goal is to illuminate pairs of cards that go together, a word (e.g., bike) and its referent (e.g., a picture of a bike). Each time a match is made, there is positive reinforcement in that the two cards disappear and there is a bell sound. If the child makes all six matches in an efficient fashion, Reader Rabbit appears and does a little dance. Because there are different levels of each game (e.g., the easiest version of matching involves matching of pairs of pictures, so that matching two pictures of bicycles is reinforced; a somewhat harder version involves matching identical words, so that finding the two "bike" cards is reinforced), it is possible to find a level for most children that results in a high rate of correct responding and thus high reinforcement. Skinner and programmed instruction enthusiasts would feel good about *Reader Rabbit*. It is apparent that reinforcement can go far in educational computing from children's great enthusiasm for *Reader Rabbit* and other programs.

Skinner never lost his intellectual commitment to programmed instruction (e.g., 1987, Chapter 8). He recognized that many educational computer programs had been informed by his thinking on programmed instruction. He also recognized that during the 1960s, programmed instruction got out of hand as many commercial outfits entered the arenas with bad programs (e.g., those programmed units sold in the supermarkets). Skinner had great insights about education and was profoundly reflective about what can be learned in classrooms and how it might be taught. Thus, those who read Skinner's (1987, Chapter 8) essay will find elegant defenses about being clear about what is being taught, with the ultimate goal the development of *intuition* (many readers might not imagine that Skinner would have used so cognitive a term) about the content area. Few would argue with Skinner's analyses of the need to teach many content areas with an eye toward development of prerequisite knowledge before expecting students to acquire advanced ideas. One of the most important ideas about education promoted by Skinner was that students should not be required to advance at the same rate: "We could double the efficiency of education with one change alone—by letting each student move at his or her own pace" (Skinner, 1987, pp. 123–124). That idea will come up at a number of points in this books, although many educational theorists who are coming to the same conclusion often fail to realize that Skinner espoused such a position for most of his career.

Behavior Modification and Token Economies   One of the most salient interventions that evolved from behavioral conceptions of learning, behavior, and development was behavior modification. No new principles are required to understand this intervention. The main idea is to reinforce behaviors that are valued. If people are not capable of those behaviors at present, reinforce behaviors they are capable of performing that are in the direction of the desired response, gradually increasing the criterion for reinforcement until the person can emit the desired response (i.e., shape the response). Thus, if a child does not do homework, find out what reinforcements matter to the child and provide those contingent on the completion of homework. If children in a class are not completing work carefully, provide reinforcements for carefully completed work. Sticker charts are used widely in American classrooms, with stickers earned for good grades on daily assignments. Such stickers are a form of **token reinforcement.** Other token reinforcements sometimes include chips that can be accumulated and eventually traded in for goodies or privileges.

Some behavior modification programs also include aversive components (i.e., punishment), although aversive stimulation was never an approach in favor with Skinner. The aversive stimulation that sometimes occurs as part of behavior modification has been the subject of much criticism and part of the reason for sensationalism with respect to such treatments. There are types of behavior modification that include, for example, use of cattle prods or other forms of electric shock on children. In the defense of these approaches, however, such aversive stimulation is provided in an attempt to eliminate more seriously injurious behavior. Thus, children who self-stimulate by beating their heads against a wall are in grave danger of doing permanent and serious neurological damage. Even a mild electrical shock can sometimes disrupt such behaviors (e.g., Lovaas, Schaeffer, & Simmons, 1965; Merbaum, 1973; Tate, 1972). When aversive stimulation is used to eliminate behaviors as serious as self-mutilation, it is defensible.

Other punishments sometimes are acceptable as well. For example, if a teacher has set up a token economy in which children are rewarded for particular appropriate behaviors, it is reasonable for there to be a response cost in the form of forfeited tokens when the child engages in inappropriate behaviors. Another alternative acceptable in many settings is **time-out,** in which a child is physically removed from the other children or activities for a short period of time. Time-out can involve moving a child to an isolated corner of the classroom, to another room, or to a hallway. Sometimes it involves having a child sit on a chair while classmates are permitted to continue roaming free in the setting.

Good behavior modification environments often have other features as well. Correct and preferred behaviors are consistently modeled by staff. Adult attention, which is a powerful reinforcement for many children, is provided for appropriate action rather than inappropriate action. Thus, if the teacher wishes to reduce aggression in a child, the child does not get attention when aggressive (which often occurs in many schools where aggression is met by teacher attention in the form of disapproval), but rather the teacher interacts with the child when the child is being good.

Behavioral contracting is another behavior modification option, in which the child makes an agreement with the educator to attempt to reach a particular goal. Usually the contract is negotiated, with the student involved in deciding what the goal will be, what reinforcement might be earned, and how much progress toward the goal is required before there is any reinforcement. Opportunities for rehearsal of new behaviors in nonthreatening, reinforcing environments often are provided. For example, children who may not know socially appropriate behaviors are taught them and provided opportunities to rehearse them with feedback. Often, classroom behavioral programs are complemented by parent training, in which parents are taught how they can use behavioral principles in order to provide reinforcement consistent with the school's program. Thus, if a teacher is reinforcing a child for bringing homework into school, the parent can be trained to reinforce the child at home for doing homework.

When reinforcement systems are used, almost invariably they are deployed on an intermittent basis, if for no other reason than it is hard for a classroom teacher to monitor and reinforce every appropriate response by all of the students in a classroom. An important goal of any token economy is to increase the ratio or interval between reinforcements, until the desired behaviors are occurring given only typical classroom reinforcements, such as praise. The gradual reduction in reinforcement is known as **fading.** Again, this is a principle that will come up at several points in this text, sometimes with a differ-

ent label (e.g., in the next chapter as "scaffolding" of instruction).

Behavior modification and token economies of various sorts enjoy a long track record of success (e.g., see Hobbs & Lahey, 1983). Full-blown token economies are most often used with special populations, often in institutional settings. Brief review of one of the more famous ones can provide some idea about how encompassing such operations can be. Achievement Place was established in the late 1960s and early 1970s by faculty at the University of Kansas as a residential-style halfway house for juvenile delinquents (Phillips, 1968; Phillips, Phillips, Fixsen, & Wolf, 1971). A main assumption of the Achievement Place developers was that their delinquent clients had not acquired many of the constructive social behaviors needed to function in society as productive, nondelinquent citizens. In their Achievement Place home, residents were reinforced for doing all those little things that are simply part of normal life for most people, but that were never learned by these youth, presumably because of unfortunate home and family environments in which normal and positive social behaviors were much too infrequent.

At first, the residents received points for everything from making their beds to arriving clean at a meal to reading the newspaper, with more points earned for more demanding tasks. There were also response costs—and hefty ones at that—for socially inappropriate behaviors, such as being late or lying. The points could be traded in for privileges and tangible rewards, including particular snack foods and telephone privileges. With the passage of time and the acquisition of increasingly sophisticated social behaviors, the daily point system was faded and replaced by a weekly point system, which also eventually was faded, until the resident functioned well without a point system. Eventually the resident exited the setting in a program of transition to home. Fading was possible because the previously reinforced behaviors had become reinforcing themselves (e.g., reading newspapers and listening to the news really are enjoyable once one starts to do it— the tokens and other features of Achievement Place only got the residents started). Moreover, the more appropriate the resident's social behavior, the greater the freedom at Achievement Place. Freedom was extremely reinforcing, especially after losing one's freedom via court action, as was the case for Achievement Place residents.

Did Achievement Place work? There were multiple indicators that it did. Compared with otherwise comparable delinquents treated in other settings (e.g., more restrictive environments) or in other ways (e.g., probation), Achievement Place graduates were in school more following release from Achievement Place, were in trouble less with the law, and did better academically (Fixsen, Phillips, & Wolf, 1973). In retrospect, it really is not surprising that such an intervention would be effective. With everyone being reinforced for prosocial behaviors, there was a great deal of modeling of prosocial and appropriate conduct by peers, for everyone was trying to be good. As will be reviewed in the next section, exposure to such modeling is a powerful learning opportunity. In addition, the treatment had many components, including caring house parents and a transition mechanism that permitted the homeward-bound resident to come back from time to time to consult and talk with Achievement Place staff.

Even if an educator does not wish to have a full-blown token economy or be completely committed to behavior modification, there are well-validated, theoretically sensible practices developed by behavioral psychologists that have great appeal to many teachers. A teacher who provides attention to students only when they are disruptive is simply asking for more disruptions! Thus, many skilled teachers ignore misconduct and pay great attention to positive behaviors. Unless the errant behavior causes harm to either the perpetrator or other children, ignoring the infraction is often a viable option. Contracting with students is almost commonplace in many school settings today. All teachers should be aware of their power as social models (also see next subsection) and behave accordingly. It can be damaging to a child to be exposed to a teacher who is a negative role model. For example, teachers who model sexism are shaping sexism. Teachers who smoke in front of their pupils are definitely encouraging smoking. The list goes on and on. One way a teacher can shape positive behaviors is by modeling positive behaviors. (As a preview, many of the principles that were developed as part of behavior modification are discussed in the next subsection on classroom management.)

Special educators and special education researchers, in particular, continue to have a great deal of interest in application of behavioral principles to education, with many specific applications to a variety of special populations being studied. Although many special education journals provide information about such research, the stature of this research in the field of behavioral psychology is apparent from the fact that much of the space in the pretigious *Journal of Applied Behavior Analysis (JABA)* is dedicated to problems of special education. As a sampler, consider that in the past few years, there have been studies of the effects of behavioral rehearsal and feedback on the generalization of question-asking behaviors from special education settings to regular classrooms (Knapczyk, 1989; Secan, Egel, & Tilley, 1989) and observational learning (see next subsection as well) of language by severely retarded children through modeling (Charlop & Milstein, 1989; Goldstein & Mousetis, 1989). For an excellent discussion of many ways that behavior modification is and can be used with mentally deficient students, see Kiernan (1985).

The practicality of behavioral teaching is obvious from the work in *JABA*, with studies about how to teach everything from clearly academic tasks such as the basic arithmetic facts (e.g., Dunlap & Dunlap, 1989; Van Houten & Rolider, 1989), to life skills tasks, such as banking (McDonnell & Ferguson, 1989) and acting in socially appropriate ways in employment settings (e.g., Park & Gaylord-Ross, 1989). That behavioral methods are more prominent in special education than regular education does not imply that there are not important applications and research in regular education. For instance, a number of fine programs aimed at focused but important behaviors have been developed. For example, behaviorists have been active in developing effective procedures for teaching children how to fend off potential sexual abuse and abduction (Miltenberger & Thiesse-Duffy, 1988; Poche, Yoder, & Miltenberger, 1988).

One knock on behavior modification in school is that the reinforcements are "bribes." Dr. Roger Ulrich, one of the pioneering researchers in the area of classroom behavior modification, provided an elegant response:

TEACHER: But you said that possibly we could give him money or something for making his numbers.

People shouldn't always expect to get something for the things they do. For one thing, this might lead to bad habits later on, such as getting people to do things they shouldn't, just for money.

DR. ULRICH: That's probably true in terms of getting people to do things for money that society says in general they shouldn't receive money for doing. And, in a sense, that's what bribery is. But is that what you're doing here? Why don't you get that dictionary and let's see what it says bribery really means.

TEACHER: Okay, the dictionary says that bribe means "any gift or emolument, used corruptly to influence public or official action, anything that seduces or allures, an allurement. Also, any valuable consideration given or promised for corrupt behavior in the performance of official or public duties."

DR. ULRICH: It's quite common for people to refer to reinforcement as bribing, especially when we use it for children. According to the dictionary definition, however, it doesn't seem to fit. It wouldn't seem that our efforts to get Billy to write his numbers better is really an example of trying to get him to do something illegal or something which goes against what is generally looked upon as being acceptable by our culture. Besides, Billy isn't a public official. Actually, writing numbers seems to be a good thing to be able to do and when you do good things, you often get rewarded for them. (Ulrich, Wolfe, & Bluhm, 1970)

Ulrich went on to counter another suggestion by the teacher that students should be self-motivated. His response consisted of pointing out to the teacher how often she in fact did provide reinforcement to children without thinking about it, as when she gave positive attention for desirable academic responses. Not surprisingly, given Ulrich's great commitment to behaviorism, he argued that such classroom reinforcements are natural, in the sense that all behavior can be affected by reinforcing contingencies. The real cincher came, however, when he pointed out that the teacher was teaching for reinforcement—a paycheck. Come to think of it, if the university stopped giving us paychecks, we probably would stop showing up.

Tangible reinforcement of children often is defensible if other reinforcements, such as attention, do not work. Such reinforcers should be faded when it is possible to do so, however. If the behaviors being encouraged by reinforcement are really functional and important ones for the child, they should become reinforcing in themselves. Think back to Achievement Place. Acquiring prosocial behaviors permitted entry into many social situations not permitted to those who had only delinquent behaviors. Similarly the student who is more proficient at school tasks has more time for other things, can gain access to important information that is not available to the student lacking fundamental literacy and numeracy skills, and is generally perceived as more "with it" by peers and teachers. Those are powerful reinforcers, and children can be weaned from tangible reinforcers once their behaviors develop to the point that they can function well and enjoy the many typical reinforcements offered in school (e.g., free reading time when work is completed; access to the classroom microcomputer once other assignments are submitted).

Behavior modification is one of those success stories for psychology. It is possible to redesign many aspects of an institutional or classroom environment into token economies, with substantial evidence that academic achievement can be improved (see Pitts, 1971; Thoreson, 1972; and Ulrich et al., 1970, for many examples of behavior modification in classrooms). Even so, classrooms that are set up along behavior modification lines are rare. Nonetheless, many principles of classroom management and instruction have emerged from work on behavioral applications in classrooms, with behavioral psychology at the center of most contemporary approaches to classroom management.

Classroom Management Before it is possible to teach anything academic, it is essential that the teacher take control of the class. For generations of teachers, there was conventional wisdom that included such truisms as, "Don't smile until November," "Never threaten unless you are prepared to make good on your threat," and "Spare the rod and spoil the child." It takes little reflection to recognize the inadequacy of such conventional thought. If nothing else, if acted upon, it would make school a dreary and threatening world and set the teacher up as an adversary. A perspective developed throughout this book is that school should be anything but threatening; another is that the teacher is a collaborator, who is helpful, rather than a taskmaster. Modern principles of classroom management provide teachers with a great deal of guidance about how to maintain order in the classroom without creating an aversive environment. For excellent, brief reviews that informed what follows in this subsection, see Doyle (1986) and Evertson (1989).

Classroom management starts before the year begins. One essential is to arrange the physical classroom so that order can be maintained and students can be monitored easily. Thus, in many elementary classrooms, much of each morning will be comprised of small reading groups meeting with the teacher in one section of the room while the rest of the class does seatwork. It is essential that the furnishings of the classroom be positioned so the teacher can conduct the reading group and easily look up to scan the rest of the classroom. The teacher also needs to establish early the rules and procedures of the classroom. The beginning of the school day, including the opening activities and the morning's administrative activities (e.g., taking attendance, collecting lunch tickets) should be routinized so they can be carried out automatically and quickly. Some teachers group students by rows and establish that movement is by rows. The point of these movement routines is not only quiet and order, but also rapid transition. Time spent in transition is time lost, and student achievement in school depends on the amount of time students are engaged in instruction. More than anything, the expectations must be clear. Students must be made aware of what is permitted and what is prohibited.

Providing students positive reinforcement when they are consistent with classroom rules is a must. Teacher praise, such as, "Row 2 has really been working hard this morning—way to go!" is common in well-managed classrooms. Providing students feedback about their behavior as well as the adequacy of their academic performances is critical.

A true story can illustrate how badly things can go in a classroom when expectations and feedback are not clear. This involved a preschool teacher who had a "work" period as part of the school day, a school day that, for the most part, permitted students free choice, including the choice to play. During this "work" period, however, students were to work on some academic content. One little boy just did not get it. He roamed from classmate to classmate. The teacher reported to the parent some concern about the child's lack of interest in academic work, reflected by the roaming during work period. Once advised, the parent sat down with the preschooler and explained that during the work period, the child should do one of the academic activities in the classroom rather than roam. The child was somewhat amazed, indicating to the parent, "That's what I'm supposed to do during 'work'?" From that day on, the child did not roam but rather engaged in academic work during the work period. The expectations and feedback in this classroom were anything but clear.

Good teachers signal their expectations. They signal when they are concerned about classroom misconduct well before the misconduct accelerates into a situation requiring sanctions. The good teacher constantly monitors the classroom and the activities of students. When sanctions are necessary, the good teacher deals with the situation quickly and as unobtrusively as possible. Good teachers are effective at dispensing mild punishers, such as telling eye contact and gentle touches to move students away from distractions. Persistent misconduct is dealt with more harshly but efficiently and with little, if any, disruption of the class. A skilled teacher informs a student of detention in less than a couple of seconds, with the student's behavior quickly improving in recognition of the teacher being in control of the situation. The student probably also expects that if he or she does not shape up, an even greater sanction will be administered, an expectation built up through consistent policies.

Good teachers are models of self-control and on-taskedness. They not only do things such as reinforce students for reading outside books and doing well in math, but also they make obvious their own enthusiasm for reading and mathematics. Good teachers model that they find their own academic competencies to be rewarding and that students can reap the same types of rewards by learning the lessons offered in school. Students in well-managed classrooms learn a great deal about how to achieve life's long-term rewards as well as how to achieve short-term reinforcements, such as positive teacher attention for carrying out assignments in ways consistent with classroom policies.

Implementing behavior management in schools continues to be researched. For example, Gottfredson, Gottfredson, and Hybl (1993) studied how conduct in middle schools improved when school rules were made clearer, consequences for violating them were more certain, classrooms were organized and managed more efficiently, parents were kept informed about the good behavior and misbehaviors of their children, and reinforcement was increased for good conduct. If we have a complaint about this type of research, there still is little information available about how such management affects student and teacher perceptions about school—that is, it has been too behavioral and not enough cognitive. There is much to be learned about how students think about and make decisions in schools that are managed well versus those that are managed poorly. We urge such research because of our strong perception that students much prefer well-managed schooling environments. We doubt that students feel they are being "behavior managed" in such settings so much as they feel they are being better educated.

Punishment   For the most part, behaviorism is a positive approach to student learning and development. The emphasis is clearly on catching the students doing well and reinforcing them for it. If the students cannot do well given current competencies, reinforce them for whatever behaviors are in the right direction and gradually shape up more complete and adequate responses. This emphasis on the positive is directly due to Skinner's theory and philosophy. Chapter 12 in *Science and Human Behavior* (Skinner, 1953—Skinner's best-known and most definitive summary of his views on the relevance of behavioral principles to human behavior) was a complete indictment of punishment. He made the case there that reductions in the frequency of undesirable behaviors using punishment were short-lived. Skinner also argued that punishment led to undesirable byproducts, such as anxiety. Even so, punishment has come to be part of the behaviorist's repertoire of methods. Ever responsive to his environment, Skinner (1953, Chapter 12) in response to behaviorists commited to punishment argued that if punishment is to be used, there should be an alternative behavior available that can be reinforced. This became known as **differential reinforcement of other behavior (DRO)** (e.g., see Ross, 1981), an important principle of behavior change.

A number of other behaviorists have studied parameters that affect the potency of punishment. In general, many of these psychologists were more sanguine than Skinner was that punishment can have enduring effects on elimination of undesirable behaviors without enduring side effects (see Walters & Grusec, 1977, for a review). A number of investigators have studied ways of supplementing punishment, with researchers such as Cheyne and Walters (1969), Parke (1969, 1974), and LaVoie (1973, 1974) establishing that rationales for obeying a prohibition can make punishment more effective. In many cases, rationales alone are as effective or more effective than punishments, with a number of researchers believing that rationales help children internalize prohibitions (e.g., Hoffman, 1970; Kanfer & Zich, 1974). Although rationales presented to young children (e.g., preschoolers) need to be concrete (e.g., you might break this toy if you played with it because it is fragile), abstract rationales that focus on the rights and feelings of others (e.g., the owner of this toy will feel bad if you play with it) are increasingly effective with advancing age during childhood (LaVoie, 1974; Parke, 1974; for a review, see Walters & Grusec, 1977, Chapter 5), consistent with Piagetian theory that concrete thinking precedes abstract thinking developmentally. The literature on rationale effects provided a good deal of support for the general position that undesirable behaviors can often be suppressed without resorting to punishment.

Still punishment exists in schools. Mild sanctions as part of a larger program of classroom management are not troubling. Even more taxing punishments can be appropriate, especially if they are used in ways that increase their effectiveness. Two of our favorite studies in this arena involve real-school punishment of real-school misbehaviors, with the investigators evaluating punishments that were designed to take advantage of the power of rationales for not misbehaving. In Blackwood (1970), junior high students who had misbehaved copied essays as punishment. The manipulation was that some students copied essays emphasizing the negative effects of classroom disobedience, and control subjects copied an essay about steam engines. The students who copied an essay emphasizing why misbehavior was problematic were less likely to misbehave following the punishment than were students who copied the control essay. MacPherson, Candee, and Hohman (1974) conducted a similar study with elementary students who had misbehaved in a cafeteria. Again, post-punishment behavior was better for students who had copied essays providing rationales for obeying school rules.

What is troubling is that much more severe sanctions than essay writing often are meted out in American schools, despite the fact that there is no compelling evidence that such actions lead to better behaved students (Edwards & Edwards, 1987). Corporal punishment is still legal in more than half of the U. S. states, and it is used frequently in many jurisdictions (Hyman, 1990; Hyman & Wise, 1977). Every day children in the United States are flogged by their teachers with paddles and straps. No one with an understanding of learning theory could endorse such actions.

Skinner (1977) delivered a scathing indictment of the practice, concluding with an easily defensible claim that corporal punishment teaches that might makes right: "The punishing teacher who punishes teaches students that punishment is a way of solving problems" (p. 336). Many other behaviorists have elaborated on that analysis, offering the compelling view that brutal punishment in school sends all the wrong messages to children (Edwards & Edwards, 1987): There is no teaching of appropriate behaviors by beating another human being! What is promoted is the lesson that retaliatory aggression is fine. There is also the possibility of reinforcing undesirable behaviors such as leaving school—we suspect many troubled high school students would rather abandon an institution than risk a severe paddling. A bad message to convey to a youngster who may already be troubled or aggressive is that aggression is sometimes okay to deploy, and that message comes through loud and clear during a spanking in the principal's office.

B. F. Skinner was a psychologist who cared greatly about students and wanted to eliminate some of the worst practices in education in favor of more effective, humane techniques. His was one of the most powerful voices ever raised to promote the development of schools with strongly positive atmospheres in which students are reinforced for getting better—consistent with the important motivational principle we favored in Chapter 5 of eliminating classroom competition in favor of improvement from baseline (to use terms Skinner would have been comfortable with).

Closing Comment The behaviorists offered many prescriptions about and much research relevant to classroom learning. Powerful methods for maintaining order and attention to academic tasks have emerged from behavioral analyses, with the fruits of these efforts apparent in everything from modern educational computer programs to the way Miss Jones keeps the rest of the class busy at seatwork while the Bluebirds meet for reading group. No one studying learning in educational settings should neglect behavioral contributions to education, nor should they view behaviorism as conceptually dead because behaviorists continue to offer important insights into academic behaviors.

For instance, Eisenberger (1992) offered a fascinating analysis of academic industriousness. When a student works hard and is reinforced for it, the reinforcement comes while the student is aware of their effort—often painfully aware of it. Because the feelings accompanying effort are experienced when reinforcement is provided, those feelings can come to have secondary reinforcing qualities. That is, because the exhaustion of mental effort precedes the occurrence of reinforcement for the effort, feelings of exertion come to be reinforcing themselves. Think about it, as you are working hard at a task and getting closer to the goal, you know the reinforcement is eventually coming, and thus all the cues that you are working hard are also reinforcing. This analysis provides teachers with a powerful incentive to make certain that students do experience explicit rewards for their hard work—a history of such rewards can lead to learned industriousness, with students working hard simply to have the feeling that they are working hard. Experiencing a secondary reinforcer is extremely reinforcing. Eisenberger has provided an important insight as to how some students come to be so dedicated to working hard despite the fact that effort is not on the face of it reinforcing—only reinforcing when it has been paired with other reinforcements for accomplishment.

Cognition and Behaviorism

If Skinner was so humane and concerned with education, why does his name and the label behaviorism so often elicit negative reactions from educators? One explanation is that Skinner was often misunderstood. Recall that reinforcements are perceived by some to be bribes. Mild electrical shocks used during some forms of behavior modification to eliminate much more painful behaviors (e.g., head banging, self-mutilation) are portrayed in the worst possible light by some critics of behaviorism: Therapists are described as herding their patients with cattle prods, rather than as using electrical shock so mild it is barely perceptible. Skinner's critics have never hesitated to engage in hyperbole when criticizing behavioral approaches.

The more important reason, however, that Skinner is not much in favor with educators was offered in the introduction to this section and deserves reiteration as this section is closed. Educational psychology has largely become a cognitive psychology of education (as we hope is apparent by this point in the book). This clashes with a powerful anticognitive stance that typified Skinner's thinking throughout his career but especially during his later years, as his theory and worldview gave way to the cognitive revolution. That is, Skinner was not just indifferent to cognitive psychology and its constructs; he was hostile. His last public statement (Skinner, 1990), a speech given to the American Psychological Association 8 days before his death, was largely an indictment of cognitive psychology.

Skinner believed strongly that cognitive psychology did not pay enough attention to the role of the environment in determining the behaviors of individuals. He believed strongly that his theory was consistent with evolutionary perspectives, that the species survive to reproduce largely because they are appropriately responsive to their environment. Skinner was certain that his emphasis on the environment as a determinant of behavior was more consistent with evolutionary thinking than cognitive psychology:

> Cognitive science takes the traditional position: Behavior starts with the organism. We think and then act; we have ideas and then express them; we intend, decide, and choose to act before acting. Behaviorists, in contrast, look at antecedent events in the environment and the environmental histories of both the species and the individual. The old stimulus-response formula was an attempt to give the environment an initiating role, but it has long been abandoned. The environment *selects* behavior. Ethologists study the species-specific behavior attributable to contingencies of survival in natural selection. Contingencies of operant reinforcement select the behavior of the individual in a similar way, of course, on a very different time scale. (Skinner, 1987, p. 94)

Skinner believed that many cognitive explanations could be translated into behavioral terms, and he often did so. For example, cognitive scientists maintain that what we perceive from an array of visual stimulation is affected by prior knowl-

edge. Skinner's explanation of the same is in terms of reinforcement:

> Everyday perception is the product of a vast number of experiences in which fragmentary patterns of light, resembling those of the moment in many different ways, have been present when behavior has had many reinforcing consequences. (Skinner, 1987, p. 96)

No constructs are more sacred to cognitive psychology than cognitive representations and rules. Skinner reduces those rules to reinforcement histories in his theory:

> Cognitive scientists presumably appeal to the storage and retrieval of representations and rules because they can then explain behavior by pointing to conditions that are present at the time when behavior occurs. The rat was changed when pressing the lever was reinforced, but it presses now "because it knows that pressing brings food." That knowledge is a current surrogate of the history of reinforcement. (Skinner, 1987, p. 101)

Skinner's complete disdain for the cognitive approach comes through in the conclusion to the essay that provided the three quotes just presented:

> *I accuse* cognitive scientists of misusing the metaphor of storage. The brain is not an encyclopedia, library, or museum. People are changed by their experiences; they do not store copies of them as representations or rules.
>
> *I accuse* cognitive scientists of speculating about internal processes which they have no appropriate means of observing. Cognitive science is premature neurology.
>
> *I accuse* cognitive scientists of emasculating laboratory research by substituting descriptions of settings for the settings themselves and reports of intentions and expectations for action.
>
> *I accuse* cognitive scientists of reviving a theory in which feelings and states of mind observed through introspection are taken as the causes of behavior rather than as collateral effects of the causes.
>
> *I accuse* cognitive scientists, as I would accuse psychoanalysts, of claiming to explore the depths of human behavior, of inventing explanatory systems that are admired for a profundity more properly called inaccessibility.
>
> *I accuse* cognitive scientists of relaxing standards of definition and logical thinking and releasing a flood of speculation characteristic of metaphysics, literature, and daily intercourse, speculation perhaps suitable enough in such arenas but inimical to science. (Skinner, 1987, p. 111)

Fortunately for behaviorism, others found points of contact and ways that behavioral and cognitive psychologies can complement one another. There are many situations in which reinforcement can play a powerful role in learning and acquisition of *knowledge,* even if Skinner might be uncomfortable with such a term. Many of the principles identified by Skinner occur in other theoretical traditions that are in greater favor with educators in the 1990s—for example, fading of reinforcement contingencies looks a lot like scaffolding of instruction, which will be taken up in the next chapter. Thus, many of the educator behaviors Skinner favored endure even if his explanation of their effectiveness does not.

COGNITIVE BEHAVIOR MODIFICATION

Many who were well educated with respect to Skinner's theory found greater favor with cognitive theory than Skinner did, largely because they recognized that many "behavioral" interventions had a strong cognitive component. In this section, there is brief coverage of the work of two scholars who offered books summarizing interventions with both behavioral and cognitive components. In doing so, they helped to make obvious the power of combining the two traditions, that the two traditions were tapping complementary, powerful competencies, rather than providing alternative explanations for the same competencies as Skinner argued (i.e., Skinner believed that many cognitive constructs could be explained via reinforcement mechanisms).

Mahoney's *Cognition and Behavior Modification* (1974)

During the 1950s, 1960s, and 1970s, a number of behaviorists were investigating and validating various types of behavior therapies (i.e., showing the therapies worked in eliminating undesirable behaviors)— therapies that clearly had cognitive components. Thus, Ellis (e.g., 1970) put forth the notion that many emotional disturbances were due to irrational ideas that could be replaced with more rational thoughts. Much of overcoming emotional torment in Ellis' view involves replacing irrational thoughts with more rational ones. Thus, a large part of coming to control one's emotions is overcoming the belief that emotions cannot be controlled and replacing it with the belief that one can take charge of

destructive emotions. Wolpe (e.g., 1958) developed **systematic desensitization** for overcoming fear of particular objects and experiences. Desensitization involved instructing clients to create relaxing images while dealing with fear-invoking stimuli. Wolpe (e.g., 1958, 1969) was also working with a therapy called "thought stopping," which was intended to eliminate thoughts that interfered with functional behaviors. Homme (1965) was teaching patients to use both thoughts and external reinforcements to curb bad habits. Thus, if a smoker had the urge to smoke, the patient was taught to think things such as, "Smoking causes halitosis" and "I'll save money by not smoking," and then to reward not smoking a cigarette by having a cup of coffee.

Cautela (1967) was urging his subjects to construct even more striking internal mediators. Thus, overweight people were taught to imagine scenes such as the following as part of treatment designed to eliminate high-caloric foods from their diet:

> I want you to imagine you've just had your main meal and you are about to eat your dessert, which is apple pie. As you are about to reach for the fork, you get a funny feeling in the pit of your stomach. You start to feel queasy, nauseous and sick all over. As you touch the fork, you can feel some food particles inching up your throat. You're just about to vomit. As you put the fork into the pie, the food comes up into your mouth. You try to keep your mouth closed because you are afraid that you'll spit your food out all over the place. You bring the piece of pie to your mouth. As you're about to open your mouth, you puke; you vomit all over your hands, the fork, over the pie. It goes all over the table, over the other people's food. Your eyes are watering. Snot mucus is all over your mouth and nose. Your hands feel sticky. There is an awful smell. As you look at this mess you just can't help but vomit again and again until just watery stuff is coming out. Everybody is looking at you with a shocked expression. You turn away from the food and immediately start to feel better. You run out of the room, and as you run out, you feel better and better. You wash and clean yourself up and it feels wonderful. (Cautela, 1967, p. 462)

In short, cognition was everywhere in behavior therapy! Clients were imagining reinforcing themselves and imagining models performing particular actions. Clients were being told to talk to themselves and to think. Behavior theory did not adequately capture these therapies, although many elements of classical behavior theory were present in them, including reinforcement, modeling, punishment, and classical conditioning. Thus, the overweight individual who imagined throwing up was anticipating a punishment and experienced reinforcement in the form of an imagined cleansing once the pie had been escaped. An integration of cognitive and behavioral perspectives was necessary to make sense of therapies that included images and thoughts of punishment and reinforcement or self-instructions to verbalize negative consequences of engaging in a behavior (e.g., saying that "smoking causes halitosis").

Michael Mahoney's (1974) *Cognition and Behavior Modification* was a careful analysis of the state of behavioral theory, cognitive theory, and therapies being proposed by behaviorally oriented clinical psychologists. Mahoney recognized that the predictive power and the conceptual breadth of a cognitive-behavioral theory would be much greater than the predictive power and conceptual breadth of the radical behaviorism of B. F. Skinner. Mahoney recognized that organisms did not simply respond to stimuli but stimuli as perceived (i.e., interpreted). Thus, Dulaney (1968) demonstrated that blasts of hot and cold air functioned as reinforcers and punishers only if they were labeled as such by an experimenter. A blast of hot air that felt bad did not suppress the behavior that preceded it unless the subject believed the blast of cold air signified an incorrect response. In fact, it could increase a response that preceded it, if the subject was informed that the blast of hot air signaled a correct response. He recognized that words were not physical stimuli but filled with meaning, meanings that made a difference even in basic learning tasks such as classical conditioning. For example, if a painful electrical shock follows presentation of the word "hare," subsequent presentation of the word "rabbit" will produce classically conditioned arousal (Maltzman, 1968). Only an organism whose memory was filled with rich semantic interconnections would behave that way. Mahoney also knew that learner awareness of learning contingencies often contributed to the learning of contingencies (Dulaney, 1962, 1968; Spielberger & DeNike, 1966). Radical behaviorism as Skinner conceived of it provided no role for perception, semantic factors in verbal conditioning, or awareness.

Perhaps most damaging of all, an enormous literature that had been produced by the prominent behaviorist Albert Bandura and his colleagues, reviewed in the next section, had appeared, making clear that people could learn by watching others. A key assumption in Skinner's theory was that responding was necessary for learning to take place. Studies documenting the power of observational learning, however, made obvious that responding was not necessary for learning to occur. There was indeed a great deal of reason to question Skinnerian psychology based on data by researchers who generally were sympathetic with Skinner's position.

Mahoney offered three mediational models. The first was simple. The external stimulus in the environment stimulated a covert (i.e., internal, cognitive) response, which served as a covert stimulus to the organism that elicited an external response. Thus, the mouse hears a meow, which stimulates an internal representation of a cat, which serves as a stimulus that causes the mouse to run! The second mediational model was termed an information processing model. A stimulus elicited attention (actually selective attention because only part of the physical stimulation is part of the focus of attention), which resulted in encoding into short-term memory, which communicated with long-term memory. Long-term memory serves up a response. This second model is compatible with most of the information processing theory presented in this book thus far. This second model included the possibility of strategies to help maintain a stimulus in short-term memory and the classical mechanisms affecting long-term memory (e.g., **decay** of memories with time, **interference** between similar memories). The executive processes of the mind were acknowledged and represented in this model.

The third model, the **cognitive learning model,** was the most ambitious of the three models. The integrative nature of this model comes through in Mahoney's introduction to it:

> . . . Man is viewed as a complex organism capable of impressive adaptation. He is in a continuous reciprocity relationship with his environment. . . . Behavior changes are influenced by the current physiological state of the organism, his past learning history, the existing environmental situation, and a variety of inter-dependent cognitive processes (e.g., selective attention, anticipated consequences, etc.). (p. 145)

Mahoney's view was that humans are anything but passive with respect to the environment and the effects of the environment on behavior: "The 'raw data' of experience are selectively filtered, transformed, categorized, and stored" (p. 146). Cognitive mediation was viewed as central to behavior, permitting learning to occur over long periods of time, inferences about the regularities and commonalities of experience, the formation of expectations about reinforcements and punishments that might follow particular actions, and complex problem solving. Particularly important, however, were cognitive strategies, with Mahoney recognizing that many times dysfunction could be explained as lack of a repertoire of strategies. The solution in those cases is to teach new strategies, including self-verbalization and imagery strategies, among others. One of the most important directions recognized by Mahoney was teaching people to self-instruct themselves to apply cognitive strategies well matched to task demands.

Without a doubt, the scientist who did the most to advance the self-instructional position, both with his research and writing, has been Donald Meichenbaum, whose discussion of self-instruction in his 1977 book went well beyond Mahoney (1974). Although Mahoney's (1974) integrative contribution must be mentioned in any scholarly review of the cognitive basis of instruction, Meichenbaum's volume has had a much more direct impact on educators, perhaps because Meichenbaum was particularly interested in a dysfunctional population commonly encountered in school: hyperactive students.

Meichenbaum's *Cognitive Behavior Modification* (1977)

Meichenbaum was aware of a large American and Soviet literature establishing that self-speech did and could be used to organize behavior. Thus, the prominent cognitive-developmental psychologist Lawrence Kohlberg (Kohlberg, Yaeger, & Hjertholm, 1968) had reported self-verbalizations by preschoolers that served to organize complex behaviors. Meichenbaum (1977, p. 19) cited the following example of child speech that had a directive function during the construction of a tinker toy car:

> The wheels go here, the wheels go here. Oh, we need to start it all over again. We have to close it up. See it closes up. We're starting it all over again. Do you know why we wanted to do that? Because I needed it to go a different way. Isn't it pretty clever, don't you think? But we have to cover up the motor just like a real car. (Kohlberg et al., 1968, p. 695)

Prominent Soviet psychologists such as Gal'perin (1969) and Vygotsky (e.g., 1962; see Chapter 8 of this volume) had argued that mature thinking was largely inner speech and dialogue representing the end product of a developmental process that began with external speech, including external dialogue with others that evolved into external speech to self. External speech that directed behavior eventually internalized in the Soviet models, with inner speech playing a major role in thinking.

Sokolov (1975) had presented substantial data in support of the inner speech model by demonstrating that when people are given difficult problems, they often manifest self-speech that can be recorded. Even if the speech is not audible, there are psychophysically measurable tensions in the musculature of the vocal apparatus during complex problem solving.

The power of speech-for-self in the regulation of children's behavior had been demonstrated in a number of studies in the 1970s. For example, Patterson and Mischel (1976) had taught preschoolers to resist a temptation by teaching them to tell themselves not to pay any attention to the distractor.

Wozniak (e.g., 1972) had provided thorough conceptual analysis of how speech-for-self could regulate preschoolers' motor behaviors. He especially analyzed how speech-for-self could be mobilized to inhibit impulsive responding.

In short, Meichenbaum was aware of an enormous body of research supporting the position that speech-for-self could organize behavior. Although there were indicators, such as Kohlberg et al. (1968), that young children often used such speech on their own, there was also a body of data (e.g., Patterson & Mischel, 1976; Wozniak, 1972) substantiating that young children often benefit from explicit instruction to self-verbalize, especially with respect to the inhibition of impulsive responses. The potential of speech-for-self to inhibit behaviors was important to Meichenbaum because he was particularly interested in increasing reflective behaviors in populations of children who are impulsive, who respond without thinking about their responses.

Meichenbaum and Goodman (1971), in what is now a classic study in cognitive-developmental psychology, demonstrated that the impulsive responding of hyperactive second-graders could be reduced through teaching children to instruct themselves to go slowly and reflect before responding. Using teacher modeling, guided practice, and the gradual fading of teacher cuing, the students were taught to make self-verbalizations consistent with this ideal model of self-instruction during a copying task:

> Okay, what is it I have to do? You want me to copy the picture with the different lines. I have to go slowly and carefully. Okay, draw the line down, down, good; then to the right, that's it; now down some more and to the left. Good, I'm doing fine so far. Remember, go slowly. Now back up again. No, I was supposed to go down. That's okay. Just erase the line carefully . . . good. Even if I make an error I can go on slowly and carefully. I have to go down now. Finished. I did it! (Meichenbaum & Goodman, 1971, p. 117)

Of course, these students were being asked to do a lot, with the self-instruction focusing the students on the definition of the problem, providing guidance to the motor behaviors required in the task, reinforcing the drawing that occurs (e.g., all those "goods"), and cuing coping when there were difficulties (Meichenbaum, 1977, p. 32).

Using Meichenbaum's approach, the teacher first described and modeled self-verbalization. Then the teacher provided external support and guidance as a student attempted to apply the approach to problems. The student was encouraged during this process to internalize the self-verbalizations, with the teacher eventually guiding the student to whisper rather than talk aloud and then eventually only to think about the problem definition, task focusing and guiding directions, and self-reinforcement as they performed the task. This is consistent with two general principles of instruction that will recur in subsequent chapters: (1) Instruction should be designed to encourage internalization of strategies. (2) Teachers can do so by prompting internalization and gradually fading their guidance of processing, intervening only on an as-needed basis.

The most striking data confirming that this type of instruction reduced impulsive responding were obtained on an instrument known as the Matching Familiar Figures Test (MFFT), which involves presentation of a picture that matches one of six similar pictures. The test taker's task is to identify which of the six pictures exactly matches the standard. Reflective and careful feature-by-feature comparisons of the standard to the six alternatives is the preferred strategy; rapid responding that does not include systematic comparisons (i.e., impulsive responding) under-

mines performance on the MFFT. In general, initially impulsive children in the Meichenbaum and Goodman (1971) study, who were trained to self-instruct, made fewer errors on the MFFT than control children who were also impulsive but who were not taught how to instruct themselves verbally to perform tasks requiring reflection.

Enthusiasm for self-instruction was fueled by a number of follow-up studies with various child populations who were impulsive. Data produced at a number of sites and with a number of tasks were consistent with the conclusion that self-instructional training could reduce impulsive responding (e.g., Bender, 1976; Bugenthal, Whalen, & Henker, 1977; Camp, Blom, Hebert, & van Doornink, 1977; Douglas, 1972; Douglas, Parry, Marton, & Garson, 1976; Finch, Wilkinson, Nelson, & Montgomery, 1975; Glenwick, 1976; Guralnick, 1976; Kagen, 1977). See Pressley (1979) for a review of these and related studies; Meichenbaum (1977) provided extensive commentary on the relevance of some of these investigations (as well as of other data) to his position that impulsive responding could be overcome with self-instructional training. More recently, Fjellstrom, Born, and Baer (1988) provided especially impressive evidence that children as young as preschoolers can learn to self-question while performing an intellectual task, with the self-questioning dramatically affecting performance.

Meichenbaum (1977) inspired many classroom researchers to develop and study interventions with self-instructional components. Manning (1991), based largely on her own previous research (e.g., Manning, 1988, 1990), has elaborated the self-instructional model so that it is applicable in elementary classrooms. An important component in Manning's model is a teacher who consistently models self-control using self-instruction.

Anyone who has ever taught knows the frustration of trying to figure out what is wrong with the overhead projector. A self-instructing teacher might cope as follows: Consistent with Meichenbaum's research, the teacher would first define the problem verbally, followed by self-verbalizations to direct appropriate actions: "Why won't this overhead turn on? Let me see. I'll try all the switches again. This arrow points to the right. Did I turn left or right. Try again." When frustrated (which typically occurs when working with an overhead projector—especially the kind that are programmed once they have been switched off to remain shut off until they are cooled), the teacher models coping via self-instruction: "It's easy to get frustrated. Take a deep breath and relax. There must be a solution." Once a solution is found, the teacher self-reinforces: "Hey! I stuck with it and found the outlet is faulty. I'll try this other outlet. Yay! It works." If there is no success, the teacher models more coping and adapting: "I've tried all I know. I'll either show you this information by putting it on the board or call the media specialist to help fix the machine. Which would be fastest?" (Manning, 1991, p. 134). Of course, there are many opportunities for a teacher to model such self-control, with the teacher who does so projecting the clear message that such self-instruction and reasoning is a mature way to approach problems.

The self-instructing teacher also models for students how to cope with problems and temptations to behave impulsively or inappropriately. Thus, the teacher might model the following sequence for a student who is unprepared and caught attempting to cheat, again starting with a verbalization of the problem and proceeding to model self-direction and self-coping until a solution is achieved that can be self-reinforced: "I forgot to study for my test. Should I look at my friend's test? I can see her paper easily. But, is that right? Just do my best. I'll feel better about myself if I don't look. This is hard. I know my answers are wrong. That's okay. I've done the best I can. Next time I won't leave my book at school. I'm glad I didn't take answers that didn't belong to me. I feel good about that!" (p. 135).

Manning's (1991) book is filled with suggestions as to how to structure the classroom environment to foster self-instruction. She discusses how teachers and peers can model self-instruction and how self-instruction can be practiced in the context of games and school tasks. In short, Manning (1991) provides a compelling discussion of how to translate the self-instructional framework developed by basic researchers into classroom practice. Many of the cognitive strategies for reading, writing, and mathematics that will be discussed in subsequent chapters could be self-instructed. Some self-instructional models have already been devised, including interventions to promote important academic competencies such as student writing (see Graham & Harris, 1989a, 1989b; Chapter 15, this volume), arithmetic (e.g., Keller & Lloyd, 1989), and higher-order problem solving (e.g., King, 1991). Teacher modeling of

self-instruction and self-control also will be evident in discussions of reading instruction in Chapter 14. The potency of self-instruction with academic content makes obvious the potential importance of Manning's model, which is the most complete conception of how to promote competence via self-instruction in the classroom. Anyone interested in conducting research on classroom self-instruction or in devising curriculum based on self-instruction should consult the Manning (1991) book as an essential resource detailing the state-of-the-art with respect to theory, research, and classroom practice.

Manning has conducted both true experiments (e.g., 1988) and intensive case studies (e.g., 1990). The experiments are essential to making the case that teaching self-instruction is a causal factor in improving classroom performance; the cases provide insights into the dynamics of this approach. In the 1988 experiment, the most behaviorally inappropriate grade-1 and grade-3 children in a school were assigned to either a self-instructional treatment group or a control condition that received additional instruction and attention except that the instruction did not include a self-instructional component. For example, when the experimental condition students saw a teacher self-instruct to inhibit inappropriate behaviors, control students received additional explicit instruction in the school rules prohibiting the inappropriate behaviors. Both experimental and control subjects received 8 hours of instruction, with the classroom teachers blind as to the condition assignment of the children involved in the study. The data were striking both immediately after training and 3 months later. The students receiving self-instructional training were perceived as more self-controlled by their teachers, were assessed to be on task more during a series of formal assessments involving academic tasks, and believed themselves to be more in control of their behaviors. In the 1990 paper, Manning described how cognitive self-instruction was used to increase the on-task behavior of a grade-4 girl. At the beginning of the intervention, Jill (the student) was on-task during school assignments only 15 percent of the time. Following training in self-instruction, Jill was on-task 80 percent of the time, with high on-task behavior still evident 3 months after the self-instructional training had occurred. Results such as these make clear that cognitive self-instruction is worthy of educational researcher and practitioner attention.

Cognitive self-instruction is an arena that is exceptionally exciting because both basic and applied research continue. Zentall (1989) summarized much of the basic research in recent years relating to self-control training with hyperactive and impulsive children, the population that Meichenbaum originally targeted for self-instruction. Some of the highlights of the research-based conclusions offered by Zentall (1989) include the following:

- Although treatment of impulsivity using reinforcement, punishment, and DRO (see discussion earlier in this chapter) can produce some reductions in classroom impulsivity, the gains last only as long as reinforcers and punishers are applied and do not result in changes in academic performance. More than reinforcement and punishment is needed to affect academic competence, with self-control training that integrates behavioral and cognitive mechanisms more powerful than behavioral training alone. This is consistent with the general conclusions of Mahoney, Meichenbaum, and others that purely behavioral theories are not as powerful as behavioral and cognitive theories combined.
- Zentall and colleagues (e.g., Zentall, Gohs, & Culatta, 1983) have observed more spontaneous self-verbalizations by impulsive and hyperactive children than would be expected based on Meichenbaum's model. Zentall et al. (1983) also observed, however, much less inaudible verbal activity by hyperactives than normals while performing academic tasks, raising the possibility that one problem for hyperactive students may be that they have not internalized appropriate self-verbalizations. See Douglas (1980) for additional evidence that hyperactive students are less capable at performing tasks that require task analysis, planning, and monitoring.
- Hyperactives attend to different cues than normals and, in particular, focus more on global cues than detail cues (Zelniker & Jeffrey, 1976; Zentall & Gohs, 1984). They also seem to be attracted to salient cues, even if these are not task relevant.

In general, Zentall (1989) concludes that effective self-instruction with hyperactive children focuses attention on planning and coordination of cognitive responses to external stimuli, especially features of stimuli that hyperactives might not attend on their own. Zentall also reviewed research supporting some of the specific components of self-instruction, including teaching students (1) to recognize when they are at risk for behaving in a noncontrolled fashion, (2) that there are more appropriate behaviors than the ones they are using to solve problems, (3) how to interrupt impulsive responding (e.g., by making comments such as, "What am I supposed to do here?"), (4) the standards that apply to a task (i.e., that define effective performance of the task), (5) to self-monitor, (6) to cope, and (7) to self-reinforce. The support for Meichenbaum's general model of self-instruction seems to be growing.

Summary

Instructions that include both behavioral and cognitive components are more powerful in many situations than ones that include simply behavioral components. As will be detailed in the next section and in subsequent chapters, it is necessary to know how to do something and to be motivated to do it. Learning "how" is more of a cognitive problem that can be addressed by interventions stimulating cognitive processes well matched to task demands; motivating use of such processes can be affected by behavioral interventions. Theorists such as Mahoney and Meichenbaum clearly recognized the need for creating instruction that produces know-how and the desire to use that know-how. Both knowing how to learn and perform cognitive tasks and the motivation to perform cognitive tasks are necessary for people to perform at high levels of competence, a theme resounded throughout this book.

SOCIAL LEARNING THEORY

What is seen and heard can contribute to complex understandings and development of complex knowledge about intricate relationships in the world. Bandura and colleagues (e.g., Bandura & Walters, 1963) proposed **observational learning theory.** The main tenet of this theory is that much can be and is learned from observing others (i.e., **behavioral models**). There have been many demonstrations over the years of the potency of observational learning. A perusal of the social development chapters in the last two editions of the *Handbook of Child Psychology* (Mussen, 1970, 1983) turns up studies of observational learning of aggression, altruism, sex-typed behaviors, attachment behaviors, and social independence—with studies documenting the potency of observational learning even in children as young as 1 year of age (e.g., Hanna & Meltzoff, 1993). Because observation is a powerful method for acquiring many types of social behaviors and because learning in this framework is by watching other people, the term **social learning** came to replace observational learning. Social learning theory has also evolved as a broader perspective than observational learning theory, encompassing some of the learning mechanisms identified in other theories of learning, most notably operant analyses of behavior.

Main Processes of Social Learning

How does learning proceed according to social learning theory?

1. *When an action is followed by a positive consequence, the action often is more likely in the future.* That is, the positive consequence is a **reinforcer** for the action it preceded. B. F. Skinner (e.g., 1953; see the discussion earlier in this chapter), in particular, provided substantial data that reinforcements can be used to **shape** behaviors. The mechanisms underlying reinforcement effects are not entirely understood, although some ways that reinforcements improve performance are by (1) imparting information and (2) motivating the behaviors that preceded them (Bandura, 1977b, p. 17).

Thus, when a professor's class asks interesting questions following a well-prepared lecture, the professor is reinforced for preparing and delivering the lecture. The attention of the class is a reinforcement that informs the professor that he or she did a good job and motivates careful preparation of lectures in the future.

On days when professors are not prepared, they are often punished by students looking blankly at them and not taking notes. This is informative feedback that hopefully motivates not putting off lecture preparation in the future until it is too late. That is, such **punishment** should, if anything, reduce the likelihood of behaviors that preceded it.

If reinforcement or punishment were required for all learning to occur, learning would be much less efficient and certain than it is. For a reinforcement or punishment to occur, the behavior that is to be reinforced or punished must occur. When a person is incapable of that behavior, it is sometimes possible to reinforce a less demanding behavior that is part of or prerequisite to the desired behavior. Thus, when first learning to drive a car, the good

driving instructor reinforces for behaviors that skilled drivers do not even think about. Thus, the student who checks carefully to see the brake is on, the car is in park, and the seat belt is fastened is reinforced for these behaviors, even though he or she may not really know what to do after turning the key! Once the student has mastered these preliminary steps, it takes more to get reinforced. So after several weeks of driving lessons, there may only be reinforcement if the day's drive was entirely smooth.

It is not possible to wait for some behaviors to occur to punish them because the behaviors are too dangerous. Thus, most people are never punished for driving over 100 miles an hour, and yet few people drive that fast. What is critical is that people know there are potential punishments for driving fast. They know because they have observed others be punished for such actions (e.g., they have seen wrecks by the roadway, listened to news reports of serious accidents involving high-speed driving, and know of others who have received citations and suspensions for fast and reckless driving). That brings the discussion to the most important mechanism for learning according to social learning analyses.

2. *People learn by watching others.* Until last month, I [MP] had never been on a television talk show. Even so, I knew exactly how to act as a guest because I had observed so many guests on talk shows over the years. One child we know had never played basketball before he received an indoor hoop and ball for his third Christmas. The first thing he did was to pick up the ball and throw it toward the hoop and scream "Basket!" when it went in. He had learned a lot from watching older boys play basketball at the park and by viewing basketball games on television.

3. *People learn what to expect if they perform an action by observing others.* Consider the following. How many different ways do you know for murdering a person? When we ask undergraduates this question, it is not unusual to receive over 100 responses, from the commonplace (e.g., shooting) to the creatively malicious (e.g., putting ground glass in food) to the extraordinarily inventive and specialized (e.g., using dissolving suture material in a heart surgery that requires the nondissolving variety). What a knowledge base all of us have for destroying other people! Most of the knowledge has been built up by observing murders on television, seeing them in movies, or reading about them in books. There have been many

observational learning opportunities for learning about murder, and they have made a difference in people's long-term knowledge.

Even so, murders are statistically rare. Why? In part because people expect that if they murder someone else, they will be punished. This **expectancy** has been established through years of observing that bad guys on television, in the movies, or in novels are caught and punished for their wicked deeds. Moreover the punishments are usually severe (i.e, they have great negative **value**), ranging from extreme personal remorse and guilt to execution. Whether a person performs a given behavior, one that she or he learned observationally, depends on expectations of rewards or punishments for performing the behavior and the value of the rewards and punishments. The **probability of performing a behavior X is a function of the expectancy of reward or punishment for X *and* the value of the reward or punishment;** this is sometimes expressed as $P_{behavior} = F$ ($E_{reinforcement/punishment} + V_{reinforcement/punishment}$). For murder, expectancy of punishment is high: Most people would feel terribly guilty about the act for the rest of life, even if they did not go to prison. The negative values associated with extreme guilt and potential imprisonment are high. Thus, most people do not commit murder.

Consider another possibility. We have watched many people over the years adopt diet and exercise regimens and build up extensive knowledge bases about how to conduct such regimens based on their observations. People are both reinforced for dieting and exercising (i.e., by losing weight) and punished for it (i.e., suffering from perceived starvation and experiencing physical exhaustion). Both authors of this book engage in diet and exercise off and on. We always expect it will reduce weight. What varies is the value of reinforcers and punishers. The heavier we get, the more valuable weight loss is. The heavier we get, the more likely the reinforcements from weight loss are greater in value than the punishments associated with going hungry and sweating. Our willingness to diet varies from day to day and situation to situation. The expectancy of a good time by going out to dinner with friends at a convention so outweighs the long-term reinforcements associated with weight loss that we often go out to dinner with friends when at conventions. We also expect the punishments associated with working up a sweat to be greater at a convention than at home—when we exercise in the morning of a convention day, legs often give out before the end of the day. Thus, whether diet or exercise occurs depends on the situation—what reinforcements and punishments we can expect in the situation and what those reinforcements and punishments mean to us. Today, author MP's weight is up a little; he expects that holding off on food and running at noon would bring his weight down some; he also expects that eating a meal at the student union would not be reinforcing anyway. With those factors combined, he is not eating lunch today and jogging instead.

We discussed expectancy X value theory in Chapter 5 already. The important additional point in this context is that expectancies are often acquired through observational learning. Of course, that is adaptive in the case of terrible punishers. We are better off acquiring an expectation that touching a high tension wire will induce death or severe injury than acquiring such knowledge from direct experience. We are better off acquiring an expectation that driving at high speeds will result in a serious accident than being involved in a near-fatal collision.

We provided these home-spun examples illustrating expectancy-value theory because our years of teaching this concept have made clear to us that it is a difficult one for students to understand how performance varies as a function of both the expectancy of a reward or punishment and the perceived value of the reinforcer or punisher. (Even 4-year-olds understand the main idea of expectancy X value theory intuitively, and their willingness to exert effort is definitely a function of both expectancy of reinforcement/punishment and the value of the incentive [O'Sullivan, 1993].)

If you do not completely understand $P = F(E + V)$ at this point, go back and review all of point 3. Once you think you understand expectancy X value theory, try this little test of your understanding of the concept:

1. You expect that studying for a test will make it likely you will pass a test. The test does not count in your grades and is over boring content. Do you study or not?
2. You expect that studying for a test will not increase the likelihood you will pass or earn a better grade. Your entire semester's grade depends on this test. Do you study or not?

3. You expect that studying for a test will increase your grade, you like the content, and the grade in this course is important to you. Do you study or not?

For situation (1), you probably do not study because the value of reinforcement is low and there is a negative value (boredom) associated with studying. For (2), you do not study because your expectation of reinforcement following studying behavior is low. For (3), you study because the expectation of reward for studying is high and there are two sources of positively valued reinforcement (i.e., the pleasure of processing this material and an important course grade). (4) *In the last chapter, we described briefly how some emotional responses can be learned via* **classical conditioning**, *such as aversions to foods that are eaten before experiencing illness.* Because fears learned via classically conditioning are often dysfunctional, these have been studied especially carefully. Thus, there is little debate that if a child approaches a dog and the dog counters aggressively, there is the possibility that the child will be fearful at the sight of the dog in the future, with the potential of the fearful response generalizing to other dogs so a phobia develops with respect to dogs (see Bandura, 1969, for an extensive analysis).

Fortunately, such emotional responses can sometimes be undone through observational learning opportunities. Thus, if children who are afraid of dogs have opportunities to see models approach and have contact with dogs with no adverse effects, negative emotional responding sometimes **extinguishes,** with the children able to approach and interact with dogs just as the models they had observed approached and interacted with dogs (e.g., Bandura & Menlove, 1968).

In summary, social learning can occur via reinforcement, punishment, classical conditioning, or observation, with these mechanisms flexibly combining in many instances to affect children's learning. Thus, a child might acquire a classically conditioned aversion to collies, an aversion that is based in part on punishment for approaching a collie (i.e., after approaching a collie, the collie's negative reaction is a punisher that elicits negative emotion, which is subsequently elicited by the sight of a collie alone). Such a negative reaction can be modulated in the future by observation of other children having fun with collies and reinforcement from a parent for the child approaching and playing with a pet collie. Throughout this sequence, the child's expectancies about reinforcements and punishments change. Before approaching the offending collie, there is an expectancy of positive reinforcement that is valued (i.e., playing with a collie). After encountering the aggressive collie, the expectations change, so punishment for approaching the collie is now expected. As the child observes other children having a good time with collies, expectancies about reinforcement increase. When the expectation of reinforcement exceeds the expectation of potential punishment, the child is likely once again to approach the collie, although there may be some conflict (i.e., this is known as an **approach-avoidance** situation, one in which both potential reinforcements and punishments can be anticipated, and thus there are both reasons to approach a stimulus and reasons to avoid it.

Although people sometimes experience reinforcements and punishments themselves, it is often the case that they learn through **vicarious** experiences: They see others experience reinforcements and punishments and thus form expectations about reinforcements or punishments that might accrue to them for performing particular behaviors through observational mechanisms. The social learning perspective is that much of human behavior is acquired via observation.

Example of Observational Learning of Behaviors and Expectancies: Classic Research Conducted by Bandura

No one has done as much to advance social learning theory as Bandura. His research on how and when people learn behaviors and expectancies through observation is now considered classical work in psychology. At least a 100-page chapter would be required to do justice to this research program. We do not have the luxury of such space here. Fortunately a lot can be learned by reviewing some prototypical research conducted by Bandura and his co-workers.

In Bandura (1965), young children viewed a film in which a child exhibited some novel physical and verbal aggressive behaviors toward a set of toys. At the completion of the film, the child model was either punished for the aggression (i.e., the child was spanked and verbally rebuked for the aggression), reinforced for it (i.e., given soft drinks, candy, and praise for the aggressive behaviors), or provided no consequences. After watching the film, the subjects were left alone in the room where the film was made with an opportunity to play with the toys seen in the film. When children watched the film involving reward or no consequences for the aggression, they were much more likely to exhibit the aggressive behaviors when interacting with the toys than if they viewed the film in which the model was spanked. Then, all children in the experiment were offered stickers and fruit juice if they would show the experimenter the aggressive behaviors that the film model had exhibited. The children had little difficulty in reproducing the behaviors.

What was going on in this situation? The children had clearly learned the aggressive behaviors in question because they could reproduce those behaviors when given an incentive to do so. They were less likely to perform the aggressive behaviors after viewing the punished model because they also learned to expect punishment from seeing the model punished. Performance of a behavior depends on knowing a response as well as expectation of reinforcements that are valued by the performer. When punishments are expected, performance often will not occur unless there are offsetting reinforcements. For many children in the Bandura (1965) study, the fun of playing with the toys aggressively was not worth the risk of getting a spanking.

During the late 1950s and 1960s, Bandura performed many experiments that shared features with his 1965 study. His work, continued into the 1970s, in general aimed at elaborating his view that observational learning is a powerful factor in the development of human behavior. The result is a highly cognitive account of social learning via observation, one that all students of educational psychology must understand.

Cognitive Mechanisms Mediating Social Learning Via Observation

Bandura's (1977b) *Social Learning Theory* was a book-length summary of the mechanisms underlying social learning and is still a well-regarded analysis. Bandura's (1986) *Social Foundations of Thought and Action* was a much longer analysis of social learning, relating it to many traditions in psychology. For students who need a short course in social learning theory that is more thorough than what is covered here, the 1977 book is recommended; for students who want to achieve professional-level understanding of social learning, the 1986 book is must reading.

At the heart of both of these books is a model of observational learning that includes **attentional, retentional, motor reproduction,** and **motivational processes.** Each of these four categories of processes is considered in detail by Bandura, with each category comprised of multiple inter-related processes.

Attentional Processes   What is attended to (i.e., observed) depends on characteristics of the model and characteristics of the observer. For example, not everyone has equal access to the same types of models. Children who are reared in environments with gentle people have more opportunities to view gentle behaviors than children who are raised in environments filled with aggressive people. Even so, all of us have some control as to the social models who are available to us and attended. Thus, when a person elects to go to college, he or she selects to be surrounded with students who model scholarly behaviors of various sorts. People who elect gang life rather than college select themselves into situations in which aggression is modeled.

In both the college and the gang situation, some of the people will command greater attention than others. Thus, the president of a fraternity is more likely to be observed and imitated than a pledge. The leader of a gang is much more likely to be watched and imitated than someone who is not as respected by gang members. The observer is more likely to attend to the behaviors of the fraternity president or the gang leader if they have been reinforced in the past for imitating such figures, which, of course, occurs often.

Advertisers have definitely figured out that high-status models are more likely to be imitated than low-status models. The power of stature to affect behavior is especially obvious when it is considered how much American presidents and their families can affect the behavior of Americans in general. How many rocking chairs were sold because Kennedy was often photographed in his rocker? More than a few of our more conservative friends had Nixon and Reagan haircuts. Older American women have been much more comfortable in simple styles of dress since Barbara Bush lived in the White House.

When researchers have looked (e.g., Yussen, 1974), it has proven easy to demonstrate that what is attended is more likely to be learned than what is not attended. Such analyses have also made clear that sometimes learners benefit from instructions about what to watch. What is attended cannot be taken for granted by those wishing to teach via observational learning.

Retentional Processes Once a person attends to a behavior, it must be remembered if it is to affect future behaviors. As we mentioned in Chapter 3, Bandura's view is that imaginal and verbal coding of observed behaviors is critical to long-term memory of observations. Consistent with much of the thinking of the 1970s about memory (see Chapter 2), Bandura also considered rehearsal processes to be critical to improving memory of observed behaviors.

Bandura did not rely simply on the classical memory literature to make his case that imagery and rehearsal processes are mediators of observational learning. Rather Bandura supervised a program of research documenting the potency of verbal, imaginal, and rehearsal processes in coding of observations (e.g., Bandura, Grusec, & Menlove, 1966; Bandura & Jeffery, 1973; Bandura, Jeffery, & Bachicha, 1974). Bandura's work was complemented by others who provided data demonstrating the criticality of encoding processes for observational learning (e.g., Coates & Hartup, 1969; Gerst, 1971). One important lesson from these studies was that instructions to construct imagery and verbal codes as well as instructions to rehearse often enhance learning of what was observed. Again, as was the case with attention, it is often important to provide explicit information about how to retain what is observed if one wants to teach using observational learning opportunities.

Motor Reproduction Processes Not only must a person perceive and remember a behavioral sequence, but also they must be able to produce it themselves. In some cases, the sequence that is observed is readily reproducible. In other cases, the observer can carry out components but not the entire action. It is often necessary for individual components to be acquired before the entire sequence can be executed. For example, a skilled gymnast can sometimes watch another gymnast's routine (e.g., on the balance beam) and copy most or all of it immediately. Less skilled gymnasts often would have to break the routine into segments (e.g., practicing the mount over and over again, practicing a particular type of handstand over and over, practicing the dismount over and over) before attempt-

ing to integrate the segments. For some of us, it would never be possible to execute a routine on a balance beam.

Thus, reproduction following observation is often a demanding process, especially when it involves a skilled performance. Although the performance in question may be impossible for some, often it is attainable, although a great deal of practice may be required for that to occur. Moreover, additional observational learning opportunities may be necessary. We recall a Little League coach repeatedly demonstrating to an aspiring infielder how to position one's body to field a ground ball. Consistent with Bandura's position, this young player was being provided both feedback about his performance and additional observational learning opportunities for a part of a larger sequence (i.e., fielding the ball and throwing it to first base):

> Skills are not perfected through observation alone, nor are they developed solely by trial-and-error fumbling. A golf instructor, for example, does not provide beginners with golf balls and clubs and wait for them to discover the golf swing. In most everyday learning, people usually achieve a close approximation of the new behavior by modeling, and they refine it through self-corrective adjustments on the basis of informative feedback from performance and from focussed demonstration of segments that have been only partially learned. (Bandura, 1977b, p. 28)

This quote from Bandura provides an opportunity to emphasize a point that will come up several times in this book. There are major debates between those who believe in discovery learning of various types and those who believe in learning through more direct instruction and explanation. There are also debates between those who believe that skills should be mastered first and those who believe that tasks should be tackled as wholes. Bandura clearly favors instruction via modeling over discovery. He also sides with the development of skills as a prerequisite to attempting the whole task.

Although we agree with Bandura in favoring instruction over discovery, the skills versus whole-task debate is somewhat overblown. That little boy who was drilled on how to position himself for a ground ball during infield practice spent the second half of practice playing in an actual game. There are many people who play entire rounds of golf after a bucket of balls at the driving range and 100 attempts on the practice putting green. Learning discrete skills and learning how to perform a whole task often can occur together; there are good reasons why they should: People are much more motivated to play whole baseball games and whole rounds of golf than to acquire component baseball or golf skills. In fact, the only motivation to learn the skills is to improve performance during a whole baseball game or round of golf, so that the "whole" task provides motivation for mastering subtasks. The way subtasks are combined in a baseball game or a round of golf is enormously complex. Learning how to combine skills flexibly as they are needed in the context of an actual game requires many years of practice. If the whole is ever to be accomplished, learners must have extensive experience participating at a level that requires coordination of all elements of the game. The reason there are Little Leagues and golf handicaps is so that people can participate in the whole activity while they are still mastering the skills that compose the activity.

Motivational Processes   People can see an action, one that they are capable of doing, remember it, and still not perform it—such as the children who failed to perform the aggressive actions after seeing the aggressive model be punished. Performance depends on motivation, which in turn follows from an expectation of a valued reward if the behavior in question is performed. Sometimes this expectation follows from observing reinforcement of others who perform the behavior (i.e., vicarious reinforcement). Sometimes the expectation follows from a personal history of reinforcement for performing the behavior, as when a person continues to run in marathons simply to experience the runner's high and the congratulations from friends and strangers at the finish line. Sometimes the reward is expected because the person will reinforce themselves for performing the action. Thus, we know a writer who will only permit himself to relax in the evening by watching television once he has completed four pages of writing for the day.

Summary   All of us are constantly being exposed to behaviors, ones that we could learn and imitate. Of course, only some of the behaviors that are observed are learned, and few that are learned are performed. For a behavior to be observationally learned and performed requires attention to the behavior. Often, several exposures to the behavior are required, even to the point of breaking the behavior into parts that are modeled over and over as part of the learner at-

tempting to master the complex sequence that is the total behavior in question. The performance of a previously observed behavior depends on retention of the behavior in memory. Imagery codes are especially emphasized by Bandura as critical in guiding performance of complex behaviors. Performance of a golf swing can be guided by an image of a previously modeled golf swing. In fact, one of the most interesting areas in sports research from the point of view of cognitive psychology is the study of how imagery can affect skilled motor performances. The evidence is growing that having an image of a to-be-performed action improves performance of the intended action (see Suinn, 1993). Whether an observationally learned action occurs is very much a matter of intention, however. The motivation to carry out an action depends on the expectancies of the learner with respect to reinforcements for performing the action. The probability of any behavior, including those learned by observation, is a function of the expectancy of reinforcement and the value of the reinforcement to the performer.

The social in the phrase "social learning theory" is intended to emphasize that learning often occurs by observing others or through the reinforcement or punishment of others. What sometimes is obscured by the term social learning is that decidedly cognitive and academic behaviors can be acquired through observational mechanisms. In fact, from the perspective of this book, some of the most exciting work conducted within the social learning framework involves acquisition of conceptual and linguistic competencies.

Observational Learning of Conceptual and Linguistic Competencies

Awareness of the relevance of social learning theory to intellectual development was increased greatly with the 1978 publication of Rosenthal and Zimmerman's *Social Learning and Cognition*. During an era dominated by Chomsky's theory, which emphasized the innate determination of language acquisition, Rosenthal and Zimmerman (1978) specified how syntactical constructions could and often were acquired via social learning mechanisms. During an era dominated by Piaget's theory that much of conceptual learning was determined largely by biologically mediated stagelike progression, Rosenthal and Zimmerman (1978) specified how Piagetian concepts (e.g., conservation) could and often were acquired via social learning mechanisms. During an era dominated by Kohlberg's thinking that moral judgmental competence is determined by stagelike progression that mirrors the stagelike progression of Piaget's stages, Rosenthal and Zimmerman specified how moral judgmental competence could and often was acquired via social learning mechanisms. And the worst part of it for those favoring Chomsky, Piaget, and Kohlberg's theories was that Rosenthal and Zimmerman (1978) were able to cite massive databases supporting their social learning analyses!!

When Rosenthal and Zimmerman's book appeared in the fall of 1978, it was obvious that they had done much to advance social learning theory, especially with respect to education and educational psychology. The timing of the book was an important ingredient in its success. Bandura's (1977b) book, a decidedly cognitive account of social learning theory, was receiving a great deal of attention. Brainerd's (1978b) *Piaget's Theory of Intelligence* appeared at about the same time as the Rosenthal and Zimmerman volume. Brainerd's book was the most complete critique of Piaget's theory ever published. Brainerd made the case that there was a massive database disconfirming Piaget's theoretical preferences. Brainerd also made clear that, in contrast, learning and social learning analyses of concept acquisition were well supported by existing data. A chapter by Brainerd published in the same year (Brainerd, 1978a) was a powerful and visible statement of how learning principles could better account for conceptual acquisitions such as conservation than did Piaget's theory. And, if that was not enough, Whitehurst and Zimmerman (1979) edited a volume the following year that included a number of chapters specifying additionally the great support for social learning analyses of conceptual and language acquisition compared to more biologically oriented approaches, such as the theories of Chomsky, Piaget, and Kohlberg.

In this section, we briefly describe the social learning perspective with respect to language acquisition, conceptual acquisition, and development of moral judgmental competence. We emphasize how the social learning perspective differed from the more biologically oriented positions. A sampler of empirical studies will be reviewed as well, all supportive of the conclusion that social learning mechanisms are important in the development of language, conceptual understanding, and moral judgment ability.

Language Chomsky's nativist position was discussed briefly in Chapter 6. The most critical part of the theory for this discussion is the assumption that humans have biologically determined language capacities. Strong versions of this theory and theories of language development emanating from it include the tenet that learning mechanisms simply do not play much of a role in language acquisition (e.g., Brown, 1973). Thus, psycholinguists in the 1960s, 1970s, and 1980s often rejected imitation as a mechanism mediating language acquisition, with their view of imitation as mimicry (Whitehurst & Vasta, 1975).

In contrast, sophisticated learning theorists view imitation as anything but mimicry. Imitation involves inducing rules from multiple exposures to examples of a phenomenon and using the rules that are constructed via induction to guide future behavior:

> . . . [O]bservers extract the common attributes exemplified in diverse modeled responses and formulate rules for generating behavior with similar structural characteristics. Responses embodying the observationally derived rule resemble the behavior the model would be inclined to exhibit under similar circumstances, even though observers have never seen the model behaving in these new situations. (Bandura, 1977, p. 41)

Bandura's (1977b) book is absolutely clear that this general formulation concerning rule induction through observation was intended to apply to language. He was on firm ground, for by that time a substantial body of evidence was accumulating that many grammatical rules can be learned via learning and social learning mechanisms (I. Brown, 1979; Rosenthal & Zimmerman, 1978, Chapter 2). For example, I. Brown (1976) established that nursery school children could induce the grammatical rules governing the production of passive constructions if they were presented a sample of passive sentences accompanied by enactments of the actions specified by the sentences. After hearing 50 such sentences with enactments, the nursery children were able to understand passive constructions involving different materials than had been used during the 50-sentence training. In fact, presentation of the sentences with enactments produced about 80 percent correct comprehension compared with 50 percent comprehension for controls who did not receive the 50-sentence training. What was most impressive were the large gains owing to exposure and enactment by children who had little understanding of passives at the beginning of the study. (Several other conditions were included in this study besides the exposure plus ennactment and control conditions. These permitted elimination of alternative explanations of the findings, so the conclusion that understanding of the passive construction was induced via observational learning was well supported.)

If there was doubt in the past about the teachability of language and the potential for learning mechanisms to mediate language acquisition, little doubt remains now: There is widespread agreement that the language structures acquired by a child are a function of the structures the child hears in the world (Speidel & Nelson, 1989). There is increasing understanding about how parent-child interactions can foster language learning. For example, there is detailed understanding about how parents can recast, expand, and reduce the utterances of their children so as to increase the likelihood that children will induce important language rules. There is increasing understanding of how exposure to models with varying degrees of language competence can promote language development. There is also evidence that positively reinforcing children to use language, in fact, increases their competent use of it (e.g., Whitehurst & Valdez-Menchaca, 1988).

One of the most important shifts, however, is in the rehabilitation of the term "imitation" by psycholinguistic researchers. Consider the introductory comments of G. E. Speidel and K. E. Nelson (1989) in *The Many Faces of Imitation in Language Learning:*

> In this book we take a fresh look at imitation. With the knowledge of some 20 years of research after Chomsky's initial critique of the behavioristic approach to language learning, it is time to explore imitation once again. How imitation is viewed in this book has changed greatly since the 1950s and can only be understood by reading the various contributions. This reading reveals many faces, many forms, many causes, and many functions of imitation—cognitive, social, information processing, learning, and biological. Some views are far removed from the notion that an imitation must occur immediately or that it must be a perfect copy of an adult sentence. But the essence of the concept of imitation is retained: Some of the child's language behavior originates as an imitation of a prior model. (p. v)

What impressed us most about this book was the sophistication of current thinking about imitation. For instance, Meltzoff and Gopnik (1989) make the case that imitation is innate, based largely on work on facial imitations by newborns reported by Meltzoff and Moore (e.g., Meltzoff, 1985; Meltzoff & Moore, 1977, 1983). Within hours of birth, infants who observe an adult opening his or her mouth or sticking out his or her tongue respond by opening the mouth or sticking out the tongue. Meltzoff and Moore's explanation is that the infant somehow internally represents the mouth opening and tongue protruding that is observed and uses this internal representation to guide mouth openings and tongue protrusions. Others (see Anisfeld, 1991) are not as sanguine about neonatal imitation, however, and offer alternative explanations of the behaviors that Meltzoff and Moore consider indicative of imitation. At a minimum, the Anisfeld analysis makes clear that imitation during the neonatal period is anything but easy to produce; if imitation occurs at all, it occurs given only extremely exacting conditions (see also Bjorklund, 1987a, who in acknowledging that imitation in neonates is greatly affected by situational factors, is more sympathetic to the interpretation that innate imitation is observed at the beginning of postpartum life).

In acknowledging the biological basis of imitation, there is no neglect of the importance of the environment and environmental differences between children in determination of language competence via imitation. In fact, Nelson, Heimann, Abuelhaija, and Wroblewski (1989) conclude the book by emphasizing the need to understand better differences in language imitation propensities of children and their parents: Children differ dramatically in their tendencies to imitate and what they will imitate. So do parents. Some imitations have more effect on language acquisition than others. The fascinating studies that are appearing to address such issues, many of which are summarized in Speidel and Nelson (1989), suggest that imitation as part of language learning will be one of the most vital fields of research on children's learning in the next decade. Indeed, as we have come to understand that there are dramatic increases in imitation during the preschool years—especially imitation deferred until sometime after a behavior has been witnessed (e.g., Kuczynski, Zahn-Waxler, & Radke-Yarrow, 1987)—there is increasing understanding that imitation is a decidedly interesting capacity that plays an expanding role in learning and development from birth onward.

Piagetian Concept Acquisition No idea in Piagetian theory was researched more than the hypothesis that children in the preschool years do not conserve, whereas older children do. That is, Piagetians believe that with development, there is increasing understanding from the preschool-age to the elementary-age years that the amount of a substance does not change because its appearance does—that amount changes only if something is taken away or added. Thus, a conserver knows that pouring water from one container to a different-shaped container does not change the amount of water; a conserver knows that seven beans in a 7-inch row (i.e., 1-inch spacing) is the same number of beans as seven beans in a 2-inch row (i.e., approximately a quarter-inch spacing); a conserver knows that a ball of clay does not change in weight or volume when it is reshaped as a pancake. In contrast, the classic Piagetian view was that preschoolers would claim that the amount of water would vary with the dimensions of its container, that the number of elements in a row would vary with the spacing in the row, and that the weight and volume of clay varies with shape of the clay.

Particularly critical here was the long-held Piagetian stance that conservation could not be taught and that attempts to do so would invariably disrupt natural development of the understanding of conservation. Americans studying the possibility that changes in conservation might be stimulated through instruction produced data that clashed with the Genevan assertion that cognitive restructuring could occur only through equilibration. Americans had little difficulty establishing conservation using conventional learning procedures (Rosenthal & Zimmerman, 1978, Chapter 4)—at least to their satisfaction (Field, 1987; see comments that follow in this subsection on the issue of criteria for concluding a child is conserving).

Brainerd (1978a) provided a review of four learning approaches that increased conservation:

- *Simple correction.* Give a nonconserver repeated trials on conservation tasks, and tell them whether their answers are right or wrong. For example, after pouring liquid from a tall glass into a wide glass, provide positive feedback if the child indicates that there is still the same amount of liquid in the wide glass as had been in the tall glass. Provide negative feedback if a child indicates the liquid changes in quantity when it is poured from one glass to the other.

- *Rule learning.* Teach the child a rule (e.g., when correcting a failure to conserve, tell the child, "I did not add or subtract anything.").
- *Observational learning.* Expose the child to a model who performs conservations perfectly.
- *Conformity training.* Have a nonconserving child work on conservation problems with a conserving child; referred to as conformity training because the child who begins as a nonconserver becomes a conserver. In general, a great deal of evidence has accumulated that children's understanding of Piagetian concepts increases by doing Piagetian problems in interaction with peers, with this general claim true up to early adulthood with college students working problems requiring application of formal operations (e.g., Dimant & Bearison, 1991).

For much of the American researcher community, the evidence favoring these teaching procedures with nonconservers (for reviews, see Rosenthal & Zimmerman, 1978, Chapter 4; Brainerd, 1978a, 1978b) was viewed as powerful evidence against the Piagetian theory of cognitive development. Particularly relevant here, two of the four procedures identified by American researchers involved clear imitative learning. The observational learning studies on Piagetian conceptual acquisitions were similar in structure and outcome to other observational learning studies: One group observed a person performing conservation and was more likely to exhibit conservation in the future than another group who had not observed conservation. The conformity training subjects were also exposed to a model doing conservation problems well—the more mature child in the dyad could and did perform the conservation tasks at a high level of competence in the presence of the nonconserving child. This database is certainly consistent with the general conclusion that imitation can play a powerful role in acquisition of cognitive concepts.

Naturally the Genevans did not concur that these American studies were all that telling, for example, arguing that the training favored by Americans did not produce general conservation but only conservation limited to a specific type of problem (Brainerd, 1978a). This objection does not convince, however. For example, although Piaget originally expected that once conservation ability developed it would be manifest across many different types of problems, that turned out not to be the way conservation develops (e.g., Brainerd, 1978b, Chapter 6). Some conservations develop early. For example, most 7-year-olds know that two rows of seven buttons that differ in length still contain the same number of buttons (i.e., most 7-year-olds recognize that length of a row does not determine the number of elements in it). There are many conservations that 7-year-olds cannot perform, however. For example, they often fail to realize that a wad of clay has the same volume whether shaped as a ball or a pancake (i.e., they do not conserve volume). **Horizontal décalage** was the term used by the Genevans to summarize that a cognitive ability, such as conservation, might be applicable in some domains and with some problems before it is applicable in other domains and with other problems. Given that horizontal décalage is the normal state of affairs with respect to the development of conservation, it hardly seems fair to criticize those teaching conservation for failing to produce generalized conservation. Our view is that the American work on training of conservation is a powerful strand of evidence supporting the power of observational learning and imitation, although those with a Piagetian orientation still find much to criticize, for example, focusing on the failure of learning researchers in many of their studies to measure conservation long after training occurred (Field, 1987).

Moral Judgment   As was the case for virtually all cognitive acquisitions, Piaget believed that children's moral judgments improved with development in a stage-like fashion. In particular, Piaget (1932) proposed two stages of moral judgment. Although there were a number of differences in the thinking of children in the less and more mature stages, Piaget focused on how children in the two stages assigned responsibility for action. Children in the less mature stage focused on the objective consequences of actions and disregarded intentions. More mature subjects evaluated the morality of actions by considering the intentions of the actors, with those intending to do harm viewed as less moral than those accidentally doing harm.

Piaget (1932) discovered these two stages using two different methods. Piaget spent a great deal of time observing children during game-playing situations, paying attention in particular to the children's conceptions of rules of games. Much of this effort was directed at analyses of the game of marbles, a game in which the rules are decidedly fluid. In addi-

tion, Piaget (1932) conducted studies in which children were presented stories that required moral judgments. One of the most famous of these involved asking children to evaluate the morality of a child who intentionally broke one cup versus the morality of a child who accidentally broke 15 cups. Children in the less mature stage viewed the child who broke 15 cups as "naughtier," because the child had done more damage. Children in the more mature stage viewed the child who intentionally broke a single cup as naughtier, focusing on why the child committed damage rather than the amount of damage that occurred.

Piaget's belief was that movement from the less mature to the more mature stage required cognitive conflict, completely consistent with his general commitment to cognitive conflict as critical to cognitive development. In particular, Piaget believed that something like the conformity training described in the last subsection was particularly critical to the development of more mature moral outlooks. He believed that when a less mature child argued out moral issues with a child with a more mature outlook, the arguments of the more mature child would produce conflict for the less mature child. Such conflict would lead to disequilibrium, which would motivate additional analyses of the more mature arguments. Eventually, equilibrium would be reestablished, now at a higher level, so the initially less mature child would now make more mature judgments. (Of course, this is a specific instance of the general Genevan position on education reviewed earlier in this chapter, that only instruction that stimulates equilibration is likely to produce cognitive change.)

Once social learning theorists began to examine the development of moral judgmental abilities, they had little difficulty teaching children with immature outlooks to make more mature judgments. One of the most famous studies in this arena was conducted by Bandura and McDonald (1963). The children in the study were initially assessed to determine how they made judgments with respect to stories like the one involving the broken cups. Those children who could clearly be classified as making judgments based on consequences (i.e., the amount of damage done) and as making judgments based on intentions (i.e., why the damage occurred) participated in the actual study.

Each child in one condition of the study was exposed to a model who was presented morality stories and made judgments, always making judgments opposite to the type of judgment favored by the child subject during the preexperiment assessment. The model received reinforcement for these judgments. The subjects, who had heard the model's judgment and observed the reinforcement, were then presented morality problems and reinforced for making judgments opposite in type to the judgments made during the preexperimental assessment. Thus, in this condition, subjects who focused on intentions during the assessment viewed a model who made judgments based on objective consequences and was reinforced for doing so; then the child subject was reinforced for making judgments based on objective consequences. In contrast, subjects who had focused on objective consequences during the assessment saw and were reinforced for judgments based on intentions.

In a second condition, the child subject observed a model making opposite judgments and receiving reinforcements for doing so (as had occurred in the first condition that was described). When the child attempted the problems, however, no reinforcement was provided in this second condition. In a third condition (a control condition), the child did not see a model but was reinforced for making opposite-type judgments when attempting to resolve the moral dilemmas.

The outcome of this study was unambiguous. The two conditions involving modeling produced dramatic shifts in the children's moral judgments, much more striking than occurred in the control condition. Rosenthal and Zimmerman (1978, Chapter 3) reported a number of subsequent studies that supported the conclusion that moral judgments could be shifted through learning mechanisms.

Summary A great deal of evidence has been generated that social learning mechanisms, and in particular observational learning, can produce changes in intellectual competence. The claims made by social learning theorists are at least as defensible, based on available evidence, as the claims made by others interested in problems of language, Piagetian conceptual development, and moral judgment. That is not to dismiss the potential of mechanisms such as cognitive conflict to produce intellectual change. In fact, at several subsequent points in this book, cognitive conflict will be considered again as a mechanism promoting growth, with the perspective offered at those points that cognitive conflict can be an important factor in motivating and causing cognitive change.

Concluding Comments

People learn a great deal by observing others, an adaptive capacity because there are many things people need to learn that could never be learned by direct experience (e.g., one trial of learning via naturalistic punishment not to walk in front of speeding cars would certainly eliminate such behaviors, but the side effects would be intolerable—an organism requiring such direct consequation of behavior for any learning to occur would not survive long). Bandura and his associates have done an admirable job in analyzing the cognitive underpinnings of observational learning. Their analyses leave little doubt that observational learning is a decidedly cognitive phenomenon.

There is a tendency by theorists of other persuasions to discount learning by imitation as simplistic. We are not persuaded by their arguments. Observational learning and imitation is a tremendously complex and decidedly higher-order capacity. For instance, despite an enormous amount of effort aimed at establishing that observational learning and imitation occurs in animals other than man, for the most part, the evidence that animals imitate is either inconclusive or negative (Galef, 1988), even in primates (Visalberghi & Fragaszy, 1990). Understanding of imitation in lower animals will undoubtedly become more complete in the coming decade, given a great deal of interest in this problem (see Zentall & Galef, 1988). For the present, it is fair to conclude that humans are the only animals whose imitation skills are so advanced that it is easy to demonstrate they exist.

CONCLUDING COMMENTS

As promised at the outset of this chapter, the theories offered here are filled with assumptions about biology: Gibson and Piaget emphasize the inherently active nature of humans and their inherent motivations to learn. Gibson's concern is especially with the types of stimulation that particularly catch the attention of humans, the types of information to which they are particularly sensitive because of genetic predisposition. Piaget proposed four stages that represent a biological unfolding; although Piaget always gives lip service to environment, stagelike progression is an inevitable consequence of biological maturation in his theory. Skinner believed that being susceptible to classical and operant conditioning provided biological advantages. That is, organisms that respond to feedback from the environment are more likely to survive than organisms that do not respond to environmental input. The Darwinian reasonableness of this claim is obvious. Bandura focuses on human's ability to learn by watching and the inherited mechanisms that permit cognitive representation of what is observed. The cognitive-behaviorists accept all of the biological proclivities specified by the behaviorists (i.e., sensitivity to input from the environment) and cognitivists (i.e., biological mechanisms for representing information considered in previous chapters of this book).

Both the Gibsons and Piaget believed that most environments human children experience provide more than enough stimulation for their biological heritage to play out. In making that claim, however, we are aware that a particular child's perceptual learning depends on specific environmental inputs. Thus, many perceptual experiences with the letters of the Cyrillic alphabet permit abstraction of the distinctive features defining letters in that alphabet. Although Piaget always downplayed the differences in speed of acquisition associated with richer versus more impoverished environments, the associations between qualities of environment and Piagetian conceptual status are striking. The behavioral work on environmental determination of conservation ability did much to make these associations particularly clear: Children who are provided high-quality observational learning and cognitive conflict experiences with respect to concepts such as conservation are likely to acquire such concepts before children who do not receive such input.

Indeed, the qualities of environments and the quantities of environmental stimulation are critical determinants of learning and conceptual development according to behavioral theories. What a child learns depends on observational opportunities according to Bandura and the cognitive behaviorists. What a child does depends on which behaviors are reinforced and punished according to both the observational learning theorists and the operant theorists. The cognitive behaviorists especially contend that children's learning and performance depend greatly on whether they are taught explicitly how to regulate their learning and behavior.

In general, when these theories are considered collectively, the case builds that high-quality environments sustained for long periods of time are absolutely essential if children's learning and conceptual development are to be optimized: Perceptual learning continues throughout life. Whenever there are new distinctions that are critical for thinking and performance, there is a need for long-term, high-quality perceptual learning opportunities. Think back to the radiologists who were discussed in Chapter 4. Tens of thousands of trials in reading x-rays seem to be required before a physician becomes expert in radiological diagnosis. In Chapters 12 and 13, the cases will be made that concrete conceptual experiences and opportunities to reflect on those experiences are essential for development of sophisticated scientific and mathematical understandings. It will be apparent during those discussions that it takes a long time to develop the conceptual understandings that compose scientific and mathematical understanding. Of course, we could go on and on. Perhaps if readers reflect on the many behaviors they have acquired observationally, it will become obvious that behavioral theories of learning and development are theories of long-term change. For example, despite having watched thousands of hours of football and playing the game recreationally for many hours, we continue to learn new things by watching NFL and college games.

An important conclusion that emerges from the theories and evidence considered in this chapter is that many different types of experiences and input are necessary during the development of the mind. Our view is that development of the mind and sophisticated behavioral repertoires involve all of the mechanisms reviewed in this chapter. Moreover, there is a great deal of commonality in the mechanisms proposed by the various theories. For instance, **discrimination** is required to abstract distinctive features in perceptual input. It is also required to learn that one occasion will lead to reinforcement for a behavior and another occasion will lead to punishment. Discrimination is also part of cognitive conflict in that cognitive conflict requires recognition that one's expectations are not consistent with the way the world actually works.

Consider a second common mechanism: **Feedback** is necessary for perceptual learning to occur, in that a child would never learn to discriminate a *b* from a *d* if there were no positive consequences for doing so. When one changes some Piagetian conceptual expectation, the feedback provided by the environment makes clear the greater adequacy of the new conception (e.g., an initially preoperational child receives more positive feedback from the world when he or she begins to predict that pouring a liquid makes no difference with respect to quantity than when the child predicted that the amount of liquid would change when pouring from one type of beaker to another). Whether something that is observationally learned is performed depends on expectations about future reinforcement based on the feedback received previously in the form of reinforcements or punishments for performing the behavior. Finally, consider a third mechanism—**practice.** Gibsonians advocate practice, as do Piagetians, as do behaviorists. In short, all of these theories specify that practice making discriminations with feedback has important effects on learning and development. There are important underlying commonalities across these theories.

Before closing this chapter, we want to emphasize that our commitment to information processing is a commitment to a theory of information processing that includes healthy respect for biological determination and the cultural specificity of learning and development. Information processing is enabled by biology; it is developed largely in a social context. Any successful theory of learning, development, and instruction will have to capture the mechanics of learning in terms of both biology and culture. Such a view will continue to emerge in the chapters that follow.

Social Interactional Theories of Learning and Development

People learn from other people, with some research documenting this claim reviewed in previous chapters (i.e., research on social learning and imitation). Some types of human interaction are more likely to foster learning and development than are other interactions, however, with a large number of researchers interested in recent years in determining qualities of interpersonal relationships that contribute to the development of sophisticated cognition. Without a doubt, one of the most influential theorists in this arena has been Lev Vygotsky, who lived in the first half of the 20th century in the former Soviet Union. Knowledge of Vygotsky's theory of the development of the mind is essential for the contemporary student of educational psychology, with many educational interventions being inspired by it and many other educational practices sensible in light of Vygotskian accounts of development.

SOCIOCULTURAL APPROACHES TO THE MIND: VYGOTSKY AND BAKHTIN

There has been some awareness of Vygotsky and his perspective on the development of the mind throughout the modern cognitive era, owing in part to the availability of a widely distributed English translation of *Thought and Language* (Vygotsky, 1962). Even so, until the late 1970s, as far as Western researchers

and educators were concerned, Vygotsky was just one of those other theorists concerned with learning and development. Vygotsky certainly was not accorded the attention given to Piaget, Skinner, or Bandura. That changed in 1978 with the translation of Vygotsky's (1978) *Mind in Society: The Development of Higher Psychological Processes* and the promotion of Vygotsky's views by important developmental psychologists interested in education, in particular Ann Brown (e.g., Brown & French, 1979) and James Wertsch (e.g., 1985, 1991). We present an overview in this section of the most important Vygotskian ideas.

Developmental Relationship Between Thought and Speech

For many years, the only Vygotskian perspective known well in the West was his view about relationships between thought and speech, which vary with developmental level.

Thought and Speech in Adults   Vygotsky (1962) believed that for adults, **inner speech** was an important mechanism involved in thought. Inner speech is different from outer speech according to Vygotsky. In particular, inner speech is abbreviated and fragmentary, with the meaning of complex thoughts captured in few words. Most prominent in inner speech are predicates. The interrelatedness of thought and speech comes through in the quotes that follow, in which Vygotsky makes the case that thoughts often can only be completed via words, and words often play a role in shaping thought:

> The relationship of thought to word is not a thing but a process, a movement from thought to word and from word to thought.... Thought is not expressed but completed in the word ... Any thought has movement. It unfolds. It fulfills some function or resolves some task. This flow of thought is realized as an internal movement through several planes, as a transition from thought to word and word to thought....
>
> Speech does not merely serve as the expression of developed thought. Thought is restructured as it is transformed into speech. It is not expressed but completed in the word. (Vygotsky, 1987, p. 250–251)

You might be able to get a feel for what is meant here by interrelationships between thought and speech if you find a somewhat complicated task to do, one that requires some thinking. Thus, yesterday author CM put together a boom box with separable speakers. She was fumbling to figure out how to attach a speaker to the box when suddenly she noticed the tongue and groove structures on the speaker and amplifier. CM said to herself something like, "That's it ... " and began to jiggle the speaker into place, thinking and mumbling to herself an abbreviated, "Move it this way." It slid on from that point. For the other speaker, CM said to herself, "Get it turned correctly," did so, and then slid the speaker on without any awareness of additional inner speech, which was unnecessary because there now was no problem to be solved. Because of the experience with the first speaker, CM knew the tongue-and-groove relationship existed and simply slid this speaker on without much thought except to get it properly oriented.

Although thought and speech are intertwined to such a degree that they are difficult to separate, thought and speech are separable:

> Thought does not consist of individual words like speech. I may want to express the thought that I saw a barefoot boy in a blue shirt running down the street today. I do not, however, see separately the boy, the shirt, the fact that the shirt was blue, the fact that the boy ran, and the fact that the boy was without shoes. I see all of this together in a unified act of thought. In speech, however, the thought is partitioned into separate words. Thought is always something whole, something with significantly greater extent and volume than the individual word. Over the course of several minutes, an orator frequently develops the same thought. The thought is contained in his mind as a whole. It does not arise step by step through separate units in the way that his speech develops. *What is contained simultaneously in thought unfolds sequentially in speech.* Thought can be compared to a hovering cloud which gushes a shower of words. (Vygotsky, 1987, p. 281)

The simultaneous-sequential distinction that Vygotsky identified has been recognized by a number of other researchers and theorists (e.g., Das, Kirby, & Jarman, 1979). When we read this passage by Vygotsky, we thought about Paivio's dual coding theory as well, discussed in Chapter 3. Paivio (1971) argued that there is an imagery system (which is holistic) and a verbal system (which is sequential) that are constantly in communication, much as thought and word are constantly interacting according to Vygotsky. This distinction between holistic and sequential is an important distinction in understanding the mind, whether thought of as a distinction between thought and word as Vygotsky did or as a distinction between imagery and verbal codes, which is Paivio's interpretation.

Some extremely important research in Soviet psychology has focused on when people subvocalize (i.e., use inner speech to mediate performance) and when they do not, with a summary of such work in English translation provided by Sokolov (1975), who was strongly influenced by Vygotsky. Sokolov summarizes studies, many of which were his own, in which subvocalization was measured using sophisticated psychophysical methods that involve measuring muscle tension in the vocal apparatus. Sokolov provides a substantial amount of evidence that whether subvocalization occurs or not depends on the difficulty of the problem facing a person, with more subvocalization when problems are taxing. Thus, Sokolov (1975, Chapter 7) reported how subvocalization increases when adults do mental arithmetic calculations. More subvocalization was recorded with problems requiring more complex calculations. When subjects were given the same problems repeatedly, subvocalization decreased on later trials compared with earlier trials. Sokolov also reported subvocalization during reading, with the intensity of subvocalization varying with the difficulty of the text being read and with the task assigned to the reader (e.g., requiring the reader to attempt to memorize what is being read increases the intensity of subvocalization). This brief discussion in no way, however, does justice to the impressive body of evidence presented by Sokolov in support of the interdependencies of thought and speech. For example, Sokolov reports fascinating studies in which thought is impaired when conditions are such that a person cannot subvocalize (e.g., they are required to recite an overlearned verbal sequence while attempting to solve a problem); he also reported interesting work in which inducing people to vocalize appropriately improved their performances—manipulations that may be reminiscent to readers of this book who recall the discussion of Meichenbaum's research in Chapter 7. A brief discussion of Meichenbaum's work permits a transition from this discussion of thought and speech in adults to a consideration of thought and speech in children.

Thought and Speech During Childhood   Meichenbaum was influenced greatly by the Soviet data that were just discussed. The Soviet position that self-verbalization plays a critical role in thinking led Meichenbaum to develop interventions based on self-verbalization and self-control of behavior via self-verbalization. One aspect of Sokolov's results is especially pertinent here. Sokolov reported that subvocalization increased in intensity when subjects were given a new task, that speech involvement is especially important in deciding how to get a task started. Indeed, if you review Meichenbaum's self-instructional approach (Chapter 7), you will see that many of the self-verbalizations taught to subjects were intended to get appropriate actions started. That Meichenbaum encourages people to do less overt self-verbalization as they become practiced with a task is also understandable in light of the Soviet data: Recall that with each additional trial on a problem or task, Sokolov observed less subvocalization.

Why did Meichenbaum teach impulsive children to self-verbalize? He believed that such children somehow had not developed regulative self-verbalization on their own, that somehow their development was different from typical development according to Vygotsky. Vygotsky believed that inner speech and thought came to be increasingly coordinated during childhood. That is, the coordinations between thought and subvocalizations observed by Sokolov represented an end point in development, a highest stage in a sequence of developmental stages.

Vygotsky's theory of the development of thought and speech specifies four stages. During the first 2 years of life, thought is nonverbal (largely sensorimotor as Piaget claimed) and speech is nonconceptual with no relationship between thought and speech. With the development of language (i.e., beginning at about age 2), thought and speech begin to merge, with the most obvious manifestation being a child who can label many objects by their "names" and with the development of verbal communications with others. Self-speech is not used in any sense to direct thinking during this second stage, however, although the speech of others can and often is directive (see Luria, 1982). Although 2-year-olds are often reputed to be terrible, many times they really will "come" when you ask them to come, something that is not likely in younger children, unless there is a good deal of nonverbal cuing about the appropriateness of coming, such as an adult offering outstretched arms (see Service, Lock, & Chandler, 1989).

The role of self-speech in directing thought and behavior begins to emerge in the third stage, which is characterized by **egocentric speech.** When preschoolers do things, they often talk to themselves about what they are doing. Piaget argued that this represented a deficit in preschoolers, that they could not communicate meaning to others, a point of view that is contradicted by voluminous research that preschoolers more often than not do communicate successfully when they talk with others (see commentary in Chapter 7, this book, on the inadequacies of Piaget's views concerning egocentric speech).

In contrast to Piaget, Vygotsky viewed the emergence of egocentric speech to be an advance, with such speech beginning to influence what the child thought and did. How many times did author MP hear Timothy say between 2 and 4 years of age, "I'm going to play with ____," before he went and played with ____; how many times did MP hear him say, "I'm going to ____," before Tim went and did ____? Often such utterances came when Tim was trying to figure out what to do, an observation completely consistent with Vygotsky. In fact, Vygotsky carried out studies with preschoolers in which the preschoolers were given tasks that were complicated by some obstacle (e.g., when a colored pencil, or paper, or paint that was needed was missing). When difficulties occur, the amount of egocentric speech is much greater than when preschoolers do the same tasks without obstacles. As an example, consider this monologue produced by a preschooler faced with a task difficulty:

> Where is the pencil? I need a blue pencil now. Nothing. Instead of that I will color it red and put water on it—that will make it darker and more like blue. (Vygotsky, 1987, p. 70)

Speech produced by this child was clearly part of thinking.

During the fourth stage, the egocentric speech that was overt becomes covert and abbreviated, with the inner speech progressively reflecting predicates more than any other part of verbalizations, as in this example: "Where's the pencil? Need blue. Will use red, add water." The actions, specified by the predicates, are much more prominent in inner speech than in egocentric speech. It was this fourth stage in the Vygotskian sequence that Sokolov studied.

For many years, this four-stage conception of the development of thought and speech was Vygotskian theory as far as Western readers were concerned. There were social contributions to this development, in that inner speech was considered to be internalized dialoguing. That is, the dialogue skills that began to develop in stage two affected the development of egocentric speech, which often involves a child conducting a monologue that can be heard by others, with this monologue eventually internalized. Markovà (1990) elegantly summarized the developmental progression considered in this subsection:

> . . . [D]ialogue was the starting point for the study of speech, arguing that inner speech is intrinsically social. For Vygotsky, too, dialogue was the starting point for the study of speech. In child development, speech is originally external to the child in the sense that he or she speaks in order to address others but not him- or herself. Only when speech has become *externally* established, for others, can it then also become *internalized*, i.e., *for oneself*. In other words, the child can have a *monologue* with him- or herself only after he or she has developed the ability of holding a *dialogue* with others. Thus, internalized or monological speech in the child is not egocentric in the Piagetian sense, but is social speech that has reached a higher stage, being for self.

Vygotsky's conception of how others play a role in the development of a child's thinking abilities became apparent to many in the West with the publi-

cation of *Mind in Society*. Although other early 20th century theorists offered sociogenetic explanations of the development of the mind that share features with Vygotsky's theory—most notably, the French psychologist Pierre Janet (Van der Meer & Valsiner, 1988), their contributions are forgotten as scholars for the last 15 years have pored over Vygotsky's writings. The ideas presented in *Mind and Society*, taken up in the next subsection, deserve the attention of every educational psychologist.

Sophisticated Thought of Individuals Develops from Interactions Between Individuals

Adults often assist children in thinking about problems they are confronting (e.g., how to solve a puzzle, trying to figure out how many "big sleeps" until Christmas). What goes on in these interactions is thinking, thinking that involves two heads. The child could not work through many problems without assistance, but with parental support makes fine progress. Years of participating in such interactions leads to internalization by the child of the types of actions once carried out between the child and the adult. That is, thought processes that were once interpersonal become intrapersonal. Probably the most frequently quoted statement by Vygotsky is his summary of this developmental progression:

> Any function in the child's cultural development appears twice, or on two planes. First, it appears on the social plane, and then on the psychological plane. First, it appears between people as an interpsychological category, and then within the child as an intrapsychological category. This is equally true with respect to voluntary attention, logical memory, the formation of concepts, and the development of volition. . . . Social relations or relations among people genetically underlie all higher functions and their relationships. . . . In their private sphere, human beings retain the functions of social interactions. (Vygotsky, 1981, p. 163–164)

According to Vygotsky, cognitive development moves forward largely because the child is in a world that provides assistance when the child needs it and can benefit from it. The responsive social world lets 2- or 3-year-olds solve for themselves those problems that they can handle. The child plays an important role in ensuring some autonomous functioning: Any parent of a preschooler knows all too well the phrase, "I can do it myself!" There are other tasks that a 2- or a 3-year-old could never perform, no matter how much assistance was provided. A responsive social environment does not even try to encourage children to do such tasks, and in fact, often discourages child attempts at behaviors far outside the range of preschooler competence (e.g., when a father physically lifts his son from the driver's seat of the car as the youngster urges the father to teach him to drive). Critical developmental interactions occur with tasks in between these two extremes, tasks that the child could not do independently but can do with assistance. The responsive social world provides assistance on these tasks that are within the child's **zone of proximal development** according to Vygotskian theory. In fact, the "zone" is defined as behaviors beyond a child's level of autonomous functioning but within reach with assistance and as such reflect behaviors that are developing. Children learn how to perform tasks within their zone by interacting with more competent and responsive others who provide hints, prompts, and assistance to the child on an as-needed basis. These hints and prompts encourage the child to process the task appropriately, with such processing eventually internalized by the child—that is, the child ultimately performs the task without assistance, a development stimulated by the supportive interactions with others before autonomous functioning is possible.

What is critical is that more competent others **scaffold** (Wood et al., 1976) instruction about the task as they interact with the child. Scaffolding was introduced in Chapter 1, with this social-interactive model of teaching discussed at a number of points in the book. Recall that a scaffold is used when a building is being erected and is gradually removed as the building becomes self-supporting. So it is with the prompts and hints provided by an adult or older child to a younger child. It is important to provide enough support and assistance so the child does not fail (i.e., fall), with that support removed as the child is capable of performing autonomously.

These ideas can best be understood by using an example. Reading Recovery (see Chapter 14) is a method for remediating primary-grade children who are experiencing reading difficulties. Advocates of Reading Recovery (e.g., Clay & Cazden,

1990) instruction is provided within the child's zone of proximal development, with the competent Reading Recovery teacher permitting the child to do as much as the child can do independently, intervening with hints and supports that can lead the child to process effectively when he or she stumbles. The following dialogue (Clay & Cazden, 1990, p. 214, adapted) illustrates how an adult tutor scaffolded the instruction of a tutee, Larry:

LARRY: THE GREAT BIG ENORMOUS TURNIP. ONCE AN OLD MAN PLANTED A TURNIP.
TEACHER: Good. (The teacher ignores omission of, "Once upon a time.") [I believe she did so because the focus of this lesson was getting the meaning of the text, and the omitted phrase was not essential to understanding the text.]
LARRY: HE SAID GROW, GROW LITTLE TURNIP, GROW (pauses at the next word).
TEACHER: How does that word start? Can I help you start it off? How does it start? s_____ He tells it to grow sw_____ sweet.
LARRY: GROW LITTLE TURNIP, GROW S_____.
TEACHER: How else does he want it to grow? He wants it to grow sweet and he wants it to grow str_____.
LARRY: STRONG
TEACHER: Good boy, that's lovely. Grow strong.
LARRY: AND THE TURNIP GREW UP SWEET AND STRONG AND—
TEACHER: What's the other word that begins with *e*? Enor_____.
LARRY: ENORMOUS.
TEACHER: Good.

And so it goes, with the teacher continuing to provide hints and support as needed, in this case, hints aimed at encouraging the student to apply word attack skills to decode words. The teacher is scaffolding this instruction in that input is provided only when the child experiences difficulty, never when the child is capable of proceeding on his own. During Reading Recovery, the child rereads texts until he or she can proceed through a text with 90 percent successful decoding. Less and less teacher input occurs on each rereading, with the teacher supporting independent functioning by the child by not intervening. Once a child can read a text at the 90 percent level, another text is selected, one that is within the child's zone of proximal development, in that the child will not be able to read the text fluently without support but can get through the text if provided hints and prompts.

Bakhtin's Theory

Vygotsky was not the only Soviet theorist to offer perspectives on the importance of culture on cognitive development and intellectual functioning. M. M. Bakhtin was a contemporary of Vygotsky, although they probably never met (Wertsch, 1991). Bakhtin's influence within literary critical circles has been much greater than his impact on psychology. Wertsch (1991), however, has analyzed the importance of Bakhtin's ideas for those interested in cognitive development and education of students. A few of Bakhtin's more critical ideas will be summarized here, with the focus on ones particularly important to education.

When we speak at a professional conference, either at the podium or in one-to-one interaction with scholarly peers, our speech is different than when we speak to old friends. When we sit on administrative committees concerned with fiscal matters and program mechanics, our speech is different than on other occasions. Our voices are decidedly friendlier and more casual, for instance, when we are out with old friends from undergraduate school or chums from the office. Bakhtin recognized this as a typical state of affairs. People use different **social languages** in different situations—they **ventriloquate** to use Bakhtin's (1981) term or are **multivoiced** to use Wertsch's (1991) vernacular.

Bakhtin's view is that the voices we have show up in our expressions of ideas, and thus, in a very real sense, nothing we say or write is really just our own but rather reflects internalized social understandings. For instance, when we use the term "stonewall," there is something of Nixon's voice in us and something of attitudes and values embraced by the former president. When we use the phrase "softer and gentler," we feel some of the political dissembling that George Bush personified when he coined the term. We are forever shaping our ideas through the speech of others, so that the language of others affects our thinking:

> The word in language is half someone else's. It becomes "one's own" only when the speaker populates it with his own intention, his own accent, when he appropriates the word, adapting it to his own semantic and expressive intention . . . the word . . . exists in other people's mouths, in other people's concrete contexts, serving other people's intentions: it is from there that one must take the word and make it one's own. (Bakhtin, 1981, 293–294)

Whenever someone produces an utterance, the most obvious question from Bakhtin's perspective is, "Who is doing the talking?" (Wertsch, 1991), with the answer always being one's own voice and at least one other voice. Think back to our presentation of Skinner's theory. Who was doing the talking? We were, but so were the many people who had taught us Skinnerian theory, such as Jack Michael, and of course, Skinner's voice was in the text we generated as well because he spoke to us through his writing. It is impossible for us even to think about concepts such as negative reinforcement without thinking about B. F. Skinner. Every sentence in this book has multiple authorship! From a Bakhtinian perspective, we do not flatter ourselves too much in believing that some of you will speak with some of our voice in the future when you have occasion to talk about educational psychology.

The social voices we have internalized determine in part what we can say and think. Thus, when we see aversive stimulation end because of a person's action (e.g., the person pulls the plug on a radio blasting heavy metal music or a child lifts her hand from a hot stove), we immediately think about negative reinforcement. The behaviorist voice we learned years ago continues to affect our thinking, but so does the cognitive psychological voice we acquired later (and thus, we think about people's cognitive representations of negative reinforcement sometimes when we see negative reinforcements occur) and the physiological psychological voice as well (and thus, we think about how neurology mediates the pleasure produced by noise reduction or cessation of pain). Multivoicedness is inevitable, and although we are only now understanding how the voices we acquire affect our thinking, this is an important direction for educational researchers (see Wertsch & Minnick, 1990). What is certain from this perspective is that the social environment surrounding a person will come to color consciousness and thought: "All that touches me comes to my consciousness . . . from the outside world, passing through the mouths of others (from the mother, etc.), with their intonation, their affective tonality, and their values" (Bakhtin, quoted in Todorov, 1984, p. 96). If you spend time in the culture of baseball, you will come to think on some occasions as baseball players do. If you spend some time in the culture of policemen, some of your thought some of the time will reflect the predominant thought patterns of policemen. If you live in a Quaker community, you think like a Quaker much of the time. The amazing thing is that if you spend time in a Quaker community and then a Catholic community and then a Jewish community, ultimately your thought will reflect all three perspectives. Moreover, sometimes when you speak, you will speak like a Quaker would, sometimes like a Catholic, and sometimes like a Jew.

Mind reflects culture according to Vygotsky and Bakhtin, and society has a much greater impact on mental functioning than other factors. This perspective completely clashes with some of the perspectives presented previously, for example, some of the biological conceptions of thinking and development presented in Chapter 6. Think back to Chapter 6 and the biological traditions reviewed there and then contrast the thinking in that chapter with this quote from Bakhtin:

> There is no such thing as abstract biological personality, this biological individual that has become the alpha and omega of contemporary ideology. There is no human being outside of society . . . it is not enough to be born physically—that is the way of animals. A second birth, *social* this time, is necessary as it were. A human being is not born in the guise of an abstract biological organism, but as a landowner or a peasant, a bourgeois or a proletarian, and that is of the essence. Then, he is born Russian or French, and finally he is born in 1800 or in 1900. Only such a social and historical localization makes man real and determines the content of his personal and cultural creation. (Quoted in Todorov, 1984, pp. 30–31)

Many educators and educational theorists have resonated to the themes developed in this passage. With respect to instruction, many who find sociocultural approaches to the development of the mind appealing believe that one form of instruction is superior to others, a form of instruction that emphasizes social interactions between an apprentice student and an expert other.

Before moving on to the discussion of apprenticeship, we must point out that our own perspective is that both biological and sociocultural variables play important roles in the development of the mind—that good information processing depends on and is shaped by both nature and nurture. Although it is sometimes useful scientifically to study biological and sociocultural variables as insulated from one another, ultimately the socioculturalist is interacting with a child born with particular biologically determined capacities and constraints, just as the biologist is interacting with a person whose particular capacities and behaviors have been shaped by the social environment that favors some biological predispositions and capacities more than others.

Apprenticeship

How did we become professors—how did we learn to do what professors do, to react as professors react? Yes, we went to school, took courses that included examinations and papers, and earned degrees. Although it is necessary to do that to become a professor, it is far from sufficient. We learned how to be professors by spending time around professors, as students and then as assistant professors. So it is with many professions and trades. People learn how to build houses by working with experienced builders as an apprentice. Airline captains learn how to fly from the left side of the plane by years of flying on the right side of the plane, as first officers working with captains. Medical residencies are apprenticeships, opportunities for young physicians to learn both the formal and the informal knowledges possessed by senior physicians through direct contact with the senior physicians. (And, of course, the Hardy boys apprenticed with Fenton Hardy, famous detective!)

Given how common apprenticeship experiences are in education, it is something of a wonder that educational researchers have only recently attempted to understand the nature of learning in such situations. Those who have begun to examine formally the nature of apprenticeship are concluding that it is a powerful approach to instruction, one that should be used not only to train young professionals and craftsmen, but also children in school as they tackle reading, writing, and problem solving.

An important idea here is that of **situated cognition** (e.g., Brown et al., 1989), which was introduced in Chapter 3. When students learn how to read, write, and problem solve in school, their understandings of reading, writing, and problem solving are largely tied to schooling environments. This is problematic because schooling environments are so different from the places where the reading, writing, and problem solving learned in school are to be put into practice. In contrast, trade and professional apprenticeships are highly situated, so that a young man who learns the art and science of beekeeping by apprenticing with a beekeeper develops knowledge that is connected to the situations in which beekeepers must work. A person who acquires an understanding of beekeeping from taking a community college class on apiary science that involves three laboratory experiences with a beehive will not have the same situated knowledge. A real challenge is to make schooling sufficiently like the real world, so that reading, writing, and problem solving learned there are tied to important real-world situations. Many believe school should be reconstructed so students serve as apprentices to people doing real reading of real books, real writing for real purposes, and solving of real problems. The best-known theoretical discussion of apprenticeship in school to date is Collins, Brown, and Newman (1989), although extensive discussion of apprenticeship in general is provided in Rogoff's (1990) book-length treatment of the topic. We relied on these sources in constructing what follows.

What do apprentice learners do? (1) They **observe.** Thus, as graduate students, we observed senior professors in many settings, both informal and formal. For example, we learned how to submit a manuscript to a journal by watching a senior colleague do so, one who provided commentary about journal submissions over the course of a number of submissions and several years. In this relationship, we learned that it was all right to react negatively to a reviewer's comments in the privacy of one's office, but in the letter to the editor specifying how the reviewer's comments were handled, it is important to make the point that the reviewer comments were helpful and to make obvious to the editor that a good faith effort was made to accommodate to the reviewer.

(2) Apprentices receive **coaching** from their mentors. Thus, when it came time to submit our first manuscripts to a journal, our graduate school mentor (the same individual for MP and CM) went over drafts of our papers, giving us pointers, helping us decide where to submit, and providing input and feedback about the form of the submissions. By the time a package left for the journal, we knew very well that the editor who was receiving it insisted on a ribbon copy in addition to the three xerox copies! We also knew that the editor receiving it had no patience for overly long abstracts or any departures from APA style, and our submission reflected this knowledge, which was passed from the mentor to us.

(3) Apprentices **practice** the tasks that are expected in the profession, although always being coached by the mentor. Thus, as graduate students, we did research and writing with our mentor coaching us along the way. A good mentor "scaffolds" (Wood et al., 1976) his or her input, providing assistance when it is needed but not so much that the student becomes dependent on it nor so little that the apprentice falters. Just as the scaffold of a building is removed as the building becomes freestanding, so it is with mentor scaffolding, with less of it provided as the apprentice is able to go it alone. There came a time when we were submitting papers on our own.

Apprenticeship for Elementary-Age Students　It is not difficult to imagine an apprentice graduate student. But is it really sensible to think about teaching grade-school children within an apprentice relationship? Collins et al. (1989) think it is, and so do we. Studies of expert tutoring have provided important insights as to what high-quality tutoring can look like, and what it looks like is scaffolding.

One of our favorite examples was provided by Lepper and colleagues (Lepper, Aspinwall, Mumme, & Chabey, 1990). In this study, six expert tutors of elementary arithmetic were observed as they worked with individual students in grades 2 through 5. What did they do? For one, they consistently let their students know that the task they were doing was a difficult one, but also that the students had great ability that could be applied to this task. There is a good reason for this. If the student fails, it is easy enough then to blame the difficulty of the task, a type of attribution that should not discourage the student (e.g., see Weiner, 1979). If they succeed, it is possible to highlight how bright the student is, an attribution that should encourage the student

(Weiner, 1979). What is really interesting from the perspective of scaffolding is that the tutor makes these attributions indirectly rather than directly— that is, the tutor provides support but not so much that the student will become dependent on it. Thus, after a student successfully completed a problem, a tutor might say, "I guess we'll have to try to find an even harder one for you," a subtle way of making the point that the last problem was hard and yet the student succeeded on it.

There are many more subtleties in the tutors' interactions with their students. There is little overt corrective feedback and little in the way of overt diagnoses about what the student is doing wrong. Indeed, 95 percent of the time errors are not labeled as such. There is little direct help and rarely do the tutors give students the answers to the problems. What the tutors did when students made errors or were having difficulties was to provide hints of three sorts:

- Questions or remarks implying that the previous move was an incorrect one.
- A suggestion about a potential direction the student might take with the problem, often in the form of a question.
- A hint about the part of the problem the student might want to think about, often in the form of a question.

What these tutors did when their students were in trouble was to ask them questions. (Readers with some knowledge of the history of education might be experiencing flashbacks about Socrates on one end of a log and one of the youth of Athens on the other end.) As an example, consider that when a student added 36 and 36 and came up with 126, the tutor commonly inquired, "Now how did you get that 6?" When this did not work, hints in the forms of questions became increasingly specific: "Which column do we start in? Where is the 1 column?"

"Subtlety" is a word that comes to mind a lot when reviewing lessons taught by skilled math tutors. The tutor is not someone waiting to pounce on an error or full of directions. Rather, the tutor is much more laid back, providing pretty good hints to students, hints that are just full of information. Consider this dialogue from McArthur, Stasz, and Zmuidzinas (1990):

TEACHER: Okay, do you want to start on number 17? I don't know, have you done these before ever? [The equation is $x/3 = b/2 + c/6$]
STUDENT: I think we have. I don't remember.
T: Now usually the thing that bothers most students is fractions. They could without them. So let us get rid of the fractions.
S: Okay.
T: Let us multiply every single term by what we refer to as the least common multiple, something all that can divide evenly into. What do you think that would be?
S: 6
T: 6. So, I'm going to divide. . . . And then it will turn into something you'll feel more comfortable with. Okay. Now, when I say, "Multiply each term by 6," I'm going to write in parentheses next to the object 6, okay? I'm multiplying each thing by 6. Three into 6 goes how many times? [T points to the 3 under x, then the parenthesized 6 above it.]
S: 2
T: So what are you going to have left?
S: [No response]
T. 2x. [S writes 2x below the x/3]
S: 2x.
T: 2 equals . . . 2 goes into 6 how many times? [T points to the 2 under the b, then the parenthesized 6 above it.] (McArthur et al., 1990, p. 210–211)

Now go back through this dialogue and look for some of the subtleties that Lepper et al. (1990) reported are part of scaffolded tutoring. Notice how the tutor provided prompts about potential directions the student might take. Were such hints in the forms of questions as Lepper et al. (1990) reported? Did the teacher give hints about the part of the problem the student might want to think about? Looking at this dialogue in this way makes obvious that there probably is a common core of behaviors that are part of expert math tutoring, behaviors that are what Wood et al. (1976) considered to be **scaffolding.** If we have a reservation about the Lepper et al. (1990) tutors, it is that they do not do much explaining, which is something that is often observed when a tutor works with a student.

Consider another example from McArthur et al. (1990), with an eye toward identifying elements of scaffolding (i.e., questions, hints, explanations):

T: Okay, what we have here is mx − 4 = 2a. And the reason I asked you prior to this if you had any difficulty solving equations is because the procedure we are going to use here is exactly like everything you've done before. Before you came with two variables. The first thing you want to know . . . it says solve for x. This is the object, or you might say the *variable* you want to isolate. [T boxes the x.] You want to get it all by itself. Therefore, your objective is to get rid of everything about it. You'll notice the 4 here. [T points to the 4.] Do you know how to eliminate the 4?

S: Yes, subtract it from both sides.

T: Okay, when you say "Subtract it," have you heard of something call the *additive inverse?*

S: Yes.

T: What is the opposite of −4?

S: +4, positive. . . .

T: Okay, let's add the additive inverse. Add +4 to both sides. Why don't you do that? [S puts +4 below both sides of the equation.] (McArthur et al., 1990, p. 218)

McArthur et al. (1990) was exceptionally thorough in cataloguing the types of hints and explanations math tutors sometimes provide, including the following:

- Descriptions of problems.
- Comments about how a current problem is similar to a previous problem.
- Comments about how a current problem is different from a previous problem.
- Goals at various levels of specificity (e.g., now your objective is to get *x* by itself, I think you want to put all the *x*s on one side and all the *b*s on the other).
- Models of ideal reasoning (e.g., if you have 4 of something and I have 8 of something and we have exactly the same amount, the only thing we can have is absolutely . . .)
- Answers.
- Comparisons of alternative approaches to a problem.
- Task management leading student to do problem either in the head, by forming an alternative type of representation of the problem, or by showing work.
- Prompts about what to do or how to do it.

- Point of the lesson (. . . the lesson to be learned here is . . .).
- Questions about whether the student feels confident.
- Assessments of performance, from indications of correct to indications that a method is okay but may not be optimal to suggestions a method is off target to suggestions that the student should practice. Sometimes students are questioned about whether they know how to do a problem or are asked to explain how they did a problem or justify their method of doing it.
- Remediation, from letting the student continue to focusing the student on the locus of the error to urging the student to "try again" to suggesting a better procedure to explanation about the student's source of error to changing the problem so that an incorrect answer is in fact correct to showing how a student's reasoning is illogical. Sometimes teacher gives student an easier problem that is similar in structure.
- Drills.
- Attention-focusing prompts to salient and important features of a problem.
- Discussion of concept behind a problem.
- Answers to student questions.
- Comments intended to motivate student (e.g., I think you can do that well). (Based on Appendix B of McArthur et al., 1990)

The point of this long list is to make the case that scaffolding is complicated. Good tutors know when and where to provide the hints, prompts, explanations, and modelings that they provide, and it is all contingent on the emerging needs of the student. This scaffolding is complex, even in the context of one teacher with one student and fairly easy arithmetic. Only people who are cognitively capable of attending vigilantly to several ongoing activities are likely to be good at scaffolding, and many people do not have such multiple-attention skills (Copeland, 1987). Scaffolding is going to be presented a number of times in this book, largely because there is a growing consensus that this is a good way of teaching and different from much of the teaching that is now going on. For example, when experienced math teachers work with individual students under the pressure of a mandated curriculum requiring that particular content be covered, teacher sensitivity to student difficulties is not always as obvious as teacher actions intended to make certain the required content is covered at least nominally (e.g., Putnam, 1987).

That was a long aside about scaffolding, which is only one part of apprenticeship. It was worth it, however, because in every analysis of academic apprenticeship, such scaffolding is at the heart of the relationship. Increasingly, American educators believe that the apprenticeship model is the right one for elementary and secondary instruction.

Rogoff (1990) provided an exhaustive summary of the literature on apprenticeship, making the argument that such participation occurs in many cultures and may be a universal of human life. She reviews the literature documenting that apprenticeship adult-child relations are the principal means of passing on knowledge about the intellectual tools valuable in the culture, typically tools complex enough that years of apprenticeship are necessary. Thus, there are societies in which apprenticeships provide education in agriculture, hunting, fishing, weaving, and healing. Although there are cultural variations in the specific behaviors constituting apprenticeship relationships, Rogoff contends that there is great similarity across various types of apprenticeship:

- During an apprenticeship, the master provides bridges from what is known by the apprentice to the unknown. The master interprets the task into terms the apprentice can understand, and the master makes demands on the apprentice that the apprentice can meet, although the ante is always going up, with the apprentice required to learn more as subskills are mastered. That is, the master structures the task for the apprentice. Rogoff refers to this as a situation in which there is **guided participation** of the apprentice, with the guidance provided by the master.
- The master gradually transfers responsibility. Scaffolding is the key term here, with the master providing as much support as the apprentice needs to function but not more than enough, until support is entirely withdrawn because the student can do it alone.

In many cultures, apprenticeship is what Lave and Wenger (1991) refer to as **legitimate peripheral participation.** The apprentices are learning skills that are legitimately valued in the culture—skills that are directly valuable to the culture in contrast to much of school learning that is only indirectly valuable. For example, a high school student's learning of Latin in high school is not legitimate as Lave and Wenger use the term, although if there is a young monk somewhere learning Latin from a master so as to be able to participate fully in monastery life, that would be legitimate participation. Through the apprenticeship, the young monk would be able to participate somewhat in a community organized around Latin-based activities. Participation would not be as full as a master's participation and hence the appropriateness of the descriptor "peripheral" for the apprentice role. Why would the master monk scaffold Latin teaching for the younger monk? Because it is important to the monasterial culture that young monks learn Latin. A key attribute of situations in which apprenticeship is common is that there is a great cultural need for the apprenticed skills to be acquired.

But more than skills are acquired. Think back to Bakhtin and his notion of social languages, which are acquired by being thoroughly imbued in and surrounded by a culture. Legitimate peripheral participation "gobbles up" the apprentice and is all-consuming, and as a result, everything changes for the person, including acquiring a social language and a complex transformation of behaviors and attitudes. Lave and Wenger (1991) put it this way:

> An extended period of legitimate peripherality provides learners with opportunities to make the culture of practice theirs. From a broadly peripheral perspective, apprentices generally assemble a general idea of what constitutes the practice of the community. This uneven sketch of the enterprise (available if there is legitimate access) might include who is involved; what they do; what everyday life is like; how masters, talk, walk, work, and generally conduct their lives; how people who are not part of the community of practice interact with it; what other learners are doing; and what learners need to learn to become full practitioners. It includes an increasing understanding of how, when, and about what old-timers collaborate, collude, and collide, and what they enjoy, dislike, respect, and admire. In particular, it offers exemplars (which are grounds and motivation for learning activity), including masters, finished products, and more advanced apprentices in the process of becoming full practitioners. (p. 95)

Legitimate peripheral participants have access to the experts in a culture that is not available to others, with the experts revealing much to the apprentices that they would never reveal to others. All of this is intended to reproduce new members of the culture that possess important skills for the culture, with the product someone who talks and thinks differently not because they are acting but because they have really changed. Some of the examples provided by Lave and Wenger (1991, pp. 105–109) are telling. For example, members of Alcoholics Anonymous learn how to talk as members of that community (see Jordan, 1989). Young repair men learn "war stories" that serve to change their thinking about how to do particular repairs (see Orr, in press). Learning to talk as the master talks is an important part of apprenticeship that can change the way one thinks in ways consistent with the community the apprentice is entering, a thoroughly Bakhtinian idea.

We are beginning to get some idea about how students in school can be apprentice readers, apprentice writers, and apprentice mathematicians (as well as apprentice scientists, geographers, and so forth), with the models that are developing taken up at various points in this book. As a preview, however, consider that the apprenticeship model requires that teachers be real readers, writers, mathematicians, scientists, and social scientists, rather than people who talk about reading, writing, mathematics, science, and social science. Educational theorists such as Lave and Wenger believe that too much of school is talking about reading, writing, mathematics, science, and social science and not enough of talking within cultures of readers, writers, mathematicians, scientists, and social scientists. There is a challenging educational theory here, a whole new way of thinking about how learning in school might be accomplished.

In the last few years, we have been fortunate to be with teachers who are real readers and can let their students know about real reading (see Chapter 14). These teachers let their students know how excited they are about reading particular authors and provide their students with many insider hints about how to get the most out of books.

For every teacher we have met who brings real reading to the classroom, we have met 10 who bring real writing, for there has been a dramatic rethinking in the last decade about the teaching of writing in school. One strand of the new thinking is that to teach writing, have people write a lot. That includes the teacher, with the best teachers ones who really identify as writers and are "into" writing in a big way. One thing that real writers do is publish, and that happens often in American schools these days. How many class books have we seen students publish, with this activity sometimes tied to introducing children to computing via word processing. How about that for across-content situated learning! Children's eyes light up when the final book is unveiled. Those students are every bit as thrilled at seeing their product in production as we will be when the first copies of this book arrive at our offices. We are certain that a generation of writers is being groomed out there in American schools, with apprentice opportunities in writing now available from nursery school on up. More about that in Chapter 15 on writing.

We have also encountered many math teachers in recent years whose enthusiasm and commitment to mathematics are motivating them to reform the curriculum offered to their students so their students are caught up in solving real problems. Consider something we saw in a kindergarten a month or so ago. The class had made necklaces out of acorns. What was interesting was all of the math that had been taught and practiced around this idea, with the students figuring out how many acorns would be needed for the project, estimating how large a wheelbarrow would be required to carry the acorns, how much paint would be needed to paint the necklaces, and so on. There were many problems that came up, with the teacher apprenticing his students about how to solve them, permitting the students to be legitimate peripheral participants in the problem-solving process. (That is, the teacher lined up the actual wheelbarrow used to gather the acorns, but only after the consultant team of kindergarten children had rendered a credible advisory about the minimum size that would be needed to carry the acorns for all 20 children in the class.)

Components of Apprenticeship The richness of apprenticeship can be appreciated by elaborative commentary on Collins et al.'s summary of its components, which expands on their three-part conceptualization of apprenticeship used to introduce this subsection:

- *Modeling:* Experts show their apprentices how to do tasks that are important and explain the subtleties of such tasks to their charges. The expert tutor will make obvious to students his or her actions, often making overt actions that they normally would carry out automatically and covertly. The student sees the actions and hears a rationale as to why the actions were taken.

- *Coaching:* The master watches the student attempt a task and offers hints, feedback, and guidance. Sometimes the coach offers additional modeling or explanation. Coaching is pervasive during apprenticeship, so much so that if the apprenticeship process had to be described in a single word, the most appropriate single word would be coaching.

- *Scaffolding:* The master offers support, guidance, and reminders. The master does not offer too much support, however, pulling away as the apprentice is able to function independently. Scaffolding requires great diagnostic skills on the part of the master, both determining when the apprentice is in need of help and offering appropriate redirection. The master must understand the many different types of errors that apprentices can make and how to deal with such errors. The flexibility of Lepper et al.'s (1990) and McArthur et al.'s (1990) math tutors is an enormous accomplishment, with such flexibility of input a hallmark of apprenticeship. Experts size up the needs of the apprentice in light of their expert knowledge of the demands of the task and make decisions about how to provide guidance so the apprentice can proceed and learn how to cope with the task in question.

- *Articulation:* Articulation is a form of testing. Masters require their apprentices to explain what they are doing. Thus, an expert math teacher may require the tutee to explain how he or she went about solving a problem and why the particular solution method was used over alternative methods.

- *Reflection:* Apprentices are encouraged to compare their work with that of others, including the master and other apprentices. This aspect of the apprenticeship relationship has received an enormous amount of attention in recent years, largely because of Schön's (1983, 1987) influential writing about the role of reflection in the development of professional competence. Thus, young teachers often watch videotapes of themselves teaching and reflect on their teaching, perhaps discussing their teaching actions with more expert teachers or fellow apprentice teachers. Reflection by apprentice writers in grade-2 classrooms occurs when they have a conference with their teacher about a rough draft or have fellow students react to a draft during a peer conference. Thinking about how one is doing with the long-term goal of improving is an important component of apprenticeship.

- *Exploration:* Apprentices cannot be mere copies of their mentors. Thus, those who mentored our scholarship did not intend that we would simply spend our careers replicating their work but would instead strike out on our own. The apprenticeship relationship permits safe exploration. Thus, when we were graduate students, we tried out some really crazy ideas in pilot studies. We still try out crazy ideas, but now we are more sophisticated in how to do such work. Part of what we learned in graduate school was how to explore. Good mentors teach their apprentices how to explore and encourage them to do so.

That apprenticeship is a powerful perspective on education is apparent from the many references to it in recent years. Whether one is reading about the education of typical students (e.g., high school students in *Horace's Compromise* by Sizer, 1984) or the development of the most creative minds in science, humanities, and arts (see John-Steiner, 1985, especially Chapter 2), there are endorsements of coaching as a form of instruction and apprenticeship as a method of development. That apprenticeship is a powerful form of teaching is a hypothesis that has face validity to many with well-informed opinions about education at its best.

Research Validating Soviet Sociohistorical Positions

Vygotskian and Bakhtinian theory are inspirational, with many educators now couching their innovations in Vygotskian terms. Educators report that they are scaffolding instruction to students who are presented tasks that are within their zones of proximal development (i.e., just a little bit more difficult than what they are able to do on their own right now). Although we are enthusiastic about these theoretical directions, we share the concerns of many that the research support for many sociohistorical ideas is thin at best and nonexistent for some tenets of the theory.

Jeanne D. Day and her colleagues (1983; Day, Cordon, & Kerwin, 1989; Kerwin & Day, 1985), more than any others, have examined critically the research supporting sociohistorical instructional recommendations and found it wanting. Thus, do adults provide children with instruction for behaviors that are in their "zone of proximal development," that is, acquisitions that are now just forming and can be displayed by the child only with the assistance of an adult? Do adults assume the more demanding roles in such interactions to reduce the workload for the child, consistent with Vygotskian theory? Do adults eventually cede control of tasks to their students?

Day correctly points out how difficult it can be to generate research that is relevant to such questions:

> How are we to determine for instance that an adult provided just enough assistance and not too much assistance? How are we to know that the child is practicing nascent skills and not ones that have already been internalized? How can we show that the child ceded control quickly enough? (Day et al., 1989, p. 86)

Even so, researchers have tried to do so, with some success. Thus, researchers have demonstrated that adults regularly do provide instruction to children consistent with Vygotsky's thinking that adults should be supportive but not overly intrusive (e.g., Gardner & Rogoff, 1982; Heckhausen, 1987), and Day was able to identify instances in which adults reduce the workload for children as a function of their developmental level and ability (e.g., Childs & Greenfield, 1980; Wertsch, 1979), consistent with the scaffolding perspective. For example, academic tutors provide more support to younger students (e.g., 7-year-olds) than older students (e.g., 11-year-olds) (Ludeke & Hartup, 1983). When expert weavers teach weaving, they intervene more with younger and less experienced learners (Greenfield, 1984). The best evidence that adults actively seek to adjust the workload demands comes from the studies documenting that adults are more likely to intervene when children are experiencing difficulties with a task than at other times (e.g., Greenfield, 1984; McNamee, 1979).

One of the most analytical studies demonstrating parental scaffolding during problem solving appeared since Day's review: Freund (1990) observed that mothers vary their support as a function of difficulties experienced by their children during problem solving. Using a true experimental design,

Freund (1990) demonstrated that the parental scaffolding had an enduring effect on the children's problem solving, with the children who experienced scaffolding better able to perform a similar problem-solving task on their own than control children.

Unfortunately, however, instructional theorists who are attracted to Vygotskian theory have made stronger claims about the superiority of scaffolding compared with other forms of instruction than are justified based on the available data. In her own research, Day has obtained mixed evidence that children who receive scaffolded instruction from an adult learn faster or better than children who receive less competence-and-progress sensitive instruction (for positive evidence, see Day & Cordon, 1993; for more negative evidence, see Day et al., 1989). In experiments on scaffolded instruction, Day and her colleagues (personal communication, December 1991) have found that scaffolding had at best a small effect on learning. About the only consistent evidence of scaffolding effects on children has been reported by Rogoff and colleagues, who have observed that when an adult and child work together on a task in a scaffolded fashion, the child is more likely to be planful when given other problems to solve (e.g., Gauvain & Rogoff, 1989; Radziszewska & Rogoff, 1988).

Just as Day has, Gelman, Massey, and McManus (1991) provided data suggesting overstatements by Vygotskian theorists. They designed a study aimed at elucidating the types of instruction that parents provide to their children during museum visits. Gelman et al. (1991) observed a number of different approaches to parent-child teaching besides scaffolding, not all of which could be considered good teaching. First, the types of interactions between parents and children varied with the type of exhibit. Thus, in an interactive grocery store exhibit, parents prompted, requested, and ordered their children to do things for much of the time. Certainly, in this setting, the adults provided support for their children, although there was little indication that the support was fine-grained—that is, adjusted to the level of the child's competence. Worse, in an exhibit intended to develop number skills, adults rarely helped their children despite the intention of the designers of the exhibit that it be approached as a parent-child interactive activity. Gelman et al. (1991) speculated that the adults may have felt more competent to assist their children in the more familiar grocery setting than in a math exhibit because math is an area in which many adults do not have stateable knowledge of many fundamental concepts. Gelman et al.'s (1991) pessimistic evaluation, that parents often do not scaffold instruction to their children when they could do so, was reinforced when she and her colleagues became involved in designing an exhibit intended to stimulate experimentation. Little scaffolded interaction was observed when children visited the exhibit with their parents. Other investigators as well have observed much less than universal scaffolding by parents to children in their charge (e.g., Pratt, Kerig, Cowan, & Cowan, 1988).

Summarizing across a great deal of research, we conclude that children receive a mix of different types of instruction (some scaffolded and some not). This is not particularly surprising because scaffolding is extremely difficult to do (Day et al., 1989). It also is time consuming and effortful. Based on existing data, it is also not clear that efforts to scaffold make that much difference relative to less scaffolded instruction.

Consistent with our conclusion, the National Research Council (1991, Chapter 4) reviewed the case for encouraging cognitive apprenticeship and concluded that this was an approach fraught with difficulties:

> ... [C]ertain strategies of learning can be easily modeled ... but the rationale for an expert's choice of strategies or solution routes may not be obvious, especially if a great deal of content knowledge is needed. Furthermore, monitoring a student's own understanding demands complex processing, and it is not clear that this is undertaken normally by tutors. Indeed, there is some evidence that teachers in a tutoring situation do not necessarily provide "intelligent" coaching and scaffolding, presumably because they have not monitored the student's understanding accurately. In fact, Putnam (1987) observed six teachers tutoring students in a one-on-one situation and found that they did not systematically diagnose students' misunderstanding and tailor feedback accordingly. Instead, they seemed to follow a structured and prescribed sequence of presenting subject-matter content to their students. (pp. 74–5) (See comments on Putnam's study earlier in this chapter.)

Think about this set of concerns with respect to what was presented in previous chapters. We make the case throughout this book that it is not enough to learn strategies. One must also learn when and where to use them. Thus, we find disturbing the

conclusion by the National Research Council that it is difficult to discern why a model is executing a strategy. More positively, in some of the successful tutoring that will be reviewed later in this and subsequent chapters, experts make clear their reasons for doing what they do, perhaps because they are sensitive to the difficulties that students have in inferring such information.

This National Research Council point about monitoring another person's understanding makes contact with work discussed earlier as well. Recall in Chapter 2 that we established that monitoring is difficult, period. People often do not know how much they are learning when they are studying or even if they have figured out the main idea of a text. In light of these failures of people to monitor their own performances, is it surprising that teachers have difficulty monitoring how students are doing? Not really. Diagnosis of student difficulties (and the underlying problem causing the manifest difficulties) is hard even if an adult can work with a student in a one-on-one situation (see Flavell, 1972). Imagine the diagnostic challenges when there are 30 students in a classroom. Even so, we will present teachers in later chapters who do seem to do a great deal of monitoring of student performance "on the run." Such teachers have built up long-term knowledge of their individual students' strengths and weaknesses as well as substantial craft and content knowledge (e.g., after years of teaching writing, one knows the errors that come up again and again and can spot them instantly). Thus, although the challenges of monitoring students and diagnosing their instructional needs must be acknowledged, we are convinced that such challenges are overcome at least by some skilled teachers.

A related difficulty with scaffolding is that children differ in their abilities to interpret teacher's appraisals and hints. In particular, children in the early grade-school years are less likely than older children to interpret accurately teacher's comments about and actions in response to their academic behaviors (e.g., Lord, Umezaki, & Darley, 1990). What this means is that during the early grade-school years, scaffolding teachers must be especially sensitive about whether the messages they are sending to their students are getting through—the younger the child, the less reason there is to believe that the student understands subtle (and sometimes not so subtle) signals that her or his processing is off target.

Finally the closing comment in the National Research Council quote that teachers sometimes follow a predetermined sequence of instruction is critical. Scaffolded instruction is anything but tightly sequenced and predetermined, rather changing as the needs of the student change. Teachers are offered many sequences and scripts, especially by textbook publishers, sometimes with the message that the scripted lesson is more effective than anything a teacher would create, so teachers are intimidated into following the sequence specified by the script. Teaching at its best involves a teacher who is aware of pupils and their needs, who knows the content area so well that many adaptations of content teaching are possible, and who is committed to expending the mental energy required to monitor student performance as students attempt tasks. Such teaching is never tightly sequenced or scripted.

In summary, while acknowledging the existence of many demonstrations of adult-child apprenticeships (see Rogoff, 1990, for a summary of the data), it is also necessary to acknowledge that parent-child and teacher-child scaffolding is anything but universal. Moreover, it is not clear that instruction that includes scaffolding is far superior to other forms of instruction, as supposed by many who find Vygotskian theory to be compelling. For example, there is always the possibility that children will attribute the help offered by the scaffolding adult as an indication that they are not capable, and thus the adult assistance might undermine academic self-esteem and long-term academic achievement motivation (e.g., Graham & Barker, 1990). In a large classroom, the scaffolding teacher must depend on students to send signals that they need help. As it turns out, the students needing the help most may be the least likely to let the teacher know they need assistance (e.g., by asking questions; Newman & Goldin, 1990).

We are struck as well that scaffolding of instruction is just one of many important behaviors of excellent teachers. For example, Dillon (1989) describes an excellent secondary reading teacher who projects that he cares about his students' culture, has established a risk-free classroom and encourages active involvement in learning, assigns interesting materials, and carefully plans and structures lessons, but he also scaffolds a lot, individualizing instruction to children's difficulties and needs. Miller, Leinhardt, and Zigmond (1988) described a school that was extremely successful in keeping at-risk secondary students in school. Although teacher scaffolding occurred, there were many other forms of support provided as well, including policy accommodations (e.g., flexibility in attendance policy), careful selection of curricular items, and grading/testing policies that rewarded effort. Scaffolding is in high-quality instruction, but it is only one component in capable teaching.

We are struck, as Day was, that there have been so few analytical studies pertaining to Vygotskian theoretical conceptions of instruction. Moreover, little of what has been offered has been really programmatic research. There has been some, however, with the work of Palincsar and Brown on reciprocal teaching the most obvious example of a research program that is often cited as pertinent to Vygotskian principles of instruction as they apply to an important type of elementary instruction: teaching of reading comprehension.

Reciprocal Teaching

Reciprocal teaching (e. g., Brown & Palincsar, 1989; Palincsar & Brown, 1984) involves instruction of comprehension strategies in the context of a reading group. Thus, students are taught to make predictions when reading, to question themselves about the text, to seek clarifications when confused, and to summarize content. The adult teacher initially explains and models these strategies for students, but the most unique part of reciprocal teaching is that quickly students are leading the group. That is, one student is assigned the role of group leader for a lesson, and this individual supervises the groups' generation of predictions, questions, and summaries as reading proceeds. The group leader also solicits points that need to be clarified and either provides clarifications or elicits them from other group members. The group interactions are cooperative. The adult teacher provides support on an as-needed basis—that is, he or she scaffolds. Brown and Palincsar summarized a typical discussion of text in a reciprocal teaching group:

> The dialogue leader begins the discussion by asking a question on the main content and ends by summarizing the gist. If there is disagreement, the group rereads and discusses potential candidates for question and summary statements until they reach consensus. Summarizing provides a means by which the group can monitor its progress, noting points of agreement and disagreement. Particularly valuable is the fact that summarizing at the end of a period of

discussion helps students establish where they are for tackling a new segment of text. Attempts to clarify any comprehension problems that might arise are also an integral part of the discussion. And, finally, the leader asks for predictions about future content. Throughout, the adult teacher provides guidance and feedback tailored to the needs of the current discussion and his or her respondents. (p. 413)

Such instruction is just full of good things from the perspective of the sociohistorical models, other social-interactive views, and even more purely cognitive views of learning and development (Brown & Palincsar, 1989). First, students are presented with multiple models of cognitive processing: The teacher models and explains. Every day the group comes together and executes a sequence of strategies well matched to the processes required to understand text, and thus peers in the group are continuously modeling reasoning about text. With respect to learning of content, students are led to make the types of elaborations and inferences that should facilitate learning of text (see Chapters 10 and 14)—that is, predictions, inferences required as part of question generation and elaboration, and summarization. The discussions permit various points of view to be aired and require students to justify and back up their claims (see the section on instructional conversations later in this chapter). These discussions permit review and commentary about the strategies being learned as well as the content being covered, so reciprocal teaching offers opportunities to learn new content as it offers opportunities to learn how to process new content.

Perhaps most critical from the perspective of Vygotskian theory is the assumption that the teacher is progressively less involved as the students gain competence. The assumption is that by participating in the group, students will eventually internalize use of the four strategies encouraged as part of reciprocal teaching. That is, the processing that was once carried out between persons in the group will come to be carried out within the individual students, consistent with the Vygotskian perspective that individual cognitive development develops from participation in social groups.

The dialogue from a sample lesson, one involving low-achieving middle-school students, should help to make clear what occurs during a reciprocal teaching reading group. The dialogue that follows was generated by a group of students who had had 13 days of experience with the method and thus were accustomed to it. The students had just read the following brief text:

TEXT: In the United States salt is produced by three basic methods: solar (sun) evaporation, mining, and artificial heat evaporation. For salt to be extracted by solar evaporation, the weather must be hot and dry. Thus, solar salt is harvested in the tropic-like areas along our southern ocean coasts and at Great Salt Lake.

STUDENT LEADER (STUDENT C): Name three different basic methods how salt is produced.

STUDENT A: Evaporation, mining, evaporation . . . artificial heat evaporation.

STUDENT LEADER: Correct, very good. My summary on this paragraph is about ways that salt is produced.

TEACHER: Very good. Could you select the next teacher. (Student C does so, selecting Student L, with the reading continuing.)

TEXT: The second oldest form of salt production is mining. Unlike early methods that made the work extremely dangerous and difficult, today's methods use special machinery, and salt mining is easier and safer. The old expression "back to the salt mine" no longer applies.

STUDENT LEADER (STUDENT L): Name two words that often describe mining salt in the old days.

STUDENT K: Back to the salt mines?

STUDENT LEADER L: No. Angela?

STUDENT A: Dangerous and difficult.

STUDENT LEADER L: Correct. This paragraph is about comparing the old mining of salt and today's mining of salt.

TEACHER: Beautiful!

STUDENT LEADER L: I have a prediction to make.

TEACHER: Good.

STUDENT LEADER L: I think it might tell when salt was first discovered, well, it might tell what salt is made of and how it's made.

TEACHER: OK. Can we have another teacher?

TEXT: Table salt is made by the third method—artificial evaporation. Pumping water into an underground salt bed dissolves the salt to make a brine that is brought to the surface. After purification at high temperatures, the salt is ready for our tables.

STUDENT LEADER K: After purification at high temperatures the salt is ready for what?

STUDENT C: Our tables.

STUDENT LEADER K: That's correct. To summarize: After its purification, the salt is put on our tables.

TEACHER: That was a fine job, Ken, and I appreciate all the work, but I think there might be something else to add to our summary. There is more important information that I think we need to include. This paragraph is mostly about what?

STUDENT A: The third method of evaporation.

STUDENT B: It mainly tells about pumping water from an underground salt bed that dissolves the salt to make a brine that is brought to the surface.

TEACHER: Angela hit it right on the money. The paragraph is mostly about the method of artificial evaporation and then everything else in the paragraph is telling us about the process. OK. Next teacher.

TEXT: For thousands of years people have known salt—tasting it, using it for their lives' needs. Sometimes it has been treasured as gold; other times it has been superstitiously tossed over the shoulder to ward off bad luck. Somehow people and salt have always been together, but never is the tie more complete than when the best people are called "the salt of the earth."

STUDENT LEADER C: My question is, what are the best people called?

STUDENT L: The salt of the earth.

STUDENT LEADER C: Why?

STUDENT L: Because salt and the people have been together so long.

TEACHER: Do you have something to add to that? OK. It really isn't because they have been together so long; it has to do with something else. Brian?

BRIAN: (reading) "People and salt have always been together but never has the tie been so complete."

TEACHER: All right, but when we use the expression, "That person is the salt of the earth," we know that means that person is a good person. How do we know that?

STUDENT B: Because we treasure salt, like gold. (pp. 421–422)

There are several interesting things about this lesson, not all of them reflecting positively on reciprocal teaching as a model. All students were participating, with a real structure to the participation. Even so, after 13 days of reciprocal teaching, there were no requests for clarification, despite the fact that some of the students were experiencing difficulties understanding the text. In addition, the questions generated in reaction to text by the student leaders required only low-level responses—they were all literal questions. Such questions do not stimulate people to think beyond the surface structure of the text. In addition, there seemed to be little scaffolding of the processing by the teacher here, with the teacher more someone who monitored whether the students were understanding the passage and providing clarification of the content as needed.

Our view of reciprocal teaching as operationalized by Palincsar and Brown (1984) is reserved. They have focused their efforts on low-ability readers and created a participation structure that invites these often passive students to take part in reading. We have watched many reciprocal teaching lessons in which there has been a preponderance of literal questions and little in the way of evidence that students are monitoring when they understand and when they do not understand, which is obvious from the striking lack of clarification questions in many reciprocal teaching lessons. Because reciprocal teaching so emphasizes that the teacher fade support, there are often long pauses in lessons with students fumbling because the teacher is uncertain whether to enter into the conversation and provide input.

That said, however, the evidence generated to date is more supportive of reciprocal teaching than not. An even-handed analysis provided by Rosenshine and Meister (1992) is particularly helpful here. They identified 19 experimental studies of reciprocal teaching (i.e., those that included both groups of students experiencing reciprocal teaching and groups experiencing some other form of instruction). Most of these interventions were brief, from 6 to 30 sessions—or a little more than a week of instruction to 6 weeks of instruction. Three investigations involved longer treatments, with two of these spanning 50 sessions and one more than 100 sessions. Of course, the studies varied in other particulars, with some distinctions crucial in understanding the effects of the intervention: (1) Nine of the studies involved only reciprocal teaching (henceforth referred to as RT studies) in that the children were brought together and taught to dialogue as just described. The comprehension strategies were introduced as students first experienced dialoguing as a form of participation in reading instruction. In the 10 remaining studies, students received explicit teaching about how to execute the comprehension strategies before they began reciprocal teaching (henceforth referred to as ET/RT studies for explicit teaching and reciprocal teaching).

(2) Some investigations focused on students having decoding problems; others involved students who had no decoding difficulties but who experienced comprehension problems; still others involved students of all abilities. (3) Some studies included standardized tests; some used experimenter-generated tests, which typically tapped the processes encouraged by the four strategies; and some included both types of measures.

Generally the effects of reciprocal teaching were greater when explicit teaching of the comprehension strategies occurred before participation in reciprocal teaching (i.e., the size of the effect was greater in studies evaluating ET/RT than in studies evaluating RT). In general, when the main effects were considered, the effect of reciprocal teaching was about the same for all three ability types. When standardized tests were used, the effect of reciprocal teaching was modest, with the effects on standardized comprehension tests extremely modest with below-average readers, especially if they did not receive predialoguing instruction in execution of the four strategies (i.e., the effects were more modest in the RT than in the ET/RT studies for weaker readers when standardized measures were the criterion); with experimenter-constructed measures tapping the processes stimulated by the strategies, the effects of reciprocal teaching were quite striking, with the effect particularly striking in the ET/RT studies. The effects of reciprocal teaching did not seem to vary with the age or grade of the students: Most studies were conducted with students in the grade-school years, although several used the approach with adults. Ten of the investigations taught the 4 comprehension strategies favored by Palincsar and Brown (1984), with the other 11 studies involving between 1 and 10 strategies. There was no discernible effect of the number of strategies taught on the effects of reciprocal teaching.

This analysis of all available data on reciprocal teaching is important because it makes clear that even a small amount of reciprocal teaching of comprehension strategies (i.e., from a week of sessions to 6 weeks of sessions) can affect comprehension processing (i.e., students begin to use the comprehension strategies taught). It also makes clear that reciprocal teaching is not a panacea, however, because the effects on standardized comprehension were not consistently striking. This latter outcome is particularly important to emphasize because Brown and Palincsar (1989; also Brown & Campione, 1990) have made much of large standardized achievement gains (i.e., 2 years or more) by a few students who experience a month or so of reciprocal teaching. True enough (e.g., Brown & Palincsar, 1989, p. 424, Figure 13.1), although almost as many control students experience such gains, suggesting that many of the largest gains are due to practice effects with the test. A realistic appraisal is that a week to a month and a half of reciprocal teaching has some discernible positive effects on the comprehension of elementary students, especially if measures directly tapping the comprehension strategies taught are the criteria (e.g., construct a summary of text, make predictions).

We think reciprocal teaching deserves further study, especially with respect to its long-term effects. Research now under way (principally designed and carried out by Marilyn Marks; Marks et al., 1993) highlights the flexibile use of reciprocal teaching by some teachers. Marks et al. (1993) studied three teachers who were using reciprocal teaching in their classrooms on a long-term basis: Sharon Craig (SC) used the method as part of grade-1 reading. Wanda Rose (WR) used it with grade-6, grade-7, and grade-8 special education students who were experiencing mild difficulties in school. Rosalie Gardner (RG) used it in her grade-11 and grade-12 literature courses. Thus, a first conclusion emanating from the study was that the method can be adapted to diverse groups of students.

What must be emphasized is the word *adapted*, for in all cases, the reciprocal teaching Marks et al. observed was consistent in many ways with Palincsar and Brown (1984) but also differed from their operationalization of it. Thus, it took about 2 months of preliminaries (e.g., introducing the students to the individual strategies) before SC's grade-1 students began participating in reciprocal teaching dialogue groups. In contrast, WR's special education students became facile at participating in about a month, which was still longer than reported by Palincsar and Brown (1984), who worked with a comparable population of students. RG's high school students learned how to participate in reciprocal teaching in a matter of a few days.

In all three cases, the teachers experienced a difficulty pointed out earlier. When asked to generate questions, the students generated low-level literal questions. All three of the teachers came up with a remedy, in this case, the same remedy. They taught the students how to generate inferential questions using a question-generation intervention well known in Maryland, where the study was conducted. Frank Lyman of the University of Maryland has devised a series of "Think Trix," which are cues for generating inferential questions (e.g., What are the advantages and disadvantages of ___?; What was the cause of ___?). Students in all three classes used the Think Trix as they developed questions to ask their fellow students during reciprocal teaching sessions.

In contrast to reciprocal teaching as Palincsar and Brown (1984) deployed it, the three teachers studied by Marks et al. (1993) regularly had their students read the selections before coming to the reciprocal teaching group, preparing questions in advance as well as identifying points that needed clarification in advance of class. Although Palincsar and Brown (1984) devised an intervention for comprehending a text on first reading, these teachers all used reciprocal teaching as a discussion format, going over text already covered.

In both SC's (grade-1) and WR's (special education) classes, the interactions in the reciprocal teaching groups were pretty much as Palincsar and Brown (1984) described. The only salient difference was that in both classes, the teachers had devised cue cards to remind students about how turn taking should proceed. This permitted greater student self-regulation of turn taking. In RG's high school class, the structure was considerably different. First, students met in small groups, with one of the small group members assuming the role of the teacher. The small groups discussed the text. Then, the entire class came together, with RG selecting one of the small groups to present questions generated in small group to members of one of the other small groups. This started a discussion that permitted seeking of clarification and eventually the generation of a summary. The class concluded with students offering predictions about what might occur in upcoming text.

What impressed Marks et al. (1993) was that the three adaptations seemed to work well, in that each teacher's classes had a discernible structure that permitted efficient use of class time. Even the grade-1 students in SC's class knew exactly what their roles were and they performed them. Part of the success at the grade-1 level may have been that SC prepared students so well for reciprocal teaching, covering all the strategies in other activities before reciprocal teaching groups were organized. Also, SC did not start students in reciprocal teaching until they

seemed ready for it, so that the highest-level students began reciprocal teaching in November, with average-achieving students starting later in the year, and the slowest students still working in May on the preliminaries leading up to reciprocal teaching.

Why did the teachers adapt the reciprocal teaching structure? Some adaptations reflected the teachers' identification of problems with the original formulation, with the best example being the need to teach students how to generate inferential questions. Others represented structural constraints. Thus, whole-class discussion and interaction is common in high school classes, so that RG's adaptations to high school literature made reciprocal teaching more consistent with the high school ecology.

We emphasize in concluding this discussion of reciprocal teaching that although various types of data suggest that reciprocal teaching can play a role in reading comprehension instruction, there is nothing in these data that permits great confidence that it is the Vygotskian aspects of the intervention that are potent. Even the most analytical of these studies (e.g., a study summarized in Brown & Palincsar, 1989, Figure 13.3) only provided a comparison between a condition in which the four comprehension strategies were taught using all of the reciprocal teaching components and another condition in which the four strategies were taught using conventional classroom explanation. That the reciprocally taught group outperformed the conventionally taught group could reflect the scaffolding of instruction by the teacher (which would probably be the Vygotskian interpretation) or the effects of the cooperative relations between peers in the reading groups (i.e., an interpretation that might be favored by cooperative learning theories; see Chapter 5) or a combination of scaffolding and cooperative learning.

The effects obtained in the many short-term studies of reciprocal teaching are not so dramatic that it is fair to conclude that short-term reciprocal teaching can dramatically alter the reading achievement of elementary students or even elementary students experiencing difficulty in reading, an interpretation that seemed to be invited by many of the early publications pertaining to reciprocal teaching. More positively, some educators at least are finding ways to put reciprocal teaching into long-term practice (e.g., some of WR's special education students had had 3 years of reciprocal teaching). Our hope that serious study of long-term reciprocal teaching will continue is consistent with a hypothesis that will be developed in this and later chapters (e.g., Chapter 14): Long-term instruction may be required for there to be striking general effects of strategies instruction. (As this text was being completed, author MP and Thommie DePinto were finishing data collection on a year-long comparative study at the grade-5 level of educator-adapted reciprocal teaching, with the descriptive data on reciprocal teaching presented here consistent with the descriptive data collected in this more recent investigation.)

Summary

The sociohistorical approach stimulated by Vygotsky's and Bakhtin' analyses is one of the most important theoretical directions in contemporary educational psychology. Conceptually attractive teaching constructs are associated with this approach, such as scaffolding and the zone of proximal development. Unfortunately the research generated by those interested in these theoretical ideas has not been analytical, limited to demonstrations that at least sometimes adults teach in a scaffolded fashion and that intervention packages that include scaffolding have some positive effects on performance.

In addition, questions about the conceptual uniqueness of some of the most important sociohistorical ideas (at least with respect to issues of instruction) are possible. For example, scaffolding seems similar to what the behaviorists refer to as fading. Fading involves provision of reinforcement and modeling when it is needed, with both reinforcement and modeling withdrawn as the learner becomes more adept. With scaffolding, what is withdrawn is modeling and hints and prompts, some of which arguably serve as feedback that functions as reinforcement.

We have sympathy with our behaviorist friends, who believe that there is some conceptual plagiarism by the Vygotskians, especially when we consider how other theoretical persuasions have dealt with the zone of proximal development idea. According to the Vygotskians, instruction will go best if it is aimed at acquisitions that are in the "zone," acquisitions just a bit beyond where the learner now is. Concepts and behaviors in the zone are in their formation stage, and thus, additional instructional input aimed at zone items will be more successful than instruction aimed at concepts and behaviors that are beyond the zone—that are not now in the process of acquisition. But is there any

theory of learning that would not predict that concepts and behaviors already partially acquired would not be learned more easily than concepts and behaviors that have not been partially acquired? Indeed, a hallmark of many instructional theories, including Piaget's, is the principle of teaching just a bit beyond the current competency of the child (see Chapter 7 especially for discussion of this idea).

The point that there may be less unique in the sociohistorical theories than Vygotskian proponents might believe will be driven home more as this chapter proceeds. In the next section, we will present some interactional theories of teaching and learning that are viewed by some as different from Vygotskian perspectives. We will develop the case, however, that there really is quite a bit in common between these approaches and those inspired by Soviet theories of learning and development. Although extremists of various persuasions (e.g., dyed-in-the-wool Vygotskians and behaviorists) make much of the subtle differences between their own perspectives and other viewpoints that they do not favor, from the perspective of developing a psychology of instruction, it is heartening to find common recommendations flowing from a variety of theories. Indeed, there is what Mathison (1988) calls theoretical triangulation for instructional ideas such as scaffolding and teaching in the zone of proximal development. That is, when different groups with different epistemological standards and methods come to similar conclusions about instruction, it increases confidence in those conclusions.

DIRECT INSTRUCTION AND EXPLANATION

If things are going well in a reciprocal teaching group, the adult teacher's presence should be hardly noticeable. The instructional theory is to reduce the teacher's input as much as possible, with student control of the interactions in the group an important part of eventual internalization by the students of the strategies being taught. In addition, there is a concern that the students construct content knowledge for themselves in the group, that the knowledge they construct via making predictions, generating questions, seeking clarifications when confused, and summarizing text will be more meaningful to them than if the teacher intervenes and provides information pertaining to the text. Those who identify with sociohistorical approaches to instruction are extremely concerned that the teacher cede control to the students as soon as possible.

Other perspectives on teacher-student interaction are not nearly so concerned with reducing the teacher's role quickly, although we will argue after reviewing these perspectives that scaffolding occurs in the teaching captured by these models and that such instruction is usually offered in what the Vygotskians refer to as the zone of proximal development. Although many of the sociohistorical types consider the perspectives covered in this section to be antithetical to Vygotskian principles, our view is that there is much less distance between the instructional theories covered in this section and those reviewed in the previous section.

Direct Instruction

Although a number of researchers have contributed research on direct instruction, one name more than any other is associated with such teaching: Barak Rosenshine. Rosenshine (e.g., 1979; Rosenshine & Stevens, 1984) has provided the most complete and blunt appraisals of the variables that are associated with achievement gains in classrooms, especially gains related to reading and mathematics during the elementary years. There can be little doubt in reading Rosenshine that his emphasis is much more on behaviors of teachers and students (i.e., objective performances) than on internal changes in students. In this era when cognitive and sociocognitive theories are dominating discussions of instruction, this emphasis on behavior is one reason many are turned off by Rosenshine's analyses of effective teaching. Even so, the scientific evidence pertaining to direct instruction is consistent with Rosenshine's conclusions.

What produces high levels of classroom learning according to Rosenshine? First, the more content covered, often measured in terms of time on academic tasks, the greater achievement. Rosenshine (1979) was particularly impressed with Bloom's (1976) conclusion, based on analysis of 15 studies, that the amount of time that students spent academically engaged was especially predictive of achievement (also Stallings & Kaskowitz, 1974): If there is one thing that is certain about direct instruction, most students are on task most of the time (e.g., Frick, 1990). Rosenshine (1979) concluded that learning was best accomplished in classrooms that were academically focused and teacher directed, ones in

which academic content was presented in a sequenced, structured fashion. Direct instruction involves clear specification of goals to students. There is sufficient time for instruction, with continuous and extensive coverage of content. Student performance is monitored. Questions are asked that are at a level that students can handle them, so that lower-level and more literal questions are directed at weaker students, and more demanding questions are given to better students. Feedback is provided immediately and is academically oriented. Even with all of this academic work going on, Rosenshine's preferred classrooms are convivial and warm, democratic and cooperative. Although positive affect alone does not make a good classroom, positive affect when combined with an academic outlook does make for academic progress.

All of this should sound good, even to nonbehaviorists. So why the reservations about Rosenshine's proposal? One reason is that he made it sound so dreary. He found no problems with teaching in large groups, emphasized the teacher as decision maker rather than the student (e.g., in limiting the materials students can work with), embraced orderliness, endorsed asking questions that students can answer rather than questions that challenge them and require reflection, and recognized that drill and overlearning often have a place in school. For those many educators who are child centered or discovery oriented, Rosenshine's description was grim. In addition, it was unidimensional with respect to outcomes embraced, focusing on measurable student achievement (Peterson, 1979), ignoring that students have individual needs and talents that sometimes are not obvious on standardized assessments.

We are more enthusiastic about Rosenshine's approach than many commentators because it seems unlikely that things would go as well as they seem to go in direct instruction classrooms if the teachers were not highly responsive to the students. Indeed, there are plenty of provisions for such responsivity. For example, a key feature of direct instruction is to provide ample time. In many direct instruction classrooms, the teacher arranges schedules so slower learners are permitted the time they need. In contrast, faster students are ushered into other academic content that goes beyond the minimum curriculum. To provide timely feedback, it is critical to be sensitive to students and their individual differences in needs and expression of needs and learning. For a teacher to ask questions that are likely to be answered correctly, he or she must be extremely aware of what students know already and be committed to taking their knowledge and perspectives into account in leading classroom discussions. Teachers who lack such sensitivity to student needs do not have classrooms that are convivial and warm. Thus, our guess is that Rosenshine's preferred classrooms are more responsive than he describes. We are certain that he was relying on data sets that were not particularly sensitive to how teachers made decisions about students or provided feedback to them.

Even if direct instruction teachers are more student oriented than Rosenshine portrayed them, repackaging of the direct instruction approach was necessary if it was to be attractive to educators in the 1980s and now the 1990s. The cognitive revolution in education forced a real concern with developing strategies, knowledge, metacognition, and motivation in students. The direct explanation approach developed by Duffy, Roehler, and their colleagues at Michigan State went well beyond the direct instruction conceptualization of effective instruction, providing an attractive cognitively oriented theory of instruction that retained many of the best features of direct instruction.

Direct Explanation

There have been innumerable studies in which an adult has explained to a child how to do something and the child has been able to do it (see Pressley, Heisel, et al., 1982, for many examples involving memory strategies). As should be obvious by this point in the book, such explanations alone are not likely to result in the child continuing to use a strategy. If the teacher models the strategy for the student, it helps, as does having the student model the strategy for the teacher with feedback. Long-term maintenance and transfer is more likely if instruction includes information about when and where to use the strategy being taught as well as opportunities to practice the strategy and practice adapting it to new situations. All of these components are included in what Roehler and Duffy (e.g., 1984) have referred to as direct explanation.

Any strategy can be taught with direct explanation. It is an extremely fluid approach to teaching, usually beginning with teacher explanations and modeling and then proceeding to student practice. Practice is monitored with additional explanations

and modeling provided as needed, with such feedback and instruction reduced as the student becomes more independent (i.e., direct explanations and feedback are provided in a scaffolded fashion). An important part of this instruction is what Duffy and Roehler refer to as **mental modeling** (e.g., Duffy & Roehler, 1989), which is simply showing the students how to apply the strategy by thinking aloud. (Mental modeling in this sense should not be confused with Johnson-Laird's mental models, which were covered in Chapter 3.) Another extremely important idea in this approach to instruction is **responsive elaboration:** That is, the information provided to students depends on the particular problems the students are encountering and the particular ways that their understandings are deficient. Reinstruction and reexplanations as well as follow-up mental modeling are responsive to student needs and usually are an elaboration of student understandings up until that point.

The best way to convey the nature of direct explanation is by going through an example. Consider the following dialogue collected as part of a lesson on a prefix-pronunciation strategy:

INTRODUCING THE BASAL TEXT LESSON: Today we are going to read a story about a monkey that lived in the zoo. How many of you have been in the zoo? What do you see in the zoo? . . . Now in this story there are some hard words that you have never had before. Here's one right here (shows students). Here's another. I'm going to teach you a strategy for figuring out these words and others like them so that, when you come to them in the story, you will be able to figure them out yourselves and go right on finding out about what happens to the monkey.

INTRODUCING THE STRATEGY: Sometimes when you are reading, you run into a word you don't recognize. . . . So we need to stop and figure out the word. . . . This strategy will help you figure out the pronunciation of prefixed words so you can continue getting the author's meaning despite these hard words. In order to do this, you need to look for the root word, then look for the *dis-* or the *un-*. Then you separate the two, pronounce each one separately, then say the prefix and the root word together.

MENTAL MODELING: I'll explain how I figure out words like these. You'll do this in a moment, so pay attention to the way I figure these words out.

[Mental modeling follows.] Let's say that I'm reading along in my basal story and I run into the word *unhappy*. If I've never seen this word before, I say to myself, "Oh, oh. I need to figure this word out if I'm going to continue getting the author's meaning." So I stop, look at the word and think about what strategy I can use to make sense out of this word. I see that it is a prefixed word, so I think about a prefix strategy. I find the root [circles it]. I separate the root from the prefix [draws a line between them]. Then I pronounce the prefix—*un-*. Then I pronounce the root—*happy*. Then I say the two parts together—*unhappy*. Then I put the word back into the sentence in the story to make sure it makes sense. Now let's review what I did. You tell me the steps I followed, and I'll list them up here on the board. Susie, what did I do first? Yes, first I [writes on board] . . . then I . . . [writes on board] . . . [etc].

MEDIATING STUDENTS' INITIAL ATTEMPTS TO APPLY THE STRATEGY USING DIRECTIVES AND CUES: Can you use my strategy to figure out unrecognized words? . . . You have . . . things to help you: the steps in the strategy listed on the board here [points] . . . Mary, show me how you use the strategy to figure out this word. [Mary does so successfully—that is, she mentally models her use of the strategy.]

INTERACTION WITH QUESTIONS AND FADED CUES: Now let's see if you can do the same thing when I give you less help. I'm going to erase from the board the steps of my strategy, and you see if you can use a strategy of your own that is like mine. . . . [Teacher is attempting to fade support some here. Puts new word on board.] Now, Sam, what would you do first to figure out this word? Can you show me how you'd figure out the word? [Sam responds by just pronouncing the word.] . . . [The teacher responds with responsive elaborations, ones tailored to the teacher's perceptions of Sam's needs.] You said the word correctly, Sam, but I don't know whether you were doing the thinking correctly. What did you do first? [Teacher cues the student to mentally model in what follows.] Talk out loud so I can hear how you figured that word out. [Sam responds, stating the steps he used.] That's good, Sam. You stated the steps you used to figure out the word correctly. This strategy doesn't work all the time, because some of our words look like words with prefixes but really aren't. [Illustrates the word *under*.] See if this word can be pronounced using our prefix strategy. [Leads stu-

dents through the process showing them where the strategy doesn't work and why. Scaffolding occurs in that the interaction that follows involves fewer cues; eventually there is interaction with supportive feedback but no cues.]

SETTING PURPOSES FOR READING THE BASAL SELECTION: Now we are going to read the story about the monkey named Clyde. . . . There are some hard words in this story, which you haven't seen before. [Mental modeling follows.] When you come to these words, say to yourself, "Oh, oh. I'm going to have to figure this word out." Then see if your prefix strategy will work, and, if the hard word does have a prefix, use what we learned about figuring out prefixed words to figure out the word in the story. [Silent or oral reading follows.]

DISCUSSION: [Leads discussion in which questions are posed about both the content and the application of the prefix strategy while reading the story. The intent is to assess whether students understood the content and the application of the prefix strategy.]

LESSON CLOSURE: [Closes the lesson by having students summarize what happened in the story and how the prefix strategy was used to help understand the story . . .] All right. Now that you have successfully used the prefix strategy to figure out hard words in the basal text story, we have to be sure to use it in other things you read. [Teacher is providing some metacognitive information about the strategy—that is, information about when and where to use the strategy.] What other things do you read where you could use this strategy? What if you ran into an unknown word when reading in . . . (another) book? Could you use this strategy in this situation? Can you tell me how you would use the prefix strategy in reading a newspaper? (Adapted with permission of the authors from Example 13.1, pp. 228–229, Duffy & Roehler, 1989)

Duffy, Roehler, Sivan et al. (1987) produced an extremely well-designed study of the effects of direct explanation strategy instruction on grade-3 reading. They taught grade-3 teachers to explain directly the strategies and processes that are part of skilled grade-3 reading, for example, the prefix pronunciation strategy covered in the example. The teachers were taught first to explain a strategy and then to mentally model use of the strategy for students. The mental modeling showed students how good readers apply the strategy when they read.

Then came guided student practice with the students initially carrying out the processing overtly so the teacher could monitor their use of the new strategy. At first, there was substantial assistance, which was reduced as students became more proficient. It must be emphasized, however, that reexplanations and remodeling and prescription of additional practice were on an as-needed basis. Thus, although there was scaffolding of instruction, the teacher was not at all reluctant to provide additional input when students needed it.

Teachers were also taught to encourage transfer of strategies by going over when and where the strategies being learned might be used. Teachers cued use of the new strategies when students encountered situations in which the strategies might be applied profitably, regardless of when these occasions arose during the school day. Cuing and prompting were continued until students autonomously applied the strategies they were taught.

A year of this type of instruction had an impact on grade-3 students. Students receiving direct explanations were more aware of lesson content and the strategic nature of reading at the end of the year than were control students receiving more conventional instruction. Even more important, however, was that the students in the direct explanation condition outperformed the control students on a number of measures of reading. In short, a full year of direct explanation of reading strategies made substantial difference in the reading achievement of grade-3 students.

Direct Explanation Compared with Direct Instruction   How is this similar to Rosenshine's direct instruction? Direct explanation classrooms are certainly more teacher than student directed. Direct explanations are well structured, and the goals of lessons are clear. Duffy, Roehler, and their colleagues are certainly concerned with using students' time well, with direct explanation and practice involving intensive academic engagement. Students are not rushed, however, with reexplanations and additional modeling occurring as needed. Thus, one of the most important roles for the direct explanation teacher is to monitor students—decisions to reexplain or remodel follow from teacher perceptions of student understandings and difficulties. The tasks (including questions) given to students are ones they can handle, at least with some support from the teacher. Direct explanations provide a great deal of feedback to students, and it is immediate academic

feedback. Finally, but not least important, direct explanation classrooms are friendly places. There can be little doubt that there is much in common between direct instruction and direct explanation.

There are also enormous differences, however, at least at a conceptual level. The direct explanation teacher's decisions are a function of the perceived needs of the students, needs that often are revealed by students' thinking aloud. The think-alouds are revealing about the students' cognitive processing. Direct explanation teachers care much more about process than products, whereas direct instruction, at least as it is described, is product oriented. (We emphasize *as described*, for we sincerely believe that many direct instruction teachers monitor process as well—it is just that the direct instruction theorists and researchers never bother to pay attention to how the teachers are sensitive to student processing.) All of the mental modeling and explaining during direct explanations are aimed at making certain that the student understands what is being learned. Student understanding is not discussed much in direct instruction circles. (Again, however, many of the performances so valued by the direct instruction types would not be possible without understanding, so direct instruction often must increase understanding, although such understanding is not the main concern of direct instruction theorists and researchers.) Duffy's direct explanation model is certainly a cognitive model, with the concern being deep understanding of strategies and when and how to use them. Although we believe that direct instruction often creates such understandings, its failing as a conceptual model of instruction is that it considers academic performances more than how those academic performances are achieved—and if there is anything that committed cognitively oriented educators (who are everywhere these days) care about, it is *how* academic performances are achieved.

Direct Explanation Compared with Reciprocal Teaching   We have argued since first reviewing reciprocal teaching and direct explanation that the two conceptions of instruction are similar (see Pressley, Snyder, & Cariglia-Bull, 1987). Both involve teaching of cognitive processes for coming to terms with text. Both involve modeling and explanation of strategies. During both, students have an opportunity to see multiple models of cognitive processing because during both types of groups, a number of students are going to be using the cognitive processes that are being instructed. The discussion of content that occurs during both reciprocal teaching and direct explanation, as students practice strategies, should increase incidental learning of the content covered in the readings used to practice the strategies being learned. Both involve teacher scaffolding of instruction—the teacher monitors what is going on and offers supportive instruction on an as-needed basis. The teacher's scaffolding of instruction necessarily results in a student-sensitive approach to instruction and a cooperative, supportive atmosphere in the reading group. The assumption in both approaches is that participating in the instructional group and receiving the scaffolded instruction will result in long-term internalization of the cognitive processes being fostered by the group, so that the teacher is progressively less involved as instruction proceeds. As striking as these similarities are, however, the differences between reciprocal teaching and direct explanation are also striking.

Reciprocal teaching was developed with respect to the teaching of four particular strategies: predicting, questioning, seeking clarification, and summarizing. Although it is possible to teach reciprocally with other strategies as the focus of instruction, most investigations of reciprocal teaching to date have involved the original four strategies used by Palincsar and Brown (1984). Direct explanation is more generic, in that it is easy to see how direct explanation could be applied with almost any strategy, including ones pertaining to reading, writing, or mathematical content. Indeed, our opening comment about direct explanation in this section was that there have been many studies in which adults have explained to children how to do something.

The most important difference between reciprocal teaching and direct explanation, however, is with respect to the saliency of the teacher. Those committed to reciprocal teaching are committed to reducing quickly the adult teacher's control. The belief is that if students are to internalize decision making with respect to cognitive processes, they need to be the ones controlling the cognitive processes. In contrast, the teacher is much more visibly in charge as part of direct explanations, although always with the goal of reducing teacher input—that is, direct explanation teaching really is scaffolded, with the teacher cutting back as soon as it is possible to do so.

There is an important consequence of this difference in saliency of the teacher in reciprocal teaching and direct explanation, one that, in our view, favors

the direct explanation approach. For the teacher to be able to step back during reciprocal teaching, what is set up is a fairly rigid sequence. Go back to the sample reciprocal teaching lesson. Each time, after the text was read, the student leader of the moment posed a question for peers. The peers attempted to respond. Then the student leader proposed a summary. During reciprocal teaching, there are always questions and summaries from the student leaders, with other students encouraged to seek clarifications by posing questions. Predictions about upcoming text are offered. Those who favor reciprocal teaching point out correctly that a great deal of flexible discussion of text and issues in text can be covered with this framework. Moreover, they correctly argue that the particular processes are ones that are critical to comprehension of text (e.g., Baker & Brown, 1984). We contend, however, that the flexibility of discussion is greater during direct explanations and that the four processes favored during reciprocal teaching do not exhaust the strategies a good reader needs to deploy to understand text (see Chapter 14, this volume).

Impact of the Direct Explanation Model We have been extremely impressed by how much impact Duffy and Roehler's (e.g., 1989) work on direct explanation is having on others who are attempting to devise cognitive process interventions for reading comprehension, a point that will be elaborated in Chapter 14. We personally believe that the most theoretically compelling instructional position developed in this chapter is Duffy and Roehler's direct explanation model, one that incorporates ideas such as scaffolding and the zone of proximal development (i.e., the processes being directly explained are just a bit beyond what the students can do now) but keeps up front that student understanding of the processing is critical, understanding that permits autonomous functioning. Our belief is that the most important strengths of direct instruction and reciprocal teaching are represented in direct explanation, with direct explanation having some advantages that are not in the reciprocal teaching and direct instruction models.

Summary: Direct Explanation and Apprenticeship We close in emphasizing that direct explanation at its best is cognitive apprenticeship. Someone who is definitely an expert in reading (or writing or mathematical problem solving) passes on expertise to the next generation. All of the elements of apprenticeship specified by Collins et al. (1989) are there—there is extensive modeling and scaffolding by a teacher who acts like a coach once students begin to practice the processes being explained. The students are required to be able to explain what they are doing (i.e., there is articulation of processing by students). Students have opportunities to compare how they are processing with how other students are approaching a task. Reflection on one's own processing is encouraged by the teacher/coach, as the teacher/coach provides feedback tailored to the difficulties the student may be having. Moreover, the teacher/coach strongly encourages the student to try out the newly learned processes in new situations and to use the processes being learned flexibly—that is, the students are encouraged to explore how the processes they are learning through direct explanations can be applied broadly. We predict that as cognitive apprenticeship in school is translated into practice, that practice is going to look a lot like direct explanation as Duffy and Roehler have conceived of it.

INSTRUCTIONAL CONVERSATIONS

Probably no form of human interaction is more common than conversation, and so it is in classrooms as well. Of course, the direct instruction, reciprocal teaching, and direct explanation approaches considered thus far in this chapter involve particular types of conversations, with the nature of these conversations taken up later in this section, after consideration of some of the most "classic" work on classroom discourse as well as emerging directions in research on conversations in classrooms.

Conversations as They Usually Occur in School: Initiate-Response-Evaluation Cycles

Conversations that are structured like the following occur every day in school:

TEACHER: Where is the Tomb of the Unknown Soldier? (Initiation)
STUDENT: In Arlington Cemetery?? (Response)
T: That's right. (Evaluation) And what might you see at that tomb? (Initiation)
S: There's always a guard of honor there. (Response)
T: Yes. (Evaluation) Do you remember what is interesting about this guard? (Initiation)

S: Uh, uh, no. (Failed response)
T: Someone else? (Implied evaluation, initiation)
S2: He's a member of the Old Guard. Really hard to get into the Old Guard. (Response)
T: Correct. (Evaluation) What else is at Arlington Cemetery? (Initiation)
S: President Kennedy's grave. (Response)
T: Anything else? (Implied acceptance, initiation)
S: President Kennedy's brother's grave. It's over the hill a little bit down from the turning flame. (Response)
T: Eternal flame. (Implied evaluation) Yes, near President Kennedy's grave. (Evaluation)

The teacher initiates an interaction, often with a question; the student responds; and the teacher evaluates the response before making another initiation. We are certain all readers can recall many such interactions during their schooling. How pervasive initiate-response-evaluation (IRE) sequences are became clear with Mehan's (1979) classic analysis of classroom lessons. Teachers and students know how to interact with each other in this way. For example, teachers send clear nonverbal signals to students that such a sequence of questioning is about to begin and that student responses are expected, nonverbal signals that a teacher's students understand very well (see Cazden, 1988, Chapter 3).

Cazden sees such interactions as part of classroom management. To the extent that students do not have to think much about nonacademic aspects of their interactions (i.e., they know what is expected of them in IRE cycles because of participating in so many cycles during a school year), their attention can be to the content of the academic conversation. Moreover, it is possible for teachers to go through a lesson in an orderly fashion and make certain the points he or she considers important are "covered." The main motivation for many traditional classroom conversations is to cover a vast amount of content rather than to air alternative perspectives on the content being covered (e.g., Alvermann, O'Brien, & Dillon, 1990) and is a tendency that is difficult for teachers to overcome even if they attempt to do so (Alvermann & Hayes, 1989).

Some of the negatives of such interactions are apparent, however. For example, questioning often tends to be lower level, filled with literal, factual questions. (Recall this was a criticism of direct instruction, and, of course, direct instruction is filled with IRE cycles.) Because only one student can be active at a time, this is a passive approach to learning for many students (for analysis, see Bowers & Flinders, 1990, Chapter 5). We suspect many readers remember such conversations as boring. Such criticisms resurface again and again in discussions of IREs (e.g., Cazden, 1988, Chapter 3).

For those who prefer students learning to control their thinking (and, of course, many if not most educators embrace such a goal), such recitation structures are particularly unattractive, for IRE cycles are almost completely teacher controlled. This is one aspect of these interactions that some sociolinguists (i.e., scientists who study social factors in communications) consider to be particularly objectionable. Sociolinguists argue that how teachers interact with students and how dialogues are structured send powerful messages to students. In particular, the IRE structure provides teachers with many more options than students, rendering students powerless to do anything except bidding to answer and then answering questions that they had no part in formulating (Bowers & Flinders, 1990, Chapter 5). Students are being sent the message that education is receiving knowledge from an authority rather than working with knowledge to understand it in ways that are personally meaningful and in fashions that engender new knowledge. We believe, as do many others, that the message to send to students is that knowledge is something that is actively constructed by people just like them (and including them) rather than received from an external authority. Fortunately, there are other ways of dialoguing in school than IRE cycles. There is a great deal of contemporary interest in determining how to promote these alternatives to IRE cycles so as to empower teachers and students to participate in such discussions in ways that maximize educational benefits, including the construction of knowledge during academic discussions.

True Dialogues in School

In natural conversations, there are evolving meanings and real attempts to inform and persuade as participants try to understand what is going on. Consider the following snippet of conversation author MP had with his wife over an upcoming schooling decision affecting their son:

MIKE: Did you call X School back? (Donna infers correctly that Mike is interested because this is a school he liked when he visited.)

DONNA: Yes, and we *are* going to go over for an interview . . . it's on the 23rd. I'll do that. (MP inferred that Donna wanted to make certain she can size up the school without MP present to highlight the features that excited him.)

MIKE: I feel bad because I'll be going to Chicago that day so I won't be able to take care of Tim at all. (Mike is trying to let her know that it is all right if she wants to go it alone for this interview.)

DONNA: What's in Chicago? (Change of topic, legitimately curious.)

MIKE: The basal publisher . . . (Mike consciously deciding to mention the business part of the trip as well as deciding to omit reference that he will be seeing some old friends on the trip as well and will probably be having a good time while Donna has a particularly hassled day.)

DONNA: I know you have to do these things. If you could keep the trip as short as possible I'd appreciate it . . . although I know it is often easier just to stay over night after completing business. (Donna correctly inferring that Mike is going to have a good time, explicitly designing a comment to guilt trip him a bit but at the same time not make a big deal out of what she knows he will do no matter what she says.)

What a lot going on here! Two people who are very familiar with one another, including each other's habits and dispositions as well as biases and opinions, made powerful inferences based on prior knowledge, going well beyond the surface level of the conversation. There was strategy here motivated by particular goals (e.g., Mike was motivated to keep Donna from getting ticked off, as she might if he made it clear that he was going to be having a good time as she spent the day juggling the school interview, Tim, and her job). The particular choice of wording involved coordinating Mike's prior knowledge and Donna's prior knowledge with metacognition about which rhetorical tactics have worked in the past. Strategy, knowledge, metacognition, and motivation are all at work here—the same four elements emphasized since Chapter 1 of this book—with the outcome the type of outcome valued throughout this book: Both participants learned quite a bit from the conversation.

The Nature of More Natural Classroom Dialogues

The analysis of the Mike-Donna conversation makes it easy to see why educators believe that conversations more natural than IRE cycles might go far in promoting learning in school. There are four important structural differences between "natural" classroom conversations and Mike's chat with Donna, however (see Cazden, 1988, Chapter 4, for some of these): (1) More people are typically involved. (2) Although students and teachers often know each other well, many of the relationships in the group will not even approximate the intimacy of knowledge shared by Mike and Donna. (3) One of the players in the classroom conversation is often someone who is much more knowledgeable and has the resources to exert control if he or she wishes—that is, of course, the teacher. (4) The topic of discussion shifts within narrower boundaries in instructional conversations. So if the discussion of the day is about dinosaurs, it stays on dinosaurs rather than switching to how the local baseball team is doing. Natural conversations are much more far-ranging, as with Mike and Donna's conversation starting with comments about Tim's school and switching to a discussion of the Chicago trip.

Example of a Naturalistic Academic Conversation
Although study of more natural academic conversations is an emerging area of research, it is already clear that students and teachers in interaction can create conversations in which the teacher is much less in control, with the comments of students stimulating other students to participate in real interactions. Consider this example of conversation generated as kindergarten students and teacher discuss the story, "Tico and the Golden Wings," by Leo Lionni:

TEACHER: I don't think it's fair that Tico has to give up his golden wings.
LISA: It is fair. See, he was nicer when he didn't have any wings. They didn't like him when he had gold.
WALLY: He thinks he's better if he has golden wings.
EDDIE: He is better.
JILL: But he's not supposed to be better. The wishing bird was wrong to give him those wings.
DEANNA: She has to give him his wish. He's the one who shouldn't have asked for golden wings.
WALLY: He could put black wings on top of the golden wings and try to trick them.
DEANNA: They'd sneak up and see the gold. He should give every bird one golden feather and keep one for himself.
TEACHER: Why can't he decide for himself what kind of wings he wants?

WALLY: He has to decide to have black wings.
(Cazden, 1988, p. 55, from a lesson taught in Vivian Paley's kindergarten class)

What a difference from IRE cycles! The students did not raise their hands to participate. The teacher did not evaluate their responses and decide who would next get a turn to answer a question. What happened instead is that these children applied their prior knowledge to this story and interpreted it. It is a good bet that the individual students reading alone would not have come up with many of the interpretations that emerged during the discussion and a certain bet that no one reader would have thought of all the counterarguments that were put on the table. There were so many **elaborations** of student knowledge and **inferences** in this few minutes of conversation. Many educational theorists are now thinking about the implications of encouraging such conversations in school.

Distributed Nature of Cognition in Naturalistic Classroom Conversations One of the most important analyses of naturalistic instructional conversations is that they are excellent examples of **distributed cognition**. The cognition—the thinking—that goes on here is not a product of one head but a product of *several heads in interaction* with one another (e.g., Bereiter, 1990; Hutchins, 1991). By heads coming together in such a fashion, it is likely that extremely powerful interpretations and understandings will emerge. First, the different heads have different prior knowledge. Moreover the different heads have attended to different aspects of the information being considered. As the talk in the group proceeds, connections are made. Something Susie says connects with knowledge activated in Billy, who in turn responds. In doing so, Billy may combine some of what he knows in common with Susie and something Susie said that he did not know previously to produce a new inference. This inference might trigger something in Tommy, and so it goes.

What does the teacher do in all of this? He or she provides conversational starters and perhaps nudges the group one way or another with questions, as the kindergarten teacher did in the example. Those who study such groups (such as Hutchins, 1991) recognize that a powerful figure in a group can do much to shape the group opinion. One of the challenges for the teacher is to shape the group opinion to get some messages that are particularly important across to students but not to shape so much as to stifle creatively constructive and appropriate interpretations. This may be a difficult role for many teachers, especially those accustomed to IRE cycles during which they are in control of what happens in the group as well as the information that will receive positive evaluation. Electing to conduct real dialogues is electing to give up some of what has been a teacher's traditional power.

Let us now diverge for two paragraphs to point out how such research is making contact with one of the more abstract theoretical ideas developed earlier in Chapter 3. Hutchins's (1991) research has to do with applying connectionist models to the study of interaction in conversations. Thus, it is possible to construct simulations on computers in which all participants (computer-simulated minds) in a group have similar prior knowledge or all have different knowledge. That is, a computer program is constructed with group members, each of whom has a set of connections. Then a problem for discussion that connects with some parts of these knowledge bases is given to the "group members" for "discussion." It is possible to figure out much about the dynamics of the discussion and how an interpretation evolves from running such a program. The outcome differs, for instance, if the programming was done by a group of equipotent peers versus a group that has one figure more powerful than others (e.g., such as a teacher). Some of Hutchins's simulations seem to capture what happens when humans interact and discuss, and thus we think there are important implications of connectionist models of knowledge for research on classroom communications.

Consider an example. What if everyone does come to the group with the same knowledge—the same connections, to use the term preferred by many neural network theorists. What a connectionist model predicts is that a group interpretation will emerge quickly once "discussion" begins and that interpretation will not change, and that is what happens when an artificial intelligence program is run in which "everybody" thinks alike. When computer-simulated people think differently, conclusions do not come nearly so rapidly as those minds interact, with many more novel inferences.

The idea that cognition can be distributed across members of a group, with novel interpretations reached when the group members enter into **transactions** with one another, has been of great interest to organizational psychologists (e.g., Levine & Moreland, 1991; Schrage, 1990, provided a nice pop-

ular summary; Wegner, 1987). No one in an organization can know everything about it. Parts of the organization come together and combine their expertise to arrive at solutions for problems, solutions that could not be produced by anyone working alone.

Thus, author CM is currently working on getting a proposal through her university. There was a meeting with an associate dean, a dean, a department chair, and several members of CM's department. They came up with a plan, with the associate dean adding elements that would salve the central administration of the university, department members putting a spin on the plan so that other departmental colleagues would feel comfortable with the proposal, and the department chair and dean offering their input designed to keep the other departments in the college subdued. Thinking was definitely distributed across the group. We offer this example because it is one that has proved compelling to other professors who want to understand the nature of **socially distributed cognition** or what is sometimes called **socially shared cognition** (Resnick, Levine, & Teasley, 1991)—committee work is socially shared and involves cognition, although there is a single product. The point is that this product never could have been crafted by any one of the minds on the committee thinking alone.

Effects of Naturalistic Academic Conversations—The Exercise of Distributed Cognition—on the Learning and Thinking of Individual Students Hatano and Inagaki (1991) provided important research substantiating the educational potential of interpretive discussion. Their starting premise was that a group of students interacting would understand a problem at a high level as a group. The issue for Hatano and Inagaki was whether the processing carried out by the group would transform the thinking of the individuals in the group. Specifically, Hatano and Inagaki explored an instructional procedure developed by another Japanese educator, Itakura (1967), a method referred to as hypothesis-experiment-instruction: The pupils are presented a question with several alternative answers. Each pupil chooses what they believe to be the correct answer, followed by a show of hands to determine how the various members of the group thought. The pupils then explain and discuss their choices, followed by another opportunity for individual students to select the correct answer. Pupils then have an opportunity to test their alternative by observing an experiment pertaining to the problem posed or by reading a passage concerning the problem. Here is how one teacher initiated such a sequence:

> Mr. Shoji started the lesson with a question: "Suppose that you have a clay ball on one end of a spring. You hold the other end of the spring and put half of the clay ball in water. Will the spring (a) become shorter, (b) become longer, or (c) retain its length. (Hatano & Inagaki, 1991, p. 337, based on an example from Inagaki, 1981)

Before the discussion, 12 children in the group selected (a), 8 selected (b), and 14 selected (c). The discussion clearly shifted individual student understanding, as evident by second attempts at the problem. This time 21 students selected the correct alternative, (a), with 5 selecting (b) and 8 selecting (c). The shifts to response (a) were almost certainly mediated by arguments presented during the discussion. Consider the following arguments in favor of alternative (a) made by supporters of response (a):

> [To a student who had selected (c)]: Your opinion is strange to me. You said, "The weight of the clay will not change because it is only half immersed in water." But you know, when a person's head is above the water, his weight is lighter in water.
>
> I don't agree with the idea that the clay ball is as heavy in water as in air. I think that water has the power to make things float.
>
> If the clay is a very small lump, I think the water can make it float. (Hatano & Inagaki, 1991, p. 338, based on an example from Inagaki, 1981)

Although shifts in perspective following such arguments are supportive of the position that opportunities to participate in group discussions can shift the thinking of individual students in the group, Hatano and Inagaki (1991) wanted more analytical information and, in particular, wanted to know if individual students' reasoning shifted as a function of participation in group discussions. That is, shifts in choices might reflect some change in understanding but not change sufficient to permit students to articulate why they changed their minds. Being able to explain why one has changed an opinion is a much more impressive accomplishment than simply changing an opinion. (The Inagaki, 1981, result is reminiscent of the conformity training reviewed in Chapter 7—when nonconserving children interact with conserving children on a conservation problem, they shift from claiming that the amount of a substance changes with a perceptual

transformation to the position that the amount of something does not vary with perceptual transformations that do not involve adding or subtracting something.)

In Inagaki and Hatano (1989), fifth-graders read a passage about animal characteristics and lifestyles. Lions and moles were discussed as examples. Then the students were given a multiple-choice problem about the characteristics of a monkey, such as, "Do the thumbs of monkeys' forefeet oppose the other 'fingers' (like in human hands) or extend in parallel to other 'fingers' (like in human feet)? How about the thumbs of their hind feet?": (a) the thumbs are never opposing; (b) the thumbs are opposing only in the forefeet; or (c) the thumbs are opposing in both the fore and hind feet (pp. 341–342). [(c) was the correct response.] The students in a group discussion condition first made a choice individually, followed by group discussion, followed by a second opportunity to respond to the question. The students then read a passage that provided the correct answer but did not provide an explanation about why the answer might be correct. Students in the control condition made an initial choice of an answer and then read the passage containing the answer.

The most interesting outcome in this experiment was that the subjects in the group discussion condition provided more elaborate defenses of their answers, when prompted to do so, than did control students. Moreover, those subjects who had talked more during the discussion provided more elaborate answers than subjects who had talked less. In short, the data in this study converged to support the position that participating in the group discussions promoted learning by the individual participants in the group.

Confidence in Hatano and Inagaki's (1991) outcome is high because it complements a growing correlational and experimental literature documenting that when students in groups construct explanations about information they are learning, their acquisition and understanding of information are more certain. For example, Webb (see 1989, for a review) has conducted a number of studies in which students solved problems as group members. The students who did the explaining in the groups learned more (as determined by measures of individual achievement) than did students who were content to listen. Anderson, Wilkinson, and Mason (1991) observed that grade-3 students learned most during reading group when they were reading aloud and answering teacher's questions.

Although there are alternative explanations for the effects reported by Hatano, Inagaki, and Webb than that they reflect the positive effects of generating explanations (e.g., more able students might be expected to lead group discussions), such alternative explanations do not apply to experiments conducted by Alison King (e.g., 1989) and her colleagues. In King's studies, students have talked about to-be-learned content in groups. In some conditions of her experiments, subjects are taught how to generate thought-provoking questions by providing them with question frames with open slots. Thus, students are encouraged to generate questions over the content using frames such as the following: How would you use ____ to ____? What is a new example of ____? Explain why ____. How does ____ affect ____? Do you agree or disagree with this statement? Such question frames do stimulate discussions that involve considerable interaction and generation of new ideas, more so than if students are involved in unstructured discussion of content. In addition, learning of the to-be-learned content is improved when students are taught to use the question frames to structure discussion. See Pressley, Wood, Woloshyn, Martin, King, and Menke (1992) for a review of the relevant literature.

In summary, group discussions can result in ideas related to content that would not have occurred to individual members of the group working alone. If learning is the goal, content seems to be better learned through group interaction, particularly if the situation is structured so there is substantial participation by each member, as in the studies reported by Hatano and Inagaki (1991) and those conducted by King. That the structure of discussion groups may be particularly critical for productive discussions that lead to new ideas and increase learning by the group has been a theme in theoretical analyses of interpretive discussions. Although the research literature pertaining to how group structure can affect thinking and learning is thin at present, there is a rich body of hypotheses emerging, ones that we believe will be evaluated extensively in the coming years.

Factors Promoting Effective Academic Discussions

Haroutunian-Gordon (1991) has offered a particularly reflective analysis of factors that can inhibit and promote productive classroom conversations. One way to stifle interaction is for the teacher to believe that there are certain issues, perspectives, or opinions that must emerge during the group discussion—that any reasonable discussion would cover particular points! Haroutunian-Gordon refers to conversations in which the teacher attempts too much to control the discussion as "phony conversations." Although it is appropriate for teachers to steer such conversations gently so students stay on topic, interpretive discussions at their best probably involve issues that the students value and ideas that the students find intriguing. Discussions around such issues have a much better chance of being perceived as "genuine" (Haroutunian-Gordon, 1991, Chapter 5) by students.

Often tension develops, however, because interpretations that the teacher believes are important do not get out on the floor and others that the teacher might consider to be misinterpretations are embraced by the group! Consider a discussion between Haroutunian-Gordon and Ms. Spring about the progress of a discussion group they are "leading" about Shakespeare's *Romeo and Juliet:*

S: What is to be done if the students leave this classroom with an erroneous vision of the play and Shakespeare's message? What have they learned in such a class?

H-G: Well, one thing we can say is that they have begun to do the job that they are supposed to do when reading the play, right? They have begun to construct a story that allows them to connect the events in the play to one another in a meaningful way. That means they will remember those events, that the story they use to connect them will allow them to bring the events up so as to, perhaps at some point, connect them to their lives.

S: Yes, but that story about Benvolio was all wrong—

H-G: Wrong? By what criteria? It is not your story–

S: It is not Shakespeare's story!

H-G: Well perhaps not, I agree. But is yours Shakespeare's story?

S: Look, I don't claim to have any corner on his views. What I do know is that those two girls have made an interpretation of Benvolio that cannot really stand up to the text in its entirety.

H-G: You may well be right about that. But don't they now have a view to modify at least? And won't there be another class tomorrow?

S: Yes, but the question is, what should I do then? I can't tell them the truth, as we said a long time ago. They won't hear it. And they won't entertain conflicting evidence—that much we have seen.

They even resist the questions I ask to get them to rethink their perspectives.

H-G: Maybe you ought to forget about Edna and Abby. Maybe things will straighten out.

S: Maybe. But what they need is a new perspective on Benvolio, another way of looking at him.

Many interesting points are raised in this conversation. Haroutunian-Gordon clearly thought that students were getting a lot from the class discussions in learning that people should read plays critically and interpretively. A theme that will be reiterated in Chapter 14 is that such discussions have high potential for increasing student understanding that intellectual activity is crucial for learning, understanding, and problem solving. Interpretive class discussions will be difficult for teachers to the extent that they fail to accept that there are alternative interpretations and that their own interpretations may be inadequate. Once such discussions get going, it will be difficult for many students to accept the validity of "standard" interpretations because they will have begun to discover the many alternative ways of looking at the content.

One of the clearest messages in the Haroutanian-Gordon (1991) book is that it takes a while for a group of students to be able to engage in interpretive discussion. Years of participating in IRE cycles have not prepared students for this! In addition, it may take a while for the students to make interesting inferences regarding new content. Thus, it was several sessions before the students in Ms. Spring's and Haroutunian-Gordon's *Romeo and Juliet* discussion group were making sophisticated comments about the play, ones reflecting deep understanding about the characters and their situation. How sensible, however! It is difficult to make sophisticated interpretations until one has sufficient background knowledge, the type of background built up in the first act or two of a play.

Perhaps one of the most important points raised by Haroutunian-Gordon (1991) is how critical it is to get students to relate their personal knowledge to academic content. Interpretive discussions permit mixing of each student's personal understandings with information in the text. This is also a theme that will come up again in this textbook, and it is directly related to schema theory, covered in Chapter 3. People come to understand new content through the schemata they already possess. Finding similarities between new content and what one knows already

produces deep understanding (see Chapter 10 discussion on understanding as a means to learn).

Organizational psychologists, who study how committees of people function and how productive collaborations proceed, provide important insights as to factors that make it more likely that interpretive discussions will fare well (e.g., see Schrage's, 1990, summary): A cooperative outlook rather than a competitive one must be fostered. Things go better when it is clear that it is all right to take risks and that there is no "right" answer but rather a variety of alternative possibilities (e.g., alternative interpretations, alternative ways to solve a problem)—when participants know that the goal of the discussion is to consider and argue about alternatives as well as to adapt the various possibilities that are considered. Discussion is not for deciding who has the best idea but for the group to take ideas that are on the floor and to pick and choose strengths and weaknesses until a consensual point of view begins to emerge. Candor is valued in such groups more than politeness, when politeness is construed as not being contentious. Such candor is possible because there is trust, trust that nonsupportive comments are not personal insults but simply directed at the ideas under consideration. These are academic arguments rather than personal disputes.

Some physical environments are more conducive to collaborative dialogue than others. Thus, productive classroom discussions often take place around a table or with students in a circle, so it is easy to watch and listen to the speaker who has the floor as well as to monitor reactions from others to the ideas now being discussed.

Potential Problems with Real Classroom Dialogues

Giving up control, including assurance that standard interpretations will be aired, is an insurmountable difficulty for some teachers. In addition, there are no small numbers of teachers and administrators who are concerned that collaborative dialogues do not force individual students to think on their own. In the current educational accountability system, most student achievement is measured by testing individual students working alone. In addition, many forms of standardized testing tap standard interpretations and understandings. Recall the earlier discussion of the cultural literacy movement (Chapter 4). If students are held accountable for standard interpretations and particular pieces of information, many would argue that schooling that emphasizes discussion undermines student achievement because discussion does not guarantee coverage of the sanctioned perspectives and key factual content. Another concern voiced by some parents is that cooperative, collaborative discussions hold back the "best" students in the class—that they spend their time in interaction with weaker students. These parents believe their talented children are getting little from the interactions, whereas the weaker students are getting quite a bit.

Reasons for Dismissing the Potential Concerns
Collaborative discussion is an exceptionally important form of instruction, one definitely acceptable (in fact, preferred) by students as a way to learn (e.g., Thorkildsen, 1989, 1991). From a Vygotskian perspective, the opportunities to participate in groups that dialogue about important content should have profound long-term effects on cognitive development. The Vygotskian theory is that opportunities to engage in interpersonal problem-solving and thinking stimulate the development of personal problem solving and thinking skills, in that many of the processes that the group carries out together eventually are internalized by individual members of the group. That is, there are long-term cognitive advantages from years of arguing with others about important ideas, reflecting as a group on strengths and weaknesses of proposals, elaborating as a group the good ideas of group members and rejecting the bad ones. Eventually the participant in such a group can construct arguments for himself or herself and has gotten in the habit of reflecting on ideas.

In addition, much of mature thinking is collaborative thinking (Resnick et al., 1991; Schrage, 1990). Flying an airliner requires several minds in collaboration to produce a safe flight. Controlling a large ship requires many more minds in interaction. Surgeons, anesthesiologists, and nurses think together to perform a complicated surgery. Innovative new products are not the inventions of individuals but the result of teamwork and groups of people reflecting and thinking together to create a better idea than any one of them could have produced on their own. Given the value of collaborative thinking in the modern world, it makes sense to foster such thinking in schools.

Although most student assessment is individual assessment, that is not to say that assessments of collaborative thinking could not be developed. Indeed, some of the new performance assessments are ex-

actly of this type (see Chapter 17). Given the many advantages of collaborative thinking, it would be exceptionally foolish to sacrifice such instruction because it does not mesh with current tests.

Finally, we definitely do not believe that better students are disadvantaged by interactions with other students varying in competency. First, the data from researchers such as Webb and King make obvious that there are clear advantages from opportunities to explain to others. In addition, there is a large literature on tutoring going back to the 1970s (see Allen, 1976) establishing that when stronger and weaker students are placed in interaction with one another, as during tutoring, both tutor and tutee benefit—that is, both the stronger and the weaker students learn from interactions involving stronger and weaker students. In fact, the stronger student often gets more out of the interaction than the weaker student (see Chapter 11 discussion of peer tutoring).

Summary All things considered, it is difficult not to be enthused about involving students in interpretive discussions with one another. General thinking skills are probably encouraged, and there is often increased learning of the specific content covered in such discussions. That does not mean, however, that it is well understood how to conduct such groups at present or that if the goal is to teach some particular content, it is certain the content will be learned as intended.

Eichinger, Anderson, Palincsar, and David (1991) reported a study of collaborative discussion that did not do everything its designers had intended. The students were enrolled in a science course that used a series of lessons that involved presentation of problems that were solved by students considering and discussing a situation as a group. For example, one of the problems near the end of a unit on the three states of water was the following:

> Imagine you are a scientist who has been assigned to a team whose job is to build a space colony on the moon. Your group is given this task: the astronauts will need to take water with them for the space flight. You must decide whether the water should be taken in the form of a solid (ice), a liquid (water), or a gas (vapor) in order to take the greatest amount of water that has the least weight. You must decide which state of water is best and *you must give reasons for your answers.* Use what you have learned about water in the last few lessons to help you solve the problem. (Anderson et al., 1991, msp. 3)

Students in each group first considered the problem on their own and wrote down a solution, which they brought to a discussion group. The group's task was to come to a consensus with supporting reasons, with about 20 minutes allocated for this. Anderson et al. (1991) analyzed in detail the dialogues in one group of students given the problem about the form of water that should be taken into space. In general, much went well in this group: Although none of the five students participating in the group arrived at group with a particularly good rationale for taking one form of water versus another, the group generated a sophisticated argument, one that was agreeable to all five group members by the end of the discussion. The students were able to defend their choice of liquid as a preferred state for space travel, based on volume considerations. During the discussion, some misconceptions were corrected as well.

Close analysis of the dialogue revealed some disturbing properties to the exchange, however. First, although this was near the end of the unit consisting of a series of such exercises involving states of water, most of the students in the group did not appear to be facile in applying ideas about weight, volume, and molecular properties in the discussion. There were misconceptions expressed in the discussions—ones flying in the face of ideas covered during the unit. Use of terms was anything but precise. Although a sophisticated argument developed in the group, when the individual students had to write out a reason for their belief that liquid was the appropriate state for space travel, the reasons they provided were far less compelling than the best arguments of the group—raising the question of how much conceptual growth had occurred for individual students during the interaction. Finally, all five members in the group did not have equally high-quality educational experiences as group participants. The students who were articulate and intellectually aggressive participated more and received more feedback.

We close this subsection by reflecting on what happened in the group Anderson et al. (1991) described and what such an interaction tells us as educational psychologists about more naturalistic academic discussions. First, there is a great deal of need to study carefully in the coming decade just what can be done to increase the quality of intellectual discussions, a prospect that is worth exploring because of

the potential of such discussion activities to stimulate long-term reasoning abilities and learning of content in the short term. Anderson et al. (1991) clearly shared this view, with their paper providing many suggestions as to potential mechanisms for increasing the quality of interaction during scientific dialogues, mechanisms they expected to explore in their own research. Second, that the students in Anderson et al. (1991) were not applying the content covered in the unit near the end of the unit, despite the participation in a number of previous problem-solving dialogues, points not so much to a difficulty with Anderson et al.'s (1991) instruction in particular but to the nature of education required for people to be able to apply what they have learned. Understanding concepts well enough to apply them to new situations requires extensive, elaborated knowledge of the concepts. Such knowledge requires long-term exposure and practice with concepts. Again and again in this book, the theme will be reiterated: Application, transfer, and creative use of what has been learned do not follow from short-term instruction. The development of powerful thinking and flexible use of knowledge is a long-term affair. Why focus on the structure of individual lessons then? Because it is a good bet that some types of individual lessons are more certainly going to lead to powerful thinking capacities and deeper understanding in the long term than are other arrangements. The many bits and pieces of evidence supporting the efficacy of true dialogues in classrooms that have been generated in research to date go far in suggesting that student dialoguing about content is one approach to individual lessons that may do much to foster impressive intellectual competence.

CONCLUDING COMMENTS

In presenting the argument in this chapter that much changed with the translation in 1978 of *Mind in Society*, we do not want to imply that Western researchers were completely oblivious to the potential impact of social interactional factors on cognitive development before that translation. In addition to the social learning theorists, who provided many experimental demonstrations in the early 1970s that children's thought could be affected by observations of and interactions with more competent others, there was much correlational data substantiating that growing up with parents who were responsive to their children's intellectual needs made a difference in intellectual outcome.

For example, Hess and Shipman (1965) found higher conceptual and linguistic functioning in children coming from homes in which parents encouraged their children to reflect before acting and to consider carefully before making choices. In homes producing more competent children, children were encouraged to size up a situation before acting rather than to apply a rigid rule. By the end of the 1960s, considerable evidence had amassed that some parents spent a great deal of time doing what is now thought of as scaffolding, providing children with intellectually engaging experiences, mediating these experiences so children were not frustrated as they dealt with appropriately challenging intellectual content (e.g., Hess, Shipman, & Jackson, 1965; Jensen, 1968; Katz, 1967). That is, some parents read books to their children and help their children come to understand the content of those books; they reason with their children about why it is necessary sometimes to stop and think before acting; they play counting games with their children, help them do the puzzles in children's magazines, and talk to them about important categories of experience (e.g., which animals can be seen at the zoo and which ones live on farms). Unfortunately, it is only some children who receive such input, with profound differences in cognitive development for those children who receive such scaffolding compared with those who do not.

Work in this tradition continued in the 1970s and 1980s (e.g., Laosa, 1978, 1980, 1982), with more demonstrations that some parents provide much more positive reinforcement and praise for their children than others, some ask more questions of their children, and some are more certain to assist their child in doing a task rather than simply doing the task for the child or leaving the task undone. Again, consistent correlations between such child-rearing behaviors, all of which are part of scaffolding, and intellectual outcomes were observed.

Other things equal, rank ordering of intellectual competence is going to favor children who have enjoyed sensitive intellectual input from parents and teachers. What theorists such as Vygotsky and Bakhtin suggest is that humans internalize cognitive processes first experienced in rich social situations—such as the favorable parent-child interactions just described—and that the ways of thinking in the surrounding social milieu become one's own ways of thinking. For that reason, it is important to do all possible to encourage parents to interact constructively with their children. (Recall the review of evidence in Chapter 6 about the efficacy of programs that encourage parent-child interactions for children at risk.) It is also important that school culture be a rich intellectual world. Thus, a value of reading groups in which children predict, ask questions about text content, seek clarifications when confused, and generate summaries is that eventually the individual members of the group predict, question, seek clarification, and summarize when they read. What happens when children can be apprentices to avid readers, real writers, and capable mathematicians in school? They come to think like real readers, real writers, and real mathematicians in that the apprentices learn to attack academic tasks as experts do; the apprentices come to talk like the experts; and the apprentices adopt the intellectual attitudes and preferences of the experts.

In this chapter, we reviewed a number of different social interactional approaches to instruction. In some of these (e.g., IRE cycles, direct instruction), if there is scaffolding of learning, those concerned with developing and studying the form of instruction paid scant attention to the scaffolding that goes on. In contrast, scaffolding is at the center of apprenticeship, reciprocal teaching, and direct explanation models of teaching and learning. We have already made the point that scaffolding requires detailed knowledge of the strengths and weaknesses of particular students and the potential misconceptions in the instructed domain. What we emphasize in closing is another dimension of difficulty that must be considered with respect to scaffolding.

Scaffolding is just plain hard work. Teachers must be tremendously motivated to do it. What is apparent to us is that some feminist scholars have hit on an important instructional ingredient not touched on in this book thus far, an ingredient that is essential if teachers are going to be willing to do the hard work that is scaffolded instruction. They have to care about their students (e.g., Noddings, 1984, especially Chapter 8). Noddings discusses how caring is at the center of a teacher-student apprenticeship situation and that this is a wonderful and fulfilling situation for the teacher:

... The teacher works with the student. He becomes her apprentice and gradually assumes greater responsibility in the tasks they undertake. This working together, which produces both joy in the relation and increasing competence in the cared-for ... needs the cooperative guidance of a fully caring adult.... The ... caring ... teacher ... has two major tasks: to stretch the student's world by presenting an effective selection of that world with which she is in contact, and to work cooperatively with the student in his struggle toward competence in that world. (pp. 177–178)

Throughout Noddings' discussion is the necessity of the teacher caring for the student, and she recognizes how difficult it is to do, so difficult that many believe it cannot be part of teaching:

> The sort of relatedness and caring I have been discussing is often dismissed as impossible [for the teacher] because of constraints of number, time, and purpose. Richard Hult, in his discussion of "pedagogical caring," notes that such requirements seem to require in turn close personal relationships.... He says, "While these may sometimes occur and may be desirable, most pedagogical contexts make such relationships implausible if not undesirable." He concludes that caring ... "cannot be the kind of caring demanded of teachers." I insist that it is exactly the kind of caring ideally required of teachers. (p. 179)

What fascinated us in reading Noddings (1984, Chapter 8) is that so many of the themes discussed in this chapter are there. She urges teachers to give up some of their control and to foster trust between them and their students. She urges true dialogue and argues that it promotes deep contact with the ideas presented in the curriculum and stimulates the development of an active thinker. Noddings urges dialogical situations that permit and encourage students to take intellectual risks. But sensitive teaching that includes caring does something else that has not been covered henceforth: it passes on an ethic of caring for others to the next generation.

We closed this chapter with Noddings to emphasize how frequently the main ideas in this chapter are encountered. Remember how we made the case earlier that many of the Vygotskian ideas overlap with behaviorist models of education as well as Piagetian thinking about the stimulation of cognitive development. That such ideas also resonate with feminist scholars should make apparent their broad appeal. Ideas such as scaffolding, apprenticeship, teaching in the zone of proximal development, and dialoguing ought to receive much more attention from educational practitioners and researchers. Many educational theorists have come to the conclusion that these are powerful concepts that should be applied during instruction—there is theoretical triangulation here (Mathison, 1988), with Soviets in the early 20th century, American behaviorists in the mid-1900s, and feminists with an eye on the 21st century all professing faith in the advantages of matching instruction to student competence, providing just enough input so educational progress occurs for every student. This will not be easy, but if we care about our children, it is a conceptually sound route to effective education that increases the likelihood of academic success for many children.

In Chapter 9, we will conclude our sojourn through the grand theories of educational psychology. We will encounter there as well some extremely important feminist ideas about education, ones that prompt reflection on some traditional notions of education, including whether theoretical commitment to biological inevitabilities (e.g., the logical inevitability of cognitive stage progression in a particular order according to a rationalistic-biological-universal conception of thinking and development) may blind educators and researchers to important social determinants of thought. Consistent with the decision to feature more biologically deterministic theories first in this discussion of grand theories (i.e., in Chapter 7 more than in Chapters 8 or 9), the ultimate conclusions reached in Chapter 9 will be that the social environment is an important determinant of the quality of thought. Just as was the case in this chapter, however, there will always be the message that there is something humanly universal about social forces as determinants of mind—that somehow we are hard-wired to be susceptible to such forces, and thus biological and social determinants of cognitive advance are inextricably intertwined.

9

Preparing Students to Think Responsibly About Difficult Social Problems

Some young Americans personally will confront issues such as whether to have an abortion or give birth to a child. Many in our generation made decisions about whether or not to fight in a war they viewed as unjust. The day comes for many people when they discover a serious dishonesty perpetrated by a friend, perhaps even a criminal act, with a decision required about whether or not to report the offense. As youth mature, they increasingly take on roles that require them to solve societal problems: Some will sit on school boards balancing the needs of teachers for higher salaries against those of parents demanding more neighborhood schools; some will help decide if it is right that younger employees be cut first when there is a budget crisis in their firm; some will join with other jury members to determine the fate of another individual that they have just judged to have committed a serious crime. As a society, we want young people to emerge from school ready to make such decisions responsibly. Such responsibility is a valued outcome, and many agree that educating students to be socially responsible should be a central mission of schooling (e.g., Wentzel, 1991a, 1991b). A big bonus from the perspective of this book is that education for responsibility can contribute to cognitive development, with this a major theme in this chapter.

Knowing how to read, write, and calculate can sometimes help with social decision making, but such knowledge is not sufficient to tackle the moral dilemmas that await each generation, not sufficient to ensure responsible thinking about important social issues that cannot even be imagined during a person's student years. For example, middle-aged readers will recognize that there was no ozone crisis, AIDS epidemic, Dr. Kevorkian, or organ transplants during their student years. The social issues that will fill the pages of *Time* and *Newsweek* in 2005 are anybody's guess, but somehow we must prepare youth to be ready to think about those issues and make decisions with respect to them. Fortunately, although development of academic competencies is not sufficient to ensure social responsibility, there are strong correlations (e.g., Hanson & Ginsburg, 1988; Wentzel, 1991a, 1991b) between academic competence and social responsibility, suggesting that there is nothing incompatible about academic education and education for societal responsibility.

There is substantial theory and research on complex, socially responsible problem solving. A great deal of the most credible theory-driven research on social problem solving was generated in reaction to Lawrence Kohlberg's analyses of moral judgment.

DEVELOPMENT AND EDUCATION OF MORAL JUDGMENT ACCORDING TO KOHLBERG'S THEORY: A COGNITIVE-DEVELOPMENTAL APPROACH IN THE TRADITION OF PIAGET

Kohlberg advanced two important theories of moral judgment. One is a largely descriptive theory of the different stages of moral reasoning. The other is a theory about how to advance moral reasoning through the stages, a theory of moral education. The developmental theory was proposed and studied first and logically must be understood before the educational theory is presented. Before Kohlberg, however, there was another developmentalist with an enduring perspective on moral judgment—Jean Piaget.

Piaget's Theory of the Development of Moral Reasoning

Piaget's (1965) theory of the development of moral judgment was informed by his observations of children playing games, especially marbles. Naturally, there were some conflicts over rules as play proceeded. Piaget formulated hypotheses about children's moral understandings based on children playing by the rules, cheating, and changing rules. He then tested these hypotheses by asking children to reason for him about social dilemmas that he presented to them as short stories ending in a question. One of the more famous of these dilemmas involved children reasoning about whether a child who accidentally broke 15 cups was naughtier than one who intentionally broke 1 cup. Piaget eventually proposed a two-stage developmental description of two types of morality he had observed on the playgrounds and heard about in interviews, one reflecting the conceptions about rules held by preschoolers and children in the early primary years (stage of heteronomous morality) and the other reflecting the thinking of older children about rules (stage of autonomous morality).

Heteronomous and autonomous moralities differ from one another qualitatively. The heteronomously moral child focuses on the "objective" consequences of an action and thus concludes that the child breaking 15 cups is naughtier because more cups were destroyed by that child than by the one who intentionally broke 1 cup. In contrast, the autonomously moral child makes decisions based on the intentions of the actors, therefore concluding

that breaking one cup intentionally is much worse than accidentally destroying many more cups. The heteronomously moral child respects and obeys those in control, those with the power. The autonomously moral child plays fairly (i.e., according to the rules) with other children, recognizing that the rules have been agreed on by the players, that obeying the rules of the game is a form of social contract. The heteronomous child views rules as sacred, as if they were written by the finger of God, never to be reconsidered. The autonomously moral child recognizes that rules are inventions of people and can be changed if people will it.

Similar to all Piagetian stages, there is an invariant order of development: The child must manifest heteronomous morality before autonomous morality. As is the case for all of cognitive development according to the Piagetian perspective (see Chapter 7), equilibration (cognitive conflict) is the main mechanism of cognitive change (i.e., movement from heteronomous to autonomous morality). Conflicts with peers that stimulate cognitive conflict are especially helpful (e.g., arguments about the rules of marbles). Such conflicts can be real mind stretchers, moving the child from viewing rules as given from above and inalterable to seeing them as agreements that the kids playing marbles can change by a show of hands or a chorus of protesting voices. Piaget's perspective that cognitive conflict was important in growth of moral thinking would be preserved in Kohlberg's theory, which elaborated and expanded the two stages of moral thinking favored by Piaget.

Kohlberg's Stage Theory

Kohlberg (e.g., 1969, 1981, 1984) posited progression through an invariant sequence of six stages. The first two of these are referred to as stages of **preconventional morality** because they represent thinking that is certainly not what would be acceptable to most adults. Stages three and four are **conventional morality,** representing the type of moral thought most typically observed in adults. Stages five and six, the stages of **post-conventional morality,** are reached by some but not all adults. Thus, the stages are invariant in that to get to stage four, one must go through stages one, two, and three. Achieving four, however, in no way guarantees achievement of five or six (nor does achieving two ensure further progress to three, or three to four).

In Kohlberg's original research establishing the stages, moral dilemmas in the form of stories were presented to adolescent boys and thus Kohlberg's main research tactic was similar to one used by Piaget. One of the most famous of Kohlberg's dilemmas involved a character named Heinz:

> In Europe, a woman was near death from a special kind of cancer. There was one drug that the doctors thought might save her. It was a form of radium that the druggist in the same town had recently discovered. The drug was expensive to make. He paid $400 for the radium and charged $4000 for a small dose of the drug. The sick woman's husband, Heinz, went to everyone he knew to borrow the money and tried every legal means, but he could only get together about $2000, which is half of what it cost. He told the druggist that his wife was dying, and ask him to sell it cheaper or let him pay later. But the druggist said, "No, I discovered the drug and I'm going to make money from it." So having tried every legal means, Heinz gets desperate and considers breaking into the man's store to steal the drug for his wife. (Kohlberg, 1984, p. 640)

An interview tapping a subject's thinking about the dilemma then occurred, which required the subject in the study to respond to the following questions:

1. Should Heinz steal the drug? 1a. Why or why not?
2. Is it actually right or wrong for him to steal the drug? 2a. Why is it right or wrong?
3. Does Heinz have a duty or obligation to steal the drug? 3a. Why or why not?
4. If Heinz doesn't love his wife, should he steal the drug for her? (If he favors not stealing the drug:) Does it make a difference in what Heinz should do whether or not he loves his wife? 4a. Why or why not?
5. Suppose the person dying is not his wife but a stranger. Should Heinz steal the drug for the stranger? 5a. Why or why not?
6. (If the subject favors stealing the drug for the stranger:) Suppose it's a pet animal that he loves. Should Heinz steal to save the pet animal? 6a. Why or why not?
7. Is it important for people to do everything they can to save another's life? 7a. Why or why not?
8. It is against the law for Heinz to steal. Does that make it morally wrong? 8a. Why or why not?
9. In general, should people do everything that they can to obey the law? 9a. Why or why not? 9b. How does this apply to what Heinz should do?
10. In thinking back over the dilemma, what would you say is the most responsible thing for Heinz to do? 10a. Why? (Kohlberg, 1984, pp. 640–641)

What mattered in the interview was not whether the subject thought Heinz should steal the drug but the reasons the subject gave for Heinz's actions, with the reasons varying from stage to stage. In stage one, the reasons focused on obedience and avoiding punishment. Staying out of trouble is the concern that is more important than all others for the stage one thinker, exemplified by these rationales (all stage rationale quotes from Kohlberg, 1984, Tables 1.5 and 1.6, pp. 49–53, based on data reported originally by Rest, 1968): In favor of stealing the drug: "If you let your wife die, you will get in trouble. You'll be blamed for not spending the money to save her and there'll be an investigation of you and the druggist for your wife's death." Of course, a case also can be made that the best way to stay out of trouble is not to steal the drug: "You shouldn't steal the drug because you'll be caught and sent to jail if you do. If you do get away, your conscience would bother you thinking how the police would catch up with you at any minute." The stage one thinker is worried only about protecting his or her own hide—avoiding punishment.

The stage two thinker is only a slight advance, concerned only about his or her own pleasures. What is right is what brings pleasure to the self. Self-interest comes through clearly in this stage two justification for stealing the drug: "If you do happen to get caught, you could give the drug back and wouldn't get much of a sentence. It wouldn't bother you much to serve a little jail term, if you have your wife when you get out." Self-interest can be used to justify not stealing as well: "He may not get much of a jail term if he steals the drug, but his wife will probably die before he gets out, so it wouldn't do him much good. If his wife dies, he shouldn't blame himself; it isn't his fault she has cancer." By now it should be obvious why stage one and two thinking is considered preconventional. Any adult offering such justifications would be viewed with horror by most other adults, who long ago rejected such narrow self-interest as legitimate in decision making.

The stage three thinker is sometimes thought of as displaying "good boy–good girl" thinking, concerned with helping and pleasing others. This is conformist thinking in the sense of wanting to go along with the majority. Although saccharine, we suspect most readers know people who might offer stage-three justifications. Consider this example in favor of stealing the drug: "No one will think you're bad if you steal the drug but your family will think you are an inhuman husband if you don't. If you let your wife die, you'll never be able to look anyone in the face again." The concern for the opinion of others comes through in this justification for not stealing the drug as well: "It isn't just the druggist who will think you're a criminal, everyone else will, too. After you steal it, you'll feel bad thinking how you've brought dishonor on your family and yourself; you won't be able to face anyone again." Something important to note is that this form of conventionality is decidedly not as advanced as stage four thinking according to Kohlberg's model. This is critical to remember because later we will take up an important dispute over Kohlberg's theory—whether Kohlberg's theory is sexist in part because stage three thinking, which some view as more consistent with women's way of thinking than men's approaches to morality, is considered less sophisticated than stage four thinking, which the critics claim is more consistent with men's perspective on the world than with women's approach to it.

Although the stage three conventional thinker is concerned with the subjective perceptions of others, the stage four thinker is concerned with being in synchrony with the codified standards of his or her society—stage four thinkers have a deep respect for law and order. The stage four thinker is concerned with doing his or her duty to country, God, spouse, or whatever else commands allegiance by societal standards. This rationalization in favor of stealing the drug in reaction to the Heinz dilemma is based on the perception of duty to family members that is expected by society: "If you have any sense of honor, you won't let your wife die because you're afraid to do the only thing that will save her. You'll always feel guilty that you caused her death if you don't do your duty to her." Consistency with the laws of society comes through in this opposition to stealing the drug offered by another stage four thinker: "You're desparate and you may not know you're doing wrong when you steal the drug. But you'll know you did wrong after you're punished and sent to jail. You'll always feel guilty for your dishonesty and law breaking."

After some experience with conventional thinking, some come to reject it. The stage five postconventional thinker views rules and laws in terms of a contract, which is intended to protect the will and rights of others. One enters into this contract and obeys rules as part of a social understanding, rather than because of fear of retribution, respect for authority, or sense of duty. If the social purpose for the rules cannot be fulfilled by obeying them, it is all right to dispense with the rules according to stage five thinkers, as reflected in this opinion in favor of Heinz stealing the drug: "The law wasn't set up for these circumstances. Taking the drug in this situation isn't really right, but it's justified to do it." The social contract orientation also comes through in this stage five advisement against stealing the drug: "You can't have everyone stealing when they get desperate. The end may be good, but the ends don't justify the means."

Although there was certainly room for debate over the adequacy of the data supporting stages one through five (e.g., Kurtines & Grief, 1974), without a doubt, the greatest challenges were launched at Kohlberg's proposals about a stage six. The stage six thinker did not compromise in respecting the sanctity of life and human freedom. Kohlberg especially was influenced by Rawls' (1971) *Theory of Justice* in his portrayal of the stage six thinker, who is described as the ultimately just individual, one who could rationally make decisions without taking self-interest into account. That is, stage six thinkers decided dilemmas as if they knew they were one of the characters in the dilemma but did not know which one they were, with the result that these just individuals attempted to make decisions that would be viewed as fair as possible by all parties. That this stage was hypothetical became obvious when Kohlberg admitted in print that there was no convincing evidence for it (see Kohlberg, Levine, & Hewer, 1983). This stage six conceptualization in terms of justice continues to be important, however, in that contemporary critics of Kohlberg point to his embrace of rationally determined justice as the highest of moral ideals to be narrow and specifically to reflect a masculine bias in his thinking.

Kohlberg and his colleagues argued that moral stage affects thinking with respect to many types of social problems. Over the years, the most popular illustrations with students in our classes about how moral stage affects thinking about social dilemmas were provided by Gilligan, Kohlberg, Lerner, and Belensky (1971; all quotes from this study based on selections made by Lickona, 1974, pp. 39–42). Gilligan and her colleagues asked high school juniors to reason about the morality of sexual relationships and identified stagelike differences in the reasoning of students in their reactions to dilemmas such as the following:

> A high school girl's parents are away for the weekend and she's alone in the house. Unexpectedly, on Friday evening, her boyfriend comes over. They spend the evening together in the house and after a while they start necking and petting: (1) Is this right or wrong? Why? Are there circumstances that would make it right or wrong? (2) What if they had sexual intercourse? Is that right or wrong? Why? (3) Does the way they feel about each other make a difference in the rightness or wrongness of having sexual intercourse? Why? What if they are in love? What does love mean and what is its relation to sex? (Gilligan et al., 1971, p. 151)

Some reactions reflected preconventional thinking, with its emphasis on rewards and avoidance of punishment: "There's nothing wrong with intercourse because I think people can do whatever they want," and "It would be wrong if they had intercourse without thinking about pregnancy—a child can cause a lot of trouble to high school kids" illustrate preconventional responses emphasizing reward and avoidance of punishment. There were good boy–good girl responses, reflecting stage three thinking: Stage three defenses for having sex included, "It's OK as long as you do it as an act of love rather than as an act of sex—if you do it with an emotional tie," and "It's someone you like to be with no matter what you do," and "Sex is part of showing you care. It should be for a special relationship." One stage three reason for abstaining from sex was, "You can get away with it, but you're not, like, clean anymore." The respect for authority, laws, and order that is stage four thinking comes through in this rationalization: "It would be wrong in our society—how will they fit in?" The social contract orientation of stage five was reflected in the following response: "Sex is OK if they are honest with each other, if they know each other's motives."

Here is another dilemma from the Gilligan et al. (1971) investigation:

> A boy and girl fall in love in high school and get married right after graduation. They have never had sexual relations before marriage. After they are married, the girl finds she doesn't like having sexual intercourse; it just makes her feel bad and she decides not to have intercourse with her husband. Was it right for the wife to do that? Would it be right for the husband to threaten separation? Seek a divorce? Have sexual relations with another girl that he meets? (Gilligan et al., 1971, p. 152)

The reinforcement perspective that typifies stage two thinking comes through clearly in this response to the dilemma: "She should give him sex; he has to earn the living." The goody-goody thinking of stage three is apparent in this analysis, "If she loves him, she would want to have sex; she's hurting him." One stage three justification in favor of extramarital sex was, "Maybe it will save their marriage and make them happier in the long run." Some stage four justifications emphasized the husband's "right in marriage" to sex. Postconventional thinking was reflected in responses suggesting that trust and loyalty were what really mattered, and the couple could agree to whatever arrangement they wanted to agree to. Gilligan et al. (1971) were able to provide a nice demonstration that there are differences in moral thinking with respect to moral dilemmas about sexual relations faced by most young people—that Kohlbergian stagelike thinking could be observed for more than just hypothetical dilemmas such as Heinz's problem with the druggist.

Before concluding this discussion of moral reasoning stages, a few points need to be made. Classifying a person into a stage was never clear cut, with many revisions of the Kohlberg scoring scheme. If you need evidence that the moral judgment interview approach produces ambiguous data, simply respond to the Heinz interview presented earlier. As you struggle attempting to classify the various responses you have to the dilemma, then realize that Heinz was one of nine dilemmas and interviews. Each interview resulted in a mass of data. It was not uncommon at all for subject protocols to reflect what became known as **stage mixture,** with the assignment of a subject to one particular stage based on the modal response category. Using the Kohlberg manuals, arriving at a diagnosis of someone's stage level took days and weeks of scoring in some cases!

Fortunately, others such as James Rest (see 1979; also Rest et al., 1986) and William Gibbs (Gibbs et al., 1984; Gibbs, Basinger, & Fuller, 1992; Gibbs & Widaman, 1982; Gibbs, Widaman, & Colby, 1982) validated adaptations of the moral judgment interview that could be scored reliably and more easily than the original Kohlberg instrument. As with the Kohlberg measure, within-person variability in responding was the norm, however, so that a person might offer stages three, four, and five responses across dilemmas, with stage mixture even for the same dilemma not uncommon. Stage mixture should be remembered because later in the chapter, when we take up the debate regarding possible sexism in Kohlberg's thinking, new evidence of how people's moral judgments can include a mix of rationale types will be presented. Readers should recall at that point that diverse reasoning is more the rule than the exception in reaction to moral dilemmas.

Another important point to emphasize in closing this discussion of Kohlberg's (e.g., 1984) stage theory is that Kohlberg believed that in coming to the postconventional stages, people acquired an understanding of the universal applicability of particular values. These values include the sanctity of human life, personal property, and civil liberties. Kohlberg's stage six thinker would never be able to justify the taking of a life (e.g., Kohlberg was profoundly opposed to capital punishment; Kohlberg & Elfenbein, 1976) and requires great justification for the denial of civil liberties. Kohlberg's confidence that identification with such positions reflected moral sophistication was bolstered by his understanding of the lives of exceptionally moral individuals, from Christ, Socrates, and St. Thomas More to Gandhi and Martin Luther King (e.g., Kohlberg & Power, 1981). All of these ultimate moral thinkers lived lives reflecting the universal values of life, liberty, and truthfulness, so much so that they were killed because of their commitments to such values.

Education and the Development of Moral Judgment

The scientific literature on moral education that accumulated in the 1960s until the early 1980s was competently summarized by Enright et al. (1983). They concluded as follows about two popular approaches to moral education:

1. One is to offer a philosophy course in ethics to students. Learning ethics as the philosophers think about the topic does not improve moral reasoning, at least not for long as measured by the Kohlberg reasoning instruments. Courses in social studies dealing with topics such as civil rights and overcoming prejudice do little for moral reasoning as well. Didactic instruction about moral behavior does not seem to affect people's abilities to reason in a sophisticated fashion about moral issues.
2. What works better is to have students discuss and reason about moral dilemmas—that is, for them to experience real cognitive conflict as part of discussions about moral issues. This is some-

times referred to as the **plus-one approach** because it results in each student being exposed to information from a stage beyond him or her, which is considered an optimally motivating discrepancy in Kohlbergian theory between current level of functioning and level of input to the student. Such an optimal discrepancy is likely to induce cognitive conflict, which will motivate reflection on the new information, reflection that often results in coming to understand the adequacy of the slightly more advanced position relative to the position currently held by the student (see Chapter 5, this volume).

The first and most famous study in the plus-one tradition was Blatt and Kohlberg (1975) with junior and senior high school students. The teacher presented moral dilemmas to students, who debated the pros and cons of various resolutions to the dilemmas. Although the teacher sometimes clarified and summarized arguments and challenged low-level reasoning, the teacher definitely did not provide a resolution to the dilemma. The moral discussions included a mixture of opinions, with some at a higher stage than others, so that everyone in the class was exposed to thinking at least a bit beyond them. (The teacher provided opinions in the discussion that were in advance of the most sophisticated student.) As was the case in a number of follow-up studies, students who participated in discussions of moral dilemmas reasoned at higher levels during moral judgment interviews than they did before experiencing the moral conflict discussions. Positive effects of plus-one moral reasoning discussions have been obtained both with short interventions—a single session—and long ones—full-semester courses (see Enright et al., 1983, for a summary).

Kohlberg was a man of great vision. One was to imagine large-scale environments—entire cultures—that would stimulate moral reflection. He believed that there was the potential for moral growth from community participation, in the sense of the traditional New England town meeting, participation that could be operationalized in schools and other institutions dedicated to improving their clients' thinking and morality. Thus, Kohlberg and his co-workers created "just communities" within the boundaries of institutional settings (see Power, Higgins, & Kohlberg, 1989, for a complete review of this approach).

For example, Kohlberg, Kauffman, Scharf, and Hickey (1974) took over part of a women's prison.

The just community way of doing business was for decisions to be made in town meetings, including the development of rules for the prison community. Rather than discipline being a matter overseen by guards, juries took up offenses against the community, with these juries composed of both staff and inmates and reaching decisions based on discussion and reflection. Rather than letting the community slip into a lull of satisfaction with the rules as established by the community, there was continuous review of rules. Did living in such a community increase moral judgment skills as defined by the Kohlberg interview measures? Yes, a little.

Just communities were also set up in several schools, with both elementary and secondary just communities created. Town meetings and self-enforced discipline via reflective discussion were the order of business in these schools as well. Did attending a just-community school increase moral judgment skills as defined by the Kohlberg interview measures? Yes, a little.

In addition to collecting evidence of moral judgment abilities with the standard Kohlbergian interviews, students in eight just-community high schools were also asked to reason about dilemmas that occur in school settings, covering difficult topics such as drugs in school, stealing, and group consequences for harmful actions by particular members of the school community (Power et al., 1989, Chapter 9). Just-community students tended to give more responsible responses to such dilemmas than did students in comparison (conventional) high schools: The responses of the just-community students reflected more concern for meeting the needs of others, thinking about the consequences of one's own actions on others and valuation of friendship, family, and community.

This Kohlbergian approach to moral education is far from dead, with just communities implemented in schools (Higgins, 1987; Power & Power, 1992; Rulon, 1992), institutions serving emotionally disturbed adolescents (Blakeney & Blakenay, 1990), and prisons (Powell, Locke, & Sprinthall, 1991). In addition, there are many other settings providing students with experiences discussing difficult issues, consistent with the plus-one approach. The best-informed proponents of this type of instruction still are inspired by Piagetian and Kohlbergian thinking about the cognitive growth provided by cognitive conflict, although increasingly plus-one discussions occur in the context of educational environments designed to promote moral judgment and

behavior using a variety of mechanisms (see especially Lickona, 1991, especially Chapters 12 through 15, and the discussion of Lickona's analysis presented later in this chapter).

New Twists on Plus-One and Just-Community Approaches Some new ways of operationalizing cognitive conflict discussions are being developed and used as part of contemporary plus-one interventions (Lickona, 1991, Chapters 12 and 13). For example, kids can be asked to deal with real moral issues, both ones in the news (e.g., should murderers receive capital punishment?) and ones pertaining to the school (e.g., how should students be punished for transgressions of school rules?). Important content dealing with civil liberties can be covered using such discussions. For example, we know of one Baltimore high school teacher who has a course on civil liberties. Rights and morality are debated by students and teacher as they consider court cases and decisions that have fleshed out the rights defined by the Bill of Rights and amendments to the Constitution. Evidence is accumulating that students can recognize situations that are controversial (e.g., whether the United States should spend more on health care and less on space exploration) from those that are not (e.g., whether astronauts should be warned about potential life-threatening flaws in the space shuttle) and understand the need for reflective consideration of multiple perspectives on controversial issues (e.g., Nicholls & Nelson, 1992).

One of the most ambitious models of school reform in the 1990s has as its most important feature that students participate in a living, breathing democracy. In many ways, the "micro-society" approach (e.g., Sommerfeld, 1992) to schooling is the ultimate just community:

> Micro-society schools are exactly what they sound like—schools that operate miniature civilizations complete with all the trappings of the real world: a legislature, courts, banks, post offices, newspapers, a host of entrepreneurial businesses, and even an Internal Revenue Service. Students hold jobs and are paid salaries in an ersatz currency, which they use to pay simulated taxes and tuition and to purchase a variety of goods and services at the school's marketplace. (Sommerfeld, 1992, p.14)

When there is a crisis, such as when the school's legislature cannot pay its bills, the members of the society must wrestle with the problems that are created, including dealing with "civil servants" who are without paychecks and the potential consequences of deficit spending. Micro-society is intended, in part, to provide hands-on experience with many aspects of economics but in doing so requires its members to engage in real community problem solving. One goal of micro-society educators is to create citizens who are fully prepared to be responsible members of democracy. The approach is intended to increase moral and ethical reasoning abilities as it provides in-depth experiences with the institutions of the real world. Whether there is moral growth and increased understanding of ethical versus unethical conduct as a function of participating in micro-society schools is a question that is fertile for educational psychologists in the 1990s.

Cognitive Conflict Models in Historical Perspective

By this point, it should not be surprising that cognitive conflict and social interactions, such as the ones experienced in just communities, would lead to cognitive advance. What should be emphasized, however, is that Piaget and Kohlberg recognized the potential for peer interactions to stimulate mental growth long before American educators rediscovered Vygotsky.

Kohlberg's understanding of the power of such interactions was the result of his thorough grounding and reflection on Piagetian and Soviet theory, but also was influenced by some decidedly American thinking—John Dewey, the 20th century philosopher who is considered the father of the progressive movement in education. Dewey embraced the notion of stagelike progression, with cognitive conflict a prime mover in intellectual development. Dewey especially advocated schooling that produces active mental engagement and experimentation with ideas by the student, including confronting the difficult moral dilemmas that are part of life. (Dewey would have loved the idea of a micro-society school!) Progressive educators in the Dewey tradition want to develop students who can and do reason cooperatively with, are sympathetic to, and are respectful of others as they try out different ways of thinking and alternative methods of approaching problems. Progressive educators aim to develop citizens who reject conventionally arbitrary thinking and who are fully prepared to be active in democratic communities and institutions (Robertson, 1992).

In one of his most famous essays, Kohlberg and Mayer's (1972) "Development as the Aim of Education: The Dewey View," three alternative educational schemes were considered. The **romantic approach** is laissez-faire, trusting that the child's biology ensures an unfolding that will result in healthy development. Educators should simply get out of the way and let nature take its course according to this perspective. The second is the predominant model in American education, **cultural transmission,** with the schoolmaster's role to fill the heads of the youth with the knowledge that is valued by the culture. Not surprisingly, Kohlberg and Mayer (1972) rejected these two models, in favor of **progressivism**—the developmental approach inspired by Dewey's philosophy of education based on learning by doing. That is, Kohlberg and Mayer (1972) rejected educational models with no society (i.e., all inevitable biologically mediated development) and all society (i.e., all environment, either in terms of information transmitted in school or experienced in society, or both) in favor of one emphasizing interactions between children and other members of society, consistent with Dewey's thinking (i.e., development involves interactions between biology and experience, consistent with the theoretical thrust in this text that both biology and experience are critical determinants of behavior and thinking; see also Gardner, 1991).

Up until this point the discussion of Kohlberg's perspective has been positive except for the intimations earlier that the theory might be sexist. The possibility of such sexism has fueled a reexamination of the moral judgments of males and females, one that is yielding new insights about the ways that both males and females reason about difficult issues. This work is making clear that educating people to be just in their thinking is not enough: Mature moral reasoning also reflects care about others and appreciation of connections that are more than the cold social contracts of Kohlberg's stage five thinker or the just outlooks emphasized by Kohlberg's stage six.

Discussion: Piaget Compared with Kohlberg

Although both Piaget and Kohlberg devised stage theories of moral judgment, and Kohlberg claimed his theory was an elaboration of Piaget's, there are some striking differences (Kavathatzopoulos, 1991). Nowhere in Piaget is there an argument for universal themes—such as reverence for life, liberty, and justice—the logic of which presumably becomes compelling with advancing development.

Kavathatzopoulos (1991) believes this represents a greater commitment to constructivism by Piaget: If people largely construct their own cognition through interactions between biological endowment and the environment, through interactions between the child's thought and the child's actions, as Piaget claimed, it would be unlikely that everyone would come to embrace the same principles of morality.

Both Piaget and Kohlberg offered theories of thinking, rather than theories of moral action. Kohlberg was especially aware that moral stage of thinking did not predict well a person's moral behavior, although he believed that correspondence between moral thinking and behavior probably increased with higher moral level—that is, for a stage five person, moral considerations are more important in determining behavior than for a stage two person. For all people, however, behavior is determined by more than just moral considerations and hence low correspondence between moral thinking stage and moral behavior (e.g., Kohlberg & Candee, 1984). For example, whether someone steals something depends in part on their expectations of gratification if they steal the desired object as well as their expectations about consequences if they are caught (Pearl, Bryan, & Herzog, 1990), expectations developed through past reinforcements and punishments they have either received or witnessed (Rotter, 1954). Because Piaget and Kohlberg were principally interested in thinking, the lack of a correspondence between moral thought and action was an irritation they could live with. For educators who are concerned at least as much with affecting moral behavior as moral thought, interventions that affect thinking alone are not enough. The lack of impact of moral-cognitive interventions on moral behavior is one of the reasons that more pragmatic moral educators design interventions that capitalize on diverse mechanisms to influence morality, with Lickona's work, which is summarized later, an excellent example of the blending of behavioral interventions aimed at improving moral action and more cognitive interventions that affect thought. Education for morality requires more than the obsession with cognition that largely motivated Piaget and Kohlberg's efforts; it requires more than cognitive conflict, which more certainly affects thinking than behavior.

Although both Piaget and Kohlberg studied children's reactions to hypothetical moral dilemmas, both also studied moral reasoning in the world. There was a subtle but important difference between their real-world studies. Piaget was interested in children's understanding of rules that already existed, specifically the rules of games like marbles; Kohlberg studied how groups invented new rules, as they do in just-community schools (Kavathatzopoulos, 1991). Logically, of course, the two are related, with this obvious in both the Piagetian and Kohlbergian data (e.g., children sometimes do change the rules of marbles; there is consideration of conventional rules of conduct as students in just-community schools design their legislation and adjudication policies). Given that most important changes in society's rules involve salient consideration of fairness and the impacts of existing laws and conventions compared with the potential impacts of new legislation, it would be good to see more explicit attention paid to how people reflect on and weigh traditional versus alternative ways of dealing with moral problems.

Finally, we reiterate that interest in moral reasoning and education as inspired by Piagetian and Kohlbergian theory is an ongoing enterprise. The theory is inspiring analyses of family characteristics and interactions that promote moral judgment. For example, Powers (1988) documented how family discussions of issues can increase moral cognition of children. Such discussions especially are educative if they support the sharing of perspectives, permitting the give-and-take of disagreements in viewpoints. It is also inspiring analyses of why institutional environments that promote moral judgment (e.g., college) do so. For example, Rest (1988) sifted through a variety of evidence supporting the possibilities that moral judgment improves during college because of generalized increases in social understanding, opportunities to engage in discussions about moral dilemmas, or because the students who elect to go to college are committed to improvement in their reflective abilities.

Challenge of Kohlbergian Educational Models

Kohlberg's educational theory also is inspiring analyses of how difficult it is to carry out Kohlbergian-type programs of moral instruction. For example, Sharp (1987) made the case that the types of discussions required in just communities of inquiry demand much of students. According to Sharp, they must be capable of all of the following:

listen to others attentively, take another's ideas seriously, accept corrections by peers willingly, build on one another's ideas, develop own ideas without fear of rebuff or humiliation from peers, revise one's own view in light of reason from others, show concern for the rights of others to express their own views, detect underlying assumptions of ideas presented in discussion, show concern for consistency when arguing a point of view, ask relevant questions, verbalize relationships between ends and means, show respect for persons in the community, show sensitivity to context when discussing moral conduct, ask for reasons from one's peers, discuss issues with impartiality, and ask for criteria. Sharp's analysis of the complexity of plus-one exchanges makes clearer why moral discussions have not been successful with elementary students (Enright et al., 1983).

If plus-one is challenging for students, it is even tougher for many teachers. There is increasing evidence that many teachers do not feel comfortable serving as models of moral cognition or they do not understand at all how to carry out Kohlberg's educational vision, identifying much more with the cultural transmission approach to moral education (e.g., Bergem, 1990; Cox, 1988; Kutnick, 1988, 1990).

Concluding Comment

Our view is that there is a lot in Kohlberg's models for contemporary educational psychologists to consider and explore. This will become even more apparent when Kohlberg's perspective is contrasted with more recent analyses of moral reasoning, ways of thinking that reflect not only fairness and justice, but also concern for others, ways of thinking that reflect not only masculine, but also feminine perspectives.

The original Kohlbergian model was presented in terms of universals, reflecting the influence of Piaget on Kohlberg: Biology constrains stagelike progression according to Piaget and hence all of thinking, with humans prepared at different stages to manifest different reasoning abilities. Themes of universalism have given way over the years as it became increasingly obvious that stage six was a philosophical preference of Kohlberg's rather than an empirically documented reality and as the effects of social factors on moral judgment were taken more seriously, especially by feminists.

Lest readers think that the concerns in this chapter are totally divorced from good information

processing, note that Stewart and Pascual-Leone (1992), consistent with neo-Piagetian theory (see Chapter 7), believe that the critical determinant of moral reasoning ability is mental capacity (i.e., short-term capacity). In their one study of the problem, mental capacity as they measured it was an important determinant of the complexity and level of moral reasoning. Like Piagetians, neo-Piagetians view mental capacity as a developmentally expanding resource (see discussion of Case's theory in Chapter 7). Thus, they expect developmental improvement in moral reasoning because of increasing mental capacity.

SEX DIFFERENCES IN MORAL REASONING: THE DIFFERENT VOICE IDENTIFIED BY GILLIGAN

Freud argued that men have stronger superegos (i.e., consciences) than women because of differences in the processes of sex-role identification for boys and girls: The Oedipal fantasies experienced by a boy that motivate identification with the male role, including the threat of castration by a jealous father in retaliation for the son's sexual desire of the mother in the family, are extremely traumatic. They are more traumatic than the corresponding Electra fantasies experienced by a girl that motivate her sex-role identification. After all, the little girl cannot be castrated by her mother for desiring the father of the household. Thus, Freud reasoned that the identification with the fantasized aggressor (i.e., the father for the son, the mother for the daughter)—which is what sex-role identification is all about in Freud's theory—is much stronger for the son than for the daughter. With sex-role identification comes the adoption of the moral standards of the aggressor in the form of the superego. Because sex-role identification is stronger for boys than for girls because of differences in fantasized trauma, it makes sense that boys have stronger superegos than girls. Not surprisingly, this view of moral development, which is definitely biologically deterministic, is offensive to many contemporary women.

The salience of Freud's sexist vision of differences in the development of conscience between males and females heightened the sensitivity of many to any claims of moral superiority for males compared with females, including some sex differences favoring boys in a few reports of moral judgment in the Kohlberg tradition (e.g., Holstein, 1976).

The sensitivity of scholars interested in women's thinking was particularly high in the case of Kohlberg's theory because much of Kohlberg's writing was based on a study that included only midwestern boys (see Kohlberg, 1969), with claims of universality of the stages based on this sample (i.e., according to Kohlberg, the moral development of males and females all over the world was captured by the stage progression observed in his males from Chicago). During the 1980s, scholars in women's studies have offered both compelling theoretical analyses and interesting studies to bolster their contention of bias or neglect of important themes in earlier studies of moral reasoning.

Gilligan's Analyses

Carol Gilligan (1982) forcefully summarized women's concerns about Kohlberg's theory in a scholarly book that received widespread attention, *In a Different Voice: Psychological Theory and Women's Development.* The perspectives developed by Gilligan (1982) were informed by a thorough understanding of Kohlberg's theory based on a long-term scholarly relationship with him (e.g., recall the Gilligan and Kohlberg collaborative work reported earlier on reasoning in reaction to sexual dilemmas). Gilligan's perspectives were also shaped by her own research and that of her colleagues at Harvard, including three studies that provided illustrations for many of the points made in the 1982 book. One was a study of the development of identity and moral thinking during the college years. The second tapped the moral thinking of young women as they contemplated having an abortion. The third was a study of thinking about rights and responsibilities, one conducted across the life span.

A main conclusion reached by Gilligan was that females were much more likely than males to consider issues of interpersonal caring and person-to-person connections as they reasoned about moral dilemmas, consistent with other feminist thinking that care is a much more important issue for women than for men (e.g., Brabeck, 1989; Noddings, 1984; see Chapter 8). This conclusion was based on an examination of reasoning by males and females over many issues involving moral decisions. The differences between reasoning that considers the interpersonal effects of decisions versus thinking that is concerned more with coming up with rational, just solutions can be illustrated by responses to the

Heinz dilemma presented earlier. Female responses are much more likely than male responses to include arguments such as, "... I ... think he [the druggist] had the moral obligation to show compassion in this case ... (p. 54)," "... if she [Heinz's wife] dies, it hurts a lot of people and it hurts her ... (p. 28)," "... you have to love someone else, because you are inseparable from them ... [t]hat other person is part of that giant collection of everybody (p. 57)," and, "who is going to be hurt more, the druggist who loses some money or the person who loses her life?" (p. 95). Compassion, connection, and concerns about minimizing hurt were issues raised by females in Gilligan's studies.

Gilligan, who was intimately familiar with Kohlberg's scoring scheme, recognized that, if anything, raising issues of care would reduce one's score in Kohlberg's traditional assessments. Her analysis was that the scoring scheme devised by Kohlberg was sensitive to a masculine strategy based on rationality and justice but insensitive to feminine thinking strategies in which dilemmas are analyzed in terms of the human, interpersonal consequences of the various possible actions by the actors in a dilemma. Gilligan contended that, at a minimum, the traditional analyses of moral judgment missed the rich diversity of thinking about moral issues, something apparent in studies conducted in response to Gilligan's (1982) book.

Johnson (1988) substantiated two different moralities (she referred to them as strategies) in the moral reasoning of adolescents. The subjects in her study were presented two Aesop's fables, including *The porcupine and the moles:*

> It was growing cold, and a porcupine was looking for a home. He found a most desirable cave but saw it was occupied by a family of moles.
>
> "Would you mind if I shared your home for the winter?" the porcupine asked the moles.
>
> The generous moles consented and the porcupine moved in. But the cave was small and every time the moles moved around they were scratched by the porcupine's sharp quills. The moles endured this discomfort as long as they could. Then, at last they gathered courage to approach their visitor. "Pray leave," they said, "and let us have our cave to ourselves once again."
>
> "Oh no!" said the porcupine. "This place suits me very well." (Johnson, 1988, p. 71)

Following the presentation of each story, the subject was interviewed, first responding to the question,

"What is the problem?" and then, "How would you solve it?" Follow-up questions were given to clarify responses, and countersolutions were presented for subject reactions. After subjects provided a spontaneous solution to a problem, they were also asked to identify the best solution to it considered during the discussion.

Consistent with Kohlberg's theory, themes of rights and justice were apparent in the reasoning about the fables, including the following responses by participants:

> The porcupine has to go definitely. It's the mole's house.
> It's their ownership and nobody has the right to it.
> Send the porcupine out since he was the last one there. (Johnson, 1988, p. 53)

So were themes of response to others and of connection and caring, however, as in the following example:

> The both of them should try to get together and make the hole bigger. (Johnson, 1988, p. 53)

There were also responses that reflected both rights and response to others:

> They should help the porcupine find a new house.
> I think the moles should just ask him again to leave and if he says no, they should ask him, why not. If he says, "I can't find another place to live," then they should maybe enlarge their home. If he says, "I just don't feel like it," then maybe they should send him out. (Johnson, 1988, p. 53)

More than three-fourths of the time, the spontaneous solutions of males reflected the rights orientation. In contrast, rights predominated in the spontaneous solution of females about half the time. The overall proportions were similar for males with respect to best solution. With females, however, the preference for a best solution that responded to the needs of the actors in the fable was apparent in more than 80 percent of the cases. That is, there were sex differences in moral reasoning that were consistent with Gilligan's theory.

Lyons (1988) asked adults, "What does morality mean to you?" She also asked them to describe themselves in relation to others and to talk about their own real-life moral conflicts and issues. Consistent with Kohlberg's work, she found that her subjects talked about objective relations between people, duties and obligations, rules and stan-

dards—a morality of justice. She also found evidence of a morality of response and care, however, consistent with Gilligan's theory. Consistent with Gilligan, the morality of justice predominated in men's responses, whereas response and care predominated in women's answers. In fact, about one-third of men made no references to response and care, and about one-third of women made no references to justice issues. Two-thirds of the subjects, however, represented both moralities in their responses, so that a scoring scheme based on justice alone would have misrepresented the moral reasoning of two-thirds of the men and all of the women.

Gilligan and Attanucci (1988) obtained evidence of a sex difference as well in a series of three studies involving upper-middle-class adolescents and adults. The participants were asked to identify an occasion when they were in a moral conflict and describe what they did, followed by reflection on whether their action was appropriate and why they thought their actions were justified or should have been different. The interview data were then analyzed for the types of moral considerations expressed by the subjects. Justice considerations predominated in the responses of two-thirds of the males, with all but one of the remaining third offering a mixture of justice and care considerations. In contrast, slightly more than one-third of females focused on issues of care, a little less than one-third focused on justice considerations, and the remaining third offered a mixture of care and justice considerations. If the data had been scored only for consideration of justice issues, the reasoning of one-third of the males and two-thirds of the females would have been misrepresented.

Gilligan and her associates believe that the identification of the two "voices" in their research on moral reasoning has far-reaching implications for education. Although their message of a sex difference is what has captured the most attention, the larger message seems to be that analyses of moral reasoning that only are rational, just, and attentive to rules and duties are narrow in their conceptualization of the world. There is another way to look at things, one emphasizing interconnections, caring, and responsibility for others.

Some implications of the recognition that rationality and caring both have a place in sophisticated thought became apparent to the faculty and staff at Emma Willard School for girls during its participation in a study carried out by the Gilligan group (Gilligan, Lyons, & Hanmer, 1990; Lyons, 1987). In particular, the faculty reported greater awareness and appreciation of the female voice and greater recognition that their curriculum was too much loaded in favor of rationality, with learning equated to acquiring and respecting information of various sorts rather than making connections between the academic content and the human condition. One teacher, Nancy Cushman, put it this way:

> As I began to teach Introduction to Psychology from a text which seemed little changed since my college years, I was immediately struck by the different approaches to learning that girls in my class seem to adopt. Young women whom I would characterize in the rights mode seemed interested in the theoretical concepts in and of themselves. They were eager to learn the vocabulary and master the theory. Girls in the response mode were delighted to find that the concepts explained a dear friend or relative and eager to spend class time relating specific personal experiences as examples of various theories. Had I not had this approach validated by the Gilligan research, I would have enjoyed these stories yet harbored an uneasy feeling that these were diversions. With a new sensitivity, I realized I was faced with the challenge of making the material available to each student in a way that was meaningful to her. (Gilligan et al., 1990, p. 304)

The value of collaborative learning opportunities became more apparent to a math teacher, who observed that some of the students could approach math with less tension when doing difficult problems in a group, whereas others seemed more comfortable working alone. That is, some felt better doing math in the context of social connections, whereas others saw math as an individual enterprise. Because of the awareness of the two ways of thinking created by Gilligan's study in their school, the math faculty were extremely open to a variety of collaborative student experiences, ones that had not occurred before the Gilligan study took place.

The Emma Willard faculty had new insights into their students, for example, why they seemed so brutally competitive in athletics against other schools but much more humane when competing against schoolmates intramurally. The coaches realized that the intramural competition was between people who had valued connections with one another but that the extramural games were *against*

other students that the Willard girls did not know or care about. The administration of the school also became more aware as a function of participating in the study that it was critical to hire teachers sensitive both to rights-oriented students and socially responsive students. They now want to hire faculty who appreciate both occasions when students act individually and in ways that seem duty bound and when students work together in ways intended to foster social connections.

In short, everything in the school changed as a function of coming to appreciate that both rational thinking bent on meeting objective criteria and socially oriented thinking focused on strengthening human connections are important. According to Gilligan's research, both types of thought should be appreciated and fostered. We expect because of Gilligan's work that the socially responsive voice will be given more credit in 21st century schools than it was previously.

Other Perspectives on "Different Voices" in Moral Reasoning

One reason there will be a great deal of additional research on sex differences in moral cognition is that Gilligan's conclusions are extremely controversial. Indeed, there is no more prominent issue in cognitive-moral and moral-education research of the 1990s than whether, in fact, there are gender differences in moral reasoning and, if there are, whether gender differences are the only differences in voice.

Why is this so? Most analyses of conventional moral judgment data—that is, data based on typical scoring of Kohlbergian or similar dilemmas—do not reveal striking sex differences (e.g., Gibbs, Arnold, & Burkhart, 1984; Rest, 1979; Rest et al., 1986; Walker, 1984, 1989). That is, as far as the conventional moral judgment data are concerned, it is fair to charge that Gilligan overattended to studies reporting sex differences.

Less conventional analyses also suggest less striking differences between males and females in their reasoning than Gilligan and her colleagues observed. In a test of Gilligan's hypothesis about sex differences in moral reasoning, Johnson, Brown, and Christopherson (1990) asked adolescents to talk about real-life moral dilemmas they face. Although both males and females described dilemmas in the context of human relationships, the males emphasized much more the effect of the conflict on themselves, whereas females emphasized the relationship aspect of conflicts much more. When Mellor (1989) administered instruments to males and females that were designed to determine how they identify themselves, females were slightly more likely to identify themselves by reference to connections to others than were males. Although the outcomes in these studies were consistent with Gilligan's conclusion that connectedness is a more important part of female than male thinking, the effects were not large.

Others using unconventional analyses have generated data even less consistent with analyses by Gilligan and her Harvard colleagues, however. For example, Galotti (1989) asked undergraduates: "When faced with a moral dilemma, what issues or concerns influence your decision?" Using analyses like the ones employed by Gilligan (1982), Galotti found little evidence of sex differences in response to this question, with both males and females including both masculine and feminine themes in their responses. (The only sex difference was that males were more likely to report that they reason systematically when working on a moral problem.) Galotti, Kozberg, and Farmer (1991) administered both conventional and unconventional moral judgment dilemmas to students in grades 8 and 11 as well as college sophomores. Again, male and female thinking was much more similar than different, although females tended to be more concerned with what others think about their judgments and the effects of their decisions on themselves, including personal guilt and social reactions. When Lawrence and Helm (1987) asked nurses to reason about ethical dilemmas they might face in their profession, the predominant theme in their reasoning was the concern for consistency with the law—that is, concern for rationality and justice rather than one of caring. Although Bebeau and Brabeck (1987) observed more similarities than differences in the moral reasoning of dental students about ethical dilemmas in their profession, they did not observe differences between males and females with respect to their concern for care, as defined by Gilligan, with respect to the dental patients. Lonky, Roodin, and Rybash (1988) found that androgynous males reasoned in a more caring fashion than other males; they also ob-

served that when people were urged to reason from their own perspectives, they were more likely to evidence stage three thinking—consistent with female perspectives—than if they reasoned from a more "objective" perspective. In short, whether one's reasoning reflects more masculine or feminine themes depends on sex-role orientation and how one approaches the task. It just is not as simple as Gilligan and her colleagues supposed. The conflicting data to date will inspire additional analyses [see Witherell, 1991, for a sampler of theoretical reactions to the inconsistencies in data regarding gender effects during the first decade since publication of Gilligan's (1982) book].

Something more noble is also going to motivate more work on the feminist vision of moral education: There is a lot that is attractive about the feminist perspective on moral education, with a complete education requiring the development of both masculine and feminine characteristics (Wingfield & Haste, 1987). Although the masculine view is that the self is related to others, the feminist view is that the self is connected to others. The masculine perspective favors consideration of rules in the abstract; the feminine perspective favors interpretation of rules in context. The masculine emphasizes independence and duties; the feminine emphasizes maintaining relationships and responsibilities. The masculine call for defined boundaries is complemented by the feminine preference for flexible boundaries. We could go on: individual responsibility versus communal responsibility, competition versus cooperation, deference to authority versus respectful communication with authority, and equality regardless of need versus consideration of need. The fact is that some situations call for relatedness to others, abstract rules, independence, duty, defined boundaries, individual responsibility, competition, and equality; other situations call for connectedness to others, contextual considerations, maintenance of relationships, flexibility, communal response, cooperation, and differential authority. Both masculine and feminine ways of thinking are worthwhile, and both should be nurtured in school.

If you need convincing that the feminist vision of morality deserves a place in the curriculum, see if you can find anyone who can provide legitimate reasons for not educating students about these moral actions, all of which can be considered more feminine than masculine:

> Students need to learn how to be good neighbors. . . . They need the history of families, housing arrangements, food production, child-raising, volunteer work, social reform and religion. They should learn about the heroism of women and men who have worked for reform in our treatment of the insane, aged, immigrants, slaves, prisoners, workers, children and animals (Noddings, 1987, p. 185).
>
> All students also need to study and practice the . . . caring for children, the sick, the elderly and needy; they need to learn how to initiate and maintain stable and gratifying relationships and how to run households in a way that nourishes bodies, minds, and spirits. (Noddings, 1987, p. 187)

Our guess is that society so expects schools to develop such propensities in students that there will be no stopping additional feminization of moral and practical curricula. Given the voluminous attention to feminist perspectives in education, we also expect that educational psychologists will be there to document the differences made by feminist influences on schooling.

The feminists are not the only ones in the 1990s offering data challenging Kohlberg's thinking about universality, however. In particular, there now is an active cross-cultural psychology of moral cognition and education, with prominent studies from Asia and Israel in the literature (Gates, 1990; Iwasa, 1992; Luhmer, 1990; Maosen, 1990; Thomas, 1990; Tzuriel, 1992; Walker & Moran, 1991). In general, although the general Kohlbergian pattern of development is observed, there are often differences in moral thinking that reflect the socialization pressures of the culture. For example, Chinese communists endorse practices such as capital punishment more readily than do many Westerners, emphasizing the benefits for the collective rather than focusing on the individual rights of the victim (Walker & Moran, 1991). Also, Chinese are reluctant to claim that arguments made in response to a particular dilemma imply any general way of thinking (i.e., they seemed not to be case-based reasoners to the extent Western people are). Even relatively sophisticated Chinese thinkers believe more in analyzing the concrete specifics of situations in making moral judgments than do Western thinkers, at least according to Kohlbergian analyses. Of course, a fair criticism of Kohlberg's approach is that he ignored his subjects' attention to contextual factors affecting judgment, which, of course, was exactly Gilligan's main point. Just how similar Western and Asian thought are regarding moral issues may become more apparent as analyses such as Gilligan's are taken into account by cross-cultural researchers. Much remains to be discovered about both the natural and the instructed development of moral judgment capabilities, both in Western societies and elsewhere.

FROM DUALITY TO RELATIVISM TO COMMITMENT: THE MODELS OF PERRY AND ERIKSON

Mature people know who they are, defined largely by what they believe in. But the firm beliefs of the 40-year-old were not always held by him or her. How people develop from not even knowing about alternative beliefs to embracing particular beliefs was the focus of theories proposed by William G. Perry and Erik Erikson.

Perry's Theory of Intellectual Development

Perry set out to determine whether there were any fundamental changes during the college years in the ways that students think about issues. Although the study was conducted in the 1950s and 1960s, it remains an important examination of undergraduate thinking.

Perry's conclusions clashed with much of the 1960s thinking about thinking. Recall that Piaget had proposed that formal operations were the peak of intellect and were achieved during the adolescent years (Chapter 7). Kohlberg, writing in the 1960s (e.g., 1969; see the discussion earlier in this chapter), claimed that postconventional thinking, the highest form of moral reasoning, was within reach of high school students. Thus, by claiming striking shifts in thinking between 18 and 22 years of age, Perry (1970) was anything but consistent with the intellectual opinions of the time.

Perry was one of the first voices in what became a multipart chorus dedicated to proclaiming that much intellectual development remains for the 18-year-old. The case is made throughout this book that intellectual power continues to expand so long as people learn new strategies, knowledge, and metacognition, with that likely so long as they are in renewing and challenging environments. For example, we discovered many new strategies for writing a long, integrated book over the course of composing this book, despite the fact that we both were proficient writers at the beginning of the task.

Perry's study began with his observations in the counseling center at Harvard that students reacted differently to the **relativism** they encountered at the university—to the presentation of diverse points of view, including differing values systems, and arguments that right versus wrong was not the way to think about perspectives but that the appropriateness of a perspective often depended on contextual variables. Some students were shocked as their favored perspectives were presented as one viewpoint among many legitimate possibilities; others were much more comfortable with the idea of multiple positions. Such differences in reactions to multiplicity of opinion were striking to an academic counselor such as Perry because success at Harvard requires relativistic thinking. For example, when freshman examination questions in government, history, English literature, and foreign literatures were analyzed for what they demanded of students, many required students to represent alternative perspectives respectfully. Making claims that one perspective was right and another wrong (i.e., **dualistic thinking,** to use a term favored by Perry) often did not earn points at Harvard.

Perry administered a questionnaire to a large sample of Harvard freshmen, one that determined where a student fell on a continuum from dualistic (i.e., engaging in "right-wrong" thinking) to relativistic (i.e., accepting a multiplicity of views and recognizing that the appropriateness of perspectives depends on the situation). Students falling at the extreme ends and the mean of the scale were selected to continue in the study. At the end of each of their four undergraduate years, these students were interviewed in an open-ended fashion. The initial question in each year's interview was, "Why don't you start with whatever stands out for you this year?" When students offered general conclusions about the year's events, there were requests for examples and elaborations. For example, interviewers sometimes asked students to explain their thoughts by role playing what they would advise other students to expect, such as with, "If you had a cousin, say, who was coming here next year, and asked you

what to expect and so on, how do you think you might answer?" After the open-ended questions, students were shown the written questionnaire responses they had produced at the start of the study, and participants were asked to indicate if there was any difference in their thinking now compared with when they filled out the questionnaire. The idea was for students to explain how they found meaning in their lives during the preceding academic year. The interviewers did everything possible not to suggest potential responses to the students. The interviewers were genuinely interested in knowing what the students thought, with Perry believing that the participants sensed the researchers' genuine interest, which motivated the students to continue in the project and provide as elaborate responses as they could to the interview items.

Students provided information about their views of knowledge, how they studied, beliefs about social relationships, and their moral values. There was evidence of dualism in the thinking of freshmen, which is not surprising because part of the sample had been recruited into the study because they were extreme in endorsing dualistic positions on the screening questionnaire. Only 3 or 4 of the 50 students who were interviewed in depth proved to be consistent with what Perry referred to as "position 1," which was defined as right-wrong, yes-no, dualistic thinking: People agreeing with me are right; those disagreeing are wrong. The position 1 thinker views education as learning the right answers, with memory and hard work seen as the route to success in college. There are authorities out there with the answers, and there are absolute truths. A few years ago, author MP was teaching a course on cognitive theories. A student at the end of the term asked, "Why did we go through all those different theories? Why didn't you simply tell us the right one?" Those questions reflect position 1 thinking.

Dualistic thinkers are challenged, however, during bull sessions in the dorms and in class discussions. For example, the God-fearing Christian may be confronted by agnostics for the first time in his or her life. Such confrontations have an impact. For example, one freshman on the screening questionnaire indicated that it was easy to disagree strongly with the following claim: "One thing is certain: even if there is an absolute truth, man will never know about it and therefore must learn to choose and venture in uncertainty" (Perry, 1970, p. 69). By the spring interview of freshman year, this same participant agreed with this item. Immersion in a college world with many opinions reduces confidence in the righteousness of one's own beliefs.

Students who conform to Perry's position 2 are in advance of position 1 in that they realize there is a multiplicity of views. Their view is that these alternatives are alien and that those who hold them are wrong and confused. As a student, the game is to know the perspectives advanced by the professor, although the student may not identify with the professor's outlooks. Position 3 students still believe there are right answers but have doubts about whether authority figures (e.g., their teachers) have figured them out. Because authority figures have not yet figured out the answers (and because there is the growing perception that all opinions have a legitimate claim on correctness), students perceive that they are evaluated simply for the form of their test answers, papers, and so on—not for the particular positions they advance because their teachers are too tentative about the various positions to feel confident in discriminating between students based on the positions they take.

Position 4 students embrace multiplicity in that it is believed that anyone has a right to their own opinion, although the multiple perspectives are seen as just that—personal opinions. They view authority as "wanting" them to think relativistically. Position 4 students do not yet recognize that the world really is inherently relativistic.

In contrast, students in position 5 believe that at least part of the world is relativistic—things are not true or false but true or false relative to a particular situation: That is, some students believe that some subdisciplines are relativistic (e.g., literature), whereas others are not (e.g., physical sciences); other position 5 students apply relativism more generally. Position 5 is clearly the swing stage in Perry's theory, the end of dualism and the beginning of relativism.

Students in position 6 accept relativism as the way of the world. A psychologically healthy position 6 outlook is to look forward to eventual commitments to particular positions with respect to religion, politics, friendships, social endeavors, and values. Thus, for example, a person comes to understand whether he or she prefers a wide range of friendships or a few. A less healthy outcome is retreating from commitment, perhaps through resentment of multiplicity of views or habitual negativism

or rebellion against the perspectives of authority figures. Some position 6 students avoid commitment by taking an attitude of "anything goes." Position 7 students are making initial commitments for themselves, recognizing the legitimacy of others' commitments. The process continues in position 8. By position 9, students are "in" their life in the sense that they have made commitments to some perspectives. Thus, a position 9 student may be committed to going to law school, practicing Catholicism, and staying single, while feeling perfectly comfortable and accepting of a friend who has decided on investment banking, converted to Judaism, and is marrying the girl back home or another acquaintance who is going to teach grade school and continue to be an agnostic.

In short, what Perry observed was that there was a general movement during the undergraduate years from dualism to relativism—an increasing recognition of a variety of legitimate perspectives in the world. Some students begin to make commitments, tentatively in the beginning and advancing eventually to more complete commitments. Others become intent on avoiding commitments, recognizing the multiplicity of perspectives but unwilling to identify with any of them. In the original research, Perry (1970) reported that about three-fourths of the students he studied were making commitments by the end of their undergraduate years. In recent years, workers at Harvard have thought that a much lower percentage of students in the 1980s moved toward commitment as undergraduates (Pascarella & Terenzini, 1991, p. 30). In arguing that students make commitments, that does not imply that growth is concluded or nearly so because there is the possibility of changing commitments and making new commitments across the life span (Perry, 1981).

Although there has not been a tremendous amount of follow-up research on Perry's model per se, there is a substantial literature documenting that with increasing higher education, thinking is increasingly relativistic (see Pascarella & Terenzini, 1991, Chapter 4). For example, college seniors are much more likely than freshmen to understand and appreciate the validity of alternative perspectives on an issue like abortion (e.g., Winter, McClelland, & Stewart, 1981). As far as the development of commitments is concerned, however, the most prominent research has been conducted in reaction to Erik Erikson's (1968) theory of identity development.

Before taking up Erikson's work, we point out that Perry's theory is decidedly a social cognitive one, with thinking shifting as a function of exposure to alternative perspectives. Cognitive development takes place in classes, informal discussions in the dorms, and as part of serious confrontations of differences between college-age lovers. There is no biological inevitability here. Rather, college life offers many opportunities for exposure to alternative perspectives and reflection on how one's own beliefs differ from those of others.

Erikson's Theory of Identity Development

Erikson proposed a life-span theory of development. People pass through eight stages according to Erikson. Each involves a central conflict, with either a positive or negative resolution of the conflict possible. These conflicts, and roughly when they happen, are as follows:

- Trust versus mistrust: During infancy, the child either forms a trusting relationship with an adult or does not. Failing to interact with an adult who can be trusted to meet the infant's needs results in long-term mistrust.
- Autonomy versus shame and doubt: During the early preschool years, children begin to do things on their own, and if they succeed in establishing some autonomy from others, that is a positive outcome. Part of autonomy is self-control, with much of the conflict involving self-control occurring during toilet training. If there are difficulties in establishing self-control and autonomy, there is the possibility of shame in not being more independent and doubt about whether one can be so.
- Initiative versus guilt: As the preschool years proceed, there are many more initiations into the world and trying on of new roles. If the child is overly punished for his or her burgeoning initiative, there is the potential for guilt.
- Industry versus inferiority: With the schooling years, the child is expected to begin to master the skills of the culture. For example, in Western culture, children are expected to develop fundamental literacy and numeracy skills. Success in doing so leads to a sense of industry; failure to do so can lead to a sense of inferiority.
- Identity versus identity confusion: During adolescence and early adulthood, the central crisis is the identity crisis. During this period, people struggle with determining who they are, what they believe in, and what they want to become. There are issues of sex-role identity and vocational identity to resolve. A positive outcome requires trying various possible identities and struggling with them. The successful outcome is emergence from the struggle with an understanding of one's sexual preferences, career aspirations, and intellectual commitments. Those who come to such conclusions without the struggle (e.g., they do as their parents expect) are at great risk for identity confusion later, confronting the fact that they are playing at roles that are not them; others simply continue to drift from role to role, with their identity confusion painfully obvious to those around them. From the perspective of Erikson's theory, it is a healthy pattern not to be committed early in adolescence but to come to commitments after experimenting with differentroles and ideas.
- Intimacy versus isolation: After youth, a person either achieves intimacy with others, usually a marital partner or the equivalent, or is at risk for feeling psychological isolation.
- Generativity versus stagnation: Adulthood either is a period of contributing to society and to the development of the next generation, or there is a risk of stagnating.
- Integrity versus despair: If one resolves all of life's crises in apositive fashion, it is likely that he or she will be able tolook back and feel a sense of integrity. Disgust and despair is a possibility if one fails to resolve positively one or more life crises.

Without a doubt, the most prominent crisis in Erikson's theory is the identity crisis, with it receiving more research attention than any of the other stages. According to Erikson's theory, during adolescence and youth, there are subcrises with respect to the identity issues that occur throughout life. These crises occur in part because of the quantum leap in intellectual sophistication that occurs with the onset of formal operations (see Piaget's theory, Chapter 7), permitting introspection and reflection on alternative possibilities, which is at the heart of the identity crisis. That is, there are identity-related conflicts during adolescence and youth with respect to development of trust versus mistrust, autonomy versus shame and doubt, initiative versus guilt, industry versus inferiority, intimacy versus isolation, generativity versus stagnation, and integrity versus despair. As part of these subcrises, adolescents and youth struggle to determine what they believe with respect to sexual orientation, intellectual interests, life philosophy, vocation, religion, and so on, with these struggles made possible by the intellectual power provided by formal operations—the power to think about hypothetical situations and to compare hypotheticals, a power that often increases doubt in what one has always believed (Boyes & Chandler, 1992).

One of the most prolific investigators in this area has been James Marcia. Marcia generated substantial support for the conclusion that adolescents and youth make many choices and often come to commitments about important issues. In particular, he identified four different identity statuses (Marcia, 1966), reflecting the degree to which adolescents have experienced and resolved their identity crises. In our years of teaching undergraduates, we have had few students who have not been able to think of schoolmates who fit into each of the following four identity statuses:

- People in **diffusion** have not experienced crises in that they (1) have not tried out, nor are trying out, new roles and (2) have made no commitments. Youth and adolescents in diffusion often are perceived to be living lives without personal meaning. They are viewed as reluctant to make commitments to positions, avoiding close relationships, and unpredictable and changeable (Mallory, 1989).
- Youth in **foreclosure** have come to commitments without experiencing any crises. The stereotypical example is the young man or woman who follows the life plan devised by their parents (e.g., to go to a prestigious college followed by law school, accepting a place in the family firm, while settling down in the same community and going to the same church as parents). They often have conservative values, are moralistic, conventional, sex-appropriate in their behaviors, and are satisfied with themselves (Mallory, 1989).
- People in **moratorium** are actively exploring. This is a healthy and appropriate status for adolescents and youth according to Erikson's theory. Young people who are in moratorium are viewed as introspective, anxious, philosophically concerned, and valuing independence (Mallory, 1989).

- Those who are **identity achieved** have gone through crises and made choices. These people are perceived as productive, consistent, and independent.

The healthy progression according to Erikson's theory is into moratorium, with identity eventually achieved. Much less healthy is to come to an identity without conflict (i.e., moratorium) or never to experience conflict or identity (i.e., diffusion).

Our analysis of the four identity statuses in terms of Perry's theory is that diffusion and foreclosure reflect dualistic thinking; moratorium clearly involves relativism, and identify achieved is commitment as Perry conceived of it. If so, there should be more upperclassmen than freshmen in moratorium and identity-achieved stages, and, in fact, that seems to be the case.

Pascarella and Terenzini (1991, Chapter 5) reviewed the evidence pertaining to whether there was movement toward identity achievement during college—that is, increasing commitments with respect to vocation, lifestyle, and philosophy from freshmen to senior years. Their conclusion, based on a dozen studies inspired by Marcia's original work and another dozen testing Erikson's theory but not as follow-ups to Marcia's work, was that commitments develop during the college years. They speculated that college produced movement into moratorium followed by eventual identity achievement because the setting introduced students to diverse possibilities, a speculation supported by correlations between changes in identity status and exposure to diverse students (e.g., Henry & Renaud, 1972; Komarovsky, 1985; Madison, 1969; Newman & Newman, 1978). Nonetheless, because few of the studies examined the identity status of comparably aged students not attending college, and when there were such controls, there were other interpretive problems with the studies, it is impossible to conclude unequivocally that the college setting is what produces the development of identity as Erikson defines it—just as it is not possible based on Perry's work to conclude that college is the determining factor in the movement from dualism to relativism.

We close this subsection by emphasizing that identity achievement is anything but certain by the end of the college years. For example, Waterman and Goldman (1976) observed that only a little more than half of the college seniors they studied had achieved identity with respect to religious or political philosophies, a result consistent with other data reviewed by Pascarella and Terenzini (1991). Pascarella and Terenzini (1991) were especially conservative in concluding that all aspects of identity are worked out for many students by the end of he college years: ". . . if identity is defined as the *simultaneous* achievement of an identity in the occupational, religious, political, and sexual realms, then it [identity] remains a relatively infrequent occurrence during the traditional college years" (p. 183).

With its roots in Freudian theory and some Piagetian overtones, there is little doubt that Erikson's outlook about human development was in part biologically deterministic. Even so, resolution of the eight life crises was determined by social factors. Biological stages of life determine the crisis currently most prominent in life. Contextual variables are important in determining whether one's responses to a crisis are developmentally adaptive or result in long-term psychic pain.

Concluding Comments

The college years are a time for sorting out values issues, including religious, philosophical, and political orientations as well as other commitments, such as to vocation and family life. A consistent speculation is that college does so by forcing confrontation with alternatives not encountered before by students who have come from generally less diverse worlds. It is interesting that Kohlberg speculated (and Rest, 1988, confirmed) that college affected movement from conventional to postconventional reasoning about moral issues in part because in college settings, students are exposed to moral arguments never encountered before by them. Such exposure produces cognitive conflicts not experienced previously, conflicts that stimulate extensive thinking about moral choices and eventual reorganization of moral thought. The consistency of Kohlberg, Erikson, and Perry's thinking about the role of college in stimulating the development of thinking about values comes through in this quote from Kohlberg (1984, p. 203), who uses both Erikson's and Perry's terms as he explains moral growth in college: "One factor that appears to have precipitated the beginning of this [moral reasoning] shift was the college moratorium experience of responsibility and independence from authority together with exposure to openly conflicting and relativistic values and standards."

Up to this point in the chapter, the main concern has been with describing various shifts in thought about values and social issues and ways of thinking about them. Virtually all of this work was conducted within developmental psychological frameworks. The task of educators to facilitate development of complex thinking requires them to consider the development of complex thinking more broadly and, in particular, to identify mechanisms increasing the likelihood that students will become increasingly adept at reasoning about social issues and thinking in responsible ways. In the 1990s, there is great interest in designing educational environments that maximize the likelihood that students will emerge from school able to tackle society's problems in intelligent ways, with the remainder of this chapter dedicated to consideration of prominent alternatives for educating competent thinking about social issues.

MANY MECHANISMS FOR STIMULATING SOCIALLY RESPONSIBLE THINKING AND BEHAVIOR: THE INTEGRATIVE APPROACH OF LICKONA

As important as Kohlberg's contribution was to heightening awareness of moral thinking and how such thinking could be developed in school, his perspectives can be construed as narrow. Kohlberg was so taken by Rawls's thinking about justice that he failed to appreciate the validity of other rationales for social action, such as responsive care that fosters connections to other people. He was strongly influenced by Piagetian theory, which resulted in an exclusive focus on moral growth through cognitive conflict. Fortunately, there has been a great deal of other research and theory pertaining to moral and ethical development. There are many ways to increase the moral sensitivities and thinking abilities of youth.

Thomas Lickona (1991), who has long been sympathetic to Kohlberg's perspective (Lickona, 1976), compiled what is without a doubt the most comprehensive sourcebook on techniques for moral education. The book is exceptionally well informed by both research and classroom practice. Cognitive conflict and just community–type interventions are considered along with many other approaches by Lickona (1991), including the following:

- **Teacher modeling of moral behavior and reasoning.** Teachers who model moral behavior and reasoning are more likely to have students who act in moral ways and can reason in a sophisticated fashion about moral issues. There is an enormous body of research on social learning of prosocial behavior and moral thinking tactics (see Rosenthal & Zimmerman, 1978; see Chapter 7, this volume), with voluminous support for the conclusion that moral behavior and reasoning are affected by observational learning experiences (e.g., Bandura & McDonald, 1963; see Chapter 7, this volume).

- **Guest speakers.** Consistent with the social learning perspective that people learn how to be better than they are by exposure to people who are exemplary, expose students to real ethical models whenever it is possible to do so.
- **Storytelling and using literature.** People can learn from symbolic models, either television characters or characters in books (Bandura, 1969, 1977b). *Aesop's Fables* have survived for 2 millennia because they are effective in increasing moral understanding. Much can be learned about moral behavior and thinking through reading about the lives of Jesus, Socrates, Thomas More, Martin Luther King, and other morally courageous figures.
- **Influencing television viewing.** Social learning researchers established clearly in the last four decades that both anti-social and prosocial behaviors can be learned from television (see Comstock & Paik, 1991). The wise teacher does all possible to encourage viewing of television in which positive behaviors are featured, through specific assignments, parent conferences, or whatever is required to reduce the amount of time spent watching aggressive cartoons and increase the amount of time spent viewing PBS and worthwhile network specials depicting honorable, heroic, and moral lives.
- **Discussion of controversial, societal-scale issues.** Students can learn that controversial issues are many-sided and complex by discussing them in class. This can include systematically seeking out and learning factual information relevant to the issues as well as considering the alternative perspectives of various stakeholders in the issues. Such debates can sometimes fit into social studies (e.g., whether the 1991 Gulf War involvement was justified; views of alternative political candidates) or science (e.g., the ethics of genetic engineering) as well as the intersection of social studies and science (e.g.,

whether there need to be tougher governmental standards for pollution; whether defense applications should be part of the space program). This stance in favor of including discussion of controversial issues in classrooms clashes with the official policies of far too many contemporary schools, which attempt to eliminate controversial topics from the curriculum to avoid the clashing of alternative cultural perspectives represented in their communities (e.g., differences in the feelings of middle-class and lower-class students on the expansion of police rights, alternative stances by Catholics and non-Catholics on contraception and abortion rights, stances by smokers and non-smokers on the propriety of no smoking laws). Eliminating such topics from the curriculum does much to undermine the education and development of students (Strike, 1991). The next section of this chapter will take up such thoughtful discussions in greater detail.

- **Direct teaching.** As we have reviewed throughout this book, direct explanations are often effective in changing student behavior. Teachers can make a substantial difference by communicating clearly that values matter. For students who may not know how to interact positively with others, teaching them social interaction skills can help. Lickona favors teaching students that everywhere in society, there is high regard for both justice and caring and that it is a good thing to be just and to care.
- **Mentoring and individual guidance.** Development of close relationships with students can have a tremendous influence on moral and ethical development.
- **Asking students to be more ethical in their conduct; explaining why they should be.** It has been known for a long time that there are associations between prosocial behaviors and receiving explanations about why antisocial behavior is unacceptable compared with prosocial behavior. Children who may not think about the consequences of their unethical behaviors on their own can come to understand the effects of their behavior on others when an adult explains those effects, with a history of such explanations associated with prosocial conduct in the long term (see Hoffman, 1970).
- **Cooperative learning and fostering cooperation in general.** The evidence is growing that the ethical and mental health climates of cooperative environments are better than competitive

environments (see Chapter 5; Davidson & Worsham, 1992).

- **Negative consequences for unethical conduct; positive consequences for the ethical, fair, and altruistic behavior.** Punishment and reinforcement affect the acquisition of many behaviors (Chapter 7). Use them to promote the development of positive behaviors and to discourage immoral, antisocial behaviors. A variety of behavioral consequation techniques can be helpful, including encouraging students to chart their misbehaviors to increase their awareness of how salient their unwanted conduct is and to provide them with tangible evidence of improvement when positive change occurs.

- **Using the curriculum to encourage moral growth.** When opportunities arise to teach responsibility, do it. For example, the class pet (i.e., rabbit, hamster, ant farm) can be used in many ways for lessons in caring and responsibility. When history, social studies, or science lessons permit opportunities for relating the content to issues of respect, care, and justice, help students to see the linkage. Make ethics an important theme in the school day.

- **Idealism.** Emphasize the moral responsibility to work and contribute cooperatively to society. Do not send the message that workaholism is expected but rather work, friends, family, recreation, community service, and development of the human spirit are all worthwhile parts of a responsible, full life.

- **High expectations.** As we will review in Chapter 11, effective schools have high expectations for their students. Send the message that there are high expectations about the moral, ethical, and civic development of students in the school, and then actually expect high moral, ethical, and civic responsibility.

- **Reject ethics as simply matters of personal opinion.** One movement in moral education, values clarification, encourages teachers not to make value judgments about student stances on ethical issues. Lickona, consistent with most in the Kohlbergian tradition, rejects this thinking, believing there are some clearly moral and immoral stances that are not controversial at all. (More on this later in the chapter.) The teacher should make clear to students when they voice ethical positions that are contrary to stances that are acceptable in society or when they engage in behavior that would be considered unethical by a moral person.

In summary, Lickona (1991) reviewed the different theoretical perspectives on moral education and the research related to them. He also visited and studied a number of moral education programs. The result is a book that is an impressive summary of many complementary approaches for increasing moral thinking. The text is really refreshingly integrative when it is viewed in light of the rhetoric that predominated in the scholarly literature for a number of years: When behaviorists produced evidence of observational learning or reinforcement effects on moral thinking skills, they often critized cognitive-developmental models. The cognitive developmentalists, in turn, argued that the behavioral interventions produced superficial change rather than changes in students' deep understanding of moral issues. Devotees of Kohlberg were fond of pointing to behavioral interventions as examples of the cultural transmission approach to education, which, as we reviewed earlier, they rejected. In contrast, Lickona's (1991) interpretation is that there are multiple mechanisms for producing advancement in moral thinking, and the effective moral educator constructs an environment that incorporates many of them. Alternative approaches can work together, and some approaches will work better in some contexts than others. Lickona is not alone in coming to that recognition (e.g., see Marantz, 1988, analyses of preschool environments promoting prosocial behaviors and attitudes).

Lickona's perspective is consistent with the point of view favored throughout this book that effective instruction is complex but understandable. Although the whole of moral education may be greater than the sum of the parts, the parts are generally recognizable as variations on observational learning, cooperative learning, direct explanation, the plus-one strategy (i.e., cognitive conflict), and so on. In addition, Lickona clearly believes it important to stimulate the development of both rational, just thinking and interpersonal care and connection to others.

As cognitive psychologists, we are particularly aware of proposals that moral education might be rendered even more effective by explicitly teaching students important critical thinking skills. For example, Baron (1990b) has proposed that moral reasoning would improve if students were made aware of people's bias to favor information consistent with their own perspectives and weigh more heavily immediately available information. Baron also argues for teaching students more about probability and interpretation of quantitative information, to counter other biases in information processing (e.g., biases resulting in reasoning that loss of 500 of 600 lives is less of a catastrophe than the loss of 100 of 100 lives). In addition, Baron contends students would be well served if taught to wait for additional information before deciding, avoid irreversible decisions, and make contingency plans. Baron's hypotheses deserve the attention of educational psychologists, given that research related to them would undoubtedly increase understanding of both critical thinking skills and the nature of effective moral education.

Penn (1990) advanced a similar hypothesis and provided an initial test of it. He has examined the effects of a college-level ethics course that involved teaching explicitly the skills of logical argument, role taking, and various ways of conceptualizing justice: Students in the course learned to discriminate when someone was arguing for a benefit to themselves, a benefit to a group to which they belonged, or to humankind. They were taught about the universal ethical principles that Kohlberg embraced as consistent with stage six thinking. Students did exercises in the class to build their logical analysis skills and were exposed to classical writings pertaining to morality, with the works of Socrates, Aquinas, Rawls, and Martin Luther King, among others, analyzed.

Did Penn's course improve moral reasoning? In fact, there was a substantial jump from the beginning to the end of the term in moral reasoning with respect to moral dilemmas, a much larger increase than typically obtained for ethics courses or plus-one interventions (see the summary of Enright et al.'s [1983] analyses presented earlier). Moreover, compared with students in other classes that were taught ethics in a different way at the same university, the gain in moral reasoning was large. One reaction, of course, is that Penn's (1990) course involved a great deal of teaching to the test, with people getting better in reasoning about moral dilemmas because they were given a great deal of practice during the course in reasoning about moral dilemmas. Alternatively a case can be made that the intervention simply involved excellent explanations about the nature of dilemmas and guided practice applying the new knowledge about the structure

and nature of moral arguments to actual moral problems. Viewed in this light, the result is consistent with the many other demonstrations of direct explanation and scaffolded practice improving cognitive performance. Our perspective is that Penn has breathed new life into an old hypothesis, that teaching of ethics should improve moral reasoning. His version of that hypothesis is that teaching the logic of moral reasoning and requiring students to analyze various types of sophisticated and unsophisticated moral arguments is part of such instruction if it is to be effective in improving moral reasoning. This is one of those problems that we hope some readers of this book take up in their own research, for we suspect there are multiple ways that Penn's intervention affects moral understanding and reasoning, consistent with Lickona's general position that educators should use multiple mechanisms to promote moral growth.

THOUGHTFUL HIGH SCHOOL CLASSES AT THE END OF THE 20TH CENTURY: THE WORKS OF NEWMANN, ONOSKO, BROWN, AND VOSS

All of the researchers considered in this chapter viewed adolescence and young adulthood as a period of great importance in the development of moral reasoning, reflection on values and beliefs, and the development of perspectives. Thus, it is not surprising that educational researchers would be interested in whether secondary schools are designed to promote thinking about alternative positions, ones that are important for students to understand for them to be able to make informed progress toward the development of identities, moral stances, or long-term commitments. Although there are many places in the curriculum that can contribute to the development of thoughtfulness in students, social understandings, and citizenship values, such human concerns have traditionally been viewed as a central mission of social studies instruction. Thus, Fred M. Newmann of the University of Wisconsin at Madison and Joseph J. Onosko of the University of New Hampshire have been examining whether high school social studies classrooms in particular are thoughtful learning environments (Newmann, 1988, 1990a, 1990b, 1991a, 1991b, 1991d; Newmann, Onosko, & Stevenson, 1990; Onosko, 1989, 1991,

1992; Onosko & Newmann, 1994; see also Chapter 11, this book).

First, Newmann and Onosko propose a model of cognitive components that contribute to in-depth understandings of social studies issues. This model includes all four of the main components of good information processing cited in this book: (1) At the heart of the social studies curriculum is content, and hence, to think about social studies issues, one must have knowledge of content (e.g., historical facts; important sociological, economic, and political science concepts; and principles of various types of governments). Some of what Newmann and Onosko view as knowledge spills over into strategies, including knowledge of formal and informal thinking tools (see Nickerson, 1988). (2) Excellent social studies instruction promotes the development of skills, some of which also might be thought of as strategies, including identification of problems; formulation of hypotheses and recognition of hypotheses when they are presented; and the detection of biases, logical consistencies, and inconsistencies. (3) Dispositions for thoughtfulness are necessary as well, with these tantamount to motivation to engage in extensive thinking. Those with such a disposition consistently want arguments to be supported by reasons, enjoy reflecting on new information in light of what they already know, are curious, and habitually try to determine what type of thinking might be applied to present situations. (4) Although Newmann and Onosko do not list metacognition as a separate component, metacognition is included as part of their other components, including the disposition to monitor thinking, knowing when and where to use skills, and important beliefs about the mind (e.g., knowledge is socially constructed, knowledge can be revised in light of new data, some things cannot be known, and extensive thinking often leads to solutions of problems).

Newmann and Onosko developed a perspective on what a thoughtful social studies classroom might be like, one likely to increase knowledge, thinking skills and strategies, dispositions to think, and metacognition. This perspective was informed in part by observations of social studies classrooms in effective schools and by knowledge of the cognition and instruction literature, especially cognitive theoretical claims about effective instruction. The characteristics of effective classrooms identified by Newmann and Onosko will have a familiar ring to students who have read this book from its beginning:

- There is sustained examination of a few topics. Newmann and Onosko are well aware of the tendency of textbooks and curriculum to be full of information and believe that an approach that covers everything ends up covering very little in sufficient depth for students to develop deep and connected knowledge. (Compare this "less-is-more" perspective to a similar one in another content area, science; see Chapter 12.)

- Lessons are substantive and coherent and build on previous knowledge.

- Students are permitted time to think, for example, time to formulate answers before responding to questions. (Compare this to the ideas about wait time presented in Chapter 11. Also, think about this characteristic of effective classrooms in comparison to other effective instruction considered in this book: The pace of effective instruction is always such that students respond only after they have reflected.)

- Teachers pose challenging questions to students and give them challenging tasks. (How many times in this book has the idea come up that it is good to present information and tasks to students that are just a bit in advance of the students?)

- Teachers model thoughtfulness and flexibility in thinking. Teachers make a point of letting students know how they are thinking about a problem, making clear as they do so that the thinking processes behind a final decision are important. Good teachers let students know how difficult it can be to make decisions. They pick up on student ideas and encourage alternative approaches to problems. (Again and again in this book, there has been support for the social learning perspective that teachers should model effective thinking for their students, with such modeling including explanations of the thinking processes demonstrated to students.)

- Students explain their thinking and provide reasons for their conclusions. The message is sent consistently to students that the validity of a solution depends on being able to support it in a well-reasoned fashion. (How many times in this book has explanation been presented as key to effective learning and thinking—from demonstrations of the effectiveness of elaborative interrogation in promoting learning of facts to correlations between providing explanations in problem-solving groups and growth in problem-solving competence.)

Newmann (1990b, 1991c, 1991d) studied 56 high school social studies classrooms across the United States, including observations of teaching and interviews of the teachers. Not surprisingly, he found variability with respect to the promotion of thoughtfulness in these classrooms. Schools that set the promotion of thinking skills as a priority, however, tended to have classrooms that were more thoughtful according to the Newmann criteria. Although there was more thoughtfulness in classrooms with generally higher-ability students, thoughtful instruction was offered to students at all ability levels in schools committed to stimulating the thinking abilities of their students. Teachers presiding over thoughtful classrooms tended to be committed to promotion of thinking as an important goal of social studies instruction; they tended to be less committed than other teachers to having great breadth in their coverage. Schools with leaders (i.e., principals, department heads) committed to promoting thinking in the curriculum tended to have more thoughtful classrooms. (Compare this finding with the finding in the effective schools literature that good schools have a strong principal; Chapter 11.) Perhaps most important, a variety of indicators suggested that thoughtful classrooms were more engaging for students (see especially Newmann, 1991b; see Chapter 11, this book): That is, students really did spend more of their time thinking about the content in more thoughtful compared with less thoughtful classrooms; students viewed such classes as more challenging, engaging, worthwhile, and interesting.

With Newmann's summary rating of thoughtfulness calculated on a 5-point scale, only one-fourth of the classrooms observed scored a 4 or higher. This was despite the fact that the study was intentionally biased in a number of ways to make it likely that a high proportion of the classrooms studied would be thoughtful. The obvious conclusion is that only a minority of American high school social studies classrooms promote thoughtfulness in the ways Newmann surveyed. This is only one of many sets of data and analyses confirming that relatively few American classrooms stimulate students to think deeply about issues (e.g., Brown, 1991; Cuban, 1984; Goodlad, 1984; Morrissett, 1982; Perrone & Associates, 1985; Powell, Farrar, & Cohen, 1985; Sizer, 1984).

Some students might be interested in determining how social studies classes they encounter (e.g., perhaps ones in the school where they teach) would fare on Newmann's scale. A rough gauge can be made by observing a class and responding to the six items that follow. For each, rate the class from 1 to 5, with a rating of 1 given if the class is not at all like the stated criterion and a 5 if it definitely meets the criterion:

1. In this class, there is sustained examination of a few topics, rather than superficial coverage of many.
2. In this class, the teacher asks challenging questions or structured, challenging tasks are assigned (given the ability level and preparation of the students).
3. In this class, students offer explanations and reasons for their conclusions.
4. In this class, the teacher carefully considers explanations and reasons for conclusions.
5. In this class, students assume the roles of questioner and critic.
6. In this class, students generate original and unconventional ideas, explanations, hypotheses, or solutions to problems. (Newmann, 1991a, p. 395)

Add all six scores together and then divide by six. An average of four or higher would be consistent with the best 25 percent of the classrooms in Newmann's studies.

Rexford Brown (1991) devised another set of criteria. The more items that can be answered "yes," from the following list, the more thoughtful the classroom (adapted from pp. xiv–xv):

1. Reference materials are available.
2. There is a lot to look at and touch in the schoolroom environment, including student work.
3. Students move around to gather information and work in groups.
4. There are few interruptions (e.g., by public address system).
5. Many students participate in discussions.
6. Students address one another in discussions.
7. The teacher permits enough time for students to respond to questions.
8. The teacher seems to be a learner as well as the students.
9. Students and teachers ask questions that call for analysis, synthesis, interpretation, or evaluation.

10. Questions encourage deeper understanding of material.
11. The teacher encourages student questions.
12. The teacher encourages students to expand on their ideas.
13. The teacher represents concepts several different ways (e.g., verbally and graphically) to ensure that many students understand them.
14. The teacher provides conceptual bridges from students' current understandings to new understandings; teachers try to lead students away from incorrect to correct understandings of content.
15. Students provide supporting evidence for their discussion comments and questions.
16. Teachers and students synthesize during discussions.
17. There is sufficient time for good discussion.
18. Teachers and students critique discussions.
19. Most students are alert and engaged.
20. Teachers and students listen carefully to one another and interact politely; they acknowledge and support each other's ideas.
21. There is humor and good will in the classroom.
22. Teachers praise student responses.
23. Teachers and students talk about thinking and the quality of it in their class.
24. Students can describe their thinking and strategies.
25. Students take notes and intend to use them later in a reflective fashion, revising or reorganizing them if necessary.
26. Multiple perspectives are accepted and encouraged.
27. Some uncertainty and ambiguity is accepted.
28. Students explore and brainstorm.
29. Students are encouraged to make mistakes—to take risks—and benefit from their mistakes.

If you do analyze a classroom using these scales, great care should be exercised in presenting a conclusion to a classroom teacher observed or to others, however, for you are untrained in making such ratings. It is likely that Newmann's and Brown's trained observers would score the teaching you observed at least slightly differently than you would. Still, looking at a classroom with these scales provides a good exercise that should increase understanding of what a thoughtful classroom looks like, and we strongly encourage readers to do it. If the classroom you observe is not thoughtful, thinking about it with respect to these criteria should make obvious what is missing that could be there; if the classroom is thoughtful, looking at it with respect to these criteria should make an impression about the sophisticated interactions and thinking that occur during thoughtful instruction. Thoughtfulness is a function of a number of social-contextual variables, with high-quality interactions around important issues an important ingredient in producing thoughtful young adults.

What difference does it make when students encounter such engaging instruction? There are a variety of higher-order thinking skills that Newmann (1991a) believes may be affected by thoughtful teaching of the social studies, including the following:

- The ability to empathize with people in other circumstances and cultures.
- Transfer of abstractions—that is, understanding how abstract social studies concepts apply in life—may be promoted by thoughtful instruction. For example, thoughtful instruction might be expected to increase understanding of constitutional principles, how racism affects social stratification, how Martin Luther King's analyses of nonviolent protest might apply in the 1990s.
- Students' abilities to make inferences and predictions from social data would be expected to improve. Social studies educators want students to be able to move beyond facts (e.g., the Iraqis continue to cross the border into Kuwait in early 1993; the Bush presidency will soon end as this is being written; Bush wants to be remembered as ending Iraqi aggression) to anticipate what might happen (e.g., Bush may strike against the Iraqis in the next few days). (Bush, in fact, did on January 13, 1993, 2 days after our prediction was put to paper: Thoughtful instruction can provide students with a crystal ball of sorts, the ability to infer what is likely in the future based on what is known today.)
- People prepared for full participation in democracy can engage in critical discourse. They can dissent when they do not believe in a position taken by the government or a neighbor. They can debate another person who adopts a morally despicable position. Thoughtful classrooms are classrooms in which such discourse is a way of life.

Our review of Newmann and Onosko's data is that they are not analytical enough to permit firm conclusions about whether thoughtful classrooms really do influence these student outcomes. There is important educational research waiting to be done here. To be sure, Newmann and Onosko's hypotheses are in the tradition of Kohlberg, especially their positions that thoughtful interactions can lead to empathy with others (i.e., improved understanding of other people's perspectives and thinking) and better preparedness to participate in democracy. All of the cognitive benefits of thoughtful education are the same presumed benefits of active, progressive education in general.

Is schooling likely to change in the direction of greater thoughtfulness—even if a great deal of additional data accumulates documenting provable benefits of such teaching? Are we likely to see movement toward the development of many more thoughtful classrooms in thoughtful schools? Newmann and Onosko are realistic in recognizing that there are many challenges to the development of thoughtful classrooms. Others, notably Rexford G. Brown (1991, Chapter 8) and James Voss (1991), who favor the idea of thoughtful classrooms—ones in which students think about important issues in depth, perhaps in the context of analyzing an important social problem (e.g., what were the options not considered during the Cuban missile crisis; was Truman's thinking about the Korea crisis as well informed and on target as it could have been?)—also have concluded there are challenges in implementing such teaching. The barriers to thoughtful education perceived by Newmann, Onosko, Brown, and Voss include the following:

- Thoughtfulness is not appealing to many of those in charge of education, because it entails questioning conventional thinking and questioning fundamental societal assumptions. Brown (1991, p. 233) observed that schools that were thoughtful for students were also thoughtful environments for teachers and administrators, with open communication, inquiry, debate, problem solving, and collaboration. Too many schools are just the opposite, ones in which unquestioning deference to authority is the norm, and questioning that occurs goes on in secret. Perhaps as bad, many educators are isolated from other educators, with their days so full of demands in their classrooms that there is little opportunity to interact with their colleagues, to engage in reflection with intelligent others.

- There are few states or even school districts that have the development of thoughtfulness as a goal. (This is changing, with many states intrigued by programs such as "Dimensions of Thinking" [see Chapter 11], sometimes mandating such programs and often requiring achievement tests that are sensitive to critical thinking processes [see Chapter 17].)

- Critical discussion is hard work for students but also requires hard mental work by teachers. Often it is easier for students to memorize and reproduce; often it is easier for teachers to present material and oversee examinations that require only recall than ones that require reflective understanding and interpretation.

- Teachers often lack the in-depth knowledge required to be effective facilitators of classroom discussions of real-world problems.

- Teachers do not know how to conduct thoughtful education. They never saw it when they were in school. They were not taught it in teachers' college. There are no examples of such teaching in their own school. There are no in-services.

- The current generation of social studies textbooks is not matched to an in-depth discussion approach, rarely providing detailed information about even a single social problem. School libraries are often poor sources of information as well.

- In thoughtful classrooms, knowledge is constructed as part of active problem solving, discussion, and writing. Such construction takes time, with partial understandings and corrections along the way. One goal is to think critically about important social assumptions; another is to do more with knowledge than simply learn it (e.g., carry out projects, create integrative essays, publish books). Construction of knowledge and products based on knowledge involves taking intellectual risks and advancing ideas that sometimes conflict with conventional thinking. All of these activities may seem counterintuitive to students, parents, and teachers who have deeply held beliefs that: "(a) Most knowledge is certain, rather than problematic, (b) knowledge is created primarily by outside authorities, not within oneself, (c) knowledge is to be comprehended and expressed in small, fragmented chunks, (d) knowledge is to be learned as quickly as possible, rather than pondered, (e) knowledge may seem counterintuitive or mysterious with respect to one's experience, but it should be believed anyway, and (f) arguments and conflict about the nature of knowledge are personally risky, because winners are favored over losers" (Newmann, 1991a, p. 393).

- There are many forces favoring breadth of coverage, and it is thus painful for many to contemplate cutting out some content to permit greater attention to fewer topics, which is essential for thoughtfulness. The knowledge transmission model is embraced by many as an ideal. Knowing facts is equated with knowing for many educators. (The enthusiasm by some for the "Cultural Literacy" [see Chapter 4] movement in education is one sign of this.)

- The reality of classroom life in American high schools is that 30 students of diverse abilities and interests come together for social studies classes. Teachers are responsible for four to six sections. The size of any one class makes reflective discussion challenging; overseeing ambitious projects or reflective writing exercises for so many students would challenge many teachers' personal resources. The study of many social problems requires more than knowledge from books and discussions; often contact with the real world would be helpful, with such contact typically difficult to arrange. The class is over when the 50-minute period ends, even though some reflective exercises and projects do not fit the 50-minute model well. Some projects (e.g., serving an internship in a community setting) might not be consistent with taking seven courses at a time. In short, school is an institution with a rigid structure, one not necessarily consistent with what is required for students and teachers to interact as they work on projects meaningful in scope.

- Many educators do not believe their students are intelligent enough to participate in a thoughtful classroom. (We do not believe this, however. We think about the hundreds of Chapter-1 primary students participating in thoughtful discussions of literature as part of the SAIL program [see Chapter 14] as we consider this objection to the creation of thoughtful classrooms. There is a great deal of data documenting that diverse populations react positively to intellectually rich and interesting environments, with data in support of this claim distributed throughout this book.) A corollary of this belief is that educators often have low expectations for their students, with some such as Voss (1991) believing that educator expectations that students will learn how to deal with social problems are even lower than their expectations that their students will learn science and mathematics.

- It is harder to grade thoughtfulness than performance on objective examinations. It is not impossible to do so, however, with new forms of assessment (see Chapter 17) being devised that are more sensitive to the processes that compose thoughtfulness.

So the answer to the question of whether widespread movement to thoughtful classrooms is likely is probably no. It is tragic that there are so few just communities, micro-societies, or even progressive schools, given almost a century of urging from Dewey, Kohlberg, Newmann, and like-minded progressives. We suspect that often progressive models of education seem incomprehensible to many teachers and potential teachers. One of our desires in writing this textbook was to ensure that a much higher proportion of the next generation of teachers and professional educators would understand the foundations of progressive education—or at least our cognitive instructional version of it—well enough that it seems do-able and desirable.

Based on the barriers to transforming schools into communities that promote thoughtfulness, rational morality, and caring, it would be easy to give up in despair (see Cuban, 1991, if the earlier list of challenges was not discouraging enough). We resist the temptation to despair, however, continuing to hope that the expanding knowledge about powerful educational reforms will eventually be too great to ignore (see also Chapter 11). At the very least, research documenting the nature of thoughtful schools provides an envisionment of what schooling might become. Some of the schools that have developed exemplary thoughtful instruction serve challenging populations: This is not just a model that works in financially privileged environments that can afford extra staffing and resources of various types.

Brown (1991), for example, presented a series of case studies of thoughtful schools in what might seem unlikely places to many readers. Brown analyzed schooling in a traditional small town in the South, on an Indian reservation, in a major American urban district, and in a multicultural Canadian setting. More research documenting the benefits of as well as research establishing how teachers can learn how to carry out thoughtful education can only help the greater educator community understand thoughtful classrooms. Even if it is a long shot that thoughtful education will become widespread, we believe it is one worth researching because the potential gains for American students are great. We do hope that some readers of this book will be educators making such gains happen and that other readers will dedicate their careers to studying such innovations.

As this chapter is being written in January, 1993, there is additional reason to hope that education for thoughtfulness might get additional support in the near future. When Bill Clinton was Governor of Arkansas, education was a high priority. Then Governor Clinton was aware of the need for more thoughtful schools and, in fact, was much taken with the thinking of Rexford G. Brown about promoting thoughtfulness in education:

> Rexford Brown's *Schools of Thought* captures the breadth, depth, and urgency of education reform . . . I recommend it to other policy-makers, whether they be in the midst of reform, as Arkansas is, or contemplating it. (Bill Clinton, dust jacket of *Schools of Thought*)

Perhaps the new leadership will send the message better than the old leadership did that knowing facts is not enough, that deep knowledge that can be reflected on and is reflected on is a laudable goal for education. Of course, that will not be enough, something understood all too well by Newmann, Onosko, Brown, and Voss, but it would help much more than the many federal government suggestions of the 1980s that boiled down simply to teaching much more content superficially (e.g., cultural literacy) rather than encouraging students to learn in depth. The United States has favored for too long knowledge that is not connected and inert over deep knowledge that is connected to other knowledge and usable (Whitehead, 1929). The evidence is accumulating as the century concludes that whether students leave school as superficial, inert thinkers or deep, connected thinkers depends more on the type of schooling environment in which they are immersed than on the innate qualities of their minds.

CONCLUDING COMMENTS

Educators have long tried to create a more ethical, thoughtful, and caring citizenry through the design of school materials and schooling environments. It is no accident that the first mass-produced primers were catechisms, beginning with Luther's *Little Catechism* in 17th century Sweden (Resnick, 1991). Understanding of liberty was promised by Elhanan's (1796) *Political Catechism, Intended for Use of Schools in the United States* (Resnick, 1991). Who could miss the moral education intentions in the instruction provided by sources such as the 1839 *New England Primer* (Chandler Press, 1988):

> In Adam's Fall, We sinned all.
> Thy life to mend, God's book attend . . .
> A dog will bite, A Thief at Night . . .
> The idle Fool Is Whipt at School . . .
> My Book and Heart, Shall Never Part.
> Job Feels the Rod, Yet Blesses God . . . (p. 11)

Dewey's progressive school movement is well known, but others also experimented with schools designed to encourage reflection (Tyler & Smith, 1942; see Cuban, 1991). Long before the current wave of efforts to increase thoughtfulness in school, governmental agencies sponsored programs to encourage the development of more thoughtful education (e.g., National Science Foundation, 1978; see Cuban, 1991). Even so, in the 1990s, we are faced with schools that are producing students whose abilities to think about social problems in realistic ways seem limited. Perhaps worse, the potential changes in schooling that might increase student thoughtfulness seem unworkable to many.

Many developmental theorists (e.g., Piaget, Erikson, Kohlberg) have offered the conclusion that reflective thinking is something that becomes possible with adolescence (i.e., the onset of formal operations). Thus, education to stimulate reflection, morality, caring, and thoughtfulness has much more been targeted at adolescents than younger students, much more a secondary school intervention than an elementary-level approach. Although some successes in improving high school education so thoughtfulness is increased have been identified, they are not disseminated widely. One possibility is that the organizational characteristics of secondary schools may make them especially resistant to reform (Cuban, 1991), with content-driven curricula so completely accepted by so many secondary educators that process-oriented approaches simply do not have a chance. Another possibility is that despite the long history of schools attempting to influence values and social decision-making skills, there really is something too controversial about teaching students how to reason better about moral issues, consider issues of rationality versus care, and deliberate about the problems faced by their home communities and nation, perhaps even about working together.

Consistent with this possibility, David Purpel (1989, Chapter 3), who has long identified with the movement to educate students to think about social issues (e.g., Purpel & Ryan, 1976), concludes that there are many pressures in society against educating the new generation to reflect on moral and social issues.

For example, 1. individual thinking and accomplishment seems more valued now than ever, with the collective activities that are at the heart of the educational visions of Kohlberg, Newmann, and others discussed in this chapter at odds with the predominating individualistic, narcissistic focus (Lasch, 1979). The competition that is valued in our society and critical to conventional education is inconsistent with the cooperative educational options presented in this chapter.

2. Many educators regard control of students as something that is essential to maintain; they really believe there are right ways of thinking, right answers, and right values. A great deal of control is given up with all of the educational options considered in this chapter. Communities in which patriotism is a high value might feel uncomfortable with schools that debated the ethics of government decision making. Schools located in religiously conservative areas of the United States might feel more comfortable transmitting particular views of morality than permitting the nature of morality to be a matter of debate. How many educators have we met who take pride in the peace and quiet in the hallways of their schools? There is much less peace and quiet when students are interacting and engaging each other in thoughtful conversations, debates, and projects.

3. Since the 1963 decision to ban prayer in U.S. public schools, any curriculum item suggesting that religion is being injected in schooling—and any curriculum in which universal values are considered is at risk for being viewed as somewhat religious—has produced discomfort in some school officials. Some educators hide behind the 1963 decision as a defense for not teaching values or even providing students with opportunities to think and talk about value-laden issues. Teachers are uncomfortable in making decisions about which values to teach (Boyd, 1988; Cox, 1988).

Even though the interventions considered in this chapter fly in the face of many social pressures affecting American schools, Purpel (1989, Chapter 4) believes that many of the values and understandings promoted by such interventions are ones that are not debatable (although not all agree; e.g., Cox, 1988). Who would debate that it is not a good thing to deepen understanding of democratic principles, which is a key outcome of interventions such as the just-community approach? The United States is founded on and dedicated to principles of individual rights, justice, and political equality. The interventions considered in this chapter are concerned with deepening awareness of these principles and how they apply in life. On reflection, does it not make sense to do so? Many would argue that qualities such as forgiveness, mercy, and care are as American as apple pie. If they are, does it make sense for schools not to develop them? Perhaps most convincing of all, however, is Purpel's claim that our intellectual heritage is consistent with characteristics that are affected by thoughtful values and moral education:

> We value freedom of inquiry and expression, we revere creativity and originality, and we urge ourselves to be open and tolerant in the force of conflicting and differing ideas. We . . . esteem a strong critical capacity. . . . We admire clarity as well as the provocative and the evocative. We recognize that the paths to truth are many, that they sometimes crisscross, and that we need to both challenge these paths as well as affirm them. Our culture values . . . the pursuit of knowledge. (Purpel, 1989, pp. 71–2)

What many of the interventions reviewed in this chapter were about is that pursuit, learning how to reason about the complicated issues that will be reencountered throughout life.

We must point out, too, that there are those who believe the interventions reviewed in this chapter do not go nearly far enough with respect to educating different ways of thinking about society and personal management. For example, Jane Roland Martin (1992, Chapter 3) advances the perspective that boys' propensity for rationality needs to be curbed somewhat by education that promotes males' capacity to care. In contrast, females' too-great propensity to care needs to be reeducated so that they are less likely to help others when the cost is great to themselves. Her proposal for implementing such education is part of what she calls the "schoolhome," which endeavors to provide much more teaching for living than is assumed by the current curriculum, teaching aimed at producing people who are more sensitive to the needs of both themselves and others. Based on Gilligan's analyses, she concludes this requires different education both for girls and boys than they are currently receiving. That Gilligan's work fuels the enthusiasm of some dedicated to radical alternatives like the schoolhome concept may be one of the reasons that any movement toward thoughtful schools is scary to many conventional educators. Once thoughtfulness begins, it may become apparent that there is need for great change.

Our perspective is that if the schoolhome, or any other alternatives designed to educate more thoughtful people, are put into practice, educational psychologists should be there to assess the impact of these interventions. The goals of the educators devising these programs are noble; if they succeed, we must know and document the differences their interventions make on students' lives during the schooling years and afterwards.

A great accomplishment of cognitive research was reviewed in this chapter. It has provided a window on sophisticated value-laden thinking, revealing its rational and caring sides and illuminating the reverence of the mature thinker for alternative positions as well as the ways good thinkers can come to commitments to some positions over others. Educational options were reviewed in the chapter as well, ones aimed at increasing the proportions of students who can systematically apply their understandings of justice, care, and diversity of ideas to the problems of tomorrow. We sincerely hope the future teachers reading this book use the instructional ideas in their classrooms; we also hope that at least a few burgeoning researchers are sufficiently stimulated by the hypotheses summarized in this chapter to expand on them as they develop and evaluate new approaches for increasing responsible and empathetic thinking in students.

There were assumptions in both Kohlberg's and Erikson's theories about how biology greatly biases people to think in particular ways and places some constraints on the potential sophistication of thinking at particular points in development (e.g., some forms of moral thought supposedly depend on formal operations). Kohlberg and Erikson and many others were aware, however, that how people think depends greatly on the social world in which they live. A main message emanating from the three chapters covering the grand theories in educational psychology is that biological and social forces are both powerful determinants of thought. Those who exclude either biology or social forces in their explanations of learning and cognition (and there have been many instances in the history of educational psychology of theorists and researchers who did) fundamentally misunderstand much about the nature of mind and how it develops.

Even so, because educators have much more opportunity to manipulate environmental than biological variables, most of what follows in this book is concerned with environment without much consideration of biology. Even so, as our knowledge about the limited biological determination of gender and race differences has increased, it has become apparent that some traditional biologically inspired hypotheses about learning, cognition, and instruction as a function of student diversity were, in fact, in error: There is no compelling reason to believe that there are biological differences between males and females or between the races that should affect what different people are taught or how they are taught. Thus, some work on biology makes it clear that the design of high-quality educational environments for all students is a sensible direction. We are going to follow that compass as we consider various interventions for improving learning and academic performance in the chapters that follow.

Part

3

Important Empirical Contributions in Educational Psychology

10

Basic Mechanisms Affecting Learning

Learning and cognition researchers have identified many mechanisms affecting learning and improving performance. In this chapter, some of the most important ones will be discussed. The work reported in this chapter is a varied lot, ranging from the oldest of ideas in traditional learning theory and research to the most important insights emerging from artificial intelligence. The claims made here also differ with respect to the amount of support they enjoy, from a century of data to a few studies buttressed by theoretical analyses. The chapter is organized into two sections: The first deals with ways of increasing memory and understanding. The second is concerned with the effects of practice on learning.

MECHANISMS AFFECTING MEMORY, COMPREHENSION, AND LEARNING

Historically, much of memory research in the 20th century focused on learning of discrete information, such as the items on lists, vocabulary and their definitions, and countries and their capitals. Such research often was conducted in laboratory studies. Increased concerns in the last decade with generating information that is more certainly relatable to school learning and reflective of the demands of school have resulted in declining interest in such laboratory-based research in general. Even so, important conclusions and principles of learning have

emerged from the traditional laboratory work, with this section featuring some of the more telling results produced by basic memory researchers.

As this section proceeds, there is movement from learning of more discrete content (i.e., some would say, more "artificial" materials) to acquisition of more connected and meaningful material. Although memory for connected materials (i.e., prose) also has occurred during much of the 20th century (e.g., Bartlett, 1932), it is fair to say that the more natural the content being learned, the more recent the bulk of the research on the problem. The late 1970s and early 1980s was a period of transition away from traditional investigations of learning and memory and toward more educationally valid studies.

Depth of Processing (Semantic Orientation)

One of the most important papers in the last 25 years in cognitive psychology was Craik and Lockhart (1972). They argued that what was remembered during a learning task depended on what the learner did during learning. Suppose, for example, that you are asked to process a list of words. Would you remember more of the words later if (1) you checked each word to determine whether it had an *e* or a *g* in it or (2) you rated the pleasantness of each word? As you probably guessed, you remember many more words following the pleasantness-rating task (Hyde & Jenkins, 1973). Try another one. When do people remember more from a paragraph describing a person:

when they read it to determine whether it describes them accurately or when they check for spelling errors (e.g., Reder, McCormick, & Esselman, 1987)? People remember more when they are concerned with the accuracy of the text's meaning.

One explanation of such differences in learning is that they reflect different depths of processing, with checking for spelling involving superficial processing of the meaning of material compared with instructions forcing orientation to meaning (e.g., pleasantness ratings or evaluating whether an article describes oneself). Craik and Tulving (1975) eventually came to the conclusion that **semantic orienting** directions are effective in promoting memory because they increase the number of elaborations to the material that is processed—the material is related more extensively to prior knowledge when learners perform a semantic orienting task than when they focus on physical features of material they are processing.

That is not to say, however, that physical features cannot be processed deeply. Thus, Bower and Karlin (1974) provided a well-known demonstration of how memory for faces was affected by attending to meaning of faces rather than to physical features. When people rated whether faces were "honest," they remembered more of them than when they rated physical features of faces.

What can be done to increase depth of processing, other than providing instructions to process materials meaningfully? One thing is to make learning more difficult by increasing **contextual interference** (e.g., Druckman & Bjork, 1991, Chapter 3). Consider two examples: If a person is attempting to learn three different motor skills, do not permit practice of one until it is mastered, then the next one, and then the next one. Rather make the person practice one skill for a little bit, then another, back to the first skill task, try the third, back to the second, some more practice on the first, and so forth. Shea and Morgan (1979) observed that such random practice of three motor skills produced much better long-term learning of the skills than massed practice, a finding consistent with the distributed practice effect reported later in this chapter. That learning the tasks was more difficult with distributed practice was apparent in the number of errors during the learning phase of the study: There were many more with random presentation than with massed presentation of the practice trials. Simply repeating the

same action over and over probably requires less attention to the task than executing one of three tasks, which at a minimum requires the learner to discriminate which of the three procedures is appropriate.

The second example of contextual interference increasing learning by increasing depth of processing comes from research on text learning. Mannes and Kintsch (1987) demonstrated that long-term memory of an article can be increased by having subjects first study an outline of it that is inconsistent with the structure of the actual text (i.e., relative to learning when people are first exposed to an outline consistent with the structure of the text). This was despite the fact that short-term memory of the text was improved by presentation of the consistent outline. The inconsistent outline probably stimulated more elaborate processing than the consistent outline—people exposed to a consistent outline would be better prepared for the messages in the text, and hence reading of and learning from the text should be easier for them than subjects expecting a different organization than what was presented. In short, factors that make learning more difficult initially often increase long-term retention, with this effect probably due in part to increased attention to and analysis of material being processed. This is a generally robust effect (for more examples, see Druckman & Bjork, 1991, Chapter 3).

Although a great deal of important research on the effects of semantic orientation on memory has been conducted in the last 20 years, Craik and Lockhart (1972) *re*discovered semantic orientation rather than discovered it. Soviet psychologists were studying depth of processing effects decades ago. For example, Zinchenko (1981; also see Smirnov, 1973, Chapter 2) presented adults with cards, each of which had a picture and a number on it. When the learners were given a task requiring categorization of the pictures, subsequent recall of the pictures was better than recall of the numbers. When subjects were asked to arrange the numbers in ascending order, subsequent recall of the numbers was greater than recall of the pictures. What is attended and processed meaningfully is what is learned!

Zinchenko's work is one example of many research efforts in the former Soviet Union aimed at establishing relationships between what people do and what they comprehend and remember—sometimes referred to as activity theory in the Soviet psychological literature. Readers who are interested in depth of processing should examine Smirnov's (1973) summary of the relevant Soviet literature for many examples of how orientation to information affects what is learned from it. Wertsch (1981) also provided translations of many fine essays by Soviet researchers interested in how meaningful activities affect learning and memory.

An appropriate way to sum up depth of processing is to recall the frequent teacher admonition to, "Pay attention." Such a command takes on meaning only when it is clear what should be attended. If students meaningfully process what is presented to them and attend to semantically rich aspects of the material, they are going to learn the meaning better than if they attend to physical features only. The head remembers what the head does (Jenkins, 1974).

An interesting new twist in depth of processing research has been introduced by educational psychologists. Recall from Chapter 5 that some classrooms are competitive and ego oriented and others are task oriented. In Graham and Golan (1991), children in grades 5 and 6 processed lists of items in either a "shallow" condition (i.e., for each word, they indicated whether the given word rhymed with another word) or in one of two "deep" conditions (i.e., indicating whether a word represented a particular class—such as whether *dog* is an animal, *doll* is an animal; indicating whether a word fit a sentence frame that was provided, such as, "She spilled the ____"). One-third of the participants were given task-oriented instructions as they performed these tasks (i.e., to view the task as a challenge and enjoy mastering it), one-third were given ego-oriented instructions (i.e., the task is to determine how good you are relative to other children), and one-third were given no motivational information as they processed the list. The most important finding in the study was that memory in the deep conditions was better given the task-oriented rather than the ego-oriented instructions. Deep, meaningful processing of material may be more certain when students are not worried about doing better than their classmates. If the Graham and Golan (1991) outcome is replicable, it would be additional powerful evidence in favor of shifting classroom motivational structures away from the competitive model and toward a cooperative, task-focused approach to motivation. An old idea from the list-learning tradition may be reveal-

ing about the effects of competition versus cooperation on the development of the mind in school.

Mnemonics

There have been many reports of magnificent feats of memory when people have used mnemonics (i.e., memory tricks) to assist their learning. Indeed, at least since the 13th century when Raimond Lullé dazzled France (Desrochers & Begg, 1987), some performers have made a living by using mnemonics to perform difficult memory tasks. Lullé and other early mnemonists (e.g., Lambert Schenkel in the 16th century) recognized the potential of mnemonics for learning of academic content. Detailed, systematic accounts of how to improve memory using imagery mnemonics and other techniques have been in print since the early 19th century, when Fenaigle (1813) published his *New Art of Memory*. Yates (1966) provided a scholarly summary of the history of memory devices based on imagery, an overview making clear that imagery mnemonics and related procedures have been understood intuitively for about 2000 years.

What may be amazing, however, is that scientific analysis of imagery mnemonics has been undertaken only in the last 30 years or so in the West. There were several reasons for this. First, for much of this century, thinking and mental phenomena were taboo in North American psychology, with the study and measurement of overt behavior viewed as the only scientifically respectable pursuit for academic psychologists. (Recall Skinner's harsh words regarding cognitive psychology in Chapter 7.)

Second, for a phenomenon to be studied, there must first be a theory. There was no compelling theory about mnemonics until Miller, Galanter, and Pribram's (1960) *Plans and the Structure of Behavior*. Miller et al. (1960) discussed imagery effects in terms of information processing, then a new direction in psychology that seemed at the time especially promising and exceptionally scientific. Miller et al.'s (1960) main claim was that behavior is guided by cognitive plans, which are intentions to perform behaviors and a rough idea about how to carry out the plans. Such plans guide all of behavior:

> . . . [Y]ou do not draw out long and elaborate blueprints for every moment of the day. You do not need to. Rough, sketchy, flexible anticipations are usually sufficient. As you brush your teeth you decide that

you will answer that pile of letters you have been neglecting. That is enough. You do not need to list the names of the people or to draft an outline of the contents of the letters. You think simply that today there will be time for it after lunch. After lunch, if you remember, you turn to the letters. You take one and read it. You plan your answer. (pp. 5–6)

Imagery mnemonics are plans according to this framework. Miller et al.'s (1960) explanation of it to an academic guest for dinner is memorable:

> . . . "But what exactly is a Plan?" [the guest] asked. "How can you say that *memorizing* depends on Plans?"
>
> "We'll show you," we replied. "Here is a Plan that you can use for memorizing. Remember first that:
>
> one is a bun,
> two is a shoe,
> three is a tree,
> four is a door,
> five is a hive,
> six are sticks,
> seven is heaven,
> eight is a gate,
> nine is a line, and
> ten is a hen."
>
> "You know, even though it is only ten-thirty here, my watch says one-thirty. I'm really tired, and I'm sure I'll ruin your experiment."
>
> "Don't worry, we have no real stake in it." We tightened our grip on his lapel. "Just relax and remember the rhyme. Now you have part of the Plan. The second part works like this: when we tell you a word, you must form a ludicrous or bizarre association with the first word in your list, and so with the ten words we recite to you."
>
> "Really, you know, it'll never work. I'm awfully tired," he replied.
>
> "Have no fear," we answered, "just remember the rhyme and then form the association. Here are the words:
>
> 1. ashtray
> 2. firewood
> 3. picture
> 4. cigarette
> 5. table
> 6. matchbook
> 7. glass
> 8. lamp
> 9. shoe
> 10. phonograph
>
> The words were read one at a time, and after reading the word, we waited until he announced that he had the association. It took about 5 seconds on the av-erage to form the association. After the seventh word he said that he was sure the first six were already forgotten. But we persevered. (pp. 134–6)

The dinner guest went on to recall the list, with him describing recall as "no sweat."

With a simple mnemonic plan, what had seemed like it would be a difficult task turned out to be a simple one. Anecdotes like this one have done more than their share to stimulate interest in imagery mnemonics in both researcher and practitioner communities.

Imagery research did take off in the years following publication of the *Plans* volume. Important basic research on imagery was conducted by Paivio and his colleagues at Western Ontario as well as by Bower and his associates at Stanford, with this fueling interest in applications of imagery, including mnemonics. Jensen and Rohwer at Berkeley would do research on the closely allied concept of **verbal elaboration,** especially in the context of associative learning, demonstrating huge effects on associative learning when learners place verbal pairs (e.g., *turkey-rock*) into meaningful verbal contexts (e.g., generating the sentence, "The *turkey* sat on the *rock*"). Some of Jensen and Rohwer's students at Berkeley, such as Joel Levin and Dan Kee, became particularly interested in mnemonics, with their work also influenced strongly by the research conducted by Paivio during the 1960s. The conceptual overlap between verbal elaboration and constructing imagery mnemonics to link paired associates (e.g., making an image of a "turkey standing on a rock") was obvious—both involved taking arbitrarily paired items and creating a meaningful context that embedded the two elements in the pair, a context that could later be used in retrieving one of the two items given the other (i.e., presentation of *turkey* brings to mind the linking image, permitting recall of the *rock*).

Over the course of 30 years, Rohwer, Levin, Kee, and their students generated a large number of basic research studies concerned with verbal and imagery mnemonics, a body of data that proved to be coherent, sensible, and relevant to many important questions in memory development (Kee, in press; Schneider & Pressley, 1989). For example, one important question was whether young children could generate mnemonic images (i.e., imagery elaborations of paired associates), a specific instantiation of a general issue in memory development concerning the susceptibility of young children to strategy instruction. Whether imagery instructions for paired-associate learning promote learning depends in part on the age of the learner, something covered briefly in Chapter 2. Preschool children and children in the early elementary grades often experience difficulty in constructing images embedding paired associates, or at least if they construct imagery elaborations, the images do not mediate their learning.

For example, Pressley and Levin (1977b) presented 6- to 7-year-old children with paired associates, ones involving paired items not obviously related to one another (e.g., *turkey* and *rock* are not related to one another, whereas the pair *balloon-pin* involves an obvious semantic relation). When the pairs were presented at a relatively rapid rate (5 seconds per pair), instructions to generate linking images did not facilitate paired-associate learning relative to control instructions. Much more positively, however, the learning situation can be engineered so images can be produced. Thus, in Pressley and Levin (1977b), when paired associates were presented at a much slower rate (i.e., 10 seconds per pair), the 6- to 7-year-olds benefited from the imagery instruction. Their analysis, based on both descriptive and experimental data, was that the 5-second presentation rate did not permit subjects enough time to determine and imagine a meaningful relationship between the paired items—recalling that Miller et al.'s (1960) adult dinner guest required 5 seconds to construct linking images, isn't it sensible that 6- to 7-year-olds might need at least that much time to construct and imagine a linking relationship between two items not having any obvious relationship to one another?

Once beyond the early grade-school years, the evidence is actually quite strong that people often can generate imagery mnemonics when learning verbal associates (see Pressley, 1977). Even adults, however, do not generate mnemonic elaborations reliably in the absence of instruction, although there is an increase in the likelihood of students using verbal and imagery elaboration on their own with increasing age during adolescence (Beuhring & Kee, 1987). That people can be taught to use mnemonics but do not use them autonomously in the absence of instruction has stimulated intensive study of how to teach people to generate mnemonics that might be useful in learning educational content, with one approach receiving more attention than any other.

Keyword Mnemonics Richard Atkinson's (1975) *American Psychologist* article was a turning point in the history of mnemonics. Atkinson summarized a series of studies conducted at Stanford (with Michael Raugh) on the **keyword method.** The keyword method, introduced in Chapter 2, involves transforming some part of one of two to-be-associated pieces of information into what he called a "keyword," one familiar to the learner. For example, foreign vocabulary words and their definitions are frequent to-be-associated pieces of information for students in high school and college, with the foreign words the elements that are transformed into keywords because the foreign words are unfamiliar to the learners and a keyword can transform an unfamiliar item into a familiar English concept. For example, to learn that *carlin* means *old woman*, first the learner identifies a word that sounds or looks like some part of *carlin:* Either *car* or *Carl* could serve as **keywords** for *carlin.* A concrete referent for the keyword would then be imagined in interaction with the definition referent. Thus, the learner might imagine an *old woman driving a car* or *Carl Yastremski, the Boston Red Sox Hall of Famer, giving his autograph to an old woman.* In general, Atkinson (1975) made the case that the keyword method facilitated the foreign language vocabulary acquisition of college students.

Something like the keyword method has been known at least since Bacon's description of mnemonically mediated learning (Bacon, 1862; see Desrochers & Begg, 1987). Indeed, some extremely well-regarded minds have concluded that transforming a new word into a more familiar phrase can be mnemonically powerful. Consider this episode in the life of Benjamin Franklin (Watson, 1830):

> My aged friend, Samuel Preston, tells some anecdotes of Dr. Franklin when he was at the Indian treaty at Easton in 1756. Preston's father, then there, much admired Franklin's ready wit. When the old Indians came in their file to speak to the Governor, he would ask their names; then the governor would ask Ben, as he called him, what he must think of to remember them by. He was always answered promptly. At last one Indian came whose name was Tocarededhogan. Such a name! How shall it be remembered? The answer was prompt:—Think of a wheelbarrow—to carry a dead hog on. (p. 515) (We are grateful to Dr. Gary G. Price of the Department of Curriculum and Instruction at the University of Wisconsin-Madison for referring us to this example.)

Although the power of imagery mnemonics was apparent to Franklin and many others throughout history (Yates, 1966), in the mid-1970s little was known about whether such procedures might work with children facing an associative learning task. This seemed an important problem because children are often asked to learn the definitions of vocabulary, the associations between countries and their attributes, information about famous people, and so on. Indeed, if anything, children are asked to do more intentional associative learning than are adults.

Thus, Pressley (1977) set out to determine whether grade-school children could benefit from keyword method instruction if they were provided mnemonic pictures. Thus, to learn that the Spanish vocabulary item *carta* means *letter*, Pressley provided elementary-level students with a picture of a letter in a shopping cart. The effects of these mnemonic pictures on learning were large for both grade-2 and grade-6 students: When given the foreign words on a test and the requirement to recall their definitions, the children seeing the keyword pictures were much more likely to remember the definitions than were the control subjects.

In a follow-up investigation, Pressley and Levin (1978) determined that providing pictorial support was much more critical with grade-2 than with grade-6 students: At the grade-2 level, keyword-method effectiveness varied with the amount of pictorial support provided; that is, complete mnemonic pictures produced better learning than provision of separate pictures of keyword and definition referents, which produced better learning than attempted keyword application given only the vocabulary word, its meaning, and the verbal keyword. (Readers might compare this finding with the Pressley & Levin, 1977b, data discussed earlier in this subsection; both sets of data substantiate that imagery mnemonic instructions do not reliably facilitate the learning of 6- to 8-year-olds.) At the grade-6 level, however, students could easily generate their own linking images provided only the vocabulary word, its meaning, and a verbal keyword.

One of the most dramatic demonstrations of the potency of keyword-mediated learning was provided by Pressley, Samuel, Hershey, Bishop, and Dickinson (1981), who presented 10 Spanish words to 3-, 4-, and 5-year-olds, with each word presented one time. When left to their own devices to learn the words given one presentation of them (i.e., at 15 seconds per word), the children could recall about 2 of the 10 meanings on a posttest (i.e., given the Spanish word *pato*, there was only a 20% chance of remem-

bering that the word meant *duck*). When same-age children were presented pictures depicting keyword referents (e.g., *pot* for *pato*) in interaction with definition referents (e.g., a *duck* with a *pot* on its head), about 70% of the vocabulary meanings could be recalled after one presentation. That is, learning was $3^1/_2$ times better when the keyword-interactive pictures were provided as an aid to learning than when the students attempted to learn the words on their own without the support of the transformational mnemonic pictures.

Levin (e.g., 1982, 1983, 1985, 1986) and his associates at Wisconsin as well as Mastropieri, Scruggs, and their colleagues at Purdue (e.g., Mastropieri & Scruggs, 1991), in particular, have produced many demonstrations of the utility of the keyword method for diverse students learning many types of factual content—contents requiring students to remember linkages between one type of information and other pieces of information. States and capitals can be remembered with the keyword method (e.g., for Madison, Wisconsin, imagine a *maid* [keyword for Madison] using a *whisk broom* [keyword for Wisconsin]). Artist and painting associations can be learned using the keyword method (e.g., imagine those huge Campbell Soup cans in a *war* to remember they were created by Andy Warhol; see Carney, Levin, & Morrison, 1988). Facts about American presidents can be encoded easily when the information is encoded in mnemonic pictures (e.g., many facts can be related to a mnemonic image of a *ray gun*, a keyword for Reagan, to remember information about the 40th president). The keyword mnemonic can be adapted so that hierarchies of scientific concepts are learned and interrelated (e.g., Levin & Levin, 1990).

Some especially striking keyword-method effects have been observed in prose-learning studies. McCormick and Levin (1987) presented short biographies to college students, with subsequent recall of name-biographical fact associations required (e.g., what did Charlene McKune do?). Subjects in the study attempted to learn biographies such as the following:

> Born and raised on a dairy *farm* where she helped take care of the cows, *Charlene McKune* has always been used to hard work. When she was a child, McKune enjoyed creating homes for her pets out of her toy *building blocks*. To earn extra money and because of her hatred for dirt of any kind, McKune began *washing cars* for her parents' friends. . . . (p. 400).

Control students were left to their own devices to learn the passages. Mnemonic keyword subjects were instructed to use a keyword for Charlene McKune (*racoon*) and to construct an image linking the most important factual elements of the passage (e.g., an image of a pet *racoon* outside a *farmhouse* jumping over a row of *building blocks* with some kids *washing cars* nearby). Memory of the name-fact associations was much better in the mnemonic keyword condition than in the control condition, with this finding representative of many others in which keyword-mnemonic intervention conditions have been contrasted with a variety of control procedures.

Despite the many demonstrations of improved learning via the keyword method, many educators are reluctant to try mnemonics. One of their concerns is that the method involves "artificial" learning, learning that is not deep because the method does not require the learners to think about the meaning of the association. One way that imagery enthusiasts have responded to this concern is with development of imagery-based procedures that do not involve keyword transformations, which more certainly represent the original meaning of the to-be-learned information.

Nonkeyword, Mnemonic Imagery The imagery mnemonics described in the last subsection all involve some transformation of the to-be-learned material that introduces elements not meaningfully related to the original to-be-learned material (e.g., conversion of a foreign vocabulary word to a keyword, which only physically resembles part of the to-be-learned content). Powerful mnemonic images sometimes can be constructed that do not require keywords, however.

Woloshyn, Willoughby, Wood, and Pressley (1990) asked Canadian university students to construct representational images as they read paragraphs containing facts about particular Canadian universities, such as the following:

> The land on which McGill University stands was donated by a fur trader. The university's first faculty was a medical faculty. The university is also recognized for establishing the first medical faculty in Canada. The psychology department at the school is internationally acclaimed. The school has an extensive puppet collection. Many students consider the university's athletic facilities to be old and small. (p. 523)

The students in the imagery condition of the study were instructed to learn each fact about McGill by imagining the fact occurring in the school's geographical location. Thus, the mnemonic processing involved constructing relations consistent with the conceptual meaning expressed in the passage—that is, for McGill, students constructed images relating information about McGill to McGill's setting, which is Montreal. This imagery instruction studied by Woloshyn et al. (1990) dramatically increased recall of the facts for each school relative to performance in an uninstructed control condition.

One potential glitch for the imagery strategy studied by Woloshyn et al. (1990) is that its use depends on prior knowledge—in the case of Canadian universities, knowledge of the geography of various parts of the country. Some students will lack that knowledge, as was the case when Pressley and Brewster (1990) attempted a similar imagery strategy with middle-school Canadian students. Even so, it was still possible to adapt the imagery procedure so these students could make use of it.

Pressley and Brewster (1990) required the students in their study to learn facts about each of the Canadian provinces. For half of the subjects in the study, the experimenters first presented one prototypical scenic picture for each province and required the students to learn the association between the prototypical scene and the name of the province in question (e.g., a picture of Lake Louise for Alberta; a wheat field for Saskatchewan). When students learned these picture-province name associations before presentation of the critical to-be-learned facts about the provinces, they benefited substantially from instructions to construct images—instructions to imagine each to-be-learned fact occurring in the prototypical setting associated with the province. Students who had not learned the picture-province name associations first benefited little from the mnemonic imagery strategy.

Others have also been studying interventions that involve imagery transformations that relate to the meaning of the to-be-learned information, most notably Mastropieri and Scruggs. They have been devising mnemonics for teaching content, such as social studies. One type of imagery mnemonic they have devised requires the learner to engage in what they call *mimetic reconstruction* once the image is retrieved. Thus, a piece of factual information such as, "Early bridges often rotted and washed away," might be accompanied by a drawing of a rickety bridge with a woman in settler's clothing watching as the bridge beneath her feet is swept away by the rushing water of a stream. Later, by remembering the picture, the learner can reconstruct the more abstract fact—that bridges in the days of the settlers often did not hold up and were swept away by water. Another type of imagery Mastropieri and Scruggs have devised involves *symbolic reconstruction* at recall. Thus, an illustration accompanying text about American isolationism before to World War I might involve Uncle Sam standing on a depiction of North America and looking toward fighting on a depiction of Europe. Uncle Sam could be saying, "Its not my fight" (Mastropieri & Scruggs, 1989, p. 97). Recalling this image later would permit reconstruction of the fact that the United States stayed out of the conflict in Europe for some time. To date, all indications are that embellishing texts with such mimetic and symbolic transformational mnemonic pictures increases learning of content.

In addition, mimetic and symbolic memory aids can be combined with pictures incorporating keyword mnemonics. Scruggs and Mastropieri are generating important studies establishing the effectiveness of embellishing traditional content with a variety of types of mnemonic pictures (e.g., Scruggs & Mastropieri, 1989, provided several months of social studies instruction to learning-disabled students using various sorts of mnemonic pictures, producing large gains in performance).

In closing, we emphasize that experimental work has established that there are many ways of representing and transforming information into mnemonic pictures and images that can increase learning of new factual content. Moreover the gains in learning often are striking, especially with populations that are otherwise difficult to teach, such as the learning-disabled. One of the most attractive features of imagery is how flexible it is. Thus, although young children sometimes have difficulties generating their own images when asked to do so, it is, nonetheless, possible to devise mnemonic pictures that provide learning benefits (e.g., see the earlier discussion of Pressley, Samuel, et al.'s [1981] provision of keyword-mnemonic pictures to preschoolers learning foreign vocabulary). Young scholars reading this book should note that new research on old and established interventions often can do much to move the field beyond the traditional approach. (What educational intervention could be more established than mnemonic imagery with its 2000+ year history! [Yates, 1966]) Providing new insights about traditional approaches often attracts positive

attention. There is much educational benefit from imagery and related pictorial interventions and much study of imagery phenomena left to be done.

Enactment

When people are asked to remember actions, their memory is typically better if they carry out the actions rather than simply verbally rehearse their names. For example, if a list of actions such as, "Bounce the ball, drink from the cup, climb the tree . . . cut the paper," is presented to a person, he or she is more likely to recall the actions if each act is mimicked by the student as it is named than if the student only listens and tries to remember the list (Cohen, 1989). A likely explanation is that a form of dual coding (e.g., Paivio, 1971, 1986; Chapter 3, this book) is mediating the increase in memory owing to the actions. That is, hearing the list stimulates a verbal coding; hearing the list and acting it out stimulates verbal and motoric coding (Cohen, 1989).

Another possibility, however, is that acting out to-be-remembered items stimulates three codings—verbal, motoric, and imaginal—for motor processes have been hypothesized for a long time to increase the formation of images (e.g., Piaget & Inhelder, 1971). For example, recall from the last subsection that young elementary-school children often fail to learn more paired associations in reaction to imagery instructions than when left to their own devices to learn. Wolff and Levin (Wolff & Levin, 1972; Wolff, Levin, & Longobardi, 1972) hypothesized that imagery instructions might be more effective in the early grade-school years if students were encouraged to act out the elaborative actions preschoolers and kindergarten children were attempting to imagine (e.g., act out with their hands a cow chasing a dog for the pair, *cow-dog*). In fact, imagery and motor instructions combined did increase associative learning at these developmental levels, with Wolff, Levin, and their colleagues concluding that the motoric actions stimulated the development of imagery.

Baker-Ward, Hess, and Flannagan (1990) offered interesting new data suggesting that it may not be the motor activities per se. In that study, children's memories of activities were enhanced if they carried out the action rather than watched the action be carried out—unless the other person doing the action was familiar to them (i.e., a classmate). Recall was as high when grade-3 children watched a classmate perform actions as when they performed actions themselves and higher than when they watched an unfamiliar peer perform the action. Somehow, performing oneself and watching a friend perform creates deeper, richer encodings than watching a stranger. Regardless of the exact mechanism underlying enactment effects, however, it is clear that enactment often—although not always—is a powerful way to facilitate learning, with the benefits of enactment obtained across the life span, from preschool (e.g., Heindel & Kose, 1990) to old age (e.g., Knopf & Neidhardt, 1989).

Learning by Understanding: Relating New Information to Prior Knowledge

Learning can often be enhanced if learners understand the content they are being asked to learn. Educational psychologists have produced substantial evidence that understanding can affect memory of information dramatically. Although the effects on problem solving have been studied less completely, there is a growing database substantiating that problem solving also can be improved through manipulations that relate a current problem situation to prior knowledge.

Effects of Understanding on Learning and Memory
Try reading and learning the following passage so you can look away from the book and recall it:

> The procedure is actually quite simple. First, you arrange the items into different groups. Of course one pile may be sufficient depending on how much there is to do. If you have to go somewhere else due to lack of facilities that is the next step; otherwise, you are pretty well set. It is important not to overdo things. That is, it is better to do too few things at once than too many. In the short run this may not seem important but complications can easily arise. A mistake can be expensive as well. At first, the whole procedure will seem complicated. Soon, however, it will become just another facet of life. It is difficult to foresee any end to the necessity for this task in the immediate future, but then, one can never tell. After the procedure is completed one arranges the materials into different groups again. Then they can be put into their appropriate places. Eventually they will be used once more and the whole cycle will have to be repeated. However, that is part of life. (Bransford & Johnson, 1972, pp. 722)

Most people experience a great deal of difficulty remembering the details of the procedure described in this passage. The points made seem so uncon-

nected and arbitrary. If the title of the passage, "Washing Clothes," had been provided before you read the material, however, it would have permitted ready comprehension of the paragraph. The title would have activated all of the schemata (see Chapter 3) possessed by you about washing clothes, ones that would permit understanding of the paragraph content. These activated schemata would have permitted you to make sense of each part of the passage and the passage as a whole.

People often understand "new" material in terms of prior knowledge (e.g., Anderson & Pearson, 1984; Chapter 3, this book). The catch is that learners must activate their prior knowledge if it is to affect current comprehension and learning. Often the to-be-learned content includes cues associated with prior knowledge so strongly that relevant schemata are activated automatically. That is the case when college students are provided the title, "Washing Clothes." Once activated, the schemata affect interpretation of all that follows. Thus, the sentence, "That is, it is better to do too few things at once than too many," would have many meanings out of context. When encountered while reading a story entitled, "Washing Clothes," the interpretation is, "It is better to wash only a few pieces of clothing at once rather than overloading the washer." Knowing the title, the reader **infers** that the text is about washing a few pieces of clothing and the concern is with overloading the washer. The activated schemata also direct the **allocation of attention.** Thus, once the washing clothes schema is activated, the reader goes looking for elements of text related to washing clothes.

In short, once schemata are activated, they guide attention to text and permit inferences, with the result a mental representation of the text by the reader that is not identical to what was presented in text. For the present example, the representation is likely to include text information central to the washing clothes schema. More ambiguous information in the text will be translated into information about washing clothes (i.e., inferences will occur reconciling the ambiguous information with the rest of the text so that the entire representation is consistent with a clothes-washing framework). Part of the reason that recall of a text is not perfect is because activated prior knowledge supports the acquisition of some parts of to-be-learned content more than others and distorts other to-be-learned content to be consistent with activated schemata. That a learner's representation of a text is not an exact copy of the text has been understood for a long time (e.g., Bartlett, 1932).

Schemata affect more than encoding. They have an impact on retrieval as well. By thinking about washing clothes, the learner can think about each part of the washing clothes schema and recall whether that part of the schema was represented in the passage. If it was represented, the schema can aid recall additionally. Thus, as you thought about loading the washer, you might remember that the passage said it was better to do only a few things at a time and that complications arise if you do too many things at once. Those memories in turn might cue long-term knowledge of what can go wrong with a washer, stimulating memory of the hassles of overflows—which, in turn, might remind that the text said mistakes could be costly. Memory using this approach would not be perfect, although it would be better than without activation of the clothes-washing schema at recall.

Some errors at retrieval will be errors of inference. So, if the washing clothes schema was used to guide recall of the washing clothes passage, some learners might infer that the passage mentioned detergent and "recall" that detergent was used. Such distortions are common, reflecting that recall involves **reconstruction** of to-be-learned information based on prior knowledge. Even so, all that is remembered are not reconstructions. Some of what is recalled is "in the memory trace."

The main point here, however, is that people's understanding of to-be-learned content in terms of prior knowledge affects both encoding and retrieval (see Anderson & Pearson, 1984, for extensive commentary). It makes a great deal of sense to do all possible to increase understanding of content by encouraging students to relate to-be-learned information to prior knowledge.

Even so, understanding material superficially often is not sufficient to ensure that new content will be learned. John Bransford, who generated so much of the research supporting models of encoding and retrieval based on schemata, also provided data substantiating that superficial understanding is not enough to ensure high memory, at least in some situations.

Bransford and his colleagues (e.g., Bransford et al., 1982; Stein & Bransford, 1979) reported a series of studies in which the subjects read sentences. Read the following and ask yourself as you are doing so whether each sentence can be understood:

> The short man bought the broom.
> The brave man gave money to the robber.
> The fat man read the sign.
> The tall man bought the crackers.
> The thin man found the scissors.
> The rich man picked up the chair.
> The sad man looked at his new boat.
> The kind man ate dinner.
> The smart man went to work.
> The bald man used the phone.
> The artistic man put down the knife.
> The frightened man ironed the sheet.
> The sleepy man bought the mug.
> The evil man wound up the clock.
> The blind man hit the flea.
> The bearded man threw out the coupon.
> The crippled man flicked the switch.
> The dying man used a feather.
> The religious man used the saw.
> The long-haired man looked for the pole.
> The Irish man counted the leaves.
> The weak man thanked the checkout girl.
> The patriotic man memorized the words.
> The dishonest man looked closely at the wrapper.
> (Sentences used by Pressley, McDaniel, Turnure, Wood, & Ahmad, 1987, p. 300)

It was easy to understand each of the sentences in that list. Does understanding the sentences make it inevitable that they will be remembered? Here's a test. Without looking back, What did the sad man do? . . . the sleepy man? . . . the crippled man? . . . the fat man? . . . the Irish man? . . . the evil man? Did understanding the sentences result in inevitable memory of them? As should be obvious by this point, for most readers, the answer is no. It is usually difficult for adults who read such sentences to remember which man did what. Even though each sentence can be understood as it is read, the relationship specified by the sentence is arbitrary. When so much arbitrary information is presented together, it is difficult to keep the arbitrary relationships sorted out. Understanding individual pieces of information does not ensure memory of the pieces.

More positively, learners often possess a great deal of prior knowledge that they can relate to arbitrary pieces of information and, if they do so, render the material more meaningful and more memorable. In the case of the "man" sentences, learners can be asked to think about why the relationship specified in each sentence makes sense—they can be asked to think about "why" each man did what he did and especially why it is significant that a man with the specified characteristic performed the action indicated. When an instruction like that is provided to learners, the sentence, "The short man bought the broom," results in rationales such as, "Maybe it is a low room that needs to be swept," and "He could see how good the bristles were because he was so close to them." The sentence about a crippled man flicking a switch elicits rationales such as, "It's a switch on an electric wheelchair," and ". . . in a building with an elevator fully designed for the handicapped."

When university students are instructed to respond to such why-questions while reading such man-facts, their learning increases dramatically. For example, when university students read "man" sentences without being told in advance that there would be a memory test (i.e., in a study of **incidental learning;** Pressley, McDaniel, et al., 1987, Experiments 1 and 2), answering why-questions improved memory by more than 280 percent. When the students were aware they were reading the sentences in preparation for a memory test (i.e., in a study of **intentional learning;** Pressley, McDaniel, et al., 1987, Experiments 1 and 3), the improvement was less dramatic but still striking (i.e., more than 30 percent).

A series of experiments followed the initial Pressley, McDaniel, et al. (1987) finding. These studies established that why-questioning (referred to by Pressley and colleagues as **elaborative interrogation**) improves learning of facts, both when presented in lists and when presented in expository passages (e.g., Pressley, Symons, McDaniel, Snyder, & Turnure, 1988; Woloshyn, Pressley, & Schneider, 1992). The benefits of elaborative interrogation can be obtained with middle school–age students as well, although the effects seem not to be as large as those obtained with adults (Wood, Pressley, & Winne, 1990).

The most important research in this series of studies, however, has pinpointed the cause of the elaborative interrogation effect. On the face of it, why-questioning might promote learning by encouraging greater effort by learners *or* increasing arousal *or* forcing more extensive and meaningful processing of to-be-learned content relative to what control subjects would be doing as they simply read facts. Pressley and collaborators believed, however, that elaborative interrogation was effective because it prompted learners to activate prior knowledge related to the to-be-learned facts, prior knowledge that would not be activated by reading alone—for people often do not automatically access knowledge they possess that could be related to new information (e.g., Prawat, 1989).

Martin and Pressley (1991) produced evidence in favor of the prior knowledge activation hypothesis. In their study, Canadian students learned facts about Canadian provinces. In four conditions of the study, the subjects were asked why-questions, with the why-questions varying from ones that directed attention to related prior knowledge to questions that directed attention away from relevant prior knowledge. If activation of prior knowledge is the active mechanism accounting for elaborative interrogation effects, performance in these four why-questioning conditions should have varied with the degree that questions oriented learners to relevant prior knowledge. Alternatively, all of the question types should have increased attention to the to-be-learned facts relative to reading alone; all question types should have increased arousal as well; and all question types should have increased meaningful processing. Thus, if increased attention, arousal, or meaningful processing account for elaborative interrogation effects, to-be-learned materials should have been learned better in all four questioning conditions relative to a reading control condition.

Martin and Pressley (1991) found that performance in the why-questioning conditions varied with the degree the why-questions forced attention to prior knowledge (e.g., "Why would the largest percentage of unionized workers be in British Columbia" orients toward prior knowledge supporting the claim that the largest percentage of unionized workers are in British Columbia; "Why is it surprising that the largest percentage of unionized workers are not in some other province" orients toward prior knowledge supporting the same fact much less so). In fact, for the questions that least directed attention to prior knowledge, there was little if any evidence of facilitation owing to elaborative interrogation. See Miller and Pressley (1989) for additional evidence that why-questions that direct attention away from critical content and toward not-so-critical information can undermine learning of essential information.

For additional evidence that prior knowledge plays a critical role in mediating the effectiveness of elaborative interrogation, see Woloshyn, Pressley, and Schneider (1992), who demonstrated that performance in why-questioning conditions depends greatly on the amount of prior knowledge possessed by learners pertaining to to-be-learned content. In their study, when Germans used elaborative interrogation to learn new information about Germany, they did better than when they attempted to learn new information about Canada using elaborative interrogation; when Canadians attempted to learn new information about Canada using elaborative interrogation, they did better than when they attempted to learn new information about Germany using elaborative interrogation.

When all of the data on elaborative interrogation are considered (for a review, see Pressley, Wood, Woloshyn, Martin, King, & Menke, 1992), it is apparent that learners often fail to relate what they already know to new material unless they are prompted to do so—such as when they are asked to answer why-questions pertaining to the material. As Ellen Langer (1989) puts it, people often process information "mindlessly." An important consequence of such mindlessness is that new content is understood less completely than it could be, and thus it is not as easily learned or remembered as it might be if the learner related prior knowledge to the task. Elaborative interrogation forces more extensive connection of new material to prior knowledge and hence greater understanding of the new to-be-learned content, with the consequence that learning is much better.

Effects of Understanding on Problem Solving   Understanding the significance of information affects not only memory, but also problem solving. One of the things that good learners do as they learn new ways to solve problems is that they construct explanations to themselves about the problem—that is, they relate a current problem to their prior knowledge. Chi, Bassok, Lewis, Reimann, and Glaser (1989; see also Chi & Bassok, 1989), for example, studied how physics students learn from worked-out example problems (see Chapter 3, this volume). The students were asked to think aloud as they went through the worked-out examples. There were large differences between students in the extent that they explained to themselves the significance of the sequence of steps in the worked-out

problems. Moreover, there were clear correlations between the number and quality of self-explanations generated and success in solving subsequently presented problems that were analogous to the sample problems.

Of course, one reaction to Chi et al.'s (1989) finding is that more intelligent and better students would be more likely to generate explanations than would weaker students, so there is no causal relationship between generation of the self-explanations and subsequent performance. That there might be ability differences between the good and poor problem solvers was suggested by clear differences in awareness of understanding by the good and poor problem solvers while processing the sample problems. The good problem solvers indicated much more often than the poor problem solvers when they were understanding the moves in the example and when they were not understanding the example moves. Thus, it could be that the more able students coming into Chi et al's (1989) study explained examples to themselves more, monitored their understanding of examples more, and solved problems better, without any necessary causal connections between self-explanations, monitoring, and subsequent performance.

There are, however, experimental data that permit stronger claims about cause-and-effect relationships between self-explanations that increase understanding and problem solving. For example, in Mayer and Cook (1981), adults listened to an expository passage about radar. For all subjects, there were pauses after every 4 to 7 seconds. Some participants in the study were required to say back the content they just heard; other subjects were instructed to try to understand the passage during these pauses by reflecting on the passage.

After listening to the passage, the subjects were asked to use the information in the passage in a new way. Subjects in the reflective condition did better on this test than did repetition subjects. During recall of the original passage, much more of the explanative material in the passage was recalled by reflection condition participants than by repetition condition subjects, although there was no difference between the two conditions for recall of other types of material in the passage. In general, it seemed as if the reflective group focused on the explanations more than did the repetition group, with this difference in attention between the two conditions the potential cause of the difference in problem-solving performance between the two conditions.

Consistent with research on elaborative interrogation, Mayer (e.g., 1980) has also demonstrated that asking readers to answer inferential questions about text they are reading (i.e., questions requiring them to compare content in one part of a text with content in another part of a text, relate content in a text to a familiar situation) results in more certain application of knowledge gained from text. That is, readers who answer such questions are more likely to be able to solve problems requiring application of the text content in situations not specifically covered by the text. During learning of the original texts, subjects who answered inferential questions were more likely to focus on and remember the explanatory parts of the texts than were subjects who read the text as they normally would in preparation for a test (see Mayer, 1985). In general, Mayer's research is strongly supportive of the importance of encouraging learners to process parts of text that provide explanations that can increase understanding of the relationships covered in text. Answering integrative questions is one approach to doing so; simply asking learners to attempt to understand text can also improve learners' abilities to apply knowledge acquired from text.

Bielaczyc, Pirolli, and Brown (1991) provided an especially compelling experiment confirming that self-explanations can positively affect use of material read to solve subsequently presented problems. The university students in the study read lessons concerned with LISP programming. In previous research, Pirolli and Bielaczyc (1989) had determined that the best problem solvers following such lessons tended to (1) determine the main idea presented in lessons, (2) determine the meaning of the LISP code presented in examples, and (3) connect ideas in text with moves in the examples. Thus, in their study, subjects in the experimental condition were taught to look for the main ideas in text and to focus on the meaning of examples and how the examples related to the text. That is, the trained subjects were taught to generate self-explanations about relations between examples and text. Such instruction occurred in a socially interactive, scaffolded (see Chapters 1 and 8) fashion that began with the subjects watching a videotape in which the self-explanation strategies were applied aloud by a student. The instruction that was provided was sensitive to difficulties experienced by particular students and attempted to remediate difficulties. The self-explanation instruction also included teaching subjects to use a series of self-questions aimed at increasing learner awareness of whether they understood the lessons and increasing ability at finding particular pieces of information in text and understanding ideas. The self-questioning structures taught to the experimental participants were reminiscent of Meichenbaum's self-instructional approach (Chapter 7). Control subjects in the study spent the same amount of time in interaction with the experimenter, with the focus of their instruction being memory and recall of the content of the lessons.

As expected, the self-explanation instruction increased self-explanations dramatically, with much less pretest to posttest increase in self-elaborations in the control condition: The instructed students increased their identification of main ideas in lessons from the beginning to the end of the study; they were also more likely at the end of training to provide meaning-oriented elaborations explaining the significance of some aspect of an example, including elaborations connecting text and examples. The instructed subjects also monitored more, indicating more often when they understood text versus when they did not understand it.

Most important, self-explanation training improved students' abilities to apply the programming skills they had learned in the lessons to new problems. This experimental effect (i.e., difference between experimental and control conditions favoring the experimental condition) was complemented by within-condition differences. Within both the control and the experimental conditions, the subjects who were most self-explanative following training performed best on the programming exercises. All of the outcomes in this study were consistent with the general position that increasing the likelihood that students explain relations between text and problems—and hence try to understand how the coverage in the text maps onto the coverage in the problems—increases effective problem-solving.

In summary, there is consistent evidence that trying to understand material—by searching prior knowledge for relationships between the new content and prior knowledge—can improve memory of the material (especially when there is salient between-item interference, as when many related facts are presented) and application of the content to new problems. Unfortunately, there is also substantial evidence that students often do not try to understand relationships presented in new material, failing to relate what they already know to new content or content covered in text through worked-out examples (Mayer, 1985; Woloshyn et al., 1992). Thus, substantial efforts are being made to determine how to increase student understanding of text (e.g., through self-questioning, including why-questioning), with the goal of eventually teaching such strategies so that students internalize them and subsequently use the strategies in a self-regulated fashion—thus, the scaffolded teaching in Bielaczyc et al. (1991). One impetus for continuing such research is striking correlations between generation of explanations as part of learning and subsequent memory and problem solving (see Webb's [1989] review of studies in which the explainer in small groups learned more than other members of the group). Another is consistent experimental outcomes in which learners taught to generate and respond to inferential questions requiring explanatory responses understand and remember text better than control subjects not taught to generate and answer such questions (e.g., King, 1989, 1990, 1992). Another way of encouraging students to relate new information to prior knowledge is taken up in the next subsection.

Processing Advance Organizers

Before reviewing the theory and research pertaining to advance organizers, we offer a warning. The term "advance organizer" has a checkered history (Corkill, 1992). Although Ausubel (e.g., 1960) was the original theorist describing advance organizers and what he considered to be their potential effects on learning from text, the concept has undergone considerable reformulation since then. One reason is that research inspired by Ausubel's work, but not necessarily consistent with Ausubel's conception of advance organizer, failed to produce consistently positive results. That is, when people processed "advance organizers" that researchers claimed were consistent with Ausubel's formulation, there was often little if any improvement in comprehension and recall of text relative to when readers were not presented advance organizers before they read. A second reason for the reformulation of the concept of advance organizer is that cognitive theory in general shifted since Ausubel's theory was proposed. Researchers such as Richard Mayer and Sharon Derry reformed the concept of advance organizer to be consistent with one of the most prominent of these new directions.

Ausubel's Original Formulation and the Research It Inspired One difficulty with Ausubel's conception of an advance organizer was that it was extremely vague. It was clear that advance organizers should be processed by readers before they encounter to-be-learned content (and hence the "advance" part of the concept). Exactly what was to be presented in advance of reading was something of a mystery except that it was supposed to be at a ". . . higher level of abstraction, generality, and inclusiveness" (Ausubel, 1968, p. 148), than the to-be-learned content. Ausubel believed that advance organizers could be used to mediate learning of both familiar and unfamiliar content, with familiar material defined as related to prior knowledge possessed by a learner.

In a series of experiments with college students, Ausubel claimed to have validated the advance organizer concept: In each study, Ausubel reported that students who read advance organizers before reading passages containing new content understood and remembered more of what they read than students who read passages not accompanied by advance organizers. One difficulty in interpreting the original Ausubelian results, however, is that the actual advance organizers used in the study were not provided in the reports (see Corkill, 1992). Such operational vagueness on Ausubel's part resulted in different readers of Ausubel's theory and studies conceiving of advance organizers differently. The result was a flurry of studies involving different prereading manipulations, all of which were identified as advance organizers by the researchers doing the work.

The concept of advance organizer was variously conceived as instruction to students to generate passage or paragraph headings, instructions to readers to predict the content of upcoming text, pictures summarizing the relations depicted in text, semantic maps of upcoming text, prequestions, outlines, and summaries presented at the beginning of a passage (Corkill, 1992). Enthusiasm for the concept of advance organizers waned because, more often than not, the operations passed off as advance organizers failed to produce improved understanding or memory of text content, with the flood of negative evidence transparent to the entire profession with the publication of a review in the prestigious *Review of Educational Research* of 32 studies purporting to test the hypothesis that advance organizers improve learning of text, with only 12 deemed to have improved comprehension (Barnes & Clawson, 1975).

Other prominent psychologists, most notably Richard Mayer (1977), were more critical than Barnes and Clawson about how various researchers had defined the concept of advance organizer but nonetheless agreed that: "Advance organizers, as presently constructed, do not facilitate learning" (Barnes & Clawson, 1975, p. 651; quoted by Mayer & Bromage, 1980, p. 210).

Mayer and Derry's Revised Definition of Advance Organizer and Research Related to It

Shortly after the Barnes and Clawson's (1975) review, schema theory emerged as the leading model of text comprehension (e.g., Anderson, Spiro, & Anderson, 1978; see Chapter 3, this book). When it did, the notion of advance organizer was rethought, with a number of new studies inspired by this reformulation. Mayer (1979) proposed that a good advance organizer would activate prior knowledge (i.e., schemata) that would increase the likelihood that the learner would be able to understand new information by relating the new content to prior knowledge (i.e., the learner would assimilate the new content to prior knowledge). Derry's (1984) addition to this definition was that learning the new content would result in an accommodation (i.e., "correction") of the original schemata.

Mayer and Bromage (1980) offered a test of the potency of advance organizers consistent with the new definition. Undergraduate students read a seven-page text explaining a simple computer language, with the text explaining command statements in the language and the operations defined by the command statements with respect to particular locations in the computer (i.e., input stack, memory, program, output) and objects operated on (i.e., number, pointer). For example, "FIND" could define an operation on the input stack involving a number: Find the number on the next data card waiting at the input stack. Alternatively, "FIND" operated on memory of a number: Find the number in the memory space indicated in the READ statement. "MOVE" could operate on a number in the input stack: Move the data card through the input stack to the finished pile. "MOVE" also could operate on a pointer with respect to the program: "Go on to the next statement."

The advance organizer that Mayer and Bromage (1980) created for this text was a diagram and text relating the computer locations to objects familiar to the readers:

The "input window" was likened to a ticket window, "memory scoreboard" was described as an erasable scoreboard with eight spaces, the "program list" and "pointer arrow" were described as a shopping list, and the "output pad" was described as a pad of message paper. (Mayer & Bromage, 1980, p. 217)

The manipulation in the study was whether subjects were presented this information before reading the text (i.e., in the advance organizer condition) or after they read it. Mayer and Bromage (1980) predicted different effects on learning as a function of this manipulation. In particular, they believed that if the organizer was presented before a text was read, the passage would activate prior knowledge in the readers that would aid their comprehension of the passage. Because prior knowledge would not be activated *before* the text was read when the information was presented after the reading, the expectation was that readers would not relate the content of the text to the prior knowledge reminded by the organizer in the after-passage condition.

In general, there was strong support for the hypothesis that presentation of the information in advance of reading affected understanding of the text. For example, when advance organizer subjects recalled information from the text, they were more likely to report integrations of ideas across the text. In contrast, the after-reading subjects kept the ideas in the text more clearly separated from one another during recall. Advance organizer students also were less likely to report inappropriate inferences in their recall (i.e., draw incorrect conclusions from the reading). This study would be one of the earliest in a substantial number of studies during the 1980s that would produce data consistent with a schema-based conception of advance organizers.

In Derry (1984), undergraduates read a text conveying the Greek mythological conception of creation. Here is part of the text that the undergraduates attempted to learn in the study:

Before Prometheus could get there, he [Epimetheus] gave away all the best gifts: strength and swiftness and courage and shrewd cunning, fur and feathers and wings and shells and the like—until no good was left to work with, no protective covering and no outstanding qualities. Too late, as always, he was sorry for he thought the elders might be displeased. He couldn't think of what to do, so he asked his brother's help. Prometheus, then, took over the task and thought out a way to make the next creations superior. He took ore and fashioned them in a noble form. And then he went to Nirvana where the sun was within reach, and there he lit a torch and brought down fire. (Derry, 1984, p. 100)

Students either read the passage accompanied by an advance organizer contrasting four themes in the myth with Biblical themes, which were presumably consistent with the students' prior knowledge, or they read the passage without the benefit of the advance organizer. Here is part of the advance organizer used in the study:

> Man created in God's image . . . the similarities between the Greek myth and Old Testament version of creation are striking. After beasts are made, Man is created by a kind, all-knowing heavenly father who strives to make humans superior to all animals. This is not an easy task in the Greek myth because of how beasts were created. But the father of Man does two things to insure Man's superiority. Like in the Old Testament, he fashions them from an earthly substance, in his own image. But the Greek myth also relates another account of how man was raised in status: the story of fire. (Derry, 1984, pp. 99–100)

The posttest required memory of the text, with some items requiring verbatim recall. Other items, however, involved selecting among potential answers, with some answers implied by the text only and some consistent with a modification of the text to accommodate the information in the advance organizer. One such question was the following:

> Prometheus took over the task of creation because
> a. Zeus asked him to because he was the wisest god.
> b. Epimetheus couldn't think of what to do.
> c. The gods had failed in their experiments with metals and called on Prometheus to help.
> d. Prometheus wanted to play a trick on Zeus.
> e. Prometheus wanted men to stand upright and be superior to beasts.

Selection of choice "e" would signal an advance organizer–modified representation of the text content; selection of "b" could be made based on the text alone. Derry's (1984) most striking result was that e-type answers were more common for students reading the advance organizers than for controls reading the same mythological text without exposure to the advance organizer.

Corkill (1992) reviewed all of the evidence pertaining to advance organizers effects, focusing on the studies conducted in the 1980s. She concluded that advance organizers can facilitate learning from text in some circumstances: when "(a) subjects will not make appropriate connections between prior knowledge and the to-be-learned material without assistance, (b) attend to the advance organizer, (c) have adequate time to study the advance organizer and the to-be-learned material, and (d) are tested for recall after at least a brief delay." In general, advance organizers that are written out in paragraph form seem to be more potent than briefer organizers. Many of the studies met these conditions, with advance organizers in the successful studies often provided to students in well-written paragraphs.

Reviewing Advance Organizers Before a Test Corkill, Glover, Bruning, and King (1988) hypothesized that reviewing advance organizers just before taking a test over material covered in a text that included advance organizers would increase recall of the text on the test. Such facilitation was observed when the test occurred sometime after the text had been read (1 day to 2 weeks later). In the language of cognitive psychologists, advance organizers are terrific retrieval cues, and if a text includes them, reading them over just before a test is a smart study strategy.

Summary Although our reading of the literature is that advance organizer effects often are not large, there does seem to be consistent effects on learning of text that is accompanied by advance organizers that are 50 or more words in length. Corkill (1992) concluded that positive effects of advance organizers have been produced in diverse content areas, when subjects have read texts varying in length, under a range of testing conditions, and with delays of up to 2 to 3 weeks after reading of text.

One constraint that we would add, however, is that there has been relatively little study of advance organizer effects below the high school level. Given that other adjunct aids (e.g., questions posed before reading of a text, postquestions) have more limited effects on children's learning than adult learning (see Chapter 14), it may be that the gains for adults produced by advance organizers would not be obtained in the elementary years.

Notetaking

Notetaking is common, at least for college students (Hartley & Marshall, 1974; Nye, Crooks, Powley, & Tripp, 1984; Palmatier & Bennett, 1974), the primary means for creating an external, long-term record of what went on in class. No one doubts that taking notes aids college-level learning, for information contained in notes is much more likely than information not noted in lecture to be recalled later on tests (Aiken, Thomas, & Shennum, 1975; Bretzing & Kulhavy, 1981; Einstein, Morris, & Smith, 1985; Kierwa & Fletcher, 1984).

Educational psychologists have been particularly interested in determining when learning occurs during notetaking, however. DiVesta and Gray (1972) suggested that both the act of taking notes (i.e., encoding) and the subsequent review of notes increase learning. A number of studies have examined the effects of encoding notes without the opportunity of review, with the clear majority of studies favoring the conclusion that taking notes per se has a positive effect on learning; a number of studies have also examined the value of review of notes taken, with the majority of those studies favoring the conclusion that review of notes also increases learning, even if the notes were produced by someone else (Hartley, 1983; Kiewra, 1985, 1989a, 1989b; Kiewra, DuBois, Christian, & McShane, 1988; Ladas, 1980).

Like other academic activities, notetaking requires self-managed coordination of strategies, prior knowledge, and cognitive resources such as attentional capacity (Strage, Tyler, Rohwer, & Thomas, 1987). For example, self-regulation of strategies during notetaking is apparent as students focus on important compared with unimportant information in constructing notes (e.g., Kiewra, Mayer, Christensen, Kim, & Risch, 1991) and when students reorganize a lecturer's message as they take notes on it (e.g., Einstein, Morris, & Smith, 1985).

Despite advances in our knowledge about the dynamics of student notetaking through true experimentation, Van Meter, Yokoi, and Pressley (1994) believed that the notetaking studies to date failed to capture many of the interesting complexities that are part of self-regulation during notetaking. One problem is that many of the controlled studies of notetaking occurred in artificial situations. That is, rather than attending a live lecture, students in the study took notes from a videotaped or audiotaped lecture. Usually the lecture was an isolated experience rather than one of a series of lectures in a course that meant something to the students. Typically the test on the lecture content occurred shortly after the lecture, rather than days or weeks or months later as is the case in courses. Factors that might make a big difference in notetaking typically were held constant in the experimental studies of

notetaking. Thus, often one rate of presentation was used in a notetaking study, typically a pace deemed to be moderate by the experimenter (see Cook & Mayer, 1983). Often the relation of lecture content to student prior knowledge was held constant by presentation of material unfamiliar to all subjects in the study. When factors such as rate and relation to prior knowledge are held constant in this fashion, there is no possibility of determining how notetaking is affected by them.

Van Meter et al. (1994) reasoned that notetaking requires conscious, complex problem solving on the part of the notetaker—that is, conscious decisions about which parts of lecture should be noted, how notes should be organized, and how notes should be used after class. Humans often have detailed knowledge they can report with respect to those situations requiring conscious decision making (e.g., Diaper, 1989; Meyer & Booker, 1991; Scott, Clayton, & Gibson, 1991). Thus, Van Meter et al. (1994) decided to ask undergraduates at the University of Maryland about their notetaking using ethnographic interviewing techniques.

Specifically, Van Meter et al. (1994) asked undergraduates to talk about their perceptions of notetaking, including their knowledge of factors affecting notetaking, their regulation of notetaking, and the functions of notetaking for them. The study began with focus groups involving up to seven or eight students discussing notetaking with the investigators. Broad questions were posed to these groups initially, such as, "How do you take notes?"; "When do you take notes?"; "How do you know what to write?"; and "What do you do with your notes outside the classroom?" Students in these focus groups were permitted to take the conversation in any direction they pleased as they responded to these questions, so long as their comments were pertinent to notetaking. The researchers sometimes followed up student remarks for clarifications or expansions. The focus group responses were used to develop more formal interview questions that were posed to individual students. Specifically the researchers identified the many different types of comments and claims made in the focus groups and developed individual interviews tapping the issues identified by the focus group members as pertinent to notetaking. There were several rounds of individual interviewing, each involving different students, with each new round aimed at seeking clarification about issues raised in the previous round. This exercise continued until it was clear that no new issues or clarifications were emerging during interviews. More than 200 University of Maryland undergraduates, representing all four undergraduate classes and many different majors, participated in the study, so the responses represented the entire undergraduate student body.

Both qualitative and quantitative analyses of these interview data were conducted. These analyses suggested complexities not identified in previous analyses of student notetaking. First, students have diverse goals when they take notes in class. Notes can be taken as study aids for upcoming examinations or to assist the solving of homework problems (e.g., worked examples of problems) or completion of writing assignments (e.g., Benton, Kiewra, Whitfill, & Dennison, 1993). Notetaking can be undertaken to increase understanding *during* class (i.e., some students believe that constructing notes helps them understand what the lecturer is saying) or as a means of forcing attention in class (i.e., staying awake!). Second, the Maryland students definitely perceived that lecturers differ in whether their style is compatible with effective notetaking. Lecturers who are easy to take notes from talk more slowly and are better organized, perhaps even providing an explicit outline of the lecture but at least separating their points clearly. Such lecturers permit students to use the notetaking strategies they most prefer (with these varying from student to student) and to develop notes that represent relationships between the concepts covered in lecture. In contrast, fast-talking, disorganized professors require much adjustment by the student, with students shifting their notetaking style to accommodate the professor's style, including the type of information the professor taps on examinations. Third, students reported that it was easier to take notes in courses presenting information related to their own prior knowledge. Fourth, notes were reported as varying depending on the type of content in the course, with verbatim notes more likely when material covered was specific and exact (e.g., definitions, names, dates), examinations emphasized verbatim memory, and students feared that paraphrasing might distort the lecturer's meaning. Fifth, students believe that they became more skilled in notetaking with increasing experience in college. Sixth, the most common postclass activity involving notes is review, although some students recopy their notes, and others rewrite them to include elaborations and

reorganizations of content. Seventh, notes play a more important role in studying when the lecturer's style permits good notes to be taken. When the lecturer's style does not permit good notes, other resources are relied on more during study, including consulting past examinations, seeking information from teaching assistants, and especially seeking clarifications from classmates.

Van Meter et al. (1994) proposed a model of student notetaking based on their own results and outcomes reported by others: Because virtually all college students take notes in all classes, every student is self-regulating his or her notetaking to some extent. Students' overarching goal of passing the course is served by notetaking, which supports the subgoals of passing examinations, completing homework assignments, and keeping the student alert in class. Good notetakers have a variety of notetaking strategies, from verbatim to highly paraphrased and abbreviated notes, from taking of scattered notes to highly organized notes. The experienced college notetaker has extensive metacognition about where and when to use the various notetaking strategies (e.g., as detailed in the previous paragraph, when and where it is appropriate to take verbatim notes). This metacognition guides student selection of to-be-noted content, with the good notetaker aware not only that important information should be encoded in notes, but also that unfamiliar material and material that might be especially difficult for him or her deserves special emphasis in notes. No two notetakers construct the same notes, with one important individual differences variable that mediates notetaking being the relationship between the learner's prior knowledge and the content in the lecture.

Even so, there is more than the notetaker who determines what notes are taken. Some lecturers inspire more homogeneous notes than others—they lecture at a pace that permits students to get the material in their notes, and they signal well to the students what they consider important. For example, by asking conceptual prequestions pertaining to upcoming content, the lecturer can stimulate more elaborate, effective notes by notetakers (Rickards & McCormick, 1988).

Also, more than the notetaker determines what the notetaker does with the notes taken in class: Good lecturers provide notes that are more likely to be used later by students in preparation for examinations and completion of other assignments than are the notes taken from poorly organized lecturers. Thus, in a very real sense, the good lecturer's control of student behavior extends past the lecture hour more reliably than does the poor lecturer's control of the student.

The good notetaker is constantly reflecting, for example, on whether notes taken were helpful on an examination. When the notes were not beneficial, the good notetaker may change notetaking strategies. When effective methods of notetaking are identified in one course, the good notetaker extends them to other courses, with the outcome of improved notetaking skills across the college years. Thus, how a college student takes notes in a course today is determined by multiple factors, including distant variables, such as a long history of experiences with courses, extending back to junior high school or earlier. It is also determined by more proximal variables, such as experiences with the examinations in this course as well as contemporary variables, such as signals the lecturer is sending as he or she presents information.

What the Van Meter et al. (1994) model does is open up a range of possibilities not considered previously in research on notetaking. Educational researchers concerned with notetaking were so obsessed with determining if both notetaking per se and review of notes increase learning that they lost track of the much bigger picture. The result is that the experimental literature on notetaking is silent about self-regulated notetaking, including the diverse goals supporting notetaking, the factors affecting the types of notes taken, and the growth of the notetaker as a strategist both within courses and across courses. The Van Meter et al. (1994) study suggests that there is a great deal to discover about the notetaking strategies students use, how those strategies develop, how use of those strategies depends on metacognition and prior knowledge, and what motivates virtually every college student to take notes in virtually every class. (This motivational function is interesting, given that we can think of no other example of an academically supportive strategy that is at least attempted on virtually all occasions when it might prove helpful.) Most textbooks leave the readers with the message that research supports the conclusion that notetaking improves learning at the high school and college levels. Our message is that there is much more to learn about this behavior that is so common in the life of virtually every college student.

We close this section on notetaking by pointing out one other notetaking problem that has been relatively neglected by educational psychologists, but to the extent that it has been studied, the data have been consistent with other data supporting important individual differences in processing as a function of expertise. There has been little study of how people take notes from texts that they read, even though this is an academic activity of great consequence not only for school learning, but also whenever someone is attempting to assemble evidence from texts. The data that do exist suggest great variability in notetaking from texts as a function of prior knowledge and academic experience.

For example, Hidi and Klaiman (1983) studied how more and less experienced students—graduate students compared with junior and senior high school students—take notes. Their participants were asked to think aloud as they took notes. The experts tended to preview the text before reading it and took notes selectively, based on their perceptions of the importance of the ideas in the text and how well the ideas in the text meshed with the reader's personal reasons for going through the text. The experts also paraphrased the content and tended to link it to their prior knowledge. Experts were conscious of their notetaking strategies. In contrast, the younger students had more difficulty verbalizing their notetaking strategies, with less selectivity and more verbatim copying apparent in their notetaking. The adolescents tended to read the text from beginning to end, in contrast to the graduate students who went back and forth in text.

Hidi and Klaiman (1983) also explored whether forcing younger students to preread text would produce better notetaking. Unfortunately, little changed with this requirement. Because of the usefulness of notetaking from text as a strategy, we believe it is a problem worth expending research resources on in the next decade. Because notetaking does involve complex coordination of goals, the relationship of prior knowledge to text content, strategies, and other constraints (e.g., amount of time available to process the text), it would not surprise us that teaching effective notetaking will not be easy. Even so, we shudder when we realize that many study skills programs are being offered to elementary and secondary schools that have not been validated at all, with notetaking from text always a prominent skill in these packages. That schools buy such programs reflects students' needs. If those needs are to be served well, researchers must develop a psychology of notetaking for the elementary and secondary years, one that includes detailed study of how to teach notetaking.

Summary

Many of the various mechanisms described in this section that can affect learning, memory, and cognition can be thought of as processes that can be used strategically: Deciding to process deeply is strategic in that attention is directed to more meaningful rather than less meaningful aspects of to-be-learned content. The strategic value of imaginally elaborating arbitrary associations has been recognized for centuries. Acting out a sequence of events to fix the sequence in memory is also a strategy, as is attempting to relate new information to prior knowledge. A student can think hard about an advance organizer or pass over it in favor of getting on with the reading, with the former action certainly more strategic than the latter action. The evidence is growing that notetaking is a reflective, strategic activity on the part of college students.

The mechanisms reviewed in this section can also be thought about with respect to nonstrategic knowledge, another of the four most important components of good information processing. Thus, deep processing is enabled by a knowledge base that connects with the meaningful elements of new content. For example, deep processing of "beast" connects to images in long-term memory of many hideous creatures as well as to verbal associations from *Beauty and the Beast* to scripture references to the devil as a beast. Mnemonic elaborations require a great deal of prior knowledge. For example, to use the keyword method to learn foreign vocabulary, it is necessary to know first-language vocabulary that can be used as keywords. In addition, the interactive relationship between the keyword and definition referents cannot be arbitrary: If it is not meaningful, the interaction will not be retrievable later when the learner is tested. Acting out actions requires prior knowledge of the actions. All methods of relating new information to prior knowledge depend on rich prior knowledge. Advance organizers work only if they activate prior knowledge that can, in turn, be related to the new content in the to-be-learned passage. Notetaking is easier when students possess prior knowledge that can be related to lecture content.

In short, the mechanisms reviewed in this section can all be thought about with respect to strategy and knowledge components in interaction, completely consistent with the good information processor model. Because each mechanism affects only particular learning situations, students must have substantial metacognitive knowledge about where and when each mechanism can be applied. Because each mechanism requires effort to carry out, and in some cases substantial efforts, such as when elementary students construct mental images, autonomous use of the mechanisms covered in this section is unlikely without strong motivation, including motivational beliefs about the potency of the mechanisms covered here in general and confidence that intelligent use of the mechanisms covered here can improve learning and performance. The work discussed in this section is all sensible from the perspective of the model featured in this book, that good thinking reflects interactions between strategic mechanisms (i.e., procedures), knowledge, metacognition, and motivation.

MANAGING OPPORTUNITIES TO LEARN: THE EFFECTS OF SIMPLE PRACTICE, DISTRIBUTED PRACTICE, AND TESTS

When new content is presented, there are many different possible ways to structure opportunities to learn. The case made in this section is that practice opportunities can greatly enhance learning of new ideas, especially if the presentations and practice are repeated on several different occasions. We will close the section establishing that people often organize their opportunities to learn in light of their expectations about tests, and hence it is important that students know the accountability demands they face.

Simple Practice

If practice does not make perfect, it certainly improves learning and performance. For example, writing a word over and over does help in learning to spell the word (e.g., Thomas & Dieter, 1987). Nonetheless, the demands of practice are not always appealing to learners. One way to increase the likelihood that a great deal of practice will occur is to set the learning criterion high. Thus, if the student is to learn a list of Latin words, require that the student remember the definitions of all words on five different occasions. If the goal is to teach a luge sledder how to shift weight going into an omega turn, require that the slider perform the weight shift correctly 30 times in a row before moving on to some other luging skill. A great deal of practice is required to meet high criteria. This practice is worth it in the long term because retention is definitely increased by a high degree of original learning (see Druckman & Bjork, 1991, Chapter 3, for a review).

Practice has other effects beyond long-term retention, especially with respect to learning of procedures. Do you remember when you first learned to start a car? You intentionally buckled your seatbelt, checked to see if the parking brake was still on, put the car in park or set the stick into the first position, depressed the clutch (if driving a standard), turned the key, and so forth. Could you think about anything else when you were first learning how to start a car? The likely answer is no, or if you were able to think about other things, it was a "mental hassle" to do so. Compare how you started a car then with how you start it now. Do you intentionally go through each step, conscious of completing each one before proceeding to the next? Can you carry on a conversation easily as you start a car? The answers to these two questions are undoubtedly no and yes.

A sequence of procedures that once required conscious processing (**controlled** processing) can now be done automatically (Schneider, Dumais, & Shiffrin, 1984; Schneider & Shiffrin, 1977; Shiffrin & Schneider, 1977). **Automaticity** is one of the byproducts of practice. As procedures become automatic, less attention (i.e., short-term capacity) is required to carry them out, so it is possible to do other things simultaneously or at least do them more comfortably. With practice, there is also an increase in consistency. When a luge slider is first taking omega turns, every trip down the track is a new adventure filled with unique adaptations to the demands of the course. With great practice, the trips look alike. Think about it. Do you ever do anything different when you get in and start the car now—not really, unless there is a glitch, which can result in a return to conscious processing and execution of the procedures that constitute the ignition sequence.

Much about practice and its effects on learning has been understood for a long time (see Annett, 1989, for a review): (1) At first, there are rather large gains in proficiency owing to practice; even though the amount of improvement is less dramatic as practice continues, there is still improvement that is detectable after many trials and years (e.g., Crossman, 1959). (2) What is at first carried out as a sequence of distinct steps eventually becomes "chunked" (Newell & Rosenbloom, 1981), so that originally separate steps become a whole.

Many of the changes that occur with practice have been summarized in a model of procedural learning proposed by Anderson (1983; Singley & Anderson, 1989) as part of ACT* theory (Chapter 3). When new procedures are first learned, they are encoded as declarative knowledge—knowledge that can be stated. Thus, many students learn in driver's education classes how to talk about and describe various aspects of driving. Indeed, they learn many if-then statements about driving, for example, "If the safety belt is fastened and if the car is in park, then it is all right to turn the key." Such information can be used to mediate driving at first, with the student driver recalling each step in the sequence of steps required to get the car to go. Driving is difficult at this point, requiring a great deal of conscious attention to recall the steps and carry them out. There are also many of errors, in part because people often experience difficulty holding in short-term memory all that must be considered to recall declarative knowledge and apply it in a particular situation (Anderson, 1983; Chapter 6, this book). With practice, there is what Anderson (1983) refers to as **knowledge compilation** (first introduced in this book in Chapter 2): Productions are created from the declarative statements specifying a process. Productions can only be acquired by performing the actions specified by the productions. How can one know that compilation has taken place?: The actions occur more rapidly. There is less verbalization as the cognitive action proceeds. The process occurs more as a whole, rather than as one step at a time.

Consider some think-aloud data generated by a geometry student working on right triangle side-angle-side/side-side-side problems. This student possessed declarative knowledge about application of the side-angle-side and side-side-side postulates. Note how long it takes the student to solve the problem. Note how much verbal restatement occurs, especially of the principles just being learned. Note that the application of the side-angle-side postulate is done in a piecemeal fashion:

> If you look at the side-angle-side postulate (long pause) well, RK and RJ [Note: names of the longest sides of two triangles sharing the side RS] could almost be (long pause) the missing side. I think somehow the side-angle-side postulate works its way into here. (long pause) Let's see what it says: "two sides and the included angle." What would I have to have to have two sides. JS and KS are one of them. Then you could go back to RS = RS. So that would bring up

the side-angle-side postulate. (long pause) But where would angle 1 and angle 2 are right angles fit in (long pause)—wait, I see how they work . . . OK, what does it say—check it one more time. "If two sides and the included angle of one triangle are congruent to the corresponding parts." So I have got to find the two sides and the included angle. With the included angle you get angle 1 and angle 2. I suppose (long pause) they are both right angles, which means they are congruent to each other. My first side is JS to KS. And the next one is RS to RS. So these are the two sides. Yes, I think it is the side-angle-side postulate. (pp. 232–233)

Now compare the solution just presented with the solution to another problem, a solution generated by the same student after a little more practice with side-angle-side problems:

Right off the top of my head I am going to take a guess at what I am supposed to do—angle DCK = angle ABK. There is only one of two, and the side-angle-side postulate is what they are getting to. (p. 234)

That this problem is solved more rapidly without overt verbalization of the procedures being learned and in a holistic fashion rather than a piece-by-piece fashion supports the conclusion that compilation is occurring: The declarative representations of the side-angle-side problem-solving procedure are evolving into procedural knowledge.

Knowledge compilation includes two subprocesses according to Anderson (1983). **Composition** involves taking a sequence of productions and collapsing them into a single production. Thus, for a child only beginning to learn how to dial telephone numbers, dialing might be conceived in terms of the following productions:

If the goal is to dial LV telephone number, and if digit 4 is the first digit of the number, then dial digit 4.

If the goal is to dial LV telephone number, and if 4 has just been dialed, and if 9 is after the 4 in the number, then dial 9.

(Continuing until all 7 digits have been dialed; based on an example in Anderson, 1983, p. 235)

Once compiled, the production operates much more like the following:

If the goal is to dial LV telephone number, and if the number is 495-1212, then dial 4 first and then 9 and then 5, etc. (Again, based on an example provided by Anderson, 1983, p. 235–236)

A **macroproduction** has been formed, one that collapses into one operation what was initially an or-

dered sequence of operations. Eventually, if the LV phone number is dialed frequently enough, the entire sequence fires off automatically once it is initiated. **Proceduralization** is said to have taken place. This can be represented as the following:

If the goal is to dial LV telephone number, dial 4-9-5-1-2-1-2.

Once proceduralization occurs, there is no need to retrieve the number from long-term memory or hold it in working memory. The fingers dial it almost without the person thinking about it. Thus, when a person's goal is to retrieve his or her voice-mail messages, he or she moves the left hand over to the phone and the dialing happens without retrieving the access codes consciously from memory or holding them in working memory. The fingers have danced over the buttons so many times that they "know" the dance.

The sure signs of composition and proceduralization are speeded performance, reduced verbalization (reflecting less need for conscious processing), and increased execution of a task as a whole rather than as parts. An important benefit of knowledge compilation is that much less conscious capacity must be expended to carry out a compiled procedure relative to a sequence of productions. Once compiled, it is still possible to represent a procedure declaratively and to execute the steps consciously—the point is that it is no longer necessary to do so to accomplish the action captured by the compilation. The criticality of such **automaticity** to skilled performance often will be apparent in the chapters that follow (e.g., automatic decoding of words permits freeing up of capacity required to comprehend text; automatic retrieval of simple math facts, such as $3 + 2 = 5$, allows the mathematical problem solver to focus on higher-order aspects of problems).

Practice is often costly in terms of time and effort, and thus there has been substantial research on whether the benefits of practice can be obtained in the absence of practice. A number of studies have been conducted in which actual practice has been compared with **mental practice.** Some of these studies have also evaluated the efficacy of combining actual and mental practice. The effects of practice for acquiring a number of different skills have been evaluated, from being able to speak quickly (e.g., MacKay, 1981, 1982) to tying knots (Annett, 1988) to completing peg boards (Hird, Landers, Thomas, & Horan, 1991). Feltz, Landers, and Becker (1988) provided a meta-analysis of the studies conducted up until that point in time. As previous reviews (e.g., Richardson, 1967; Singer, 1972; Weinberg, 1982) had concluded, Feltz et al. (1988) reported that mental practice produced better performance than no practice. Mental and physical practice combined was better still. Actual practice alone produced better performance than either physical and mental practice combined or mental practice alone. Although it is anything but clear what mechanisms mediate mental practice effects (Annett, 1989), that mental practice can improve linkages of a sequence of behaviors makes obvious that the effects of practice probably involve cognitive components—that the compilation that occurs when tying a knot improves with practice is not a compilation of actions alone but a compilation of representations that mediate execution of the motor task.

Practice with Feedback

In general, if learners are provided feedback about when they are right and wrong, learning is more rapid than if they are not provided feedback (e.g., Lhyle & Kulhavy, 1987). Although feedback can be construed in behavioral terms as reinforcement, the more popular interpretation of feedback by cognitive psychologists is that feedback provides information about what has been learned and what remains to be learned. The more that feedback stimulates the learner to reflect on their errant responses in comparison to correct alternatives, the more likely it is to be effective. (Recall the discussion earlier in this chapter about reflection on errors.) Feedback involving explanations to the learner about the reasonableness of the correct approach compared with the learner's answer is more effective than other types of feedback, especially if the feedback results in the learner constructing a new, more adequate understanding of the material being learned (Bangert-Drowns, Kulik, Kulik, & Morgan, 1991). Simply telling a person when they are right or wrong is feedback but much less effective in improving performance.

Although the literature on the timing of feedback is somewhat confusing, immediate feedback seems to promote learning more than delayed feedback. The effects of immediate feedback in studies conducted in actual classrooms have been especially consistent, however, and thus we have no hesitations in recommending that immediately after giving a test—

preferably during the same class period—provide feedback about what constitutes a correct answer and what constitutes an error (Kulik & Kulik, 1988).

Total Time Spent Learning or On Task

Both basic (e.g., Bugelski, 1962) and applied (e.g., Brophy, 1988) researchers in educational psychology have observed that the total amount of time spent learning correlates with the amount and degree of learning. The proportion of classroom time engaged in academic activities predicts classroom achievement level. Even so, an important lesson reiterated throughout this book is that time spent learning and using effective strategies is going to be more productive than time spent learning and practicing ineffective procedures. It is not enough to consider just total time, but what one does with the total time!

An important consideration is that how students spend their time is under their personal control. Students who are attentive in class and when doing assignments—and who choose to engage in academic activities on their own (e.g., reading) when there is "free" time—are going to do better in school (i.e., other things being equal) than children who goof off and elect to expend free time on nonacademic activities (e.g., Alexander, Entwisle, & Dauber, 1993). One of the things that good information processors do is to elect activities that make them better information processors, with one of their choices going to be to elect to spend substantial proportions of their total available time being intellectually active.

Regardless of what one does with time and how much total time is available for learning, learning and practice opportunities can be scheduled in different ways. The temporal distribution of learning and practice opportunities is an important determinant of achievement as reviewed in the next subsection.

Spaced Learning and Distributed Practice

Suppose that you have a test on this chapter 1 week from today. Will you do better on that test if you study for $3^1/_2$ hours in one sitting or in 7 sittings of a half hour?—or perhaps will you do equally well because the total amount of study time is the same in both cases? There is little doubt that you would do better after 7 short sittings than after one long sitting. This is a specific instance of the principle of **spaced learning,** sometimes referred to as **distrib-**

uted practice, with the latter term especially appropriate if what is being learned is some procedure: If a given amount of study or practice time is distributed over several sessions, learning is greater than if the same amount of study or practice is massed into one session.

Distributed practice effects have been known for all of the 20th century, originally identified by Ebbinghaus (e.g., 1913) in his classic research on memory. The phenomenon has been demonstrated many times and across diverse materials and tasks, from basic verbal learning to acquisition of text content to motor learning (see Crowder, 1976; Dempster, 1988b; Lee & Genovese, 1988). It has been documented with children as young as preschoolers (Toppino, Kasserman, & Mracek, 1991). Educators, nonetheless, rarely seem to exploit distributed practice (Dempster, 1987b, 1988b). Why is this? One reason is that although the positive effects of distributed practice are obvious in analytical studies, they may not be so obvious to learners and teachers on those occasions when they experience spaced practice. In particular, because spaced practice requires extending instruction over a longer period of time, it may seem as if much more investment in time is being required (Druckman & Bjork, 1991, Chapter 3).

Even so, the benefits of spaced practice are often large, and endure. Bahrick and Phelps (1987) reported a study in which the critical data were collected 8 years after material was originally studied. The participants learned Spanish vocabulary words, distributed over 30 days or studied on 1 day. Eight years later, the 30-day distributed practice participants remembered twice as many Spanish words as the massed-practice subjects.

Even if the only opportunity for learning is one particular day, it is possible to obtain benefits from distributed practice. For example, in Pressley (1987), university students studied 35 Latin vocabulary words, either presented one word at a time for one time at 9 seconds per word or three times at 3 seconds per presentation of a word. Learning was 68% better with spaced practice (for converging data, see Dempster, 1987a). The total amount of time spent studying alone does not determine learning; how the study time is scheduled makes an enormous difference, a finding of great applied significance that emerged from basic research on learning.

Consider one familiar situation. Remember the many math textbooks in your career as a student.

The typical format in such books was to present a lesson on some type of operation (e.g., addition of fractions), followed by some problems requiring the operation. The next lesson was on another operation (e.g., multiplication of fractions) followed by problems requiring the operation, and so on. These texts massed practice. In contrast, practice could be distributed by providing a mix of problems after each lesson, some of which required the new operation and some operations learned previously. Thus, if the author wanted students to practice 50 addition of fractions problems, they could be presented all in one lesson or 10 could be presented in the first lesson (with 40 problems of other types), 5 in each of the next 5 lessons (with 45 problems of other types in each lesson), and 3 in the next 5 lessons (with 47 problems of other types in each lesson). With the latter format, the students not only receive distributed practice but also would get practice at identifying which of the procedures they know should be applied to each problem. No such identification is required when practice is massed—all of the problems in that case require the same operation. Because being able to recognize when to apply a procedure is extremely important in mathematics, the distributed format makes much more sense. Although we have seen some mathematics texts that distribute practice and require students to determine which operation to use (in particular, ones developed and published by renegade mathematics educator, John Saxon; see Mathews, 1993), practice is massed in most mathematics texts. In this situation, it is difficult to defend not distributing practice.

Why does distributed practice work? Researchers are not sure, but there are two probable mechanisms that underlie the effect (Hintzman, 1974; Madigan, 1969; Rundus, 1971): (1) When learning is massed, attention probably wanes over a long period of study. Thus, the total amount of attention and active attempts at learning may be greater with distributed presentation. This interpretation was especially supported in an analytical study of repeated text reading by Krug, Davis, and Glover (1990; also Glover & Corkill, 1987), who observed more waning of attention during massed than distributed repeated reading, but who also observed that attention during massed repeated reading was maintained when subjects read paraphrased versions of the same text rather than the exact same text twice. When subjects read the paraphrased versions of the same passage, memory was as high as when reading the same version of the passage was distributed; in contrast, massed reading of the same version of a passage resulted in less memory for the passage than distributed repeated reading of the same passage. The only explanation consistent with all of the effects observed in this study was that attention wanes when there is immediate reading of the same version of a passage, but is maintained if a paraphrased version is read or reading of the identical version is delayed (i.e., distributed). Differences in attention account for differences in memory associated with distributed and massed processing of a text.

(2) An alternative explanation of the distributed practice effect is that with multiple presentations, there is probably greater **encoding variability** than during a massed presentation. That is, each new presentation of something to be learned probably produces a slightly different approach to study and learning. Thus, one massed presentation likely results in continuous use of one or a few approaches, with attention during learning deployed in a particular way. This results in encoding of particular information. In contrast, several short presentations may produce attention to different aspects of the to-be-learned content and different ways of studying the content on each presentation, with the result being a richer representation of the to-be-learned content.

Practice Tests, Including Self-Tests

Practice tests improve learning of content (e.g., Foos & Fisher, 1988), even in the absence of opportunity for additional study following the practice tests. One possibility is that taking a practice test forces retrieval and review of material during the test, which strengthens memory of the material and connections between different parts of the material (e.g., Bahrick & Hall, 1991; Glover, 1989). When there is an opportunity for restudy following a practice test, the practice test can heighten students' awareness of whether there is a need to restudy (Pressley, Snyder, Levin, Murray, & Ghatala, 1987; Walczyk & Hall, 1989).

Learners can create practice tests by self-testing themselves as they attempt a learning task. To the extent self-testing has been studied, it is clear that this is not an obvious strategy to children in the early elementary years. In some situations, it increases in likelihood with increasing age during the grade-school years (i.e., during list learning; e.g., Dufresne & Kobasigawa, 1989). That adults often

have no idea whether they are ready to take a test over text that they have processed, however (e.g., Glenberg, & Epstein, 1987; Glenberg, Wilkinson, & Epstein, 1982; Glenberg, Sanocki, Epstein, & Morris, 1987; Maki & Berry, 1984; Maki, Foley, Kajer, Thompson, & Willert, 1990; Maki & Serra, 1992; Pressley, Snyder et al., 1987; Walczyk, & Hall, 1989), makes clear that people do much less self-testing than they could do. We believe that an important problem for eduational psychologists is to determine if it is possible to teach students to self-test themselves consistently as a means of deciding whether additional study is necessary. The full effects of self-testing and how to develop self-testing are poorly understood.

Test Expectancy Effects

Do you study material differently as a function of the type of test you expect on it? The possibility that students do has been evaluated extensively by educational psychologists, with the conclusion offered that examination demands play a large role in determining how and what teachers teach and students study and learn in a course (e.g., Fredericksen, 1984). What Lundeberg and Fox (1991) found when they reviewed all of the available experimental studies is that this is one problem that was not served well by laboratory studies. There were a number of laboratory studies in which students made preparations for either a recall or a recognition test and then received either a recall or a recognition test, with four possibilities: study for recall, recall test; study for recall, recognition test; study for recognition, recognition test; study for recognition, recall test. In fact, in laboratory studies, studying for a recall test when a recall test is given makes a big difference (i.e., studying for recognition—which is generally easier than recall—does not prepare a student for a recall test). Studying for a recognition test when a recognition test is given makes little difference (i.e., preparing for a harder recall test has a carryover effect such that a learner is also ready for the easier recognition test). In contrast, in real classrooms, studying for a recall test when a recall test is given makes a difference as does studying for a recognition test (e.g., multiple-choice) when a recognition test is given. Test expectancy can affect performance on classroom tests, presumably by shaping how and how much one prepares for a test. Thus, the outcomes in the classroom experimental literature suggest that it is important for students to know the type of test that will be given.

European researchers in particular have studied correlations between testing demands in courses and students' approaches to studying. Marton and Säljö (1976) proposed that students could use either **deep** or **surface** approaches to study. Deep processing entails looking for underlying meaning and linkages. (Note the use of the term "deep" to mean extensive meaningful processing, by both these European educational psychologists and North American depth-of-processing theorists, whose perspectives were reviewed earlier in this chapter.) Noel Entwisle, a Scottish researcher, and his colleagues have been particularly successful in demonstrating that the more a course demands memory during evaluations, the more surface processing is apparent (e.g., Entwisle & Ramsden, 1983). If a teacher wants students to think deeply about material, evaluations should reward students for coming up with insights that go beyond the information given, that require more than simple recall of the material. Many thoughtful educational researchers and theorists have concluded that the most potent way to affect student study strategies is through test demands, with students willing to learn how to process in ways that permit them to meet the demands of the tests they will face (e.g., Crooks, 1988; Elton & Laurillard, 1979).

Summary

More than teacher talk is required in effective educational presentations. Practice plays an important role in increasing acquisition and understanding of new knowledge; distributing presentation of content and practice opportunities across a number of occasions is supported by a broad base of evidence. An old hypothesis about time and learning was that total time (e.g., Bugelski, 1962) spent studying content—sometimes referred to as total time on task by classroom researchers (e.g., Doyle, 1983)—was a good predictor of learning. The distributed practice effect makes clear that that is not the case, however. Moreover, throughout this book, the case is made that what matters is not the amount of time spent doing something but what one does with the time. For example, a person applying an efficient strategy may learn much more in much less time than another person who uses a counterproductive strategy. What studies such as Pressley (1987) suggest is that distributed practice makes a difference whether using an efficient or an inefficient strategy. If practice makes perfect, spaced practice makes more perfect!

Some final points about time and learning derive from an analysis offered by John Carroll (1963): Students differ in the amount of time they need to learn as well as their willingness to persist until they have learned. For many students, they fail to achieve at high levels because they do not put the time in studying and practicing (i.e., their time spent attempting to learn is less than their time needed to learn). When such students are given incentives to persist, their learning and performances often improve (e.g., Gettinger, 1989). Also, most students can learn at a faster rate than they might naturally be inclined to do so (e.g., because their attention wanes). Thus, it often pays to give students incentives to stay on task and learn at a more rapid rate than they might do in the absence of incentives (Gettinger, 1989). In short, how much time it takes to learn something depends on the learner and situational variables (e.g., whether study is distributed or spaced). Incentives can be used to keep students on task who do not naturally devote enough time to material for them to learn it; incentives can also be used to increase concentration and effort and thus reduce the amount of total time a student requires to learn something. Will there be enough time for a student to learn some content? The answer is that it depends largely on the student and the situation, including potential incentives for learning in the situation.

CONCLUDING COMMENTS

There is more of an old-fashioned look to the work reported in this chapter compared with most of the coverage in this book. In fact, most of the ideas discussed in this chapter were being studied before the cognitive revolution was fully under way in the mid-1970s. That makes the principles that emerge from this work no less valuable, and, in fact, some of the principles from research in older traditions have been reformulated in information-processing terms. Thus, imagery mnemonics have been explained in terms of cognitive plans (Miller et al., 1960) and strategies (e.g., Pressley & Levin, 1978), with a variety of evidence generated by cognitive researchers suggesting that use of mnemonics depends on prior knowledge and is affected by capacity constraints (Kee, in press). In addition, explanations of advance organizers effects have been couched in schema theoretical terms (Derry, 1984; Mayer, 1979). Enactment effects have been hypothesized to be mediated by multiple representations, consistent with Paivio's dual-coding theory. Notetaking research is now being reconceived in terms of self-regulation theory.

Whenever a person is confronted with a learning task (e.g., learning the ideas in a history chapter about the Civil War in preparation for a test), there are a number of ways to react. The lesson in this chapter is that how the learner reacts will make a huge difference in memory. Thus, attempting to process text content deeply by relating it to prior knowledge should increase memory; inventing memory tricks to remember particular pieces of content improves learning of those details (e.g., one eighth-grader told us about an image of how "Lincoln dug a hole to bury his opponent in," as a way to remember that Douglas debated Lincoln); and taking notes is helpful in promoting learning, as is reviewing them later. If a student decides to spread studying out over an extended period of time (e.g., a little bit of studying each night for a week), learning is more certain than if the student attempts to cram for an examination. (Indeed, the best explanation to give to junior and senior high school students, who often have blind faith in cramming for examinations, is to explain the distributed practice effect!) That Ebbinghaus understood this principle more than a century ago—and it has endured more than a century of scrutiny by researchers—suggests the conclusion that the principle of distributed practice is one of the most certainly correct pieces of advisement offered in this book.

As an *aide memoire*, Table 10.1 summarizes practices discussed in this chapter that facilitate learning.

Table 10.1

Practices That Promote Academic Performance (Roughly in Order of Coverage in Chapter 10)

Deeply processing to-be-learned material (i.e., thinking about its meaning)

Learning with some contextual interference

Mnemonics, often based on some form of imagery

Enactment of to-be-remembered content

Learning by understanding, including by relating new information to prior knowledge, responding to why-questions (i.e., elaborative interrogation), and constructing self-explanations

Processing advance organizers, including as a review-before a test

Notetaking

Simple practice

Practice with feedback

Distributed learning

Practice tests, including self-tests

Forming accurate test expectancies that guide study (i.e., understanding accountability demands and responding to them; e.g., deep or surface processing required to meet course expectations)

11

Teaching Practices and the Development of Intellect

Despite the beliefs of many intelligence theorists that individual differences in intelligence are genetically determined (see Chapter 6), many educators retain faith in the environment as a powerful mechanism shaping the mind. In this chapter, we will explore first the idea that general intelligence as defined by IQ tests can be altered by schooling. In subsequent sections, we will turn attention to some specific teaching practices that have an impact on the development of intellect and school achievement. We will discuss characteristics of successful schools and then factors that might increase student success in any school. Finally, we will address questions that might have occurred to many of the readers of this book as they experienced higher education and this course in particular: Does college really affect intellect? What difference will this course make? Researchers have addressed both of these questions.

By the end of this chapter, it will be clear that long-term schooling can make an important difference in thinking ability and that some schooling practices and policies can make a substantial difference in achievement at school. It will also be apparent, however, that some educational interventions specifically advertised as improving thinking do not do so. Attending college and taking a course like this one, however, are not included in the list of interventions that are falsely advertised, for the section that concludes this chapter presents substantial evidence that college makes a difference in the development of intellect, and taking a course in cogni-

tive psychology results in enduring understandings about the nature and education of mind.

EFFECTS OF SCHOOLING ON IQ

Going to school is so commonplace in Western life at the end of the 20th century that it is often overlooked as a cognitive intervention. In general, when researchers have evaluated the hypothesis that schooling profoundly affects mental abilities, there has been support for the conclusion that school affects the way that people think. For example, recall in Chapter 2 that cross-cultural studies were discussed in which use of basic memory strategies was shown to be related to attendance at Western-style schools. A wealth of data within Western culture also supports the conclusion that schooling dramatically affects cognitive competence.

Stephen Ceci (1991), a Cornell University psychologist, more than anyone else has increased our awareness of the effects of schooling on the fundamental mental abilities tapped by intelligence tests. Ceci reviewed about 200 studies (many of which were conducted within the United States) that studied the relationship between schooling and IQ. What he found was a variety of evidence favoring the hypothesis that psychometric intelligence is increased by school attendance. Consider the following specific findings:

- There are high correlations (often 0.80 and greater) between the number of years of schooling completed and IQ. A high correlation is detected even when possible confounding influences, such as socioeconomic level, are removed statistically.
- Summer vacation results in a drop in psychometric intelligence in children.
- Intermittent school attendance is associated with lower IQ than regular school attendance. Some of the most interesting data on this point were collected in rural hollows about 100 miles from Washington, DC, in the Blue Ridge Mountains (Sherman & Key, 1932): IQ systematically varied with the degree that educational opportunities were available in the hollows. There is reason to shudder at this result, for even in the 1990s, there are school jurisdictions where children are not receiving schooling because the district cannot afford to provide school bussing.
- For various reasons, the onset of schooling is sometimes delayed. Such delay is associated with reduced IQ. An 8-year-old who has had 3 years of schooling will outperform an 8-year-old with 2 years of schooling on an IQ test (see Baltes & Reinert, 1969; Cahen & Cohen, 1989; Cahen & Davis, 1987).
- Leaving school before the completion of high school is associated with low IQ.
- The availability of schooling in various countries, and for various groups within countries, has fluctuated throughout the 20th century. In general, the more available schooling was during an era for particular populations, the greater the IQ scores for the group in question during that period.

Although any one of the results that Ceci (1991) examined might be explained away as artifactual (e.g., the reason students in some studies were not in school is because of low IQ), there were many attempts across the various investigations to consider alternative explanations, with many alternative explanations discounted. On the whole, the case that Ceci made is compelling, a case that is not consistent with the views of creators of IQ tests, many of whom believe such tests tap biologically determined differences, differences mapping on to competencies that are insulated from environmental influence (see Chapters 6 and 16).

Ceci's (1991) conclusion that IQ is affected by amount of schooling is compelling. As he explained:

> In summary, despite the many interpretive snarls one confronts with correlational data, when one considers the entire corpus of correlations that have been reported this century, the high correlations between IQ and schooling are difficult to account for on the basis of genetic selection or any other explanations (e.g., motivational differences or parental SES [socioeconomic status]), because these mechanisms appear far-fetched in many of the studies that were reviewed. The most parsimonious account of the correlations that have been reviewed is that of a direct causal link, namely that the processes associated with schooling influence performance on IQ tests through a combination of *direct* instruction and indirect inculcation of modes of cognizing and values associated with standardized testing. (Ceci, 1991, p. 711).

The last sentence makes clear that Ceci (1991) was not content to claim that schooling affects only the competencies somewhat vaguely defined by IQ. Rather Ceci also reviewed data supporting the conclusion that specific cognitive processes, such as fundamental perceptual abilities, conceptual capacities, and memory, are affected by school attendance. The type of evidence supporting this conclusion included the following:

- The abilities to use depth-perception cues, to disambiguate figures in a maze or in a larger scene, and to perform tasks with a high visual-spatial component all correlate with school attendance.
- Schooling is associated with the propensity to use conceptual dimensions, such as taxonomic class, rather than perceptual ones, such as color, to think about information that varies in terms of both taxonomic and perceptual features.
- Schooling influences memory performance on a variety of memory tasks, including all of the ones covered in earlier chapters of this book.

Some of the most compelling evidence that schooling can affect intelligence has been produced in studies assessing the effects of early childhood interventions on the development of economically disadvantaged children. For example, consider the Carolina Abecedarian Project (e.g., Burchinal, Lee, & Ramey, 1989; Ramey & Campbell, 1987; Wasik et al., 1990). (*Note:* Abecedarian in this context means someone who is learning the alphabet, although the Carolina Project encompasses much more than alphabet acquisition. The Abecedarian Project and its predecessor were the inspirations for the extremely successful Infant Health and Development Program described in Chapter 6.)

Experimental and control participants in Abecedarian Project began their participation shortly after birth. The experimental and control subjects were provided nutritional support, family-counseling contacts, and medical care. Most critically, however, the experimental children attended a high-quality preschool environment, attending for the entire day throughout the year. Parent meetings were held as part of this preschool program to increase parental awareness of how to stimulate child development and use community opportunities.

A total of $4^1/_2$ years of the Abecedarian Program produced moderate-sized gains in IQ (i.e., 8- to 12-point advantages at age $4^1/_2$ for experimentals over controls; Ramey, 1992).

More recently, however, the Abecedarian study has been extended so that it is possible to compare the effects of 8 years of Abecedarian intervention (i.e., through the first 3 years of schooling) with 5 years of Abecedarian intervention during the preschool years, 3 years of Abecedarian intervention during the elementary years, and no Abecedarian intervention. For children receiving Abecedarian intervention during the years of public schooling, efforts were made to maximize the likelihood of appropriate, stimulating educational experiences at school. Master teachers also visited with the students' parents and coached them about how they could stimulate their children's cognitive development. These master teachers were aware of the specific content being covered in school and provided "... literally thousands of specific activities and guides that parents could use in a gamelike manner to give their children extra practice and support in activities that were directly related to classroom performance" (Ramey, 1992, p. 247).

The outcomes in this experiment were clear at age 8: 8 years of Abecedarian intervention were superior to either 5 years of preschool Abecedarian intervention or 3 years of elementary-level Abecedarian intervention. For example, only 16 percent of the 8-year students required repetition of a grade level up until the age of 12 (i.e., 4 years after intervention had ended), much lower than in any other condition of the study. The power of even 5 preschool years of Abecedarian instruction was apparent on the intelligence data collected at age 12,

with only 12.8 percent of the students who had received 5 years of Abecedarian intervention scoring 85 or less on an IQ test compared with 44% of control children who scored below 85 on an IQ test. In general, the more total Abecedarian intervention received, the lower the failure rate and the higher the IQ at age 12 (Ramey, 1992).

Of course, the Abecedarian data are complemented by other data reviewed in this book, such as Reading Recovery in Chapter 14. The message is clear: Intelligence and academic achievement of at-risk children can be improved through intensive, long-term, academically oriented intervention. We now have the know-how for increasing the academic performances of many types of children who historically have fared poorly in school. Ramey (1992) summarized his views about this know-how. A stimulating environment during the preschool years involves high-quality adult-child transactions with the following features:

- Encouragement of exploration.
- Mentoring in basic skills (e.g., labeling, sorting, sequencing, comparing, and noting means-end relationships).
- Celebration of developmental advances.
- Guided rehearsal and extension of new skills.
- Protection from inappropriate disapproval, teasing, or punishment (e.g., for mistakes in trying out a new skill, unintended consequences of curious exploration or information seeking).
- A rich and responsive language environment.

What is especially striking to us is how much this description complements descriptions of other high-quality instruction that stimulates academic growth, taken up in the next subsection. With respect to this section, however, the Abecedarian studies are powerful evidence consistent with Ceci's general conclusion that schooling can affect intellectual development as defined by IQ measures.

SCHOOLS THAT ESPECIALLY PROMOTE INTELLECTUAL COMPETENCE

Do all Western schools have the same effects on intellectual competence? Believe it or not, many academics once thought that all schools were pretty much equal in their impact on achievement. The biggest culprit in advancing this perspective was a report issued in 1966 that became known as the

Coleman Report (Coleman et al., 1966). After controlling statistically for family background factors and some other variables, Coleman et al. (1966) concluded that differences in the qualities of schools (e.g., as measured by per pupil expenditure) accounted for little of the variability in achievement differences between students. This finding was used by many to argue against pumping resources into schools as a way to promote the academic achievement of disadvantaged students (e.g., Jencks et al., 1972).

Although it may be surprising to some, more money alone is probably not the answer. That is, Coleman et al.'s (1966) original conclusion is not so far off the mark: There have not been consistent relationships reported between the amount of money spent on pupils and intellectual attainment as measured by IQ scores (see Ceci, 1991, for a review). Rather than concluding that quality of schooling does not predict intellectual competence of pupils, however, an alternative interpretation is that the amount of money spent does not predict the quality of the educational environment: Both good and bad environments can be expensive or cheap.

There have been many studies (see Firestone, 1991, for a review) in the past two decades documenting qualitative differences in schooling environments that produce differences in IQ and other achievement measures. One wing of this group is especially visible, known as the "effective schools movement" (e.g., Edmonds, 1979). Although a number of methods have been used by those interested in effective schools, the effective schools movement has been especially interested in "outlier" schools, ones in which achievement is especially high relative to what might be expected in the school based on characteristics of its students, such as socioeconomic status (Firestone, 1991). Intensive case studies of such schools have been conducted. One famous list of characteristics of effective schools was provided by Edmonds (1979). High achievement during the elementary years is obtained by inner-city youth, ones who are at risk of school failure because of socioeconomic disadvantage, when they attend schools that have the following features:

- Strong administrative leadership.
- High expectations for all children.
- A safe, orderly but not rigid environment.
- Top priority given to student acquisition of basic school skills.

- Willingness to divert resources from other tasks to development of basic school skills.
- Frequent monitoring of pupil progress. (based on Firestone, 1991, p. 15)

A similar list of characteristics emerges from analyses of effective secondary schools. Collapsing across analyses, the following are features of high schools that work:

- A shared sense of academic purpose by faculty, parents, and community.
- Recognition of student accomplishments.
- Recognition of good teaching.
- High involvement by parents and community in school affairs.
- A sense of caring and community (i.e., students care about school affairs and educators are committed to student welfare).
- Academic emphasis (and coursework) for all students.
- Homework.
- High expectations that students can learn.
- Most class time is on-task (i.e., there is a great deal of instruction).
- School environment is orderly.
- Discipline is fair-minded.
- There is strong leadership that actively recognizes problems in the school and seeks to solve them.
- Teachers and administrators believe they are in control of the school and teaching.
- There is staff collegiality. (based on Newmann, 1991b, p. 58).

Although many criticisms can be levied against the studies of effective schools that have been done, it is difficult not to be impressed by two outcomes (Bliss, 1991; Firestone, 1991): (1) The consistency in results across studies is striking, with Edmonds's conclusions generally supported in many subsequent analyses (e.g., Bryk & Thum, 1989; Good & Brophy, 1986; Lezotte, 1986; Mortimore, 1991; Rutter, 1983; Stedman, 1988). (2) Many schools across the United States have paid attention to this research literature, with some estimates as high as 41% of U. S. schools influenced to some degree by the movement (General Accounting Office, 1989).

Others concerned with quality in education focused on what went on in particular classrooms. Rosenshine's (1979) analyses (see Chapter 8) were especially influential. Rosenshine identified classroom variables linked to high achievement: academic focus, teacher directedness, orderly presentations of material, clear goals, sufficient time for instruction, high percentage of time devoted to academic content, monitoring of student performances, questioning with responding by students, immediate feedback, conviviality and warmth, democracy, and cooperation. If this list is compared with the ones generated by Edmonds (1979) and Newmann (1991b), it is clear that the conclusions are complementary. For example, all three analyses specified that achievement was greatest in environments with a high academic focus and clear academic leadership by educators (i.e., the principal at the school level and the teacher in the classroom).

Role of Academic Engagement in Fostering Academic Achievement

How can this literature be tied to Ceci's (1991) conclusion that the amount of schooling influences cognitive competency? Newmann (1991b) has provided a linking framework (see also Chapter 9 this volume): Newmann claims that effective schools are ones that permit and foster a high degree of pupil **engagement** in learning. Engaged students are really invested in and committed to learning, understanding, and mastering what is presented in school. Engaged students concentrate on their work, are enthusiastic about it, and are deeply interested in academic content. They care about whether they are doing well in school.

Good schools do not emphasize meaningless, rote tasks, although some of this goes on in all school environments and is probably necessary to some degree. Rather, engaging educational environments present students with tasks that seem authentic to the students, lead them to inquire about important academic issues, require integration of knowledge, and produce outcomes that mean something besides the grade that results. Effective schools present their students with tasks that they "own" in part because they are involved in deciding what is done in school and how it is evaluated. There is flexibility in the pace and methods of teaching and learning, many opportunities for students to ask questions that are important to them, frequent occasions to pursue issues that students see as important, and many demands that students invent their own work—that is, create new understandings

rather than simply parrot back what the teacher has said. Engagement is fostered by academic environments that encourage risk taking—there is no disrespect for trying and failing, but rather great respect for making an effort and support for making new attempts following a failure. Engagement is fostered by environments that respect student dignity and project a message that young people are important. Not least of all, engaging environments are fun.

Presence in school is a powerful determinant of academic achievement and intellectual competence, as evidenced by the studies summarized by Ceci (1991); presence in a high-quality school that fosters engagement now and commitment to learning for the long term promotes achievement more than presence in schooling environments that do not foster learning, as evidenced by the effective schools literature. Schooling, especially schooling at its best, is a powerful factor in the determination of academic competence and the promotion of intellectual development.

Schooling as a Means of Overcoming Academic and Economic Disadvantages

A persistent hypothesis is that schooling can be used to elevate those who are now disadvantaged academically and economically. No one has performed the experiment necessary to evaluate this hypothesis. What is required is an experiment in which one group of at-risk students is provided high-quality educational input for their entire schooling career. The educational and economic outcomes for this group would be compared with outcomes obtained by students who are similar demographically and intellectually at the outset of the study but who receive instruction typically offered to the disadvantaged in the United States (i.e., instruction which is often poor by any standard).

Shorter-term interventions have been studied, however, with positive results. For example, the effects of Head Start and related preschool and extended-kindergarten interventions have been evaluated extensively. Intellectual gains (e.g., improvements in IQ) are obtained in the short term (e.g., Entwisle, Alexander, Cadigan, & Pallas, 1987). Environmental support beyond the preschool years is required, however, as is evident by the fact that Head Start students are difficult to discriminate from non–Head Start students on purely intellectual measures (e.g., IQ) by grade 3. Nonetheless, there are clear, long-term, positive effects of early childhood interventions with disadvantaged populations. Disadvantaged children receiving high-quality preschool instruction subsequently are less likely to be referred into special education, fail a grade, or be charged with delinquency (Consortium for Longitudinal Studies, 1983; Lazar, Darlington, et al., 1982). Although short-term interventions do not provide as striking long-term advantages as their developers anticipated (i.e., they had hoped the boost on measures such as IQ would be permanent), the advantages that are produced are not trivial ones. With every passing year, there is additional documentation of both long-term academic and social advantages associated with experiencing high-quality preschool environments (Field, 1991).

Longer-term educational interventions for at-risk students are being tested as this book is being written, with one of the best known of these developed by Slavin and colleagues at Johns Hopkins and dubbed "Success for All" (e.g., Slavin, Madden, Karweit, Dolan, et al., 1991; Slavin, Madden, Karweit, Livermon, & Dolan, 1990). The goal of this program is to make certain that all at-risk students entering school arrive at grade 3 performing at grade level in basic skills, especially reading. Special enriched curricula are provided beginning in preschool and kindergarten. Those grade-1 students experiencing the greatest difficulties with reading receive one-on-one tutoring. Most students require no more than a semester of such tutoring to get them on track, although such tutoring could continue for years if necessary. Family support services are provided as well, especially ones targeted at solving problems that might interfere with academic progress. There is substantial assessment of students to make certain that problems are not overlooked and their treatment delayed. The data generated to date suggest positive effects of this approach, with substantial benefits especially apparent for extremely at-risk students who have received 3 years of Success for All (Madden, Slavin, Karweit, Dolan, & Wasik, 1993).

As enthusiastic as we are about the results produced by Slavin and his associates, we must add that our own view is that it is probably wrongheaded to think that at-risk children who have received enriched instruction for the primary years are ready to go it alone. A good guess is that many will be overwhelmed by the increasing demands they face in later schooling, demands that more ad-vantaged children often can weather because of high-quality home and out-of-school environmental support.

For example, Snow, Barnes, Chandler, Goodman, and Hemphill (1991) provided data consistent with the hypothesis that for schooling beyond the primary years, high-quality educational environments are especially critical. They observed disadvantaged parents who strongly supported the education of their children but lacked the intellectual resources to provide compensatory instruction in the topics covered in the late grade-school, middle-school, and high school years when the schools did not cover the topics well for their children (see also Duran & Weffer, 1992). Snow et al. (1991) described some disadvantaged children who experienced successful years in school followed by less successful years, with the variability in success during a school year strongly tied to the quality of the teaching experienced that year. For at-risk students, the quality of school matters greatly.

We close this section by returning to the work of James Coleman, for every so often, we still see references to the 1966 Coleman Report as evidence that improving school quality would not improve the intellectual competence of students. Like all good scholars, Coleman went on to do much more research, including in-depth analyses of academic achievement in public, parochial, and other private schools. In this later work, Coleman strongly made the case that academic achievement varies with the quality of academic environment. Not surprisingly, Coleman found that achievement in private and parochial schools exceeds achievement in public schools. He also noted that daily absenteeism and cutting of classes are much more prevalent in public than in parochial or private schools. There were multiple indicators in the data that student time engaged with academic content was lower in the public than in the parochial and private schools (e.g., public students were more likely not to obey teachers; be late for school; and engage in vandalism, drug abuse, and fighting). Through a variety of statistical manipulations, Coleman was able to estimate (see Coleman, 1991, pp. 264–266) differences in academic achievement if public schools were to become as disciplined as parochial and private schools: Massive gains in academic achievement would be produced by reducing absenteeism and student antisocial behaviors that are inconsistent with academic engagement.

Although Coleman's name has been used to argue against improving school quality, it is also one of the names most frequently mentioned by those who argue for increasing school quality, especially those who argue that quality is not determined so much by the financial cost of schooling as by the way the available dollars are spent (e.g., Finn, 1991). There is plenty in Coleman's data and many other data sets to make clear that financial resources available for education can be deployed in ways that either foster achievement or undermine it.

SCHOOL AND AFTER-SCHOOL PRACTICES THAT AFFECT ACADEMIC GROWTH

Much of this book has been about school interventions that can improve academic achievement. In a sense, this section is devoted to some practices that have fallen between the cracks in the commentary presented in earlier chapters but practices that are nonetheless important to consider. Some occur daily in the classroom; others affect more the quality of intellectual life "after school."

Schooling Practices That Have Implications for Student Achievement

We proceed in this section from practices that individual teachers can control to ones that are controlled more at the level of the school or the district.

Teacher's Questioning of Students About Academic Content   At several points in this book, we discuss the effects of questioning on learning. For example, in Chapter 14 we consider whether adjunct questions in text improve learning—they do, although the effects are often not large. The elaborative interrogation strategy considered in Chapters 4 and 10 can be applied when learning a large number of facts.

One type of questioning not considered in detail at other points in this book, however, is teacher questioning. Many teachers feel compelled to ask questions all day. Who does not recall social studies, science, and literature classes that involved little more than one teacher question after another? (Recall from Chapter 8 that the most common discourse structure in school involves the teacher initiating a question, students attempting to respond, followed by a teacher evaluation—IRE cycles [Mehan, 1979].) Do the thousands of questions that students experience in school over their career make a difference in learning?

The answer is that they do. Two types of questions must be differentiated in order to appreciate fully the effects of classroom questioning on student learning. There are **higher-order questions**—ones requiring manipulation of information and reflection—and **lower-order questions**—ones requiring simple recall of information. One possibility supported in some data analyses (e.g., Brophy & Evertson, 1976) is that high proportions of higher-order questions are especially important in high-ability classes and that predominantly lower-order questioning may lead to higher gains in achievement with weaker classes. Presumably, lower-order questions increase the likelihood that weaker classes will at least learn the facts; higher-order questions stimulate those students who acquire the facts with less effort to go beyond the information given—to think through it and relate the new content to prior knowledge, something that does not occur automatically (as demonstrated by the low level of control subject performances in the elaborative interrogation studies reviewed in Chapters 4 and 10). What about "typical" classrooms that have a mix of abilities? Redfield and Rousseau (1981) meta-analyzed (see Chapter 1) studies of higher-order and lower-order questioning effects in classrooms. In general, higher-order questioning was more potent—a moderate-sized effect—in the studies reviewed by Redfield and Rousseau.

Even though lower-order questions may promote the learning of weaker students, a number of analyses have documented that teacher-controlled classrooms filled with lower-order, factually-oriented questions are filled with much less interesting and expansive discourse than classrooms in which teachers encourage more natural discussion (Almasi, 1993; Dillon, 1985, 1991; Wong, 1991). When asked for the facts, students tend to give just the facts! When asked for opinions and examples and when encouraged to follow up on peer comments, students are capable of far-ranging discussions that are filled with alternative perspectives on the topics covered by the lessons (see especially Almasi, 1993).

One variable that has been demonstrated to make a difference in questioning effects on achievement is whether teachers give students a chance to respond after they pose a question. When teachers wait for students to respond (i.e., provide **wait**

time), they give the students a chance to think before responding, with such thinking time reliably associated with increases in achievement (e.g., in math and science classes; Tobin, 1987). The wait does not have to be long to have an effect on learning, with as little as 3 seconds providing a learning advantage for students compared with when teachers demand immediate responses before providing the answer or moving on to another student.

Readers should note that at several points in this book, we reviewed interventions intended to replace teacher-controlled questioning as the predominant approach to teaching, with cooperative learning (see Chapter 5) and discussion methods (see Chapters 8 and 12 through 14) two such approaches that are extremely popular in the 1990s. As we contemplate the research needed to establish whether cooperative discussions really are effective in promoting achievement, we believe that an appropriate comparison for content learning is with the achievement that accompanies high-quality teacher questioning. Of course, one aim of cooperative discussions is to promote the long-term internalization of the cognitive processes that go on in the discussion, with the Vygotskian-theoretical notion that such dialogical processes are more akin to sophisticated thinking than are the cognitive processes that occur in response to teacher questions. The empirical issue is whether better thinkers emerge from more natural discussion-oriented instruction than emerge from more conventional teacher-controlled classrooms, with our belief that this issue is a crucial one for Vygotskian-oriented instructional theorists to address in the coming decade if their perspective on the nature of optimal classroom structure is to be defensible.

It seems likely that the quality of teacher questioning will improve because of all of the research on it and because teachers can fairly quickly learn how to improve their classroom questioning skills (Gliessman, Pugh, Dowden, & Hutchins, 1988). This is one of only a number of factors likely to improve the quality of classroom discussions in the coming years, with the research covered in the next section also expected to make a difference in the type and amount of discussion encouraged in classrooms.

Encouraging Student Questions Teachers can answer questions as well as ask them, and when they do, they often assist students to understand new material (e.g., Fishbein, Eckart, Lauver, Van Leeuwen, & Langmeyer, 1990; Ross & Balzer, 1975; Ross & Killey, 1977). The catch is that some of the students most in need of assistance often will not seek it out, wanting to be independent or believing that their efforts to seek help may be perceived as reflecting low ability (Newman, 1990; Newman & Goldin, 1990; van der Meij, 1988). For this reason, many educators encourage students to ask questions when they are not sure and send many messages in their classrooms that asking questions is not a sign of low ability but something a smart person does whenever he or she is in need of assistance.

A particularly important hypothesis is the possibility that teaching children how to ask questions about academic content can affect their processing of it. For example, Courage (1989) demonstrated that 4-, 5-, and 7-year-old students can be taught how to ask for categorical information about an object. Lyman (1992) is teaching elementary-level students to ask questions about text, tapping factual information, cause-and-effect relationships, temporal sequences, similarities and differences between ideas covered in the text, induction of generalizations from examples, and deduction of examples from generalizations. Just how such instruction affects academic processing remains to be documented, however. Evaluations of the effects of interventions that encourage student questions should be a high priority, given the popularity in the 1990s of all types of interventions that are aimed at increasing active student discussion (see Chapters 8, 12, 13, and 14).

Teacher Expectancies If a teacher expects a child to do well in school, will that child excel academically? Will the teacher's prophecy be fulfilled—perhaps because the teacher acts differently toward the child than would occur in the absence of a belief in the child's ability? In one of the most famous studies in the educational psychology literature, Harvard psychologist Robert Rosenthal and his colleague Jacobson (Rosenthal & Jacobson, 1968) reported data suggesting that teacher expectancies about student achievement were a powerful determinant of actual achievement.

Early in the school year, all children in one school were administered a standardized test that was represented as predictive of children who were about to blossom—that is, those who would be exceptionally likely to exhibit substantial intellectual growth in the next year. When the data from the test were reported to the teachers, 20% of the children in each classroom were identified as likely to make larger than typical gains during the current school year. This was a ruse, however, for these children had been selected at random, so in reality there was no objective basis for believing these children would gain any more or less during the upcoming year than other children in the school. Nonetheless, when the children were tested at the end of the school year, the children who had been identified as likely to make differentially large gains in fact made larger gains during the year than the sample of students as a whole.

With the publication of *Pygmalion in the Classroom*, Rosenthal and Jacobson's (1968) experiment became well known almost immediately: At the end of the 1960s and beginning of the 1970s, there was great interest in the possibility that a child's achievement was greatly affected by the teacher's beliefs about the child's promise and ability.

Similar to any visible piece of social science, Rosenthal and Jacobson (1986) inspired follow-up research. More often than not, other scientists did not obtain significant teacher-expectancy effects, and sometimes those expected to do poorly did well and those expected to do well did poorly (Goldenberg, 1992). Rosenthal (1985) analyzed the relevant studies and reported that significant effects were obtained in a little more than one-third of the studies inspired by *Pygmalion*. Using a meta-analytic procedure (see Chapter 1), Rosenthal (1985) argued that Pygmalion effects were real, although they tended to be small. Rosenthal's (1985) evaluation is the most positive, well-informed appraisal of the *Pygmalion* studies that we have encountered, with reports of null effects in follow-up studies accompanied by methodological criticisms of the original *Pygmalion* study (e.g., Elashoff & Snow, 1971). Teacher beliefs alone have only a small effect on student achievement, if there is any effect at all.

Readers will recall, however, that expectancies about performance were cited earlier in this chapter as potentially important in affecting academic success: Effective schools are characterized by faculty and administration who have high expectations about their students' abilities and potential for achievement. One of the reasons that tracking may have a negative effect on the achievement of students in lower tracks is that their teacher's expectancies about their achievement are low (Brophy, 1985).

Although there are many doubts about whether expectancies alone can affect achievement, there are far fewer doubts (although again the evidence is not entirely unambiguous on this point; see Hall & Merkel, 1985, for a review) that teachers do behave differently as a function of their expectancies about students based on previous outcomes achieved by those students. That is, even if teachers do not react differently to children based on test reports about the children's abilities, they do react differently when they see evidence of high and low ability in their daily interactions with students.

Brophy and Good (1970) studied the teacher-student interactions in four grade-1 classrooms intensively. They observed that classroom life was different for higher-ability and lower-ability students. Based on their own work and other research on teacher-student interactions in classrooms, Brophy and Good (1974) compiled a list of ways that the classroom environments of low-ability and high-ability students differ, with this list elaborated by Brophy (1985):

- Teachers are less likely to wait for a low-ability child to respond to questions than for a high-ability child.
- When low-ability students hesitate to answer a question, teachers are more likely to give them an answer or call on another child to respond.
- Reinforcements are less likely to be contingent on correct responding for low-ability students compared with high-ability students.
- Low-ability students are criticized more often (e.g., in response to their failures).
- Low-ability students receive less praise than high-ability students.
- When low-ability students respond publicly, they are less likely to receive feedback than are high-ability students.
- Teachers generally pay less attention to low-ability students and interact with them less.
- Teachers call on low-ability students less often than on high-ability students.
- Teachers seat low-ability students further from the teacher than they seat high-ability students.
- Teachers interact with low-ability students more privately than publicly. They structure the activities of low-ability students more and control the behaviors of low-ability students more than they control the behavior of high-ability students.

- Teachers demand less from low-ability students.
- In matters of grading, low-ability students are less likely than high-ability students to receive the benefit of the doubt on close calls.
- Teachers are less friendly in their interactions with low-ability students.
- The questions of low-ability students receive briefer responses that are not as informative as the responses to questions of high-ability students.
- Low-ability students are less likely to receive effective but time-consuming instruction than are high-ability students. (list based on Brophy, 1985, pp. 309–310)

Additionally, such differences are not only detected by skilled observers such as social scientists, but also are easily detected by other teachers and students (Babad, Bernieri, & Rosenthal, 1991): It is easy to spot which students a teacher expects to do well and which the teacher believes will be slow. Brophy and Good (1970, 1974; Brophy, 1985) believe that such gross differential treatment affects students' perceptions of themselves and their own abilities. The low-ability students come to perceive clearly that they are less likely to succeed than high-ability students—that is, they form a much more negative academic self-concept, which in turn reduces their motivation for school and learning and their levels of aspiration. Perhaps it should not be surprising given how unpleasant life is for the low-ability students that they are less well behaved than high-ability students and less likely to seek out interactions with the teacher than high-ability students (Brophy, 1985).

What is at work is probably a vicious cycle, with teachers believing that children who behave poorly are less likely to achieve academically (Bennett, Gottesman, Rock, & Cerullo, 1993), with this belief fueling teacher behavior toward the unruly child that is not as supportive of academic advancement as teacher behavior directed to better behaved children and, in fact, results in lower achievement by the ill-behaved child relative to classmates. Children who behave well in school make more academic progress than do ill-behaved children (Wentzel, 1993), perhaps mediated in part by teacher expectancies about the academic competence of well-behaved and ill-behaved students that affect teacher behaviors directed toward the children. (Recall from Chapter 1 that good information processors often behave in ways that increase the likelihood that they will experience high-quality academic interactions, and thus they play an important role in determining their own academic achievement.) In summary, there is considerable evidence that a teacher's perceptions about his or her students' academic abilities and behaviors can serve to increase differences in achievement between those students to the extent that the perceptions affect teacher behaviors toward children as outlined by Brophy (1985).

One reason why the high expectancies in effective schools are so notable is that self-fulfilling prophecies with respect to achievement undoubtedly do occur: Thus, when teachers expect much of students that many others would expect to fail, the teacher's positive expectations can influence their teaching behaviors so that their interactions with their students are more favorable. In turn, the academic self-concepts of students in such schools are improved, as are the motivational beliefs of students and ultimately their long-term academic performances.

One final twist on expectancy effects was provided by Jamieson, Lydon, Stewart, and Zanna (1987), who provided data making clear that expectancy effects in classrooms are not just one-way affairs (i.e., teachers reacting to students) but can be mediated by student reactions to teachers. Jamieson et al. (1987) convinced two classes of grade-11 students that that they were being taught by an able English teacher. These students, outperformed students in control English classes who had not been led to believe that the same teacher was exceptionally able. Jamieson et al. (1987) believed that a number of interacting effects may have contributed to the overall difference, with students in the positive-expectancy classes talking more, with this in turn affecting the teacher's perceptions, which in turn affected the teacher's behavior, and so on. Given that students in high school and college often are privileged to rumors about their teachers' competencies, we find compelling the need to understand this effect better. If it is replicable, there is good reason to think about what might be done to encourage students to believe their teachers are competent.

Even if teacher beliefs alone are not enough to create a Pygmalion from a weak student—and the evidence is mixed that such beliefs alone can even exert a weakly positive effect on student achievement—teacher beliefs and the behaviors fueled by those beliefs can go far in maintaining or even increasing achievement differences between students who are objectively strong and weak academically or objectively well behaved and ill behaved. Over the decades, social psychologists have established many times that people like to interact with and behave more favorably toward people that are like them. Capable, well-behaved students, with their commitments to things academic, are probably perceived more like comrades in intellect and behavior by teachers than are weaker or misbehaving students. Such camaraderie that serves strong and well-behaved students so well can undermine the education of weaker, misbehaving students. Given the perspective advanced throughout this book that all students are capable of learning how to learn and capable of learning a great deal when teachers construct a classroom environment that fosters learning, the behaviors of teachers toward weaker students—behaviors that certainly are not consistent with the models of good teaching featured in this book—are disturbing.

We hope that one effect of this book will be more teachers who understand that there is much reason for optimism about the education of weaker students, when such students are provided high-quality teaching that fosters the growth of strategies, powerful world knowledge, metacognitive understandings, and motivational beliefs about themselves as effective learners. Our experience has been that when young teachers enjoy success in teaching weaker students by teaching students appropriate strategies that are applied to content that is important to students, they come to understand well a point made throughout this book—that even the most at-risk students can do well if they are taught in ways that are sensitive to their current understandings, with teaching continuing in a scaffolded fashion until the student grasps the new strategies and content being presented to them. If the accountability system is such that progress is rewarded rather than performance relative to the rest of the class, there is a fighting chance that even weak students will develop positive academic self-esteem that will motivate continued effort, especially if high-quality, scaffolded instruction continues to be provided. Teachers can behave in ways that undermine the achievement of weaker students or promote it. Many of the readers of this book will face the choice of teaching in ways that perpetuate failure by some students or assure academic progress

for all students. We hope readers will do all possible to be different than the teachers studied by Brophy, who so clearly provided a less supportive academic environment for weaker compared with stronger students.

Parental Involvement in School We review in this book many pieces of evidence that academic achievement and school preparedness (e.g., Reynolds, 1991) are affected by home variables. For example, homes in which a great deal of storybook reading occurs during the preschool years prepare children better for elementary reading than homes in which storybook reading is rare (see Chapter 14). Preparedness for elementary arithmetic is affected by interactions with parents during the preschool years about things numerical (see Chapter 13). Responsive environments, with parents actively involved in stimulating their children's thinking, have both immediate and long-term positive effects on cognitive development (Bradley, Caldwell, & Rock, 1988). Particularly relevant in this chapter, Stevenson and Baker (1987) used census data to evaluate the hypothesis that parental involvement in school promotes academic achievement. What they found was that it does. Although better-educated parents were more likely to be involved with school, the overall pattern in the data suggested that involvement was the active ingredient in promoting the child's academic achievement, not the educational level of the parent per se. Such large-database conclusions are complemented by much smaller, intensive case studies of parents working with their children at home on academic tasks and thus improving the academic performances of their children in school (e.g., Goldenberg, 1989). We take up next one way that parents can be involved in school to the benefit of more than just their own children.

Volunteers in the Classroom In recent years, there has been increasing emphasis on strengthening of school-community relationships. One way of doing so is to welcome community adults into schools as volunteers, with volunteer tutoring one of the most common contributions that citizens can make to schools. Such tutoring definitely increases the achievement of tutees (Michael, 1990, Chapter 4). College students often volunteer in schools, with their efforts clearly promoting the achievement of students they tutor (Reisner, Petry, & Armitage, 1989). Many teacher education reform efforts include requiring that potential teachers participate in tutoring programs throughout their 4 years of teacher training. In addition to providing hands-on experience in real schools to prospective teachers, such requirements provide an important resource to schools. The clear benefits of tutoring provided by volunteers should stimulate additional efforts to increase the use of volunteers in school, and we hope that educational psychologists will be there to study the volunteer tutoring process and experiment with ways to increase the efficacy of volunteer tutors.

Peer Tutoring   Not only can adult volunteers tutor, but also students can tutor other students. A consistent finding in the literature going back to Vernon Allen's work in the 1970s (Allen, 1976) is that both the student tutor and tutee benefit from such interactions. If anything, long-term memory of course material is probably improved more by being a tutor than a tutee (Semb, Ellis, & Araujo, 1993), so that peer tutoring is an even more positive educational opportunity for the tutor than the tutee. Although peer tutoring is an intervention with a long history, there continue to be attempts to identify exceptionally powerful peer tutoring arrangements.

For example, Fantuzzo, Riggio, Connelly, and Dimeff (1989) evaluated the efficacy of a complex peer tutoring intervention relative to some simpler models. The complex approach was more potent than alternative approaches involving only some of the components of the complex approach. Fantuzzo et al (1989) dubbed their best approach to peer tutoring as **reciprocal peer tutoring.** In their study, students in a university-level psychology course were paired with one another for most of the term. There were examinations in the course over each unit of material. Before each examination, each partner constructed 10 multiple-choice questions on the material in the unit. The partners then met and administered the examinations to one another, followed by a discussion in which the partner writing the examination question explained to the partner taking the examination the answer for each item answered incorrectly. It is easy to understand why this treatment was so effective. First, generating questions over academic content, such as was required by constructing the practice test for the partner, increases learning (Rosenshine & Trapman, 1992). So does taking practice tests (e.g., Glover, 1989; Chapter 10, this volume), as does explaining academic content to another person (Webb, 1989).

Greenwood, Delquadri, and Hall (1989) offered an especially impressive analysis of peer tutoring, comparing a group of low–socioeconomic status students who had been in classrooms emphasizing peer tutoring all through grades 1 to 4 with an otherwise comparable group of children in more conventional classrooms. When assessed at the end of fourth grade, the children experiencing the peer tutoring–emphasis curriculum achieved at higher levels than the control children in reading, math, and language arts. The peer-tutored children were also better behaved in class and spent a higher proportion of class time engaged in academic activities. When the striking positive effects of this study and others are considered, it is clear that peer tutoring is an attractive form of instruction—as well as one that is accepted and considered fair by students themselves (Thorkildsen, 1993). Because it is completely consistent with cooperative instruction models (see Chapter 5, this volume), we expect that peer tutoring will be common in American classrooms in the decade ahead.

In addition to peers, children also have brothers and sisters. One interesting hypothesis emerging is that older siblings may be especially adept and effective as tutors, with younger tutees more attentive to and willing to interact actively with older siblings than other child tutors (Azmitia & Hesser, 1993).

Ability Grouping and Tracking by Ability Level
Ability tracking for instruction has been common in schools. It begins with three different groups for reading in grade 1 (good readers, average readers, weaker readers) and continues through the end of high school, with advanced placement courses for the best students and vocational education options for students who have not fared well academically in junior high school and the early years of high school. Special education has sometimes been offered as an extreme form of tracking, with "special"-school, "special"-classroom, and "resource room" placements given to students designated as learning-disabled or mildly retarded.

In the last two decades, the practice of ability grouping has come under attack. With respect to classified students, the law (in particular, **U.S. Public Law 94-142**) now requires that special education students be placed in minimally restrictive environments (i.e., environments as much as possible like normal schooling), which translates into a regular classroom placement whenever possible, with many efforts now to identify ways to maximize the learning of special education students in regular classrooms (for many examples, see Schloss, 1992).

Research bears out the wisdom of P.L. 94-142. Forming classrooms that are homogeneous with respect to student ability does not promote academic achievement (e.g., Oakes, 1987; Slavin, 1987a, 1990a). Putting a child in the middle or slower group guarantees different instruction relative to placement in the high group: He or she reads different materials, the pace is slower, and classmates are less capable (Juel, 1990). In particular, segregation of students with special needs has exceptionally great potential for undermining their achievement: When special education students are isolated for instruction, the instruction often is not good. Even assignment to resource rooms for part of a day, which is a much less extreme form of special placement than assignment to a separate school or a special classroom for the entire day, has a bad impact on the quality of instruction offered to students.

Allington, McGill-Franzen, Meyers, and Gelzheiser, all of the State University of New York at Albany, in particular, have documented that when students receive resource room instruction, they actually receive less total instruction (e.g., time that might have been used for instruction is eaten up shuttling from the regular classroom to the resource room). In addition, the instruction offered to the students in the resource room is not well matched to the accountability demands that special education students face. Rather than addressing the content and skills required of these students during regular instruction, lower-level instruction is offered. The time spent in the resource room, in fact, reduces the amount of instruction these students receive with respect to the content and skills they are expected to be acquiring in the regular classroom. Indeed, rather than making these students' lives better, resource room instruction can make special education students' lives worse, fragmenting their day and their instruction and providing less opportunity for them to learn the material on which they are evaluated (graded) than they would have had in the absence of the resource room instruction. Allington and McGill-Franzen's indictment of pulling children out of their regular classroom extends beyond special education placement: For example, they argue that special instruction offered to poor children through federally funded Chapter 1 services often has the same effect of fragmenting the day and reducing the

amount of instruction matched to the accountability demands the students face (Allington, 1983, 1991a, 1991b; Allington & McGill-Franzen, 1989, 1991; McGill-Franzen, 1987; Meyers, Gelzheiser, Yelich, & Gallagher, 1990). O'Sullivan, Ysseldyke, Christenson, and Thurlow (1990) have generated independent evidence supportive of the main conclusions of the Albany group.

Oakes (1985) examined tracking in 25 high schools across the United States (schools originally studied by Goodlad, 1984), ones representing the full range of diversity in students and schools that was present in the United States in the late 1970s and early 1980s. All of these high schools included some form of tracking. Oakes studied these classrooms to determine if the opportunities to acquire knowledge differed as a function of how one was tracked and if the process of education was different for students in higher and lower tracks. (This research is especially interesting from the perspective of equity issues in that the poor and minorities more often end up in the lower tracks in high schools, including the ones studied by Oakes.)

There was considerable evidence that the students in the high tracks in Oakes's (1985) study were exposed to much more important content than the students in the lower tracks—that schools offered the high-track students much greater opportunity to develop worthwhile knowledge. Although a variety of analyses were offered to support this conclusion, some of the most haunting and memorable data were in the students' own voices. Consider the following answers from students in high-track classes to the question, "What is the most important thing you have learned or done so far in this class?":

Learning political and cultural trends in relation to international and domestic events.
Things in nature are not always what they appear to be or what seems to be happening is not what is really happening.
To infer or apply the *past* ideas to my ideas and finally to the future's ideas.
We have learned the basics of the law of relativity, and basics in electronics. The teacher applies these lessons to practical situations.

Now consider answers to the same question from low-track students:

To be honest, nothing.
How to blow up lightbulbs.

Spelling, worksheets.

The most important thing I have learned in this class I think is how to write checks and to figure the salary of a worker. Another things is the tax rate. (All from Oakes, 1985, pp. 67–72)

In addition to finding that low-track students are exposed to less knowledge and knowledge that is not as valued in our culture, Oakes (1985) demonstrated that less of the total class time in lower-track classes is devoted to instruction. Students in low-track classes spend more time fooling around. They are assigned much less homework. Despite the fact that it is known that it takes longer for lower-ability students to learn content than higher-ability students (Carroll, 1963), lower-track classrooms are structured so that lower-ability students spend less time on learning than higher-ability students. In addition, there were multiple indications that the quality of school life was worse for low-ability compared with high-ability students: Teachers were less enthused about teaching them.

Teacher communications were more likely to be understood by high-ability than lower-ability students. Grades were more clearly tied to effort and achievement for higher-ability students than for lower-ability students. The high-track classes seemed better planned and organized than the lower-track classes. Teachers were more respectful of higher-track students; they were more punitive of lower-track students. Teachers were more open to questions from higher-track students than lower-track students. Even peer relations were warmer and friendlier for higher-track students than lower-track students, who seemed to take their frustrations out on each other. When we read Oakes's (1985) book, it was easy to recognize our own high schools. Perhaps that is one reason her book had so much impact—It was so believable but in being so made clear that tracking created a nastier, less educative world for weaker than for stronger students.

There has been progress with respect to integration of special education students into regular classroom settings—that is, in the 1990s, many special needs students are "mainstreamed." Progress in "untracking" students not classified as needing special education services (i.e., the types of lower-ability students studied by Oakes) has been slower, however. At the time of this writing, however, Anne Wheelock's (1992) book, *Cross the Tracks: How "Untracking" Can Save America's Schools*, was receiv-

ing a great deal of attention, and we expect that there will be substantial efforts in the next decade to reduce ability grouping in schools.

Educational psychologists need to study carefully the impact of such efforts, because it is not entirely clear that untracking will, in fact, improve schooling for disadvantaged students. For example, mainstreaming of special education students might be used as an excuse for not providing special services for them. If so, special students' needs might be met even less well when they are mainstreamed than when they receive pullout instruction—even though pullout instruction has the disadvantages we reviewed earlier. Alternatively, mixing weaker and stronger students in high schools might result in a watering down of content for stronger students. Another possibility is that there will be additional frustration for weaker students, for example, if high school teachers were to teach to the top of mixed-ability classes. Moreover, when weaker students are placed in classes with stronger students, their weaknesses are ever more apparent to them, with the possibility that daily negative comparisons with students who are doing better in school will undermine achievement efforts (e.g., Renick & Harter, 1989; Reuman, 1989). There are no guarantees with untracking, with a clear need for objective assessment of the costs and benefits it affords.

Sex-Segregated Education   Some have argued based on correlational data that single-sex educational settings may produce greater academic achievement than coeducation (e.g., Coleman, 1961). In particular, some believe that gender biases that affect girls negatively (e.g., see Chapters 12 and 13, this volume) are reduced when girls are schooled in sex-segregated settings (e.g., Willis & Kenway, 1986). Although the evidence is mixed (Marsh, 1989a, 1989b), there is probably a small positive effect (i.e., 0.1 to 0.2 SD) of sex segregation on academic achievement at least at the secondary level (Lee & Bryk, 1986, 1989).

Class Size   The typical elementary teacher in the United States has between 20 and 30 children in her or his classroom, with the average being 25 or more. The typical secondary teacher faces sections with between 25 and 30 students, with the mean closer to 30; five or more sections per day is common (National Center for Education Statistics, 1992). Virtually all reviewers of the literature on class size conclude that smaller classes boost achievement, particularly for weaker students (e.g., Cooper, 1989a; Educational Research Service, 1978; Glass & Smith, 1979; Hedges & Stock, 1983; Slavin, 1984). The debate is about how small classes must be before there are worthwhile gains in achievement, with some reviewers arguing that reducing classes to 15 pupils would make a difference (Glass & Smith, 1979) and others believing that gains are not large until class size is reduced to numbers more typical of small-group tutoring than classroom instruction (e.g., three students per teacher, Slavin, 1984; one-to-one tutoring, Slavin, 1989).

This is a problem now being attacked in true experimental studies, which permit clearer cause-and-effect conclusions than permitted by earlier research efforts on class size. In 76 schools in Tennessee, Finn and Achilles (1990) assigned kindergarten students either to small classes (i.e., 13 to 17 students) or larger classes (i.e., 22 to 25), with the presence or absence of an aide systematically manipulated in the larger classes. These class sizes and class assignments were held intact through grade 1. (Although some adjustments had to be made to deal with the realities of schools, the manipulation was reasonably clean, especially given the scope of the study.) The evidence in favor of the smaller classes was clear, with definitely greater achievement in mathematics and reading by the smaller classes at the end of grade 1. The advantages of the smaller class were especially striking for minority students. Although the presence of an aide helped, especially in grade 1, the smaller class students generally outperformed the students in larger classes taught by a teacher and an aide. The definitiveness of outcome in this study when compared with the previous efforts illustrates well the power of true experiments for illuminating important issues regarding schooling—Finn and Achilles (1990) demonstrated that large-scale experimentation is possible with respect to an important question pertaining to educational policy.

What is disappointing in reviewing this literature is that the emphasis has been so quantitative. We favor new investigations of class size that examine much more completely the diversity and types of learning opportunities occurring in smaller compared with larger classes. We suspect that new qualitative analyses might open some windows on potential class size effects not considered in previous analyses (e.g., whether the curriculum really is more individualized with fewer students, how small classes must be before it is possible to monitor and reinforce individual student growth with sensitivity). The indications to date that classroom life and achievement are improved by smaller class sizes do much to stimulate interest in analyzing as completely as possible how small class size might affect the lives of students and teachers so as to maximize student learning in classrooms.

Notably, one of the most articulate reflections on the need for more qualitative, process-oriented data was provided by Finn and Achilles (1990), who provided the most impressive quantitative analysis on this problem we have seen:

> It is clear from recent scholarly writing that students' active involvement in schooling, in various forms, is an essential requisite to the successful completion of 12 years of schooling (Ekstrom, Goetz, Pollack, & Rock, 1986; Finn, 1989; Hawkins & Lam, 1987; Wehlage, 1986). Reduced class size may be one of many ways to promote a greater variety and extent of participatory behavior. Augmenting regular classes with specialized teacher aides may be another, although we must seek to understand their roles and functions in the classroom better than we do now. In either case, it is important that the process issues— What is taught? How is it taught? How are students responding?—be addressed as well as the issues of learning outcomes. (p. 575)

See Morrow and Smith (1990) for an outstanding analysis of differences in interactions when reading instruction occurs in small groups rather than in whole classes.

Retention   Should children be retained in a grade if their academic or social progress is not at the level of other children? The answer seems to be no, with retained children rarely measuring up academically to same-grade students several years after the retention experience (Holmes & Matthews, 1984), and when they do measure up, there is no advantage (i.e., retained and nonretained students perform comparably several years after the retention experience; e.g., Peterson, DeGracie, & Ayabe, 1987). More positively, perhaps, when all of the data are examined, stereotypical perceptions that retained children's self-esteem is reduced and their attitudes toward school negatively affected by the retention experience seem overblown, with only small negative effects of retention on self-esteem and attitudes toward school (Holmes & Matthews, 1984). In some cases, the motivations and attitudes of retained children seem to improve. For example, Plummer and

Graziano (1987) studied more than 200 children (grades 2 and 5) retained in one Georgia county. They did not find across-the-board social rejection of such children. In fact, the self-esteem of retained children was higher than the self-esteem of nonretained children.

Even so, some analysts conclude that retained children do fine, and other observers catastrophize about the effects of retention on children. This is an area in which a great deal more research is required before it is reasonable to draw firm conclusions, especially because teachers endorse retention as an acceptable, helpful educational practice, especially during the primary years (e.g., Smith & Shepard, 1988; Tomchin & Impara, 1992). One problem that has received special attention has been kindergarten retention, with it not uncommon for one or two children in a kindergarten class to be retained, with younger children and boys more likely to be held back than other kindergarten students (e.g., Bryant, Clifford, & Peisner, 1991; Mantzicopoulos, Morrison, Hinshaw, & Carte, 1992). In general, kindergarten-retained children do worse in the early elementary years than do nonretained child1ren (e.g., Mantzicopoulos & Morrison, 1992; Shepard, 1989), which on the face of it suggests the practice does not promote long-term academic success. The frustration in examining these studies is that it is never known how the retained children would be doing in the primary years if they had not been held back in kindergarten. We are not certain that well-controlled work on this problem is ethical (e.g., randomly deciding which kindergarten children should be retained from among the kindergarten children who are doing poorly in school), but better controlled studies might help to clear the air about what the actual effects of retention are: Is it helpful as some teachers believe or harmful as suggested by the available correlational data?

Mastery Learning **Mastery learning** (Bloom, 1968) typically involves breaking course content up into manageable units, with students studying and taking quizzes on a unit until the test is passed at a high level of mastery (e.g., 80 to 100 percent). The course consists of the student proceeding through units, mastering each along the way. The assumption is that some students will need to study more than will others, and some will require more instruction than will others. All students, however, can end up mastering the material and earning an "A," how-ever, which is different from conventional instruction, which involves all students receiving a fixed amount of instruction and a fixed number of quizzes, with some students learning more than others and thus some making better grades than others. Mastery learning is consistent with the task-oriented, noncompetitive models of classroom motivation favored in Chapter 5.

Fred Keller (1968), a distinguished behavioral psychologist interested in education, devised a version of mastery learning he dubbed **personalized systems of instruction (PSI).** Keller favored reinforcement mechanisms more than Bloom, the other major mastery learning theorist, focusing on the consistent reinforcement for studying and learning afforded by quizzing with feedback until the student is successful.

Although mastery learning can and has been implemented in elementary and secondary schools, it is used much more frequently in higher education. When student achievement (e.g., on final examinations) in mastery courses is compared with learning and achievement in traditional courses, mastery learning boosts performance on teacher-constructed or experimenter-constructed tests approximately 0.5 SD (Kulik, Kulik, & Bangert-Drowns, 1990), a moderate-sized effect (see the discussion of meta-analysis in Chapter 1). Students in mastery courses also tend to like such courses better than traditional courses. One important factor that seems to increase the effect of mastery learning is to increase the passing criterion for the quizzes, with better final examination performance when students must perform perfectly on quizzes to proceed than when 70% on a unit quiz allows continuation to the next unit.

Although we conclude that mastery learning seems to have positive effects, we are also aware of critics who cite failures of mastery learning to improve performance on more standardized measures than teacher-constructed tests (e.g., Slavin, 1990b). Still, in a school world of teacher-made tests tapping what the teacher expects students to learn, mastery learning effects on teacher-constructed instruments are important. We find ourselves persuaded by the passionate words of Benjamin Bloom to an earlier criticism of mastery learning by Slavin (1987b), words urging additional exploration of mastery learning in the elementary years (which seems consistent with the motivational principles favored in Chapter 5, this volume):

In spite of the pessimistic view of Mastery Learning by Slavin (based on the particular set of studies he selected), there is much research evidence that Mastery Learning in some form is essential in order for the schools to improve the educational effects for the majority of students. I readily admit that the top 10 percent of the students in a class are likely to get less out of these procedures than the remaining 90 percent of the students in the same class. However, I do believe that the schools need to improve the life chances of most of the students. . . .

We must teach each child with the basic assumption that he can learn well when given the support and encouragement needed. Mastery Learning is an approach that is likely, in the long run, to bring more schoolchildren to a high level of school achievement than will a policy that gives much more to the top than to the bottom children. This is especially true at the elementary school level, where most of the children need as much support and as many rewards as possible to progress well in the elementary school and to develop the necessary confidence and interest in their learning ability for the later levels of schooling. It is a crime against mankind to deprive children of successful learning when it is possible for virtually all to learn to a high level. (Bloom, 1987, pp. 507–8)

Summary One reaction to much of what was presented in this subsection is that the conclusions are so commonsensical—that higher-order questions facilitate learning, teacher expectancies about achievement may affect teacher behaviors that in turn affect student achievement, more teaching in the form of tutoring by volunteers improves achievement, and students in lower-ability tracks are provided less rich instruction that undermines their achievement. Commonsensical or not, classroom questioning is often factual rather than higher order; negative teacher expectancies are all too common, especially with respect to disadvantaged students; many potential school volunteers remain at home; and there are many more tracked schools than untracked ones. Our understanding of factors that can improve the quality of schools is way ahead of school practice, a conclusion that we hope has been obvious at many points in this book. One of our intentions in writing this book was to inspire some of its readership to teach differently and to know why shifts away from traditional educational practices toward many of the interventions and practices considered in this book are so defensible. A second intention was to inspire other readers to continue the tradition of conducting research that extends the educational cutting edge

Summer School

A persistent speculation is that there is some forgetting of what was learned during the school year over the summer. The Sustaining Effects Study (Heyns, 1987; Klibanoff & Haggart, 1981), a huge national effort mandated by Congress to assess the effects of schooling, generally concluded otherwise. By testing large samples of students in the spring and fall, it was possible to determine that there were actually summer gains in reading. As Heyns (1978, 1987) pointed out, however, the rate of growth in reading is less during the summer months than during the school year, with disadvantaged populations experiencing less growth during the summer in the absence of instruction than advantaged populations. There were slight losses over the summer in mathematics, especially at the high school levels.

The U.S. federal government in particular invests heavily in providing summer school programs to elementary and high school students, especially to disadvantaged students. Unfortunately the effects of these short-term programs, many of which are not well integrated with the curriculum experienced during the school year, tend to be small (Heyns, 1987).

It is heartening that there is not massive loss during the summer of academic skills gained during the year. Perhaps it should not be surprising that short-term summer programs would have little impact. What cannot be lost track of, however, is that the discontinuation of schooling does have a cost in that growth during the summer is slower than during the year. There is every reason to believe that if the United States were ever to opt for year-round schooling, there would be an increase in the achievement levels of American students. Based on Heyns's (1987) analyses, we conclude that for one-fourth of the year, American students' academic growth is at about one-third the rate it is for the remainder of the year. That is, a 20 percent increase in what is learned probably could be obtained by year-round schooling compared with the current 9-month school year.

After-School Educational Practices

What goes on after the school day ends can also affect achievement. All of the after-school factors are complex in that the decisions to engage in them are made by students, educators, and parents in interaction, sometimes explicitly (as when teachers assign homework) and sometimes implicitly (as when Japanese parents encourage their children to elect after-school tutoring).

Homework For most American students, homework is a fact of life from the middle elementary grades through the remainder of their schooling. Not surprisingly, the effects of this pervasive educational "intervention" have been explored by educational researchers, who have asked whether, when, and how much homework improves academic achievement. Cooper (1989b) provided a definitive summary of the experimental and correlational research on homework. His conclusions included the following:

- Doing homework does seem to promote learning.
- The positive effects of homework are small in the upper elementary years and gradually increase until they are moderate in magnitude (see Chapter 1, this volume) during the high school years.
- Although the evidence on whether homework makes a bigger difference for some school subjects compared with others is mixed, Cooper concluded that the effects of homework on math, reading, and English were probably greater than the effects of homework on social studies and science achievement. Cooper is more optimistic about the effects of homework on simple skills that benefit from practice and repetition than more complex skills requiring integration and reflection.
- For junior high school students, 1 to 2 hours of homework per night seems optimal. High school students benefit from more homework, although it is not clear based on available data what a reasonable maximum might be.
- Just as distributed practice (spacing; see Chapter 10) works in other arenas, it works with homework. Homework that requires practicing material based on more than just today's lesson (or very recent lessons) is more effective than massed practice of today's content.

As in other areas of educational research, much work remains to be done before there would be anything similar to a comprehensive understanding of homework effects. Cooper points out that there is a need for studies of homework effects on factors other than achievement. Does homework encourage the development of better study habits or greater self-regulation? We do not know at this time. Are some types of homework assignments better than others in promoting achievement? Again, there is little relevant evidence in the literature. The effects of different types of parental involvement in homework are not understood either, despite the fact that there is increasing recognition that academic progress depends on both school and home factors. We suspect that as the electronic revolution continues, the effects of technology on homework are also going to become important to evaluate. Innovations such as "homework hotlines" in some districts (i.e., telephone numbers students can call for homework assistance) only scratch the surface of what might be possible as microcomputers become more available in the home and modems are more common. Professors across the world already consult on e-mail; it seems likely that students will be able to communicate much more broadly from their homes in the foreseeable future, expanding dramatically the possibilities for consultation and assistance with homework as well as the types of assignments that can be made to students. It seems likely that homework research and studies of educational technology will be carried out in tandem in the near future.

After-School Tutoring One way of providing remediation is to provide additional instructional time after school. For students who are slower to learn, this seems like a logical way of increasing the opportunities of such students to learn. Unfortunately, it is not elected often in the West (Rowan & Guthrie, 1989). After-school instruction is common is Japan, with *juku* instruction commonly sought out by the brightest Japanese students, who seek years of tutoring as preparation for difficult university entrance examinations (e.g., White, 1987). There is a clear perception that such after-school and weekend tutoring makes a substantial difference in the ultimate achievement levels of Japanese students. Our view is that there has been much too little attention to the possibility of extending daily and weekly instructional time through outside tutoring. Educational psychologists should be interested in such tutoring because the dynamics of it will probably be different from the dynamics operating in school. As an example of the extremely social and motivating nature of this type of instruction compared with normal schooling, consider this description of one *juku* tutor, Sagara:

> The students see him as on their side, as uncompromisingly working *with* them, and sometimes even as an ally against their parents. He constantly rewards them, and provides nurturance in the form of treats and surprises, such as getting them ice cream on a hot day or buying them books or special gifts. [One student] even received several comic books from Sagara when the young student was sick, and Sagara offered him a whole set of them if he'd promise to study hard for his high school entrance exam. Sagara's relationship with his students is of the kidding, big-brother sort. Sagara once bet his students on the answer to a very hard problem and said that if he were wrong, he'd cut his hair very short. He was and he did. He is boyish and dresses casually, and the intensity of *juku* study is mitigated by Sagara's cheerful liveliness. . . . For the graduates, the *juku* experience seems to have been more meaningful than their time in regular schools, for they say "after I graduated from *juku*. . ." instead of "after I graduated from junior high. . . ." They all say Sagara is one of the most important people in their lives. (White, 1987, pp. 148–9)

It is definitely an interesting question whether such people can make a difference in the academic achievement of their students, with the possibility that such relationships should be considered as one way to supplement schooling—or perhaps even as a means for restructuring school so it is more personal and supportive. Although there are many reasons for Japanese superiority in mathematics achievement (see Chapter 13), one likely cause is that many university-bound Japanese students spend much of their out-of-school time with *juku* tutors. Tutoring—after school and otherwise—is an intervention that works much of the time, one that needs to be explored further to understand how it works, as well as how it might be incorporated more certainly in the lives of more students. (See the discussion of programs that involve one-to-one tutoring, such as Success for All, earlier in this chapter and in Chapter 5 as well as Reading Recovery in Chapter 14.)

Extracurricular Activities Does playing sports, cheerleading, participating in drama or debate, playing in the band, and a myriad of other activities affect student achievement? If these activities took time away from schoolwork, they might interfere with school achievement (e.g., Coleman, 1961). Alternatively, they might be enriching experiences. Using data collected in more than 1000 high schools by the federal government, Marsh (1992b) determined that there were small but consistently positive correlations between extracurricular participation and a variety of academic outcomes. In addition, students participating in extracurricular activities tended to have slightly better academic self-concepts. Although it is impossible to determine from the Marsh (1992b) analysis whether such participation increases academic ability or whether more capable students elect to participate in extracurricular activities, there was nothing in the Marsh data to indict extracurricular involvement.

Holland and Andre (1987) offered an especially optimistic (and controversial; Brown, 1988; Holland & Andre, 1988; Taylor & Chiogioji, 1988) appraisal of extracurricular activities, claiming the literature supported correlations between such participation and higher self-esteem, better racial relations, more political and social involvement, feelings of greater control, lower delinquency, and higher grades and academic achievement and aspirations. One bonus finding was that students enrolled in smaller schools were more likely to partake of extracurricular activities and enjoy the benefits of such experiences.

We note, however, that much more study of extracurricular activities is needed, that the evaluations to date have generally been conceptually vacuous and methodologically questionable. Moreover, the many different types of activities, from academic after-school clubs to athletic teams, are often lumped together in analyses (Brown, 1988; Holland & Andre, 1988; Taylor & Chiogioji, 1988). Given how salient extracurricular activities are in the lives of participants, they deserve more serious consideration than they have been given to date.

After-School Employment Despite hypothesized benefits of after-school work, such as increased self-reliance, work orientation, and self-esteem, there is little evidence that students experience such benefits from such work (Steinberg & Dornbusch, 1991). Extensive work is associated with poorer school performance, more psychological distress, substance abuse, and delinquency (Steinberg & Dornbusch, 1991; Steinberg, Fegley, & Dornbusch, 1993). If students work, the hours should be limited so as not to interfere with schoolwork. Unfortunately, students who are already having difficulty in school are most likely to elect outside work, which results in even lower in-school achievement (Steinberg et al., 1993).

Recall from Chapter 1 that good information processors elect possibilities that improve their minds; unfortunately the converse is also true, such as when low-achieving students elect to spend even less time and effort on school in favor of taking outside employment.

Student Viewing of Popular Television and Interaction with Other Media One of the largest demands on the time of American students is popular television. Although there is some disagreement about how pejorative the effects of television viewing are on academic achievement, all analysts who have worked through the relevant data sets conclude that there is a negative relationship between television viewing and academic achievement (Comstock & Paik, 1991, Chapter 3). An interesting twist compared with many other negative effects, however, is that the negative effects of television viewing seem to be greater for students from more socioeconomically advantaged homes (e.g., Anderson, Mead, & Sullivan, 1986). The declines in achievement with increased television viewing are observed across virtually all academic subjects (e.g., California Assessment Program, 1988), however. Although elementary students tend to be heavy viewers of television regardless of ability levels, with increasing grades, there is a movement away from television, especially pronounced for brighter children—that is, with increasing age, brighter children are more likely than children of lower ability to engage in reading and other acitivities (Comstock & Paik, 1991, Chapter 3). Heavier viewers of television tend to spend a much higher proportion of their total viewing time with reruns of the "Dukes of Hazzard," "Saved By the Bell" and "Full House," than do light viewers, who view a mix of television weighted in favor of news and information programming (e.g., California Assessment Program, 1982). That is, smarter adolescents view less television and are more likely to watch news and other information-rich programming than are lower-ability adolescents.

The negative correlations between academic achievement/intelligence and overall television viewing cannot be interpreted as clear evidence of a causal relationship between television viewing and intellect. It is just as reasonable to argue that weaker students would choose to watch television as to argue that watching massive amounts of television reduces intellectual ability. Even so, when students watch large amounts of light-entertainment television, they are consuming time that could be devoted to activities that almost certainly improve intellect and academic achievement more than reruns of "I Love Lucy" and contemporary counterparts—activities such as reading (e.g., Williams, 1986).

A balanced appraisal of television effects on mind requires consideration of the positive effects of television viewing on academic achievement. For example, there is no doubt that when preschoolers view "Sesame Street" for an extended period of time, they learn a great deal about basic literacy and numeracy concepts, such as the names of letters and the meaning of numbers (e.g., Ball & Bogatz, 1975). In Chapter 13, we will review evidence that PBS's "Square One" television is increasing children's knowledge of mathematical concepts. The widespread availability of public television across North America has resulted in an intervention that is generally available to almost all children regardless of socioeconomic, racial, or ethnic status (Comstock, 1989; Comstock & Paik, 1991, Chapter 3)—which is not trivial given how scarce academic resources are for many of the least advantaged children.

Indeed, for most children and many teenagers, television is their only source of news. Television exposes children to occupational roles, ethnic groups, and information about settings that they would not experience otherwise—often with improvements in understanding and acceptance of diversity. Television can be used to reverse stereotypes by presenting programming in which nontraditional roles (e.g., sex roles) are portrayed in a favorable light (Comstock & Paik, 1991, Chapter 4). In short, television definitely can improve children's knowledge of the world. The trick, of course, is to encourage viewing of programming that encourages ethically desirable, prosocial attitudes and the development of knowledge that is valuable both in and out of school, while discouraging heavy viewing of genetically altered reptiles, half-hour tales constructed to be amusing rather than informative, and mind-numbing music videos.

One of the most gratifying aspects of a visit to a contemporary video store is that there is a growing library of excellent and entertaining programs that can be viewed at any time. In addition, with the development of technologies such as CD ROM and interactive videodisks (see Chapter 13), there will be increasing opportunity for teachers to use bits and pieces of video presentations selectively and for students to "construct" their own educational television programs by selectively viewing segments of programs that are matched to their interests and informational needs, much as previous generations selectively read parts of books and journals to build understandings of particular content. As these technologies become more universally available, they will compete for "out-of-school" time. In the 21st century, educational psychologists will be exploring these technologies (and the ones that follow them) to determine how new media can affect the development of intellect both in school and at home.

Although there is insufficient space to take up the many potential effects of emerging technology on cognitive development, suffice to point out here that the coming generations of educational psychologists will be charged with determining the effects of home-based computers on cognitive development (including machines that will be able to access increasingly sophisticated mainframe computers), expanded access to information afforded by new television possibilities (e.g., the more than 500 channels available on the television sets of the future), and the effects of ever more realistic computer simulations and computer-constructed images on understanding and thinking (e.g., the meanings of derivatives and integrals can already be portrayed dynamically and in three dimensions on home computers, with it a good bet that students who experience a heavy dose of such microworld interactions will emerge with different understandings of calculus than the ones carried away from the textbook-bound courses of the past). Every new medium entering the home, however, has potential for positive effects on the development of mind as well as negative effects (e.g., a home-based computer can be used to permit literacy and numeracy experiences never before available to students, or it can be used to run video arcade–type games). Educational psychologists are already busy exploring how new technologies can be used in school; we believe that they also should play a key role in determining how to promote constructive uses of the new media at home.

Summary   If the mind stops being engaged when the school bell rings at the end of the day, cognitive development is not as extensive as when the mind continues to be academically engaged through homework, tutoring, or exposure to worthwhile media activities, such as watching of news programming. Many more waking hours are spent out of school than in school, and thus there cannot be a complete understanding of education without an understanding of the educational experiences that occur before the pledge to the flag and after dismissal. Not everything that can occur between the morning and afternoon bells reliably promotes development of the mind, however, with the next section devoted to curricular options that can be seductive entries into the school day but fail to deliver everything that they promise.

EXPLICIT TEACHING OF THINKING IN SCHOOLS: THINKING SKILLS PROGRAMS

There are many packaged programs aimed at increasing the thinking abilities of students. Many are sold by professional education associations and private publishers. The particular goals of programs vary, although all assume that many students do not develop the skills stimulated by the programs on their own. Of course, this is a fair assumption in light of the evidence that has been reviewed thus far in this book. Consistent with the massive database supporting the teachability of many of these skills, including many of the studies already reviewed in this book, there is an assumption that effective thinking skills can be taught. Many of the older programs assume that the heart of thinking skills instruction should be a set of general procedures that can be applied across domains. There has been growing recognition, however, by producers of these programs that skills often are domain specific, an understanding fostered by work such as the expert-novice research reviewed in Chapter 4. There is a growing understanding that good thinking is sensitive to context, that what works in one situation will not work in other situations (e.g., see Lipman, 1991, Chapter 4). The more modern programs also seem to reflect awareness of the need to educate students so that the skills and strategies taught can be accessed easily and used flexibly and the skills and strategies be practiced until they can be executed automatically. Although many of the early efforts reflected linear and somewhat rigid application of the skills taught, there has also been increasing recognition that much of thinking is nonlinear and recursive, involving novel combinations and inventive sequencing of skills and strategies that meet the demands of particular tasks and problems (Adams,

1989; Lipman, 1991; Nickerson, Perkins, & Smith, 1985; Segal, Chipman, & Glaser, 1985).

Most of these programs are constructed by amalgamating a large number of individual instructional procedures, each of which has been validated in basic research, and thus there are claims by program developers that their inventions are based on research. At best, however, these programs have been understudied, with many never evaluated as wholes in anything even resembling an experimental or quasiexperimental evaluation. This is an extremely unfortunate gap in the educational research literature because many of these programs are implemented widely in schools. There are so many different programs that we can cover only some of the more famous ones.

CoRT Thinking Program

Edward de Bono (e.g., 1985; also Nickerson et al., 1985, Chapter 7) of Great Britain has offered a number of thinking programs over the years, with the most extensive one, *CoRT* (which stands for "Cognitive Research Trust"), intended to be implemented over 3 years of instruction (i.e., with one lesson per week). The claim is made that CoRT can be used with children as young as 8 years of age and is appropriate for all subsequent age/grade levels. The program also is proposed as appropriate for slow and bright students and useful across cultures. It is based on de Bono's (1969) description of mind at its best, as a self-organizing, self-stabilizing, and active entity.

CoRT is a program intended to teach general thinking skills. Indeed, the claim is made that the program does not depend on the acquisition of prior knowledge. The CoRT skills can be applied across a wide range of situations and are particularly aimed at changing people's perceptions of situations. The program is designed to be simple and practical, emphasizing skills that are important in real life and transferable to a range of real-life situations.

There are six sets of 10 lessons, with each covering an important aspect of thinking:

- The first emphasizes **breadth** of thinking. There is particular emphasis on examining ideas for their good, bad, and interesting points; there is also an emphasis on looking at a number of factors in a situation rather than focusing on a few, immediately salient features. Con-

sequences of strategies are introduced, as is the idea of selecting and defining thinking objectives. Setting priorities is introduced. Generating alternatives rather than simply accepting a salient possibility is emphasized. Students are encouraged to consider all points of view in a situation.

- The second set of lessons involves teaching of **organization** skills. These include labeling a situation based on key characteristics. Students are taught to divide up problems and situations in order to deal with them. They are taught about making comparisons and selecting among alternatives. Other skills include teaching how to start working on a problem, how to organize the steps of problem solving, and how to consolidate what one knows and generate conclusions.
- The third set deals with **interaction,** notably how to debate and discuss issues. These skills include examining both sides; evaluating types, value, and structure of evidence; determining how to structure evidence to increase agreements and reduce disagreements; and knowing the various ways of being right and wrong.
- The fourth set of lessons is aimed at increasing **creativity.**
- The fifth involves the roles of **information and feeling** in thinking.
- The sixth set of lessons is an **action** plan that teaches students how to use all of the skills taught in the previous lessons to produce powerful thinking. Students are taught to select a target for thinking and then to expand their thinking about the target followed by a narrowing of focus. Being clear about purpose is emphasized, as is identifying relevant inputs. Students are encouraged to generate alternative solutions to problems and to make choices among the alternatives.

CoRT lessons have a common structure (de Bono, 1983a, 1983b, 1985). Each has a focus, which is first explained by the teacher. Illustrations are provided that make clear the purpose of the lesson. There are practice items, which are accomplished in small groups. There is a great deal of feedback as part of instruction, emanating from teachers and students (i.e., to one another). There are discussions and projects involving application of the thinking skills (e.g., writing assignments requiring use of the CoRT skills). An important part of each lesson is a set of notes that is provided to students that summarizes the points of the lesson. Although the focus of each lesson is on a particular type of thinking skill, there are review lessons that integrate across lessons. de Bono is emphatic in arguing against attempting to combine the lessons with content instruction, believing that this would diminish attention to the thinking skills.

Unfortunately the evaluation of CoRT is thin at best (for a review, see Nickerson et al., 1985, Chapter 7). de Bono reports in his manuals and books that there have been experiments comparing CoRT students with students not receiving CoRT instruction. Not surprisingly, given the emphasis on production of ideas in CoRT, CoRT students produce more ideas regarding problems than non-CoRT students. There is also some evidence that the quality of ideas produced by CoRT students is better than the quality of ideas produced by non-CoRT students (e.g., CoRT students are more likely to examine several sides of an issue, rather than just one). Thus, following participation in the CoRT 1 lessons on breadth, more and slightly better ideas are generated in response to problems such as the following: "Should pupils have a say in making school rules?" and "A man is found to have stolen a huge pile of left shoes. What do you think he is up to?"

de Bono (1985) claims, however, that the outcomes of CoRT teaching are broader than simply an increase in the number of ideas produced, including that CoRT students begin to consider themselves "thinkers" and apply the CoRT thinking skills broadly, especially to important school tasks and contents. He also believes that CoRT instruction increases academic motivation. Our view is that these claims should be treated as hypotheses that deserve more evaluation, given that CoRT is being distributed worldwide at present. If CoRT does these things, it is imperative that the educator community find out because generalized use of the skills that are taught in CoRT would be an extremely attractive outcome, especially if it can be produced with one short lesson a week for 3 years! The promise is great enough to justify the resources necessary to evaluate it fully.

Productive Thinking Program

Martin Covington of the University of California at Berkeley and his associates (Covington, Crutchfield, Davies, & Olton, 1974) devised a thinking skills intervention aimed at the later grade-school years (i.e.,

grades 5 and 6). There are 15 short booklets in the program, with these telling tales about a boy and a girl who are confronted with a series of mysteries that must be solved. The stories are conveyed using text and cartoons, with the books designed to be extremely attractive and interesting to elementary students. The characters in the story engage in a variety of problem-solving methods as they tackle these mysteries, continually sending the message that strategic effort is required to solve problems, ones that may prove extremely challenging (i.e., there are failures of problem solving in the stories before there are successes). Students in the program are given many opportunities to generate solutions to problems. They are specifically taught a number of strategies for confronting the problems in the stories:

- Assemble the facts before attempting to problem solve.
- Formulate the problem carefully before attempting to problem solve.
- Generate many ideas.
- Try to think of unusual ideas.
- Consider that there are many ways to solve a problem.
- Be planful, addressing problems systematically.
- Do not stay "stuck," but rather think of new approaches when having difficulty.
- Map out the various possibilities in a problematic situation.
- Think of general ideas and then variations on these general solutions. (Based on summary by Nickerson et al., 1985, p. 210)

To the extent that the program has been evaluated—and it has been evaluated more than most thinking skills programs (for reviews, see Covington, 1985; Mansfield, Busse, & Krepelka, 1978; Nickerson et al., 1985, Chapter 7)—the effects have been mixed. When presented problems similar to the ones presented in the program itself, *Productive Thinking* students produce more ideas and at least slightly better ideas than nontrained students. When confronted with problems that are somewhat different from problems encountered in the lessons, the effects are not as striking. Nickerson et al. (1985) summarized some of the reasons that *Productive Thinking* produces little transfer:

> The answers to the "whodunit" problems [in the program] are short—the identity of the culprit and a brief

explanation—rather than complex products. The problems are given rather than found by the problem solver. The problems are very concrete. The program guarantees that a solution exists. And, finally, the program leads the students through the entire process of thought to the solution. (p. 213)

In contrast, problems in the real world are often complex; often much of the problem-solving task is problem finding and definition; and solutions are often abstract and anything but guaranteed. Perhaps a greater difficulty with the program, however, is that it simultaneously gives students too much—in that explanations of how to do the problems posed are provided ultimately—at the same time that it gives them too little—in that a narrow range of problem types is presented. Our own view is that *Productive Thinking* does about as much as could be expected in 15 lessons, for consistent with evidence reviewed throughout this book, interventions producing broad-based transfer will be implemented for years rather than months or days.

Instrumental Enrichment

Israeli Reuven Feurstein (1979, 1980; for a review see Nickerson et al., 1985, Chapter 6) believes that poor cognitive performance involves failures of encoding and lack of elaboration of information that is presented and acquired (i.e., students do not relate what they know already to new information). When information is presented, the poor learner makes sweeping perceptions, rather than detailed and analytical ones; is unplanned and impulsive; fails to comprehend because of low verbal, spatial, and temporal abilities; does not conserve in the Piagetian sense (see Chapter 7); is not precise or accurate in measurement; and cannot deal with more than one source of information at a time. Elaboration is deficient in that the poor learner is not selective with respect to the information that is attended, fails to make important inferences and generate hypotheses, and thinks in terms of particulars of a situation rather than about how a situation is representative of a broader class of situations. Poor learners' responses tend to involve much trial-and-error responding, are often imprecise, and are impulsive.

Mediated learning experiences are crucial in overcoming these deficiencies according to Feurstein's view, with "mediated learning" virtually synonymous with "scaffolded" instruction (see Chapters 1 and 8). During mediated learning experiences, more knowledgeable adults assist children, modifying input that is provided to the child so it can be comprehended by the child. The adult interprets the task for the child and points out the relevant features of the situation that need to be considered to perform tasks given to the child. Sometimes this means substantial reorganization and restructuring of a problem by the adult before the child is permitted to attempt it. The adult also assists at the response end, for example, making efforts to discourage impulsivity, so the child reflects before responding.

The instrumental enrichment program involves providing mediated learning experiences as students work on a series of paper-and-pencil exercises. The program is intended for low-functioning adolescents and is delivered 3 to 5 hours a week for 2 to 3 years. While working on the exercises, the adult works closely with the student, helping the student understand the task, how he or she is approaching it, and how the task might be accomplished differently when the student uses more appropriate processes. After a student attempts the exercises independently, often there is a small-group discussion, which is aimed especially at producing insights about how to apply the processes practiced in the exercises to both school and out-of-school tasks. (These group discussions are reminiscent of the instructional conversations considered in Chapter 8 as part of socially mediated learning; the social-interactive aspects of this intervention are as striking in many ways as the specific curriculum materials that have been developed for the program.)

As in many other thinking skills programs, the thinking skills exercises are content free and do not require any domain-specific knowledge. The exercises emphasize both perceptual and logical skills. For example, "organization of dots" involves organizing an array of dots by finding in them hidden figures that correspond to model figures shown to the learner. Feurstein's analysis of such tasks is that they require perceptual and search skills, with the task best accomplished if there is substantial planning by the learner. This task also requires inhibiting impulsivity. Because Feurstein believes that poor learners are "episodic" in their thinking, treating a current situation in an isolated fashion rather than as representative of a more general set of relations (i.e., students do not relate a current task to their prior knowledge), there are a number of exercises aimed at understanding how one situation relates to another. Thus, there are exercises designed to develop the knowledge that how something looks depends on one's perspective on it. There are exercises to increase understanding that past and future exist as well as the present. There are many opportunities in the exercises to consider alternatives, and there is a consistent emphasis on learners explaining why and how they come to problem solutions. There are exercises requiring learners to work with sets and subsets, with these requiring substantial logical skills as learners work with abstract elements.

Does this program work? At best, the evidence is mixed, and the most compelling support is difficult to interpret (see Nickerson et al., 1985, Chapter 6 for a review). Feurstein's own work (Feurstein, Rand, Hoffman, & Miller, 1979; Rand, Tannenbaum, & Feurstein, 1979) was with the children of African and Asian immigrants to Israel, groups that were decidedly out of the Israeli mainstream. As a group, these children were impoverished and low functioning relative to the general Israeli society. Progress following 2 years of instrumental enrichment was compared with progress made by comparable students who received the type of remedial instruction and enrichment typically offered to such immigrant children. After the intervention, there were clear differences between the instrumental enrichment and control students, although the effects of instrumental enrichment were not across the board but limited to particular competencies. Number, geometry, and addition skills were affected by instrumental enrichment, as was performance on some spatial and figure grouping measures. Instrumental enrichment subjects displayed better interpersonal conduct in class than controls as well as greater self-sufficiency and adaptiveness to work demands. There were some academic and social-adjustment improvements attributed to instrumental enrichment in Feurstein's own studies, with the academic improvements generally on nonverbal measures, perhaps not surprising given that many of the exercises in the instrumental enrichment program are perceptual or logical and demand little in terms of verbal competency relative to what they demand with respect to perception and logic.

What do we make of Feurstein's outcomes, especially given they were produced with a population so atypical of students in Western schools? Our view is not to make much of them, consistent with the perspectives of other reviewers (e.g., Blagg, 1991, Chapter 2; Bradley, 1983), because evaluations of instrumental enrichment with Western populations (see Arbitman-Smith, Haywood, & Bransford, 1984) have produced statistically significant but generally modest effects (e.g., 5 to 10 IQ points gained over the course of the intervention). The methods in many of the existing studies have been severely criticized, especially because many of the design decisions, such as choice of dependent variables closely resembling training materials, were biased in favor of instrumental enrichment (e.g., Burden, 1987). When school achievement data are examined, there is little evidence of effect. For example, in a controlled study in South Carolina, O'Tuel and Darby (1993) evaluated the effects of receiving instrumental enrichment for the 3 years of grades 4, 5, and 6. There were no discernible effects on reading, math, or language as measured by standardized tests.

Nigel Blagg, who conducted one of the better designed and more thorough assessments of the program (modified slightly to match the British educational environment in which the study was conducted), summed up the results of his investigation as follows:

> . . . [There was] little quantifiable evidence to suggest that the [instrumental enrichment] program had a positive influence on the 14- to 16-year-old low-attaining pupils [participating in the study] . . . there was no evidence that the . . . program produced any improvements in children's cognitive abilities . . . the . . . program did not produce any significant improvements to children's work study skills, reading or math attainments. . . . (Blagg, 1991, p. 90)

More positively, appropriate classroom participation (e.g., in discussions) seemed to be promoted by the program, although there was considerable variability in the participation gains observed. Even so, Blagg's (1991) data add to a growing body of evidence that instrumental enrichment does not have the broad-based effect on cognitive development that has been attributed to the curriculum by its developers and instrumental enrichment enthusiasts.

Philosophy for Children

Matthew Lipman (see 1985, 1991; also Nickerson et al., 1985, Chapter 10), who teaches at Montclair State in New Jersey, wrote a series of novels for students in the latter grade-school years (i.e., grades 5 and 6). In each of these, the main themes were thinking and reflecting on thinking. The core novel, *Harry Stotlemeir's Discovery* (Lipman, 1974; note the play on the name, "Aristotle") is about Harry and his friends, who spend a lot of time talking about thinking and engaging in interactions that simulate thinking processes. There is coverage of how to conduct inquiries, discovery and invention, construction of inferences, causes and effects, and so on. Teachers who use the materials are provided information about how to stimulate classroom discussions around the thinking themes in the texts. The readings and discussions are intended to encourage students to discover for themselves the thinking themes in the books, with those discoveries taking place in a classroom "community of inquiry" (see Lipman, 1991, especially Chapter 14). The types of classroom conversations that Lipman promotes are similar in design to the interpretive conversations considered in Chapter 8. How *Philosophy for Children* stimulates children's participation in authentic dialogues in the classroom has been a major focus of theoretical analyses of the intervention, with many claims that conversations about philosophical stories can foster the development of thinking abilities, moral understanding, and the existence of multiple perspectives (Lipman, Sharp, & Oscanyen, 1980; Sharp & Reed, 1992).

Does it work? The evaluations that are available are positive (see Nickerson et al., 1985, Chapter 10, for a review). Improvements as a result of reading and discussion of *Philosophy for Children* have been reported in controlled studies. *Philosophy for Children* students have outperformed controls on intelligence test items, reading comprehension, mathematics, and formal reasoning. Our own examination of *Harry Stotlemeir's Discovery* and the *Philosophy for Children* texts that followed it are that they are interesting readings for elementary-school students, full of possibilities for interpretive discussions and collaborative problem solving. These texts would seem to fit well in the social-collaborative instructional settings that are evolving in the 1990s (see Chapter 8). That consistent benefits have been obtained is encouraging, even though the effects have not always been large.

Our bottom line is that the *Philosophy for Children* books are as good as many other pieces of literature given to grade-school students to read; the interpretive conversational skills that are part of the program are also consistent with the social-interactive instruction we favor. Because *Philosophy for Children* promotes reading competence anyway, nothing is lost by assigning these texts as part of reading, and some important thinking competencies might be gained when the texts are discussed in groups. *Philosophy for Children* probably deserves a place in the elementary curriculum, although we hope that much more research and much more analytical research might occur in the coming decade. Dialogic problem solving (i.e., problem solving through group discussion and reflection), which is a main approach promoted by *Philosophy for Children*, is more popular now than at any other time since the first appearance of the program, and hence research documenting the strengths and weaknesses of *Philosophy for Children* as well as research illuminating various ways of using *Philosophy for Children* in classrooms would be timely. Nonetheless, that dialogic education is increasing may reduce the need for a specific set of materials intended to stimulate dialogic discussions because teachers are now using many more authentic materials as starters for such discussions. Lipman's idea may have been ahead of its time. As the rest of the field catches up, however, there may be less need for Lipman's specific materials, although our reading of the volumes produced by Lipman and his colleagues is that they represent sophisticated reflection on the potential of classroom dialogue for stimulating cognitive growth (e.g., Lipman, 1991; Sharp & Reed, 1992). Thus, Lipman's theoretical work and the theoretical suggestions of those inspired by Lipman deserve additional consideration even if interest in Harry Stotlemeir might wane.

Dimensions of Thinking

Marzano et al.'s (1988; Marzano, 1992) *Dimensions of Thinking* is a framework for encouraging critical and creative thinking in classrooms. According to this perspective, explicit instruction in how to form *concepts* should be provided to students, as should instruction in how to find *relationships* between concepts (i.e., principles). *Comprehension* processes should be taught, as should approaches to *problem solving* and *decision making*. Students should be taught methods of *scientific inquiry*; they should be taught how to *compose*, including written, musical, mechanical, or artistic products, depending in part on student interests and talents; and they should be provided opportunities to learn how to *talk* with other people. In addition, there are a set of thinking skills that need to be developed in every student, according to *Dimensions of Thinking*. These overlap other thinking skills programs, including the CoRT program described earlier:

- *Focusing skills*, including defining problems and setting goals.
- *Information-gathering skills*, including systematic observation and formulation of questions.
- *Remembering skills*—both encoding and retrieval strategies.
- *Organizing skills*, such as comparing, classifying, ordering, and recoding from one form to another (referred to as "representing" in *Dimensions of Thinking*).
- *Analyzing skills*, such as identifying attributes of things, relationships between elements, main ideas, and recognizing logical errors and other types of mistakes.
- *Generating skills*, including making of inferences, predictions, and elaboration of content.
- *Integrating skills*, such as summarizing and restructuring.
- *Evaluation skills*, such as establishing criteria and verifying whether criteria are met. (Based on Marzano et al., 1988, pp. 147–148)

In visits to schools, we often encounter the *Dimensions of Thinking* materials, published by the Association for Supervision and Curriculum Development. We conclude from these observations that the *Dimensions of Thinking* are on the mind of many educators, with many attempts across the United States to implement the instructional ideas supported by *Dimensions of Thinking*. Our greatest concern with this direction is that we have not seen a single convincing evaluation of packages that are comprised of a large number of strategies aimed at diverse cognitive goals, including *Dimensions of Thinking*, which is simply the most recent example of multistrategy packages. In our more cynical moments, we have referred to such programs as "dump-a-bunch-of-strategies" approaches. Most of the components in *Dimensions of Thinking* have been validated, however. Two thick edited volumes (Idol & Jones, 1990; Jones & Idol, 1990;) summarize basic research supporting various aspects of the *Dimensions of Thinking*. That the components work tells us nothing about the efficacy of the package, however:

The brand-new parts for a Ferrari can be assembled into a superb sports car, an inefficient clunker, or something that resembles an abstract sculpture that does not run at all. Whether *Dimensions of Thinking* is the sports car or clunker version of thinking skills instruction is indeterminate at this time.

Why be so pessimistic about a program that is mostly teaching of strategies? Much of the basic research already reviewed in this book makes clear that teaching strategies to students is not enough. Students must also learn when and where to apply new strategies. They must become fluent in strategy execution while they learn how to adapt the strategies to new situations. Students need to learn how to coordinate strategies and skills with prior knowledge. Unfortunately, our reading of *Dimensions of Thinking* is that there is too little concern in it with issues of transfer, coordination, and adaptation. Our own view is that development of strategic competence involves long-term instruction and development; the message of many packages is that great gains in thinking can be realized in a short period of time. More positively, a strength of *Dimensions of Thinking* is that it favors long-term teaching.

Whether educators will use and adapt it so as to make a difference in the cognitive development of students is not known. We cannot emphasize enough how important it is to begin systematic research on multistrategy, multicomponent cognitive interventional packages, if for no other reason than because they are being widely disseminated. Well-planned quantitative and qualitative studies could do much to increase our understanding of such packages, their impact, and their potential.

In closing this subsection, however, we also want to emphasize that some of the criticisms of strategies instructional programs are entirely unfounded and irrational. In particular, some fundamentalist religious groups have examined these programs and have noted some overlap between the cognitive processes they encourage and the cognitive processes that are important in Eastern religious practices (e.g., both encourage generation of images, both instruct students [followers] to focus on particular dimensions of information relative to others). The fundamentalists have concluded that thinking skills programs are "New Age" interventions, designed to encourage religious beliefs contrary to conservative Christian traditions. We have examined all of the programs in question, and have some knowledge of Eastern religions to boot, and conclude confidently that there is no Eastern religion, overt or subliminal, in these programs. These interventions unambiguously follow directly from information processing research and analyses, conceptions of thinking and mind that are far removed from Eastern or New Age outlooks. New Age cognitive processes resemble the cognitive processes in these programs because there are only so many things the mind can do. Any tradition attempting to alter the way that people think must construct interventions that include the fairly small set of processes that are carried out by the mind. A few minutes' thought about how Western Judeo-Christian traditions, such as prayer, depend on cognitive processes will make obvious that cognitive psychologists are no more New Age in their thinking about how to alter people's thinking than are Protestant ministers, Catholic priests, or rabbis who call their congregations to worship. Although we have reservations about dump-a-bunch-of-strategies interventions, it is not because of any attempt by information processing–oriented educators to sneak the New Age into schools.

Summary No one could read the literature on critical thinking and not wish for more data. There simply is not enough research on these programs, which is especially disturbing because all of the programs discussed in this section are widely distributed. It is also disturbing that many of these programs are offered as "stand-alone" programs, rather than integrated with the curriculum. There is more teaching of strategies than anything else in these packages—with neglect of coordination of strategies with prior knowledge or application of strategies to other content in the curriculum. There is a lot of faith in transfer of the strategies taught, despite the fact that a great deal of research forces the conclusion that transfer occurs infrequently unless instruction is designed specifically to promote transfer. There is not nearly enough concern in some of these packages with the development of metacognitive understandings about the appropriate use of the strategies taught. Motivation to think well and use strategies is not a prominent concern in these packages either. We hope that teachers adopting these packages would encourage their students to find ways to apply the principles learned in the programs to content-area learning, explicitly attempt to develop metacognitive understandings in their students about when and where to use the strategies taught, and make efforts to motivate coordinated use of the strategies with other knowledge.

One striking consistency across these packages, however, is the encouragement of collaborative discussion about thinking and problem solving. In that way, they are consistent with many of the other interventions favored in this book. Even so, such discussions seem less rich than others considered in other chapters of this book because there is little concern with learning content as strategies are practiced in collaborative dialogues. The abstract problems favored in Instrumental Enrichment and CoRT contrast with discussion of material that can be related to children's prior knowledge—the type of material now covered routinely in many classrooms that have moved to cooperative models of learning. Although the novels in *Philosophy for Children* and the stories in the *Productive Thinking Program* can be discussed as narratives, they are not the outstanding children's literature now prominently discussed daily in many classrooms. Although thinking skills programs favor discussion methods of learning, they seem to offer less to talk about than is offered in many classrooms now committed to collaborative discussion.

DOES HIGHER EDUCATION PROMOTE COGNITIVE COMPETENCE?

Most readers of this book will either have completed or be near the end of 4 years of college. A fair question to address as part of an educational psychology course is whether this 4-year (or 5-year or 6-year) intervention promotes cognitive development as advertised. Not surprisingly, substantial research has been directed at determining the effects of higher education on academic competence. Fortunately, for those of us who write books like this, Pascarella and Terenzini (1991; see also Astin, 1993) have compiled a 900-page summary of literature documenting how college affects students.

Thinking Skills Affected by College

Some of the positive effects of college documented by Pascarella and Terenzini (1991) include the following:

- Both general (math and verbal competence) and specific subject matter knowledge increase.

- College probably increases the likelihood that people will continue to engage in knowledge-enhancing activities following graduation. College graduates are more likely than high school graduates to read newspapers, magazines, and books; be informed about public affairs; and participate in continuing education (Hyman, Wright, & Reed, 1975). There is increased interest in classical music, reading and creative writing, theater, intellectual discussions, and the performing arts in general. Intrinsic interest in liberal education increases during the college years.
- Oral and written communication skills improve.
- Critical thinking improves, including the ability to deal with ill-structured problems and controversial issues.
- Flexibility in thinking improves (i.e., the ability to see several sides of an issue), as does the ability to deal with complex issues.
- Piagetian formal operational competence increases (e.g., Eisert & Tomlinson-Keasey, 1978; Mentkowski & Strait, 1983).
- Intellectual self-confidence (e.g., confidence in writing and math skills) increases, as does achievement motivation (e.g., Pascarella, Smart, Ethington, & Nettles, 1987).

Although the magnitudes of these effects are not always large and alternative explanations of improvements (besides college attendance) are possible in most instances, it would be difficult given the many correlations between college attendance and subsequent cognitive change not to be convinced that cognitive competence increases during the college years. The case is similarly strong that commitment to long-term intellectual participation is fostered by what happens during the college years.

Effects of Particular Majors and Courses

An extremely interesting finding is that college major can affect fundamental reasoning abilities. Lehman and Nisbett (1990) studied the reasoning abilities of University of Michigan students when they were first-semester freshmen and then again late in their senior year. A variety of reasoning tasks were administered. What they found was that majoring in a social science resulted in people who could use statistical reasoning to draw conclusions. Although there were improvements in statistical reasoning over the 4 years for students majoring in

natural sciences and the humanities, the improvements were not as great as for the students in the social sciences. Natural sciences and humanities students improved in their conditional logical abilities (i.e., in their ability to solve problems requiring only logical reasoning rather than reasoning from evidence) more than social sciences students. In addition, the verbal reasoning abilities of natural sciences and humanities students improved slightly over the 4 years compared with a slight loss in verbal reasoning skills for social sciences students. Given the differences in curricula for social sciences compared with natural sciences and humanities students, this was a sensible pattern of results. Drawing inferences from statistical evidence is at the heart of most social sciences; logical reasoning is demanded more often in the natural sciences and humanities. Four years of immersing a head in a particular type of reasoning affects the reasoning ability of that head!

Even particular courses have long-term impact on development of intellect. Bahrick of Ohio Wesleyan University is the most notable investigator who has studied the long-term effects of what is learned in high school and college courses. His 1984 study was concerned with how well people remember the Spanish they learned in school, with original learning occurring in some cases as long as 50 years ago. The answer is people remember some of what they learned in courses very well. Thus, for students who completed the equivalent of five semesters of college Spanish, there was about a 70 percent chance (collapsing across subtests) that they would be able to match the meanings of Spanish and English words—even 35 years later. More negatively, recall of the meanings of Spanish words or Spanish words given English meanings was much lower. Although there was decline across the 50 years in memory for diverse elements of Spanish, from grammar to idioms, memory was always greater than zero even after 50 years. That is, something was remembered. In summary, Bahrick (1984) observed substantial loss in knowledge of Spanish in the first 6 years, followed by a 30-year or so leveling off before there was additional noteworthy decline. At every retention interval, students receiving more training originally, in terms of the number of courses taken, had better long-term memory than students receiving less initial instruction. "A" students remembered more than "B" students. Bahrick's (1984) work makes obvious that there are long-term changes in knowledge as a function of foreign language instruction, although there is some forgetting as well.

But what about this course! Will you remember much of what was presented in a course concerned principally with cognitive psychology and education? One reason to be suspect that much might be forgotten from a single course in educational psychology is that in Bahrick's (1984) analyses, recall of Spanish vocabulary definitions (and recall of the Spanish given the English) was poor after 3 years for students who had taken only one course. Recalling a classmate in college who received a passing grade in first-year Spanish only by promising the teacher never to take Spanish again, we are aware of how difficult it is to interpret the extremely low 3-year recall of students who quit Spanish after one course. Of course, the only way to know if students will remember the content of courses such as this one is to study the long-term memories of students who have taken such a course. Conway, Cohen, and Stanhope (1991) approached that ideal study.

Conway et al. (1991) administered memory tests to former students in a cognitive psychology course (which was similar in content to much of what is covered in this book, although there was emphasis on more basic cognitive concepts rather than their applications in education). The "retention interval" (i.e., time since the course was taken) was as long as 10 years in some cases. Five different types of tests were administered:

1. Name and concept recognition: Lists of names and concepts were presented with the students required to recognize whether the names and concepts had been covered in the course. The concept list included the following: *chronometric cycle, eigen stimulus test, vector cells, quadratic activation effect, embedded figures test, texture cues,* and *preattentive processing.* (The last 3 are correct.)
2. Fact verification: True facts covered in the course were presented, as were false facts. The participants were required to distinguish the true and false facts. For example, one item was, "The behaviorists considered learning to be a passive process."
3. Concept grouping: Subjects were required to sort 24 concepts into six groups.
4. Cued recall of proper names and concepts: Items included, "E— was an early German psychologist who studied the learning of nonsense

syllables." "In p—— inhibition forgetting is caused by interference from prior learning."
5. Research methods: Two-choice questions concerning methods were presented, including the following: "An experiment that uses different subjects in each experimental condition is known as (A) a between-subjects design (B) a within-subjects design." "Data that can be ranked from best to worst is known as (A) ordinal data (B) nominal data." (Conway et al., 1991, pp. 398–399)

With the exception of the research methods and fact verification data, there were clear declines in memory during the first 3 years following the course, with memory performances leveling off after 3 years. The research methods questions were answered at a level well above chance at all retention intervals with no apparent decline as a function of retention interval. There was little decline in recognition of general facts, as indicated by both correctness of responses to these items and confidence in responses; although correct recognition of specific facts did not decline with retention interval, confidence in these responses did.

In general, there was much in Conway et al.'s (1991) data to make those of us who labor as teachers of psychology to take heart. Much seemed to be remembered. More negatively, at least for some of the more demanding measures of memory (i.e., those involving recall and conceptual grouping), there was precipitous decline in the 3 years following the course. (A colleague observed that even this did not concern him because he had previously believed that many students learned it for the test and then forgot it immediately—only true for some types of information, according to Conway et al.'s, 1991, or Bahrick's, 1984, data.)

Stanhope, Cohen, and Conway (1993) studied former students' memory for a novel covered in a university course taken up to 39 months earlier. They reported outcomes generally consistent with those observed by Conway et al. (1991). For a brief summary of the most important evidence to date on long-term retention of information learned in a university, see Conway, Cohen, and Stanhope (1991, 1992).

What the studies by Bahrick and Conway et al. established was that much of what is learned is put in some type of **"permastore,"** to use Bahrick's (1984) terminology. What the data summarized by Pascarella and Terenzini (1991) tell us is that a college education changes thinking in many ways. We definitely need more specific information, such as whether some courses may have a greater impact than others. Pascarella and Terenzini's (1991) data summary is absolutely silent about the effects of individual courses. The closest they come to such an analysis is with respect to differences produced as function of the type and perceived quality of institutions— with analyses to date suggesting that where one goes to college makes less of an impact on cognitive change than whether one goes to school at all. If those of us in higher education knew better what makes a difference in promoting long-term knowledge and thinking skills, much more intelligent decision making about university requirements and curricula might be made. That analyses of institutional differences have not produced telling conclusions to date should not be taken to mean that what goes on at college is irrelevant: Analyses such as Conway et al. (1991) and Stanhope et al. (1993) stimulate the idea that the appropriate unit of analysis here might be the course. When we have mentioned long-term study of the effects of particular courses as important research for educational psychologists to undertake, our students' heads always have nodded approvingly! Many of them are suspect that there is long-term value only to some of the courses supported by their tuition. We think the higher-education community should begin to determine which ones, with educational psychologists well equipped to participate in such an evaluation effort.

Mentors

Many universities and colleges have made great efforts to encourage faculty to mentor undergraduates: to provide personal support, encouragement, and guidance; coach them in matters academic; be a role model; sponsor and supervise in research; and socialize students into the world of academia. Both of us were fortunate to have faculty mentors in our undergraduate years, with both of us feeling these people played important roles in launching our careers as educational psychologists. Unfortunately, there is not yet a database evaluating the general effects of mentors, but we mention this factor because we believe it is potentially an important part of undergraduate education at its best. Jacobi (1991) provided an exceptionally lucid conceptual introduction to what we hope will be an important type of research in future years. We expect it will be appealing to some because there is the opportunity to document here personal and rich instruction, instruction that probably produces growth in both the mentee and the mentor. For example, we "know" we are better professors, scientists, thinkers, and human beings because of the close associations we have had with particular students, and some of them reinforce our efforts as educators by letting us know that we made a profound difference in their lives. If we can find out what needs to occur for mentoring to work well, perhaps more can be done to stimulate the development of high-quality, educationally effective, and personally gratifying experiences for larger numbers of students and the professors who teach them.

CONCLUDING COMMENTS

Schooling can make a difference in cognitive development and competence. High-quality schooling can make more of a difference than does low-quality schooling. There is plenty of evidence that schooling can be improved through translating research findings into educational practice. Once the practice is devised, researchers must follow through and make certain that the interventions they have provided are doing what was hypothesized. Unfortunately, such follow-through has not always occurred, such as with some of the thinking skills curricula. Those of us who teach at the university also have been more certain that the courses we teach have long-term impact than is justified based on the available data. There is plenty to do for future generations of researchers who are interested in identifying educational practices that already work and for those interested in devising and validating new approaches to classroom learning.

Can student learning be maximized? Can the odds be increased that future generations of students will be good thinkers? The general message in this chapter and this book is yes, with it possible to improve education in various ways. Progress has been made at the elementary and secondary levels in identifying the characteristics of educational settings that predict long-term achievement; a great deal of research has been summarized in this book establishing ways of improving particular types of learning. Whether all of this research makes a difference depends on translation of research findings into actual curricula and widespread dissemination of instruction that is informed by theory and research. We hope that this book prepares you to participate in contemporary schooling, either as an educator or a researcher. If you are like the many students we have taught over the years, at the very least, you are convinced that schooling can be done better than it has traditionally been done and that research can play an important role in school improvement. With luck, you will apply those understandings to better schooling whether you participate in it as a professional, a parent, or a policymaker. It is important that you do, for the future of the United States depends on it. If you do, in the future, it may not be so easy to write the pessimistic books on education that we alluded to in the opening lines of this book. In the spirit of collaborative discussion that we have endorsed at many points in this book, we urge you to share what you know with those who believe there is no hope for education. There is hope, and now you know it and you know why.

Because this chapter presented a mixture of interventions that definitely work to improve student learning, thinking, and performance; others that have small or inconsistent effects at best; and still others that are untested for the most part, we summarize in the table below what was covered in this chapter regarding documented efficacy with respect to stimulating student achievement.

Interventions That Provide Certain Effects and Ones That Provide Either Small and Uncertain Effects or Have Not Been Tested Completely Enough

Certain Effects

Attending school, especially "effective," orderly schools

Academically oriented, engaging classrooms

Head Start and early intervention programs

One-on-one tutoring, including as it occurs in programs such as Success for All and after school, as in the *Juku* system

Teacher questioning

Wait time during teacher questioning

Student questioning

Differential teacher reactions to students on basis of ability

Parental involvement in schooling

Volunteer tutors in classrooms

Peer tutoring

Smaller classes

Mastery learning

Homework, especially after the elementary-school years

Viewing educational television

Higher education

College major

Some college courses

Small, Uncertain, Negative, or Not Tested Satisfactorily

Teacher expectancies (mixed evidence)

Ability grouping and tracking (negative)

Sex-segregated classrooms (small)

Retention of students in a grade (negative)

Short-term summer school programs (small)

Extracurricular activities (uncertain)

After-school work (negative)

Viewing entertainment television (negative)

Thinking skills programs (not tested sufficiently)

Mentors in college (not tested sufficiently)

Part

4

Cognition and Instruction

12

Science

The scientific and science educator community have been thinking a great deal about the nature of science education. Scientists are convinced that American students do not know enough science, with one indication being poor performance on standardized tests (e.g., Education Commission of the States, 1988; Mullis, 1989). Scientists are even more acutely aware than other educators that the world is changing rapidly and that technological competence will be essential in the future. Scientists also believe that there is intrinsic intellectual value in understanding science, in being **scientifically literate** (e.g., Murname & Raizen, 1988, Chapter 2). People with a scientific world view are different from those who lack scientific understandings: The scientifically educated person construes the world as understandable and measurable. Education in science cultivates awareness of differences between the theoretical and the empirical. Scientific education permits appreciation of the systematic study, permitted by simplification and systematization. With advanced education in science, it becomes obvious that science is carried out by individuals distributed over time and across the world and that scientific knowledge is knowledge reached by broad-based consensus. Scientific education increases understanding of the significance of basic research. For example, the consequences of ozone depletion can be understood more fully when armed with knowledge of modern cell biology; earthquakes in California can be comprehended in terms of plate tectonics.

The scientific community believes that education in science can lead to habits of mind—strategies or higher-order thinking skills—that are less likely to be developed in other disciplines (e.g., Committee on High School Biology Education, 1990, Chapter 1; Murnane & Raizen, 1988, Chapter 2, p. 19): These include (1) forming hypotheses in reaction to questions and problems; (2) seeking information that pertains to problems rather than simply attempting uninformed solutions; (3) using information to solve problems, although recognizing that the quality and generalizability of information is always constrained by limits on sampling; (4) mentally playing with information and thinking about it from alternative perspectives in order to solve problems; (5) offering arguments and counter-arguments; and (6) building a consensus across individuals through collaboration and communication.

A great fear of the scientific community is that the poor performance of American students on standardized assessments probably reflects a populace that is not (1) ready for new technological demands in the workplace; (2) appreciative of some of the great insights about the world that have emerged from science, insights that permit fuller participation in the world and more informed decision making; and (3) as capable of thinking logically as a populace with more complete scientific training.

How extensive are the educational deficiencies? Who and what is to blame? The Committee on High School Biology Education (1990) concluded that just about everything that could be wrong with biology education is wrong with it and that just about everybody who contributes to science education is to blame:

- Textbooks are inadequate. They are encyclopedic, attempting to mention everything. They are filled with terms—sometimes as many as 2000 new vocabulary in a year's worth of reading. Often the texts are not factually accurate. Often the newest advances in a field are not integrated into texts to reflect how a field has advanced. If covered at all, new advances are "boxed off." Many of the authors of elementary and high school texts do not understand the advances themselves well enough to explain how they relate to more traditional content coverage. The books are often illogical, incoherent, or inaccurate (see also Sutman, 1992). Illustrations are often decorations rather than explanatory. As will be discussed in Chapter 14 (see also Staver & Bay, 1989; Wood & Wood, 1988), the readability level of texts often is mismatched to intended audiences. Textbooks do not convey well the experimental nature of biology. They are filled with conclusions rather than with information about how conclusions are generated in science. Often, they are boring! In summary, *textbooks have too much in them, with the wheat and chaff not well separated for students.* Not surprisingly, many students view science as learning lists of unrelated words, missing many of the concepts these texts are intended to convey (e.g., Koballa, 1988; Mason, 1992; Mason & Kahle, 1988). That it can be different is illustrated by Japanese and Singaporean science textbooks, which tend to cover less content and do so in a more organized fashion (Chambliss & Calfee, 1989).
- Laboratory exercises are cookbook affairs that can be accomplished without much thinking by the student. Current laboratory work does not contribute to increased understanding of biological concepts. In addition, laboratory work has been on the decline. In summary, *students need more laboratory work that involves genuine investigation and scientific thinking.*
- The standardized tests assessing scientific knowledge do not tap understanding. Because

tests are an important part of the accountability system, teachers teach to these tests, which emphasize breadth of knowledge (e.g., vocabulary) rather than depth of knowledge (see Crooks, 1988; also Wood, 1988). *New tests are needed, ones that tap understanding of science and ones matched to the scientific knowledge that is essential for the 21st century.*

- Current teacher education does not prepare science teachers well. Science teachers are not acquiring a sophisticated understanding about how to relate science to students of various ages or how to engage students in the process of science, perhaps because they do not have a good understanding of the process themselves because they are products of a system of science education in which knowing facts was emphasized more than hands-on knowledge of process. *Our understanding of how to teach the scientific process must continue to expand through teacher education research; in turn, science teacher education must be reformed to reflect insights emerging from cutting edge research on the teaching and learning of science.* The nature of in-service education and continuing education must also be rethought to shape these important educational opportunities so as to maximize their impact on reforming science education. In addition, a great deal of additional thought must be given about how to ensure that teachers know the scientific content they are being asked to teach. When teachers lack content knowledge, the result can be an emphasis on students learning facts from textbooks and workbooks. Such teachers lack understanding about how to restructure textbook content so it is more meaningful (see Tobin & Fraser, 1990), more obviously related to the real-world experiences of students (e.g., Mitman, Mergendoller, Marchman, & Packer, 1987).
- State and local policies often interfere with the effective teaching of science (see Brickhouse & Bodner, 1992, for an elegant analysis of how such constraints have an impact on beginning teachers whose education has prepared them to do better teaching than the system permits; see also Shymansky, Yore, & Good, 1991, for data related to this point in an across-national study conducted in the United States). For example, laboratory exercises often take more than 45 minutes, which is the standard class period.

Often a science teacher's day is spread across several classrooms, so it is not possible to set up elaborate demonstrations. Teachers often have far too many students to teach effectively and develop creative educational experiences for students. Often, these institutional barriers occur in an environment that presents other challenges (e.g., serious behavior problems; generally low academic achievement, literacy, and numeracy in many students). *There needs to be serious rethinking about how schools and school days are organized in order to overcome unnecessary institutional barriers.*

- Science education is often conceived of as happening in high school. The result is that elementary-school and middle-school science is poorly thought out and does not link with the high school curriculum. Sophisticated, appealing elementary-school and middle-school science instruction is needed, instruction presenting content of great value to students both now and in their futures. There need to be opportunities to make scientific observations, experience hands-on involvement, and construct personal scientific interpretations. The importance of such teaching is becoming increasingly apparent with demonstrations that high-quality lessons in the early elementary grades can continue to affect scientific understandings many years later (e.g., Novak & Musonda, 1991).

It would be easy to read this list of ills of science education and conclude that there is no hope: The textbooks are lousy, the teachers are ill prepared and underresourced, and the tests encourage learning all the wrong things! The possibility of a quick fix (e.g., 1 year of really excellent biology in high school) is out, with the realization that effective education is long term.

There is a bright side, however. We are making substantial progress in understanding how to structure science education so it is more effective, with psychologists playing an important role in the development of new curricula. Contemporary science education is informed by the nature and representation of knowledge, Vygotskian theories, and principles of motivation as well as other psychological perspectives. Readers who have digested what has been presented up until this point in the book will find interventions described in this chapter that make good sense in light of a great deal of psycho-logical theory and research. The reader should emerge from this chapter recognizing that better science texts, science teacher education, and science teaching are possible. This pessimistic introduction was presented only to provide historical perspective; science educators are determined to create more effective science education for the nation's children. Before it is possible to understand the significance of their work, however, more bad news needs to be considered.

MISCONCEPTIONS OR ALTERNATIVE FRAMEWORKS

One of Piaget's (e.g., 1929) most important insights was that people often have ideas about the world that clash with scientific viewpoints. For example, they often believe that inanimate objects are alive! Piaget believed that such **animism** was a symptom of preoperational intelligence and that with the development of concrete and formal operations, children's ideas about what is alive versus what is not alive would reflect conventional thinking about life. In a number of follow-up investigations, many of which were conducted in the 1930s and 1940s (for a brief review, see Brainerd, 1978b), it became apparent that although animism declined with development from the preoperational to the concrete and formal operational stages, it never extinguished. Animism persists throughout adulthood.

We have often conducted the following demonstration in university classes to make the point to students that animism occurs in adult thought. Students are told to close their books for a pop quiz. They are then asked to number a piece of paper from 1 to 13. As the instructor reads the name of an object, the student is to indicate whether the object is alive by writing, "Yes," or not alive by writing, "No." The instructor then reads a list of 13 objects, with these objects being identical to ones used in actual studies of animism: (1) unlighted match, (2) lighted match, (3) electric clock, (4) the sun, (5) the wind, (6) a nickel, (7) a pearl, (8) gasoline, (9) the ocean, (10) clouds, (11) lightning, (12) stars, and (13) the earth. Then students exchange papers, and the instructor asks for a show of hands for each person holding a paper with at least one "yes" on it. It never fails that at least one-quarter of the class attributes life to one or more of the 13 list items. Often the majority of students make such attributions. Many adults have animistic beliefs.

For years, the Piagetian-inspired discovery that nonscientific thinking was common in adults was largely forgotten. Then in the late 1970s and in the 1980s, contemporary scientists and science educators noted that often people have important misconceptions about physical and biological relationships. "Intuitive physics" (e.g., McCloskey, 1983) is a set of different laws than the laws of actual physics: For example, if you were running with a football and dropped the ball, what would be the trajectory of the ball as it headed for the ground? Many people have the intuition that the ball will fall straight down, because only gravity would be acting on it. In reality, however, the ball continues to move forward all the time it is moving downward, because no force has been exerted to change its forward velocity. When a discus thrower spins around in a 360-degree motion, what is the trajectory of the discus from the point of release? Intuitive physics puts a curve on the trajectory, although the actual trajectory is a straight line, consistent with Newton's first law that in the absence of a force being applied to it, an object in motion travels in a straight line. What forces operate on a baseball after it is hit into the air? According to intuitive physics, upward forces and gravity are at work, when in fact, gravity is the only force applied to the ball in flight (all of these examples based on McCloskey, 1983). For many people, upward motion implies an upward force (see Clement, 1982).

Although scientific misconceptions in physics have been studied more than other misconceptions (Pfundt & Duit, 1991), people seem to have misconceptions about every scientific arena imaginable. Table 12.1 provides a listing of just a few of the common misconceptions that Woloshyn, Paivio, and Pressley (1992) uncovered in their review of the literature, a literature now comprised of more than 2000 studies (Duit, 1991). Scientific misconceptions can have a range of consequences, including ones that are tragic. Consider the pain that has been inflicted on victims of AIDS by people holding the following misconceptions (DiClemente, Pies, Stoller, Straits, Olivia, Haskin, Rutherford, 1989; DiClemente, Zorn, & Temoshok, 1986, 1987; Price, Desmond, & Kukulka, 1985): (1) A person can get AIDS by touching someone with the disease. (2) All gay men have AIDS. (3) AIDS can be spread by using someone's personal belongings like a comb or hairbrush. (4) A person can contact AIDS by being around someone with the disease. (5) All gay women have AIDS. (6) It is easy to detect a person with AIDS. (7) All persons exposed to the AIDS virus will get the disease. (8) A person can get AIDS by attending school with a student with AIDS. (9) It is unsafe for a person with AIDS to work near children.

Even after completing science courses covering scientific concepts and passing tests on them, misconceptions persist. (Indeed, even expert scientists sometimes fail to recognize an exemplar of an elementary concept, such as acceleration [Reif & Allen, 1992].) The work of Charles Anderson at Michigan State has been especially revealing about the persistence of misconceptions following education. For example, Anderson, Sheldon, and Dubay (1990) studied college students' conceptions of respiration and photosynthesis at the beginning and at the end of a year-long biology course. At the beginning of the course, students offered grossly deficient answers, even though most students had 1 or more years of biology previously. When asked on the pretest for a definition of respiration, few students mentioned energy and fewer mentioned food, offering in many cases, simplistic definitions such as the following: "Exhaling CO_2 for humans, exhaling O_2 for plants; breathing; has lungs to breath with; and air in, air out." The same held for pretest definitions of photosynthesis, another chemical process producing energy conversion. A minority of students mentioned food or energy in their definitions, which included the following: "Plants take in CO_2 and change it to O_2"; "I remember needing to know a formula for it in high school; keeps plants green; and green plants turn sun and CO_2 into chlorophyll." Students offered the following as explanations of "food for a bean plant": "Food for a bean plant is what is necessary for it to grow, water, soil, and minerals, sunlight"; "The chemicals it receives from the sunlight, soil, and fertilizer"; "Sunlight, water, soil"; and "The nutrients in the soil. The sun, the water, other animals that died and their body becomes part of the soil." In short, these students certainly did not understand that plants manufacture their own food.

What is much more disturbing than the pretest performances, however, is that at the end of the course, many students still had misconceptions: Almost a fourth had little idea about the nature of respiration; a fifth did not understand that the essence of food is that it provides energy for metabolism and materials for growth; 40 percent did not completely understand that plants make their food; and more than half failed to understand that animals obtain energy from food, and plants obtain energy from sunlight. (Note that when stricter scoring

---

Common Scientific Misconceptions

The Sun

The sun is a living organism—it is an animate object
The sun's surface is solid
The light of the sun is made up of only a few colors, mostly yellow and orange

Rattlesnakes

The rattlesnake is very dangerous and mean
The forked tongue of the rattlesnake is of little use to the snake
The rattlesnake smells objects with its nostrils

Water

One place where water does not exist is in the air
The distance between water molecules does not change when water is frozen
Good drinking water has an odor, some taste, and a slight color

Three States of Matter

Although molecules are small, they are still visible and can be seen with a
  microscope
Heat and light are matter and take up space
Molecules in solids are always still

Plants

All plants have roots, stems, leaves, and flowers
Plants eat soil and water
Plants use light energy from the sun to help them stay warm

Blood

All organisms have blood
Blood is made of only one component, red cells
The functions of the heart include cleaning, filtering, making, and storing blood

Animals

All animals have a backbone
People are not animals
Worker bees buzz to tell other bees where there is food

Genetics

Environmentally induced factors can be transmitted to offspring
A gene can be dominant in one offspring and recessive in another
Variations in an individual are caused by developmental deficits only

---

List assembled by Woloshyn, Paivio, & Pressley (1992).

was applied, the proportions of students having misconceptions at the end of the course were considerably higher.)

Bishop and Anderson (1990) reported a similar study tapping college students' understanding of some important ideas from genetics. Again, although most students had 1 or more years of biology before taking the course in biology, at pretesting it was apparent that the overwhelming majority did not understand fundamental ideas about how new traits arise via genetic mechanisms, about how variation in traits is related to reproductive success, and how evolution is a change in the proportion of individuals with discrete traits. Again, and even worse,

at posttesting, more than one-third of the students could not answer applications questions based on these fundamental genetic principles, questions such as the following:

> While ducks were evolving webbed feet:
> (a) With each generation, most ducks had about the same amount of webbing on their feet as their parents.
> (b) With each generation, most ducks had a tiny bit more webbing on their feet than their parents. (*a* correct)
> If a population of ducks were forced to live in an environment where water for swimming were not available:

(a) Many ducks would die because their feet were poorly adapted to the environment.

(b) The ducks would gradually develop nonwebbed feet.

(*a* correct)

The populations of ducks evolved webbed feet because:

(a) The more successful ducks adapted to their aquatic environment.

(b) The less successful ducks died without offspring.

(*b* correct)

(Adapted from Bishop & Anderson, 1990, p. 418)

That many of these students could answer midterm and final examination test questions on this material during the course suggests that they "had it" at some level. Whitehurst's notion of **inert knowledge,** introduced earlier in Chapter 3, seems relevant here in that what was learned in the course seems not to generalize very far. What is absolutely certain, however, is that misconceptions held when entering a course of scientific study are not eliminated through courses, at least during conventional science instruction. There are numerous reports in the science education literature about students having a misconception before taking a course or experiencing a lesson, learning an alternative and more scientifically defensible concept during the course or lesson, and then reverting to the logic of the misconception when given a subsequent problem that could be solved by applying the scientific concept. Those who argue that more traditional science coursework is what is required to reform science education need to ponder the implications of students just experiencing conventional instruction on chemical change and then failing to think about atoms and molecules when explaining chemical reactions, treating chemical changes like physical changes (e.g., thinking of rusting as only a form of decay rather than a chemical reaction), and failing to recognize that some reactions produce invisible products such as gases. Heese and Anderson (1992) observed such reasoning in a sample of high school chemistry students after they had studied chemical reactions.

We have been using the term misconception until this point because it is used frequently in the science education literature. What we have been discussing are misconceptions in the sense that they are not consistent with scientific ideas. Some researchers take exception to the term because they believe that what we have been discussing might better be regarded as **alternative frameworks** that provide people with guidance in many situations (e.g., Driver & Easley, 1978; see Duit, 1991). Another term that has been applied to the type of thinking considered here is **children's science;** still another is **children's conceptual frameworks.** All three of these terms suggest a dignity that is lacking from the term misconception. Nonetheless, because the term misconception is used more than any of the alternative terms, we use it here, although occasionally using some of the synonyms as well, and we emphasize that misconceptions and alternative frameworks are operationally synonymous as far as we can tell (i.e., the subtleties differentiating the terms are ones that science educators may wish to debate, but most readers can ignore without loss of understanding). When Piagetians and philosophers of science talk about the phenomenon discussed here, the language of conceptual frameworks is preferred; when information processing–oriented theorists talk, they often think in terms of misconceptions (see Confrey, 1990). Our use of the term misconception reflects in part our greater comfort with information processing than with Piagetian and more philosophical points of view.

The research on alternative frameworks makes obvious that students do not arrive in science classrooms as blank slates. Rather, they often possess prior knowledge that is inconsistent with the content they will be asked to learn in the science course. Whether it is well organized or fragmented prior knowledge is a matter of debate (e.g., diSessa, 1982). Regardless of whether the errant prior knowledge forms a network of understandings, it often is so deeply entrenched that students will continue to apply alternative frameworks even after learning new science content that is inconsistent with the prior knowledge.

Why is errant prior knowledge so enduring? It has been built up over years of experience, and it is consistent with other knowledge possessed by the subject (Duit, 1991). Thus, how often have you talked about how something "burned up?" Such *language* suggests that what was burned was destroyed. It is counterintuitive for there actually to be more matter after burning than before. Nonetheless, weigh a piece of steel wool before and after it is burned, and it weighs more after. The chemical reaction during the fire created a product that weighs more than the original steel wool. Other times, *appearances are deceiving* (Eylon & Linn, 1988). The docility of a rattlesnake is not suggested by its appearance. The sun looks yellow and orange, and thus there is a perceptual basis for believing it produces mostly yellow and orange light. The *social environment* is filled with misinformation, such as the errant information about AIDS that has been spread by rumor and uninformed speculation. Finally, often *instruction provided to students is just plain wrong*, with students actually taught errant information. For example, we have encountered more than a few discussions of particle theories of light that make it seem as if light must be matter. Children live in a world that is filled with errant information, information that can seem sensible even if it is not correct. Misconceptions are connected to a great deal of other knowledge. Thus, even though we know based on recent reading and discussions that rattlesnakes generally are shy, nonaggressive creatures, our immediate thoughts when we see a picture of a rattlesnake are about the dangers and evils of snakes. Information that is well learned over time comes to mind more quickly than information that is not learned well, perhaps because it has been presented in an unconvincing fashion or simply has not been presented often. For new knowledge to replace old knowledge in the sense that the new knowledge would come to mind and be applied rather than the old knowledge, it is necessary for the learner to learn new information well.

The science educators are convinced that most instruction does not permit learning that is extensive and meaningful enough (deep enough? see Chapter 10) to permit the development of rich and strong connections to other knowledge. Part of the problem is that learners' prior knowledge leads them to process new information in biased ways. In Piagetian terms, new information is assimilated to prior knowledge rather than prior knowledge being accommodated to new information.

For example, Roth (e.g., 1991) has observed that when students read a text, they frequently "remember" information that came not from the text, but from their prior knowledge. Consider this example:

> Kevin, a seventh-grade student . . . had a rich prior knowledge about plants and food. He "knew" that plants, like people, have multiple sources of food that they take in from the external environment. He wrote on a pretest:
> Food (for plants) can be sun, rain, light, bugs, oxygen, soil, and even other dead plants. Also warmth or coldness. All plants need at least three or four of these foods. Plus minerals.
> When Kevin read a text that explained that minerals are not food for plants but that plants make their

own food during photosynthesis, he ignored the statement that minerals are not considered food (even after a second reading of the key paragraph). This allowed him to incorporate inappropriately the concept of photosynthesis into his own schema of multiple foods for plants:

> INTERVIEWER: Could you summarize where does the plant get its food?
> KEVIN: Whew, from lots of places! From the soil for one, for the minerals and water, and from the air for oxygen. The sunlight for the sun, and it would change chemicals to sugars. It sort of makes it own food and gets food from the ground. And from air. (Roth, 1990, p. 145)

What is interesting is that Kevin's response actually includes a rough definition of photosynthesis. Even so, his belief in plants getting food from the ground persists. Roth (1990) viewed this as an example of **conceptual capture** (Posner, Strike, Hewson, & Gertzog, 1982), as some of the new conceptual information was captured and integrated into the students' knowledge, knowledge that is scientifically incorrect and actually contradictory to the scientific concept being studied.

Similarly, Duit (1991) made the case that prior knowledge affects student observations, guiding them to information consistent with their own perspectives. Thus, classroom demonstrations intended to make one point can end up supporting an alternative perspective not consistent with scientific perspectives. As an example, Duit related how some students in a study conducted by Gunstone and White (1981) reacted to a demonstration involving a weight and a bucket of sand, which were in equilibrium on opposite sides of a pulley and extending downward an equal distance from the wheel of the pulley:

> A small spoonful of sand is added to the bucket. It is so small that no movement is caused. But the college students who have the idea that the bucket will sink "observe" this (well, it sinks just a little). Then so much sand is added that an accelerated movement of the bucket results. Students are asked to observe the speeds of the bucket at two positions. Students who believe that uniform speeds will occur, "observe" it. (Duit, 1991, pp. 71–72)

When presented science instruction, students often are looking to confirm what they "know" already, with the result both extremely selective attention and distortion of information provided during instruction.

Sometimes the prior knowledge is so strong that students will simply not believe what they see. Thus, when Gunstone and White pulled the bucket down, which raised the weight, students were asked to predict what would happen if the experimenter let go of the bucket. Many students predicted that the weight would drop and the bucket would return to its original position, something that of course did not happen (i.e., the equilibrium in such a system depends only on equal weight on each side of the pulley, not on the height of the two counterbalancing weights). Some of the students reacted to this outcome by trying to argue it away, claiming that somehow the pulley system in question was producing a nongeneralizable result (i.e., that there was something about the specific problem situation that resulted in a violation of the natural tendency of the bucket to return to its original height; Duit, 1991). That Gunstone and White's (1981) observation is not unusual is obvious from the many examples of working scientists who have refused to abandon deeply held scientific beliefs when confronted with evidence to the contrary (see Hull, 1988).

Another bias that reduces student comprehension of scientific content is a tendency to concentrate on big words, scientific facts, and details when reading science—to reduce learning of science to a rote exercise rather than as a task involving understanding. Here is how Roth (1991) described some middle-school students in one of her studies processing information in scientific text:

> . . . [R]eaders relied too heavily on details in the text, failing to attach any meaning to them. The details—most often specialized vocabulary words—were isolated fragments that students saw as having no relationship to one another or to their real world knowledge . . .
>
> . . . [Other] students placed too much emphasis on facts, viewing science learning as a process of developing long lists of facts about natural phenomena. Their prior experiences in school had convinced them that memorizing unrelated facts constitutes satisfactory learning. They accumulated many facts from the text and described these facts accurately. But they treated all the facts as equally important, and they never attempted to relate facts to one another or to their real world knowledge about plants. (Roth, 1991, pp. 50–51)

The result was that the students "learned" what was in the text so that they could report it back, but they could not apply it:

> . . . [T]he big words they picked up from the text were never used when they talked about real plants. Thus, school knowledge was something totally separate from the real world, and it was not expected to make sense or to relate to everyday phenomena.
>
> [One student] . . . remembered that the text described photosynthesis as the way plants make their food. However, when asked to explain how a plant sitting on the windowsill gets its food, she never mentioned photosynthesis or plants' ability to make food. (Roth, 1991, pp. 50–51)

In summary, this entire section was a downer! Not only do students have alternative frameworks, but also these alternatives are persistent and can distort processing of more credible scientific concepts. Often students process scientific content superficially, not attempting to understand it. Rather, they attempt to memorize it, a strategy that, unfortunately, often pays off, given the emphasis on rote memorization in many science courses.

There is reason for optimism, however, even when students are left on their own to process science content. Some students wrestle with science content, for example, attempting to understand the meaning and significance of science textbook presentations and actively seeking to accommodate (to use the Piagetian term) their beliefs about a phenomenon with the information in text. Roth (1991) reported how some of the middle-school students in her studies reacted to text:

> They recognized the conflicts between what the text said and their own personal theories and puzzled about these inconsistencies until they could resolve the conflict. Often, this meant changing their personal theories to accommodate scientific explanations . . . the conceptual change readers:
>
> 1. Made efforts to link text ideas with their experiential knowledge.
> 2. Recognized and thought about central text statements that conflicted with personally held ideas.
> 3. Distinguished between main ideas and supporting details, often minimizing the importance of big words.
> 4. Experienced and recognized conceptual confusion while reading.
> 5. Worked to resolve this conceptual confusion.
> 6. Were aware that their own ideas about real world phenomena were changing.
> 7. Used concepts presented in the text to explain real world phenomena. (Roth, 1991, p. 52)

In short, some students activated prior knowledge related to text but recognized that their prior knowledge was not entirely congruent with meaning presented in text. These students worked at understanding the discrepancy so their own thinking could be refined. The result is knowledge that can be applied, as exemplified by one student who used this **conceptual change strategy:**

INTERVIEWER: If I were to cover up all but one leaf of this plant, do you think the way it grows would change?

SUSAN: Yeah, it would, because there's only one leaf that can change the materials to food and regularly you have much more—and I don't think it could feed the whole plant. I just don't believe it.

The good news that some students do think about the meaning of scientific text and do attempt to correct misconceptions is complemented by more good news in the next section. A variety of instructional mechanisms have been proposed and are being investigated as means of increasing student understanding, memory, and use of scientific content, especially content that conflicts with everyday knowledge. At the heart of some of these interventions is the conceptual change strategy, with a number of science educators convinced that students can be taught to notice and resolve discrepancies between their own prior knowledge and science content, with deep understanding of science the result of such active processing.

TEACHING FOR CONCEPTUAL CHANGE

Although many science textbooks continue to be encyclopedic and many science courses continue to be traditional lecture and demonstration, science educators are increasingly convinced that new formats must be developed. Traditional science instruction is not producing a populace that is well educated with respect to science; when science content is taught that conflicts with prior knowledge, prior knowledge wins out in the long term. Even when there is no conflict with prior knowledge, students often find scientific ideas to be challenging. Some students learn little in traditional science classes; others learn at a superficial level and cannot apply what they have learned. Such students are little better educated than they were before taking science courses.

In this section, a number of interventions will be described. A word of warning is that many of these interventions have not been evaluated as completely

as we would like. The most prevalent designs used by science educators to evaluate interventions are qualitative case study approaches and uncontrolled pretest-posttest designs. Of course, there are many alternative explanations besides the efficacy of a treatment when knowledge improves in a case study or from pretest to posttest, for example, testing effects (i.e., performance is better the second time a test is administered because of practice). More positively, there have been some true experiments and quasiexperiments, and some of these will be discussed. When the literature is considered as a whole, the positive results to date are sufficient to argue for much more intense study of interventions aimed at conceptual change, but there are not enough well-controlled evaluations reporting positive effects to justify strong conclusions about conceptual change teaching at this time. With that warning, we begin the discussion with one of the most famous of the conceptual change interventions.

Conceptual Conflict and Accommodation Model

Nussbaum and Novick (e.g., 1982) proposed that to overcome a misconception, a student first needs to be aware of his or her belief. Once aware, exposure to an event that cannot be explained by the belief or is inconsistent with it has the potential for producing cognitive conflict. Consistent with Piagetian thinking, such conflict motivates efforts toward conflict resolution and, in particular, motivates efforts to understand the scientific concept explaining the observed event. That is, conflict motivates efforts toward accommodation, setting up the possibility of modification of current cognitive structures (i.e., belief) and the creation of new ones.

In Nussbaum and Novick's (1982) study, primary-school children were given a lesson on the particle theory of gases and, in particular, a lesson establishing there is empty space between molecules of air. As part of the lesson, air was sucked from a flask with a hand pump. Students' awareness of their beliefs about air was induced by having them draw pictures of the flask and its contents before and after the air was removed. Some of the student drawings and explanations were discussed by the instructor, as was the scientifically correct position that the flask contained particles of air with empty space between the particles before and only empty space after pumping. Of course, many of the students did not understand that the air molecules had empty space between them before the pumping began, for example, believing all of the space in the flask must have been occupied by air.

Then the instructor introduced a discrepant event. Students were shown syringes with equal volumes of air and water in them. The teacher attempted to compress the water, with no movement of the syringe plunger. Then, the teacher succeeded in compressing the air. If there was no space between air molecules, such compression should not have been possible. Discussion followed about how the student models of the flask situation might explain or be inconsistent with the compressibility of air but not water. The instructor's job was to help students see that the only model that could explain the evacuation of air from the flask and the compressibility of air in the syringe was the empty space theory. The success of this instruction was apparent to Nussbaum and Novick because many of the students accepted the empty space theory after such instruction, despite having no conception of empty space between air particles at the beginning of the lesson. They contended that conceptual conflict was created when errant beliefs were activated and confronted by an event inconsistent with the belief. This motivated cognitive accommodation, which operationalized as attention and openness to the scientifically correct conception.

Nussbaum and Novick's (1982) position can be criticized, however. For example, Posner, Strike, Henson, and Gertzog (1982) argued that more than just cognitive conflict is necessary for cognitive change to take place. They believe that effective instruction needs (1) to produce clear dissatisfaction with the errant belief and (2) to provide an intelligible and plausible alternative conception, and (3) the alternative must be fruitful in that it provides obvious intellectual power not permitted by the prior conception. In other words, students often need quite a bit of convincing before they give up a conception that is obviously correct to them in favor of a new one. The status of the prior conception often must be lowered (i.e., dissatisfaction induced) and the status of the new conception raised (i.e., proved useful), for the new conception to replace the old one (Hewson & Thorley, 1989).

Posner et al.'s (1982) elaboration of the conceptual conflict model is important: (1) There are many scientifically valid ideas that do not seem as plausible to students initially as their prior conceptions. For example, Clement, Brown, and Zeitsman (1989)

noted that many students find implausible that static objects exert forces (e.g., a table exerting an upward force equal to the weight of the items on it). Indeed, Osborne and Freyberg (1985) made the case that many ideas about force seem counterintuitive to young students: It is hard to accept that a ball thrown in an upward flight does not have an upward force operating on it while it is on the way up. It is hard to accept that a speeding bicycle that is no longer being pedaled does not have a forward force operating on it. (2) Often students find new conceptions to be unintelligible, with student exclamations such as, "I don't know what you're saying," or "I don't know what you mean" (Hewson & Thorley, 1989). (3) Students often prefer their prior conceptions to the new conceptions offered in school, believing that their own knowledge is consistent with the "real world" even if it is not consistent with what must be learned in school (Dreyfus, Jungwirth, & Eliovitch, 1990). If new knowledge is to prove fruitful, it often is going to have to prove more useful than everyday knowledge that the student trusts because it is grounded in experience.

Even though Posner et al.'s (1982) conditions for conceptual change learning are cited frequently and acknowledged as critical based on anecdotal and case study information, there has been surprisingly little research on them, and the work that has been completed is not analytical (see Hewson & Thorley, 1989). Moreover, there has been little translation of the model into classroom practice. Part of the problem is that Posner et al.'s (1982) rationale for their position was presented in abstract and philosophical terms.

More positively, the relevant literature that is available largely has been summarized in a meta-analysis by Guzzetti, Snyder, Glass, and Gamas (1993), who concluded that conceptual conflict instruction was effective in promoting understanding of ideas in science not consistent with prior knowledge. Posner et al.'s (1982) model is an important one. To promote understanding of science and conceptual change according to it, educators should do the following:

- Develop lectures, demonstrations, problems, and laboratory experiments that produce cognitive conflict in students. Posner et al. (1982) suggested that both homework and laboratory experiences could be used to make obvious inconsistencies between student prior knowledge and to-be-acquired scientific conceptions.

- Teachers should monitor their students' thinking about new to-be-learned concepts, being especially alert to defensive moves of students to resist accommodating their prior conceptions to scientific conceptions.
- Teachers should act as Socratic tutors, confronting students when they attempt to assimilate scientific concepts to their misconceptions rather than accommodate their current thinking to the scientific idea.
- Teachers should model scientific thinking, with them making clear to students that there must be consistency in one's beliefs (e.g., the misconception and scientific concept cannot both be true). Teachers should also make clear that beliefs should be consistent with evidence and that it is not appropriate to "explain away" evidence inconsistent with one's beliefs in an ad hoc fashion.
- Students should be presented content in multiple modes (e.g., verbal, mathematical, concrete-practical, pictorial), with relationships between the various representations made clear.
- Teachers should rely on assessments (e.g., interviews) that can be revealing about students' conceptual changes and their lack of change.

As ambitious as Posner et al.'s (1982) teaching model for conceptual change is, there are important mechanisms that are not taken up in it or are not developed well. We believe that Posner et al.'s basic instructional framework would be able to incorporate some of the other mechanisms discussed in the remainder of this section. For example, as part of being a Socratic tutor, teachers might make use of analogies to explain scientific concepts that students are not assimilating.

Analogies

Making analogies involves finding similarities between a new concept and a familiar one in order to make the new concept more understandable. One reason it is good to teach students to think analogically is that scientists think analogically (Glynn, 1991): Kepler explained planetary motion with analogies to clockwork; Priestley explained electrical force using analogies to gravitational force; and the physicist Campbell argued that particles of kinetic gases behave something like billiard balls. Powerful analogies can help teachers communicate to young minds as well and may be especially compelling when some scientific fact is difficult to comprehend to the point of being unbelievable. (See Chapter 3 of this book for additional discussion of the power of analogies in thinking; e.g., Gick & Holyoak, 1980, 1983).

Recall a point made in the previous subsection, that sometimes students find it difficult to accept that static objects exert force, so that it is somewhat unbelievable to many young students that the chair they are sitting on is exerting an upward force equal to their weight or that a table is exerting a force equal to the weight of the centerpiece, place settings, and food on top of it. Clement and colleagues (see Clement et al., 1989) had the insight that there were other physical situations analogous to static objects exerting force that are understood and accepted by many students and that these situations could be used as analogies to explain the more unbelievable idea, referring to the understandable situations as anchoring intuitions or bridging analogies. Clement et al.'s hypothesis was consistent with a report by an exceptionally talented physics teacher, Jim Minstrell (1982), that student understanding of static objects producing forces could be increased by having students consider and discuss what happens when a weight is put on a table, a hand, or a spring balance.

In Clement et al.'s (1987) study, high school physics students received instruction about forces exerted by static objects, Newton's third law of collisions (i.e., if one object exerts a force on a second object, the second exerts an equal and opposite force on the first), and frictional forces. Students in the treatment classes were presented and discussed anchoring intuitions. For the example of a rigid table exerting force on a book lying on it (i.e., of a force exerted by a static object), students considered how a book might cause a piece of foam rubber to sag if placed on it, or how a book might bend a "table" made of a flexible board (with the bending becoming less and less apparent as the board is thickened until the point when it is the thickness of a conventional table board). Students also reflected on how a spring would compress if a book were on it, and they experienced the force they exerted to hold a book in the palm of their hand. Although it took a number of discussions and bridging analogies to make the point, students in the classes receiving these analogies were better able to solve posttest problems involving forces exerted by static objects than were students receiving conventional instruction, with this advantage apparent even 2 months after instruction. Similar differences favoring analogical teaching were apparent for problems involving Newton's third law and frictional force.

Others have been able to replicate Clement et al.'s (1987) finding in true experimental comparisons (e.g., Brown, 1992; Stavy, 1991). One of the interesting features of Brown's study was the inclusion of an exceptionally difficult transfer problem requiring students to realize that when a 200-pound block is resting on a 40-pound block, the 40-pound block exerts 200 pounds of force—an idea totally foreign to those not understanding Newtonian mechanics. Brown also determined that bridging analogies establish a condition considered critical by Posner et al. (1982) in that they make Newtonian ideas more plausible to students. Given the success of bridging analogies in research studies, it is not surprising that instructional packages are now being developed that include bridging analogies. Athough these packages are generally not evaluated in anything similar to true experiments, students do experience large gains in understanding from pretests to posttests as a function of experiencing these curricula (e.g., Summers, 1992).

Analogies can be useful even if students do not possess misconceptions related to the to-be-learned idea—if for some reason the material is difficult to understand because it is from an unfamiliar or abstract domain. For example, Royer and Cable (1976) presented students with texts about comparable phenomena involving the flow of heat and the flow of electricity. In one of their conditions, the first passage students read made the flow phenomena understandable through the use of concrete analogies. In other conditions, the first passage did not contain analogies. To get an idea of the difficulty of understanding such content without the benefit of analogies, try to understand the following passage from Royer and Cable's (1976) study, one about heat flow:

> The presence of a foreign particle or impurity in the chemical composition of the metal also reduces the efficiency of heat transfer in the medium. This is because the particle produces a distortion in the structural symmetry of the crystalline lattices. The result is that some of the molecules in the medium will be moved into oblique positions, with a resultant loss of thermal agitation transfer. The impurity produces this loss of efficiency in two ways. It absorbs some of the energy instead of passing it on, and because of the fact that the impurity is not as structurally bonded as the crystal lattices, it moves erratically, thereby dis-

turbing the normal transfer of energy. (Royer & Cable, 1976, p. 207)

Now, consider how much easier the passage is to understand by replacing one of its sentences with a physical analogy:

> The presence of a foreign particle or impurity in the chemical composition of the metal also reduces the efficiency of heat transfer in the medium. This is because the particle produces a distortion in the structural symmetry of the crystalline lattices. If we were to place some sizeable object (such as a pack of cigarettes) in an orderly array of dominos, we would see that the toppling motion would be reduced around the object. The impurity produces this loss of efficiency in two ways. It absorbs some of the energy instead of passing it on, and because of the fact that the impurity is not as structurally bonded as the crystal lattices, it moves erratically, thereby disturbing the normal transfer of energy. (Royer & Cable, 1976, p. 207)

The really impressive finding is that the improved comprehension of this passage about heat via concrete analogy permitted improved understanding of the second passage read, which was an abstract passage about the effects of a magnetic field on the flow of electricity through metal. (That is, comprehension of the second passage read, which did not contain analogies, was better for subjects who had read the first passage with analogies than if they had read a first passage without analogies.) Just as Clement et al. (1989) used the term bridging analogy, Royer and Cable (1975) noted that passages containing analogies can serve as "bridge builders" (p. 121), activating information that is familiar to a learner and comprehensible to him or her and thus serving to increase understanding of subsequent abstract information that shares structural similarities with the familiar knowledge.

Sometimes more than one analogy is available, and it can make a difference which analogy is applied in a situation. Thus the flow of electricity can be understood either by analogy to flow of water (see Dupin & Johsua, 1989, for a review of evidence relevant to this point) or motion of a crowd of objects. The water flow analogy is as follows (Gentner & Gentner, 1983):

- Pipes correspond to wires, pumps to batteries, and narrow pipes to resistors.
- Water pressure is analogous to voltage, narrowness of pipes to resistance, and flow rate of water to electrical current.

- Connections in plumbing systems are like connections in electrical systems, involving pipes, pumps, and narrow pipes in the former case and wires, batteries, and resistors respectively in the latter case. Just as flow rate increases with pressure, current increases with voltage. (Based on Gentner & Gentner, 1983, Table 6.1)

In contrast, the moving crowds analogy involves objects moving through passageways with all of the attendant characteristics of such crowds. For example, when the passageway narrows, there is a slowing down at the point where the narrowing occurs. Gentner and Gentner (1983) described it this way:

> Voltage corresponds to how powerfully they [moving objects] push. Like the water analogy, the moving-crowd model establishes a distinction between current and voltage. Further, the moving crowd model allows a superior treatment of resistors. In this model we can think of a resistor as analogous to a barrier containing a narrow gate. This "gate" conception of resistors is helpful in predicting how combinations of resistors will behave. . . . However, it is hard to find a useful realization of batteries in this model. (p. 111)

Gentner and Gentner (1983, Experiment 1) analyzed how high school and college students who used water flow and moving crowd models performed on circuit problems. The most pertinent result here is that performance depended on the model used by the subjects. Water flow subjects did better on problems involving serial and parallel combinations of two batteries than on ones involving serial and parallel combinations of two resistors. Exactly the opposite pattern was observed for moving crowd thinkers.

In a second experiment, subjects were taught either the water flow or moving crowd analogy and were administered the same problems used in the first experiment. Subjects taught the moving crowd analogy performed much like the subjects who used the moving crowd analogy on their own in the first experiment (i.e., performing better than water flow subjects on the resistor problems). The water flow analogy did not produce superior performance on problems involving batteries, however. Qualitative follow-up data made clear what was going on and provided an important warning about analogies: The college students taught the water flow analogy did not understand how water behaves. *For an anal-*

ogy to work, people must understand the analogue situation. People who do not understand how water flows cannot productively use their deficient knowledge of water flow to solve problems about electrical flow—and in fact may make inferences about electricity that are not justified based on their errant understanding of water flow (see also Zook, 1991, and Zook & DiVesta, 1991). In Gentner and Gentner (1983), misconceptions about water flow produced misconceptions about electrical flow when subjects were taught to think of electrical flow as analogous to water flow.

Additional support for the claim that the analogy used makes a difference in thinking about a target concept was produced by Dupin and Joshua (1989). They observed different ways of thinking about electricity when elementary and high school students were taught a mechanical train analogy versus a heat flow analogy. Also, Halpern, Hansen, and Riefer (1990) had adults read passages about the lymph system and about enzymes. When readers were alerted before reading the passage on the lymph system that the system could be thought about as operating like water through the pores of a sponge, there was greater comprehension of the passage than when the analogy was to blood through the veins. When readers read the passage on enzymes, an analogy to ministers and judges making and breaking matrimonial bonds was more effective than an analogy to heat as producing different effects.

Caution in the use of analogies in science instruction is justified for several reasons. First, as we have already seen, analogies work only if learners understand the analogy. Second, sometimes students have a difficult time mapping the relationship specified by the analogy to the material they are processing, as when Kloster and Winne's (1989) students had difficulty relating an analogical advance organizer about abuses involving office photocopiers to a passage about computer crime, even though the designers of the analogous advance organizer built in a one-to-one relationship between the elements of the photocopier example and the information about computer crime presented in the text. A third is that analogies (and there are many analogies in science texts; Glynn, 1991) can produce misconceptions. For example, Walker and Wilson (1991) found the following analogy in a grade-4 science textbook, which induces the misconception that for raindrops to appear, a cloud must be squeezed, which is not consistent at all with the scientific explanation for why the molecules come closer together:

> You might think of the air as a sponge. A sponge holds water until it is squeezed. Cooled air is like a sponge being squeezed. As air is cooled, its molecules lose energy and slow down. They come closer together. Some of the water molecules in the air are squeezed out. (Cooper, Blackwood, Bolschen, Giddings, & Carin, 1985, p. 169)

Fourth, even the best analogies break down at some point. Thus, even though water flow is a good analogy for electrical flow, when an electrical wire breaks, the electricity does not flow out of it as water flows out of a broken pipe (see Glynn, 1991).

One solution to the inadequacy of single analogies may be to present multiple analogies. Although each analogy breaks down in some way, in that it is incomplete, misleading, or fails to focus attention on important information (see Spiro, Feltovich, Coulson, & Anderson, 1989), several analogies can cover all of the important information pertaining to a to-be-acquired concept. Also, if students do not understand one of the potential analogies or cannot map the analogous example to the to-be-learned relationship, they might understand a different analogy well enough to use it productively. This multiple-analogy approach currently is being explored for teaching of advanced concepts, such as biological information conveyed to medical students. We believe this approach should be explored in some detail for elementary science teaching as well, however. For example, recall in Clement et al. (1987) that it was possible to identify multiple analogies to explain basic physics concepts. Recall also that Clement et al. (1987) believed their intervention was successful because of the multiple analogies. Multiple analogies probably permit learner insights that single analogies cannot, highlighting different attributes of the concept (Glynn, 1991; Spiro et al., 1989) Multiple analogies also probably have persuasive force that single analogies do not.

On many occasions, however, the science teacher is only going to have a single analogy—for even a single analogy is sometimes hard to devise! Glynn's (1991) **teaching with analogies (TWA)** model has special promise in that situation. Glynn (1991) argued that to teach with an analogy, either as part of text or in a lecture, the target concept should be introduced, the retrieval of the analogue should be cued, the features shared by the target and analogue should be highlighted and the similarities mapped, the conclusions about the target intended by the analogy should be drawn, and where the analogy breaks down should be indicated. That is, one way to handle analogy breakdown is simply to warn the learner. Indeed, by explaining where an analogy breaks down, it is possible to highlight the unique features of the concept being taught, as in this explanation of the breakdown of the water flow analogy for electrical flow cited by Glynn (1991):

> The water analogy is quite useful for gaining a conceptual understanding of electric circuits, but it does have its limitations. An important one is that a break in a water pipe results in water spilling from the circuit, whereas a break in an electric circuit results in a complete stop in the flow of electricity. Another has to do with turning current off and on. When you *close* an electrical switch that connects the circuit, you allow current to flow in much the same way as you allow water to flow by *opening* a faucet. Opening a switch stops the flow of electricity. An electric current must be closed for electricity to flow. Opening a water faucet, on the other hand, starts the flow of water. Except for these and some other differences, thinking of electric current in terms of water current is a useful way to study electric circuits. (Hewitt, 1987, p. 526–527)

Glynn and his colleagues are now conducting research aimed at identifying the strengths and weaknesses of the TWA model.

In summary, analogies often can help students understand scientific concepts. Analogies have limits, however, in that the student must understand an analogue situation in order to use it to mediate learning of new content. In addition, no analogy completely captures a new concept, with analogical breakdowns having the potential for inducing misconceptions. Use of multiple analogies and presentation of explanations that warn of breakdowns may reduce the impact of this shortcoming of analogies, however. We expect considerable additional research on analogically mediated learning of science given the prominence of discussions of analogy in the science education literature. Such work has considerable promise for affecting educational practice, especially because even students as young as preschoolers can benefit from analogies at least in some cases (Alexander et al., 1989; Alexander, Willson, White, & Fuqua, 1987; Brown, 1989; Brown & Kane, 1988; Brown, Kane, & Echols, 1986; Brown,

Kane, & Long, 1989; Goswami, 1991, 1992; Vosniadou & Schommer, 1988). Research on instructional analogies can also be theoretically important, informing theories of representation in particular (see Chapter 3): Analogical thinking is often conceived of as having an imagery component (Paivio, 1986); analogies can also be considered mental models, which can be used flexibly and expanded (Gentner & Stevens, 1983). Analogical instruction of science is an exceptionally promising area of study for educational psychologists.

Refutation Text

One possible way to deal with misconceptions is simply to alert students to potential misconceptions and how the misconceptions differ from the scientific concept being taught. Consider the following example of text, which includes a refutation of potential misconceptions (highlighted here):

> A central point to be made is that the medieval impetus theory is incompatible with Newtonian mechanics in several fundamental ways. . . . To get a sense of some of the motion studies mentioned, imagine the following situation. A person is holding a stone at shoulder height while walking forward at a brisk pace. What kind of path will the stone follow as it falls? *Many people to whom this problem is presented answer that the stone will drop straight down, striking the ground directly under the point where it was dropped. A few people are even convinced that the falling stone will travel backward and land behind the point of its release. In reality,* the stone will move forward as it falls, landing a few feet ahead of the release point. Newtonian mechanics explains that when the stone is dropped, it continues to move forward at the same speed as the walking person, because (ignoring air resistance) no force is acting to change its horizontal velocity. (Hynd & Alverman, 1986, p. 444)

Adding refutational information to text has had variable effects on student learning in investigations to date. Adding refutations to text improved learning for low-achieving college students in Alvermann and Hague (1989) and Hynd and Alvermann (1986). Comparable effects with average-achieving college students have not been obtained in studies to date (Alvermann & Hynd, 1991). Perhaps less able students cling less tenaciously to their misconceptions because they are less certain of them, lacking confidence in their knowledge and abilities in general (Alvermann & Hynd, 1991).

An interesting possibility, however, is that refutation text will be more potent if efforts are made to ensure that students do in fact experience cognitive conflict as they process the text. Thus, if students are warned that they are reading about a concept for which they may possess misconceptions and are urged to activate relevant prior knowledge that is not consistent with the to-be-acquired concept, refutation text may have more of an impact (Alvermann & Hynd, 1991). The effects of refutation text, including the possibility that it may need to be complemented by other instructional components that increase cognitive conflict, should be explored in greater detail because, on the face of it, good refutations seem like a direct way to alert students to potential beliefs they may hold that are inconsistent with scientific conceptions.

Multiple and Alternative Representations

A recurring hypothesis in the science education literature is that students will learn science content better if they construct multiple and alternative representations of the content, stimulated in part by two types of reports: Distinguished scientists (Ben-Zvi, Eylon, & Silberstein, 1987; Miller, 1984) and good science students (e.g., Bowen, 1990) report constructing alternative representations as they think about scientific problems. The skilled chemist can represent a reaction with an equation, imagine the molecules interacting in his or her mind's eye, and imagine what the reaction looks like (e.g., memories of water drops on the sides of the many beakers used in classroom demonstrations of hydrogen and oxygen reacting). In contrast, many typical students do not construct multiple or alternative representations on their own (e.g., Ben-Zvi et al., 1987; Wandersee, 1988; Yarroch, 1985), for example, perhaps not thinking beyond the symbols in a chemical equation—so much so that the symbols are treated more as elements in a mathematical equation than as symbols for chemicals with physical characteristics. Consistent with expert theory (see Chapter 4), one possibility is that if students could only be taught and persuaded to construct multiple representations, their scientific learning and thinking would be improved. This hypothesis is particularly interesting because science educators have had it so long—generations of students have constructed ball and stick models in chemistry classes. Tens of millions of frogs have been dissected in hopes of increasing understanding of anatomy beyond insights produced by text and pictures. When dissection is not possible, such as in introductory courses in human anatomy, students have been presented many different depictions of the same anatomical features.

Some of the multiple/alternative representations hypotheses currently being explored in formal science education research mirror ones covered in earlier chapters: For example, to increase comprehension and recall of science, create verbal and imaginal (pictorial) representations of the same concept because concepts dually coded are more memorable than those coded verbally only or imaginally only (e.g., Vasu & Howe, 1989; Walker & Wilson, 1991). Alternatively, write about science in order to learn science (e.g., Santa & Havens, 1991).

Other multiple/alternative representation hypotheses are more unique to science education, such as the following: (1) Graphing data as they are collected increases understanding of the significance of data. For example, graphing the speed of an object as a function of time since it was thrown is a striking way of understanding acceleration, especially if it can be done quickly after the data pertaining to the physical event have been collected (e.g., Beichner, 1990; Brasell, 1987; Krajcik, 1991; Mokros & Tinker, 1987). Microcomputer technologies now exist that permit graphing of acceleration and velocity functions shortly after a movement occurs. A radar gun–type device feeds data directly into a microcomputer. Other types of physical relationships can be graphed quickly after data collection based on inputs from other probes, including thermometers as well as voltage, light, and pH meters. See Linn and Songer (1991) for an example of how such technology can be used to teach thermodynamics.

(2) Videodisc and microcomputer presentations of scientific events (e.g., chemical reactions) when combined with more conventional symbolic representational activities (e.g., writing and balancing equations) increase understanding of scientific concepts so represented (Krajcik, 1991; Smith & Jones, 1988). Videodisc visuals illustrating the particulate nature of matter are effective in combination with tutorial dialogue (Krajcik & Peters, 1989). Many such scientific **microworlds** (Pea & Kurland, 1984) are being created at present (Simmons, 1991), with it virtually certain that a great deal of research will be conducted in the near future to determine the effects of microworlds on student representation and understanding of scientific concepts. Microworlds afford the possibility of watching and rewatching scientific phenomena (e.g., chemical reactions) at various levels of analysis and from various perspectives (e.g., a time-lapse presentation of a plow rusting as well as a molecular-level animation of the molecules reacting).

(3) Scientific ideas can be rendered more understandable if students create **conceptual maps** focusing on the more important concepts and specifying relationships between more and less important terms and ideas. Because creation of conceptual maps is receiving a great deal of research attention at present, most of the remainder of this subsection is devoted to discussion of conceptual mapping research.

The hypothesis that conceptual mapping might be helpful is offered in the context of science instruction based on poorly organized textbooks and classroom instruction (Mason, 1992) that does not differentiate well between more central and less critical scientific information. Science educators such as Novak (e.g., Novak & Gowin, 1984) recommend conceptual graphing as a means of organizing scientific content that is presented initially in a poorly organized fashion. Once a decision has been made to map some content area, mapping proceeds as follows (Ault, 1985; Novak & Gowin, 1984; Okebukola, 1990):

- Key words and phrases are identified.
- Key concepts are ordered from the most general (i.e., most abstract and inclusive) to the most specific.
- The concepts are then clustered using two criteria. Concepts that interrelate are put together; concepts are classified with respect to their level of abstract (i.e., general concepts to specific ones). All of the concepts are then arranged loosely in a two-dimensional array with abstractness as one dimension and main ideas as the other.
- Related concepts are then linked with lines, with the lines labeled to specify the relationship between the concepts.

The concept maps produced by students will differ because a concept map represents an individual's construction of meaning from text. The idea is to get students to recognize not only hierarchical relationships between concepts, but also cross-linkages between various concepts. Concept maps need not capture just relations in a single text or in to-

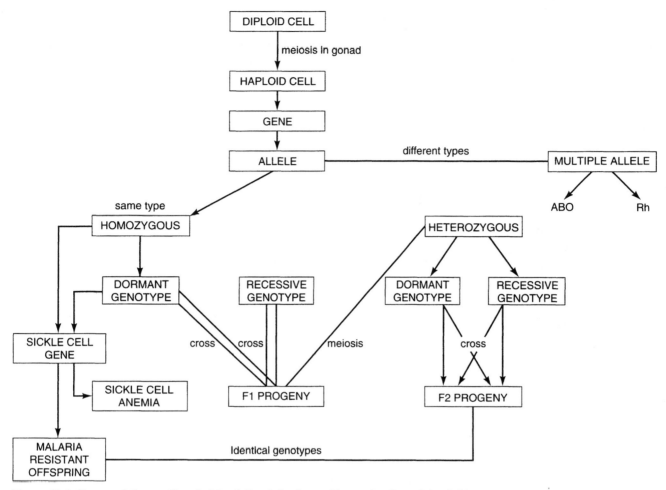

Figure 12.1 Concept Map on Simple Mendelian Inheritance Drawn by One of the Subjects
in Okebukola (1990)
(From P.A. Okebukola (1990) Attaining meaningful learning of concepts of genetics and ecology.
Journal of Research in Science Teaching, *p. 498. Reprinted by permission of the author and the*
National Association for Research in Science Teaching.)

day's lecture. Good concept maps capture relationships across courses of studies. Concept maps can be extremely elaborate.

Two examples of concept maps generated in Okebukola's (1990) research are presented in Figures 12.1 and 12.2. Readers should study these maps carefully, noting the hierarchical relationships between concepts captured by going from the top to the bottom of the concept maps. Within each level of this hierarchy, concepts are roughly equal in abstraction and importance. Linkages between ideas within concepts and between concepts are specified in the maps. The flexibility of concept mapping and the intricacies of relationships that can be captured should be apparent with a few minutes' contemplation of the sample figures. It should also be apparent that

construction of concept maps requires a great deal of active processing of content, including selective attention to and encoding of information, selective combination of information to make it interpretable, and selective comparisons of concepts to one another and to concepts known previously (Okebukola, 1990). Such selective encoding, combination, and comparisons would be expected to affect understanding and memory of scientific content.

Does concept mapping increase learning and understanding of science? The evidence is mixed (Willerman & MacHarg, 1991) at present. Some studies report significant, positive effects (e.g., Heinze-Fry & Novak, 1990; Okebukola, 1990), and others do not (e.g., Lehman, Carter, & Kahle, 1985). When we read the concept mapping studies, we

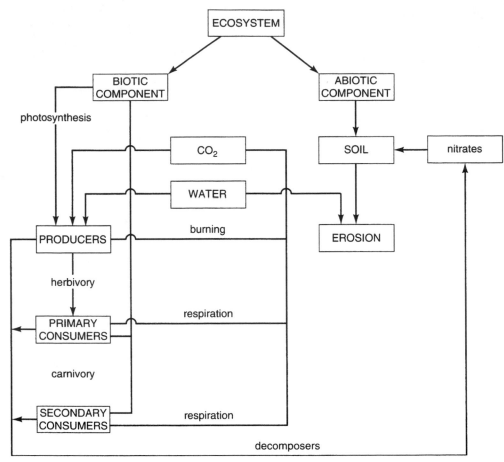

Figure 12.2 Concept Map on Ecology Drawn by Another Student in Okebukola (1990). *(From P.A. Okebukola (1990) Attaining meaningful learning of concepts of genetics and ecology.* Journal of Research in Science Teaching, *p. 498. Reprinted by permission of the author and the National Association for Research in Science Teaching.)*

were struck that even when positive effects were produced, they were often small in magnitude. One possibility might be that inconsistencies in outcomes and small overall effects reflect differential impact of mapping, with concept mapping helping some types of students but not others.

In fact, there is evidence supporting the differential-effect hypothesis: Only lower-ability students benefited from concept mapping in Stensvold and Wilson (1990). Sherris (1984) obtained concept mapping effects with students who had an external locus of control (i.e., students whose cognition and perception tend to be affected by external factors) but not with students with internal control. Students who mastered the techniques of concept mapping benefited more from construction of concept maps

than students who had not mastered the techniques in Fraser and Edwards (1985).

One group, at Texas Christian University, has reported more success than others in improving learning through mapping (Lambiotte, Dansereau, Cross, & Reynolds, 1989). They have found that providing students with maps outlining a procedure or process (e.g., flow through the digestive system) is more effective in promoting learning than maps describing details related to other concepts (i.e., maps summarizing declarative knowledge), with such maps more effective in promoting learning than text describing the same process. Consistent with other investigators, they have observed greater mapping effects with lower-ability compared with higher-ability learners.

Our guess is that the great interest in concept mapping will continue. Our suspicion as well is that these procedures will seem more effective as investigators devise measurement procedures that are more sensitive to the strengths of conceptual mapping. For example, conceptual mapping does require interpretations by students, resulting in selective attention to information and ultimately in differences in concept map representations. The richness of these interpretations has not been a focus of evaluations of concept mapping to date. If concept mapping does lead students to identify relationships they would otherwise miss and construct interpretations not obvious when mapping is not encouraged, these are important cognitive outcomes. More research, particularly more creative research (especially with respect to dependent variables), should be conducted in this area.

In general, when all of the evidence on multiple and alternative representations is considered, there is modest support for encouraging students to construct alternative interpretations. Even though effects often are reported, they are not always large, so there is nothing here to support the possibility that attempting to construct multiple representations alone leads to great expertise. When the interests in multiple representations in mathematics education (Chapter 13) and science education are combined, however, it is clear that there is considerable intellectual momentum in the direction of expanding study of multiple representations. A number of research careers will be devoted to determine when and how instruction (and what types of instruction) in the construction of multiple representations produces important gains in science achievement.

Socially Supported, Collaborative Construction of Science Concepts

Many science educators would like students to engage in pure discovery learning, consistent, for instance, with Piagetian notions of learning (i.e., natural cognitive conflict, which is viewed as a powerful mechanism for cognitive change, often accompanies discovery). Such educators believe that discovery learning produces especially deep understanding of science and improves student attitudes toward science, hypotheses that have recurred throughout the 20th century from Dewey (e.g., 1933) to articles published in the 1990s (e.g., Ajewole,

1991). That there are so many science misconceptions among students who have acquired scientific knowledge on their own makes it obvious that pure discovery learning alone is not always a good idea, however, despite its enduring attraction to some science educators. Rather than abandon entirely the constructivist ideal of discovery, many other science educators are exploring a number of socially mediated types of instruction that permit guided discovery and scaffolded student exploration of science concepts. Thus, scaffolded instruction and various types of cooperative learning are being explored in science education, although these are always part of multicomponential instruction.

Consistent with this direction, social support is consistently observed in analyses of outstanding science teaching. Kenneth Tobin of Florida State University has been especially active in studying outstanding science teaching, observing teachers nominated by teaching peers and other educators as outstanding at their craft. The findings from Tobin's studies are generally consistent with those of others studying exemplary science teaching (e.g., Garnett, 1987; Treagust, 1991).

For example, after studying 13 exemplary elementary and high school science teachers, Tobin and Fraser (1990) offered the following observations:

- Exemplary science teachers use management strategies that encourage *high student engagement*. They monitor their students and maintain control with quick, effective interventions. There is little need for teacher sanctioning, however, because there is little misbehavior. Instruction is well organized, with little time wasted moving from one activity to another. There are well-established routines in the class so students know what to do when. There is a cooperative spirit in the classroom, with students consistently helping others.
- Teachers understand well the content they are teaching.
- Teachers are concerned with improving student *understanding* of content. There are activities that require student involvement and problem solving, with adequate materials and support for these activities. Concrete examples and analogies are used to explain abstract ideas. Most critically, teachers monitor student understanding and react when there is misunderstanding, posing questions to students that stimulate thinking

in particular directions. Students elicit clarifications, and teachers react by prompting extensions of student thinking. Teachers do offer explanations on some occasions, however. That is, instruction is *scaffolded* in the sense of the term developed in Chapter 8. In particular, there are "safety nets," so students can participate without risk of embarrassment or failure. For example, teachers treat all attempts at problem solving with respect and work with all misunderstandings, attempting to lead even students who have extreme misunderstandings to scientifically defensible perspectives.

Good science teachers are like other teachers in having well-managed classrooms (see Chapter 7). They know what is happening in their class as a whole and with individual students, providing feedback and input that is tailored to student needs.

Audrey B. Champagne of the State University of New York at Albany as been a leading proponent of socially interactive instruction. Champagne (e.g., Champagne & Bunce, 1991) argues for presenting academic problems to entire classes, with each student in the class required to come up with an approach to the problem and a defense for the approach. As individual students generate problem-solving plans, they are submitted to the group for discussion. The group's goal is to identify a small number of potential problem solutions that are then tried out by the group. Through group discussion, students come to understand the problem better and what must be accomplished to solve it. Students as a group relate their prior knowledge to problems (for a compelling analysis, see Schmidt, De Volder, De Grave, Moust, & Patel, 1989), elaborating and thinking aloud in detail about various solution strategies. The teacher's role during discussion is to monitor problem-solving progress and to intervene as a coach when needed, providing hints, prompts, and information that lead the group toward a realistic problem-solving plan.

Champagne and Bunce (1991) are enthused about this approach because they believe it mirrors how actual scientists conduct themselves. As contributing educational scientists, we find their analysis credible. When a new scientific problem is presented to the educational research community (e.g., can computers be used in beginning reading instruction?), there is a great deal of discussion among scientists, with the community coming to judgment about the worth of some hypotheses versus others. Those community evaluations go far in deciding which ideas are actually tested in experiments and other types of investigations (e.g., granting agency funding committees recommend that only some projects receive support). Champagne and Bunce (1991) are also aware of the ways that such instruction falls short of actual participation in science for students. For example, scientists have more degrees of freedom than even the most fortunate students in deciding what problems they will pursue. In addition, the goal of socially interactive science instruction is to develop in students understandings that have already been nurtured in mature scientists, such as fundamental knowledge of the content area being explored and insights into the evidentiary standards of the scientific community. Still, socially interactive approaches to science teaching are growing in their appeal.

Theorists and educators such as Newman and colleagues (e.g., 1990; Newman, Griffin, & Cole, 1989) believe that socially interactive instruction permits students to experience distributed cognition (see Chapter 8)—to experience thinking in groups. Consistent with Vygotskian theory, they conceive of much of thinking happening outside the head of the student, with participation in thinking groups and in interaction with teachers who scaffold input as crucial to cognitive development and learning. Newman et al.'s (1989) commitment to Vygotskian ideas about instruction within the zone of proximal development (see Chapter 8), instruction that leads children to construct new knowledge in collaboration with others, is apparent from consideration of the title of their book: *The Construction Zone.*

One especially interesting point emphasized by Newman is that the meaning of a child's action is often determined by what follows the action, so that teachers can respond either in ways that make a child's actions meaningful or in ways that do not link the child's actions to effective problem solving. An example of responding that enhances student understanding of their own actions was provided by Newman et al. (1989) when they taught grade-4 students how to make all possible comparisons between pairs of objects. An efficient way to generate all possible comparisons is first compare objects 1 and 2, then objects 1 and 3, then 1 and 4, until 1 and n is reached; then compare objects 2 and 3, 2 and 4, and so on until 2 and n is reached; then compare 3 and 4 and so on until 3 and n is reached; continue until n-1 and n are compared. This strategy usually is not observed in the absence of instruction until adolescence (e.g., Inhelder & Piaget, 1958).

First, Newman et al.'s (1989) tutor presented the student with a stack of picture cards of movie stars with the task of generating all possible pairs of movie stars. After the student generated a response, which invariably reflected generation of less than all possible pairings, the tutor reacted: "How do you know you have all pairs?" A typical response was, "I can't think of anymore," to which the tutor responded, "Could you check to see if you have all the pairs?" When the student fails to respond, the tutor says, "Well, I have a way to check. Do you have all the pairs with Mork?" (p. 191). Then, the tutor went through a checking procedure asking about whether Mork had been paired with each of the other stars by the student, going through the deck on a star-by-star basis. Then the tutor did the same checking exercise with a second star, perhaps checking whether Mindy had been paired with every other star in the deck. Once the student understood this checking procedure, the tutor permitted the student to do it on his or her own.

When students were presented subsequent generate-all-pairs tasks, they were much more likely to be successful than they had been on the first trial in generating all possible pairings, despite the fact that they had never been taught directly to do so. What happened was that the tutor had taken the student's initial actions and rendered them more meaningful with the remarks about the checking strategy. These remarks made clear that the student's first pairings were incomplete. The comments also provided a powerful hint as to how more complete pairings might be generated. The student, however, generated the insight that the checking strategy could be used proactively. The tutor took what the student did and reacted to it so that the student would construct more powerful understandings of the inadequacy of the initial attempt and how the task might be done more effectively. Student cognitive growth occurred because of a particular reaction by the teacher in the context of supportive student-tutor interactions.

An important pedagogical principle emerges from Newman's analyses in particular. When students attempt an in-class experiment or work on problems, it is critical for there to be reflective discussion afterward. Thus, if small groups of students work on a chemistry laboratory experiment, bringing the group back together to discuss what happened makes a great deal of sense, in that alternative possibilities will be discussed with ensuing cognitive conflict. There is also the possibility for the teacher to react to what the students have done in order to stimulate them to think more about the problem. If the teacher is successful in providing hints and input that encourages students to understand the shortcomings of their problem solutions, while encouraging students to "figure out" more adequate solutions, he or she would be successful from Newman's perspective that teachers can encourage additional cognitive growth by encouraging reflection by students on their actions. If students provide such feedback to one another as well, the situation is even better. In that case, thinking would be fully distributed between teachers and students, with cognitive development of individual students stimulated by such thinking in social interaction consistent with Vygotskian ideals. Simultaneously the Piagetian ideal that knowledge is best developed through student constructions would be served. Reflective consideration of student attempts at problem solving has a lot going for it. (For another example of such socially interactive teaching in science, review the Chapter 8, this volume, discussion of Hatano and Inagaki, 1991.)

Consistent with a point emphasized in Chapter 8, socially interactive science teaching requires students to explain their thinking and justify their responses, both of which should improve learning because such explanations require students to relate new information to what they already know. Generation of such explanations overtly in a group provides many opportunities for other students and teachers to reflect on student responses and respond in turn to them in ways that can lead both the student originally generating an explanation and other students to more complete understandings.

Brown and Campione (1990) provided an example of grade-3 lower-achieving students offering explanations in group, with subsequent reactions by fellow students and teachers that stimulated additional reflection and growth in understanding by students. Thinking is really distributed across this group in interaction, who are using a version of reciprocal teaching (Chapters 8 and 14) to read and discuss science text as a group, with this discussion involving much *clarifying* and *questioning*, followed by a *summarizing* and some *predicting* (i.e., all four of the strategic processes taught in reciprocal teaching; see Chapters 8 and 14):

STUDENT 1: What does camouflage mean?

STUDENT 2: It means you invisible like GI Joe.

S1: What color can the chameleon be?

STUDENT 3: Brown.

S1: No.

S2: Green.

S1: No.

ALL: What? (Confusion)

S1: What color would it be if it was on a fire engine—red, right? And on a cab—yellow, right?

ALL: No! No!

STUDENT 4: It can only be greenish or brownish, like in nature.

S1: (Indignant) It says (reading text), "A chameleon can take on the color of its background"—so that it can be *any* color, right?

S4: No. No! It can only be colors like brown earth and green trees and yucky color like mud—like GI Joe.

S6: So he matches.

TEACHER: (Scaffolding weaker student: repeating text line): Yes, he matches. He's almost invisible.

S6: He changes colors so his enemy won't get him.

T: Good. That is right.

S1: (Question—confused) But what if he's not in the grass, what if he's a whitish kinda color?

S6: He would turn white?

ALL: No.

S1: (Question—still confused) But what if he doesn't have that color? What if he can't turn that color?

S5: He just moves on down to another spot that has his color.

S4: Only green and brown and yucky.

S1: Can it be blue like water in the forest?

S3: Water in the forest isn't blue, it's yucky colored, so chameleons can be yucky colored too.

S1: OK, OK. I summarize. It change color.

T: What does?

S1: Chameleon change color to hide from its enemies. It can be green—umh brown—yucky color (pause) so it has to stay in the forest 'cause those colors are there.

S1: (Question) I have another question. How does it change color?

T: Good question. Anyone know?

S6: It doesn't say.

T: Do we really know how it changes?

S1: No.

T: Any predictions? No?

T: (Prediction) I think it might be a chemical in its body, let's read to find out. (Adapted slightly from Brown & Campione, 1990, p. 119)

Consistent with Newman's thinking, the students and teachers consistently made more meaningful each others' comments by reacting to them. The teacher's reactions to a student's curiosity about the cause of the changing colors sets the stage for the children to be sensitive to this particular issue and the possibility that the change is caused by chemical reactions. (Imagine, for example, how different the students' orientation to the next section might be if the teacher had not reacted as she did.) Reciprocal teaching is intended as a framework for social interaction that permits reflection on academic content (i.e., before students can summarize, they must understand, which is accomplished through interactive dialogues). The teacher's role is to provide gentle prompts and support as needed, with this support, at its best, responding to student thinking at the moment, reacting to it in a way that leads the students to construct for themselves a more sophisticated understanding of the material. (For example, by alerting students to the possibility that chemicals might cause the change in colors, the teacher has set the students up to be attentive to information in text consistent with that possibility but has not told the students that the color changes are definitely caused by chemicals.)

Summarizing up to this point in this subsection, an emerging consensus in science education is that social interaction around science problems is desirable, especially if a skilled teacher collaborates with students and scaffolds input to them. Consistent with direct explanation models, such teachers sometimes explain and sometimes model scientific thinking. There is also mounting evidence that such instruction produces great student involvement in learning, with students self-regulating their participation in group problem solving so a high percentage of time is devoted to learning (e.g., see Pizzini & Shepardson's [1992] analysis of one socially interactive, problem-solving approach to science instruction; also, Amigues [1988] provided an important analysis of how interaction during physics problem solving heightened grade-10 students' self-monitoring and deliberate self-regulation).

Glynn, Yeany, and Britton (1991) in the introduction to their edited book on the psychology of science learning provided a summary of socially in-teractive instruction that captures all of its most important features:

> Teachers should require students to reason scientifi-cally. One way they can do this is by modeling scien-tific reasoning for their students. In effect, teachers and students should become collaborators in the process of scientific reasoning. Together, students and teachers should construct interesting questions about scientific phenomena; simply telling students the answers has little lasting value. Teachers and stu-dents should guess, or hypothesize, about the under-lying causes of science phenomena. Teachers and stu-dents should collect data and design scientific tests of their hypotheses. And, finally, teachers and students should construct theories and models to explain the phenomena in question. Throughout all stages of this collaboration, teachers and students should be con-stantly "thinking out loud" (Glynn, Muth, & Britton, 1990). By means of the "thinking out loud" technique, teachers can help students to reflect on their own sci-entific reasoning processes (that is, to think metacog-nitively) and to refine these processes. (p. 4)

Teachers modeling and explaining processing to students as they attempt to work it out (i.e., con-struct their own understanding of the processing) in interaction with other students should be a familiar theme by now. This is how sophisticated cognitively based instruction is occurring across the curriculum. No teacher could possibly convey all of the tacit knowledge, the know-how, that is part of under-standing any scientific concept (or any other concept for that matter). Students can acquire much tacit knowledge (e.g., Champagne & Bunce, 1991) by working out problems with help from their class-mates and their teachers.

We close this discussion with three important points about social factors in instruction. The first is that there may be many positive features not yet tapped, something suggested by a study of some ex-tremely fortunate students that was conducted by Spector and Gibson (1991). They interviewed high-achieving, middle-school students who had been enrolled in an innovative summer school program aimed at understanding water and its effect on the world. This program was loaded with great demon-strations and activities:

> . . . [I]nvestigations at the bench to determine surface tension, density, and osmolarity of both salt and fresh water; snorkeling in the gulf and bay to get an under-water perspective of marine life in its natural envi-ronment; canoeing on the Hillsborough river to ascer-tain the impact of humans on fragile river environ-ments; sailing in the bay to learn physics principles; studying the Living Seas Pavilion at EPCOT to com-pare human-made environments to natural environ-ments; and conducting soil filtration investigations in the laboratory, exploring sink holes, and inspecting Hooker's Point Waste Water Treatment Plant to un-derstand the need for and ways to supplement nat-ural processes that keep an adequate supply of fresh water available. (p. 468)

Although the students certainly appreciated the effects of these laboratory and experiential opportu-nities on their learning, and appreciated that their teachers taught them how to experiment on their own, what is noteworthy here is the social and affec-tive elements that students cited as important in pro-moting their learning: The students talked about the difference it made to be able to have fun and learn and to be with other students who shared the learn-ing experiences and cared about the topic. They rec-ognized how different the motivational orientation of their teachers and students was compared to typical schooling (i.e., there was definitely a task orientation, to use a term introduced in Chapter 5, this book).

Reading Spector and Gibson (1991) made an im-pact on us because we recognize that so much of our enthusiasm for research as graduate students was because of supportive peers. One of the things that keeps us generating scientific studies is that it is fun to interact with others over scientific issues. Yet, as we recognize that fact, we also recognize that there is little research on how immersion in a group of supportive peers affects the development of scien-tists—either young ones, such as students in middle school experiencing such groups for the first time, or old ones, such as ourselves as we mix it up with our scientific peers, many of whom are close friends with whom we have shared many adventures, sci-entific and nonscientific. Making science with peers and interacting with old friends about science is a way of life for mature scientists. Perhaps if that mes-sage were clearer to many students, science would be more appealing. There is a real need to evaluate the differences in science learning when it occurs in a world of friendship, trust, and collaborative inves-tigation rather than in a school world of competi-tion, which fosters students working in isolation to learn facts.

Our second closing point is that students getting together to help other students may be a cost-effective way to help many students cope with science content. Recall the idea introduced in Chapter 10 that total time matters with respect to learning. From that perspective, it makes sense to attempt to increase the amount of time students receive science instruction. Yet teachers and teacher time cost money. In addition, many of the difficulties are not ones that a professor many years beyond students can really understand or address. A potential solution is to provide supplemental instruction that is more on the order of peer cooperative groups than formal tutoring from a professor.

Lundeberg (1990) reported on one such effort. Chemistry majors were paid and trained to lead out-of-class discussion groups for first-year chemistry courses at a small liberal arts college: "Their role was to model the thinking involved in learning chemistry; to listen to students' questions, comments, concerns, and answers; to ask relevant questions; and to encourage students to work cooperatively in solving chemistry problems" (p. 147). The students talked about what they understood and what they did not understand. Although there were tensions at first, good students and weaker students eventually worked together, with the cooperation between students often extending to times other than when the supplemental instruction group met. Both the chemistry major leaders and the students in the elementary chemistry course learned to talk about chemistry, as they helped each other and became friends in a cooperative environment. Although nervous at first about making mistakes, students eventually became relaxed in their interactions with each other.

Did it work? The students who voluntarily attended the sessions did better in the chemistry course than the students in the course who chose not to attend the supplemental sessions. Of course, there are potential, alternative interpretations of this outcome, including that volunteers were more able or motivated than nonvolunteers. Nonetheless, we believe this approach deserves much more study based on the qualitative data in Lundeberg's (1990) report. Lundeberg perceived that the peer interaction and support had many positive effects, including reducing anxiety by increasing understanding of chemistry. Consistent with other tutoring data (e.g., Allen, 1976; see Chapter 11, this book), there were also indications that the chemistry major leaders

deepened and extended their understanding of chemistry as a function of modeling chemistry problem solving and explaining difficult concepts to the introductory students (consistent with other data substantiating the importance of explaining difficult ideas to others as part of coming to understand those ideas; e.g., Pressley, Wood, Woloshyn, et al., 1992; Webb, 1989). There are many potentially psychologically interesting effects of such peer interactions. When the cost-effectiveness of peer tutoring is considered as well, the motivation is great to study the dynamics and effects of peer-supplemented instruction thoroughly.

The third closing point is a negative one, however. It is easy for socially interactive instruction and problem solving to go awry. For example, Gayford (1989) observed that in many cooperative science-instruction groups, one person did most or all of the work. Not surprisingly, many members of such groups learn little (Gayford, 1992). Basili and Sanford (1991) found that there were good and poor cooperative group leaders, with conceptual change anything but certain in cooperative groups, especially ones with poor leaders. One difficulty in Basili and Sanford (1991) was that students often lacked critical prior knowledge that could not be remediated effectively by group cooperative discussion. What is required is not social interaction per se but social interaction in which all students participate and learn without fear or intimidation; the presence of a science expert who can detect a variety of misunderstandings that students may possess and intervene to provide remediation may be necessary for instruction in advanced conceptual areas, such as most of science.

Perlmutter, Behrend, Kuo, and Muller (1989) reported variable effects of cooperative pairing when children worked on problem solving together in a computer environment. Some children some of the time were helped by cooperation; some children some of the time were harmed by cooperation, with little basis for predicting when facilitation should be expected versus interference. Cooperative models that boil down simply to regrouping students for instruction often will fail to produce the types of high-quality social interactions considered in this section. Implementing cooperative learning alone guarantees nothing (e.g., Sherman, 1988; Tingle & Good, 1990). A big challenge for educational psychologists is to produce systematic understanding of when cooperative grouping facilitates learning of difficult science and how a group can be best arranged to maximize effects of cooperative grouping.

Closing Comments: Constructivist Nature of Conceptual Change Instruction

If there is any theme that pervades contemporary science education, it is that students must construct scientific understandings for themselves if they are really to understand at a deep level. Consistent with Piaget, science educators recognize that the conceptual understandings a student brings to a situation play a large role in determining their understanding of the situation. If new information is inconsistent with the views already held by a child, there is the possibility for cognitive conflict, which motivates efforts by the child to comprehend the new input. Such conflict opens the possibility that the student will accommodate his or her current views to the new input, resulting in a new conceptualization of the situation by the student.

Analogies can aid in the process by connecting new information with understandings already possessed by the student but ones not activated by the student naturally (e.g., reminding the student of the clear effort exerted when books are held in the palm of the hand when the student is trying to comprehend that a table must exert a force equal to the weight of the objects on it). Other methods considered in this section also increase the likelihood that students will simultaneously activate newly presented science concepts and inconsistent prior knowledge, such as refutation text and socially interactive instruction. Although these interventions increase the likelihood that the student will exert cognitive effort to attempt to understand the scientific conception, science educators believe that analogies, texts, and social interaction advance scientific understanding by stimulating cognitive conflict, which results in reflection and ultimately in construction of new knowledge.

These interventions work because humans have an intrinsic motivation to be more competent than they currently are (e.g., White, 1959). Anything that makes obvious that current thinking is probably flawed, probably not competent, stimulates efforts toward greater competence. A new piece of information that is presented as more adequate than the student's current thinking is grist for the mill in this situation. Demonstrations and text accompanying this new information are especially likely to be processed at a deep level if the student is aware that the new information is not in synchrony with prior knowledge, and there is reason to believe that the "fault" is with the student's current understanding rather than the new information.

Although both instructors and students are making efforts with respect to all of the interventions considered in this section, the efforts of the students toward construction of meaning are much more critical than the efforts of the instructors. The instructional tactics taken here are important only because they make student construction of knowledge more likely. Science educators are completely constructivist in their outlooks.

DEVELOPMENT OF SCIENTIFIC THINKING SKILLS

As far as the great theorists in educational psychology are concerned (see Chapters 7 to 9), there is no doubt who is the greatest in the eyes of the science educator community. Long after most of the cognitive developmental and educational psychologists have moved on to other ideas, the science educator community continues to find Piaget's theory helpful, which should have been obvious in the discussion of conceptual change. One of the greatest appeals of the theory is that the ultimate stage of development in Piaget's theory is formal operations, which is characterized by Piagetians as enabling the best of scientific thinking.

The classic reference on formal operations is *The Growth of Logical Thinking from Childhood to Adolescence* (Inhelder & Piaget, 1958). The formal operational adolescent's thinking is not confined to the world of concrete objects and facts as is the world of the elementary student. Adolescents are capable of reasoning about realities they have never experienced. They are capable of abstract thinking, fully hypothetico-deductive reasoning. Should the adolescent be informed that Smedleyville is west of Burgertown, and Burgertown is west of Fidlerdale, the adolescent can deduce that Smedleyville is west of Fidlerdale, with all of the reasoning going on in the student's head at a symbolic level. That is, the adolescent can make deductions given premises.

Even more impressive, the adolescent can make inductions, reasoning from evidence to conclusions. The adolescent can form hypotheses, imagining what would happen if a particular theory held.

Moreover, the adolescent can experiment, understanding how to vary single factors at a time while other factors are held constant (i.e., formal operational thinkers understand how to control variables). For example, think back to the pendulum problem described in Chapter 7. To determine the factors affecting the rate of pendulum swing, it is essential to vary the length of strings while holding the weight of the pendulum constant and to vary the weight of the pendulum while holding the string length constant.

A variety of other abilities are also hypothesized to follow from formal operations according to Piaget. One is the ability to generate all possible combinations when several factors can vary (e.g., given four binary characteristics [+ or -], the adolescent with formal operations can generate all 16 possibilities, from ---- to ++++ and everything in between: +---, -+--, --+-, ---+, ++--, +-+-, +--+, -++-, -+-+, --++, +++-, -+++, +-++, ++-+). Another is to be able to solve problems requiring comparison of several proportions. Adolescents also can understand probability, which is an extremely important competency for working scientists.

Piaget's claim was that formal operations permit all types of scientific feats that are beyond the concrete operational student (see Brainerd, 1978b, Chapter 6, for a more extensive review than could be offered here). The bad news is that many adolescents and young adults fail to achieve formal operations (e.g., Lawson, 1983; Piaget, 1972). And, it may make a difference.

A recurring hypothesis is that formal operational status will be associated with success in various types of science instruction. For example, Lawson and Renner (1975) produced a clear relationship between formal operational status and the ability to acquire scientific understandings that are not the result of direct experience (i.e., **hypothetical concepts**), such as knowing what a "gene" is or "DNA replication" or "natural selection." Such concepts were beyond all concrete operational thinkers; the more highly developed formal operational competencies were, the better the acquisition of such hypothetical concepts. More recent work by Lawson and his associates (e.g., Lawson & Thompson, 1988) has produced additional support for the conclusion that many scientific concepts are acquired more certainly by students who have attained formal operations than by those who have not, with the relationship between formal operational status and concept

acquisition obtained even when other factors such as verbal intelligence and age are controlled. Others (e.g., Gipson, Abraham, & Renner, 1989; Glasson, 1989), however, have produced evidence that Lawson may have overestimated the relationship between formal reasoning and acquisition of abstract scientific concepts, making obvious that debates about the role of formal operational competence in scientific reasoning continue.

Case's neo-Piagetian theory (see Chapter 7) is also receiving attention from the science educators, with the possibility that mental capacity as defined by Case (i.e., the neo-Piagetian version of working memory) is an important determinant of the ability to learn various types of science content. Although not all of the evidence is positive (e.g., Staver & Jacks, 1988), researchers such as Niaz (e.g., 1988, 1989) are producing evidence that mental capacity can make a difference in learning scientific content such as chemistry. In particular, Niaz produced evidence that problems vary in difficulty to the extent that they demand students hold information in working memory. In summary, many science educators continue to believe that cognitive demands of science can be understood in Piagetian and neo-Piagetian terms. Moreover, there is some evidence in support of the Piagetian and neo-Piagetian assumptions.

The most ambitious program of research on the development of scientific thinking skills in recent years has been conducted by Kuhn and colleagues, resulting in two book-length reports since 1988. Kuhn definitely begins with Piagetian thinking as a starting point, although there can be little doubt that her research significantly extends Piagetian analyses of scientific thinking and behavior. Thus, the remainder of this section on the development of scientific reasoning abilities is concerned almost exclusively with Kuhn's impressive contributions to our understanding of the development of scientific competence and the potential of her work for stimulating additional studies illuminating the development of scientific competence.

Evaluation of Scientific Evidence

Kuhn, Amsel, and O'Loughlin (1988) studied the scientific evaluation abilities of students from grade 3 through college, in some cases comparing their performances with the expert evaluations of five Ph.D. candidates in philosophy. (Well-trained philosophers have extensive knowledge about how to evaluate evidence and relate it to theory.) The method used in these studies was to present participants with a problem that some scientists wanted to solve. Although several different problems were used in these studies, the most frequently cited one was concerned with determining which of four factors affected the "servability" of balls in a paddle game that was under development:

> The subject was told that a sports company was conducting an investigation. A new game was being developed and different kinds of balls were being tried out to use in the game. All the rules of the game were not yet decided, but the game was to be played by two players, who hit a ball across a net to each other using a special kind of paddle. The interviewer also explained to the subject that the investigators at the company had tried lots of different balls and found that some resulted in good serves and some in poor serves and that there really were not any balls in between.
>
> A box of 16 sample balls was then presented for the subject to examine. The four features of the balls, size (large or small), color (light or dark), texture (rough or smooth), and presence or absence of ridges, were then described . . . [and shown to subjects]. (Kuhn et al., 1988, p. 107)

Then each subject was shown "good serve" and "bad serve" baskets, and the experimenter asked the participant which variables he or she thought determined whether balls would result in good or bad serves. The subjects were required to explain their opinions and eventually to rank order the variables with respect to the impact on serving. This permitted the experimenter to know the subject's theory of serving—that is, coming into the experiment, which variables the participant believed affected serving.

After their personal theories of variables affecting serving were assessed, subjects were presented a number of trials, each of which was "evidence" relevant to theories of servability. For example, in one of the simpler studies, on each trial, one ball was put in the good serve basket or in the bad serve basket. Then the subject was asked what the implication of the outcome was for the theoretical variable that the subject thought was most likely to be causal. Thus a subject who believed that the ridging of a ball affected the quality of serves might be asked the implications of a large, light, rough, ridged ball producing a "good serve." If that same subject believed the color of the ball had the least effect on serving, they might be asked to evaluate the impact on this belief of the same ball producing a "poor serve."

More complex presentations were made in other studies, although the goal of the study was always the same, to evaluate the impact of the evidence on hand to the subject's theory. Thus a subject holding the view that ridging was important might be presented a good serve basket containing the following balls:

- large, dark, rough, ridged
- small, light, rough, ridged
- large, light, rough, ridged
- large, light, smooth, nonridged
- small, dark, rough, ridged
- small, dark, smooth, nonridged

The same subject would be presented a poor serve basket containing the following balls:

- large, light, rough, ridged
- small, dark, rough, ridged
- small, light, smooth, nonridged
- large, dark, smooth, nonridged
- large, light, smooth, nonridged
- small, dark, smooth, nonridged

For this example, five-sixths of the evidence supports the view that ridging is a determinant of servability. Such an outcome is certainly consistent with the theory that ridging produces servability, although it does not prove it. (Recall from Chapter 1 that correlation does not imply causation.) An outcome that would not be consistent with the theory that ridging affected servability would be half the balls in the good basket were ridged and half were not ridged.

There were a variety of variations in presenting evidence and differences in the questions asked in these studies. For example, when subjects in one study were presented two baskets of six balls, they were asked to determine whether the data were more consistent with the theory that color of the balls mattered or smoothness mattered. (For the example presented earlier, there is more evidence for smoothness as a potent variable, with rough balls being slightly more servable than smooth balls; servability does not covary at all with color, with equal numbers of light and dark balls in the good and poor bins.)

By getting judgments from grade 3 through college students and philosophers on such problems, it was possible to come to a number of conclusions about how students evaluate scientific data, both the strengths and weaknesses of such evaluation efforts.

Some of the more important conclusions from this series of studies were the following:

1. There is improvement in evidence evaluation skills from childhood to adolescence to adulthood, although even college-student adults do not evaluate evidence as skillfully as philosopher experts. Thus, many of the evaluation shortcomings that follow are more pronounced in elementary students than in adolescents or in college students.

2. People interpret evidence that favors a theory they support one way and the identical evidence differently when it conflicts with a nonpreferred theory. For example, if they favor the theory that ridging affects servability, they are often quite willing to interpret a single good serve by a ridged ball as evidence of ridging as a causal variable; in contrast, if they do not favor the theory that ridging is a determinant of servability, they are less willing to accept a good serve with a single ridged ball as supportive of the theory that ridging matters in servability. Kuhn et al. (1988) concluded from such observations that people often cannot separate theory and evidence. A person who can keep theory and evidence separate permits the evidence to have equal impact on the evaluation of a theory regardless of whether the theory is one preferred by the subject. This observation is one that is reported frequently by science educators. See Johsua and Dupin (1987) for examples of elementary students who were adroit at explaining away evidence that was inconsistent with their personally held theories.

3. People often ignore evidence that is not consistent with their preferred theories. They sometimes distort evidence to make it consistent with their own theories (e.g., explaining away discrepant evidence by appealing to some third variable that must be operating to distort the situation).

4. People often make the mistake that correlation implies causation. For example, that five of the six balls in the good basket are ridged and five of the six balls in the bad basket are not ridged does not prove that ridging causes servability. An alternative possibility is that ridging covaries with some other variable—perhaps the ridged balls are made of a different material than the nonridged balls.

5. Many people do not understand the concept of covariation, for example, believing that some inference about covariation could be made given only one ball in one of the baskets. One light-colored ball or one dark-colored ball cannot be informative about the effect of color on servability—at a minimum, there must be some variation in color, which requires evidence from at least two balls. Thus a light ball in the good basket and a dark ball in the bad basket reflect covariation; covariation in the other direction would be reflected by a dark ball in the good basket and a light ball in the bad basket; noncovariation would be represented by both balls in one of the baskets.

6. People have difficulties comparing two theories at once, paying attention only to a subset of the information available. Thus, to decide whether there was more support for smoothness versus roughness as a causal variable or color (i.e., in the previous example), it is necessary to compare the ratios of smooth to rough balls in both the good and bad baskets as well as the ratios of light to dark balls in each basket. Many subjects will calculate only one of the ratios and make a decision about the relative strengths of the two potential causal variables.

7. People do not recognize that when variables do not covary, causality is not possible. (Correlation does not imply causation, but causation implies correlation.) Noncovariation for color in the six-ball example would be reflected by three light and three dark balls in each bin. If one held the theory that light balls are more servable, six light balls in the good bin and six dark balls in the poor bin would reflect perfect covariation. If there were six dark balls in the good bin and six light ones in the poor bin, it would not support the theory that light balls are more servable but certainly is consistent with the theory that color matters (i.e., covariation in the other direction). People confuse noncovariation and covariation in the direction opposite to the one they supposed might be operative.

8. People have difficulty making sense of mixed evidence. Thus, that only five-sixths of the evidence in the previous example was consistent with covariation between ridging and servability sometimes leads to the assumption that ridging and servability do not covary. The small amount of evidence not consistent with co-

variation is weighed heavily against covariation. That is, people do not understand that scientific evidence is probabilistic and often is not completely consistent with one theory or another.

In summary, Kuhn et al. (1988) produced evidence that people often failed to see relationships that existed in data. Other times they claim the existence of relationships that could not be inferred rationally from the evidence on hand. Although there were developmental improvements in the evaluation of evidence, consistent with the conclusion that children have more difficulty than adults in coordinating theories and evidence potentially relevant to theories (Kuhn, 1989), there was still great variability in the abilities of adults to interpret evidence. Philosophers rarely made logical errors; college students did not do as well as philosophers but were much better at evaluation of evidence than adults not enrolled in college. Kuhn et al. (1988) complemented this research on evaluation with research on whether people can generate evidence consistent with particular theories, with that work generating additional evidence of difficulty in separating theory and evidence.

Generation of Evidence

A critical scientific skill is knowing what types of outcomes would support a theory and what would not support it. For example, a scientist cannot begin to plan a test of a theory without knowing in advance the nature of evidence that would provide compelling support for the theory as well as the nature of evidence that would be inconsistent with the theory. For example, to evaluate the development of competence to generate scientific evidence, Kuhn et al. (1988) asked subjects to generate evidence supporting their preferred explanation of servability:

> You said that *size* makes a difference in how a serve comes out. Suppose now that the company did a test using these balls, and the results of the test proved that you're right. In other words, the results showed that *size* makes a difference in how a serve comes out. Can you show how the results would have to come out to prove that you're right? In other words, what balls would result in a good serve and what balls would result in a bad serve in order to prove that you're right that size makes a difference in how a serve comes out? Can you put them in the baskets to show me? You can use as many or as few balls in your test as you want. (Subject completes the place-

ment of balls in baskets.) Can you explain how this proves that size makes a difference in how a serve comes out? (pp. 162–163)

Subjects were also asked to generate evidence that a theory was wrong:

> Suppose now that someone else thinks you're wrong when you say that *size* makes a difference, and they believe that *size* does not make a difference. Can you show me how the results would have to come out to prove you're wrong and this other person is right? In other words, what balls would result in a good serve and what balls would result in a bad serve in order to prove that you're wrong when you say that size makes a difference in how a serve comes out? Can you put them in the baskets to show me? You can use as many or as few balls in your test as you want. (Subject completes the placement of balls in baskets.) Can you explain how this proves that you're wrong in saying *size* makes a difference in how a serve comes out? (p. 163)

In addition to generating evidence for preferred theories, subjects were also asked to generate evidence for theories they did not hold (i.e., the theories of some "other" causal variable than their preferred explanation; e.g., *color* determines servability).

In general, the outcomes were consistent with the evaluation study outcomes:

1. In general, there were developmental improvements from grade 3 to college, with college students better at generation of evidence than noncollege adults.
2. Participants were better able to produce evidence of covariation than evidence of noncovariation. Only college students were highly proficient at generating evidence of noncovariation, with a frequent error among young students generating covariation opposite in direction to their belief (e.g., claiming a nonridged ball producing a good serve and a ridged ball producing a bad serve—with the other variables held constant—is an example of noncovariation because they expected ridging to produce the good serve and nonridging the bad serve).
3. The most prevalent difficulty in generating covariation evidence was a failure to control other variables. For example, subjects were willing to make claims of a clear covariation between ridging and servability with presentation of a confounded comparison, perhaps of a large, light, rough, ridged ball producing a good serve and a

small, dark, smooth, nonridged ball producing a poor serve. Ridging is confounded (covaries) with all three other variables in this example. A two-ball example providing clearer support of covariation between ridging and servability would be a large, light, rough, ridged ball producing a good serve and a large, light, rough, nonridged ball not doing so. In general, younger subjects were not as proficient in generating evidence of covariation as they had been in evaluating evidence of covariation.

4. It was easier to generate evidence compatible with one's own theory than evidence incompatible with one's own beliefs.

Consistent with the evaluation data, there were substantial difficulties in the generation of evidence, and, in particular, there were more difficulties in working with noncovariation than with covariation. Although there was evidence in both the evaluation and the generation data that younger students in particular experience difficulties isolating and manipulating single variables (or understanding manipulations of single variables), in contrast to Piaget's (e.g., Inhelder & Piaget, 1958) theory, Kuhn et al. (1988) do not ascribe the difficulties they observed to lack of formal operations. Rather they raised the possibility that young students lack "experimentation strategies." A person with an experimenting strategy knows to focus on one variable at a time—varying that variable while holding other factors constant. Thus, information about roughness is provided when a small, dark, rough, ridged ball is compared with a small, dark, smooth, ridged ball but not if a large, dark, rough, ridged ball is compared with a small, dark, smooth, ridged ball (i.e., size and roughness or darkness are confounded in the latter comparison). The importance of having such an experimenting strategy will be considered further later in this section.

Skills of Argument

Kuhn (1991) extended the work reported thus far, examining adults' abilities to generate and evaluate arguments. Adults across the life span were presented three problems from the social sciences, all ones that are pursued actively by social scientists, although all ones that are known to be extremely complex: (1) What causes prisoners to return to crime after they are released? (2) What causes children to fail in school? (3) What causes unemployment? Kuhn

(1991) selected these problems because they tapped domains in which people are likely to have theories, if for no other reason than the prevalence and importance of these problems to society.

Each adult was interviewed to determine whether he or she had a theory regarding the problem. Thus, for the crime question, subjects were asked, "What causes prisoners to return to crime after they're released?" If they offered multiple theories, they were then asked, "Which of these would you say is the major cause of prisoners' returning to crime?" They were then probed to determine how they knew this was the cause and were asked to give evidence that might be offered to convince someone else that the causal factor they identified was correct.

An important characteristic of a theory is that it can be falsified. That is, a good theory specifies what should not be observed if the theory is correct. If these unexpected observations occur, there is reason to reject the theory, to falsify the theory (Popper, 1961). Whether people are capable of engaging in the argumentative skills required to specify a theory so that it would be falsifiable was also addressed in this study by asking subjects to indicate observations that would be inconsistent with the subject's theory: "Suppose now that someone disagreed with your view that this is the cause. What might *they* say to show that you are wrong? What evidence might this person give to try to show that you were wrong? Could someone prove that you're wrong?"

A good theoretical thinker also can respond to contrary evidence. To determine whether subjects would be able to rebut contrary evidence, they were asked the following: "Would you be able to prove this person wrong? What could you say to show that your own view is the correct one?"

Finally, subjects' theories about the nature of knowledge were examined, including whether they believed there were absolutely correct positions and that multiple perspectives could all be valid: "How sure are you about what causes prisoners to return to crime? Do experts know for sure what causes prisoners to return to crime? Would it be possible for experts to find out for sure if they studied this problem long and carefully enough? How sure are you of your view compared to an expert? Is more than one point of view possible regarding the question of what causes prisoners to return to crime? Could more than one point of view be right?"

Many of the participants in this study had a great deal of difficulty in constructing arguments, potential counter evidence, and rebuttals, and thinking about the nature of theories and arguments. Although college-educated adults were better able to think about argumentation than were adults who had not attended college, there were many shortcomings prevalent in the thinking of all participants, including the following:

- Regardless of the issue (crime, school, employment), no more than 22 percent of the participants understood that theories are products of hard cognitive work and that good theories could not possibly be absolutely right, although they are far better reasoned than mere personal opinions. Indeed, 49 percent of subjects believed there were absolute answers to the crime question, 50 percent to the school failure issue, and 65% to unemployment. The participants in Kuhn (1991) certainly did not view theories as scientists do, as tentative models, with the possibility that one model might account better for some phenomena (e.g., males returning to crime) and another model account better for related phenomena (e.g., females returning to crime). Rather, consistent with previous studies of adult thinking (e.g., Perry, 1970; see Chapter 9, this text), many of Kuhn's (1991) adult subjects believed that it is really possible to know something and that some authorities with great expertise do know the answers to problems of crime, school failure, and unemployment.
- The majority of participants were confident about the correctness of their theories, with confidence especially high when they were close to a problem area (i.e., parole officers were confident about their theories about crimes; teachers were confident about their theories about school failure). This is despite the fact that experts view all three problems to be complex and impossible to explain definitively.
- The majority of participants had a difficult time generating legitimate scientific evidence to support their positions (e.g., citing a covariation between the causal determinant they favored and the undesirable outcome). Genuine evidence was produced by 39 percent, 48 percent, and 40 percent of the subjects for the crime, school, and unemployment questions.
- Although a clear majority of participants (58 percent for crime, 69 percent for school failure, 66 percent for unemployment) could generate

theories alternative to their own, they had great difficulty generating counterarguments to their own theories (successful 48 percent of the time for crime, 52 percent for school failure, 41 percent for unemployment). Rebuttals were also difficult for the majority of subjects, with the respective percentages of successful rebuttals being 42 percent, 49 percent, and 50 percent. Integrative rebuttals, including additional support for the original theory while discounting the alternative, were much rarer, occurring 21 percent, 32 percent, and 22 percent of the time for the three issues.

Scientists and social scientists routinely pose theories, think about alternatives, and defend their own positions relative to alternatives. Such rhetorical competencies are essential to participation in the scientific community, a community that rejects the idea that there could be positions that are absolutely correct. That Kuhn was not expecting the impossible from her subjects was obvious by considering the responses of philosophers to the same questions posed to other subjects in Kuhn (1991). Philosophers could advance theories, imagine alternatives and contrary evidence, and think of ways they might respond to evidence inconsistent with their theory. A major challenge for science education is to devise instruction that will result in a much higher proportion of the adult population being able to engage in scientific argument. Given that so much of science education is memorization of facts provided by absolute authorities, such as textbooks and teachers, is it any surprise that students believe in absolute authority? When science education does not encourage questioning of authority and the generation and testing of alternative theories, is it any wonder that most adults are not able to think deeply about theories and evidence? Kuhn's (1991) data on argument skills provide plenty of motivation for rethinking the way students are taught to think about scientific theories and scientific thinking. Kuhn and her colleagues are also assuming leadership in the development of educational opportunities that might produce more capable scientific thinking, with some of her research in this arena taken up in the next subsection.

Scaffolded Practice Performing Experiments

In a number of studies, Kuhn and her colleagues have evaluated the possibility that students may learn scientific procedures through practice doing tasks requiring the procedures for success. In the two studies discussed here, subjects were provided multiple trials working on scientific problems designed to illuminate particular scientific procedures. The first was concerned with children learning how to evaluate and generate evidence. The second focused on children learning how to make unconfounded comparisons, learning how to control variables (i.e., how to make the tests Piagetians consider indicative of formal operational competence, as discussed earlier in this section). The adult experimenter provided scaffolded support in these studies, nudging the child gently to "discover" a strategy or way of thinking about data. There were substantial improvements in many children's scientific thinking skills observed in these studies.

Kuhn et al. (1988, Study 5) investigated the acquisition of evidence evaluation and generation skills in the context of the "balls" problem considered earlier in this section. Over the course of nine sessions, grade-5 and grade-6 students were asked to generate evidence to show a theory to be correct, generate evidence of theory incorrectness, evaluate insufficient evidence, evaluate theory-consistent and theory-inconsistent covariation evidence, evaluate mixed evidence, and evaluate unequal evidence for two competing theories. As subjects attempted problems, the experimenter provided prompts directing attention to important evidence that the subject ignored. For example, if the subject used only evidence from one of the two baskets to generate an evaluation, the experimenter pointed out the evidence in the basket that was ignored. Sometimes the experimenter would elicit information about potential strategies that might be used by asking the subject to reflect and respond to how someone else performed a task (e.g., Another person thought that size was what caused them to come out different. What do you think of that person's idea?).

Many of Kuhn et al.'s (1988, Study 5) students (but not all) made progress in learning how to evaluate and generate evidence. A particular strength of Kuhn et al. (1988, Study 5) was the inclusion of a control condition that did not receive practice on the balls task but did receive experimenter attention by working on another problem-solving task during the time corresponding to when the "balls" subjects worked on balls problems. Although the balls subjects and the control subjects performed identically and poorly on a pretest involving evaluation and

generation of evidence on balls problems, the balls subjects were much better able to evaluate and generate evidence on the posttest.

In Kuhn and Phelps (1982), grade-4 and grade-5 subjects who did not have an isolation-of-variables strategy were presented problems involving mixtures of chemicals producing reactions. Thus, they observed an experimenter pour three chemicals in a beaker containing a fourth chemical with a resulting reaction (liquid turns red). The experimenter then poured three other chemicals in a container with the same fourth chemical and produced a different reaction (liquid turns cloudy). The subjects were then asked to plan and carry out experiments to determine what caused the reaction producing red and what caused the reaction producing cloudiness. (In both cases, combining one of the three chemicals with the fourth chemical was sufficient to cause the reaction observed.) As the child attempted a solution to this problem, the experimenter encouraged the child to analyze what they were doing and to interpret their results. There were 11 to 13 sessions of such problem solving, with problems becoming more complicated as sessions continued (i.e., combinations of several liquids produced reactions instead of combinations of two chemicals). An optimal response in this situation included generating a genuine *hypothesis* (e.g., "It could be either B or C that is making it red," or "I want to see if D has anything to do with it"), a genuine *experiment involving manipulation* of a variable or variables of interest while holding other variables constant, and a legitimate *inference* based on the manipulation (e.g., "It's B because it turned cloudy when we tried it by itself," or "It's not C because C alone didn't do anything"). Such an optimal approach reflects understanding and use of the isolation-of-variables strategy.

At first, none of the subjects engaged in valid, efficient experimentation. By the end of the 11 to 13 trials, many subjects were performing experiments and making valid inferences. This outcome led Kuhn and Phelps (1982) to conclude that strategic experimenting behaviors (i.e., isolation-of-variables, to use the Piagetian term) can become more sophisticated when students work in a problem arena, albeit with prompts and hints and indirect feedback about how to proceed. What was also apparent in the study, however, was that figuring out how to experiment was a long-term affair with uneven progress. It was not unusual for a student to perform a true experimental manipulation during one session and then revert to less systematic testing at the beginning of the next session. Kuhn and Phelps concluded that their subjects not only were learning the new isolation-of-variables strategy, but also had to extinguish inefficient strategies (i.e., simply to proceed unsystematically, messing around) and that inefficient strategies were slow to go. (Recall from Chapter 2 the discussion of how elementary students can benefit from applying a new strategy relative to a more familiar approach and yet not use the new strategy in the future. Experiencing success with a new strategy one time is not enough to ensure that a new strategy will be adopted and used in the future.)

It was also not unusual for students to believe they understood the factors affecting the chemical reaction before they actually did so (i.e., they failed to monitor their understanding, consistent with other reports of failure to monitor discussed previously; see Chapter 2, this volume). In short, the scaffolded discovery learning that was observed here (i.e., students tried out strategies while receiving feedback from an adult) required a number of trials for students who were successful in acquiring the isolation-of-variables strategy, with these successful students manifesting a number of processing deficiencies (e.g., failing to monitor their understanding, failing to stick with a successful strategy). In addition, almost half of the students were not successful in consistently applying the isolation-of-variables strategy.

There is evidence of increases in knowledge of scientific procedures (e.g., control-of-variables strategy, rules for evaluating evidence) through scaffolded experience in attempting to evaluate and generate evidence or conduct mini-experiments. The type of teaching considered in this subsection is completely constructivist, involving adults structuring the situation so students are likely to discover how to be scientific. These studies seem important to us because they are addressing the effects of a type of learning that science educators value, students learning from personal experimentation and grappling with evidence. Moreover, this is a type of learning that has been valued by some, at least since Dewey (see Robertson, 1992). What the research reviewed in this chapter reveals, however, is that children are not nearly as facile at drawing conclusions from trial-and-error experiences as Dewey believed, and thus this work is not rewarmed Dewey but rather a whole new vision of the challenges a child faces in constructing an understanding of the world through experimentation.

Much more work of this type is needed, and we are optimistic it will get done. One reason is that scientific microworlds are becoming ever more common, and as they do, they permit a perfect opportunity for experiments in which student experiences in such worlds are structured in various ways (e.g., White, 1984). For example, it should be possible to determine if science procedures might be learned more certainly and efficiently with slightly more direct explanations and modeling. This seems likely because other researchers have succeeded in teaching students to control variables using explicit instructions and feedback, at least with respect to some traditional tasks used to tap formal operational competence. For example, Case (1974) taught 7- to 8-year-olds how to control other variables to determine factors affecting the flexibility of rods. Lawson and Wollman (1976) taught grade-5 and grade-7 students to control variables on the same task with some transfer to other Piagetian tasks observed (e.g., pendulum). In research to date (see Ross, 1988, for a review), training students to control variables has been more effective with more intense instruction of individual students than during classroom instruction and when training has occurred across contexts (e.g., school and non-school).

One extremely intriguing possibility suggested by Lawson and Wollman's (1976) analysis (also Danner & Day, 1977) is that acquisition of strategies such as control-of-variables will be easier, more certain, and more generalizable for students who have attained formal operations. Additional study of this possibility in particular could do much to illuminate when it makes sense to offer instruction in sophisticated strategies of experimentation such as control-of-variables.

As working scientists, we know that there are no more important scientific skills than understanding how to make controlled comparisons and knowing how to evaluate and generate scientific evidence. Our years of experience in teaching methodology courses to undergraduate and graduate students have made us all too aware of the number of students who cannot design a controlled comparison, confuse covariation and causality, fail to recognize that noncovariation and causality are incompatible, and cannot anticipate scientific outcomes that would support theories they hold or outcomes that would explicitly clash with their views.

As teachers of scientific methods, we are also aware, however, that there is little time in the curriculum to teach these skills. One traditional solution for experimental psychologists has been to teach methods and content simultaneously (e.g., Underwood, 1966), with scientists designing and carrying out studies related to some important content in experimental psychology (e.g., designing studies of distributed practice effects as such effects are discussed as content in a course on learning). We believe that such combined methods and content teaching ought to be possible in developing high-quality methods instruction for elementary and high school students. We are heartened by exciting attempts to do so, such as Linn, Clement, Pulos, and Sullivan's (1989) teaching of the control-of-variables strategy as content about blood pressure was taught to high school students. Carey, Evans, Honda, Jay, and Unger (1989) taught grade-7 students about the nature and purpose of science, hypothesis testing, experimentation, and evaluation of data as part of lessons on yeast. Lawson and Snitgen (1982) taught college students about how to make controlled tests as biology content was covered.

A FEW MORE THOUGHTS ON DISCOVERY LEARNING

Many science educators seem to remain committed to discovery learning experiences as part of science education, despite the fact that induction is inefficient at best and uncertain in outcome. There is no research on the horizon that is likely to identify ways of overcoming these limitations. Schauble (1990) provided an example of how even guided discovery (i.e., participation scaffolded by an adult who nudges the student in the direction of potentially important information) is associated with slow progress in coming to understand a scientific problem and a substantial percentage of students who do not solve a problem after a reasonable period of time.

Grade-5 and grade-6 students in Schauble (1990) interacted with a microworld involving racing cars (i.e., a racing game run on a microcomputer). Children planned, carried out, and evaluated experiments aimed at determining the variables affecting the speed of the racing cars. The game permitted the construction of 48 different racing cars by selecting one value for each of five features: (1) Engine: large or small? (2) Fin: on or off? (3) Wheels: large, medium, or small? (4) Color: red or blue? and (5)

Muffler: on or off? Other things equal, large-engined cars were faster (i.e., went farther given the time permitted for the race) than small-engined cars. Medium-wheeled cars were faster than small-wheeled or large-wheeled cars. Not having a fin increased the speed of large-engined cars but had no effect on the speed of small-engined cars. Neither color nor the muffler variables affected speed. The computer program permitted the racing of up to three cars at a time as well as the storage of results from experiments for review.

Of course, children arrived at the microworld with some prior beliefs about what affects speed of racing cars, and thus each child's initial theory of speed was assessed during the first session. For example, many children believed that big engines, no muffler, and either small or large wheels would increase speed. After their theories were assessed, the children were told that their task was to determine what factors did affect the speed of the racing cars, and they were showed how to design cars using the computer program and how to conduct the experimental races. After cars for the race were designed, the child was asked what would be learned from the experiment and to make a prediction about the outcome of the race. Then the child ran the race. The experimenter asked the child to explain the outcome. If the child's explanation focused only on a personal theory and failed to include evidence from the test run, the experimenter probed: "What do the road-tests tell you about (one of the features)?" Several tests were run each session, and sessions continued for 8 weeks.

Over the course of the 8 weeks, there were improvements in understanding the variables affecting the speed of the cars. In particular, 2 of the 22 participants figured out that the presence of the tail fin interacted with engine size; the number who believed the muffler was not a causal factor more than doubled from 8 students at pretest to 17 students at the end of 8 weeks; and 21 participants believed by the end of the study that medium wheels were fastest, compared with 5 who held this belief at the pretest. Increases in knowledge about the variables affecting speed permitted much better predictions at the end of the 8 weeks than at the beginning of the study.

In short, consistent with the Kuhn studies, Schauble observed that students could induce understandings by personally experimenting with variables, at least given the cuing provided by the experimenter, which included some powerful hints about what might be gained from controlled comparisons. Nonetheless, the students were not efficient in generating information, sometimes figuring out a causal relation in one session and then forgetting about it in the next session (see Hancock, Kaput, & Goldsmith, 1992, for another example of students failing to coordinate across days progress made during scientific exploration). Schauble's students were not adept at monitoring their progress in understanding the causal variables in the microworld. Some children, however, consistently made confounded comparisons (e.g., trying to interpret a comparison between a large-engined, finless, medium-tired, *red, mufflerless* car with a large-engined, finless, medium-tired, *blue, mufflered* car). Invalid inferences (i.e., from invalid comparisons) included both attributions of covariation (e.g., that a noncausal variable was causal) when covariation could not be inferred logically and failures to recognize noncovariation. Many invalid judgments reflected distortions (neglect) of evidence in ways that served to preserve the children's initial theories, with such distortions more common for children who had not acquired the control-of-variables strategy during the study.

Lest readers think that inefficiencies during discovery learning are restricted to children, reports of adult difficulties during discovery learning are published regularly. For example, Hardiman, Pollatsek, and Weel (1986) presented college students with Piaget's balance beam problems, which requires subjects to determine the rule for placing weights on a beam so that the beam balances on a fulcrum at the midpoint of the beam. (There is one solution to this problem. For each weight, calculate the product of the weight × distance from the fulcrum. Sum these products for each side of the beam. These sums must be equal on each side of the beam for the beam to be in balance.) The college students required a mean of 49 problems before they figured out the principle for balancing the beam, with the most efficient student needing only 30 trials. Even once subjects induced the rule, they sometimes reverted to solving subsequent balance beam problems with an incorrect procedure.

Given these difficulties with induction, is there any reason to continue with at least some discovery learning opportunities? Logically the answer is yes. If real science is anything, it is an inductive enterprise. The scientist's job largely is to discover the solutions to problems. There have been many examples in this text of the principle that part of learning to do complex tasks (e.g., read for comprehension, write coherent essays) is to practice doing them. It makes good sense from this perspective to give students discovery learning experiences if we want them to be able to discover in the future.

McDaniel and Schlager (1990, Experiment 2) provided evidence that experience in discovering problem solutions increases the ability to discover solutions for subsequent problems. College students were first given experiences with water jar problems:

> In a typical water-jar problem, the subject is asked to imagine a number of empty jars (usually three) on a counter, near a sink. Each jar can hold a specified volume of water, but has no graduated markings with which to hold fractional amounts. The subject is given the capacities of the three jars and an amount of water to be obtained. The object is to figure out a sequence of filling and emptying operations that will result in the goal amount residing in one of the jars. For example, the subject is told that Jar A can hold 7 units, Jar B can hold 24 units, and Jar C can hold 98 units. The goal is to obtain 60 units of water in Jar C. (McDaniel & Schlager, 1990, p. 142) [Solution to problem: Fill Jar C with 98 units of water, take out 7 units of water two times using Jar A, and remove 24 units of water one time with Jar B, resulting in 60 units in Jar C.]

All subjects in the study were given 16 practice problems, in sets of four. Each of the problems in a four-problem set could be solved using a particular "formula": (1) Fill one jar, twice remove the contents of another jar, and then add the contents of the third jar; (2) fill one jar and twice remove the quantity in one of the other jars and three times remove the quantity in the remaining jar; (3) fill one jar and remove once the quantity for one jar and twice the quantity for the other jar; and (4) fill one jar, twice remove the quantity for the other jar, and four times add the quantity of the third jar. In one condition, before attempting a set of four problems, the experimenter provided the solution rule; in the other condition of the study, subjects had to infer the rule themselves.

There were two types of transfer tasks, water jar problems involving applications of the exact rules that applied to the practice problems and water jar problems requiring discovery of novel rules. All participants were required to solve these transfer problems on their own (i.e., the experimenter did not provide the rules for solving any of the transfer problems). In general, there were small advantages for the "discovery" subjects in the speed of solving the transfer problems that involved application of previously practiced rules. More importantly, there were quite large advantages on problems requiring the discovery of new rules. The previous practice in inducing the solutions to problems seemed to increase the efficiency with which these college students grappled with problems in pursuit of a solution.

The McDaniel and Schlager (1990) data make obvious that we dare not abandon providing discovery-learning experiences as part of science education. The inefficiencies of discovery learning make clear as well, however, that if the purpose of an exercise is to ensure that all participants understand a scientific principle, more than an opportunity to discover the solution may be required. In addition, when time is a factor, and it is given the extent of the contemporary science curriculum, there are more efficient methods of conveying information than discovery learning. There is little evidence that not providing discovery experiences will limit the extent to which students can apply a procedure taught through direct explanation to situations requiring exactly that principle. (McDaniel & Schlager's [1990] subjects given direct explanation of the strategies that solved the practice problems applied those strategies quite well relative to control participants not taught the principles or provided practice with problems that could be solved with the procedures that were explained.)

Research on the appropriate balance of direct explanation and discovery experiences is badly needed. The either/or quality of this debate in the past is missing the possibility that these two approaches can both be used to accomplish different objectives in a science curriculum that includes a number of goals, including making certain that students know certain classic approaches to solving particular types of problems (which often can be accomplished using direct explanation) and guaranteeing that students are able to induce new solutions when presented new types of problems (which requires skills at discovery). In addition, much more work is needed on how the discovery process interacts with the prior knowledge the learner brings to the task. For example, Schauble, Glaser, Raghavan, and Reiner (1992), in a study of undergraduates attempting to solve electricity problems through ex-

perimentation, observed that both a student's general experimentation strategies and level of domain knowledge affected performance on the task. Discovery-learning (experimentation) strategies are similar to any other strategies in that they operate in coordination with other knowledge, although there has been much too little attention to the effects of prior knowledge on discovery in previous research.

ENCOURAGING FEMALES TO STUDY SCIENCE

Increasing the participation of women in science and mathematics is a priority of the scientific community (e.g., Committee on High School Biology Education, 1990), especially women who are members of minority groups (Task Force on Women, Minorities, and the Handicapped in Science and Technology, 1988). The main problem is not that women are not achieving at a high level when they choose to participate (e.g., women do better in college mathematics than do men, Bridgeman & Wendler, 1991), although there has been a tendency for boys to outperform girls on standardized assessments of science knowledge (e.g., Comber & Keeves, 1973; Erickson & Erickson, 1984; Levin, Sabaer, & Libman, 1991). Despite the achievement test differences, when analytical studies of basic processes directly pertinent to science have been conducted (e.g., the ability to formulate scientific hypotheses), there have not been gender differences between males and females who are talented enough to have a good chance of making it in science (Hoover & Feldhusen, 1990). The problem is probably not gender differences in scientific talent. The problem is that women are less likely than men to elect to study science and mathematics, even when they clearly have the ability to do well in technical fields (see Eccles, 1989; Jones & Wheatley, 1988; Swiatek & Benbow, 1991). The concern with increasing the science and mathematics participation of females has stimulated substantial research on potential reasons why females drop out of science and mathematics, with Jones and Wheatley (1988) providing an overview of potential determinants. Consideration of some of the more salient of the factors identified by Jones and Wheatley (which are consistent with those of others who have reviewed the same literature systematically; e.g., Eccles, 1989; Oakes, 1990; see also Chapter 13, this book) makes obvious that sex differences in science and mathematics learning and interest are probably multiply determined:

- Females have less confidence in their science abilities and are more likely to perceive science to be too difficult for them, with these feelings and perceptions apparent from the early elementary grades. Girls are more likely to perceive science as boring and irrelevant than are boys.
- The traits of successful scientists are ones considered masculine, such as independent, self-assertive, competitive, aggressive, dominant, and aloof. In contrast, females are socialized into personality patterns that undermine motivation to achieve in science. As Rossi (1965, p. 1201) put it, "A childhood model of the quiet, good, sweet girl will not produce many women engineers. It will produce the competent, loyal laboratory assistant who will not operate so readily on her own." Women consider science to be a male domain. This is reinforced by parents, teachers, and others who provide more science experiences for boys than for girls in the real world, including visits to factories and places where science is applied. Science is more likely to be an extracurricular activity for males than females (Kahle & Lakes, 1983; Kahle, Matyas, & Cho, 1985).
- Females seem to prefer activities with clear-cut rules that can be done in an exact fashion. Boys seem more comfortable with the discovery activities that are so much a part of science (e.g., Linn & Pulos, 1983).
- There are more male science teachers than female teachers, with male teachers especially likely to teach advanced and high-status courses. This reinforces media stereotypes of science being conducted by males, including depictions in science textbooks.
- Males receive more total interactions and more academic interactions with their science teachers than do females (e.g., Becker, 1982; Jones & Wheatley, 1990; Sabar & Levin, 1989; Taber, 1992; Walford, 1983), largely because boys assert themselves in science classes more than girls do (e.g., Sabar & Levin, 1989; Taber, 1992).
- Important adults in children's worlds (i.e., parents, teachers) often believe that science or math is not for females, with these beliefs negatively affecting the self-perceptions of females about

their scientific and mathematical abilities, which in turn negatively affects their performance in these areas (e.g., Jacobs, 1991).

One way to react to such a long list of determinants would be to conclude that the forces converging to shape sex differences in science and mathematics achievement and interest are overwhelming. Another way is to recognize that these multiple determinants permit multiple opportunities for intervention. Educational decision makers at all levels can elect options that decrease gender discrimination (e.g., Jacobs & Wigfield, 1989). For example, Jones and Wheatley (1988) catalogued many ways that teachers can make their teaching less sex biased. These include projecting clear expectations for science achievement by both girls and boys, doing all possible to ensure comparable interactions with girls and boys (e.g., making certain both girls and boys play active roles in science laboratory activities), and making reference to scientific contributions by both males and females. To the extent educators encourage female submissiveness, they undermine science achievement. When teachers encourage independence, self-reliance, and exploration, they encourage the development of scientific traits. Providing females with opportunities to experience science and mathematics hands-on through clubs and field trips is consistent with the development of science and mathematics participation. Teachers, counselors, and school administrators need to send the message that females can achieve in science and mathematics. (See also the summary in Chapter 13 of classroom factors that promote and undermine female motivation in technical areas.)

What is particularly encouraging at this point in time is that there is a great deal of interest in studying whether and how sex differences in science and mathematics interest and achievement can be reduced. Even more encouraging, interventions that are tried seem to work. For example, Mason and Kahle (1988) studied the effects of teaching science teachers how to create a more gender-free learning environment. The treatment did boost the interest of female students in science, with self-reported increases in participation in science activities outside of school. Martinez (1992) produced support for the hypothesis that modifying science materials and activities to enhance the interestingness of the activity and social appeal promotes the interest of girls in the activities (e.g., posing questions as part of the activity that elicit discussion, require joint answers, and sharing; personal references in the materials, such as "you"). Burbules and Linn (1988) observed that providing junior-high girls with additional experiences during laboratory exercises (i.e., enriched opportunities to examine the laboratory equipment and to generate hypotheses based on these examinations) improved their learning of scientific ideas that clashed with their misconceptions. Societies in which the organizations of the schools encourage girls to take science and mathematics (e.g., Finland, Thailand) are being studied, with evidence that girls achieve and participate at the same high levels as boys when the educational system supports the view that females can achieve in science (Klainen & Fensham, 1987; Klainen, Fensham, & West, 1989; Skaalvik, 1990). For example, in Thailand, 80% of the chemistry and 50% of the physics teachers are female; girls often participate more actively than boys in Thai science classrooms. There is a cost, however, in that some freedom is eliminated: Science is more of a "required" than an elective option in Thailand secondary schooling.

Assuming that American society is not likely to move away from elective participation in science and mathematics, it makes sense to determine factors that can increase the elective appeal of advanced sciences and mathematics. Science educators such as Koballa (1988) are doing so, determining who grade-8 girls are most likely to believe with respect to recommendations to take science. That they believe Mom and Dad suggests that a great deal of effort should be aimed at encouraging parents to encourage their daughters to take science; that they find women science teachers credible provides another vote of support for increasing the number of female science teachers who can serve as role models; and that they are likely to believe a boy high school student highlights the need to socialize students who elect science to think about science in a nonsexist fashion because the attitudes of these students may go far in encouraging or discouraging their friends, brothers, and sisters to take science. Successes in identifying ways of improving female attitudes toward science and mathematics and the great need to do so given the economic demands of the nation for a technically proficient population will combine to fuel more research on factors affecting female participation in science. This is a must-research area in the 1990s.

CONCLUDING COMMENTS

The lack of true experimentation in science education research is striking. Although the many case studies and uncontrolled pretest-to-posttest qualitative analyses conducted by the science educator community permit rich instructional theory, especially about conceptual change, there has not been enough testing of that theory in true experiments. Because most of the conceptual change interventions discussed here are not long term, at least with respect to any particular misconception, true experiments should be possible at a reasonable cost. We are heartened that leaders in the science education community share this concern. As president of the National Association for Research in Science Teaching, William G. Holliday (1990) of the University of Maryland urged more experimentation:

> People who say, "Experimental designs are out of fashion or cannot answer interesting questions in science education" are treading on thin scientific ice. Their argument is double talk because, on the one hand, experimental scientific research is the established mechanism of assessing functional relationships and is a necessary ingredient in theory development. . . . (p. 2)

In doing so, Holliday (1990) urged appropriately complex and ecologically valid designs, a point that seems essential to us:

> . . . [B]ut, on the other hand, some of the experiments of past years are incredibly uninteresting and unproductive. . . . But, researchers favoring experimental investigation need to capitalize on the opportunities by asking questions mindful of classroom context, [incorporating] valid and realistic designs, and multivariate process and performance measures. (p. 2)

A theme that appears repeatedly in the science education literature is that the amount of material covered in science should be reduced, in favor of a strategy of covering especially important concepts in depth. We recognize fully that the conceptual change instruction detailed here requires more than the typical lecture or textbook presentations that are now science education and thus agree with the general sentiment that if important concepts are to be taught thoroughly, there will probably need to be some reduction in the overall coverage. One of the reasons that science education is challenging is because to participate in scientific discourse, it is necessary to be armed with a large technical vocabulary, so it is not realistic to believe that there can be wholesale elimination of much of the factual learning that has traditionally been associated with science instruction.

A realistic psychology of science learning must be multifaceted, dealing both with deeply held misconceptions and factual information that is completely new or almost so. There are many techniques already covered in this book that are equal to the second task. In fairness to the science education community, some of their members are already studying some of the conventional mechanisms that can improve comprehension and learning of science and other things. (In fairness to the authors doing such work as well, we point out that a high proportion of the citations that follow this paragraph included better controlled evaluations than typify the science education literature as a whole.)

For example, there are demonstrations of the positive effects on learning of science from advance organizers (e.g., Healy, 1989; Willerman & MacHarg, 1991), adjunct questions (e.g., Holliday & Benson, 1991; Holliday & McGuire, 1992; Pearson, 1991), elaborative interrogation (see Chapter 10, this book; e.g., Woloshyn, Paivio, & Pressley, 1992; Wood, Pressley, & Winne, 1990), alternative types of discourse (e.g., Dhindsa & Anderson, 1992), and dual-coding through instructive illustrations and animation. Studies of the effects of dynamic pictures on learning are particularly timely because they may stimulate the construction of mental models (Mayer, 1989a; see Chapter 3, this volume). Illustrations and animations may facilitate the construction of both verbal and imaginal representations of dynamic processes (e.g., how a pump works as in Mayer & Anderson [1991, 1992], Mayer & Gallini [1990], Rieber [1990]; how a brake works, in Mayer [1989b]). Illustrations can also increase the memorability of important details (e.g., Waddill, McDaniel, & Einstein, 1988). Dee-Lucas and Larkin (1991) have demonstrated that students often can understand scientific proofs better if they are explained using ordinary language rather than mathematical equations. In addition, there have been studies of new technologies, such as interactive videodiscs (e.g., Hofmeister, Engelmann, & Carnine, 1989; Leonard, 1989, 1992) and microworlds (e.g., Faryniarz & Lockwood, 1992), technologies that permit much more "experimentation" as part of simulations compared with the experimentation permit-

ted when materials must be gathered as part of a "wet" or hands-on laboratory.

Our view is that many of these approaches that are now on the periphery of the science education discipline, which has been and is obsessed with conceptual change, should probably be moved more toward center stage. There needs to be some extensive thinking about how various methods of teaching can be combined to achieve a variety of science education goals, including conceptual change, construction of multiple representations of concepts entirely new to students, and development of scientific habits (e.g., commitment to isolation-of-variables strategies because of many demonstrations in microworlds that such a strategy permits generation of interpretable data).

As we conclude this chapter, we find ourselves especially disturbed about Deanna Kuhn's findings. Many students, including college students, cannot reason scientifically. There are no skills more valuable to a scientist than knowledge of the methods that permit creation of new knowledge and evaluation of scientific evidence. Kuhn's data make clear that much attention needs to be given to increasing a few fundamental thinking skills in the nation's students, including abilities to understand and generate experiments, understand and generate correlational data, and communicate clearly about theoretical positions.

We are encouraged that Kuhn and her associates view important scientific competencies, such as control-of-variables, as strategies that can be learned by students rather than competencies determined by factors generally considered to be out of instructional control (e.g., Piagetian stages). What is more discouraging, however, is that there has not been more thought about the important strategies that should be imparted during science teaching. Not surprisingly, given the lack of concern with procedural knowledge, there is little about metacognition in the science education literature, either. More positively, a great deal of thought about other types of knowledge has occurred, although there has been emphasis on misconceptions and conceptual change over other aspects of knowledge. Thinking about motivation is rudimentary. Yes, there are concerns about increasing motivations of females to take science and a strong belief that conceptual conflict motivates conceptual change. Even so, motivation is treated superficially compared with other treatments now in the literature. It will be awhile before it will be possible to construct an empirically defensible description of science learning consistent with the strategies-metacognition-knowledge-motivation framework that pervades this book. That there are some investigations of strategies and motivation provides hope for more; with investigations of strategies, there will undoubtedly also be investigations of metacognition, especially awareness of where and when to use strategies and the utility of the strategies being learned.

There is growing commitment to direct explanation teaching and scaffolded practice, with a great deal of theoretical commentary about the potential benefits of socially interactive forms of science teaching. Still the science educators have made less progress in validating such instruction than have workers in other areas. That exceptionally prominent cognitive scientists (e.g., Ann Brown) and science educators (e.g., Audrey Champagne) are making strong cases for such instruction fuels optimism that analytical research will follow.

We hope some readers take from this chapter the perspective that there are great opportunities here for scientists interested in instruction. There are fascinating theoretical ideas here that need evaluation and additional fleshing out with respect to more constructs than science educators have favored in the past. More sophisticated theory and excellent research in this arena might go far in increasing our understanding of how to educate more and better scientists. This is an urgent national goal, and thus the educational researchers who take on science education can be optimistic that they will be doing research that certainly will count on many fronts and be embraced by many audiences.

For readers who might wish to read more about this national crisis, Herbert Walberg (1991) provided a concise yet sweeping appraisal of the challenges facing science education as well as potential solutions. Every line of his article deserves national reflection and considered study by all interested in the scientific development of the nation, and we urge you to make the trip to the library to read his important article.

13

Mathematical Problem Solving

Many educational and cognitive psychologists are interested in mathematics education and mathematical cognition. One reason is that problem solving was one of the first arenas that information processing–oriented psychologists studied (see Newell & Simon, 1972). Although the problems given to subjects to solve in the earlier days of information processing were often artificial (e.g., how to get cannibals and missionaries across a body of water given constraints on the size of a boat and the ratio of cannibals to missionaries on any one trip likely to result in the survival of the missionaries), with every passing year, the problems studied by cognitive researchers have had a more familiar look. The cognition and instruction literature pertaining to familiar mathematics is so large, in fact, that much greater selectivity is necessary in this chapter than was the case for science. Even so, there is so much research on problem solving that this is the longest chapter in the book.

What is presented here is research that simultaneously is representative of contemporary research on mathematical problem solving and is directly pertinent to mathematics education. Because much of the most educationally relevant research has been conducted in elementary mathematics, there is a great deal of work pertaining to arithmetic. To be certain, cognitive psychologists are thinking about algebra, geometry, calculus, and probability (Nesher & Kilpatrick, 1990), but the empirical efforts in these

areas pale in comparison to the voluminous data on elementary arithmetic operations.

INSTRUCTION OF GENERAL PROBLEM-SOLVING STRATEGIES

When I [MP] was a sophomore in high school, there was a terrifying experience that occurred about every 2 weeks: Word problems would be assigned as homework in algebra II! In the midst of going over word problem homework, a classmate once posed a question that had occurred to many students in the class: "Is there anything we could read that would tell us how to solve word problems?" Of course, the students in the class expected an answer such as, "No, you just have to work at it," or "Nothing worthwhile is easy." But on that day, the teacher provided a different answer. "There is . . . a book called *How to Solve It* by a mathematician named George Polya." Unfortunately, none of the students in the class tracked down the book.

If they had, what they would have found was a set of general strategies designed to be used whenever attempting to solve a problem (adapted from Polya, 1957):

Understand the problem. Example approaches for doing so:

Ask yourself, "What am I looking for?"

Ask yourself, "What information is given in the problem?"

Try drawing a diagram to illustrate what is given in the problem and what needs to be solved.

Then, devise a plan for solving the problem. Example approaches for doing so:

Ask yourself, "Do I know a similar problem?"

Ask yourself, "Do I know an easier problem that might be related to this one or be one of the components of this one?"

Ask yourself, "Can I restate the problem?"

Try solving a related problem.

Try to solve part of the problem.

Carry out the plan.

Look back. Example approaches for doing so:

Check the calculations and result.

Try to get the same result using a different method.

Ask yourself whether this solution plan might work for another problem (e.g., in your present homework set!)

Readers of this volume should recognize some of the strengths of Polya's approach: (1) Formulating a plan and carrying it out is consistent with the perspective that tasks should be approached strategically, that people often need to reflect about potential ways of doing a task rather than jumping right in. (2) Looking back is mostly monitoring. (3) The recommendation to attempt to apply the solution plan to another problem was aimed at developing case-based knowledge of solution strategies. Because many homework assignments involve application of the same procedures, this was sound advice based on Descartes's famous insight: "Each problem that I solved became a rule which served afterwards to solve other problems" (cited by Polya, 1981, p. 1). Of course, the idea of homework assignments is to develop general understandings of the strategies that can be used to solve them efficiently, and thus Polya's advisement boils down to recommending that students reflect on their problem solving so they acquire the knowledge that the lessons and homework were intended to instill.

One obvious quagmire in the Polya four-step scheme is coming up with a plan (i.e., step 2). Isn't that the crux of the problem?: The potential problem solver does not know which processes to use to solve the problem at hand. Aware that people often do not know specific strategies that could be applied to problems they face, others devised general plans for solving problems (Newell & Simon, 1972). The most popular of these approaches became known as **means-end analysis.**

The person using the means-end plan is constantly aware of the end state he or she wishes to achieve (e.g., knowledge of how many hours is required to drive 650 miles). The person is also aware of what he or she knows now (e.g., that the speed limit for 300 of the miles is 55, the speed limit for 325 miles is 65, and the speed limit for 25 miles is 45). The idea is to make progress from the initial state to the desired end state, deciding on steps that permit progress. A first step that might be elected would be to figure out how long it takes to go through each speed zone by dividing the total distance for the zone by the speed limit: 5.45 hours for the 55-speed zone, 5.00 hours for the 65-speed zone, and 0.55 hours for the 45-speed zone. Has progress been made toward the goal? Absolutely, for at least now we have total times spent on various parts of the trip, which is progress because the final solution must be expressed in terms of total time on the road. What next? We could add the time spent on each segment: 5.45 hours + 5.00 hours + 0.55 hours = 11.00 hours. Have we come to the end? Yes, we know how long it would take to drive the 650 miles in question. The means-end problem solver is always asking how to reduce the difference in present state and desired end state and carries out operations that make progress until the end state is reached.

The teaching of general planning strategies fell out of favor in the 1970s and 1980s, however, largely because of the recognition that the most powerful problem solving in any domain is done by individuals with a great deal of domain knowledge (e.g., Owen & Sweller, 1989). Domain knowledge often includes knowledge of extremely efficient strategies for accomplishing common problems in the domain, so that working from a starting state to an ending state would be less efficient than just applying well-known approaches that are almost "rules-of-thumb." Thus, the experienced driver might recognize that the routing is mostly interstate, with the usual state-to-state variation between 55 and 65 miles an hour, which means when half the time is spent in 65 states and half in 55 states, the average speed is 60 miles an hour. The 25 miles at a speed of 45 miles an hour just slows the trip a little bit, so use

60 for the estimate and then increase the overall time estimate just a little to take the 45 mile per hour segment into account. The average speed of 60 goes into 650 a little less than 11 times (i.e., trip takes approximately 11 hours). The final figure of 11 seems reasonable because that provides some adjustment for the little bit of lost time on the 45-mile-an-hour segment. As experienced long-distance drivers, this strategy is one we have used many times when we are on the open road, and it works fine, but it is nothing like means-end analysis. Rather, it is informed by our vast experiences on interstates. The hundreds of hours we have spent every year behind the wheel, with mental calculations of this sort almost an obsession as we figure out how far it is until lunch, the next gas station, the evening's stopover, or our parents' homes, have contributed to the development of expertise in mental calculation of driving times.

By the early 1980s, it seemed questionable whether it made sense to teach general planning routines to novice problem solvers because the thinking of the day was that students should be taught to do as experts do, and experts do not use means-end analyses or other general approaches. Another difficulty also became apparent in the early 1980s. People have a difficult time abstracting specific problem-solving schemes when they use means-end analysis to solve problems (e.g., Sweller & Levine, 1982; Sweller, Mawer, & Ward, 1983). That is, they do not emerge from a means-end–mediated problem-solving experience with generalizable knowledge of the specific strategies that can be applied to the types of problems they have been solving. For example, after solving a group of distance = rate × time problems through means-end analysis, students might not know to look for the distance, rate, or time in the given information of the problem and solve for the missing value, which is the strategy that practice with such problems is intended to instill. Because the goal of problem-solving instruction is to produce students who can recognize problem types immediately and solve them using efficient procedures, encouraging students to rely on means-end as a way to "discover" specific problem-solving strategies seems unwise.

Sweller (1988, 1989) and Owen and Sweller (1989) proposed several reasons why solving problems using means-end analyses might not result in abstraction of strategies useful when encountering problems of the same type in the future: (1) Means-end focuses attention on reducing the discrepancy between what is known now and what needs to be known; it does not encourage stepping back at the end of problem solving and getting the whole picture, which is absolutely necessary if there is to be understanding of the approach used to solve a problem. (That is, when using means-end analysis, people do not seem to follow through with Polya's fourth step, which is to check their answer, including figuring out if the solution plan they devised for this problem might apply to other problems.) (2) Means-end analysis also consumes a great deal of short-term capacity (Owen & Sweller, 1985), for the present state must be held in memory and compared with the end state as the problem solver tries to figure how to reduce the difference between the present and end states. With so much mental juggling going on, there may be little capacity left over for remembering the sequence of steps that produced a problem solution.

Despite these problems with general problem-solving plans such as means-end analysis, we are not convinced that general problem-solving strategies should be abandoned entirely. Indeed, there is a great deal of evidence favoring Polya's four-step approach. That general problem-solving plans, such as Newell and Simon's means-end approach, are ineffective tells us nothing about the efficacy of the much more encompassing Polya approach!. An analysis by Burkell, Schneider, and Pressley (1990) was more informative on this point.

Burkell et al. (1990) analyzed studies in which elementary-age students had been taught successfully how to solve problems. They found in every one of the successful studies that Polya's four steps were taught, although the researchers did not always use Polya's terms. In every one of the studies, students were encouraged first to make certain they understood the problem before they attempted to solve it (Polya's first step). The specific recommendations for doing so differed from study to study: Students can attempt to understand a problem by (1) reading the problem aloud (presumably, slowly and deliberately, thinking hard about it), (2) identifying the problem being asked, (3) identifying important information specified in the problem statement, (4) defining terms, (5) paraphrasing the problem, (6) making a list or table summarizing the important elements in the problem, (7) creating a representation of the problem using objects, and (8) drawing a diagram representing the problem.

Students in the problem-solving studies identified by Burkell et al. (1990) were also encouraged to devise and carry out strategies for solving problems (i.e., follow Polya's steps 2 and 3). To this end, they were encouraged to (1) relate the present problem to easier examples they might have encountered, (2) identify a familiar pattern in the problem, and (3) construct hypotheses and potential operations for solving the problem (and, of course, then carrying out the operations). Of course, some of the operations used to understand the problem also led to generation of problem solution plans, with plans often discovered by representing the problem using concrete objects or by using a diagram or even from listing the critical information in the problem.

All of the successful problem-solving regimens also encouraged students to review and reflect on their work (Polya's fourth step). Specifically, students were encouraged to (1) check their answer, (2) compare the answer they obtained through problem solving with an estimated answer, (3) solve the problem another way, (4) summarize what they did to solve the problem, and (5) construct a problem that would be similar to the present one and require the same solution strategy.

What is important to emphasize is that more than Polya's four general strategies were taught in the studies in which problem solving improved. Rather the general Polya-type problem-solving instruction was integrated with other mathematics instruction. Review of one of the best designed and most convincing of the studies analyzed by Burkell et al. (1990) makes clear that development of skilled problem solving involves long-term teaching of general and specific problem-solving approaches.

Charles and Lester (1984) conducted their experiment in grade-5 and grade-7 classrooms. At each grade level, teachers were assigned to an experimental or a control condition. Control teachers carried on business as usual in their mathematics classes. So did the experimental teachers except that they supplemented their mathematics instruction with teaching of a Polya-like approach to problem solving.

To understand problems, experimental students in Charles and Lester (1984) were encouraged to (1) read and reread problems carefully, (2) write down what is known, (3) look for key phrases, (4) find the important information in each problem, (5) paraphrase the problem, and (6) make certain of what must be found out. For generation and execution of a strategic plan, students were taught to (1) look for a pattern resembling one they had seen in other problems, (2) draw a picture representing the problem, (3) make a list or table summarizing what is known and needs to be known, (4) use objects to depict the problem, (5) simplify the problem, (6) guess and check, and (7) write an equation. After generating an answer, students were encouraged to (1) determine whether all of the important information stated in the problem was used, (2) decide whether the answer made sense, and generally (3) check the answer.

Instruction to use these general problem-solving strategies took place over 23 weeks, with students taught to apply the strategies to the problems normally covered in their courses. Pretest and posttest assessments were made, with a great deal of evidence that the strategy instruction made a substantial difference. There were indications at posttest that the strategy-trained students were more likely than control participants to develop a plan when attempting to solve new problems, although using the general problem-solving strategies did not always translate into finding a problem solution. That is, although there was a problem-solution advantage for trained over control students, it was not huge. The trained students, however, seemed to have better understanding than control students about how and when to use the mathematical skills they were acquiring.

The recommendation to teach general problem-solving strategies, including the four steps outlined by Polya and means-end analysis, has something of a checkered history. On the one hand, such strategies are not substitutes for instruction of more specific problem-solving approaches, and solving problems using general strategies in no way guarantees discovery and acquisition of more specific skills. On the other hand, teaching of general strategies as part of mathematics instruction makes some sense, with teaching of Polya's four steps prominent in interventions that improve problem solving.

If readers return to the discussion of experts in Chapter 4, it is easy to see general problem-solving strategies in expert performances, especially when experts are confronted with difficult problems. For example, radiologists attempting to make a difficult diagnosis first make certain they understand the problem, then they evaluate alternative ways of analyzing the x-ray before advancing a tentative diagnosis, and finally they check their diagnosis

(Lesgold et al., 1988). The general understanding-planning-solving-checking sequence is informed at all times by extensive domain-specific knowledge, however, and proceeds largely because of this domain-specific knowledge. Effective problem solving for experts is an articulation of general strategies and domain-specific strategies and declarative knowledge.

Can the problem-solving of poor problem solvers be understood in terms of Polya's general model? Montague and Bos (1990) administered questionnaires, reasoning tests, and mathematics achievement tests to high-achieving, average-achieving, low-achieving, and mathematics learning-disabled grade-8 students (i.e., students whose only problem in school was with math). All students in the study were filmed as they solved five problems, so they could watch the videotape later with a researcher and explain what they were doing. The interview used to elicit student descriptions of their problem solving covered all parts of Polya's four-step problem-solving process as well as some more specific problem-solving strategies:

> Questions either pertained to general strategic performance (e.g., describe any strategies that you used to solve math problems) or focused on the following strategies specific to mathematical problem solving: (1) Reading (e.g., what did you do when you read the problem?). (2) Paraphrasing (e.g., did you try to put what you read in your own words?). (3) Visualizing (e.g., what do you do to make a picture in your mind?). [*Note:* These first three categories correspond to "understanding" in the Polya model.] (4) Hypothesizing (e.g., how did you think of the operations to use?). [Planning in the Polya model.] (5) Estimating (e.g., how did you estimate or try to guess the answer?). (6) Computing (e.g., what did you think about when you did the computation?). (7) Checking (e.g., how did you check to make sure you used all the steps you needed?)

Several aspects of the Montague and Bos (1990) data are relevant to the present discussion: First, the higher the mathematical achievement level of the student, the more of the Polya problem-solving steps evidenced during problem solving. Second, the higher the mathematics achievement, the more knowledgeable the student about strategies as reflected by responses to the interview items. Third, better students were more likely to indicate that they actually used the problem-solving strategies routinely than were weaker students. Montague and

Bos (1990) confirmed that knowledge and use of the Polya strategies varied from extensive by good problem solvers to unlikely by weaker problem solvers. Such correlational data make clear that the interventions reviewed by Burkell et al. (1990) reflect the problem solving of good students, consistent with Polya's analysis 40 years ago.

Without a doubt, however, the most extensive analysis of the general processes in skilled problem solving was a meta-analysis of 487 studies conducted between 1920 and the present (Hembree, 1992). Collapsing across studies (both experimental investigations manipulating problem-solving components, such as strategies, and correlational studies of problem solving), there were clear associations between each of the Polya strategies and problem-solving performance. For example, the correlation between comprehending a problem and performance was 0.54, between selecting the correct problem-solving operations and performance was 0.72, and between checking work and performance was 0.25. There were positive effects of performance for using a variety of specific strategies as part of problem-solving plans (e.g., $r = 0.31$ for drawing a diagram). There also were effects for teaching a variety of specific strategies (e.g., the effect size for teaching diagramming as a problem-solving strategy was 1.16 SD compared with controls).

The most interesting relationship identified by Hembree (1992), however, involved the effects of teaching the Polya heuristics. The teaching of the Polya strategies had a greater impact with advancing age, with the overall correlation between teaching of Polya strategies and performance only 0.17 for children in grades 4 to 5, increasing to 0.26 at grades 6 to 8, increasing much more to 0.72 at grades 9 to 12, and decreasing to 0.40 when postsecondary students were instructed in use of the strategies. If my high school classmates and I [MP] had obtained a copy of Polya's (1957) *How to Solve It* and taken it to heart, it might have made a striking difference for us in our algebra 2 class because high school students seem to get more out of general problem-solving instruction than do students at other grade levels.

A reading of Polya's books (e.g., 1954a, 1954b, 1957, 1981) makes clear that the effective problem solvers he considered were rich in knowledge of mathematics, and the effective problem solving he wrote about was articulation of general and domain-specific approaches. Polya's idea that students benefit from instruction to organize their application of domain-specific knowledge and strategies using general strategies is doing well in the 1990s (see Lawson, 1990), a theme that will recur in this chapter. Indeed, Hembree's (1992) review suggests that at the secondary level at least, the case in favor of teaching Polya's heuristics is already strong; both Hembree and Burkell et al. (1990) offered analyses supporting the teaching of the Polya strategies to even younger children.

What has died has been enthusiasm for a once popular general approach to problem solving, means-end analysis. The best bet based on the extant data is that effective problem-solving education will include teaching of the general strategies favored by Polya as well as instruction of domain-specific concepts and strategies, with a great deal of practice solving problems requiring articulation of Polya's general strategies and specific mathematical concepts and problem-solving procedures.

INSTRUCTION THAT PROMOTES MATHEMATICAL UNDERSTANDING

Contemporary mathematics educators believe that too much of traditional mathematics instruction has been conveying information from teacher or textbook to student. That is, the teacher or textbook attempts to give knowledge to the student rather than encourage the student to construct knowledge on his or her own. Students are taught methods of doing problems without being taught why the methods work. There is too much memorization of math facts and procedures. Math is taught as a 20- to 60-minute segment in the school day, rather than as a useful part of life, with few attempts to map mathematical concepts and procedures to real-world relationships. The result of such conventional pedagogy is less than complete understanding of the mathematics taught.

If you were to ask many contemporary mathematics educators what good mathematics instruction does—that is, how it contrasts with conventional instruction—they would tell you that it promotes understanding of mathematical concepts and procedures, understanding that is essential if mathematics is to be used broadly and flexibly. What does that mean? As it turns out, it means many things, with the following a brief catalog generated by summarizing over commentary provided by a number of mathematics educators about the na-

ture of mathematical understanding (e.g., Baroody, 1987; Fennema, Carpenter, & Peterson, 1989; Hiebert & Carpenter, 1992; National Council of Teachers of Mathematics, 1989, 1991; Scheid, 1993, Chapter 4; Schoenfeld, 1987; Schroeder & Lester, 1989; Silver, 1985, 1987; Skemp, 1989):

- Recognizing that mathematics is a way of thinking about and organizing real experiences.
- Recognizing why the mathematical concepts and procedures being learned are important.
- Recognizing how the particular mathematical concepts and procedures being learned are related to one another and are related to information already understood by the student.
- Knowing when, why, and where to apply mathematical concepts and procedures and being able to do so when confronted with situations that call for particular mathematical knowledge and use of mathematical procedures.
- Being able to explain why particular mathematical concepts and procedures are used to solve particular problems.

These views of mathematical understanding lead to certain assumptions about the teaching of mathematics:

- Learning of mathematics is best when it results from children's own mathematical activities—that is, when they generate their own understandings of problem solving and mathematics concepts rather than when problem solving and mathematics concepts are taught by a teacher or textbook. When children construct their own mathematical understandings, the knowledge is intimately related to what the children know already. As they discover new knowledge, children also gain experience self-regulating themselves as they do mathematics, which is important because self-regulated application of mathematical concepts and procedures is an important goal of mathematics education.
- Students should learn to approach problems in the fashion prescribed by Polya, involving reflection on the problem situation, planning, and monitoring the effectiveness of solution attempts. Strategies such as representing problems with diagrams (which really is effective; e.g., Lewis, 1989) and checking and reflecting on one's work stimulate deep understanding of problems and should be encouraged.

(Nonetheless, sometimes reflection on more than one problem of a given type is required—and sometimes even then a general solution strategy is not abstracted [e.g., Reed, 1989], so that there is a lot to be said for instruction that provides explicit information about how to solve particular problem types, a theme reiterated throughout this chapter, even though such instruction might seem hypocritical to the most devoted of radical constructivist mathematics educators, who unquestioningly embrace discovery approaches to learning.)

- Problem solving is a means for learning about new ways of solving problems, not just an activity that the student does after being taught methods of problem solving. That is, just as Polya prescribed, students should be encouraged to reflect on their problem solving in order to abstract general problem-solving principles and procedures from working particular problems.

- Often mathematical concepts can be grasped by children through manipulatives before they can be grasped symbolically, a conclusion supported by voluminous research (see Sowell, 1989). Understanding how mathematical symbols relate to the world can be fostered by encouraging children to connect operations performed with manipulatives to symbols (e.g., after observing a row of 8 buttons being extended by 3 buttons, resulting in an 11-button row, the symbolic equivalent of $8 + 3 = 11$ can be related to the physical representation of buttons; relating an equation to such a concrete representation is considered to be an especially effective way of increasing young children's understanding of concepts such as "addition" and "equation." In general, concrete, incomplete, and unsystematic (e.g., informal) learning of mathematics precedes abstract (i.e., symbolic), complete, systematic, and formal learning. Formal learning is at its best when it is connected and related to students' informal understanding (e.g., Putnam, Lampert, & Peterson, 1990).

- Students should be encouraged to use technology such as calculators as part of problem solving because these devices eliminate much of the lower-order computational demands of problem solving, permitting more attention to the higher-order, executive decisions.

- Instruction should emphasize how mathematical symbols are related to events and relationships in the world, especially events and relationships already understood by the child (e.g., relating the mathematical operation of division to sharing, such as when three children share six cookies, with each child receiving two cookies).

- Word problems should be used from the beginning of mathematics instruction. Word problems require students to map the relationships expressed in the problems verbally to mathematical concepts, symbols, and procedures.

- Instruction should permit students to observe how the mathematical concepts and procedures they are learning apply in a variety of situations, with such experiences necessary for students to acquire understandings about when and where to use mathematics, understandings that are essential if mathematical knowledge is to be used generally and flexibly.

- Students should experience many examples illustrating concepts and procedures they are learning.

- Much of problem solving should occur in everyday situations.

- Instruction should foster beliefs that support student behaviors likely to motivate appropriate efforts and persistence in learning mathematics. Thus, students should be encouraged to believe that it makes sense to ask questions when a concept or procedure is not understood, errors are to be expected when doing mathematics and do not reflect low ability, and the mathematics learned in school relates to everyday life.

- Teachers should question students about how they are solving problems and listen to student answers because such answers can be revealing about what students understand and do not yet grasp. This is part of ongoing assessment of student progress in understanding the mathematical ideas they are being taught.

- Problem solving in small groups is often effective, especially in getting students to explain their reasons for problem solving in particular ways, but also in exposing students to alternative solution methods, exposure that should foster understanding that problem solving is a flexible enterprise. Small-group problem solving also permits students to experience the understanding-solving-checking cycle recommended by Polya. For example, Artzt and Armour-Thomas (1992) observed groups of grade-7 students while they solved problems: The students recursively read problems, attempted to understand them, explored, analyzed, planned, carried out plans, and checked. That students can experience such high-quality problem-solving experiences in small groups is one reason that leading mathematics educators, such as Alan Schoenfeld (e.g., 1992), are emphatic that real mathematics is a social and collaborative enterprise, that it involves talking and explaining and making false starts with other people.

- Teachers should model problem solving, making obvious as they do so that problem solving is not always straightforward but often involves false starts and consideration of many factors.

These pedagogical perspectives on teaching for understanding are summarized in two volumes published by the National Council of Teachers of Mathematics (NCTM), known for short as the *Standards* (i.e., *Curriculum and Evaluation Standards for School Mathematics* [1989] and *Professional Standards for Teaching Mathematics* [1991]). These *Standards* are having a great deal of impact on mathematics education reform across the United States.

Many different psychological theories influenced NCTM as they developed their positions on teaching, including the following:

1. *Piaget:* Some of the instructional recommendations in the *Standards* are based on progressive, constructivist philosophy. It is hard to miss the Piagetian influence on recommendations to teach mathematics to young children using concrete materials. The Piagetian themes of exploration and discovery pervade the NCTM recommendations. The Piagetian emphasis that instruction should be matched to the child's level of functioning (Inhelder et al., 1974) comes through as well, with teachers urged to diagnose continually the level of functioning of the child and provide instruction just beyond the current levels of their students.

2. *Traditional learning theory and direct explanation models:* Although the mathematics educators often are reticent to admit it, elements of traditional learning theory and direct explanation are prominent in their recommendations as well. Teachers are urged to model problem solving for children and to make certain that instruction includes explanations for mathematical relationships. Indeed, our reading of the NCTM *Professional Standards for Teaching Mathematics* is that the teaching recommended there resembles in many ways the best of direct explanation approaches (see Chapters 1 and 8): Teacher explanations and modeling are provided on an as-needed basis and flexibly; the emphasis is on thorough understanding rather than on moving through the curriculum at a rapid pace.

3. *Representational theories of mind:* Contemporary mathematics educators also recognize that information is represented in various ways in the human mind (see Chapter 3, this volume), with the recommendation to present alternative representations of concepts and procedures stimulated in part by the understanding that the mind includes concrete, imaginal conceptions (e.g., a vision of a row of 8 buttons joined by a row of 3 buttons to form 11 buttons) as well as more abstract codes that are closer to formal mathematical symbolism (e.g., $8 + 3 = 11$).

4. *Network theories of representation:* Cognitive theorists and researchers recognize that people can connect related representations but often fail to do so on their own. The recognition that connections are anything but automatic, based on knowledge of cognitive theory and years of experiences with students who did not recognize mappings between equations (e.g., $x^2 + y^2 = 4$) and their concrete representations (i.e., a circle with radius of 2), resulted in the NCTM recommendation for mathematics teachers to encourage connections between alternative representations of mathematical ideas.

In short, the mathematics educators have done a good job of reading the cognition and instruction literatures and culling from them instructional recommendations. Most cognitive psychologists find much that pleases them in the NCTM *Standards*. What is even more pleasing to the psychological researcher community, however, is that some members of the mathematics education profession are conducting impressive experimental evaluations of their ideas, evaluations that are providing high-quality information about the effects of some of the instructional practices favored in the *Standards*.

Examples of Instructional Experiments Validating the Importance of Teaching Mathematics so as to Enhance Student Understanding of Mathematical Content

The experiments conducted by mathematics educators range from ones that are short term and focused to those that evaluate entire curricula implemented over an extended period of time. We consider three such studies here, to illustrate better what is meant by teaching for mathematical understanding as well as the research tactics being used by some of the more analytical researchers in the mathematics education community.

Evaluation of a Kindergarten Part-Part-Whole Curriculum A powerful mathematical understanding is that any number can be decomposed into parts (e.g., Resnick, 1983; Riley, Greeno, & Heller, 1983). Thus, 14 can be decomposed into a 10 and a 4. The number seven can be decomposed into a 4 and a 3 or alternatively into two 2s and a 3. Complete understanding of addition and arithmetic is not possible without part-part-whole understanding, with the evidence mounting that instruction of part-part-whole can increase children's understanding of basic arithmetic operations.

For example, Fischer (1990) evaluated the consequences of teaching kindergarten children the first seven whole numbers using a part-part-whole approach compared with conventional mathematics instruction. Two kindergarten classes received 25 days (20 minutes a day) of part-part-whole instruction. The children receiving the part-part-whole curriculum also counted sets of objects, but in doing so they were required to create subsets (e.g., if counting five objects, to create two subsets). The exercises emphasized counting various combinations of subsets to establish that whole numbers can be decomposed into components and that however decomposed, the parts sum to the whole.

Two control condition classes experienced a curriculum based on counting, saying, and writing the first seven whole numbers. Control students practiced counting items in sets, including verbalization of the numbers involved in counting and writing the number of items in a just-counted set. The control curriculum was rich compared with much of conventional kindergarten instruction because it was supplemented with manipulatives, and there were more total counting exercises than in many conventional textbooks (i.e., this was not a "straw-man" control). There was equivalent instruction about the whole numbers from 1 to 7 in the experimental and control classrooms. There were also the same number of opportunities to count sets of seven items and comparable work sheet opportunities.

The part-part-whole curriculum made a slight difference on a number concept posttest (i.e., part-part-whole students answered questions requiring counting and knowledge of the first seven whole numbers slightly better than control students). When asked to do some simple problems requiring dividing numbers such as 12, 14, and 15 into two sets, the part-part-whole students did slightly better than controls. A really striking advantage for part-part-whole students was observed, however, in solving simple word problems, even though neither group of students had experienced instruction in solving word problems. This is an important finding because solution of word problems requires understanding the relationships specified in the word problems and performing the arithmetic operations. Such problems often pose difficulties for older children (e.g., Morales, Shute, & Pellegrino, 1985) and sometimes even for university-level students (e.g., Lewis & Mayer, 1987).

Students receiving part-part-whole instruction were better able to understand and solve problems such as the following (Carpenter, 1985):

> Sam had 2 books. Mom gave him 4 more. Now how many books does Sam have?
> The cat has 9 kittens. Six are brown and the rest are white. How many white kittens are there?

It takes only a little thought to recognize that awareness of how parts combine to produce wholes could facilitate representation and solution of such problems. Fischer's (1990) demonstration of increased competence in mathematics when important mathematical understandings are developed is one of a growing number of such demonstrations.

Evaluation of a Grade-1 Curriculum for Increasing Understanding of Place Value Hiebert and Wearne (1992) evaluated a grade-1 curriculum covering place values, with extensive coverage of the tens-place and ones-place value and an introduction of the hundreds-place value. Understanding of place value was developed in the experimental curriculum by relating concrete representations of numbers (e.g., 56 represented as five bars of 10 units and 6 unit bars) and symbolic representations (i.e., the number 56 with a 5 in the tens place and a 6 in the units place). Hiebert and Wearne (1992) described the experimental curriculum as follows:

> The . . . lessons began by posing problems of finding how many objects there were in large sets, most sets between 50 and 100. Class discussions and suggested strategies began with counting by ones and shifted to counting more efficiently by regrouping and counting by twos, fives, and eventually, tens. One kind of

object investigated was Unifix cubes. These were eventually grouped into quasi-permanent bars of 10. Two-digit numerals were introduced as efficient ways of recording the size of sets. Discussion frequently included the two ways of interpreting the written number—as ones and as tens and ones. For example, 57 was interpreted as 57 individual objects and as 5 groups of 10 objects with 7 leftover objects. Base-10 blocks were introduced as tools, like Unifix cubes but already hooked together. Most tasks at this point were story situations that involved dealing with large sets by, for example, packaging them for sale in groups of 10. Students used base-1 blocks or pictures of the blocks or written numbers to help them solve the problems and then described the strategies they used (Hiebert & Wearne, 1992, p. 101)

Such instruction continued through coverage of two-digit addition and subtraction without regrouping (i.e., for readers from another generation, problems not requiring "borrowing" or "carrying"). Physical and symbolic representations were related to one another throughout instruction on addition and subtraction. Students shared with one another their strategies for solving problems. The teacher encouraged student reflection on the various strategies and solutions as well as emphasizing the relationships between physical and symbolic representations.

The experimental curriculum differed from the control curriculum, which was conventional grade-1 instruction, with respect to the interactions between students and the reflection encouraged by the teacher. The textbook presentation in the control condition involved showing bundles of 10 sticks to represent 10-place elements and single sticks to represent units. It continued with exercises involving different types of objects so grouped. Control students also had some opportunity to work with one actual physical representation (i.e., 10 beans glued to a stick to represent one 10 in the tens place). For two-digit addition and subtraction without regrouping, most of the instruction involved workbook pages of problems. These were introduced with "bean stick" representations of addition and subtraction and some instruction about checking addition and subtraction using estimation. Although the controls received high-quality conventional instruction, what they did not experience were the discussions intended to increase understanding of place-value concepts. These discussions covered various strategies for representing numbers and for adding and subtracting two-digit numbers, strategies requiring knowledge and use of place-value knowl-

edge. The control students were able to practice many more problems than did the experimental students because the in-depth discussion in the experimental classrooms consumed a great deal of time. Although the control students actually covered more topics in each lesson, the experimental students generated more numerous representations for each of the problems they practiced.

Did the instruction designed to inculcate understanding make a difference? Did making certain that the students understood relationships between the physical and symbolic worlds affect their ability to do problems involving place value? It did. The students in the experimental classes did better on posttest problems similar to the ones covered in class (e.g., two-digit addition and subtraction problems not requiring regrouping). More impressive, however, was that experimental students were much better able than control students to do addition and subtraction problems that required regrouping (i.e., problems requiring "carrying"), despite the fact that no instruction on regrouping had been given to them. The deep understanding of place value developed in the experimental classrooms increased transfer of addition skills especially (i.e., addition with regrouping was accomplished better by experimental students than subtraction with regrouping).

Evaluation of a Problem-Centered Grade-2 Mathematics Curriculum Cobb and his colleagues at Purdue University (Cobb, Wood, Yackel, Nicholls, Wheatley, Trigatti, and Perlwitz, 1991) compared performance in 10 grade-2 classrooms receiving arithmetic instruction consistent with NCTM recommendations (see description earlier in this section) and 8 classrooms receiving conventional instruction. Students in the NCTM classrooms solved challenging problems continuously, with students engaged in constructing solutions to the problems presented to them. The students were encouraged to reflect on their problem-solving activities and to construct knowledge about how to solve problems. The problem solving generally took place in interactive, cooperative classroom groups, groups in which the role of the teacher was to provide support and gentle guidance in the direction of productive problem solving, rather than to provide solutions or explicit instruction about how to solve problems. The grade-2 experimental curriculum focused on addition and subtraction and the development of strategies for solving such problems. Students were encouraged to believe that success in mathematics was possible through individual and collective efforts. The experimental students were encouraged to feel successful when they solved challenging problems. In short, the NCTM curriculum combined Vygotskian notions (Chapter 8, this volume) that sophisticated thinking can be developed in social interactions and contemporary motivational perspectives (see Chapter 5) that long-term motivation is most likely when students attribute success to effort and reinforce themselves for taking on and persisting with challenging tasks. Consistent with Cobb et al.'s identification with radical constructivist theories of the development of mind, which posit that socially mediated discovery and construction of knowledge is to be preferred over any form of explicit instruction, the Cobb et al. curriculum downplayed elements of direct explanation compared with other interventions consistent with the NCTM perspective (e.g., 1991).

Did the NCTM-type instruction make a difference? It did on state-administered assessments of mathematics achievement as well as on an experimenter-produced test of mathematics achievement. Differences favoring the experimental students were especially notable on items requiring application of the concepts covered in the curriculum. The students in the experimental classes reported that they valued collaboration more than did control students; the experimental students did not identify with academic competition as much as control students.

Commentary: Teaching for Understanding

The formalization of the NCTM *Standards* (1989, 1991) is stimulating substantial instructional research on mathematics education, with the constructivist-theoretical underpinnings of the NCTM perspective now being examined in ambitious instructional experiments. Although it is possible to find flaws in individual studies, the strengths are more striking. There is a growing database supportive of the proposition that mathematics instruction stimulating deep understanding of mathematical concepts and procedures promotes mathematics achievement.

Even so, the claims made by the mathematics educator community sometimes are too strong. In particular, there are frequent claims in the mathematics educator fraternity that the instruction they prescribe and embrace—often instruction promoting student discovery of important mathematical concepts through social interactions—is the best way for students to learn mathematics. Note that the

comparison conditions in the three studies discussed in this subsection were variations on conventional instruction. Note as well that conventional mathematics instruction is currently assumed not to be very effective.

Although we find credible that students receiving instruction for understanding outperform even students receiving good conventional instruction, that is no guarantee it would fare well if it was pitted against high-quality teaching inspired by models other than radical constructivism. For example, we would like to see outstanding versions of instruction intended to stimulate "understanding" of mathematics compared with outstanding instruction based on direct explanations. Of course, we believe that good instruction that includes modeling, explanations, and scaffolded practice (i.e., high-quality direct explanation teaching) includes a great deal of student construction of knowledge (see Chapter 15), so that we would view such a comparison as between two types of constructivism: radical constructivism (sometimes referred to as endogenous constructivism; Moshman, 1982, see Chapter 15, this book), which requires much more student invention, compared with exogenous constructivism (again, Moshman's [1982] term), which begins with an explanation from a teacher as a starting point and is followed by student reflection and elaboration of the concept or process as a function of attempting to apply the procedure to new problems. Our perspective is that radical constructivists such as Cobb et al. (1991) often fail to recognize the constructive activities that are stimulated by modeling and explanation (see Chapter 15, this book; Harris & Pressley, 1991; Pressley, Harris, & Marks, 1992).

We cannot emphasize enough that we do not believe that all direct explanations are effective. That the quality of explanation provided to students is critical has been made obvious in work by Perry (1991) of the University of Michigan. She taught grade-4 and grade-5 students to solve problems of the form $4 + 6 + 9 = \underline{\quad} + 9$. (In the absence of instruction, grade-4 and grade-5 children fail on such problems 90 percent of the time.) Perry varied the type of instruction provided to students. Some students received instruction that emphasized the step-by-step procedures for solving such problems:

> One way to solve a problem like this is to add up all the numbers on the left side of the problem (e.g., in the problem $4 + 6 + 9 = \underline{\quad} + 9$, the experimenter would use her hand to indicate $4 + 6 + 9$) and then subtract

the number on the right side of the problem (and then indicate the 9 on the right side of the equation).

Other students received instruction that emphasized the principle involved in solving such problems:

> The goal of a problem like this is to find a number that fits in the blank and makes both sides equal; that is, to make this side (pointing to the right side of the equation) equal to this side (pointing to the left side of the equation).

Still other students received instruction that included both procedural and principle information.

On a posttest covering addition problems similar to the ones used during instruction, Perry's procedure-plus-principle students outperformed students taught only the procedures, who slightly outperformed students taught only the principle. On a transfer task, however, involving the solution of multiplication problems of the form $2 \times 3 \times 4 = \_\_\_ \times 4$, there was a clear advantage for students who had been taught only the principle.

Perry's (1991) finding is complemented by other outcomes. Reed (1989) observed in college algebra classes that students often did not abstract general solution strategies for particular types of problems from working the problems, even if the instruction forced them to pay attention to the components of the solution procedure (see also Dellarosa, 1985). Reed concluded that abstraction of solutions is unlikely much of the time unless students first understand the principles that lead to the solutions. Also, transfer of solution strategies on calculators to problems different in structure from sample problems used to teach the calculator strategies is more likely when students are taught the principles underlying the calculation steps than if they are simply taught the steps (for a review, see Bibby, 1992). Hong and O'Neil (1992) observed that both undergraduate and graduate students in statistics courses learned a statistical procedure better if a conceptual explanation of the procedure preceded the explanation of how to carry out the procedure compared with simultaneous presentation of conceptual and procedural information. Might Perry's outcome have been different if she had sequenced the principles and procedural information?

Because high-quality direct explanations, which we favor as a means of instruction, include both conceptual and procedural information, we are fascinated by the Perry (1991), Reed (1989), and Hong and O'Neil (1992) studies and look forward to follow-up work aimed at identifying optimal ways of presenting both conceptual (i.e., domain-specific or problem-specific information) and more abstract procedural information. At present, however, readers should note that there are converging data supporting the conclusion that teaching students about underlying mathematical (problem-solving) principles is an important part of problem-solving instruction—which is another way of saying that it is important for students to understand the solution strategies they are learning at a high level of generality rather than just to memorize them. Our bet is that deep understanding of mathematics can be fostered by high-quality explanations that include both principles and the nitty-gritty, how-to-do-it information. We recognize as we state this hypothesis that a great deal of work on factors affecting the effectiveness of direct explanations needs to be completed before it will be possible to gauge just how much understanding can be produced by high-quality explanations combining principled and procedural knowledge. (Readers might note the similarity between the conclusion that follows from the work of Perry, Reed, and Hong and O'Neil and the theory of advance organizers offered by Ausubel, reviewed in Chapter 10 of this book: Deep understanding is facilitated by experiencing an abstract representation of an idea before getting buried in the details according to these perspectives.)

Even if the mathematics educators are more confident in radical constructivist teaching than scientific prudence might dictate from our perspective, their emphasis on understanding as a goal of instruction is to be applauded—and consistent with the instructional models favored throughout this book. There are far too many nominally well-educated adults, that is, people who have completed high school or beyond, who lack important mathematical understandings. That many adults do not understand even basic mathematics has been apparent in case studies of experienced teachers attempting to teach children mathematics in the ways intended by the NCTM-type reformers.

More Commentary: Teaching for Understanding: When the Teachers Do Not Understand

A real stumbling block for the mathematics education reform movement is that many of the people charged with teaching mathematics to our youth are among the adults who lack important mathematical understandings (Fennema & Franke, 1992). Perhaps it is not surprising when teachers do not understand the deductive nature of mathematical proofs or cannot discriminate adequate from inadequate proofs (e.g., Martin & Harel, 1989). The lack of understanding is much more fundamental, however.

Many primary teachers do not have exhaustive understanding of the strategies that can be used to solve simple addition and subtraction problems (Carpenter, Fennema, Peterson, & Carey, 1988). A high proportion of students preparing to be teachers cannot perform basic multiplication and division operations; many of those who can perform the operations cannot explain them; and blatant misconceptions about multiplication and division are common, such as the belief that the quotient in a division problem must be less than the dividend (e.g., Ball, 1990; Borko et al., 1992; Graeber, Tirosh, & Glover, 1989; Tirosh & Graeber, 1990). It is difficult to imagine how people who do not understand such mathematical concepts would be able to provide the support required in constructivist mathematics classrooms in which reflection on these mathematical ideas is expected to occur (Ball, 1988; Fennema & Franke, 1992; Stein, Baxter, & Leinhardt, 1990). To the extent that the issue of teacher understanding of mathematics as a determinant of student progress has been examined, teachers who understand arithmetic operations better are more likely to develop students' understanding of the basic arithmetic operations (e.g., Carpenter et al., 1988).

States and school districts can adopt policies favoring reforms such as NCTM mathematics, but how these policies are translated into practice depends on the competencies of the teachers who meet the students. It cannot be expected that teachers can be transformed instantly into constructivist mathematics educators (or high-quality direct explainers either). Most likely teachers will adapt slowly, with the early years of constructivist instructional efforts reflecting many of the practices favored during the era just completed—that is, the "basic skills" so embraced in the late 1970s and early 1980s will continue to be all too apparent in many classrooms as teachers attempt to blend in the new approaches emphasizing understanding with the basic skills approach that they were held accountable to for much of the 1970s and early 1980s (Cohen & Ball, 1990). Case studies conducted to date are filled with exam-

ples of teachers who attempt to be constructivist educators but who fall short (see the fall, 1990, issue of *Educational Evaluation and Policy Analysis* or the November, 1992, issue of *Elementary School Journal*). American teachers are taking the NCTM recommendations and assimilating them to their knowledge of mathematics and mathematics instruction, with some accommodation of their old understandings about mathematics and well-ingrained instructional practices to the new recommendations (Cohen & Ball, 1990). That is, the Piagetian principles of assimilation and accommodation (see Chapter 7) can be applied to understanding the slow changes of the teaching community. People do not abandon prior knowledge and beliefs wholesale but rather assimilate new information to their old understandings and accommodate slowly, with gradual changes in their behaviors the result.

We believe that the changes in teaching that do occur in reaction to the widespread reform efforts in mathematics education deserve serious study, especially with respect to how the reforms produce differences in students' understanding of mathematics. Carpenter, Fennema, Peterson, Chiang, and Loef (1989; Peterson, Carpenter, & Fennema, 1989) presented evidence that shifting grade-1 teachers' knowledge of the mathematics taught in grade 1 can do much to affect teaching and achievement. They provided a 1-month institute during which NCTM perspectives on addition and subtraction were presented (e.g., how to reconceptualize addition and subtraction as problems of operating on parts and wholes; the informal knowledge of addition and subtraction grade-1 children bring to school; and different types of addition and subtraction problems, as covered earlier in this chapter). No prescriptions were given with respect to teaching of addition and subtraction, however. Even so, when the teachers attending the institute returned to their classrooms, they were more likely than control teachers to use word problems in their classrooms. When they used word problems, institute teachers were more likely to discuss the problems with the class as a group, whereas control teachers assigned the problems to individual students. The institute teachers were more aware than control teachers of what their students knew about mathematics, perhaps reflecting that they were monitoring their students' understanding as a guide in deciding what and how to teach, consistent with Carpenter's model that formal mathematics instruction should build on students' informal knowledge of mathematics (e.g., Putnam et al., 1990). The institute teachers spent less time than control teachers drilling students on addition and subtraction facts. In short, problem solving occurred more frequently and was more salient in the classrooms of the institute teachers than the control teachers. Various indicators of mathematics achievement collected at the end of the academic year, including the ability to solve word problems, favored the students in classrooms of institute teachers. A month of reform-informed instruction about grade-1 mathematics did much to transform the classrooms in Carpenter et al. (1989).

Whether larger-scale reform efforts than the Carpenter et al. (1989) intervention will improve the mathematical competencies of U.S. students is not a foregone conclusion. It is an issue that can only be resolved by careful study—and there is reason to believe that the effects of reform-inspired instruction may be complex. For example, when Swing, Stoiber, and Peterson (1988) taught grade-4 teachers how to teach problem-solving skills to their students, there was not an across-the-board effect on student achievement. Rather, positive effects were greater in classrooms in which achievement was already high. When lessons were analyzed, it was clear that teachers in high-ability classrooms were more successful in conveying the strategies to their students than teachers with lower-ability classrooms. Even so, within any one classroom, the students most likely to benefit from the instruction were the lower-ability students, presumably because they were less likely than average and above-average students to use such strategies in the absence of instruction. That is, the outcomes in Swing et al. (1988) were determined by the abilities of the individual students as well as the abilities of their classmates. The effects of reform-inspired instruction may not be as pervasive as many reformers hope but depend instead on subtle factors, such as the intellectual abilities of classmates.

Careful investigation of how teachers respond to reform and how it affects student thinking could go far toward informing mathematics educators about what they can do to maximize the likelihood that their important messages will be understood and embraced by teachers. That some teachers can shift from teaching mathematics as rote rules and memorized procedures to teaching for understanding, that some classrooms can be transformed from passive to actively interactive, and that sometimes teachers give up the information transmission model in favor of scaffolded instructional interactions make obvious that it is possible for at least some teachers to change how they instruct mathematics (Wood, Cobb, & Yackel, 1991). We expect that much could be learned by studying teachers who can translate the NCTM perspective into instruction that improves student achievement.

Conventional instruction has produced many adults who lack fundamental mathematical understandings, understandings that we now wish to develop in the next generation. What is required is education at several levels. An important hypothesis that deserves detailed study is that as teachers understand mathematics better, so will students. Like many lofty and worthwhile goals, great resources will be required if a larger proportion of the high school class of 2006 is to understand mathematics better than did the classes of 1976, 1986, and 1996.

SCHOENFELD'S MODEL OF MATHEMATICAL COGNITION

Some outstanding mathematics educators, including Schoenfeld of the University of California at Berkeley, have offered models of competent mathematical cognition that are consistent with the good information processor model featured in this book. For the past decade, Schoenfeld has explored mathematical thinking and the development of mathematical abilities via instruction. What has emerged from his work is a model of thinking that includes four information processing components (Schoenfeld, 1992): (1) The knowledge base, (2) problem-solving strategies, (3) monitoring and control, and (4) beliefs and affects. A fifth component in the model is instructional practices that foster effective mathematical cognition. The information processing hardware (especially short-term memory) also figures in Schoenfeld's formulation.

Schoenfeld's Model of Mathematical Thinking

The components Schoenfeld describes overlap considerably with the components considered throughout this book. Most readers of this book will have little difficulty in recognizing Schoenfeld's complete model as an example of good information processing and mapping Schoenfeld's particular components to the components introduced in Chapter 1.

Knowledge   Schoenfeld's (1985, 1992) conception of mathematical thinking begins with mathematical knowledge, including both the declarative and procedural knowledge (see Chapter 2) required to do mathematics: There are algorithms which are procedures that the thinker can execute flawlessly and does so whenever they can be applied appropriately. Other procedures (i.e., routine procedures) are also likely to be used correctly and to be executed without great difficulties, but there is less of a guarantee than with algorithms. The good thinker articulates declarative knowledge of mathematical concepts and procedural knowledge when solving problems.

For example, the student who begins with two intersecting lines, with a point P on one of them, and constructs a circle tangential to both lines and to point B using a straightedge and a compass, applies both declarative and procedural knowledge to do so (Schoenfeld, 1985, Chapter 2; 1992, pp. 349–350). The declarative knowledge includes knowing that a tangent to a circle is perpendicular to a radius drawn to the point of tangency and that any two constructible loci are sufficient to determine the location of a point. The procedural knowledge includes understanding how to bisect an angle and drop a perpendicular to a line from a point. With a moment's thought about any mathematical problem, it is easy to identify both mathematical facts that contribute to solving the problem and mathematical procedures that do so. Try it.

Knowledge Effects on Functional Short-Term Capacity
Schoenfeld recognizes that problem-solving depends on short-term capacity, which is limited. That the long-term knowledge of mathematics is well organized and "chunkable" for the expert does much to reduce demands on capacity and is one source of expertise in mathematics: Good problem solvers are able to juggle more in their limited capacity than weaker problem solvers in part because their chunks are bigger and better organized. There have been multiple confirmations that good problem solvers have more extensive working memory capacities than weaker problem solvers, at least with respect to mathematical symbols and operations (e.g., Cooney & Swanson, 1990; Dark & Benbow, 1990). For any particular student, one reliable way to make problems more difficult is to set them up so that a great deal of working memory capacity is required to construct a solution. For example, problems that require three pieces of information be held

in memory to solve them are more difficult than those requiring two pieces of information be held in memory; those requiring computations not yet automatized are more demanding than those requiring only calculations that are automatized (e.g., Fayol, Abdi, & Gombert, 1987). When students can rapidly recall math facts as they work word problems, short-term memory demands are reduced—that is, having to reflect on $3 + 2 = 5$ consumes short-term capacity: In a study examining various factors contributing to word problem–solving ability, Zentall (1990) observed that only speed of math fact retrieval predicted performance on word problems, consistent with the hypothesis that problem solving is less certain when short-term memory is strained. In short, there is diverse evidence substantiating that short-term or working memory figures largely in skilled problem solving, consistent with Schoenfeld's theory.

Problem-Solving Strategies   At the center of Schoenfeld's conception of problem-solving strategies are Polya's strategies. Schoenfeld recognizes that these work only if the thinker is armed with a great deal of other knowledge, including strategies specialized for particular types of problems.

Schoenfeld's best-known study (Schoenfeld, 1979) involved an evaluation of the teaching of Polya-like strategies to university students in a mathematics course. The strategies included analyzing the problem (e.g., draw a diagram, try to simplify the problem), exploring it with the goal of coming up with a solution plan (e.g., relate the current problem to equivalent, slightly modified, or similar problems), and verifying the solution (e.g., checking whether the solution uses all the relevant data, is reasonable, can be obtained using another procedure). Such strategies can only be applied to specific problems by someone who knows a great deal about the specific mathematics concepts and procedures relevant to a problem being attempted. What is interesting given the current emphasis by mathematics educators on understanding, especially understanding through reflective discussion of problem solving, is that such discussion was important in the Schoenfeld intervention. Students practiced problems and then discussed how the problem-solving strategies taught in the course were applied to the practice items.

The reflective give-and-take that went on in Schoenfeld's class is illustrated in this description of how the class tackled a difficult problem:

I would ask, "What approaches or techniques might we try?" If a student made a suggestion that was clearly inappropriate, the class might explore it for a while until it was clear that the suggestion made little sense; at that point it would be pointed out that it helps to understand the problem before one jumps into its solution. The class was encouraged to generate a number of plausible ideas before committing itself to any particular one. When a few ideas had been generated, the class discussed which to pursue and why. Does Approach A look easier than Approach B? How far will A get us? What about B? If we are successful with A, how will we proceed? And the same for B? Classroom discussions focused explicitly on making informed judgments while solving problems: "We've been doing this for 5 minutes. Is it working? Should we try something else? If so, is there something in this we can salvage? When there was good reason to do something . . . we did so. (Schoenfeld, 1985, p. 113)

When we listen to outstanding elementary-level mathematics educators, such as James Hiebert and Paul Cobb, describe what they view as high-quality interactions with elementary students, we are reminded of this description provided by Schoenfeld. At the heart of contemporary problem-solving strategies instruction are reflective discussions about how to select strategies that might permit progress in solving a given problem, discussions similar in purpose and structure to the ones Schoenfeld (1979) evaluated with university-level students.

Did Schoenfeld's university-level students benefit from learning and using the general problem-solving strategies? Comparisons of problem solving before and after the strategies instruction as well as comparisons to students enrolled in another mathematics-oriented course revealed that the course had substantial impact (Schoenfeld, 1985, Chapters 6–9). There was no doubt that strategies-instructed students benefited from the problem-solving instruction they received. There were clear differences favoring trained students both in problems similar to ones covered in the course and in problems quite different from those practiced and discussed as part of the class requirements. The difficult problems included some that Professor Schoenfeld put on the final test simply because they had stumped him for some time. The students taught to analyze problems using the problem-solving strategies were less distracted by surface details of the new problems on the test than were control students. The strategies-instructed students focused more on the aspects of the problems that provided the information needed to solve the problem (Schoenfeld & Herrmann, 1982). Think-aloud protocols confirmed extensive use of the general strategies to organize application of specific mathematical concepts and procedures by the students who took the course.

Although Schoenfeld's training clearly involved some student discovery and guided discovery via teacher coaching, there is no doubt that Schoenfeld's instruction was more explicit than the instruction prescribed by many radical constructivists (e.g., see Schoenfeld, 1989b). Our interpretation of Schoenfeld's work is that it is direct explanation in the best sense of the term (see Chapter 8), in that the teacher provides the students with a good start on the processes that constitute effective problem solving, but students and teachers then work together to develop a much fuller understanding of the problem-solving strategies. Schoenfeld's students worked hard to figure out how to adapt and elaborate the strategic scheme Schoenfeld provided to them, with the result an internalization of a flexible approach to problem solving, an approach to problem solving that students constructed for themselves. Although Schoenfeld typically refers back to his training studies as evidence favoring articulation of general strategies and more specific knowledge, including specific mathematics procedures that could be thought of as task-specific strategies, there were other sets of data generated in the 1980s that also supported models of mathematical cognition that include strategies. Some of these will be touched on as the discussion of other components in Schoenfeld's model proceeds.

Monitoring and Control (Self-Regulation) Monitoring is an aspect of metacognition that Schoenfeld highlights. Schoenfeld focuses on how monitoring contributes to self-regulated use of knowledge, including procedural knowledge. Schoenfeld recognizes that an expert electing a strategy to make a first attempt at solving a problem uses metacognitive understandings to do so as part of planning a candidate problem solution. For instance, Schoenfeld (1992) reports how professional mathematicians spend a great deal of time analyzing problems before making a first move to problem solve compared with novices, many of whom spend almost no time in planning. Once a strategy is activated, the expert monitors whether progress is being made in solving the problem, with shifts in strategies when the expert senses that progress is not occurring or that there may be a better approach. Such shifts are much less common when novices attempt problems, with much less on-line monitoring of progress during problem solving by novices compared with skilled problem solvers.

Schoenfeld believes that the good math instructor can do much to foster understanding of where and when particular mathematics strategies work as well as foster a general tendency in students to monitor their progress during problem solving—to ask questions when problem solving seems not to be proceeding well or important information seems to be missing (e.g., Graesser & McMahen, 1993). This can be accomplished using scaffolded instruction as groups of students attempt to solve problems. The good mathematics teacher coaches students during their problem-solving attempts, posing questions such as the following:

> What (exactly) are you doing? Can you describe it precisely?
> Why are you doing it? How does it fit into your solution?
> How does it help you? What will you do with the outcome when you obtain it? (Schoenfeld, 1992, p. 356)

Such questions, when posed consistently as part of mathematics instruction, sensitize students to monitor their problem solving and to become aware of the effects of the strategies they are using as well as where and when positive effects can be obtained.

Schoenfeld believes (informed in part by research by Lester; see the earlier discussion of Charles & Lester, 1984) that teachers can improve student understanding of mathematics and self-regulated problem solving by modeling for students the monitored use of mathematical concepts and strategies and coaching students to monitor and self-regulate. He recognizes that the development of self-regulated problem solving requires long-term input, however, and that our understanding of how to structure classrooms and coaching interactions so as to foster best self-regulated problem solving is far from complete.

Schoenfeld is aware that students often have misconceptions and misunderstandings about when and where to use the mathematical procedures they

know (see also Confrey, 1990, and Putnam et al., 1990); sometimes their execution of strategies is systematically flawed as well, as in the case of the many subtraction bugs (i.e., consistent errors made during subtraction; van Lehn, 1990). If students are to become aware of errant metacognitive and procedural knowledge and correct it, it is essential that they monitor whether the strategies they are using are effective. From Schoenfeld's perspective, it is not surprising that there are clear correlations between problem solving and monitoring competencies (e.g., Slife, Weiss, & Bell, 1985; Van Haneghan, 1990; Van Haneghan & Baker, 1989). Consistent with this relationship, problem-solving instruction that includes monitoring is more effective than otherwise comparable instruction that does not encourage students to monitor their progress toward solutions (Delclos & Harrington, 1991). Also, students who are high on metacognition in general are better problem solvers than students who are not (Swanson, 1990).

Beliefs and Affect   Students construct beliefs about mathematics, often ones based on the experiences they have as part of mathematics instruction. These beliefs are sometimes errant in ways that undermine the development of sophisticated mathematical behaviors (Schoenfeld [1989a and 1992] provided all of the beliefs described here; see also Ball, 1988; Lampert, 1990; Schommer, Crouse, & Rhodes, 1992; Stodolsky, 1985). For example, the common beliefs that, "Mathematics problems have one and only right answer," and, "There is only one correct way to solve any mathematics problem—usually the rule the teacher has most recently demonstrated to the class," have high potential for discouraging reflective problem solving, including the generation of alternative ways of tackling particular problems. So does a belief such as, "When the teacher asks a question in math class, the students who understand only need a few seconds to answer correctly." Perhaps it should not be surprising in light of such beliefs that some students conclude that math learned in schools is, "Mostly facts and procedures that have to be memorized." Many students come to believe more in memorizing as a process underlying achievement in mathematics than in reflection, endorsing perspectives such as, "The best way to do well in math is to memorize all the formulas," and, "You have to memorize the way to do constructions (from students in a geometry class)." Moreover, by high school, students are making attributions that clearly undermine exerting effort when having difficulty with mathematics (see Chapter 5), often attributing achievement in mathematics to uncontrollable factors such as ability: "Some people are good at math and some just aren't."

The experiences that shape these beliefs include many nights of homework that has only one final answer as well as years of taking tests that require quick responding. By emphasizing speed of responding, teachers often discourage reflection and encourage the belief that if a student cannot do a problem in a few minutes, it is probably beyond the student (Schoenfeld, 1985, 1992). Of course, such teaching is the result of teacher beliefs that their job is to prepare students to work the "problem" typically covered in elementary-level arithmetic, algebra, geometry, or calculus and to work it quickly because that is what is required on the SAT and other instruments in the accountability system.

Beliefs affect motivations and hence determine behavior. Traditional mathematics instruction is rigged to encourage the beliefs that memorizing is problem solving; problems that require reflection are problems that cannot be solved; and if math does not come easily, the ability to do mathematics is not there. Such beliefs motivate memorizing and rapid responding and giving up when a problem solution is not immediately obvious. Such beliefs must be turned around if students are to become reflective problem solvers who persist in the face of difficulties during problem solving.

Practices   Just as conventional mathematics instruction undermines reflective problem solving, there are instructional practices that promote it, ones consonant with effective instructional practices we have encountered before. Students and teachers can engage in reflective dialogue, with the teacher providing challenging problems, ones that are nonetheless within reach of the students Effective teachers also provide support on an as-needed basis. In such classes, there are collaborative attempts to make sense of problems and discussions of potential alternative solutions. There are thoughtful arguments. Teachers do not tell answers or how to get them. Students and teachers cooperatively interact to construct and evaluate potential solutions.

Schoenfeld is aware of mathematics educators who manage to teach mathematics as a collaborative enterprise. He also recognizes that such instruction

is too rare and that we know too little about it. There is much research to be done here. Such work has high potential for informing the larger educator community: As we have reviewed in previous chapters, teacher-student collaborative problem solving and meaning-making are at the heart of contemporary models of learning to read and write as well as considered essential in contemporary science instruction. (More about cooperative models in mathematics education later in this chapter.)

Schoenfeld's Model and the NCTM Standards   The NCTM *Standards* (1989, 1991) address all of the factors Schoenfeld believes are important in mathematical thinking and problem solving. Problem solving is at the heart of mathematics consistent with the *Standards* calling for students to be taught the general Polya-type strategies as well as many specific procedures for particular types of problems. These specific strategies are viewed as procedures to be used flexibly and in combination with other mathematical knowledge as part of problem solving. Monitoring of performance is one of the general strategies, with students consistently encouraged to reflect on their problem solving. Such reflection is intended in part to encourage the development of sophisticated metacognition about specific problem-solving strategies and the applicability of particular mathematics concepts.

The NCTM *Standards* particularly encourage instruction that promotes beliefs that will motivate persistence and effort during problem solving as well as long-term commitment to mathematics as a way of thinking about the world that is accessible to most students. We will make the case in Chapter 17 that one way to encourage instruction of some important content is to assess it, for educators do in fact teach to whatever tests their students face. The trick is to make certain that assessments tap knowledge and beliefs that should be fostered. Thus, the *Standards* call for consistent assessment of student dispositions about mathematics, including their (1) confidence in using mathematics, (2) flexibility in doing mathematics, (3) perseverance at mathematical tasks, (4) curiosity in doing mathematics, (5) reflection on their own thinking, and (6) appreciation of the role of mathematics in applications (NCTM, 1989, Standard 10). Why assess these dispositions? Because, as Schoenfeld (1985, 1992) contends, beliefs can motivate mathematical achievement and commitment or undermine it.

Beyond encouraging assessments consistent with the NCTM goals, there are many other concrete instructional recommendations in the *Standards* for increasing student confidence in using mathematics. Virtually every part of the *Standards* encourages student understanding that mathematical thinking is flexible and that perseverance is often required to solve problems. Students are encouraged to reflect on their own mathematical problem-solving behaviors and to be curious about mathematical phenomena. Understanding that mathematics is useful in the real world is encouraged by instruction that features problems from the real world.

At the heart of the *Standards* is a model of instructional practice that is completely consistent with the instructional practices Schoenfeld favors. Compare this description about teaching from the *Standards* with the reflective discussion, described earlier, that occurred in Schoenfeld's classes:

> Teaching mathematics from a problem-solving perspective . . . involves the notion that the very essence of studying mathematics is itself an exercise in exploring, conjecturing, examining, and testing—all aspects of problem solving. Tasks should be created and presented that are accessible to students and extend their knowledge of mathematics and problem solving. Students should be given opportunities to formulate problems from given situations and create new problems by modifying the conditions of a given problem.
>
> Teachers should engage students in mathematical discourse about problem solving. This includes discussing different solutions and solution strategies for a given problem, how solutions can be extended and generalized, and different kinds of problems that can be created from a given situation. All students should be made to feel that they have something to contribute to the discussion of a problem. Assessment should focus on the notion of whether mathematics is being taught in such a way as to promote these aspects of problem solving.
>
> Teaching mathematics as an exercise in reasoning should also be commonplace in the classroom. Students should have frequent opportunities to engage in mathematical discussions in which reasoning is valued. Students should be encouraged to explain their reasoning process for reaching a given conclusion or to justify why their particular approach to problem solving is appropriate. The goal of emphasizing reasoning in the teaching of mathematics is to empower students to reach conclusions and justify statements on their own rather than to rely solely on the authority of a teacher or textbook. (NCTM, 1991, pp. 95–96)

If this type of instructional practice seems familiar to readers of this book, it should. We have encountered this type of discussion in chapter after chapter as we have considered the nature of effective instruction.

The NCTM emphasize again and again that mathematics instruction should be about how mathematics relates to, describes, and can explain the world. Such teaching requires more time than the conventional, superficial approach. It also requires more than homework problems from a textbook. Thus, when elementary children study geometric shapes, the *Standards* urge that children analyze real-world objects to identify the shapes in them (e.g., patterned rugs, furniture arrangements); when high school students learn about probability, the problems should come from the real concerns of students (e.g., what is the probability of a 60 percent shooter hitting on 9 of 10 free throws?). The *Standards* emphasize collaborative, reflective teaching and problem solving between students and teachers. Stimulating the spread of such instruction is one purpose of the NCTM *Standards*. Whether the *Standards* have such an effect is in itself an important research question for the 1990s.

Summary Schoenfeld's perspectives on mathematical cognition are consistent with what we call good information processing, which includes knowledge, strategies, metacognition, and motivational beliefs in interaction. An important mechanism in the development of good information processing is teacher-student collaborative instruction that begins with teacher modeling and explanations but that expands as teachers and students work together in applying new strategies to diverse tasks.

Author MP first summarized the nature of good information processing in mathematical cognition in an article published one year after Schoenfeld's (1985) classic, *Mathematical Problem Solving* (Pressley, 1986). The article was written in 1984 before MP encountered the Schoenfeld volume. As the years have passed, both Schoenfeld's perspectives and the points of view in Pressley (1986) have endured, with virtually every claim in both sources now more supportable than it was at the time of publication. Both have had impact on development of new models of problem-solving instruction.

For example, Derry (e.g., Derry, Hawkes, & Tsai, 1987; Derry & Kellis, 1986) cites both the Schoenfeld model and the good information processing perspective as important in her thinking as she developed her TAPS (Training Arithmetic Problem-Solving Skills) model of problem-solving instruction. She teaches middle-school, high school, and young adult populations strategies for solving simple word problems, instruction that emphasizes when the strategies taught can be applied. Derry's students are taught to react to a problem by first attempting to understand it. Then they come up with a plan based on matching strategies they have learned to the demands and constraints of the problem and monitor their problem solving. TAPS has proved effective in promoting the arithmetic word problem–solving skills in several studies and provides additional validation for both Schoenfeld's model and the good information processing perspective.

NATURAL DEVELOPMENT OF MATHEMATICAL UNDERSTANDINGS

Mathematics education researchers, such as Thomas Carpenter, Thomas Romberg, and James Moser of the University of Wisconsin; Karen Fuson at Northwestern; and Arthur Baroody of the University of Illinois, have studied extensively the natural development of young children's arithmetic competence. They contend that conventional mathematics instruction does not build on what the child knows already about numbers and mathematical operations. This is unfortunate from their perspective because they believe that children are most likely to understand completely the mathematics they are taught if it is related to prior knowledge, again a prescription encountered repeatedly in this book as part of effective instruction. Much of the research on the development of mathematical cognition has focused on preschool and primary-grade children's acquisition of addition and subtraction.

Mathematical Understandings Developed During the Preschool Years

There is substantial development of mathematical understandings during the preschool years (e.g., Baroody, 1987; Fuson, 1988, 1992; Romberg & Carpenter, 1986). We summarize in this section some of the most important discoveries of Baroody, Fusen, Carpenter, Romberg, and their like-minded colleagues. (We make no attempt in this subsection to attribute the documentation of specific competencies to specific researchers, pointing out that what follows in this subsection is an abstraction across the writings of Baroody, Fusen, Carpenter, and Romberg.)

Many 2-year-olds can report to their parent when there are two toys. Three- to 4-year-olds also can point out three cookies or four people. Recognition of such small sets seems to be based more on perceptual differences between one, two, three, and four items, rather than on a deep conceptual understanding of the concepts of number or the amounts represented by the numbers 1 through 4, with the term **subitizing** used to refer to young children's abilities to identify the number for small sets of objects. Identification of larger sets of objects by number is infrequent for 2- to 4-year-olds.

With small numbers, addition and subtraction operations are sometimes performed by preschoolers, in the sense that they can "get some more" and "lose some." Preschoolers also can conserve in the Piagetian sense when small numbers of objects are involved (Piaget, 1965): Suppose a row of three objects is shown to a child. Then the row is covered, with the middle object surreptitiously removed. When the cover is lifted, the child will definitely notice that the number of objects in the row has changed, not fooled for an instant by the fact that the row of two mice spans the same distance as the row of three mice did (Gelman & Gallistel, 1978). In contrast, with larger numbers of objects, preschoolers perceive that a 10-inch row of n objects has the same number of objects as a 10-inch row of n + 2 or n + 3 objects; also, two rows with n objects are perceived as having different numbers of objects if one row is 10 inches long and the other 13 inches long. That is, preschoolers do not conserve larger numbers—perceptual qualities other than the number of objects are used to decide equivalency and nonequivalencies of amount. With one-, two-, and three-object quantities, however, the number of objects in a set is used to determine equivalency of sets, rather than any other physical property of the sets, such as length of the row in which the set members are displayed.

Many preschoolers learn the whole-number sequence from 1 to 10, and often preschoolers acquire the sequence from 1 to 20. It is common for a child to arrive at kindergarten able to write the whole numbers to 20. Some kindergarten children learn to count to 100 or 200 as well as "by 10s" up to 100. On their way to learning these sequences, consistent errors are common, with a frequent error being that some numbers are skipped in number sequences (e.g., 13, 14, 16, 18 . . .). Much of the learning of sequences is more memory work than conceptual: Children do not recognize that 1, 2, 3, and so forth are related to 11, 12, 13, and so forth or to 10, 20, 30, and so forth, perhaps because it is not obvious how 2 is related to 12 or 20 given that the word two is not perceptually salient to the preschooler in the pronunciation of twelve and twenty.

Preschoolers begin to learn how to count objects, recognizing that they need to arrange items so each item is counted once and only once using the whole-number sequences they have learned. Even so, preschoolers sometimes do not arrange relatively large numbers of objects, and they sometimes point to an object and fail to count it or point to an object and say two numbers. By 5 years of age, it is not unusual for children to be able to count up to 20 or more objects, although it takes a lot of effort on behalf of the child. If the child attempts effort-reducing shortcuts during counting, such as simply looking at each object rather than pointing at or touching them, errors are common and likely—number sequences and the operations of counting are anything but automatic for the 5-year-old, with the result that high effort is required and errors are common. For the 5-year-old, counting is a short-term memory capacity–demanding activity.

An important acquisition is the development of understanding that the last number uttered in a count is the number of objects in the set counted (i.e., the **cardinal number**). The development of understanding of cardinality as it relates to counting is known as the **count-to-cardinal** transition. Many 5-year-olds recognize that if the count of two sets of objects end in the same number, the two sets have the same number of objects (e.g., 1,2,3,4,5,6 apples in this row is equal to 1,2,3,4,5,6 apples in that row). This is an important understanding because a cognitive prerequisite for learning simple addition and subtraction is the ability to note equivalence of two sets. Beyond having this prerequisite knowledge, kindergarten and grade-1 entry-level students often know much more, including how to add and subtract, at least in some situations.

Naturally Developed Addition and Subtraction Skills of Primary-Grade Children

As we just reviewed, children entering kindergarten or grade 1 have many fundamental mathematical understandings. In fact, they arrive at kindergarten and grade 1 already able to do much of what they are supposed to learn in primary mathematics: Even before receiving instruction in addition and subtraction, children often can do a variety of elementary addition and subtraction if they are provided concrete objects to manipulate.

Addition   In a prominent 3-year longitudinal study of children's addition and subtraction, Carpenter and Moser (e.g., 1982) and their colleagues (e.g., Carpenter, Hiebert, & Moser, 1981) evaluated how school-entry children solved two types of addition problems:

> **Joining** problems involve putting together two quantities as in, "Connie had 5 marbles. Jim gave her 8 more marbles. How many marbles did Connie have altogether?" Joining problems involve a dynamic, changing relationship.
>
> **Part-part-whole** problems require analyzing an existing quantity and decomposing it into it components, such as in, "There are 6 boys and 8 girls on the soccer team. How many children are on the team altogether?" Part-part-whole problems involve a static, descriptive relationship.

Carpenter, Moser, and their colleagues were able to discern several different strategies used by children beginning school. Some used their fingers or other concrete objects to solve the problems. Others used counting sequences; sometimes children relied on number facts they had learned (i.e., if a child "knew" $8 + 5 = 13$ based on prior experience, there was no need to use fingers or counting to solve the problem). In general, Carpenter and his associates noted that these strategies were used for both joining and part-part-whole problems, with no consistent differences in the way that the preschoolers tackled the two types of problems.

Often, strategies were combined, with **counting all with models** a strategy combination discussed frequently in the literature. This combination involves establishing two sets as the addends and then counting all of the elements, beginning the count with the whole number 1. Some of the best-known counting strategies in children's addition, ones documented since the late 1960s and early 1970s (e.g., Groen & Parkman, 1972; Suppes & Groen, 1967), also were observed. One was **counting all without models,** which is the same as counting all with models except that no concrete objects are used to represent the addends and sum. Another counting strategy observed was **counting on from first** (i.e., start from the addend mentioned first and count up by the number represented by the second addend) and **counting on from larger** (which involves starting with the larger addend and counting up the number specified by the smaller addend). Counting on from larger is often referred to as the **MIN** strategy (Groen & Parkman, 1972) because it minimizes the number of counts required to solve an addition problem when using a counting strategy.

Consistent with young children being more facile in their perception, representation, and use of small compared with large numbers, problems involving small numbers were especially likely to be solved in the studies conducted by Carpenter and his associates. In general, early in grade 1, counting all with models was the predominant strategy. By the end of grade 1, and thus following some instruction in addition, counting on was observed more than other strategies. The most important point, however, is that even at entry to grade 1, children were strategic problem solvers, able to do something that had not yet been covered in school formally.

Subtraction   Just as children entering primary school can do several types of addition problems, they can also solve different types of subtraction problems. For example, consider Romberg and Carpenter's (e.g., 1986, Table 29.2, for all examples provided in this paragraph) analysis of subtraction word problems: Some problems require **separation** of one set of objects from another, such as the following:

> Tom has 13 marbles. He gave 5 marbles to his sister Connie. How many marbles does Tom have left?

Others are **join/missing addend** problems, similar in structure to this one:

> Tom had 5 marbles. His sister Connie gave him some more marbles. Now Tom has 13 marbles. How many marbles did Connie give him?

A **compare** problem involving Tom and Connie might be the following:

> Tom has 5 marbles. His sister Connie has 13 marbles. How many more marbles does Connie have than Tom?

A **combine** problem involves specification of a total, with one of the numbers contributing to the total given and the other missing, as in this problem:

> There are 13 marbles in the bag. Five of them are red and the rest are blue. How many blue marbles are in the bag?

Several strategies were observed as grade-1 students attempted these problems. One, the **separating from given** strategy, involves constructing a set of concrete objects representing the larger number in the problem, and then separating out (i.e., by counting) the number to be subtracted from the larger number. The **counting down from given** strategy is like the separating from strategy, except no concrete objects are used. Counting down from involves starting with the larger number in the problem and counting down from that number, one count at a time, equal to the total number of counts in the smaller number in the problem. The **adding on** strategy begins with setting up the number of objects equal to the smaller number cited in the problem. Objects are then added on one at a time until the larger number cited in the problem is reached. The number of objects added on is then counted to provide the solution. A pure counting version of adding on (i.e., involving no concrete objects) is called **counting up from given.** A third strategy involving manipulation of concrete objects was termed **matching.** Two sets of concrete objects corresponding to the numbers in the problem are established. Then objects from the two sets are paired in a one-to-one fashion. When one set still has remaining items, those are counted, with that count being the correct answer to the problem.

Importance of Word Problems and Children's Use of Natural Strategies to Solve Them   All of the problems discussed in the last two subsections were word problems, consistent with the NCTM recommendation to present word problems to young children. Analysis of such word problems to produce solutions using concrete representations requires real mathematical understandings, more so than the mechanical addition and subtraction exercises that typify much conventional primary addition and subtraction problems (e.g., ones in which number sentences are set up and the student need only solve the set up problem, such as $13 - 5 =$ __, $8 + 5 =$ __, or $13 -$ __ $= 5$, exercises that are intended to develop long-term memory of the basic addition and subtraction "facts" and facility in using the facts).

Conventional thinking is that children are not ready for word problems until they have mastered the relevant addition and subtraction facts. That children can solve word problems before relevant addition and subtraction facts have been memorized and automatized is clear evidence that the conventional wisdom is wrong, at least with respect to the prerequisites for word problems. Carpenter and Moser's (1983) position is that the conventional wisdom is essentially backwards: Solution of word problems should be used to stimulate the development of knowledge of mathematical facts (i.e., knowledge of facts such as $13 - 5 = 8$, $8 + 5 = 13$, or $13 - 8 = 5$ will increase as an incidental byproduct of solving problems involving the facts); memorization of facts should not be used to set the stage for presentation of word problems. Carpenter and Moser's position is consistent with the recurring contemporary emphases on student construction of mathematical knowledge as a means of developing mathematical understandings.

Even so, we believe there is reason for caution in coming to general prescriptions about the use of word problems as children's introduction to arithmetic problems. A study by Levine, Jordan, and Huttenlocher (1992) is telling with respect to this point. They presented simple addition and subtraction problems to children ages 4 to 6. When the children were given word problems similar to the ones used in Carpenter et al. (1981), the 6-year-olds solved the problems about two-thirds of the time. The 4-year-olds and young 5-year-olds, however, rarely solved these word problems. In contrast, when 4- and 5-year-olds were presented problems comparably difficult but with concrete referents (black buttonlike disks) that could be added or subtracted, they solved many more problems, with the difference in solution rates for 4- and 5-year-olds versus 6-year-olds small when problems were presented with disks but much larger when the children attempted word problems. There may be a lower developmental limit on the usefulness of word problems in beginning arithmetic instruction, with word problems more appropriate for grade-1 and older children than for preschoolers.

Readers who experienced conventional grade-1 mathematics instruction will recognize how radically different the developmental point of view is compared with conventional outlooks about the teaching of addition and subtraction. For example, we both can remember that our grade-1 teachers did everything possible to dissuade students from solving addition and subtraction problems on their fingers. In contrast, the contemporary outlook is that the fingers are a natural set of concrete objects and that using them to solve problems involving addition and subtraction is developmentally appropriate.

Readers might also note that the use of mathematical strategies by preschoolers is consistent with previous discussions in this book about preschoolers' strategic competence (see Chapter 2, this volume). Implicit throughout this book is that use of strategies is important in the construction of declarative knowledge. The effects of children's problem-solving efforts on the development of mathematical knowledge during the preschool and primary-grade years has been of special interest to Robert Siegler of Carnegie-Mellon University.

Development of Knowledge of Math Facts: The Distribution of Associations Model

Siegler's work (covered briefly in Chapter 4, this volume) emphasizes that most children eventually abandon the counting and concrete manipulation strategies identified by Carpenter and colleagues. They come to rely on knowledge of math facts when presented simple problems (e.g., given $2 + 5 = $ ____, they retrieve the answer 7 from long-term memory). Siegler's (e.g., 1987, 1988, 1989; Siegler & Shrager, 1984) theory is that as children use strategies to work addition and subtraction problems, they develop associations between the problem statements (e.g., $2 + 5$) and the answers they generate for problems (i.e., the association between "2 + 5" and "7" is strengthened when a child solves $2 + 5$ using fingers or through counting). Of course, children do not always produce the correct answer to problems, and thus they also form associations between problem statements and incorrect answers (e.g., the association between "2 + 5" and "6" is strengthened when a child errantly generates 6 as an answer to the problem $2 + 5$). Because the most frequently experienced answer is the correct one (i.e., when children are shown complete number facts, such as on flash cards, they experience correct associations; adults or other children often correct errant answers by providing the correct answer; and the most frequent answer produced by most children in reaction to a problem is the correct answer), the strongest association between a math fact problem (e.g., $2 + 5$) and an individual number is with the number corresponding to the correct answer (e.g., 7). When the associative strength between the problem and the correct answer is sufficiently stronger than any other math fact–number association, the math fact comes to elicit the correct answer reliably. The student no longer needs to solve the problem using concrete aids or counting—they can simply "look it up" in long-term memory (e.g., Ashcraft & Battaglia, 1978; Ashcraft & Stazyk, 1981), although some students will continue to count or use other strategies "just to make certain" he or she is reporting the correct answer (Siegler, 1988). What Siegler is describing is a shift from reliance on problem-solving strategies to reliance on the knowledge base (see Chapter 4).

In general, Siegler's most important results have been replicated by others as part of analyses supporting the model developed by Siegler, in particular that development of associations between simple problems and their answers permits retrieval of correct answers to become a preferred approach when solving simple problems (e.g., Geary & Burlingham-Dubree, 1989; LeFevre, Kulak, & Bisanz, 1991). Even so, it must be remembered that Siegler's studies were of children answering "number-fact" problems devoid of external referents. This is an important limitation, for children do not seem to use the strategies Siegler studied (e.g., use of fingers) as certainly when they are confronted with problems depicted concretely (e.g., addition and subtraction problems presented with black buttons) or when presented word problems based on number facts (Levine et al., 1992). Nonetheless, given the many occasions when children are presented math fact problems without concrete supports, there is no doubt that Siegler has provided an important window on a salient part of many children's mathematical experiences. The importance of this developmental model is obvious from the amount of follow-up research it has inspired.

Additional Understandings of Basic Mathematical Skills Produced in Research Evaluating Developmental Shifts from Reliance on Computing Strategies to Reliance on Fact Retrieval

The orderly outcomes produced by the Wisconsin and Carnegie-Mellon groups have stimulated much follow-up research, with this work providing increasingly detailed understanding of basic addition and subtraction. A brief review of some of the more interesting of these studies makes obvious that this is an exceptionally active area of research. This work

also makes obvious that basic addition and subtraction competencies are enormous intellectual accomplishments. Consider the following examples:

- Children's facility in using counting as a problem-solving procedure improves considerably during the preschool years, with counting applied to an increasing range of problems from 3½ years of age onward (Sophian, 1987).

- Among the computational strategies based on counting that preschoolers use, some are more efficient than others. There have been suggestions in the literature since Groen and Parkman (1972) that with practice doing addition problems, children eventually discover and use the more efficient MIN strategy rather than less efficient procedures. Siegler and his colleagues (e.g., Siegler & Crowley, 1991; Siegler & Jenkins, 1989) reexamined this issue by observing children solve many problems and interviewing them after they solved them. They believed the preschoolers they watched discovered the MIN strategy. In short, work continues on preschoolers' use and discovery of strategies, with the aim of providing more detailed understanding of the origins and nature of preschoolers' strategic competencies. There is no doubt that preschoolers discover many strategies as they practice solving addition problems (e.g., Christensen & Cooper, 1991).

- Widaman, Little, Geary, and Cormier (1992) studied the addition competencies of students in grades 2, 4, and 6 and college. In two experiments, students were provided simple math facts, with each fact accompanied either by its correct or an incorrect answer (e.g., 2 + 5 = 7 or 2 + 5 = 8). The second experiment also included more complex problems, one involving addition of two-digit numbers with two-digit numbers (e.g., 41 + 25), again accompanied either by a correct or incorrect answer. The students' task was to decide as quickly as possible when presented a problem and answer whether the answer was correct. The reaction time data were analyzed to make inferences about strategies used by the students and shifts in use of strategies. One important conclusion was that at each developmental level, there were students using strategies to solve problems and others relying on retrieval of math facts. (See Geary & Brown, 1991, for an analysis of differences in solution strategies among grade-3 and grade-4 students; see Geary, 1990; Geary, Brown, & Samaranayake, 1991; and Geary, Bow-Thomas, & Yao, 1992, for evidence that some students are much more likely to develop a repertoire of addition strategies than are other children, and some children are more likely to come to rely on retrieval of math facts than are other students.) Although this was not surprising at the grade-2 level in Widaman et al. (1992), it was striking that nontrivial proportions of grade-6 (30 percent) and college (20 percent) students use computational strategies: Is it possible that even some college students do not know their basic addition facts, or were they computing the answer just to be sure they were right? Widaman et al. (1992) believe the answer is that fact retrieval from long-term memory is anything but certain for some adults. Complementary analyses document that for most adults, even simple addition problems require some cognitive effort to solve (Kaye, deWinstanley, Chen, & Bonnefil, 1989).

- That simple addition is problematic for some middle-grade children was illuminated by the work of Goldman and her colleagues at Vanderbilt. Goldman, Mertz, and Pellegrino (1989; also Goldman, Pellegrino, & Mertz, 1988) studied students in grades 3 and 4 who had not reached the point of being able to retrieve their math facts automatically, continuing to rely extensively on MIN and other counting strategies. Using a microcomputer program, the students were given extensive practice (i.e., sessions provided over 3 months) in generating the answers to basic single-digit addition problems. In general, student responding quickened over the period of practice, although even at the end of 3 months, virtually all participants seemed to use counting strategies (particularly MIN) at least some of the time, consistent with other data that mathematically disabled students overrely on counting strategies (Geary et al., 1992; Geary & Brown, 1991; Geary et al., 1991).
- Just as many children come to "know" addition facts and rely on retrieval of facts rather than computation when presented simple addition problems, they also come to know other math facts, with fact retrieval eventually supplanting counting strategies when presented elementary multiplication problems (Cooney, Swanson, &

Ladd, 1988; Geary, Widaman, & Little, 1986; Koshmider & Ashcraft, 1991). For example, Campbell and Graham (1985) studied the development of associations between the single-digit math problems up to 9×9 and the answers to these problems. In general, Siegler's distribution-of-associations model fit the data, with the strength of association between a problem and its answer eventually stronger than any competing associations. By grade 5, children's use of multiplication-fact retrieval resembled multiplication-fact retrieval by adults in the study.

- Widaman et al. (1992) also validated three different component skills involved in multidigit addition (Widaman, Geary, Cormier, & Little, 1989) that are performed slowly at first and eventually can become automatized. The three skills are (1) initial coding of the digits in a problem, (2) computing or retrieving the correct sum for each column from long-term memory, and (3) carrying to the next column. Others (e.g., Wolters, Beishuizen, Broers, & Knoppert, 1990), who have been studying mental addition of multi-digit numbers, have also identified ways in which long-term knowledge of addition facts is essential as part of the problem-solving process, which often depends heavily on reformulating addends into parts and adding the parts, for example, thinking of $29 + 64$ as $(30 - 1) + (60 + 4)$, which can be calculated quickly as $30 + 60 + 4 - 1 = 93$. Siegler and Shrager's (1984) insights about the use of long-term–remembered math facts to solve simple addition problems is helping to explain how people solve even more complex problems than the ones Siegler studied.

Children acquire simple problem-solving strategies before they come to school. A consequence of practicing these strategies and generating answers to problems is the development of associations between problems (e.g., $4 + 3$, $2 + 7$) and the answers generated in response to problems. Because the correct answer to a problem (e.g., 7 and 9, respectively, for the example problems) is associated with the problem more often than any other answer, this association becomes stronger than competing problem-number associations, so eventually the correct answer is elicited reliably and automatically whenever the problem is presented. By the middle elementary grades, many children are relying on retrieval of answers from long-term memory over any other strategy in generating answers to single-digit addition problems. With practice performing other operations, such as subtraction and multiplication, there is strengthening of associations between subtraction and multiplication problems and their correct answers so that by the middle-to-late elementary grades, many children rely on retrieval from long-term memory to respond to basic subtraction and multiplication problems as well as addition problems. It is important to recognize that there are individual differences, however, with respect to whether students come to use the retrieval strategy. For example, a nontrivial proportion of adults continue to rely on counting strategies to solve single-digit arithmetic problems.

Another Developmental Model of Procedural and Knowledge Contributions to Early Arithmetic Competence

Byrnes of the University of Maryland (e.g., 1992; also Byrnes & Wasik, 1991) believes that mathematical concepts and procedures are stored in separate memory systems, consistent with the ACT* model reviewed in Chapters 2 and 3 and with the specification throughout this book of procedural and declarative knowledge as distinguishable components in good information processing. Byrnes also believes, however, that mathematical procedures index pieces of conceptual knowledge that must be understood for the procedure to be carried out. For example, the procedure of "adding fractions" is indexed to the concept of "least common denominator" because a least common denominator must be found as part of the fraction addition operation. Concepts are also linked to one another in long-term memory according to Byrnes's viewpoint (e.g., "fractions" is indexed as connected to "least common denominator").

Despite these interconnections when procedures and concepts are understood well, Byrnes believes it makes sense to separate them for several reasons: One is that people can know concepts but not be able to carry out the procedures that call for them (e.g., understanding the idea of lowest common denominator without understanding how to add fractions); moreover, sometimes people can execute procedures without fully understanding the concepts relating to the procedures (e.g., adding fractions using an algorithm). Another support for

separation of conceptual and procedural knowledge is neuropsychological evidence (e.g., Keller & Sutton, 1991), substantiating that mathematical-conceptual and procedural knowledge involve different regions of the brain. Even so, most mathematical operations involve dynamic interaction and simultaneous use of procedural and mathematical conceptual knowledge.

Byrnes (1992) offered impressive evidence in favor of his perspective. He studied grade-7 students who had just received their first instruction about the concept of integers. They had been taught about the negative and positive parts of the number line, but they had not yet been taught about how to do computations involving integers (i.e., how to add and subtract positive and negative numbers). Byrnes first measured how much conceptual knowledge each of 25 students had acquired from instruction they had received thus far about integers: The conceptual knowledge measure required students to place four positive and four negative integers on a number line; the students also placed the same numbers on an analogous "staircase," which had a landing corresponding to zero and steps descending from it to the left to represent negative numbers and ascending from the right to represent positive numbers. The numbers −4 and +2 were already placed on the correct steps of the staircase. The conceptual measurement also required students to decide which of two integers presented to them was larger. Byrnes also assessed how much procedural knowledge the students possessed with respect to addition and subtraction of integers. This measurement required students to show, using a number line, the results of adding or subtracting particular integers from a particular starting point on the number line. Students also attempted a number of computational problems involving signed numbers.

After these assessments of conceptual and procedural knowledge were taken, instruction in computation (addition, subtraction, multiplication, division) of integers was provided to students. Computational skill was measured again. The most interesting relationship between pretest assessments and postinstructional computational performance was that pretest conceptual understanding of order was correlated with final computational facility. That is, children's conceptual understanding of integers was related to their ability to acquire procedural skills involving integers, consistent with Byrnes's belief that although mathematical conceptual and procedural knowledge can be separated, they interrelate to determine mathematical competence.

In a second experimental study, Byrnes (1992) manipulated adults' conceptual understanding of "prime number," teaching either a correct or incorrect definition of it. All subjects were then taught a set of mathematical operations requiring knowledge of prime numbers. There was a striking effect of conceptual knowledge on the acquisition of these novel procedures in this study: Students who had learned the errant definition of prime numbers performed the new mathematical procedures more poorly than students taught the correct definition of primes. Once again, acquisition of a mathematical procedure depended on understanding a mathematical concept. We expect more experiments from Byrnes and others specifying in greater detail how conceptual and procedural knowledge interact to affect the development of and developmental differences in mathematical competence.

Instructional Implications

There are some important instructional messages in these data. Carpenter, Romberg, and Moser's work made obvious that word problems are not beyond the capabilities of primary students, and indeed their perspective is that working such problems is much more mathematically meaningful for primary students than drilling on the basic math facts. Knowing the math facts by heart is not necessary for grade-1 students to be able to solve many word problems. Even so, retrieval of the single-digit math facts is essential for performing more complex functions (e.g., single-digit addition facts are used to solve multiple-digit addition problems), so it is disturbing that many students in the later elementary grades and even a number of adults do not automatically retrieve the answers to single-digit problems. Practice doing such problems helps, but there is no quick fix here. Even after 3 months, many of Goldman et al.'s (1989) students were still relying on counting strategies some of the time. A great deal of work remains to be done to determine how to ensure that most students will leave the primary grades "knowing" their math facts—with it likely based on the work of Carpenter and other mathematics educators that much of the instruction intended to produce such knowledge should involve

much more than drill and practice: The goal must be students who reliably retrieve facts such as $2 + 7 = 9$, understand how such facts relate to the world, and connect the mathematical facts they know to other mathematical knowledge. Both knowing math fact associations *and* understanding addition, subtraction, multiplication, and division are essential if a student is to be competent in elementary mathematics and beyond.

Although many mathematics educators seem uncomfortable with the idea of direct teaching of problem-solving skills, believing that mathematics is better learned by students constructing their own understandings, there is substantial evidence of positive effects of explicit mathematics instruction. For example, kindergarten and grade-1 students can solve some types of simple addition and subtraction problems much more reliably if they are given instruction. Problems involving comparison of one set size with another set size can be difficult for primary students who have not been taught a strategy for constructing comparisons (Riley & Greeno, 1988). One reason is that kindergarten and grade-1 students misinterpret statements such as, "Mary has 5 more marbles than John" to mean "Mary has 5 marbles" (Cummins, 1991.) Bebout (1990), however, demonstrated that with instruction primary students can learn to solve such problems. The children in her study were taught how to use concrete aids to represent the problems and then how to translate the concrete representations into symbolic representations. For example, given a comparison problem such as "Bill found 9 pennies. Rosemary found 6 pennies. How many more pennies did Bill find than Rosemary?", Bebout taught students to represent the problem with concrete manipulatives. Then students were shown corresponding number sentences capturing the important elements in the problem (e.g., $9 - 6 = \_\_$), with teacher-student interactions until the students could see how the concrete situation was represented with the number sentence. Instruction continued with students inventing word problems given number sentences (e.g., developing their own word problem that could be represented with $6 + \_\_ = 14$). In short, there was a great deal of direct instruction of how to construct number sentences. Fourteen lessons produced a great deal of improvement in the students' construction of correct number sentences for a variety of problem types.

Finally, we emphasize that the notion of strategy teaching, which is featured in this book, makes sense in the context of primary arithmetic. For example, many children do not naturally develop some effective elementary problem-solving strategies (e.g., counting up from the subtracted number to the larger number to determine a difference— such as counting up from 8 to establish that 6 digits intervene between 14 and 8 and thus represent the answer to 14 − 8). Fuson and her colleagues (e.g., Fuson & Fuson, 1991; Fuson & Willis, 1988) have demonstrated that the counting-up strategy can be taught profitably to primary students, with Fuson's group relying on direct explanation that emphasizes subtraction conceptualized as "adding on." Fuson's work and studies such as Bebout (1990) make clear that direct explanation of elementary problem solving can emphasize understanding. Such instruction can result in students who are more adept at representing the world with mathematical expressions and better able to solve math problems that are presented to them. Our view is that study of conceptually rich instruction of mathematics strategies should be a high priority in the next decade and that the models of information-processing theorists such as Siegler and Byrnes do much to inspire testable hypotheses that are advancing understanding of how children do problems and can learn to do them better. Such theoretically rich research, however, is occurring simultaneously with research that is more obviously applied in focus.

APPLIED RESEARCH INCREASING UNDERSTANDING OF EFFECTIVE MATHEMATICS INSTRUCTION

Mathematics educators are as much as any educator group "on the cutting edge" of new instructional approaches. This section covers some salient instructional and technological innovations currently being evaluated by mathematics educators and researchers interested in mathematical problem solving. Some of these interventions depend on direct explanations of content and procedures, which are intended as a starting point for additional student construction of knowledge; other interventions are more consistent with radically constructivist perspectives on mathematics teaching and learning, in that they leave more for the student to discover. Readers should reflect on the direct explanatory and radical constructivist aspects of the various interventions covered in this section.

Cooperative Learning

Cooperative learning (introduced in Chapter 5) is used for many content areas but is especially appropriate for mathematics education, given the importance that contemporary mathematics educators place on social collaboration in problem solving. Davidson of the University of Maryland and his colleagues (e.g., Bassarear & Davidson, 1992; Davidson & Kroll, 1991) have been at the vanguard in developing cooperative methods for mathematics instruction. They believe that cooperatively interacting to solve problems can be a transformative experience for many students, with the advantages including the following:

- Students come to value the process of problem solving rather than production of a correct answer. In conventional mathematics instruction, giving a wrong answer can be fearful to the point of producing paralysis. Cooperative interaction helps students come to understand that mistakes are a natural part of problem solving. Cooperative interaction in problem solving encourages growth in understanding rather than reinforcing the production of correct answers, with understanding especially fostered by the constructive feedback people provide to one another as they attempt to reach mutual goals.
- Davidson and his colleagues have observed that mathematics anxiety is reduced when students work in cooperative groups. They note that students who never ask questions in conventional mathematics classes feel they can do so as part of exploring a problem in a cooperative group.
- Cooperative instruction permits more challenging and less conventional problems to be presented to students.
- Cooperation fosters student explanations and re-explanations to one another, which is important because explaining difficult ideas to others is an effective method of forcing people to understand the ideas fully (e.g., Webb, 1989, 1991). The discussions bring to light misconceptions, which can sometimes be resolved via discussion. Students make connections to other knowledge as they discuss, with different students offering to the group differing insights

about how the mathematics being learned connects to the world.

- Multiple representations of problem situations are offered in discussions, which is important, for mathematical people realize that any situation can be represented in a variety of ways. Conventional instruction, with its emphasis on correct answers, does not foster the production of alternative representations of the same situation.
- There are many variations of cooperation. For students who have difficulty working with a group but work well with one other student, pairing is possible. For those who seem to thrive when there is a larger group, placing them in discussions with several students makes sense.

Although not all studies comparing cooperative learning of mathematics with more conventional instruction have produced significant effects favoring cooperation, many studies have done so (Davidson, 1985). The evidence is simply overwhelming that usually at least small positive effects of cooperation are obtained with respect to objective mathematics performances (e.g., students can solve problems on standardized assessments better as a function of participating in cooperative learning experiences).

Nonetheless, there has not been nearly enough systematic study of the many possible effects suggested by Davidson and other cooperative learning theorists (see Chapter 5): If cooperative learning promotes student valuation of processing rather than production of correct answers, increases student facility with multiple representations, and increases understanding that problem solving naturally involves risk taking and false starts, that would be more than enough reason to be enthusiastic about cooperative methods. Davidson's important hypotheses about the multiple positive effects of cooperative learning deserve a great deal of research attention: His position is that cooperative learning produces much deeper understanding than conventional mathematics instruction (and deeper understanding than captured by problem-solving performance measures sensitive only to whether a correct answer is produced). His view is that cooperative learning also increases the likelihood that people will enjoy mathematics, which seems essential if they are eventually to elect the calculus, probability and statistics, and matrix algebra courses required to be mathematically numerate at levels required by

many contemporary professions or, in the shorter term, to elect to try tonight's algebra I assignment.

A healthy turn in cooperative learning research as part of mathematical problem solving is the analysis of the dynamics and structures of groups. Webb (1989, 1992) has established (both in her own research and through systematic review of studies conducted by Peterson and colleagues; e.g., Peterson & Janicki, 1979; Peterson, Janicki, & Swing, 1981; Peterson & Swing, 1985) both the positive effects of generating explanations in cooperative groups and the negative effects on achievement of only being told correct answers when seeking assistance.

Webb has observed that cooperative groups have the potential of allowing only some members to benefit, however, so some caution in constituting groups is in order: Because the higher-ability students in a group are more likely to dominate interactions (also see Dembo & McAuliffe, 1987) and provide explanations, the higher-ability students in a cooperating group of students benefit more from participation in the group. With groups composed of a wide range of abilities, one interesting dynamic is that the high-ability students often form teacher-learner relationships with the lower-ability students, with the unfortunate result that medium-ability students are less involved in group interactions than other students. Medium-ability students are much more active and learn more in homogeneous groups and in groups in which the range of abilities is more narrow (i.e., in groups composed of high-ability and medium-ability students or of medium-ability and low-ability students). Homogeneously high-ability groups tend to be less engaging for high-ability students than mixed-ability groupings, perhaps because the high-ability students assume that other high-ability students do not need their assistance; homogeneously low-ability groups are filled with incorrect explanations, with the result that low-ability students benefit less from homogeneous grouping than from mixed-ability grouping. When all factors are considered, mixed-ability grouping representing less than the full range of abilities seems to be the best combination (i.e., highs and mediums together, mediums and lows together).

Webb (1984) has also studied the effects of gender balance in cooperative groups. She reported that girls were more likely to be interactive in cooperative groups that were gender balanced (i.e., equal numbers of boys and girls), with majority-boy groups resulting in girls being ignored and majority-girl groups resulting in disproportionate interactions directed at the boys in the group. Achievement was greater for girls when they participated in gender-balanced groups.

Good and his colleagues (Good, Grouws, Mason, Slavings, & Cramer, 1990) have also studied how groups operate in elementary classrooms, concentrating on grades 4, 5, and 6, but also collecting data in the primary years. What they observed was that small-group instruction was used extensively as part of mathematics instruction, although there continue to exist classrooms that rely principally on whole-group instruction followed by seatwork practice. The most frequent arrangement was for small-group, cooperative instruction to be used flexibly in conjunction with whole-group instruction, with advantages for both the whole-group and small-group portions of the lessons. For example, there was more discussion of high-level mathematics during whole-class lessons, and there was more use of manipulatives. Whole-class seatwork was more problematic with respect to task engagement, however, with much more off-task time observed than when students worked on comparable problems in small groups. The small groups afforded substantial interactions between students about mathematics. More complex and interesting mathematics tasks were assigned in classrooms with small-group activities compared with classrooms in which only whole-class instruction was used. The small-group format did not always lead to cooperative interaction, with a number of classrooms observed in which teaching occurred in small groups (much like a traditional reading group), followed by seatwork that was carried out by students working alone. Experimental data produced by Good's group (Mason & Good, 1990) suggest that noncooperative grouping may actually lead to lower mathematics achievement than whole-class instruction. There are dangers in simply teaching to smaller groups of students who are then assigned work sheets to be completed individually. The students often get less mathematics instruction because the teacher is making three presentations to different groups of students, with each presentation less extensive than a single whole-class presentation would be.

We expect much more study of cooperative-learning group dynamics, especially with the development of analyses that are sensitive to both the cognitive strategies being used in the groups and the metacognitive information conveyed by group members to one another (e.g., Artzt & Armour-Thomas, 1992). Such research is important because it is becoming apparent that group problem solving sometimes goes awry.

Stacey (1992), for instance, collected verbal protocols of students in grades 7 to 9 while they attempted challenging problems in small groups. What was disturbing was that the group members were often willing to go along with a simple and wrong method of problem solution that was put on the floor by one member of the group. Sometimes good solutions were rejected. Cooperative grouping is no guarantee of successful problem solving (see also Tudge, 1992). Much more research is needed to map in detail when groups work and what can be done so they work better. For example, perhaps adult scaffolding of cooperative learning is necessary—at least at first—for students to sort out effective and ineffective problem-solving tactics. Even as we end this subsection on a cautious note, we remind readers that cooperative learning interventions have proved effective more often than not and can be implemented successfully from the primary grades (e.g., Yackel, Cobb, & Wood, 1991) to college level (e.g., Dees, 1991). Cooperative learning theorists and enthusiasts have thought extensively about how to adapt cooperative methods to various situations, with well-written summaries of their insights now available (e.g., see Davidson & Worsham, 1992).

Scaffolded, Elaborative Teaching

We are inventing the term "saffolded, elaborative teaching" as a way to describe teaching that contrasts with the teacher-as-presenter-of-information or the teacher-as-referee-in-the-competitive-race-for-grades. Such teaching is exemplified here by the teaching of one mathematics instructor, Magdelene Lampert, who has analyzed her own teaching in detail (e.g., Lampert, 1990).

Lampert used cooperative learning methods, with five groups of four and one group of five in a class of 25 grade-5 students. How were these groups formed? The students discussed various ways of dividing the class, recognizing that groups of five would have permitted perfectly equal groups but dismissing this possibility because they believed better interactions would occur with groups of four. This discussion took place as part of the introduction to fractions for the class. That is, the decision about how to break up the class was posed to students as a real-world application of fractions, the topic they were about to study. Once the groups were formed, more discussion of fractions occurred, as students considered other potential ways of fractionating the class—into groups of girls, boys, students new to the school, and so on. Such problems connected the academic content covered in the class to the world experienced by the students.

The teacher made clear that what was valued in the class and in learning groups were clear explanations, not just answers to problems (see Chapter 8 for evidence that explaining in groups is a powerful learning mechanism). The teacher's role in all of this was as the individual with more background in mathematics than other group members. She introduced mathematical ideas and symbols to the class. The teacher provided problems to students, and the students went about solving them via discussion and interaction. Lampert did not teach the students formulas for solving the problems; rather, she let the students work as a group to discover and justify ideas about how to solve problems. The classroom environment was safe for such exploration because the teacher's stance was clear that risk taking was part of solving problems.

Formal mathematics did make its way into the classroom, however. Lampert interacted with the groups in the class in ways intended to increase their understanding of the meaning of the mathematical ideas they were constructing as they worked on problems. In particular, she provided information to the students about how their ideas related to thinking familiar to the larger mathematics community. In this role, Lampert spent a great deal of time recasting student explanations into mathematical explanations and symbolism. By doing so, Lampert taught students mathematical formalisms in ways that made sense to them and yet were consistent with conventions honored in the larger mathematics community. In general, these interactions produced understanding of the concepts covered. These interactions produced much more, however, including alternative ways of thinking about the situation, ways connected to real experiences for these children:

> By the fifth day of working on fractions of a population, many students had "invented" the familiar algorithm: given a fraction written in the conventional form, divide the population by the denominator and multiply the answer to that by the numerator . . . and almost all students could produce a drawing if called

on to do so to illustrate their procedure. . . . (Lampert, 1990, pp. 258–259)

Lampert's role was to present problems to students and to facilitate their construction of mathematical understandings. According to Lampert (1990, adapted from p. 264), the effective mathematics teacher:

- Expects students to make sensible assertions as they attempt to solve problems.
- Fosters and manages the classroom as a cooperative community of discourse.
- Keeps the discussion focused on the problems and potential solutions.
- Expects students to defend their assertions and their use of algorithms that they invent.
- Expects and supports revision of ideas.
- Represents students' assertions in language and drawings that translate individual student ideas into ones that can be grasped by the entire class and ones that are linked with symbolic representations used in the mathematics disciplinary community.
- Guides consolidation of student ideas to a public construction of the class thinking about a mathematical procedure.
- Guides the instruction toward general mathematical "truths" and discussions of when the truths hold.

There is student construction of mathematical understandings here, but it is guided so the mathematical generalizations that are important in elementary mathematics are discovered. Students are really engaged in the give-and-take of the classroom, with the teacher taking the role of a supporting, cooperating guide. Although teachers such as Lampert can inspire others, such teaching cannot be manufactured wholesale or developed with 3-hour, in-service sessions. Lampert knows mathematics well and is committed to the idea that mathematics instruction must foster understanding, a commitment undergirded by her thorough knowledge of Vygotskian theory (Chapter 8). Lampert believes that the members of student communities who problem solve together will not only learn better the specific mathematical content covered in lessons, but also eventually will internalize the problem-solving processes worked through every day by the teacher and class in interaction as they pursue mathematical understandings. Such teaching is scaffolded in the

Vygotskian sense but elaborative in the sense that the teacher elaborates the student thinking, connecting it to conventional mathematical conceptions.

Parental Help with Homework

To the extent it has been studied (i.e., in a half dozen studies with students in grades 4 to 6), parental assistance with homework is associated with improved student problem solving (Hembree, 1992). This association is striking because *assignment* of homework has only a small effect on elementary student achievement in problem solving (Hembree, 1992). Just getting assignments does not stimulate understanding; getting help with assignments from a parent does.

Learning from Examples

Although social interactions can increase mathematical understandings, there are also nonsocial ways of increasing knowledge of mathematical problem-solving procedures. We both took calculus in university. We remember almost never bothering with the textbook in math courses. Rather we purchased and studied supplementary texts filled with worked problems, believing that the way to do well in calculus was to understand the worked problems and be able to do ones like them. Research outcomes are consistent with our undergraduate intuitions about the importance of worked examples in learning how to solve problems.

One of the most important studies evaluating the role of examples in acquisition of problem solving was reported by Sweller and Cooper (1985). In their studies, grade-8 and grade-9 algebra students either were provided worked examples of problem types or practiced solving such problems on their own. The first finding was that it took subjects less time to process the worked problems than to work through the practice problems on their own.

After presentation of practice problems, the participants in the study were presented identically structured test problems. The students who had been given the worked examples during practice solved these new problems more rapidly than did the students who had worked the practice problems on their own. Moreover, the students who had received worked examples made fewer errors on the test problems than did the practice control participants (see also Cooper & Sweller, 1987). These advantages with identically structured problems did not transfer to problems that were not identical in structure, however, even though they involved the same problem-solving operations as the practiced problems. That is, the procedural competence acquired from studying the worked examples did not generalize to new problem types in Sweller and Cooper (1985), something that has been noted in other investigations of short-term instruction as well (e.g., Eylon & Helfman, 1982; Reed, Dempster, & Ettinger, 1985).

When longer-term instruction involving presentation of worked-out examples has been studied, there has been evidence of long-term retention of skills learned through worked-out examples as well as acquisition of understandings about when the skills learned should be applied. Zhu and Simon's (1987) outcome was exemplary in this regard. As part of their work in high school mathematics instruction, they studied instruction of factoring of quadratic expressions (i.e., expressions of the form $x^2 + ax + b$), multiplication involving exponents (i.e., operations of the form $a^m \times a^n = a^{m+n}$, $(a^m)^n = a^{m \times n}$, and $(ab)^m = a^m \times b^n$), geometry proofs, ratios, proportions, and fractions. In general, across their experiments, problem-solving procedures were acquired more quickly with greater final competence when students were provided worked example problems. Perhaps the most impressive achievement is that a 3-year mathematics curriculum (2 years of algebra and 1 year of geometry) has been developed based on worked-out examples. This is now being implemented in some Chinese high schools, with all indications that problem-solving achievement is higher and learning occurs more rapidly in this program of instruction than in traditional programs. This is impressive because greater overall performance in mathematics requires that students not only learn the procedures taught, but also how, when, and where to apply the procedural competence they have acquired.

Although learning from examples is a preferred mode of learning for students (e.g., Anderson, Greeno, Kline, & Neves, 1981; LeFevre & Dixon, 1986; Pirolli & Anderson, 1985), much less effortful than attempting to derive principles by working out practice problems (Paas, 1992), and simply placing examples in texts seems to make texts more effective in conveying understanding of problem-solving procedures (e.g., Reder, Charney, & Morgan, 1986), there are many subtle factors that can make a worked example more or less effective. Sweller

(1989) warned that worked examples are effective only if the to-be-learned relationships are apparent without a lot of mental juggling—without a lot of integration that consumes short-term capacity, for learning the solution is a capacity-demanding process.

Conventional worked examples, such as the following, were not effective in teaching students how to do problems in a study conducted by Ward and Sweller (1990; also see Tarmizi & Sweller, 1988):

> A car is accelerated in a straight line from rest for 10 seconds and in this time travels 100 meters. What is the final velocity of the car?
>
> Solution: $s = vt$
> $v = s/t$
> $= 10$ meters/second
> $V = 2v$
> $= 2(10)$
> $= 20$ meters/second
>
> (Sweller, 1989, p. 464)

A much better approach was to integrate the solution information into the problem so students could easily map the solution components to the problem components, as in this revised version of the same worked problem:

> A car is accelerated in a straight line from rest for 10 seconds and in this time travels 100 meters [$s = vt$; $v = s/t = 100/10 = 10$ meters/second]. What is the final velocity of the car? [$V = 2v = 2(10) = 20$ meters/second]

Although there is a great deal of work to be done to determine exactly how to design worked examples so they maximize understanding of solution processes, it is work well worth doing and is being pursued (e.g., Paas, 1992). A trip to any college book shop to survey the stacks of worked example books for every area of mathematics, physics, chemistry, statistics, and engineering makes obvious that worked examples are important instructional resources for many students.

Computer Programming Experiences

Computer programming requires problem solving. Planning before attempting to design a program is essential. Revision is to be expected because it is rare for a program to run on the first try. Scaffolding occurs in the form of "error messages" from the computer, which are intended to provide hints about

what is wrong with the program that just bombed. Eventually the program runs, although a comparison of one's own program with the one produced by a classmate attempting the same problem often reveals that the classmate used an entirely different approach. There are different ways to solve programming problems, some more efficient than others.

A recurring hypothesis in the mathematics education literature is that experiencing computer programming should enhance mathematical problem-solving abilities. Because many programs include experience with particular mathematical contents, some also hypothesize that programming experiences have positive effects on mathematical content knowledge.

One of the most popular computer programs for elementary students is LOGO. Children can construct patterned images by commanding the cursor (referred to as a "turtle" because of its triangular turtlelike shape) to move in particular directions (specified in terms of left and right and by degrees) and to go particular distances.

One mathematical content–enhancement hypothesis is that LOGO programming should increase knowledge of geometrical concepts. It does (e.g., Clements & Battista, 1989, 1990; Edwards, 1991; Lehrer, Guckenberg, & Lee, 1988; Lehrer, Randle, & Sancilio, 1989; Olive, 1991). For example, compared with grade-3 students not receiving LOGO instruction, grade-3 students who received 26 weeks of it (three times a week) learned a great deal of geometry. They were more likely to be able to draw an angle when asked to do so, draw a larger angle than a given angle, and recognize right angles. LOGO students were more likely to know the number of angles in a triangle and a rectangle. They were better able to sort quadrilaterals into piles corresponding to classic categorizations of quadrilaterals (i.e., squares, rectangles, parallelograms, trapezoids). They could explain better the concept of "shape."

Unfortunately the evidence that LOGO programming experiences produce general improvements in problem-solving competencies is less compelling (see Lehrer, 1989, for a review; also Palumbo, 1990; Pea & Kurland, 1984). When generalization of problem solving has been observed, either the effects have been subtle (e.g., Clements, 1990; Lehrer et al., 1988), or the transfer problem included salient elements shared by LOGO and the problem context (e.g., Lehrer [1989] describes a chore task that is solved better by LOGO students that involves helping a "turtle" pick up its toys given some constraints regarding the order of the chores). Such shared elements are powerful clues to apply the skills learned as part of LOGO programming.

Perhaps it should not be surprising that LOGO experience per se does not produce large general increases in problem-solving skills. Recall the discussion in Chapter 5 about how educational computing programs often do not produce intended effects because they do not motivate or require the processes that are intended. Noss and Hoyles (1992) analyzed LOGO and concluded that many versions of the program do not stimulate the type of reflection that is required to build understanding of the processes performed when the turtle follows commands to move in particular ways. Moreover, children often prefer to construct figures by approximation and guessing rather than by working out a plan mathematically—and the program works regardless of which tactic the child takes. Although Noss and Hoyles (1992) believe that the LOGO program alone is capable of providing the type of scaffolded input that promotes general problem solving, they conclude, as do others such as Lehrer (1989; e.g., Lehrer & Littlefield, 1991), that hints and prompts from live teachers (i.e., teacher scaffolding) can do much to increase student reflection on LOGO problem-solving activities. Such hinting can increase student understanding of the relationships between the symbols manipulated in the program and the movements observed on the screen. Studying the effects of LOGO programming when students receive scaffolded instruction should be a high priority, especially because mathematicians have analyzed LOGO in great detail to determine many different types of mathematical understandings that might be promoted by it (see Hoyles and Noss, 1992). Another possibility, suggested by the results of a study by Clements and Nastasi (1988), is that if children practice LOGO programming in small groups, reflection may be more likely, and that LOGO programming may be a good stimulus for interactions that promote cognitive development (e.g., experiencing social-cognitive conflict as part of trying to identify a way to program some particular movements of the turtle). In short, there are converging data suggesting that programming experiences may be a good deal more enriching if experienced with other people—but more than that, that the problem solving required by programming may encourage interpersonal interactions that stimulate the cognitive development of participants.

The evidence of generally improved problem solving following instruction in other programming languages is not much more compelling than it is for LOGO. For example, Blume and Schoen (1988) provided one of the more positive reports we have encountered, with the outcomes mixed in favor of programming effects on more general problem solving. Grade-8 participants in Blume and Schoen (1988) either learned how to program in the language BASIC or they were provided no such instruction. The criterion problem-solving test required facility in solving word problems and logic exercises. In support of the case that programming produced positive effects on problem solving, the programmers were more systematic in their problem-solving attempts and seemed to check their work more carefully. Nonetheless, the programmers did not seem to plan more and were no more successful in solving problems than were the nonprogrammers. In short, some problem-solving processes were stimulated by the programming experience, but the overall effectiveness of problem solving was not improved by learning to program in BASIC.

It must be emphasized, as the negative evidence involving effects on problem solving is considered, that programming experiences do seem to promote other general mathematical understandings, just as LOGO experiences increase understanding of geometry. For example, Oprea (1988) observed in a true experiment that 6 weeks of BASIC programming experience had a number of positive effects on the mathematical competencies of grade-6 students: The BASIC students outperformed control subjects on a test requiring understanding of mathematical combinations, exponents, number patterns, and geometrical shapes. They outperformed controls on a test requiring knowledge of programming. The BASIC students were better able than controls to evaluate simple algebraic statements and translate verbal statements into algebraic equations (i.e., they were better at algebra skills used in construction of BASIC programs). Anyone who has taught grade-6 children mathematics recognizes that growth in these areas is not trivial, so the 6 weeks of BASIC instruction provided by Oprea (1988) was worthwhile for the students in her study.

We believe that the effects of computer programming experiences deserve much additional study, if for no other reason than computer programming is an ever-more-prominent experience in education. The ability to interact with computers will be an essential 21st century skill for many jobs. Greater opportunities to interact with computers in school are being provided every year, with it realistic to believe that many children will receive many years of programming experience as part of education in the early part of the 21st century. Most elementary and secondary schools in the United States already have instructional computers in them (National Center for Education Statistics, 1992).

Analyses of programming, such as Hoyles and Noss (1992) and Lehrer (1989), are filled with important, testable hypotheses that deserve research resources. Although, at present, the hypothesis that computer programming experiences produce across-the-board improvements in problem-solving competencies is not well supported by databased inquiries, some of the modifications suggested in these new analyses might go far in promoting increased student understanding of problem solving as students program (e.g., increased teacher scaffolding as students program might enhance development of problem-solving competencies). Hembree's (1992) meta-analysis discussed earlier in this chapter was informative about when programming might be effective: He determined that the largest effects to date had been obtained with students in grades 7 and 8, although even then the effect size was moderate at best (i.e., 0.4 SD).

Another direction that should be pursued is that programming instruction may promote learning of problem solving only after some threshold of proficiency in basic aspects of programming has been achieved. Introductory programming often emphasizes syntax and acquisition of low-level skills; instruction emphasizing planning, reflection, and real problem solving comes only after some basics have been mastered (Husik, Linn, & Sloane, 1989). The problem-solving strategies of students in advanced programming classes are impressive—with differences in problem-solving strategies in these classes associated with differences in programming achievement (e.g., Rohwer & Thomas, 1989). To date, there has been much more attention paid to potential gains in problem solving in introductory computer classes; a better question might be whether advanced computing coursework affects general problem-solving competency.

Programming is not the only possibility with classroom computers. There is a great deal of software that is potentially educational even for students who cannot write a single line of program.

Mathematics/Problem-Solving Instructional Software

There are already a number of mathematical instructional software packages on the market. These have been understudied; we are not aware of a single experimental evaluation of any of the popular programs (i.e., the ones available in most commercial software stores). Because such programs are commonly encountered by many 1990s children, this is an important gap in the mathematics instructional literature, one that perhaps will be filled by some readers of this book. A few well-controlled experimental studies that included sensitive measures of processing could go far in illuminating whether, how much, and how these programs affect children's problem-solving abilities and acquisition of mathematical concepts.

There is plenty of reason to be optimistic about the potential effects of the commercially visible programs, for less popular instructional programs have been validated to some extent. For example, software packages that tutor graphing skills (e.g., *Graphing Equations*) do seem to increase students' abilities to produce and comprehend graphs (e.g., Edwards, 1992), although more rigorous, better controlled evaluations of such software are necessary for complete confidence in their effectiveness. Beyond strictly mathematical problem solving, programs are being devised that can be integrated with regular classroom instruction to stimulate skills in solving life problems (e.g., *Health Ways* program, which stimulates analysis of lifestyle variables to create a healthy environment for individuals; Woodward, Carnine, & Gersten, 1988). Our faith that such software can be effective is increased by complementary work conducted with calculators, which is described in the next subsection, establishing that opportunities to construct graphs and manipulate functions at the push of a button (or a few buttons) can increase understanding of graphing and functions.

How teachers, students, and computers interact with one another is an important problem for educational psychologists to study as the turn of the century approaches, a century in which instructional computing is likely to play an increasing role in American classrooms. This is especially likely with the appearance of analyses documenting that computer-mediated mathematics instruction is cost-effective (i.e., effective in boosting performance and less expensive than other forms of instruction; e.g., Fletcher, Hawley, & Piele, 1990).

Interactive Computer Networks

Scientists all over the world communicate and collaborate with one another by using interactive computer networks. Thus we shared sections of this book with other scientists before it was published by using E-mail. The E-mail messages were typed into the personal computers on our desks and transmitted to the mainframe computers on our campus using modems. The mainframe in turn transmitted the message to a satellite, which directed it to the computers at the home institutions of colleagues receiving the texts, with these campus-based computers delivering the messages to the "mailboxes" of our colleagues, who collected their mail through their own personal computers, which are linked by modem to the mainframes on their campus. One of the advantages of this system is that it is free to users, subsidized by governments and computer companies.

A number of scientists are now exploring the consequences of providing such networks to schools, attempting to foster across-classroom, across-school, across-nation, and across-world contacts with other students (see Scott, Cole, & Engel, 1992). The collaborative possibilities using such systems are staggering, permitting low cost to free rapid communications between students in Anytown USA or to anywhere in the global village that is on the network. We look forward to educational psychologists investigating the effects of these technologies on student-to-student interaction including during problem solving.

Calculators

Cognitive psychologists believe that the tools one uses to think can affect the way one thinks. Thus, children who use an abacus to calculate come to perform mental calculations differently than do children who use non-abacus methods, with substantial evidence that long-term use of an abacus results in an internal abacus (i.e., an image of an abacus that is used to make mental calculations; e.g., Hatano, Amaiwa, & Shimuzu, 1987; Hatano, Miyake, &

Binks, 1977; Hatta, Hirose, Ikeda, & Fukuhara, 1989; Hishitani, 1990; Stigler, 1984).

With respect to more up-to-date technology, use of electronic calculators can increase mathematical conceptual understandings, problem-solving abilities, and attitudes toward mathematics (Hembree & Dessart, 1986). For example, Russow and Pressley (1993) explored the effects produced by college-level students using a graphing calculator in a basic mathematics course that covered mathematical functions. Compared with control students who hand graphed functions, the graphing calculator students came to understand the concept of function much more completely than controls, with graphing calculator students solving more problems on final examinations that required understanding of the relationship between mathematical functions and their graphs than did control students. These results were consistent with the observations of mathematics educators who have observed student use of calculators in classroom applications without conducting formal experiments of the effects of calculator assistance (see Demana & Leitzel, 1988).

We especially expect many more studies of the effects of calculators on student mathematical cognition, for their use is strongly recommended by many leading mathematics educators (e.g., Fey, 1990). Mathematics educators recognize that these devices reduce the amount of effort required for routine calculations and thus permit students to focus more certainly on mathematical decision making and problem solving (e.g., Baggett & Ehrenfeucht, 1992). That is, students can devote their attention to the higher-order aspects of mathematics rather than worry about the lower-order tasks.

Both the quantitative and the qualitative data in Russow and Pressley (1993) were consistent with these conclusions. Although many of their students at first found using a calculator to be an additional effort, they eventually had "a-ha" experiences, recognizing that the calculator permitted easy practice of graphing and experimentation to "see what would happen if I changed this." Of course, systematic exploration of mathematical functions, which the calculator permits to be carried out with ease, should foster deep understanding of how functions relate to their graphs as well as to real-world phenomena (e.g., Reys, 1989). The shift from student perceptions of an additional burden to the perspective that the calculator is a valuable tool were only detected in the Russow and Pressley (1993) work because they studied students longitudinally over the course of an entire semester. We believe that additional longitudinal research on how student mathematical understandings change with calculator experiences would do much to deepen knowledge of the effects on mathematical cognition of this increasingly commonplace tool. The increases in mathematical competencies owing to calculator use that have been documented already provide great stimulus for additional study of this piece of "high technology" that now can be provided at low cost to all students.

Interactive Videodiscs

Interactive videodisc technology offers opportunities to present richly contexted problems to students. Students can be presented a complex set of relationships in a movielike presentation, with realistic depiction of the many features that define the complex contexts in which realistic problems can occur. It is a format that permits easy review of a section of the presentation. Thus, viewers can interact with it, reexamining the images and screenplay to gather information needed to make a decision.

The Cognition and Technology Group at Vanderbilt (e.g., 1992; Van Haneghan, Barron, Young, Williams, Vye, & Bransford, 1992) is pioneering research in applications of videodisc technology to teaching and learning of mathematical problem solving. Much of their early work involved creating problem sets to be solved in light of information in commercially made movies (e.g., *Raiders of the Lost Ark*), information that could be viewed and re-viewed as part of attempting to solve a problem. More recently, they have produced their own series of shows, dubbed the *Jasper* series, about the adventures of a character named Jasper Woodbury. The first tape in the series was a 17-minute adventure ending in a problem.

The plot of *The Journey to Cedar Creek* was as follows:

> . . . [A] person named Jasper Woodbury takes a river trip to see an old cabin cruiser he is considering purchasing. Jasper and the cruiser's owner, a woman named Sal, test-run the cruiser, after which Jasper decides to purchase the boat. As the boat's running lights are inoperative, Jasper must determine if he can get the boat to his home dock before sunset. Two major questions that form the basis of Jasper's decision are presented at the end of the disc: Does Jasper have

enough time to return home before sunset, and is there enough fuel in the boat's gas tank for the return trip? The story indicates that Jasper decides he can get home before sunset. (Van Hanaghan et al., 1992, p. 22)

The students must attempt to solve the problems Jasper had to solve in reaching his conclusion, discussing and reviewing information in the videotape in order to solve the problems. Just as real-life problems are often complex and the essential facts buried in many irrelevant details, so are the facts in the *Jasper* stories. Just as there are alternative ways of figuring out the solution to the complex problems that fill the real world, so there are alternative routes to solution in the *Jasper* problems.

The complexity of the situations presented to students is apparent from consideration of the plot outline of another Jasper adventure, *Rescue at Boone Meadow:*

> . . . [W]e see Jasper Woodbury's friend, Larry Peterson, flying his ultralight into Cumberland City, their hometown. We soon learn that Larry is not only a very good pilot, he also gives flying lessons. One of his pupils is Emily Johnson. During Emily's lessons, she (and the viewers), learns much about the ultralight, including information on landing, payload, fuel capacity, fuel consumption, speed, and how the shape of the wing produces lift.
>
> After several weeks of lessons Emily has a successful first flight, and she, Larry, and their friend Jasper celebrate at a local restaurant. During dinner, Jasper reveals that he will soon be taking his annual fishing trip. He plans to drive to Hilda's (where she has a house and her gas station), park his car, and hike about 18 miles into his favorite fishing spot, Boone's Meadow. We also learn that Larry recently flew his ultralight to see Hilda and landed the plane at the field next to Hilda's house. As they leave the restaurant, Emily and Larry stop and weigh themselves.
>
> Next, we see Jasper fishing and eating his catch. As he is eating he hears a gunshot and he investigates. He finds a wounded bald eagle and uses his CB radio to call for help. Hilda answers Jasper's call and relays the information to Emily. Emily consults the local veternarian, Doc Ramirez, and they discuss additional information on eagles, distances, etc. The map on his wall reveals there are no roads from Cumberland City (where Emily and Doc Ramirez are located) to Boone's Meadow (where Jasper and the eagle are located). Nor are there roads from Hilda's to Boone's Meadow. Doc Ramirez leaves to attend another patient but emphasizes that time is essential if they are to save the eagle.

The adventure ends with Emily posing the challenge to herself: What is the fastest way to rescue the eagle, and how long will it take? The challenge is presented to the students, and they are told that all the facts that they need to solve the problem are presented in the video. (Cognition and Technology Group at Vanderbilt, 1992, pp. 297–298)

The solution of this problem involves generating alternative rescue plans and making calculations about them. Three characters potentially can be involved in the rescue, and there are at least two vehicles available. There is information about many possible routes presented in the film. If the ultralight is chosen, there are constraints with respect to payload, including constraints on the amount of gasoline that can be put on the plane, which varies depending on the weight of the pilot. The possible complications go on and on! Students working together usually require several hours of problem solving to generate the optimal solution, including a great deal of exploration of the tape for important clues. The exploration of the tape requires students to attend to both visual and auditory information and to separate out problem-relevant and problem-irrelevant information as they build a mental model (see Chapter 3) of the problem situation. Teachers provide guidance and support on an as-needed basis (i.e., problem solving is scaffolded). After students attempt to solve the problems, they view the resolutions presented on the disc. Once the problems posed in the tape are solved, teachers present additional problems to the students, which can be solved using material in the tape.

Does experience with the Jasper problems affect problem-solving abilities? Van Haneghan et al. (1992) summarized the results of a controlled study in which the grade-5 experimental participants experienced the Cedar Creek tape and problems. Rather than working the problems related to Jasper, control students received instruction and practice on problems using conventional textbook materials, with problems relevant to competencies and topics covered during the time corresponding to the Jasper problem-solving experiences for participants in the experimental condition. The controls also received some instruction about Polya's general four-step model of problem solving and were urged to apply the Polya model while they attempted their practice problems.

There were no important differences in the problem-solving performances of experimental and control participants at the start of the study. Following problem-solving experiences with *Jasper*, however, experimental subjects performed better on a transfer task involving watching a short video and solving a problem. The think-aloud protocols of *Jasper* students reflected more sophisticated problem solving. The overall solution rate of *Jasper* students was twice that of control participants. The *Jasper* students also performed better on written word problems, despite the fact that the controls had practiced solving word problems and the *Jasper* students had not. In short, this first test of *Jasper* provided support for its efficacy in promoting problem-solving performances.

The Cognition and Technology Group at Vanderbilt (1992) reported the results of a much more ambitious evaluation of Jasper, conducted in the middle grades in 11 school districts. Five of the districts included both experimental and control condition classes, permitting an interpretable comparison of the effects of *Jasper*. The *Jasper*-site students experienced at least three *Jasper* adventures. Some sites experienced four of the adventures. Controls received practice doing word problems. Pretest measures revealed no problem-solving differences between experimental students and controls at the outset of the study.

As in the Van Haneghan et al. (1992) study, however, there were striking differences on posttests favoring students who had experienced *Jasper*. Performance on word problems was better for *Jasper* students. Because *Jasper* emphasizes planning skills, problems requiring planning were given at pretest and posttest. Although such problems were difficult for all students at pretesting, at posttesting *Jasper* students planned much more effectively than did control participants—they constructed a mental model of the problem situation and generated alternative solutions before deciding on one approach over others. A variety of attitude measures were collected as well. After experiencing *Jasper*, students were less likely to believe that math was scary, more likely to believe that mathematics has many uses, more interested in math, and more likely to enjoy the challenge of solving complex problems than were control students. In addition, the teachers liked *Jasper* and believed it facilitated students' learning of mathematics and problem solving.

Interactive videodisc presentations can be prepared that provide challenging and interesting problem-solving opportunities for students. Although *Jasper* is still in the evaluation stages, the positive outcomes to date should stimulate additional development of this technology. As interactive videodisc technology becomes more common, the commercial viability of this approach to problem-solving instruction should increase as well. The Vanderbilt-based group is continuing their creative evaluations of video presentations, extending their work upward, examining the effects of video learning opportunities for college students as they learn about complex theories and their application to real-world problems (e.g., Michael, Klee, Bransford, & Warren, 1993).

Educational Television Programming

Children's Television Workshop (CTW) has a long history of success in producing programming that positively affects children's cognitive growth, with *Sesame Street* and *Electric Company* their best known products. Both of these shows increase children's understanding of important literacy and numeracy concepts (Comstock & Paik, 1991, Chapter 3). A more recent addition to public television is CTW's *Square One,* which was designed specifically to stimulate positive attitudes and enthusiasm for mathematics in 8- to 12-year-olds, encourage development of problem-solving processes, and present important mathematical content. The program generally appears 5 days a week on public television. Math is presented via enjoyable detective stories. The show is a mathematized version of *Dragnet* in many ways, with the detectives encountering many problems that can be solved using math.

Well-designed evaluations of *Square One* television are beginning to appear. Thus, in Hall, Esty, and Fisch (1990), grade-5 children were pretested with respect to their mathematical problem-solving abilities. Some of the children then watched 30 episodes of *Square One,* with controls not exposed to the program. Careful matching based pretest scores ensured that the *Square One* viewers and controls were equal in problem-solving competence at the outset of the study. At posttesting, the students who watched the series episodes outperformed the control students on a number of measures of problem solving. The children who had watched the program manifested a greater variety of problem-solving behaviors in reaction to posttest problems, offering solutions that were more complete and more sophisticated than the solutions proposed by control

participants. *Square One* is entertaining programming that stimulates development of problem-solving competence.

Summary

A variety of methods for enriching mathematics instruction have been proposed and studied. These are not competing methods but complementary ones. Thus, what we describe as scaffolded, elaborative teaching can easily be combined with the classroom organizational structure that is cooperative learning. Interventions such as problem solving in reaction to interactive videodisc presentations would seem naturally to fit into cooperative-group arrangements, as group sifting through and selection of information from videodisc adventures is a natural part of coming up with a solution plan. Although individuals can use calculators, calculators can also be used as groups of students explore mathematics, with the calculator a device so portable that it can go anywhere that students might engage in problem solving. We have seen many occasions in school when individuals work at computer tutorial programs; we have also watched as small groups of students do so.

The instructional ideas and products that have been researched and developed have enormous potential for transforming the way mathematics education occurs. Not only are the new approaches targeting instruction of concepts and understanding of mathematical procedures, but also there is a real concern for increasing motivation to attempt and stick with mathematics. Cooperation has high potential for reducing the motivational declines experienced in conventional mathematics classrooms; when students work with graphing calculators, computers, and interactive videodiscs, they are experiencing the exciting world of high technology, technology that eliminates much of the drudgery of mathematics (e.g., long-division calculations) and provides rapid feedback about the effects of various types of mathematics manipulations (e.g., the effects of doubling the radius of a circle on the area of a circle can be observed graphically by some computer programs that provide simultaneous presentation of the areas of circles with 1, 2, 4, 8, 16, 32 . . . inch radii). A great deal of information can be generated quickly by these machines in formats that encourage student reflection. Such reflection is more likely when students work with these machines in cooperative groups or with a teacher who assumes the role of a coach. When children go home, some of them are turning on *Square One* television, television programming that is both fun and educational. The lucky ones then get help with their math homework from their parents.

In applauding the technological advances reviewed in this section, we are haunted by the reality that such advances are not distributed equitably to American schoolchildren (see Scott et al., 1992). The more expensive the technology, the more likely that its distribution to schools will widen the gap between the education offered to the rich and poor, for expensive technology goes only to the districts that can afford it. The districts that can afford it serve the children of taxpayers who can afford to pay for fine schools. The American track record on educating disadvantaged children with respect to high technology is terrible compared with the record on educating more advantaged children (e.g., Sutton, 1991). In addition, even within a school, the intellectually rich may get richer and the poor get poorer in high-technology environments, which often impose new intellectual demands on students that are easier for high-ability students to handle than low-ability students (e.g., all those little commands one must learn to use a computer; Hativa, 1988). Given that technological competence will be a requirement for more and more jobs in the coming economy, it is imperative that the nation devise plans to ensure that all children are given high-quality educational experiences involving computers, interactive videos, calculators, and whatever other electronic wizardry emerges as an important problem-solving tool in the soon-to-be 21st century. This may be easier with each passing year, both because the prices of high-technology equipment come down and such environments are always being made more user friendly, with the former factor important for economic equality of opportunity and the latter factor important for equality of opportunity for students varying in ability.

What about the question posed at the beginning of this section concerning direct explanation and radical constructivism? As it turns out, there is direct explanation with respect to every one of the interventions covered in this section, but there is also a great deal of construction of knowledge. All of these interventions require students to solve real problems, which is always going to require taking what one knows and constructing innovative solution plans. The new media products and technologies do not just give information; rather they encourage students to use ideas that are new to them in ways that really require flexibility in application and reflection before and during problem solving. Ideally, reflection occurs afterwards as well, with such post–problem-solving instruction perhaps most likely when a knowledgeable teacher such as Lampert helps children understand how their thinking about mathematics relates to the conventions of the mathematics community. Lampert, who is decidedly a constructivist, is also an explainer. Explanations stimulate new constructions, and new constructions elicit more advanced explanations when mathematics instruction is at its best, when students and teachers interact during problem solving, sometimes problem solving involving use of highly sophisticated technology. This technology at its best permits alternative ways of examining mathematics and encourages active interaction with important mathematical concepts and procedures.

Although we do not expect any school to include all of the elements covered in this section, combining powerful elements of mathematics instruction has a good track record (e.g., cooperative learning and interactive, scaffolded instruction; Hawkins, Doueck, & Lishner, 1988). We expect much mixing of the components covered in this section in the years to come in American schools.

When other cultures are examined, ones more successful in producing high percentages of excellent mathematics students than we are, it is clear that there are many converging supports in these cultures for mathematics learning. As Asian education and life is considered in the next section, readers might reflect on how Americans could exploit the new technologies and understandings about teaching that are emerging in research so as to provide mathematics instruction that is as rich and appealing as the instruction now occurring in Japan and China.

MATHEMATICS ACHIEVEMENT IN ASIAN SCHOOLS

American students do not do as well in international comparisons of mathematics achievement as do students in many other countries, notably Japan and China (National Center for Education Statistics, 1992). Harold Stevenson (e.g., 1990, 1992), a distinguished senior professor at the University of Michigan, and his colleagues (e.g., Stevenson et al.,

1990a, 1990b; Stevenson, Lee, & Stigler, 1986; Stevenson, Lummis, Lee, & Stigler, 1990; Stigler, Lee, Lucker, & Stevenson, 1982; Stigler, Lee, & Stevenson, 1987, 1990; see also d'Ailly, 1992) have studied intensively the differences between American and Asian educational systems in an attempt to understand the academic achievement differences between these cultures.

One possibility was that the achievement tests were biased in some way to favor the Asian students over Americans. Thus, Stevenson took great care to construct tests that tapped mathematical concepts covered in both cultures. Moreover, the form and administrations of the Stevenson instruments were carefully controlled so the testing experiences were as equivalent as possible for Asian and American students. After controlling potential extraneous factors that could have affected the relative mathematics performances of the Asian and American children, what Stevenson found was that the Asian students still outperformed Americans: The average American students were performing at about the levels of the weakest Asian students.

Stevenson's studies included both formal quantitative comparisons and more qualitative assessments to elucidate potential factors that might account for at least some of the achievement differences between Asians and Americans. It was also possible to eliminate some explanations of the differences that have been proposed. For example, the following probably do not account for much, if any, of the Asian-American difference:

1. Innate intelligence: There is no dependable evidence that Asians and Americans differ in intelligence. The very small differences in spatial abilities between orientals and caucasians (see Iwawaki & Vernon, 1988) could not possibly account for the large mathematics achievement differences observed between Asians and white Americans—that is, the most likely subcomponent of intelligence that might affect population differences in mathematics achievement probably does not do so.
2. Differences in preschool education: Asians do not receive greater mathematics instruction during the preschool years, so the hypothesis that Asians get a head start because of preschool curricular differences is not compelling.
3. Pushy and demanding Asian parents: Although Asian parents are more supportive of educa-

tional achievement than their American counterparts, they do not put high pressure on their children to achieve. What they do is provide a home setting that permits children time to learn, with the consistent message to sons and daughters that school achievement is important.
4. Rote learning: Asian students do not learn mathematics by rote, expending incalculable effort to pound mathematics content into their long-term memories. Rather they are taught mathematics conceptually, with construction of mathematics understandings at the center of Asian mathematics pedagogy.
5. Insane academic intensity and commitment: Some point to a high post–World War II suicide rate among Japanese youth as a sign of psychological stress induced by high achievement demands, either imposed by the students themselves or by their families. In recent years, the adolescent suicide rates in the United States and Japan have not differed much. There are no credible indications that greater proportions of Japanese or Chinese students burn out than American students.

So what might account for the differences in mathematics achievement in China and Japan compared with the United States? There are many possibilities:

- American students and parents are satisfied with lower levels of mathematics achievement than are Asians, documented quantitatively in Stevenson's studies (Crystal & Stevenson, 1991).
- The Asian curricula are more difficult in that more advanced concepts tend to be introduced earlier.
- Asians attribute successes and failures to effort; Americans are much more likely to attribute successes and failures to ability (Hess, Chih-Mei, & McDevitt, 1987; Holloway, 1988). The Asian attributions motivate high academic effort because academic achievement is controllable in their view. The American attributions do not motivate high effort as certainly, for Americans do not view mathematics achievement as controllable but as the product of an uncontrollable factor, innate ability (see Chapter 5.
- Many more hours are spent on mathematics in Asian classrooms compared with American classrooms.

- Asian students are on-task for a greater proportion of classroom time than are Americans, with Stevenson believing that this may be due to differences in scheduling of the school days in Asia so that children have more breaks for play during an overall longer school day. It is easier to be attentive during class time when there are periods of relaxation during the school day.
- Asian teachers are more energetic in class because they teach fewer hours per day than American teachers and have much greater opportunity for preparation.
- Achievement in school is much more valued in Asia than it is in the United States.
- Asian children spend more time on homework than do Americans (Chen & Stevenson, 1989).
- There are demanding, national mathematics curricula in Asian countries, in contrast to local decision making in the United States and hence greater variability in curricular expectations in the United States.
- Mathematics instruction in Asian schools involves high-level interactions and teachers monitoring students to determine whether and how well they understand. That is, Asian instruction already resembles the NCTM ideal, whereas much of American mathematics instruction still resembles the conventional instruction stereotype. The extensive seatwork given in the United States compared with Asian schools does not promote teacher-student interactions.
- Consistent with NCTM ideals is the use of many more manipulatives in Asian classrooms than in American classrooms.
- Word problems, another favored curriculum item by the NCTM, are more common in the Asian elementary experience than in the American experience.
- Feedback to students is much more common in Asian classrooms.
- Asian teachers do more to relate mathematics to the lives of their students than do American teachers.
- Asian teachers question their students more about mathematical concepts and about mathematics strategies that might be used to solve problems (Perry, VanderStoep, & Yu, 1993). Such questioning probably stimulates deeper thinking about mathematics in Asian classrooms, beginning in the primary grades at which Perry et al.

(1993) made their observations of questioning during mathematics instruction in Asian and American classrooms. (Recall the discussion of elaborative interrogation in Chapter 10—questioning often stimulates students to relate new content more completely to what they know already than students do in the absence of questioning.)

In short, it is impossible to single out a single factor as *the* cause of superior mathematics achievement in Asian schools. The most likely explanation is that there are many ways that Asian instruction differs, with the Asian curriculum filled with components that, if anything, should promote mathematics achievement. Interestingly, when Song and Ginsburg compared the mathematics achievement of Korean elementary students with American students, they observed increasing superiority with each additional year of schooling and concluded, as Stevenson and his colleagues have, that a variety of teaching practices, parental attitudes and expectations, and cultural values combined to promote achievement in mathematics (see also Holloway, 1988).

There are many lessons we could learn from the Japanese about improving the quality of mathematics instruction. At present, organizations such as NCTM are making progress in stimulating reform of mathematics education in ways consistent with the Asian instructional models. Whether our society is willing to pay the price of more teachers so that each teacher could teach fewer hours and plan more is an open question. Whether we are willing to have longer school days with more play time in order to enhance the quality of academic time is also an open question. What is less of an open possibility is the overall societal support for academic achievement. American homes do not revolve around children's educational achievement like Asian homes do. This cultural difference alone might make it unlikely that the Asian-American mathematics achievement gap could ever be closed entirely, although it might be closed somewhat by making the shifts in mathematics instruction that are possible in the American context, including use of more manipulatives, word problems, and socially interactive instruction. If readers think back to the innovations covered in the section preceding this one, they will recall that there are many new approaches to increasing mathematics learning and participation. The innovations covered in that section might better match American lifestyles and approaches to child rearing.

GENDER, RACE, AND SOCIOECONOMIC DIFFERENCES IN MATHEMATICS ACHIEVEMENT

U.S. females historically have not achieved at the same level in mathematics as U.S. males, especially when the benchmark was achievement on standardized mathematics assessments. American minorities perform more poorly in mathematics than do members of the majority culture. Poor children do not perform as well in mathematics as children from middle-class and upper-class families. The result is that females, racial minorities, and people with lower-class origins are underrepresented in the pool of mathematics majors and in professions that require mathematics competency (Maple & Stage, 1991). This is a real dilemma because occupations requiring math are among the more prestigious and rewarding of vocational possibilities. Thus, group differences in mathematics achievement are an enormous concern for policymakers and the mathematics educator community (e.g., Research Advisory Committee, 1989).

On the positive side, male-female differences in U.S. mathematics achievement are not large and have declined in recent years (Friedman, 1989; Hyde et al., 1990). As far as classroom grades are concerned, females do better than males, with male advantages confined to math achievement as defined by standardized tests (Kimball, 1989). There also have been detailed analyses of factors that promote and undermine female students' motivation with respect to mathematics, with these analyses informing the mathematics reform movement (see Chapter 5). In addition, international comparisons are making obvious that there is no inherent biological reason for female underachievement, for there are cultures in which males and females perform comparably on mathematics assessments (e.g., Walberg, Harnisch, & Tsai, 1986). There also has been some closing of the white-minority achievement gap (Dorsey, Mullis, Lindquist, & Chambers, 1988; Jones, 1984). Still, there is much gap that remains to be closed, and we expect a great deal of research in the next decade aimed at identifying mathematics instruction that works with minority students, studies that

would complement and inform efforts to involve more females, minorities, and lower-class students in science (see Chapter 12).

There is reason to be hopeful that it might be possible to produce large achievement gains for some groups. Movies such as *Stand and Deliver*, which featured one math teacher's successes in teaching advanced high school mathematics to disadvantaged students, provide some inspiration. Beyond inspiration, however, are controlled studies of interventions that produce striking gains in minority achievement. For example, Cardelle-Elawar (1990) taught Hispanic grade-6 students who were experiencing difficulties in mathematics to apply a variation of Polya's model to the solution of problems: The students were taught first to understand a problem, translating it into questions that could be answered. Essential knowledge and algorithms needed to solve the problem were then identified and a solution plan devised. Students were taught to monitor their execution of the problem-solving plan. Control students in Cardelle-Elawar (1990) received more conventional instruction, emphasizing feedback about the correctness of answers to problems. There was a huge effect of this intervention on problem-solving performance on a mathematics achievement posttest (i.e., more than 3 SD difference), with both boys and girls benefiting from the intervention.

Recall as well the demonstration by Fantuzzo et al. (1992) of the effectiveness of a math tutoring program in an inner-city elementary school, discussed in Chapter 8. Effective instruction can and is being devised, instruction that works well in schools that predominantly serve minority students.

Although Cardelle-Elawar's (1990) outcome is encouraging, what must be emphasized is that waiting until grade 6 may be waiting too long. Mathematical competency group differences favoring majority-group students can be detected at the onset of schooling (e.g., Entwisle & Alexander, 1990). At special risk are minority students whose parents dropped out of school themselves or who do not value academic achievement (Entwisle & Alexander, 1990). The differences are most striking when children are given demanding mathematics tasks for their age, such as word problems (e.g., Jordan, Huttenlocher, & Levine, 1992). (Note one more advantage of word problems with young children: They reveal group differences in mathematical competence that are not revealed when children solve problems presented using mathematical symbols only; Jordan et al., 1992.)

Can the differences detectable in mathematics competence in kindergarten and grade 1 be eradicated through instruction? We do not know at this time. As a society, we need to know what difference it makes if children receive high-quality mathematics instruction throughout their schooling, with the possibility that some who have done poorly in conventional mathematics programs might do much better if provided other instruction.

There are many reasons to conduct studies in which the mathematics achievement of girls, minorities, and economically underprivileged students is targeted. One is that different factors may determine mathematics achievement for girls, minorities, and the disadvantaged than for white, middle-class boys. For example, Ethington (1992) analyzed some of the data from the Second International Mathematics Study (Crosswhite, 1986) and concluded that for boys, mathematics achievement could be predicted from their previous achievements in mathematics and their expectations of success or failure in math. For girls, previous achievement and expectations of achievement predicted achievement but so did three other factors: (1) Ethington found that girls who were less likely to receive help in mathematics from their families suffered for it more than did boys. (2) The achievement of girls who view math as a male dominion is lower than the achievement of other girls. (3) If girls view math as difficult, it has a negative impact on their math achievement. As far as intentions to take mathematics in the future, Ethington (1991) reported that grade-8 boys' expectations of success in math and their valuation of math powerfully affected their plans to take math in the future; for girls, expectations of success had little impact on their plans, with valuation of mathematics a much more important determinant of whether they intended to take additional mathematics. In short, there are different determinants of math achievement and motivation to take mathematics for boys and girls.

Despite the fact that the gender-achievement gap has been narrowed (Hyde et al., 1990), contemporary girls still rate their math abilities lower than do boys; girls expect to do less well in mathematics than do boys; girls are less likely to attribute their successes in mathematics to ability and their failures to bad luck than do same-age boys; elementary-age girls are less likely to be confident that mathematics success can be achieved through effort than elementary-age boys; girls take less pride in their math successes than do boys; and girls are more likely to want to hide following a math failure than are boys (see Stipek & Gralinski's [1991] analyses of elementary and junior high school students' beliefs before and after mathematics examinations). We suspect that such reactions are not characteristic of girls alone and that there are complexities in the explanations of math achievement in minorities and the poor, just as there are complexities in the explanation of gender-related differences in mathematics achievement (see Reyes & Stanic, 1988, for extensive commentary on this point). We hope some readers of this book resolve to disentangle some of these complexities. Once the determinants of math achievement are better understood for females, minorities, and the poor, it might be easier to devise interventions targeted at factors that are critically important determinants of math achievement in these groups.

In Chapter 12, we argued that intensive, accelerated programs for gifted science students deserve more research attention. The same is true with respect to mathematics programs, particularly because such programs may be especially likely to affect the long-term development of mathematically talented females. Swiatek and Benbow (1991) reported 10-year follow-up data on students who had attended accelerated math courses during their middle-school years. Compared with equally high-ability students who did not elect such classes, the students attending these accelerated classes achieved at higher levels during their college years and were more likely to go on to graduate school. The positive effects on achievement of the accelerated math classes were especially pronounced on girls. Although there are alternative interpretations to the data (e.g., students willing to elect an accelerated math course may differ in a number of subtle ways from students who would not elect such a course, ways not captured by the instruments used to document the comparability of the accelerated-class and control samples), such an outcome highlights the possibility that enrichment opportunities deserve much more intensive study than they have received in the past. They may be potent educational experiences for many students and, in fact, may make a huge difference for some students.

In arguing for greater attention to the math achievement of underrepresented groups, we do not want to send the message that there is no real concern with the achievement of whites and males. The fact is that too few Americans are becoming highly proficient in mathematics, with this claim true for whites and males as well as other groups (Maple & Stage, 1991). Much more research on how to increase all students' mathematics achievement and interest in mathematics is needed. The intervention research discussed in this chapter is only a start.

CONCLUDING COMMENTS

Mathematical cognition and teaching of mathematics are being studied from a variety of perspectives in the 1990s. One reason is that it is so easy to document poor problem solving even in university-level students (Perkins & Simmons, 1988), including use of trial-and-error rather than planful analysis, persevering with approaches that are leading nowhere or quitting once a difficulty is encountered, guessing, and equation cranking (a mindless form of working backwards from a solution, looking only for equations that yield the solution rather than for equations that correspond to elements in the problematic situation). We close by reviewing the most important ones and by touching on some emerging approaches to the study of mathematical thinking and the teaching of mathematics.

Understanding Mathematical Concepts

The emphasis on understanding that is so prominent in the thinking of contemporary mathematics educators really is different than previous conceptions of learning mathematics. Davis (1992, pp. 226–228), summarized the differences between the old and new views:

- Although the old view was that ". . . mathematics is about symbols written on paper," the new perspective is that, ". . . 'mathematics' is a way of thinking that involves mental representations of problem situations and of relevant knowledge, that involves dealing with these represen-

tations, and that involves heuristics. It may make use of written symbols . . . but the real essence is something that takes place within the student's mind."

- The old view was that ". . . knowledge of mathematics is constructed from words and sentences. . . ." The new view is that knowledge of mathematics is built up from "previous experience." "This often means concrete experience. . . ." Although "words may be used . . . to guide the construction of mental representations, . . . the mental representations themselves are *not* built out of words."

- The conventional perspective was that teaching meant ". . . getting students to write the right thing in the right place on the paper. . . ." The current conception is that ". . . 'teaching mathematics' is a matter of guiding and coaching the student's own development of his/her repertoire of basic building blocks (from which mental representations can be constructed), and helping students to develop skill in building and using mental representations."

- It once was thought that ". . . the point of learning mathematics . . . [was] to learn a few facts. . . , a few standard algorithms . . . , and a few definitions" and that ". . . advanced mathematics . . . [involved] . . . memoriz[ing] a few proofs." In contrast, the reason for studying mathematics today ". . . is to learn to think in a very powerful way. . . ."

- It was once thought that ". . . students would not be able to invent algorithms themselves." Now, it is acknowledged that ". . . students often invent their own algorithms, even though they may conceal them from view of adults who would probably diapprove." (See Rohwer, 1980b, for commentary on children's invention of powerful algorithms that they carry out in secret.)

Of course, Davis (1992) painted extremes. Much of conventional mathematics instruction is not as incomplete or mindless as Davis or other radical constructivists (e.g., Cobb, Wood, Yackel, & McNeal, 1992) imply. For example, elementary teachers do not just follow the book but more typically emphasize topics they perceive to be particularly important or difficult for their students (Freeman & Porter,

1989). Even so, there is no doubt that too much of mathematics instruction in the United States is teacher transmission of information followed by students individually practicing problems as seat-work or board work (e.g., Stodolsky, 1988; Stodolsky, Salk, & Glaessner, 1991).

Regardless of the problems with conventional mathematics, many of the claims about the constructivist approach are not as well grounded in research as we would like. Indeed, we often think that the mathematics educators have done a better job of specifying the problems with mathematics education than they have in producing an alternative that can be recommended with confidence. If we were charged with writing a chapter summarizing credible research consistent with the radical constructivist instructional agenda, this would be a short chapter. In fact, the vague terms of reference used by many constructivist theorists, such as Davis's "way of thinking," his allusions to mathematical representations by specifying what they are not (*not* words) rather than what they are, and his advancement of extremely general goals (e.g., "thinking in a very powerful way"), undermine research in mathematics education. We find much attractive about talking in more concrete terms, such as those offered by other perspectives, some of which will be considered in the remainder of this section. At the same time, the commitment of the likes of Thomas Carpenter, Paul Cobb, and James Hiebert to models of mathematics education emphasizing understanding ensures much more research in this tradition. We look forward to it, for the work to date is advancing the understanding of the nation about how theoretically inspired mathematics education can make a difference in what students learn about fundamental mathematical ideas and their application in the world.

Situated Knowing About Mathematics

There also is progress in understanding the social-environmental contributions to mathematical thinking, with a growing number of scholars conceptualizing mathematical cognition as situated knowing (Greeno, 1991, 1992). A heuristic study for this perspective was conducted by Carraher, Carraher, and Schliemann (1985). They identified young Brazilians who make a living as entrepreneurs in city streets. As part of their business operations, these children

perform complex calculations efficiently. When given problems in a formal testing situation, however, ones requiring exactly the same computations as the problems worked in the street, these children falter. Their mathematical competence is situated, tied to the world in which the mathematical operations typically are carried out. People develop nonstandard ways of doing the math that the world requires of them (see also Saxe, 1988).

Greeno's (1991) analysis is that these children probably use mental models (Chapter 3) as they calculate, ones that operate on mathematical concepts grounded in real-world understandings. That is, the children have some knowledge of prices and create on the spot a set of operations on that knowledge to generate the price they need. Consider how the price of 10 coconuts might have been determined:

> The price of 3 coconuts might have been known [by a child seller] . . . 105 crusados. . . . [This figure] . . . was . . . put into the mental model. This was replicated, and the two objects together, representing 3 coconuts and 3 more coconuts, were associated with the combined amounts of money, 210 crusados. The 6 coconuts now accounted for were compared with the 10 coconuts specified in the problem [facing the young merchant during the business transaction], with the inference that 4 more coconuts had to be accounted for. Then one more 3-coconut object was added to the model, with its 105 crusados, giving a total of 315 crusados, and the problem was completed by adding the remaining coconut of the 10 and a quantity of money, 35 crusados, to the price. (p. 194)

Such math works for a coconut seller when calculating the price of coconuts. It fails when problems are stripped of concrete familiarity. When asked to solve the problem 10×35 out of the context of street merchandising, it is not obvious to the young Brazilian merchants that they could relate the problem to selling of coconuts. Sound familiar? As we have observed earlier (e.g., in Chapters 2 and 3), people do not always apply knowledge they have when confronted with problems in unfamiliar domains—or even in situations that are simply different from those in which the knowledge is typically used. (Recall the failure of Gick & Holyoak's subjects to transfer a solution from a military problem to an analogous medical problem.) Failing to relate decontextualized problems to prior knowledge, street sellers do not come up with answers to abstract multiplication problems.

Context matters in math, with subtle contextual factors often having a huge effect on student success. For example, asking a student to calculate a price is more likely to be related to knowledge of money if the numbers in the problem are consistent with the money system in the culture (Baranes, Perry, & Stigler, 1989). Thus, in the United States and Canada, numbers such as 100, 50, and 25 are more likely to elicit use of real-world money-management strategies from children than are numbers such as 95, 60, or 15. The numbers 100, 50, and 25 in a problem calling for nonmonetary operations (e.g., dividing a set of marbles), however, do not result in the student relating the problem to prior knowledge of the monetary system. That is, whether prior knowledge is activated depends on salient cues in a problem relating to that knowledge, with a mixture of situationally relevant and situationally irrelevant cues less reliably resulting in use of prior knowledge than when all cues in the problem are situationally relevant (Baranes et al., 1989).

Given the general interest of cognitive psychologists in situated learning (see Chapter 3) and the compelling demonstrations to date of context effects in academic cognition, we expect much more of such work. We believe that analyses of situational factors will only enrich understanding of the instruction and processing models favored throughout this chapter and book.

Good Information Processing and Its Development Via Instruction

Although research on mathematical cognition and instruction is being framed with respect to a number of exceptionally modern theoretical frameworks, including contemporary neuropsychological, situational, and constructivist theories, both the instructional and the cognitive-theoretical models featured in this book fare well when considered in light of the research conducted by math educators and psychologists interested in mathematics.

Direct Explanation Theories Recall the analysis of effective problem-solving studies conducted by Burkell et al. (1990): Effective problem-solving instruction includes teaching specific problem-solving competencies in the context of explanations and efforts to insure that students first attempt to understand problems, then formulate and carry out problem-solving plans, and conclude by monitoring the

adequacy of their solutions (although, of course, these are recursive processes, so linear progress from understanding to planning to calculating to checking is approximate at best). Good mathematics instruction is multicomponential, like all of the effective instruction featured in this book. We emphasize this point because some reform-minded mathematics educators, in the name of constructivism, sometimes argue for instruction that is not explicit in directing students and not filled with the components observed in studies of effective problem solving. We agree wholeheartedly with the reformers' goal that students should understand the mathematics they are learning; we disagree that understanding is most likely when students receive largely nondirective and discovery-oriented instruction.

The direct explanations we favor are just a starting point for students—enough information that they can at least make some progress on routine problems. Additional instruction is provided in the form of hints and clues and elaborations (scaffolding) as the effective direct explanation teacher pushes her students on to more challenging problems. That is, the teacher explanations are only a beginning for students who construct much more elaborate conceptions of the instructed ideas and procedures as they work on mathematics problems. Explanations about mathematical concepts and procedures were provided to students in many of the more successful instructional studies reviewed in this chapter. We emphasize as well that the best of direct explanation research is as situationally contexted as instruction favored by constructivist educators—that excellent mathematics strategy instructors present problems from the real world to students. Although many math educators, and even some educational psychologists (e.g., Derry, 1992), view strategy instructional models as different from constructivist, situated teaching, we know of enough examples of strategy construction in authentic situations following instruction to be confident that at least some strategy instruction is constructivist and situated.

In contrast, less directive instruction has been less studied, and when it has been examined, nondirective approaches often have been compared to instruction known to be ineffective. (Recall our discussion of the instructional studies designed to make the case that increasing students' conceptual understanding of mathematics would improve mathematics achievement.) The empirical case in favor of nondirective, radical constructivist instruction is not extensive nor strong compared with the empirical case favoring teacher presentation of high-quality explanations followed by scaffolded opportunities to apply the mathematical knowledge to meaningful problems. Then there are the many explanations that occur when students cooperate to solve problems: Explaining to other students how to do mathematics is an approach that increases the understanding of the explainer as well. Despite constructivist attacks on explanation models of instruction, there is plenty of evidence justifying resistance to those attacks.

Good Information Processing   Just as the instructional perspectives featured in this book are consistent with much of the evidence in the mathematics education literature, so is the model of thinking that we favor consistent with models embraced by many mathematics educators. Earlier in the chapter, we made the case that Schoenfeld's perspective was consistent with good information processing. We close by returning to the theorist whose ideas opened the chapter, George Polya (1954a, 1954b, 1957, 1981), whose description of how highly effective mathematicians think is wholly consistent with the good information processing model.

Strategies are everywhere in Polya. These range from particular strategies—such as focusing attention on the unknowns, data, and conditions of a problem to drawing figures to enhance problem comprehension to looking for analogies with other problems to decomposing a problem into subproblems—to the higher-order problem-solving strategy for which Polya is best known (i.e., attempting to understand, solve, and check a problem, with understanding, solving, and checking processes applied recursively). Polya recognized that use of these problem-solving strategies improves with practice: "Problem solving is a practical skill like, let us say, swimming. We acquire any practical skill by . . . practice" (Polya, 1957, p. 4).

Polya understood the importance of metacognition, such as the criticality of knowledge about where and when to use particular strategies, as illustrated by this quote:

> Look out for such features of the problem at hand as may be useful in solving problems to come—try to disclose the general pattern that lies behind the present concrete situation. (Polya, 1981, p. 116)

There are many instances in Polya's writings when he instructs students to determine whether a present problem might be analogous to a previous problem that the student already knows how to solve (e.g., Polya, 1957, pp. 110–112; Polya, 1981, pp. 81–82). In short, Polya emphasizes that students should always be attempting to increase their understanding of when and where particular problem solutions can be applied, and they should always be sizing up new problems to determine if they might already know how to solve the problem at hand.

Another aspect of metacognition that is important in good information processing is monitoring. Polya recognized that such awareness of cognitive actions and how they affect problem solving is salient in the thinking of good problem solvers. Here is how Polya on one occasion described what is referred to in this book as monitoring:

> You keenly feel the pace of your progress. . . . Whatever comes to your mind is quickly sized up: "It looks good," "It could help," or "No good," "No help" . . . such judgments are important to you personally, they guide your effort. (Polya, 1954b, pp. 145–146)

What contemporary educational psychologists think of as metacognition pervades Polya's descriptions of effective problem solving.

Polya also understood how declarative knowledge can be critical to problem solving and how such knowledge must be used in conjunction with procedural competence in order to solve problems. For example, Polya (1981, p. 37) explained how it would be impossible to solve a problem about iron spheres floating in mercury without a great deal of knowledge about both iron and mercury.

Motivation is in Polya, too. He believed that good problem solvers really "get into" problem solving, to use a contemporary expression. He believed that motivated intensity such as the following was typical during effective problem solving:

> [As you solve a problem,] . . . [y]our mind becomes more selective; it becomes more accessible to anything that appears to be connected to the problem, and less accessible to anything that seems unconnected. You eagerly seize upon any recollection, remark, suggestion, or fact that could help you to solve your problem, and you shut the door upon other things. When the door is so tightly shut that even the most urgent appeals of the external world fail to

reach you, people say that you are absorbed. (Polya, 1954b, p. 145)

All of the elements of good information processing have been in Polya's writings for more than 40 years. Polya's perspectives are even more relevant today than they were in the 1950s, however, for there now exists a more substantial database to support his theories about instruction and mathematical thinking. The good information processing perspective gets a big boost of support from Polya's theories, just as it does from Schoenfeld's more contemporary approach and the expanding database in mathematical cognition documenting that strategies, metacognition, nonstrategic knowledge, and motivation are key determinants of success in mathematical problem solving. We expect that as work on mathematical thinking inspired by traditions such as neuropsychology, situationism, and constructivism proceeds, new understandings about the physical and social determinants of strategies, metacognition, nonstrategic knowledge, and motivation to do mathematics will be identified. We expect the new theoretical lenses being applied to mathematical thinking and mathematics education to provide complementary explanations of thinking and learning rather than competing ones.

Literacy I: Reading

In recent years, American political leaders and the citizenry have concluded that there is a literacy crisis. The shock wave began with the 1975 publication of *The Adult Performance Level Study* (Northcutt, 1975). The shock magnified with *A Nation at Risk* (U.S. Department of Education, National Commission on Excellence in Education, 1983). The literacy deficiencies of the nation have also been apparent in the "nation's report card," the National Assessment of Educational Progress (NAEP; e.g., Kirsch & Jungeblut, 1986): Many Americans lack fundamental literacy skills. Both political liberals (e.g., Shor, 1987; Simonson & Walker, 1988) and conservatives (e.g., Hirsch, 1987; Finn, 1991) in the United States agree that something needs to be done.

Why is there so much concern? Bowsher (1989, Chapter 1) cited some of the economic consequences created by low literacy and illiteracy:

- Many citizens cannot qualify for productive employment. Those who cannot read are at greater risk for being on welfare rolls than those who can read.
- Many Americans do not have the literacy skills necessary to participate in new technologies that could increase the international competitive edge of the United States.
- Other indicators of social malaise are linked to illiteracy, such as drug and alcohol abuse.

Perhaps the government's most powerful statement regarding the economic risks of illiteracy was

Workforce 2000 (Johnson, Packer et al., 1987). That report concluded: There will be few new jobs in the emerging economy for those who cannot read and write or have low literacy skills. In fact, more than 40 percent of the new jobs will require the highest levels of literacy skills tapped on tests like the NAEP, requiring postsecondary education.

There are personal costs as well. Arguably the most poignant publication ever produced by the U.S. Department of Education was Eberle and Robinson's (1980) *The Adult Illiterate Speaks Out: Personal Perspectives on Learning to Read and Write.* Consider the fate of the illiterate:

- A landlord can claim anything is in the lease when dealing with an illiterate.
- Illiteracy produces dependency on others who must read for the illiterate.
- Privileges available to others are denied to illiterates. For example, in some jurisdictions, obtaining a driver's license depends on being able to read.
- Self-esteem is continually threatened. Imagine being an illiterate parent whose 7-year-old discovers that mother or father cannot read. The fear of being discovered is acute: "Just the idea of telling somebody that I couldn't read was painful" (Cole, 1976, p. 46).

In short, literacy is power. According to case studies and statistical analyses, the evidence is overwhelming that illiterates and low literates are less likely to fulfill their personal dreams and ambitions than are those who are fully literate.

We suspect that many of our readers are thinking at this point, "It cannot be that bad for the youth of the nation! I cannot remember anyone in my high school class who could not read at all." In fact, that is correct. By age 17, virtually 100 percent of current American students can perform the most simple of literacy tasks: They can write a simple description of a job they would like; they can locate a single piece of information in a newspaper article of moderate length; they can select words, phrases, or sentences to describe a simple picture (Kirsch & Jungeblut, 1986). The problem, of course, is that much more is demanded in our ever more complex society, and only a small proportion of students seem to be able to carry out literacy tasks equal to these new demands (Mikulecky, 1987). For example, less than 5 percent of 17-year-olds can extend and work with ideas in specialized, complex text. That is, most students have a tough time with demanding scientific materials, critical essays, historical source documents, and technical materials such as those experienced in the workplace. They have trouble linking ideas in more complex essays and are not facile at making generalizations based on such texts.

To get a feel for what these most demanding items on the NAEP are like, try the following two items. Read each passage and answer the multiple-choice question that follows it:

> In the years between 1940 and 1960, literature, the arts, and culture in general became increasingly oriented to the many. In an economy of high productivity, deluging millions of people daily with movies, magazines, books, and television programs, American culture achieved a degree of homogeneity never dreamed of before. However, if such cultural homogeneity spelled loss of individuality—which it undoubtedly did—and if mass culture was often produced primarily for profit and only secondarily for aesthetic reasons, nevertheless mass production of "art" made available to millions of people what in previous times had been the privilege only of the aristocratic few. Good radio and phonograph music was available where there had been no music before; there were more symphony orchestras and chamber music groups than ever; and toward the end of this period more Americans purchased tickets to classical concerts than to baseball games. Paintings and items of sculpture were being turned out en masse in moderately good reproductions. The world's literature was being distributed in inexpensive paperback editions in every bookshop, drugstore, and transportation ter-

> minal. On balance it seemed that mass production, while it might not raise culture, would not destroy the growth of genuine taste either.

> What does the passage imply the arts were before 1940?
> A. Homogenous B. Generally enjoyed C. Oriented to an elite D. Oriented to the average person E. I don't know

> There is a myth, very popular these days, that the Court is divided into "liberal" and "conservative" wings, or as some would put it, into "activists" and those who practice "judicial constraint." Labels of this kind are convenient but not accurate. Members of the Court, applying general constitutional provisions, understandably differ on occasions as to their meaning and application. This is inevitable in the interpretation of a document that is both brief and general by a human institution composed of strong-minded and independent members charged with a grave and difficult responsibility. But the inappropriateness of these labels becomes apparent upon even the most perfunctory analysis.

> In line 6, what does the word "their" refer to?
> A. Citizens B. Conservatives C. Liberals D. Members of the Court E. Provisions F. I don't know (NAEP, 1985, pp. 26–27)

If you did not identify C and E as the correct answers to these two sample questions, respectively, you are not alone. Items at this level of difficulty can be completed by only the most sophisticated of high school seniors. Such students are also among the few who can search documents when multiple constraints must be met. For example, when given a city bus schedule, about 5% of students can determine when the next bus would arrive on one particular street corner on a Saturday afternoon if the 2:35 bus had just departed. Given the prevalence of much more demanding search tasks in the workplace—and that search of text is the predominant literacy activity in the workplace (Guthrie, 1984)—it is easy to understand why the government is worried about the literacy of the workforce. Of course, remember the statistic presented earlier: 40 percent of the new jobs in the economy will require literacy competencies tapped by these most difficult NAEP items.

The shock wave produced by the many analyses suggesting Americans are much less literate than they need to be contributed in part to the great interest in the last two decades in reading. The information processing theory emphasized in this book also had an impact, with information processing analyses of many aspects of literacy produced in the last 20 years. Other theories of literacy and how to promote it flourished as well in the 1970s and 1980s. For example, "whole language" theorists considered the acquisition of literacy in terms of natural language development in the context of a linguistically rich environment. Social constructivist views of cognitive development (e.g., Vygotsky) contributed to new conceptualizations of preschoolers as emergent literates.

In general, this chapter is mostly about reading (Chapter 15 is devoted to writing), organized developmentally, with discussion of reading in the preschool years followed by discussion of elementary-level reading and reading by adolescents and youths. Some thoughts on the challenges in promoting adult literacy will then follow. Before setting out on this developmental description, we begin with a description of what really good reading looks like.

NATURE OF GOOD READING

Good reading is like other types of good information processing and can be described using many of the same terms (e.g., strategies, metacognition, nonstrategic knowledge, motivation). Consider some of the attributes of good readers confirmed by information processing research and summarized by Oakhill and Garnham (1988):

- Their eyes take in text in an efficient fashion. There are **fixations** and **saccades** (i.e., pauses of about a quarter of a second apiece and jumps accomplished in a twentieth of a second). The movements are planned: The next saccade is determined during this fixation, with some perception of the next 15 or so letters to the right of the point of the current fixation point. Most of the time, the next jump is forward, but some of the time, there are regressive saccades.
- Letters and words are recognized automatically, as the good reader has knowledge of many words in a **mental lexicon,** containing the many words the reader has learned in his or her lifetime. One theory proposed by Morton (1979) is that each word is represented as a **logogen.** When the good reader encounters enough visual evidence for a particular word, the internal representation (i.e., the logogen) is activated. Thus, when one of us sees l_g_g_n, a logogen for the word logogen is activated, just as it

would be if logog_n, _ogogen, logogen, LOGOGEN, or lOgoGeN were encountered. If an unfamiliar word occurs in text, the good reader can sound it out efficiently or decode the word using other strategies.
- The good reader's knowledge of syntax is so complete and used so automatically that even the most difficult syntactic constructions can be rendered sensible.
- The good reader has sufficient working memory to be able to hold "in mind" some of what was read previously as new information now fixated is taken in. What has been read and what is being read can be integrated in working memory to permit the good reader to understand the text's meaning (e.g., Dixon, LeFevre, & Twilley, 1988; Just & Carpenter, 1992).
- The good reader has extensive background knowledge that permits inferences (also represented well by some of the data in Dixon et al., 1988), ones that elaborate on the stated meanings in the text and others that permit linkages between ideas in the text and between this text and other texts the reader has encountered in the past (Hartman, 1992). This knowledge base also permits **instantiation** of concepts in text (i.e., more specific interpretations than explicitly stated in the text). Thus, readers instantiate the word "container" with "bottle" when they read, "The *container* held the cola" (Anderson & Ortony, 1975).
- Their knowledge includes knowledge of text structures (i.e., the typical elements in narratives and expositions), which permits good readers to abstract main points and important details from text.

Given the emphasis on strategies and metacognition in this book, it should not surprise readers that strategies and monitoring play prominent roles in skilled reading and work in concert (e.g., Baker, 1989; Walczyk, 1990). Moreover, the best bet is that strategic and monitoring competence continue to grow well into adulthood (Baker, 1989).

When we were undergraduates, we used to go to the campus library. Early in our university careers, we became aware of the existence of academic journals—the periodicals rooms at Northwestern (MP's alma mater) and Purdue (CM's alma mater) were nice places to study, but we never realized that the archival volumes were the lifeblood of scholarship. The journals were all around us, however, and sometimes we would sneak a peek. They seemed to be filled with arcane and difficult-to-read articles. As we progressed through school, we were gradually introduced to journal articles through courses and even had occasions to use the periodicals room as more than a study hall. The articles we were assigned were rough going at first. When we entered graduate school, many of our assignments included reading of journal articles, and the expectation of our professors was that we would be reading the leading journals in the field. We did and noticed that as the years went by, reading of journal articles became less difficult. Both of us feel that our reading of such articles continued to improve for years into our careers (remember that skills just keep getting better with practice). The long trek from initial exposure to journals as underclassmen to our feeling like expert readers is consistent with the arguments about the development of expertise advanced in Chapter 4.

That it took as long as it did provided some inspiration to me [MP] with respect to research: One way to find out what really good reading looks like, especially reading of difficult text, might be to study how professors read journal articles. Some of my students and I did just that. What we found out is that although such reading is complicated, it can be understood in terms of the good information processing model featured in this book.

Wyatt, Pressley, El-Dinary, Stein, Evans, and Brown (1992) asked 15 accomplished social science professors to select a journal article that would be interesting to them and in an area of great expertise for them. These professors were required to think aloud as they read their article, with their verbalized thoughts audiotaped for later analyses. Their behaviors as they read were recorded as were any markings on the articles. Despite the fact that these professors came from different areas of competence and were reading different articles, there were great similarities in the way they read. At least 12 of the 15 professors used each of the following comprehension strategies:

- Anticipated or predicted information in text.
- Looked for information relevant to personal goals, such as their own research, writing, or teaching.
- Went backwards and forwards in text looking for particular pieces of information.

- Reread information when uncertain about meaning.
- Attended closely to tables and figures.
- Varied their reading style according to the relevance of the text to their reading goals.
- Paraphrased and explained what was in the text and gave examples illustrating text content.
- Summarized.

Other strategies were observed as well, although these were not as frequent (i.e., used by at least 5 of the 15 participants but by less than 12 of the professors):

- Decided early in the reading that they were looking for specific information.
- Noted parts of the text to be read later or particular citations in the text to be looked up later.
- Related content in one part of text to content in another part.
- Watched for particular information throughout the reading.
- Read the article's reference list to activate prior knowledge.
- Decided to read parts of the text in a particular order.
- Noted relations among parts of an argument in the text.
- Underlined or made other markings.
- Read aloud.

Monitoring, which is so critical to regulation of strategies (see Chapter 2,), was observed as well. At least 12 of the 15 professors monitored their reading and comprehension in the following ways:

- Noted how difficult or easy the text was to read.
- Noted when text content was already known or not known.
- Evaluated the relevance of text information to reading goals.

Other types of monitoring occurred, although less frequently (i.e., used by between 5 and 11 of the 15 professors):

- Indicated awareness of personal biases about text content.
- Noted when something was worth or not worth knowing.
- Noted when content was taken from another source.
- Adjusted attention depending on relevance to reading goals.

- Noted when the text contradicted a belief held by them.

Finally the professors experienced great affect as they read—consistent with the perspective that the entire range of human affective responses can be produced in response to text (e.g., Goetz, Sadoski, Olivarez, Calero-Breckheimer, Garner, & Fatemi, 1992). In particular, the professors produced affectively charged evaluation as they read. Eighty percent of the professors did the following:

- Reacted to information in the text based on their prior knowledge, often their own theories, writing, or personal contacts with the author of the text being read.
- Evaluated the quality of the text (e.g., the quality of the literature review, theoretical perspectives, methods, analyses, results, conclusions, discussion, writing or editing style, or biases of the author).
- Expressed negative affective reactions, including anger, weariness, or boredom.
- Expressed interest in the text.

Less frequent evaluative reactions included the following:

- Expressed surprise by what was in the text.
- Responded evaluatively using nonverbal expression (laughed, looked puzzled, made gestures, gave the raspberry, scratched the chin, slapped the forehead).
- Swore.
- Expressed positive affect about the text content.

What Wyatt et al. (1992) demonstrated was that good readers are active readers. Good readers use diverse strategies, they monitor their understanding in many different ways, and they react to what they are reading. Good readers separate the wheat from the chaff as they read, expending more effort to process parts of text that are important than parts of text covering information not well matched to the reader's needs (e.g., Reynolds, 1992; Reynolds, Shephard, Lapan, Kreek, & Goetz, 1990). They evaluate the sensibility of text in light of what they already know (see Baker & Brown, 1984). One of the most interesting aspects of the Wyatt et al. (1992) data was the great correlation between use of monitoring strategies and evaluations ($r = 0.77$). The correlation between use of comprehension strategies in general and evaluations was much smaller ($r = 0.45$,

and $r = 0.31$ when the relationship between use of comprehension strategies and monitoring was taken into account): Good readers assess the worth and credibility of what they read as they process text in their area of expertise.

Documenting the many comprehension strategies and monitoring tactics used by good readers has been a cottage industry of sorts for educational psychologists, with most strategies lists generated by psychologists (e.g., Afflerbach, 1990; Lundeberg, 1987; Pritchard, 1990; Wade, Trathen & Schraw, 1990). Documenting that readers with extensive prior knowledge make interpretive evaluations of what they read is a related scholarly activity carried out by rhetoricians (i.e., those interested in how scholarly arguments are constructed), with a number of rhetorical analyses of experts reacting to text in their domain (e.g., Bazerman, 1985; Charney, 1993; Geisler, 1991; Haas & Flower, 1988; Schwegler & Shamoon, 1991; Wineberg, 1991a, 1991b). The strength of Wyatt et al. (1993) is that it captured the strategies and monitoring favored in psychological analyses as well as the interpretive processes that have been the concern of rhetoricians.

An Example of Good Reading

The richness of the skilled reading captured in Wyatt et al.'s (1992) analyses can be appreciated by considering how one participant in the study went through the text he read. JK, a professor in education, interwove strategic, monitoring, and evaluative reactions with other behaviors to make sense of the journal article he was reading.

Before and during reading, JK made conscious decisions about how he was going to read the text. For example, he mentioned specific information he would be watching for throughout the article. He also mentioned his intention to read sections in a specific order:

> So what I'm going to do is I'm gonna start looking at the background and theory because I want to see what kind of a, where this person comes at from his theoretical perspective.

When JK began reading the article, he selectively skipped the abstract. He related the following to the researcher at the moment he decided to pass over the abstract:

> I tend to ignore abstracts. I don't know why; I just do. Uh, sometimes because they're so short that it doesn't tell me much.

Before reading the article carefully, JK briefly surveyed it. Following the survey, JK's overall reading pattern was front-to-back, line-by-line. There were, however, many specific instances when JK jumped ahead or back, sometimes briefly and sometimes for a longer period of time (i.e., several minutes). JK reported skipping around to look for information in another section of the article or to clarify a statement he had just read, such as in the following report:

> So now that I looked at the instruments they used, I'm gonna go back and look at the design a little bit more because I didn't really look very closely at the design or at the instruction. So I went back.

JK frequently mentioned specific information he was looking for in the article. For example, he looked for information in the introduction, references, and results sections; JK also evaluated whether what he was reading was the information he was seeking. Furthermore, JK frequently mentioned looking for information relevant to his professional writing, and he evaluated whether the article was relevant to his own writing. This comment is typical of the goal awareness statements made by JK:

> One of the reasons that I'm reading this paper is so that I can write . . . [a] paper, looking at how they're defining problem solving, which is right down here.

JK showed awareness of differences in importance of parts of the text, carefully reading some parts of the article but skimming others, depending on relevance to his reading goals. JK talked about his expectations of the text and mentioned a bias he had toward the text:

> So, my guess is that this isn't the same paradigm that I work out of. I think it's an old paradigm; I don't think it's very fruitful to keep investigating this.

More than once, JK anticipated information that would appear in the text, including anticipating where he might find information if he looked back in the article. For example, JK read the references and talked about expectations based on what he knew:

> So I'm back here in the reference section now and, and it seems like he's citing some of these neo-Piagetian studies, 'cause he cited this Pascual-Leone, who I believe everyone refers to as a neo-Piagetian. He's also citing Niaz and Lawson on balancing chemical equations: The role of developmental level and mental capacity, and he's also citing Karplus—science teaching and development of reasoning. There's

also another Lawson article in here, who works out the Piagetian research paradigm in science education.

JK tested his predictions by acknowledging when he found information he had anticipated.

JK also studied tables and noted parts of text that he might go back to later if he wanted more information or clarification. JK adjusted his attention to the text, reading more slowly when he came to a part that seemed relevant to one of his goals. During the reading, JK often explicitly decided to continue reading although he said in other circumstances (i.e., if he did not have the pressure of writing a chapter hanging over him), he might have stopped, based on what he had seen so far:

> So that tells me something real quickly about the theoretical background which might tell me that I don't know if I really want to get involved in this thing. But anyway, I'm gonna now go ahead and read it. I'll skim parts of this just to see what they have to say because it's so important for me to know what this article is about, because of this chapter that I'm gonna write this critique for.

On multiple occasions, JK mentioned whether he understood the text, whether it was puzzling, whether he knew it before, whether it was worth knowing, or whether the information was based on another source.

JK frequently related new information in the article to something he knew already. For example, JK reacted to information in the article based on his background knowledge of the authors of the article, authors cited, methods, analysis procedures, and the content of the paper.

JK frequently expressed his affective reactions about the text both verbally and nonverbally. He gestured, throwing his hands in the air. He gave a raspberry to something in the text. And he frequently used slang when talking about the text:

> You know, so they know very little about balancing equations before and very much after. Well, that's baloney. They know how to mechanically solve those problems afterwards. It's not that they know a lot afterwards.

His evaluations included noting when the article contradicted his own beliefs:

> And so, you know, I'm sitting here now thinking this paper does everything that I think it shouldn't do. For instance, it really doesn't measure in any kind of detail the students' conceptual understandings.

His prior knowledge of methods in the discipline was his main basis for evaluation of the methodology:

> Not only that, so this thing does not measure the impact of conceptual knowledge, but then they sort of ignored treatment. And the treatment that they do is fairly terrible.

JK often integrated information from different parts of the text, for example, by comparing the text to the tables and verbally connecting different parts of the text:

> I'm looking at Table 6. I believe it's that regression equation that they were talking about where it came out that, uh, the only significant F was the pretest variable.

JK elaborated on the text by constructing conclusions beyond those provided in the article. He frequently explained and paraphrased parts of the text, interpreted results and tables, gave examples to elaborate on the article, and made summary interpretations of issues in the text:

> And I'm looking at the scores on the prior knowledge test. And you'll notice they're fairly high. It's 13 out of a possible 15. So, you know, you wonder: What did that really measure? Looks like it kinda topped out.

JK also went beyond the information given by looking at the article from other people's perspectives:

> I'm wondering to myself why they would do this—these guys are some fairly good researchers—why they're using this instrument.

After reading the article, JK wrote many notes on a computer in reaction to the entire paper:

> I'm here now behind my computer, which I usually do. I, typically, I never write with a pen or pencil and paper because if I do I can't read it the next day. I usually sit down behind my computer and I develop some key points. But anyways, I'm sitting here thinking right now about what are the main points that are in the [says authors' names] article related to this review that I'm doing.

JK's reading was active and strategic, with strategies carried on as extensive prior knowledge permitted ready evaluation of the text in a fine-grained fashion. We emphasize that all of the readers in the Wyatt et al. (1992) study demonstrated similar complexity in their responses, although all readers' responses could be coded mainly as strategies, monitoring, and evaluations.

One of the more striking differences between student readers and domain experts is that student readers are much more accepting of what is in a text than are readers more experienced in a domain (e.g., Haas & Flower, 1988; Wineberg, 1991a, 1991b)—really good readers question what is in text rather than believing it all; good readers realize that there are often messages in text not apparent on first reading (Schommer, 1990). Domain experts in particular recognize that the truth value of advanced articles and books is often debatable—that the experts writing articles often advance opinions; student readers are more likely to assume that those writing in prestigious outlets such as journals and books know what they are talking about and can advance claims that are beyond debate. Ask yourself the following question: Have you believed most of what has been presented in this book, or do many points seem debatable to you? During the development phase of this book, many students and colleagues read this text. Summarizing over many conversations, students often told us that most of what was in the book was sensible. Summarizing over many other conversations, many of our colleagues debated perspectives we took although, fortunately for us, usually could understand why we adopted the stances taken here. When experts read something, expect an evaluation; when nonexperts read, there is a better chance that text content will be accepted as presented by the author.

Still not all reading is so serious. Good readers read differently for different purposes, recognizing that what we do to understand what is read varies with the reading task as does the amount of concentration required to carry out various reading tasks (Reed & Schallert, 1993). Lorch, Lorch, and Klusewitz (1993), in a study of young adults' knowledge of reading strategies and when various strategies are used, identified 10 different reading purposes that corresponded to different strategic approaches to reading: (1) examination preparation, (2) reading to research (e.g., in preparation for a term paper), (3) class preparation, (4) reading to learn (e.g., reading an English book to learn how to construct a particular type of essay), (5) reading to apply (e.g., reading of how-to books in anticipation of a task requiring some know-how), (6) search for information, (7) reading to self-inform (e.g., a nonfiction book or a biography of an important person in the news), (8) intellectually challenging reading (e.g., reading news magazines), (9) reading for stimulation (e.g., reading horror or romance stories), and (10) light reading (e.g., going through the campus paper). As an example of differences in strategies depending on purpose, Lorch, Lorch, and Klusewitz's (1993) participants recognized that reading for an examination requires slow reading, self-testing, and use of outside supports (e.g., class notes). While preparing for an examination, there is careful attention to what is in the text. In contrast, reading for class involves quicker reading and less concern with detail. Good readers are extremely metacognitively sophisticated in that they know exactly when to apply the many strategies they know to the various reading tasks they face.

Good Reading Compared to Expert Problem Solving

Skilled reading by domain experts shares many similarities with problem solving by domain experts (Chapter 4, this volume), and perhaps it should because abstracting meaning from complicated text is a form of problem solving:

- Domain experts use their prior knowledge extensively during problem solving, recognizing large patterns and strong connections with previous experience. So it was in Wyatt et al. (1992).
- Experts are opportunistic during problem solving, using clues they encounter while solving a problem to assist in deciding next moves. So it was in Wyatt et al. (1992)—for example, when readers moved forward and backward in text to find particular pieces of information they considered important.
- Experts exhibit flexibility as they solve problems. So it was in Wyatt et al. (1992), with diverse tactics used by the social scientists as they came to terms with text.
- Experts monitor their performances (Baker, 1989). So it was in Wyatt et al. (1992), with monitoring of understanding, difficulty of text, and pertinence of a text to the reader's goals.
- Experts process "deeply" as they solve problems, using prior knowledge in conjunction with strategies, continually monitoring progress in understanding the problems. So it was in Wyatt et al. (1992).

It is a long developmental trip to expert reading, however. We begin now at the beginning of that journey.

EMERGENT READING DURING THE PRESCHOOL YEARS

Not so long ago, a common question asked by parents and educators was, "Is my child ready to read?" Typically, this question was posed once the child had reached 5 or 6 years of age. Whatever happened before that was viewed simply as "getting the child ready to read." That is not how many contemporary educators think, however. Rather, there is a recognition that a great deal of literacy development occurs during the preschool years, that this is a period of **emergent literacy,** a term coined by Marie Clay (1966, 1967), a prominent New Zealand reading educator. Elizabeth Sulzby's (1988) definition is a good one: Emergent literacy is reflected in the reading and writing behaviors during the preschool years that precede and develop into conventional literacy.

Literacy begins in infancy according to this perspective; it is a home and school thing, something that develops anywhere young children are. Children are seen as active in the development of their own literacy, seeking out and initiating many behaviors that are literate and literacy fostering. The social environment can support and facilitate such literacy activities. Unfortunately, however, not all children live in worlds that are as supportive as they could be: Environments that support emergent literacy include (1) rich interpersonal experiences with parents, brothers and sisters, and others; (2) physical environments that include literacy materials, from plastic refrigerator letters to story books to writing materials; and (3) high positive regard by parents and others for literacy and its development in children (Leichter, 1984; Morrow, 1989).

Insights about the factors supporting emergent literacy can be gained by considering the characteristics of homes in which children learn to read before they start school (Briggs & Elkind, 1973; Clark, 1976; Durkin, 1966; King & Friesen, 1972; Morrow, 1983; Plessas & Oakes, 1964; Teale, 1978):

- The children were interested in and experienced paper-and-pencil activities, letters, and words at an early age.
- Parents read to the children, helping them with their "reading" and "writing." Parents frequently read themselves, valuing reading as a source of pleasure.
- There were books everywhere around the home.
- Parents took their children to libraries and bookstores.

- Early readers tended to come from smaller families.
- The literacy richness of the environment was more important than parental education or economic status (Hansen, 1969).
- Television viewing was limited.

In short, for these children, literacy often began before the first birthday, perhaps through experiences with plastic "bathtub" books filled with colorful pictures or from mothers and fathers who read nursery rhymes to their children as they rocked them to sleep. These early beginnings expand into a rich array of literacy experiences, from scribbling letters to grandma to experiencing stories on grandma's lap. Such experiences are so important that entire programs of research have been devoted to them, as exemplified by research on storybook reading.

Storybook Reading

Scientific interest in storybook reading predates the concept of emergent literacy. See Sulzby and Teale (1991) for a review of the literature establishing correlations between amount of storybook reading during the preschool years and vocabulary and language development, children's interest in reading, and success in early reading. In recent years, research on storybook reading has been substantially more analytical (Sulzby & Teale, 1991).

What do we now know about storybook interactions? Whether storybook reading occurs at home or at school, there are rich discussions and animated conversations between the reader and the child. The adult and child work out the meaning of the text, and they have a lot of fun doing it (Morrow, 1989). There is questioning, both by the adult and the child; there is modeling of dialogue by adults, with children sometimes participating; the adult praises the child's efforts to get meaning from the pictures and print; adults offer information to children and respond to children's reactions to text; and both adults and children relate what is happening in the text to their lives and the world around them (Applebee & Langer, 1983; Cochran-Smith, 1984; Flood, 1977; Pellegrini, Perlmutter, Galda, & Brody, 1990; Roser & Martinez, 1985; Taylor & Strickland, 1986).

Consistent with the Vygotskian ideas about scaffolding described in Chapter 8, parents seem to encourage children to participate as much as possible in storybook interactions, providing support as children need it, providing input that children can

understand (e.g., DeLoache & DeMendoza, 1987). With increasing age during the preschool years, parents do more of the reading—the children are attentive to longer sections of text (Heath, 1982; Sulzby & Teale, 1991). With increasing experience reading storybooks, adults and children have more complex discussions about text (Snow, 1983; Sulzby & Teale, 1991). Children who experience a lot of storybook reading are accustomed to interacting with an adult about story content; they are appropriately attentive during storybook reading, much more so than same-age children who have not experienced storybook reading (Bus & Van Ijzendoorn, 1988).

There has been some attention to differences in style of storybook reading and the effects of such variation on cognitive development. There is better vocabulary development for children who interact with adults who are skillful at eliciting verbal interactions from their children during reading (e.g., Ninio, 1980). Heath (e.g., 1982) established a correlation between the degree to which parents prompted and provided elaborations of book content and the eventual literacy attainment of their children: Children who experienced rich elaborations of text meaning did better on higher-order comprehension tasks than other children.

This correlational evidence favoring the hypothesis that quality of storybook reading affects long-term literacy development is bolstered by evidence from an impressive experiment conducted by Whitehurst et al. (1988). In that study, the parents of 14 children between 1¾ years and 3 years of age participated in a 1-month intervention designed to improve interactions between parents and children during storybook reading. Parents were taught to asked more open-ended questions and more questions about the functions and attributes of objects in stories as they read stories with their preschoolers. The parents were also given instruction in how to respond appropriately to their children's comments during story reading and how to expand on what the children had to say. The parents in this treatment group were also taught to reduce the amount of straight reading that they did as well as to eliminate questions that the child could answer simply by pointing to something in an illustration. Fifteen other children and their parents served as control participants in the study, with these families encouraged to continue reading storybooks as they normally did with their children.

First, the intervention parents were able to implement the treatment. That is, they could learn to interact differently with their children during story-book reading and in ways that increased the qualities of interactions between the children and their parents. Although there had been no differences between intervention and control children at the beginning of the study with respect to language variables, there were clear differences at the end of the month of treatment, ones favoring the intervention participants: At the end of the study, the intervention participants outscored the control subjects on a standardized measure of psycholinguistic ability and on two vocabulary tests. What was most striking in this study was that when the same measures were repeated 9 months later, the intervention subjects still had an advantage over the control participants, although the differences were not as large on the 9-month follow-up as at immediate posttesting. In general, however, everything in Whitehurst et al. (1988) was consistent with the hypothesis that high-quality storybook reading can have a positive impact on long-term language development, which is a critical emergent literacy ability. Notably, Valdez-Menchaca and Whitehurst (1992) replicated and extended the Whitehurst et al. (1988) finding with Mexican children.

As Sulzby and Teale (1991) concluded, most of the storybook reading data have been interpreted with respect to Vygotsky's theories of scaffolding and gradual internalization of cognitive skills: Within the context of the adult-child dyad, the child learns how to attend to text and how to participate in discussions of complex issues about stories, such as cause-and-effect in story sequences. A lot is learned in these interactions—including both procedural knowledge, such as how to identify the main ideas in stories (Lehr, 1988), and declarative knowledge, such as cultural information incidentally conveyed in high-quality literature (e.g., Cornell, Sénéchal, & Broda, 1988). Much is learned largely because parents help the child as needed and "up the ante" when the child is ready for it (i.e., read longer sequences to the child, urge the child to sit still for more). Another significant emergent literacy experience comes out of it as well: The children begin to "read" the storybooks themselves, doing independent reenactments.

Independent Reenactments

Ask a child to "read" one of their familiar books and the child produces a reading. This reading is not like any other speech the child utters but rather shares a

lot of properties with the language patterns in books. It is a different syntax than the child normally uses; different words are used than occur in a conversation (Pappas, 1987; Sulzby, 1985, 1988). Even 2-year-olds' readings are constrained by what is in the text; by 5 or 6 years of age, many children actually read. Sulzby and Teale (1991) summarized the changes in such "reading" that can be observed during the preschool years:

> . . . [C]hildren were seen to move from (a) strategies of labeling and commenting on items in discrete pictures, to (b) weaving an oral account over the pictures in order, to (c) creating a story with the prosody and wording of written language, to (d) using print in preconventional way to read the story, and finally to (e) reading the story conventionally. (p. 735)

Preschoolers learn a great deal about reading books, what is in books, and how to interact with book content if they are in an environment supportive of emergent literacy. They also learn from their friends on *Sesame Street*.

Sesame Street

Since fall, 1969, American preschoolers have had *Sesame Street* in their living rooms, with a typical audience of about 10 million homes (e.g., Palmer, 1984). Every evaluation ever conducted of *Sesame Street* (e.g., Anderson & Collins, 1988; Ball & Bogatz, 1970; Bogatz & Ball, 1971) has concluded that children learn a great deal about the alphabet and language from watching the program, much more so than from entertainment television, with *Sesame Street* making contributions to the development of literacy over and above family interactions and other sources of stimulation (e.g., Rice, Huston, Truglio, & Wright, 1990). *Sesame Street* is designed to grab children's attention through use of elements such as animated films, second-person address, and lively music (Campbell, Wright, & Huston, 1987), with the result substantial learning of the material featured on the show.

Concluding Comment

The more parents interact verbally with their children, the more verbally competent the children are (e.g., Huttenlocher, Haight, Bryk, Seltzer, & Lyons, 1991); watching Ernie, Bert, Big Bird, and Cookie Monster can stimulate some fundamental literacy understandings as well. Preschoolers especially seem to learn a great deal about literacy when adults read to them and when 2- to 5-year-olds "read" on their own (e.g., they come to understand what words are and how they function from such interactions with elders and books; Roberts, 1992). Not surprisingly, 5-year-olds who are more emergent literate—reflected by greater competence in re-enacting stories, writing individual words, "writing" stories, and "reading"—tend to outperform less emergent literate 5-year-olds in reading during the primary grades, which can be interpreted as a validation of sorts for emergent literacy experiences (Barnhart, 1991): That is, emergent literacy competence at age 5 predicts later more conventional reading competence. We believe, as did Feitelson (1988), who had studied early reading instruction around the world, ". . . informed opinion as well as the results of experimental studies seem to indicate that a particularly good way to use the years *before* children enter school may be to emulate what middle-class parents seem to have been doing intuitively all along, namely reading intensively to their children" (p. 153).

A great deal is being learned about how to structure children's worlds to increase their emergent literacy experiences. For example, more emergent literacy experiences are observed when children's play areas include props that encourage literacy. Thus, labeling of objects in the child's world can stimulate interaction with print and words. The world of play can include paper, pencils, and pens; "stores" and "offices" in play settings can include "order forms" and letters, appointment books, and message pads; and children's attempts at drawing and writing can be displayed. The presence of magazines and books as well as cozy corners in which to read them also stimulate emergent reading and writing activities (e.g., Morrow, 1990; Morrow & Weinstein, 1986; Neuman & Roskos, 1992).

READING DURING THE ELEMENTARY YEARS

Elementary reading, especially beginning reading, has fueled enormous controversies. A quarter of a century ago, the whole word versus phonics debate was detailed by Chall (1967) in *The Great Debate*, although data then and now (e.g., Byrne, Freebody, & Gates, 1992; Freebody & Byrne, 1988) support the phonics approach much more than whole-word reading. The winds of war between beginning reading camps stir again in the 1990s with extremely rancorous debates about the relative merits of whole

language, which emphasizes comprehension and does not include explicit decoding instruction (e.g., Goodman & Goodman, 1979) and instruction that includes explicit teaching of decoding skills.

We are not going to waffle between whole language and decoding positions here but rather come down squarely on the side of explicit decoding instruction. The evidence is simply overwhelming that explicit decoding instruction benefits most children and might be essential for many if they are to make rapid progress in becoming readers during the elementary years (e.g., Adams, 1990). Given the scientific stance taken in this text, we have no choice but to emphasize the decoding literature in the discussion that follows. In arguing for explicit phonics instruction, however, we caution that we do not dismiss the many potential advantages of whole language. In fact, we believe that excellent beginning reading instruction includes many of the elements favored by whole language enthusiasts. Before elaborating on that conclusion, however, we cover some of the best science that is informing the teaching community about the importance of phonemic awareness and explicit decoding instruction in beginning reading.

Research on Phonemic Awareness

Emergent literacy experiences such as book reading do not produce all of the competencies that are essential for success at reading during the elementary years. One such critical competency is **phonemic awareness,** which is awareness that words are composed of separable sounds (i.e., phonemes) and that phonemes are combined to say words. Phonemic awareness is one of the best predictors of success in early reading in school (e.g., Adams, 1990; Bond & Dykstra, 1967; Scarborough, 1989). Children who fail to learn to read during the first several years of schooling often lack phonemic awareness (e.g., Pennington, Groisser, & Welsh, 1993; Stanovich, 1986). Children who lack phonemic awareness have a difficult time learning to spell and to develop understanding of letter-sound relationships (Griffith, 1991; Juel, Griffith, & Gough, 1986). Poor phonemic awareness at 4 to 6 years of age is predictive of reading difficulties throughout the elementary years (Juel, 1988; Stuart & Masterson, 1992). Poor readers at all age levels often are less phonemically aware than same-age good readers (e.g., Pratt & Brady, 1988), with low phonemic awareness, which persists despite instruction, almost certain in dyslexic readers (e.g., Bruck, 1992; Bruck & Treiman, 1990; Pennington, Van Orden, Smith, Green, & Haith, 1990).

In normal readers, for phonemic awareness to develop, formal instruction in reading seems essential (i.e., only a small proportion of children develop phonemic awareness in the absence of such instruction; e.g., Lundberg, 1991). Notably the one emergent literacy experience that predicts phonemic awareness is parental teaching of letters and their sounds (Crain-Thoreson & Dale, 1992). Many parents, however, do not engage in such teaching, so education that has an impact on phonemic awareness typically occurs in school.

Without a doubt, the best-known experimental study of the effects of instruction aimed at increasing phonemic awareness was conducted in England by Lynette Bradley and Peter Bryant (e.g., 1983), although it was not the first (see Williams, 1980). They hypothesized, based on analyses of correlations between children's rhyming and alliteration skills (which require understanding that words are comprised of sounds; i.e., phonemic awareness) and later reading achievement (e.g., Calfee, Chapman, & Venezsky, 1972; Calfee, Lindamood, & Lindamood, 1973), that providing instruction to children about how to categorize words based on their sounds would increase phonemic awareness and hence long-term reading achievement.

An important principle emphasized in the Bradley and Bryant (1983) training was that the same word can be categorized in different ways based on sound when it is in different sets of words. Thus, if *hen* is in a group of words that includes *hat, hill, hair,* and *hand,* it would make sense to categorize all of these words together as starting with *h,* especially in contrast to other words starting with another letter (e.g., *b* words such as *bag, band, bat*). If *hen* were on a list with *men* and *sun,* however, these three words could be categorized as ones ending in *n.* If *hen* were on a list of words that included *bed* and *leg,* it would be possible to categorize the words as ones with *short e* in the middle.

The training involved 40 10-minute sessions spread out over 2 years, although a more recent version of the instruction was implemented over a period of 4 months (Bradley, 1988). During the first 20 sessions, 5- and 6-year-olds who initially lacked phonemic awareness were taught to categorize words based on common sounds using pictures of the objects (i.e., pictures of a *hen, men,* and a *leg*). For example, in one lesson, a set of pictures representing the letter *b* was shown to the child who named the objects. The child repeated the names with the teacher urging the child to listen to the sounds. The child then was asked if he or she could hear a sound common to each word. This continued until the child could identify the common sound, with the adult providing help and hints if the child experienced difficulty doing this.

The sound identification task was repeated a number of times during training, and there were variations (e.g., presentation of *bus* with the child required to pick out a picture starting with the same sound from an array of pictures; presentation of *bus* with the direction to pick out pictures starting with a different sound than the one at the beginning of *bus*). Children were given sets of pictures and asked to group them together based on common sounds, with them also required to justify their classifications. Odd-one-out was played, with the child required to eliminate a word starting (or ending or containing) a sound different than the other pictures in a set. Many such exercises were given for each sound (e.g., *b*), with the teacher moving on to a new sound only when the child seemed to be proficient with the sound previously introduced. Of course, as new sounds accumulated, the difficulty of tasks increased (e.g., there can be depictions of items starting with many different sounds rather than just one or two, as is the case at the beginning of training).

The 20 sessions with pictures were followed by 20 sessions with words, with children required to determine whether words rhymed or began with the same sound (alliteration). After the child was proficient at this task, there were lessons on end sounds (e.g., odd-word-out exercise requiring elimination of the word ending in a sound different than the others). After the child could manage categorizing based on final sounds, there was instruction of categorization based on middle sounds in words.

Pictures yielded to purely aural presentations in this training. Various discrimination exercises eventually gave way to production exercises, so that children had to recall words containing particular sounds in particular positions. In the latter half of the curriculum, children were required to spell words using plastic letters, with the teacher providing help as needed, up to and including spelling the word for the child if that was what was needed to move the lesson along. Spelling exercises included sets of words sharing common features. Thus, for a set involving *hat*, *cat*, and *rat*, an efficient strategy was simply to change the first plastic letter as each new word was requested. The saliency of many different sound patterns was illustrated with such spelling lists.

This training produced substantial gains in standardized reading performance (i.e., about a year advantage) relative to a control condition in which children were trained to categorize pictures and words conceptually (e.g., *cat*, *bat*, and *rat* are all animals). The sound categorization–trained students were even further ahead of control participants, who had received no supplementary categorization training. Even more striking, however, were the results of a 5-year follow-up. Even though many of the control subjects had received substantial remediation during the 5-year interval following participation in the study, there were still striking reading advantages for students who had experienced the sound categorization training when they were in the primary grades. See Bradley (1989) and Bradley and Bryant (1991) for discussion of these data.

Since the appearance of the Bradley and Bryant (1983, 1985) study, there have been other experimental evaluations of the hypothesis that phonemic awareness training is effective in promoting reading achievement. Such instruction does affect reading positively:

- In Lundberg, Frost, and Peterson (1988), classrooms of 6-year-olds were provided daily phonemic awareness training (i.e., rhyming exercises; dividing words into syllables; identifying phonemes, including segmenting words into phonemes and synthesizing phonemes into words), every day for 8 months. Control classrooms received no such training. The most dramatic evidence of training effectiveness was that 3 years later, students in trained classrooms continued to perform better on reading and spelling tasks than students in control classrooms.
- Ball and Blachman (1988) provided instruction to 5-year-olds. In the phoneme awareness condition, kindergarten students met in small groups for 20 minutes, 4 days a week for 7 weeks. Students moved counters to represent the sounds in words, were exposed to letter names and their associated sounds, and performed categorization tasks like the ones used in Bradley and Bryant's work. In the language activities control condition, students were given

vocabulary lessons, listened to stories, and practiced semantic categorization activities. They also received instruction in letter names and sounds that was identical to that provided to the phoneme awareness participants. There was also a no-instruction control condition in the study. The most important result was that the phoneme awareness group outperformed the two control groups on a word reading test—despite the fact that no word reading had been taught in the phoneme awareness condition. In follow-up studies with kindergarten students, the phoneme awareness treatment again produced superior word recognition and spelling compared with control performance (Ball & Blachman, 1991; Blachman, 1991; Tangel & Blachman, 1992).

- Lie (1991) taught Norwegian grade-1 students to analyze new words with respect to their phonological structure. This training promoted reading and spelling as measured in grade 2, compared with control students not receiving phonological training. Weaker readers benefited more from the training than did stronger students.
- Cunningham (1990) compared two approaches to increasing the phonemic awareness of kindergarten and grade-1 children. One approach was "skill and drill," with emphasis on segmentation and blending of phonemes. In the second approach, there was discussion of the value of decoding and phonemic awareness and how learning to segment and blend phonemes could be applied in reading. This latter condition was metacognitively rich, providing children with a great deal of information about when, where, and why to use the knowledge of phonemes they were acquiring. Although both forms of instruction were effective, the metacognitively rich instruction was more effective at the grade-1 level. We view this as an especially important study, with it complementary to studies discussed previously in this book that established that metacognitive embellishment of strategy instruction (segmentation and blending are procedures that could be considered strategic for young readers) increases general application of the procedures learned (e.g., O'Sullivan & Pressley, 1984; see Chapters 2 and 5).

When these data, along with the outcomes in related training studies (e.g., Treiman & Baron, 1981) are considered, it is hard to resist the conclusion that increases in phonemic awareness have a causal influence on subsequent successful reading. That is not to suggest, however, that that is the only relationship between phonemic awareness and reading. Both Wimmer, Landerl, Linortner, and Hummer (1991) and Perfetti (1992), for example, have presented evidence that phonemic awareness is increased by reading, with the implication that reading-induced increases in phonemic awareness in turn influence subsequent reading. Research on the role of phonemic awareness in reading may simply be getting started. The box score to date for this research is prompting a lot of serious thinking about various relations between awareness and reading. Readers of this text can be certain that there will be more of this work in the late 1990s.

At present, however, robust associations between phonemic awareness (sometimes used synonymously with the term phonological awareness, as in the next quote) and learning to read have been established in both manipulative (i.e., experimental) and nonmanipulative (i.e., correlational) studies. Goswami and Bryant 1992 elegantly summarized the findings:

> There can be little doubt that phonological awareness plays an important role in reading. The results of a large number of studies amply demonstrate a strong (and consistent) relationship between children's ability to disentangle and to assemble the sounds in words and their progress in learning to read. . . . There is also evidence that successful training in phonological awareness helps children learn to read. . . . Put together, these two sets of data are convincing evidence that phonological awareness is a powerful causal determinant of the speed and efficiency of learning to read. . . . The enterprise of establishing the importance of phonological awareness . . . has immediate educational implications, and it will also undoubtedly play a great part in theories about learning to read. However, it is only a first step. (p. 49)

We concur and follow up on Goswami and Bryant's (1992) opinion that there is more to early reading than phonemic awareness: In the next section, various mechanisms that have been implicated in early reading are reviewed. Learning to read is an elegant intercoordination of a number of processes.

Other Processes in Learning to Read Words

This section is arranged with respect to the complexity of the mechanisms that permit decoding of individual words, with the less complex mechanisms presented first. One possibility is that the simpler mechanisms would be operative before the more complex ones, so that moving from the beginning to the end of this list would be a rough developmental progression. We resist that conclusion, for some mechanisms that appear complex seem to be used by quite young children under at least some circumstances (e.g., analogy; Baron, 1977; Goswami & Bryant, 1992). Although perhaps it goes without saying at the beginning of a section on other processes, we emphasize from the outset that there is more than one way to read a word (see Ehri, 1991, which informed much of what follows, for elaborate discussion of this point). We also emphasize that how beginning and skilled readers read words is an extremely active area of research, and there is much debate. What is not debated is that such decoding is extremely complicated. Thus, what is presented in this subsection is an overview of some of the more important ideas, with no attempt to present exhaustive coverage of the mechanisms defining either beginning or skilled decoding.

Logographic reading **Logographic reading** (sometimes referred to as **visual cue reading;** e.g., Ehri, 1991) involves using only salient visual characteristics of a word rather than relying on letter-sound correspondences. There is an association for these children between the visual cue and the word. This generation of children often can read the word "Apple" on a computer or the same word on television when it is accompanied by the company's multi-colored apple with a bite out of it; the word *Jello* has a memorable shape; *STOP* is read correctly by some children so long as it is in the middle of a red hexagon; many 5-year-olds can read the words SCHOOL BUS on the back of a large, yellow vehicle; and what 4- to 5-year-old has trouble decoding Disney's signature, even though it is written in script.

Gough (reported in Gough, Juel, & Griffith, 1992) presented 4- to 5-year-olds with four words to read, one on each of four flashcards. One of the flashcards had a blue thumbprint on it. The participants went through the deck of cards until they could say each word given its card. Then came the interesting part. Could the children say the word that had been presented with the blue thumbprint if they were shown the word on a clean card devoid of the thumbprint? No. Could they say the word if they were shown just the blue thumbprint? Yes. In days of old, when verbal learning was popular, this would have been explained as a case of the blue thumbprint being a functional stimulus for saying the word. Gough et al. (1992) refer to this as **selective association,** which is another name for logographic reading or visual cue reading. Regardless of what it is called, it is the same process.

Alphabetic Reading   Traditional decoding instruction emphasizes sounding out words using letter-sound relations. This mechanism is operative in both reading and writing well before the time when children know *all* of the letter-sound correspondences (e.g., Ehri & Wilce, 1985; Huba, 1984; Scott & Ehri, in press). For example, preschoolers who know some letter-sound correspondences use what they know to attempt invented spellings of familiar words. When readers know some letter-sound relationships, they are capable of doing what Ehri (1991) refers to as **phonetic cue reading.** Ehri (1991) contrasted such reading with logographic reading using the following example:

> . . . [L]ogographic readers might remember how to read *yellow* by the "two sticks" in the middle (Seymour & Elder, 1986). In contrast, phonetic cue readers might see the two l's in *yellow*, hear their name in the pronunciation, and use this information to connect the spelling to the word in memory. (p. 391)

To be certain, however, such reading has its hazards. If the same letter cues are used for several words or a cue used to decode some word is experienced in a new word, there may be mix-ups. For example, it is not uncommon for a child to misread a sight word, referring to it as another word that is known to the child that is similar in length and shares common letters (e.g., *yellow* read for *pillow*; Ehri's [1991] interpretation of Seymour & Elder's [1986] data; Ehri & Wilce, 1987a, 1987b). Of course, phonetic cue readers have a devil of a time if asked to learn a set of words that share letters (e.g., *pots, post, spot, stop*; e.g., Gilbert, Spring, & Sassenrath, 1977).

Eventually, young readers learn all of the letter-sound relationships. They acquire what Gough and colleagues (e.g., Gough et al., 1992) refer to as the **cipher,** which is a code mapping the sounds of a language (i.e., **phonemes**) onto its alphabet. The complexity of the cipher is clear from this brief description of it:

> The orthographic cipher of English (in short, the cipher) is very complex. Simple cipher would map each

letter onto a single phoneme and each phoneme onto a single letter. But English has only 26 letters to map into more than three dozen phonemes, so it could not be simple; either a letter must represent more than one phoneme, or some phonemes must be represented by more than one letter. . . .

> Consider only the mappings of the initial letters onto initial phonemes. For only a minority of the letters (*b, d, f, l, n, r, v, z*) is it possible to identify the phoneme it represents. For the other 19, at least one additional letter must be identified before the identity of the word's first phoneme can be determined; in some cases, at least four more letters are required (compare *chord* and *chore*). The vast majority of the letter-sound correspondences of the English cipher are context dependent. (Gough et al., 1992, p. 39)

Acquiring the cipher and using it increases speed and accuracy in reading of unfamiliar words.

Before students acquire the cipher, they must understand the **alphabetic principle**—"that all twenty-six of those strange little symbols that comprise the alphabet are worth learning and discriminating one from the other because [they stand] for . . . the sounds that occur in spoken words" (Adams, 1990, p. 245). Once these realizations occur, there are a number of specific decoding "rules" that must be acquired as part of cipher learning. Some are easy because they require only one piece of information: The letter *b* is pronounced the same regardless of context; the same is true for *d, f, l, n, r, v, z*, the easy initial letters cited in the previous Gough et al. (1992) quote. Other letters sound differently, depending on other letters in the word, with the most common example being that vowels are long if there is a final *e* in a syllable and short if there is not. Another example is that *c* is pronounced differently if followed by an *e* or an *i* than if followed by an *a, o*, or *u* (e.g., compare the pronunciation of the *c* sounds in *celestial, city, cat, cot*, and *cut*). In general, conditional rules (i.e., involving consideration of more than one letter to determine the sound of a particular letter) are acquired later than rules involving one letter-sound association (e.g., Venezky & Johnson, 1973).

An important point to emphasize here is that knowing about letters, their names, and sounds may not be sufficient, if the student does not possess phonemic awareness (i.e., thorough understanding that words are composed of sequences of sounds). Thus, Tunmer, Herriman, and Nesdale (1988) observed that grade-1 children were especially likely to make good progress in decoding instruction if they possessed both phonemic awareness and high levels of letter-name knowledge. Even more relevant was Byrne and Fielding-Barnsley (1990, 1991), who observed that preschoolers with phonemic awareness who also knew the sounds associated with letters were particularly adept at decoding unfamiliar words. Alphabetic reading may depend on phonemic awareness—a proposition that seems reasonable when it is understood that alphabetic reading involves mapping sounds onto letter sequences that must be decomposed. Such decomposition would seem to depend on understanding first that there is a sequence of sounds in each word that can be separated.

Explicit Phonics-Rule Application Much of this early reading is probably rule-based decoding, if for no other reason than that much of early reading instruction involves teaching of phonics rules. Every morning in grade-1 classrooms across the United States, children experience letter-sound association drills. There are then opportunities to experience the letter-sound associations in the contexts of real words, with stories in phonics-based reading programs filled with regularly spelled words, preferably ones containing the letter-sound relations already presented to the children.

Students in phonics-based programs are taught other rules as well ("When two vowels go walking . . . ", "When there is an *e* at the end of a syllable . . . "). There are a manageable number of such rules (e.g., Clymer, 1963, listed 45 rules). Although termed rules, phonics generalizations never hold 100 percent of the time. For example, "Two vowels go walking . . . " works about 66 percent of the time according to Clymer. Thus, it almost always works when *oa* is the vowel combination as in *boat;* it rarely works for *ui* (i.e., it works for *suit* but not for most other *ui* words, such as *build, quill*). The final *e* rule really is a host of rules of varying utility: "When there is one *e* in a word that ends in a consonant, the *e* usually has a short sound" works about 76 percent of the time (e.g., for *leg* but not *blew*). "In many two-and three-syllable words, the final *e* lengthens the vowel in the last syllable" works 46 percent of the time (e.g., for *invite* but not *gasoline*).

Although whole-language enthusiasts and theorists disagree, the consensus based on an analysis of the scientific data is that such instruction is extremely profitable for many children, assisting them in learning to read (Adams, 1990; Anderson, Hiebert, Scott, & Wilkinson, 1985; Ehri, 1991).

"Sounding out" of words is more likely among children receiving explicit phonics instruction than among children receiving no such instruction (e.g., Barr, 1974–75). The value of phonics instruction is in giving students a good start. Although the phonics rules do not always work, they seem good enough.

Sight Word Reading We doubt that anyone reading this text has had to sound out a single word in this chapter except perhaps for unfamiliar proper names such as Ehri. Every word in it is in readers' sight vocabularies. There probably was a time when each and every word covered in this chapter was sounded out. Many trials of successfully sounding out a word, however, increase the connections between the letter pattern defining the word and the word in memory (Adams, 1990, Chapter 9; Ehri, 1980, 1984, 1987, 1992; see the discussion of connectionism in Chapter 3, this book). Thus, on initial exposure to a word like *frog*, the word is sounded out. Such sounding out begins a process in which the connections between each letter and adjacent letters are strengthened (e.g., between *fr* and *og*) and connections defining the entire sequence of letters and letter combinations in the word (strengthening of the connection between *fr* and *og*). Eventually the spelling is represented in memory as a unit consisting of *frog*. By repeated reading, there is also a strengthening of the connections between this visual stimulus and the conceptual understanding in long-term memory that defines a frog, so that eventually even the briefest exposure to the word *frog* elicits thoughts of a green, jumpy thing.

Orthographic Reading This can occur only after a child has experience with alphabetic reading. Eventually, meaningful letter strings are perceived as wholes (i.e., repeated co-occurrence of *i, n,* and *g,* in that order, results eventually in *-ing* being perceived as a unit; e.g., Stanovich & West, 1989). Prefixes and suffixes are obvious examples, but there are other recurring combinations, many of which are root words (e.g., *-take, mal-, ben-, rog-, do-*). When familiar orthographic patterns are encountered, it is not necessary to decode alphabetically. Rather, there is a direct connection with the sound sequence in memory and probably direct connections with meaning as well. For example, when author [CBM] encountered the word *maleic acid,* she really had no idea what the substance was but was certain at first glance—based on the "mal-" part—

that there was something bad about it. (There is, by the way—it stinks!)

There are tremendous advantages when words can be read by sight and orthographic chunks can be processed as wholes, with these advantages addressed in what LaBerge and Samuels (1974; also Samuels, Schermer, & Reinking, 1992) dubbed as **automaticity theory.** Two tasks are required to get the meaning out of a word: (1) It must be decoded. (2) What is decoded must be comprehended. Both require use of short-term memory, that extremely limited resource that can be thought of as one's attentional capacity. Decoding operations and comprehension processes can be thought of as competing for such capacity.

Alphabetic decoding or phonics rule application requires a great deal of attention on the part of the reader. Walk into any grade-1 classroom on any morning and there will be children during round-robin reading who will have all of their mental energy and attention devoted to the task of sounding out the words when it is their turn to read. If all of the attentional capacity is consumed by decoding, there is nothing left over for comprehension, with the result that the word may be pronounced but not understood. One solution for the slow alphabetic decoder might be to decode first and then comprehend. The cost of this is enormous: It is slow. Because decoding and comprehending are done in sequence, the phonological representation of the word must be held in short-term memory, which involves reduction of capacity that is needed for comprehension. No matter how the alphabetic reader approaches the task, there is strain on short-term capacity.

Automatic sight word reading and automatic recognition of orthographic chunks, in contrast, requires little effort or attention, and thus there is substantial mental capacity left over for comprehension when decoding is automatic. Indeed, for many sight words and orthographic chunks, there are probably automatic connections between the sight words and the chunks, the phonological representations of the word and the chunks, and the meanings of the words and the chunks (e.g., Baron, 1977). The result is faster, more accurate, and less effortful reading with experience and development (e.g., Horn & Manis, 1987). That is right. A paradox of slow, high-effort alphabetic reading is that it is less certain to result in accurate decoding than fast, low-effort automatic decoding via sight words and orthographic chunks, with the reader who recog-

nizes orthographic regularities automatically especially advantaged when words are encountered in isolation (e.g., Barker, Torgesen, & Wagner, 1992; i.e., there are no external context clues about the word or its meaning).

Reading by Analogy Words that sound the same often have the same spelling patterns. Thus a child who knows how to pronounce *beak* could make a good guess at *peak* the first time it is encountered simply by decoding by analogy (i.e., this is like *beak* only it starts with a *p*). That same *beak*-word knower would have a fighting chance with *bean, bead,* and *beat* as well using the analogy strategy. Adams (1990, pp. 210–211) provided the example that good readers quickly pronounce the word *kail* to rhyme with *ail, bail, tail, Gail,* and *hail.* Adams (1990 Chapter 9) in particular favors the connectionist theories (see Chapter 3) to explain such decoding by analogy. Each time a word with *-ail* in it is encountered and pronounced with the long *a* sound, there is a strengthening of the association between *-ail* and the long *a* sound. Thus, when *kail* is encountered by someone who has had many exposures to the *-ail* and long *a* association, there is automatic activation of *kail* and the word is pronounced correctly almost without thinking.

For the most part, analogy has been considered an advanced strategy used only by children who have been reading a while or by adults, with Marsh and his colleagues especially strong advocates of this position (e.g., Marsh, Desberg, & Cooper, 1977; Marsh, Friedman, Desberg, & Saterdahl, 1981; Marsh, Friedman, Welch, & Desberg, 1981). Although there are procedural aspects of these studies that reduce confidence in Marsh's conclusions about the advanced nature of analogy (see Goswami & Bryant, 1992), we concentrate here on the positive evidence produced by others that analogy is a tactic available even to beginning readers, focusing, in particular, on evidence produced by Goswami and Bryant (see 1992, for a review) because it is particularly convincing.

In one study (Goswami, 1986), 5- to 8-year-olds were asked to read words that were either analogous or not analogous to "clue" words such as *beak,* which was shown and pronounced for the child. Although children were not instructed how to use the clue words, they were better able to read words that were analogues to the clue words than words that were not analogues. Even nonreaders were able to do this in some cases (i.e., with respect to words sharing simple endings such as *-at*). Goswami (1988) replicated this finding.

One especially interesting aspect of Goswami's results is that analogies based on word endings are especially likely to be made by young children (i.e., words that rhyme are decoded as such). We like this finding because it connects to historically important work on what children remember about words they encounter, with children frequently confusing words that they have heard in a learning task with words that rhyme (e.g., Bach & Underwood, 1970). The historical learning research established that children are attentive to rhyme; Goswami's research establishes that they are inclined to use rhyme to figure out new words. Goswami and Bryant (1990, 1992) are developing a theory that children's rhyming categories (which are established early in life, including in the context of learning nursery rhymes and playing word games) are the basis of orthographic categories that permit decoding by analogy.

In closing this subsection, we must point out again that Goswami's results are controversial. For example, Ehri and Robbins (1992) found that only children who already had some phonological decoding skills were able to decode words by analogy, a finding inconsistent with Goswami's conclusion that nonreaders can decode by analogy; Peterson and Haines (1992) produced results complementary to the Ehri and Robbins outcome. In addition, Bruck and Treiman (1992) demonstrated that even when young children can use analogies, they rely greatly on decoding of individual phonemes and orthographs in decoding new words they encounter. Given the commitment of Goswami, Ehri, Bruck, Treiman, and their associates, we suspect there will be substantial additional research addressing the issue of whether decoding by analogy depends on being able to decode using letter-sound associations.

Using Semantic Context Clues When Words Are Presented in Meaningful Text A popular hypothesis with whole-language theorists and enthusiasts (e.g., Goodman, 1967; Smith, 1971) is that when words are read in context, decoding is really a "psycholinguistic guessing game." That is, reading of isolated words (which is frequently how decoding was studied in the investigations summarized in this section) is nothing like reading of words in real text, for real text offers many cues about the meaning of words that facilitate decoding. The classic

study supporting this position was Goodman (1965), who demonstrated that children's reading accuracy for words improved 60 to 80 percent when the words were in text compared to when the same words were presented on lists.

There have been a number of follow-up investigations with generally consistent results. When there have been positive effects of context on reading of words, the effects have generally been smaller than the effects obtained by Goodman (1965). Nicholson's work, in particular, has been informative with respect to this issue. What Nicholson found (Nicholson, 1991; Nicholson, Bailey, & McArthur, 1991; Nicholson, Lillas, & Rzoska, 1988) was that younger children in the primary years are more likely to benefit from context than older primary-level readers; poor readers benefit more than better readers. Goldsmith-Phillips (1989) and Schwantes (1991) also reported that reliance on context was a strategy used by younger grade-school readers much more than by more mature readers. Nicholson (1991) and Goldsmith-Phillips (1989) interpreted these results in terms of compensation (Stanovich, 1980): Poor readers rely on context in an attempt to compensate for poor decoding skills. See Stanovich (1986) for a review of other evidence, which is massive, supportive of this conclusion. Although Corley (1988) was not willing to rush to the conclusion that relying on semantic cues undermines the development of sound-analysis and syntax-analysis skills, she also observed weaker readers who relied too much on meaning cues as they processed sentences and not enough on phonological and syntax-analysis skills.

Summary Except for the youngest of readers, who might know only some logographs, readers do not use only one approach to decoding of words, although there is no doubt that with increasing experience, students use a greater variety of word-level strategies and do so more flexibly (e.g., Rayner, 1988). One popular theory of flexibility in decoding that emerges from much of the research (Baron, 1977; Barron, 1981, 1986; Bryant & Bradley, 1980; Coltheart, Davelaar, Jonasson, & Besner, 1977; Frith, 1979; Treiman & Baron, 1983) is **dual route theory.** Ehri (1992) summarized this perspective as involving knowledge of some words based on their visual representation versus derivation of a word's pronunciation when the word is not visually familiar and then matching this pronunciation to an item in the mental lexicon. The visual route, of course, is faster than the phonological route, not requiring linear processing of the letter and sound relationships. An interesting new development is that Ehri (1992) believes that the faster visual route probably still involves some phonological decoding. She makes a case in her 1992 chapter that there is a need to study carefully exactly what happens when reading seems direct and is fast.

Still, for the present, the more extreme version of the dual route theory is a good way to organize the processes covered in this section. When readers engage in logographic decoding, sight word reading, or orthographic reading, their processing is more on the side of faster, more direct, visual accessing of the lexicon (although there may still be some phonological coding as part of this process); when readers engage in alphabetic reading or phonics rule application, their processing is more of the slower, less direct, extensively phonological sort. Reading by analogy could be either.

When good readers read text that is easy for them, much of it is sight word reading. On other occasions, skilled reading involves other mechanisms. Thus, when an adult sees a Russian can of Pepsi, there is logographic reading of Pepsi. When teachers read the roll the first day, much of the reading of unfamiliar last names involves alphabetic reading and sometimes reading by analogy (e.g., guessing the pronunciation of *Baser* given its resemblance to *laser*). The full repertoire of decoding strategies taken up in this section is available to good readers. That is not the case with young reader. It takes the young reader a while to build up a sight vocabulary. It takes a while to build up sufficient knowledge of orthography to use analogy strategies to the full extent. That there is so much to learn in order to decode reliably and so much practice required in order to decode most words reasonably automatically has been respected in school for years: Most of the first 3 years of formal reading instruction is dedicated more to decoding instruction than anything else; decoding instruction continues through the grade-school years and in many cases into the middle school. Some specific mechanisms that have been proposed as means of making decoding instruction more efficient are taken up in the next section.

Before leaving this subsection, however, we think it important to point out one of the important discoveries of the last 15 years: When good readers read, they process the words in a text thoroughly. Studies of eye movement during skilled reading have established that not only are good readers reading every single word when they are trying to learn what is in text (e.g., McConkie, Zola, Blanchard, & Wolverton, 1982; for a discussion, see Carver, 1990, Chapter 5), but also they are processing every single letter (e.g., Rayner, Inhoff, Morrison, Slowiaczek, & Bertera, 1981) (for commentary and reviews, see Adams, 1990, Chapter 6; Stanovich, 1986). A good college-level reader has no difficulty reading at a rate of 200 to 300 words per minute, at least when reading easy text (Carver, 1990). Such a reader is processing an enormous amount of information quickly—30 or so letters a second. Years of reading are required before such an information processing feat is possible. And feat it is, for when the reader first starts to read, often all attentional capacity is fixated on single letters, with several seconds sometimes spent on a letter (Samuels, Miller, & Eisenberg, 1979). Think about it, from several seconds to process a single letter (and then sound it out correctly only some of the time) to 30 milliseconds or less with 100 percent accuracy (Carver, 1990).

Instructional Methods That Improve the Acquisition of Decoding Abilities as Documented by Research

In addition to the methods for teaching decoding alluded to in the previous subsection (e.g., learning explicit decoding rules), there are many others prescribed in the reading education literature. We confine our coverage here to a few that are defensible based on research, largely to make the point that although early reading instruction is an old field, it is still possible to break new ground (or make clear the reasonableness of some traditional practice) with telling experimental and correlational research.

Repeated Readings According to LaBerge and Samuel's (1974) automaticity theory, comprehension of a word is more likely the more automatic its decoding. The more quickly and effortless the words of a text can be decoded, the more cognitive capacity can be devoted to comprehension (also consistent with Perfetti and Lesgold's [1977] **verbal efficiency theory,** which specifies that comprehension is more likely if lower-order processes such as decoding are accomplished efficiently).

One method for increasing automaticity of decoding of the words in a story is to have children read the story multiple times, with the children required to keep reading until they demonstrate some level of fluency as defined by accuracy and speed of decoding (i.e., **method of repeated readings;** Samuels, 1979). Once the child gets good with a passage, then another more challenging passage is presented. Sometimes this approach is combined with audio presentation of stories initially, especially for slow readers (Dowhower, 1987).

As far as reading of the specific words in a passage is concerned, there is little doubt that repeated readings produce faster reading. More general increases in reading speed have not been obtained, however, such as being able to read other stories faster (Fleisher, Jenkins, & Pany, 1979; Rashotte & Torgeson, 1985; see Carver, 1990, Chapter 17, for an analysis) or even other words sharing features with the items read repeatedly (Lemoine, Levy, & Hutchinson, 1993). An additional limitation is that the method may send the message to students that reading is just decoding and that meaning is not important. O'Shea, Sindelar, and O'Shea (1985) considered this possibility and created a repeated readings condition in which students were informed that comprehension was extremely important. Both comprehension and decoding improved with this instruction.

Computer-Based Decoding Instruction If current instructional computers do anything well, they are great at providing drill and practice at low cost in terms of human instructional time and without the fatigue a human teacher inevitably experiences when required to carry out rote drills. Joseph Torgeson (1986), a leading figure in devising microcomputer applications for early reading, puts it this way: "Computers have the capacity to deliver motivating, carefully monitored, individualized and speed oriented practice in concentrations far beyond those available in traditional instructional formats" (p. 159).

One of the most exciting new directions in this arena is directed at development and validation of computer programs that increase phonemic awareness of prereaders. Torgeson and colleagues (Torgeson, Foster, & Foster, 1992) have generated true experimental data on one program (*The Daisy Quest Program*) that seems to do just that, work that complements other instructional work by Torgeson (e.g., Torgeson & Morgan, 1992; Torgeson, Morgan, & Davis, 1992) aimed at increasing children's phonemic awareness.

Daisy Quest is designed to train children to be able (1) to identify individual sounds in intact words (**analytical phonological skills**) and (2) to blend individual sounds into recognizable real words (**synthetic phonological skills**). For the former, the program requires the student to identify rhyming words; to make comparisons of words based on first, middle, and last sounds; and to count the number of phonemes in short words. There are also two activities in the program to stimulate blending skills. The program "talks" and the graphics are colorful as the children "search" for clues to where Daisy the Dragon is hiding.

After 20 sessions of the program, *Daisy Quest* players outperformed control subjects (all participants were $4\frac{1}{2}$ to $6\frac{1}{2}$ years of age) on tasks involving matching words based on first sounds and identifying which of four words has a different last sound. They could also segment and blend words better. In short, the program seemed to promote phonemic awareness. Qualitative data collected by the researchers suggested that this program might be an inviting way for prereaders to experience exercises aimed at increasing phonemic awareness. Torgeson et al. (1992) reported that children enjoyed interacting with *Daisy Quest* and its graphics, could follow the directions, and understood and liked the speech used in the program. Only one of the youngest children in the study did not want to finish the 20 sessions. *Daisy Quest* is engaging instructional material that works.

Integrated Picture Training Ehri, Deffner, and Wilce (1984) tested a clever mnemonic method for teaching letter-sound associations to preschoolers and kindergarten children. First, children are given some exercises to ensure they "know" the sounds they will be learning. Thus, if the lesson includes the *h* sound, the child is told the name *Harry* and asked to pronounce the initial sound, with this continuing until the child can identify the initial sound reliably. Then, for each sound taught, a word is provided that starts with the sound (e.g., *house*), with presentation of these words continued until the child can confidently tell the initial sound for each word presented. Then the child is introduced to the letter (lower-case form in the study) and a mnemonic picture in which the letter is used as part of a picture of the object beginning with the letter (e.g., a *house*, with windows and a door under the arch of the letter and the part of the left side of the letter extending higher than the arch serving as a chimney). Children who were provided such integrated pictures learned more letter-sound relations than control children who studied the letter-sound associations without the integrated pictures. This is an application of mnemonic strategies (Chapter 10) that we have seen used in actual classrooms.

Just Reading More   One of the best ways to increase competence with respect to many aspects of reading is to read more. The evidence substantially suggests that better readers do in fact read more (see Allen, Cipielewski, & Stanovich, 1992; Allington, 1977; Cipielewski & Stanovich, 1992; Cunningham & Stanovich, 1990, 1991; Juel, 1988; Samuels et al., 1992; Stanovich, 1986). By doing so, they make themselves even better readers (Taylor, Frye, & Maruyama, 1990) and more knowledgeable people in general (Stanovich & Cunningham, 1993). To appreciate the literacy advantages that a good reader creates for himself or herself, consider the following numbers generated by Nagy and Anderson (1984): A middle-school student who is not motivated to read may read 100,000 words a year. An average-achieving, average-motivated, middle-school reader might read 1 million words a year. In contrast, the best and most voracious readers will read between 10 million and 50 million words a year.

There are important concerns that American children read little outside of class (e.g., Anderson, Wilson, & Fielding, 1988), often favoring other activities such as heavy watching of television (e.g., Beentjes & Van der Voort, 1988; Neuman, 1988), and it makes a difference. Good readers become better readers largely by deciding to read (e.g., Anderson et al., 1988). Stanovich (1986) provided an elegant summary of how voracious readers make themselves better readers:

> Children who become better readers have selected (e.g., by choosing friends who read or choosing reading as a leisure activity rather than sports or video games), shaped (e.g., by asking for books as presents when young), and evoked (e.g., the child's parents noticed that looking at books was enjoyed or perhaps just that it kept the child quiet) an environment that will be conducive to further growth in reading. Children who lag in reading achievement do not construct such an environment. Anbar (1986) noted the importance of these active and evocative organism-environment correlations in her studies of children who acquired reading during school: "Once the parents began to interact with their children around the reading activities, the children reciprocated with eagerness. The parents then intuitively seemed to follow the child's learning interests and curiosity, sensi-

tively responding to requests for aid. Once could say, therefore, that the parents facilitated the child's natural course of development" (p. 77). (Stanovich, 1986, p. 382)

Of course, Stanovich and everyone else who has studied the effects of amount of reading on reading achievement believe that such practice affects a number of reading competencies, not just adequacy of decoding. Thus, this is a good jumping-off place with respect to coverage of decoding. The long-term goal of reading instruction is not the training of readers so they can "say" words but the development of readers who can construct meaning—who can comprehend. Because prior knowledge facilitates comprehension, and additional reading increases prior knowledge enormously (Stanovich & Cunningham, 1993), reading a great deal affects long-term comprehension abilities by permitting readers to relate new content to their knowledge of the world, which was constructed in part by reading important content in the past. Just as there have been exciting research findings in the last two decades about how decoding occurs, there have been exciting research findings with respect to comprehension, with much of the research aimed at increasing comprehension instruction during the elementary years.

Comprehension Strategies Instruction

One of the most important research studies about reading comprehension instruction was conducted by Durkin (1978–79). She observed that elementary reading instruction included little teaching aimed at fostering comprehension. Instead of teaching comprehension, teachers seemed to be testing it all of the time, asking lots of questions about what had been in the text, with Durkin noting many IRE cycles (see Chapter 8) but little information provided to students about how they might prepare themselves to answer questions about text they were reading.

That study did much to motivate research on how to increase reading comprehension. An important assumption was that comprehension could be increased if students were encouraged to create coherent representations of text. Recall from Chapter 3 the various ways that scientists have thought about representations in memory. Such theories inspired a number of instructional interventions.

Much of the research on comprehension strategies instruction was of the following form: A researcher believed that if students constructed a particular type of representation (e.g., mental images representing the story told in a narrative, summaries) or reacted to texts in a particular way (e.g., relating it to prior knowledge, explicitly seeking clarifications when unsure of meaning), comprehension and hence long-term memories of text would be improved. The experimenters testing these strategies usually had reasons to believe that students were not already engaging in such processing when reading, or they were doing so less systematically and completely than they could.

In these studies, the reading comprehension of students receiving instruction typically was measured by some type of objective test of understanding (e.g., multiple-choice items over literal and potentially inferred messages in text). The performances of instructed subjects on such tests were compared with the performances of students not receiving strategy instruction (e.g., control subjects permitted to read as they normally would in preparation for an objective test). If the strategy-trained students outperformed the control students on the test, there was support for the conclusions that the students (1) probably were not using the trained strategy on their own or were not using it systematically, but (2) more positively, that they can be taught to do so. In addition, (3) there was some additional validation of the theory of representation of knowledge that gave rise to the intervention (e.g., when imagery instructions improved learning, it bolstered confidence that people really can represent material with images).

There were many such experiments in the 1970s and 1980s, producing evidence that students could benefit from instructions to use a number of individual strategies aimed at improving learning from text (see Haller, Child, & Walberg, 1988; Pearson & Dole, 1987; Pressley, Johnson, Symons, McGoldrick, & Kurita, 1989). We illustrate these interventions and the research on them with brief discussion of summarization, mental imagery, and story grammar training.

Summarization   Kintsch and van Dijk's (e.g., 1978; van Dijk & Kintsch, 1983) theory was that good readers store the main ideas presented in text, the macropropositions. In contrast, children are much less likely to store the main ideas of what they read (e.g., Brown & Day, 1983; Brown, Day, & Jones, 1983). A number of reading researchers reasoned that if children were taught to extract the main ideas

and summarize text, their comprehension and memory of text should improve.

Summarization strategies were devised and tested and proved their worth in controlled studies. For example, Brown and Day (1983) devised an intervention based on the summarization principles that mature readers use, as specified in the van Dijk and Kintsch (1983) framework (see Chapter 3). Brown and Day's summarization rules were to (1) delete trivial information, (2) delete redundant information, (3) substitute superordinate terms, (4) integrate a series of events with a superordinate action term, (5) select a topic sentence, and (6) invent a topic sentence if there is none. Bean and Steenwyk (1984) successfully instructed grade-6 students in the use of these rules. After the students were taught to apply such rules to paragraph-length texts, their performances on standardized reading comprehension tests, which generally involves reading short texts, improved.

A number of other summarization interventions have also improved the comprehension and memory of grade-school students:

1. Taylor and associates (Taylor, 1982; Taylor & Beach, 1984) taught students to outline text using text headings and subheadings. Main idea statements were generated for every paragraph and embedded in this outline.
2. Rinehart, Stahl, and Erickson (1986) taught children to produce summaries that included main ideas and important supporting details. Their instruction involved Brown and Day's (1983) summarization rules and instruction to relate the various parts of text in a hierarchical outline form, as in Taylor's instruction.
3. Berkowitz (1986) taught students to construct maps of passages. Students wrote the title of the passage in the middle of a page and then identified a half dozen or so main ideas in the passage. These were placed in boxes surrounding the title. Each of these boxes was then filled with supporting details for the main idea placed in it.
4. Armbruster, Anderson, and Ostertag (1987) taught students the problem/solution structure, which is characteristic of many social studies texts: Students were taught to summarize the problem covered by a passage and the actions taken to resolve the problem.

That memory and comprehension were consistently improved by summarization instruction has done much to stimulate the teaching of summarization in elementary classrooms. Sometimes summarization is taught alone, but a more defensible approach is to teach it as one of several strategies that is used in combination with others. Theoretically, this makes sense because in any particular text, there are both specific pieces of information and relations between different facts, with discrete information and relational information acquired in different ways (McDaniel & Einstein, 1989). For example, discrete pieces of information in a text can be encoded via imagery. In contrast, attending to story grammar elements definitely focuses attention on key elements in stories and how they relate to one another.

Mental Imagery   At least after the age of 8, memory and understanding of text improve when children are instructed to create images depicting what they have read (e.g., Gambrell & Bales, 1986; Pressley, 1976), possibly because of dual-coding of what is read (i.e., construction of both verbal and imagery codes; see Chapter 3, this volume; Paivio, 1971). Often the gains in learning due to imagery instructions are not large, but they are consistent (see Pressley, 1977, for a review; also Pressley, Borkowski, & Johnson, 1987). The exception to this generalization is when the learner is required to learn material that includes many relationships that might seem arbitrary. If there are a lot of them, such situations have high potential for interference. The construction of an image for each confusing fact seems to reduce interference and thus greatly increases the likelihood that learners will keep the various facts straight. Pressley, Symons, McDaniel, Snyder, and Turnure (1988) provided an example of such facilitation.

In their Experiment 1, Pressley, Symons et al. (1988) asked university students to learn sentences about things that various types of men had done—like the sentences presented in chapter 10 that were used in Bransford's research. Thus, when presented the sentence, "The bald man used the phone," they were to imagine a bald man using a phone. When presented, "The crippled man flicked the switch," they were to imagine that. The effect of imagery on learning was huge. Subjects who constructed images remembered a mean of 18.45 of the 24 sentences compared with controls who remembered 9.15 of 24 sentences on average—more than a 100 percent improvement in learning owing to the

use of imagery. Thus, when learning confusing content, construction of images that represent as exactly as possible the meaning of the text has the potential to produce large learning gains.

If representational imagery usually does not produce large effects on learning of text, why worry about teaching it to students? The most compelling response to this question comes not from cognitive psychology but from literary (reader) response theories (e.g., Rosenblatt, 1978). One of the principal ways that good readers respond to text is that they construct images of the meanings conveyed by the text. These images are interpretive and personal. Images are important forms of aesthetic response to text. Indeed, many texts are written explicitly to elicit vivid images in readers. Unfortunately, however, not all readers respond as intended by authors, with the potential consequence that readers will miss the point of many tales they read.

Much of Sadoski's work (e.g., 1983, 1985) has been directed at the consequences of readers constructing images in reaction to text, images that are essential for deriving important understandings from text. In his research, students in the middle elementary grades read stories, ones that have a climax. For example, the grade-5 students in Sadoski (1983) read "Freddie Miller, Scientist":

> The story concerns the plight of a boy scientist whose frequent home experiments go awry and get him into trouble. In the end, the boy becomes the family hero when he aids his sister, who has become locked in a closet, by constructing a home-made flashlight and lowering it to her through the transom vent above the closet door. The story contains three illustrations. Two depict experiments at the beginning and middle of the story, and the third is a diagram of the home-made flashlight. The illustration shows only the flashlight and does not illustrate the climactic event in which the flashlight was used. (pp. 111–112)

One important finding in this research is that about half of the children reported images at the point of climax in this story (a finding replicated with grade-3 and grade-4 children in Sadoski, 1985). Moreover, understanding of the story varied in an interesting way with whether subjects reported climax imagery or not. The subjects who reported climax imagery were much more likely than subjects who did not to be able to provide the theme of the story during their recall of it (a finding replicated in Sadoski, 1985). This is powerful evidence in favor of reader response claims that imagery reactions are a part of acquiring a deep understanding of what is read.

Sadoski and Quast (1990; also Sadoski, Goetz, & Fritz, 1993a, 1993b) extended the previous work. In Sadoski and Quast (1990), college students read feature articles from popular magazines (e.g., *Time, Newsweek*). They found that college students still remembered quite a bit from such articles when they were tested 16 days after reading them. What was interesting was the parts of the texts that were recalled: The sections of the text that were most easy to imagine were more likely to be remembered than other sections of the text. This contrasted with no significant relationship between the importance of the information and memory. In Sadoski et al. (1993a, 1993b), adults read biographical texts: How easy it was to generate an image of the text predicted recall of the text much better than did the rated interestingness of the material or even its familiarity to readers. Sadoski's work supports the conclusion that texts evoking powerful images are more memorable than texts that do not invoke such images.

Although psychologists have emphasized memory in their research on imagery, some of the most exciting thinking about imagery pertains to its role in understanding of text. Literary response theorists such as Iser (e.g., 1978) believe that the "image" of a story unfolds as readers proceed through text—and that images are highly personal, reflecting prior knowledge and personal interests (see Sadoski, Goetz, & Kangiser, 1988, for data confirming this view of reader imagery). Such images are the heart of aesthetic understanding, with thinking that parallels Iser's prominent in theoretical analyses of comprehension.

For example, Langer (1986, 1990) believes that how a reader's **envisionments** of text content change can be extremely revealing about how the reader is relating prior knowledge to text or constructing and understanding the underlying morals of tales. At their best, these envisionments are extremely dynamic and rich, including deep understanding of character motivations and suppositions about why the plot is unfolding as it is. (See Wittrock and Alesandrini, 1990, for additional evidence that summarization-integration and imagery processes are related.) Any student who is looking for an important research direction to pursue could study how imagery as conceptualized by more information processing–oriented researchers, such as Sadoski and Paivio, relates to conceptions of text un-

derstanding emerging from literary response theory. Complete understanding of representational imagery and its effects on understanding both particular parts of texts and the emerging messages in text will require investigations that are sensitive to both dual-coding and literary response theories.

Story Grammar Training   Some children do not possess knowledge of story grammar (see Chapter 3). Short and Ryan (1984) reasoned that teaching such children the elements of a story and to use these elements to understand text would improve comprehension and memory of stories. They taught grade-4 poor readers to ask themselves five questions in order, questions corresponding to the elements of story grammar, as they read stories:

1. Who is the main character?
2. Where and when did the story take place?
3. What did the main characters do?
4. How did the story end?
5. How did the main character feel?

Students who received this training were able to recall more of stories they read than students who did not receive training. The facilitation was large, great enough to improve the reading of the poor grade-4 readers to the level of skilled grade-4 readers.

Other research has been conducted since Short and Ryan's (1984) pathbreaking study. Idol (1987; Idol & Croll, 1987) taught 9- to 12-year-old poor readers to construct a story map as they read stories, a map containing the elements of story grammar: setting, problem, goal, action, and outcome. Memory of stories improved following this training. Nolte and Singer (1985) taught students to ask themselves questions as they read, questions focusing attention on the story grammar elements of stories. The students were taught to ask themselves about the setting, the main characters, the goals of the characters, and the obstacles encountered on the way to the goal. This instruction had a large effect on students' ability to answer short-answer questions over text.

Other Single Strategies   Other strategies have been evaluated, including the following: (1) **Mnemonic imagery:** Construction of images that transform text meaning in some way to make it more memorable (e.g., when reading a biography of Charles Dickens, imagining each of the events occurring to a "Mr. McGoo" Scrooge in order to remember these were events in Dickens' life, rather than events from some other biography; see Chapter 10, this volume): (2) **Question generation:** Thinking of questions about the meaning of text as reading proceeds (e.g., Rosenshine & Chapman, 1992). (3) **Prior knowledge activation:** Relating what one already knows to information encountered or expected in text (e.g., Anderson & Pearson, 1984). If this activation occurs before reading, it often involves prediction of text content (e.g., as in reciprocal teaching; Palincsar & Brown, 1984, which was introduced in Chapter 8).

What resulted from these studies was a collection of strategies that could be applied before (e.g., making predictions based on prior knowledge), during (e.g., imagery generation), and after (e.g., summarization) reading (Levin & Pressley, 1981). Even so, this research was not aimed at coordinated use of strategies before, during, and after reading but rather was aimed at the validation of particular individual strategies. More complicated studies of strategies instruction were required, for many sophisticated models of thinking specified that multiple strategies could help students make sense of the world, including worlds created in texts (e.g., Baron, 1985; Brown et al., 1983; Levin & Pressley, 1981; Nickerson et al., 1985). A few prominent investigations of this type were conducted in the 1980s.

Multiple-Strategies Instruction   Scott Paris and his University of Michigan associates (e.g., Paris & Oka, 1986) developed a set of strategies lessons that could be used across a year of elementary reading instruction. The curriculum included instruction of many of the individual strategies validated in research as well as some attention to metacognitive and motivational components in strategy use. Although approximately 20 weekly lessons resulted in improved performance on some of the specific tasks covered in the curriculum, more general changes, such as improvements on standardized reading comprehension tests, did not occur.

Others, however, also reported improvements in student reading as a function of teaching multiple strategies. The best-known multiple-strategies intervention developed during the 1980s was reciprocal teaching of comprehension strategies, perhaps because it was the first report of a classroom-deployed, multiple-strategies intervention that seemed to promote reading comprehension (Palincsar & Brown, 1984). As discussed in Chapter 8, this intervention, which involves teaching students to predict, self-question, clarify when confused, and sum-

marize, produced consistent increases in lower-ability students' use of the processes taught (i.e., prediction, seeking clarification, question-generation during reading, and summarization); often, this type of instruction also produced at least modest gains on more general measures (e.g., standardized reading comprehension; Rosenshine & Meister, 1992).

Yuill and Oakhill (1988) improved the comprehension of weaker 7- to 8-year-old readers by teaching them to generate questions about text, make predictions about text content, and analyze individual words in text as a clue to overall text meaning. In Duffy et al. (1987), grade-3 teachers recast the skills taught during grade-3 reading as strategies, with the teachers providing many direct explanations about how to attack text and comprehend it (see Chapter 8). Collins (1991) improved comprehension in grade-5 and grade-6 students by providing a semester (3 days a week) of lessons on reasoning skills. The students were taught to seek clarification when uncertain, look for patterns and principles, analyze decision making that occurs during text processing, problem solve (including the use of backward reasoning and visualization), summarize, predict, adapt ideas in text (including rearranging parts of ideas in text), and negotiate interpretations of texts in groups. Although the trained students did not differ from controls before the intervention with respect to standardized comprehension performance, there was a large difference between treated and control conditions on the posttest. Bereiter and Bird (1985) demonstrated that students in grades 7 and 8 benefited from instructions to use a few comprehension strategies used by older, more sophisticated readers (i.e., restate difficult text, backtrack as necessary, watch for pertinent information in text, and resolve apparently anomalous information in text). Their findings could be combined with Duffy et al.'s (1987) and Collins's (1991) data to produce optimism that instruction of multiple strategies is an intervention that is potentially effective during most of the elementary-school years.

Notably, Duffy et al. (1987), Collins (1991), and Bereiter and Bird (1985) all involved extensive direct explanations of strategies by teachers to students, with these direct explanations conveying both information about how to carry out strategies and metacognitive information about the role strategies play in thinking and when they can make a difference in comprehension (see Meloth, 1990). In all three studies, the teachers made visible otherwise invisible mental processes by thinking aloud (i.e., mental modeling; Duffy, Roehler, & Herrmann, 1988). In all three cases, students had extensive practice opportunities, with teacher assistance provided during practice as required by students. In all three cases, there was opportunity for gradual acquisition of the repertoire of strategies and long-term instruction about the coordination of the strategic competencies acquired.

Summary By the end of the 1980s, there had been substantial success in demonstrating that instruction of some individual cognitive processes improves comprehension of text. In addition, a few investigators succeeded in teaching multiple strategies in ways that improved reading comprehension. The multiple-strategies approach is especially appealing theoretically because learning from text involves remembering specific items mentioned in text as well as how the various pieces of information in text relate—such generative processes at multiple levels are more likely when readers apply both strategies that increase memory and understanding of particular parts of text and ones that promote integration across various parts of the reading (McDaniel & Einstein, 1989; Wittrock, 1990).

What was missing in this research, however, was information about how real educators might translate strategies instruction into effective educational practice. Indeed the true experiments just discussed were not at all revealing about the instructional dynamics of lessons—the interweaving of teacher and student behaviors that is instruction. They did not answer some extremely important questions, such as "What do complete strategies instruction lessons look like?" and "What do years of such lessons look like?" Getting answers to such questions was important because widespread dissemination and acceptance of effective strategies instruction would be unlikely in the absence of high-quality knowledge about how strategies can and should be taught. Fortunately, analyses of important reading programs, including strategies-based ones, are now available, with some of these reviewed in the next subsection.

Before moving on, however, we point out that an emerging direction in reading comprehension research is to find ways to increase comprehension by manipulations that decrease the demands on short-term memory. For example, when text is presented more rapidly than readers normally read, more of the text can be held in short-term memory than is normally held, with increases in comprehension

(e.g., Breznitz, 1987; Breznitz & Share, 1992). Thus a new twist on reading strategies is probably going to be to teach young readers how to make the most of their short-term capacity, which will probably include teaching children to read more quickly than they are inclined to do so naturally. Part of this effort will involve familiarizing students with many more vocabulary so that the words can be rapidly accessed when encountered in text, consistent with the observation that functional short-term memory is greater for familiar words than for unfamiliar ones (Engle, Nations, & Cantor, 1990).

Reading Programs

The three reading programs reviewed here are covered in "developmental order," with whole language being implemented from the onset of schooling, reading recovery applied when decoding problems are evident (i.e., at end of grade 1), and transactional strategies instruction appropriate for children who can decode, with its focus on comprehension.

Whole Language **Whole language** is difficult to define (e.g., see Watson, 1989, for an entire article on the challenges of defining it). Whole-language educators are determined that the integrity of language be preserved in literacy education, that children deal with "whole" language rather than be presented language skills instruction. There is reading of "whole" texts and writing of "whole" texts as well. Language instruction is done within the context of the "whole" life of the child. If it is not clear what is whole about whole-language instruction, try rereading from the beginning of this paragraph and substituting "authentic" for every appearance of "whole" (Weaver, 1990, p. 6). If whole language is difficult to define, it is not difficult to identify its chief advocate—Kenneth Goodman of the University of Arizona, who has written extensively on how whole-language philosophy is consistent with a broad range of scientific and philosophical traditions, from psycholinguistic analyses of language development to Dewey's methods of education through real-world problem solving to integrated curricular perspectives on language arts (i.e., language arts across the school day).

Some of the tenets of whole-language instruction include the following (adapted from Weaver, 1990, p. 6):

- Children learn to read and write as they learned to talk, which means as a gradual and natural process, one in which instruction is down-played. (Much of traditional instruction is presumably not natural.) The teaching role is that of someone who assists rather than instructs the child.

- Children are encouraged as they work with language rather than discouraged. For example, creative inventive spellings that reflect the sounds of the language are to be praised rather than corrected.
- Children read real stories, poems, and books every day.
- Children write something for a real audience every day (e.g., they write a story that will be read to classmates or be read by classmates).
- Reading and writing occur across the school day as part of art, social studies, science, and so on. (Learning to decode, familiarization of vocabulary to the point of automaticity, and acquisition of new vocabulary meanings are presumed to be a byproduct of extensive, authentic language activities.)

Our view is that whole language is an important approach to literacy instruction that should be evaluated in a serious fashion by the research community, if for no other reason than its prevalence in American and Canadian education. No movement has had a greater impact on the education of children in recent years than has whole language.

Although supporters of whole language (e.g., K. Goodman, 1989; Weaver, 1990, Chapter 6) make the case that there already exists a scientific database supporting whole-language philosophy and practice, it is not large. There are only a handful of studies comparing whole-language approaches directly with other approaches to literacy instruction (e.g., basal reader programs, which have predominated in early literacy education for the last half century). Moreover, the comparisons that have been made do not favor whole language over other instruction (Stahl & Miller, 1989). Particularly disturbing, however, is that there are at least hints in the literature that whole language may make little difference for average-ability or high-ability readers and actually negatively affect the reading progress of weaker students (Stahl & Miller, 1989).

That whole language has the potential for doing harm is really the greatest concern with the approach. In particular, there is substantial evidence that explicit teaching of phonics and explicit at-

tempts to increase phonemic awareness benefit students who are at risk for difficulties in learning to read because the home environments did not support and encourage emergent literacy during the preschool years (Adams, 1990). The problem is that such explicit teaching of decoding is seen as skills instruction by whole-language advocates and considered inconsistent with the development of reading via authentic approaches. Our view is that the scientific database favoring explicit instruction in decoding for at-risk primary students far outweighs the database favoring whole-language instruction with such students. Indeed, the assumption that reading and writing should or could be acquired naturally, without instruction, by most students seems flawed. It is based on an analogy to the acquisition of a first language. Although the natural learning of first language is well established, there is no credible scientific evidence that humans have evolved so that learning to read and write is an inevitable consequence of experience with print and other authentic language and literature experiences (Bertelson & De Gelder, 1989; Liberman & Liberman, 1990).

Even so, there is still much that is attractive about the whole-language approach. Who could argue that reading fine literature is not a good thing for children to do? Who could argue with daily writing? Our guess is that such experiences have profound effects on children, ones that may not be captured readily by standardized tests such as those used in evaluations to date. The challenge for whole-language researchers is to design evaluations that are convincing to the scientific and educational policy-making communities, evaluations that include measures sensitive to the advantages whole language might confer on young readers.

For example, tests sensitive to the development of prior knowledge about contemporary children's authors should reveal advantages for whole-language students over participants in basal programs because of the whole-language emphasis on exposing students to texts by the best children's writers. In short, our view is that the scientific analyses of whole language have barely begun, but that thorough analyses are needed because of the widespread dissemination of the approach based on claims made by advocates such as Kenneth Goodman. Although some in the whole-language movement believe such research is not possible, necessary, and perhaps even destructive (e.g., Edelsky,

1990), we think that legitimate and fair inquiry is possible and essential.

Reading Recovery Many grade-1 students make little progress in learning how to read. Such students are at long-term risk for academic difficulties. An important program aimed at such children was developed by New Zealand educator Marie Clay (e.g., 1985). It involves daily one-teacher, one-child sessions for 10 to 20 weeks, with each session lasting approximately 30 to 40 minutes. The goal is to help the student catch up with peers. The starting assumption is that students may be learning too narrow a range of strategies for dealing with print and may not be flexible in their use of the strategies they have acquired. For example, students may attempt to sound out every word, when in fact a variety of strategies (see the earlier discussion in this section) can be applied during the identification of words in texts.

Much of reading recovery is teaching students strategies, which are defined by Clay (1985; Pinnell, 1989) as the processes required to read, including the following:

- Reading left to right on a page.
- Using a return sweep from the right-hand side of the page rather than a slow return to the left side.
- Monitoring whether what is being read makes sense.
- Using cross checks on meaning-making processes, such as illustrated by the following:

  A reader might use one kind of information to predict a word but will check that prediction by using another source of information. For example, glancing at a picture of the Billy Goats Gruff going across a bridge, a young reader might predict the word "water" in the text. Checking the print, however, the reader might notice that the word "stream" is not visually consistent with that prediction. This cross-checking may lead to a self-correction or other indication from the child of an awareness of a discrepancy. (Pinnell, 1989, p. 166)

- Searching for cues to meaning from pictures, language structures, and visual cues in print.
- Rereading when meaning is unclear.
- Self-correction rather than waiting for teacher correction of errors.

The emphasis on strategies in Reading Recovery comes through in the following:

> . . . [A]ttention of teacher and child must be on strategies or operations—mental activities initiated by the child to get messages from a text. If the teacher becomes involved in teaching items rather than strategies—particular letter-sound correspondences or sight vocabulary words, for example, rather than the strategy of checking a word that would make sense in the context against the information in the print—the prospect of accelerated learning is seriously threatened. Letter-sound correspondences and spelling patterns are learned, but in the course of reading and, especially, writing meaningful text, RR teachers praise children for generative strategies, not for items learned. (Clay & Cazden, 1990, p. 208)

There is a common structure to each Reading Recovery lesson: (1) The child rereads two or more short, familiar books. (2) The child reads a book introduced the day before, with the teacher keeping track of errors that are made. This provides baseline information, with the goal of the child eventually reading the book with 90% accuracy on subsequent days as part of step (1). (3) There is a letter identification exercise involving plastic letters that attach to a metal board. Once children know letters, this step is deleted, or other decoding or vocabulary teaching is substituted. (4) The child composes and writes out a story. (5) The child reassembles the story after the teacher cuts it up into pieces. (6) A new book is introduced and read by the child.

The interaction that goes on around composing and reading of the new books is definitely scaffolded, with the student receiving hints and support as needed (Clay & Cazden, 1990). For example, during writing, the teacher calls attention to the sounds of words and spelling patterns by urging the student to listen carefully to words that will be written, prompting the child to write out a new word several times so that it will be memorable, praising progress, and so on. Consistent with Clay's (1991) perspective that reading instruction should develop inner control (i.e., internalized use of strategies taught to children), such support is faded as the child is able to function independently, with additional support provided as more challenging texts and tasks are presented following success with easier texts and tasks.

Does Reading Recovery work? Evaluations have been conducted in both New Zealand and in Ohio (see Pinnell, 1989). In both settings, most (at least two-thirds is the lowest estimate we have seen) of the Reading Recovery students catch up with their classmates. More impressively, 2 or 3 years later, Reading Recovery students are reading pretty much like other students. These are impressive outcomes, and many are excited about Reading Recovery as an intervention, as they are about other one-to-one tutoring programs that seem to be effective (see Wasik & Slavin, 1993; also the discussion of "Success for All," in Chapter 11, this book).

Critics, however, point to the cost of one-to-one tutoring for half a year. Our reaction is that it is a small price to pay relative to the long-term costs when students do poorly in school, and it is a good bet that a fair proportion of students who go through Reading Recovery would have done much worse in school without the intervention. Wasik and Slavin (1993) offered a reflective discussion of the cost-effectiveness of one-to-one tutoring that complements our perspective.

Conceptually, we find Clay's (1991) analysis of reading as the development of inner control to be appealing, with it similar to other ideas about internalization of cognitive processes such as those offered by Vygotsky (1978; see Chapter 8, this text). We also find the Reading Recovery results reported thus far to be compelling evidence of the program's efficacy. Even so, we are also struck that some are finding ways to improve on it, such as Iversen and Tumner (1993) who produced quicker improvement when reading recovery was complemented with more explicit instruction about phonology and decoding. We are also struck that some much less expensive approaches to one-to-one tutoring, such as parental tutoring, have the potential to encourage inner-controlled reading by primary students who had previously experienced difficulty with grade-1 reading (e.g., Mudre & McCormick, 1989).

Transactional Instruction of Comprehension Strategies I [MP] knew of a number of sites where comprehension strategies instruction was documented to be done well. At the end of the 1980s, I began visiting these sites. I visited Michigan State to deepen my understanding of Annemarie Palincsar's work and Gerry Duffy and Laura Roehler's direct explanation model. I had frank conversations with Carl Bereiter about the Bereiter and Bird research. My trips included a visit with Deshler and Schumaker's (e.g., 1988) group at the University of Kansas, who were responsible for a learning strategies curriculum that was disseminated nationwide and that was researched extensively as it was developed. Margo Mastropieri and Tom Scruggs (e.g., 1991) welcomed me to Purdue for detailed explanations of their work on teaching learning-disabled students to use elabo-

ration strategies to remember academic content. In addition, there were trips to many individual teachers who were doing what they could to implement strategies instruction based on what they could glean from the existing literature.

After the visits came a series of qualitative investigations in two settings. One was Benchmark School near Philadelphia, which serves bright elementary-school children who experienced great difficulty learning to read in regular schools. At the heart of the Benchmark curriculum is the teaching of cognitive strategies, so that study of the school's approach to teaching and learning was ideally informative about how strategies instruction might be implemented, especially because of the school's long track record of success with children who had failed elsewhere. A large-scale interview study was conducted at Benchmark (Pressley, Gaskins, Cunicelli et al., 1991), as was an intensive case study of a semester in one Benchmark classroom (Pressley, Gaskins, Wile, Cunicelli, & Sheridan, 1991) and an analysis of the classroom discourse at Benchmark (Gaskins et al., 1992; see Chapter 8). The second set of studies was conducted in a public school strategies instruction program (i.e., *Students Achieving Independent Learning* [SAIL]), which was targeted at Chapter 1 students and seemed to produce impressive outcomes (based on quasiexperimental achievement evaluations conducted by the school district) relative to other Chapter 1 interventions. As at Benchmark, the SAIL teachers participated in interviews, observations, and case studies (e.g., El-Dinary, Pressley, & Schuder, 1992; Pressley, El-Dinary, Gaskins et al., 1992; Pressley, Schuder, SAIL Faculty and Administration, Bergman, & El-Dinary, 1992).

When the visits and the qualitative analyses were combined, it was clear that there was great commonality of philosophy and method across the Benchmark and SAIL settings. The developers of these programs operate on the following assumptions about skilled reading: Good readers make decisions about reading rate and focus; which basic processing strategies to use (e.g., word-for-word reading, skimming); and how to coordinate strategies for monitoring, problem solving, and evaluation. Good readers anticipate what might happen subsequently in a text, evaluate their expectations as reading proceeds, generate questions about the text content, visualize the meanings conveyed in the text, seek clarifications when confused, identify main ideas, and selectively attend to important and interesting parts of the material. Good readers are generally active as they read, making associations between their prior knowledge and content encountered in text. Good readers evaluate the text (e.g., whether they like it, whether it is serving its intended purpose). Good readers possess extensive metacognition about the strategies they use (e.g., Flavell, 1985, Chapter 4; Chapter 2, this book), especially recognizing where and when those strategies can be applied profitably (see Pressley, Borkowski, & O'Sullivan, 1984, 1985). Such metacognition is crucial to the regulation and appropriate use of the strategies learned in the curriculum. (Comparing the list of reading behaviors summarized here with those reported by the expert social science readers, discussed earlier in this chapter, reveals great consistency between the educators' understandings of skilled reading and the skilled reading observed in analytical investigations of good reading, such as Wyatt et al., 1993.)

The strategies instruction programs that colleagues evaluated used direct explanation and mental modeling to teach students the processes that compose capable reading. Thus, students in these programs are taught a manageable number of comprehension strategies. For example, students in the SAIL program are taught to predict, visualize, and summarize as they read. Generally, active processing of text is stimulated by having SAIL students think aloud during reading instruction, with associations to background knowledge encouraged as part of thinking aloud. Such thinking aloud is expected to reduce impulsive responses and encourage planning before and during reading. This use of language to support cognitive actions is consistent with theoretical positions developed by Vygotsky (1978, 1987) as well as Meichenbaum (1977), ones reviewed in Chapters 7 and 8. That is, thinking aloud about cognitive processes can promote self-regulation of those processes: Thinking aloud during application of reading strategies should promote student control of attention, the contents of thoughts, and the use of strategies. In addition, thinking aloud gives the teacher and other members of the reading group access to a student's thought processes, so that members of the reading group are continually modeling active thinking about text for their peers. This is critical, for such mental modeling by peers can influence those exposed to it (e.g., Bandura, 1986; Duffy, Roehler, & Herrmann, 1988).

Because SAIL students always receive reading instruction in texts at or above grade level, they are taught problem-solving strategies for dealing with difficult words when reading for gist. For instance, when encountering a new word in text, students are taught that it could be sounded out, skipped, or guessed, or context clues could be used to infer its meaning, rereading if necessary for additional clues.

What Pressley and his colleagues observed in their studies at Benchmark and in the SAIL program was teachers modeling and explaining comprehension strategies as part of regular reading group lessons. The teachers used outstanding children's literature from trade books, magazines, or basal reader anthologies as they did so. A lesson might begin with the teacher reading first and, thinking aloud about how the text ought to serve his or her purposes and how its content and structure might relate to prior knowledge. The teacher might make predictions; report images stimulated by the text; or note consistencies and inconsistencies between text content, text structure, and reader expectations. Then the teacher might invite students to try using the strategic procedures with the text. Members of the reading group would take turns reading aloud. Throughout the process, student interpretations of text are encouraged, and thus reading group participants are exposed to a variety of interpretations of text and the processes for constructing and evaluating those interpretations.

Pressley, El-Dinary, Gaskins, et al. (1992) refer to this type of instruction as **transactional strategies instruction,** so dubbed because what happens during reading group is co-determined by a teacher and student in interaction with a text (Bell, 1968; Bjorklund, 1989, pp. 228–231; Sameroff, 1975), and, in particular, the interpretations of text are co-determined by teacher-student-text transactions (e.g., Rosenblatt, 1978). Years of transactions involving predictions, questioning, clarifications, visualizations, associations, and summaries are intended to produce independent, successful readers who engage in such processes on their own. For example, the average Benchmark student stays at the school for 4 years, with some attending for up to 7 years; SAIL is implemented in grades 1 through 5. Internalizing the cognitive processes taught as comprehension strategies and learning how to use such processes in a flexible fashion with diverse types of texts is an impressive intellectual accomplishment that cannot be accomplished in a few lessons or a few months.

For detailed commentary about the nature of transactional strategies instruction lessons, see

Pressley, El-Dinary, Brown et al. (in press-a, in press-b). We note in closing this section that an important part of transactional strategies instruction is the motivational component. Students are taught about strategies and encouraged to use them in contexts that do much to maximize academic motivation, with the teachers in these settings aware of and using many of the motivational recommendations presented in Chapter 5. Some consideration of these motivational features will highlight again a theme running through this book, that there is no one component that defines effective instruction. Rather, effective instruction promotes strategies well matched to task requirements (e.g., such as prediction, self-questioning, seeking clarifications, summarization), development of nonstrategic knowledge (e.g., the type of information that might be acquired from the fine literature read in the transactional strategies instruction classrooms), enhancement of metacognition about strategies learned (e.g., knowledge of when and where to use strategies that follows from practice using them in many contexts, the practice that can occur over multiple years of instruction), and motivation to use what one knows to accomplish academic tasks.

Pressley, El-Dinary, Marks, Brown, and Stein (1992) identified some of the features of good strategies instruction classrooms:

- Task involvement and task orientation are encouraged rather than ego orientation (Nicholls, 1989). Each student's improvement is emphasized rather than how students are doing relative to one another. (See Chapter 5, this volume.)
- Success is ensured when strategies are taught and practiced, largely through scaffolding. (See Chapter 8, this volume.)
- Teachers reinforce thinking that reflects strategic engagement. It is not the correctness of answers that is reinforced but how students generate responses.
- The utility of strategies—how they help students—and when they help is emphasized (see Chapter 2). Teachers do all possible to identify many occasions when strategies being taught might be helpful to students (e.g., prediction is helpful in math and science as well as in the context of reading group).
- Students practice strategies with authentic, appropriately challenging (i.e., not too difficult but not too easy), and interesting tasks. The tasks are made more interesting because the strategies are applied as part of the process of personally interpreting the task. (See Chapter 5)
- There is little criticism in these classrooms. The overall environment is positive.
- An exceptionally important characteristic of this instruction is that student choice is emphasized. Transactional strategies instruction teachers do not tell students to do this strategy or that one but rather remind students of the comprehension strategies they know and urge them to choose a strategy that is appropriate for a current comprehension demand. When a reader encounters a problematic word, the teacher might remind the student of the various problem-solving strategies in the student's repertoire of strategies but would not prescribe one over another. The message is that the student is in control and that self-regulation of cognition is being developed. Students are not learning to take orders from teachers; they are learning to make the types of choices good readers make, similar to the choices their teachers, who are good readers, model for them.

Our view is that it may be absolutely necessary for strategies instructional environments to promote student motivation. Strategies instruction benefits may be more likely when (1) there are clear messages to students that improvement is the goal of schooling rather than student performance relative to other students; (2) there are efforts to match various aspects of strategies instruction and other teaching to particular student interests and abilities; and (3) instruction occurs in a generally cooperative atmosphere, one in which students help one another in the application of strategies and in the development of understandings (e.g., interpretations of texts).

Effective comprehension instruction is multicomponent. Students are taught a small repertoire of powerful comprehension strategies. Teaching takes place over a number of years via explanations, modeling, and practice opportunities. As the strategies are practiced by students, metacognition that permits their informed use develops (i.e., students discover when the strategies help them and when they do not). Motivation develops as students come to understand the utility of strategies in an instructional environment that sends the message that students can become better learners, especially if they learn the strategic procedures and other knowledge taught in school.

Concluding Comment In the 1990s, there has been substantial study of important reading interventions that are based on psychological analyses of reading. Even so, much more about the effects of various types of reading instruction could be known. Reading instructional programs are dynamic, evolving entities that have been affected by research in the past and will be affected by research in the future.

Before leaving elementary reading, it is hard not to be struck by how much instructional good is coming from understandings produced in basic research. There is now a firm scientific database supporting explicit decoding instruction, especially for students who enter school without phonemic awareness. Teaching students to apply flexibly a few powerful comprehension strategies (e.g., prediction, self-questioning, seeking clarification, summarization), all of which were evaluated in basic research studies, stimulates much active reading and increases the likelihood students will get the big ideas from text. Teaching text analyses strategies (e.g., to analyze stories into story grammar components; expositions into their logical structures such as cause-and-effect), again strategies validated in basic studies, can aid reading comprehension and permit a reading-writing connection (i.e., using the same analyses strategies to plan and generate stories and expositions).

Those who might question whether basic research can provide knowledge that is translated into important educational practices and policies should study how elementary reading has changed in recent years: Groan-and-grunt phonics instruction has been replaced by well-validated methods of decoding. The vacuum in comprehension instruction identified by Durkin (1978–79) has been filled by instruction stimulating the comprehension processes used by exceptionally sophisticated readers. Educational scientists studying elementary reading have definitely made an impact on elementary reading education.

READING DURING ADOLESCENCE AND EARLY ADULTHOOD

In contrast to the admirable research efforts at the elementary-school level, there has been much too little study of literacy and literacy instruction during middle school, high school, and college. This is regrettable because it is clear that there is still a great need for reading and writing instruction after elementary school: Far too many students receive high school diplomas even though their literacy skills are weak compared with what they should or could be; far too many students arrive at universities ill prepared for the demanding reading and writing expected of college students, with deficiencies in such skills predictive of difficulties in college (e.g., Royer, Marchant, Sinatra, & Lovejoy, 1990). Although a number of practitioners are designing instructional practices that mesh with secondary instruction (see Alvermann, Moore, & Conley, 1987; Lapp, Flood, & Farnan, 1989; any issue of the *Journal of Reading*), critical, empirical evaluations of interventions are infrequent, and when they are conducted, often the treatments and outcomes are reported in ways that make it difficult to understand why the treatments might work.

Why the neglect of research on reading and writing during the middle-school, high school, and college years? Perhaps the main reason is that the principal educational goal at these levels of schooling is not the development of basic competencies but instruction of specific contents—literature, social studies, history, and sciences. Although reading educators are developing methods of reading instruction that can be implemented as part of and complementary to content-area instruction (Lapp et al., 1989), there is little reason to believe that most content-area teachers are responding to this input.

More positively, there have been some exceptionally distinguished analyses of literacy and literacy instruction after childhood. Those will be featured in this section.

Comprehension

Alvermann and Moore (1991) provided an exceptionally complete summary of secondary school reading. One of the most important aspects of their review was an analysis of the adequacy of the existing literature to inform educational practice. They were generally pessimistic about the usefulness of this literature, given design decisions made by investigators: Many studies were conducted outside of classrooms. Many of the interventions and their evaluations were not informed by classroom teachers. Many of the studies were conducted on texts not representative of what students actually must read as part of their schoolwork. A number of studies involved brief strategy instruction, much shorter in duration than instruction that students might typically receive in school.

Despite these difficulties, Alvermann and Moore (1991) were able to generate some important conclusions about comprehension instruction. When their conclusions are combined with ones that can be abstracted from Weinstein and Mayer's (1986) review of learning strategies research as well as a few other sources, it is possible with some confidence to generate a list of strategies that can promote comprehension and memory of text by postelementary students. These are mentioned briefly here, as they have been described in previous chapters and sections of this chapter:

- **Using/analyzing text structure** to abstract main ideas.
- **Summarizing, outlining, and mapping** of text, if substantial instruction is provided about how to do it.
- **Notetaking**.
- **Self-questioning,** although the benefits seem greater for lower-ability students. This can include self-questions designed to prompt students to look for main ideas and elaborate on them.
- **Elaborations of text** of various sorts, including representational imagery, relating to prior knowledge, and thinking about why the relationships specified in text hold (see Pressley, Wood et al., 1992).
- **Creating mnemonic images** (e.g., an image capturing many of the features of the Whiskey Rebellion, which also incorporates a big bottle of whiskey as a distinctive encoding cue), which are proving especially effective with special education populations (e.g., Masteropieri & Scruggs, 1991), although there is no reason to limit their use to such populations.

One especially interesting point is that some strategies recommended widely in the studies skills literature simply do not seem to be effective:

- **Rehearsal** of complex materials seems effective only if the greater amount of time required to rehearse (e.g., copy a passage) is ignored. Also, rehearsal may depress more conceptual analyses of text. Tobias (1987) offered an interesting twist on this theme, demonstrating that students do not benefit much if left on their own to choose what to reread. If they are in a computerized instructional environment that mandates rereading of the parts of text that are important or that they are not understanding (i.e., as evidenced by performance on adjunct questions accompanying the reading), rehearsal is effective. In general, however, because high school students are not effectively selective in what they reread, there is usually little if any gain produced by rereading.
- **Underlining** of text produces small, inconsistent improvements in learning at best.
- **SQ3R** (Survey, Question, Read, Recite, Review), although recommended in many studies skills courses, does not have a track record of exceptional effectiveness (Forrest-Pressley & Gilles, 1983).

What might be noted about all three of these less effective techniques is that they involve largely simple rehearsal (attention) to material rather than extensive recoding and relating of new content to other knowledge. In contrast, all of the unambiguously effective procedures require more of the learner with respect to the meaning of the text. The learner works with the text content, analyzing relationships between elements of the text as given or considering the text that is given in light of other knowledge already possessed by the learner.

Important insights about comprehension strategies instruction are still emerging. For example, one of the real challenges for high school and college-level students is to read expository texts in their content area courses, especially science (see Chapter 12). Cook and Mayer (1988) studied one approach for improving comprehension of scientific texts. They taught students the types of ideas that can appear in a scientific text and how these ideas are structured in scientific texts, including (1) generalizations, (2) enumerations, (3) sequences, (4) classification, and (5) comparison-and-contrast structures. Junior college students who were given instruction about these types of text structure, along with some practice in identifying such structures as part of trying to understand text, in fact, were better able to comprehend scientific texts than were uninstructed control students. The basic research significance of such a finding is high: As any student of the rhetoric knows, the expository structures taught by Cook and Mayer are basic argument structures. Teaching students to look for such structures and use them to understand text is a strategy that should be of great general utility. Whether it is or not is a question that remains to be studied, perhaps one that some readers of this book will tackle. For another example of a sequence of processes that can be taught profitably to college students for improving comprehension of content area text, see Simpson, Hayes, Stahl, Connor, and Weaver's (1988) analysis of PORPE, which involved teaching students to *p*redict, *o*rganize, *r*ehearse, *p*ractice, and *e*valuate.

One of the intriguing aspects of the postelementary comprehension data is that a good deal of effort has been made to establish which procedures facilitate comprehension and memory of text, but that relatively little effort has been put into determining *how* to teach comprehension strategies. There are no theoretical or empirical analyses that correspond to the analyses of reciprocal teaching, direct explanation, and transactional strategies instruction in the elementary literature. The most frequent method of instruction used in the secondary and college years is to teach a large number of strategies in a relatively short period of time, such as in the context of a studies skills course. There are few evaluations of such courses. The ones that do exist suggest small to inconsistent effects. Unfortunately, most of the attempted validations of such courses contain methodological problems serious enough to undermine confidence in the conclusions emanating from the studies. Such warnings are especially telling when it is realized that careful, longer-term, scaffolded instruction is often required to ensure that students can carry out particular strategies in the curriculum (e.g., the summarizing, outlining, and mapping strategies cited earlier in this subsection).

We have talked with many studies skills counselors who firmly believe that building up repertoires of strategies is essential for many high school and college students. They also recognize that traditional studies skills courses provide too much, too fast. Our view is that it makes a great deal of sense to take what we have learned about individual strategies that work and think seriously about how high school and college students could receive systematic instruction in ways that would complement rather than threaten the content-driven curricula that compose secondary and postsecondary education. At present, we are probably failing large numbers of students who could be better learners if they were taught powerful comprehension tools in ways that made sense to them (e.g., slowly enough that

the strategies can be understood, in the context of realistic assignments)—something brought home by strong correlations between reading ability and achievement in college-level courses (e.g., Royer, Abranovic, & Sinatra, 1987). That college-level achievement in general might be increased by thorough teaching of comprehension strategies in high school and early in a college career is a hypothesis that could keep more than one newcomer to the field of educational psychology extremely busy. Perhaps some readers of this book will take up the challenge.

READING INSTRUCTION DURING ADULTHOOD

This chapter began with frank admissions about the literacy inadequacies of a large number of Americans. Low literacy and illiteracy are problems in many parts of our diverse society. Consider this partial listing of adults who might benefit from high-quality literacy instruction during adulthood:

- Adults who never learned to read. Many had inadequate opportunities to do so. Some suffer from an organic impairment, such as dyslexia (see Chapter 6, this volume).
- Adults reading far below where they could read with additional instruction, especially those for whom it is vital to acquire additional skills (e.g., poor readers who are unemployed or underemployed because of low literacy).
- Adults for whom English is a second language.
- Recent immigrants.
- Adults with learning disabilities.
- High school dropouts.
- High school students at risk for dropping out.
- Minorities—who are overrepresented in all groups just cited.
- Women (re)entering the labor force, who, after years of being out of the workplace, often require retooling.
- Working class women, who "suffer disproportionately from economic marginality, unsatisfying jobs . . . and alienation from the American mainstream. Limited education and limited experience outside the home have held these women back" (Hunter & Harman, 1979).
- Poor people.
- Older adults who frequently lack important literacy and life skills.

- Prisoners—half of whom are illiterate.
- People who can read— and could read to advantage—but won't (Thimmesch, 1984).

On the positive side of the ledger, there are many institutions and groups attempting to provide literacy instruction to adults, including the following (e.g., Newman & Beverstock, 1990, Chapter 7):

- Conventional schools, especially those serving adults who are functioning below their potential. These range from universities with large proportions of students possessing poor language and study skills to elementary and high schools engaged in work with students at risk for adult illiteracy or underachievement.
- Adult and continuing education units at universities and colleges, often branches administering programs different from conventional postsecondary education, tailored to the perceived needs of middle-aged to older adults.
- Prisons.
- Educational groups and classes administered by organizations concerned with adult literacy, such as Laubach Literacy Action and Literacy Volunteers of America.
- Reading clinics, some private and some public.
- Libraries.
- Workplace literacy programs.

Also on the positive side of the ledger, these groups receive considerable support from private foundations, businesses, business associations (e.g., booksellers), state governments, and distinguished Americans, perhaps the most notable of which is former First Lady Barbara Bush. Mrs. Bush has been deeply committed to promoting literacy for a long time, with her presence in the White House from 1989 to 1993 doing much to heighten national awareness of the need for adult literacy initiatives. One of America's most persistent critics of education played an important role as well: Jonathon Kozol's (1985) *Illiterate in America* dramatically portrayed the extent of illiteracy in America (i.e., 25 million adult Americans who cannot read at grade-5 level and another 35 million who cannot read at grade-9 level according to Kozol). In particular, Kozol made the case that there is no less powerful group than illiterates:

> We are told in school that, when we have a problem or complaint, we should write a letter "to our representative in City Hall". . . . [This] . . . is denied the

man or woman who cannot participate in print society. Neither the press release nor the handwritten flier that can draw a crowd into a protest meeting at a local church lies within the reach of the nonreader. . . . Even the rock-bottom levels of political communication—the spray paint and graffitti that adorn the walls of subways and deserted buildings in impoverished neighborhoods—are instruments of discourse which are far beyond the fringe of the illiterate American. Walking in a ghetto neighborhood . . . we see the sprawl of giant letters that decry the plight of . . . other persecuted groups. We read no cogent outcries from illiterates. (Kozol, 1985, pp. 32–33)

Exclusion from the printed word renders one third of America the ideal supine population for the "total state" that Auden feared and Orwell prophesized: undefended against doublespeak, unarmed against the orchestrated domination of their minds. Choice demands reflection and decision. Readers of the press at least can stand back and react; they can also find dissenting sources of opinion . . . it is the illiterate who has been rendered most susceptible to . . . entire domination . . . (Kozol, 1985, p. 34).

With all of this going for the adult literacy movement, it would seem that success should be likely.

Continuing with the positive side of the ledger, when researchers have looked, they have found discernible improvements in the literacy of adult literacy program participants. All of the programs reviewed by Diekhoff (1988), for example, produced gains in reading achievement—for instance, 1.35 grade levels for 82.6 hours of instruction (Darling, 1982), 1.5 grade levels for 75 hours of participation (Darling, 1984), 1 grade level for 51 days of teaching (Pasch & Oakley, 1985), and 1.6 grade levels achieved during a 9.8-month course (Diekhoff & Wigginton, 1987).

On the negative side of the ledger, however, few people became functionally literate or improved their literacy by a practical amount in these programs: The vast majority of participants chose to drop out, with Diekhoff (1988) claiming that only 20 percent of the matriculants in such programs stay as long as a year. Even though participants make reasonable gains in reading for the amount of time spent—consider, for example, that a year of gain in reading at the elementary-school level usually requires 200 or more hours compared with approximately 50 hours of teaching when adults are the students—these programs fail because they cannot retain their clients. One of the biggest challenges for adult literacy programs is to be sufficiently motivating to retain students for the long time required to develop reading and writing skills. Often students enter adult literacy programs expecting miracles rather than understanding that the road to literacy is a long one that requires sustained dedication on their part (Taylor, 1989).

Why are there motivational problems? Schlossberg, Lynch, and Pickering's (1989) analyses of the challenges in educating adults are telling here: Many adults simply cannot imagine themselves as students and believe the role is demeaning. Moreover, family and work demands are often great for those who need adult education most. Sometimes these families and employers are supportive of educational efforts, but many times they are not.

Another factor is that the instruction offered is simply not interesting. Mezirow, Darkenwald, and Knox (1975) provided an early, now classic analysis of adult literacy programs in six U.S. cities. What they found were many lonely students, often knowing no other students in their programs. (Imagine for a moment attending college and having no peers as friends.) When there were larger classes of students, often they varied greatly in competence, making instruction difficult. The educational settings were often decidedly second class—dirty, cramped, uncomfortable. Often the instruction was childish (for additional commentary on this point, see the review by Singh, Singh, & Blampied, 1985). There was drill and recitation on demand, with the instruction often routine and boring. Adults were often required to perform at the chalkboard, a situation making their literacy difficulties ever more public. There was a lot of concern with preparing students to take standardized tests such as the high school equivalency examination. There was much less concern with providing literacy skills that might be perceived as useful by students. Although there has been some improvement since Mezirow et al.'s (1975) work (see Newman & Beverstock, 1990, Chapter 5), many of the same problems were detected in studies conducted in the 1980s (e.g., Fingeret, 1985). What is most striking, however, is that little progress has been made in analyzing the characteristics of programs that do seem to hold their students (see Taylor, 1989).

Adult literacy is an arena in which a great deal of high-quality research is desparately needed, especially with respect to the development of literacy education programs that are effective in the sense that students make progress and stay in the programs. There are exciting directions here for researchers with differing orientations and interest in human learning and cognition. Consider these exciting possibilities:

- Leading researchers such as Sticht (1988) are arguing for adult literacy instruction that is targeted at both the adults and children in a family. The idea is to transform illiterate adults into literates as their children learn to read. See Newman and Beverstock (1990, Chapter 5) for a review of such programs, which at present are promising but not proven.

- Computer technologies for providing adult literacy instruction have been developed (Lewis, 1989). There is great opportunity here for studies of how illiterate adults react to such computerized instruction and how these resources can be managed and adapted to maximize their effectiveness.

- Other technologies provide great opportunities for improving literacy at low costs. A favorite example is the use of captioned television. Because many programs are now captioned for the deaf, all that is required is an inexpensive decoder attached to the home television. As the person watches television, they are provided a print version of what is being said. In studies to date, there does seem to be incidental learning of vocabulary and improved ability to comprehend text from exposure to such captioning (Neuman & Koskinen, 1992). The effects of such inexpensive interventions that can be incorporated into everyday events should be explored in detail.

Although there are resources for increasing adult literacy and a great national need to do so, there has been much less progress in understanding how to promote learning in these populations than in other groups. One hypothesis, borne out by reviewing the major handbooks in adult education (e.g., Merriam & Cunningham, 1989; Titmus, 1989), is that researchers in adult literacy have not made much contact with the basic learning and cognition literatures (i.e., the work featured in this book) or even the reading research literatures (i.e., work featured throughout this chapter) and thus are not aware of many of the most important advances in learning theory and research.

More positively, when relevant basic research is examined, there is much more reason for optimism than pessimism about adult learning. Yes, there are some declines in capacities that are critical to learning and development of reading competence, such as reduced working memory (short-term memory) capacity (see Cohen, 1988). Such a reduction in capacity is especially apparent when older adults compared with younger adults are required to process demanding texts. For example, older adults are less likely than younger adults to detect subtle anomalies in text content (e.g., statements such as "Homes near airports are quiet," and "A girl with a broken arm went swimming"; Cohen, 1979) or to link relationships across various elements in text (e.g., Light and Capps, 1986). Much more importantly, however, even though there are declines in some cognitive resources, older adults are still able to learn complex cognitive skills and strategies (e.g., Baltes & Willis, 1982; Smith & Baltes, 1990) and progress is being made in identifying ways of minimizing the impact of short-term capacity limitations—or other biologically mediated declines (e.g., speed of accessing knowledge of words)—on reading comprehension. For example, one way to make up for low capacity or slow access is simply to read more slowly, and adults do seem to regulate their reading to compensate for their own capacity deficiencies (e.g., Walczyk, 1993). There is no reason to give up on the person who did not learn essential skills during the typical years of schooling, for the evidentiary base is growing in support of the conclusion that learning can occur across the life span.

Perhaps the biggest challenge for the science is to identify methods for teaching important literacy skills to adults that are motivating or require little in terms of motivation to be effective (e.g., close-captioned television). Perhaps the biggest challenge for society is to determine new means of assisting those adults who desperately need to be more literate. We close this section by discussion of a point that makes clear that literacy enhancement really is best thought about as a life-span and intergenerational problem.

An important risk factor for a child is growing up in a home in which parents do not read or write. Such a child is at much greater risk for illiteracy or low literacy than a child coming from a more advantaged environment (e.g., recall the discussion of differences in phonemic awareness at the beginning of schooling as predictive of success in reading). If parents can become readers and be encouraged to support the literacy development of their offspring, there is great potential for breaking this intergenerational cycle of illiteracy. Teaching adults to read has the potential for multiplier effects: Their children are more likely to be readers. If their children learn to read, grandchildren are more likely to be readers, and so on.

MODIFYING TEXTBOOKS SO THEY ARE EASIER TO READ AND UNDERSTAND

A great deal of effort has been expended by information processing researchers attempting to devise ways to modify texts so that the information in them is easier to comprehend or remember (Glynn, Andre, & Britton, 1986). Four approaches to text modification have been studied in more detail than others: signaling, adding elaborations and connections, adjunct questions, and illustrations.

Four Approaches to Text Modification

Signals Meyer (e.g., 1975) has provided some of the most explicit arguments in favor of putting **signals** in text. Types of signals include the following:

- Use of text conventions that flag the structure of the text. For example, when a cause-and-effect relationship is specified in the text, signal the cause with the introductory clause, "The cause of X is. . . ." Sequences of events can be signaled with "first," "second," "third," and "fourth," or with (1), (2), (3), and (4).
- Advance organizers summarizing a main point can be provided, with these sometimes in the form of a summary statement early in the passage (see Chapter 10).
- Summary statements can be put at the end of sections of text.
- A variety of words specifying the information considered important by the author can be placed in text, such as "Of less consequence . . . ," "More to the point . . . ," "An exceptionally important consideration is . . ." and "Just as an aside, consider . . ."

In general, signaling seems to provide at least slight comprehension advantages to readers (e.g., Lorch, 1989; Meyer, Brandt, & Bluth, 1980). Even more explicit signals are being studied by some investigators, such as providing a graphical outline of the text summarizing the main points in the text and how the points relate to one another (e.g., Armbruster, Anderson, & Meyer, 1991; Guri-Rozenblit, 1989). One important conclusion supported by some studies is that signaling is especially helpful in making difficult conceptual information comprehensible and useful—for example, permitting readers to solve problems related to the topic of a passage (e.g., Loman & Mayer, 1983). More negatively, although signals promote learning of the content and its organization, rarely are there any carry-over benefits to other parts of text (Lorch, 1989; Lorch, Lorch, & Inman, 1993). One way to overcome that limitation, however, is to organize the entire text well: Texts with clear hierarchies, topical structures, sequences, and causal chains are understood better than texts lacking salient organization (Calfee & Chambliss, 1987; Chambliss & Calfee, 1989).

Elaborations and Connections   In a series of investigations, Beck and associates at the University of Pittsburgh (Beck, McKeown, Sinatra, & Loxterman, 1991; McKeown, Beck, Sinatra, & Loxterman, 1992) have claimed that textbooks used by elementary-level students often fail to provide enough information so students can detect and understand the interconnections between ideas. Often the students lack prior knowledge assumed by the texts; in addition, many textbook passages are poorly written if not downright incoherent.

The Pittsburgh group (as do others—Britton, Van Dusen, & Gülgöz, 1991; Britton, Van Dusen, Gülgöz, & Glynn, 1989; Duffy et al., 1989; Graves & Slater, 1991) believes that the solution is to modify textbooks so essential background information is contained in readings and linkages between ideas in text are made more explicitly (i.e., to **add elaborations and connections** to text). Thus, consider a text for use in grade-4/grade-5 American history:

The French and Indian War

In 1763 Britain and the colonies ended a 7-year war with the French and Indians. As a result of this war France was driven out of North America. Britain would now rule Canada and other lands that had belonged to France. This brought peace to the American colonies. The colonists no longer had to fear attacks from Canada. The Americans were happy to be a part of Britain in 1763. Yet a dozen years later, these same people would be fighting the British for independence, or freedom from Great Britain's rule. This war was called the War for Independence, or the American Revolution. A revolution changes one type of government or way of thinking and replaces it with another. (Beck et al., 1991, p. 275)

Now, consider this elaborated version which fills in some gaps in information and increases the connectedness of the text in general:

The French and Indian War

About 250 years ago, Britain and France both claimed to own some of the same land, here, in North America. This land was just west of where the 13 colonies were. In 1756, Britain and France went to war to see who would get control of this land. Because the 13 American colonies belonged to Britain, the colonists fought on the same side as Britain. Many Indians fought on the same side as France. Because we were fighting against the French and Indians, the war has come to be known as the French and Indian War.

The war ended in 1763. Britain won the war. Now Britain had control of North America, including Canada. The French had to leave North America.

The colonists were glad that Britain had won. They now felt safer in their homes. Before the war, Indians had often attacked colonists who lived near the borders. Now Britain owned these lands where the Indians lived. The colonists were sure that Britain would protect them.

The colonists were happy to be part of Britain, but that was about to change. They began to decide that they would rather have their own country, independent from Britain. So a dozen years later, the colonists would be fighting the British for freedom from Great Britain's rule. This later war would be called the War for Independence, or the American Revolution. (Beck et al., 1991, p. 275-6)

Beck and her associates have reported modest increases in learning owing to revisions. If Beck and her associates are correct that what elementary students need are longer, more explicit, and more connected texts, extensive thought will be needed about what content should be retained and what should go from future textbooks: Only by deleting content would it be possible to produce elementary-school textbooks of reasonable length, if the amount of writing required to convey each important piece of content is greater than the length used to convey an important piece of information currently (Guthrie & Pressley, 1992). Recall, however, that there are content-area educators who are beginning to think that less may be more with respect to presentation of content information to young students (e.g., see Chapter 12, this book, on science). Also, if anything, the benefits of revision at the high school and college levels that have been obtained have been greater than the gains at the elementary level (Britton et al., 1989, 1991; Duffy et al., 1989; Graves & Slater, 1991), which is important because content coverage is more important in high school and college than in the elementary years. The idea of writing more complete texts that explain important ideas more completely is appealing from a number of perspectives.

It particularly makes sense to construct texts that do not require students to make inferences that they may not be able to make based on their prior knowledge (Britton & Gülgöz, 1991): For example, a contemporary high school text writing about 1965 is probably not well written when it contains phrases like "air war in the North," at least compared to this more explicit phrasing that does not require as much prior knowledge: "air war in North Vietnam."

Adjunct Questions Another classic way to increase learning of text content is to place **adjunct questions** in the text (e.g., Rothkopf, 1966, either before the text [prequestions] or after the text [postquestions]). The outcomes produced in studies of adjunct questioning were orderly (Anderson & Biddle, 1975). Both prequestions and postquestions enhance memory for material covered by questions. Prequestions either do nothing to enhance learning of other information in the text, or they actually reduce memory of nonquestioned information. A prequestion directs attention to questioned information and thus reduces attention to other information in the passage. In contrast, postquestions improve learning of both questioned and nonquestioned material. Postquestions seem to increase review and reflection of more than just the information that answers the postquestion, although the types of information tapped by postquestions over present content can increase differential attention to the same type of information in subsequent sections of text (e.g., Mayer, 1975; McConkie, Rayner, & Wilson, 1973; McGaw & Grotelueschen, 1972; Sagerman & Mayer, 1987). In general, however, it should be noted that adjunct questioning effects typically are not dramatically large, consistent with the general tendency of most text modifications to produce small effects. In general as well, adjunct question effects tend to be smaller with children than with adults (see Pressley & Forrest-Pressley, 1985). Still, textbooks that include a variety of signals or adjunct questions should promote learning at least slightly, making it easier for readers to comprehend and remember the messages in the text.

Illustrations The fourth approach is to provide **illustrations** as accompaniments to text. Memory of text is improved to the extent that illustrations overlap the meaning conveyed by the text (Levin, 1982, 1983; Levin & Lesgold, 1978; Pressley, 1977), consistent with Paivio's (e.g., 1971) dual-coding theory (see Chapter 3). Pictures also sometimes stimulate inferences that would not occur if the text alone were read (e.g., Holmes, 1987). The only consistently negative effect of pictures on learning that has been reported is with beginning readers. Pictures can reduce decoding demands for these readers and thus reduce their attention to the words they are reading. If children read words accompanied by their illustrations, their acquisition of the words as sight vocabulary is less likely than if they read them without accompanying illustrations (Samuels, 1970)—that is, a great deal more attention to and analysis of the words, "a boy rides the bike," when the sentence is read alone than when it is read in the context of a picture depicting a boy riding a bicycle.

Should Text Be Made Easier to Comprehend?

Chall, Conard, and Harris-Sharples (1991) produced one of the most thoughtful analyses of the entire issue of text design and difficulty, attempting to answer the question, *Should Textbooks Challenge Students?*. Those authors make the case that debates about textbook difficulty have gone on for more than 60 years. They often focus on the **readability** of the text, which is based on word difficulties, word lengths, and sentence lengths of texts. As the century progressed, traditional concerns about readability yielded to concerns about the degree that readings reflected text structures well understood by children (e.g., story grammar, Stein & Glenn, 1979; see the discussion earlier in this chapter), the cohesion of text (e.g., Freebody & Anderson, 1983), and the propositional density (i.e., the number of ideas expressed given a particular number of words; Kintsch & Vipond, 1979). Chall et al. (1991) also noted the shift from concern with difficulty alone to difficulty in relation to the child's level of ability and the amount of instructional support provided (i.e., according to theorists such as Vygotsky, optimally difficult text is challenging to the child, with the child able to negotiate it, however, if provided appropriate instruction). Despite more sophisticated theoretical analyses of text difficulty, publishers continue to rely on quantitative measures of vocabulary difficulty and readability as well as the subjective evaluations of teachers and other educators.

Chall et al. (1991) generated several important conclusions about the difficulty of textbooks:

- Content-area texts tend to be more difficult than same-grade basal readers and other language arts instructional materials. They tend to be from one to as many as four grade levels in difficulty above the grade level for which they are intended. In general, science textbooks tend to be written at a higher level of difficulty than social studies texts.

- Both elementary and secondary teachers are concerned that the difficulty of text materials be matched to their students' abilities and needs.
- Many more teachers perceived science and social studies content text to be too difficult than perceived them to be too easy.
- Teachers believed that their best students should be presented more challenging reading than contained in textbooks; for below-average students, teachers favored the difficulty level of current books or wanted easier texts. That is, teachers perceived that the reading levels of textbooks were inappropriate for many students, a point appreciated by other investigators as well (e.g., see Ciborowski, 1993, Chapter 3).
- Both science and social studies texts play prominent roles in instruction, serving as the primary instructional tools in many science and social studies classes.
- When comprehension tests are administered to students, the best grade-4, grade-6, grade-8, and grade-11 students have little difficulty understanding and remembering content from books intended for their grade level. In contrast, the weakest students have great difficulty.

What the Chall et al. (1991) data establish is that proposals to modify textbooks may be missing the mark. What is needed is not some optimal textbook for a given content area at a particular grade level but different textbooks for different students, depending on their reading ability. Even science textbooks written above grade level are too easy for the best students; such textbooks devastate weaker readers. Recall the motivational principles covered in Chapter 5: There is little challenge for the best students—they are not being asked to read materials that are just a bit beyond them. There is no realistic challenge for the weaker students, with them being asked to do tasks that are completely out of reach.

We note that the idea of not relying on a single textbook at a given grade level is entirely consistent with a number of educational philosophies, including whole language covered earlier in this chapter. The whole-language approach emphasizes trade books and authentic literature. Within that framework, students select (and teachers gently guide students to) texts that are appropriate to their interests and abilities. Given the mix of abilities within any given classroom, such an approach makes good sense. Although such an approach might seem foreign in conventional classrooms in which all students are expected to be learning the same content, if the motivational principles of Chapter 5 are considered, it is a reasonable approach. Recall the arguments made there that motivation is maximized by emphasizing student improvement rather than students doing well relative to one another. If students are in environments in which texts are matched to their competencies, improvement should be more certain, with it likely that such gains will motivate additional engagement in academic learning. When students have a fighting chance to do well (as they do when processing appropriately difficult texts), they are more likely to stay with reading than when struggling with texts that are well beyond them and consequently receiving feedback that they are not "getting it" nearly as well as other students in the class.

Even if the motivational principle of providing information a bit beyond the reader is followed, it makes some sense to do all possible to improve the organization and saliency of the organization of textbooks. Roller (1990) provided a telling analysis of the importance of well-structured text when students are processing moderately unfamiliar content: If content is familiar and easy, students will comprehend it regardless of whether the text is well organized. If content is too difficult, students will not understand it even if the text is well organized. When content is moderately familiar (or unfamiliar, depending on how you look at it), organization and clues to text organization make a huge difference (see Spyridakis & Standal, 1987, for a complementary analysis of how signaling improves comprehension of optimally difficult text more than text that is easy or difficult for a reader). Thus, if we had our way, students in classes would receive texts varying in readability and content (with students given texts that are moderately challenging to them), but in all cases the texts would be well organized, with the organization made apparent through signals.

Complete Analysis of Textbook Modification

Although we are not as enthused about attempts to create one-size-fits-all textbooks as are some educational psychologists, we cannot deny that regardless of the difficulty of the text, it is often possible to modify books based on guidance from cognitive theory and research. One of the more complete analyses of this process has been provided by Ciborowski (1993). Her analyses summarize well current thinking about what a good textbook is like and what it does for students:

- The book stimulates connecting textbook content with student prior knowledge. There are sometimes explicit directions and questions to students aimed at activating prior knowledge, such as "Have you ever seen a tumble weed?" Good texts flag for teachers what students need to know or should review (be reminded of) before attempting to understand a new text, such as material covered in previous chapters relating to the upcoming text (Glover, Dinnel, Halpain, McKee, Corkill, & Wise, 1988). They might provide suggestions for telling demonstrations related to the phenomena covered in the reading. Perhaps not surprisingly, organizational devices that stimulate connections between prior knowledge and new text, in fact, are more effective with students having high prior knowledge in the content domain covered in the text (e.g., Wilhite, 1989). If students do possess relevant prior knowledge, however, organizational supplements often improve the comprehension and learning from text for weaker students more than they improve the performance of stronger students (Yuill & Joscelyne, 1988).
- Good textbooks contain excellent illustrations that convey important content and clarify difficult concepts. These might include concept maps relating important vocabulary and ideas to one another.
- They encourage general thinking skills as they teach content.
- They are well written, appealing, and well organized (i.e., coherent).
- There is explicit structure, producing **"considerate text"** (Anderson & Armbruster, 1984). There are accurate and helpful titles and subtitles, headings and subheadings; main ideas in topic sentences; short but well-written previews and summaries; and pointer words (such as, "My first point . . . ," "A second consideration . . . ," and "The third and final concern . . . "). The structures of texts are obvious, such as comparison-and-contrast organizations, problem-solu-tion points, specifications of cause-and-effect, and lists and sequences.
- Excellent textbooks can convey information about how to think about and remember content (e.g., they provide instruction about comprehension strategies), although at present many textbooks fail to do this.
- Especially with weaker students, even the best textbooks cannot stand alone. Teacher-student collaborative learning is often going to be required for weaker students to get the most out of textbooks. Weaker students especially require explicit instruction about how to understand what they read and get the most out of reading. Extended direct explanations about use of comprehension strategies will often be necessary with weaker students.

Summary

A good deal is now known about how to modify textbooks so as to increase the comprehensibility/learnability of them, although the types and amounts of gain vary depending on the modifications made. Interestingly, textbooks that are modified in ways to increase their learnability are obviously clearer: When asked to evaluate a variety of textbooks (Britton, Van Dusen, Gülgöz, Glynn, & Sharp, 1991), 95 percent of college students were able to discriminate texts that were constructed to be highly learnable from texts that were not carefully constructed with respect to comprehensibility and learnability. An important understanding that is emerging, however, is that textbooks are not difficult or easy in and of themselves, but only relative to the abilities, prior knowledge, and motivations of their readers. Consistent with this, many believe that what is important is to provide textbooks that are appropriately challenging for each reader, which means different texts for different students. Such texts seem like a good bet for maximizing the likelihood that students can and will engage text and will learn more than if one textbook is provided to all students. Whether that bet is a winner or loser may be determined in the next decade. One interesting possibility in such research is to ask students to think aloud as they process such textbooks, with Sawyer (1991) making the case that this approach could provide great insights into the processes stimulated by various types of text modifications. Given the insights about information processing during text learning generated in think-aloud studies to date (see the discussion earlier in this chapter), we believe think-aloud methodology should be considered seriously as a source of information by anyone planning research on text modification in the future. Moreover, we hope that at least a few readers of this book decide to take up the challenge of identifying ways to make textbooks more effective.

CONCLUDING COMMENTS

There is a long history of claims that reading can be improved. Many are unlikely, including assertions that phonics and decoding can be learned by only listening to jingle-filled audiotapes and that people can learn to read thousands of words per minute by enrolling in a course that meets for a few hours a night for 10 to 20 weeks (e.g., 600 words per minute is probably the maximum a person can read given physiological constraints; Carver, 1990, Chapter 19). In contrast to such claims, the benefits as a result of the instruction summarized in this chapter are more credible. Notably, there were no quick fixes in this chapter. Years of high-quality, theoretically reasonable instruction is a potential solution to many of the literacy problems of the nation.

Broad-based conclusions about reading that emerge from the well-conducted, systematic study of important reading problems and processes include the following:

1. There are concerns about inadequate reading skills at every age level in the U.S. population. Some children go through their preschool years without exposure to emergent literacy experiences. Many children arrive at grade 1 lacking phonemic awareness. National tests document lower than desired levels of literacy throughout the elementary and secondary years. Life opportunities for many adults are reduced by illiteracy or low literacy.

2. There are psychologically sound (or at least promising) interventions for every age level. There is voluminous evidence that literacy instruction works across the life span, although there is also evidence at every age level that some types of instruction are more effective than others. Understanding how good readers read has done much to increase understanding about how to devise interventions that promote the literacy of lower-achieving readers. Despite increases in knowledge about how to foster literacy, we suspect a minority of children receive literacy instruction even approximating the best practices described in this chapter. More positively, there are greater commitments to high-quality emergent literacy experiences and reading comprehension instruction than there were a decade ago, largely because of the understandings produced by research reviewed in this chapter.

3. We have come to understand that good reading is a specific instance of good problem solving: Both involve strategies, metacognition, knowledge, motivation, capacity, and constructive social interactions. Teaching of general problem-solving strategies would not produce good readers, however, for effective readers have developed strategies that are exceptionally well matched to the particular demands of reading.

4. Effective reading instruction is definitely long term, with instructional packages conceptualized in terms of months and years more than often than days or weeks. In the best of all possible worlds, a newborn would experience high-quality literacy experiences matched to needs, interests, and abilities for every day of her or his life.

5. Meaning construction is the emphasis in contemporary reading instruction. How to teach decoding and comprehension strategies in order to foster efficient abstraction of meaning from text is the overarching issue. Skills and drills are not the orders of the day. Rather the concern is with students coming to understand the cognitive processes that constitute skilled reading so that those processes can be used to derive meaning from texts and create new meanings in new texts.

6. Direct explanation, including modeling, of effective reading processes, which is then followed by scaffolded student attempts to use the processes, emerges as a sound method of teaching reading. Rich teacher-student interactions aimed at encouraging students to become interpreters of text, to construct their own understandings of text, are gaining in prominence. As will be considered in detail at the conclusion of the next chapter, student construction of knowledge about reading is key. Students can be assisted to learn how to read, but they are the ones who figure out how to do it. Good direct expla-

nations with follow-up scaffolding encourage construction of knowledge, with students made ever aware that the processes modeled by the teacher are flexibly adaptive.

7. The interdisciplinary nature of reading research is striking, with brain scientists (see Chapter 6), experimental psychologists, curriculum specialists, literary critical theorists, and social constructivists all playing a role. For the young researcher who enjoys the opportunity for intellectual breadth while pursuing a specialization, it would be difficult to imagine an area of study permitting more opportunity for wide-ranging interactions and contact with biological and social sciences. Many educational psychologists have made their careers as literacy researchers, permitting the lengthy synopsis that is this chapter; they have created a vital science that undoubtedly will be inviting to many readers of this book.

We recognize that a large amount of information was covered in this chapter. One way that our students found it helpful to organize the various topics covered is with respect to whether the research on them is revealing about decoding or comprehension or both. Although such a separation is an artificial one—for example, when a word is decoded by a skilled reader, comprehension processes are operating as well—it does seem to help make a large and potentially difficult-to-organize literature more comprehensible. Thus, we conclude the chapter with Table 14.1 as a summary.

Table 14.1

Organization of Reading Research with Respect to Whether Decoding or Comprehension Was the Main Focus

Decoding

Research on phonemic awareness and its development through instruction

Research on logographic reading, alphabetic reading, phonics rules, sight words, orthographic reading, reading by analogy, and use of semantic context cues to infer words

Research on various forms of experience (e.g., repeated readings, just reading more) that promote decoding competence

Study of fixations and saccades and other word-level processes

Comprehension

Cognitive processes apparent in think-aloud analyses of good reading

Comprehension strategies instruction (e.g., imagery, summarization), including instruction of coordinated use of multiple comprehension strategies (e.g., transactional strategies instruction)

Whole language

Secondary and college-level reading

Textbook modification

Both Decoding and Comprehension

Emergent literacy experiences (e.g., decoding: plastic letters, alphabet song; comprehension: reenactments, joint meaning construction during storybook reading)

One-on-one tutoring such as Reading Recovery and Success for All

Abilities that need to be fostered so that more adults can participate in the economy of the 21st century

Reading instruction for adult illiterates and adults in need of additional instruction in reading

15

Literacy II: Writing

In the past 15 years, there have been intense analyses of the nature of good writing. In part, this was due to growing awareness that most students left American schools unable to communicate their ideas clearly in writing (e.g., Beach, 1976; Emig, 1971; Shaughnessy, 1977). We begin this chapter with an overview of the nature of good writing. This will be followed by discussion of writing instructional research and commentary about reading and writing connections.

NATURE OF GOOD WRITING

Although there are some disagreements about details, there is little disagreement among investigators in this field about the essentials of excellent writing. Rohman's (1965) early model of writing, involving three stages, proved to be nearly on the mark: Rohman conceived of writing as involving (1) prewriting (planning), (2) writing (composing a draft), and (3) rewriting (editing and revising). The only problem with this perspective was its linearity. People do not plan, write, and revise. Rather, they plan a little, write a little, plan some more, and write some more. Perhaps as they revise some of what they have already written, the need for more planning and writing becomes obvious, and so on. Flower and Hayes (1981) noted this recursive property of good writing: Planning occurs before and during writing, revision can occur from the moment something is first written, and a final draft may re-

quire many trips through planning-writing-revision cycles before a composition is ready.

According to the Flower and Hayes (1980) model, writing can be understood by considering the author's long-term memory, the environment the writer inhabits, and the composition being developed. How long-term memory, the environment, and the composition interact will become clearer by considering the writing subprocesses of **planning, translating,** and **revising** in more detail.

Good writers spend a lot more time planning than do weak writers, with their planning activities focusing on the higher-order meanings that the composition is intended to convey (Bereiter & Scardamalia, 1987). There are three subprocesses to such planning, with these occurring recursively. First, it is necessary to **generate the information** that might go in the composition. This can be done by retrieving information from long-term memory or by seeking information in the environment, such as when a reporter interviews witnesses to an accident or a student searches a library for material that might go in a paper. Second, planning involves **setting writing goals.** Occasionally a goal is provided, such as when a teacher assigns an essay topic such as, "What I Did on My Summer Vacation." More often, however, it is up to the writer to decide on the topic of the composition and what effect the writer wishes to have on readers. For example, an essay on a condemned killer could be written to elicit sympathy from readers, acceptance of capital punishment as necessary, or political action from readers in the form of protest to the governor. Often, what the goals should be becomes clear only as planning proceeds (e.g., deciding to write an essay on how behaviorism is not incompatible with doctrines of free will can occur only after the writer discovers that the behaviorism–free will controversy exists and determines that this seems like a fairly interesting topic compared with the other information about behaviorism that was covered in trips to the library). The third aspect of planning is **organizing the information** retrieved, a large part of which is selecting information that is relevant to the writing goals that have emerged during the planning phase.

Think about the last term paper that you wrote. Was the start of the paper much like what was described in the last paragraph, involving fumbling around for an idea, which might have become clear after a few hours of reading in the topic area? Once the big idea for the paper became evident, did planning become more focused, with attention directed at identifying information consistent with the main idea of the paper and organizing that information so that an outline of the paper began to take shape? If you could answer "yes" to the two questions posed in this paragraph, you were engaging in planning of your paper as defined in the writing process literature.

The translating phase of composing is transforming the sketch of a paper that emerges from planning into standard English sentences, ones that go together reasonably well to form paragraphs and represent the arguments intended by the writing plan. Sometimes, deficiencies in the plan become evident during the translating phase, in which case more planning occurs. Although good writers plan before they write, they also do a lot of planning once writing has begun (Humes, 1983), fixing up and elaborating the plan in light of what they discover as they write, including changing their writing goal (Flower & Hayes, 1980; e.g., discovering that they really do not believe that behaviorism and free will are compatible after all and thus changing the topic of their essay to the incompatibility of Skinner's psychology and freedom). Often, additional planning is required because a gap in knowledge becomes evident as the author tries to craft a coherent essay. Thus the reporter might discover during writing that nothing is known about the judge who sentenced the condemned convict, with the reporter having a hunch that this might be a critical part of

the overall story. The tone of the article might be different with a "hanging judge" versus one who had sentenced only one person to death—the condemned person featured in this article. The reporter might call the judge as part of additional planning or talk to defense attorneys in the town where the judge sits.

Revision is usually considered to begin once a draft is completed, although, of course, it can begin earlier with the decision to scrap a paragraph, word, or sentence that one has just written during the translating phase. There are essentially two subprocesses to revision: reading what has been written and editing. Editing involves looking for technical errors, such as noun-verb disagreements and punctuation errors. If a reading of the draft creates the sense that the message is not getting across, the point of editing is not technical accuracy but getting the meaning more in line with the intentions of the writer. The writing goals are always in mind during revision. If the draft falls far short of meeting the goals, substantial additional planning and rewriting may be required.

Challenges of Planning, Translating, and Revising

When we teach educational psychology courses, students easily remember that skilled writing involves planning, translating, and revising. They often fail to appreciate what a revolutionary perspective the Flower and Hayes (1981) model is—somehow forgetting years of schooling that emphasized good spelling and correct punctuation as the heart of good writing—or how complex planning, translating, and revising are. Brief review of some subprocesses of planning, translating, and revising that have been studied as problems in their own right will make clear how challenging composition is. We particularly highlight here subprocesses research that has been conceptualized in psychological terms.

Planning   One subprocess of planning is searching for information that might be placed in an essay. After years of using university libraries, we are still learning new ways of accessing information. A student wishing to write on behaviorism and its philosophical implications (e.g., for doctrines of free will) might start at a library card catalog, which will serve up some book-length references. More telling arguments might be expected to be in the archival journal literature. A person, however, does not simply go to the periodicals room and start thumbing the journals. Rather, there are now computerized indices (e.g., *Psychological Abstracts*) that can generate lists of articles that meet narrow criteria. For example, by putting in the keywords "behaviorism," "philosophy," and "free will," it is likely that these indices could direct the searcher to relevant material. (If you are not familiar with these indices, see the reference librarian at your school immediately, for you are missing out on an essential low-cost resource.)

There are clear individual differences between students in how they search for information in a large-scale environment like a library. For example, Nelson and Hayes (1988) studied how college students search for material for term papers. Some students went to the library shortly before the due date for the paper, and completed their search in one afternoon and evening, with their selection of books anything but exhaustively systematic. Other students headed to the library much more in advance of the deadline and were extremely systematic and selective in their choice of references.

Suppose for the moment that the student is far enough along with the project to have a fairly clear goal (e.g., discussing why behaviorism is compatible with doctrines of free will even though it may appear not to be so at first glance) and has photocopies of some articles identified by the computerized abstracts as relevant. Will the student find the information he or she is seeking—even if the article has been retrieved, photocopied, and read? Guthrie and colleagues (e.g., Guthrie, 1988; Guthrie, Bennett, & Weber, 1991; Dreher & Guthrie, 1990) have determined that search of documents is extremely complex, involving the following steps:

- **Goal formation,** in which an objective is specified. For example, to discover information supporting the thesis that behaviorism and free will are compatible.
- **Category selection,** in which relevant parts of the document being read are identified. Thus, if an article contained only some sections containing information about free will, it is important to find those sections.
- **Extraction of information,** involving the identification of the critical information within relevant sections of a text. Thus, if there is a section discussion of how some church leaders make a

case for behavior modification as a way of enhancing the quality of life and freedom in the long run (e.g., patients whose fear of flying is extinguished through behavior modification are free to fly in the future), the student author might want to record it for possible inclusion in the essay under development.

- **Integration** of the new information found with prior knowledge and other relevant information in the document.

Of course, this is not a linear process but one that is also recursive. Thus, it may become obvious when reading one section of an article that has been categorized as potentially relevant that it is not relevant at all. This might stimulate reconsideration of the other sections of the text that have been singled out for more detailed search. In addition, some information found in the third or fourth section of the text searched might make clear that something read earlier was more relevant than the writer thought it was, stimulating a search for the material that was dismissed when covered previously.

Finding information in a text is difficult even for bright high school and university students. Often they fail to identify the information they are seeking in a text even though it is there (e.g., Guthrie & Dreher, 1990). Often people will read the relevant information and not recognize that that is what they are looking for (Symons & Pressley, 1993) or understand it (Grabe, 1989). The document search problems of students have been demonstrated in the National Asssessment of Educational Progress as well, which includes data on Americans up to 21 to 25 years of age. About one-third of young adults can find a piece of information in a newspaper article that involved consideration of three features (e.g., many young adults would have a tough time reading an article on Republican versus Democratic policies and identifying a position endorsed by both parties but difficult for former President Bush to accept, even though there is explicit reference in the article to endorsements by Republican and Democratic parties and specific mention of Bush's dissatisfaction with the position.) Perhaps most readers would not be surprised to learn that the college students who went to the library near the paper deadline in Nelson and Hayes (1988), which was discussed earlier in this section, were also ineffective when it came to searching in the texts they located. They tended to do a lot of copying of quotes from sources without reflecting much on the appropriateness of the quotes. In short, document search is challenging but an essential part of planning when writers must retrieve information from archival sources in order to have sufficient information to write an essay.

Researchers in writing have documented a number of other difficulties during planning (see Harris & Graham, 1992, for commentary): A common one is that some student writers do not plan but rather simply write, doing what Bereiter and Scardamalia (e.g., 1987, Chapter 1) refer to as **knowledge telling,** illustrated by this description of writing by one 12-year-old:

> I have a whole bunch of ideas and write down until my supply of ideas is exhausted. Then I might try to think of more ideas up to the point when you can't get any more ideas that are worth putting down on paper and then I would end it. (Bereiter & Scardamalia, 1987, p. 9)

Some writers have a great deal of difficulty generating ideas for compositions and cannot zero in on an appropriate topic (Morocco & Neuman, 1986). Some have a lot of information in their heads about their writing topic but seem not to be able to access it or do so inefficiently (see Englert & Raphael, 1988; Graham & Harris, 1989a).

Translating Any trip to a bookstore will confirm that there are many writing style manuals, most of which are filled with technical rules, detailing everything from when to use a semicolon to how to cite a reference. Readers of this book who continue their study of psychology will undoubtedly be exposed to the *Publication Manual of the American Psychological Association.* There are plenty of rules of writing in that source. It would be easy to get the impression from sources such as the American Psychological Association (APA) *Manual* that good writing required only knowledge and application of such rules, a perspective reinforced for years by educators who emphasized such rules. Knowledge of such rules does not produce good writers or even people who can translate a writing plan into good prose. In fact, overconcern with such rules might interfere with the construction of text that conveys what the author wants to say. (e.g., Bereiter & Scardamalia, 1987, Chapter 4). There has been ample documentation that students often receive negative feedback about technical problems in their writing, with such negative feedback discouraging rather than encouraging additional student efforts to write

(Daiker, 1983, 1989; Dragga, 1986; McCarthy, 1987; Rose, 1985, 1989). Think back to the issues of self-efficacy discussed in Chapter 5, and the motivational implications of persistent negative feedback should be obvious. Recall the limits of short-term memory and it is easy to imagine that if much of short-term capacity is consumed with attending to technical matters, there may be little short-term capacity left over to attend to developing the meaning of the text—so much effort is put into punctuating and capitalizing correctly by some writers that they forget what they want to say (see Bereiter & Scardamalia, 1987, Chapter 4).

The real challenge in text production is developing text that expresses the intended meaning—that is what good writers can do and poor writers cannot do. Thus, there has been increasing emphasis in developing writers who can write what they mean. (Some of the most important of this work will be taken up later in the chapter.)

One important difficulty in creating texts that convey meaning is that authors must respect what Nystrand (1986) refers to as the **reciprocity principle.** In constructing a text that makes sense, the author must be aware of what the potential reader knows already. Thus, when one of us writes the introduction to a technical article in educational psychology, we do not spell out the meanings of all of the terms we use—as we have been doing while we write this text for you. It is safe for us to assume that readers of our technical articles would be familiar with most of the terminology in our introductions. In fact, to define such terms in such an article might be seen as an insult to the readership. If we were not to define our terms in the chapters in this book, few of you would be reading this book because few instructors would have deemed it appropriate for students. Good writers keep their audience in mind as they construct text. Because the reader is not there to ask questions of the author as the composition is created, the author must anticipate the questions that readers might have and answer those questions (see McCutchan & Perfetti, 1983; Scardamalia & Bereiter, 1986) as part of constructing the text. Psychologists think of this as a problem of **social cognition:** Good writers are aware of the state of the readers' minds and adjust their writing so that readers can understand the meaning intended by the writer.

Revising Revision has proved to be an extremely intriguing problem for psychologists. Again, getting the meaning of the text right is what is critical in revision. Worrying about the mechanics alone does not result in effective revisions (e.g., Graham, Schwartz, & MacArthur, 1991; McArthur & Graham, 1987; McArthur, Graham, & Schwartz, 1991).

Suppose that a writer is confronted with a text in need of revision because it does not convey the intended meaning or does so poorly. Why might the writer fail to revise?: The writer may not detect that there is a problem with the text. More positively, if someone else points out that there is a difficulty, writers are often capable of fixing up problems they initially fail to detect (e.g., Beal, 1987; see Beal, 1989, for additional discussion), although there are developmental differences such that the ability to correct initially undetected problems (i.e., once they are pointed out) increases during the grade-school years (Beal, 1990). Also, students can be taught to monitor whether there are inconsistencies in a piece of writing. For example, Beal, Garrod, and Bonitatibus (1990) taught grade-3 and grade-5/6 children to self-question themselves about drafts of narratives using a set of questions that any complete and consistent narrative should be able to answer: Who are the people in the story and what are they like? What is happening in the story? Why are they doing what they did? Where does the story take place? When does the story take place? Such instruction increased detection of errors and construction of revisions. Even more effective detection and revision was obtained with grade-3 students when the instruction they were given about revision included exposure to example stories containing parts that should be revised. Beal et al. (1990) provided compelling evidence that detection of problems in stories can be taught so that young children can identify when to make revisions—although the main point here is that in the absence of instruction, children often fail to detect difficulties with text.

Writers may fail to identify problems because they lack adequate criteria about what makes a piece of writing appropriately communicative (e.g., McCormick, Busching, & Potter, 1992). For example, based on much of the feedback about writing given in school, students sometimes accept text as adequate if the mechanics of the writing (i.e., spelling, punctuation, capitalization) are fine and the writing is neat. Alternatively, they may be seduced by interesting details (see Chapter 5). For example, they may believe a text is communicative because they like the examples used in the text (e.g., anecdotes about pets), failing to recognize that the anecdotes are not good illustrations of the phenomena being explained in the text.

Even when writers detect problems, sometimes they do not know how to revise to express the meaning they intend. Some students do not know how to make additions, deletions, substitutions, and text rearrangements as revisions (e.g., Fitzgerald & Markham, 1987).

Fortunately, some people do learn how to revise well. A number of studies have been conducted in which think-aloud data have been collected as writers revise. Fitzgerald (1992) summarized how good revisers approach the task. First, they keep the overall meaning of the text in mind and what the reader needs to get out of the text (Berkenkotter & Murray, 1983; Hayes, Flower, Schriver, Stratman, & Carey, 1987). If there is a particular writing style that they want reflected in the writing, that is considered prominently as revision proceeds (e.g., Graves, Slater, Roen, Redd-Boyd, Duin, Furniss, & Hazeltine, 1988). They do not worry about problems at the sentence and word level as much as they worry about problems at a higher level of organization—for example, concentrating more on the overall organization of the text than the construction of individual sentences (Hayes et al., 1987). Although attention to higher-order meaning takes precedence, expert revisers also evaluate grammar and spelling and some writing maxims, such as to use parallel constructions and to avoid wordiness (Hayes et al., 1987; Hull, 1987).

In short, expert revisers have a repertoire of strategies that they apply while they are revising, from ones that are directed at the main messages of the text to others that are directed at details of grammar, spelling, and punctuation. Throughout Fitzgerald's (1992) review of revision, she keeps returning to Nystrand's (e.g., 1986) reciprocity principle: Good revisers are aware of the needs of the reader. For that reason among others, a popular instruction option is for students to revise in small groups, with peers reading one another's work and reacting with constructive criticism. Consistent with Vytgotskian theory (Chapter 8), many who favor revision groups believe that participating in such discussions will lead to long-term internalization of the revision processing carried out in the group (e.g., DiPardo & Freedman, 1988).

Good Writing Compared to Expert Problem Solving

Just as good reading is an example of expert problem solving (see Chapters 4, 13, and 14), so is good writing:

- Domain experts use their prior knowledge extensively during problem solving. So it is with skilled writers who have a great deal of knowledge about the specific topics they are writing about and ways of expressing their ideas.
- Experts are opportunistic during problem solving, using clues they encounter while solving a problem to assist in deciding next moves. So it is with skilled writing, with writing plans changing as writers encounter gaps in the texts they are creating.
- Experts exhibit flexibility as they solve problems. So it is with skilled writing, with the good writer juggling the plan until it seems right, experimenting with different ways of expressing a thought and revising by applying multiple criteria simultaneously.
- Experts monitor their performances. So it is with good writers, who size up when they need to plan more as they experience difficulties with writing and who explicitly approach revision as an exercise involving error detection and correction (see Beal's [1989] analysis).
- Experts process "deeply" as they solve problems; that is, expertise in problem solving produces a complex thinker who does not simply apply readily available prior knowledge to a problem but rather uses prior knowledge in conjunction with strategies, continually monitoring progress in understanding the problems. So it is with writing, with the skilled author thinking extensively about the essay and how it can be crafted best to express intended meaning. For example, author [MP] once explicitly kept track of how many revisions he made to manuscripts before submitting them for publication to a journal. In some cases, the first draft was followed by more than 40 revised drafts. All writers know that essays in construction can require enormous cognitive resources—the essay that is not going well can be on the author's mind during meals and social events, can prevent an author from falling asleep, and can result in authors foregoing weekend or holiday

activities to "hole up" in the library to formulate a new writing plan.
- Finally, expertise in problem solving takes a long time to develop. So it is with writing. Good writers write a lot (Applebee, 1984; Applebee, Langer, & Mullis, 1986).

Good writing is so much a problem solving process that Linda Flower has produced a college-level introductory writing textbook, entitled *Problem-Solving Strategies for Writing* (1989). We strongly recommend this volume as a tutorial for those who wish a full-blown exposition on how writing can be accomplished using strategies. Her summary of the nine steps and strategies provides a review of many of the points made in this section:

Step 1. Explore the rhetorical problem. (Figure out the writing assignment.)
Step 2. Make a plan.
Step 3. Generate new ideas. (This includes brainstorming and eventually resting and allowing the various ideas to "incubate.")
Step 4. Organize your ideas.
Step 5. Know the needs of your reader.
Step 6. Transform your writer-based prose into reader-based prose. (That is, express your ideas in a form that potential readers will be able to understand.)
Step 7. Review your paper and purpose. (Review your goals and the meanings expressed in your paper. Diagnose discrepancies between goals and meanings in the paper. Revise.)
Step 8. Test and edit writing. (Edit for economy and to create a forceful style.)
Step 9. Edit for connections and coherence. (Make connections between sentences that are presented in a listlike fashion; make the inner logic of the paragraphs salient.)

Closing Comment on Good Writing

The analyses of skilled writing presented here were intended to make obvious that writing can be understood in terms of information processing but that being able to explain it in such terms does not diminish the enormity of the task. Good writing involves the integration of a number of skills that require a great deal of time and experience to develop. What is shocking is that American education traditionally has required little writing of students, a point forcefully made by Applebee (1984). Consider the following claims from the conclusions section of that study of high school writing in the United States:

> The majority of school assignments provide little room for writing of even paragraph length.
>
> When more extended writing is required, it still tends to be rather limited in scope. The typical assignment is a first-and-final draft, completed in class, and requiring a page or less of writing. Topics for these assignments are usually constructed to test previous learning of information or skills; hence the students' task is to get the answer "right," rather than to convince, inform, or entertain a naive audience. (pp. 183–184)

How could we expect to develop excellent writers in such a schooling environment? Fortunately, since Applebee's (1984) study, and in part because of it, there has been renewed interest in increasing the amount of writing done in school, with some of the most important discoveries about the effects of such writing instruction considered in the pages that follow. As a preview of what is to come, we simply say that writing opportunities and writing instruction are a concern at all levels of contemporary schooling, and the development of competent writers is of great interest to both educators and researchers.

EMERGENT WRITING DURING THE PRESCHOOL YEARS

If a child can hold a crayon, it is likely that he or she will engage in writing at some level according to the emergent literacy perspective. There is a clear developmental progression during the preschool years for children who live in an environment supportive of writing (Sulzby, 1985): Drawing and then scribbling are significant precursors to conventional writing. Eventually, scribbling is not random, with letterlike features observed in both drawings and scribbling. The child will learn to draw some letters, such as the ones in his or her name, although often the letters are far from perfect or in the correct order (e.g., how many times did TIM come out MIT?). With time and experience, the child can write many more, often inventing spellings based on the sounds of the word (e.g., GNYS for GENIUS; Bissex, 1980). Invented spellings gradually approximate conventional spellings, until there comes a time that spelling is completely conventional.

When invented spelling is allowed, the child is free to write much more than if adults are hung up about conventional spelling. Preschools and kindergartens are now filled with writers. It is not unusual in fact to see all types of writing in any given kindergarten, from drawings and scribbling to short sentences and phrases written with conventional spelling (Allen et al., 1989; Sulzby & Teale 1991). Variations on writing such as invented spelling persist into the early elementary years. An assumption of many language arts educators who are committed to positions such as "whole language" is that letting the kids write as they will and can is essential if children are to be motivated to be writers.

Recall the point made earlier in this chapter about how overconcern with mechanics can interfere with writing and reduce the motivation to write. IMURJENT RITing iS A WUNDuRFULL IDiR!

WRITING DURING THE ELEMENTARY YEARS

Walk into an American elementary classroom on any given morning, what are the three most likely events to occur? One is the pledge to the flag, an American institution (or singing of *O Canada* north of the border). The second is reading group, a staple of elementary education for more than a century. The third is **Writers' Workshop,** which is only about a decade old (Atwell, 1987; Calkins, 1986) but is becoming as commonplace as the pledge and reading group. Children are learning that to write every day is natural.

Writers' Workshop is designed to be motivating: For example, students often are permitted to choose their own topics for writing rather than writing to some teacher-prescribed topic. Students control other aspects of their writing as well, such as how long their essays will be and how they will revise. Just as good readers experiencing transactional strategies instruction are taught that they must make choices for themselves, so it is with Writers' Workshop participants, something hypothesized to increase the likelihood of eventual self-regulated writing.

Why do we write? Our most important motivation is to affect students like you—to have an impact on your development as educators, psychologists, or simply well-educated people. As part of the writing process, we often submit drafts to student groups, who respond to the work. Over the years, we have discovered what works and what does not work in writing for student audiences. Analogously, students in Writers' Workshop receive feedback from their peers, with a great deal of sharing of writing between students. We have many memories of children listening to peers and then explaining what it is they like about a peer's essay, what they do not understand, and what might be a good way to extend the piece. Students do much to teach each other how to communicate effectively as part of the Writers' Workshop experience.

That students provide feedback to one another does not deny the role of the teacher in instruction, however. One prominent instructional role for the teacher is to listen to student essays just as the peers do and provide the same type of feedback, about strong points and aspects that might be elaborated or clarified.

When students reach the end of this process, many Writers' Workshops provide another lesson in writing—a lesson about another important reason that authors write. The completed essay is "published," perhaps in a class book or for display on a bulletin board. In some classes we have seen, students use a special word processing program and higher-quality font and paper to produce the final draft of their paper. The opportunity to publish is so motivating that we have seen children who clamor to stay in at recess to publish their paper on the computer. (Although we have missed no recesses in writing this book, the motivation to see it in print is so great that many movies, sporting events, and parties were neglected in favor of the word processor. Seeing one's words in print must be a powerful motivator!)

In describing these salient features of Writers' Workshop, many of which are explicitly aimed an increasing both knowledge of writing and motivation to write, we have downplayed one of its most important components. In many Writers' Workshops, teachers provide a great deal of direct explanation and modeling about the writing process, with the Flower and Hayes (1981) model considered earlier in this chapter (and variations of it) guiding much of contemporary writing instruction. As it turns out, there is great need for such instruction.

Deficiencies in the Writing of Elementary Students

There are five potential problems that students can have with writing (Harris & Graham, 1992; Langer,

1986; Scardamalia & Bereiter, 1986). They can fail to do the following:

1. Establish a writing goal. They do not establish whether the task is to be persuasive or to tell a tale; they fail to identify their audience, etc. More positively, there are age-related increases in student awareness of the communication possibilities that writing permits, although these understandings of communication possibilities are much less developed in the elementary years compared with the high school years (Langer, 1986, Chapter 3).

2. Generate enough content: They may fail to search their memories or environments completely for information that could be put in an essay.

3. Organize what they write: They do not plan enough, often only doing what Scardamalia and Bereiter (1986) refer to as "knowledge telling," which is simply writing without planning or reorganizing.

4. Do the mechanics of writing efficiently. Their writing, spelling, or sentence construction is weak, *or* they get so hung up on the mechanics that they pay little attention to the meaning and organization of what is being written. That children often are overly concerned about mechanics probably reflects that many schooling environments overemphasize mechanics such as spelling and sentence construction skills (Langer, 1986, Chapter 3).

5. Revise, including shifting goals if that seems appropriate based on what was discovered during planning, drafting, and previous revisions (see Fitzgerald, 1987).

In short, elementary student writing is often deficient with respect to the processes associated with good writing. More positively, elementary writing instruction is an area in which there have been many successes. Students can learn to write well.

Writing Instruction

Although Scardamalia and Bereiter (e.g., 1986) generated the first large-scale systematic program of investigations of writing instruction during the elementary grades, there is a growing fraternity of process-oriented writing researchers. Graham and Harris are particularly prominent members of this group, having identified a number of ways that the writing performance of elementary-age learning-disabled students can be improved. Based on their own research on writing, especially with learning-disabled students, and the research of others concerned with writing by elementary students, Harris and Graham (1992; but also Graham & Harris, 1988, 1992; Graham, Harris, MacArthur, & Schwartz, 1991; Sawyer, Graham, & Harris, 1992) provided a particularly thorough review of their perspectives on writing instruction. According to Harris and Graham, writing should proceed as follows:

> First, students could be urged to concentrate on topic choice, planning, and content generation [planning stage in the Hayes & Flower framework]. Once a first draft is generated [writing stage], students could then concentrate on revising their paper with an eye focused on content and organization [revision stage]. When students feel comfortable that their paper is complete, then editing for mechanical errors could take place. A routine of this nature focuses students' efforts on content and meaning.... Hence, they will not be needlessly distracted by errors of mechanics and usage.... However, students do not forget that the paper will eventually need to be edited.... As students master such a routine, they should further be encouraged to see the various processes recursively.
>
> It is not only critical that students become comfortable with the various stages involved in writing, they also need to develop effective strategies for executing these processes. Within the Writers' Workshop, one way teachers can help students develop these strategies is to model the pertinent strategies and the thought processes involved in executing them. For instance, a teacher may demonstrate how to gather raw material, mentally rehearse ideas and images to write about, talk to others to gain information, or use brainstorming and webbing activities to generate content for a topic. Modeling will not be enough.... Current research ... suggests that ... contextualized and explicit instruction is highly effective in promoting the development of cognitive and self-regulation skills central to academic success (Duffy & Roehler, 1986). (Harris & Graham, 1992, pp. 314–315)

There it is: Plan, write, and revise, with direct explanation and modeling of strategies for each of these stages. The strategies that can be applied during planning, writing, and revision include the following:

- *Strategies predominantly addressing the planning stage.* Because students sometimes do not search their memories thoroughly for everything they might know about a topic (see Scardamalia & Bereiter, 1986, for an analysis) either before or while they write, strategies that promote more thorough search of memory for ideas can increase the quantity of material written on a topic. For example, Humes (1983) recommended providing sets of question prompts that would stimulate systematic search of memory for relevant content. (Such prompts are a specific instance of **procedural facilitators** [Scardamalia & Bereiter, 1986], in that they make more likely execution of procedures that will result in a more complete and well-organized piece of writing.) Thus, if the student were writing about a sequence of events, the questions included the following: What happened first? What happened next? Next? What happened last? When did it happen? Where did it happen? To whom did it happen? Similarly, Harris and Graham (1985) taught students a routine for searching their memories to find action verbs, adjectives, and adverbs that would be sensible in their essays, with this search routine increasing the amount written and the quality of the text. Bereiter and Scardamalia (1982) provided students with sentence openers such as, "One reason ... ," "Even though ... ," "For example, ... ," and "I think...." Perhaps the most intuitively obvious approach, however, is simply to ask the child who writes a short essay to "write some more" (Graham, 1990; Scardamalia & Bereiter, 1986), a command that children can internalize and make to themselves if they are taught to do so (Graham & Harris, 1987).

- *Strategies predominantly addressing the writing stage.* Students can learn to instruct themselves to respond to a series of probes that are matched to the information contained in essays in the genre. Thus, to write a short persuasive essay, students can be taught to respond to the following four prompts in order: (1) Generate a topic sentence. (2) Note reasons. (3) Examine the reasons and ask if readers will buy each reason. (4) Come up with an ending (Graham & Harris, 1988). A second example is a set of questions for generating a narrative with conventional story grammar (Harris & Graham, 1992): Who is the main character? Who else is in the story? When does the story take place? Where does the story take place? What does the main character do or want to do? What do other characters do? What happens when the main character does or tries to do it? What happens with other characters? How does the story end? How does the main character feel? How do the other characters feel?

- *Strategies predominantly addressing the revision stage.* After teaching students the elements of a good essay, Graham and MacArthur (1988) taught learning-disabled students to revise by cycling through six steps: (1) Read the essay. (2) Find a specific sentence that tells what the student believes and wants to say. (3) Add two reasons to the essay for the belief. (4) Scan each sentence of the essay. (5) Make changes on the computer (or paper, if handwritten). (6) Reread and make final changes. Fitzgerald and Markham (1987) taught grade-6 students to approach revision as a problem-solving task, one that could be solved by making additions, deletions, substitutions, and rearrangements. Graham and MacArthur (1988) taught students to revise by adding details, examining the clarity and cohesiveness of the paper, and fixing mechanical errors. Peers can be asked to give feedback on the content and the structure of the paper (e.g., MacArthur, Schwartz, & Graham, 1991). (Recall as well the description earlier in this chapter of the self-questioning strategy taught to elementary students by Beal et al., 1990.)

We assume by this point that it is obvious to readers that there is much to be learned in order for a student to plan, write, and revise an essay. Not surprisingly, writing instruction is a long-term process, although it is often possible to observe some benefits after a few weeks or months of some specific type of strategy instruction. (Harris & Graham, 1992). The time such instruction requires is well spent, with Harris and Graham consistently observing maintenance of training (i.e., continued application of the strategies taught when doing the same writing task), sometimes measured as long as 16 weeks after the instruction was completed. In addition, Harris and Graham (1992) have observed some transfer of the strategies they have taught, for example, to different settings (teachers) and writing genres.

Harris and Graham (1992) not only spend a good deal of time instructing students (which is essential for students to learn writing strategies, especially learning-disabled students, who are their particular concern), but also they teach according to a model of instruction that is consistent with many other types of effective strategies instruction (including a number already reviewed in this chapter): (1) There is an initial conference with students to explain the goals of the strategy instruction and why such instruction is important (i.e., benefits of instruction are explained). (2) Prerequisite skills are taught to students who may be deficient. For example, if knowing conventional story grammar is critical to execution of the strategy, students who may not understand the conventional structure of stories can be taught what they need to know. (3) There is initial discussion of the strategy, during which the instructor explains each step and its significance to the overall process. (4) The teacher models use of the strategy being taught. As part of this, the teacher talks aloud about his or her problem that might be solved with the writing strategy. The teacher self-evaluates as his or her writing proceeds, correcting errors and providing self-reinforcement (e.g., Hey, this is really coming along!) as the essay develops. (5) The student memorizes the steps of the strategy. (6) The student receives scaffolded instruction from the teacher while practicing the strategy. (7) Eventually the student can execute the strategy independently, with talk-aloud data reflecting use of all of the steps of the strategy. (8) The student and teacher discuss how to apply the strategy in other settings and with other tasks, and then the student attempts to use the strategy during the regular school day.

We assume readers have no difficulty discerning the by now familiar pattern of explicit explanation and modeling followed by scaffolded practice until the student is ready for independent performance. This is a winning formula, although one that can take years to complete, as illustrated by one of the most important instructional studies of student writing reported to date.

Englert, Raphael, Anderson, Anthony, and Stevens (1991)

Englert and colleagues at Michigan State set out to teach grade-4 and grade-5 students (both regularly achieving students and special education students) how to construct particular types of expositions: explanations and compare-and-contrast essays. The study took place over the course of an entire academic year. They dubbed their approach **Cognitive Strategy Instruction in Writing (CSIW)**.

CSIW has much in common with other Writers' Workshop approaches: (1) There is direct explanation of writing strategies and modeling of their use. (2) There is daily writing, usually on topics selected by the students. (3) Procedural facilitators are provided to increase the likelihood that children will execute completely the processes they have been taught. (4) Peers evaluate each other's papers and provide revision comments. (5) Teachers and students have frequent writing conferences. (6) There is "publication" of student papers.

First, the text structures that students were learning were introduced using examples (see Chapter 3), ranging from extremely well-structured ones to completely disorganized passages. As part of this introduction via examples, students were provided information about the types of questions the text structure in question addresses and the types of text signals that authors can build into such text to make the text work as intended. There was discussion of appropriate ways to begin such an essay, how to construct opening sentences that catch the attention of readers. As the teacher went over the good and bad examples, he or she thought aloud for students in ways that were revealing about strengths and weaknesses of the text (e.g., "I wonder how the author got into this situation?") or structural elements the student should note (e.g., "Did the author address what is being explained?"; "Who is involved?"; "What materials are needed?"; "Did he or she explain where it was taking place?"; and "What are the steps?"). As examples continued, students played an ever-increasing role in these analyses activities, doing so at the invitation of the teacher, who scaffolded their participation in the analysis process.

Second, teachers modeled the writing of texts conforming to the structure being instructed. They talked aloud as they did so, informing students what they were doing and how they were doing it. While thinking aloud, teachers provided information about when to use the text structure under instruction and the text-construction strategies being modeled. For example, a teacher modeling the construction of an explanation-type text would first think aloud about planning: "Who am I writing for?" "Why am I writing this?" "What do I know about this?" "How can I organize all of this?"

Third, the teacher introduced a "planning think sheet," a type of procedural facilitator, something intended to assist planning of the essay. Thus the planning think sheet for explanation essays included the types of questions the teacher previously modeled as part of his or her planning:

WHO: Who am I writing for?
WHY: Why am I writing this?
WHAT: What do I know? (Brainstorm)
HOW: How can I group my ideas?
    How will I organize my ideas?: _____
    comparison/contrast, _____ problem/solution
    _____ explanation _____ other

Students then wrote class papers in dialogue with the teacher, with the teachers and students using the planning sheets collaboratively to construct essays. As this writing proceeded, the students took more and more responsibility. That is, instruction was scaffolded, with the teacher providing no more help than needed. After the group construction efforts came attempts by students to construct their own essays, again with scaffolded instruction from teachers. The students worked collaboratively with one another as they worked on essays. Essay writing continued in this fashion until the student was ready to prepare an essay that could be published in the class book. Throughout the process, however, whenever students needed additional explanations or modeling, they received it.

CSIW was evaluated in a quasi-experiment in which comparable control students and teachers carried on their instructional business as usual. The control students were receiving high-quality language arts instruction, including some instruction in process writing (i.e., the controls were learning to plan, draft, and revise as part of writing). That the instruction in the control classrooms was good teaching bolsters confidence in the claims of effectiveness made by Englert et al. (1991)—Englert et al. had a challenging control condition rather than a "straw man" control.

On the posttest, participants in the study were asked to explain in writing how to do something they were familiar with (e.g., how to play a game or make some object), keeping in mind that the reader would know little about the topic before reading the essay. They also wrote a compare-and-contrast paper, comparing two different people, places, or things. A third writing assignment required the students to write about something that they knew a great deal about, which was a transfer task because CSIW students had never been taught a text structure strategy for such writing.

In general, the posttest essays of CSIW students were superior to those of controls, both when judged holistically (i.e., readers rated the overall quality of the essay) and with respect to important characteristics of explanatory (i.e., introduction of topic; a sequence of steps; key words such as first, second, third; and closure, approximately in that order) and compare-and-contrast (i.e., identification of two things compared; similarities; differences; key-words such as alike, different, but; and conclusion, roughly in that order) essays. Three other outcomes were important as well, however: (1) The texts of CSIW students were more sensitive to the needs of readers as reflected by more interesting introductions, explicit statements of purpose, anticipating and answering potential reader questions, and an explicit author voice indicating that personal opinions were being expressed, with the writer's personality injected in the essay in various ways. (2) The CSIW students wrote better "expert" papers as well, even though they were not taught text structure strategies for such texts. Englert et al. (1991) intepreted this as evidence of transfer of writing strategies to a novel writing task. (3) At posttest, students in CSIW had much more metacognitive knowledge about the writing process than control students: For example, they could talk about writing as a process involving planning, writing, and revising. They understood the importance of essay organization and that revising was to establish coherence (i.e., rather than to correct grammar, spelling, and so forth) and knew more ways of producing coherence (e.g., putting closely related ideas in the same paragraph).

In general, there was a great deal of evidence in Englert et al. (1991) supporting the general conclusion that a year of expository writing instruction benefited students. CSIW students produced better organized, more interesting essays at the end of the year of instruction than did control students experiencing otherwise high-quality language arts instruction. The effects were pronounced both for normally achieving students and for learning disabled students.

The plan-write-revise framework can be taught to grade-school students of varying abilities, including those who are experiencing special education interventions because of previous difficulties in language arts. A number of specific approaches have been developed to address each of the three recursive phases of writing. Good instruction provides students with a repertoire of specific procedures for facilitating planning, writing, and revising and permits a great deal of scaffolded practice of expository writing. Procedural facilitators in the form of lists of elements that should be in an essay are used frequently as part of writing instruction. Even short-term writing instruction aimed at improving some specific writing competency occurs over hours and days; impressive writing gains, such as the transfer documented by Englert et al. (1991), occur after weeks and months of instruction. Fortunately, long-term writing instruction is part of many educators' conceptions of high-quality language arts instruction, instruction that is decidedly multifaceted.

(See Zellermayer, Salomon, Globerson, & Givon, 1991, for an evaluation of computerized scaffolding and provision of procedural facilitators to high school students, one in which 20 hours of interaction with the computerized "writing partner" improved the quality of students essays.)

Integrated, Process-Oriented Language Arts Instruction

So far in this chapter and the previous one, decoding instruction, comprehension, and writing have been described separately. High-quality, process-oriented instruction has been described that can be applied to each of these processes. Although such compartmentalization of language arts competencies can aid scientific study of each one—and it has proved worthwhile to study decoding, comprehension, and writing separately—eventually it is necessary to think about how decoding, comprehension, and writing instruction can be meshed. Although teacher educators do not yet understand how to prepare a nation of teachers who can do it, and language arts researchers do not understand all of the effects of integrated instruction, we are convinced it can happen because some outstanding elementary teachers are already doing it.

Lynn Coy-Ogan has been teaching as part of the Montgomery County SAIL program for five years (see Chapter 14). She is an outstanding grades-1/2 SAIL teacher, explaining and modeling comprehension strategies as part of lessons in which students practice these same procedures. Lynn's language arts instruction is much, more, however.

Lynn's grade-1 students as well as the few grade-2 students still experiencing difficulties with phonics receive explicit phonics instruction tailored to their needs. As part of this, Lynn employs mnemonic-phonics materials similar to those studied by Ehri and Wilce (1985) and covered earlier in Chapter 14. Her whole-class reading lessons also provide some coverage of phonics and decoding. For example, when one of us (MP) visited her class on November 12, 1991, the students had a whole-group lesson on identification of long vowels in words, the decomposition of compound words, and contractions. This whole-group lesson was offered in preparation for seatwork assignments requiring students to work with long vowels, to decompose compound words, and to construct contractions.

Writing happens every day, with every student having a writing folder in which their completed work and writing in progress are stored. Student essays are regularly displayed in the class. Author MP was impressed with the quality of passages he read. Lynn believes her students are such good writers because they write and edit about one story a week. Lynn is fortunate in that five parent volunteers have been assigned to her room. She has trained them to carry on reading conferences with individual students, so her students receive substantial adult feedback about their writing.

Some of the writing is tied to the SAIL comprehension instruction. For example, a frequent assignment is for students to write summaries of stories read in the reading group using the SAIL strategies.

Lynn's Writers' Workshop is definitely process oriented, with students taught how and why to write and provided explicit strategies for planning essays. For example, Lynn's students had lessons early in the year on reasons for writing: (1) persuasion, (2) provide information, (3) express feelings, and (4) tell stories. Later in the year, they had lessons on story structure (i.e., stories contain characters, a setting, a problem, and a solution) and how the elements of a story can facilitate story construction. In April, 1992 author MP observed a lesson during which students were taught to construct a "web" of ideas in anticipation of writing. Lynn and her students constructed a web in preparation for writing on the topic of "spring." Lynn put the word "spring" in an oval on the chalk board with spokes coming off the oval. Students brainstormed for information about spring that might be put in an essay. Along the way, Lynn explained to students that when the essay was actually written, more organization of ideas would be required; she also let them

know that every idea generated during the brainstorm might not show up in every student's essay. The students also were urged to personalize their paragraphs. Then Lynn sent them off to their desks to write a rough draft on scratch paper, which was to be followed by scheduling a teacher appointment so the paper could be edited. The students were reminded that the rough draft did not need to be especially neat and that the way to write the essay might be to identify the most important ideas and then expand on each of these. As students planned and drafted, Lynn circulated in the room, providing mini-lessons matched to the specific difficulties displayed by each student: She gave students hints about how they might proceed next in planning or writing their essay; she suggested to one student that he might think about how some of the ideas on the spokes might be combined; and when she encountered a student who was constructing causal linkages between the brainstormed ideas about spring (e.g., It gets warmer, which makes new leaves form on the trees and birds return from the south), Lynn thought out loud (so that all the students could hear her), "John is really clever telling the reader that getting warmer causes new leaves and the return of the birds."

During her SAIL reading lessons, a great deal of information about literature and how to process literature is provided to students. Thus, students learn that predictions about a book can often be made if another book by the same author was read previously. This idea permitted a mini-lesson on intertextual connections. Use of the SAIL strategies also permitted other instruction. Thus a clarification about the use of the word "nail" in a text led to a discussion of its several definitions. While thinking aloud, Lynn was able to relate a vocabulary word in a story to other content being covered in science (i.e., "Carnivores . . . I know where I've seen that word before. Many dinosaurs were carnivores"). In addition to modeling and cuing use of the strategies, Lynn provides plenty of metacognitive information about the strategies. For example, as students read one story, Lynn let her students know that visualization was especially useful for stories without pictures, especially if the story provided detailed descriptions. During summarization of the same story, students were reminded that summarizing after reading a story was usually a good idea, permitting a little more attention to the most important information in the story.

When MP visited Lynn's classroom in April, 1992, he also observed small groups of children (up to five) reading stories and carrying out the SAIL strategies without teacher assistance. Lynn had initiated these teacher-independent groups as a step toward more self-regulated use of the comprehension strategies. She reported that pairs of students sometimes read together, again using the SAIL strategies to do so.

Lynn encourages good information processing in a number of ways in her classroom: (1) She teaches both reading (decoding and comprehension) and writing strategies. (2) There is ample metacognitive discussion highlighting when and where to use the strategies being learned and what advantages the strategies can provide. In addition, children have numerous opportunities themselves to experience the advantages of the strategies because students read and write daily in Lynn's classroom. (3) A great deal of nonstrategic knowledge is conveyed, from specific vocabulary to information about authors and genres. The knowledge ranges from what can be gleaned from analyses of individual words (e.g., nature of compound words and relationships between words with similar roots) to reading and comparing a series of books by the same author. (4) The happy, nonthreatening atmosphere in Lynn's classroom is meant to make literacy inviting. No one who sits for a morning in Lynn's class can doubt that her students are "into" reading and writing. Her kids rush to reading corner when it is their turn. They eagerly seek out advisement from peers about how to fix up essays.

A relatively new emphasis with respect to process instruction is to extend it beyond integrated reading and writing to encompass the entire curriculum (e.g., Walmsley & Walp, 1990). Thus, it is not unusual at all for Lynn's students to apply their reading and writing strategies in social studies or science. For a detailed description of how strategies instruction was extended across an entire school day in a grade-4 classroom, see Pressley, Gaskins, Wile, Cunicelli, and Sheridan (1991). Those investigators observed a semester of instruction during which students first learned to analyze expository text with respect to its structure (e.g., cause and effect, description, explanation, temporal sequence) in order to comprehend it. Students practiced such analyses with a variety of text types, including science and social studies. What was especially interesting was

that the students also learned how to plan and write texts using these same expository text structures, again doing so to produce writing in several content areas—understanding the nature of exposition is a critical component in composing well-organized expositions (Cox, Shanahan, & Sulzby, 1991; Spivey & King, 1989; Wright & Rosenberg, 1993). Reading was taught in the service of writing, and the reading and writing strategies acquired in the Benchmark classroom served learning of other content.

Summary

The work reviewed in this section has been produced by cognitive scientists and psychologists, specialists in curriculum and instruction, rhetoricians, and special educators. Various specialists have combined basic ideas from cognitive psychology with their knowledge of the literacy needs and capabilities of students to design interventions that improve children's writing. What is gratifying to cognitively oriented educational psychologists is that it is now possible to walk into classrooms and see theoretically-motivated practice that is effective and received enthusiastically by students and teachers alike.

If there is a "secret" here, it is that a lot can be had from simple but powerful ideas: When students learn to plan, write, and revise compositions—and specific ways to accomplish each of these stages of composition—they have learned important literacy lessons. Good text does not just happen but rather is a human construction, one usually accomplished only with hard work and many reworkings.

WRITING DURING ADOLESCENCE AND EARLY ADULTHOOD

Without a doubt, the two most prominent researchers studying secondary-school writing and writing instruction are Applebee and Langer (e.g., Applebee, 1984; Langer & Applebee, 1987). Their work and that of their colleagues at the federally sponsored National Center for the Study of Writing have involved a number of methods, from detailed case studies of student writing and the teaching of writing to analyses of the writing samples of hundreds of students and the collection of questionnaire data from teachers across the United States. A coherent set of important conclusions emerged from their analyses.

Nature of Student Writing

Much of the writing done by students is to convince the teacher that they have learned content that has been taught. Often this writing is in the form of a short-answer response on a test. Such writing is undemanding, with teachers rarely worried about whether answers are communicative so long as the student touches on the points that he or she was to learn for the examination.

More positively, there are clear developments in writing skills moving from the elementary years through the high school years, largely in response to new demands made by schooling. Thus, during the elementary years, children in Applebee's and Langer's (e.g., Langer, 1986) studies could write simple reports and simple stories, narratives containing story grammar elements and other features common in stories (e.g., starting with, "Once upon a time. . . " and ending with, "They lived happily ever after. . . "). (Given the increased prominence of writing instruction in the elementary years since Applebee's and Langer's investigations, much more might be expected from grade-school students if the study were to be repeated now.) By the end of the grade-school years and in the middle-school years, students are writing book reports. These are typically not more than a page or two in length, requiring description of the text and some evaluative commentary. Although most students learn to cope with these styles and offer acceptable stories and book reports, individual differences in qualities of text are evident even with respect to these simple forms of writing. For example, some students will provide interpretations of books they have read, whereas others will simply offer evaluative commentary (Durst, 1984).

In contrast, high school requires more analytical forms of writing. Thus, English and social studies courses include assignments in which students must present a thesis and defend it. Science courses include laboratory reports. Although students experience difficulties in learning how to produce such essays, they eventually succeed (Durst, 1984). What is somewhat disturbing, however, is that they seem to learn a formula for generating the writing required for specific classes. Once that formula is understood

and mastered, it is followed (Applebee, 1984; Marshall, 1984b).

For example, students learn that thesis essays open with a paragraph stating the thesis, followed by several paragraphs (often three) supporting the thesis. Each of the supporting points is explicitly tied to the main idea of the thesis. There is a concluding paragraph that ties up the essay, offering a conclusion or perhaps a generalization. Students' understandings of this frame are so specified that many seem to have the goal of writing paragraphs that are precisely three sentences long, a minimum prescribed length for paragraphs in some middle-school and high-school textbooks presenting information to students about how to write effective thesis-type essays. Similarly, students learn that science laboratory reports include (in order) the following: statement of purpose, hypothesis, materials, procedures, results, and conclusions. Once the basic form is mastered, students generate essays consistent with the form (Durst, 1984; Marshall, 1984b).

The positive side of all of this is that students can produce essays of different types. In addition, many students do understand the necessity of revising, especially with respect to longer essays that are developed over a period of time, with good high school writers often first revising to produce a clear meaning, worrying about revisions involving mechanics only near the due date for the essay (Butler-Nalin, 1984). Even so, many students do not revise or do not do so effectively; many high school students have learned skills rather than strategies, formulas that are applied rigidly rather than heuristics that are creatively adapted, expanded on, and applied in new ways in new settings and with new tasks (Applebee, 1984; Durst, 1984; Marshall, 1984a, 1984b). Applebee believes that the rigid use of writing formulas largely reflects ineffective writing instruction in high school.

Writing Instruction

Applebee and Langer clearly subscribe to the plan-write-revise model presented earlier in this chapter. Moreover, they are convinced that effective writing instruction must be scaffolded. Consistent with the Vygotskian principles discussed in Chapter 8, their view of writing instruction is that it should possess the following characteristics (Langer & Applebee, 1987, Chapter 9):

- Students should recognize that they are not simply to obey the instructions presented to them. They need to understand why they are learning a writing process and how it can help them. Instruction must send a message that writing is for students to say what they mean. Writing instruction should permit students to codify their own ideas, with the result that students have a sense of **ownership** about the essays they write.
- The writing tasks should be at an **appropriate level of challenge,** not so easy that no effort is required but not so difficult that they are beyond students even if the students are given teacher support.
- Teacher support should be aimed at making the structure of the writing task clear. Teachers need to convey that the strategies being taught can be used to produce a variety of texts and that the purpose of the instruction is to prepare students to produce texts in the future. Students need to be impressed that the **purpose** of writing instruction is for them to learn how to convey meaning rather than for them to acquire low-level skills (e.g., punctuation, grammar, knowledge of a writing formula that can be applied mechanically).
- Good writing instruction is **collaborative,** with teachers **scaffolding instruction:** They provide the support and assistance needed by a student but no more.
- The goal is **internalization** of the writing strategies taught. What this requires is for the teacher to let go of the student when the student can proceed autonomously. Teachers must understand that they are successful to the degree that they exert less and less control over students.

Unfortunately the writing instruction that Applebee, Langer, and their associates found in schools was far from this ideal. First, most writing was brief and intended to let the teacher know that particular content was learned. Such a situation does little to inspire a sense of ownership. This situation was caused in part by textbooks filled with assignments requiring knowledge of content. A second cause was teachers' concerns with accountability—if writing contains the "right" information, it is easier to defend a grade than if writing is more creative, interpretive, or evaluative. Third, teachers provided little instruction in writing as the creation of meaning, with much attention instead devoted to the mechanics of writing. Fourth, even teachers who taught according to some form of the plan-write-revise model were only partially consistent with the model: Their concern with evaluation led such teachers to emphasize the correctness of information in essays over the creation of a novel writing product (Marshall, 1984-a): That is, the correctness of the final product (e.g., a science laboratory report) was more important than the writing process that produced it.

Why is writing instruction like this? Langer and Applebee (1987, Chapter 9) offered analyses consistent with the realities of contemporary schooling: (1) Plan-write-revise strategies promote in-depth learning (see next subsection). In contrast, the schooling accountability system emphasizes breadth of learning and, in particular at the high school level, emphasizes knowledge of content. The science teacher recognizes that his or her students must know a lot of science facts at the end of the year; whether they can write inventive, reflective laboratory reports or essays about science is not captured by the conventional evaluation system. (2) The easiest way to grade a student essay is to check off the points made that are consistent with points that should have been made in an essay on a particular topic. This approach to grading is consistent with the ongoing accountability system but stifles student ownership of writing. (3) The textbooks on writing are woefully inadequate and not consistent with the modern approaches to writing instruction considered in this chapter. (4) High school teachers are overloaded with work; reading student essays puts a heavy demand on already hectic programs. (5) Many teachers are not good writers themselves with respect to the genres of their discipline.

There are many aspects of contemporary schooling and school life that make it difficult for classrooms to be communities of writing scholars rather than acquirers of information that is to be remembered and will be tested. Langer and Applebee's (1984) clear opinion is that if writing instruction is to improve, "The role of the teacher must shift, from an evaluator of what has already been learned to a collaborator who can help the student accomplish more complicated or sophisticated purposes" (p. 179). The teacher who scaffolds student writers who are trying to create their own meanings does this;

the teacher who evaluates grammar, punctuation, and correctness of content does not.

Learning from Writing

Langer and Applebee are concerned that teachers are too much evaluators of student knowledge and not enough developers of creative writing competence, but this does not mean they are not concerned with learning of content. In particular, Langer and Applebee (1987) reported a series of studies designed to elucidate what is learned when students write in various ways.

High school students in these studies read passages and responded in writing in one of several ways across the three studies: writing answers to study questions, notetaking, writing a a summary of the essay, or constructing a written analysis of the essay. There were control participants in two of the three studies who simply read and studied the same content. Think-aloud data were collected as the participants did the tasks. Learning was measured at various intervals, from immediately after processing of the passage to as long as a month later. A variety of memory and recall measures were taken, from ones tapping recall of specific pieces of information in the text to others requiring recall of "everything you can remember about the passage" to others requiring the construction of a coherent argument summarizing the points made in the reading.

Although not all of the effects were large, there were clear variations in what was remembered and what students could do later as a function of what was written during study. Students who had written essays at study were better able to construct essays on the posttest; students who wrote essays were also slightly better at remembering text content when they were simply asked to recall what was in the essay they had read. More negatively, writing essays tended to reduce memory of some of the specific information in text, although whether posttest questions requiring recall of specific information were answered correctly varied somewhat with how much was written at study: Students who had written longer essays at study or longer answers in response to comprehension questions presented at study remembered slightly more specific pieces of information on the posttest than students who wrote shorter essays or shorter responses to comprehension questions at study.

What Applebee, Langer, and their associates have demonstrated is that writing can affect what is learned in school. In general, this is an extremely important direction in research that requires much more study, for students are often assigned writing tasks intended to increase their learning in a content area. How writing does so and how much learning is affected are not well understood at this point. This is one of several problems that are of great concern to researchers interested in reading and writing connections.

Reading and Writing Connections

That reading and writing instruction now occur together with increasing frequency in school would be more than enough reason to study potential reading and writing connections. Such analyses make sense theoretically as well, however, for example, with respect to consideration of common information processes in reading and writing. Information processing theorists, who believe that individual differences in fundamental processing are responsible for individual differences in many areas of functioning, could produce a great deal of support for their positions if they could identify meaningful relationships between reading and writing that reflect the operation of fundamental processes (e.g., monitoring, active use of strategies). Without a doubt, the most complete review and commentary on potential reading-writing connections was provided by Shanahan and Tierney (1990), both prominent literacy researchers. They have identified three approaches to the study of reading and writing connections.

1. *Reading and writing require common knowledge and share common processes.* According to this perspective, there should be correlations between writing and reading competence because of common components in the two tasks: They both require knowledge of vocabulary, syntax, and understanding of text organization alternatives. Competent reading and writing both require monitoring, predicting and idea generation, revising of thinking, and so on. Consistent with this hypothesis, there are in fact correlations in reading and writing ability, although these tend to be small to moderate in size (i.e., 0.30 to 0.40 with a maximum of 0.60). Because such correlations could be due to the relationship of reading and writing to a third factor

such as general intelligence, the significance of these correlations is not entirely clear. Other evidence of common processes affecting reading and writing simultaneously has been produced in studies in which learning to read better has improved writing *or* learning to write better has promoted reading. Unfortunately, however, Shanahan and Tierney (1990) estimate that such conjoint improvement has been obtained only in 30 percent of the studies in which researchers have looked for simultaneous improvement. Although armchair task analyses of reading and writing suggest that there are connections between reading and writing, such connections have not been easy to demonstrate, and promoting reading through writing instruction and promoting writing through reading instruction are much less certain than proponents of this position would like.

2. *Reading and writing both involve communication skills.* "Writers anticipate the needs of potential readers, and . . . readers use their thinking about authors to enhance their reading comprehension" (Shanahan & Tierney, 1990, pp. 18–19). Some of the most persuasive evidence that communication skills are an important reading and writing connection is that interventions designed to increase writers' awareness of audience needs do seem to improve the quality of writing (Black, 1989; Cohen & Riel, 1989; Greenlee, Hiebert, Bridge, & Winograd, 1986; Schriver, 1986). Another type of evidence supportive of links between literacy and communications comes from think-aloud data generated during reading. When readers experience difficulty understanding a text, they often report attempting to think about the author's intentions, perspectives, and meanings (e.g., Flower, 1987; Tierney, LaZansky, Raphael, & Cohen, 1987). The communications hypothesis would be especially compelling if there were data establishing that learning to think about readers during writing improves reading or learning to think about writer's during reading affects writing. No such data exist at this point.

3. *Reading and writing are used jointly to accomplish some tasks.* If students are asked to take notes, write answers to questions, or construct essays in response to reading, they sometimes learn more (e.g., Marshall, 1987; Newell, 1984;

Newell, Suszynski, & Weingart, 1989), although the exact mechanisms mediating the learning gains are not well understood and may reflect only greater total reading time when written responses to text are required (Shanahan & Tierney, 1990). Such activity does not always lead to greater learning and may in fact reduce learning (e.g., if summary essay writing is required and memory for details in text is later tested). It seems that whether writing during reading aids learning probably depends on what the student must recall or do later: If memory of detail is critical, writing answers to detail questions or notetaking may help a little; if recall of the big ideas of the text is important or using the big ideas of a text to frame an argument is the task the student must do later, more integrative writing in reaction to text that is read helps more (see the earlier discussion of Langer & Applebee, 1987).

Some of the most interesting research on reading and writing together has been conducted at Carnegie-Mellon University, although work on coordination of reading and writing is also being conducted at other institutions as well (e.g., McGinley, 1992; Nash, Schumacher, & Carlson, 1993). Flower and colleagues (Flower et al., 1990) provided book-length coverage of their work on this problem with CMU freshmen. In the CMU studies, students are given several texts about a topic to read with the assignment of constructing an integrative essay of some sort. Although all of the students attempted to get the main ideas of the passages that were read, university students nonetheless differed in their reading strategies: (1) Some students did what Flower et al. (1990) referred to as gist and list. They simply listed the main ideas in the text in preparation for writing. (2) Others were more selective and evaluative, deciding whether the information being processed was true, important, or something they agreed with (i.e., they used the "true, important, I agree" strategy [TIA]). This strategy has a lot of power, providing the reader-writer with ideas that are appealing and worth putting in an essay from the perspective of the reader-writer. The problem, of course, is that the student reader-writer's perspective can predominate rather than the messages that the writers of the text intended or emphasized. (3) The third strategy, the dialogue strategy, involved the student reader-writer comparing the texts being read (i.e., creating a dialogue between the authors of the texts), generating counterexamples to information in text (i.e., debating the ideas in the text), imagining occasions when the point made in the text might hold, and a fourth and extremely complicated form of dialogue: statements synthesizing " . . . two claims by qualifying both or at least putting them into relation with one another." These qualifications were sometimes insights and sometimes counterexamples.

Once the reading was done in Flower et al. (1990), it was time to write the essay. Students differed in how they planned their essays: (1) Some hardly planned at all, simply writing an essay that reflected the ideas they had come up as they gisted and listed, TIAed, or dialogued during reading. (2) Others relied almost exclusively on the ideas generated during reading but were more planful in the sense of carefully classifying and organizing the content. The difficulty with both approaches (1) and (2), however, is that really are simply what Scardamalia and Bereiter (e.g., 1986; Bereiter & Scardamalia, 1987, Chapter 1; see the discussion of knowledge telling by children presented earlier in this chapter) refer to as "knowledge telling" strategies. This is the strategy of an elementary-school student. When more is expected, as it is of university student writers, knowledge telling is not a good strategy. Unfortunately, it was the strategy of choice for the majority of the freshmen in Flower et al.'s (1990) study.

(3) A better approach, used by about 40 percent of the Flower et al. (1990) sample, is to do **constructive planning.** Constructive planners " . . . spent time thinking about not only the content, as did everyone, but about the goals for the paper, about criteria for judging it, about problems in designing it, and/or alternative ways to handle the task. They became reflective, strategic thinkers, looking at their writing as a rhetorical problem and a constructive act. . . . Constructive planning . . . often came as a response to a problem" (p. 240). Yes, the constructive planner uses the knowledge gained from the texts that were read, but the constructive planner tries to go beyond those texts, creating elaborations that permit a more creative essay. One of Flower et al.'s (1990) subjects provided the following protocol, which is representative of constructive planning:

Unless I just restate a lot of this stuff, talk about the fact that, you know, it is important . . . but that's not what they want. They want me to assimilate this, come up with some conclusions, they [should] be related to something. . . . [He rereads his assignment and appears to conceive a new goal.] I guess I'm gonna have to deal with how, how to attack the problem of time management. It sounds good, write this down and attack problem. Yeah! Great! Things I can think of off hand, you got to put in there about. . . . [At this point he begins to review notes, to search the text and to rethink his response. . . . A few minutes later he returns to his plan.]

I guess I can do a little bit more than restate what they have in the text. I can relate to my situation as a college student. It would be easier to relate to a college student! Well, wonderful. (p. 241)

Spivey and King (1989), in another study conducted at Carnegie-Mellon, examined how grade-6, grade-8, grade-10 students write from sources. The students were given three encyclopedia articles on the topic of "rodeo," with the assignment to write a report about rodeos. The most important finding in this study was that although there were some improvements in organization of writing and the resulting texts with increasing grade level, there was a much more striking effect for reading ability, with more able readers planning more and spending more total time writing, with the result better organized and more compelling texts. Writing from multiple sources—a typical student writing activity—is greatly affected by reading ability.

Summary The search for reading and writing process connections, including ones based on communication functions, is an active area of interest for researchers, including both applied researchers and those interested in the most fundamental properties of mind (e.g., its monitoring capacities, strategic tendencies). In many ways, however, the most interesting and challenging reading and writing connection work may be the studies in which the articulation of reading and writing are studied. So many important tasks depend both on understanding and an interpreting text and then conveying our reactions to texts to others. Think about it. A letter arrives that angers you. To react to it intelligently, you must make certain you understand the letter and your interpretation of it, including its emotional effect on you. Then, if you wish to write back, it is important to plan carefully, using the information in the original correspondence as you craft a reply that presents your position in the best possible light. Such cycles of reading and constructing a written response are common in life. They also can be a great consequence. As a student, for example, whether you earn A's or C's on your papers depends greatly on use of constructive planning rather than knowledge telling. Parroting back will not impress many professors. To the extent that the problem has been studied analytically, the evidence supports the conclusion that reading and writing together produces deeper thinking about content than either reading or writing alone (e.g., Tierney, Soter, O'Flahaven, & McGinley, 1989). That even Carnegie-Mellon students (i.e., freshmen at a highly selective university) are sometimes prone to uncreative reading and writing strategies, such as gist and list, and the majority engage in knowledge telling is depressing.

Rose's (1989, Chapter 7) commentaries on his work at the tutorial center at University of California, Los Angeles (UCLA), illustrate that if anything, however, the situation is worse at less selective universities than CMU. Most of the students he worked with at UCLA had done well in beleaguered urban high schools:

> They were the kids who held class offices and saw their names on the honor role; they went out for sports and were involved in drama and music and a variety of civic and religious clubs. If they had trouble with mathematics or English or science, they could depend on the fairness of the system that rewarded effort and involvement: They participated in class discussions, got their work in on time, helped the teacher out, did extra-credit projects. In short, they were good academic citizens, and in some high schools—especially beleaguered ones—that was enough to assure them a B. (p. 172)

Despite succss in their high schools, at UCLA these students end up in remedial courses or receive poor grades in their freshmen work. Their self-esteem suffers—they begin to think that they are stupid. They feel isolated in the university and alienated from it. What is offered currently to these students does little—the remedial skills programs consist of dumping a bunch of strategies on them, without scaffolded instruction (or sensitive instruction of any kind) about how to use the strategies. The inabilities of these students (e.g., not being able to identify the theme of a piece of unfamiliar poetry) are striking in the context of UCLA, where students

are supposed to be able to identify the main themes in sophisticated writing produced by the likes of Jacob Bronowski and Thomas Szasz.

Moreover the traditions of disadvantaged students often make the intellectual tasks of higher education more difficult. For instance, Rose (1989, pp. 183–185) described an immigrant student who had been raised in a family adhering to unquestioning Catholic authority, a background that made it emotionally and intellectually difficult for her to analyze required texts with unorthodox themes at their core. Black English emphasizes elegance, whereas white middle-class English emphasizes precision, with this difference in emphasis definitely favoring well-educated mainstream citizens over citizens who have internalized the best language traditions of their own nonmainstream culture (e.g., Dillard, 1972, Chapter 7). Trying to use the language of the mainstream while learning the advanced content covered in university-level courses puts poor and minority students at great disadvantage. Consider the insights of one teacher about her minority students:

> [Professor X] . . . who taught anthropology at a Negro university . . . analyzed her students' language in comparison to their success in giving the right answers to . . . [essay test] . . . questions. She found . . . that those whose language was most nearly Standard English made the lowest grades. Those whose writing had few or no Non-Standard structures tended to put down very little real anthropological material on the 3-hour written examination—something no more than a page or two . . . the ones who let themselves go grammatically and concentrated on what they wanted to say managed to get in some anthropology, if not much "grammar" by the standards of the average English teacher. Those who struggled with the unfamiliar system of Standard English were unable to concentrate on anything else and thus, succeeded in writing very little (Dillard, 1972, p. 276).

It is difficult even for many good students coming from culturally different backgrounds to be prepared to navigate the requirements of the modern research university, and if they do navigate the many obstacles, it is likely to be more emotionally scarring than for majority students. There is a great need for much additional research on how to increase the reading and writing competence of bright university students who come from backgrounds that do not prepare them for the literacy demands of university study. One reason to conduct such research is that many of these students are within reach—several years of high-quality enrichment might do much to make up for previous educational disadvantages. We conclude this section with commentary on a program of research and development that makes clear that it is possible to devise and disseminate on a large scale cognitive instruction for adolescents and youth that makes conceptual sense and can be validated.

Kansas Strategies Instruction Model

Deshler, Schumaker, and their colleagues at the University of Kansas (Deshler & Schumaker, 1988; Schumaker & Deshler, 1992) have devised reading (e.g., paraphrasing) and writing (e.g., paragraph writing) strategy interventions aimed at improving important academic competencies in high school students, with learning-disabled students the target population for their interventions. We cover the Kansas work here because it provides a model of how to devise, validate, and distribute cognitively based instruction that can promote the literacy of large numbers of secondary students, including their abilities to acquire, store, and communicate important information.

There are five phases in the Kansas curriculum development model, with these occurring roughly in the following order:

1. *Identification phase.* This involved determination of the demands placed on students in school. As part of this effort, the Kansas group spent time in high school settings determining what high school students are asked to do. This information was combined with knowledge of deficiencies of weaker students, such as their memorizing, organizing, reading, and writing problems as documented in the research literature and evident in schools studied by the Kansas group.

2. *Design phase.* Once a performance goal is targeted (e.g., to increase learning-disabled students' abilities to write paragraphs), the literature is searched for information about strategies that may have already been identified in meeting the need. Often there have been. Once a strategy has been identified as profitable to teach, step-by-step instruction is devised, as are methods of measuring whether students are learning the strategy. For example, when the goal was to teach students how to write paragraphs (see Schumaker & Lyerla, 1991), a strategy involving the writing of paragraphs that in-

tegrated topic sentences, detail sentences, and clincher sentences was devised. Explicit descriptions of the strategy were created as were methods of modeling the strategy. Various types of scaffolded practice were designed into the instructional package (i.e., Kansas uses a direct explanation model of strategy instruction). There was clear understanding at the outset about the type of paragraph writing that was expected at the end of the instructional unit and specification about how students could be taught to generalize the paragraph strategy across their school day once they had learned to construct such paragraphs as part of controlled instruction.

3. *Pilot-test phase.* The intervention is tried out with a small number of students, with the researchers attempting to determine whether the instruction is sound, the measures reliable, and the strategy practical for students.

4. *Research phase.* One or several formal research studies are carried out. Typically the research is school based with teachers teaching the strategy package. The strategy may be revised (or abandoned) in light of the data generated in the formal studies. See Schumaker and Deshler (1992) for a review of the research studies supporting their model.

5. *Refinement phase.* The goal is to make the intervention as useful as possible for a number of different settings. Feedback from teachers who have used the intervention is helpful during this phase. Once this phase is completed, the package is ready for widespread dissemination.

There are some exceptionally important features to the research approach used by the Kansas team: (1) The goals of the instruction are socially valid ones (i.e., the strategies meet demands students actually face). (2) Conventionally accepted research designs are used, often the multiple-baseline procedures developed as part of research on behavior modification (see Chapter 7, this volume). (3) The research and development is conducted in school settings. (4) Every effort is made to design instruction that teachers will accept and be enthused about, for without teacher acceptance, there will be no dissemination. (5) The criterion measures are ones tapping valuable outcomes; they are the indicators of school success and failure that are routinely collected in school. For example, the goal is not to produce statistically significant effects but effects that are significant in the lives of the students. Thus, improving grades a little bit can be statistically significant with enough subjects in the research study. That would not be enough. Going from F's to B's on school assignments (e.g., ones involving writing of paragraphs) is the type of shift that the Kansas researchers attempt to produce (and often do produce).

Kansas instruction is not a quick fix, with a new strategy learned over a period of several months. Years of participation are required for students to acquire a repertoire of strategies providing diverse means of acquiring, retaining, and writing about academic content. The instruction is developed by teachers who have received intensive instruction about how to use direct explanations, modeling, and guided practice during the initial acquisition of strategies and as part of teaching for generalization. Teacher training is offered by a national network of trainers, with teachers often participating in such instruction for several years. Because of the concern with learning-disabled secondary students, most of the instruction has been provided by special education teachers. What is exceptionally exciting, however, are successful efforts to teach strategies to junior college and university students as well as minority students (Bulgren, McKnight, Deshler, & Schumaker, 1989; Denton, Seybert, & Franklin, 1988; Moccia, McKnight, Deshler, & Schumaker, 1990; see Schumaker & Deshler, 1992, for a review). Basketball fans might want to note that Deshler and Schumaker do their bit for the Kansas basketball program, which is a perennial contender for national ranking. They teach members of the team how to apply learning strategies in their university courses, providing a valuable source of assistance to student athletes who are often at academic risk but who always need to get the most out of the study time that is available to them during the season (Hock, Deshler, & Schumaker, 1991).

Despite the effort required by teachers to learn the Kansas model and the amount of time required by students to acquire a repertoire of strategies, such instruction is extremely well received by teachers, administrators, parents, and students, with the learning and performance gains that result from the program worth the investment in instructional resources and student efforts. Although reservations about some of the particular validation studies are sometimes expressed, no one could examine the entire body of evidence generated by Deshler,

Schumaker, and their colleagues and not conclude that they have devised important instructional programming that is effective. The completeness of their approach is unprecedented in the history of the design, validation, and implementation of curricula based on scientific analyses. The list of strengths is longer than the list of strengths for any other intervention discussed in this book. Their work is distinguished by (1) careful assessment of students needs; (2) well-informed design of strategies based on extensive knowledge of the cognitive, behavioral, special education, and educational psychology literatures; (3) validations in actual school settings; (4) attention to acceptability issues; (5) design of instructional methods that work to ensure acquisition and increase the likelihood of transfer; (6) design of effective teacher education; and (7) distribution and administration of teacher training across the United States and Canada. As far as the research-based curriculum development community is concerned, the Kansas group is the best of us. The rest of us can learn much from them. Students contemplating careers as curriculum designers should study the Kansas work carefully for guidance about how to devise instruction that works and will be used by the educator community.

For the most part, the need for better reading and writing instruction for adolescents and young adults is great. What the Kansas group teaches us is that it is possible to do research and development that is scientifically credible and has an impact on instruction in the nation. It is particularly important that Deshler, Schumaker, and their colleagues are now working with young adults, because no one has done for young adults what the Kansas researchers have done for adolescents: No one has conducted complete analyses of adult literacy needs that stimulate development of instruction that transforms the lives of low-literate and illiterate adults.

WORD PROCESSING AND ITS EFFECTS ON WRITING

Concomitant with the theoretical revolution in how composing is conceived in terms of higher-order planning, writing, and revising processes rather than lower-level (i.e., sentence and word level) processes, there has been a technological revolution in writing. When Flower and Hayes were generating their first versions of the plan-draft-revise model of writing, most Americans had not heard of word processing, and far fewer had actually word processed. In the 1980s, word processing became a way of life and word processors are now everywhere, including in many elementary classrooms. A number of researchers interested in writing have evaluated the impact of word processing on writing, including student writing.

Cochran-Smith (1991) summarized the available literature on word processing effects in elementary-level classrooms, with her review capturing much of the literature pertaining to older students as well. Some of her most important conclusions included the following:

- Students are positive about word processing and writing in a word processing environment.
- Word processing permits young writers to think about the meaning of what they are writing, with many of the low-level processes (e.g., printing by hand) no longer a focal concern of writing.
- One potential low-level hassle unique to word processing is keyboarding. Although it is slow at first, the evidence is compelling that most children become good enough at keyboarding that they can work with a word processor shortly after being introduced to it. One possibility is that career hunt-and-peckers are being created, but because many people (including ourselves) are extremely efficient at hunting and pecking, this seems not to be an important risk. It is important, however, when students are first introduced to word processing, that they be given time and practice at the keyboard to become familiar with it.
- Word processing makes planning, drafting, and revision a more fluidly recursive process. Because the low-level cost of drafting and revision is eliminated (i.e., labor-intensive writing by hand is eliminated), planning does not need to be as extensive before starting to draft and changing plans in light of the direction an argument is taking is not nearly as big a hassle (i.e., minor adjustments in what was written previously can be dealt with easily on a word processor). Alternatively, however, word processing may interfere with some types of revisions, because it is impossible to hold more than one screen-full in view at a time, whereas with a handwritten copy, it is easy to juxtapose material from the beginning, middle, and end of a piece. (Of course, as we have learned from revising this text—and we suspect many students eventually learn—a great way to revise on a word processing file is with a hard copy of the document being revised in hand.)
- Word processing increases the number of revisions. Cochran-Smith correctly points out that much needs to be learned before coming to conclusions about the desirability of increased revisions in word processing environments. Perhaps people are more planful when they compose with pencil and paper compared with the word processor; often "more" revisions boil down to tiny corrections, many of which are compensations for poor keyboarding skills (i.e., lousy typing).
- Educators and educational researchers are working to devise instruction that increases student awareness of the many revising options permitted by word processors, instruction intended to encourage students through prompts and hints to experience writing as real writers do. Consistent with Vygotskian notions, it would be expected that long-term teacher or word processor prompts about revision possibilities would lead to internalization of the prompts and eventual self-prompting. With a word processor, teachers and students can explore many different ways of modifying text—at a low cost in terms of effort—with students able to experience how good writers often move and alter large sections of text as they juggle bits and pieces of arguments in an attempt to construct a coherent message. The word processor makes it possible for much more realistic instruction in revision to be provided, with a great deal of opportunity for practice that does not include the great efforts involved in completely rewriting a piece or in physically cutting and pasting it to reorder important parts.
- Writing instruction in a word processing environment undoubtedly creates a much different social milieu than is in place when writing is taught with handwritten plans, drafts, and revisions. We need to understand much more about the social dynamics of these alternative situations, the strengths and weaknesses of both. In

addition, it seems likely that teaching in a word processing environment changes as teacher (and student) competency with word processing and computing in general improves. There has been too much attention to the nature of instruction and learning when word processing is first introduced and too little research attention to the nature of writing instruction when teachers and students are computer literate and computer facile.

In short, Cochran-Smith's (1991) review heightens awareness about how instructional theories and technology can interact. The plan-draft-revise conception of writing has evolved at a point in time when a new technology well matched to it was developing. It is clear that writing and writing instruction are different when students are using the word processor than when they are using pencil and paper. Because computer expertise will be so important in the 21st century and classroom computing is rapidly expanding, it seems transparent to us that if a young researcher must choose between studying writing in a word processing environment or a more conventional desk-bound setup, study the young writer working at the computer.

There is much to be learned about how master writers, powerful composing machines, and writing novices interact to stimulate the growth of the young writer, with it transparent that we understand little about what is undoubtedly an exceptionally dynamic instructional situation. Some cognitive theorists (e.g., Bereiter, 1990) conceive of the thinking that goes on in such situations as distributed across people and the machine. Given the emerging interest in such distributed cognition (Chapter 8, this volume; Resnick et al., 1991), studies of writing instruction in computer environments have particularly high potential for informing theory. We are particularly struck by Bereiter's (1990) conception that much of thinking may be highly contextualized such that particular thinking can occur only in particular contexts (i.e., with contextual support), and thus some thinking is modularized (i.e., thinking and context are inseparable, part of a module that is more than is enabled by its parts in interaction). The observation that planning, drafting, and revision is much more fluid and recursive in word processing environments is supportive of the modularization idea—the cognition that is writing is different when a person is in a paper-and-pencil environment with thinking distributed across the person and paper compared with when the same person is in a word processing environment with thinking distributed across the person and the computer.

CONSTRUCTIVIST NATURE OF LITERACY STRATEGIES INSTRUCTION

A criticism of strategy instruction that has been made by some (e.g., Poplin, 1988a, 1988b) is that it is reductionist, stimulating students to copy the processing of others rather than constructing their own approaches to important cognitive tasks, such as reading and writing. We do not concur with these evaluations because of the documentation that strategy instruction done well is student sensitive, stimulating students to experiment with strategies and to construct their own personalized versions of efficient information processing. Adaptation of strategies occurs continually occurring as they are used flexibly in coordination with diverse knowledge to accomplish diverse goals in diverse situations (Harris & Pressley, 1991; Pressley, Harris, & Marks, 1992; for other versions of the perspective that what is taught by the teacher is a beginning point for student construction of knowledge, see Elbers, 1991; Iran-Nejad, 1990; Wittrock, 1992).

None of the strategy instructors considered in Chapters 14 and 15 expect students to carry out mechanically the strategies that are explained and modeled by the teacher. One of the reasons that teaching and practice extend over a long period of time is so that students can explore how the strategies can be flexibly adapted to different tasks, so they can observe how their execution of the strategies is both similar to and different from the strategic efforts of classmates. Moreover, teacher modeling of strategies is certainly not algorithmic. In fact, often it happens on the run, when an academic task calls for it. Such opportunities to model rarely afford "canned" responses but rather require creative application, modification, and combination of strategies.

If the explanations of strategies do not make clear the personalized nature of such processing, the reexplanations offered in light of student difficulties certainly should. Reexplanations and additional modeling invariably require the teacher to model "gerry-rigging" of strategies. These reexplanations are dialogic, with the student and teacher working together to figure out how to apply strategies to a situation that poses difficulty for the student. The teacher is not content until he or she believes the student understands what he or she is doing; that is, the reexplanations are aimed at helping students "figure out" the situation rather than simply directing them about how to make correct responses.

Strategies are not forced on students. Rather, the students are taught procedures that permit them greater success with less effort. Students come to value the strategies because they recognize that strategies are intellectually empowering. Good strategy instruction sends the message that students can control how they do academically, with much gained by creatively applying the cognitive strategies that are taught to them. Good strategy instruction encourages student reflection, permitting powerful tools for reflective "meaning-getting" from texts, creation of reflective stances via writing, and reflective decision making about whether and how to use strategies they know to tackle new situations.

A variety of characteristics of and constraints on human communication abilities make it inevitable that students will construct their understanding of strategies from strategy instruction:

- Teachers' understandings of strategies differ, so their explanations will differ. In addition, any one teacher's approach to a particular strategy will vary from situation to situation.
- In making a good faith attempt to explain a strategy, even experienced, exceptionally competent strategy teachers do not cover a strategy completely or provide exhaustive information about where or when to use the strategy or completely cover all of the benefits of deploying the strategy. Thus, there is always plenty left for the student to figure out. If the teacher's presentation is so deficient that students cannot even begin to understand and apply the strategy, the teacher will be cued by students to provide more input (e.g., reactions such as "huh?" or looks of puzzlement).
- When students ask questions of teachers about the strategies they are attempting to learn, there are always a variety of responses. The teacher who is scaffolding instruction provides enough of a response that students can then begin to make progress on their own in applying and understanding strategies.

Pressley, Harris, and Marks (1992) summarized the inevitability of student construction of knowledge during strategies instruction as follows:

Teacher-student interactions during strategy instruction are not tightly scripted in advance, but rather worked out as instruction proceeds. The good strategy teacher tries to provide instruction about strategies that is clear and can be grasped by students. No matter how well the teacher expresses her or his knowledge of a strategy, the student's understanding of the procedure will differ somewhat from the teacher's conception. The teacher and student will have exchanges throughout the instructional process, with the nature and content of these exchanges determined largely by the student's progress in coming to understand the strategy and how to execute it, as well as the teacher's perceptions of the student's progress. Exactly what is taught and learned during strategy-instructional sequences is a function of many reactions and adjustments during teacher-student exchanges, adjustments that often represent best guesses by the teacher and student about what the other one means or understands. . . . what a student experiences during good strategy instruction and what he or she takes away from the experience varies enormously from student to student and from class to class. Strategies are not rigidly formulated, exacting cognitive rules; rather, they entail personal interpretation. . . . (pp. 15–16)

What we emphasize most here, however, is that when the teaching procedures of those who profess to be constructivist teachers (e.g. Ferreiro, 1985; Petitto, 1985; Pontecorvo & Zucchermaglio, 1990) are analyzed and compared with good strategy instruction, there are remarkable similarities:

- Students interact with teachers attempting to construct understandings for the student, with both agreements and disagreements during these interactions, with the interactions going smoothly sometimes and not so smoothly other times.
- There is group instruction, with peers providing input and feedback to one another.
- Teachers continuously monitor the student's understanding of what is being taught, with additional instruction provided on a personalized, as-needed basis. The better the student's progress, the fewer the reexplanations and the less the remodeling of strategies.
- Dialogues between students and teachers are not scripted.
- Teachers continuously encourage students to apply what they are learning to new situations.
- Individual differences in students' rates of progress are permitted.

- It is clear that teacher explanations and modeling of strategies are intended to be transformed by students; students know that they are not just to mimic the teacher's actions but rather to use the teacher's actions as a starting point for the construction of personalized actions.
- There is great emphasis on learning through understanding. Understanding is the most valued educational outcome.

There is, of course, a difference between instruction provided by professed constructivists and good strategy instructors. Good strategy instructors are much more explicit in their explanations. Even though they expect that students will interpret and adapt the procedures that are explained and demonstrated, the good strategy teachers do offer explicit explanations and demonstrations. Our view is that how learning begins is not what is critical. What counts is that students come to understand the procedures they are learning, coming to know the procedures in ways that permit them to use the procedures flexibly to accomplish goals that are important to students. Our view, consistent with many perspectives on mind (e.g., Piaget, 1970; White, 1959) is that humans inevitably construct understandings from input that is presented to them, that they are highly motivated to do so. The extent to which they are successful in coming to sophisticated understandings depends on the input with which they work, however, with exceptional understanding more likely with high-quality instruction that stimulates student construction. As Resnick (1987) concluded, good instruction provides ". . . the 'material' upon which constructive mental processes work" (p. 47). Good strategy instructors provide the best explanations they can and then encourage their students to take it from there, providing additional assistance as they can as students work it out. Our view, along with others (e.g., Graham & Perry, 1993), is that it is exceptionally important to understand more about students' knowledge when they are first beginning to learn something— how the beginnings of understanding motivate students to work on constructing additional understanding. (See Moshman, 1982, for an exceptionally lucid discussion of the range of instruction that is constructivist, from discovery approaches to explicit instruction models that lead students to construct their own understandings.)

We provide this input about the constructivist nature of strategy instruction at this point in the book because we believe that enough information about strategy instruction has been provided by now to permit understanding of our perspective on the constructivist nature of strategy instruction. From this point on, additional allusions will be made to the constructivist perspective. One of the most irritating characteristics of constructivist educators is that the constructivist nature of the instruction they provide is emphasized repeatedly, overshadowing many other properties of effective instruction. Although we are constructivists, our recognition that many other factors play an important role in intellectual advancement compels us not to provide obsessive discussions of the constructivist nature of the instruction considered in this book. Still, much of it is constructivist, and readers should keep that in mind as they consider what follows and reconsider material covered earlier.

CONCLUDING COMMENTS

Meaning construction is the emphasis in contemporary writing instruction. How to teach writing so that writers can communicate ideas that are important to them is the overarching question in writing instructional research. Understanding how good writers write has done much to stimulate the development of such instruction. Just as good reading is an instance of good problem solving, good writing is good problem solving. Just as with reading, writing can be understood in terms of strategies, metacognition, knowledge, motivation, capacity, and constructive social interactions. Just as with effective reading instruction, effective writing instruction is long term, lasting years. Just as direct explanation followed by scaffolding was a sound approach to reading instruction, it is also a sound approach to writing instruction.

The historical tendency to treat reading and writing separately is yielding to the study of reading and writing connections and instruction designed to foster reading and writing connections. Just as literacy is both reading and writing, we expect that much of the future research on literacy will capture reading and writing simultaneously. Because literacy is essential to learning in content areas, there is also a breaking down of historically prominent barriers between reading instruction and teaching in the content areas, with some of these new directions touched on in the chapters on math and science education in this book.

In closing, we emphasize that the high quality literacy instruction featured in Chapters 14 and 15 is aimed at teaching strategies well matched to the demands of literacy tasks: For example, comprehension strategies that enhance understanding and memory of text; also, writing strategies that increase the likelihood that compositions are comprehensible. The high-quality strategy instruction featured in these chapters is intensive and long-term, permitting many opportunities for students to learn when and where to use the strategies they are learning and permitting many opportunities for students to practice adapting strategies to new situations. High-quality literacy instruction is designed to make reading and writing enjoyable experiences for students, experiences that make sense to students. The goal is not to get the "right" interpretation from text but to process and build one's own meaning; the goal is not to produce an essay that is just "good English" but rather an essay that says something important, with mechanics considered after the meaning is established. High-quality literacy instruction undoubtedly builds other knowledge as well. Students are reading excellent texts with important messages, messages that are more likely to be understood and reflected on because of the strategy instruction. When students write, they are often writing about important content; information used to create new texts is going to be thought about in a "deep" fashion, increasing the likelihood that the student writer will make connections to prior knowledge. Good literacy instruction enhances the good information processing that is the focus of this book, increasing knowledge of strategies, metacognitive understandings, other knowledge, and important motivational beliefs about what counts in school and in literacy. Such instruction deserves the research attention of the next generation of educational researchers, such as some of the readers of this text, for this already rich instruction has much potential for extension as it continues to be translated into educational practice.

Part
5

Assessment and Individual Differences

16

Traditional Assessments and Conceptualizations of Intelligence and Academic Competence

Much of this book is about individual differences and how differences affect competency: People perform differently on memory and comprehension tasks depending on the strategies they know and use; differences in metacognition predict differences in strategy use; knowledge differences between experts and novices influence problem solving; and differences in motivational beliefs affect the willingness to attempt academic tasks. Our view is that future study of individual differences will be attuned to the types of differences highlighted in this book. Traditionally, however, the term "individual differences" in psychology has been used most often to refer to differences in competencies tapped by psychometric instruments, such as traditional intelligence tests.

Issues of assessment and individual differences are often seen as dull and far removed from education by many students in educational psychology courses. One of the best ways to dispel these impressions is to cover an educational assessment students know well because they have experienced it, one that has made a difference in their lives. The two tests covered in the next section are important assessments faced by readers of this book—tests that are often feared and despised!

HIGHER EDUCATION ADMISSIONS TESTS

Admissions to college or graduate school invariably involve standardized testing. Students often do not understand well the entrance examinations they are asked to take, however. (Perhaps even more distressing is that many people involved in the admissions decision process do not either.) Most students new to educational psychology find the information that follows to be enlightening.

Scholastic Aptitude Test

Many readers of this book will have taken the Scholastic Aptitude Test (SAT). (Others will have taken the American College Test [ACT], which in many ways in similar in design to the SAT.) The SAT is usually taken in the junior year of high school or early in the senior year. There are typically five sections on the test, divided between math and verbal sections. The math section includes traditional high school mathematics problems. The verbal section taps knowledge of vocabulary (e.g., verbal analogies) and comprehension (i.e., reading passages and answering questions about the meaning of texts). Both the verbal and math scores can range from 200 to 800. An excellent review of the SAT, its history, and the controversies surrounding it was provided by Hanford (1991), a former President of the College Entrance Examination Board, which administers the SAT. Much of what follows about the SAT is covered in Hanford's autobiography, which we recommend for students who wish an insider's understanding of academic admissions tests.

In the late 19th century, only some colleges had admissions tests. Each college that had a test created its own test. The problem this created for secondary schools was enormous as they attempted to prepare their students for admissions to many different colleges with different expectations and admissions criteria. In 1900, a group of U.S. East Coast colleges attempted to solve the problem by establishing the College Entrance Examination Board at Columbia University. At first, the College Board administered essay examinations, tapping a prescribed high school curriculum. Thus, two benefits of the early tests were that students could apply to more than one school without taking multiple admissions tests and what would be tested became more predictable.

The test evolved throughout the 20th century. During World War I, the U.S. Army conducted research on an intelligence test (the Army Alpha Test), which involved multiple-choice questions. Brigham of Princeton University applied this new multiple-choice approach to the SAT. At about the same time, there was a movement away from a curriculum-based assessment to testing of general verbal and math abilities that might be expected to develop given a variety of high school curricula. Multiple-choice SAT testing of general math and verbal abilities was in place by the mid-1920s—that is, the SAT began to resemble the test administered today.

In those days, the administrators of the test could have reverted back to essay examinations if the multiple-choice format had proved unsatisfactory, for only a select group of students attempted to enter college. As the century progressed, more and more students would aspire to college, so that more than 2 million students take the SAT annually. Hanford estimated that if essay examinations were administered today, the SAT would have to rent out Madison Square Garden to seat all of the readers employed to correct it! A computer-scored, objective test is the only option when so many students are tested at once. Thus, a third advantage of the SAT is that it can be administered economically to many

students, with quick reporting of results (usually 1 to 2 months after the testing date).

A fourth advantage is that an SAT score until 1994 meant the same as a SAT score from the 1950s, 1960s, 1970s, and 1980s. The meaning of a SAT score remained constant from 1941 to 1994. First, the higher a score was on the 200 to 800 scale, the better the score was. Second, a score of 500 in 1991 meant the same as it did 50 years ago—the student was exactly in the middle of the range of 1941 performances. A 600 placed the student at about the 84th percentile of the 1941 distribution of performances. A 700 score meant that 98% of the 1941 sample performed more poorly than the 1990s student in question. That is, SAT scores were figured for most of the past 50 plus years with respect to how a student performed relative to the 1941 sample. Because of declines in overall performance on the SAT, however, a 500 score in 1991 was well above the average for students taking the test in the 1990s. We emphasize this latter point because of many high school counselors we have encountered who believe that 500 was the mean score on the SAT and thus send signals to 500-scoring students that they have average SAT scores. In 1991, the mean verbal SAT score was 422 and the mean math score was 474 (*Chronicle of Higher Education,* 26 August 1991, p. 9). A 500 score on either the verbal or math scale was above average relative to the scores of the current cohort of students. In part because of this problem, in 1994 500 was set as the mean SAT score. Thus, from now on a 500 performance is an average performance.

A fifth advantage of the SAT is that the test has excellent psychometric properties. First, the test is **reliable.** What that means is that if a student takes one form of the test today and a second form of it tomorrow, there is a good chance that the scores for the two sittings will be within 30 points of one another (actually about a two in three chance). Indeed, SAT scores are often thought of and expressed as ranges, so that a score of 470 means that there is a good chance (two in three) that the student's **true score** is in the 440 to 500 range.

In addition, the SAT is a **valid** predictor of academic performance in college. In fact, it predicts about as well as high school grades. When high school grades and SAT scores are used together in statistical formulas for predicting grades, prediction is better than when either is used alone—that is, even when high school grades are already taken into account, the SAT improves the prediction of college grades. Many colleges have conducted studies of how well high school grades and SAT scores predict success at their institutions, with the consensual conclusion that the SAT is useful in deciding who might do well at a given college and who is likely to do poorly. To be certain, such predictions are not perfect. For example, collapsing across 685 colleges, the combined verbal and math SAT score correlates 0.42 with freshmen grades, which is roughly comparable to the 0.48 correlation between high school grades and freshmen grades. When SATs and high school grades are combined, they predict freshmen grades with a correlation of 0.55 (Anastasi, 1988, Chapter 11). Although not perfect, admissions tests and high school grades are the best predictors available.

One exceptionally interesting strength of the test is how well it predicts exceptionally talented people. If the test is given to grade-7 and grade-8 students, those scoring in the top quarter of 1 percent of the population taking the math test (i.e., the absolute top scorers on the test) do much better in high school, college, and graduate school than those who are in the top 1 percent of test takers but not in the top quarter of 1 percent of the distribution (Benbow, 1992).

With so many advantages, what is the down side of the SAT? First, there has been an overall decline in absolute performance in recent years, with some believing the decline reflects the increasing irrelevancy of the SAT. There are more than 80 possible alternative explanations for the decline, however, with two of the most likely of these being the following: The College Board believes much of the decline is due to a broadening of the range of people taking the test, a conclusion based on careful study of the populations of students taking the test between 1963 and 1977 (Donlon, 1984; Turnbull, 1985; Wirtz, 1977). The decline also may reflect a shift in the courses students take in high school. A natural reaction is that perhaps the test should be renormed with samples more typical of today's test takers and college aspirants and be updated to be more congruent with contemporary curricula rather than the curricula in place in the 1940s.

A second negative for the SAT is that some groups do better on the test than do other groups. Whites do better than minorities; men do better than women. For example, whites enjoyed at least a 50-point advantage on both verbal and math SATs in 1991 over American Indians, blacks, Mexican-Americans, Puerto Ricans, and Hispanics (*Chronicle*

of Higher Education, 26 August 1992, p. 9). One possibility is that this reflects bias in the test. The College Board points out in its defense that the SAT is a good predictor of college success for all groups, however (see Reynolds & Kaiser, 1990a, 1990b, for a brief review of the relevant issues and literature). That is, when only blacks are considered, those blacks who score better on the SAT are more likely to do well in college than blacks who score poorly. That is, the test is a valid predictor of college success for blacks just as it is a valid predictor of college success for whites. The College Board also discourages the use of its test data in ways that are blatantly discriminatory—for example, it opposed a New York State Regents plan that provided scholarships based on SAT scores because such a policy would discriminate against women and minorities.

A third negative aspect perceived by some is that the test does not provide enough of a boost in predictability over high school test scores to justify its expense. Countering this claim are arguments that standardized tests are great equalizers. Every college "knows" certain high schools better than others because of proximity or a long history of alumni from the high school proceeding to the college. It is easy to prove biases toward particular high schools and toward particular groups of people by some colleges. The SAT is the one hurdle faced by all applicants, giving the student from a backwoods or distant high school a chance to distinguish himself or herself (see Jensen, 1981, Chapter 1). In addition, the SAT is used by some national scholarship agencies to identify talented youth. Many such youth would be overlooked in other types of talent searches.

Even though the SAT is a psychometrically sophisticated instrument (i.e., it is reliable and valid), it is subject to many of the same criticisms as other tests, most notably bias against particular groups of people. That it is predictive of college outcomes for all groups is what saves it. One interesting direction in higher-education research is to determine whether the strategy-use perspective detailed in this book is more predictive of college success than tests such as the SAT. For example, Britton and Tesser (1991) examined whether reported use of study time management strategies (i.e., responses to a questionnaire tapping whether students plan their study time, make good use of available study time, and make long-range plans to complete papers and prepare for examinations) predicted overall success in college as reflected by grade-point averages.

Consistent with the perspective in this book that strategies are an important determinant of academic success, strategic study time management accounted for four times as much variance in predicting college success as did the SAT. Although the SAT is a benchmark, it is a benchmark that may be surpassed in predictive validity as more sophisticated measures of strategic engagement in college are developed.

We cannot leave our discussion of the SAT without commenting on a frequent question posed to us—whether it is possible to improve SAT scores through specific educational experiences, such as taking widely advertised test-preparation courses. Short-term courses produce only small effects (Becker, 1990). Courses that involve long-term participation have greater effects. The best preparation for SAT tests, however, is taking a demanding curriculum throughout the high school years (Messick & Jungeblut, 1981).

Graduate Record Examination

The General section of the Graduate Record Examination (GRE) includes math and verbal sections (see Anastasi, 1988, Chapter 11). Although more advanced than the corresponding SAT sections, there is a great similarity between the GRE and SAT, including with respect to scoring. In addition to the General sections, there are Subject Tests for many areas of university study (e.g., psychology, history, mathematics, education).

The GRE is scored with reference to a 1952 sample of seniors at 11 colleges. Thus a score of 500 means that the test taker would have been in the middle of the 1952 sample. The test is reliable with 0.90 correlations between scores obtained at different administrations of the test. In general, GRE scores are slightly better predictors of graduate school performance than is undergraduate grade point average, although best prediction of graduate school performance is obtained by statistically combining GRE scores and undergraduate grades. Readers of this book enrolled in graduate study in psychology might be interested that the correlation between the GRE Psychology Subject Test and the likelihood of completing the Ph.D. in psychology is 0.34. That is, there is a modest but positive relationship between the Subject Test score and making it through graduate school (Anastasi, 1988). What is amazing about the SAT and GRE tests is that 3-hour assessments predict future educational achievement almost as well as the years of grades summarized on high school and undergraduate transcripts.

Do not fear if all of the ideas covered in this section are not yet clear. The most important concepts introduced here will be expanded on in the next section, with the SAT and GRE examples referred to in the next section in order to provide readers with somewhat familiar examples.

PSYCHOMETRIC QUALITIES OF TESTS

A first requirement of a test is that it be **reliable;** without reliability, it cannot possibly be **valid.** Reliability and validity are concepts that must be understood by all students of educational psychology. Only tests that are reliable and valid for the purpose of the tester should be administered. The SAT has survived so long and is used so widely largely because it is extremely reliable and it validly measures what admissions committees are interested in determining—the likelihood of academic success in college (i.e., it is valid). What follows is a distillation of the most important ideas regarding reliability and validity found in most leading psychometric textbooks (e.g., Anastasi, 1988; Cronbach, 1990; Jensen, 1980; Nunnally, 1978; Sattler, 1992). For those students desiring more information, an outstanding low-cost publication providing definitive professional-level information about test construction is the *Standards for Educational and Psychological Testing* (American Psychological Association, 1985). An interesting historical perspective on test validity is provided by Geisenger (1992b).

Reliability

To understand reliability, it is essential to understand that any **observed score** on a test can be decomposed into two scores, the **true score** and **error.** The following equation summarizes this relationship: **observed score = true score + error.**

Error represents the part of the score that is due to irrelevant and chance factors. If the same test could be administered to a person many times with each testing independent of the other (i.e., under the impossible constraint that taking a test on one occasion would not affect test performance on a second occasion), the errors would cancel each other out over the many test administrations so that the mean score would reflect the subject's true score for the test. On any single testing occasion, however, the observed score includes error, so that on some occasions performance is higher than it typically would be, and on other occasions, it is lower than it typically would be.

Consider the following example. Suppose that you consider 10 games of a baseball player's batting performance, using each day's performance as an estimate (i.e., a test) of batting average, with batting average for any one day = number of hits on that day/number of at bats on that day):

Game 1: 2 hits for 5 at bats: Day's average = 0.400: error = −0.150

Game 2: 1 hit for 6 at bats: Day's average = 0.167: error = −0.083

Game 3: 0 hits for 5 at bats: Day's average = 0.000: error = −0.250

Game 4: 3 hits for 5 at bats: Day's average = 0.600: error = +0.350

Game 5: 1 hit for 5 at bats: Day's average = 0.200: error = −0.050

Game 6: 0 hits for 5 at bats: Day's average = 0.000: error = −0.250

Game 7: 2 hits for 5 at bats: Day's average = 0.400: error = +0.150

Game 8: 2 hits for 5 at bats: Day's average = 0.400: error = +0.150

Game 9: 0 hits for 5 at bats: Day's average = 0.000: error = −0.250

Game 10: 1 hit for 2 at bats: Day's average = 0.500: error = +0.250

Overall: 12 hits for 48 at bats: 10-game average = 0.250

The best estimate of true score (i.e., the player's real batting average) in this case would be the average over many games (e.g., 10 games), which is 0.250 for the example. With that estimate of true score, it is possible to determine the error for each day, which is the difference between a day's average and the overall average (e.g., for game 8, 0.400 − 0.250 = +0.150). Note that the "errors" cancel each other out in that they add up to 0 over the 10 games.

Suppose that you have a large number of people taking a test. Their observed scores will vary, which can be expressed as a quantity known as the **observed score variance.** True scores and error scores also vary between individuals, so that there is also **true score variance** and **error variance,** with the following relationship holding: **observed score variance = true score variance + error variance.** The re-

liability of a test is then defined as the following: **reliability = true score variance/observed score variance,** which can be expanded as follows: **reliability = true score variance/(true score variance + error variance).**

What should be obvious from this final equation is that reliability varies inversely with error. That is, the greater the error, the less the reliability. Thus, to the extent that how well a batter hits on any given day depends on other factors besides batting ability—for example, the specific pitcher, the opposing team, the particular ball park, the weather, and game time (i.e., day or night)—the greater the error and the less reliable is day-to-day performance. For example, if all 10 games used to construct a batting average could be played against the same opponent who fielded the same pitcher every game and played the game in the same park beginning at one o'clock on sunny afternoons, there would be less variability in the daily averages than if all of these factors vary from game to game. Thus, one way to increase the reliability of a test is to do all possible to hold testing conditions constant for all people taking the test. Tests that have high reliability only when all conditions are equal have an important shortcoming, however: We cannot know if the test would be reliable or valid if another set of conditions held. Even so, the reliabilities of many tests are tied to specific conditions. Thus, SAT and GRE reliabilities were calculated with group administration of the tests; particular time constraints holding; and students not permitted to interact with one another or consult notes or open textbooks. If a student took the SAT with notes and open books, it would be inappropriate to infer that the published reliability and validity information would hold under the new circumstances.

Because an observed score is not equal to a true score, many psychometricians have adopted the practice of providing a **confidence band** instead of a single score. This confidence band specifies a range of scores such that there is a two-thirds likelihood that the true score is in the confidence band. To calculate the confidence band, it is necessary to have the student's observed score, the standard deviation for the test, and the reliability of the test (r) defined by the following formula:

confidence band = observed score ± [Standard deviation × $\sqrt{1 - \text{reliability}^2}$

Note that the greater the reliability, the narrower the confidence band. That is, the greater the reliability, the more likely it is that the observed score is close to the true score. Think back to the SAT example. Recall that the confidence band for that test was the observed score ± 30 points. With a little algebra, it is easy to derive the reliability of the SAT test because it is known that both the verbal and math subscales have standard deviations of 100:

$$\text{observed score} \pm 30 = \text{observed score} \pm [100 \times \sqrt{1 - \text{reliability}^2}]$$
$$30 = 100 \times \sqrt{1 - \text{reliability}^2}$$
$$0.3 = \sqrt{1 - \text{reliability}^2}$$
$$(0.3)^2 = 1 - \text{reliability}^2$$
$$\text{reliability}^2 = 0.91$$
$$\text{reliability} = 0.95$$

(Because the College Board rounds, this estimate of 0.95 is bit high. A fairer estimate of the reliability of the SAT is about 0.90 or perhaps a little higher, depending on the method used to calculate the reliability [Donlon, 1984].)

In actual practice, how is reliability determined? A complete discussion of this topic is worthy of an entire book itself. What follows is a distillation of the best thinking on the topic with respect to the educational assessments that are common in schools (e.g., SAT, IQ, achievement tests).

One method of determining a test's reliability is simply to administer the same test twice, with the correlation in the scores between the two testings defined as reliability using this **test-retest** method. There are a number of problems with this method, however. One is that the reliability will differ depending on the retest interval, with reliabilities generally greater for retests closer in time. Often, lower correlations at greater intervals are due to factors other than chance variation, for example, changes in rank orderings between people taking the test because of different rates of development. Thus, the longer the interval, the less a test-retest correlation provides reliability information alone. For this reason, if the test-retest method is used to estimate reliability, it is essential that the interval between testings be specified. A second problem with test-retest is that performance often improves from the first to the second testing session because of practice taking the test the first time. Even without the practice effect, with a short retention interval, people remember the answers they gave previously. The test-retest reliability estimate will be inflated to the extent that answers are given from memory on the second test.

Alternate-forms reliability can be assessed when there are multiple forms of a test, such as with the SAT and GRE examinations. People are assessed with two forms of the measurement. The correlation between performances on one form of the test and the other form is the reliability for the test. As with test-retest reliability, the correlation can be affected by the length of time between the two testings, so it is important to specify this interval when reporting alternate-forms reliability. The likelihood of high alternative forms reliability is increased the more the alternative forms of a test are really parallel. If the alternative forms cover the same content with the same number of items for each topic covered by the test and with care taken to ensure that items covering particular contents are roughly equal in difficulty, there is reason to be optimistic of high alternate-forms reliability. The likelihood of high alternate-forms reliability also is increased if the two forms of the test are taken close in time (e.g., one form today, the other tomorrow), the directions and examples are comparable, and the testing settings are similar or identical.

Estimates of the reliability of a test are even possible if only one form of a test is available, a form that is administered only once. An historically prominent approach was to calculate the **split-half reliability.** A test was literally split in half using this method, for example, constructing scores based on the odd items and the even items on the test. The correlation between the half-test scores was the estimate of reliability. The problem with this approach is that the estimate of reliability will vary depending on how the items are split, so in most cases the correlation between odd-even halves would differ from a correlation based on halves produced by randomly assigning items to half-test scores. Cronbach (1951) proposed a solution: **coefficient alpha,** which is the mean of all possible split-half reliabilities. A variation of the procedure, the **Kuder-Richardson 20 formula** (Kuder & Richardson, 1937), can be used if all items on the test can be scored as either right or wrong. Although the formulas for these methods are presented in all psychometrics texts, in practice, most people generate them using computer programs, with these reliability indices available on most commercially produced advanced statistics packages. The point we emphasize here is that reliability of a test can be calculated even if only one version of the test exists.

Heteroscedasticity and Homoscedasticity   The reliability of some tests also varies depending where on the scale the respondent falls. Thus, for the SAT (Hanford, 1991), the reliability for the midrange of the scale (i.e., 400–700) is greater than the reliability for the lower end of the scale (i.e., 200–400) or the upper end of the scale (i.e., 700–800). Indeed, the test was designed to have this characteristic—known as **heteroscedasticity,** which contrasts with **homoscedasticity** (i.e., equal reliability at all parts of the scale). Such heteroscedasticity is acceptable for the SAT because most students taking the test are in the middle range of the scale. The way that this is accomplished is by having many more items that are moderate in difficulty than items that are very easy or very difficult. Thus, for students scoring over 700, the only items that discriminate between them are the few difficult items because 700+ students would correctly respond to all or most moderate and easy items. With only a few discriminating items, chance factors have less opportunity to equal out, with the result that a score of 750 is not as reliably different from a score of 720 as is a score of 550 from 520. At the lower end of the scale, the least-able students will do no better than chance on the moderate and difficult items, so the only basis for discriminating between the students in the 200 to 400 range will be the relatively few easy items.

Length of Test   This discussion of heteroscedasticity makes salient a test characteristic that greatly influences the reliability of a test. In general, the longer a test, the more reliable it is. In general, if the reliability of a test is known, the reliability of increasing a test by a factor b can be determined with the following formula (Nunnally, 1978, Chapter 7): **reliability$_{longer\ test}$ = (b × reliability)/(1 + [(b − 1) × reliability]).** For example, if the reliability of a test is 0.80 and it is doubled in length, the reliability of the new, longer test would be 0.89. If the reliability of a test is 0.80 and it is tripled in length, the reliability increases to 0.92. In providing this formula, we recognize, however, that often people want to shorten a test rather than lengthen it. For example, in educational research, participant time is often precious, so an hour long vocabulary test might not be acceptable given time constraints. Reducing the test to 15 minutes by giving only one-fourth of the items might better fit the available research time with each participant. If the original test had a reliability of 0.90, the shortened test would have a reliability of 0.69, which is lower than many psychometricians would consider acceptable. If participants took half of the original vocabulary test, however, the reliability of the vocabulary measure would be 0.82. The extra 15 minutes of testing might well be worth the gain in reliability in this case.

Although exact guidance on acceptable reliabilities is difficult to provide, in general, reliabilities above 0.70 are viewed as adequate for many purposes. One important factor that educational researchers should keep in mind is that if a test is being used as a dependent variable in a study, it is more difficult to produce statistically significant results with an unreliable compared with a reliable instrument. Think back to Chapter 1. The error terms in test statistics such as the t test are constructed based on within-cell variability. Such variability is higher for unreliable compared with reliable assessments because this variability largely reflects measurement error. When conducting a study with relatively few subjects (e.g., five) per condition, it is especially important to make certain that tests used in the study are reliable in order to have a good chance of detecting a significant effect. Thus, if we were conducting a study of vocabulary knowledge with five subjects per condition, we would do everything we possibly could to have participants take the full hour test with the 0.90 reliability. If we had 100 subjects per condition in the same study, the 15-minute test would be more acceptable.

Ceiling or Floor Effects   If the test is so easy that many people get everything right or so difficult that few people get anything right, the reliability of the test will be low because there will be little variability in the test scores. In general, a good test produces a range of performance, with few people (if any) scoring zero (i.e., on the floor of the scale) or achieving a perfect score (i.e., at the ceiling of the scale).

Other Factors That Reduce the Reliability of Tests   Jensen (1980, Chapter 7) generated our favorite list of ways to increase the unreliability of a test. (Of course, to make a test more reliable, do the converse.) Here are some of the more useful points made by Jensen:

- The more subjective the scoring of the test items, the lower the reliability.

- Restrict the ability range of people taking the test, and the reliability of the test goes down. The wider the range of abilities taking the test, the greater the reliability.
- If some questions on the test suggest the answers to other questions, the reliability of the test will be lowered.
- If the test is taken by people with similar backgrounds (other things being equal), reliability will be higher than if the test is given to people with diverse backgrounds.
- Tricky questions reduce the reliability of a test.
- Poorly worded questions reduce the reliability of a test.
- Poor directions reduce the reliability of a test.
- If the people taking the test are tired, anxious, excited, sick, or do not care about the test, reliability will be lowered.

Generalizability Theory Cronbach and colleagues (e.g., Cronbach, Gleser, Nanda, & Rajaratman, 1972; for a readable introduction of the theory, see Shavelson & Webb, 1991) have adopted a different stance with respect to reliability than the traditional approach just covered here. **Generalizability theory** rejects the idea that a person taking a test could have a single true score or that there is some single reliability coefficient that reflects the dependability of the test. According to generalizability theory, what traditional psychometricians consider error is not really error at all. Rather, when a test is given, who gives it, where it occurs, and so on determine test scores in a systematic fashion. What traditional psychometricians do is ignore these systematic sources of variability in test scores, sweeping them under the rug of error variance, assuming that the effects of these factors are random rather than systematic. The big problem, of course, is that users of tests are often interested in its suitability as a function of when the test is given (e.g., at grade 1 or grade 2), who gives it (e.g., a same-race examiner as the test taker or a different-race examiner than the test taker), and where it occurs (e.g., in a classroom group or in the guidance counselor's office with individual administration). A generalizability study of a test attempts to measure how various important factors may affect a test score and the reliability of the test. Although generalizability studies have not been conducted for many tests, largely because of the demanding data collection and formidable mathematics involved in such studies, students of educational psychology should realize that this alternative approach to assessing a test's psychometric characteristics exists.

Although traditional psychometricians have not embraced generalizability theory, they are aware that the reliability of tests often varies with the sample of test respondents. For example, IQ assessments with preschool children usually are not as reliable as IQ assessments with adults. For many important tests, there are norms for different populations (e.g., grade-level norms). When these exist, the psychometric characteristics of the test for the target population should be what is considered in deciding whether to use a test rather than across-population statistics.

Summary Tests that are not reliable cannot be trusted. An unreliable measure produces different scores today and tomorrow. Thus the primary indicator of the trustworthiness of an assessment instrument is whether it is reliable. Although there are a variety of methods of assessing reliability, we encounter alternate-forms and Cronbach's alpha more than others because these approaches have fewer problems than other approaches.

Understanding principles of reliability can aid the educator in many ways. For example, every teacher must construct tests. One principle that emerges from reliability theory is that longer tests are better. A corollary is that extremely short tests reveal nothing dependable. Thus, we recall "pop quizzes" in school, sometimes consisting of as few as one question. Suppose that the pop quizzer's regular 50-item examinations were highly reliable (i.e., 0.90). What would be the reliability of a one-question pop quiz?: Approximately 0.15. A test with such low reliability inspires no confidence. We urge students to study carefully the list of factors affecting reliability. Jensen's list in particular provides excellent guidelines about how not to make up tests.

The reliability of a measurement is not enough, however. The measurement must also be valid for its purpose. Thus, although we can measure the circumferences of children's heads with high reliability, head circumference is not a valid measure of intelligence (see Gould, 1981), with even proponents of such measurement able to produce only low correlations between head girth and intelligence (e.g., Rushton, 1992). We will make the case in the next subsection, however, that a measurement can be no more valid than it is reliable, so issues of validity and reliability must be considered simultaneously by test developers.

Validity

Does this assessment measure what it is supposed to measure? That is the main validity question. More exacting validity questions are posed, however, depending somewhat on the nature of the characteristic being assessed. The various ways that validity can be construed are considered briefly in the three subsections that follow. For readers who wish an expansive discussion of contemporary perspectives on test validity, see Shephard (1993).

Content Validity   Does this test cover the content it is supposed to cover? Suppose we want to devise a test of high school mathematics achievement. What should our test include? A content-valid assessment would include items from general mathematics, algebra, geometry, trigonometry, and calculus. Depending on the test's purpose, the proportions of such items might vary. Thus, if the desire was to do a good job of discriminating whether students had obtained the most basic numerical competencies required of citizens, the test might consist entirely of general math items. If the test is to decide who should be selected as a finalist for scholarship consideration in mathematics, there would be a much greater proportion of calculus and trigonometry items than general math items; challenging algebra and geometry problems might also be included on such a test.

When devising an educational achievement test, content validity is often a paramount concern. Thus, when test developers are devising a subject area test to assess knowledge in some undergraduate major area (e.g., GRE in psychology), they first plan carefully about what should be covered and in what proportions. Thus, the test developers might lay out all of the subfields of psychology that they wish to cover, such as experimental, social, clinical, physiological, statistics, educational, and so on. Then they decide the proportions of items for each subfield, using some conception about which areas deserve emphasis relative to others (e.g., areas that would be covered by all psychology majors would receive more emphasis than completely elective areas). Within a subfield (e.g., educational psychology), additional decisions are made about what topics to cover (e.g., theories about learning, assessment and individual differences, motivation), with the pro-

portions of items for each of these topics decided based on the centrality of the topic to the subdiscipline (e.g., for educational psychology, many more items about cognitive theories than personality).

If a test developer is planful, there is no excuse for not achieving content validity. All that is required is laying out what topics should be covered by a test and in what proportions.

A related form of validity is **face validity:** Does this test look like it measures what it is supposed to measure? Often, if people are to be cooperative in taking a test, the test must seem to measure what it is purported to measure. We recall from our student days the frustrations of some fellow graduate students as they attempted to have older adults perform Piagetian concrete operational tasks (e.g., deciding whether the weight of a ball of clay is the same when shaped like a ball and when reshaped as a pancake). The hypothesis was that some older adults "lost" some of their operational competence with advanced age. The problem for these researchers was that many adults refused to be tested on a childish task involving the stuff of child's play—clay. They found incredible that such tasks could be tapping logical competence. This was a problem of face validity.

Criterion Validity   Does this test make the discriminations it is supposed to make? For example, does the SAT discriminate between students who will be successful in college and those who will not be successful? It does (as discussed earlier in this chapter): There is a positive correlation between SAT performance and grades in college. When the criterion is prediction into the future, as it is when the SAT is used to predict college grades, the criterion-related validity is referred to as **predictive validity.** When both a measure and its criterion can be collected close in time, criterion-related validity is sometimes referred to as **concurrent validity.**

At this point, it is possible to explain exactly, in psychometric terms, why the reliability of a measure limits the validity of the measure. First, the correlation between a test and its criterion is its **validity coefficient.** Second, this correlation is limited by the reliabilities of both the test and the measurement of the criterion: The correlation of any measurement with another measurement cannot exceed the square root of the product of their reliabilities. For example, suppose that college grade points were perfectly reliable and that the reliability of the SAT is 0.90. The maximum validity coefficient for the SAT would be 0.95

(i.e., $\sqrt{0.90 \times 1.00}$). Of course, this is not too bad at all. Consider, however, if the reliability of the predictive test is 0.20 and the criterion is 0.50. Then the maximum validity coefficient would be 0.32 (i.e., $\sqrt{0.20 \times 0.50}$). In short, the top value of the validity coefficient is much less than 1 because of the unreliability of the test and criterion measure. Validity depends on reliability.

A little bit of trickery that psychometricians sometimes use is to **correct for attenuation** of a correlation because of unreliability of the scores used in calculating the correlation. What this does is to provide an estimate of what the correlation might have been had the reliabilities of the measures been perfect. This is done by dividing the obtained correlation (in this case, a validity coefficient) by the square root of the product of the reliabilities. Thus, suppose a correlation is calculated between the predictive test with a reliability of 0.20 and the criterion measure that has a reliability of 0.50, with a correlation of 0.13 resulting. To "correct" this correlation for the unreliability of the scores correlation, 0.13 would be divided by 0.32 (i.e., $\sqrt{0.20 \times 0.50}$). The "corrected" correlation would be 0.41. We certainly have seen many instances of validation coefficients reported that were corrected for attenuation. The discerning reader always remembers that there is some trickery involved with such coefficients. Young researchers would be well advised to work hard to create reliable measures so that there is a reasonable chance of obtaining a high validity coefficient without correcting for unreliability of measurement.

Construct Validity Does this test measure the construct it is intended to measure? To understand this question, it is first necessary to define a construct. Many psychological variables are abstract rather than concrete (Nunnally, 1978). "Ability" cannot be observed directly nor can "intelligence." **Constructs** must be inferred from behavioral observations. Thus, "mathematical ability" is inferred from consistent, exceptional mathematics performance. "Anxious personality" is inferred from many instances of anxiety in situations that do not provoke anxiety in others. Intelligence is inferred from performances on intelligence test items.

If a test developer is attempting to create a new test for a construct measured by existing instruments—for example, attempting to create a short intelligence test that can be given in groups and thus one that can be administered much less expensively than psychometrist-administered, individual tests of intelligence—construct validation requires demonstrating that the new test correlates with the accepted tests assessing the construct. Again, because the maximum values for such correlations are constrained by the reliabilities of the measurements correlated, it is essential that the new measure be reliable (presumably the old, accepted measure is reliable, or it would not have attained the status of a standard).

In addition to creating new tests to measure familiar constructs, psychologists are forever attempting to validate new constructs. Campbell and Fiske (1959), in a classic paper, provided exceptionally clear guidance as to how to do this. First, establishing the reliability of the measures of the new construct is essential. Second, it is necessary to demonstrate that the new construct is not identical to another construct. That is, that it does *not* correlate with other familiar constructs. (If there is a high correlation, it is difficult to make the case that a unique new construct is being tapped by the new measure.)

For example, one set of test developers wanted to make the case that they were measuring "psycholinguistic ability." The claim has not been widely accepted because their measure correlates highly with psychometric intelligence, suggesting that their test is really tapping IQ rather than some unique psycholinguistic ability (see Sattler, 1992, pp. 345–347). Because many intellectual tests do correlate with IQ, demonstrating a low correlation with IQ is a standard for some in establishing the **discriminant validity** of a measurement claiming to tap a new cognitive construct (e.g., Mischel, 1968).

Rigid insistence on such a standard would not be reasonable, however, in many cases, such as when the unique construct might be expected to affect intelligence test performance. Thus, reading disability is likely to affect performance on IQ tests, which are filled with verbal competence items so that years of reading disability should depress IQ. Another possibility is that the unique competence depends on intelligence, so that creativity may only be possible given at least moderate intelligence (see Haensley & Torrance, 1990).

In the best of all possible psychometric worlds, Campbell and Fiske also specify a third criterion that is met for establishing the validity of a construct: More than one measure of the construct is created, with the two measures correlating highly (and, of course, neither of the two measures correlates with other, familiar constructs). When two or more measures of a construct correlate highly with one another, there is said to be **convergent validity** for the construct. Thus, a construct such as attention deficit/hyperactivity is convergently validated because various measures of attention deficit and hyperactivity correlate with one another (i.e., performances on maze, attention, and frustration measures correlate with classroom observational scales indicative of poor attention and hyperactivity). At the same time, there is no pattern of performance on standardized IQ tests that is a sure tipoff of hyperactivity, providing some discriminant validation for the hyperactivity/attention deficit construct (see Sattler, 1992, Chapter 20).

Summary and Concluding Comments Good tests are well-validated ones, although there is flexibility in making claims of validity, something implied in this section emphasizing the various ways validity is construed. Familiar tests that have survived the test of time almost always have been validated in many different ways. Unfortunately, there are many other tests on the market with questionable validations at best. Before adopting a test for a particular purpose, educators have an obligation to their students to obtain validation information about an instrument. This information is often supplied by publishers of reputable tests. If it is not, an invaluable source of information is the *Buros Mental Measurements Yearbook*, which publishes reviews specifying the psychometric characteristics of many tests.

Before covering the most famous psychometric assessments of all, IQ tests, one more concept needs to be discussed. Sometimes tests are not homogeneous with respect to what they tap or the processes/knowledge that affects performance on them. When that is the case, performances on some items may correlate more highly with one another than performances on other items. **Factor analysis** is a way of making sense of the intercorrelations between items. The starting point for factor analysis is a correlation matrix identifying how performance on each item of a test (or perhaps how the score on each subtest of a test) correlates with performance on each other item (or subtest) on the test. For example, if every time a student is correct on item 12, he or she is correct on item 16, and every time a student is wrong on 12, he or she is wrong on 16, the correlation between 12 and 16 would be 1 (i.e., performance

on 16 can be predicted perfectly from performance on 12). If there is a 50% chance a person who gets 12 right will get 16 right and a 50% chance that someone who gets 12 wrong will get 16 right, the correlation between 12 and 16 would be 0 (i.e., it is impossible to predict performance on 16 from knowing performance on 12). If there are 50 items on a test, there will be 1225 correlations in this matrix.

What factor analysis does is identify clusters of items that correlate with one another, with several "factors" often emerging from the analysis. The investigator can then look at the variables that "load" on each factor to identify what might be causing the correlations. One of the most common outcomes when intelligence test data are analyzed is for all of the items or subtests to "load" on one common factor, which has become known as **g** for general intelligence. Much more about g as well as the concepts of reliability and validity will be presented as the chapter proceeds, so that it should become apparent that reliability, validity, and factor analyses are working concepts for test developers.

INTELLIGENCE ASSESSMENT

Psychometricians are exceptionally aware of their history, how contemporary psychometric theory and practice have been influenced by well over a century of theoretical and test-development work. The history is a rich one, although charged with controversy from its beginning. An exceptionally interesting history of the *mismeasurement* of intelligence was provided by anthropologist Stephen Jay Gould (1981). Block and Dworkin (1976) provided a documentary history of the checkered history of mental tests and their interpretation. Excellent shorter histories are provided by Brody (1992, Chapter 1); Kaufman (1990, Chapter 1); Plomin, DeFries, and McClearn (1990); and Sattler (1992, Chapter 3 and frontleaf), all of which informed the short history that follows.

The origins of psychometric intelligence theory often are traced back to Galton's (1869) *Hereditary Genius: An Inquiry into Its Laws and Consequences*. He made the important observation that exceptionally bright people often had exceptionally bright offspring. Using rudimentary ideas about the normal curve, Galton argued that blood relationships between geniuses were much closer than would be expected by chance. To support his case, he analyzed the lives of eminent individuals of the day from a variety of walks of life, discovering for example that the 1000 most eminent men he could identify came from only 300 families. This statistic is striking given the 1 in 4000 chance of attaining eminence in Galton's analyses. Within these families, Galton was also able to show that eminence was more likely in close relatives than in distant relatives. For example, eminent men often had eminent fathers, with about a 1 in 4 probability. They were less likely (1 in 12 probability) to have eminent grandfathers. Galton concluded from these probabilities that genius was inherited.

Although Galton's strong claims about the heritability of genius did not hold up, Galton's contributions to the scientific analysis of intelligence were enormous. For example, he devised a rudimentary individual differences test based on reaction time, strength, eyesight, and motor abilities. He also devised rudimentary correlation coefficients as well as medians and percentiles to analyze the data he collected. Galton performed the first twin studies in an attempt to separate the contributions of heredity and environment in determination of individual differences. Although Galton did not develop an instrument resembling contemporary intelligence tests, others provided more refined approaches to statistical analyses, and Galton's twin studies were merely precursors of what studies of twins would be, Galton's thinking was a source of stimulation for both European and American workers who were interested in individual differences in intellectual abilities.

European interest in individual differences in intelligence grew in the late 19th century (e.g., Binet & Henri, 1896), concomitant with the birth of what is now recognized as the discipline of psychology, signified by the opening of a psychology laboratory at Leipzig by Wundt in 1879. In the United States, Cattell (1890; Cattell & Farand, 1890) established a mental testing laboratory at the University of Pennsylvania, collaborating with Wissler (1901) at Columbia University, using correlation to identify mental measurements that were related to one another.

An extremely important advance was Spearman's (1904) paper, which conceptualized intelligence as consisting of multiple factors, one general factor (g) and the others more specific (s): Every item on an intelligence assessment was assumed somehow to be related to general intelligence, with the degree of correlation to g varying among measures.

Every measure of intelligence also tapped specific functions s independent of g. Spearman definitely understood that intelligence was a construct, something that had to be inferred. He also understood that powerful inferences could be made based on intercorrelations of measurements and developed the statistical methods that permitted analyses of large numbers of correlations so that factors giving rise to patterns of correlation could be identified. The pattern of correlation giving rise to g was that every mental test correlated somewhat with every other mental test: The fundamental importance of this discovery is obvious in that no one has ever devised a mental test that does not correlate positively with other mental tests (see Jensen, 1992).

Spearman was a theoretical giant, with his conception of intelligence fueling theoretical debates about the nature of intelligence for much of the first half of the 20th century. Thomson, for example, argued that the single factor g was a statistical artifact and deflected attention from the true nature of intelligence, which was a large set of independent bonds in the mind. Thurstone emphatically made the point that a "factor" could emerge in a correlation matrix because of similarities in test items that had nothing to do with any abstract factor (e.g., verbal test items are similar in many ways besides their relevance to verbal intelligence; spatial test items share similarities besides tapping spatial abilities). Thurstone's position was that there are several important factors underlying intelligence, not just g and a collection of myriad characteristics specific to each of the many items on intelligence assessments. Based on a large battery of tests administered to hundreds of subjects, Thurstone (1938) concluded that the **primary mental abilities** were spatial, perceptual, numerical, verbal, memory, word fluency, inductive, arithmetical reasoning, and deduction factors.

The early years of the 20th century witnessed the proliferation of intelligence tests, including Binet and Simon's (1905a, 1905b, 1905c) intelligence scale for children; Terman's revision of the Binet-Simon scale, which was carefully normed on American children (i.e., the Stanford-Binet scale; Terman & Childs, 1912); and the Army Alpha and Beta tests, which were a group-administered adaptation of the Binet test (Yoakum & Yerkes, 1920). It is impressive that there remains a great deal of resemblance between these early tests and contemporary intelligence assessments, although it must be emphasized that these tests were the survivors, for a number of other tests of intelligence were proposed and dismissed or discontinued after a short period of use. That Terman's test and the Army tests were derived from Binet's scales makes clear that the testing giant in the early 20th century was Binet. Theoretical thinking was driven by Spearman; testing applications were stimulated by Binet.

Why were intelligence tests developed? Binet was charged by the Minister of Public Instruction in Paris to find a way to discriminate between normal and retarded children. Terman shared Binet's vision that useful discriminations could be made between normal and low intelligence children but also thought the tests could be useful in identifying feebleminded adults. The Army tests were designed to discriminate the mentally unfit from those who attempted to fake stupidity to avoid World War I. These tests proved able to make discriminations in ability, with some validations exceptionally convincing. For example, performances on the Army tests generally were better for higher-ranking than lower-ranking troops (Yoakum & Yerkes, 1920).

In the 1930s, Wechsler began work on the test that would become the standard for the assessment of adult intelligence, the *Wechsler Adult Intelligence Scale–Revised (WAIS-R)*. He borrowed liberally from previously validated tests, although his instrument was unique in its balance of nonverbal and verbal items (i.e., verbal items had predominated in most previous assessments). Because this is the most frequently used assessment of adult intelligence, educational psychologists must be familiar with it. An overview of the *WAIS-R* illustrates many of the conceptual ideas already developed in this chapter.

Wechlser Adult Intelligence Scale–Revised

Wechsler's first intelligence test was the *Wechsler-Bellevue Intelligence Scale* (Wechsler, 1939), revised in 1955 as the *Wechsler Adult Intelligence Scale (WAIS)*, and revised again in 1981 as the *WAIS-R*. Although there was substantial overlap in items from version to version, there was also some updating to modernize the test with respect to cultural considerations (e.g., the WAIS-R includes new items that mention prominent black Americans). In addition, *WAIS* items that produced floor or ceiling effects were eliminated from the *WAIS-R*. Although there are

many sources of information about the *WAIS-R*, we recommend (and used in the writing of this chapter), the *WAIS-R Manual* (Wechsler, 1981), Kaufman (1990), and Sattler (1992).

The test can be administered to adults between 16 and 75 years of age. It is administered to one person at a time by a psychometrist or psychologist. The test is composed of six Verbal Scales and five Performance Scales. The Verbal Scales include the following:

1. Information: 29 questions tapping general knowledge from literature, history, and geography.
2. Digit Span: lists of digits (up to 9 for forward digit span and 8 for backward digit span) that must be recalled either in order of presentation (forward span) or reverse order of presentation (backward span).
3. Vocabulary: 35 words that the examinee is asked to define.
4. Arithmetic: 14 problems that the examinee is asked to solve.
5. Comprehension: 16 questions dealing with organization of the government, the nature of law, health standards, social relations, and proverbs.
6. Similarities: 14 pairs of words, with the examinee asked to explain the similarity between the words in each pair.

The Performance Scales are the following:

1. Picture Completion: 20 drawings of well-known objects are presented, each of which is missing some essential component, with the examinee asked to indicate the missing part (timed).
2. Picture Arrangement: examinee is asked to sequence series of pictures logically, with 10 problems of this type (timed).
3. Block Design: examinees are shown red-and-white pictures of designs and must construct a matching design with red-and-white plastic blocks (timed).
4. Object Assembly: examinee solves four jigsaw puzzles to produce pictures of well-known objects (timed).
5. Digit Symbol: examinee must copy symbols presented as paired with numbers—that is, after presentation of the digit-symbol pairings, 93 digits alone are presented with the subject required to copy the appropriate symbol for each one (timed).

The *WAIS-R* manual specifies in detail how to derive an IQ score from performance on these 11 subtests. Mean performance on the test is set at 100 with a standard deviation of 15 (normed with a national sample of 1900 respondents representative of the racial, gender, and regional mix of people in the United States). If the distribution in IQ were normally distributed (as described in many textbooks), less than 2 percent of the population would have an IQ less than 70, approximately 14 percent would have an IQ between 70 and 85, 68 percent would have IQs between 85 and 115, 14% would score between 115 and 130, and 2 percent would have scores greater than 130. The reason for the *if* is that the distribution of intelligence is not entirely normal, with a slightly greater proportion of people in the tails of the distribution (i.e., less than IQ of 70 and greater than IQ of 130) than if it was a normal distribution (see Brody & Brody, 1978). One reason for this is that people do not marry by chance, with exceptionally smart people more likely to marry other exceptionally smart people and feeble-minded people more likely to married one another than would occur by chance (Gilger, 1991; Neale & McArdle, 1990). Even so, thinking about IQ as normally distributed is close enough for most purposes, with the following intelligence classifications attached to various IQ ranges for the *WAIS-R* (and other Wechsler scales):

- 130 and above: very superior
- 120–129: superior
- 110–119: high average
- 90–109: average
- 80–89: low average
- 70–79: borderline
- 69 and below: mentally retarded for the *WAIS-R*; mentally deficient for the *WISC-R* and *WPPSI* (described later)

One the of strengths of the *WAIS-R* is that it has extremely high reliability (0.97). That the reliabilities of each of the 11 subtests are lower than the overall reliability is due in part to the fact that scores based on more items (i.e., full-scale IQ is based on all items from all subscales) are more reliable than scores based on fewer items. (Remember the point made earlier in the chapter that longer tests are more reliable than shorter tests.) There is about a two in three chance that the IQ score obtained for a person with the *WAIS-R* is within 5 points of the score the person

would obtain on a retesting (i.e., the confidence band for the test is 10 points, IQ score ± 5 points).

The concurrent validity (and to some extent the construct validity as well) of the *WAIS-R* was determined by correlating *WAIS-R* IQ with IQs obtained with other tests, including the 1955 *Wechsler Scale* and the *Stanford-Binet* (Thorndike, Hagen, & Sattler, 1986) scales. In general, these correlations were high (e.g., 0.94 with the *WAIS* and 0.85 with the *Stanford-Binet*). Factor analyses were used to determine that all of the subtests load on the g factor.

Males average 2 points better on the *WAIS-R* than females. There is about a 2-point advantage for urban dwellers compared with rural residents. There is a 2- to 3-point advantage for people living in the Northeast and Western United States compared with the Midwest and South. None of these differences cause much alarm, however. The population difference that is striking is that white Americans outperform black Americans by about 15 points on the test (i.e., 101.4 for whites compared with 86.8 for blacks), a result that is, nonetheless, consistent with historical white-black differences in IQ. (There is great controversy surrounding the interpretation of such differences, with the alternative perspectives considered later in this chapter.)

The *WAIS-R* is a good test with excellent psychometric properties. It is an adult scale, however, and thus not appropriate to administer to children, who are the concerns of many educators. A downward extension of the test, the *Wechsler Intelligence Scale for Children–Revised* (*WISC-R*) is appropriate for school-age children and is taken up next.

Wechsler Intelligence Scale for Children–Revised

The *Wechsler Intelligence Scale for Children* (*WISC*) was published in 1949 (Wechsler, 1949), with the revision, the *WISC-R*, published in 1974. (Many clinicians we know pronounce the abbreviated test name like "whisker.") The tests were based on the *WAIS* and *WAIS-R*, and thus there is a great deal of similarity between the *WAIS-R* and the *WISC-R*. What follows is based on the *WISC-R Manual* and Sattler's (1992) article on the *WISC-R*.

The *WISC-R* is appropriate for children 6½ to 16½ years of age. Similar to the *WAIS-R*, there are Verbal and Performance Scales. Child-relevant versions of the 11 subtests of the *WAIS-R* are included on the *WISC-R*, with one additional Performance test: A mazes subtest requires subjects to complete a series of mazes. The full-scale IQ for the *WISC-R* is based on only 10 of the subtests, however, with the digit span and mazes data eliminated from the computation. Similar to the *WAIS-R*, the mean for the *WISC-R* is 100, and the standard deviation is 15. There is a two in three chance that an IQ score is within $6^{1}/_{2}$ points as determined by a *WISC-R* retest (i.e., 13-point confidence band, IQ ± 6.5 points). Often, educators think about intelligence data in terms of **mental age,** which can be calculated with the *WISC-R*.

The reliability is high (i.e., 0.96 for test-retest). As with the *WAIS-R*, none of the subscales have as great reliability as the full-scale IQ. Concurrent validity is also high, with the test correlating with other standardized measures of intelligence including traditionally well-regarded measures of children's intelligence (e.g., correlation with the *Stanford-Binet* was 0.80). It correlates with the *McCarthy Scales of Children's Abilities* (0.72), the *Kaufman Assessment Battery for Children* (0.70), and the *Peabody Picture Vocabulary Test* (0.68). Performances on five subtests of the *WISC-R* are strongly associated with g (i.e., Vocabulary, Information, Similarities, Block Design, Comprehension); four are moderately associated with g (i.e., Arithmetic, Object Assembly, Picture Completion, Picture Arrangement); and three are correlated weakly with g (i.e., Digit Span, Mazes, Digit-Symbol). (Notably, two of the three subtests that load weakly on g are not included in the calculation of the full-scale score.)

Males have about a 2-point advantage over females on the *WISC-R*. There is about a 2-point advantage for urban compared with rural children. The Northeast and West enjoy a 2-point advantage over the Midwest and about a 6-point lead over the South. The 15-point advantage for whites over blacks on the *WAIS-R* is also observed on the *WISC-R*.

The *WISC-R* has desirable psychometric properties but is limited to the grade-school years. Because many decisions must be made about children during the preschool years, Wechsler (1967) developed a test for younger children.

Wechsler Preschool and Primary Scale of Intelligence (WPPSI)

The *WPPSI* (see Sattler, 1992; Wechsler, 1967; *WPPSI* pronounced "whipsey" by many users of the test) is

appropriate for children 4 to $6^{1}/_{2}$ years of age. It has eight subtests that are similar to the *WISC-R* (Information, Vocabulary, Arithmetic, Similarities, Comprehension, Picture Completion, Mazes, Block Design) and three subtests unique to it:

1. Sentence: examinee repeats sentence read by tester.
2. Animal House: examinee places colored cylinders in a board with holes, with matching of cylinders and holes based on matching of four different animals.
3. Geometric Design: examinee copies geometric designs from printed cards.

Similar to the other Wechsler tests, the mean IQ on the *WPPSI* is set at 100 with standard deviation of 15. The test was normed on a sample of 1200 children (200 at each of six age levels), balanced to reflect the racial, gender, and regional mix of the United States. Mental ages can be calculated from the test data.

The reliability for full-scale IQ is 0.96. At all age levels, there is a 2 in 3 chance that the reported full-scale IQ is within 6 points of an IQ score obtained on a retest. The test also has good concurrent validity, correlating highly with other intelligence scales used with children. Yule, Gold, and Busch (1982) also demonstrated the predictive validity of the *WPPSI*, with *WPPSI* scores predicting *WISC-R* scores obtained 11 years after the *WPPSI* was administered (i.e., $r = 0.86$ between the intelligence rank orderings at $5^{1}/_{2}$ and $16^{1}/_{2}$ years of age). See Sattler (1992, Chapter 9) for review of several other studies that also reported long-term prediction of intelligence differences from *WPPSI* scores. These predictive studies provide especially impressive support for use of the *WPPSI* as a meaningful measure of intellectual ability. All of the *WPPSI* subtests are strongly related to g.

Sex differences in full-scale IQ are trivial on the *WPPSI*. Rural test takers have a 1-point advantage over urban children. The mean *WPPSI* full-scale IQ for the Western United States is reported as 105, compared with 102 for the Northeast and Midwest and 98 for the South.

Despite the fact that the *WPPSI* is administered to an age range that has often been considered difficult to assess reliably, the *WPPSI* does well as a measure. The predictive validity data on the *WPPSI* as well as the substantial overlap for subtests on the

WPSSI, WISC-R, and the *WAIS-R* suggest that if for some reason it is desirable to have longitudinal intelligence data on children (and often it is for both clinical and research purposes), a reasonable strategy would be to administer the *WPPSI* during the preschool years, the *WISC-R* during elementary and the early to mid high school years, and the *WAIS-R* during the late high school and adult years. David Wechsler made an enormous contribution to the assessment of individual differences in intelligence.

Other Intelligence Tests

There are many intelligence tests (sometimes going by other names, however) that have been published. Some are as well designed and validated as the Wechsler (e.g., *McCarthy Scales of Children's Abilities, Stanford-Binet Intelligence Scale*), and these scales are the ones used much of the time by competent examiners, such as professional psychometrists and psychologists. If we had the space to provide information about these tests, the write-up would share many points with the write-up of the Wechsler scales: good reliability, concurrent validity, perhaps even predictive validity, and high loadings on g. Unfortunately, there are many other published instruments purporting to measure intelligence that have not been prepared or studied with the same care as the Stanford-Binet and the Wechsler scales. If there is a need for intelligence test data on a child, the best bet is to go to a well-qualified professional who will identify an appropriate instrument and know how to administer it.

When educators are presented "intelligence test" data (or other data that are equivalent to IQ in meaning, such as general ability data, mental maturity, and academic potential; Anastasi, 1988, p. 322), the score should be interpreted with respect to its source. If it is a Wechsler or Stanford-Binet score that was generated by a qualified testing professional, there is good reason to believe the number reflects psychometric intelligence. If the score comes from a test of unknown (or low) reliability or validity or was generated by someone other than a professional psychometrist or psychologist, there is reason to be cautious in putting any faith in the score.

At the same time, we emphasize that there are some group tests of mental ability (i.e., they can be administered to groups of children by guidance counselors or other educator professionals) that have been carefully validated and are reliable. Tests such as the Otis-Lennon School Ability Test (OL-SAT), the Cognitive Abilities Test (CogAT), the Detroit Tests of Learning Aptitude (DTLA), and School and College Ability Tests (SCAT) provide a great deal of helpful data to teachers and school personnel at low cost (see Sattler, 1992, for reviews of these tests). Typically, students are provided a response book or answer sheet and mark their answers in the booklet or on the sheet. The directions for these tests have been carefully prepared, and most students can understand them. Items on these tests call for students to make classifications, solve analogies, comprehend relationships (e.g., mark the picture that shows a cat under a chair), solve number series, and solve problems (see Anastasi, 1988, Chapter 11). Educators should take care to read manuals and supporting materials carefully before they administer such tests or attempt to interpret the scores.

There are also many useful and well-validated measures that are designed for particular populations and purposes. Some of the better-known indices (ones with at least moderately good psychometric characteristics) of "intellectual ability" broadly construed include the following (Sattler, 1992):

- *Brazleton Neonatal Behavioral Assessment Scale.* This scale can be administered to newborns to evaluate reflexes and responsivity to the environment. One of its notable characteristics is that it predicts performance on the most common infant mental and motor development scale, the *Bayley*—that is, the newborn differences in reflexes and responsivity predict differences in mental and motor development many months later (Francis, Self, & Horowitz, 1987).
- *Bayley Scales of Infant Development.* This is a test of motor skills and mental abilities that can be administered to children 2 months to 2½ years of age. This is an excellent measure of mental and motor development except that it does not correlate highly with intelligence in later childhood, with the correlation between Bayley scores and childhood intelligence especially low for Bayley scores obtained in the first year (e.g., Goodman, 1990).

• *Visual habituation paradigm.* Fagan (e.g., 1991; Fagan & McGrath, 1981; Thompson, Fagan, & Fulker, 1991) has determined that infant susceptibility to **habituation** predicts intelligence in childhood, with individual differences in habituation obtained during the first year of life correlating with individual differences in intelligence at ages 5 to 7 (see Goodman, 1990, for a review). Sometimes the correlations have been as high as 0.60, which is impressive in comparison to the 0 to 0.10 or 0.20 correlations obtained for correlations of the Bayley with childhood intelligence. (These correlations are especially impressive given the small number of "items" on the habituation tests in many cases [see Fagan, 1985].)

In one variation of the habituation paradigm (i.e., the preference paradigm), an infant is shown two identical visual stimuli, such as two copies of the same face. Then two more pictures of faces are shown, one identical to the original faces and one a new face. The measure of habituation is the degree of preference for the new face. The correlations between habituation and later intelligence suggest that children who process information more efficiently during early childhood are the ones most likely to process information more efficiently in later childhood, with Fagan believing that the habituation paradigm is telling about infants' abilities to form and remember mental representations, which are, of course, critical information processing skills throughout life. Fagan has developed an apparatus that is being sold to hospitals and other infant assessment professionals that simulates the testing conditions in his original studies and provides information about individual differences in infant habituation.

Given both the predictive validity of Fagan's measurements and the predominance of information processing as a perspective for understanding mental processing in the 1990s, it seems likely that Fagan's approach to measurement of individual differences in intellectual abilities of infants will become much more popular than it is now. See Rose (1989) for discussions of extensions of Fagan's work and an illuminating perspective on the psychometric challenges of devising infant intelligence measures (e.g., low Cronbach alphas when habitua-

tion is measured with several different type of visual stimuli). See Ruff, Lawson, Parrinello, and Weissberg (1990) for research using other attention paradigms confirming long-term stability of individual differences in attention from infancy to the preschool years, with evidence that attention-deficit disorders during childhood are detectable in infancy; Rose, Feldman, Wallace, and McCarton (1991) generated evidence that some recognition memory measures during infancy may predict later intelligence. In short, some information-processing differences in infancy predict intelligence differences in later childhood and possibly during adulthood (DiLalla et al., 1990; for an integrative review of all of the available evidence, see McCall & Carriger, 1993).

• *Blind Learning Aptitude Test.* This is a nonverbal test to assess the learning abilities of blind children.

• *Leiter International Performance Scale.* This is an IQ test that can be administered nonverbally. It can be used with children who have sensory or motor difficulties or who cannot speak or read.

• *Hiskey-Nebraska Test of Learning Aptitude.* A cognitive abilities test for deaf children.

• *Kaufman Assessment Battery for Children.* This is a processing-oriented intelligence scale, developed to tap "how" children tackle intellectual problems rather than simply whether they are successful or not. Because the Mental Processing scales are nonverbal, this test is aimed at providing a fair assessment of minorities, bilinguals, and children with language difficulties (see Anastasi, 1988; also, Kamphaus, Kaufman, & Harrison, 1990).

• *Raven's Progressive Matrices.* A test that can be used to measure the nonverbal abilities of culturally diverse individuals as well as language-impaired and hearing-impaired children and children with cerebral palsy (Naglieri & Prewett, 1990).

Several important generalizations emerge from review even of this short list of tests. First, there are tests that are sensitive to the needs of diverse groups of children, including minority, handicapped, and the very young. Second, processing theories are making an impact on the development of new assessments (more about this later in the chapter), with Kaufman and Fagan's measures inspired by information processing theory and research. Readers should emerge from this section on intelligence testing aware that an extensive, sophisticated testing technology exists, with this technology influenced deeply by a rich heritage of intellectual assessment (e.g., many *WAIS-R* items are updated versions of items on the earliest intellectual assessments) as well as new psychological theory.

WHY TEST INTELLIGENCE? WHAT DOES PSYCHOMETRIC INTELLIGENCE REVEAL ABOUT THE DEVELOPMENT OF THE MIND?

Psychometric intelligence is useful both to practitioners and researchers. In general, the careful work involved in developing these tests has paid off in that orderly, replicable relationships between intelligence and other variables are common: The high reliability of intelligence assessments makes it possible for respectably high correlations with other variables.

Educational Success

There is voluminous evidence that IQ correlates with current and future successes in school, with Brody (1992) estimating that overall the correlation between IQ and school performance and achievement is about 0.50. It is impressive that success in reading at grade 6 correlates 0.45 or higher with intelligence as measured in kindergarten (Butler, Marsh, Sheppard, & Sheppard, 1985; Feshbach, Adelman, & Fuller, 1977). The *WISC-R* validation data includes report of a 0.39 correlation between performance on the *WISC-R* and school grades (Sattler, 1992); there are a number of reports of *WPPSI* performance in the preschool, kindergarten, and grade-1 years predicting performance on academic achievement tests several years later (Sattler, 1992); and the *WAIS-R* correlates (typically, 0.6 or higher) with academic achievement as measured by psychometric assessments (Sattler, 1992).

The amount of schooling completed also varies with IQ. For example, consider the following data for the *WAIS-R* reported by Reynolds, Chastain, Kaufman, and McLean (1987):

College graduates: Mean IQ = 115, IQ range = 87–148 95% have IQ of 96 or higher

Some college: Mean IQ = 107, IQ range = 76–139 95% have IQ of 89 or higher

High school graduate: Mean IQ = 100, IQ range = 63–141 95% have IQ of 81 or higher

Some high school: Mean IQ = 96, IQ range = 59–146 95% have IQ of 72 or higher

Elementary graduate: Mean IQ = 91, IQ range = 65–125 95% have IQ of 76 or higher

Some elementary school: Mean IQ = 82, IQ range = 53–139 95% have IQ of 59 or higher

Although there are high-ability individuals in every one of the categories of educational completion, low-ability individuals are rare at the college completion level. What these data (and other data on the relationship of intelligence to completion of schooling; see Kaufman, 1990, Chapter 6) suggest is that there is a minimum amount of intelligence required to complete each level of education, with the minimum increasing with more advanced educational level. Overall, Kaufman (1990) estimated about a .60 correlation between IQ and level of education completed.

IQ predicts the occupational status that one will achieve as well. Harrell and Harrell (1945; summary data reproduced in Brody & Brody, 1978) measured the intelligence level of a number of professions. There was a clear relationship between IQ and mean educational status, although there was also clear evidence in the data that high intelligence did not guarantee a high-status occupation. Consider the following examples:

Lawyer:
Mean IQ = 127.6,
IQ range = 96–157

Chemist:
Mean IQ = 124.8,
IQ range = 102–153

Bookkeeper:
Mean IQ = 120.0,
IQ range = 70–157

Salesperson:
Mean IQ = 115.1,
IQ range = 60–153

Machinist:
Mean IQ = 110.1,
IQ range = 38–153

Mechanic:
Mean IQ = 106.3,
IQ range = 60–155

Bartender:
Mean IQ = 102.2,
IQ range = 56–137

Chauffeur:
Mean IQ = 100.8,
IQ range = 46–143

Truck driver:
Mean IQ = 96.2,
IQ range = 16–149

What is especially striking in these data is that as the status of a job and the years of education required to perform a job decline, the lower the intelligence of the least intelligent people performing the job and the lower overall intelligence of all the people in the occupation. Even so, there are people with high intelligence performing every one of the jobs just listed—and in fact, every one of the jobs in Harrell and Harrell's (1945) study. Brody and Brody's (1978) interpretation seems correct to us: "... [I]ndividuals who score low on intelligence tests have limited opportunity to enter more prestigeful occupations" (p. 95). The psychometrically smart in our society have more opportunities and more freedom of choice than the less intelligent.

A traditional conclusion (see Brody & Brody, 1978) based on some work by Ghiselli (1966, 1973) was that even though intelligence predicted occupational level, it did not correlate with success within an occupation. Hunter and Hunter (1984) reanalyzed the studies and data considered by Ghiselli and reached a different conclusion based on more modern and sensitive statistical methods. Their conclusion was that occupational success, based on measures such as supervisor ratings, correlated 0.53 with intelligence, a substantial relationship. The smarter one is in a psychometric sense, the more likely one is to do well at one's job.

IQ is a proven predictor of important life outcomes, including success at school, level of educational and occupational attainment, and success within an occupation. When decisions are being made about the allocation of scarce and valuable resources—for example, high-tech training opportunities in the military—using IQ as one indication of who should receive the resources is fully justified. When employers are attempting to determine who to hire, many factors weigh in. That there is a moderate relationship between IQ and occupational success makes clear that taking the intelligence of a potential employee into account as part of the hiring decision is justified. There is simply no other measure that does as well as IQ in predicting school and life success.

Intellectual Competencies Across the Life Span

Studies of human intelligence have played a prominent role in producing contemporary views of intellectual functioning across the life span. Analysis of intelligence functions is one of the most salient areas of research in the area of life-span cognitive development.

Early Childhood to Adulthood   Although it has been known for some time that IQ scores at age 7 will correlate at least 0.6 or 0.7 with IQ scores at age 18 (see Brody & Brody, 1978), the general conclusion has been that test data generated during the first year of life have no predictive value and that the correlations between preschool measures and intelligence at 18 fall far short of the 0.6 to 0.7 level. That seems to be changing with the development of new measures. Thus, the predictive correlations that Fagan is reporting on measures taken in the first year of life excite many interested in intelligence. The generally high correlation between the *WPPSI* and later measures is striking to researchers interested in the long-term stability of intelligence. Much more research on infant and preschool intelligence and its relationship to later intelligence seems certain (e.g., Diamond, 1991).

Across the Adult Life Span   One stimulus to the study of intelligence across the adult life span was an exceptionally unbelievable conclusion that was believed by many people. For many years, a classic introductory-psychology-textbook conclusion was that intelligence as measured by psychometric tests decreases with increasing age during adulthood. After age 20, it was all downhill! We are certain that many readers—especially those who are no longer in their 20s—immediately question the credibility of this conclusion. Consider, however, the following mean IQ scores as a function of adult age for the *Wechsler-Bellevue* (*WB*), the *WAIS*, and the *WAIS-R* (from Kaufman, 1990, Table 7.1, p. 185):

20–24 years of age: WB = 103.1, WAIS = 99.8, WAIS-R = 97.2

25–34 years of age: WB = 100.2, WAIS = 99.9, WAIS-R = 98.2

35–44 years of age: WB = 95.4, WAIS = 97.5, WAIS-R = 93.5

45–54 years of age: WB = 90.6, WAIS = 93.4, WAIS-R = 91.8

55–64 years of age: WB = 87.6, WAIS = 89.6, WAIS-R = 87.6

65–69 years of age: WB = —, WAIS = 85.5, WAIS-R = 84.4

70–74 years of age: WB = —, WAIS = 78.5, WAIS-R = 81.7

75+ years of age: WB = —, WAIS = 72.9, WAIS-R = —

It is easy to understand why researchers might conclude from data such as these that intelligence declines with increasing age during adulthood.

Some German developmental psychologists understood, however, that there was an important confounding factor in such data (e.g., Baltes, 1968; Baltes, Reese, & Nesselroade, 1977, Chapter 13; Schaie, 1980; Schaie & Labouvie-Vief, 1974): The data were generated in cross-sectional studies. That is, different people provided the intelligence data at each age level, and thus there was a confounding of age level and cohort of people providing the data. Thus, it could be that the 55- to 64-year-olds have not declined to high-80s intelligence. Rather 55- to 64-year-olds might never have been able to obtain a score in the high 90s or at a mean of 100 if tested against the people currently taking the test. A little more explanation will clear up what must seem terribly confusing.

With every generation, there are increased educational and cultural opportunities. Thus, many of today's 25-year-olds have had richer and broader educational experiences than today's 50- to 70-year-olds. For example, a 15-year-old of today is more than twice as likely as a contemporary 55-year-old person to have completed college (Kaufman, 1990, Table 7.3, p. 187). If somehow it were possible to obtain data on the same test when today's 50- to 70-

year-olds were 25, it seems likely that the performance of today's 25-year-olds might be higher than the hypothetical performance of 25-year-olds of yesteryear. If that were true, it would be expected that if intelligence data were collected longitudinally—thus eliminating the confounding between age level and the particular cohort of people tested—the decline in IQ might be less dramatic than it seems when cross-sectional data are examined.

There now have been a number of such longitudinal investigations (see Schaie, 1990, for a review), and the consensus is that a simple conclusion of across-the-board decline in psychometric intelligence is unjustified. A little review of the composition of intelligence tests and a little theory will help move this discussion along.

Recall that the Wechsler tests have two scales, Verbal and Performance. The verbal scales tap knowledge that an individual has; the performance scales require quickness and flexibility in mental functioning. Many intelligence tests have items that can be thought of as tapping either knowledge or ability to process quickly and adeptly.

Cattell (e.g., 1987; also, Horn, 1985) has argued that g should be thought of as two separate factors, which he labeled **fluid** and **crystallized ability.** Fluid intelligence is the biological ability to acquire knowledge and adapt to new situations and is presumably tapped by tests such as those on the Performance Scale of the Wechsler tests. Any task tapping visualization, ability to discern figural relations between elements, make inferences, short-term memory, or sensory discrimination would be expected to "load" on the fluid factor. Although all of these abilities depend heavily on a fully functioning nervous system, proposed revisions of Cattell's original approach have played down the biological claims, claiming that fluid intelligence is simply a summary label for nonverbal reasoning and reflects learning as well as biological endowment (e.g., Horn, 1985).

Crystallized ability is influenced more by acculturation according to the classic Cattellian formulation, with revisionists such as Horn (1985) relaxing the emphasis on the environmental determination of crystallized intelligence in favor of both biological and environmental influences. Vocabulary knowledge is the premier crystallized intelligence task, with the vocabulary a person possesses determined largely by their environmental experiences according to Cattell's reasoning.

With respect to development during the childhood and adolescent years, Cattell claimed that both fluid and crystallized abilities increase. In fact, that is the case. For example, both the proportions of Verbal and Performance Scale items on the Wechsler scales that are answered correctly increase during childhood and adolescence (Sattler, 1992). During adulthood, however, there are important differences in the course of fluid and crystallized intelligence.

There is one certain fact about the human nervous system: It declines with advancing age during adulthood. Recall from Chapter 6 that adults lose something like 50,000 neurons a day. Thus, it would make sense that intellectual functions that depend strongly on biological integrity would decline with advancing age. Consistent with this supposition, a variety of longitudinal and cross-sectional evidence supports the conclusion that fluid intelligence declines with advancing age during adulthood (see Brody, 1992, Chapter 8; Kaufman, 1990, Chapter 7). This translates into dramatic reductions in the ability to reason about new problems and to be able to execute quickly the many operations that often must be executed quickly to solve demanding problems (see Salthouse, 1982, 1985, 1988, 1992).

For crystallized intelligence, it is a different story. One of the most dramatic findings in Schaie and Labouvie-Vief's (1974) report of 14 years of longitudinal intelligence data was that some indicators of crystallized intelligence actually improved with advancing age into the seventh decade of life. For example, there were one-half standard deviation improvements over 14 years on measures such as vocabulary.

Some impressive evidence in favor of the view that crystallized intelligence increases was produced by Hertzog (1989), who statistically adjusted crystallized performance measures to eliminate individual differences in processing speed with advancing age (i.e., to control statistically for declines in fluid abilities). With speed of processing controlled, there was evidence for increases in crystallized abilities until age 70.

Kaufman and associates (Kaufman, Reynolds, & McLean, 1989; see also Kaufman, 1990, Chapter 7) also addressed whether differences in education between cohorts could account for the appearance of decline in IQ across adulthood. What they discovered was that once age was controlled statistically, there was still substantial decline with advancing age in cross-sectional fluid intelligence measures; with edu-

cation controlled statistically, there was little decline with advancing age in crystallized abilities. Kaufman (1990, p. 191) summarized the result this way:

> Regardless of chronological age (and, hence, *when* people were educated), adults with the same amount of formal education earned about the same mean sum of scaled scores on the Verbal Scale. . . . This relation maintained whether the adult was 25, 50, or 65, and whether he or she was educated in the 1910s, 1930s, or 1950s. . . . Unlike Verbal sums, Performance sums *decreased steadily* [with increasing chronological age] within each educational category. . . .

When the developmental functions for the various Verbal subtests are examined in Kaufman's analyses, which controlled for different levels of education at the various age levels, there is strong support for the supposition that knowledge continues to grow through most of the adult life span. For example, the peak age for performance on the Information subtest was 62; for Vocabulary, 72; and for Comprehension, 62.

Even if older people cannot respond as quickly and perform cognitive processes as adeptly, they "know" more information. This is despite the fact that intelligence test items, if anything, are biased toward younger generations with respect to the particular information tapped on information, vocabulary, and comprehension subtests, reflecting the type of information prevalent in contemporary schools. Because standardized testing is more prevalent now than it was earlier in the century, contemporary students may also benefit from better general test-taking skills. Because there are these reasons for believing that crystallized measures are loaded in favor of the young, it is especially impressive that people do better with advancing age on items tapping crystallized intelligence. If anything, the analyses documenting life-span increases in crystallized knowledge probably underestimate such increases.

That the thinking of older adults prevails in the larger culture, despite clear declines in fluid abilities—for example, how many political leaders in the world are old—may reflect that knowledge really is intellectual power. Knowledge often boils down to "knowing" the solutions to problems based on previous experience rather than having to reason about a problem situation because the problem (or one like it) has not been encountered before. Case-based reasoning (see Chapter 3) rather than reasoning using only logical abilities becomes much more possible as knowledge of cases increases through experience in the world. A pessimistic way of looking at the life-span intelligence data is that it is difficult to teach old dogs new tricks. More optimistically, old dogs already know so many tricks that they have no need of easily learning new ones to stay ahead of a pack of puppies that have intact nervous systems but little experience tackling the challenges of the kennel.

A case can be made that most creative work in many fields (athletics to mathematics and physical sciences to biological and social sciences) is produced by young people (e.g., Mattarazzo, 1972; Simonton, 1990). Kaufman (1990, p. 229) believes that this may reflect the relatively intact fluid abilities of younger people, arguing that creative flexibility is determined by fluid factors.

We believe that an important direction in intelligence theory in the near future will be to tease out more completely the role of general reasoning and other fluid abilities versus knowledge and crystallized abilities at different points in the life span. Such work has already permitted great insights, such as debunking the myth that it is all downhill intellectually after the 20s: Even though thinking will be slower as a person ages, people tend to know more with advancing age. Given the importance of knowledge built up over many years in many forms of expertise, it seems likely that future analyses may be emphasizing the strengths of such thinking (e.g., the nature of wisdom, Simonton, 1990) rather than the weaknesses of it.

The model of thinking that emerges from Schaie, Cattell, and Horn's work is more compatible with the perspective that has dominated this book than is g theory: Intelligent functioning is due to a number of factors in interaction, with much of intellectual development and functioning explained by development of knowledge through environmental input, although this knowledge always depends on biological resources. As knowledge increases with advancing age, however, it is less necessary to rely on biological resources to reason through situations, which is fortunate because biological capacities decline with increasing age.

Analyses of Individual Differences Leading to Conceptions of Intelligence That Dovetail with Information Processing Analyses

Much of cognitive research involves comparisons of mean performances—how people do on average under one set of conditions (e.g., instructions) versus another set of conditions. Within any condition, however, there are always individual differences in performance. When the concern is with comparing means, these individual differences are treated as error. In contrast, for researchers interested in individual differences, it is this within-cell variability that is really interesting. Individual differences theorists believe that much about the human mind can be learned by explaining differences in performance between people. Intelligence testing forces attention to individual differences, and as theorists and researchers have attempted to understand the nature of intelligence as measured by intelligence tests, they have stimulated much thinking about the many processes involved in thinking. Two of the more prominent traditions in the cognitive analysis of intelligence data are taken up in this subsection.

Factor Analytic Approaches Implicating Cognitive Processes Thurstone (e.g., 1938, 1947) conducted some especially thorough factor analyses of intelligence tests, concluding in the first half of the 20th century that intelligence test data reflected the operation of at least nine **primary mental abilities:** inductive reasoning, deductive reasoning, practical problem reasoning, verbal comprehension, associative short-term memory, spatial abilities, perceptual speed, numerical competence, and word fluency (see Horn & Hofer, 1992, for a concise, informative history of this work and research stimulated by it). Subsequent analyses by others hypothesized many more factors, with Guilford (e.g., 1967), who worked from this model, eventually proposing that there might be 120 primary mental abilities defined by five types of operations × six types of products × four types of products matrix.

Cattell and Horn (e.g., Horn & Cattell, 1967; Horn, 1968; Cattell & Horn, 1978) and their colleagues (e.g., Hakstian & Cattell, 1978; Horn & Stankov, 1982) also conducted research within this framework, producing the theory of fluid and crystallized intelligence presented earlier in this section. As it turns out, however, those are only two of nine factors these investigators believe to be implicated in intelligence. Horn and Hofer (1992) summarized the nine factors as follows:

1. Fluid reasoning (G_f) measured in tasks requiring inductive, deductive, conjunctive, and dis-

junctive reasoning to understand relations among stimuli, comprehend implications, and draw inferences.

2. Acculturation knowledge (G_c) measured in tasks indicating breadth and depth of the knowledge of the dominant culture.

3. Quantitative knowledge (G_q) measured in tasks requiring understanding and application of the concepts and skills of mathematics.

4. Short-term apprehension-retrieval (G_{sm}), also called short-term memory, measured in a variety of tasks that mainly require one to maintain awareness of, and be able to recall, elements of immediate stimulation—that is, events of the last minute or so.

5. Fluency of retrieval from long-term storage (G_{lr}), also called long-term memory, measured in tasks that indicate consolidation for storage and mainly require retrieval, through association of information stored minutes, hours, weeks, and years before.

6. Visual processing (G_v), measured in tasks involving visual closure and constancy, and fluency in "imaging" the way objects appear in space as they are rotated and flip-flopped in various ways.

7. Auditory processing (G_a), measured in tasks that involve perception of sound patterns under distraction or distortion, maintaining awareness of order and rhythm among sounds, and comprehending elements of groups of sounds such as chords and the relations among such groups.

8. Processing speed (G_s), although involved in almost all intellectual tasks (Hertzog, 1989), measured most purely in rapid scanning and responding in intellectually simple tasks (in which almost all people would get the right answer if the task were not highly speeded).

9. Correct decision speed (CDS), measured in quickness in providing answers in tasks that require one to think (Horn & Hofer, 1992, pp. 56–57).

What is important at this point is that such an analysis points out that the cognitive products that are counted up as part of calculating an IQ are the results of processes, each of which is performed better by some people than others. Presumably, if we knew how well a person could perform each of the individual processes specified by the nine factors considered critical by Horn and his colleagues, we would be in a good position to estimate how well the person would do on an IQ test. The estimate would not be perfect because intelligence is the result of the coordinated use of the nine processes, not simply the sum of the nine processes.

More process-oriented factor analyses of individual differences in psychometric intelligence (and explanations of intelligence factors in terms of processes) stimulated a great deal of theory and research aimed at elucidating individual differences in cognitive processes, with many workers in this arena believing that if individual differences in information processing components are understood, individual differences in intelligence will be understood (Das, 1992; Hunt, Frost, Lunneborg, 1973): For example, psychometric intelligence is related to differences in speed of information processing (see Chapter 6), with speed differences related to g (and hence highly heritable; e.g., Baker, Vernon, & Ho, 1991; Jensen, 1982; Vernon, 1983, 1985; for comprehensive reviews, see Vernon, 1987). There are also strong relationships between working memory capacity/functioning (perhaps best thought of as attentional capacity/functioning; e.g., Tomporowski & Simpson, 1990) and IQ (e.g., Necka, 1992).

Triarchic Theory of Intelligence Yale cognitive psychologist Robert Sternberg has proposed a **triarchic theory** of intelligence. At the heart of Sternberg's theory (e.g., 1985) **are components,** which are elementary information processes that operate internal representations of objects or symbols (Sternberg, 1977; 1980; 1985, pp. 97–98). Components can ". . . translate a sensory input into a conceptual representation, transform one conceptual representation into another, or translate a conceptual representation into a motor output" (Sternberg, 1985, p. 98). The theory is referred to as triarchic because there are three main types of components involved in intelligent functioning:

1. "**Metacomponents** are higher-order executive processes used in planning, monitoring, and decision making in task performance" (Sternberg, 1985, p. 99). These include the following (Sternberg, 1985, pp. 99–105):

   a. Deciding what the problem is that requires solution.

   b. Selecting a set of lower-order components to solve the problem.

c. Selecting one or more organizations or representations of information for other components to work on.

d. Selecting a strategy for combining lower order components.

e. Deciding how to allocate short-term memory (i.e., limited-capacity attentional resources).

f. Monitoring solution of the problem as processing proceeds.

g. Attending to and processing feedback.

2. **"Performance components** are processes used in the execution of a task" (Sternberg, 1985, p. 99). These include the following (Sternberg, 1985, pp. 105–106):

a. Encoding components that are involved with initial perception and memory of new information.

b. Combination and comparison components, which are involved in integrating and comparing pieces of information.

c. Response components involved in outputting solutions once they are determined.

3. **"Knowledge-acquisition components** are processes used in gaining new knowledge" (Sternberg, 1985, p. 107). These include the following:

a. Selectively encoding by sifting relevant from irrelevant information.

b. Selectively combining selectively encoded information into a coherent whole.

c. Selectively comparing new information with information with information acquired in the past.

The components of intelligence can also be classified in another important way, with respect to their level of generality. **General components** are required to perform all tasks. **Class components** can be sed for a number of similar tasks but do not apply to all tasks. **Specific components** apply to individual tasks.

Sternberg believes that the factors identified in factor analyses by intelligence theorists can be explained in terms of components. For example, individual differences in general components lump to produce a g factor: Many metacomponents are general components because planning and monitoring are required for many if not all tasks. Some knowledge acquisition and performance components ap-

ply across most tasks as well (e.g., most problems require encoding and responding). A second example is Sternberg's explanation of crystallized and fluid intelligence in terms of component: Crystallized intelligence is the product of knowledge-acquisition components. That is, those who are better at acquiring knowledge will have more of it as reflected by vocabulary and general information subtests on IQ scales. Fluid ability depends more on the performance components. Because both crystallized and fluid intelligence depend on the operation of metacomponents, crystallized and fluid intelligence should be correlated somewhat, which they are.

Is there any reason to be cautious about enthusiasm for this conceptually appealing approach to individual differences in intelligence? One good reason for caution is that correlations between information processing components and psychometric tests generally have proved small (see Sternberg, 1983, 1991). Cognitive components work has not succeeded in explaining IQ differences among people.

Summary and Concluding Comments   Intelligence data have inspired information processing analyses to explain them. Work such as Thurstone's provided powerful insights about the complexities of thinking that a theory of information processing would have to explain. Although some information processors now talk as if psychometric intelligence theory and research on it are passé, we are impressed that psychometric intelligence theory seems healthy. Our suspicion is that both psychometric intelligence approaches to mind and information processing approaches will continue to cross-fertilize one another. Indeed, there will be substantial discussion in the next chapter about how information processing theory is stimulating the development of new types of psychometric instruments. One reason psychometric and information processing conceptions both will continue to exist is that it has not yet been proven possible to "explain" intelligence in terms of the information processing components favored by Sternberg or others (i.e., with high correlations between information processing and intelligence individual differences a necessary starting point for such explanations).

We cannot close this short section on the relationship of psychometric intelligence theory to information processing theory without discussing the good information processing model featured in this book. Strategies, metacognition and monitoring, knowledge, and short-term memory show up in all information processing analyses as they do in the good information processing model. An important difference, however, between other information processing frameworks and good information processing is that motivation is highlighted in good information processing. Another important difference between other information processing perspectives and good information processing is that good information processing research has been aimed at tasks considerably more complex than the tasks on intelligence tests—and considerably more valid (see Sternberg, 1991, for discussion of the limitations of information processing approaches to intelligence that focus on explaining performance differences on tasks traditionally appearing on IQ tests).

Our confidence in traditional psychometrics research and information processing analyses of psychometric intelligence is undermined by the lack of measurement of educationally realistic reading comprehension, writing, and problem solving by those doing such work. One reason that the alternative assessments considered in the next chapter are stimulating so much interest is that testing is finally taking on tasks that are educationally valid, such as reading comprehension, writing, and problem solving similiar to that expected in school. One challenge is to devise tests measuring educationally valid processes that have psychometric properties rivaling the scales developed by traditional intelligence testers such as Wechsler. This is an enormous challenge and one that will require a marriage of psychometric specialists who know the technical aspects of measurement and cognitive instructional psychologists who know what to measure and can provide some insights to the psychometrists about how to do it. If these new assessments prove to be predictive of school achievement, they might also correlate with psychometric intelligence because psychometric intelligence correlates with school achievement. If that happens, great progress will have been made in identifying the long-sought theoretical linkages between information processing and intelligence.

Concluding Comments About the Value of Intelligence Tests

Intelligence tests permit insights about individual students, providing excellent data predicting the probability of academic success. Such tests must not be seen as providing an inevitable prediction, however. Correlations between IQ and academic success are never perfect because there are other determinants of individual differences. Indeed, much of this book has been about environmental interventions that can increase academic success.

Years ago, one of us [MP] had an English teacher who every year visited the school office before the school year began to review the intelligence test data for her incoming students—to know what each student was capable of. Such a practice is not defensible. That same teacher concluded that MP should be able to get a B in writing based on her analysis of the intelligence data. By learning some writing strategies and working hard, however, MP earned an A in writing and now depends on writing for a large proportion of his income. The IQ test was not a good predictor, in part because it was a group-administered, short-form test, given on the day that MP was concerned about finishing quickly to make the bus for an away basketball game. An IQ score is not a perfect predictor, with some IQ scores much better than others (i.e., those generated by testing professionals using the best available tests outpredict cheaper, quicker assessments most of the time).

The evidence in this section has been consistent with a main theme in this book, that intellectual performance is multiply determined, with both biology and environment critical in the formation and development of competence. Many of the process-oriented investigators conducting the research covered in other chapters of this book have shunned psychometric intelligence analyses. Our view is that there is more than enough room for both perspectives and that these two perspectives will do more than coexist: Psychometric theorists and information processing theorists will goad each other on to make testing more informative to the issues favored by information processors and to make information processing analyses more informative about what sophisticated tests may be testing. In fact, psychometric research also has stimulated the development of information processing theories of mind. Indeed, as will become even clearer in Chapter 17 on alternative assessments, testing and information processing research traditions are interacting in the 1990s.

There is another reason besides theoretical advance that psychometric conceptions of intelligence are more out of favor today than they once were. For many, there is a dark side to testing. They believe testing is biased against some groups of people. The depressed performances of some groups compared with others on IQ tests have enormous potential for stimulating discrimination, something that is apparent to many critics of testing and all too often ignored by advocates of testing. This dark side of psychometrics is taken up next.

BIAS IN MENTAL TESTING

In the fall of 1969, author MP was a freshman at Northwestern University. It was an exciting time to enter college, with the debate over the Vietnam War acted out almost daily in various ways on campus and in American life. The Chicago 7 trial, which resulted in acquittal for seven leaders of protests at the 1968 Democratic Party convention in Chicago, stimulated additional discussion and protests. Then there was the Jensen controversy. The cries of protest over the war and the injustices of the seven trial are memories; the debates sparked by Jensen continue, from the hallways and classrooms of the finest universities to Congressional hearing rooms and courtrooms to popular magazines and television programs.

In 1969, Arthur Jensen, a Berkeley psychologist who had devoted most of his previous scholarly efforts to studies of laboratory learning, published an article in the prestigious *Harvard Educational Review* (Jensen, 1969): "How much can we boost IQ and scholastic achievement?" touching off an explosion. Author MP remembers vividly one session in the Scott Hall Grill, which was then what sufficed for a student union at Northwestern, in which blacks and whites, both students and faculty, together vehemently denounced the Jensen article as racist and intelligence tests as tools of the establishment for keeping blacks down. For the first time in his life, MP realized that what was in educational research journals could really stir the souls of people.

What was so disturbing about the Jensen article? Although most academics concerned with intelligence testing had known for a long time that blacks traditionally score much lower than whites on IQ tests (i.e., usually about a standard deviation of 15 points for most IQ measures), this article (more correctly, second-hand reports of it in the media) made many more Americans aware that the measured intelligence quotients of blacks were on average quite a bit lower than the IQs of whites. For many Americans in 1969, IQ was an unquestionably valid measure of intellectual ability. Jensen's em-

phasis on the black-white difference came at a time when Lyndon Johnson's Great Society programs, many of which were aimed at increasing the economic well-being of minorities, were taking a beating. Many of those who had put Richard Nixon in the White House were all too ready for news confirming their biases, one of which was that Great Society programs could not work because poor people were poor largely as a result of their own lack of talent and effort.

If Jensen's article had only increased awareness of the 15-point difference in the average IQs of whites and blacks, that would have been bad enough. It went much further, however, making the case that the 15-point difference reflected an essential biological difference between blacks and whites, one favoring whites with respect to intelligence. By that time, there was substantial study of the heritability of IQ, including the work of Burt (e.g., Burt, 1966), a strong advocate of the position that intellectual differences reflect genetic differences. Most of the work had been conducted with white populations, with the conclusion that within these populations, differences in intelligence were largely inherited. Jensen (1969) extrapolated from the within-white-population claims of heritability to explain between-population differences in mean intelligence: He concluded that the 15-point disadvantage for blacks compared with whites on IQ tests was not due to socioeconomic disadvantage or culturally biased tests (alternative hypotheses that might explain at least part of the 15-point difference) but due to genetic differences between blacks and whites. MP remembers one extremely bright minority woman he knew going into a rage at Scott Grill, shouting at a Jensen supporter, "Tell me I'm inferior! Tell me my genes are not as good as yours! Tell me I can't better myself!" Her rage was the rage of many.

Our view is that that rage was justified. It has been understood for a long time that within-population estimates of heritability cannot be generalized to estimate between-population differences (e.g., see Plomin et al., 1990, Chapter 14). We explain this to classes using our version of a well-known example among behavior geneticists.

Suppose we take the seeds from a watermelon. Make two piles. Plant both piles of watermelon seeds in side-by-side plots with equally good soil, excellent fertilizer, appropriate amounts of water, and weekly weeding of both plots. Is it likely that better watermelons are going to be produced in one plot or the other? No, the two piles of seeds are biologically equivalent, and the environments are equivalent. Now, what if we had started with the same two piles of seeds. Instead of putting them in identical plots with identical care, suppose one pile is treated as described earlier in this paragraph. Suppose the other is put in a plot with inferior soil and denied fertilizer. Suppose as well that the inferior plot is put under a translucent tent that cuts out most of the sunlight and precludes rain from falling directly on the plot. Which plot will yield the better melons? All students recognize that there will be different yields when the plot environments differ. Then, we ask, "why the difference?" Everyone claims it is environment. No one ever claims it is innate difference in the seeds. That is the point, of course: There can be massive differences between two groups who have essentially the same genetic endowment, differences that must be due entirely to environment.

That environment may make a difference in IQ is suggested by the consistent correlation observed between IQ and socioeconomic status, a correlation observed within both white and black groups (e.g., Jensen, 1973, Chapter 6; Sattler, 1992, Chapter 4). One possibility is that the inferior environment has caused depression in intelligence, a position attractive to the detractors of IQ testing and biological explanations of between-population differences in IQ (e.g., Mensh & Mensh, 1991). Alternatively, of course, it may be that less intelligent people simply do not do as well in this world, and thus they end up worse off than others, an explanation of socioeconomic differences acceptable to supporters of IQ testing and biological explanations of between-population differences in IQ. One attack on the intellectual problem of determining whether racial differences in intelligence might be wiped out if socioeconomic differences between blacks and whites could be eliminated is to control statistically for socioeconomic status in analyses of intelligence data. When that is done, some of the difference is wiped out (perhaps a third; see Jensen, 1973), but there is still an 8- to 10-point discrepancy. Another possibility is to look at the types of items that high and low socioeconomic populations answer correctly and determine if the overall pattern of black-white performance differences on the various subtests of IQ scales are similar to the pattern of differences between high and low socioeconomic populations: They are not (see Jensen, 1992).

The most obvious case to make against the part of the black-white discrepancy that cannot be explained as due to socioeconomic-mediated differences is to argue that the test is unfair: IQ tests are biased against various groups, including blacks and other minorities. (Such bias may exist even for some white populations. Many students who have taken testing courses at graduate schools in the South undoubtedly recall discussions of "Yankee bias." These discussions are stimulated by test items pertaining to concepts such as "snow" and consistent with regional differences in mean IQ scores favoring the Northeast and West over the South, as reviewed earlier in this chapter.) The possibility of test bias against minorities has been raised repeatedly, informally in protests at places like Scott Grill and formally in many courtrooms (e.g., see Jensen, 1980, Chapter 1; Reynolds & Kaiser, 1990a, 1990b). For many, racial or ethnic differences in IQ scores is proof enough of test bias (see Reynolds & Kaiser, 1990a, 1990b, for a review). There is much more to proving bias than that, however.

Potential Sources of Test Bias

Bias can be introduced in a number of ways, with those reviewed by Reynolds and Kaiser (1990a, 1990b) overviewed here. First, and most obvious to many, is that the content of items can tap concepts and experiences more familiar to some racial and ethnic groups than others. There are many possible variations on this theme, such as differing answers to the same item in different cultures and failure to use vocabulary in testing a concept that is familiar to all people taking the test. Although a great deal of effort is expended by many test constructors to eliminate bias, it is definitely not clear how to ensure that tests are content unbiased. One of the greatest difficulties is that even experts in a culture cannot identify reliably items that will pose difficulty for children in their culture— with judges disagreeing between themselves and judges' rating of item difficulties for their culture correlating poorly with actual item difficulties for members of their culture (Jensen, 1976; Sandoval & Mille, 1980). Test constructors have generated a great deal of evidence that weighs against the claim of gross cultural bias in well-constructed intelligence tests: For example, across a number of well-designed tests, there are high correlations (i.e., 0.94 and above) in the difficulty level of items across populations (see Reynolds

& Kaiser, 1990b). If there were many culturally-loaded items, such high correlations would seem unlikely.

A second possible bias is with respect to the constructs measured by the test: The test might measure one thing for one population and something different for another population (e.g., intelligence for the majority population and language proficiency for minorities). If that is the case, one might expect different factor analysis outcomes for different racial and cultural groups: Attempts at identifying differences in the factors underlying the IQ performances of different groups have generally produced comparable factors for the groups studied (Reynolds & Kaiser, 1990a, 1990b), however.

A third possible bias is with respect to predictive validity, with tests predicting educational or other types of successes better for some groups than others. Again, that has been investigated for a variety of good tests, including IQ and SAT tests, with the general conclusion that these tests predict equally well across racial and cultural groups. Even when test means differ between populations and even when the correlations between the predictor (i.e., test score) and predicted outcomes (e.g., educational attainment) differ between groups, it is possible statistically to construct equations that minimize the number of errors in decision making for all groups in question (e.g., Cleary, Humphreys, Kendrick, & Wesman, 1975)—and that is what is required for a test to be unbiased in a predictive validity sense: For example, if the test is asked, "Will this person do well in this college?," it is unbiased if the answer it generates is "right" the same proportion of times for all groups. For a test to be right with equal probability for various groups can require a different prediction equation for each group in question, but such equations can be constructed if the test is reliable and representative, and sizable norming samples have been generated for each of the populations in question.

A fourth potential source of bias is with respect to the standardization samples. Examination of a volume such as Sattler (1992), which provides extensive norming information, makes clear, however, that more recent, generally well-constructed tests are aware of the need for representative, national norming samples, and they generate such samples. Examination of a volume such as Sattler (1992) also makes clear, however, that there are many tests on

the market that have not been normed with representative samples.

A fifth potential source of bias is mismatch between the race or culture of the examiner and the test taker. This hypothesis has been studied extensively with respect to race, however, with little evidence that the race of an examiner makes a difference in the test score earned by a person being examined (Graziano, Varca, & Levy, 1982). An examiner variable that does seem to matter is familiarity between examiner and person being tested, with personal familiarity between tester and examinee slightly boosting examinee performance. What is especially important in this context is that the familiarity effect seems to be especially large for lower socioeconomic populations (Fuchs & Fuchs, 1986).

Test constructors are extremely sensitive to many ways that tests can be biased and are attempting to devise unbiased tests. Testing at its best involves instruments without blatant cultural bias in content, tests normed with representative samples and demonstrated to be measuring the same constructs in various cultures. These tests are administered by examiners who do all possible to make certain that blatant cultural differences do not interfere with a fair assessment (e.g., language differences between the tester and the student). At the other extreme, however, are tests that are terribly biased with respect to content (e.g., dated tests often have content bias) and that have not been normed with data generated by populations being tested with the instrument. Sadly, there are examiners who simply are insensitive to problems that minorities may face in taking a test and do not hesitate to report low test scores as valid despite many indications during testing of language barriers or failures of the student in question to cooperate with the tester or to understand the consequences of the assessment. Of course, the closer an assessment is to the first description, the more weight should be given to the test data; it is essential that the educator community do everything possible to eliminate assessments made with instruments of uncertain reliability and validity or conducted by examiners who ignore examinee characteristics that might preclude a valid assessment. If such tests cannot be eliminated, they should, at least, be ignored in decision-making processes.

Mean differences between racial and cultural groups on various tests exist. On the one hand are those who claim that the mean differences reflect true differences between the groups: They point to the efforts to construct fair tests and the sophistication of those who are involved in constructing such tests. A great deal of wrath has been produced by the claim that the mean differences reflect differences in the innate abilities, especially of blacks and whites. Arthur Jensen is one of the most prominent social scientists advocating such biological determinism, although he is joined by the likes of Harvard psychologist Richard Hernstein (e.g., 1971, *IQ and the Meritocracy*) and Britain's Hans Eysenck (e.g., 1971, *Race, Intelligence and Education;* 1973; *The Inequality of Man*), with this fraternity pressing their case on many fronts, from academic journals to university talks to appearances on talk shows.

On the other hand, there are those who conclude that the tests really are biased against minorities—with the mean difference proof enough of bias—despite all of the precautions to make the tests unbiased. They point again and again to the indeterminancy of the heritability of group differences from within-population estimates of heritability. Their view is often couched in political terms, viewing IQ tests as the tools of the political right wing who are determined to maintain class distinctions and legitimize historical discriminations, with advocates of this position including Harvard biologist R. C. Lewontin and Princeton psychologist Leon J. Kamin (e.g., Lewontin et al., 1984, *Not in our Genes: Biology, Ideology, and Human Nature*). This view gains legitimacy from analyses that debunk some of the data favored by the biological determinists: One of the best examples was Kamin's (e.g., 1974) analyses of Burt's work, one of the most historically prominent of the biological determinists, producing an appealing argument that much of Sir Cyril's data were fabricated: The data were too good; the data were attributed in part to assistants who probably did not exist; and a mysterious additional 32 pairs of twins reared apart appeared in Burt's writing after 1955, during a time in Burt's life when he could not have collected such data. (Although Kamin's perspective has been supported by some analyses [Hearnshaw, 1979], see Joynson's [1989] fascinating book, *The Burt Affair*, in which the author provides an analysis that might explain away Kamin's and Hearnshaw's analyses, clearing Burt's name if correct.) A second excellent example of debunking is distinguished anthropolo-

gist Stephen Jay Gould's history of intelligence assessment, *The Mismeasure of Man*, that presents examples of overblown claims, indefensible methods, and aggressive assertions about intelligence advanced by geneticists over more than a century.

As it turns out, whether tests are biased is an exceptionally important debate in psychology with enormous stakes, becoming more evident as we consider just a few of the issues surrounding the testing of Hispanics in the United States.

Testing Hispanics

The Hispanic population of the United States has increased dramatically in size in the last 15 years and is projected to continue increasing in size, one factor motivating critical examination of the appropriateness of standardized testing with Spanish-speaking Americans. The issues are so urgent that the American Psychological Association provided funds for a conference series that resulted in a book-length treatment, *Psychological Testing of Hispanics* (Geisenger, 1992a), a volume we strongly recommend for those with a need to know the many sides of testing issues affecting Americans of Spanish descent.

There are three main potential sources of bias in the eyes of many well-informed test developers who are concerned with measurement of Hispanic students (e.g., Rodriguez, 1992): (1) Many students of Spanish descent do not speak English well, if at all. Until recently, there were laws in some parts of the United States—ones now stricken down by courts, litigation, and changing professional standards— requiring that all children be tested in English, with decisions about school placement into special education or giftedness classes based on such tests (e.g., Donlon, 1992; Rodriguez, 1992). When the same score is used to decide on the allocation of special education and enriched education for all populations, it is easy to understand why disproportionately high numbers of Spanish-speaking children end up in special education and disproportionately low numbers of Spanish children experience accelerated offerings. Any given IQ score generated by an English-speaking examiner with a test in English does not mean the same thing when earned by an English-first-language student as by an English-second-language student or a student who cannot speak English at all (e.g.,

Donlon, 1992; Pennock-Román, 1992; Schmeiser, 1992).

(2) The second source of bias is potential sociocultural differences between the samples used to norm standardized tests (e.g., predominantly white, English-speaking, predominantly of non-Hispanic background) and the Hispanic community and, in particular, sociocultural differences in understanding what it means to take a test and what the long-term implications of tests are, summarized elegantly by Rodriguez (1992):

> ... [T]est-taking behaviors are culturally learned behaviors. Thus, at a basic level, the argument may be advanced that most Hispanics are not "test wise." Steeped as immigrants in a traditional culture where test taking is not customary, Hispanics come to the testing situation with a cultural disadvantage. Hispanics do not have a cultural knowledge of the mechanics of testing (e.g., there are several choices, but only one correct choice; the correct answer must be recorded in a given slot and within a given allotment of time), nor do they necessarily adhere to the advanced industrial norms and values encapsulated by the general belief in the legitimacy of the testing enterprise as the standard by which to assess performance ... a traditionally minded Hispanic is at a disadvantage in not understanding the implications of tests for future life chances. (pp. 13–14)

One counter to this concern is that it will be reduced as Hispanics become acculturated to American life, and thus, for those Hispanics who are already so acculturated, this concern may no longer be valid. There are important difficulties with this counter: Many important decisions must be made about Hispanic students before that occurs. Measurement of acculturation is fraught with difficulties, especially in the case of Hispanics (e.g., Marín, 1992). Often, tests assume students have prior knowledge that many Hispanic students do not possess, with clear negative impact on the test performance of Hispanics relative to students from the majority culture (e.g., Garcia, 1991).

(3) The third concern is that standardized test performance is known to vary with socioeconomic status. Because Hispanics are disproportionately represented at the poverty levels of American society, there is a real concern that many Hispanics will be victims of the socioeconomic bias in tests.

On the positive side, progress has been made in eliminating the abuses of tests with non–English-speaking minorities, with the *Standards for Educa-tional and Psychological Tests* (American Psychological Association, 1985) making clear that the scores of many standardized tests may be distorted because of language problems if the tests are administered to non–English-speaking minorities. For example, ability tests administered in English to Spanish-speaking students sometimes correlate 0.00 with ability tests administered in Spanish (Pennock-Román, 1992). That is, the distortions are sometimes massive to the point of transforming a test that is highly valid and interpretable with English-speaking students to one that is of no value for assessing minority students. The *Standards* makes recommendations to test developers and users about how to avoid such distortions, although there are contentions that the standards are still not explicit enough (Donlon, 1992). The 1985 *Standards* are a start. It is realistic to believe that some members of the generation of students reading this book will make an important part of their work in educational psychology the refinement of the *Standards* in light of future research in psychometrics, much of which will probably be conducted by the generation of young psychologists who are the target of this book.

Returning to the present, however, there is additional reason for optimism. Because of litigation, there is much more protection for the Spanish-speaking student (Donlon, 1992; Rodriguez, 1992; Schmeiser, 1992): The ruling in *Diana vs. California State Board of Education* (1970) was that students must be tested in their native language (Geisenger, 1992a). In this case, an English-administered IQ test had been used to place Spanish-speaking students in special education. The Court ruled that all Spanish-speaking and Chinese-speaking children in the state who were in classes intended for retarded children had to be retested using procedures that did not discriminate based on language. The Court also ruled that the retesting had to eliminate test items tapping vocabulary and general information that might not be encountered in the minority cultures. The retesting determined that seven of the nine students who had brought the case were much more intelligent than originally assessed (i.e., more than 15 points better, a full standard deviation; Constantino, 1992). The students were taken out of the classes for retarded students after the new, fairer assessment data were collected. The California legislature subsequently passed new laws to prevent the abuses that had produced the *Diana* case (Geisenger, 1992a), and there has been additional court action in

California to prevent overrepresentation of minorities in special education classes (Constantino, 1992).

Another important case was *Larry P. vs. Riles* (1979) in which a federal judge ruled that California's mandate that IQ tests be used to decide special education placements for blacks and minorities was inappropriate. Tests that have been normed without sufficient samples of minorities are being rejected as a reasonable basis for making decisions about minorities (e.g., *Rivera vs. City of Wichita Falls*, 1982). Courts are recognizing when tests are being used with the intent to segregate students and are rejecting the use of tests in this way (e.g., *Morales vs. Shannon*, 1975).

Even so, when tests are reliable and valid and are not being used intentionally to discriminate, they are being upheld as appropriate, even if disproportionate numbers of minorities fail the test, such as the *National Teacher Examination* (*United States of America vs. State of South Carolina* 1978); the courts are not rejecting wholesale the use of tests, with clear court support for tests that clearly tap competencies that are relevant to the selection process (e.g., competencies clearly required to do a job that are measured by a test used to discriminate potential employees from those who are not qualified; e.g., *Washington vs. Davis*, 1978). That conventional standardized tests are not rejected across the board with respect to placement of minorities is obvious from a decision involving a case similar to *Larry P.*: In *Parents in Action on Special Education vs. Joseph P. Hannon et al.* (1980), a federal judge upheld the use of standardized tests for classification of minority children in Chicago as mentally retarded (see Koocher & Keith-Spiegel, 1990, Chapter 3; also, Oakland & Parmelee, 1985). Student readers of this book should note that leading measurement professionals have been in the midst of the legal battles surrounding testing, so that students relishing academic problems that will thrust them into the arenas of public policy, legislative, and courtroom debates might find the field of measurement to be especially appealing.

As with African-American populations, the mean differences in IQ between Mexican Americans and members of the white majority culture have been used to argue for biological deficiency in Hispanics (Constantino, 1992; Garth, 1923). The case is strong that such tests have been used to label Hispanic children unfairly as retarded and to deny access to gifted educational alternatives (Constantino, 1992). In addition, there is substantial evidence that many barriers to the effective education of Hispanic children persist and that testing is misused to maintain such educational barriers (Constantino, 1992). More positively, however, there is more sensitivity now than ever before about how IQ tests and other standardized measures can be misused in their application with minorities, such as Hispanics, and there is greater legal protection for minorities than ever before.

Although it is possible to devise tests on which minority students perform better (e.g., Mercer's [1979] *System of Multicultural Pluralistic Assessment* [*SOMPA*]; Williams' [1972] *Black Intelligence Test of Cultural Homogeneity* [*BITCH*]), such tests have not proved valid. For example, they are not very good predictors of academic achievement (Constantino, 1992; Sattler, 1992).

Testing of multicultural individuals is an area in which certain conclusions are difficult to draw. We are sympathetic to the concerns of minorities, however, with history as our guide. For example, two of the earliest intelligence tests (Army Alpha and Beta) were used by the United States Army during World War I, with psychologist Carl Brigham analyzing the data produced by hundreds of thousands of young recruits and conscripts. Brigham (1923; *A Study of American Intelligence*) emphatically presented the conclusion that the testing proved recent immigrants to the United States were not as intelligent as white people born in the United States. The proof was that recent immigrants had not done as well on the Army tests as whites born in the United States. There was a clear threat to the intelligence of the United States by continuing to permit such people to immigrate, for it was known that intelligence was biologically determined. The folly of Brigham's argument is transparent, for the 1990s descendants of those Irish and Italian and Swiss immigrants who performed so poorly on IQ tests shortly after their immigration do just fine when their intelligence is assessed.

The point of the Brigham-Army intelligence example is that there has been an historical tendency in the United States to denigrate the intelligence of minorities and to conclude that their minds are somehow biologically inferior. Such arguments lead quickly to arguments that immigration should be restricted to protect the quality of the American mind or even that eugenics should be practiced (i.e., control of breeding through encouragement of marriages between highly intelligent people; creation of sperm banks containing the genetic material of extremely intelligent people; sterilization of people of below average intelligence). Ideas of inherited intelligence and social programming to enhance intelligence have been tied since the earliest work on intelligence assessment, with Galton a strong advocate of eugenics. For stirring history and commentary about how biological determinists have participated in efforts to discriminate against those they consider to be biologically inferior, it is hard to beat Daniel J. Kevles's (1985) *In the Name of Eugenics: Genetics and the Uses of Human Heredity.* That Hispanic and other minorities have every right to be concerned about how they are assessed and how assessments are used to determine their futures will be apparent to any conscionable person who studies the historical ties between biological determinist intelligence theorists and movements to restrict the inclusion of minorities in American society. The biological deterministic intelligence theorists have had more than a scientific agenda. There is plenty of reason to pause and wonder whether the political leanings of these theorists may have influenced their willingness to embrace and emphasize evidence favoring the biological determinist position as they discounted and attempted to discredit evidence of environmental effects on intelligence. The wonder of it all, to many, is that the debate continues at all, for there is an intermediate alternative that is extremely appealing and scientifically defensible that has been presented in bits and pieces throughout this book: Biology provides potential, with environment determining how much and how well that potential is realized.

CONCLUDING COMMENTS

Some tests are as American as apple pie. It is difficult to grow up in America without experiencing standardized achievement tests. For example, many readers will have taken the *Iowa Test of Basic Skills* during their elementary years. Those who aspire to higher education invariably take either the *SAT* or the *ACT*. Postgraduate work requires *GREs* or the *Law School Aptitude Test (LSAT)* or the *Graduate Management Aptitude Test (GMAT)* or a similar examination. All of these examinations have characteristics similar to the *SAT* and *GRE:* They have been normed on large, nationally representative samples. They are reliable and valid in predicting future academic achievement. Indeed, school grades and standardized test performance together provide greater predictive power than any other predictor.

For many years, intelligence assessment was almost as prevalent as other forms of standardized testing, with many school jurisdictions routinely administering group tests of intelligence to their students. Such tests are not as widespread as they once were: It has become recognized that abuse of such data was common, especially because many teachers who had access to such numbers were not trained in the proper interpretation of psychometric assessments. Also, that minorities often perform at lower levels than members of the majority population on such assessments has reduced their attractiveness to many educators who have been under substantial pressure in the last two decades to be sensitive to minority concerns.

Nonetheless, IQ testing is still extremely common as part of the assessment of children referred for assessment and treatment. Whenever there is a need to do a complete assessment of a person (e.g., attempting to determine the cause of a student's difficulty in learning to read), IQ testing is likely to occur. Indeed, many mental health classifications require psychometric assessment of intelligence. For instance, classification of learning disabilities is in terms of academic performance relative to what would be expected based on intelligence, with academic performance lower than expected based on intelligence the telltale sign of learning disabilities.

It is essential for students of educational psychology to understand standardized tests because such tests are used to make many important decisions, such as whether a student should be placed in special education or enrolled in a gifted program. This chapter summarizes the essential points about reliability and validity that all educational psychology professionals should understand. The student who understands the various types of reliability and validity discussed in this chapter would be able to understand much of the commentary in technical write-ups accompanying many tests or articles in sources such as the *Mental Measurements Yearbook* or Sattler (1992).

An important type of statistical analysis with respect to tests is factor analysis, which is a way of identifying pools of test items that intercorrelate. Inspection of the intercorrelating items often suggests a way they are similar and points to some underlying competency that could be mediating the intercorrelations. An important point with respect to factor analysis is that different factors and different numbers of factors can emerge depending on specific assumptions and decisions made as part of the analysis procedure.

Factor analysis is notable because it has stimulated theory about intelligence. Analyses of every intelligence test to date have yielded a factor that has come to be known as g: That is, all intelligence test items intercorrelate with one another to some extent, presumably reflecting general intelligence. The separation of intelligence test items into those tapping fluid and those tapping crystallized intelligence was critical to development of a theory of life-span intelligence separating biological and cultural factors as determinants of intellectual competence at different points in the life span. The identification of primary mental abilities was a precursor to modern approaches to identify the information processes that underlie intellectual performances. Factor analysis has played a prominent role in advancing understanding of the nature of intelligence.

Scholars interested in standardized assessments are immersed in historically prominent issues, including the relative roles of nature and nurture in development, the appropriateness of using intelligence assessment with nonmainstream populations, and continuities and discontinuities in the nature of the mind across the life span. A variety of extremely sophisticated tools are used to answer such questions, including the twin and adoption methods of behavior genetics (see Chapter 6, this volume) and the longitudinal experimental designs of interventionists interested in the long-term effects of high-quality educational experiences. Such work affects both the development of new educational theory and practice.

Although measurement professionals are aware of the intellectual foundations of their work, foundations that permit a strong case for standardized testing and traditional intelligence assessment, these same workers are always looking for new ways to assess competence. A variety of new methods have been inspired by theory and new technology as well as by new societal demands. Some of the most intriguing of the new approaches to assessment of individual differences will be taken up in the next chapter.

17

Alternative Assessments

Chapter 16 covered assessments that most readers of this book had probably heard of before taking a course in educational psychology. SATs and IQ scores have been part of American life for most of the 20th century. As the 20th century nears its end, however, there is much rethinking about how to measure competence. Many new measurements are providing important ways of thinking about learning, thinking, and intelligence. Some of the measures are having enormous impact on scientific understanding of intellect; others are having great impact on public policy and public perceptions about education and American students; and some may be much more useful to teachers than traditional measures were. In this chapter, many of the most prominent of these "new" assessments, with new defined as having been developed in the last quarter century or so, are explored.

NATIONAL AND STATE ASSESSMENTS

American students are tested extensively, with the National Commission on Testing and Public Policy 1989 estimating that American students take on average three standardized tests a year. Many are conventional standardized achievement tests that have been normed in a rigorous fashion such as the SAT, described in Chapter 16. Their purpose is to provide information about the progress of individual students, although many jurisdictions use them to make

decisions about whether their schools are doing well or not. Perhaps, more accurately, the test data are used by school officials to make the case that their particular schools are doing well: As it turns out, by carefully selecting tests and the norms used to interpret them (i.e., there are many sets of published norms for some tests) as well as by repeatedly using the same standardized tests (i.e., so teachers learn how to teach to them), it is easy to make the case that most American schools are doing better than average. As educators become more familiar with the tests and prepare students more completely to take them, scores rise. Because most people are not aware of the diverse sets of norms and how to use norms to interpret tests, smart administrators have no difficulty juggling their test scores to convince others (and sadly often themselves as well) that their students are more than okay—their students are above the national average. In two books, John Cannell (1987, 1989), a physician by training, particularly pointed out this "Lake Wobegon effect," so named because all the children in Garrison Keillor's famous hometown are "above average." Our confidence that the United States really is a lot like Lake Wobegon in evaluating its students can be high because Cannell's commonsensical approach to determining if kids everywhere are reported as above average (i.e., he contacted each state for information on academic achievement) has been complemented by a technically sophisticated confirmation of the Lake Wobegon effect conducted by top evaluation specialists (Linn, Graue, & Sanders, 1990).

Given the great alarm about eroding educational standards and students who are not making the grade compared with previous generations (e.g., *A Nation at Risk*), however, not surprisingly, the federal government and state governments are interested in determining how well schools are doing. Thus, many U.S. states as well as Canadian provinces conduct state-wide and province-wide assessments of student competence. So does the federal government, with the *National Assessment of Educational Progress (NAEP)* the best known of the national testing efforts. This section includes an overview of the *NAEP* because it is such a prominent test, with statistics from it presented almost continuously in the media. All Americans should have at least a general understanding of the *NAEP*.

This section will also discuss some of the newer, more innovative assessments being developed for use at the federal and state levels. Testing is being transformed from conventional multiple-choice into radical visions that attempt to measure academic abilities more directly than the traditional assessments. These visions are especially important because they are being created with the explicit goal of reshaping what is taught in school. The theory is that if the new assessments directly tap particular academic skills, schools will teach those skills.

By beginning with the *NAEP*, this section will proceed from more conventional to less conventional tests, although the *NAEP* also has many innovative aspects to it. Before proceeding, however, there is one important point. Most national and many state assessments are aimed at evaluating the performance of educational institutions through assessments of their students. That is, the focus in many national and state assessments is not on the achievement of the individual student, as it was for the assessments covered in Chapter 16 and later in this chapter. Rather, the focus is on group differences: How do minority students fare compared with white students? How do students living in various types of urban environments do compared with students living in rural areas? How do the performances of public and private school students compare? How do students in Our County fare compare with students in Their County?

Even so, in some cases, state assessment data are reported as student scores; also, some new forms of assessment, such as student portfolios, are not only being developed for state assessment exercises, but also as a new way of evaluating students in general. As such, portfolios are much more individualized assessments and indicators of unique individual differences than any of the other tests considered either in Chapter 16 or in this chapter.

National Assessment of Educational Progress

The *NAEP* is billed as "The Nation's Report Card" by Educational Testing Service (ETS), its most visible analyst. There are few readers who would not agree, however, that report card grades often distort. We will make the case here that there are reasons to be cautious about accepting all of the claims made based on *NAEP* data, although generally we applaud the indicators it provides to the United States about the achievement (or, unfortunately, underachievement) of the nation's students.

Development and Administration   The Congress mandated the *NAEP* with legislation in the late 1960s. The original assessment was devised by the National Commission of the States to provide information to policymakers about the state of education in the United States. This was done under the direction of Ralph Tyler, one of the great curriculum and measurement figures of the 20th century. There are periodic assessments of 9-, 13-, and 17-year-olds in school, with data collected biannually; there are also assessments of young adults, up to 35 years of age. Exactly which subject areas are tested varies from assessment to assessment. Over the years, reading, writing, mathematics, science, social studies, literature, art, music, citizenship, computer skills, and career development have been evaluated. ETS goes to great lengths to ensure content validity of the examination, using a broad base of experts to generate and evaluate items before the test is used. Every effort is made to make certain that the test covers content that students should know (or processes they should be able to carry out) without them having to use some particular textbook or experience some particular curriculum. Items are reviewed carefully to make certain they are not offensive to some subcultural groups. Measurement specialists review items in detail to ensure that they are constructed properly. In addition to testing student knowledge, there also are items asking students about their educational experiences, including how much and what type of instruction they have received in the content area

(Anderson et al., 1990; Mitchell,1992). Such information about instruction is invaluable in research efforts to determine how national achievement is related to the instruction provided to students.

Once the test is constructed, great efforts are made to identify and test a nationally representative sample. For example, the 1988 civics assessment (Anderson et al., 1990), which will be used in this subsection to represent the type of outcomes generated by the *NAEP,* was administered to 11,000 students in more than 1000 public and private schools distributed across the United States. The sampling was sufficient to permit meaningful comparisons across demographic, school, and home characteristics.

Sample Test Items from the 1988 Civics NAEP   Most of the items on the civics NAEP were multiple choice in format. Among the easiest items on the test (passing rate = 71 percent at grade 4, 94 percent at grade 8, and 99 percent at grade 12) were the following:

> Who would become President of the United States if the President dies?
> A. The Secretary of State
> B. The Speaker of the House
> C. The Chief Justice of the Supreme Court
> D. The Vice-President
>
> Suppose a person has just been arrested because the police have evidence that he or she has stolen some money. Does the accused have the right to know what he or she is accused of?
> A. Yes
> B. No
> C. I don't know (Anderson et al., 1990, p. 31)

These items are slightly more difficult (passing rate = 10 percent at grade 4, 61 percent at grade 8, 89 percent at grade 12):

> In the United States, an individual citizen has the right to:
> A. Impeach the President
> B. Vote for government officials
> C. Make new laws
> D. Collect taxes
>
> Under the law, United States citizens may work or change government policy by doing all of the following *except:*
> A. Making public speeches
> B. Writing letters of protest
> C. Persuading legislators to change laws
> D. Refusing to pay taxes (Anderson et al., 1990, pp. 34–35)

These are even more challenging (passing rate < 1 percent at grade 4, 13 percent at grade 8, 49 percent at grade 12):

> How is the Chief Justice of the United States Supreme Court selected?
> A. By a national election with approval by a majority of state governors
> B. Through a majority vote by the existing Supreme Court justices
> C. By constitutional amendment and presidential signature
> D. Through appointment by the President with the consent of the Senate (Anderson et al., 1990, p. 36)

These were among the most difficult items on the test (passing rate < 1 percent at grades 4 and 8, 6 percent at grade 12):

> Bicameralism is best defined as a
> A. Government composed of two principal branches
> B. Multilevel judicial system containing a higher court of appeals
> C. System of checks and balances between two branches of government
> D. Legislative system composed of two houses or chambers
>
> In the execution of its responsibilities, which of the following is *least* likely to be influenced by lobbying?
> A. The Supreme Court
> B. The House of Representatives
> C. The Senate
> D. A state governor (Anderson et al., 1990, p. 39)

In addition to the multiple-choice questions, students at grades 8 and 12 responded to an essay question requiring them to name the President and to write during a 15-minute period a description of his responsibilities.

Outcomes for the 1988 Civics NAEP   NAEP data are analyzed so as to provide indications of how students across the United States are doing, with a variety of comparisons possible. For example, the civics test confirmed a steady increase in civics knowledge from grades 4 to 12. There were small, inconsistent gender differences. Whites outperformed African Americans and Hispanics. Students residing in urban advantaged environments outperformed rural students, who did better than students from urban disadvantaged backgrounds. Children with parents who were more highly educated outperformed children from homes with less educated parents. Having both parents at home was associated with better performance than living with one parent; children living with one parent outperformed those living with people other than their parents. There were only small differences associated with maternal employment. Grade 12 students enrolled in academic programs (i.e., rather than vocationally oriented programs) and those planning to attend postsecondary education outperformed other students. The only consistent regional difference was that students in the Southeast performed slightly worse than students in other regions of the United States. (Although this evaluation of the 1988 *NAEP* did not break down outcomes on a state-by-state basis, analyses for *NAEP*s collected from 1990 on do so, with such data first released in 1991.)

Some controllable aspects of the home environment proved to be telling determinants of achievement. The more reading material reported to be at home, the higher the test score. At the upper two grade levels, television viewing was predictive of poorer performance, with heavier viewers doing worse than lighter viewers. At grade 4, more than 6 hours of viewing a day produced poorer performance than more moderate viewing (see the discussion of television effects in Chapter 11, this volume). These findings complement earlier *NAEP* data (e.g., Applebee, Langer, & Mullis, 1986, 1988; Educational Testing Service, 1985; Pikulski, 1991): Students tend to engage less in academic activities, such as reading and writing, on their own with increasing age, with less engagement in such activities associated with lower academic achievement. When all of the *NAEP* data are considered on this point, it is clear that students not achieving academically are choosing to spend their time doing nonacademic things rather than activities that might advance their intellect more.

The test was also revealing about curricular features. For example, students at grades 8 and 12 knew more about rights and responsibilities than they did the political process, political institutions, or the purposes of government. Students who experienced social studies three or four times a week did better than those receiving less instruction. Receiving civics instruction was associated with better performance on the civics *NAEP*. This outcome was consistent with a general conclusion based on *NAEP* data across tests that receiving instruction in the area tested increases achievement on the test, with the more instruction received the greater the test score (e.g., Dorsey, Mullis, Lindquist, & Chambers, 1988). At the two higher grade levels, stu-

dents who received homework assignments outperformed those who did not. There was an especially clear effect at the high school level, with students who did more than 3 hours homework a week outperforming those who did 2 hours, who outperformed students who did 1 hour, who did better than students with no homework (or who did not do homework; see Chapter 11, this book). At all grade levels, reading more than five pages a day was predictive of better performance on the civics test. An especially disturbing finding was that African-Americans and Hispanics receive less social studies instruction than whites. Extensive information also was collected about the particular topics covered as part of civics instruction at each grade level, with detailed topic-by-topic breakdowns provided for each grade level.

An interesting outcome was that opportunity to participate in mock elections, trials, and related activities was predictive of *NAEP* performance. A more disturbing outcome was that few students reported experiencing such participation. Indeed, what emerged from the analysis of instruction was a heavy reliance on textbooks to convey knowledge rather than writing or more creative activities. This outcome is consistent with a general pattern in *NAEP* data—that the most innovative and potentially effective curricular innovations, such as ones reviewed in this book, are not encountered frequently in school (e.g., process approaches to writing such as those described in Chapter 15, this book; use of group discussion as part of reading instruction [see O'Donnell, 1991; Ruth, 1991; Chapters 8 and 14, this book]). There are some indicators that the situation is improving, for example, data confirming that students have more conferences with their teachers as they write and revise, consistent with plan-write-revise models of writing such as those covered in Chapter 15 (Applebee, Langer, Jenkins, Mullis, & Foertsch, 1990).

The responses to the essay question on presidential responsibilities produced evidence of low knowledge—or possibly low ability in expressing knowledge—for the majority of grade-8 students and for a substantial proportion of grade-12 students. The essays were scored for completeness of response in the following fashion:

- Elaborated response: Thoughtful response with a mix of specific examples and discussion (7.3

percent of grade-8 students, 19.0 percent of grade-12 students).

- Adequate: One or two examples of presidential responsibilities with little discussion (34.0 percent at grade 8, 40.0 percent at grade 12).
- Minimal: Generalities given or list of responsibilities included errors (49.9 percent at grade 8, 34.6 percent at grade 12).
- Unacceptable: Not on topic, incorrect, or no attempt (8.8 percent at grade 8, 6.4 percent at grade 12).

One aspect of the essay data provided one of those shocking tidbits of information that the media often pick up and report: 11 percent of grade 8 and 6 percent of grade 12 students did not know that Ronald Reagan was President of the United States (at the time the test was taken). Close analyses of the civics *NAEP* revealed that many students do not know much of the vocabulary pertaining to civics, lack knowledge of many important political processes, and are deficient in their understandings of many aspects of government history and tradition.

These *NAEP* civics data made clear that efforts to increase student exposure to academic content pay off. Home environments that do not include reading materials and that permit extensive television viewing result in poorer performance than home environments in which books are salient and the television is turned off. Schools that foster learning by offering more classwork on civics, more homework, and opportunities to participate in mock political events produce higher achievement. These conclusions based on the civics assessment generally are consistent with conclusions that have emerged from other *NAEP* assessments.

NAEP Outcomes in General and What They Mean
There are several important general conclusions that emanate from *NAEP* data, with these frequently reported in the media. We make the case in this section that there is reason to be cautious in making too general claims based on this test, however.

Poor Performance of Contemporary Students.
A consistent trend over the years has been for American students to perform at lower levels on *NAEP* assessments than is desirable (e.g., review the discussion of NAEP performance levels in reading that were covered in Chapter 14)—at least in the eyes of some prominent policymakers who publish analyses of *NAEP* data along with stinging criticisms of American students and the schools that are

educating them (e.g., Bennett, 1984; Cheney, 1987; Ravitch & Finn, 1987). A theme in such commentaries, and those of like-minded politically conservative thinkers (e.g., Bloom, 1987; Hirsch, 1987), is that schools are not preparing students as well as they used to be prepared.

Whittington (1991) decided to examine critically that claim, responding specifically to Ravitch and Finn's *What Do Our 17-year-olds Know?*, which decried the poor performance of the U.S. students on recent American history and literature *NAEPs*. She examined student performance on American history tests going back to 1915, when the multiple-choice test first appeared and was applied to assess American student competence in history (Tryon, 1927). Here is what she found:

- A 1915 objective test of American history administered to five school districts, two teachers' colleges, and at the University of Texas: Mean test performance ranged from 21 to 45 percent correct depending on the sample.
- A test reported in 1920 given to 23 schools in nine cities, containing items such as "Who was the first president of the United States?" and "What was the historical significance of the Articles of Confederation?": Eleventh-graders averaged 72 percent. Twelfth graders averaged 90%.
- An objective test administered in Wisconsin in 1920 to high school students produced means ranging from 27 to 77 percent.
- A 1922 report from South Bend, Indiana, claimed that high school students there averaged between 48 and 59 percent on an objective test of American history knowledge.
- A mean of 41 percent correct was provided in a 1924 report for a test administered in six states.
- When students in 15 cities were administered a 200-item factual test in the early 1920s, the mean correct was 40 percent.
- A national standardized test of American history administered from 1936 to 1965 produced means of 34 percent for high school students, 45 percent for adults, and 69 percent for social studies teachers.

One conclusion that is immediately obvious from these results is that it is not fair to assume that student knowledge about American history was ever great—at least for the first two-thirds of this century. Whittington (1991) examined the tests carefully for items comparable in content to ones on the history *NAEP*. Her conclusion was that student knowledge of history then and now was not all that different:

> One major implication of the results of this study is that the perception of a decline in the "results" of American education is open to question. Indeed, given the reduced dropout rate and less elitist composition of the 17-year-old student body today, one could argue that the students of today know more American history than did their age peers of the past. . . . Advocates for reform of education and excellence in public schooling should refrain from harkening to a halcyon past (or allow the perception of a halcyon past) to garner support for their views. (Whittington, 1991, p. 778)

As scholars who have dedicated much of our careers to designing ways to improve student learning, over the years we have been sensitive to many references, even in historical documents, about the need for students to read, write, and study better. Thus, we never found credible the claim that there once was a time in the United States when all students (or even most students) learned to read, write, and think with great proficiency.

Wyatt (1992) systematically reviewed some of the references we had encountered over the years. She identifies claims about underprepared college students, ones not able to read college-level texts or write college-level essays, throughout the last two centuries—with these reports emanating from elitist institutions such as Yale, Chicago, Wisconsin, Michigan, Indiana, Minnesota, Cornell, Dartmouth, and Harvard. Remedial courses of various sorts were offered at many of these institutions in the 19th century. We believe that Maxwell (1979, p. 279) made an accurate assessment of the situation, one that should be kept in mind when reading books such as *What Do Our 17-year-olds Know?*: "It seems that every generation at some point discovers that students cannot read as well as they would like or as well as professors expect."

Narrowing of the Gap Between Black and White Achievement. *NAEP* data have been analyzed for racial differences in performance since this testing program started. Whites always outperform blacks. Even so, the gap in black-white performance differences has been narrowing, with the most prominent analyses for reading and mathematics (Jaynes & Williams, 1989, Chapter 7; Mullis, Owens, & Phillips, 1990). Although there has also been a narrowing of

black-white differences in performance on tests such as the *SAT* during this same period, the *NAEP* data are seen as more telling because these data are more representative of the entire population, as the *SAT* is a test elected only by those interested in postsecondary education.

Not all who examine this closing of the gap are sanguine about it (Darling-Hammond & Snyder, 1992; Secada, 1992). First, at least for some of the *NAEP* assessments, the narrowing represents both a decline in white achievement and a gain in black achievement, so that focusing on the black-white difference misses the point that there have not been especially striking improvements in black performance. In addition, when there is close analysis of the pattern of performances within tests, much of the black performance improvement (e.g., in mathematics) is with respect to lower-level competencies rather than the more advanced competencies tapped by the test (Jaynes & Williams, 1989, Chapter 7; Kirsch & Jungeblut, 1986). The critics of these tests argue that the closer one looks at *NAEP* data, the more clear it is that there is a long way to go if minorities are to perform at the higher level of competencies tapped by these tests, levels of competency that reflect the ever-increasing literacy and numeracy demands of modern life. Those who focus simply on the narrowing of the black-white gap are missing the point that education is still failing to be effective with many more minority than white majority children.

Other Potential Failings of the NAEP, Analyses, and Interpretations of It. Besides the danger of projecting an overly pessimistic outlook on the current generation compared with past generations, there are a number of other failings of the *NAEP*, at least in the eyes of its critics. These include the following:

- The *NAEP* tests basic skills much more than higher-order skills, with this driving the curriculum toward drill and practice to ensure students could perform the competencies tapped by the test (Squire, 1991). Many of the content items require only superficial acquaintance with the material (e.g., knowing who wrote what) rather than the deep understanding that comes from critical reading, reflecting, discussing, and acting on important content (Rosenblatt, 1991). Somewhat paradoxically, to the extent that the *NAEP* measures higher-order thinking skills— and every *NAEP* test does so to some degree— such skills are lacking in American students, with the critics believing that the national (and state) tests to some extent are the cause of the apparent failures to teach higher-order processes and strategies. The prominence of the thinking that standardized assessments such as the *NAEP* are stifling real educational reform was dramatized by the cover of the September 1992 *Teacher* magazine. The following was in bold print: "Testing: Our obsession with standardized multiple-choice tests is impeding educational innovation." The article on testing that followed was entitled, "The Enemy of Innovation."

- The *NAEP* data are used by policymakers to leverage for reforms consistent with their agendas (e.g., Darling- Hammond & Snyder, 1992; Early, 1991; Farr & Beck, 1991; Ruth, 1991), which are not always consonant with educator agendas. One of the most debatable of these is the push by conservative groups for a common curriculum, one based on what they perceive to be the great Western ideas (e.g., Finn,1991; Hirsch, 1987), but not one considered broad enough by many nor necessarily representative of the best of all thought and ideas. Moreover, it seems to be an agenda that is decidedly focusing on lower-order skills. These include memorizing and rote learning rather than the higher-order reading, writing, and problem-solving skills that educators believe are important. Another conservative agenda fueled by *NAEP* data is the push for the advancement of private schools because of the consistently higher scores on standardized tests by private compared with public school students (e.g., Finn, 1991).
- There are some important sampling problems with the *NAEP*. In particular, only children who are enrolled in school are measured. Because minorities and members of economically disadvantaged groups tend to drop out in larger proportions from school, they may be underrepresented in the high school data especially (Secada, 1992). In addition, students whom school officials believe would have difficulty with a standardized test because of language proficiency problems (e.g., English-as-a-second-language students) sometimes do not take the test (Secada, 1992). Thus, the *NAEP* may be substantially overestimating how well minorities and the poor are doing in academic achieve-

ment because many of the worst off in minority and poor groups are not tested. Ignoring such sampling bias may be choosing to underestimate the educational needs of some groups.

- Some claims made in light of the test data may be flagrant overstatements (e.g., the conclusion that American students lack higher-order thinking skills). One possibility is that the higher-order thinking skills that students possess will not be evident in all situations, with a standardized testing situation being one in which reflective, higher-order thinking may not occur as readily as it would in other situations (Newkirk, 1991). Dyson and Freedman (1991) express their concerns about the validity of the *NAEP* writing assessment as follows:

"These national writing assessments all evaluate relatively short samples of writing collected under formal testing conditions. Thus, the samples present the same validity problems as the impromptu writing scored for school, district, and state assessments. Only *NAEP* has published claims about the state of writing in our nation, and these claims must be interpreted with great caution, given that their students' performance on impromptu writing is completed in 15 minutes. . . " (p. 759)

In short, even when the *NAEP* deviates from multiple-choice formats in an attempt to provide a more valid assessment, there are major questions about whether they succeed in tapping the higher-order competencies they seek to measure with their non–multiple-choice items.

Although there are many other data supporting the conclusion that students' higher-order skills are not as well developed as they could be, perhaps the case made based on *NAEP* scores is too extreme. This is an important point to consider because the higher-order skills presumably tapped by the *NAEP* are ones deemed essential for a high proportion of the population in the new technologically advanced economy of the 21st century: If the *NAEP* data are on target with respect to extreme underdevelopment of many advanced academic skills, there is reason for great concern. To the extent that the lack of higher-level competencies reflects measurement inadequacies, the happier the situation is for the United States. In general, to the extent that the *NAEP* taps too thin a slice of the education day and the competencies developed during that day, its credibility as an indicator of the national failure of education goes down (e. g. Sizer, 1984).

Summary   Although the *NAEP* is an impressive assessment achievement yielding voluminous, but generally orderly, data for the last quarter of a century, there are doubts. As was the case with the standardized assessments covered in Chapter 16, there are doubts about how well minority populations are measured by the *NAEP*, although some of the specific concerns differ from the ones raised about IQ testing. In addition, just as many believe that IQ testing is a tool of the political right, the *NAEP* raises suspicion that it is a political lever of reactionary America: The political right publicly embrace *NAEP* data more uncritically than others and seem to use it to push their own agenda toward a curriculum emphasizing American and Western knowledge and values.

Without a doubt, however, there has been more discussion about *NAEP* conclusions regarding higher-order thinking than about almost any other topic. Too few students are scoring near the top of the *NAEP* scales; too few are getting the most difficult items on the tests correct. One possibility is that most U.S. students are not developing higher-order academic skills, such as being able to coordinate strategies to find information in texts; plan, write, and revise texts; and understand, plan, and carry out complex solutions in an attempt to solve problems. Alternatively, perhaps the tests simply are not good at assessing these competencies. This possibility is one impetus for the development of new assessments that tap higher-order skills more directly, with such assessments taken up in the next subsection.

Before closing this subsection, however, we point out that the *NAEP* is a tremendous force in education. Presidents, Secretaries of Education, Governors, and state-level education department officials have accepted its conclusions; so have legislators. These politicians, their appointees, and employees of the executive departments they control have designed new federal and state policies, ones that have changed what is taught in school. As consultants for textbook companies, we remember many conversations with materials producers about how cultural literacy might be incorporated into texts, largely stimulated by policymaker reactions to *NAEP* data: For example, some state textbook adoption boards have set clear policies about the need for cultural literacy coverage in basal readers used in

their state. *NAEP* data are a steady feature in those colored graphs in *USA Today* and in other newspapers across the United States; the newest *NAEP* data often make the network radio and television broadcasts. This is information that parents and teachers receive all the time; we believe it has made a difference, for example, in stimulating parents to clamor for instruction in higher-order thinking skills for their children (i.e., skills that are deficient according to the test), teachers to teach those skills (i.e., skills students will be tested on), and school districts to buy critical-thinking programs such as the ones reviewed in Chapter 11. Do not underestimate the importance of the NAEP and other government-mandated tests in the lives of children.

Performance Assessments

There are substantial data documenting that if students are tested on particular content, teachers will teach to that content (e.g., Darling-Hammond & Snyder, 1992; F. Smith, 1986, Chapter 6; M. L. Smith, 1991a, 1991b). What is also interesting, however, is that they will teach some processes that they believe will be useful on the test: They teach students how to take the test, most prominently test-taking skills and strategies, from those with only implications for test taking, such as eliminating obviously incorrect multiple-choice answers before making a guess if not sure, to those that have some educational value beyond the test, such as converting story problems into equations that can be solved (Smith, 1991a).

One of the rationales behind performance assessments is that this powerful tendency of teachers to prepare their students for national, state, and other standardized assessments can be exploited for some good (Popham, 1987)—if the tests require processing abilities that are valuable in and of themselves: Performance assessments are being designed explicitly to force change in what students are learning in school, with performance assessment one of the most active areas in measurement research and development. Policymakers who have been influenced by educational researcher findings have decided that it is a good thing for students (1) to learn how to plan, write, and revise essays, with the result that performance assessments are being devised that require students to demonstrate how they write; (2) to perform scientific experiments, from hypothesis formation to hypothesis testing, with the outgrowth the development of assessments that require students to conduct experiments from hypothesis formation to actual experimentation to writeup of the outcomes of the experiment; and (3) to learn the skills necessary to work mathematics problems and explain them at a conceptual level, stimulating the creation of math assessments in which students must explain their answers and how the answer was generated (O'Neil, 1992).

Some examples of performance assessments will make more obvious how different these assessments are from the standardized tests considered in Chapter 16 and in this chapter thus far. For readers who wish many more examples and extensive descriptions of performance assessments, Mitchell's (1992) *Testing for Learning: How New Approaches to Evaluation Can Improve American schools* is an excellent and accessible sourcebook, a book we strongly recommend to any reader with a need to be informed about modern approaches to educational accountability. This book also provides substantial input about the many different groups who are working on development of performance assessments; it is an excellent history of this short-lived movement that is expanding its intellectual scope as the 1990s proceed, with many more jurisdictions coming on board as political support for new assessments increases.

Maryland Reading-Writing Assessment (Maryland State Performance Assessment Project)   Many leading literacy theorists believe that reading and writing should be taught together and are naturally related activities (see Chapter 15). One way to encourage teachers to teach that way is to use assessments that require simultaneous and coordinated reading and writing, which is one of the approaches used in the Maryland State Performance Assessment Project (MSPAP).

Consider an assessment used at grade 8 (Mitchell, 1992, pp. 47–49; also see *Educational Leadership,* May 1992, p. 17): Each student is given some texts (Jack London's classic story, "To Build a Fire," and a short piece from a book by Robert Pozos and David O'Born, *Hypothermia: Causes, Effects, and Prevention).* Each student also receives a map of North America including Alaska and Canada's Yukon Territory. They also receive a response book into which they write their answers during the assessment.

The students are asked first to think about when they have been cold. They are given 10 minutes to

write about their experiences being cold in the response journal. This is followed by reading of the London story, with students then responding to a series of comprehension questions. Some questions can be answered by constructing drawings; most require written responses. One question asks them to compare their own experiences with the cold with those of the dying man in "To Build a Fire." The students also assess how difficult the reading was for them; they are asked to write about the reading strategies they employed while reading the story by responding to a question about what they did when they came to a word or reference that they did not understand. That is day 1.

The test continues on Day 2. First, students write a 5-minute letter to the dying man in "Fire," advising him about what to do to save his life. What follows is a class discussion of this topic, with the teacher recording on the board student ideas, especially in response to some of the words in the story (succumb, insidious). Students then read the piece from the book on hyperthermia and respond in writing to a series of comprehension questions, some of which can be answered by constructing pictures and diagrams.

Day 3 is concerned with integrating the information in the two pieces that were read. Students are required to write one of three types of responses:

- An essay informing friends what they need to do to be safe on a weekend trip.
- A poem, story, or play capturing the feelings associated with extreme states of heat, cold, hunger, or fatigue.
- A speech attempting to persuade people not to travel to the Yukon.

The teachers of students, however, do not know which of these types of writing will be required, although they have been informed in advance that students will be required to construct one of these three types of responses. The idea, of course, is to encourage teachers to teach students how to compose essays, poems, stories, plays, and persuasive speeches. The idea is to force the curriculum to cover particular types of writing processes in reaction to material that is read.

As they construct their Day 3 writing, students are required to show their process. They are required to list words they have brainstormed in planning the essay or record in their journal a semantic web of ideas used in planning the essay. Then they write a rough draft. They revise. The examination concludes with them using a proofreading guide sheet to check their final copy.

All of this material is graded on two criteria. One is for comprehension of what was read. That is, there is scoring of whether the student seemed to understand what was read. In addition, there is scoring of the quality of writing and how the writing task was done.

Connecticut Science and Mathematics Assessments
Policymakers have decided that learning how to cooperate and create group products is important, consistent with principles and data considered in Chapters 5 and 8 of this book. Thus, some performance assessments, such as the Connecticut Science and Mathematics Assessments, require cooperative action. In addition, science and mathematics educators are extremely concerned that students develop conceptual understandings rather than the superficial understandings promoted by rote use of formulas or recall of factual knowledge only (see Chapters 12 and 13). In response to the need for science and mathematics education reforms that promote such conceptual understandings, the Connecticut Assessments require students to provide conceptual explanations and to problem solve in a reflective fashion. Although there is no doubt that these assessments are meant to force changes in education, readers of this text should understand that there is a broad base of consensus that the new performance assessments in science and mathematics are much better matched to the thinking skills that scientists and mathematicians believe should be stimulated than are traditional assessments (see Kulm, 1990; Murnane & Raizen, 1988; again, see Chapters 12 and 13).

For example, some questions on the assessments are the following (Mitchell, 1992, p. 72):

- What does it mean that one supermarket has lower prices than another? All items are lower? If only some, which ones? What kinds of math are needed to figure out what this means?
- Determine the energy costs in taking a shower. Design an alternative shower using less energy.
- Figure out which mixture of antifreeze and water has the highest boiling point, making it suitable for extreme climates.
- Construct vivid comparisons to make the magnitude of the Valdez oil spill disaster obvious. (Adapted from Mitchell, 1992, p. 72)

A worked-out example from the assessment illustrates how such assessment occurs in practice. Students are presented the following problem:

> Your principal has recently become concerned over the issue of lead poisoning in your school. He has asked your class to study and report back to him on safety of the school's drinking water. . . . You will design an experiment to determine that amount of lead present in your school's drinking water. You will also study factors which affect the amount of lead in the water . . . the source of the water (i.e., from various faucets or drinking fountains, the temperature of the water, the pH of the water, and the length of standing time of the water in the pipes). (Mitchell, 1992, p. 72).

Just as was the case with the Maryland reading-writing assessment, this task requires 3 days to complete. The ultimate performance for the students was to make a group presentation of their findings to the principal, with each member of the group required to contribute to the oral presentation. The teacher observes the process and completes a checklist about what happened during problem solving; students also complete a checklist, indicating their contribution to the task.

In addition, each student prepared a written report for the principal. This contained analysis of the lead in the school's water versus the allowable amount of lead in water, based on the data generated by the student's group as well as the data generated by the entire class. The letter contained an explanation about how the amount of lead in the school water was determined. Students also indicated how confident they were in their results. Recommendations were made by the student about how to improve the safety of the school's water. That is, the student was required to produce a writeup comparable to the type of writeup required at the end of any scientific inquiry.

More About Mathematics and Science Performance Assessment Such assessments are different from conventional assessments because there is observation of the decision-making process, either decision making in groups of students or by individual students (Berk, 1986; Webb, 1992). For example, if attempting to assess students' measurement skills, performance assessment at its best involves observation of students as they use rulers, tape measures, different types of scales, and so on. That is, they are not shown a drawing of a ruler next to an object and asked to read off the length from the depiction. The assessor sizes up the procedures used and the attitudes and confidence of students as they proceed with problem solving.

Mathematics educators are also working on performance assessments that are paper-and-pencil assessments, although ones with a difference: These assessments require students to reveal their understanding of process. Consider the following example, which involves presentation of this problem and the solution attempted by another student:

> A bowl contains 10 pieces of fruit (apples and oranges). Apples cost 5 cents each and oranges cost 10 cents each. Altogether the fruit is worth 70 cents. We want to find out how many apples are in the bowl. Kelly tried to solve the problem this way:

$10 \times 5 = 50$	$8 \times 5 = 40$
$2 \times 10 = \underline{20}$	$3 \times 10 = 30$
70	$4 \times 10 = 40$
	$6 \times 5 = 30$

> There were 30 apples in the bowl. (Szetala & Nicol, 1992, p. 44)

The student taking the assessment is then asked to evaluate the performance of the student whose answer is shown, by responding to the following questions:

1. Is Kelly's way of solving the problem a good one? Tell why you think it is or is not a good way.
2. Did Kelly get the right answer? Explain why she did or did not. (Szetala & Nicol, 1992, p. 44)

Most readers will have figured out that Kelly's solution contained serious errors (e.g., 30 apples as a response makes no sense when there are only 10 pieces of fruit total in the bowl; the correct solution is 6 apples, with Kelly's error that she copied the wrong piece of information from her computations and failed to check her answer against the reality of the situation). To evaluate Kelly's solution, a student must be able to represent the problem and compare his or her representation with Kelly's. The questions posed about Kelly's solution require that students reveal their thinking about the problem.

Szetala and Nicol (1992) provided a list of a variety of methods that require students to communicate about their thinking, which included the following:

- Present a problem and part of its solution, with the student required to complete the solution.
- Present a problem that includes some irrelevant facts. Have students evaluate the quality of the problem and remove incongruous information.
- Have students explain how they did a problem using only words.
- After solving a problem, have students create a new problem using the same problem structure but a different context. (Adapted from Szetala & Nicol, 1992, p. 44)

Those devising such questions are also devising methods for scoring them in a fashion other than right or wrong, ranging from no credit for a response that misses the point of the problem completely to partial credit for showing some appropriate reflection and progress toward solution to full credit for a fully reflective answer with detailed commentary on the processes required to respond to the request made by the test item (Szetala & Nicol, 1992).

Closing Comments on These Examples and Testlike Performance Assessments   A diverse range of competencies can be tested via performance assessment. A major question, however, is how good these tests really are: Are they reliable and valid? Shavelson and associates (e.g., Shavelson, Baxter, & Pine, 1992) have been evaluating science performance assessments for grade-5 and grade-6 science. For example, in one, students were asked to test three different types of paper towels to determine which soaked up the most and least water. In addition to the towels, the students were provided water, beakers, a scale, a timer, and other utensils. In a second assessment, students were "given" mystery boxes containing circuit components in a MacIntosh computer microworld simulation. Using wires, batteries, and bulbs, they were to determine what was in these boxes. The students were apprised that each box had (1) two batteries linked into the circuit (2) a wire in the circuit, (3) a light alone, (4) a battery and light, or (5) nothing. In a third assessment, students experimented with sow bugs to determine the bugs' environmental preferences, with the bugs and manipulations carried out in a MacIntosh simulation. They were to determine whether the bugs liked damp or dry environments and light or dark environments. In all three assessments, students were required to keep records of what they did and report their conclusions.

Could student performances be assessed reliably with these tests? Yes and no. On the positive side of the ledger, it was easy to get agreement between raters with respect to the scoring of individual assessments. It was harder to produce consistent results across tasks, however, with some students performing better on one assessment than another. What this latter result means is that to obtain reliable performance assessment data, a number of tasks will have to be included in such assessments. This is a formidable demand given that the expenses in developing, administering, and scoring single performance assessments are high. More positively, it did seem in Shavelson's studies that reliable scoring of student writeups of their assessments was possible; in addition, presentation of the problems on a microcomputer with subsequent experimentation in the simulation environment (and recorded by the program) also seemed satisfactory. Thus, there do appear to be cost-saving shortcuts to actual hands-on student performances observed and scored by raters.

With respect to validity, Shavelson et al. (1992) expected that students who had been enrolled in "hands-on" science courses that taught process would outperform students in traditional textbook-oriented courses. That proved to be the case. In addition to testing subjects with the performance assessments, Shavelson's group also tested other students with paper-and-pencil tests designed to assess the experimental competencies measured in the performance assessments. The most interesting finding with respect to these tests was that they did not differentiate students with hands-on science instruction from those receiving traditional instruction, although the performance assessments had done so, which, of course, provides some validation for the performance assessments.

One of the main messages of Shavelson's work is that the development of good performance assessments is going to take time. Former President Bush indicated he wanted such tests in schools by 1993. That was unrealistic given the reliability and validity studies needed to ensure that such assessments are measuring what educators and policymakers want measured. If readers review the dates presented in this chapter and the last one, it will be obvious that care in development of a test is warranted: Tests seem to stick around with small modifications once they are established (e.g., contemporary IQ tests resemble the ones developed at the beginning of the 20th century; Wolf, Bixby, Glenn, & Gardner, 1991).

One of the other concerns with performance assessments is their expense relative to traditional assessments. As professionals who have been close to groups developing such tests, it is striking how much time and effort—many committees and many pilot assessments—go into the development of performance assessment items. Then, there are the administration costs, with these tests extending over days of school rather than over hours of school. Finally, there is scoring, which requires many person-hours of effort compared with the rapid machine scoring permitted by multiple choice. Mitchell (1992) estimated that these tests may be 10 times more costly than conventional assessments. Although research such as Shavelson et al. (1992) suggests some cost-saving possibilities, such as reliance on journals and written products rather than actual observations of students, there are also indicators that more resources may have to be put into future assessments than present ones: Recall that Shavelson et al. (1992) observed that a large number of items would be required for reliable performance assessments, which involves the costs of designing the items and then administering them. If Shavelson et al. (1992) are right, the 3-day tests that are performance assessments in the early 1990s may seem like "quickies" compared with future performance assessments. Extensive thinking about whether what is gained by performance assessment is worth the cost of it is needed.

The one gain that is mentioned most often is that performance assessment increases the likelihood of schools deciding to teach the complex processes tapped by the assessments. In fact, there are indicators of test-driven effects on instruction. The most frequently cited of these comes from California: After the state initiated its process writing assessment, teachers reported increasing their instruction of process-oriented writing (California Department of Education, 1990). Author MP worked with Maryland schools when many of them scrambled to put in place process-oriented curricula with the advent of the *MSPAP* assessments; author CBM observed great interest in strategies-based instruction in South Carolina with increasing state assessment of process.

Our awareness of the complexity of skilled reading, writing, and problem solving heightens our personal doubts about the possibility of devising testlike performance assessments that capture the complexity of thought that school at its best would develop. The problems students have been presented on performance assessments to date often are simple or contrived compared with the types of problems we would like students to be able to solve; the essays that emanate from the writing assessments are short and without feeling compared with the essays educators want to stimulate their students to write. In short, our perception of testlike performance assessments is that they are not authentic enough. That is one reason another form of performance assessment, portfolios, covered in the next subsection, is much more appealing to us. Portfolios include authentic student products, students' best efforts, efforts most likely to reveal their competence. Even so, we will conclude the section on portfolios with a continuation of this discussion of reservations about new forms of assessment.

Portfolios: A Form of Long-Term Performance Assessment

A few years ago, one of us had the occasion to hire a commercial photographer for a project. Several candidates were interviewed, each bringing his or her portfolio to the meeting. A photographer's portfolio consists of samples of his or her best work assembled over a long period of time. It is intended to permit potential future employers to make evaluations—positive ones—and hence every effort is made to include strong efforts. Assessment portfolios in education are much like these photographers' portfolios (Bird, 1990): It is a file of a student's best work in writing, math, science, or any area of competence that is the target of education (Collins, 1992; Y. Goodman, 1991; O'Neil, 1992).

Educational portfolios are intended to provide information so that inferences can be made about student knowledge, ability, and their attitudes toward their work. Educators are thinking hard about how student portfolios can and should be used, what should be included in portfolios for various educational tasks and contents (e.g., science, writing, mathematics), and how complete such files should be. Ultimately the portfolio is a collection of objects, often a file of completed projects. Some portfolios might be more specific than others, such as Collins's (1992) suggestion that physics students could be asked to develop portfolios of evidence over some

set period of time to verify their understanding of some physics concept (e.g., a file of examples of how physics impacts everyday life). Some portfolios designed to evaluate teachers more than students might be summaries about how a school year was spent, including examples of outstanding student performances (e.g., essays, projects) to illustrate various facets of the curriculum. In short, portfolios are **collections of objects assembled for a purpose** (Bird, 1990; Collins, 1992). The purpose must be clear before setting out to develop a portfolio.

Because of the focus on measurement of students in this chapter and Chapter 16, the examples of portfolios we provide next are student portfolios (i.e., rather than the teacher portfolios mentioned in the previous paragraph). These examples illuminate the diversity that is portfolio assessment as well as some of its benefits besides providing assessment data. The examples are followed by coverage of how portfolio assessment is already used in large-scale standardized assessments and how it is being developed by the *NAEP* and some states as a performance assessment.

Portfolio Examples from the Classroom   As part of Hansen's Literacy Portfolios Project in Manchester, New Hampshire, fourth-grade students prepare portfolios to document their literacy, with Hansen (e.g., 1992) believing such folders provide students as much opportunity to know themselves and how rich their literacy lives are as they provide opportunity for educators to get to know and understand students and their literacy better.

What is in a grade-4 literacy portfolio? Scott's is an example: (1) a drawing; (2) a draft of some writing Scott had published as a "book" in the resource room; (3) a piece of writing from this year; (4) a list of books he can read; (5) his favorite book, *The Little Engine That Could*; (6) his grade-3 report card; (7) a photo of his father, and (8) a photo of his grandparents (Hansen, 1992, p. 66). These objects are all critically important to Scott, representing that he (1) can now draw, write, and read, when before he could not; (2) can now earn passing grades; and (3) has family members who are dear to him.

Literacy portfolios in New Hampshire often contain evidence of reading and writing outside of school as well as inside school because children often engage in significant literacy that is not school reading and writing. Hansen and her colleagues recognize the importance of documenting such activity if an assessment is to be a comprehensive representation of a child's literacy. The purpose of the portfolios is not only to document reading and writing growth of the child, but also to be an expression of who the child is, both as a literate person and more broadly: Thus, one grade-1 student's portfolio includes a book about a character who has trouble speaking, a book important to the child because he has a speech problem, too. One junior high student's portfolio includes a book about a juvenile who had stolen a car, went to prison, and reformed. This book meant something to the young reader because he had been thrown out of a previous school for misconduct and found the story inspirational as he attempted to make good in a new school.

Hansen (1992) and colleagues believe it important that portfolios capture children's perspectives on their literacy, at least some of the reasons why reading and writing are important to them, and why some books they read and some things they write are more important to them than others. One reason is that such a literacy portfolio provides a great deal of information to new teachers the student will encounter, information that can be used to aid in planning a literacy curriculum that is sensitive to student needs, concerns, and interests.

Collins (1992) provides a description of potential grade-4 science portfolios. There are four classes of objects in such a portfolio: (1) *artifacts,* such as written reports of experiments and tests; (2) *reproductions,* such as a photo of a bulletin board display created by the student; (3) *attestations,* which are appraisals of the student by someone other than the student and his teacher who reviews the portfolio, with examples being letters of gratitude for something a student did (e.g., organized an environmental clean-up day) or a note from other members of the students' cooperative learning group praising a particular contribution made by the student; and (4) *productions,* objects prepared especially for inclusion in the portfolio, including goal statements from the teacher about the purpose of the portfolio, reflective statements by the student indicating the importance and relationship of the various documents in the portfolio, and captions attached to each document in the portfolio to describe what the object is and why it is significant.

One fourth-grade teacher's goal was for students to document that they had acquired balanced science knowledge during the year. Thus, students were required to include documentation about their learning in the content area they liked best during the year of science instruction, two thinking skills they had mastered, and evidence that they had learned about some topic of public concern. (These three categories mapped the particular instructional objectives the teacher had for the class during the year: to develop in-depth knowledge about a range of topics, to increase thinking skills, and to stimulate awareness of the social relevance of science.) To do so, the portfolios could include work sheets from problem-solving activities, diagrams or pictures that had been graded, and products from group work. The number of pieces of evidence was limited, and students were required to develop captions for each exhibit and a reflective statement summarizing how the various exhibits related to one another. The individual students consulted with their teacher about what ought to be included in their portfolio, with the construction of the portfolio a dynamic experience, permitting review of the year's work and increased self-understanding by the students:

> Knowing the purposes of the portfolio and its structure, students have saved their work throughout the year.... Now, as the year ends, they sit in teams with all their evidence spread before them discussing which topic was their favorite and why, or which assignment from that topic best illustrates their mastery; they have all their problem-solving sheets and can see how their skills have changed; they recognize that each has different strengths—the future artist, future mechanic, and future author. As the students write their reflective statements, they integrate their experiences in science class with their experiences from other classes. (Collins, 1992, p. 462)

Such a science portfolio provided a great deal of information about what had been accomplished by the student for that year and was especially rich documentation for parents about their own student's progress. The grade-4 teacher was able to make evaluations of individual students and assign grades for the year, with the portfolios extremely helpful in this process. The portfolios as a collection provided the next year's teachers with a rich fund of evidence about the science coverage experienced in grade 4. The portfolios provided assessment information for this grade-4 science teacher, a rich educational experience for the students, and a window on the students' knowledge for subsequent educators.

Pam Knight (1992) is a middle-school mathematics teacher in California. She had her students keep exhaustive files of their work for the year, including some long-term projects, notes they had taken, tests, problems of the week, homework, and journal remarks about especially difficult examination problems. At the end of the year, she had them go through their folders and select five items that would represent their knowledge of math and the efforts they had expended during the year. The students attached a personal statement to each of these exhibits. Here is an example of one set of comments:

> I chose three papers for my portfolio because they show my best work and my worst work. They portray both sides of my academic performance in math this last semester.
>
> The 45 percent math test is in my portfolio because it shows that I have some problems in math. It shows my bad work. It shows that sometimes I have a bad day. It shows also that I forgot to study (ha, ha, ha).
>
> I can sum up three papers in this paragraph. Those are the Personal Budget, the James project, and the $2000 lottery project. On all of these papers, I did really well. That shows I do much better on those projects, especially the creative ones. I have a bit more fun doing them rather than doing just normal take home math assignments. These papers definitely show me at my best. (Knight, 1992, p. 72)

One of the most immediately obvious effects of this new form of assessment for Knight was that it did what performance assessment is intended to do: It changed her teaching:

> As a result of trying to implement portfolio assessment, my classroom has definitely changed. It became apparent early on that if I wanted variety in my children's portfolios, I had to provide variety in assignments. I have changed my curriculum to include more problem-solving opportunities with written explanations. I have also had my students do two long-term situational problems. In the past, although I knew my algebra classes found such problems entertaining, I had questioned their lasting value. Now I see that these problems are the ones the kids remember the most. (Knight, 1992, p. 72)

The portfolios were used as part of assessing students in the course, providing about 20 percent of the total grade. Knight believed that the portfolio provided her with increased understanding of student maturity, self-esteem, and writing. She also believed that student self-assessment was an important gain from construction of the portfolios, with the portfolio construction project forcing them to re-view their strengths and weaknesses and what had been accomplished in the class.

In closing this subsection on examples of evaluations with portfolios, we emphasize that these reports are typical of many we have been encountering, in published accounts of teacher use of portfolios and as we interact with teachers in the field. The three essential steps to construction of a portfolio are the following: Students (1) collect their work over a reasonable period of time; (2) review it at some point, selecting some "best" work or most representative work for inclusion in a portfolio; and (3) assemble the portfolio, including reflective, integrative commentary about the pieces selected and their significance. Typically, teachers provide criteria to students to help them select and reflect on their work.

Many teachers believe portfolio construction increases student review and reflection on their work; as an assessment device, it informs them as teachers about strengths and weaknesses of their curriculum and is informative to parents and future teachers about the curricular accomplishments of individuals as well as groups of students. In the remainder of this subsection, we turn attention to large-scale attempts to use portfolio assessment, attempts that are generating additional enthusiasm for this form of **authentic assessment.** (Authentic assessment is a term used by psychometric types whenever the test is a direct measurement of the competency being measured—such as looking at student writing to determine whether a student is a good writer.)

NAEP and Portfolio Assessment: The 1990 Writing Portfolio Pilot Study

Although the *NAEP* has been criticized for relying too much on multiple-choice tests, it also has a distinguished track record for integrating new and innovative methods into large-scale assessments (e.g., the presidential responsibilities essay on the civics test). *NAEP* is now studying the possibility of national portfolio assessment of writing, with Gentile (1992) reporting the results of a 1990 pilot study related to that effort.

NAEP has been conducting writing assessments for some time. The typical format for these assessments is for students to be provided a writing assignment that can be completed in 15 minutes. A great failing of this type of assessment is that much of writing requires more than 15 minutes. Indeed, most of the process writing instruction that is favored by writing researchers and theorists—and is being translated into instruction in many schools—involves multiple sessions of planning (perhaps including library or other research) and revisions after the completion of a first draft. These revisions often involve student conferencing with teachers, peers, or parents. Given the growing commitment of many educators to plan-write-revise models, the *NAEP* is questioning the validity of its 15-minute, first-and-final draft writing assessment. Consistent with their commitment to research-based conclusions, however, *NAEP* has decided to study the situation as part of piloting portfolio assessment of writing rather than simply concluding that the 15-minute format is inadequate. We applaud such a commitment to research rather than armchair analyses of assessment.

The portfolio project involved grade-4 and grade-8 students who had participated in the regular *NAEP* writing assessment. The teachers of these students were contacted and asked to assist the students in selecting one piece of their *best* writing from the grade-4 or grade-8 school year. More than 1000 students were tapped at each age level. (One reason this was a pilot is that the sample ended up not being as carefully constructed with respect to national representation issues as other *NAEP* samples, although none could read the description of the sampling without thinking that the study was adequate to permit at least tentative conclusions about the writing of American grade-4 and grade-8 students.)

Once the essays arrived at *NAEP*, a great deal of effort was devoted initially to determining how to analyze them. One of the first analyses was to examine exactly what type of writing was submitted. There were some surprises. First, more than half of the writing samples (51 percent at grade 4, 59 percent at grade 8) were informative essays. The second most common type of writing was narratives (36 percent at grade 4, 30 percent at grade 8). An especially striking finding was that there was little persuasive essay writing, striking to the *NAEP* because their assessments so often ask students to write persuasive essays. (Thus, a first major finding was that a type of essay frequently tapped on more traditional *NAEP* writing assessments probably is not practiced much in school writing.) There was also little poetry, few letters, and almost no research reports. One disturbing finding was that 7 percent of the grade-4 and 5 percent of the grade-8 submissions were skill sheets, with teachers indicating that they had not started writing instruction by the

spring. (Thus, another important finding is that despite the claim in Chapter 15 that writing instruction is almost as common as the pledge to the flag in American elementary schools, there are some schools where it does not happen or does not happen until late in the year.)

The papers were assessed for several other features early in this analysis process, with substantial important information emerging from these analyses. First, almost all of the papers were written to an unspecified audience, despite the fact that many believe skilled writers write to specific audiences and shape essays according to audience background knowledge and need. Second, fewer than half of the papers showed evidence of using the plan-write-revise approach. The most common process that was evident was minor revision. Although the *NAEP* had requested that drafts accompany the submissions, they recognized the possibility that many teachers sent best drafts and that their assessment of process on this pilot might underestimate the amount of process students use. They gathered more extensive information about process in their 1992 portfolio assessment, which was planned in part by considering the difficulties with the 1990 pilot. (Results not yet available when this book went to press.) Third, the most frequently used resource for papers were students' own ideas rather than material from sources. Fourth, only 2 percent of the papers were written on computers, suggesting a low level of computer use for word processing in schools. Fifth, the majority of papers were written in response to general prompts from the teacher, such as "write about Thanksgiving" or "write about bicycles." A great deal about student writing in the United States was discerned from even these preliminary assessments.

After reviewing the papers systematically, the *NAEP* came up with ways of scoring the various types of writing to reflect the characteristics of good versus poor writing. Thus, the worst narratives described only a single event, often minimally with a list of sentences. Then came undeveloped stories, followed by stories that contained all of the main story grammar elements (i.e., a series of events carried out by characters confronting problems; see Chapters 3 and 14, this book). It was also possible to discern better developed stories, with these classified as extended stories, developed stories, and elaborated stories (with elaborated the best of these three, which included all of the story grammar elements with elaborated problems and resolutions to problems). Similar scoring schemes were developed for informational essays and persuasive writing, with the weakest examples of each genre scored as 1's (e.g., single events in the narrative category) and the best examples scored as 6's (i.e., elaborated stories for narratives). A critical part of this analysis work was establishing the reliability of these scoring schemes: Two different raters agreed on the exact rating for an essay more than three-quarters of the time; two different raters were within one category (e.g., one gave it a 3, the other a 4) a minimum of 96 percent of the time, ranging up to 100 percent of the time (i.e., for grade-4 narratives and informative essays). The scoring was reliable.

The outcome was not entirely different from other *NAEP* assessments, however, including the writing assessments used to generate the *Writing Report Cards* for the United States to date. First, most students performed on the low end of the scale. Collapsing across all types of writing, 88 percent of grade-4 students and 70 percent of grade-8 students received a 1, 2, or 3. Virtually none of the students received 6's. Only 1 percent of the grade-4 narratives received a 5; only 2 percent of the grade-4 informative essays did so; there were no grade-4 persuasive essays earning a 5. Only 8 percent of the grade-8 narratives earned a 5; only 8 percent of the grade-8 informative essays did so; no grade-8 persuasive essays earned a 5.

A critical question for the *NAEP* was whether students would score differently on this portfolio assessment compared with the more traditional *NAEP* writing assessment. At the grade-4 level, if they did poorly or well on the portfolio assessment, they did the same on the *NAEP Writing Report Card* assessment 77 percent of the time. The corresponding figure at the grade-8 level was only 55 percent, however. That is, the grading of students on the two assessments was more similar at the grade-4 than at the grade-8 level. When there was a discrepancy in student performance at either grade level, students were more likely to score well on the portfolio assessment than on the 15-minute, first-and-last-draft assessment. Our reading of these data is that the portfolio was providing unique information at both grade levels and, if anything, information that is more informative to the United States about the type of writing that many educators wish to foster.

Although there were glitches in the 1990 *NAEP* portfolio pilot, such as the need for more extensive information about the processes students used to produce their portfolio essay, the assessment process seemed to have proceeded smoothly with this new format, producing data directly relevant to contemporary writing instruction and models of excellent writing instruction. That the *NAEP* is planning a 1992 assessment with refinements over the 1990 pilot is indicative of their commitment to this new type of assessment tool, one that promises to deliver a more interesting and probably more valid writing report card to the United States in the future.

State Portfolio Assessments A number of states are now developing portfolio assessments, with Vermont one of the most visible efforts (Mitchell, 1992, Chapter 5). In Vermont, students take standardized writing and math tests, but they also construct portfolios, including a "best" piece of work for each subject. Statewide committees of teachers developed these portfolio approaches, piloted them, and grade them. There is a reliable evaluation scheme, one communicated to all teachers in the state so they know what counts in this assessment. The scoring is sensitive to whether there is evidence of process writing instruction and whether mathematics teaching encourages exploration and trying alternative approaches. Schools are evaluated with respect to whether they are developing in students process writing and mathematics skills. Portraits of achievement in math and writing for the entire state are developed, capturing what children in the state are being taught and what they can produce in writing and mathematics. An especially appealing feature of the Vermont assessment is that schools hold town meetings once the results are available to present and discuss the school, its students, and their academic accomplishments.

The amount and quality of information generated in the Vermont assessments can be appreciated by considering the various ways that mathematics portfolio products are scored. There are evaluations of student performance on all of the following dimensions (Mitchell, 1992, pp. 118–120):

- Understanding of mathematics tasks: Includes separating relevant from irrelevant information.
- Quality of strategies used to solve problem.
- Reasons for student decision making as problems are solved.
- Quality and extent of decisions, findings, conclusions, observations, and generalizations made.
- Use of mathematical language.

- Use of mathematical representations: graphs, charts, tables, diagrams, manipulatives, and so on.
- Clarity of presentations: Is the portfolio presentation organized, coherent, and clear, so that others could follow it?

We should point out that the initial data generated in Vermont suggest, as did the *NAEP* pilot study, that much change in Vermont mathematics instruction is needed. For example, the portfolios included a great deal of traditional homework and skills sheets (Mitchell, 1992). Of course, an important goal of the portfolio assessment developers is to stimulate schools to provide better instruction. That the state-level portfolio assessments have a fighting chance of making it is encouraged by the fact that there is one national portfolio assessment that has been around for 20 years.

Advanced Placement Studio Art (College Entrance Examination Board)

Can you imagine a paper-and-pencil test to determine whether a student should receive advance placement in studio art? Such a test would be the stuff of a *National Lampoon* parody of testing. The College Board recognized that the only way to determine the placement status of someone in studio art would be to look at their studio art.

There are two different types of portfolios that students can prepare as part of the Advanced Placement Studio Art test, one a general portfolio and the other a drawing portfolio (Mitchell, 1992, Chapter 5). A general portfolio contains four original works, no larger than 16 by 20 inches; slides, films, or videotapes depicting work on a single theme; and a set of slides to illustrate breadth, with slides illustrating student abilities in color, design, sculpture, and drawing. A drawing portfolio has 6 drawings, up to 20 slides on a theme, and up to 20 slides illustrating the student's breadth. Students provide written information about what they have chosen to send and why. They also have to explain how they came up with the idea for the work and disclose technical assistance they received.

All of the materials for all 4500 students submitting portfolios are examined by 18 judges whose evaluations are weighed and averaged to produce an overall evaluation about whether the student deserves advanced placement in studio art. In essence, this is a jury method, one that takes a gymnasium to perform because of the number of submissions and a large staff, but it can be done. Similar to other port-

folios, it influences education, with many high school studio art courses emphasizing student preparation of a portfolio, including a concentration project and the development of a breadth of competencies. (Mitchell's [1992] account of the studio art assessment is particularly interesting.)

Concluding Comments

Portfolio assessment is stimulating a great deal of interest among teachers and those responsible for national assessments. One of its great appeals is that the assessment and the educational product are the same; the items placed in the portfolio are ones that should be produced in a high-quality educational environment. Of course, in some cases, the portfolio assessment stimulates teachers to require their students to do the type of high-quality work required for a successful portfolio. That tests such as Advanced Placement Studio Art have influenced educational practice encourages those interested in using assessment to leverage the educational system to change what is taught in school.

The effects portfolios have on students and teachers need to be studied closely, however: If portfolios have the positive effects on self-esteem suggested by some of the educators discussed in this subsection, that is an important benefit. If they stimulate student understanding of their work and how it fits together, that is an important benefit. If they lead to more effective review of material covered in a course, that is also a benefit that needs to be documented. The research opportunities are great here, both for those interested in testing and for those more concerned with instruction.

Our general enthusiasm for portfolios is held in check, however, by many concerns about performance assessment in general. One way to think about the concerns, however, is as challenges to overcome. If the benefits of portfolios can be documented better, there is every reason to believe that educators and educational researchers will devise ways to overcome obstacles. Our guess is that for portfolios, the obvious external validity of this form of assessment is going to have tremendous appeal to many constituencies, and thus thinking about how to overcome concerns is more appropriate than trying to make the case that defensible portfolio assessment is impossible.

One critical concern is that portfolios, similar to other performance assessments, are capturing only a small part of academic achievement. There are many sources of information that teachers have available to them that provide information about whether their students are making progress. For example, for primary teachers who are charged with the development of literacy in their students, they observe (1) changes in how students respond to stories, (2) whether students engage in independent reading, and (3) the development of oral reading fluency. Teachers obtain data about student reading achievement throughout the school day (e.g., Chittenden, 1991). When these many sources of information about children's literacy are considered, it is clear that even the richest portfolios are going to miss a lot. Thus, one reaction we have to portfolios is to applaud that they are more comprehensive than traditional assessments and more authentic to boot; another reaction is that they could be even more comprehensive and tap a broader range of authentic classroom experiences. We sincerely hope that some clever assessment types, perhaps student readers of this book, will take on the challenge of documenting how more expansive portraits of student accomplishments might be assembled, ones that would permit more complete conclusions about the progress of students in the United States toward literacy and numeracy than any existing assessments. A first step in such work might be some serious research documenting the many possible indicators of performance available in school settings (see Berger, 1991).

Are New State and National Assessments a Good Idea at All?

There is a perception of crisis in American education, fueled largely by what are perceived to be poor performances by American students on standardized assessments, including assessments that permit international comparisons. When comparisons with other countries are made, there always seems to be a lot of other countries that do better than the United States! Everyone is worried, including the President (e.g., Bush, 1991). The argument is that if children do not learn more in school than the current cohort of students, the United States will not be able to keep up because it will lack the literate and numerate workforce required to staff the economic opportunities of the 21st century. Tests, which helped bring on this sense of crisis, have been part of the plan for improving education for the last quarter century. In particular, the new performance assessments are de-

signed to stimulate teaching of the best instruction developed to date, to inculcate the information processing that has proved beneficial in many research studies about how children can read, write, and problem solve well.

As much as we support the type of instruction reviewed in this book, we also recognize that this is the state-of-the-art for the early 1990s. Will it be so a decade from now? Probably not. If performance assessments such as those envisioned are put into place and have the longevity of their predecessor assessments, there is a good chance that the instructional technologies that are so much at the cutting edge today will continue to influence education even after new technologies are developed that surpass them because the cutting-edge instruction of the 1990s is institutionalized in standardized assessments.

There are other concerns as well. High-stakes testing brings out behaviors in many educators that would not occur otherwise because many educators are anxious about the perceived consequences of their students doing poorly on a standardized assessment. Such behaviors range from the ethical—such as teaching test-taking skills, checking answer sheets to make certain students have filled them out correctly, and attempts to increase student motivation to do their best on the test—to the unethical—such as teaching to the test, making certain low achievers are absent on the day of the test, and telling the students the test items before they take the test (Haladyna, Nolen, & Haas, 1991; Smith, 1991a, 1991b). It is the unethical practices that concern us. Teachers are powerful figures in children's social learning (see Chapter 7). Observing a teacher cheat sends a powerful message that cheating is okay and that any means of beating the system is legitimate. Some otherwise ethical teachers sometimes compromise when it comes to standardized testing of their students and do so in ways that increase student perceptions that it is appropriate to attempt to rig the outcomes of a test.

Although attempts to improve results using unethical tactics are made harder by assessments such as portfolios, the potential is still there. For instance, one of the chief concerns of the *NAEP* in its development of the writing portfolio assessment is that the essays submitted are created by the students who are being assessed rather than others (Gentile, 1992). Because high-stakes tests are as much evaluations of the educators as the students, the classroom teacher cannot police the system as persons free of interest in the assessment outcomes, however.

This subsection of the potential dangers of testing could be long, but space pressures mandate that it not be. Thus, we present an unelaborated list of concerns about standardized testing of all sorts, ones that we find especially compelling (Haney, 1991; Perrone, 1991a):

1. It puts unneeded pressure on students.
2. A great deal of class time is spent preparing students for tests and administering them. Such time could be used better.
3. The thin slice of the curriculum covered on the tests receives much more emphasis in instruction than it should.
4. Those advocating for national tests often fail to realize the limitations of them, believing that assessments designed to reveal the competencies of the United States as a whole are flexible enough to be used to make decisions about the competencies of school personnel and the fitness of students to attend college.
5. Those with vested interests in the development of assessments tend to ignore the many other ways of evaluating the quality of schools, such as graduation rates, the success of alumni, and the development of young citizens committed to living constructive lives.
6. Schools are already constrained by too much government red tape; national assessments and the accountability policies associated with them simply add to a laundry list of federal and state requirements that divert resources from the real mission of schooling, which is the education of students.
7. Test scores reliably correlate with socioeconomic status of those examined; most standardized testing thus guarantees that schools serving the least advantaged jurisdictions will be knocked one more time.
8. Teachers rarely use the information provided by standardized assessments to affect instruction, viewing tests as mismatched to the curricula and important educational goals they have for their students.
9. These tests are attempting to force a national curriculum or, in the case of state tests, a state curriculum and thus reduce educator power to make decisions about how best to educate the students they serve.
10. Teachers want tests that tell them something about their own students, information that can assist in their decision making and development of instruction; they do not care how their school compares with the rest of the United States.
11. The motivational theory behind national and statewide testing is naive. There are substantial data making clear that assessments that provide negative information (as the statewide assessments do) fail to motivate attempts at improvement; often, especially if negative feedback is consistent, those receiving it become helpless and fail even to try to improve their teaching (see Chapter 5). When educational researchers examine closely the motivational effect of standardized tests on students, they find much more evidence of these tests undermining student effort than evidence of tests increasing academic motivation in students (e.g., Paris, Lawton, Turner, & Roth, 1991).
12. National and statewide assessments usually occur at only a few grade levels, generating little information that is useful to many other grade levels. Moreover, testing at these three grade levels often translates into pressures for "reforms" only at those grade levels, with explicit pressure for teachers whose children will be tested to provide instruction to prepare their students for tests that are imminent.
13. The resources being used to develop and disseminate assessments could be used to develop and disseminate more effective instruction. After all, the goal of school is to teach children well, not test them well. With better instruction, there would be more interesting outcomes to assess. As Perrone (1991b) put it: "If teaching is skill sheets, textbooks, basal readers, and simplified explanations, a larger view of assessment is not likely to take root. Who wants, for example, a portfolio of skill sheets?" (p. 166)

(By the way, this is our favorite of the criticisms leveled at national and statewide testing.)

Finally, no one could read the new assessment literature without discerning contempt by some of the new assessors about old assessment practices (e.g., Wolf et al., 1991). Our own view is that the new assessments represent an evolutionary development that has benefited enormously from the psychometrics work that preceded it. For example, the evaluations of new assessments in terms of reliability and validity are informed by years of work in standardizing traditional instruments. We fear that some extremely useful, more traditional tests may be dismissed too readily, however, if the aggressive anti–standardized testing rhetoric of the new assessors becomes the politically correct position, which is pretty clearly a goal of many of the new breed of testers. (There is no quicker way to elicit turned-up noses from many testing reformers than to mention IQ!)

One of the old assessment practices that comes under attack is measuring individual students at all. The result is that many performance assessment products are team products, such as a group of students conducting experiments together, with their collaborative efforts and products examined. This reform raises some important questions: Are children well served by never measuring how they perform as individuals, given that individualized accounting systems await them outside of school? Isn't it important to know if some students are more in need of help than others? Indeed, given the limited remedial resources available, it is often necessary to make a strong case based on objective measurement that students who are receiving special assistance need it more than others in a school. We worry that individual students might be forgotten more easily in schools that orient exclusively to the testing of group performances rather than individual children. The dynamics of individual children's learning and intelligence still seem important to us, with the work of some like-minded testing reformers considered in the next section. What is really interesting is that the assessments considered in the next section permit measurement of individuals without neglecting the role of social factors in performance, so what follows is an intermediate point between traditional assessment in which the lonely student does a test on his or her own and some of the most radical of performance assessments that examine only group processing and performances: The dynamic assessments in the next section emphasize measurement about how students respond to instruction from social agents who try to be sensitive to their needs and processing deficiencies.

One last comment, however, before leaving this section on national and state assessments. Many readers are probably feeling that they have been buffeted between information favoring new testing and information critical of it. That is exactly the feeling we wanted to create. There is a substantial ongoing national debate about how testing should be done and what role it should play in decision making and curriculum reform. This section was intended to prepare students to be aware of the many sides of that controversy and to experience the barrage of arguments that educators are experiencing as they grapple with national and state assessment pressures.

DYNAMIC ASSESSMENT (LEARNING-POTENTIAL ASSESSMENT)

Those who identify with the dynamic assessment movement are concerned that traditional IQ measures underestimate the competencies of many children. They view an IQ test like an achievement test—that is, a measure of skills and knowledge already acquired. The assumption of those constructing IQ tests is that smarter people will have acquired more than same-age people of lesser intelligence because the smarter people learn more quickly. This assumption is filled with additional assumptions about equal opportunity, however, assumptions that clearly do not hold for many segments of society: For example, children living in poverty do not have the same opportunities for exposure to the type of information tapped on IQ tests as do majority children (Budoff, 1987b).

For more than 30 years, intelligence researchers such as Budoff (e.g., Budoff & Friedman, 1964) have argued that a fairer test of intelligence would measure speed of learning more directly, that high intelligence would come to be defined as being able to benefit from experience readily, and low intelligence would be reflected by inability to benefit from environmental experiences. The general approach taken by Budoff was to design assessments that involved a teaching component. Students are tested, then taught, followed by retesting. For example, a student might be given a problem to solve; after failing to solve it, be provided problem-solving instruction, with subsequent retesting on the problem. If the child benefits from a short period of training, the inference is made that the child profits from experience. (Readers should note that this is a different approach to linking assessment to teaching than performance assessment, with learning potential assessment directly assessing whether the child can benefit from instruction.)

In much of Budoff's work, a block design task (Kohs, 1923) was used in the assessment. In this task, the subject is provided a picture of block design involving red, white, blue, yellow, blue-yellow, and red-white sides. The task is to duplicate the depicted design with blocks that are provided. A subject is presented 15 of these problems, increasing in difficulty as testing during the first session proceeds. Then there is coaching, which includes the following:

1. Maximizing success by the possibility of working down to the simplest elements in the design.
2. Freely offering praise and encouragement.
3. The strategy of motorically checking the construction, block by block, against the design card to encourage an active, planned, and systematic work approach and to allow the subject to see concretely the success he or she is achieving.
4. Emphasis on the concept of two-color blocks as the elements composing the design (e.g., by teaching the process of building a stripe and the concept of orientation of the blocks in a design by constructing a diamond). (Budoff, 1987a)

One day and one month after the coaching session, student performance on the designs is tested again.

Budoff and Friedman (1964) were able to demonstrate in a true experiment that retarded children benefited from the training they provided. More importantly, regardless of IQ, some subjects benefited more from training than did other subjects. In addition, there were indicators in subsequent work that those who gained the most from training achieved at a higher level in school than did low gainers (Babad & Budoff, 1974; Budoff, Gimon, & Corman, 1974). One of the most impressive demonstrations of the predictability of learning potential classification was conducted at the middle-school level. Gainers acquired more from a science unit on electricity than did nongainers (with IQ controlled statistically). In short, Budoff and colleagues provided substantial data to support the hypothesis that susceptibility to instruction, which is what learning potential is, predicts academic achievement. Budoff's work has done much to fuel enthusiasm for dynamic assessment in North America.

The approach favored by Budoff has been "discovered" by other intelligence theorists working in other cultures, which is perhaps a testimony to its appeal. Thus, Feurstein (e.g., 1979) developed dynamic assessment approaches to measure Israeli juveniles who had been living outside mainstream Israel, including many post–World War II immigrants. Feurstein's (1979) test includes many items that resemble traditional IQ test items, although ones that presumably require high-order thinking to accomplish. For example, consider the "Organization of Dots" task. A subject is given a card with dots on it, with the dot patterns varying from item to item on the test. The subject is also shown geometric figures. The task is to find the same figures in the dot patterns and connect the dots. Feurstein (e.g., 1979) contends that this task involves a number of higher-order processes, including discriminations of form and size, restraint of impulsivity, planning, and systematic search and comparison among others.

As with Budoff's test, subjects are tested first and then provided some training in the strategies and principles required to perform the test task. This instruction is individualized to deal with particular problems that subjects may encounter. Thus, teaching is not rigidly standardized but flexible. The teaching phase is followed by retesting. The focus is on the processing strengths of the person being assessed (i.e., the peaks in their performances).

The main finding from Feurstein's work (e.g., Rand & Kaniel, 1987) is that performance on test items does improve with training: Posttraining performance of socioculturally deprived children often approaches the level of performance of mainstream children. Feurstein (1979) believes that this pattern of results confirms one of his most important claims—that static measures of IQ (e.g., simulated with the learning potential pretests, which are always lower for deprived children compared with mainstream populations) underestimate the competencies of socioculturally deprived populations. Moreover, Feurstein and colleagues (e.g., Tzuriel & Feurstein, 1992) contend that their studies confirm that children who initially test poorly can improve dramatically if given high-intensity, responsive teaching at a high level of abstraction, teaching that emphasizes strategies and principles. (See the discussion of instrumental enrichment in Chapter 11.)

Soviet psychologists developed testing procedures consistent with dynamic assessment as well (e.g., Luria, 1961). One important Soviet idea that has been linked to dynamic assessment, by Feurstein (e.g., 1979) originally but more recently by Campione and Brown (1987), is the zone of proximal development: Vygotsky (e.g., 1978; see Chapter 8) argued that much of learning is mediated by interactions with others, who provide support for the young child attempting to acquire new concepts and procedures. There are some things that a child can do unaided. There are others that the child can accomplish if provided some assistance from an adult. There are still other skills and competencies that are beyond the child at present. Those competencies that can be carried out by the child with assistance define the child's zone of proximal development. ("Proximal development" refers to the assumption that those skills that the child can perform with assistance are partially developed already—the child's development is in the proximity of these capacities, although not yet achieving them.) An important measure of individual differences is the "width" of this zone, with more capable children able to perform many more tasks with assistance than less capable children (i.e., more capable children have wider zones of proximal development than do less capable children). A critical assumption is that the width of the zone can change for a child, for example, after high-quality instruction has begun following years of neglect, so that today's appraisal of the width of the zone may be invalid in a few weeks or months depending on what happens in the child's environment (see Campione & Brown, 1987).

Campione and Brown's (1987) approach to dynamic assessment is similar in many ways to Budoff's and Feurstein's, although there are also unique elements. Their studies involve variants of traditional psychometric tasks (e.g., matrix problems). Subjects are pretested; then they receive instruction about ways to solve the problems; then they are tested again, with maintenance problems (i.e., identical in format to pretest items) and transfer problems (i.e., items related in format to pretest items but requiring slightly different operations). Thus, if subjects are trained to solve matrix problems that require using one of three rules, maintenance problems would require using one of three rules, but transfer problems might require using two rules simultaneously.

Some of the research from Campione and Brown's group was conducted with preschool children (e.g., Bryant, 1982; Bryant, Brown, & Campione, 1983). The preschoolers were given simple matrices tasks. Consistent with Campione and Brown's findings in general in this area (as well as others such as Budoff), static measures of ability (i.e., IQ) did predict learning and transfer to some degree. In particular, Campione and Brown's group found that higher-ability children required fewer hints to learn during training than did the lower-

ability participants. Moreover, higher-ability subjects as defined by IQ required fewer hints to do the transfer tasks than did lower-ability subjects. Importantly, however, even when IQ was controlled, there were still relationships between the pretest-to-posttest gain scores (i.e., the index of learning potential) and the number of hints required at transfer. What Campione and Brown's (1987) data suggest is that both the static and the dynamic measures are useful in predicting transfer. People with high psychometric intelligence transfer more readily (i.e., with less hints) than people with lower psychometric intelligence; after intelligence is accounted for, however, there are differences in how quickly people learn. Those who learn more quickly transfer more readily (i.e., require fewer hints to apply skills learned on one task to another related task).

The Campione and Brown emphasis on predictive validity as reflected by transfer data is important. Good thinkers can use what they know broadly—they can transfer. That there is a relationship between the susceptibility to instruction and transfer makes clear that by measuring differences in learning when given instruction, the assessor is tapping into competencies at least related to the broad use of what has been learned.

We view the predictive validity issue as especially critical with respect to dynamic assessment. After all, one of the reasons traditional intelligence tests have endured is that they are predictively valid: They predict well who will succeed in school. A reasonable expectation is that alternative measures that might be proposed as replacements for traditional assessments would have greater predictive validity than IQ. Besides the Budoff studies and the work of Campione, Brown, and their associates, there are other data consistent with the perspective that dynamic measures provide better predictions of academic achievement (at least in some situations) than do other measurements. For example, Luther and Wyatt (1989) reported that dynamic assessments predicted the school success of English-as-a-second-language students better than did traditional IQ. Dynamic assessments predicted better than conventional intelligence test data which preschool handicapped students would do well enough in school so that 2 years later they would be in regular classrooms rather than in special education placements (Samuels, Killip, MacKenzie, & Fagan, 1992). Shochet (1992) reported that for disadvantaged students entering college, traditional static measures did a reasonable job of predicting the success of students who proved less modifiable in dynamic assessments; the success of students proving more modifiable in dynamic assessments was not predictable from static assessments. Guthke and Wingenfeld (1992) reported that among disadvantaged children in particular dynamic assessments did a better job of predicting academic achievement longitudinally than did static tests.

Detailed discussion of the differences between a dynamic and a static assessment with respect to a now familiar issue (i.e., early reading; see Chapter 14) might make clearer the advantages of dynamic assessment. Before doing so, we point out that one variation of dynamic assessment involves the progressive provision of cues and hints about how to do tasks that students cannot perform when they are first presented. The assumption is that students who are more modifiable will catch on with fewer hints. This approach has the advantage of being considerably less cumbersome than the test-teach-retest approach, and we expect it will be attractive to many test developers as they work to create dynamic assessments that can be used efficiently and economically.

Spector (1992) was interested in predicting success in kindergarten reading. You might recall from Chapter 14 that phonemic awareness measures are often predictive of success in early reading and seem to do better than other measures in doing so. Thus, at the beginning of the kindergarten year, Spector administered some traditional measures of phonemic awareness, such as children's ability to divide pronounced words into sound segments and to delete phonemes (e.g., what word remains if the $/j/$ sound is deleted from *jam?*). An invented spelling measure was administered as well, which produced higher scores for children who represented the sounds of words pronounced to them in their invented spellings of the words. In addition to these static measures of phonemic awareness, Spector included a dynamic measure. The starting point for the dynamic measure was the phoneme segmentation measure. If a child was unable to segment a word correctly, he or she was given progressively more explicit prompts about how to do so, with more points awarded the fewer the prompts required for the child to segment the word:

No prompts: 6 points awarded for the item if correct.
Prompt 1: Pronounce the target word slowly; 5 points awarded for the item if correct.

Prompt 2: Ask the child to identify the first sound of the word; 4 points awarded for the item if correct.
Prompt 3: Cue the child with the first sound; 3 points awarded for the item if correct.
Prompt 4: Cue the child with the number of sounds in the word; 2 points awarded for the item if correct.
Prompt 5: Modeling segmentation using pennies placed in squares to represent the number of sounds in the word; 1 point awarded for the item if correct.
Prompt 6: Modeling segmentation as above, but working hand over hand with the child while pronouncing the segments; 0 points.
Prompt 7: Repeating prompt 6; 0 points. (Adapted from Spector, 1992, p. 355)

The most striking outcome in the study was that the dynamic measure of phonemic awareness predicted children's word recognition abilities in the spring, but the static measures of phonemic awareness did not. Consistent with the pattern observed by Campione and Brown in their work, the spring dynamic measure of phonemic awareness was a slightly better predictor of word recognition than was psychometric intelligence, although not a significantly better one (our reanalyses).

Why might the dynamic measure of phonemic awareness be a better assessment than the static measure? Any test item involves more than just the competency being tested. Spector (1992) argued, and we find the argument compelling, that static test items are more likely to place demands on students not relevant to the competencies being assessed. Spector (1992) put it this way:

> ... [T]he dynamic measure was ... a "cleaner" ... measure of phonemic awareness. Analysis of the static conditions suggests the possibility that task demands unrelated to phonemic awareness prevented many students from achieving greater success. For example, on both deletion and static segmentation, some students may have had difficulty maintaining the target word in working memory while relating in order the sounds they heard. In the dynamic condition, on the other hand, the children were asked to identify the initial sound only and were then asked for each succeeding sound, prompting each response by repeating sounds that the child had already given. The dynamic condition clearly placed fewer demands on working memory than did the static segmentation and deletion tasks. (Spector, 1992, p. 360)

An outcome such as Spector's, which suggests that dynamic assessment might shine new light on relationships considered exceptionally important by contemporary educational psychologists, fuels a lot of enthusiasm. The intense social interaction between tester and the person being assessed during dynamic assessment should permit more complete understanding of how students process information (see Tzuriel & Haywood, 1992), permitting even better hypotheses about how processes measured in an assessment (e.g., of phonemic awareness) might relate to valued intellectual outcomes (e.g., learning to read). Thus, dynamic assessors are claiming that the tester-examinee interactions can provide a window on (1) emotional difficulties that might interfere with academic achievement (e.g., Barr & Samuels, 1988; Kaniel & Tzuriel, 1992); (2) the degree to which subjects organize, plan, and are flexible in their processing of academic content (e.g., Samuels, Lamb, & Oberholtzer, 1992); and (3) motivations of subjects that might dampen academic performances (e.g., Kaniel & Tzuriel, 1992; Samuels et al., 1992). One especially positive outcome is that when teachers dynamically assess handicapped students, they form a better impression of them than when they administer more standard assessments: The learning phase of the assessment highlights that the students can learn (e.g., Delclos, Burns, & Kulewicz, 1987).

Even so, we believe a great deal of work needs to be done before firm claims can be made about the value of dynamic assessment. First, there are issues of reliability, with little attention to this critical psychometric consideration in the dynamic assessment literature to date (Laughon, 1990; Samuels, Tzuriel, & Malloy-Miller, 1989). Second, much more work needs to be done on the predictive validity of dynamic assessment relative to conventional assessment. The few data that are available, however, are supportive of the conclusion that dynamic measures are better predictors of achievement than static measures. A second problem is that there are only a few studies examining prediction of real-school academic performance, which, of course, is the predictive validity of greatest concern.

Without a doubt, the most frequent type of study conducted by dynamic assessors involves demonstrating that after teaching students how to process test items, test performances of many students are much higher than before process teaching of the items (for review of many examples, see Haywood & Tzuriel, 1992b; Lidz, 1987). One inference that is made and seems justified is that this suggests great plasticity in many students who initially perform poorly on psychometric assessments. Other claims seem more tentative to us, such as arguments that performances by disadvantaged children following testing that are comparable to the performances of advantaged children before testing suggest that the discrepancies in the abilities of disadvantaged and advantaged children have been exaggerated in the past. Our view is that no such claim is valid without also looking at the performance following item-process teaching of advantaged children, a comparison that generally has been ignored by dynamic assessors. Claims that the teaching that goes on during dynamic assessment may make long-term impact on the cognitive processing of students in ways that affect academic performances meaningfully also seem far-fetched (e.g., reviewers of Spector's piece offered such speculation with respect to the dynamic phonemic awareness measure, a claim that she viewed—and we agree—was unlikely given the long-term training required to increase phonemic awareness; e.g., Bradley & Bryant, 1983). With additional research, it should become clear what dynamic assessment does and what it does not do. If it proves only to be more predictive of important academic outcomes than static assessment, however, that is quite a bit.

Dynamic assessment is extremely attractive to many who are concerned about disadvantaged students, believing that such students are discriminated against by conventional assessments. For example, some of those fighting the legal battles to prevent standardized assessment from being used to assign minority children to special education view dynamic assessment as potentially fairer to minority children, permitting more certain identification of students who would benefit from particular types of educational interventions (Elliott, 1992; Utley, Haywood, & Masters, 1992).

One possibility with dynamic assessment is for the assessor to try a variety of teaching methods during the teaching phase of the test-teach-retest cycle, until the assessor zeroes in on methods that work with this particular student. If dynamic assessors can succeed in reliably identifying treatments that work for particular students but not others, this would be a tremendous accomplishment (e.g., Utley et al., 1992). What an exciting approach to assessment this would be compared with more conventional approaches, which are aimed largely at gauging who will make it and who will not in conventional school. Consistent with this general direction, the next section describes some approaches for deciding whether particular forms of instruction are working for particular students as they face real-school academic demands.

CURRICULUM-BASED ASSESSMENT AND MEASUREMENT

Many of the measurements detailed in Chapter 16 and in this chapter have involved tasks and materials removed from actual classroom tasks and materials, with the most conspicuous exception being portfolio assessment. Not surprisingly, the recommendations that emerge from such assessments often are not helpful in instructional decision making. Classroom-based assessment/measurement contrasts with most other approaches to assessment with respect to the classroom authenticity of the materials used in the evaluations and generation of recommendations that are explicitly relevant to the curriculum the student is experiencing.

Shinn, Rosenfeld, and Knutson (1989), based in part on Deno (1987), defined classroom-based assessment as, "... *any* set of measurement procedures that use direct observation and recording of a student's performance in the local curriculum as a basis for gathering information to make instructional decisions" (p. 300). They go on to describe some variations on this approach, concluding that there are four different models of assessment that qualify:

1. *Curriculum-based assessment for curriculum design* was proposed by Gickling and colleagues (e.g., Gickling, Shane, & Croskery, 1989). Consistent with the motivational principle of optimal levels of challenge (see Chapter 5, this volume), Gickling believes that students are best served if they are being asked to learn material that is just a bit beyond them, material that presents some challenge but is not overwhelming. The key is to test students to find out where they are in the curriculum, to determine which tasks they can do with little challenge, which can be done only with hesitation or with assistance, and which are completely beyond them. Thus, a student is in the appropriate reading level according to this model if he or she can do the skill and drill exercises for the level with 70 to 85 percent correct responses and recognizes 93 to 97 percent of the words in the reading. Note that such levels of cor-

rectness permit the student to do well much of the time, although there is still some learning for the student to master the level.

Gickling and Armstrong (1978) studied the academic achievement and behaviors of students who were matched well to curricular level versus those provided tasks beyond their current competence and those presented tasks that were too easy. Students given assignments that were too difficult did not do as much work as well-matched students, with more off-task behaviors by the overchallenged mismatched students. Off-task behavior was common when tasks were too easy as well. Academic engagement was greatest with appropriate matching to difficulty level.

The assessments conducted by a teacher to determine level of placement are constructed from course materials. Once the initial placement is made, based on determining which part of the curriculum offers optimum challenge, there is ongoing assessment to determine whether the student is making progress. If the student masters the current level, he or she moves on in the curriculum. If not, there may be reason to consider alternative instruction from what is being provided. In short, such assessment is for instructional planning. Many readers will certainly have noted that it is "dynamic" (see Haywood, Tzuriel, & Vaught, 1992, who make an explicit case that curriculum-based assessment is dynamic). Shinn et al. (1989) acknowledged its potential for determining who should be referred for special educational services versus students who can make progress in the regular education environment: That is, if students do not make progress given current instruction that is aimed at a level matched with their current level of functioning, that is a sign that other instructional measures are appropriate. Because such an assessment is grounded in the curriculum for which the student is accountable and because the focus is on whether and how the student can learn, it is an admirable form of dynamic assessment.

2. *Curriculum-based measurement,* favored by Deno (e.g., 1986; also Fuchs & Fuchs, 1990), involves assessing students continuously with respect to a long-term goal. Perhaps the goal is for a student to be able to read at a second-grade, second-semester level one year from now. Beginning now and throughout intervention, there will be measurement of the student's reading of grade-2, second-semester materials, perhaps including responses to comprehension questions, ability to retell what has been

read, or oral fluency. The teacher often will graph the student's progress so the student can have visual evidence of improvement when it occurs. If improvement is not occurring, it is a signal to the teacher to make some changes in the instruction that is occurring, and such monitoring does seem to increase the number of curricular adjustments that teachers make (Fuchs, Fuchs, Hamlett, & Stecker, 1991). This type of measurement is entirely forward looking, with students expected to do poorly at first because they are responding to material far beyond them. The goal is to be able to perform capably in the long term the tasks that are frustrating today.

3. *In criterion-referenced models (also known as mastery learning approach),* students are tested on content they are currently learning, with large chunks of content often broken down into smaller units (Fuchs & Fuchs, 1990; see the discussion of mastery learning in Chapter 11, this book). If the students meet some predetermined criterion for a unit test (e.g., 80 percent of the comprehension questions correct)—one devised by the teacher over unit content—they are deemed to have learned the material for the unit and can move on in the curriculum to the next unit. If the students fall below the criterion on the mastery test, there is additional teaching and subsequent retesting.

4. *Curriculum-based evaluation* is the last model of assessment. Howell and Morehead (1987) argued that good teachers should, ". . . test what you teach and teach what you test," contending that alignment of instruction and assessment was one way to increase learning. Those favoring this approach emphasize breaking tasks down into their subskills. During the initial assessment, students are asked to perform the task of interest to the assessor (e.g., subtraction of multidigit numbers). The student errors are analyzed by the assessor in order to generate hypotheses about what the student might be doing wrong while working problems (e.g., the student cannot regroup during subtraction). Assessments are then designed that tap the presumed problems the student is experiencing (e.g., a number of subtraction problems requiring regrouping are constructed, with student performance explicitly compared on otherwise similar problems that do not require regrouping). Decisions are made from these follow-up tests about the deficiencies of the student so that appropriate instruction can be planned to remediate the shortcomings.

In summary, curriculum-based assessment/measurement is actually a family of procedures that share similarities. First, the assessments are based on the curriculum and viewed as informing instruction. The assessments tend to be brief and inexpensive, or at least no more expensive than any other teacher-made tests. All of these approaches are sensitive to student improvement and when students fail to improve signal that there is a need for change in instruction or, at least, additional instruction. In general, the evidence is growing that use of curriculum-based assessment has a positive effect on the students measured in that their progress is more certain if they experience curriculum-based assessment as an integral part of instruction than if they do not (e.g., Deno & Fuchs, 1987; Fuchs, Fuchs, & Maxwell, 1988; Marston & Magnusson, 1985).

As with dynamic assessment, there is an assumption that most students can learn and improve and that one role for the assessment process is to stimulate the identification and development of instruction that works with particular children. In contrast to standardized assessments conducted by professionals from outside the classroom using measurements not reflecting classroom tasks, curriculum-based assessment is teacher controlled and administered and tied to actual curricula. There is high content validity here.

Unfortunately, other reliability and validity issues have been neglected in the development of curriculum-based measurements. In addition, much of the concern is with short-term gains, with notable exceptions such as Deno's curriculum-based measurement, which entails monitoring progress toward long-term goals. The most promising, most up-to-date approaches to curriculum-based assessment, however, combine approaches identified by Shinn et al. (1989): These combined approaches include monitoring of progress toward long-term goals, assessing short-term gains, and diagnosing weaknesses in current abilities (e.g., Fuchs, Fuchs, Hamlett, & Stecker, 1990; Shapiro, 1990). That the four approaches identified by Shinn et al. (1989) can be combined makes clear that the four approaches tap different, complementary information.

Great efforts are now being made to train young teachers in curriculum-based assessment (e.g., Howell & Morehead, 1987; Salvia & Hughes, 1990), with these textbooks providing examples and stimulating the practice of curriculum-based assessment/measurement across the entire curriculum. Although some teachers perceive that curriculum-based measurement is costly in terms of time (King-Sears, Richardson, & Ray, 1992), once teachers learn how to do it, their perceptions improve (King-Sears et al., 1992). Moreover, there are some shortcuts, such as students monitoring one another (e.g., Bentz, Shinn, & Gleason, 1990).

Our view is that this commonsensical approach to assessment deserves the attention of both teachers and educational researchers. The hypothesis that curriculum-based assessment increases academic achievement deserves much more research attention, for such assessment is intervention that could be delivered by most classroom teachers at low cost. This approach also puts control of much of assessment back into the hands of the teachers, stimulating professional decision making on their part. For all of these reasons, we expect the journals throughout the 1990s to include much new information about classroom-based assessment as a method of improving teaching and learning.

In closing this subsection, we must show our hand about how enthused we really are about this approach to assessment. Recall from Chapter 5 the motivational benefits from focusing on student improvement. Curriculum-based assessment/measurement makes improvement salient. Teachers who do it can defend grading practices based on improvement because there are objective records. Curriculum-based assessment may be an important development in the eradication of the competitive classroom, a classroom structure that undermines academic motivation. In making this conjecture, we note that at present, curriculum-based assessment is used much more in special education than regular education. There is nothing, however, about this combined assessment and intervention that limits its use to special education populations. We hope that regular educators begin to use this approach to monitor sensitively the progress of students as well as to identify their students' instructional needs.

NEUROPSYCHOLOGICAL ASSESSMENTS

Before proceeding with a discussion of neuropsychological assessments, the difference between **structure** and **function** must be appreciated (see Chapter 6). In a complete diagnosis of a brain disorder or injury, information would be produced about the parts of the brain involved (i.e., brain structure) and the processing (i.e., functioning) that is disrupted. An extremely important point is that there is not a one-to-one relationship between brain structures and functions. Often, functions normally accomplished by one region of the brain sometimes can be taken up by another region of the brain, with the ability of the brain to compensate in this way inversely related to age (i.e., younger children are more likely to exhibit compensation than older children or adults; see Chapter 6, this book).

For example, the two largest structures in the brain are the right and left cerebral hemispheres. Different regions in these structures are normally associated with different functions, for example, the frontal lobes with planning and carrying out higher-order functions (see Chapter 6). A particularly important functional distinction is that the right hemisphere often is involved more with nonverbal abilities than is the left hemisphere, which specializes in verbal functions. Often, if the right hemispheric structure is damaged, there is functional loss of depth perception, spatial reasoning, and recognition of faces. Left-hemisphere injuries are more likely to result in loss of speech, reading, or writing abilities. The extreme plasticity of the brain with respect to function—at least when brain injury occurs early in life—is illustrated by outcomes in some cases of left hemisphere removal, usually because of a tumor. When adults lose their left hemisphere, there is massive loss of language functioning. When young children lose the left hemisphere, however, they occasionally (e.g., Dennis & Whitaker, 1977; Woods, 1980) develop into adults with normal language and intellect (e.g., McCarthy & Warrington, 1990, Chapter 1; McFie, 1961; Smith & Sugar, 1975). That is, the right hemisphere performs some of the functions normally performed by the left hemisphere. A complete neuropsychological assessment of such a patient documents well exactly the structures that have been damaged or removed as well as the neuropsychological functions that are normal versus those that are disrupted. Historically, medical diagnoses have provided structural information (see medical approaches to such assessments discussed in Chapter 6), and neuropsychological diagnoses have provided functional information.

Less extreme examples make the point how important complete and complementary medical and psychological diagnoses are. It is not at all unusual for even young people to experience small strokes, with some damage to small areas of brain tissue. The presenting symptom that brings the victim to the emergency room in many cases is something like loss of speech or sudden onset of blindness. Such symptoms stimulate physicians to perform diagnostic procedures that produce images of the brain (see Chapter 6), which often provide definitive information about the location of the problem in the brain. Additional medical tests usually are done to attempt to determine the underlying cause for the stroke (e.g., atherosclerosis, hypertension; Brust, 1991). Neuropsychological diagnoses are routinely done as the patient is recovering to assess functional losses. What is important to emphasize is that often there is spontaneous recovery of function, so that the individual appearing at the emergency room unable to talk will be talking normally a month later. The brain has found another way for the function that was disrupted by the small stroke to be performed, a not uncommon occurrence. Extensive neuropsychological diagnoses can often determine the completeness of such functional recovery, with this information critical in determining whether there is a need for long-term rehabilitative interventions. The focus in this section is on such assessments.

Neuropsychological test batteries are more recent developments than traditional intelligence tests or the SAT (although notably the Wechsler scales can be used for neuropsychological assessment; Golden, Zillmer, & Spiers, 1992; Sattler, 1992, Chapter 22), but they are not that new. For example, the Halstead-Reitan Neuropsychological Test Battery was developed in the 1940s (Halstead, 1947). The Luria-Nebraska Neuropsychological Battery was developed in the 1970s by Golden and colleagues, although it was based on tests developed by Luria, the great Soviet neuropsychologist who developed his assessments many years earlier (see Luria, 1966, 1973). Both of these important adult scales have been adapted for use with children (see Sattler, 1992, Chapter 22). The Halstead-Reitan Battery consists of a series of cognitive (e.g., concept formation, expressive and receptive language, memory) and perceptual-motor (e.g., finger tapping, marching, rhythm, tactile form recognition) tests. The Luria-Nebraska not only includes basic cognitive and perceptual-motor tasks, but also tasks that are recognizably academic tests, such as reading, writing, and arithmetic scales. In addition to these batteries, there are large numbers of neuropsychological tests designed to tap specific functions (see Spreen & Strauss, 1991).

What these tests do well when administered by well-qualified neuropsychologists is to discriminate between people who are brain-injured or suffering from some serious brain disorders (e.g., aphasias of various sorts, which are receptive and productive language disorders; epilepsy; dyslexia; short-term memory loss) and those who have normally functioning brains (Golden, Zilmer, & Spiers, 1992). In making this generalization, however, it must also be pointed out that great skill is often required for the diagnostician to differentiate various types of brain dysfunctions and brain dysfunctions in general from other disorders, for example, hearing loss, delayed speech, autism, or various forms of psychoses, such as schizophrenia (Golden et al., 1992; Sattler, 1992). What the skilled diagnostician does is to compare patterns of performance across tests and within tests to come to an assessment decision. There is a great deal of flexibility in the assessment procedure, with the assessor often deciding in the middle of the assessment to test some function that emerged as suspect in subtests already administered. This flexibility is described aptly by Golden et al. (1992):

> The flexible approach to neuropsychological testing, often referred to as the hypothesis testing approach, is based on the idea that each exam should be adapted to the individual patient. Rather than employing a standard battery of tests, clinicians choose the tests and procedures within an exam, based on hypotheses made from impressions of the patient and information available about the patient from other sources. As a result, each exam may vary considerably from patient to patient. The clinician may use standard tests, or tests may be altered and adapted as the clinician attempts to form an opinion on the nature of the deficits. . . . (p. 71)

Such tailoring is necessitated, in part, because of the length of time required to present an entire battery of tests—up to 6 hours or more for the Halstead-Reitan. Many perfectly healthy patients would have a tough time putting up with so many questions; people suspected of brain damage often have little energy and patience for a grueling day of testing. Although the shorter test administered by the hypothesizing psychologist may be more humane, there are risks, including that if the psychologist's hypothesis is only partially correct, there may be only a partially correct diagnosis: With more tests administered, additional dysfunctions might have been identified. An especially serious problem is that of reliability of ad hoc assessments: The reliabilities of the full neuropsychological batteries are not as great as the reliabilities of tests such as the Wechsler; a shorter test will have lower reliability, and with the test battery customized for each patient, it is impossible to gauge the reliability of the assessment provided to any particular person.

There are many children who require neuropsychological assessments, with possible brain damage suffered by some children prenatally (see Chapter 6) and by others who contract disease, experience physical trauma, or are exposed to hazardous environmental agents, including some illicit drugs. In most cases, the neuropsychological assessment is part of a much larger assessment that includes extensive medical evaluation. By examining the patterns of performances on the various subtests in light of medical outcomes, the neuropsychologist often can make credible predictions about brain damage and functioning. Because a great deal of knowledge has accumulated about how specific brain injuries and disorders are related to important academic competencies such as reading, writing, calculation, and problem solving (see McCarthy & Warrington, 1990), neuropsychologists believe such knowledge is invaluable in educational planning. It should not only increase awareness of the potential limitations of brain-injured students, but also, more importantly, increase awareness of functions that are unimpaired, functions that might be exploited to compensate for other dysfunctions (e.g., knowing that the ability to read sight words is intact for a child even if her or his ability to decode using letter-sound rules is missing might be extremely helpful in planning reading instruction for the student).

What is suggested by neuropsychologists (e.g., Hooper & Willis, 1989, Chapter 8) is that children with certain types of disorders should respond to certain types of treatments, whereas children with other functional disorders would respond favorably to other treatments (an aptitude X treatment interaction hypothesis; see Chapter 1, this book). Workers in the area of learning disabilities have been especially avid enthusiasts for the possibility of **subtype X treatment** (i.e., subtype is the aptitude) interactions, meaning that by categorizing learning-disabled children with respect to their processing

strengths and weaknesses using neuropsychological batteries, treatment effects will be maximized by matching students to treatments that require them to use their intact functions and bypass their weaker functions. As appealing as the hypothesis is that different treatments will have different effects depending on specific brain disorder, however, there are scant data to support it, with one of the great challenges for researchers in neuropsychology to generate more support for this important claim that neuropsychological data can be predictively useful in developing educational interventions (see Lewandowski, 1992).

It is important to emphasize that neuropsychological assessments often are not one-shot affairs and not simply useful in deciding how to intervene: The initial assessment is often treated as a baseline so that improvements in functioning, either spontaneous improvements (and there often are striking improvements in functioning as time passes following an injury) or responses to treatment, can be documented. Thus, neuropsychological assessments also can provide valuable data in intervention studies about the efficacy of a treatment: That is, neuropsychological data have the potential to be both "independent" variables, defining different populations that receive treatment, and dependent variables, providing information about whether the assigned treatments worked as intended.

In closing this subsection on neuropsychological tests, we emphasize that these tests are largely still in development. It seems virtually certain that how these tests are used is going to change in the coming years as a function of development of other assessments, such as neural imagery (see Chapter 6), with the role of neuropsychological assessments in research likely to diminish as cutting-edge brain scientists continue to develop new technologies for assessing cognitive processes. Nonetheless, many of the "high-tech" measures are far from ready for widespread deployment, and many have serious drawbacks. For example, many of the new measurements are limited in what they reveal, excellent at providing only particular information. A second problem is that some of the measures are thousands of dollars for a single measurement. A great deal of more conventional neuropsychological assessment can be bought for that kind of money. We believe it a good bet that the neurological test batteries, which generate many different types of information at relatively low cost, will continue to be developed and play a role in clinical diagnosis and in research studies.

CONCLUDING COMMENTS

A number of measurement approaches were considered in this chapter and in Chapter 16. Individual differences are assessed in different ways for different purposes. Thus, some tests provide information about the promise of individual students based on what they have learned so far. These include conventional IQ assessments and SATs. Others provide information about differences in student susceptibility to instruction and different types of instruction. Both dynamic assessments and curriculum-based assessments are suited to this purpose. Some assessments are designed to determine how well schools are doing, with aggregate statistics summarizing individual student performances a window on school impact. The *NAEP* and the state assessments do this, with these measurements increasingly attempting to capture whether students have acquired important procedural knowledge—important strategies for reading, writing, and scientific and mathematical problem solving. Some of the most "high-tech" of assessments are designed to illuminate the biological foundations of human competence.

In classifying tests with respect to purpose, as we did in the last paragraph, that is not to deny flexibility in purpose. For example, we suspect that biologically based assessments of individual differences in intelligence are possible. Moreover, portfolio assessments, which are being used at the state and national level to characterize achievement at the school level, can be modified and used by individual teachers to assess individual students, with examples of portfolios used in this way included in this chapter. In addition, results from tests such as the SAT are often aggregated over populations or regions to provide composite information. That is, good tests can do a lot of good: For example, the SAT has proved useful to students as they plan for college and to colleges as they select their classes. It also is an indicator of national patterns of academic achievement and as much as any test has provided a wake-up call of sorts to educators and the policy community about the possibility of declining achievement in American schools. Because tests pro-

vide so much helpful information, we generally are enthused about their use and development.

Standardized testing, however, has also been associated with harm to some groups. For example, minority groups have often made the case that tests are biased against them. In the sense that some minority groups consistently score lower on such assessments than do members of the majority culture, there is bias. Some extreme proponents of testing argue that such differences are real and reflect a fundamental, and perhaps biological, difference between members of the majority and minority communities. We not only do not identify with that sentiment, but also find compelling that tests are better matched to the majority culture than they are to many minority cultures, and this mismatch might account for much of the differences in performance observed between majority and minority cultures.

Dana (1993) summarizes the case that many minorities have different world views that can affect their responses in testing situations. For example, the Anglo-American perspective of personal control and responsibility is not shared by Native Americans, which can undermine propensity to problem solve. Native Americans may be disadvantaged on assessments calling for active problem solving because of this difference in style. In addition, many minorities do not have a strong commitment to cultural assimilation, resulting in acquisition and display of behaviors appropriate in their setting but not captured or valued by assessments matched to the culture they are resisting. Finally, it is difficult to escape that even if tests were culture free (which they are not), there would still be some racism in some individual assessors. For example, it is racist when a psychologist tries to determine if a white student's poor showing on an assessment might be accounted for by motivational or ameliorating factors (e.g., illness) but on the same day is willing to accept low scores from a black child at face value. Readers should be assured that good training programs do all possible to educate psychologists about the inappropriateness of such differential assessment; even so, many of the racist tendencies in the larger society will be reflected in any professional activity, including psychologist assessment. Competent psychologists, however, recognize the ambiguities in the measurement of minorities and take those ambiguities into account when they generate competency reports and make recommendations with respect to treatment.

In closing this chapter on alternative assessments, we urge readers never to lose track of the basics with respect to assessments. It is necessary always to be asking whether a test is valid for the purpose for which it is being used. One strength of newer assessments is that their purpose is more immediately obvious from the operations of the test. Thus, math portfolios are obviously related to math achievement and more certainly so than performance on a standardized math test. A few years ago, author MP worked with an undergraduate who amassed quite a portfolio of accomplishments in his last 2 years of college, including earning A's in graduate-level statistics and performing the statistical analyses on some published papers. What a surprise when this student scored in the 300's on the Graduate Record Examination in mathematics. Because of this student's extreme test anxiety, the GRE was not a good measurement of mathematical aptitude. Several faculty worked with this student to develop a portfolio of accomplishments that was sent with graduate school applications. The happy ending is that the student was accepted at a top graduate school and is now completing a postdoctoral fellowship in a leading psychology department with a long list of professional accomplishments to his credit and a bright future. Tales like this one do much to convince us that the newer assessments, which have high content validity, should be explored carefully.

The other basic is reliability, which is often ignored by psychologists as they use measurements (Rushton, Brainerd, & Pressley, 1983). As we pointed out at the beginning of Chapter 16, assessments with low reliability cannot be valid. Thus, many of the current science performance assessments that have only one, two, or three unreliable items cannot be valid (Shavelson et al., 1992). Indeed, because most individual test items are unreliable, measurements based on only a few items are rarely valid. Fortunately the measurement errors for items tend to cancel one another out when there are a large number of items. Thus, one ready solution for low reliability is simply to increase the number of items. This is a problem for the new performance assessments only because many of the single items on these assessments take a long time to complete.

Psychologists have shot themselves in the foot many times by relying on low-reliability tests: The lower the reliability of a test, the more difficult is it for the test to prove telling in an experimental study. That is, it is more difficult to obtain statistically significant differences with low-reliability compared with high-reliability measurements. The reason is simple. The error term in significance tests is a function of the reliability of the variable being tested; the lower the reliability, the greater the error term (which is in the denominator of t and F ratios) and hence the smaller the t or F assuming that other things are equal. Rushton et al. (1983) provide a review of many examples of investigators failing to find significant effects because of low reliability of measurement; important scientific discoveries have followed in many instances simply by replacing less reliable measurements with more reliable measurements. Making certain that measurements are reliable can do much to reduce frustration for individual investigators and ensure that scientific tests of an idea are valid tests (i.e., tests based on unreliable measurement cannot be valid).

Psychological measurements are used to come to conclusions about individuals and groups. At the individual level, academic evaluations frequently are made to determine whether students are retarded or normal, learning-disabled or retarded, learning-disabled or normal, or gifted. Because of the importance of classifications of students in terms of intellectual abilities, the third and concluding chapter on individual differences takes up retardation, learning disabilities, and giftedness.

18

Various Types of Learners

By this point, it should be clear that what assessment is about is measurement of differences between people. One byproduct of this assessment enterprise has been the creation of entire new fields of inquiry aimed at understanding particular types of learners. The purpose of this chapter is to provide an overview of some of the types of learners and learner differences that have captured the attention of educational psychologists. Throughout the chapter, there will be attention to the ways that various groups differ and the similarities in information processing across groups.

The first part of the chapter reviews three classifications commonly used with learners with special needs: mental retardation, learning disabilities, and giftedness. What then follows is an overview of various types of children who are at risk for school difficulties. These include children living in poverty (including economically disadvantaged minorities) and those with a native language other than the majority language. The chapter concludes with discussion of an individual differences dimension that affects all of us: cognitive changes during the adult years.

MENTAL RETARDATION

All psychological classifications are inexact, with mental retardation no exception (Clarke, and Clarke, & Berg 1985). The American Association on Mental Deficiency reflected extensively on the vari-

ous factors involved in retardation in attempting to construct a definition of the disorder (Grossman, 1983). Three points must hold for a person to be considered retarded by their criteria:

- There is significantly subaverage general intellect, which is usually operationalized as IQ of 70 or lower (i.e., 2 standard deviations below the mean; see Chapter 16, this book).
- There are deficits in adaptive behaviors, which means that their personal and social behaviors are atypical given their age and culture.
- Retardation is manifested during the developing years (i.e., the first 18 years of life).

Various professionals interested in retardation emphasize these three criteria differently, although low IQ often is pointed out as the most telling characteristic of retardation (e.g., Zigler, Balla, & Hodapp, 1984).

There is tremendous diversity within the population of the retarded, with more than 200 types of retardation now identified. A frequent convention is to consider those with IQs between 50 and 70 to be mildly retarded and those with IQs below 50 as severely retarded (Richardson & Koller, 1985). In general, the long-term prospects for independent functioning vary with the degree of retardation, with most severely retarded individuals requiring substantial social services and support their entire lives. Many mildly retarded individuals manage to live reasonably independent lives as adults. That many mildly retarded individuals navigate the world outside of school is indicative that IQ is a much better predictor of success at school than it is a predictor of successful functioning in the larger world. There are a number of wage-earning jobs that do not require high IQ. Even so, mildly retarded people as a group are at much greater risk than other populations to become involved in socially dysfunctional or criminal activities (Richardson & Koller, 1985).

In providing guidelines relating level of IQ to retardation status, we emphasize that there is nothing magical about the IQ = 70 cutoff. For example, there is a long history of considering people who have IQs between 70 and 85 as borderline for retardation, with these individuals at greater risk for failure in school than individuals with average intelligence (i.e., about IQ = 100). The one magical aspect of the IQ = 70 cutoff may be that its existence in definitions of retardation may have force reduced attention to borderline groups (Zetlin & Murtaugh, 1990), which is not trivial given that there are four times more people with IQs between 70 and 85 than people with IQs of 70 or less.

Another important distinction within the retarded population is between those who are retarded because of known organic causes and those who are socially/culturally retarded, with such a breakdown of the subnormal population recognized as early as the late 19th century (Burack, 1990). There are a number of causes of organic retardation, including the following:

- Chromosomal anomalies, including Down syndrome, which usually is due to three copies of chromosome 21 (rather than two, which is normal; i.e., trisomy 21). An important and still emerging direction is the identification of abnormalities on chromosomes, including abnormal genes and "fragile" sites (e.g., Evans & Hamerton, 1985). Evidence is accumulating that many such disorders are inherited.
- Prenatal factors, including disease and infection, such as syphilis, measles, cytomegalovirus, and toxoplasmosis; exposure to radiation; malnutrition; maternal PKU; and exposure to alcohol and other drugs (e.g., Berg, 1985; Stern, 1985).
- Injury at birth, including oxygen deprivation and mechanical injury (e.g., Berg, 1985).
- Premature birth, with factors such as greater susceptibility to injury (e.g., hemorrhage in the brain) playing a role (e.g., Berg, 1985).
- Neonatal hazards, including disease (e.g., meningitis), head injury, chemical assault (more about this later), and disorders induced by malnutrition, such as beriberi and pellagra (e.g., Berg, 1985; Stern, 1985).
- Inborn errors in metabolism (i.e., genetically determined enzyme deficiency), with these often resulting in structural damage to the nervous system caused by profound biochemical abnormalities (e.g., Stern, 1985).
- Childhood psychosis, including autism, schizophrenia, and neuroses, although separating out the cause and effect of retardation in such cases is often difficult (Clarke, 1985).

Being able to point to the many causes of organic retardation does not mean that the cause of retardation will be known for every child diagnosed as retarded. Some disorders require extremely sensitive tests (e.g., of metabolism). In other cases, the retardation is diagnosed only long after the precipitating event (e.g., many cases of mild retardation are not diagnosed until the child enters school), making the determination of cause much more a probabilistic venture. For example, everyone who works with retarded children knows of multiple instances of the attribution of retardation to some head injury during infancy (e.g., the infant fell on its head). Often these explanations are by default, in that other possibilities have not been detected, and the head-dropping story is the one situation that the parent remembers that seems a plausible cause.

Sociocultural retardation tends to run in families, although it is extremely difficult to draw firm conclusions as to why this is so. One obvious possibility is heredity, with parents of below-average intelligence more likely to give birth to children of lower intelligence than are parents of average intelligence (i.e., parents at the lower end of the normal distribution of intelligence provide a genetic endowment to their children that puts them at the lower end of the normal distribution). There is always the possibility, however, that sociocultural retardation is not just the lower end of the normal distribution but due to some inherited but undetected organic disorder. The difficulty with drawing any conclusion based on biological endowment, however, is that parents of lower intelligence often provide less stimulating environments for their children than do parents of higher intelligence. In short, there probably are multiple determinants of familial retardation. That is, when an unfortunate genetic endowment encounters the nonstimulating environment provided by parents who are of low intelligence themselves, the result is that the child ends up at the bottom of her or his reaction range of intelligence, which from the moment of conception was a lower range compared with many other children born of parents with more fortunate genetic characteristics.

Determining the prevalence of retardation is extremely difficult, dependent on factors such as the exact definition used and the age level considered. Even so, Richardson and Koller (1985) were able to construct an estimate of the prevalence of severe retardation based on a survey of the world literature on retardation, concluding the overall rate was 4 in every 1000 children (see also Zigler & Hodapp, 1986, Chapter 5). The prevalence rates for mild retardation are much more variable from setting to setting, ranging from 3 or so per 1000 children in some urban areas to 70 or 80 per 1000 in some poor and rural areas. About 75 percent of all retardations are of the nonorganic type, with the more common nonorganic retardation presenting much less severe impairment than organic retardation. One good ballpark number to remember is that at most 1 in 100 people are severely retarded, with most of these organically caused. Another 2 to 3 100 are mildly retarded, with more of these representing sociocultural retardation than organic retardation. In the most unfortunate of populations, the rate of retardation runs as high as 8 in 100 people, with sociocultural retardation predominating in these groups.

Information Processing in the Retarded

There has been extensive study of many aspects of retarded children's information processing. This research provided windows not only on the processing of retarded people, but also on the information-processing determinants of intelligent behavior in general.

Strategies and Metacognition   In the absence of instruction, retarded individuals are less likely to develop a variety of strategies than are normally intelligent individuals (see any of a number of chapters in Ellis, 1979). Even so, there have been many demonstrations of retarded individuals being able to carry out basic memory strategies following instruction in the processes composing the strategies. Retarded children can be taught to rehearse during list learning, use categories to cluster categorizable lists that are to be memorized, and construct elaborations that mediate paired-associate learning (e.g., Blackman & Lin, 1984; Brown, 1978; Taylor &

Turnure, 1979). Such training demonstrations suggest much greater competence than is apparent from the typical memory performances of retarded individuals (i.e., how they remember on their own in the absence of instruction).

An important hypothesis advanced by Brown and her colleagues (e.g., Brown, 1974; Brown & Campione, 1978) was that retarded children could carry out strategies but often do not do so on occasions when it would be appropriate—even when it is ensured through training that they know relevant strategies. Brown argued that retarded children have an executive deficiency: They do not regulate their use of strategies they know.

Belmont, Butterfield, and Ferretti (1982) offered an analysis supporting this executive deficiency hypothesis, but also making clear that with more elaborate instruction, retarded children can improve the regulation of their use of strategies. Belmont et al. (1982) examined more than 100 strategies training studies conducted with mentally handicapped students, identifying seven investigations that included some evidence of transfer. In six of these seven studies, not only had a strategy or strategies been trained, but also students had been taught how to self-regulate their use of the strategy using a variant of the self-instructional approach originally devised by Meichenbaum (1977; see Chapter 7). That is, when presented with a memory task, these students were taught to do the following:

- Decide on a goal.
- Make a plan to attain the goal.
- Try the plan.
- Ask themselves after their attempt: "Did the plan work?"
- If yes, no more is required; if no, ask: "Did I actually follow the plan?" If no, try the plan. If yes, ask: "What was wrong with the plan?" Devise a new plan and try it. (Adapted from Figure 2, Belmont et al., 1982)

That teaching students to self-regulate their use of strategies increases transfer of rehearsal, elaboration, and problem-solving procedures provides important support for Meichenbaum's (1977) perspective that explicitly teaching disadvantaged students how to self-regulate can increase their use of know-how they acquired through instruction (see Chapter 7). There is a great deal of know-how (i.e., strategies) that retarded children can acquire, but for them to use such know-how broadly, they often have to be taught much more than simply how to carry out the operations that define the strategic process.

Why might self-instruction work? One possibility is that use of strategies in such a self-controlled fashion increases metacognition about the strategies (e.g., Borkowski & Kurtz, 1987). Because retarded students are often impulsive in their responding, they do not naturally plan as extensively as normals. By forcing such planning, as self-instruction does, the learner must reflect on his or her actions and the characteristics of the situation. When students check their performance outcomes following use of a strategy, they are attending to utility information, which is important in promoting maintenance of strategies being learned (see Chapter 2). Attempting to devise a new plan when an old plan fails also forces attention to information about when and where the strategies being learned are helpful. Thus, the research on higher-order, self-regulated strategies instruction is also consistent with the perspective that improved metacognition about strategies increases transfer of newly learned procedures (see Chapter 2).

When students transfer procedural knowledge they have acquired, it is an excellent sign that they are self-regulating, which is an important marker of competence. Indeed, a mainstream theory of mental retardation is that retardation is a self-regulatory disorder (e.g., Whitman, 1990), with language critical to self-regulation: Language can be used to formulate cognitive plans (e.g., Asking oneself: "Have I seen a problem like this one before?"), to cue oneself to do something (e.g., "First I should do this and this and then this), and to organize one's thoughts (e.g., "These are *farm* animals and those are *zoo* animals, so they're different types of animals). Whitman (1990) believes that one reason retarded people do not self-regulate as normals do is because of their language deficiencies, although he also recognizes that relative to normals, retarded children are strategy deficient, less metacognitively developed, and less likely to have an extensive knowledge base, with all of these factors probably contributing to self-regulation failures in the retarded.

In pointing out these deficiencies, we also emphasize that the potential is great, for retarded people can learn a great deal and do so, especially when provided long-term exposure to material that is functionally important to them. For example, many retarded individuals learn important life scripts (e.g., washing hands, how to prepare and eat meals appropriately, getting off to school in the morning; Soodak, 1990). In addition, although there is variability in reading achievement in retarded populations, it is not unusual for middle school–age retarded children to be decoding near grade level with some evidence of comprehension (Rynders & Horrobin, 1990). Although more explicit prompting and more support may be required than with normal children, the retarded can learn many behaviors via scaffolding and reinforcement of correct responding (e.g., Butterfield & Nelson, 1991; Day & Hall, 1988; Demchak, 1990). Other behavioral learning mechanisms work with retarded children as well, such as punishment (see Mulick, 1990), classical conditioning (e.g., Ross & Ross, 1976), and observation and imitation (e.g., Kreitler & Kreitler, 1990)—that is, the four mechanisms that permit social learning by normally intelligent people (see Chapter 7) affect the learning of the retarded.

Although there have been attempts to discredit studies demonstrating cognitive gains in retarded children and children at risk for retardation when these children are exposed to environments providing stimulation and enriched opportunities for learning (e.g., Spitz, 1986a 1986b), such gains are not easily explained away (see Garber, Hodge, Rynders, Dever, & Velu, 1991; also Storfer, 1990). There are multiple indications in the literature that retarded children can learn quite a bit when placed in environments carefully engineered to foster learning. Such careful engineering is more critical with retarded children than with normally intelligent students, however, for left on their own, the retarded often undermine their own learning, for example, by making attributions that reduce effort, as taken up in the next subsection.

Motivation Retarded children's attributions about their own academic performances are likely to discourage future intellectual efforts (see Chapter 5, this volume; Merighi, Edison, & Zigler, 1990; Zigler & Hodapp, 1986, Chapter 6). When retarded children fail at tasks, they tend to blame themselves more than do normally intelligent children (e.g., MacMillan & Knopf, 1971). Retarded children's failures lead them to doubt whether they could possibly solve problems presented to them and increase their dependency on others to provide solutions to them (e.g., Achenbach & Zigler, 1968; Zigler & Balla,

1982), although they also tend to be more wary of potentially helpful adults than are other children (Merighi et al., 1990). Retarded people often have little confidence in themselves as learners or problem solvers.

More positively, some motivational interventions work extremely well with the retarded (e.g., Kiernan, 1985). Behavior modification, which involves the provision of reinforcements (see Chapter 7) for appropriate behaviors, has been used with great success with retarded populations. Retarded individuals can be taught self-help skills (e.g., self-feeding) and self-regulation (e.g., neat eating rather than sloppy eating) with behavior modification; there have been a number of behavior modification successes in improving communication skills, increasing attention span, decreasing hyperactivity, and increasing social interaction. Punishments (e.g., time-out) and reinforcements can be used to eliminate undesirable behaviors (e.g., aggression), with **differential reinforcement of other behavior** (i.e., reinforcing a desired behavior while punishing a nondesired behavior) working well with retarded populations. What the behavior modification literature demonstrates is that the retarded population is susceptible to motivation interventions, with a variety of reinforcers (e.g., from opportunities to interact with others to money) proving to be powerful motivators for behavior change in the retarded.

One important direction that needs to be explored is how retarded individuals' feelings about themselves as learners—that is, their feelings of competence—change as a function of improved behavior owing to behavior modification. On the one hand, provision of reinforcement has the potential for damaging belief in one's own abilities: People can come to believe they are performing well only because they are being rewarded (e.g., Weiner, 1979). On the other hand, knowing that you can do well at all might give a big boost to self-esteem if that success follows a long history of failure in other settings (with retarded individuals, that is usually the case).

Whitman (1990) recognized how critical motivation is if retarded individuals are to learn how to self-regulate. He argued that any instruction that would succeed in increasing self-regulation would need to produce high success in retarded students. Influenced by his Notre Dame colleague, John Borkowski, Whitman also recognized the need for retarded individuals to come to understand that they can control their academic outcomes to some degree by exerting effort in the execution of effective strategies—and that failure often reflects lack of effort and failure to use task-appropriate strategies. That is, retarded learners need to acquire beliefs that are likely to motivate cognitive effort and strategy use rather than persist with beliefs that support passivity (e.g., "I am dumb," and thus, there is little reason to try).

Processing Efficiency: Interactions Between Working Memory, Speed of Processing, and Knowledge Tasks that are presumed to require substantial working memory to be performed well—typically requiring recall of information presented rapidly without the opportunity for reflective study (e.g., digit span)—are performed much more poorly by retarded than by normally achieving people (for a review of data, see Torgesen, Kistner, & Morgan, 1987). There is substantial evidence that working memory capacity probably is more limited in retarded people than in normally achieving individuals (Hulme & MacKenzie, 1992), although it is difficult to know for certain whether there is really less neurological capacity or it only seems so because the capacity is used inefficiently: There is inefficiency because the information processing of retarded individuals is slower than the processing of nonretarded individuals (Brewer, 1987; Detterman, 1979; Nettlebeck & Brewer, 1981; Torgesen et al., 1987). Although the retarded can learn to do many tasks faster with practice, they remain far slower than normally intelligent individuals given equivalent practice (Brewer, 1987). The efficient use of working memory capacity is further undermined in the retarded because they are often less fully attentive to task-relevant information than are normals (e.g., Ross & Ross, 1984; Zeamon & House, 1979). Retarded individuals do not possess nearly as much knowledge of the world and academic content areas as normally intelligent people, so that information that can be "chunked" into larger units by normally intelligent people—and thus be easier to hold in short-term memory—cannot be chunked by the retarded. A variety of factors combine to reduce the efficiency of processing by retarded individuals compared with normal individuals, with the evidence clear that other things being equal, retarded individuals do not process as much in any given instant of time as do normally intelligent individuals. If the actual working memory capacity of retarded people is not less than normals, their functional short-term capacity certainly is.

Summary When the thinking of the retarded is conceived in terms of strategies, metacognition, knowledge, and motivation, it is obvious why enormous efforts are required to improve the functioning of the retarded. It will not be enough to teach strategies alone or only embellish strategy instruction with metacognition or only increase content knowledge or only shift motivational beliefs. All of these factors must be attended to and much more intensively than with normally intelligent children who are underperforming.

In addition, other possibilities besides cognitive training alone should be pursued, including the design of environments that maximally stimulate retarded individuals and provide great cuing to them about appropriate cognitive actions (Baer, 1990). Reinforcement can be used to increase the independent functioning of the retarded (e.g., Baer, 1990; Kendall, 1990). One of the heartening aspects of much of contemporary special education intervention research is that cognitive, environmental, and behavioral interventions are being combined (e.g., Kendall & Braswell, 1985).

We close this section on information processing by emphasizing that we favor much more work on the development and evaluation of treatments that combine all of our best thinking about how to improve mental functioning by the mentally retarded. This includes creating rich environments filled with reinforcement for appropriate behaviors and cognitive stimulation to maximize the acquisition of strategies, metacognition, and other knowledge. As Pressley (1990) put it:

> What would happen: If retarded children were immersed in environments where important social and academic procedures were taught using detailed explanations and modeling? If extensive feedback and corrective, constructive, and elaborative commentary were provided—even if such scaffolding were imperfect because of poor cues from retarded children or limited patience by teachers? If important metacognitive information about when and where to use academic strategies was emphasized as well? If educators consistently presented important world knowledge in digestible quantities? If retarded students were taught that appropriately directed effort (i.e., use of

strategies and application of knowledge that they already have or could acquire) determines performance more than does ability or other uncontrollable factors . . . ? Some work evaluating such a large-scale intervention might provide important guidance to the educational community about how to promote self-regulation in the very next cohort of retarded children. (Pressley, 1990, p. 370)

Even as we are sanguine, however, we remain open to the possibility that even the most favorable of instruction and environments might not be able to overcome some of the biological limitations (e.g., speed of processing) that seem to be inherent in retardation.

Progress in Understanding Cognitive Processing Differences: Research on Down Syndrome

Because much of the discussion of retardation has been general, we present here a summary of some specific research findings pertaining to one visible group of mentally retarded students, those with Down syndrome. This is a genetically mediated disorder, caused by three copies of chromosome 21 rather than the usual two. Because chromosome 21 is a small chromosome compared with most of the other 22 chromosomes, and because only a small part of chromosome 21 seems to be implicated in Down syndrome, the massive defects that define Down syndrome are the result of less than 0.5 percent of the genetic material (Wishart, 1988). It is the most common of the severe mental handicaps, with about 7000 new Down syndrome children born each year in the United States (Wishart, 1988). Down syndrome children are recognizable by distinctive facial features, including slanted eyes and a broad nose; their posture and gait are distinctive as well; the hands of people with Down syndrome are often stubby with some apparent webbing. Often, people with Down syndrome have congenital heart difficulties, which are treatable. What is now being discovered as more individuals with Down syndrome survive longer is that brain pathology resembling Alzheimer's disease is common by age 35 in people with Down syndrome (Nadel, 1988, p. 1).

We now know a great deal about people with Down syndrome that we did not know 20 years ago. Perhaps the most striking finding is that children with Down syndrome function at much higher levels when reared in supportive and rich home environments than when reared in institutions (Carr, 1975, 1985). Many with Down syndrome can function at least in the borderline retarded range when they are appropriately stimulated (Wisniewski, Miezejeski, & Hill, 1988). What is also apparent, however, is that even parents of children with Down syndrome have a natural tendency not to stimulate these children as they would other children. For example, if a person believes the child they are playing with has Down syndrome, they use more verbal commands and engage in less interactive questioning (e.g., Krasner, 1985). Adults often send the message to children with Down syndrome that not much is expected of them and that the adult expects to provide more help for these children than normal children. This may contribute to a tendency to avoid cognitive challenge that has been detected in children with Down syndrome as early as the first 2 years of life—they seem to turn off to stimulation when it is more than minimally challenging, in contrast to normal children, who are turned on by content that is just a bit beyond them (Wishart, 1988; see Chapter 5).

Researchers have been able to identify whether (and how well) children with Down syndrome process academically relevant content. Some examples illustrate the breadth and depth of this research:

1. Children with Down syndrome have more difficulties in moving beyond the one-word stage of language development (i.e., use of single words to communicate a variety of messages) than do normally intelligent children (Fowler, 1988), evidencing a variety of language production problems (Miller, 1988). Down syndrome children have particular difficulties with acquisition of grammar (Fowler, 1988).
2. Meyers (1988) reported on how computers with speech output can be used as a language intervention with Down syndrome toddlers, producing increases in their receptive language capabilities, with the possibility of accelerating the language development of children with Down syndrome using computer instructional environments. Another possibility is to use the computer as a prosthetic device to assist the production of language (Meyers, 1988; Nadel, 1988).
3. There is substantial evidence that Down syndrome children are much more disadvantaged with respect to mathematical competencies than verbal and reading abilities (e.g., Rynders & Horrobin, 1990; Wisniewski, Miezejeski, & Hill, 1988).
4. For example, Gelman and Cohen (1988) report that when presented problems that require counting for solutions, normals are more likely than children with Down syndrome to self-correct their false starts. They are more likely to vary their approach to a problem depending on problem characteristics. Down syndrome children need more explicit and extensive hints to solve many problems. In addition, Down syndrome children's counting seems much more like the acquisition of a rote, associative sequence rather than a reflection of deep understanding about how sequences of numbers relate to one another.
5. Processing of auditory information is more impaired than processing of visual information (Courchesne, 1988; Pueschel, 1988).

As in other areas of cognition, there also have been substantial advances in understanding the neurological factors mediating Down syndrome (Kemper, 1988). For example, there is much more extensive loss of small neurons in the hippocampus and the neocortex in children with Down syndrome than in other people. There are also some irregular groupings of neurons in the cerebral cortex. A great deal of attention is being given to the similarities and differences in brain structure of middle-aged people with Down syndrome and older normal adults with Alzheimer's disease (Courchesne, 1988; Nadel, 1988; Thase, 1988). Both Down syndrome and Alzheimer's disease involve chromosome 21, and there are some similar neurological structures in Down syndrome 35-year-olds and elderly with Alzheimer's disease. One of the most striking differences, however, is that most 35-year-old people with Down syndrome do not exhibit dementia, whereas virtually all Alzheimer's patients are demented.

Our summary of Down syndrome can be somewhat personal. Author MP had his first hands-on experience in psychology at a state home for the mentally retarded in the summer of 1968. Many of the residents had Down syndrome. The expectations for these people were minimal; so was their functioning. But why not? The institutional environment was more like a prison than a hospital. MP can reflect back on the school in this institution as one of the least stimulating educational environments he has encountered. In contrast, in 1992, it is now commonplace to see citizens with Down syndrome holding down gainful employment and living a life not so different from other lives. Although neither of the authors have encountered any A students with Down syndrome in our work in schools, we have encountered a number who are doing reasonably well in the mainstream curriculum, especially in reading.

A quarter century ago, little was known about the biology of Down syndrome other than its chromosomal determination and its gross physical consequences. The model that most had about people with Down syndrome was that they were deficient, deficient, and deficient. There is now much more emphasis on what these people can do and learn.

Most people with Down syndrome are extremely friendly and kind toward those around them. If we lived in a world in which humanity was valued more than intelligence, it would be us who would be retarded and many with Down syndrome considered the elite. One great benefit of more people with Down syndrome living in the community rather than in institutions is that more of them are models of good nature as they maneuver a demanding world. All of our lives are enriched because people with Down syndrome are now raised differently than they once were, now brought up in environments that stimulate them to perform nearer the top of their reaction range for intelligence rather than nearer the bottom of the range determined by their abnormal genetic endowment.

Concluding Comment

The cognitive model featured throughout this book can make retardation comprehensible, with our discussion of retardation here in terms of strategies, metacognition, knowledge, motivation, and short-term capacity (i.e., the elements of information processing that explain normal thinking). The commitment to instruction as an important determinant of functioning that has been reiterated throughout this book is supported further by the work on retardation. The performance of retarded individuals is affected by high-quality instruction and enriched environments: Regardless of biological endowment, there is a range of possible outcomes for a retarded individual, with exceptionally good instruction an important environmental factor that can result in re-

tarded students performing at the higher end of their reaction range. Our confidence in both the good information processing model and the role of instruction in affecting academic competence will increase as other types of individual differences, classifications, and dimensions are reviewed.

LEARNING DISABILITIES

The term learning disabilities came into being in the late 1960s and early 1970s (Wiederholt, 1974). Since its inception, definitional debates over learning disabilities continued to rage (see Kavale & Forness, 1992; Stanovich, 1991; Torgesen, 1991), although a majority view has emerged:

> Learning disabilities is a general term that refers to a heterogeneous group of disorders manifested by significant difficulties in the acquisition and use of listening, speaking, reading, writing, reasoning, or mathematical abilities. The disorders are intrinsic to the individual, presumed to be due to central nervous system dysfunction, and may occur across the life span.
>
> Problems in self-regulatory behaviors, social perception, and social interaction may exist with learning disabilities but do not by themselves constitute a learning disability.
>
> Although learning disabilities may occur concomitantly with other handicapping conditions (for example, sensory impairment, mental retardation, serious emotional disturbance) or with extrinsic influences (such as cultural differences, insufficient or inappropriate instruction), they are not the result of those conditions or influences (National Joint Commission on Learning Disabilities, Memorandum, 1988; reported in Torgesen, 1991, p. 21)

What does this definition imply? About the only thing obviously wrong with the learning-disabled student is that he or she is having trouble in some academic area. If academic difficulties can be explained as symptoms of other handicapping conditions or environmental deprivations, the problems do not reflect learning disabilities. The use of the conjunctive *or* in the list of problem areas is important. Learning disabilities are specific to one or two competencies or to a cluster of closely related competencies (e.g., reading and writing). Although terms such as general learning disabilities have been used to classify children who are having difficulties in most academic areas, many would argue such use of the term learning disabilities is a euphemism for below-average intelligence, mild retardation, or behavioral/emotional disturbance (e.g., Gajar, 1980).

What should be obvious from the conjunction *or* is that learning disabilities is a family of disorders, something that makes research on learning disorders per se extremely difficult or impossible. Indeed, one of the most critical sections in any learning disabilities journal article is the subjects subsection of the methods. Although it is important in any scientific article to specify who was studied, the need is especially urgent with respect to learning disabilities. In general, to make the case that a sample of children is learning-disabled, it is necessary to establish they are performing below expected levels in some academic arena but that other functioning is within expected levels of achievement for age or grade. In many articles, mean intelligence scores will be reported with the claim made of normal intelligence despite low performance in the deficit area.

The assumption of central nervous system dysfunction is often exactly that, supported at best by "soft signs" of neurological impairment, including the following:

- Speech/language delay.
- Motor clumsiness.
- Perceptual deficits.
- Poor right-left orientation.
- Meaningless and hyperactive motor behavior.
- Awareness that only one hand is being touched when both are being manipulated (especially applicable after age 8).
- Inability to copy simple geometric forms.
- Sloppy writing and copying.
- Faulty hand-eye coordination. (Based on Gaddes, 1985, pp. 12–13)

These signs are tapped by neuropsychological assessments and can be combined with other measures (e.g., patterns of differences on subscales of intelligence measures and standardized neuropsychological assessments such as the Halstead-Reitan and the Luria-Nebraska; see Chapters 16 and 17, this book) to make a case for learning disabilities.

Although more direct measures are possible, such as neurological surgery or neuroimaging (see Chapters 6 and 17), these are rarely used to diagnose learning disabilities. Readers may recall from Chapters 6 and 17, however, that progress in research has been made in identifying neurological abnormalities (especially for reading disabilities) us-

ing such procedures. For example, through a variety of techniques—from studies of cerebral blood flow to autopsies—abnormal structures and dysfunctions of the left hemisphere have been detected in the reading disabled (e.g., Flowers, Wood, & Naylor, 1991; Galaburda, Sherman, Rosen, Aboitz, & Geschwind, 1985; Gross-Glenn, Duara, Yoshii, Barker, Chen, Apicella, Boothe, & Lubs, 1988; Hier, LeMay, Rosenberger, & Perlo, 1978; Johnson & Myklebust, 1967). Although it was a controversial study (see Lyon, Newby, Recht, & Caldwell, 1991), Duffy, Denckla, Bartels, and Sandini (1980; see also Duffy & McAnulty, 1990) used an electroencephalogram (EEG) procedure to provide preliminary evidence of different patterns of left-hemisphere electrical activity in dyslexics and normal readers. Abnormal electrical activity in reaction to visual information (e.g., Conners, 1971; Harter, 1991) has been recorded with reading-disabled students. There are spikes in EEGs when normal readers read silently and aloud that are less pronounced when dyslexic readers read silently and aloud (Galin, 1989). One interesting finding produced using magnetic resonance imaging (MRI) technology is that regions of the brain implicated in language processing tend to be smaller in reading-disabled students than in normal learners (Hynd & Semrund-Clikeman, 1989); MRI studies have also detected abnormal brain structures at the back of the left hemisphere of dyslexics (Jernigan, Hesselink, Sowell, & Tallal, 1991; Larsen, Hoien, Lundberg, & Ødegaard, 1990). In addition, there also are abnormalities of blood flow in the frontal lobes of attention-deficit children (Lou, Henriksen, & Bruhn, 1984), which is sensible in light of the criticality of the frontal lobes in self-control and self-regulation (see Chapter 6, this volume).

These new and sophisticated measures also shed light on the issues of plasticity and recovery. For example, it has proven possible to document cases of massive structural abnormalities in the left hemisphere, with no apparent disruption of function for the affected child (e.g., Bigler & Naugle, 1985; Kolb, 1989). One possibility is that large structural abnormalities "force" the brain to reorganize more certainly than do smaller structural irregularities or breakdowns (Bigler, 1992; Kolb, 1989). Thus, because learning disabilities are often caused by small differences in structure, the brain may not be forced to reorganize, with the smaller brain disorders producing learning disabilities more certain to affect behavior and development in the long term than some more encompassing brain differences.

One point about biology and learning disabilities especially deserves commentary. For many years, learning-disabled students were referred to as "minimally brain damaged," reflecting the assumption that some unknown brain trauma had occurred at some point in life. One form of support for this supposition was that known brain damage does sometimes produce the same intellectual impairments experienced by learning-disabled students. Nonetheless, the best physiological data now suggest that these children are brain different—usually in the left hemisphere (i.e., at least for language/reading deficiencies, which have been studied most extensively using advanced physiological techniques)—not brain damaged.

That learning disabilities involve biological differences is also supported by behavior genetics research. For example, Smith and Pennington and their colleagues (e.g., Smith, Pennington, Kimberling, & Ing, 1990) have experienced some success in determining the chromosomal locations of genes affecting reading ability and disability. Some of the most theoretically interesting data have been produced in twin studies, however, with reasonable heritability estimates for individual differences in phonological processing, including the ability to sound out novel words (see Stevenson, 1992, for a review). In contrast, there is little heritability for individual differences in the ability to read sight words (Stevenson, 1992). Readers of this book should recall the discussion in Chapter 14 about the importance of phonemic awareness and decoding ability. The evidence is mounting that there is an inherited biological basis for differences between children in their ability to analyze words and sound them out. What is also apparent is that such heritabilities are in the 0.40 to 0.75 range, meaning that there is a substantial environmental component and thus every reason to expect that environmental interventions can be developed that improve phonological processing, even for those children who may have a biological endowment that supports phonological processing less than does the biological endowment of other students.

In concluding that there are biological factors in the determination of learning disabilities, that is not to say that environment plays no role. In fact, there is growing evidence that some parental behaviors probably are dysfunctional in that they lead to maladaptive outcomes for children who may be at risk for various forms of learning disabilities. For example, Jacobvitz and Sroufe (1987) studied children who manifested attention deficit disorder in school at 6 years of age. These children were part of a larger longitudinal study that involved taking many measures on the children and their interactions with their parents. When these children were observed during the preschool years in problem-solving situations with their parents (e.g., solving an Etch-a-Sketch maze-tracing problem), the interactions were different than were the interactions between other parents and children. The parents of children who eventually would be diagnosed as attention deficit tended to overstimulate their children as they solved problems, either physically touching them or interacting with the child in ways that more provoked or teased than helped. In general, during daily interactions, these same parents were more likely than parents of other children to interfere with the child's ongoing activity without taking into account the child's state, mood, or interest. Buhrmester, Camparo, Christensen, Gonzalez, and Hinshaw (1992) also observed that parents of hyperactive children have more provocative and interfering interactions with their children than do parents of normal children. Such observations suggest that the parents may have played a role in shaping the child's attention deficit, which is a source of difficulty in performing the academic demands of schooling.

Generating reliable incidence figures for learning disabilities is impossible, precluded largely by the debates over definition and the uncertainty in many cases about whether a child is actually learning-disabled or simply manifesting symptoms consistent with learning disabilities, symptoms caused by some as yet undiagnosed alternative causal factor. When more than 100 experts in learning disabilities were polled in 1983, all offered estimates between 0 and 5 percent of the school-age population (*Journal of Learning Disabilities*, January 1983, Volume 15). Even so, there was little agreement within that range as to what the incidence might be. Figures can be provided for the percentage of students classified as learning-disabled in schools, with this figure often between 4 and 5 percent of the population of children in school (see Kavale & Forness, 1992). As Kavale and Forness (1992) point out, there are a myriad of reasons for students being classified as learning-disabled, with some, such as government funding formulas (i.e., formulas determining what percentage of the school population is eligible for special education funds), prompting suspicion that too many students are currently being classified as learning-disabled. For example, teachers taking our graduate classes have frequently told us that the only way to obtain needed services for some students is to have them classified as learning-disabled, although there is no reason to believe that these students have learning disabilities (e.g., the evidence more suggests that the students are far behind in school because their parents did not provide academic stimulation during the preschool years). In recent years, with increasing pressure from the federal government to identify no more than 2 percent of the total school-age population as learning-disabled, there has been a trend to reduce the number of students so classified.

In closing this subsection on the definition of learning disabilities, we want readers to appreciate the turmoil and debate that continue over determining who is learning-disabled and who is not. An article appearing in the prestigious *Journal of the American Medical Association* (Shaywitz, Shaywitz, Fletcher, & Escobar, 1990) dealt with differences in diagnosis of learning disabilities depending on who does the classification. The authors, who were outside the school system, individually assessed 445 children from kindergarten through grade 3. Whether participants were reading disabled was determined by examining whether their reading performance on a standardized reading measure was less than would be expected based on their IQ (i.e., was there a discrepancy between reading performance and intellectual ability, consistent with definitions of learning disabilities?). The authors compared whom they identified as reading disabled with those identified by the schools as learning-disabled. There was a striking difference in the classifications using the individualized assessment and the school assessment. First, fewer boys were identified as reading disabled with the individual assessment than by school authorities; second, more girls were identified as reading disabled with the individualized assessment than the school assessment. The typical pattern of two to four times as many boys being identified as reading disabled than girls was replicated in the school-provided data; the individual assessments suggested approximately equal numbers of boys and girls having reading disability.

Shaywitz et al. (1990) offered an explanation of the difference between the school appraisals and the categorizations emerging from the individual assessments. School-identified children may have been referred because they were hyperactive and behavior problems—the school-identified children were high on these characteristics. Because boys are more likely to evidence these problems than girls, they are more likely to be referred for assessment of reading disability, with some proportion of these assessed as reading-disabled. Girls, who are less likely to be hyperactive and behaviorally problematic, are less likely to be referred, and hence fewer of them end up diagnosed as reading-disabled. The point of this example is that the prevalence of learning disabilities in any group of children and the particular children diagnosed as reading-disabled will depend on how the children are screened and assessed. The Shaywitz et al. (1990) findings, if replicable, would suggest a terrible sex bias in the provision of service by schools: Boys who are not reading-disabled are labeled as such and taught like reading-disabled children are taught. Some girls who are reading-disabled and might benefit from treatment are missed by a school screening system that passes over well-behaved children.

Before coming to the conclusion that educator assessments of learning disabilities are harshly biased against some children, something else should be considered. In fact, learning-disabled students who also manifest behavior problems are more at risk than learning-disabled children without behavior problems: McKinney and Speece (1986) reported that learning-disabled students with behavior problems progressively declined in achievement relative to normally achieving peers (i.e., with time, the gap in academic achievement between learning-disabled and normally achieving peers widened); learning-disabled children who were not also behavior problems did not evidence comparable progressive decline, with the difference in their achievement level from the level of normally accomplished students constant over a 3-year period. What these data suggest is that more than the current academic deficiency must be considered in deciding whether a student should be referred for service, for those who are low in achievement and high in behavior problems are at much greater risk than well-behaved children with learning disabilities.

A final consideration in this section on definition is that many readers may have the impression that one type of learning disability—dyslexia, which is the inability to decode words well despite intensive educational efforts—is all learning disabilities. Dyslexia accounts for only a small proportion of all learning-disabled. Again, incidence figures are difficult to gauge, but a fair guess is that no more than half of 1 percent of all people suffer from dyslexia. What that means is that if a school district is classifying 4 percent of its students as learning-disabled, about one in eight of these children might be dyslexic. Learning disabilities is more than dyslexia, including difficulties in comprehending once decoding is accomplished, difficulties in remembering what has been read, and nonverbal disabilities, such as extreme difficulties in calculating (i.e., dyscalculia).

Problems of definition and diagnosis abound in the area of learning disabilities. Even so, the more that is learned about biological and behavioral differences between learning-disabled and normal students, the more defensible is the category of learning disabilities. We expect that as additional research on structural and physiological differences accumulates, there will be even more justification for considering some students to be learning-disabled. One possibility is that neurophysiological assessments now used only in research will become more common in the not-too-distant future, permitting more certain diagnosis of whether a person is learning-disabled as well as determination of their particular problem.

Information Processing by Learning-Disabled Students

There has been a great deal of description of the deficiencies of students with various types of learning disabilities (e.g., how the mathematical computations by people with dyscalculia differ from the mathematical computations of people who are normally achieving in arithmetic). There has also been progress in understanding the processing differences between the learning-disabled and normal achievers. Indeed, learning-disabled students have been studied intensely as part of attempts to build models of effective and ineffective cognition (e.g., Larson & Gerber, 1992). In part, these efforts were stimulated by persistent hypotheses offered by learning disabilities theorists about the probable causes of learning disabilities, with a number of single factors proposed as determinants of learning dysfunctions over the years (Willis, Hooper, & Stone, 1992).

Although some of these single-factor theories have contributed to scientific progress, not all have. Worden (1983) offered a summary of the range of opinion about what might account for learning difficulties in otherwise normal children:

> Current theories of causation range from the reasonable to the incredible: learning disabilities have been attributed to genetic factors ... incomplete hemispheric lateralization ... environmental and nutritional deprivation ... biochemical anomalies, food allergies, vitamin deficiencies, children's TV, fluorescent lights, cigarette smoke, and aerosol sprays.... (p. 132)

As discussed in the previous subsection, there is increasingly sophisticated genetics evidence linking genetic and biological factors to some forms of learning disabilities. Not all biologically oriented theories have fared well on examination, however. Orton (1928, 1937) contended that learning disabilities reflected delay in establishing functional dominance of one hemisphere, supported by his observations that there was a correlation between ambidextrousness and learning problems. Although this position was important in stimulating research on possible contributions of the two hemispheres to learning disabilities, it is now clear that the causes of learning disorders cannot be reduced to this one factor. The physiological data reviewed in the last subsection establish that there are a number of brain structures and mechanisms implicated in learning disabilities.

Over the years, many have proposed that visual-perceptual problems were the cause of learning disabilities. Such a position was supported by correlations between perceptual disorders and learning disabilities (see Kavale, 1982), such as erratic eye movements during reading in learning-disabled readers compared with normal readers (e.g., Pirozzolo, 1979). A variety of data combined to undermine the hypothesis that the perceptual dysfunctions caused the learning dysfunctions, however. For example, interventions designed to improve reading by modifying eye movements fail to do so (Daneman, 1991).

An alternative to the perceptual deficiency hypothesis is that learning disabilities are due to underlying problems in processing of language, with Vellutino (1979) offering a book-length summary of the evidence supporting the claim that verbal information processing deficiencies underlie dyslexia. Of the single-factor theories offered, this one certainly has the greatest support, continuing to mount with advances in neuropsychology: When neuropsychological correlates of reading and learning disabilities have been detected, more often than not they have been in the left hemisphere and often in areas of the brain known to be implicated in processing of language.

Regarding the other potential causal factors, although our general concern for the environment and good health urges nonuse of aerosal sprays or cigarettes, and we support wholeheartedly efforts to ensure adequate and balanced nutrition for children, and we believe the social learning effects of television viewing alone are sufficient to cause concerns about the effects of television on social behaviors, we have no reason to believe that any of these factors contribute to learning disabilities. Even so, given that learning disabilities is a visible academic problem that affects large numbers of students, we also expect continued media coverage of theories attributing learning disabilities to incredibly unlikely sources. Readers of this book should be armed with knowledge that will permit them to inform those around them of more likely causal determinants, such as biological differences in language processing.

Even if differences in parts of the brain underlying language competence prove to be the most fundamental cause of many learning disorders, it is important to understand learning disabilities at a psychological level, for information processing models have proved important in designing treatments that dramatically affect the learning and performance of learning-disabled students. Again, thinking about learning disabilities in terms of the elements of good information processing makes them more comprehensible.

Strategies and Metacognition   Some of the earliest analytical research on learning disabilities focused on the use of strategies by learning-disabled students as they attempted the types of basic memory tasks that had been studied extensively in normal children (see Chapter 2). Learning-disabled students proved less likely than normally achieving students to use strategies such as rehearsal and category reorganization during list learning (e.g., Bauer, 1977a, 1977b; Dallago & Moely, 1980; Kastner & Rickards, 1974; Tarver, Hallahan, Cohen, & Kauffman, 1977; Tarver, Hallahan, Kauffman, & Ball, 1976; Torgesen, 1977; Torgesen & Goldman, 1977). More positively, learning-disabled students are able to carry out these strategies and others when instructed to do so (e.g., Bauer, 1977b; Tarver et al., 1976, Experiment 2;

Torgesen, 1977), making clear that their deficiencies did not prevent them from carrying out processes such as rehearsal and categorical reorganization of material.

One of the leaders of this basic research thrust, however, Torgesen (1979, 1980; Torgesen & Houck, 1980), led the way in urging the study of processing with tasks better matched to the ones learning-disabled students faced in school. In the 1980s, studies of strategy use and strategy instruction in basic task situations gave way to studies of strategy use and strategy instruction in exactly the types of situations confronted by learning-disabled students in school. The concern of learning disabilities researchers for improving the processing of problem learners in school has done much to move the entire field of cognition and instruction, with learning disabilities researchers generating some of the best and most ecologically valid research on strategies instruction.

The strength of that research already might be apparent to readers in that it has been featured in previous chapters of this book. Thus, reciprocal teaching of prediction, questioning, clarification, and summarization strategies was designed to teach middle-school students with reading problems how to increase their comprehension (see Chapters 8 and 14). The most convincing data to date on the effectiveness of transactional instruction of comprehension strategies have been generated with weak readers (Chapter 14). Some of the best writing intervention studies, including research by Englert, Raphael, Harris, and Graham, were produced with learning-disabled students, with the case strong that students experiencing specific learning deficiencies can learn complex strategies. For example, students who have difficulties in language arts can learn to use plan-write-revise approaches to composition (see Chapter 15). Deshler, Schumaker, and their associates at Kansas (Chapters 14 and 15) in particular have validated and disseminated a number of comprehension, writing, memory, and problem-solving strategies designed explicitly for use with the learning-disabled.

When these strategy instructional packages are examined, there is always extensive attention to metacognition, emphatic efforts to increase student awareness of when and where the strategies being learned can be used, and many prompts encouraging students to monitor their performance. The reason for this is that there have been many demonstrations in the literature that weaker students, and learning-disabled students in particular, often are not as aware as normally achieving students of their cognition. As Larson and Gerber (1992) summarized it:

> ... [P]oor readers are found to be less aware of the purpose of reading as meaning-getting, less knowledgeable about strategies for decoding, comprehending, and reading for a specific purpose, less sensitive to important parts of text, and less aware of text inconsistencies. ... In the area of spelling, learning-disabled students have difficulty with ... error monitoring. ... In the area of math, learning-disabled students have been described as having significant difficulties selecting correct algorithms ... using strategies correctly ... and monitoring procedures. (pp. 128–129).

Of course, as emphasized throughout this book, if learners are to make the most of the strategies they are learning and know, they must know when and where the procedures apply, which is often reflected by effective selection of strategies; they must also monitor whether the tactic they are taking at present is paying off or whether some other approach might work better. Certainly, learning-disabled students are not unique in their lack of awareness of the appropriateness of various strategies or their awareness of the status of their cognition, for a variety of evidence has been presented in this book of how increasing metacognition in normal learners can increase the use and generalization of new strategies. Moreover, there has been a variety of evidence presented about how normal learners vary in metacognitive status and use of metacognition (e.g., elementary children may use what they know about the relative effectiveness of strategies only when prompted to do so; people tend to monitor how they do during testing much more than they monitor their performances during learning; see Chapter 2, this book).

Just as Torgesen led the way in urging more ecologically valid study of strategies, he provided some of the earliest thinking on the possible role of metacognition in mediating learning disabilities. Torgesen (1975, 1977), in noting the passivity of learning-disabled students relative to other students, proposed that these students were not as aware as other students about the value of planning and monitoring or of the situational value of strategies they might know and be able to use. Differences in such metacognitive understandings overlap with differences in the motivational beliefs held by learning-disabled students, with their motivational beliefs actually another form of metacognition (i.e., knowledge of the value of cognitive activities), which is often deficient in ways that undermine active attempts to tackle academic tasks.

Motivation Learning-disabled children often are caught in a terrible cycle. Because they have done poorly in school, they begin to think of themselves as academic failures—they begin to believe they are stupid. Such a belief does nothing to motivate academic effort, which results in additional failure, which, if anything, strengthens the perception of low ability (e.g., Borkowski et al., 1990; Licht, 1983, 1992; Torgesen, 1977; see Chapter 5, this book). The evidence is simply overwhelming that compared with normally achieving children, learning-disabled students lack academic self-esteem (e.g., Licht, 1992; Rogers & Saklofske, 1985; Winne, Woodland, & Wong, 1982). They expect to do poorly in school (e.g., Butkowski & Willows, 1980; Rogers & Saklofske, 1985). The instruction they are receiving does not make sense to them, and they know it has not been effective in the past (e.g., Kos, 1991). In general, conventional remedial instruction does not reduce the gap in academic self-esteem between normally achieving students and those with learning disabilities (e.g., Chapman, 1988).

Rather, conventional schooling does much to reinforce the negative academic self-esteem of children with learning disabilities. American classrooms are filled with reminders to students who are doing poorly that they are experiencing difficulties: Their papers are not displayed with the A papers, their names are not part of the "Geographer of the Week" display, they are not honored by placement on the classroom's "Tip-Top Speller" list, and they are not members of the reading group that includes all the smartest children in the class. The more the classroom publicly honors its high achievers, the worse the social comparison for the low achievers (Ames & Archer, 1988; Stipek & Daniels, 1988). If anything, the situation is worse for girls because boys more readily explain away their failures as caused by factors other than their low ability (e.g., the teacher doesn't like me; the tests aren't fair; Licht, Kistner, Ozkaragoz, Shapiro, & Clausen, 1985; see Chapter 5). Hyperactive children seem to be especially likely to believe that academic matters are out of their control (e.g., Hartsfield, Licht, Swenson, & Thiele, 1989).

This situation is not hopeless, however, with growing evidence that as students are taught ways of tackling academic tasks that improve their task-related performances, they can also be taught to attribute their task-performances to use of the strategies they are learning (for reviews, see Borkowski et al., 1990; Licht, 1992; also Chapter 5, this book). Borkowski and colleagues have experienced substantial success in increasing the long-term commitment of learning-disabled students to use of new strategies they are learning by making certain their students understood as part of instruction that their performances were improving because of their use of strategies (see Chapter 5).

There are also other instructional procedures that increase sense of competence and control (Licht, 1992). Bandura and Schunk (1981) reported that focusing students' attention on successful attainment of concrete and immediate goals (e.g., getting today's problems correct) increases student **self-efficacy,** which is their term for learners believing that their performances are under their own control. Focusing on progress toward long-term goals (e.g., thinking about today's performance with respect to how many days it will take to cover the entire unit of material) has much less of an impact on self-efficacy. When students perform strategies in ways that make it salient that they are doing something to attempt to perform a task (e.g., they self-verbalize the strategy), self-efficacy seems to be enhanced as well (Schunk & Cox, 1986). When children see another person like themselves coping with a task, but finally accomplishing it, their self-efficacy is likely to improve (Schunk, Hanson, & Cox, 1987). In addition, children seem to have greater self-efficacy, more positive feelings of competence, and better performance in classrooms emphasizing improvement rather than performance relative to peers (e.g., Nicholls, 1989).

What is really heartening is that review of the academic interventions with learning-disabled and low-achieving students featured in previous chapters (e.g., Deshler and Schumaker's work on a variety of learning strategies, Graham and Harris' writing interventions, transactional reading comprehension instruction) makes clear that such interventions are rich with instruction to shift motivational beliefs that might undermine academic effort. Students are taught that their performances can improve through use of strategies that are under their control. They receive substantial here-and-now feedback about improvement. Their improvements are emphasized rather than their absolute level of performance or their standing relative to classmates. Students see models coping and struggling to apply the strategies being taught. At least initially, they perform strategies using self-verbalization, which really makes obvious *how* they are coping with the academic task. That successful instructional packages do include these motivational components provides some validation of the theoretical stance that it is essential to alter the dysfunctional motivational beliefs of learning-disabled students if great progress is to be made in advancing the academic achievements of learning-disabled students.

It must be emphasized in closing, however, that altering motivation is not enough. Programs that are effective with learning-disabled students teach strategies, teach metacognition about those strategies, and have students apply their newly learned information processing tools to content worth learning, content that can stimulate increases in a student's declarative knowledge base. The consistent message throughout this book is that academic success is a mixture of factors, most notably strategies, metacognition, other knowledge, and motivation.

Processing Efficiency: Interactions Between Working Memory, Speed of Processing, and Knowledge
Memory span tasks—typically requiring recall of information presented rapidly without the opportunity for reflective study (e.g., digit span)—often are performed much more poorly by learning-disabled than by normally achieving students (e.g., Torgesen & Houck, 1980):

1. The verbal processing difficulties experienced by many learning-disabled children are a factor in memory span, with the phonetic coding demands of such tasks interfering with performance (e.g., simply saying "four, seven, nine, one, three, five, and two" may require substantial effort for a child with language/learning difficulties).

2. Although the pervasive slowness of processing observed in the retarded is not evident in the learning-disabled, learning-disabled students are slower for some processes than are normally achieving students (e.g., initial processing of sequentially presented information, such as saying the to-be-remembered items to oneself).

3. The efficient use of working memory capacity also is undermined in some learning-disabled

students because of attention problems (e.g., Shaywitz & Shaywitz, 1992).

4. To the extent that academic prior knowledge has been reduced by the learning disability (i.e., learning-disabled children learn less content in school because of their learning disability), there also is reduced ability to recode information into larger meaningful chunks efficiently—to do so requires prior knowledge that makes clear which particular pieces of new information relate to one another.

One of the more interesting observations about working memory and learning-disabled children is that reading-disabled children may have a more generalized impairment in working memory than other learning-disabled children. Siegel and Ryan (1989) observed that reading-disabled children had difficulty with a memory span task involving processing of sentences and another working memory task requiring counting. In contrast, arithmetic-disabled children had difficulty only with the working memory–counting task. The possibility of working memory difficulties varying with type of learning disability (see also Siegel & Ryan, 1988) deserves further study.

Although processing inefficiencies in children with learning disabilities are not as pronounced as in the retarded, there is less efficient use of limited capacity working memory by learning-disabled students compared with normally achieving students, at least some of the time. Most analyses are consistent with the conclusion that, if anything, learning-disabled students and many students experiencing academic problems (e.g., weaker readers) have less working memory or short-term capacity than do normal achievers (e.g., Hulme & MacKenzie, 1992; Swanson, 1992; Swanson & Cooney, 1991). As is always the case in analyses of working/short-term memory, however, it is impossible to be absolutely certain that there is really less capacity for the learning-disabled. It may only seem that way because of processing inefficiencies: For example, so much effort can be expended phonetically coding the to-be-remembered digits that there is little capacity left over for the memory part of the task. So much attention can be diverted from the task by irrelevancies in the environment that little of the total capacity is available for the memory demand. Lacking prior knowledge prohibits the learning-disabled from forming meaningful "chunks," such as recoding the

sequence 7-4-7 as "747 jet," 4-1-1 as "directory assistance," or 2-8-2-7 as the "score of a football game in which both teams scored four touchdowns and one missed one extra point."

Summary Relative to normally achieving classmates, learning-disabled students are likely to use fewer strategies, be less metacognitively aware, to possess more dysfunctional beliefs, and to know less in general. New advances in assessment are permitting increased understanding of the information processing approaches of learning-disabled compared with normally achieving students, which is taken up in the next subsection.

Progress in Understanding Cognitive Processing Differences: New Directions in Assessment

Meltzer (e.g., 1987, 1991, 1992) and her associates (Meltzer, Solomon, Fenton, & Levine, 1989) have devised assessment tools (*Survey of Educational and Problem-Solving Skills*) that are revealing about the information-processing strengths and weaknesses of 9- to 14-year-olds. These are individually administered tests, so detailed measurement is possible, including observations of processing and interviews about how students approach academic tasks. Students perform academic tasks, such as problem solving, reading, spelling, composition, and math, as part of the assessment. The strategies used by students are scored as they perform such tasks; so are students' monitoring and correction of errors. Students' awareness of the strategies they are using is measured; whether they can explain their use of strategies is tapped. Much is learned about student thinking by combining these observations of process with performance outcomes, including evaluations of (1) cognitive flexibility, (2) working memory, (3) strategy use, and (4) automaticity of strategy use. Meltzer and associates have demonstrated that these variables predict differences in academic performance during the elementary-school and middle-school years.

What we hope is clear by this point is that learning disabilities are being conceived of in terms of the models at the heart of this book. (For example, much of the conceptual justification for Meltzer's assessment refers to the articles that inspired Chapter 1 in this book.) We believe that this conceptualization has great potential for eliminating or reducing the definitional conflicts that have plagued the field of learning disabilities. From this perspective, the possibility of learning disabilities is assessed when there is low academic achievement in some important academic domain but not in others. What is expected is that such low achievers will use fewer and less efficient strategies than normally achieving learners as they attempt tasks in the deficiency domain. The strategies they do use will be applied less flexibly than when normally achieving students use strategies. Limited working memory may be apparent, especially in the deficiency domain, in that learning-disabled students can do fewer tasks simultaneously than can other students. Although it is likely that these information processing differences ultimately relate to biological differences, at least at present, knowledge of information processing differences is permitting greater progress in the development of interventions to improve the functioning of learning-disabled children than is new knowledge of physiological and anatomical differences between learning-disabled children and other children.

Progress in Understanding Cognitive Processing Differences: Studies of Exceptionally Effective Educational Environments

If information processing analyses of learning disabilities are correct, and theories of education based on information processing are correct, it might be expected that educational environments that have been developed in light of information processing theory might be especially effective. Formal study of such environments has only begun, but the data generated to date inspire additional confidence in information processing approaches to instruction with these children.

Benchmark School, outside of Philadelphia, is dedicated to the education of otherwise normal children who have already experienced great difficulties in school. The typical entry-level student has done poorly in 2 years of regular schooling, with the most common problem being failure to learn to read. Formal assessments have been conducted and determined that the child is at least average and more typically above average in intelligence.

During the first year or two at Benchmark (see Gaskins & Elliot, 1991, for a book-length description of the school, its programs, and students), students are taught to decode, using an approach to decoding

developed at the school. Lessons on decoding continue throughout the elementary years. Right from the start, however, Benchmark students learn that reading is not only sounding out words, but also "meaning-getting." As decoding skills develop, students read increasingly challenging literature; they are taught to tackle such challenging reading by using the comprehension strategies that work for all elementary children (see Chapter 14). In addition, there is daily instruction in writing, again involving instruction of higher-order strategies, such as the planning-translation-revising strategies featured in Chapter 15. Content-area instruction is not neglected but rather the strategies that the student learn to use to read, write, and problem-solve are applied to social studies and science texts (Pressley, Gaskins, Wile, Cunicelli, & Sheridan, 1991).

The Benchmark model of instruction is consistent with the model of instruction favored throughout this book (Pressley, Gaskins, Cunicelli, et al., 1991)—long-term instruction of strategies well matched to important academic tasks; development of metacognition about strategies through direct explanation, modeling, and scaffolded practice; reinforcement for improvement rather than for outperforming other students in a class, with every effort made to encourage healthy motivational beliefs (e.g., I can do well if I apply the right strategies, the ones being learned in school); and expansion of content knowledge.

Does it work? Although no true experiment of Benchmark has ever been conducted (or ever could be), the case is nonetheless strong that Benchmark makes a difference for its students: An 8-year-old who cannot read, which is the status of most entry-level Benchmark students, is a great risk for long-term academic failure. In contrast, most Benchmark students leave the school in an average of 4 years (some stay as long as 7 years) to return to normal schooling. When they do so, typically they are at least average students or better. Virtually all Benchmark alumni graduate from high school; many go on to college.

Irene Gaskins and some of her Benchmark associates started their school in a church basement a quarter century ago. What they have done consistently is apply the best research-based ideas of the day about instruction to the education of learning-disabled children. The result is a school that is at the cutting edge of education, a model for the United States of what schooling at its best can look like—

and what outstanding instruction can do to improve the thinking and academic performances of students who are at extremely high risk for academic failure. Our perspective is that exceptionally effective educational institutions such as Benchmark deserve careful study because they have the potential of informing the United States about how schooling can be done well, schooling that more certainly produces desirable outcomes than what is conventional instruction in many U.S. schools (see also Chapter 11). The success of Benchmark illustrates that learning-disabled students can achieve in school when they are offered high-quality instruction.

GIFTEDNESS

The intellectually gifted are a great societal resource. Our lives certainly are fuller and better because of the presence of genius among us: How different life would be if there had been no Mozart, Van Gogh, Edison, or Steven Jobs (one of the founders of Apple Computer). Some of the gifted become great writers; physicians; statesmen; and business, academic, and industrial leaders. Although not all of the gifted achieve at the level of greatness, we are touched daily by the accomplishments large and small of the exceptionally talented.

Genius and high academic ability have been fascinations for psychologists since Galton's early work in high intelligence and achievement (see Chapter 16). We know quite a bit about highly intelligent people: The gifted are a diverse group. First, one distinction is between prodigies, who are talented in one particular domain, and people who are generally smart but not exceptionally talented in any one area. As Feldman (1986, Chapter 1) put it, the gifted include specialists and generalists. One of Feldman's hypotheses, borne out by other analyses (e.g., Howe, 1990; Radford, 1990; see Chapter 4, this book, for discussion of Bloom, 1985), is that prodigious genius is more fragile than generally high intelligence. The prodigy will thrive in particular environments but not others, whereas general intelligence is fostered in a greater range of settings. We also point out that there is nothing inimical between prodigious genius and high general intelligence, and, in fact, many prodigious geniuses have high general ability.

So who is gifted? What defines a gifted student? There is great debate over these questions (Hoge, 1988). One criterion is IQ, although many different IQ cutoff points have been used as the starting point for giftedness. Often scores of 130 to 140 are considered the lower part of the gifted range. In many school districts, however, scores as low as 115 are taken as the beginning of the gifted range, which means that approximately 10 percent of all children would be considered gifted (Grinder, 1985). Of course, high IQ alone is not sufficient to define giftedness. For example, there are underachievers, students who perform well below what they are capable of based on psychometric intelligence. Some students are much stronger on some subscales of intelligence tests than on other subscales, so that an overall IQ score does not represent adequately their giftedness. Not surprisingly, there have been diverse pressures to expand the definition of giftedness beyond being a label for the upper end of the IQ distribution (e.g., Richert, 1991). Recall, for example, the discussion of Gardner's **multiple intelligences** (see Chapter 6, this volume). A person can have much greater intelligence in music, in math, or for physical activities than for other competencies. Even if their specialized competence is not so great as to be considered prodigious, there is often little doubt that these people have better ability in one area than in others.

What does it mean to be prodigious? We favor a definition offered by Radford (1990, Chapter 11, p. 200): "Statistically, a prodigy comes at the extreme end of a distribution of achivement in a particular activity. . . ": Thus, in recent National Hockey League all-star games, Wayne Gretsky has clearly been the best of the best, a hockey prodigy if there ever was one, with his talent apparent since he first showed up at the neighborhood rinks in Brantford, Ontario. Liona Boyd received a guitar for Christmas when she was 12 and as a young adult established herself as the first lady of classical guitar. Stevie Wonder was a successful songwriter and singer at age 12 and continues at the top of the profession today. Prodigies have generated a great deal of attention in the last decade, with several book-length treatments of their accomplishments.

Prodigies

A main question posed by many studying prodigious genius is how to foster the giftedness of such individuals: What environmental variables have an impact on whether a person with a great talent becomes a leading figure in a field of specialization? If the talent is there, how can we increase the odds of producing a great mathematician, scientist, or artist? Although each reviewer of the lives of prodigies comes up with a slightly different list, and although each reviewer has a factor or two they view as particularly critical, the following are mentioned often as important to the development of prodigious genius (e.g., Bloom, 1985; Feldhusen, 1986; Feldman, 1988; Radford, 1990; Renzulli, 1986; Tannenbaum, 1986):

- High general intellect.
- A distinctive aptitude or aptitudes (although some authors dispute whether such aptitudes are innate, emphatically arguing that many aptitudes can be rendered "special" by high-quality instruction and experience, pointing to data supporting their claim; see Howe, 1990, pp. 31–34).
- Instruction related to exceptional abilities, with this often extensive to the point of mentoring.
- Often there are a series of teachers of increasing sophistication that coach the student in the area of giftedness.
- Parents who are generally nurturant and supportive, but also supportive of the development of the particular talent; parents are often seen as playing a guiding role in the nurturance of high talent, recognizing it and identifying resources that can foster the talent in their child.
- Long-term motivation to develop the ability—often to the point of being uncontrollably "turned on" by the activity or obsessively devoted to the field; doing the activity is as much play as work: Some adjectives that apply are "dogged, persistent . . . hardworking, attentive, strong-willed, self-directed, independent, enthusiastic, energetic. . . " (Howe, 1990, p. 181).
- Prodigies are multiply rewarded for engaging in the activity; for example, consider the multiple rewards for child piano prodigies early in their careers: "The children were encouraged by the progress they had already made, by the knowledge that playing the piano was an opportunity to be special, and to do something that others of their age could not achieve, and by the attention and applause they were given . . . " (Howe, 1990, p. 186)
- A great deal of practice of the special ability or abilities.
- Confidence in their special ability.

- The high ability must be meshed with a field in which recognized accomplishment is possible; it helps if it is a developing field, not so advanced that it cannot be mastered in a reasonable period of time and not so developed than it is closed to new ideas (e.g., a young genius in the calculus will have a tougher time coming to a new insight than will a burgeoning genius in computer programming). One's talents must match the needs of a field at a particular point of development (see especially Feldman, 1986).

A moment's thought about this list makes it clear that prodigious talent is the happy coincidence of many factors, something borne out not only in the rich biographic studies that inspired the list we just presented, but also in harshly quantitative analyses of high achievement based on data sets in which the prodigious are anonymously represented to the researchers (e.g., Benbow & Arjmand, 1990; Reynolds & Walberg, 1991; Tomlinson-Keasey & Little, 1990). The right genes are born into a supportive family (or at least the family fosters a talent that can be developed by the child); the child is excited by the special competency and dedicated to developing it; and the talent is one that is needed by society, one matched to the state and needs of the world at the time. Prodigy is not just intellect or special talent. There are factors that are at least partially non-intellectual, such as motivation; there are factors external to the individual, such as family support and historical circumstance. For example, would Steven Jobs have been a prodigy if he had been born in the late 19th century? Perhaps his ability to work inventively with complex relationships would have translated into genius resulting in turn-of-the-century inventions complementing the work of Edison, and then again maybe his innate abilities would not have been as powerfully matched to the level of development and the needs of that era of invention as they were to the level of development and the needs of the modern computing age. A lot of prodigy is probably lucky coincidence of genes and resources and the state of the world—consistent with a general perspective that intelligence is a product of both an individual's competencies and the opportunities afforded by his or her society (Kornhaber, Krechevsky, & Gardner, 1990).

Some are pessimistic that school can play much of a role in all of this (e.g., Howe, 1990, Chapter 4), recognizing correctly that real prodigies will rarely experience a prolonged contact with regular school teachers who have the talent themselves to foster great talent, let alone the time or the motivation to do so. We are not so pessimistic, believing that extensive thinking and research are needed on exactly what schools can do to identify and foster specialized and generally high talent. For the child who does not have parents who are committed to developing his or her talent, school usually is society's best shot at directing the talent appropriately. Our guess is that emerging genius is often going to require some creative linking of resources to educate well, with the need for resourcefulness especially great for students who have little in this world except their impressive innate abilities. Conventional educational options may not serve well the brilliant grade-5 computer programmer. Perhaps a solution for such a child would be to match him or her with community members who are excellent programmers or at least interested in computing. Such individuals may be able to introduce an exceptional student to a much larger world of computing than anyone in the school could offer. Our point here is that there is no reason to look at the list of factors that traditionally have aligned when prodigious talent has flourished and conclude that little can be done if the child does not have a supportive family with substantial resources. It is definitely in the best interests of society to find ways to increase the odds that great talent comes to fruition. Although it would not be possible, or necessary from our perspective, to customize the education of all 10 percent of those children with IQs above 115, or even all of the 2½ percent of children with IQs above 130, it seems not too much to ask that schools think about how best to maximize the educational development of those in the top 1 percent of the distribution, and if not that many, those in the top one-tenth of 1 percent.

People Who Are Generally Highly Intelligent

Suppose that we accept IQ = 130 as the cutoff for high general ability. With that figure representing roughly only 2½ percent of the population, it is obvious that general intelligence is a scarce resource but not so rare that most educators are not going to be dealing with it on a regular basis. If a person is teaching 125 students a day at a high school with an absolutely average group of students, 3 or 4 of that teacher's students would have IQs exceeding 130.

Teachers who teach in socioeconomically advantaged communities could have a much higher percentage of such pupils, because socioeconomically advantaged communities tend to have a larger proportion of residents of above-average intelligence. Thus, all educators should have a working understanding of such people.

Unfortunately, the literature on giftedness is anything but complete, with learning-disabled and retarded children studied much more completely and in many more investigations than are the gifted. In the remainder of this subsection on giftedness, we will summarize some of the most important information that has been obtained in studies of gifted students. Any such discussion must include coverage of one of the most distinguished longitudinal studies ever conducted, a study that began in the 1920s by Lewis Terman (i.e., the Stanford professor who developed the Stanford-Binet IQ test; see Chapter 16, this book), a study that continues to generate new analyses and perspectives today (e.g., Schuster, 1990; Shurkin, 1992; Tomlinson-Keasey & Little, 1990).

Terman's Kids Genius fascinated Lewis Terman. During the years when he was developing the Stanford-Binet test, Terman encountered a number of children who scored in the 140 range or higher; he was fascinated by the tales the parents of these children told of their sons and daughters reading and writing early. Terman knew of the stereotypes—that geniuses were quirky, eccentric, and even unhealthy. Terman also recognized as he became acquainted with geniuses firsthand that he was meeting a well-adjusted and happy group of people, whose sole peculiarity was that they were exceptionally smart. Word spread throughout the Stanford community of Terman's interest in child brilliance, and the faculty made it a point of bringing around new examples. The more of these people he met, the more convinced Terman was that brilliance and good mental health were complementary (Shurkin, 1992, Chapter 2, for this and other points in this subsection; Terman, 1925; Terman & Oden, 1947; Terman & Oden, 1959).

In the early 1920s, he sought and received funding to begin a longitudinal study of exceptionally bright children. To do so, he administered intelligence tests and other assessments to a large number of children throughout California, many of whom had been nominated by their teachers as exceptionally bright. Others were nominated in a haphazard fashion by those acquainted with the study; some were brothers and sisters of nominated children. In the end, a sample of 643 children was identified as gifted in the sense of having IQ scores of 135 or higher. Other children from outside the geographical areas searched were added to the sample, as was a group of children with special talents, so that the final sample was comprised of more than 1500 children.

A not infrequent complaint about this study is with the method of sampling. For example, teacher nominations may have been biased toward nomination of well-adjusted children, ones doing well in a conventional school; there may have been bright kids who were not nominated because they did not do well in school, an institution mismatched to their thinking skills and talents. Although some precautions were taken so as to reduce bias owing to language and cultural differences, review of these precautions does not bolster confidence that the screening procedures were unbiased with respect to ethnic and language minorities, especially because the total sample included much lower proportions of minorities than were present in California in the 1920s. The initial sample was biased toward more boys, and many aspects of the study as a whole suggest great sex bias on Terman's part. A charitable evaluation might be that he was less familiar with the ways that women might excel, and thus Terman was unable to devise a study sensitive to the achievements of the Terman sample females. There was a decided middle-class and upper-middle-class bias in the sampling.

Terman's kids were studied extensively, including evaluations of their health and physiques, with them proving both healthy and physically normal. They were more healthy and slightly superior physically to the population as a whole, contrary to stereotypes of the day. Terman's subjects were excelling in school, and often moved ahead in the curriculum. Half of the sample were able to read before they began school. They read more than other children; they read "better" books than other children, and their reading interests were more diverse than the interests of the typical child. Their zeal for the written word remained high into high school and college and adult life, with more than three-quarters of the sample reporting as adults that they read "literature." They tended to graduate from high school early and enter college at a young age, with most "Termites" going to college or wanting to go (90 percent went relatively early in life, 70 percent grad-

uated relatively early in life). The Terman kids excelled in college, outperforming their classmates. This was true even for the students who attended the highly selective Stanford—the Terman kids did better than other students admitted to one of the West Coast's best colleges. A high proportion of Terman's subjects made Phi Beta Kappa. Despite their academic successes, these gifted people were socially adept and accepted; they were well-behaved and had the normal sexual urgings. The exceptions—the nerds—were among the very brightest in the sample, however.

Terman's adults were more likely to earn doctorates and professional degrees than members of the general population, with the majority of the sample eventually earning graduate degrees. Their incomes were well above population averages. They published many more books than any random sample of 1500 adults (200 + books). They averaged more than 1 published article per person (i.e., 2500 + articles). They produced 350 patents. Quite a few earned fame in their fields, even if very few earned widespread recognition. Alcoholism was low for the group; so was criminality. Their mental abilities during adulthood, as measured by conventional psychometric instruments, continued to be impressive relative to the general population.

The majority were satisfied with their life and life's work. Family was important to them, as was joy of life. In general, personal satisfaction was more important than occupational satisfaction. Terman's subjects married other bright people and gave birth to children with IQs that were well above average. An intriguing outcome, from the perspective of the sexually liberated 1990s, is that the majority of Terman's women became nonincome-producing homemakers. Even so, in twilight of their lives, the Terman men and women who remain alive seem happy as a group.

One of the more interesting differences involved comparison of very successful Terman kids with less successful Termites. The successes were more likely to have parents who pushed them to achieve in school and to go to college. Thus, as with prodigies, parents seemed to play a guiding, shaping role in the lives of successful people with high intelligence. Ability alone does not produce great success; ability is fostered by supportive family and friends.

The Terman study is admirable if for no other reason than so many people were studied for so long, with Shurkin (1992) expecting data collection on Terman's kids to continue until the last one of them dies. We expect secondary analyses to continue for some time after that. Although this study provided many measures of the participants' competence, it was not as analytical as studies directed at specific aspects of information processing, with more focused studies providing essential data about the good information processing of gifted individuals compared with the population at large.

Information Processing Cognitive theorists (e.g., Borkowski & Peck, 1986; Jackson & Butterfield, 1986; Sternberg, 1986, 1991) concerned with giftedness cite the factors highlighted in this book as critical to gifted performances:

- Strategies: repeated observations of great facility by the gifted in combining information and working with knowledge to produce new ideas and products (e.g., Feldman, 1982; MacKinnon, 1978); use of more advanced strategies than average-intelligence age mates on a variety of academic tasks (e.g., Jackson & Butterfield, 1986; Robinson & Kingsley, 1977; Zimmerman & Martinez-Pons, 1990); enhanced ability to translate problems into mathematical expressions (e.g., Dark & Benbow, 1990).
- Metacognition: superior in regulating and coordinating cognitive processes and knowledge (Sternberg, 1981; Zimmerman & Martinez-Pons, 1990); gifted children are more likely to transfer new strategies they have learned from one task to another task that can be mediated by strategies (Borkowski & Peck, 1986; Jackson & Butterfield, 1986); when asked questions tapping knowledge of cognition in general, gifted children outperform children of average intelligence (Borkowski & Peck, 1986).
- Knowledge: early mastery of the knowledge required for the field in which the person is gifted (Feldhusen, 1986); deeper and broader knowledge than people of normal intelligence (e.g., Gagné & Dick, 1983; Rabinowitz & Glaser, 1985; Sternberg, 1981; Tannenbaum, 1983).
- Motivation: high commitment to excellent performance in one or more fields (Feldhusen, 1986; Feldman, 1979; Terman & Oden, 1959); high self-concept (e.g., Feldhusen, 1986; Feldhusen & Kolloff, 1981; Ketcham & Snyder, 1977; Ringness, 1961), although a minority of gifted children greatly underestimate their abilities, perhaps reflecting parental underestima-

tion of their children's talents (e.g., Phillips, 1987).

One important point relating to good information processing is that gifted people process information more efficiently than do more typical people, for example, being able to scan a set of items being held in memory more rapidly than people of average intelligence (i.e., they can decide more quickly than normals whether a particular letter is included in a set of letters being held in memory; Keating & Bobbitt, 1978; McCauley, Kellas, Dugas, & DeVillis, 1976). The gifted tend to have superior short-term memory for material pertaining to their area of great competence—for example, highly gifted mathematics students have better short-term memory for digits than do people gifted in other arenas (Dark & Benbow, 1990, 1991). Gifted individuals also can retrieve information more rapidly than can people of average intelligence (i.e., the speed difference in deciding that two physically identical letters are same [e.g., AA] and deciding that two physically different letters have the same name [e.g., Aa] is small relative to average-ability people; e.g., Borkowski & Peck, 1986; Hunt, Lunneborg, & Lewis, 1975; Jackson & Myers, 1982; Keating & Bobbitt, 1978). Another index of retrieval efficiency is the speed of deciding whether two objects are members of the same category; gifted people perform such categorizations more rapidly (e.g., Goldberg, Schwartz, & Stewart, 1977) and certainly (Rabinowitz & Glaser, 1985) than others: Gifted students process information more efficiently than do less talented people, with their superior efficiency freeing up more of their short-term capacity for consideration and manipulation of strategies and other knowledge.

In short, relative to comparably aged individuals, gifted people have more and better strategies, metacognition, other knowledge, and motivation (at least with respect to fields in which their giftedness is expressed). In addition, their information processing is faster and more efficient. Gifted people transfer what they know how to do more readily to new situations than less talented people. Their extensive knowledge permits insights that elude others, ways of seeing relationships that are novel (Sternberg & Davidson, 1983).

One information processing characteristic of the gifted is extremely important. Gifted people do not just solve problems; they discover new ones (e.g.,

Perkins, 1981)—sometimes they invent entire new arenas of inquiry. For example, Jean Piaget was a great psychologist because he made the world aware of the developing mind. John Flavell is a great developmental psychologist because he pioneered the study of strategies and metacognition in development. An entire new area of inquiry was opened up after George Miller wrote about the 7 ± 2 chunks of memory. Think about the impact of Edison with his light bulb, Marx and his views of economics, or Jefferson and his ideas about democracy. The gifted often invent concepts that change the world. They identify new technologies and ideas that become the passions and concerns of many others. Giftedness is intellectual leadership.

Given the enormous potential of the smartest and most creative among us, there is much reason for expanding substantially the resources devoted to understanding how best to educate the most talented of future generations. The gifted have great potential for becoming great information processors (see Barell, 1991). It is time to find out how to maximize that potential. We do not envision that such education will be strange or lonely. The gifted like being with one another (e.g., Feldhusen, 1986). They are not introverts in general (Richardson & Benbow, 1990; Schuster, 1990; Tomlinson-Keasey, 1990). Rather their social relationships are normal, with gifted often more interpersonally adept than their less talented classmates (e.g., Schneider, Clegg, Byrne, Ledingham, & Crombie, 1989). Smart people learn a lot from their smart friends, so the social interactions of gifted information processors are a stimulus for even better information processing. We expect that the many suggestions about socially interactive instruction introduced earlier in this text are applicable with the gifted as well and if anything might work even better, with real intellectual live wires chatting away in cooperative learning.

Comparison of the Information Processing Characteristics of Retarded, Learning-Disabled, Normally Achieving, and Gifted Students

The processing of retarded, learning-disabled, normal, and gifted children has been studied with respect to the information processing components featured in this book. In general, evidence of strategy use increases going from retarded to learning-disabled to normally achieving to gifted students, as does evidence of metacognition, extensive world knowledge, and motivation supporting academic behaviors. In addition, there is increasingly efficient information processing in terms of speed moving from retarded to gifted students. Although it is not possible to know if the amount of neurological capacity allocated for short-term processing differs between these classifications, functional short-term capacity certainly does, with performance on short-term memory tasks improving steadily going from retarded to learning-disabled to normally achieving to gifted classifications.

We emphasize, however, it is not just that better learners have "more" of each of the components of skilled processing. The coordinated use of information processing components is also more certain for gifted achievers than for normally achieving students, who articulate their cognitive components more effectively than do learning-disabled or retarded students. Also, it should be noted that although the retarded versus normally achieving comparison is a main effect in that normally achieving students are generally better off than retarded students, both learning disabilities and giftedness often reflect particular deviations from typical abilities and performances. That is, an otherwise normally achieving student who does poorly in math is math disabled; an otherwise normally achieving person who is superior in mathematics is mathematically gifted. Thus, in the cases of learning disabilities and giftedness, it might be expected to see vast differences in information processing from normally achieving students for the particular disability or gift, but otherwise observe strategies, metacognition, knowledge, and motivations typically observed in the general population. The information processing model featured so prominently in this book is a powerful way of thinking about learner differences, with this becoming more evident as other dimensions of learner differences are considered.

What is disappointing is that despite much scientific progress in understanding such individual differences, schools generally do not use cutting-edge knowledge in classifying students, with great variability in how decisions are made from district to district (e.g., Singer, Palfrey, Butler, & Walker, 1989). The reasons for this neglect range from ignorance to exploitation: As one school administrator admitted to author MP a few years ago, "If there is state funding for 2 percent of the total school population to be educated as learning-disabled, we find 2 percent of the kids to be LD. If we can economically support G and T [gifted and talented] instruction for 10 percent of students, 10 percent of students are designated at G and T." The distance between science and practice in many diagnostic decisions is staggering. We hope the situation will change as the research just covered is disseminated and better understood.

POPULATIONS AT RISK FOR SCHOOL DIFFICULTIES AND FAILURE: CHILDREN LIVING IN POVERTY AND NON–ENGLISH-SPEAKING CHILDREN

This section focuses on two of the most salient groups of at-risk students in American education, groups that overlap in their composition: the poor and non–English-speaking Americans. For the most part, the literatures relevant to the populations are not as extensive as the literatures pertaining to the mainstream culture. Even when there has been substantial study, however, it usually has not been informative with respect to the factors we consider critical to efficient thinking—strategies, metacognition, other knowledge, and motivation. Thus, this section is not as orderly or complete with respect to information processing as the previous commentary in this chapter. What is presented here are some of the main issues and ideas with respect to each of these two categories of difference.

Poverty

One in 5 American children lives in poverty; 1 in 10 Canadian children does so. The U. S. poor are worse off than the impoverished of previous generations, largely because the federal social safety net disappeared during the Reagan-Bush years. States have not made up the difference, often unable or unwilling to do so even when mandated to serve the poor by federal fiat. The transformations of the economy in the last 15 years have not only increased the number of poor, but also have made it more difficult to escape poverty through personal effort (Eitzen, 1992). The more successful programs for poor children, such as Head Start, serve only a fraction of the children who need assistance. In past decades, doing well in school was a passport for many from poverty to the middle class; that routing is much less certain in the 1990s. It should not be surprising that there is a great deal of frustration in schools serving the poor as well as a great deal of indiffer-

ence, for the institutions have too few resources to meet the needs of the children in them, and there are perceptions by many students that schooling can do little to improve their life chances.

No matter what the academic standard, poor children fare worse in school and in cognitive matters than do children living well above the poverty line. Poor children are less likely than age mates to master basic skills and less likely to be orderly in the classroom. The traditional reaction to such disadvantaged students has been to provide them more instruction in basic skills, which means below-grade-level instruction. Often, remediation is provided in small doses during trips to resource rooms. Many such programs are offered under the governmental program known as Chapter 1, which is intended to improve the education of children in poverty. On the positive side, there have clearly been increases in the basic skills of poverty-level children. On the negative side, critics contend that such instruction fragments the school day for children in poverty, places heavier academic demands on them than on other children (i.e., the Chapter 1 students are accountable for both the resource room material and what is covered in regular class), and reduces the total amount of instruction given to children in poverty as well as the amount of instruction devoted to grade-level skills and knowledge (e.g., Allington, 1991a, 1991b; Peterson, 1988). That such instruction has no effect on higher-order competencies is apparent in that test scores tapping higher-order competencies have been unmoved by compensatory education (Means & Knapp, 1992).

In recent years, however, the movement has been away from long-term, low-intensity doses of basic skills instruction. The current thinking is to find powerful ways to provide basic skills instruction intensively at the lower primary levels, at great enough intensity to produce clear improvement quickly (e.g., see the discussion of Reading Recovery in Chapter 14). Then high-quality instruction aimed at developing higher-order competencies is provided. For example, the SAIL comprehension strategies were developed in Chapter 1 schools (see Chapter 14). Providing only lower-level computational practice to students experiencing difficulties in school while their classmates receive higher-order problem-solving skills is no longer acceptable or recommended. Rather mathematics instruction that emphasizes conceptual understanding is now seen as the right instructional model for all students

(Porter, 1991; Secada, 1991; Chapter 13, this book). In addition, rather than providing one-size-fits-all instruction for the poor, there is growing recognition that poor children differ in their instructional needs and with respect to the treatments that work with them (e.g., Corno, 1988; Peterson, 1988), so that there is need to assess students' aptitudes and current achievements and match instruction to the children's competencies and proclivities. The evidence is growing that poor children are quite capable of acquiring advanced thinking skills if they are provided high-quality instruction, such as Stanley Pogrow's HOTS (*Higher-order thinking skills*) program, which begins by teaching thinking skills in the abstract and then encourages students to apply these skills to grade-level content (e.g., Pogrow, 1992).

Recall that the recommendations for effective schools presented in Chapter 11 were derived largely from study of exemplary schools serving poor children. There is a real sense in the United States that orderly schools, ones requiring high academic engagement, and ones with parental and community involvement can make a difference for children of poverty. The need for consistent, excellent instruction for poor children is much greater than is the need for such instruction with more advantaged students. Middle-class and upper-class children are much more likely to have backups if school does not provide effective instruction. For example, economically advantaged parents can often provide tutoring even into high school when their children experience difficulties with school work; such assistance is much less likely after the primary grades for children living in poverty because many poor parents lack the skills and knowledge taught in the upper-elementary grades and beyond (see Snow et al., 1991). Unfortunately the poor, who are in greatest need of quality schooling, are the least likely to receive it (e.g., Kozol, 1991). We believe that excellent schooling for the most needy will occur consistently only when excellent schooling is universal. Because many of the studies reviewed in this book have involved poor children benefiting from instruction based on sound cognitive theory, instruction provided in a student-sensitive and supportive fashion, we are confident that poor children can be taught in ways that will produce much more learning and academic accomplishment than results from conventional instruction.

One of the real frustrations, however, is that so many of the poor children in the United States are educated in rural districts that are the least likely to know about educational innovations and reforms, let alone implement them (DeYoung, 1991; Schmuck & Schmuck, 1992). If excellent education is to be universal, and if excellent education is to be available to high proportions of children living in poverty, a real challenge is to reach such districts to transform the minds and hearts of the educators running them. It is a terrible secret that many rural schools in the United States differ little from schools in the first half of the 20th century, with the poor of the nation disproportionately represented in them. One reason it is still a secret, however, is because educational researchers have generally ignored rural populations (DeYoung, 1987). We hope some readers of this book will see the need to fill this gap and commit their careers to doing so.

Economically Disadvantaged Minorities   On average, economically disadvantaged minorities, including blacks and Hispanics, do not do as well in school as mainstream youngsters. Traditionally, academic differences between whites and others often have been conceived of in simple terms, for example, as a debate between heredity and environment. As reviewed in Chapter 6, however, most sophisticated scholars do not think in such either/or terms. There is recognition of the massive contributions of the environment in producing achievement differences between groups who are poor and those who are well off. An additional consideration is gaining increasing credibility, however: The environment that is school may be mismatched to the personal characteristics and proclivities of minorities in ways that reduce academic achievement and full participation in the schooling community.

For example, the work of Beth Harry (e.g., 1992) of the University of Maryland is illustrative of the potential miscommunications between schools and minority parents, miscommunications that reduce the likelihood of positive relationships between schools and families. Harry (1992) studied the interactions between schools and 12 Spanish-speaking, Puerto Rican–American families whose children were enrolled in special education. She conducted interviews with these families, made observations, and studied the school records as part of a large-scale effort to understand how these families interacted with the schools and understood those interactions. The approach was qualitative, with the researcher moving back and forth between the data and new observations.

The findings were quite striking:

1. The American school seems impersonal and uncaring to the parents studied compared with schools they remembered in native Puerto Rico. The American schools often made errors in classification of the students in these families, with these errors doing nothing to increase parental trust (e.g., children were "promoted" by mistake and subsequently returned to their previous grade level). Because these parents often deferred to the authority figures, their concerns often were not aired. Ironically the respect of these parents for the professionals they encountered in the school, respect that resulted in the parents not challenging the professionals, increased the lack of trust by parents.

2. The written communications from the schools were off-putting to these parents, in part because the letters were in English, which required finding someone to interpret them. The letters were also filled with educational jargon, embedded in text that was above the readability level of many parents.

3. Parents often thought they had not received critical information about their students. Sometimes the information had in fact been provided but was not understood. Other times it was provided incompletely. Sometimes there were mixed messages.

4. Many of the parents withdrew from interactions with the school and increasingly felt alienated.

Such an analysis is shocking, especially when it is recognized that the effective education of disadvantaged children is most likely to be successful when there are coordinated efforts between families and schools. More positively, educators are beginning to understand how to educate disadvantaged minorities: Franklin (1992) summarized a set of beliefs of many educators about how to be successful in educating students from diverse cultures. These include the following (pp. 116–117), adapted by us to emphasize the compatibility of these recommendations with the perspectives offered in this book:

- Instruction should incorporate elements of the students' cultural environment. (Our view of this recommendation is that instruction that relates to student prior knowledge is more likely to be successful than instruction that cannot be understood in terms of prior knowledge. Of course, instruction consistent with the culture of students is more likely to relate to student prior knowledge and hence more likely to be successful.)

- Special education should not be the primary way of dealing with minority children. (Minority children are disproportionately represented in special education; see Chapter 14.)

- African-American differences should not be interpreted as genetic deficiencies. (The racist belief that racial differences are biological deficiencies is rampant in American society. As we reviewed in Chapter 6, the claim that academic differences between races are due to biology alone is not supportable.)

- Good teachers exploit children's strengths and interests. (All children bring extensive knowledge to school, with this knowledge available as a starting point for building new, more powerful understandings.)

- Teachers need to be sensitive to the possibility of misunderstandings because of differences between school language and student dialects and language.

- New skills and strategies should be taught in culturally sensitive ways. (For example, powerful reading and writing strategies can be used to understand and create culturally important messages, such as interpretation of literature from one's own culture and creation of new literature reflecting one's culture and interests.)

Although we certainly applaud practices such as the ones advocated by Franklin and believe they can make some difference in the lives of disadvantaged, cultural minorities, we also believe that much more is needed. First, much of school is structured so that those who are behind are guaranteed to stay behind. For example, competitive grading practices all but assure that many minorities will receive poor marks in school. Such grading practices cause great pain to disadvantaged students and do much to discourage them (e.g., Hill, 1991). A humane system, vested in maximizing the achievement and happiness of all students, would abandon competitive grading in favor of reinforcement of improvements (see Chapter 5). One of the reasons we so strongly endorse evaluations that are based on student improvement is that such systems give those who start at the bottom a chance to be rewarded (see Chapter 5).

Second, the interventions that work with disadvantaged children, indeed all children, such as high-quality strategy instruction, often require a high degree of teacher monitoring and instruction directed at particular student needs. Such instruction is unlikely when teachers are confronted with classrooms of 25, 30, or more diverse students.

Third, there are powerful political forces at work that argue against instruction that builds on what multicultural students already know, arguing instead for immersion in the best of Western thought (e.g., the cultural literacy movement; see Chapters 1 and 3); there are also forces that are downright hostile to instruction that is in anything except English (Fillmore, 1992). In short, there are those ready to wage wars to make certain school is structured in ways that would make learning harder for minorities and achievement less certain.

Fourth, the way that schooling is financed in the United States (i.e., largely through local property taxes) assures that children living in the poorest communities will have the worst school buildings, fewest and most dated materials, least equipment, and most poorly paid teachers (Kozol, 1991). Potential reforms, such as voucher systems, have as many dangers as promises, with many believing that vouchers will reduce the income to schools serving the least advantaged children and increase the incomes of schools serving the richest children: The vouchers are not sufficient to permit extremely poor people to buy alternative schooling, but they will provide new revenues to schools that are good enough to hold their students.

Poor children are caught in a schooling structure that in many ways is hostile to their interests. Dramatic restructuring would be required to overcome the structural problems of the schooling institution if it is to work for disadvantaged children. Even if such restructuring efforts are expensive and difficult, we nonetheless believe they should be undertaken. As we argue in favor of educational reforms that logically seem as if they should make schooling more effective with minority children, we are painfully aware of how little research there is documenting factors that really do make a difference in the achievement of economically disadvantaged children (Grant, 1992). More positively, to the extent that many of the powerful interventions in this book have been examined with minorities (e.g., various forms of strategy instruction), disadvantaged children have experienced great benefits. Our own position is that the human mind works the

same for rich and poor alike: The difference is that the rich often have greater opportunities to learn potent strategies and other knowledge in environments supportive of their long-term motivations. In addition, the strategies and knowledge acquired by the majority population are often better matched to the demands of school than the strategies and knowledge acquired by minority children, with the differences in strategies and knowledge between mainstream and minority children often characterized as differences in style. For example, Shade (1982) made the case that school requires sequential, analytical, and object-oriented strategies, comparable to the strategies fostered in the majority culture. In contrast, black children learn survival skills in their environment, a world that shapes up intuitive and person-oriented strategies, ones not valued or valuable in school.

What needs to be investigated from our perspective is how to maximize the likelihood that minorities have high-quality educational experiences. Such experiences must be presented and structured so as to be meaningful for students with diverse backgrounds and motivating to all children, both in the short term and the long term. That our perspective on offering high-quality, higher-order cognitive instruction to disadvantaged children is consistent with others who specialize in minority achievement was emphasized to us by a list of recommendations provided by Means and Knapp (1992).

Can you think of specific interventions already reviewed in this book that meet Means and Knapp's (1992, pp. 286–289) recommendations? We provide hints in the parentheses following each recommendation:

- Focus on complex meaningful problems. (Comprehension of whole stories and performing experiments are two examples of meaningful problems.)
- Embed basic skills instruction in the context of more global tasks. (How many basic skills are practiced when composing an essay or doing a story problem?)
- Make connections with students' out-of-school experiences and culture. (As we listen to tapes of SAIL lessons, the lives of the children come through in their interpretations of stories.)
- Model powerful thinking strategies. (This has been encouraged in this book since the discussion of *The Hardy Boys* in Chapter 1.)

- Encourage multiple approaches to academic tasks. (Students choosing their own strategy is included in many of the interventions reviewed in this book.)
- Provide scaffolding to enable students to accomplish complex tasks. (Who could have missed scaffolding in chapter after chapter?)
- Make dialogue the central medium for teaching and learning. (Again, there have been many instances in which we have discussed children and teachers constructing powerful understandings through dialogue. We do not believe that children ever copy somebody else's strategies or approaches—rather they interpret procedures they observe and discover and use these strategies as a starting point to construct much more powerful understandings.)

We doubt that it will be possible to offer disadvantaged minorities consistent and sufficient high-quality instruction (such as the instruction suggested by Means & Knapp, 1992) without substantial reform of schooling, however. The need for reform is obvious when it is recognized how much difference there is between the ideal sketched in the preceding paragraph and the predominating methods in urban elementary education (Haberman, 1992). Urban teachers largely give information, administer tests, maintain order, and assign grades. Student compliance is the ideal rather than student involvement with learning; low-level factual knowledge is emphasized rather than big ideas and major concepts; memory is emphasized rather than comparison of ideas, analysis, synthesis, evaluation, generalization, and development of critical thinking skills; and the texts and materials students work with are more akin to the 1960s than to the 21st century. The shocking discrepancy between typical instruction in urban schools and what is possible and necessary to educate children well provides great motivation for us to endorse rapid reform. Our strong opinion is that reforms should be informed and accompanied by research documenting the effects of changes in school structures and policies on achievement. Reforms and research on them are essential if the economically disadvantaged are to have a shot at the American Dream. If more poor and minority students succeed in school, the United States will be better off, for a much greater proportion of Americans will have the skills essential to participate in the economy of the 21st century.

Finally, we believe there is good reason to be confident that many multiculturals will do well in school. Diversity has always been a fact of life of schooling in the United States, and there have always been tensions between preserving diversity and the demands of schools that students meet common standards (Fass, 1989). Schools have generally served the disadvantaged well, with both public and private institutions (i.e., largely the nation's Catholic schools) making enormous efforts to provide nonmainstream groups with education that would permit productive participation in American society. The record is clear that schools historically have been exceptionally humane institutions with respect to cultural minorities. That 1990s educators are continuing to give much thought to issues of multicultural education leads us to believe that schools will continue to be one of the most humane parts of the melting pot, doing all possible to provide matriculants of varied backgrounds with the literacy and numeracy tools and cultural knowledge essential for productive participation in 21st century American life.

Children Whose Native Language Is Not the Majority Language

It is not unusual in major urban environments in the United States and Canada to have 20 to 40 different first languages in a school population. All of the points made with respect to multiculturals and people in poverty hold for many of the children with a first language different than English. In addition, these children are faced with the challenge of learning English as a second language (or French in some parts of Canada). There are a few extremely important conclusions that have emerged from sophisticated cognitive analyses of second-language learning and second-language learners.

Challenge of Second-Language Learning for Children A well-known hypothesis (Lenneberg, 1967) is that learning a second language is much easier for children than adults. Despite the popularity of this hypothesis, there is really no evidence to support it. In fact, the evidence is consistent with exactly the opposite hypothesis, that second-language learning is more challenging for young children than for adults (Hakuta, 1986, Chapter 6; McLaughlin, 1984, Chapter 3). Even so, on average those who learn a second language during childhood are more likely to sound like natives once the second language is acquired, and they will have better grammar (Hakuta, 1986, Chapter 6). Although true, on average, it must be emphasized that there are many adults who acquire a second language, with little if any detectable accent.

Attitudes About and Motivation to Learn the Second Language Some of the most important research on second-language learning in school contexts has been conducted in Canada. Lambert of McGill University and Gardner of the University of Western Ontario (e.g., Gardner & Lambert, 1972) have provided the premier analyses of the relationship between attitudes about a target second language (i.e., French in the Gardner and Lambert investigations) by first-language-English students and learning of the second language. Using several clever measures of attitude (e.g., personality ratings of French and English speakers), Lambert and Gardner documented clear individual differences among English-speaking Canadian students in their attitudes toward the French language. (Anyone who has spent time in Canada immediately recognizes the validity of this claim. There are intense feelings about language in Canada, an officially bilingual country, which nonetheless has many more monolingual enclaves than regions that are truly bilingual.) Important in this context, the differences in attitudes about French by English-speaking Canadians are associated with differences in success in learning French (Gardner, 1980). By measuring the language attitudes of members of the students' families, Gardner and Lambert have been able to make the case that the causal direction is from attitude to achievement: Better attitudes about French cause higher achievement in French, with students who have a negative attitude about French coming from families who foster negative feelings toward French language and culture (Gardner, 1983). These Canadian findings provide plenty of reason for pause when it is recognized that relations between American bilingual minorities and English-speaking Americans are often hostile. The contemporary political climate favoring multiculturalism rather than assimilation may in fact do much to undermine the motivations of individual non–English-speaking students to learn and use English.

Intelligence, School Achievement, and Bilingualism The literature contains the contradictory hypotheses (and contradictory data) that bilingualism reduces intelligence and that bilingualism increases intelligence (e.g., Hakuta, 1986, Chapter 2). Such a mix of positions and results does not inspire confidence for either position, however, and conclusions about the relationship of cognitive competence to bilingual status should be avoided. In fact, the data are contradictory even within individual investigations, with Hakuta (1987) reporting that bilingualism improved cognitive functioning in the grade-school years, with corresponding effects not detectable during the middle-school years. Any real or enduring effects of bilingualism on intellectual processing are probably small at best and possibly fleeting.

One of the most important tasks facing a second-language child is learning to read in the second language. Verhoeven (1990) studied this process as Turkish immigrant children learned Dutch in the Netherlands and concluded that learning to read in Dutch was facilitated by learning to speak Dutch. For primary-grade children, both word recognition and comprehension in Dutch were related to oral proficiency in Dutch. This study highlights the importance of encouraging spoken language skills in the majority language as a determinant of success in learning to read in the majority language.

Immersion Programs Immersion programs were developed in Canada and have been adapted by Americans. In the primary years of immersion, most of the school day is spent in the second language. Beginning at about grade 3, the day is more evenly split between instruction in the second language and instruction in the first language. By high school, the majority of instruction is in the first language, although a large proportion of the day (e.g., 40 percent) is spent in classes conducted in the second language. The immersion model is intended to stimulate the development of both the first-language and second-language skills. Although the outcomes are complex, acquisition of both first and second languages is generally satisfactory. Academic achievement seems not to be reduced when it is provided in the second language (Genesee, 1985).

Canadian-type immersion programs are unique in that there is a substantial database available for them (including U.S. data). A number of other types of second-language programs are now being explored in the United States (see Ovander & Collier, 1985). The relative benefits of these are difficult to assess at the time of this writing, with a clear need for extensive evaluation of the various alternatives. To the extent that program alternatives have been evaluated in the United States, the evaluations have been weak methodologically (Lam, 1992).

There are many pressures for increased bilingual instruction, including legal ones. For example, in *Lau v. Nichols* (1974), the U.S. Supreme Court ruled that non–English-speaking children had to be provided instruction that permitted their participation in school, including the possibility of instruction in English or instruction in the native language. In addition, the Bilingual Education Act, originally passed in 1968, has been amended considerably since then, each time increasing the pressures on educators to provide bilingual education.

Particularly heartening from the perspective of this book, second-language educators are exploring how students can be taught strategies for learning second language as well as the metacognition to regulate use of strategies, with substantial evidence that many of the strategies useful for mainstream students are also useful for second-language students (e.g., Langer, Bartolome, Vasquez, & Lucas, 1990; O'Malley & Chamot, 1990). Consistent with the good information processing model, however, such strategies are often more evident with materials related to the reader's background (i.e., their cultural schemata; e.g., Malik, 1990). Second-language education is an area of research in which it is especially likely there will be great progress in research in the near future, and we suspect that many of the processes reviewed in this book will prove important in reshaping education of bilinguals so it is increasingly effective.

Concluding Comments

In closing this section on at-risk students, a frank admission is that schools probably often do much to increase the likelihood that poor and minority students fail. Kagan (1990, adapted from pp. 110–111) provided an analysis:

1. Students at risk for school failure are asked fewer questions by their teachers, are responded to in a more authoritarian fashion, are given less praise, and receive more criticism.
2. Teachers initiate less with them.
3. Teachers expect less of them.
4. School less often encourages higher-order strategies in low achievers.
5. Low achievers are less likely than average and above-average students to understand directions provided to them by teachers.
6. They receive lots of cues that they are inadequate.
7. Their peers pay less attention to them during academic interactions; they tend to pay less attention to them at other times as well.
8. Because of difficulties in communication skills, students at risk for low achievement often do not engage in as productive communications during group learning.

What seems to happen is that some children get behind early, with poor and minority students more likely to experience early failure than other students. Once behind, these students tend to stay behind. They associate more with one another than with more successful students, which is accentuated in many schools by tracking systems that segregate based on academic ability. The most behaviorally aggressive of these low achievers are especially likely to invoke sanctions during their interactions at schools, so school is even more aversive for them than for more prosocial low achievers, with their risk for dropping out, delinquency, and other adverse outcomes ever increased (e.g., Moffitt, 1990). Female low achievers are at greater risk for pregnancy than their high-achieving peers, with adolescent pregnancy in itself a factor increasing the likelihood for school dropout (e.g., Cairns, Cairns, & Neckerman, 1989).

In short, school is not a pleasant place for the low achiever, many of whom were disadvantaged before they arrived at the schoolhouse gate. Low achievers are more likely than high achievers to have experiences that undermine their academic growth and lead them to drop out of school. What happens at school to low achievers reduces their academic self-esteem and long-term motivation to learn more than it enhances it. Thus, even though this is a chapter on individual differences, there is no reason to assume that at-risk status is a "person" variable. Rather, at-risk status is an interaction between students with particular characteristics and educational environments.

What is tragically ironic in considering the school contributions to failure for minority students is that the families of such students are often supportive of schooling and more committed to their children doing well in school than are majority parents (e.g., Delgado-Gaitan, 1992). They are more likely to be supportive of homework, comparative achievement testing, and longer school days. These family values translate into students who try hard to do well in school, although their efforts are often not sufficient to overcome institutional barriers to achievement by minorities (Duran & Weffer, 1992). That schools are failing the poor and minorities is not due to wholesale lack of minority community support for the institution.

It is heartening that there are some effective schools serving the poor and non–English-speaking communities (see Chapter 11). We need to understand better why such schools are effective and attempt to create many more educational environments that better promote both academic achievement and academic self-esteem in at-risk students. The effective schools movement discussed in Chapter 11 is an excellent start in that direction, although studies of effective schools have not been sensitive to "what" is taught—for example, are strategies taught? We suspect that many of the instructional strategies and tactics being validated by research in regular and special education could go far in making schooling more effective for diverse populations.

DIFFERENCES IN THINKING ABILITIES ACROSS THE LIFE SPAN

Now more than ever, education occurs across the life span. It is not unusual at all for university-level and graduate students to be in their 30s, 40s, and 50s. Many universities now have programs for "golden agers," people in their 60s and older. Many of these people are returning to school, perhaps fulfilling an educational dream that was suspended some years before in favor of marriage or children or because of the economic infeasibility of pursuing higher education during youth. In addition to college-level returnees, there are many who seek to complete high school equivalency work. Others are remediating basic skills deficiencies, with national efforts now under way to reduce adult illiteracy. There are parts of the United States in which 10 to 20 percent of the population are illiterate in the sense that they cannot read at a grade-4 level with comprehension. There is a real need for 21st century educational psychologists to understand adult thinking and learning abilities.

Two groups have historically been interested in adult development. There is a substantial adult education community, a community that is growing rapidly with the increasing demand for additional educational opportunities for middle-aged and elderly students. Scholars in this area have studied educational programs operating in diverse settings, from colleges and junior colleges to libraries to community drop-in centers to prisons to the workplace. Much of the concern of the adult education community has been with identifying what works with adult learners. A guiding assumption is that the needs and abilities of middle-aged and older students differ from younger adults, adolescents, and children in more traditional school settings.

A second group of scholars interested in adult learning refer to themselves as life-span developmentalists. Their starting point is developmental psychology, with the hypothesis that there are complex changes in learning and cognitive abilities across the life span (e.g., the nature of psychometric intelligence; see Chapter 16). Fortunately, from the perspective of this book, much of their work has been conceptualized in terms of information processing. For this reason, the life-span development work will be considered more extensively in this subsection than will the research produced by adult educators. Relying on this literature introduces an important bias in this section, however: Life-span developmentalists have studied the late end of the life span more completely than points in between youth and retirement. Thus, there will be more discussion of the elderly than the middle-aged in what follows. The voluminous data on young adults and the elderly highlight what we believe is one of the most understudied problems in education: How do middle-aged adults learn? We hope some readers of this book make this problem their research problem because the need for such information is great given the large middle-aged population that needs retraining and is seeking additional education.

Strategies

A large number of studies have been conducted in which elderly were presented some basic memory task, such as paired-associate or list learning. Subjects in one condition were taught a strategy well matched to the task (e.g., making interactive images for paired associates, organizing list materials by categories); control subjects were left to their own devices to process the material. Consistently in these studies, the elderly who were given the strategy instruction outperformed control subjects (for a review, see Meyer, Young, & Bartlett, 1989, Chapter

2; also, Roberts, 1983). What is clear is that typically, if left to their own devices, the elderly are not as strategic as they could be. Nonetheless, they are quite capable of carrying out a number of strategies if provided brief instruction about how to do so.

When these studies have included younger adults as well, a common finding is that younger control participants outperform elderly controls and that younger strategy-trained subjects outperform elderly strategy-trained subjects. That is, although it is not uncommon for strategy-trained elderly to outperform young adult controls, strategy-trained elderly do not perform anywhere near the level of strategy-trained young adults. Cognitive strategy training can improve the functioning of the elderly, but it usually does not permit the levels of performance that are possible during youth and younger adulthood.

For example, in Kliegl, Smith, and Baltes (1990), when younger and older adults performed a serial learning task under control instructions, the older subjects remembered about 12 percent of the list items, and the young adults recalled about 25 percent. Following a type of imagery mnemonic instruction (i.e., a one-is-a-bun pegword strategy; see Chapter 10, this volume), the recall of the elderly increased to the 40 percent level; the recall of the younger participants, however, soared to 75 percent. Under control instructions, there was substantial overlap in the scores of older and younger subjects (i.e., some older subjects outperformed some younger participants). Under the imagery instruction, few of the elderly outperformed any of the younger adults. After a lot of practice with the imagery mnemonic strategy, the elderly were able to boost their learning to about 50 percent; the youngers went over the 80 percent level with practice.

There was another striking finding in the Kliegl et al. (1990) study. Large gains owing to strategy training occurred for the elderly only when lists were presented slowly (i.e., 10 seconds per item or more). In contrast, younger subjects experienced great gains even at a faster rate (i.e., 5 seconds per item) and some gains at a much faster rate (i.e., 1 to 3 seconds per item). When all of the Kliegl et al. (1990) data are combined (see also Kliegl, Smith, & Baltes, 1989, as well as Baltes & Kliegl, 1992), what is apparent is that although the imagery strategy is helpful for the elderly, it is more helpful for younger adults and can be used by younger adults in more situations. Perhaps it should not be surprising that

the elderly are less likely than younger adults to want to continue using imagery strategies they are taught (Brigham & Pressley, 1988; see Chapter 2, this book), for strategies produce greater benefits for younger adults than for the elderly.

A fair criticism of the adult literature on strategies is that there has been far too little evaluation of strategy use with ecologically valid materials. More positively, some such work is appearing. An example is Meyer et al.'s (1989) development and evaluation of a complex text learning strategy.

Meyer et al. (1989) Many adults, both younger and older, do not know how to process expository texts as efficiently as such texts can be processed. Meyer et al. (1989) were aware of a number of analyses of adult deficiencies in expository text processing; they were also aware of a number of successful attempts to teach young adults to analyze the structure of expository texts (i.e., determine whether the text is descriptive, a sequence of events, a cause-and-effect sequence, a problem-solution structure, a comparison, or a listing of related elements) and to use the structural cues to guide reading and learning from text (see Meyer et al., 1989, Chapter 2). They were interested in whether older adults could be taught to identify the structures in expository text and use this information to increase their learning from text. Meyer et al. (1989) evaluated the value of their training in a true experiment involving both younger (mean age = 24) and older (mean age = 68) subjects.

Participants in the strategy-training condition were taught "The Plan Strategy." This involved identifying the writing plan of the author of an expository piece. For each type of expository structure, participants were taught the structure and words in a text that could signal the use of the structure. The **signals** for each of the expository writing plans were as follows:

- *Descriptive text* is signaled by phrases such as the following: for example, which was one, this particular, for instance, specifically, such as, attributes of, that is, namely, properties of, characteristics are, qualities are, marks of, in describing.
- *Temporal sequence* is signaled by phrases such as the following: afterwards, later, finally, last, early, following, to begin with, as time passed, continuing on, to end, years ago, in the first place, before, after, soon, more recently.

- *Causation* is signaled by phrases such as the following: as a result, because, since, for the purpose of, caused, led to, consequence, thus, in order to, this is why, if/then, the reason, so, in explanation, therefore.

- *Problem/solution* is signaled by phrases such as the following: (1) problem signals: problem, question, puzzle, perplexity, enigma, riddle, issue, query, need to prevent, the trouble; (2) solution signals: solution, answer, response, reply, rejoinder, return, comeback, to satisfy the problem, to set the issue at rest, to solve these problems.

- *Comparison* is signaled by phrases such as the following: not everyone, but, in contrast, all but, instead, act like, however, in comparison, on the other hand, whereas, in opposition, unlike, alike, have in common, share, resemble, the same as, different, difference, differentiate, compare to, while, although.

- *Listing* is signaled by phrases such as the following: and, in addition, also, include, moreover, besides, first, second, third, etc., at the same time, another, and so forth. (Based on Meyer et al., 1989, Table 3.3, pp. 47–48)

Thus, knowledge of the signals is a form of metacognition, tipping off the reader about the type of text the author composed. Armed with this understanding, the reader then expects and seeks out information consistent with that structure. Thus, if the phrases "to begin with," "continuing on," and "finally" are spotted, the reader is alert to information about temporal sequence and attempts to construct a temporal sequence as the main idea of the passage. If the reader sees "in contrast" and "on the other hand," these are signals that the main idea is a comparison and that it is appropriate to set up the main idea as a comparison-and-contrast structure to aid understanding and memory of the passage.

Other metacognition about strategies is developed as well, with instruction provided about when the Plan Strategy works: It works when readers want to be able to recall the most important information in a text. It is not a useful strategy when the goal is simply to find some particular piece of information in a text. Thus, the training of the Plan Strategy was rich in information about when and where to use the plan as a whole and where and when to use particular expository structures to analyze text.

During training, participants applied the Plan Strategy to advertisements at first, with examples from television programs, newspapers, and stories employed in the instruction. There was cooperative learning in pairs during training, with practice in identifying the structures of various passages and applying the Plan Strategy in its entirety to some passages. Near the end of training, using the plan both at study of a passage and to guide later recall was emphasized. Although this instruction was complex, it was completed in five sessions.

There were two conditions in the study besides the Plan Strategy–training condition (henceforth, the strategy-training condition). A practice control condition (henceforth, the practice condition) practiced reading and remembering texts during the time corresponding to training in the Plan Strategy condition. There was also a no intervention/no practice control condition (henceforth, the control condition).

A number of dependent measures were collected in this study. Participants read and recalled a number of passages. They took standardized measures of reading achievement. Participants were asked to sort passages according to their organization, identify the main ideas in passages, and complete questionnaires about reading strategies.

The findings were orderly and striking. Whether subjects used one of the expository structures to organize their recall of text was examined. The only pretest-to-posttest increases in the use of such structures occurred in the strategy-training condition for both younger and older participants. In general, there was slightly more pronounced evidence of pretest-to-posttest shifting in the younger than in the older sample, although the increases were quite striking for both younger and older participants. There were also posttest measures of the ability to identify types of passage structure, with strategy-trained subjects outperforming practice and control subjects. Again the tendency was for younger subjects to be at least slightly more proficient in making such identifications. In addition, the strategy report questionnaire data confirmed predominant use of the Plan Strategy in the strategy-trained condition, although there was slightly more reported use of it among younger than older subjects.

Strategy training increased recall of passage ideas in the elderly (from 21 percent at pretest to 32 percent at posttest) and in the young (from 20 percent at pretest to 35 percent at posttest). Much of this gain may have been due simply to the practice component, however, for there was a 18 to 25 percent increase in recall in the elderly practice condition and a corresponding 23 to 30 percent increase in the young adult group. More importantly, however, the strategy-trained subjects were more likely to recall higher-order information than were the subjects in the practice and control conditions. Also, when asked to identify the main ideas in passages, the trained subjects were slightly better at it than the practice or control participants.

What to make of the results of this study? First, brief training did seem to move use of strategies visibly without producing earthshaking changes in the level of performance. Although the differences between trained elderly and younger subjects were never large, these comparisons tended to favor the trained younger participants. That so many participants were able to apply this complex strategy at all given the brevity of the training is heartening to us, although we note that fairly short passages were used in the tests in this study. That the strategy training did not produce huge increases in performance is also not surprising. Recall the discussion of comprehension strategy instruction with children in Chapter 14. Our belief is that effective comprehension instruction will take a long time. What the Meyer et al. (1989) results suggest to us is that there is good reason to believe that the investment in long-term comprehension strategy instruction with adults might pay off, for the positive effects of training were consistent even if they were not large. In addition, two-thirds of the elderly subjects in the strategy-instruction condition claimed their interest in reading had increased because of the training, a much larger percentage than claimed increased interest because of participation in the other two conditions of the study. Meyer et al.'s (1989) data offer the possibility that expository comprehension strategies instruction is possible for older adults, beneficial for them, and engaging as well. It is hard to ask for more than that except perhaps larger effects on recall. Larger effects might have occurred if participants had been provided more instruction and practice using the procedures. Meyer et al. (1989) was an exceptional study of strategy instruction with young and elderly adults that deserves a great deal of follow-up. Many adults are faced with the need of getting information from expository materials. Unfortunately, in the absence of instruction, many adults are not armed with the strategies to extract such information efficiently.

Rehabilitative Cognitive Strategy Training One important limitation of Meyer et al.'s study is that all of the participants were healthy, with no evidence of degenerative brain disease. Not all elderly are so lucky. A particularly exciting area of strategy instruction with adults and the elderly is aimed at populations who have experienced substantial brain damage because of disease or injury.

Alzheimer's disease is a common cause of dementia in the elderly. The most important symptom is clear intellectual decline, including poor memory, reduced thinking abilities, poor judgment, and breakdowns in impulse control (Branconnier, 1986; Nebes, 1992). Although it seems that both new learning and retention are impaired in patients with Alzheimer's disease, these patients are capable of some learning (Camp & McKitrick, 1992). Some of the strategy interventions that are successful with healthy elderly are not nearly as successful with patients with Alzheimer's disease, however. Thus, imagery mnemonics are acquired rather easily by normal elderly. In contrast, patients with Alzheimer's disease experience a great deal of difficulty even remembering the steps required to execute imagery mnemonic strategies (Hill, Evankovich, Sheikh, & Yesavage, 1987). Indeed, the evidence is mounting that patients with Alzheimer's disease have severe difficulties whenever they are required to remember intentionally (e.g., Nebes, 1992) and that there are severe impairments with Alzheimer's disease in the ability to coordinate several cognitive processes (e.g., as is required to execute many strategies), possibly because of Alzheimer's disease–associated impairments in working memory (e.g., Baddeley, Logie, Bressi, Della Sala, & Spinnler, 1986). One speculation is that the difficulties in carrying out internal cognitive procedures prompt many with Alzheimer's disease to use external memory aids (e.g., notebooks, relying on family members to remember for them).

There has been greater success in cognitive training with people who have experienced other types of neural loss (i.e., losses other than those caused by Alzheimer's disease, such as due to diseases such as cancer or to accidents). Such individuals are frequently able to carry out imagery-mnemonic and rehearsal strategies when they are instructed to do so (e.g., Wilson, 1987; Ylvisaker, Szekeres, Hartwick, Tworek, & Wingate,1991), although there has been much less success in teaching brain-injured adults to use newly learned strategies generally—perhaps because there have been few attempts to develop appropriate metacognition during strategy training or teach students how to apply the strategies they have learned across a variety of settings (Pressley, 1993).

An appropriate aside given the discussion in Chapter 17 of alternative methods of assessment is that progress is being made in diagnosis of brain disease and injury using modern technologies. Computed tomography (CT) scanning is routinely used to locate structural anomalies in the brain; both CT scanning and MRI are proving useful in identifying structural changes in the brain with the onset of Alzheimer's disease (e.g., Goldman & Coté, 1991; Riege, Harker, & Metter, 1986). Positron-emission tomography scanning to measure glucose metabolism is being studied as a means of detecting age-related declines in brain activity, including degenerative diseases such as Alzheimer's disease (de Leon, George, & Ferris, 1986; Goldman & Coté, 1991).

Summary There is substantial evidence of plasticity in human cognition across the adult life span (Lerner, 1990)—that thinking and performance can vary depending on conditions, with one important condition that can improve thinking being instruction. Life-span researchers have made this point through studies of strategy instruction. Strategies can be taught across the life span, within the constraint that the learner possesses a normally healthy brain. Strategy instruction is not a magic bullet, however, eradicating age differences completely. Younger people using a strategy often outperform older people using the same strategy. What is particularly optimistic is that adults can learn complex strategies that have real-world value, such as Meyer et al.'s (1989) Plan Strategy. One reason such instruction works, however, is that many adults do not use such strategies on their own before receiving explicit instruction. (It should be apparent to readers of this book by this point that adult thinking is often far from what it can be—that there is a need for instruction long after the completion of formal schooling.)

One important reservation that we have about the strategy instructional research across the adult life span is that it is an upward extension of strategic processes studied with children and young adults. This is disturbing because there is a good possibility that older adults approach some tasks in ways that are qualitatively different from the ways young adults approach them.

Labouvie-Vief and her colleagues (e.g., Adams, Labouvie-Vief, Hobart, & Dorosz, 1990; Jepson & Labouvie-Vief, 1992; Labouvie-Vief, Schell, & Weaverdyck, 1981) have pursued this possibility, believing that older adults are more integrative when they process text. Thus, when younger and older adults are asked to recall information from texts they have read, younger adults tend to be quite literal in their memories, recalling information stated in the text. Older adults are much more likely to include in their recall the integrative moral themes of the passages and much more likely to give personal interpretations. As readers may recall from Chapter 14, we view generation of integrative interpretations to be an indication of exceptionally capable processing of material. Much fuller study of adult abilities to generate interpretations needs to occur, with it likely that such studies would provide insights about how to encourage all readers to orient toward integrative understanding of text: Such work should also be enlightening about whether it is accurate to think about aging only in terms of decline, which is often the focus in studies of memory. Just as knowledge increases across the adult life span (see Chapters 3 and 16), it seems possible based on the work of Labouvie-Vief and her associates that the tendency to abstract global themes and universal morals from texts increases with age. Rather than looking at models of youthful thinking only for guidance about efficiency, we believe there are good reasons to examine the thinking patterns of the elderly for guidance about how to design new instruction that could be applied across the life span.

One of the nicest aspects of Jepson and Labouvie-Vief's (1992) study was that a middle-aged sample was included, with substantial evidence of these people also generating integrative themes as they remembered text. Perhaps getting the big point and the universal themes in text is an adult thing, whereas focusing on literal understanding is a youthful folly. (See the discussion of Brigham and Pressley's [1988] study in Chapter 2, this book, for additional evidence that older people are much less concerned with objective memory of information than are younger individuals.)

We pointed out at several points in this subsection the need for metacognitive input in strategy instruction with adults (consistent with all of our previous discussions of instruction). There is reason to be more concerned about metacognition in older adults than in younger students for several reasons, however, with some of the peculiarities of metacognition that occur toward the end of the life span taken up next.

Metacognition

Because decline in memory with increasing age has been a particular concern of life-span developmental psychologists, metamemory has been assessed more often than other types of metacognition in life-span studies. One of the most important ways that metacognition has been examined in adulthood has been with metacognitive questionnaires. For example, here are some items that appear on one questionnaire:

1. How would you rate your memory in terms of the kinds of problems you have?
2. How often do you need to rely on your memory without the use of remembering techniques, such as making lists, when you are engaged in . . . (a) social activities?
3. How is your memory compared to the way it was . . . (b) one year ago?
4. How often do these present a problem to you . . . (a) names?
5. As you are reading a novel, how often do you have trouble remembering what you have read . . . (a) in the opening chapters once you have finished the book?
6. How well do you remember things that occurred . . . (a) last month?
7. When you actually forget in these situations, how serious a problem do you consider the memory failure to be . . . (a) names?
8. How much effort do you usually have to make to remember in these situations?. . . . (a) names. (Adapted from Gilewski & Zelinski, 1986, Table 11.7, and Kausler, 1991, Table 9.3).

There are a variety of metamemory questionnaires now available, with them tapping adults' knowledge of strategies, task variables affecting memory, and understanding of capacity and capacity limits. There are also questions about how people perceive their memory abilities changing with development, how much having a good memory means to them, whether they are anxious about memory, and whether they believe they can exert control over their intellectual performances (Kausler, 1991, Chapter 9).

The most striking finding in this literature is that older adults are extremely pessimistic about their memory capabilities (e.g., Devolder & Pressley, 1991) and attribute difficulties they are experiencing to mental decline: To use a term from the motivational literature that has been adopted by metacognitive theorists and researchers interested in memory across the life span, there is a decline in **memory self-efficacy** (e.g., Berry, West, & Dennehey, 1989; Hertzog, Hultsch, & Dixon, 1989). One possibility is that reduced memory self-efficacy undermines motivation to remember and hence memory itself. That is, believing that you have a poor memory as a result of aging, which is out of your control, would not motivate efforts to remember, efforts that if made would improve memory (e.g., Bandura, 1989). It is not clear, however, that these beliefs, in fact, undermine motivation to attempt to remember new information, with mixed evidence of relationships between pessimism about memory and objective memory performances (Kausler, 1991, Chapter 9). We note, however, that leading contributors to the instructional literature with the elderly are now calling for studies in which strategies are taught as measures are taken to increase older adults' expectations about their intellectual abilities (e.g., Best, Hamlett, & Davis, 1992).

Another metacognitive possibility raised in the literature on aging is that older adults do not monitor their memories as well as do younger adults, with this often measured by examining the difference in how people believe they will perform a task and how well they actually perform the task. The literature is extremely mixed on this possibility as well, however, with some studies reporting declines in accuracy and others reporting equally accurate monitoring in younger and older adults (see Devolder, Brigham, & Pressley, 1990, for a review of the various studies).

Metacognition and monitoring are important to the extent that they are determinants of performance and efforts to affect performance. Thus, if a learner monitors that he or she has not yet mastered a task and reacts to that perception by working on the task some more, monitoring has played an important role in cognitive control. One possibility is that objective performances and perceptions of objective performances are not as critical in determining the behaviors of older learners compared with younger learners (see the discussion of Brigham & Pressley, 1988, in Chapter 2, this book).

Strong conclusions about monitoring in the elderly and its role in the cognition of the elderly are not possible based on the extant data. We are struck, however, by how salient efforts to increase metacognitive understandings are in successful training studies with the elderly (e.g., Meyer et al., 1989), consistent with successful intervention packages reviewed throughout this book.

Knowledge

One well-known measure of knowledge, the crystallized intelligence factor, was discussed in Chapter 16. Crystallized intelligence increases across the adult life span, an unsurprising finding on reflection. What is more interesting, however, are potential qualitative differences in the knowledge possessed by younger and older people, with developmental psychologists searching for such differences. The conclusion based on a large body of work at this point, however, is that the commonalities in the qualities of knowledge possessed by younger and older adults are greater than the differences.

One problem of great interest to life-span psychologists is whether there are differences in the scripts (see Chapter 3) possessed by younger versus older adults. When younger and older adults are asked about common activities, both groups provide descriptions that are recognizable as the activity. That is, their scripts are similar. Nonetheless, the scripts of older adults are more idiosyncratic in content than the scripts of younger adults (e.g., Hess, 1992; Light, 1992; Ross & Berg, 1992). The scripts provided by older adults reflect peculiar experiences and perspectives more clearly than do the scripts of younger adults. Consider how one elderly woman responded to the question, "What happens when you go on an airplane trip starting with the decision to take the trip and ending when you are called to enter the plane?":

> Son sends the ticket. Get ticket. Become paralyzed with fear. Cut off appointments for 2 weeks. Tell people when I'll be gone. Look through my clothes to find the nicest. Put clothes on the davenport. Look at clothes. Pack by process of elimination. Take out what looks too shabby. Take out what looks too small. Take out suitcase. Take out the list of what I brought before. Judge by the list what I will need now. Put the list with the ticket. Wait for the day I go. Ask friend to take me. He takes me there 1 hour early. Get there. They assign a seat. They put me in a wheelchair because the distance is long. They ask me which

> seat I prefer. Get an aisle seat. They write the number of my seat. Sit. Read. They open the door to the plane. (p. 39)

The significance of such quirky knowledge is that it can affect other learning. Thus, when Ross and Berg (1992) presented younger and older adults with script-type information to learn, they found that adults at both age levels had an easier time learning script-type information consistent with the idiosyncracies of their scripts. Even so, it seemed likely that the younger adults were making use of their personalized scripts to encode new material more than did the older adults, for the difference in recall between information consistent with idiosyncratic versus nonidiosyncratic scripts was greater for younger subjects than for older subjects.

Another possible difference in the knowledge of younger and older adults is with respect to semantic network organization, which would be reflected by different associations to vocabulary items. Thus, if given "table," different semantic organizations in long-term memory would be assumed if one person responded "chair" and another responded "legislation." One hypothesis, supported in some studies, but not in ones in which level of education and vocabulary knowledge are carefully controlled (see Kausler, 1991, Chapter 9, for a review; also, Light, 1992), is that the semantic networks of older adults are more idiosyncratic than the semantic networks of younger adults. If so, many more younger adults would offer a first response of "chair" given "table," than would older adults who would offer a variety of first responses to "table." The problem is that in some studies they do and in some studies they do not. That they do not in the more carefully controlled studies encourages the conclusion that the organization of concepts in memory may not differ dramatically during adulthood as a function of age. Other methods (besides word association) that potentially might reveal differences in semantic organization also have failed to produce evidence of age-related differences in conceptual relations.

Regardless of whether semantic memory is organized differently as a function of age during adulthood, there is little doubt that older adults make less use of their semantic memory to organize study and recall than do younger adults. For example, when studying lists of words that could be grouped into categories, the recall of older compared with younger adults is less likely to be organized with respect to the categories (see Kausler, 1991, Chapter 7). In addition, there is some evidence that the ability to retrieve information from long-term memory may decline with advancing age. One type of information supportive of this conclusion is that recognition memory shows less decline with advancing age than does recall, which implicates retrieval as a possible causal factor in the decline of recall because greater retrieval is required for recall than recognition. Similar differential declines with advancing age have been noted in other tasks that differ in the role of retrieval, with greater retrieval requirements associated with greater decline over the adult life span (see Salthouse, 1992, for a review of the relevant data).

When all of the data are reviewed, most suggest qualitative similarity in the structure of knowledge in younger and older adults, with the organization of concepts and the structure and content of scripts and schemata studied more completely than other types of knowledge. The more striking difference between young adults and the elderly is that knowledge is more certainly accessed and used to assist the accomplishment of new tasks by the young compared with the elderly. One possibility is that if new material is saliently consistent with schemata possessed by the elderly person, the information is processed relative to the schemata and memory is fine—for example, if to-be-learned information is presented in an organized picture that is easily related to a schema possessed by the older adult (e.g., recognition of a kitchen setting given an organized picture of a kitchen and the objects in it). If some effort is required to identify schemata that might be used to organize the information presented (e.g., to-be-learned kitchen items are presented in a disorganized picture), older adults are less likely to expend the effort required to identify and use schemata that might facilitate the learning of the material (Hess & Slaughter, 1990).

Motivation

A variety of motivational hypotheses have been advanced to explain, at least in part, the lower performances of older compared with younger adults. Only some of these have received support (Kausler, 1990, 1991; Willis, 1985). The following ideas about motivation in the elderly enjoy some support:

- Older adults have slightly less need for cognitive stimulation than do younger adults, result-

ing in at least slightly less engagement in cognitive activities by the elderly (Salthouse, Kausler, & Sault, 1988).
- Older adults have difficulties inhibiting task-irrelevant behaviors and thoughts relative to younger adults (e.g., Hasher, Stoltzfus, Zacks, & Rypma, 1991). That is, the problem is not an age-related difference in motivation to do something; it is an age-related difference in staying on task (i.e., a volitional difference; e.g., Corno, 1989; see Chapter 5, this volume).
- Older adults are more likely than younger adults to believe their performances are out of their control (i.e., older adults are more likely to attribute their cognitive difficulties to impaired ability, whereas younger adults attribute performance differences to controllable factors, such as effort and use of inappropriate strategies; e.g., Devolder & Pressley, 1992), with correlations between believing that cognitive performances are under personal control and objective performance levels (e.g., Devolder & Pressley, 1992).

Other potential motivational explanations of age differences have not been supported:

- Potential age differences in performance-disruptive anxiety (i.e., older people are more anxious and hence more likely to experience anxiety-related disruption of performance) have not been observed reliably.
- The need to achieve does not reliably decline with increasing age during adulthood as hypothesized by some. Enjoying learning for the sake of learning does not seem to vary with age during adulthood either.
- Older adults do not seem to be underaroused by cognitive tasks relative to younger adults, as proposed by some theorists interested in aging; nor do they seem to be overaroused reliably relative to younger adults, an hypothesis offered by some other workers in aging.

In short, some of the obvious ways that motivation could differ between older and younger adults have not proved telling. The more promising age-related motivational differences are understudied at this point, however. If older adults really do not enjoy thinking as much as younger adults, if they are less likely to stay on task, and if they are less likely to believe that they can control their performances, these are serious deficiencies that adult educators should be aware of. Based on attribution-retraining successes with other populations (e.g., learning-disabled; see Chapter 5, this book), we would be optimistic that dysfunctional attributions might be reduced through instruction; given the success of self-instructions in keeping other populations on task (e.g., see Chapter 7), we think it possible that inhibition can be developed in the elderly if inhibition is indeed a serious problem for older adults. We expect educational psychologists to be active in studying academic motivation across the life span, including investigation of ways to modify instruction so that older adults are more likely to try hard to undertake a task and stay with it.

Processing Efficiency: Developmental Changes During Adulthood in Speed of Processing and Working Memory

One of the best substantiated findings in the literature on aging is that with advancing age, processing of information slows (e.g., Salthouse, 1982). In addition, although the data are not completely conclusive, slowing with increasing age during adulthood probably translates into decline in functional short-term capacity with advancing age (e.g., Hertzog, 1989; Salthouse & Babcock, 1991). Regardless of whether speed underlies declines in short-term or working memory, however, the evidence is mounting that short-term or working memory capacity decreases with advancing age (e.g., Kausler, 1991, Chapter 8). For example, recency effects in list learning (i.e., recall of the last few items from a list that has been studied), which are determined mostly by short-term memory factors, vary with age, with older adults less likely to recall the last items in a list than are younger adults (for a review of the relevant studies, see Kausler, 1991, Chapter 8). Campbell and Charness (1990) studied how young, middle-aged, and older adults perform mathematical computations in their head. With advancing age, there are many more errant substitutions, deletions, and omissions in performing calculations, errors that are due to short-term processing difficulties rather than long-term knowledge of mathematics facts and procedures. When older people retell stories, they are more likely than younger adults to make references to characters or events in ways that it is unclear which particular characters or events are intended, a failure of working memory: The frequency of such errors correlates with working memory differences

in the elderly (Pratt, Boyes, Robins, & Manchester, 1989).

In addition to behavioral slowing, other factors contribute to decline of functional capacity. For instance, older adults are less likely to use their prior knowledge to chunk information into fewer, more meaningful pieces—that is, older adults are less likely than younger adults to use their knowledge to render demanding cognitive tasks easier (e.g., Taub, 1974; see also the earlier comments in the Knowledge subsection). In short, several factors combine to undermine the efficiency of thinking by older adults compared with younger adults.

Concluding Comment

Something that is striking is that the differences in the thinking of the young, healthy adult and the older, healthy adult are not great. A number of subtle differences, nonetheless, combine to reduce the overall performance of older adults compared with younger adults: The older adults are not as quick in their thinking; they are less likely to adopt newly offered strategies; they do not apply prior knowledge to tasks as certainly; their motivation for many tasks is less than that of younger adults; and their recall tends to be filled both with quirky irrelevancies and broad generalizations, whereas younger adults focus more on the objective and particular in their recall.

The value of a healthy brain in effective thinking is only too apparent when older adults with Alzheimer's disease are compared with healthy age mates or younger adults. Huge individual differences in the integrity of the nervous system in the final decades of life make it impossible to provide generalizations about educability near the end of life. For the healthy elderly, there is "reserve capacity" to use the terminology of the German life-span developmentalists (e.g., Kliegl et al., 1990); the old can learn new tricks. That many adults want to learn new tricks is apparent from the numbers now seeking additional education during middle and late adulthood. The increasing participation of adults in education makes it apparent that 21st century educational psychology must be broader than 20th century educational psychology: The predominant study of children and college-age adults in educational psychology studies in the past must increasingly be complemented by many more investigations that inform about learning and cognition across the life span.

Finally, we note in closing that stereotypes about the elderly as cognitively unproductive ignore the many important contributions of the elderly to life—including scientific contributions. For example, many of the most prominent educational psychologists have remained productive long after they started receiving retirement checks, including such greats as James Angell, Edwin Boring, James Cattell, John Dewey, Arnold Gesell, G. Stanley Hall, Sidney Pressey, Robert Woodworth, Robert M. Yerkes, and Lewis Terman (Charles, 1989). With the increased longevity afforded by contemporary health care, we are optimistic that there are readers of this book who will be working away at problems of educational psychology at the middle of the 21st century and beyond.

CONCLUDING COMMENTS

Within each individual differences classification considered here (i.e., retarded, learning-disabled, or gifted; various categories of students considered at risk; male and female; younger adults and older adults), there are distributions of abilities. Little is known about a person by knowing any of the classifications considered in this chapter relative to what must be known to make informed judgments about that person, their thinking qualities, or interventions that might be effective with them. Thus, our view is that knowledge of individual differences as discussed in this chapter is useful with respect to understanding how psychology has illuminated ways that people can differ from one another. What is presented in this chapter is useless, however, in making decisions about individuals.

Decisions about individuals require extensive information about how that person performs various tasks and what the person's needs are. Often, classroom teachers can gather that information using informal assessments, teacher-made tests, and so on. In cases in which a child or adult has exceptional difficulties, more formal assessments can be helpful, sometimes including the intelligence or neuropsychological assessments detailed in Chapters 16 and 17 or other standardized measures of academic achievement. When information from these tests is considered by a professional psychologist working with educators who know the person well, there is good reason to believe that testing can provide some important data that can supplement other information (e.g., classroom performance and behavior) in making educational decisions about the person in question. The value of such standardized assessments is apparent when an important insight emerges that was not apparent to family members or teachers previously (e.g., that a person may be suffering from a sensory impairment, such as hearing loss, that accounts for poor achievement; when a child does very well on an IQ test when evaluated by a psychologist who overcomes a child's shyness to reveal the active mind that lives behind a reticent veneer).

In concluding this chapter on individual differences, we feel frustrated. Although there has been much progress in understanding many groups of people for whom school is a challenge, there are other groups that are virtually ignored, groups that represent nontrivial proportions of the school-age population. We do not yet have an educational psychology that assists teachers in dealing with students who exhibit recalcitrant behavior problems, including in the 1990s those who bring guns to school and use drugs. We do not know much about how to reduce the likelihood of students dropping out of school or how to design educational alternatives that might be appealing enough to keep them in school. Although the challenges of studying such marginal students are great, it seems timely to do so. About all that we know now is that schools with rigid schedules, demands, and offerings do not work well for these students, if they work at all (Sinclair & Ghory, 1987). One of the next missions for educational researchers interested in learner differences should be to attempt to understand students like the inhabitants of "Blackboard Jungle" as well as we understand students in the Beaver's neighborhood. It is time for researchers to get to know many more types of learners than they have known in the past, for the 21st century demands that we educate better people of color, those challenged by poor health, and adults attempting to learn new skills required by technological advances as well as kids in leather jackets experimenting with drugs and exhibiting unacceptable behaviors. We will all benefit if school works for everyone, and it is more likely to do so if there is more extensive study of how all of us can succeed in school. We hope some readers found inspiration in this book to join us and other educational psychologists in the research and application challenges that are ahead.

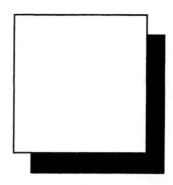

References

Abrami, P. C., Cohen, P. A., & d'Apollinia, S. (1988). Implementation problems in meta-analysis. *Review of Educational Research, 58,* 151–179.

Ach, N. (1910). *Uber deb willensaks und das temperament.* Leipzig Germany: Quelle & Meyer. (Cited in Corno, 1989.)

Achenbach, T., & Zigler, E. (1968). Cue-learning and problem-learning strategies in normal and retarded children. *Child Development, 3,* 827–848.

Adair, J. G., Sharpe, D., & Huynh, C-L. (1989). Hawthorne control procedures in educational experiments: A reconsideration of their use and effectiveness. *Review of Educational Research, 59,* 215–228.

Adams, C., Labouvie-Vief, G., Hobart, C. J., & Dorosz, M. (1990). Adult age group differences in story recall style. *Journal of Gerontology: Psychological Sciences, 45,* P17–P27.

Adams, M. J. (1989). Thinking skills curricula: Their promise and progress. *Educational Psychologist, 24,* 25–77.

Adams, M. J. (1990). *Beginning to read.* Cambridge, MA: Harvard University Press.

Afflerbach, P. P. (1990). The influence of prior knowledge on expert readers' main idea construction strategies. *Reading Research Quarterly, 25,* 31–46.

Ahern, S. K., & Beatty, J. (1979). Physiological signs of information processing vary with intelligence. *Science, 205,* 1289–1292.

Ahern, S. K., & Beatty, J. (1981). Physiological evidence that demand for processing capacity varies with intelligence. In M. Friedman, J. P. Das, & N. O'Connor (Eds.), *Intelligence and learning.* New York: Plenum Press.

Ahn, W. (1987). *Schema acquisition from a single example.* Unpublished master's thesis. Urbana, IL: University of Illinois, Department of Psychology.

Ahn, W., & Brewer, W. F. (1988). Similarity-based and explanation-based learning of explanatory and nonexplanatory information. *Proceedings of the Tenth Annual Conference of the Cognitive Science Society* (pp. 524–530). Hillsdale, NJ: Erlbaum & Associates.

Ahn, W., Mooney, R. J., Brewer, W. F., & DeJong, G. F. (1987). Schema acquisition from one example: Psychological evidence for explanation-based learning. *Proceedings of the Ninth Annual Conference of the Cognitive Science Society* (pp. 50–57). Hillsdale, NJ: Erlbaum & Associates.

Aiken, E. G., Thomas, G. S., & Shennum, W. A. (1975). Memory for a lecture: Effects of notes, lecture rate, and information density. *Journal of Educational Psychology, 67,* 439–444.

Ajewole, G. A. (1991). Effects of discovery and expository instructional methods on the attitude of students in biology. *Journal of Research in Science Teaching, 28,* 401–409.

Aks, D. J., & Coren, S. (1990). Is susceptibility to distraction related to mental ability? *Journal of Educational Psychology, 82,* 388–390.

Alexander, K. L., Entwisle, D. R., & Dauber, S. L. (1993). First-grade classroom behavior: Its short- and long-term consequences for school performance. *Child Development, 64,* 801–814.

Alexander, P. A., & Judy, J. E. (1988). The interaction of domain-specific and strategic knowledge in academic performance. *Review of Educational Research, 58,* 375–404.

Alexander, P. A., Willson, V. L., White, C. S., & Fuqua, J. D. (1987). Analogical reasoning in young children. *Journal of Educational Psychology, 79,* 401–408.

Alexander, P. A., Willson, V. L., White, C. S., Fuqua, J. D., Clark, G. D., Wilson, A. F., & Kulikowich, J. M. (1989). Development of analogical reasoning in 40 5-year-old children. *Cognitive Development, 4,* 65–88.

Allen, J. B., Clark, W., Cook, M., Crane, P., Fallon, I., Hoffman, L., Jennings, K. S., & Sours, M. A. (1989). Reading and writing development in whole language kindergartens. In J. Mason (Ed.), *Reading and writing connections* (pp. 121–146). Needham Heights, MA: Allyn & Bacon.

Allen, L., Cipielewski, J., & Stanovich, K. E. (1992). Multiple indicators of children's reading habits and attitudes: Construct validity and cognitive correlates. *Journal of Educational Psychology, 84,* 489–503.

Allen, V. L. (Ed.) (1976). *Children as teachers: Theory and research on tutoring.* New York: Academic Press. Allington, R. (1977). If they don't read much, how they ever gonna get good? *Journal of Reading, 21,* 57–61.

Allington, R. L. (1983). The reading instruction provided readers of differing ability levels. *Elementary School Journal, 83,* 548–559.

Allington, R. L. (1991a). Effective literacy instruction for at-risk children. In M. S. Knapp & P. M. Shields (Eds.), *Better schooling for the children of poverty: Alternatives to conventional wisdom* (pp. 9–30). Berkeley, CA: McCutchan Publishing Co.

Allington, R. L. (1991b). The legacy of "slow it down and make it more concrete." In J. Zutell & S. McCormick (Eds.), *Learner factors/teacher factors: Issues in literacy research and instruction: Fortieth Yearbook of the National Reading Conference* (pp. 19–29). Chicago: National Reading Conference.

Allington, R. L., & McGill-Franzen, A. (1989). School response to reading failure: Chapter 1 and special education students in grades 2, 4, & 8. *Elementary School Journal, 89,* 529–542.

Allington, R. L., & McGill-Franzen, A. (1991). *Unintended effects of educational reform in New York state.* Unpublished paper. Albany: State University of New York, School of Education.

Almasi, J. F. (1993). *The nature of fourth graders' sociocognitive conflicts in peer-led and teacher-led discussions of literature.* Unpublished dissertation. College Park, MD: University of Maryland, Department of Curriculum and Instruction.

Alvermann, D. E., & Hague, S. A. (1989). Comprehension of counter-intuitive science text: Effects of prior knowledge and text structure. *Journal of Educational Research, 82,* 197–202.

Alvermann, D. E., & Hayes, D. A. (1989). Classroom discussions of content area reading assignments: An intervention study. *Reading Research Quarterly, 24,* 305–335.

Alvermann, D. E., & Hynd, C. R. (1991). The effects of varying prior knowledge activation modes and text structure on nonscience majors' comprehension of physics text. *Journal of Educational Research.*

Alvermann, D. E., & Moore, D. W. (1991). Secondary school reading. In R. Barr, M. L. Kamil, P. B. Mosenthal, & P. D. Pearson (Eds.), *Handbook of reading research,* Vol. II (pp. 951–983). New York: Longman.

Alvermann, D. E., Moore, D. W., & Conley, M. W. (Eds.) (1987). *Research within reach: Secondary school reading.* Newark, DE: International Reading Association.

Alvermann, D. E., O'Brien, D. G., & Dillon, D. R. (1990). What teachers do when they say they're having discussions of content area reading assignments: A qualitative analysis. *Reading Research Quarterly, 25,* 296–322.

Alvermann, D. E., Smith, L. C., & Readence, J. E. (1985). Prior knowledge activation and the comprehension of compatible and incompatible texts. *Reading Research Quarterly, 20,* 420–436.

American Psychological Association (1985). *Standards for educational and psychological testing.* Washington, DC: American Psychological Association.

Ames, C. (1984). Competitive, cooperative, and individualistic goal structures: A motivational analysis. In R. Ames & C. Ames (Eds.), *Research on motivation in education,* Vol. 1 (pp. 117–207). New York: Academic Press.

Ames, C. (1990). Motivation: What teachers need to know. *Teachers College Record, 91,* 409–421.

Ames, C. (1992). Classrooms: Goals, structures, and student motivation. *Journal of Educational Psychology, 84,* 261–271.

Ames, C., & Ames, R. (1981). Competitive versus individualistic goal structures: The salience of past performance information for causal attributions and affect. *Journal of Educational Psychology, 73,* 411–418.

Ames, C., & Archer, J. (1988). Achievement goals in the classroom: Students' learning strategies and motivation processes. *Journal of Educational Psychology, 80,* 260–270.

Ames, C., & Felker, D. W. (1979). Effects of self-concept on children's causal attributions and self-reinforcement. *Journal of Educational Psychology, 71,* 613–619.

Amigues, R. (1988). Peer interaction in solving physics problems: Sociocognitive confrontation and metacognitive aspects. *Journal of Experimental Child Psychology, 45,* 141–158.

Anastasi, A. (1988). *Psychological testing* (sixth edition). New York: Macmillan.

Anastasiow, N. J. (1990). Implications of the neurobiological model for early intervention. In S. J. Meisels & J. P. Shonkoff (Eds.), *Handbook of early childhood interventions* (pp. 196–216). Cambridge, UK: Cambridge University Press.

Anbar, A. (1986). Reading acquisition of preschool children without systematic instruction. *Early Childhood Research Quarterly, 1,* 69–83.

Anderson, B., Mead, N., & Sullivan, S. (1986). *Television: What do National Assessment results tell us!* Princeton, NJ: Educational Testing Service.

Anderson, C. W., Sheldon, T. H., & Dubay, J. (1990). The effects of instruction on college nonmajors' conceptions of respiration and photosynthesis. *Journal of Research in Science Teaching, 27,* 761–776.

Anderson, D. R., & Collins, P. A. (1988). *The impact on children's education: Television's influence on cognitive development.* (Office of Research Working Paper No. 2). Washington, DC: U.S. Department of Education, Office of Educational Research and Improvement.

Anderson, J. R. (1978). Arguments concerning representations for mental imagery. *Psychological Review, 85,* 249–277.

Anderson, J. R. (1983). *The architecture of cognition.* Cambridge, MA: Harvard University Press.

Anderson, J. R. (1984). Spreading activation. In J. R. Anderson & S. M. Kosslyn (Eds.), *Tutorials in learning and memory: Essays in honor of Gordon Bower* (pp. 61–90). San Francisco: W. H. Freeman & Co.

Anderson, J. R., & Bower, G. H. (1973). *Human associative memory.* New York: Wiley.

Anderson, J. R., Greeno, J. G., Kline, P. J., & Neves, D. M. (1981). Acquisition of problem-solving skill. In J. R. Anderson (Ed.), *Cognitive skills and their acquisition* (pp. 191–230). Hillsdale, NJ: Erlbaum & Associates.

Anderson, L., Jenkins, L. B., Leming, J., MacDonald, W. B., Mullis, I. V. S., Turner, M. J., & Wooster, J. S. (1990). *The civics report card.* Washington, DC: U.S. Department of Education, Office of Educational Research and Improvement.

Anderson, R. C., & Biddle, W. B. (1975). On asking people questions about what they are reading. In G. Bower (Ed.), *The psychology of learning and motivation,* Vol. 9. New York: Academic Press.

Anderson, R. C., Hiebert, E. H., Scott, J. A., & Wilkinson, I. A. G. (1985). *Becoming a nation of readers.* Washington, DC: National Institute of Education.

Anderson, R. C., Mason, J. M., & Shirey, L. (1984). The reading group: An experimental investigation of a labyrinth. *Reading Research Quarterly, 20,* 6–38.

Anderson, R. C., & Ortony, A. (1975). On putting apples into bottles: A problem of polysemy. *Cognitive Psychology, 7,* 167–180.

Anderson, R. C., & Pearson, P. D. (1984). A schema-theoretic view of basic processes in reading. In P. D. Pearson (Ed.), *Handbook of reading research.* New York: Longman.

Anderson, R. C., & Pichert, J. W. (1978). Recall of previously unrecallable information following a shift in perspective. *Journal of Verbal Learning and Verbal Behavior, 17,* 1–12.

Anderson, R. C., Reynolds, R. E., Schallert, D. L., & Goetz, E. T. (1977). Frameworks for comprehending discourse. *American Educational Research Journal, 14,* 367–382.

Anderson, R. C., Shirey, L. L., Wilson, P. T., & Fielding, L. G. (1987). Interestingness of children's reading material. In R. E. Snow & M. J. Farr (Eds.), *Aptitude, learning, and instruction, Volume 3: Cognative and Affective Process Analyses* (pp. 287–299). Hillsdale, NJ: Erlbaum & Associates.

Anderson, R. C., Spiro, R. J., & Anderson, M. C. (1978). Schemata as scaffolding for the representation of information in connected discourse. *American Educational Research Journal, 15,* 433–439.

Anderson, R. C., Wilkinson, I. A. G., & Mason, J. M. (1991). A microanalysis of the small-group, guided reading lesson: Effect of emphasis on global story meaning. *Reading Research Quarterly, 26,* 417–441.

Anderson, R. C., Wilson, P. T., & Fielding, L. G. (1988). Growth in reading and how children spend their time outside of school. *Reading Research Quarterly, 23,* 285–303.

Anderson, T. H., & Armbruster, B. B. (1984). Content area textbooks. In R. C. Anderson, J. Osborn, & R. J. Tierney (Eds.), *Learning to read in American schools* (pp. 193–226). Hillsdale, NJ: Erlbaum & Associates.

Anglin, J. M. (1977). *Word, object, and concept development.* New York: Norton.

Anisfeld, M. (1991). Neonatal imitation. *Developmental Review, 11,* 60–97.

Annett, J. (1988). Motor learning and retention. In M. Gruneberg, P. Morris, & R. Sykes (Eds.), *Practical aspects of memory 2.* Chichester, UK: John Wiley & Sons.

Annett, J. (1989). Training skilled performance. In A. M. Colley & J. R. Beech (Eds.), *Acquisition and performance of cognitive skills* (pp. 61–84). Chichester, UK: John Wiley & Sons.

Applebee, A. N. (1984). *Contexts for learning to write.* Norwood, NJ: Ablex.

Applebee, A. N., & Langer, J. A. (1983). Instructional scaffolding: Reading and writing as natural language activities. *Language Arts, 60,* 168–175.

Applebee, A. N., Langer, J. A., Jenkins, L. B., Mullis, I. S., & Foertsch, M. A. (1990). *Learning to write in our nation's schools.* U.S. Department of Education: Office of Educational Research and Improvement.

Applebee, A. N., Langer, J., & Mullis, I. (1986). *The writing report card: Writing achievement in American schools.* Princeton, NJ: Educational Testing Service.

Applebee, A. N., Langer, J., & Mullis, I. (1988). *Crossroads in American education: A summary of findings.* Princeton, NJ: Educational Testing Service.

Arbitman-Smith, R., Haywood, W. C., & Bransford, J. D. (1984). Assessing cognitive change. In P. Brooks, R. Sperber, & C. M. McCauley (Eds.), *Learning and cognition in the mentally retarded.* Hillsdale, NJ: Erlbaum & Associates.

Armbruster, B. B., Anderson, T. H., & Meyer, J. L. (1991). Improving content-area reading using instructional graphics. *Reading Research Quarterly, 26,* 393–416.

Armbruster, B. B., Anderson, T. H., & Ostertag, J. (1987). Does text structure/summarization instruction facilitate learning from expository text? *Reading Research Quarterly, 22,* 331–346.

Armstrong, F. D., Seidel, J. F., & Swales, T. P. (1993). Pediatric HIV infection: A neuropsychological and educational challenge. *Journal of Learning Disabilities, 26,* 92–103.

Armstrong, J. M. (1985). A national assessment of participation and achievement of women in mathematics. In S. F. Chipman, L. R. Brush, & D. M. Wilson (Eds.), *Women and mathematics: Balancing the equation* (pp. 59–94). Hillsdale, NJ: Erlbaum & Associates.

Arnaudin, M. W., & Mintzes, J. J. (1985). Students' alternative conceptions of the human circulatory system: A cross-age study. *Science Education, 69,* 721–733.

Arnheim, R. (1971). *Visual thinking.* Berkeley: University of California Press.

Artman, L., & Cahan, S. (1993). Schooling and the development of transitive inference. *Developmental Psychology, 29,* 753–759.

Artzt, A. F., & Armour-Thomas, E. (1992). Development of a cognitive-metacognitive framework for protocol analysis of mathematical problem solving in small groups. *Cognition and Instruction, 9,* 137–175.

Asarnow, J. R., & Meichenbaum, D. (1979). Verbal rehearsal and serial recall. *Child Development, 50,* 1173–1177.

Ashcraft, M. H., & Battaglia, J. (1978). Cognitive arithmetic: Evidence for retrieval and decision processes in mental arithmetic. *Journal of Experimental Psychology: Human Learning and Memory, 4,* 527–538.

Ashcraft, M. H., & Stazyk, E. H. (1981). Mental addition: A test of three verification models. *Memory & Cognition, 9,* 185–196.

Aslin, R. N. (1981). Experimental influence and sensitive period in perceptual development: A unified model. In R. N. Aslin & F. Peterson (Eds.), *The development of perception* (Vol. 2, pp. 45–93). Orlando, FL: Academic Press.

Astin, A. W. (1993). *What matters in college? Four critical years revisited.* San Francisco: Jossey-Bass.

Atkinson, R. C. (1975). Mnemotechnics in second-language learning. *American Psychologist, 30,* 821–828.

Atwell, N. (1987). *In the middle: Reading, writing, and learning from adolescents.* Portsmouth, NH: Heinemann.

Ault, C. S. (1985). Concept mapping as a study strategy with earth science. *Journal of College Science Teaching, 15,* 38–44.

Ausubel, D. P. (1960). The use of advance organizers in the learning and retention of meaningful verbal learning. *Journal of Educational Psychology, 51,* 267–272.

Ausubel, D. P. (1961). Learning by discovery: Rationale and mystique. *Bulletin of the National Association of Secondary School Principals, 45,* 18–58.

Ausubel, D. P. (1968). *Educational psychology: A cognitive view.* New York: Holt, Rinehart, & Winston.

Azmitia, M., & Hesser, J. (1993). Why siblings are important agents of cognitive development: A comparison of siblings and peers. *Child Development, 64,* 430–444.

Babad, E., Bernieri, F., & Rosenthal, R. (1991). Students as judges of teachers' verbal and nonverbal behavior. *American Educational Research Journal, 28,* 211–234.

Babad, E. Y., & Budoff, M. (1974). Sensitivity and validity of learning potential measurements in three levels of ability. *Journal of Educational Psychology, 66,* 439–447.

Bach, M. J., & Underwood, B. J. (1970). Developmental changes in memory attributes. *Journal of Educational Psychology, 61,* 292–296.

Bachevalier, J. (1990). Ontogenetic development of habit and memory formation in primates. In A. Diamond (Ed.), *The development and neural bases of higher cognitive functions* (pp. 457–484). New York: New York Academy of Science.

Bacon, J. H. (1862). *The science of memory.* London: Simpkin & Co.

Baddeley, A. (1986). *Working memory.* New York: Oxford University Press.

Baddeley, A., Logie, R., Bressi, S., Della Sala, S., & Spinnler, H. (1986). Dementia and working memory. *Quarterly Journal of Experimental Psychology, 38A,* 603–618.

Baer, D. M. (1990). Why choose self-regulation as the focal analysis of retardation? *American Journal of Mental Deficiency, 94,* 363–364.

Baggett, P., & Ehrenfeucht, A. (1992). What should be the role of calculators and computers in mathematics education? *Journal of Mathematical Behavior, 11,* 61–72.

Bahrick, H. P. (1984). Semantic memory content in permastore: Fifty years of memory for Spanish learned in school. *Journal of Experimental Psychology: General, 113,* 1–29.

Bahrick, H. P., & Hall, L. K. (1991). Preventive and corrective maintenance of access to knowledge. *Applied Cognitive Psychology, 5,* 1–18.

Bahrick, H. P., & Phelps, E. (1987). Retention of Spanish vocabulary over 8 years. *Journal of Experimental Psychology: Learning, Memory, and Cognition, 13,* 344–349.

Bakan, P. (1969). Hypnotizability, laterality of eye movement, and functional brain asymmetry. *Perceptual and Motor Skills, 28,* 927–932.

Baker, L. (1989). Metacognition, comprehension monitoring, and the adult reader. *Educational Psychology Review, 1,* 3–38.

Baker, L., & Brown, A. L. (1984). Metacognitive skills and reading. In P. D. Pearson, R. Barr, M. Kamil, & P. Mosenthal (Eds.), *Handbook of reading research* (pp. 353–394). New York: Longmans.

Baker, L. A., Vernon, P. A., & Ho, H-Z. (1991). The genetic correlation between intelligence and speed of information processing. *Behavior Genetics, 21,* 351–367.

Baker-Ward, L., Hess, T. M., & Flannagan, D. A. (1990). The effects of involvement on children's memory for events. *Cognitive Development, 5,* 55–69.

Baker-Ward, L., Ornstein, P. A., & Holden, D. J. (1984). The expression of memorization in early childhood. *Journal of Experimental Child Psychology, 37,* 555–575.

Bakhtin, M. M. (1981). *The dialogic imagination: Four essays by M. M. Bakhtin* (Edited by Michael Holquist; Translated by Caryl Emerson & Michael Holquist). Austin: University of Texas Press.

Bakwin, H. (1973). Reading disability in twins. *Developmental Medicine and Child Neurology, 15,* 184–7.

Ball, D. L. (1988). *Knowledge and reasoning in mathematical pedagogy: Examining what prospective teachers bring to teacher education.* Unpublished doctoral dissertation. Michigan State University.

Ball, D. L. (1990). Prospective elementary and secondary teachers' understanding of division. *Journal for Research in Mathematics Education, 21,* 132–144.

Ball, E. W., & Blachman, B. A. (1988). Phoneme segmentation training: Effect on reading readiness. *Annals of Dyslexia, 38,* 203–225.

Ball, E. W., & Blachman, B. A. (1991). Does phoneme segmentation training in kindergarten make a difference in early word recognition and developmental spelling? *Reading Research Quarterly, 26,* 49–66.

Ball, S., & Bogatz, G. A. (1970). *The first year of "Sesame Street": An evaluation.* Princeton, NJ: Educational Testing Service.

Ball, S., & Bogatz, G. A. (1975). Some thoughts on this secondary evaluation. In T. D. Cook, H. Appleton, R. F. Conner, A. Shaffer, G. Tamkin, & S. J. Weber, *"Sesame Street" revisited.* New York: Russell Sage Foundation.

Baltes, P. B. (1968). Longitudinal and cross-sectional sequences in the study of age and generation effects. *Human Development, 11,* 145–171.

Baltes, P. B., & Kliegl, R. (1992). Further testing of limits of cognitive plasticity: Negative age differences in a mnemonic skill are robust. *Developmental Psychology, 28,* 121–125.

Baltes, P. B., Reese, H. W., & Nesselroade, J. R. (1977). *Life-span developmental psychology: Introduction to research methods.* Monterey, CA: Brooks/Cole.

Baltes, P. B., & Reinert, G. (1969). Cohort effects in cognitive development in children as revealed by cross sectional sequences. *Developmental Psychology, 1,* 169–177.

Baltes, P. B., & Willis, S. L. (1982). Plasticity and enhancement of intellectual functioning in old age. In F. I. M. Craik & E. E. Trehub (Eds.), *Aging and cognitive processes* (pp. 353–389). New York: Plenum.

Bandura, A. (1965). Vicarious processes: A case of no-trial learning. In L. Berkowitz (Ed.), *Advances in experimental social psychology*, Vol. 2 (pp. 1–55). New York: Academic Press.

Bandura, A. (1969). *Principles of behavior modification*. New York: Holt.

Bandura, A. (1977a). Self-efficacy: Toward a unifying theory of behavioral change. *Psychological Review, 84*, 191–215.

Bandura, A. (1977b). *Social learning theory*. Englewood Cliffs, NJ: Prentice-Hall.

Bandura, A. (1982). Self-efficacy mechanism in human agency. *American Psychologist, 37*, 122–147.

Bandura, A. (1986). *Social foundations of thought and action: A social cognitive theory*. Englewood Cliffs NJ: Prentice-Hall.

Bandura, A. (1989). Regulation of cognitive processes through perceived self-efficacy. *Developmental Psychology, 25*, 729–735.

Bandura, A., & Cervone, D. (1983). Self-evaluative and self-efficacy mechanisms governing the motivational effects of goal systems. *Journal of Personality and Social Psychology, 45*, 1017–1028.

Bandura, A., & Cervone, D. (1986). Differential engagement of self-reactive influences in cognitive motivation. *Organizational Behavior and Human Decision Processes, 38*, 92–113.

Bandura, A., Grusec, J. E., & Menlove, F. L. (1966). Observational learning as a function of symbolization and incentive set. *Child Development, 37*, 499–506.

Bandura, A., & Jeffrey, R. W. (1973). Role of symbolic coding and rehearsal processes in observational learning. *Journal of Personality and Social Psychology, 26*, 122–130.

Bandura, A., Jeffrey, R. W., & Bachicha, D. L. (1974). Analysis of memory codes and cumulative rehearsal in observational learning. *Journal of Research in Personality, 7*, 295–305.

Bandura, A., & McDonald, F. J. (1963). Influence of social reinforcement and the behavior of models in shaping children's moral judgments. *Journal of Abnormal and Social Psychology, 67*, 274–281.

Bandura, A., & Menlove, F. L. (1968). Factors determining vicarious extinction of avoidance behavior through symbolic modeling. *Journal of Personality and Social Psychology, 8*, 99–108.

Bandura, A., & Schunk, D. H. (1981). Cultivating competence, self-efficacy, and intrinsic interest through proximal self-instruction. *Journal of Personality and Social Psychology, 41*, 586–598.

Bandura, A., & Walters, R. H. (1963). *Social learning and personality development*. New York: Holt, Rinehart, & Winston.

Bangert-Drowns, R. L., Kulik, C-I. C., Kulik, J. A., & Morgan M. (1991). The instructional effect of feedback in test-like events. *Review of Educational Research, 61*, 213–238.

Banks, M. S., & Salapatek, P. (1983). Infant visual perception. In M. M. Haith & J. J. Campos (Volume Ed.) and P. H. Mussen (General Ed.),

Handbook of child psychology, Vol. II, *Infancy and developmental psychobiology* (pp. 435–571). New York: John Wiley & Sons.

Baranes, R., Perry, M., & Stigler, J. W. (1989). Activation of real-world knowledge in the solution of word problems. *Cognition and Instruction, 6*, 287–318.

Barclay, C. R. (1979). The executive control of mnemonic activity. *Journal of Experimental Child Psychology, 27*, 262–276.

Barell, J. (1991). Creating our own pathways: Teaching students to think and become self-directed. In N. Colangelo & G. A. Davis (Eds.), *Handbook of gifted education* (pp. 256–270). Boston: Allyn & Bacon.

Barker, G., & Graham, S. (1987). Developmental study of praise and blame as attributional cues. *Journal of Educational Psychology, 79*, 62–66.

Barker, T. A., Torgesen, J. L., & Wagner, R. K. (1992). The role of orthographic processing skills on five different reading tasks. *Reading Research Quarterly, 27*, 334–345.

Barnes, B. R., & Clawson, E. U. (1975). Do advance organizers facilitate learning? Recommendations for further research based on analysis of 32 studies. *Review of Educational Research, 45*, 637–659.

Barnett, M., & Andrews, J. (1977). Sex differences in children's reward allocation under competitive and cooperative instructional sets. *Developmental Psychology, 13*, 85–86.

Barnhart, J. E. (1991). Criterion-related validity of interpretations of children's performance on emergent literacy tasks. *Journal of Reading Behavior, 23*, 425–444.

Baron, J. (1977). Mechanisms for pronouncing printed words: Use and acquisition. In D. LaBerge & S. J. Samuels (Eds.), *Basic processes in reading: Perception and comprehension* (pp. 175–216). Hillsdale, NJ: Erlbaum & Associates.

Baron, J. (1985). *Rationality and intelligence*. Cambridge, UK: Cambridge University Press.

Baron, J. (1988). *Thinking and deciding*. New York: Cambridge University Press.

Baron, J. (1990a). Reflectiveness and rational thinking: Response to Duemler and Mayer (1988). *Journal of Educational Psychology, 82*, 391–392.

Baron, J. (1990b). Thinking about consequences. *Journal of Moral Education, 19*, 77–87.

Baroody, A. (1987). *Children's mathematical thinking*. New York: Teachers College Press.

Baroody, A. (1989). Kindergartners' mental addition with single-digit combinations. *Journal for Research in Mathematics Education, 20*, 159–172.

Baroody, A. J. (1992). The development of kindergartners' mental-addition strategies. *Learning and Individual Differences, 4*, 215–235.

Barr, H. M., Streissguth, A. P., Darby, B. L., & Sampson, P. D. (1990). Prenatal exposure to alcohol, caffeine, tobacco, and aspirin: Effects on fine and gross motor performance in 4-year-old children. *Developmental Psychology, 26*, 339–348.

Barr, P., & Samuels, M. (1988). Dynamic assessment of cognitive and affective factors con-

tributing to learning difficulties in adults. *Professional Psychology: Research and Practice, 19*, 6–13.

Barr, R. C. (1974–75). The effect of instruction on pupil reading strategies. *Reading Research Quarterly, 10*, 555–582.

Barrass, R. (1984). Some misconceptions and misunderstandings perpetuated by teachers and textbooks of biology. *Journal of Biological Education, 18*, 201–206.

Barron, R. W. (1981). Development of visual word recognition: A review. In G. E. MacKinnon & T. G. Waller (Eds.), *Reading research: Advances in theory and practice*, Vol. 3 (pp. 119–158). San Diego: Academic Press.

Barron, R. W. (1986). Word recognition in early reading: A review of the direct and indirect access hypotheses. *Cognition, 24*, 93–119.

Barsalou, L. W. (1982). Context-independent and context-dependent information in concepts. *Memory and Cognition, 10*, 82–93.

Bartel, N. R., & Thurman, S. K. (1992). Medical treatment and educational problems in children. *Phi Delta Kappan, 74*, 57–61.

Bartlett, F. C. (1932). *Remembering*. Cambridge, UK: Cambridge University Press.

Basili, P. A., & Sanford, J. P. (1991). Conceptual change strategies and cooperative group work in chemistry. *Journal of Research in Science Teaching, 28*, 293–304.

Bassarear, T., & Davidson, N. (1992). The use of small group learning situations in mathematics instruction as a tool to develop thinking. In N. Davidson & T. Worsham (Eds.), *Enhancing thinking through cooperative learning* (pp. 235–250). New York: Teachers College Press.

Bauer, P. J., & Fivush, R. (1992). Constructing event representations: Building on a foundation of variation and enabling relations. *Cognitive Development, 7*, 381–401.

Bauer, P. J., & Mandler, J. M. (1989). One thing follows another: Effects of temporal structure on 1- to 2-year-olds' recall of events. *Developmental Psychology, 25*, 197–206.

Bauer, P. J., & Mandler, J. M. (1992). Putting the horse before the cart: The use of temporal order in recall of events by one-year-old children. *Developmental Psychology, 28*, 441–452.

Bauer, P. J., & Thal, D. J. (1990). Scripts or scraps: Reconsidering the development of sequential understanding. *Journal of Experimental Child Psychology, 50*, 287–304.

Bauer, R. H. (1977a). Memory processes in children with learning disabilities. *Journal of Experimental Child Psychology, 24*, 415–430.

Bauer, R. H. (1977b). Short-term memory in learning disabled and nondisabled children. *Bulletin of the Psychonomic Society, 10*, 128–130.

Bazerman, C. (1985). Physicists reading physics: Schema-laden purposes and purpose-laden schema. *Written Communication, 2*, 3–23.

Beach, R. (1976). Self-evaluation strategies of extensive revisers and nonrevisers. *College Composition and Communication, 27*, 160–164.

Beal, C. R. (1987). Repairing the message: Children's monitoring and revision skills. *Child Development, 58*, 401–408.

Beal, C. R. (1989). Children's communication

skills: Implications for the development of writing strategies. In C. B. McCormick, G. Miller, & M. Pressley (Eds.), *Cognitive strategy research: From basic research to educational applications* (pp. 191–214). New York: Springer-Verlag.

Beal, C. R. (1990). The development of text evaluation and revision skills. *Child Development, 61,* 247–258.

Beal, C. R., Garrod, A. C., & Bonitatibus, G. J. (1990). Fostering children's revision skills through training in comprehension monitoring. *Journal of Educational Psychology, 82,* 275–280.

Bean, T. W., & Steenwyk, F. L. (1984). The effect of three forms of summarization instruction on sixth graders' summary writing and comprehension. *Journal of Reading Behavior, 16,* 297–306.

Bebeau, M. J., & Brabeck, M. M. (1987). Integrating care and justice issues in professional moral education: A gender perspective. *Journal of Moral Education, 16,* 189–203.

Bebout, H. C. (1990). Children's symbolic representation of addition and subtraction word problems. *Journal for Research in Mathematics Education, 21,* 123–131.

Bechtel, W., & Abrahamsen, A. (1991). *Connectionism and the mind.* Cambridge, MA: Basil Blackwell.

Beck, I. L., McKeown, M. G., Sinatra, G. M., & Loxterman, J. A. (1991). Revising social studies text from a text-processing perspective: Evidence of improved comprehensibility. *Reading Research Quarterly, 26,* 251–276.

Becker, B. J. (1990). Coaching for the Scholastic Aptitude Test: Further synthesis and appraisal. *Review of Educational Research, 60,* 373–417.

Becker, J. R. (1982). Differential treatment of females and males in mathematics classes. *Journal for Research in Mathematics Education, 12,* 40–53.

Beckwith, L., & Parmelee, A. H., Jr. (1986). EEG patterns of preterm infants: Home environments and later IQ. *Child Development, 57,* 777–789.

Beentjes, J. W. J., & Van der Voort, T. H. A. (1988). Television's impact on children's reading skills: A review of research. *Reading Research Quarterly, 23,* 389–413.

Beichner, R. J. (1990). The effect of simultaneous motion presentation and graph generation in a kinematics lab. *Journal of Research in Science Teaching, 27,* 803–815.

Bell, R. Q. (1968). A reinterpretation of the direction of effects in studies of socialization. *Psychological Review, 75,* 81–95.

Belmont, J. M., Butterfield, E. C., & Ferretti, R. P. (1982). To secure transfer of training: Instruct self-management skills. In D. K. Detterman & R. J. Sternberg (Eds.), *How and how much can intelligence be increased* (pp. 147–154). Norwood, NJ: Ablex.

Benbow, C. P. (1992). Academic achievement in mathematics and science of students between ages 13 and 23: Are there differences among students in the top one percent of mathemati-

cal ability? *Journal of Educational Psychology, 84,* 51–61.

Benbow, C. P., & Arjmand, O. (1990). Predictors of high academic achievement in mathematics and science by mathematically talented students: A longitudinal study. *Journal of Educational Psychology, 82,* 430–441.

Ben-Chaim, D., Lappan, D., & Houang, R. T. (1988). The effect of instruction on spatial visualization skills of middle school boys and girls. *American Educational Research Journal, 25,* 51–71.

Bender, N. (1976). Self-verbalization versus tutor verbalization in modifying impulsivity. *Journal of Educational Psychology, 88,* 347–354.

Bennett, F. C. (1987). The effectiveness of early intervention for infants at increased biologic risk. In M. J. Guralnick & F. C. Bennett (Eds.), *The effectiveness of early intervention for at-risk and handicapped children* (pp. 79–112). Orlando, FL: Academic Press.

Bennett, R. E., Gottesman, R. L., Rock, D. A., & Cerullo, F. (1993). Influence of behavior perceptions and gender on teachers' judgments of students' academic skills. *Journal of Educational Psychology, 85,* 347–356.

Bennett, W. L. (1984). *To reclaim a legacy: A report on humanities in higher education.* Washington, DC: National Endowment for the Humanities.

Benton, S. L., Kiewra, K. A., Whitfill, J. M., & Dennison, R. (1993). Encoding and external-storage effects on writing processes. *Journal of Educational Psychology, 85,* 267–280.

Bentz, J., Shinn, M. R., & Gleason, M. M. (1990). Training general education pupils to monitor reading using curriculum-based measurement procedures. *School Psychology Review, 19,* 23–32.

Ben-Zvi, R., Eylon, B., & Silberstein, J. (1987, July). Students' visualization of a chemical reaction. *Education in Chemistry,* 117–120.

Bereiter, C. (1990). Aspects of an educational learning theory. *Review of Educational Research, 60,* 603–624.

Bereiter, C., & Bird, M. (1985). Use of thinking aloud in identification and teaching of reading comprehension strategies. *Cognition and Instruction, 2,* 131–156.

Bereiter, C., & Scardamalia, M. (1982). From conversation to composition: The role of instruction in a developmental process. In R. Glaser (Ed.), *Advances in instructional psychology,* Vol. 2 (pp. 1–64). Hillsdale, NJ: Erlbaum & Associates.

Bereiter, C., & Scardamalia, M. (1987). *The psychology of written communication.* Hillsdale, NJ: Erlbaum & Associates.

Berg, C. A. (1989). Knowledge of strategies for dealing with everyday problems from childhood through adolescence. *Developmental Psychology, 25,* 607–618.

Berg, J. M. (1985). Physical determinants of environmental origin. In A. M. Clarke, A. D. B. Clarke, & J. M. Berg (Eds.), *Mental deficiency: The changing outlook* (4th edition) (pp. 99–134). New York: Free Press.

Bergem, T. (1990). The teacher as moral agent. *Journal of Moral Education, 19,* 88–100.

Berger, R. (1991). Building a school culture of high standards: A teacher's perspective. In V. Perrone (Ed.). *Expanding student assessment* (pp. 32–39). Alexandria, VA: Association for Supervision and Curriculum Development.

Berk, R. A. (1986). *Performance assessment: Methods and application.* Baltimore: Johns Hopkins University Press.

Berkenkotter, C., & Murray, D. (1983). Decisions and revisions: The planning strategies of a publishing writer and responses of a laboratory rat—or being protocoled. *College Composition and Communication, 34,* 156–172.

Berkowitz, S. J. (1986). Effects of instruction in text organization on sixth-grade students' memory for expository reading. *Reading Research Quarterly, 21,* 161–178.

Berliner, D. (1986). In pursuit of the expert pedagogue. *Educational Researcher, 15 (7),* 5–13.

Berliner, D. C. (1988). *The development of expertise in pedagogy.* Washington, DC: American Association of College for Teacher Education.

Berndt, T. J., & Miller, K. E. (1990). Expectancies, values, and achievement in junior high school. *Journal of Educational Psychology, 82,* 319–326.

Berry, J. M., West, R. L., & Dennehey, D. M. (1989). Reliability and validity of the memory self-efficacy questionnaire. *Developmental Psychology, 25,* 701–713.

Bertelson, P., & De Gelder, B. (1989). Learning about reading from illiterates. In A. M. Galaburda (Ed.), *From reading to neurons* (pp. 1–23). Cambridge, MA: MIT Press.

Best, D. L. (1993). Inducing children to generate mnemonic organizational strategies: An examination of long-term retention and materials. *Developmental Psychology, 29,* 324–336.

Best, D. L., Hamlett, K. W., & Davis, S. W. (1992). Memory complaint and memory performance in the elderly: The effects of memory-skills training and expectancy change. *Applied Cognitive Psychology, 6,* 405–416.

Best, D. L., & Ornstein, P. A. (1986). Children's generation and communication of mnemonic organizational strategies. *Developmental Psychology, 22,* 845–853.

Beuhring, T., & Kee, D. W. (1987). Developmental relationships among metamemory, elaborative strategy use, and associative memory. *Journal of Experimental Child Psychology, 44,* 377–400.

Bibby, P. A. (1992). Mental models, instructions, and internalization. In Y. Rogers, A. Rutherford, & P. A. Bibby (Eds.), *Models in the mind: Theory, perspective, and application* (pp. 153–172). London: Academic Press.

Bielaczyc, K., Pirolli, P., & Brown, A. L. (1991, March). *The effects of training in explanation strategies on the acquisition of programming skills.* Presented at the annual meeting of the American Educational Research Association, Chicago.

Bigler, E. D. (1992). The neurobiology and neuropsychology of adult learning disorders. *Journal of Learning Disabilities, 25,* 488–506.

Bigler, E. D., & Naugle, R. I. (1985). Case studies in cerebral plasticity. *International Journal of Clinical Neuropsychology, 7,* 12–23.

Binet, A., & Henri, V. (1896). La psychologie in-dividuelle. *L'Annee Psychologique, 2*, 411–465.

Binet, A., & Simon, T. (1905a). Sur la necessite d/etablit un diagnostic scientifique des etats inferieurs de l'intelligence. *L'Annee Psychologique, 11*, 163–190.

Binet, A., & Simon, T. (1905b). Methodes nou-velles pour le disagnostic du niveau intellec-tual des anormaux. *L'Annee Psychologique, 11*, 191–244.

Binet, A., & Simon, T. (1905c). Application des methodes nouvelles au diagnostic du niveau intellectual chez des enfants normaux et anor-maux d'hospice et d'ecole primaire. *L'Annee Psychologique, 11*, 245–336.

Bird, T. (1990). The schoolteacher's portfolio: An essay on possibilities. In J. Millman & L. Darling-Hammond (Eds.), *Handbook of teacher evaluation: Elementary and secondary personnel, second edition* (pp. 241–256). Newbury Park, CA: Sage.

Bishop, B. A., & Anderson, C. W. (1990). Student conceptions of natural selection and its role in evolution. *Journal of Research in Science Teaching, 27*, 415–427.

Bissex, G. (1980). *GNYS at work: A child learns to write and read.* Cambridge MA: Harvard University Press.

Bjorklund, D. F. (1985). The role of conceptual knowledge in the development of organiza-tion in children's memory. In C. J. Brainerd & M. Pressley (Eds.), *Basic processes in memory de-velopment: Progress in cognitive development re-search* (pp. 103–142). New York: Springer-Verlag.

Bjorklund, D. F. (1987a). A note on neonatal imi-tation. *Developmental Review, 7*, 86–92.

Bjorklund, D. F. (1987b). How age changes in knowledge base contribute to the develop-ment of children's memory: An interpretive review. *Developmental Review, 7*, 93–130.

Bjorklund, D. F. (1988). Acquiring a mnemonic: Age and category knowledge effects. *Journal of Experimental Child Psychology, 45*, 71–87.

Bjorklund, D. F. (1989). *Cognitive development.* Monterey, CA: Brooks/Cole.

Bjorklund, D. F., & Buchanen, J. J. (1989). Developmental and knowledge base differ-ences in the acquisition and extension of a memory strategy. *Journal of Experimental Child Psychology, 48*, 451–471.

Bjorklund, D. F., & Harnishfeger, K. K. (1987). Developmental differences in the mental ef-fort requirements for the use of an organiza-tional strategy in free recall. *Journal of Experimental Child Psychology, 44*, 109–125.

Bjorklund, D. F., & Harnishfeger, K. K. (1990). The resources construct in cognitive develop-ment: Diverse resources of evidence and a theory of inefficient inhibition. *Developmental Review, 10*, 48–71.

Blachman, B. A. (1991). Phonological awareness: Implications for prereading and early reading instruction. In S. A. Brady & D. P. Shankweiler (Eds.), *Phonological processes in lit-eracy: A tribute to Isabelle Y. Liberman* (pp. 29–36). Hillsdale, NJ: Erlbaum & Associates.

Black, J. E., & Greenough, W. T. (1991). Developmental approaches to the memory process. In J. L. Martinez Jr., & R. P. Kesner (Eds.), *Learning and memory: A biological view,* 2nd ed. (pp. 61–91). San Diego: Academic Press.

Black, K. (1989). Audience analysis and persua-sive writing at the college level. *Research in the Teaching of English, 23*, 231–253.

Blackman, L. S., & Lin, A. (1984). Generalization training in the educable mentally retarded: Intelligence and its educability revisited. In P. H. Brooks, R. Sperber, & C. McCauley (Eds.), *Learning and cognition in the mentally retarded* (pp. 237–263). Hillsdale, NJ: Erlbaum & Associates.

Blackwood, R. (1970). The operant conditioning of verbally mediated self-control in the class-room. *Journal of School Psychology, 8*, 257–258.

Blagg, N. (1991). *Can we teach intelligence?: A comprehensive evaluation of Feurstein's instru-mental enrichment program.* Hillsdale, NJ: Erlbaum & Associates.

Blakenay, R., & Blakenay, C. (1990). Reforming moral misbehaviour. *Journal of Moral Education, 19*, 101–113.

Blatt, M., & Kohlberg, L. (1975). The effects of classroom moral discussion upon children's level of moral judgment. *Journal of Moral Education, 4*, 129–161.

Bleakley, M. E., Westerberg, V., & Hopkins, K. D. (1988). The effect of character sex on story interest and comprehension in children. *American Educational Research Journal, 25*, 145–155.

Bliss, J. R. (1991). Strategic and holistic images of effective schools. In J. R. Bliss, W. A. Firestone, & C. E. Richards (Eds.), *Rethinking effective schools research and practice* (pp. 43–57). Englewood Cliffs, NJ: Prentice-Hall.

Block, N. J., & Dworkin, G. (Eds.) (1976). *The IQ controversy.* New York: Pantheon.

Bloom, A. (1987). *The closing of the American mind: How higher education has failed democracy and impoverished the souls of today's students.* New York: Simon & Schuster.

Bloom, B. S. (1968, May). Mastery learning. In *Evaluation comment* (Vol. 1, No. 2). Los Angeles: UCLA, Center for Evaluation of Instructional Programs.

Bloom, B. S. (1976). *Human characteristics and school learning.* New York: McGraw-Hill.

Bloom, B. S. (1985). *Developing talent in young people.* New York: Ballantine Books.

Bloom, B. S. (1987). A response to Slavin's Mastery Learning reconsidered. *Review of Educational Research, 57*, 507–508.

Bloom, L. (1973). *One word at a time.* The Hague, Netherlands: Mouton.

Blume, G. W., & Schoen, H. L. (1988). Mathematical problem-solving performance of eighth-grade programmers and nonpro-grammers. *Journal for Research in Mathematics Education, 19*, 142–156.

Blumenfeld, P. C. (1992). Classroom learning and motivation: Clarifying and expanding goal theory. *Journal of Educational Psychology, 84*, 272–281.

Bogatz, G. A., & Ball, S. (1971). *The second year of "Sesame Street": A continuing evaluation.* Princeton, NJ: Educational Testing Service.

Bogen, J. E. (1975). The other side of the brain. VII: Some educational aspects of hemispheric specialization. *UCLA Educator, 17*, 24–32.

Bolles, R. C. (1970). Species-specific defense re-actions and avoidance learning. *Psychological Review, 77*, 32–48.

Bomba, P. C., & Siqueland, E. R. (1983). The na-ture and structure of infant form categories. *Journal of Experimental Child Psychology, 35*, 294–328.

Bond, G. L., & Dykstra, R. (1967). The coopera-tive research program in first-grade reading instruction. *Reading Research Quarterly, 2*, 5–142.

Borko, H., Eisenhart, M., Brown, C. A., Underhill, R. G., Jones, D., & Agard, P. C. (1992). Learning to teach hard mathematics: Do novice teachers and their instructors give up too easily? *Journal for Research in Mathematics Education, 23*, 194–222.

Borko, H., & Livingston, C. (1989). Cognition and improvisation: Differences in mathemat-ics instruction by expert and novice teachers. *American Educational Research Journal, 26*, 473–498.

Borkowski, J. G. (1985). Signs of intelligence: Strategy, generalization, and metacognition. In S. R. Yussen (Ed.), *The growth of reflection in children* (pp. 105–144). Orlando, FL: Academic Press.

Borkowski, J. G., Carr, M., Rellinger, E. A., & Pressley, M. (1990). Self-regulated strategy use: Interdependence of metacognition, attri-butions, and self-esteem. In B. F. Jones (Ed.), *Dimensions of thinking: Review of research* (pp. 53–92). Hillsdale, NJ: Erlbaum & Associates.

Borkowski, J. G., & Kurtz, B. E. (1987). Metacognition and executive control. In J. G. Borkowski & J. D. Day (Eds.), *Cognition in spe-cial children: Comparative approaches to retarda-tion, learning disabilities, and giftedness* (pp. 123–152). Norwood, NJ: Ablex.

Borkowski, J. G., Levers, S., & Gruenenfelder, T. M. (1976). Transfer of mediational strategies in children: The role of activity and awareness during strategy acquisition. *Child Development, 47*, 779–786.

Borkowski, J. G., & Muthukrishna, N. (1992). Moving metacognition into the classroom: "Working models" and effective strategy teaching. In M. Pressley, K. R. Harris, & J. T. Guthrie (Eds.), *Promoting academic competence and literacy in schools* (pp. 477–501). San Diego: Academic Press.

Borkowski, J. G., & Peck, V. A. (1986). Causes and consequences of metamemory in gifted children. In R. J. Sternberg & J. E. Davidson (Eds.), *Conceptions of giftedness* (pp. 182–200). Cambridge, UK: Cambridge University Press.

Borkowski, J. G., Weyhing, R. S., & Carr, M. (1988). Effects of attributional retraining on strategy-based reading comprehension in learning-disabled students. *Journal of Educational Psychology, 80*, 46–53.

Bornstein, M. H., Kessen, W., & Weiskopf, S. (1976). Color vision and hue categorization in young infants. *Journal of Experimental Psychology: Human Perception and Performance, 2,* 115–129.

Bouchard, T. J., Jr., & McGue, M. (1981). Familial studies of intelligence: A review. *Science, 212,* 1055–1059.

Bowen, C. W. (1990). Representational systems used by graduate students while problem solving in organic synthesis. *Journal of Research in Science Teaching, 27,* 351–370.

Bower, G. H. (1972). Mental imagery and associative learning. In L. Gregg (Ed.), *Cognition in learning and memory* (pp. 51–87). New York: Wiley.

Bower, G. H., & Clapper, J. P. (1989). Experimental methods in cognitive science. In M. I. Posner (Ed.), *Foundations of cognitive science.* Cambridge, MA: MIT Press.

Bower, G. H., & Hilgard, E. R. (1981). *Theories of learning,* 5th ed. Englewood Cliffs, NJ: Prentice-Hall.

Bower, G. H., & Karlin, M. B. (1974). Depth of processing pictures of faces and recognition memory. *Journal of Experimental Psychology, 103,* 751–757.

Bowers, C. A., & Flinders, D. J. (1990). *Responsive teaching: An ecological approach to classroom patterns of language, culture, and thought.* New York: Teachers College Press.

Bowlby, J. (1969). *Attachment and loss,* Vol 1. *Attachment.* New York: Basic Books.

Bowsher, J. E. (1989). *Educating America: Lessons learned in the nation's corporations.* New York: John Wiley & Sons.

Boyd, D. R. (1988). Perspectives on moral education within the Canadian multicultural mosaic. *Journal of Moral Education, 17,* 148–160.

Boyes, M. C., & Chandler, M. (1992). Cognitive development, epistemic doubt, and identity formation in adolescence. *Journal of Youth and Adolescence, 21,* 277–304.

Boysen, S. T., & Berntson, G. G. (1990). The development of numerical skills in the chimpanzee (*Pan troglodytes*). In S. T. Parker & K. R. Gibson (Eds.), *"Language" and intelligence in monkeys and apes* (pp. 435–450). Cambridge, UK: Cambridge University Press.

Brabeck, M. M. (Guest Ed.) (1987). Special Issue: Feminist perspectives on moral education and development. *Journal of Moral Education, 16* (3).

Brabeck, M. M. (Ed.) (1989). *Who cares? Theory, research, and educational implications of the ethic of care.* New York: Praeger.

Bracht, G. H., & Glass, G. V. (1968). The external validity of experiments. *American Educational Research Journal, 5,* 437–474.

Bradley, L. (1988). Making connections in learning to read and to spell. *Applied Cognitive Psychology, 2,* 3–18.

Bradley, L. (1989). Predicting learning disabilities. In J. Dumont & H. Nakken (Eds.), *Learning disabilities,* Vol. 2, *Cognitive, social, and remedial aspects* (pp. 1–18). Amsterdam: Swets Publishing.

Bradley, L., & Bryant, P. E. (1983). Categorizing sounds and learning to read—a causal connection. *Nature, 301,* 419–421.

Bradley, L., & Bryant, P. (1985). *Rhyme and reason in reading and spelling.* International Academy for Research in Learning Disabilities Series. Ann Arbor, MI: University of Michigan Press.

Bradley, L., & Bryant, P. (1991). Phonological skills before and after learning to read. In S. A. Brady & D. P. Shankweiler (Eds.), *Phonological processes in literacy: A tribute to Isabelle Y. Liberman* (pp. 37–45). Hillsdale, NJ: Erlbaum & Associates.

Bradley, R. H., Caldwell, B. M., & Rock, S. L. (1988). Home environment and school performance: A ten-year follow-up and examination of three models of environmental action. *Child Development, 59,* 852–867.

Bradley, R. H., Caldwell, B. M., Rock, S. L., Ramey, C., Barnard, K. E., Hammond, M. A., Mitchell, S., Gottfried, A. W., Siegel, L., & Johnson, D. L. (1989). Home environment and cognitive development in the first 3 years of life: A collaborative study involving six sites and three ethnic groups in North America. *Developmental Psychology, 25,* 217–235.

Bradley, T. B. (1983). Remediation of cognitive deficits: A critical appraisal of the Feurstein model. *Journal of Mental Deficiency Research, 27,* 79–92.

Brainerd, C. J. (1978a). Learning research and Piagetian theory. In L. S. Siegel & C. J. Brainerd (Eds.), *Alternatives to Piaget: Critical essays on the theory* (pp. 69–109). New York: Academic Press.

Brainerd, C. J. (1978b). *Piaget's theory of intelligence.* Englewood Cliffs, NJ: Prentice-Hall.

Brainerd, C. J. (1978c). The stage question in cognitive developmental theory. *Behavioral and Brain Sciences, 1,* 173–213.

Branconnier, R. J. (1986). A computerized battery for behavioral assessment in Alzheimer's disease. In L. W. Poon (Ed.), *Handbook for clinical memory assessment of older adults* (pp. 189–196). Washington, DC: American Psychological Association.

Bransford, J. D., & Johnson, M. K. (1972). Contextual prerequisites for understanding: Some investigations of comprehension and recall. *Journal of Verbal Learning and Verbal Behavior, 11,* 717–726.

Bransford, J. D., Stein, B. S., Vye, N. J., Franks, J. J., Auble, P. M., Mezynski, K. J., & Perfetto, J. A. (1982). Differences in approaches to learning: An overview. *Journal of Experimental Psychology: General, 111,* 390–398.

Brasell, H. (1987). The effect of real-time laboratory graphing on learning graphic representations of distance and velocity. *Journal of Research in Science Teaching, 24,* 385–395.

Brennan, W. M., Ames, E. W., & Moore, R. W. (1966). Age differences in infants' attention to patterns of different complexity. *Science, 151,* 354–356.

Bretzing, B. H., & Kulhavy, R. W. (1981). Notetaking and passage styles. *Journal of Educational Psychology, 73,* 242–250.

Brewer, N. (1987). Processing speed, efficiency, and intelligence. In J. G. Borkowski & J. D. Day (Eds.), *Cognition in special children:*

Comparative approaches to retardation, learning disabilities, and giftedness (pp. 15–48). Norwood, NJ: Ablex.

Brewer, W. F. (1989). The activation and acquisition of knowledge. In S. Vosniadou & A. Ortony (Eds.), *Similarity and analogical reasoning* (pp. 532–545). Cambridge, UK: Cambridge University Press.

Brewer, W. F., & Liechtenstein, D. H. (1982). Stories are to entertain: A structural affect theory of stories. *Journal of Pragmatics, 6,* 473–486.

Breznitz, Z. (1987). Increasing first graders' reading accuracy and comprehension by accelerating their reading rates. *Journal of Educational Psychology, 79,* 236–242.

Breznitz, Z., & Share, D. L. (1992). Effects of accelerated reading rate on memory for text. *Journal of Educational Psychology, 84,* 193–199.

Brickhouse, N., & Bodner, G. M. (1992). The beginning science teacher: Classroom narratives of convictions and constraints. *Journal of Research in Science Teaching, 29,* 471–485.

Bridgeman, B., & Wendler, C. (1991). Gender differences in predictors of college mathematics performance and in college mathematics course grades. *Journal of Educational Psychology, 83,* 275–284.

Briggs, C., & Elkind, D. (1973). Cognitive development in early readers. *Developmental Psychology, 9,* 279–280.

Brigham, C. C. (1923). *A study of American intelligence.* Princeton, NJ: Princeton University Press.

Brigham, M. C., & Pressley, M. (1988). Cognitive monitoring and strategy choice in younger and older adults. *Psychology and Aging, 3,* 249–257.

Britton, B. K., & Gülgöz, S. (1991). Using Kintsch's computational model to improve instructional text: Effects of repairing inference calls on recall and cognitive structures. *Journal of Educational Psychology, 83,* 329–345.

Britton, B. K., & Tesser, A. (1991). Effects of time-management practices on college grades. *Journal of Educational Psychology, 83,* 405–410.

Britton, B. K., Van Dusen, L., & Gülgöz, S. (1991). Reply to "A response to 'instructional texts rewritten by five expert teams.'" *Journal of Educational Psychology, 83,* 149–152.

Britton, B. K., Van Dusen, L., Gülgöz, S., & Glynn, S. (1989). Instructional texts rewritten by five expert teams: Revisions and retention improvements. *Journal of Educational Psychology, 81,* 226–239.

Britton, B. K., Van Dusen, L., Gülgöz, S., Glynn, S. M., & Sharp, L. (1991). Accuracy of learnability judgments for instructional texts. *Journal of Educational Psychology, 83,* 43–47.

Brody, E. B., & Brody, N. (1978). *Intelligence: Nature, determinants, and consequences.* New York: Academic Press.

Brody, N. (1992). *Intelligence.* San Diego: Academic Press.

Brophy, J. (1981). Teacher praise: A functional analysis. *Review of Educational Research, 51,* 5–32.

Brophy, J. (1985). Teacher-student interaction. In

J. B. Dusek (Ed.), *Teacher expectancies* (pp. 303–328). Hillsdale, NJ: Erlbaum & Associates.

Brophy, J. (1986, October). *On motivating students.* Occasional Paper No. 101. East Lansing: Michigan State University, Institute for Research on Teaching.

Brophy, J. (1987). Socializing students' motivation to learning. In M. L. Maehr & D. A. Kleiber (Eds.), *Advances in motivation and achievement: Enhancing motivation,* Vol. 5 (pp. 181–210). Greenwich CT: JAI Press.

Brophy, J. (1988). Research linking teacher behavior to student achievement: Potential implications for instruction of Chapter 1 students. *Educational Psychologist, 23,* 235–286.

Brophy, J., & Evertson, C. (1976). *Learning from teaching: A developmental perspective.* Boston: Allyn & Bacon.

Brophy, J., & Good, T. (1970). Teachers' communication of differential expectations for children's classroom performance: Some behavioral data. *Journal of Educational Psychology, 61,* 365–374.

Brophy, J., & Good, T. (1974). *Teacher-student relationships: Causes and consequences.* New York: Holt, Rinehart, & Winston.

Brown, A. L. (1974). The role of strategic behavior in retardate memory. In N. R. Ellis (Ed.), *International review of research in mental retardation,* Vol. 7. New York: Academic Press.

Brown, A. L. (1978). Knowing when, where, and how to remember: A problem of metacognition. In R. Glaser (Ed.), *Advances in instructional psychology,* Vol. 1. Hillsdale, NJ: Erlbaum & Associates.

Brown, A. L. (1989). Analogical learning and transfer: What develops? In S. Vosniadou & A. Ortony (Eds.), *Similarity and analogical reasoning* (pp. 367–412). Cambridge, UK: Cambridge University Press.

Brown, A. L., Bransford, J. D., Ferrara, R. A., & Campione, J. C. (1983). Learning, remembering, and understanding. In J. H. Flavell & E. M. Markman (Eds.), *Handbook of child psychology,* Vol. III, *Cognitive development* (pp. 77–166). New York: Wiley.

Brown, A. L., & Campione, J. C. (1978). Permissible inferences from cognitive training studies in developmental research. In W. S. Hall & M. Cole (Eds.), *Quarterly Newsletter of the Institute for Comparative Human Behavior, 2 (3),* 46–53.

Brown, A. L., & Campione, J. C. (1990). Interactive learning environments and the teaching of science and mathematics. In M. Gardner, J. G. Greeno, F. Reif, A. H. Schoenfeld, A. DiSessa, & E. Stage (Eds.), *Toward a scientific practice of science education* (pp. 111–139). Hillsdale, NJ: Erlbaum & Associates.

Brown, A. L., & Day, J. D. (1983). Macrorules for summarizing texts: The development of expertise. *Journal of Verbal Learning and Verbal Behavior, 22,* 1–14.

Brown, A. L., Day, J. D., & Jones, R. S. (1983). The development of plans for summarizing texts. *Child Development, 54,* 968–979.

Brown, A. L., & French, L. (1979). The zone of proximal development: Implications for intelligence testing in the year 2000. *Intelligence, 3,* 253–271.

Brown, A. L., & Kane, K. J. (1988). Preschool children can learn to transfer: Learning to learn and learning from example. *Cognitive Psychology, 20,* 493–523.

Brown, A. L., Kane, M. J., & Echols, K. (1986). Young children's mental models determine analogical transfer across problems with a common goal structure. *Cognitive Development, 1,* 103–122.

Brown, A. L., Kane, M. J., & Long, C. (1989). Analogical transfer in young children: Analogies as tools for communication and exposition. *Applied Cognitive Psychology, 3,* 275–294.

Brown, A. L., & Palincsar, A. S. (1989). Guided, cooperative learning and individual knowledge acquisition. In L. B. Resnick (Ed.), *Knowing, learning, and instruction: Essays in honor of Robert Glaser* (pp. 393–451). Hillsdale, NJ: Erlbaum & Associates.

Brown, A. L., & Smiley, S. S. (1978). The development of strategies for studying texts. *Child Development, 49,* 1076–1088.

Brown, B. B. (1988). The vital agenda for research and extracurricular influences: A reply to Holland and Andre. *Review of Educational Research, 58,* 107–111.

Brown, D. E. (1992). Using example and analogies to remediate misconceptions in physics: Factors influencing conceptual change. *Journal of Research in Science Teaching, 29,* 17–34.

Brown, I. (1976). Role of referent concreteness in the acquisition of passive sentence comprehension through abstract modeling. *Journal of Experimental Child Psychology, 22,* 185–189.

Brown, I. (1979). Language acquisition: Linguistic structure and rule-governed behavior. In G. J. Whitehurst & B. J. Zimmerman (Eds.), *The functions of language and cognition* (pp. 141–173). New York: Academic Press.

Brown, J. S., Collins, A., & Duguid, P. (1989). Situated cognition and the culture of learning. *Educational Researcher, 18 (1),* 32–42.

Brown, M. C., Hopkins, W. G., & Keynes, R. J. (1991). *Essentials of neural development.* Cambridge, UK: Cambridge University Press.

Brown, R. (1973). A first language: The early stages. Cambridge, MA: Harvard University Press.

Brown, R. G. (1991). *Schools of thought.* San Francisco: Jossey-Bass.

Brown, R. T., Armstrong, F. D., & Eckman, J. R. (1993). Neurocognitive aspects of pediatric sickle cell disease. *Journal of Learning Disabilities, 26,* 33–45.

Brown, R. T., & Madan-Swain, A. (1993). Cognitive, neuropsychological, and academic sequelae in children with leukemia. *Journal of Learning Disabilities, 26,* 74–91.

Brownell, W. A. (1928). The development of children's number ideas in the primary grades. *Supplement to Education Monographs,* No. 35.

Bruce, B. (1983). A new point of view on children's stories. In R. C. Anderson, J. Osborn, & R. J. Tierney (Eds.), *Learning to read in American schools* (pp. 153–174). Hillsdale, NJ: Erlbaum & Associates.

Bruck, M. (1990). Word-recognition skills of adults with childhood diagnoses of dyslexia. *Developmental Psychology, 26,* 439–454.

Bruck, M. (1992). Persistence of dyslexics' phonological awareness deficits. *Developmental Psychology, 28,* 874–886.

Bruck, M., & Treiman, R. (1990). Phonological awareness and spelling in normal children and dyslexics: The case of initial consonant clusters. *Journal of Experimental Child Psychology, 50,* 156–178.

Bruck, M., & Treiman, R. (1992). Learning to pronounce words: The limits of analogies. *Reading Research Quarterly, 27,* 374–398.

Bruner, J. S., Olver, R. R., & Greenfield, P. M. (1966). *Studies in cognitive growth.* New York: Wiley.

Brust, J. C. M. (1991). Cerebral circulation: Stroke. In E. R. Kandel, J. H. Schwartz, & T. M. Jessel (Eds.), *Principles of neural science* (pp. 1041–1049). New York: Elsevier.

Bryant, D. M., Clifford, R. M., & Peisner, E. S. (1991). Best practices for beginners: Developmental appropriateness in kindergarten. *American Educational Research Journal, 28,* 783–803.

Bryant, N. R. (1982). *Preschool children's learning and transfer of matrices problems: A study of proximal distance.* Unpublished master's thesis, University of Illinois, Urbana. (Reported in Campione & Brown, 1987.)

Bryant, N. R., Brown, A. L., & Campione, J. C. (1983, April). *Preschool children's learning and transfer of matrices problems.* Paper presented at the Society for Research in Child Development meetings, Detroit.

Bryant, P. E., & Bradley, L. (1980). Why children sometimes write words which they do not read. In U. Frith (Ed.), *Cognitive processes in spelling* (pp. 355–370). San Diego: Academic Press.

Bryk, A. S., & Thum, Y. M. (1989). The effects of high school organization on dropping out: An exploratory investigation. *American Educational Research Journal, 26,* 353–383.

Budoff, M. (1987a). Measures for assessing learning potential. In C. S. Lidz (Ed.), *Dynamic assessment: An interactional approach to evaluating learning potential* (173–195). New York: Guilford Press.

Budoff, M. (1987b). The validity of learning potential assessment. In C. S. Lidz (Ed.), *Dynamic assessment: An interactional approach to evaluating learning potential* (pp. 52–81). New York: Guilford Press.

Budoff, M., & Friedman, M. (1964). Learning potential as an assessment approach to the adolescent mentally retarded. *Journal of Consulting Psychology, 28,* 434–439.

Budoff, M., Gimon, A., & Corman, L. (1974). Learning potential measurement with Spanish-speaking youth as an alternative to IQ tests: A first report. *Intraamerican Journal of Psychology, 8,* 233–246.

Bugelski, B. R. (1962). Presentation time, total time, and mediation in paired-associate learning. *Journal of Experimental Psychology, 79,* 383–384.

Bugenthal, D. B., Whalen, C. K., & Henker, B. (1977). Causal attributions of hyperactive children and motivational assumptions of two behavior-change approaches: Evidence for an interactionist position. *Child Development, 48,* 874–884.

Buhrmester, D., Camparo, L., Christensen, A., Gonzalez, L. S., & Hinshaw, S. P. (1992). Mothers and fathers interacting in dyads and triads with normal and hyperactive sons. *Developmental Psychology, 28,* 500–509.

Bulgren, J. A., McKnight, P., Deshler, D. D., & Schumaker, J. B. (1989). *The 1989 INROADS program report.* Lawrence, KS: University of Kansas, Institute for Research in Learning Disabilities.

Burack, J. A. (1990). Differentiating mental retardation: The two-group approach and beyond. In R. M. Hodapp, J. A. Burdack, & E. Zigler (Eds.), *Issues in the developmental approach to mental retardation* (pp. 27–48). Cambridge, UK: Cambridge University Press.

Burbules, N. C., & Linn, M. C. (1988). Response to contradiction: Scientific reasoning during adolescence. *Journal of Educational Psychology, 80,* 67–75.

Burchinal, M., Lee, M., & Ramey, C. (1989). Type of day-care and preschool intellectual development in disadvantaged children. *Child Development, 60,* 128–137.

Burden, R. L. (1987). Feurstein's Instrumental Enrichment program: Important issues in research and evaluation. *European Journal of Psychology of Education, 2,* 3–16.

Burgess, D. M., & Streissguth, A. P. (1992). Fetal alcohol syndrome and fetal alcohol effects: Principles for educators. *Phi Delta Kappan, 74,* 24–30.

Burkell, J., Schneider, B., & Pressley, M. (1990). Mathematics. In M. Pressley & Associates, *Cognitive strategy instruction that really improves children's academic performance* (pp. 147–177). Cambridge, MA: Brookline Books.

Burt, C. (1966). The genetic discrimination of differences in intelligence: A study of monozygotic twins reared together and apart. *British Journal of Psychology, 57,* 137–53.

Bus, A. G., & Van Ijzendoorn, M. H. (1988). Mother-child interactions, attachment, and emergent literacy: A cross-sectional study. *Child Development, 59,* 1262–1272.

Buschke, H., & Schaier, A. H. (1979). Memory units, ideas, and propositions in semantic remembering. *Journal of Verbal Learning and Verbal Behavior, 18,* 549–564.

Bush, G. W. (1991). *America 2000: An educational strategy.* Washington DC: U. S. Department of Education.

Butkowski, I. S., & Willows, D. M. (1980). Cognitive-motivational characteristics of children varying in reading ability: Evidence for learned helplessness in poor readers. *Journal of Educational Psychology, 72,* 408–422.

Butler, S. R., Marsh, H. W., Sheppard, M. J., &
Sheppard, J. L. (1985). Seven-year longitudinal study of the early prediction of reading achievement. *Journal of Educational Psychology, 77,* 349–361.

Butler-Nalin, K. (1984). Revising patterns in students' writing. In A. N. Applebee (Ed.), *Contexts for learning to write: Studies of secondary school instruction* (pp. 121–133). Norwood, NJ: Ablex.

Butterfield, E. C., & Belmont, J. M. (1977). Assessing and improving the executive cognitive functions of mentally retarded people. In I. Bialar & M. Sternlicht (Eds.), *Psychological issues in mental retardation* (pp. 277–318). New York: Psychological Dimensions.

Butterfield, E. C., & Nelson, G. D. (1991). Promoting positive transfer of different types. *Cognition and Instruction, 8,* 69–102.

Byrne, B., & Fielding-Barnsley, R. (1990). Acquiring the alphabetic principle: A case for teaching recognition of phoneme identity. *Journal of Educational Psychology, 82,* 805–812.

Byrne, B., & Fielding-Barnsley, R. (1991). Evaluation of a program to teach phonemic awareness to young children. *Journal of Educational Psychology, 83,* 451–455.

Byrne, B., Freebody, P., & Gates, A. (1992). Longitudinal data on the relations of word-reading strategies to comprehension, reading time, and phonemic awareness. *Reading Research Quarterly, 27,* 140–151.

Byrnes, J. P. (1988). Formal operations: A systematic reformulation. *Developmental Review, 8,* 1–22.

Byrnes, J. P. (1992). The conceptual basis of procedural learning. *Cognitive Development, 7,* 235–257.

Byrnes, J. P., & Wasik, B. A. (1991). Role of conceptual knowledge in mathematical procedural learning. *Developmental Psychology, 27,* 777–786.

Cahan, S., & Cohen, N. (1989). Age versus schooling effects on intelligence development. *Child Development, 60,* 1239–1249.

Cahen, S., & Davis, D. (1987). A between-grade-levels approach to the investigation of the absolute effects of schooling on achievement. *American Educational Research Association, 24,* 1–13.

Cairns, R. B., Cairns, B. D., & Neckerman, H. J. (1989). Early school dropout: Configurations and determinants. *Child Development, 60,* 1437–1452.

Calderhead, J. (1983, April). *Research into teachers' and student teachers' cognitions: Exploring the nature of classroom practice.* Paper presented at the annual meeting of the American Educational Research Association, Montreal.

Calderhead, J., & Robson, M. (1991). Images of teaching: Student teachers' early conceptions of classroom practice. *Teaching & Teacher Education, 7,* 1–8.

Calfee, R. C., & Chambliss, M. J. (1987). The structural design features of large texts.

Calfee, R. C., Chapman, R., & Venezsky, R. (1972). How a child needs to think to learn to
read. In L. W. Gregg (Ed.), *Cognition in learning and memory.* New York: Wiley.

Calfee, R. C., Lindamood, P., & Lindamood, C. (1973). Acoustic-phonetic skills and reading—kindergarten through twelfth grade. *Journal of Educational Psychology, 64,* 293–298.

California Assessment Program (1982). *Surveys of sixth grade school achievement and television viewing habits.* Sacramento: California State Department of Education.

California Assessment Program (1988). *Annual report: 1985–86.* Sacramento: California State Department of Education.

California State Department of Education (1990). *California Assessment Program.* Sacramento: California State Department of Education.

Calkins, L. M. (1986). *The art of teaching writing.* Portsmouth, NH: Heinemann.

Camp, B. W., Blom, G. E., Hebert, F., & van Doornick, W. J. (1977). "Think aloud": A program for developing self-control in young aggressive boys. *Journal of Abnormal Child Psychology, 5,* 157–169.

Camp, C. J., & McKitrick, L. A. (1992). Memory interventions in Alzheimer's-type dementia populations: Methodological and theoretical issues. In R. L. West & J. D. Sinnott (Eds.), *Everyday memory and aging: Current research and methodology* (pp. 155–172). New York: Springer-Verlag.

Campbell, D. T., & Fiske, D. W. (1959). Convergent and discriminant validation by the multitrait-multimethod matrix. *Psychological Bulletin, 56,* 81–105.

Campbell, D. T., & Stanley, J. C. (1966). *Experimental and quasi-experimental designs for research.* Chicago: Rand-McNally.

Campbell, J. I. D., & Charness, N. (1990). Age-related declines in working-memory skills: Evidence from a complex calculation task. *Developmental Psychology, 26,* 879–888.

Campbell, J. I. D., & Graham, D. J. (1985). Mental multiplication skill: Structure, process, and acquisition. *Canadian Journal of Psychology, 39,* 338–366.

Campbell, T. A. (1987). Form cues and content difficulty as determinants of children's cognitive processing of televised educational messages. *Journal of Experimental Child Psychology, 43,* 311–327.

Campbell, T. A., Wright, J. C., & Huston, A. C. (1987). Form cues and content difficulty as determinants of children's cognitive processing of televised education messages. *Journal of Experimental Child Psychology, 43,* 311–327.

Campione, J. C., & Brown, A. L. (1987). Linking dynamic assessment and school achievement. In C. S. Lidz (Ed.), *Dynamic assessment: An interactional approach to evaluating learning potential* (pp. 82–115). New York: Guilford Press.

Cannell, J. J. (1987). *Nationally normed elementary achievement testing in America's public schools: How fifty states are above the national average.* Daniels, WV: Friends for Education.

Cannell, J. J. (1989). *How public educators cheat on standardized achievement tests.* Albuquerque, NM: Friends for Education.

Cantor, N., Markus, H., Niedenthal, P., & Nurius, P. (1986). On motivation and self-concept. In R. M. Sorrentino & E. T. Higgins (Eds.), *Motivation and cognition: Foundations of social behavior* (pp. 99–127). New York: Guilford.

Caplan, D. (1992). *Language: Structure, processing, and disorders.* Cambridge, MA: MIT Press.

Capron, C. (1987). Analyse génetique et méthode des adoptions. *Psychologie Francaise, 31,* 267–274.

Capron, C., & Duyme, M. (1989). Assessments of effects of socioeconomic status on IQ in a full cross-fostering study. *Nature, 340,* 552–553.

Cardelle-Elawar, M. (1990). Effects of feedback tailored to bilingual students' mathematics needs on verbal problem solving. *Elementary School Journal, 91,* 165–175.

Cardon, L. R., DiLalla, L. F., Plomin, R., DeFries, J. C., & Fulker, D. W. (1990). Genetic correlations between reading performance and IQ in the Colorado adoption project. *Intelligence, 14,* 245–257.

Carey, S. (1985). *Conceptual change in childhood.* Cambridge, MA: MIT Press.

Carey, S., Evans, R., Honda, M., Jay, E., & Unger, C. (1989). "An experiment is when you try and see if it works": a study of grade 7 students' understanding of the construction of scientific knowledge. *International Journal of Science Education, 11,* 514–529.

Cariglia-Bull, T., & Pressley, M. (1990). Short-term memory differences between children predict imagery effects when sentences are read. *Journal of Experimental Child Psychology, 49,* 384–398.

Carlson, J. S., & Widaman, K. F. (1987). Elementary cognitive correlates of g: Progress and prospects. In P. A. Vernon (Ed.), *Speed of information-processing and intelligence* (pp. 69–99). Hillsdale, NJ: Erlbaum & Associates.

Carney, R. N., Levin, J. R., & Morrison, C. R. (1988). Mnemonic learning of artists and their paintings. *American Educational Research Journal, 25,* 107–125.

Carpenter, T. P. (1985). Learning to add and subtract: An exercise in problem solving. In E. A. Silver (Ed.), *Teaching and learning mathematical problem solving: Multiple research perspectives* (pp. 17–40). Hillsdale, NJ: Erlbaum & Associates.

Carpenter, T. P., Fennema, E., Peterson, P. L., & Carey, D. A. (1988). Teachers' pedagogical content knowledge of students' problem solving in elementary arithmetic. *Journal for Research in Mathematics Education, 19,* 385–401.

Carpenter, T. P., Fennema, E., Peterson, P. L., Chiang, C-P, & Loef, M. (1989). Using knowledge of children's mathematics thinking in classroom teaching: An experimental study. *American Educational Research Journal, 26,* 499–531.

Carpenter, T. P., Hiebert, J., & Moser, J. M. (1981). Problem structure and first-grade children's initial solution processes for simple addition and subtraction problems. *Journal for Research in Mathematics Education, 12,* 27–39.

Carpenter, T. P., Hiebert, J., & Moser, J. M. (1983). The effect of instruction on children's solutions of addition and subtraction word problems. *Educational Studies in Mathematics, 14,* 55–72.

Carpenter, T. P., & Moser, J. M. (1982). The development of addition and subtraction problem-solving skills. In T. P. Carpenter, J. M. Moser, & T. A. Romberg (Eds.), *Addition and subtraction: A cognitive perspective* (pp. 9–24). Hillsdale, NJ: Erlbaum & Associates.

Carpenter, T. P., & Moser, J. M. (1983). The acquisition of addition and subtraction concepts. In R. Lesh & M. Landau (Eds.), *The acquisition of mathematics concepts and processes* (pp. 7–44). New York: Academic Press.

Carr, J. (1975). *Young children with Down syndrome.* London: Butterworth.

Carr, J. (1985). The effect of the family of a severely mentally handicapped child. In A. M. Clarke, A. D. B. Clarke, & J. M. Berg (Eds.), *Mental deficiency: The changing outlook* (4th ed.) (pp. 512–548). New York: Free Press.

Carr, M., & Borkowski, J. G. (1989). Attributional training and the generalization of reading strategies with underachieving children. *Learning and Individual Differences, 1,* 327–341.

Carr, M., Borkowski, J. G., & Maxwell, S. E. (1991). Motivational components of underachievement. *Developmental Psychology, 27,* 108–118.

Carr, M., Kurtz, B. E., Schneider, W., Turner, L. A., & Borkowski, J. G. (1989). Strategy acquisition and transfer: Environmental influences on metacognitive development. *Developmental Psychology, 25,* 765–771.

Carraher, T. N., Carraher, D. W., & Schliemann, A. D. (1985). Mathematics in the street and in schools. *British Journal of Developmental Psychology, 3,* 21–29.

Carroll, J. (1963). A model of school learning. *Teachers College Record, 64,* 723–733.

Carson, M. T., & Abrahamson, A. (1976). Some members are more equal than others: The effect of semantic typicality on class-inclusion performance. *Child Development, 47,* 1186–1190.

Carter, K. (1990). Teachers' knowledge and learning to teach. In W. R. Houston (Ed.), *Handbook of research on teacher education* (pp. 291–310). New York: Macmillan.

Carter, K., Cushing, K., Sabers, D., Stein, P., & Berliner, D. (1988). Expert-novice differences in perceiving and processing visual classroom information. *Journal of Teacher Education, 39,* 25–31.

Carter, K., Sabers, D., Cushing, K., Pinnegar, S., & Berliner, D. C. (1987). Processing and using information about students: A study of expert, novice, and postulant teachers. *Teaching & Teacher Education, 3,* 147–157.

Carver, R. P. (1990). *Reading rate: A review of research and theory.* San Diego: Academic Press.

Case, R. (1974). Structures and strictures: Some functional limitations on the course of cognitive growth. *Cognitive Psychology, 6,* 544–573.

Case, R. (1985). *Intellectual development: Birth to adulthood.* Orlando, FL: Academic Press.

Case, R. (1991). A developmental approach to the design of remedial instruction. In A. McKeough & J. L. Lupart (Eds.), *Toward the practice of theory-based instruction* (pp. 117–147). Hillsdale, NJ: Erlbaum & Associates.

Casserly, P. (1980). An assessment of factors affecting female participation in advanced placement programs in mathematics, chemistry, and physics. In L. H. Fox, L. Brody, & D. Tobin (Eds.), *Women and the mathematical mystique* (pp. 138–163). Baltimore: Johns Hopkins University Press.

Cattell, J. M. (1890). Mental tests and measurement. *Mind, 15,* 373–380.

Cattell, J. M., & Farand, L. (1890). Physical and mental measurements of the students of Columbia University. *Psychological Review, 3,* 618–648.

Cattell, R. B. (1987). *Intelligence: Its structure, growth, and action.* Amsterdam: North-Holland.

Cattell, R. B., & Horn, J. L. (1978). A check on the theory of fluid and crystallized intelligence with description of new subtest designs. *Journal of Educational Measurement, 15,* 139–164.

Cautela, J. R. (1967). Covert sensitization. *Psychological Reports, 20,* 459–468.

Cavanaugh, J. C., & Borkowski, J. G. (1979). The metamemory-memory "connection": Effects of strategy training and maintenance. *Journal of General Psychology, 101,* 161–174.

Cazden, C. B. (1988). *Classroom discourse: The language of teaching and learning.* Portsmouth, NH: Heinemann.

Ceci, S. J. (1991). How much does schooling influence general intelligence and its cognitive components? A reassessment of the evidence. *Developmental Psychology, 27,* 703–722.

Ceci, S. J., & Liker, J. K. (1986). A day at the races: A study of IQ, expertise, and cognitive complexity. *Journal of Experimental Psychology: General, 115,* 255–266.

Ceci, S. J., Ross, D. F., & Toglia, M. P. (1989). *Perspectives on children's testimony.* New York: Springer-Verlag.

Celano, M. P., & Geller, R. J. (1993). Learning, school performance, and children with asthma: How much at risk? *Journal of Learning Disabilities, 26,* 23–32.

Chall, J. S. (1967). *Learning to read: The great debate.* New York: McGraw-Hill.

Chall, J. S., Conard, S. S., & Harris–Sharples, S. (1991). *Should textbooks challenge students? The case for easier and harder books.* New York: Teachers College Press.

Chambliss, M. J., & Calfee, R. C. (1989). Designing science textbooks to enhance student understanding. *Educational Psychology, 24,* 307–322.

Champagne, A. B., & Bunce, D. M. (1991). Learning-theory-based science teaching. In S. M. Glynn, R. H. Yeany, & B. K. Britton (Eds.), *The psychology of learning science* (pp. 21–41). Hillsdale, NJ: Erlbaum & Associates.

Chan, C. K. K., Burtis, P. J., Scardamalia, M., &

Bereiter, C. (1992). Constructive activity in learning from text. *American Educational Research Journal, 29,* 97–118.

Chandler Press (1988). *Early American school books.* Maynard, MA: Chandler Press.

Chapman, J. W. (1988). Cognitive-motivational characteristics and academic achievement of learning disabled children: A longitudinal analysis. *Journal of Educational Psychology, 80,* 357–365.

Chapman, M., & Lindenberger, U. (1989). Concrete operations and attentional capacity. *Journal of Experimental Child Psychology, 47,* 236–258.

Chapman, M., Skinner, E. A., & Baltes, P. B. (1990). Interpreting correlations between children's perceived control and cognitive performance: Control, agency, or means–ends beliefs? *Developmental Psychology, 26,* 246–253.

Charles, D. C. (1989). The old age of some eminent psychologists. *Educational Psychology Review, 1,* 369–380.

Charles, R. I., & Lester, F. K., Jr. (1984). An evaluation of a process-oriented instructional program in mathematical problem solving in grades 5 and 7. *Journal for Research in Mathematics Education, 15,* 15–34.

Charles, R. I., & Silver, E. A. (Eds.) (1989). *The teaching and assessing of mathematical problem solving,* Vol. 3. Hillsdale, NJ: Erlbaum & Associates and National Council of Teachers of Mathematics.

Charlop, M. H., & Milstein, J. P. (1989). Teaching autistic children conversational speech using video modeling. *Journal of Applied Behavior Analysis, 22,* 275–285.

Charness, N. (1989). Expertise in chess and bridge. In D. Klahr & K. Kotovsky (Eds.), *Complex information processing: The impact of Herbert A. Simon* (pp. 183–208). Hillsdale, NJ: Erlbaum & Associates.

Charney, D. (1993). A study in rhetorical reading: How evolutionists read "The Spandrels of San Marco." In J. Selzer (Ed.), *Understanding scientific prose.* Madison, WI: University of Wisconsin Press.

Chase, H. (1973). The effects of intrauterine and postnatal undernutrition on normal brain development. *Annals of the New York Academy of Sciences, 205,* 231–244.

Chase, W. G., & Ericsson, K. A. (1981). Skilled memory. In J. R. Anderson (Ed.), *Cognitive skills and their acquisition.* Hillsdale, NJ: Erlbaum & Associates.

Chase, W. G., & Ericsson, K. A. (1982). Skill and working memory. In G. H. Bower (Ed.), *The psychology of learning and motivation,* Vol. 16. New York: Academic Press.

Chase, W. G., & Simon, H. A. (1973). Perception in chess. *Cognitive Psychology, 4,* 55–81.

Chen, C., & Stevenson, H. W. (1989). Homework: A cross-cultural examination. *Child Development, 60,* 551–561.

Chen, Z., & Daehler, M. W. (1989). Positive and negative transfer in analogical problem solving by 6-year-old children. *Cognitive Development, 4,* 327–344.

Chen, Z., & Daehler, M. W. (1992). Intention and outcome: Key components of causal structure facilitating mapping in children's analogical transfer. *Journal of Experimental Child Psychology, 53,* 237–257.

Cheney, L. V. (1987). *American memory: A report of the humanities in the Nation's public schools.* Washington, DC: National Endowment for the Humanities.

Cheyne, J. A., & Walters, R. H. (1969). Intensity of punishment, timing of punishment, and cognitive structure as determinants of response inhibition. *Journal of Experimental Child Psychology, 7,* 231–244.

Chi, M. T. H. (1978). Knowledge structure and memory development. In R. S. Siegler (Ed.), *Children's thinking: What develops?* (pp. 73–96). Hillsdale, NJ: Erlbaum & Associates.

Chi, M. T. H., & Bassok, M. (1989). Learning from examples via self-explanations. In L. B. Resnick (Ed.), *Knowing, learning, and instruction: Essays in honor of Robert Glaser* (pp. 251–282). Hillsdale, NJ: Erlbaum & Associates.

Chi, M. T. H., Bassok, M., Lewis, M., Reimann, M., & Glaser, R. (1989). Self-explanations: How students study and use examples in learning to solve problems. *Cognitive Science, 13,* 145–182.

Chi, M. T. H., Feltovich, P. J., & Glaser, R. (1981). Categorization and representation of physics problems by experts and novices. *Cognitive Science, 5,* 121–152.

Chi, M. T. H., Glaser, R., & Farr, M. J. (1988). *The nature of expertise.* Hillsdale, NJ: Erlbaum & Associates.

Chiesi, L., Spilich, G. J., & Voss, J. F. (1979). Acquisition of domain-related information in relation to high and low domain knowledge. *Journal of Verbal Learning and Verbal Behavior, 18,* 257–273.

Childs, C. P., & Greenfield, P. M. (1980). Informal modes of learning and teaching: the case of Zinecanteco weaving. In N. Warren (Ed.), *Studies in cross-cultural psychology,* Vol. 2 (pp. 269–316). London: Academic.

Chipeur, H. M., Rovine, M. J., & Plomin, R. (1990). LISREL modeling: Genetic and environmental influences on IQ revisited. *Intelligence, 14,* 11–29.

Chittenden, E. (1991). Authentic assessment, evaluation, and documentation of student performance. In V. Perrone (Ed.). *Expanding student assesment* (pp. 22–31). Alexandria, VA: Association for Supervision and Curriculum Development.

Chomsky, N. (1965). *Aspects of the theory of syntax.* Cambridge, MA: MIT Press.

Chomsky, N. (1980a). Initial states and steady states. In M. Paittelli-Palmarini (Ed.), *Language and learning: The debate between Jean Piaget and Noam Chomsky* (pp. 97–130). Cambridge, MA: Harvard University Press.

Chomsky, N. (1980b). Rules and representations. *Behavioral and Brain Sciences, 3,* 1–61.

Christensen, C. A., & Cooper, T. J. (1991). The effectiveness of instruction in cognitive strategies in developing proficiency in single-digit addition. *Cognition and Instruction, 8,* 363–371.

Churchland, P. S., & Sejnowski, T. J. (1992). *The computational brain.* Cambridge, MA: MIT Press.

Ciborowski, J. (1993). *Textbooks and the students who can't read them: A guide for teaching content.* Cambridge, MA: Brookline Books.

Cipielewski, J., & Stanovich, K. E. (1992). Predicting growth in reading ability from children's exposure to print. *Journal of Experimental Child Psychology, 54,* 74–89.

Clandeinin, D. J. (1986). *Classroom practice: Teacher images in action.* London: Falmer Press.

Clark, E. V. (1973). What's in a word? On the child's acquisition of semantics in his first language. In T. E. Moore (Ed.), *Cognitive development and the acquisition of language* (pp. 65–110). New York: Academic Press.

Clark, H. H., & Clark, E. V. (1977). *Psychology and language.* New York: Harcourt, Brace, Jovanovich.

Clark, J. M., & Paivio, A. (1991). Dual coding theory and education. *Educational Psychology Review, 3,* 149–210.

Clark, M. M. (1976). *Young fluent readers: What can they teach us?* London: Heinemann.

Clarke, A. M. (1985). Polygenic and environmental interactions. In A. M. Clarke, A. D. B. Clarke, & J. M. Berg (Eds.), *Mental deficiency: The changing outlook* (4th ed.) (pp. 267–290). New York: Free Press.

Clarke, A. M., Clarke, A. D. B., & Berg, J. M. (1985). *Mental deficiency: The changing outlook* (4th ed.). New York: Free Press.

Clay, M. M. (1985). *The early detection of reading difficulties: A diagnostic survey with recovery procedure.* Portsmouth, NH: Heinemann.

Clay, M. M. (1991). *Becoming literate: The construction of inner control.* Portsmouth, NH: Heinemann.

Clay, M. M., & Cazden, C. B. (1990). A Vygotskian interpretation of Reading Recovery. In L. C. Moll (Ed.), *Vygotsky and education: Instructional implications and applications of sociohistorical psychology* (pp. 206–222). Cambridge, UK: Cambridge University Press.

Cleary, T. A., Humphreys, L. G., Kendrick, S. A., & Wesman, A. G. (1975). Educational uses of tests with disadvantaged students. *American Psychologist, 30,* 15–41.

Clement, J. (1982). Students' preconceptions in introductory mechanics. *American Journal of Physics, 50,* 66–71.

Clement, J., with the assistance of Brown, D., Camp, C., Kudukey, J., Minstrell, J., Palmer, D., Schultz, K., Shimabukuro, J., Steinberg, M., & Veneman, V. (1987). Overcoming students' misconceptions in physics: The role of anchoring intuitions and analogical validity. In J. Novak (Ed.), *Proceedings of the second international seminar: misconceptions and educational strategies in science and mathematics,* Vol. III (pp. 84–97). Ithaca, NY: Cornell University Press.

Clement, J., Brown, D. E., & Zeitsman, A. (1989). Not all preconceptions are misconceptions: finding 'anchoring conceptions' for grounding instruction on students' intuition. *International Journal of Science Education, 11,* 554–565.

Clements, D. H. (1990). Metacomponential development in a Logo programming environment. *Journal of Educational Psychology, 82,* 141–149.

Clements, D. H., & Battista, M. T. (1989). Learning of geometric concepts in a LOGO environment. *Journal for Research in Mathematics Education, 20,* 450–467.

Clements, D. H., & Battista, M. T. (1990). The effects of LOGO on children's conceptualizations of angle and polygons. *Journal for Research in Mathematics Education, 21,* 356–371.

Clements, D. H., & Nastasi, B. K. (1988). Social and cognitive interactions in educational computer environments. *American Educational Research Journal, 25,* 87–106.

Clifford, M. M. (1975). Validity of expectation: A developmental function. *Alberta Journal of Educational Research, 21,* 11–17.

Clifford, M. M. (1978). The effects of quantitative feedback on children's expectations of success. *Journal of Educational Psychology, 48,* 220–226.

Clifford, M. M. (1984). Thoughts on a theory of constructive failure. *Educational Psychologist, 19,* 108–120.

Clifford, M. M. (1991). Risk taking: Theoretical, empirical, and educational considerations. *Educational Psychologist, 26,* 263–297.

Clymer, T. (1963). The utility of phonic generalizations in the primary grades. *Reading Teacher, 16,* 252–258.

Coates, B., & Hartup, W. W. (1969). Age and verbalization in observational learning. *Developmental Psychology, 1,* 556–562.

Cobb, P., Wood, T., Yackel, E., & McNeal, B. (1992). Characteristics of classroom mathematics traditions: An interactional analysis. *American Educational Research Journal, 29,* 573–604.

Cobb, P., Wood, T., Yackel, E., Nicholls, J., Wheatley, G., Trigatti, B., & Perlwitz, M. (1991). Assessment of a problem centered second-grade mathematics project. *Journal for Research in Mathematics Education, 22,* 3–29.

Cochran-Smith, M. (1984). *The making of a reader.* Norwood, NJ: Ablex.

Cochran-Smith, M. (1991). Word processing and writing in elementary classrooms: A critical review of related literature. *Review of Educational Research, 61,* 107–155.

Cognition and Technology Group at Vanderbilt (1992). The Jasper series as an example of anchored instruction: Theory, program description, and assessment data. *Educational Psychologist, 27,* 291–315.

Cohen, D. K., & Ball, D. L. (1990). Relations between policy and practice: A commentary. *Educational Evaluation and Policy Analysis, 12,* 249–256.

Cohen, G. (1979). Language comprehension in old age. *Cognitive Psychology, 11,* 412–429.

Cohen, G. (1988). Age differences in memory for texts: Production deficiency or processing limitations? In L. L. Light & Burke D. M. (Eds.), *Language, memory and aging* (pp. 171–190). New York: Cambridge University Press.

Cohen, J. (1988). *Statistical power analysis for the behavioral sciences,* Revised ed. Hillsdale, NJ: Erlbaum & Associates.

Cohen, M., & Riel, M. (1989). The effect of distant audiences on students' writing. *American Educational Research Journal, 26,* 143–159.

Cohen, R. L. (1989). Memory for action events: The power of enactment. *Educational Psychology Review, 1,* 57–80.

Cole, E. (1976). *The experience of illiteracy.* Dissertation. Yellow Springs, OH: Union Graduate School.

Coleman, J. S. (1961). *The adolescent society.* New York: Free Press of Glencoe.

Coleman, J. S. (1991). *Equality and achievement in education.* Boulder, CO: Westview Press.

Coleman, J. S., Campbell, E. Q., Hobson, C., McPartland, J., Mood, A. M., Weinfield, F. D., & York, R. L. (1966). *Equality of educational opportunity.* Washington, DC: Office of Education, U.S. Department of Health, Education, and Welfare.

Collins, A. (1992). Portfolios for science education: Issues in purpose, structure, and authenticity. *Science Education, 76,* 451–463.

Collins, A., Brown, J. S., & Newman, S. E. (1989). Cognitive apprenticeship: Teaching the crafts of reading, writing, and mathematics. In L. B. Resnick (Ed.), *Knowing, learning, and instruction: Essays in honor of Robert Glaser* (pp. 453–494). Hillsdale, NJ: Erlbaum & Associates.

Collins, A. M., & Loftus, E. F. (1975). A spreading-activation theory of semantic processing. *Psychological Review, 82,* 407–428.

Collins, A. M., & Quillian, M. R. (1969). Retrieval time from semantic memory. *Journal of Verbal Learning and Verbal Behavior, 8,* 240–247.

Collins, A., & Stevens, A. L. (1982). Goals and strategies of inquiry teachers. In R. Glaser (Ed.), *Advances in instructional psychology,* Vol. 2 (pp. 65–119). Hillsdale, NJ: Erlbaum & Associates.

Collins, C. (1991). Reading instruction that increases thinking abilities. *Journal of Reading, 34,* 510–516.

Collins, W. A., Wellman, H., Keniston, A. H., & Westby, S. D. (1978). Age-related aspects of comprehension and inference from a televised dramatic narrative. *Child Development, 49,* 389–399.

Coltheart, M., Davelaar, E., Jonasson, J. T., & Besner, D. (1977). Access to the internal lexicon. In S. Dornic (Ed.), *Attention and performance VI* (pp. 535–555). Hillsdale, NJ: Erlbaum & Associates.

Comber, L. C., & Keeves, J. P. (1973). *Science education in nineteen countries.* Stockholm: Almqvist & Wiksell.

Committee on High School Biology (1990). *Fulfilling the promise: Biology education in the nation's schools.* Washington, DC: National Academy Press.

Comstock, G. (1989). *The evaluation of American television.* Newbury Park, CA: Sage.

Comstock, G., & Paik, H. (1991). *Television and the American child.* San Diego: Academic Press.

Confrey, J. (1990). A review of the research on student conceptions in mathematics, science, and programming. In C. B. Cazden (Ed.), *Review of Research in Education,* Vol. 16 (pp. 3–56). Washington, DC: American Educational Research Association.

Connelly, F. M., & Clandenin, D. J. (1985). Personal practical knowledge and the modes of knowing: Relevance for teaching and learning. In E. Eisner (Ed.), *Learning and teaching the ways of knowing (84th yearbook of the National Society for the Study of Education, Part II,)* (pp. 174–198). Chicago: University of Chicago Press.

Conners, C. K. (1971). Cortical visual evoked response in children with learning disorders. *Psychophysiology, 7,* 418–428.

Conrad, C. (1972). Cognitive economy in semantic memory. *Journal of Experimental Psychology, 92,* 149–154.

Consortium for Longitudinal Studies (1983). *As the twig is bent.* Hillsdale, NJ: Erlbaum & Associates.

Constantino, G. (1992). Overcoming bias in the educational assessment of Hispanic students. In K. F. Geisinger (Ed.), *Psychological testing of Hispanics* (pp. 89–98). Washington, DC: American Psychological Association.

Conway, M. A., Cohen, G., & Stanhope, N. (1991). On the very long-term retention of knowledge acquired through formal education: twelve years of cognitive psychology. *Journal of Experimental Psychology: General, 120,* 395–409.

Conway, M. A., Cohen, G., & Stanhope, N. (1992). Very long-term memory for knowledge acquired at school and university. *Applied Cognitive Psychology, 6,* 467–482.

Cook, L. K., & Mayer, R. E. (1983). Reading strategy training for meaningful learning from prose. In M. Pressley & J. R. Levin (Eds.), *Cognitive strategy research: Educational applications* (pp. 87–131). New York: Springer-Verlag.

Cook, L. K., & Mayer, R. E. (1988). Teaching readers about the structure of scientific text. *Journal of Educational Psychology, 80,* 448–456.

Cook, T. D., & Campbell, D. T. (1979). *Quasi-experimentation: Design and analysis issues for field studies.* New York: Rand-McNally.

Cooney, J. B., & Swanson, H. L. (1990). Individual differences in memory for mathematical story problems: Memory span and problem perception. *Journal of Educational Psychology, 82,* 570–577.

Cooney, J. B., Swanson, H. L., & Ladd, S. F. (1988). Acquisition of mental multiplication skill: Evidence for the transition between counting and retrieval strategies. *Cognition and Instruction, 5,* 323–345.

Cooper, E., Blackwood, P., Bolschen, J., Giddings, M., & Carin, A. (1985). *Science,* level 4. Orlando, FL: Harcourt, Brace, Jovanovich.

Cooper, G., & Sweller, J. (1987). Effects of schema acquisition and rule automation on mathematical problem-solving transfer. *Journal of Educational Psychology, 79,* 347–362.

Cooper, H. M. (1989a). Does reducing student-to-instructor ratios affect achievement? *Educational Psychologist, 24,* 79–98.

Cooper, H. (1989b). *Homework*. New York: Longman.

Copeland, W. D. (1987). Classroom management and student teachers' cognitive abilities: A relationship. *American Educational Research Journal, 24*, 219–236.

Corkill, A. J. (1992). Advance organizers: Facilitators of recall. *Educational Psychology Review, 4*, 33–67.

Corkill, A. J., Glover, J. A., Bruning, R. H., & King, D. (1988). Advance organizers: Retrieval context hypotheses. *Journal of Educational Psychology, 80*, 304–311.

Corley, P. J. (1988). A developmental analysis of sentence comprehension abilities in good and poor readers. *Educational Psychologist, 23*, 57–75.

Cornell, E. H., Sénéchal, M., & Broda, L. S. (1988). Recall of picture books by 3-year-old children: Testing and repetition effects in joint reading activities. *Journal of Educational Psychology, 80*, 537–542.

Corno, L. (1988). More lessons from aptitude-treatment interaction theory. *Educational Psychologist, 23*, 353–356.

Corno, L. (1989). Self-regulated learning: A volitional analysis. In B. J. Zimmerman & D. H. Schunk (Eds.), *Self-regulated learning and academic achievement: Theory, research, and practice* (pp. 111–141). New York: Springer-Verlag.

Corno, L., & Kanfer, R. (1993). The role of volition in learning and performance. In L. Darling–Hammond (Ed.), *Review of research in education*, Vol. 19 (pp. 301–341). Washington, DC: American Educational Research Association.

Courage, M. (1989). Children's inquiry strategies in referential communication and in the game of twenty questions. *Child Development, 60*, 877–886.

Courchesne, E. (1988). Physioanatomical considerations in Down syndrome. In L. Nadel (Ed.), *The psychobiology of Down Syndrome* (pp. 7–50). Cambridge, MA: MIT Press.

Covington, M. V. (1985). Strategic thinking and fear of failure. In J. W. Segal, S. F. Chipman, & R. Glaser (Eds.), *Thinking and learning skills*, Vol. 1, *Relating instruction to research* (pp. 389–416). Hillsdale, NJ: Erlbaum & Associates.

Covington, M. V. (1987). Achievement motivation, self-attributions, and the exceptional learner. In J. D. Day & J. G. Borkowski (Eds.), *Intelligence and exceptionality* (pp. 355–389). Norwood, NJ: Ablex.

Covington, M. V., Crutchfield, R. S., Davies, L. B., & Olton, R. M. (1974). *The productive thinking program: A course in learning to think*. Columbus, OH: Merrill.

Covington, M. V., & Omelich, C. L. (1979a). It's best to be able and virtuous too: Student and teacher evaluative responses to successful effort. *Journal of Educational Psychology, 71*, 688–700.

Covington, M. V., & Omelich, C. L. (1979b). Effort: The double-edged sword in school achievement. *Journal of Educational Psychology, 71*, 169–182.

Covington, M. V., & Omelich, C. L. (1981). As

failures mount: Affective and cognitive consequences of ability demotion in the classroom. *Journal of Educational Psychology, 73*, 796–808.

Covington, M. V., & Omelich, C. L. (1984). Task-oriented versus competitive learning structures: Motivational and performance consequences. *Journal of Educational Psychology, 6*, 1038–1050.

Cox, B. D., Ornstein, P. A., Naus, M. J., Maxfield, D., & Zimler, J. (1989). Children's concurrent use of rehearsal and organizational strategies. *Developmental Psychology, 25*, 619–627.

Cox, B. E., Shanahan, T., & Sulzby, E. (1991). Good and poor elementary readers' use of cohesion in writing. *Reading Research Quarterly, 26*, 47–65.

Cox, E. (1988). Explicit and implicit moral education. *Journal of Moral Education, 17*, 92–97.

Craik, F. I. M., & Lockhart, R. S. (1972). Levels of processing: A framework for memory research. *Journal of Verbal Learning and Verbal Behavior, 11*, 671–684.

Craik, F. I. M., & Tulving, E. (1975). Depth of processing and the retention of words in episodic memory. *Journal of Experimental Psychology: General, 104*, 268–294.

Crain-Thoreson, C., & Dale, P. S. (1992). Do early talkers become early readers? Linguistic precocity, preschool language, and emergent literacy. *Developmental Psychology, 28*, 421–429.

Crandall, V. C. (1969). Sex differences in expectancy of intellectual and academic reinforcement. In C. P. Smith (Ed.), *Achievement-related behaviors in children*. New York: Russell Sage Foundation.

Craver-Lemley, C., & Reeves, A. (1992). How visual imagery interferes with vision. *Psychological Review, 99*, 633–649.

Crawford, M., & Chaffin, R. (1986). The reader's construction of meaning: Cognitive research on gender and comprehension. In E. A. Flynn & P. P. Schweickart (Eds.), *Gender and reading: Essays on readers, texts, and contexts* (pp. 3–30). Baltimore: Johns Hopkins Press.

Cronbach, L. J. (1951). Coefficient alpha and the internal structure of tests. *Psychometrica, 16*, 297–334.

Cronbach, L. J. (1957). The two disciplines of scientific psychology. *American Psychologist, 12*, 671–684.

Cronbach, L. J. (1990). *Essentials of psychological testing*, 5th ed. New York: Harper & Row.

Cronbach, L. J., Gleser, G. C., Nanda, H., & Rajaratman, N. (1972). *The dependability of behavioral measurements: Theory of generalizability of scores and profiles*. New York: John Wiley.

Cronbach, L. J., & Snow, R. E. (1977). *Aptitudes and instructional methods: A handbook for research on interactions*. New York: Irvington.

Crooks, T. J. (1988). The impact of classroom evaluation practices of students. *Review of Educational Research, 58*, 438–481.

Crossman, E. R. F. W. (1959). A theory of the acquisition of speed skill. *Ergonomics, 2*, 153–156.

Crosswhite, J. F. (1986). President's report: Better teaching, better mathematics: Are they enough? *Math Teaching, 7*, 572–580.

Crouter, A. C., MacDermid, S. M., McHale, S.M., & Perry-Jenkins, M. (1990). Parental monitoring and perceptions of children's school performance and conduct in dual- and single-earner families. *Developmental Psychology, 26*, 649–657.

Crowder, R. G. (1976). *Principles of learning and memory*. Hillsdale, NJ: Erlbaum & Associates.

Crutcher, K. A. (1991). Anatomical correlates of neuronal plasticity. In J. L. Martinez Jr., & R. P. Kesner (Eds.), *Learning and memory: A biological view*, 2nd ed. (pp. 93–146). San Diego: Academic Press.

Crystal, D. S., & Stevenson, H. W. (1991). Mothers' perceptions of children's problems with mathematics: A cross-national comparison. *Journal of Educational Psychology, 83*, 372–376.

Cuban, L. (1984). Policy and research dilemmas in the teaching of reasoning: Unplanned designs. *Review of Educational Research, 54*, 655–681.

Cummins, D. D. (1991). Children's interpretations of arithmetic word problems. *Cognition and Instruction, 8*, 261–289.

Cunningham, A. E. (1990). Explicit versus implicit instruction in phonemic awareness. *Journal of Experimental Child Psychology, 50*, 429–444.

Cunningham, A. E., & Stanovich, K. E. (1990). Assessing print exposure and orthographic processing skill in children: A quick measure of reading experience. *Journal of Educational Psychology, 82*, 733–740.

Cunningham, A. E., & Stanovich, K. E. (1991). Tracking the unique effects of print exposure in children: Associations with vocabulary, general knowledge, and spelling. *Journal of Educational Psychology, 83*, 264–274.

Cunningham, J. G., & Weaver, S. L. (1989). Young children's knowledge of their memory span: Effects of task and experience. *Journal of Experimental Child Psychology, 48*, 32–44.

Dabbs, J. (1980). Left–right differences in cerebral bllod flow and cognition. *Psychophysiology, 17*, 548–551.

Daiker, D. (1983). *The teacher's options in responding to student writing*. Paper presented at the Conference on College Composition and Communication, Washington, DC.

Daiker, D. (1989). Learning to praise. In C. M. Anson (Ed.), *Writing and response: Theory, practice, and research* (pp. 103–113). Urbana, IL: National Council of Teachers of English.

d'Ailly, H. H. (1992). Asian mathematics superiority: A search for explanations. *Educational Psychologist, 27*, 243–261.

Dallago, M. L. L., & Moely, B. E. (1980). Free recall in boys of normal and poor reading levels as a function of task manipulations. *Journal of Experimental Child Psychology, 30*, 62–78.

Dana, R. (1993). *Multicultural assessment perspectives for professional psychology*. Needham Heights, MA: Allyn & Bacon.

Daneman, M. (1991). Individual differences in reading skills. In R. Barr, M. L. Kamil, P. B. Mosenthal, & P. D. Pearson (Eds.), *Handbook of reading research*, Vol. II (pp. 512–538). New York: Longman.

Danner, F. W., & Day, M. C. (1977). Eliciting formal operations. *Child Development, 48,* 1600–1606.

Dark, V. J., & Benbow, C. P. (1990). Enhanced problem translation and short-term memory: Components of mathematical talent. *Journal of Educational Psychology, 82,* 420–429.

Dark, V. J., & Benbow, C. P. (1991). Differential enhancement of working memory with mathematical versus verbal precocity. *Journal of Educational Psychology, 83,* 48–60.

Darling, S. (1982). *Adult education projects that work.* Unpublished manuscript.

Darling, S. (1984). Illiteracy: An everyday problem for millions. *Appalachia, 18,* 21–28.

Darling-Hammond, L., & Snyder, J. (1992). Curriculum studies and the traditions of inquiry: The scientific tradition. In P. W. Jackson (Ed.), *Handbook of research on curriculum* (pp. 41–78). New York: Macmillan.

Das, J. P. (1992). Beyond a unidimensional scale of merit. *Intelligence, 16,* 137–149.

Das, J. P., Kirby, J. R., & Jarman, R. F. (1979). *Simultaneous and successive cognitive processes.* New York: Academic Press.

Davidson, N. (1985). Small-group learning and teaching in mathematics: A selective review of the research. In R. Slavin, S. Shara, S. Kagan, R. Hertz-Lazarowitz, C. Webb, & R. Schmuck (Eds.), *Learning to cooperate, cooperating to learn* (pp. 211–230). New York: Plenum.

Davidson, N., & Kroll, D. L. (1991). An overview of research on cooperative learning related to mathematics. *Journal for Research in Mathematics Education, 22,* 362–365.

Davidson, N., & Worsham, T. (Eds.) (1992). *Enhancing thinking through cooperative learning.* New York: Teachers College Press.

Davis, R. B. (1992). Understanding "understanding." *Journal for Research in Mathematics Education, 11,* 225–241.

Day, J. D. (1983). The zone of proximal development. In M. Pressley & J. R. Levin (Eds.), *Cognitive strategy research*, Vol. 1, *Psychological foundations* (pp. 155–175). New York: Springer-Verlag.

Day, J. D., Borkowski, J. G., Dietmeyer, D. L., Howsepian, B. A., & Saenz, D. S. (1994). Possible selves and academic achievement. In L. Winegar & J. Valsiner (Eds.), *Children's development within social contexts.* Hillsdale, NJ: Erlbaum & Associates.

Day, J. D., & Cordon, L. A. (1993). Static and dynamic measures of ability: An experimental comparison. *Journal of Educational Psychology, 85,* 75–82.

Day, J. D., Cordon, L. B., & Kerwin, M. L. (1989). Informal instruction and development of cognitive skills: A review and critique of research. In C. B. McCormick, G. Miller, & M. Pressley (Eds.), *Cognitive strategy research: From basic research to educational applications* (pp. 83–103). New York: Springer-Verlag.

Day, J. D., & Hall, L. K. (1988). Intelligence–related differences in learning and transfer and enhancement of transfer among mentally re-

tarded persons. *American Journal of Mental Deficiency, 93,* 125–137.

de Bono, E. (1983a). *CoRT thinking: CoRT I, II, III, IV, V: Teacher's notes.* Oxford: Pergamon Press.

de Bono, E. (1969). *The mechanism of mind.* New York: Simon & Schuster.

de Bono, E. (1983b). *CoRT thinking: Notes.* Oxford: Pergamon Press.

de Bono, E. (1985). The CoRT thinking program. In J. W. Segal, S. F. Chipman, & R. Glaser (Eds.). *Thinking and learning skills*, Vol. 1, *Relating instruction to research* (pp. 363–388). Hillsdale, NJ: Erlbaum & Associates.

deCharms, R. (1968). *Personal causation.* New York: Academic Press.

Deci, E. L. (1971). Effects of externally mediated rewards on instrinsic motivation. *Journal of Personality and Social Psychology, 18,* 105–115.

Decker, S. N., & Vandenberg, S. G. (1985). Colorado twin study of reading disability. In D. B. Gray & J. Kavanaugh (Eds.), *Biobehavioral measures of dyslexia* (pp. 123–135). Baltimore: York.

Dee-Lucas, D., & Larkin, J. H. (1990). Organization and comprehensibility in scientific proofs, or "Consider a particle p. . . ." *Journal of Educational Psychology, 82,* 701–714.

Dee-Lucas, D., & Larkin, J. H. (1991). Equations in scientific proofs: Effects on comprehension. *American Educational Research Journal, 28,* 661–682.

Dees, R. L. (1991). The role of cooperative learning in increasing problem-solving ability in a college remedial course. *Journal for Research in Mathematics Education, 22,* 409–421.

Deese, J. (1961). From the isolated verbal unit to connected discourse. In C. N. Cofer (Ed.), *Verbal learning and verbal behavior.* New York: McGraw-Hill.

Deese, J. (1962). On the structure of associative meaning. *Psychological Review, 69,* 161–175.

Deese, J. (1965). *The structure of associations in language and thought.* Baltimore: Johns Hopkins Press.

DeFries, J. C., Fulker, D. W., & LaBuda, M. C. (1987). Evidence for a genetic aetiology in reading disability of twins. *Nature, 329,* 537–539.

de Grazia, A., & Sohn, D. A. (Eds.) (1964). *Programs, teachers, and machines.* New York: Bantam Books.

de Groot, A. D. (1965). *Thought and choice in chess.* The Hague: Moutone.

de Groot, A. (1966). Perception and memory versus thought: Some old ideas and recent findings. In B. Kleinmuntz (Ed.), *Problem solving* (pp. 19–50). New York: Wiley.

de Groot, A. M. B. (1983). The range of automatic spreading activation in word priming. *Journal of Verbal Learning and Verbal Behavior, 22,* 417–436.

Delclos, V. R., Burns, M. S., & Kulewicz, S. J. (1987). Effects of dynamic assessment on teacher's expectations of handicapped children. *American Educational Research Journal, 24,* 325–336.

Delclos, V. R., & Harrington, C. (1991). Effects of strategy monitoring and proactive instruction

on children's problem-solving performance. *Journal of Educational Psychology, 83,* 35–42.

Delgado-Gaitan, C. (1992). School matters in the Mexican-American home: Socializing children to education. *American Educational Research Journal, 29,* 495–513.

de Leon, M. J., George, A. E., & Ferris, S. H. (1986). Computed tomography and positron emission tomography correlates of cognitive decline in aging and senile dementia. In L. W. Poon (Ed.), *Handbook for clinical memory assessment of older adults* (pp. 367–382). Washington, DC: American Psychological Association.

Dellarosa, D. (1985). *Abstraction of problem-type schemata through problem comparison* (Tech. Report No. 146). Boulder: University of Colorado, Institute of Cognitive Science.

DeLoache, J. S., Cassidy, D. J., & Brown, A. L. (1985). Precursors of mnemonic strategies in very young children's memory. *Child Development, 56,* 125–137.

DeLoache, J. S., & DeMendoza, O. A. P. (1987). Joint picturebook interactions of mothers and 1-year-old children. *British Journal of Developmental Psychology, 5,* 111–123.

Demana, F., & Leitzel, J. (1988). Establishing fundamental concepts through numerical problem solving. In A. F. Coxford & A. P. Shulte (Eds.), *The ideas of algebra K-12: 1988 yearbook of the National Council of Teachers of Mathematics.* Reston, VA: National Council of Teachers of Mathematics.

Dembo, M. H., & McAuliffe, T. J. (1987). Effects of perceived ability and grade status on social interaction and influence on cooperative groups. *Journal of Educational Psychology, 79,* 415–423.

Demchak, M. (1990). Response prompting and fading methods: A review. *American Journal of Mental Deficiency, 94,* 603–615.

Dempster, F. N. (1985). Short-term memory development in childhood and adolescence. In C. J. Brainerd & M. Pressley (Eds.), *Basic processes in memory development: Progress in cognitive development research* (pp. 209–248). New York: Springer-Verlag.

Dempster, F. N. (1987a). Effect of variable encoding and spaced presentations on vocabulary learning. *Journal of Educational Psychology, 79,* 162–170.

Dempster, F. N. (1987b). Time and the production of classroom learning: Discerning implications from basic research. *Educational Psychologist, 22,* 1–21.

Dempster, F. N. (1988a). Retroactive interference in the retention of prose: A reconsideration and new evidence. *Applied Cognitive Psychology, 2,* 97–113.

Dempster, F. N. (1988b). The spacing effect: A case study in the failure to apply the results of psychological research. *American Psychologist, 43,* 627–634.

Dempster, F. N. (1992). The rise and fall of the inhibitory mechanism: Toward a unified theory of cognitive development and aging. *Developmental Review, 12,* 45–75.

Dennis, M., & Whitaker, H. A. (1977). Hemisphere equipotentiality and language acquisition. In S. J. Segalowitz & F. A. Gruber (Eds.), *Language development and neurological theory*. New York: Academic Press.

Deno, S. L. (1986). Formative evaluation of individual programs: A new role for school psychologists. *School Psychology Review, 15,* 358–374.

Deno, S. L. (1987). Curriculum-based measurement. *Teaching Exceptional Children, 20,* 41.

Deno, S. L., & Fuchs, L. S. (1987). Developing curriculum-based measurement for special education problem solving. *Focus on Exceptional Children, 19* (8), 1–16.

Denton, P. H., Seybert, J. A., & Franklin, E. L. (1988). Ideas in practice: A content-based learning strategies program. *Journal of Developmental Psychology, 11,* 20–24.

Derry, S. J. (1984). Effects of an organizer on memory for prose. *Journal of Educational Psychology, 76,* 98–107.

Derry, S. J. (1992). Beyond symbolic processing: Expanding horizons for educational psychology. *Journal of Educational Psychology, 84,* 413–418.

Derry, S. J., Hawkes, L. W., & Tsai, C. (1987). A theory for remediating problem-solving skills of older children and adults. *Educational Psychologist, 22,* 55–87.

Derry, S. J., & Kellis, A. (1986). A prescriptive analysis of low-ability problem-solving behavior. *Instructional Science, 15,* 49–65.

Deshler, D. D., & Schumaker, J. B. (1988). An instructional model for teaching students how to learn. In J. L. Graden, J. E. Zins, & M. J. Curtis (Eds.), *Alternative educational delivery systems: Enhancing instructional options for all students* (pp. 391–411). Washington, DC: National Association of School Psychologists.

Desrochers, A., & Begg, I. (1987). A theoretical account of encoding and retrieval processes in the use of imagery-based mnemonic techniques: The special case of the keyword method. In M. A. McDaniel & M. Pressley (Eds.), *Imagery and related mnemonic techniques: Theories, individual differences, and applications* (pp. 56–77). New York: Springer-Verlag.

Detterman, D. K. (1979). Memory in the mentally retarded. In N. R. Ellis (Eds.), *Handbook of mental deficiency: Psychological theory and research* (pp. 727–760). Hillsdale, NJ: Erlbaum & Associates.

Devine, T. G. (1987). *Teaching study skills: A guide for teachers*. New York: Allyn & Bacon.

Devolder, P. A., Brigham, M. C., & Pressley, M. (1990). Memory performance awareness in younger and older adults. *Psychology and Aging, 5,* 291–303.

Devolder, P. A., & Pressley, M. (1991). Memory complaints in younger and older adults. *Applied Cognitive Psychology, 5,* 443–454.

Devolder, P. A., & Pressley, M. (1992). Causal attributions and strategy use in relation to memory performance differences in younger and older adults. *Applied Cognitive Psychology, 6,* 629–642.

Dewey, J. (1913). *Interest and effort in education*. Boston: Riverside.

Dewey, J. (1933). *How we think: A restatement of the relation of reflective thinking to the education process*. Boston: Heath.

DeYoung, A. J. (1987). The status of American rural education research: An integrated review and commentary. *Review of Educational Research, 57,* 123–148.

DeYoung, A. J. (1991). Economic underdevelopment and its effects on formal schooling in southern Appalachia. *American Educational Research Journal, 28,* 297–315.

Dhindsa, H. S., & Anderson, O. R. (1992). A model of the effects of rate of teacher communication on student acquisition of information. *Science Education, 76,* 353–371.

Diamond, A. (1985). Development of the ability to use recall to guide action, as indicated by performance on AB. *Child Development, 56,* 868–883.

Diamond, A. (1990a). Developmental time course in human infants and infant monkeys, and the neural bases, of inhibitory control in reaching. In A. Diamond (Ed.), *The development and neural bases of higher cognitive functions* (pp. 637–676). New York: New York Academy of Science.

Diamond, A. (1990b). Rate of maturation of the hippocampus and the developmental progression of children's performance on the delayed non-matching to sample and visual paired comparison tasks. In A. Diamond (Ed.), *The development and neural bases of higher cognitive functions* (pp. 394–433). New York: New York Academy of Science.

Diamond, A. (1990c). The development and neural bases of memory functions as indexed by the A[not]B and delayed response tasks in human infants and infant monkeys. In A. Diamond (Ed.), *The development and neural bases of higher cognitive functions* (pp. 267–317). New York: New York Academy of Science.

Diamond, A. (1991). Frontal lobe involvement in cognitive changes during the first year of life. In K. R. Gibson & A. C. Petersen (Eds.), *Brain maturation and cognitive development: Comparative and cross-cultural perspectives* (pp. 127–180). New York: Aldine de Gruyter.

Diamond, A., & Gilbert, J. (1989). Development as progressive inhibitory control of action: Retrieval of a contiguous object. *Cognitive Development, 4,* 223–249.

Diamond, M. C. (1988). *Enriching heredity: The impact of the environment on the anatomy of the brain*. New York: The Free Press.

Diamond, M. C. (1991). Environmental influences on the young brain. In K. R. Gibson & A. C. Petersen (Eds.), *Brain maturation and cognitive development: Comparative and cross-cultural perspectives* (pp. 107–124). New York: Aldine de Gruyter.

Diamond, M. C. (1992, October). Plasticity of the brain: enrichment versus impoverishment. In C. Clark & K. King (Eds.), *Television and the preparation of the mind for learning*. Washington, DC: U.S. Department of Health and Human Services.

Diamond, M., Scheibel, A., Murphy, G., & Harvey, T. (1985). On the brain of a scientist: Albert Einstein. *Experimental Neurology, 88,* 198–204.

Diana v. State Board of Education, C-70-37 RFP (N. D. Cal. June 18, 1973) (stipulated settlement).

Diaper, D. (Ed.) (1989). *Knowledge elicitation: Principles, techniques, and applications*. New York: John Wiley & Sons.

DiClemente, R. J., Pies, C. A., Stoller, E. J., Straits, C., Olivia, G. E., Haskin, J., & Rutherford, G. W. (1989). Evaluation of school-based AIDS education curricula in San Francisco. *The Journal of Sex Research, 26,* 188–198.

DiClemente, R. J., Zorn, J., & Temoshok, L. (1986). Adolescents and AIDS: A survey of knowledge, attitudes, and beliefs about AIDS in San Francisco. *American Journal of Public Health, 76,* 1443–1445.

DiClemente, R. J., Zorn, J., & Temoshok, L. (1987). The association of gender, ethnicity, and length of residence in the bay area to adolescents' knowledge and attitudes about acquired immune deficiency syndrome. *Journal of Applied Social Psychology, 17,* 216–230.

Diekhoff, G. M. (1988). An appraisal of adult literacy programs: Reading between the lines. *Journal of Reading, 31,* 624–631.

Diekhoff, G. M., & Wigginton, P. K. (1987). *Factors of success in an adult literacy program*. Unpublished manuscript.

DiLalla, L. F., Thompson, L. A., Plomin, R., Phillips, K., Fagan, J. F. III, Haith, M. M., Cyphers, L. H., & Fulker, D. W. (1990). Infant predictors of preschool and adult IQ: A study of infant twins and their parents. *Developmental Psychology, 26,* 759–769.

Dillard, J. L. (1972). *Black English: Its history and usage in the United States*. New York: Vintage Books.

Dillon, D. R. (1989). Showing them that I want them to learn and that I care about who they are: A microethnography of the social organization of a secondary low-track English-reading classroom. *American Educational Research Journal, 26,* 227–259.

Dillon, J. T. (1985). Using questions to foil discussion. *Teaching and Teacher Education, 1,* 109–121.

Dillon, J. T. (1991). Questioning the use of questions. *Journal of Educational Psychology, 83,* 163–164

Dimant, R. J., & Bearison, D. J. (1991). Development of formal reasoning during successive peer interactions. *Developmental Psychology, 27,* 277–284.

DiPardo, A., & Freedman, S. W. (1988). Peer response groups in the writing classroom: Theoretic foundations and new directions. *Review of Educational Research, 58,* 119–149.

DiSessa, A. (1982). Understanding Aristotelian physics: A study of knowledge based learning. *Cognitive Science, 6,* 37–75.

DiVesta, F. J., & Gray, G. S. (1972). Listening and notetaking. *Journal of Educational Psychology, 63,* 8–14.

Dixon, F. W. (1972). *The Hardy Boys detective handbook*. New York: Grosset & Dunlop.

Dixon, P., LeFevre, J–A., & Twilley, L. C. (1988).

Word knowledge and working memory as predictors of reading skill. *Journal of Educational Psychology, 80,* 465–472.

Dobbing. J. (1974). The later growth of the brain and its vulnerability. *Pediatrics, 53,* 2–6.

Doman, R. J., Spitz, E. B., Zucman, E., Delacato, C. H., & Doman, G. (1960). Children with severe brain injuries. *Journal of the American Medical Association, 174,* 219–223.

Donlon, T. F. (Ed.) (1984). *The College Board technical handbook for the Scholastic Aptitude Test and achievement tests.* New York: College Entrance Examination Board.

Donlon, T. F. (1992). Legal issues in the educational testing of Hispanics. In K. F. Geisinger (Ed.), *Psychological testing of Hispanics* (pp. 55–78). Washington, DC: American Psychological Association.

Dooling, D. J., & Lachman, R. (1971). Effects of comprehension on retention of prose. *Journal of Experimental Psychology, 88,* 216–222.

Dorsey, J. A., Mullis, I. V. S., Lindquist, M. M., & Chambers, D. L. (1988). *The 1986 mathematics report card.* Princeton, NJ: Educational Testing Service, National Assessment of Educational Progress.

Douglas, V. (1972). Stop, look, and listen: The problem of sustained attention and impulsive control in hyperactive and normal children. *Journal of Behavioral Science, 4,* 259–276.

Douglas, V. I. (1980). Higher mental processes in hyperactive children: Implications for training. In R. M. Knights & D. J. Bakker (Eds.), *Treatment of hyperactive and learning disabled children* (pp. 65–91). Baltimore: University Park Press.

Douglas, V. L., Parry, P., Marton, P., & Garson, C. (1976). Assessment of a cognitive training program for hyperactive children. *Journal of Abnormal Child Psychology, 4,* 389–410.

Dowhower, S. L. (1987). Effects of repeated reading on second-grade transitional readers' fluency and comprehension. *Reading Research Quarterly, 22,* 389–406.

Doyle, W. (1983). Academic work. *Review of Educational Research, 53,* 159–199.

Doyle, W. (1986). Classroom organization and management. In M. C. Wittrock (Ed.), *Handbook of research on teaching,* 3rd ed. (pp. 392–431). New York: Macmillan.

Dragga, S. (1986). *Praiseworthy grading: A teacher's alternative to editing error.* Paper presented at the Conference on College Composition and Communication, New Orleans.

Dreher, M. J., & Guthrie, J. (1990). Cognitive processes in textbook search processes. *Reading Research Quarterly, 25,* 323–339.

Dreyfus, A., Jungwirth, E., & Eliovitch, R. (1990). Applying the "cognitive conflict" strategy for conceptual change–some implications, difficulties, and problems. *Science Education, 74,* 555–569.

Driver, R., & Easley, J. (1978). Pupils and paradigms: a review of literature related to concept development in adolescent science students. *Studies in Science Education, 5,* 61–84.

Druckman, D., & Bjork, R. A. (Eds.) (1991). *In the mind's eye: Enhancing human performance.* Washington, DC: National Academy Press.

Duda, J. L., & Nicholls, J. G. (1992). Dimensions of achievement motivation in schoolwork and sport. *Journal of Educational Psychology, 84,* 290–299.

Duemler, D., & Mayer, R. E. (1988). Hidden costs of reflectiveness: Aspects of successful scientific reasoning. *Journal of Educational Psychology, 80,* 419–423.

Duffy, F. H., Denckla, M. B., Bartels, P. H., & Sandini, G. (1980). Dyslexia: Regional differences in brain electrical activity by topographic mapping. *Annals of Neurology, 7,* 412–420.

Duffy, F. H., & McAnulty, G. (1990). Neuropsychological heterogeneity and the definition of dyslexia: Preliminary evidence for plasticity. *Neuropsychologica, 28,* 96–103.

Duffy, G. G., & Roehler, L. R. (1986). *Improving classroom reading instruction: A decision-making approach.* New York: Random House.

Duffy, G. G., & Roehler, L. R. (1989). Why strategy instruction is so difficult and what we need to do about it. In C. B. McCormick, G. Miller, & M. Pressley (Eds.), *Cognitive strategy research: From basic research to educational applications* (pp. 133–154). New York: Springer-Verlag.

Duffy, G., Roehler, L., & Herrmann, G. (1988). Modeling mental processes helps poor readers become strategic readers. *Reading Teacher, 41,* 762–767.

Duffy, G. G., Roehler, L. R., Sivan, E., Rackliffe, G., Book, C., Meloth, M., Vavrus, L., Wesselman, R., Putnam, J., & Bassiri, D. (1987). Effects of explaining the reasoning associated with using reading strategies. *Reading Research Quarterly, 22,* 347–368.

Duffy, T. M., Haugen, D., Higgins, L., McCaffrey, M., Mehlenbacher, B., Burnett, R., Cochran, C., Sloane, S., Wallace, D., Smith, S., & Hill, C. (1989). Models for the design of instructional text. *Reading Research Quarterly, 24,* 434–457.

Dufresne, A., & Kobasigawa, A. (1989). Children's spontaneous allocation of study time: Differential and sufficient aspects. *Journal of Experimental Child Psychology, 47,* 274–296.

Duit, R. (1991). Students' conceptual frameworks: Consequences for learning science. In S. M. Glynn, R. H. Yeany, & B. K. Britton (Eds.), *The psychology of learning science* (pp. 65–85). Hillsdale, NJ: Erlbaum & Associates.

Dulaney, D. E. (1962). The place of hypotheses and intentions: An analysis of verbal control in verbal conditioning. In C. W. Eriksen (Ed.), *Behavior and awareness* (pp. 102–129). Durham, NC: Duke University Press.

Dulaney, D. E. (1968). Awareness, rules, and propositional control: A confrontation with S-R behavior theory. In T. R. Dixon & D. L. Horton (Eds.), *Verbal behavior and general behavior theory* (pp. 340–387). Englewood Cliffs, NJ: Prentice-Hall.

Duncker, K. (1945). On problem solving (L. S. Lee, Trans.). *Psychological Monographs, 58,* 407–416.

Dunlap, L. K., & Dunlap, G. (1989). A self-monitoring package for teaching subtraction with regrouping to students with learning disabilities. *Jounral of Applied Behavior Analysis, 22,* 309–314.

Dupin, J. J., & Joshua, S. (1989). Analogies and "modeling analogies" in teaching: Some examples in basic electricity. *Science Education, 73,* 207–224.

Duran, B. J., & Weffer, R. E. (1992). Immigrants' aspirations, high school process, and academic outcomes. *American Educational Research Journal, 29,* 163–181.

Durkin, D. (1966). *Children who read early.* New York: Teachers College Press.

Durkin, D. (1978–79). What classroom observations reveal about reading comprehension instruction. *Reading Research Quarterly, 14,* 481–533.

Durst, R. K. (1984). The development of analytic writing. In A. N. Applebee (Ed.), *Contexts for learning to write: Studies of secondary school instruction* (pp. 79–102). Norwood, NJ: Ablex.

Duyme, M. (1987). La méthode des adoptions: Evolution des problématique et des procédures. *Psychologie Francaise, 31,* 261–265.

Duyme, M. (1988). School success and social class: An adoption study. *Developmental Psychology, 24,* 203–209.

Dweck, C. S. (1986). Motivational processes affecting learning. *American Psychologist, 41,* 1040–1048.

Dweck, C. (1987, April). *Children's theories of intelligence: Implications for motivation and learning.* Presented at the annual meeting of the American Educational Research Association, Washington, DC.

Dweck, C. S., & Leggett, E. L. (1988). A social-cognitive approach to motivation and personality. *Psychological Review, 95,* 256–273.

Dweck, C. S., & Licht, B. G. (1980). Learned helplessness and intellectual achievement. In J. Garber & M. E. P. Seligman (Eds.), *Human helplessness: Theory and applications.* New York: Academic Press.

Dyson, A. H., & Freedman, S. W. (1991). Writing. In J. Flood, J. M. Jensen, D. Lapp, & J. R. Squire (Eds.), *Handbook of research on teaching the English language arts* (pp. 754–774). New York: Macmillan.

Early, M. M. (1991). Major research programs. In J. Flood, J. M. Jensen, D. Lapp, & J. R. Squire (Eds.), *Handbook of research on teaching the English language arts* (pp. 3–17). New York: Macmillan.

Ebbinghaus, H. (1913). *Memory.* New York: Teachers College.

Eberle, A., & Robinson, S. (1980). *The adult illiterate speaks out: Personal perspectives on learning to read and write.* Washington, DC: U.S. Department of Education.

Eccles, J. S. (1985). Sex differences in achievement patterns. In T. Sonderegger (Ed.), *Nebraska Symposium on Motivation,* Vol. 32. Lincoln: University of Nebraska Press.

Eccles, J. S. (1989). Bringing young women to math and science. In M. Crawford & M. Gentry (Eds.), *Gender and thought: Psychological perspectives* (pp. 36–58). New York: Springer-Verlag.

Eccles, J. S., & Blumenfeld, P. (1985). Classroom experience and student gender: Are there differences and do they matter? In L. C. Wilkinson & C. B. Marrett (Eds.), *Gender influences in classroom interaction* (pp. 79–114). New York: Academic Press.

Eccles, J. S., & Jacobs, J. (1986). Social forces shape math participation. *Signs, 11,* 367–380.

Eccles, J., MacIver, D., & Lange, L. (1986, April). *Classroom practice and motivation to study math.* Presented at the annual meeting of the American Educational Research Association, San Francisco.

Eccles-Parson, J., Adler, T. F., & Kaczala, C. M. (1982). Socialization of achievement attitudes and beliefs: Parental influences. *Child Development, 53,* 310–321.

Eccles-Parson, J., Kaczala, C. M., & Meece, J. L. (1982). Socialization of achievement attitudes and beliefs: Parental influences. *Child Development, 53,* 322–339.

Edelsky, C. (1990). Whose research agenda is this anyway? A response to McKenna, Robinson, and Miller. *Educational Researcher, 19,* 8–11.

Edmonds, R. R. (1979). Effective schools for the urban poor. *Educational Leadership, 37 (1),* 15–24.

Education Commission of the States (1988). *The impact of state policies on improving science curriculum.* Denver, CO.

Educational Research Service (1978). *Class size: A summary of research.* Arlington, VA: Educational Research Service.

Educational Testing Service (1985). *The reading report card.* Princeton, NJ: Educational Testing Service.

Edwards, H. (1973). *Sociology of sport.* Homewood, IL: Dorsey Press.

Edwards, L. D. (1991). Children's learning in a computer microworld for transformation geometry. *Journal for Research in Mathematics Education, 22,* 122–137.

Edwards, L. D. (1992). A comparison of children's learning in two interactive computer environments. *Journal of Mathematical Behavior, 11,* 73–81.

Edwards, R., & Edwards, J. (1987). Corporal punishment. In A. Thomas & J. Grimes (Eds.), *Children's needs: Psychological perspectives* (pp. 127–131). Washington, DC: National Association of School Psychologists.

Ehri, L. C. (1980). The development of orthographic images. In U. Frith (Ed.), *Cognitive processes in spelling* (pp. 311–338). London: Academic Press.

Ehri, L. C. (1984). How orthography alters spoken language competencies in children learning to read and spell. In J. Downing & R. Valtin (Eds.), *Language awareness and learning to read* (pp. 119–147). New York: Springer-Verlag.

Ehri, L. C. (1987). Learning to read and spell words. *Journal of Reading Behavior, 19,* 5–31.

Ehri, L. C. (1991). Development of the ability to read words. In R. Barr, M. L. Kamil, P. B. Mosenthal, & P. D. Pearson (Eds.), *Handbook of reading research,* Vol. 2 (pp. 383–417). New York: Longman.

Ehri, L. C. (1992). Reconceptualizing the development of sight word reading and its relationship to recoding. In P. B. Gough, L. C. Ehri, & R. Treiman (Eds.), *Reading acquisition* (pp. 107–143). Hillsdale, NJ: Erlbaum & Associates.

Ehri, L. C., Deffner, N. D., & Wilce, L. S. (1984). Pictorial mnemonics for phonics. *Journal of Educational Psychology, 76,* 880–893.

Ehri, L. C., & Robbins, C. (1992). Beginners need some decoding skill to read words by analogy. *Reading Research Quarterly, 27,* 12–27.

Ehri, L. C., & Wilce, L. S. (1985). Movement into reading: Is the first stage of printed word learning visual or phonetic? *Reading Research Quarterly, 20,* 163–179.

Ehri, L. C., & Wilce, L. S. (1987a). Does learning to spell help beginners learn to read words? *Reading Research Quarterly, 18,* 47–65.

Ehri, L. C., & Wilce, L. S. (1987b). Cipher versus cue reading: An experiment in decoding acquisition. *Journal of Educational Psychology, 79,* 3–13.

Eichinger, D. C., Anderson, C. W., Palincsar, A. S., & David, Y. M. (1991, April). *An illustration of the roles of content knowledge, scientific argument, and social norms in collaborative problem solving.* Presented at the annual meeting of the American Educational Research Association, Chicago.

Einstein, G. O., Morris, J., & Smith, S. (1985). Note–taking, individual differences, and memory for lecture information. *Journal of Educational Psychology, 77,* 522–532.

Eisenberger, R. (1992). Learned industriousness. *Psychological Review, 99,* 248–267.

Eisert, D., & Tomlinson–Keasey, C. (1978). Cognitive and interpersonal growth during the college freshman year: A structural analysis. *Perceptual and Motor Skills, 46,* 995–1005.

Eitzen, D. S. (1992). Problem students: The sociocultural roots. *Phi Delta Kappan, 73,* 584–590.

Ekstrom, R. B., Goertz, M. E., Pollack, J. M., & Rock, D. A. (1986). Who drops out of high school and why? Findings from a national study. *Teachers College Record, 87,* 356–373.

Elashoff, J. D., & Snow, R. E. (1971). *Pygmalion reconsidered.* Worthington, OH: Jones.

Elbaz, F. (1983). *Teacher thinking: A study of practical knowledge.* New York: Nichols Publishing.

Elbers, E. (1991). The development of competence and its social context. *Educational Psychology Review, 3,* 73–94.

El-Dinary, P. B., Pressley, M., & Schuder, T. (1992). Becoming a strategies teacher: An observational and interview study of three teachers learning transactional strategies instruction. In C. Kinzer & D. Leu (Eds.), *Forty-first Yearbook of the National Reading Conference.* Chicago IL: National Reading Conference.

Elliott, E. S., & Dweck, C. S. (1988). Goals: An approach to motivation and achievement. *Journal of Personality and Social Psychology, 54,* 5–12.

Elliott, R. (1992). Larry P., PASE, and social science in the courtroom: The science and politics of identifying and educating very slow learners. In H. C. Haywood & D. Tzuriel (Eds.), *Interactive assessment* (pp. 470–503). New York: Springer-Verlag.

Ellis, A. (1970). *The essence of rational psychotherapy: A comprehensive approach to treatment.* New York: Institute for Rational Living.

Ellis, N. R. (Ed.) (1979). *Handbook of mental deficiency: Psychological theory and research.* Hillsdale, NJ: Erlbaum & Associates.

Elton, L. R. B., & Laurilland, D. M. (1979). Trends in research on student learning. *Studies in Higher Education, 4,* 87–102.

Emig, J. (1971). *The composition process of twelfth graders.* Urbana, IL: National Council of Teachers of English.

Engle, R. W., Nations, J. K., & Cantor, J. (1990). Is "working memory capacity" just another name for word knowledge? *Journal of Educational Psychology, 82,* 799–804.

Englert, C., & Raphael, T. (1988). Constructing well-formed prose: Process, structure, and metacognitive knowledge. *Exceptional Children, 54,* 513–520.

Englert, C. S., Raphael, T. E., Anderson, L. M., Anthony, H. M., & Stevens, D. D. (1991). Making strategies and self-talk visible: Writing instruction in regular and special education classrooms. *American Educational Research Journal, 28,* 337–372.

Enright, R. D., Lapsley, D. K., & Levy, V. M. (1983). Moral education strategies. In M. Pressley & J. R. Levin (Eds.), *Cognitive strategy research: Educational applications* (pp. 43–83). New York: Springer-Verlag.

Entwisle, D. R., & Alexander, K. L. (1990). Beginning school math competence: Minority and majority comparisons. *Child Development, 61,* 454–471.

Entwisle, D. R., Alexander, K. L., Cadigan, D., & Pallas, A. M. (1987). Kindergarten experience: Cognitive effects or socialization. *American Educational Research Journal, 24,* 337–364.

Entwisle, D., & Hayduk, L. (1978). *Too great expectations: The academic outlook of young children.* Baltimore: Johns Hopkins Press.

Entwisle, N. J., & Ramsden, P. (1983). *Understanding student learning.* London: Croom Helm.

Epstein, W., Glenberg, A. M., & Bradley, M. M. (1984). Coactivation and comprehension: Contribution of text variables to the illusion of knowing. *Memory and Cognition, 12,* 355–360.

Eraut, M. (1985). Knowledge creation and knowledge use in professional scientists. *Studies in Higher Education, 10,* 117–133.

Erickson, G. L., & Erickson, L. J. (1984). Females and science achievement: Evidence, explanation, and implications. *Science Education, 68,* 63–89.

Ericsson, K. A., Krampe, R. Th., & Tesch-Römer, C. (1993). The role of deliberate practice in the acquisition of expert performance. *Psychological Review, 100,* 363–406.

Ericsson, K. A., & Polson, P. G. (1988). An experimental analysis of the mechanisms of a memory skill. *Journal of Experimental Psychology: Learning, Memory, and Cognition, 14,* 305–316.

Ericsson, K. A., & Simon, H. A. (1984). *Protocol analysis.* Cambridge MA: MIT/Bradford.

Ericsson, K. A., & Staszewski, J. J. (1989). Skilled memory and expertise: Mechanisms of exceptional performance. In D. Klahr & K. Kotovsky (Eds.), *Complex information processing: The impact of Herbert A. Simon* (pp. 235–267). Hillsdale, NJ: Erlbaum & Associates.

Erikson, E. H. (1968). *Identity, youth, and crisis.* New York: W.W. Norton.

Estrada, M. T. (1990). *Improving academic performance through enhancing possible selves.* Unpublished master's thesis. University of Notre Dame, Notre Dame, IN.

Ethington, C. A. (1991). A test of a model of achievement behaviors. *American Educational Research Journal, 28,* 155–172.

Ethington, C. A. (1992). Gender differences in a psychological model of mathematics achievement. *Journal for Research in Mathematics Education, 23,* 166–181.

Evans, J. A., & Hamerton, J. L. (1985). Chromosomal anomalies. In A. M. Clarke, A. D. B. Clarke, & J. M. Berg (Eds.), *Mental deficiency: The changing outlook* (pp. 135–213). New York: Free Press.

Evertson, C. M. (1989). Classroom organization and management. In M. C. Reynolds (Ed.), *Knowledge base for the beginning teacher* (pp. 59–70). New York: Pergamon Press.

Eylon, B., & Helfman, J. (1982, February). *Analogical and deductive problem-solving in physics.* Paper presented at the annual meeting of the American Educational Research Association, New York.

Eylon, B., & Linn, M. (1988). Learning and instruction: An examination of four research perspectives in science education. *Review of Educational Research, 58,* 251–301.

Eysenck, H. J. (1971). *The IQ argument: Race, intelligence and education.* New York: Library Press.

Eysenck, H. J. (1973). *The inequality of man.* London: Temple Smith.

Eysenck, H. J. (1987). Speed of information processing, reaction time, and the theory of intelligence. In P. A. Vernon (Ed.), *Speed of information processing and intelligence* (pp. 21–67). Norwood, NJ: Ablex.

Fagan, J. F. (1985). A new look at infant intelligence. In D. K. Detterman (Ed.), *Current topics in human intelligence, Vol. 1, Research methodology in human intelligence* (pp. 223–246). Norwood, NJ: Ablex.

Fagan, J. F. (1991). The paired-comaprison paradigm and infant intelligence. In A. Diamond (Ed.), *The development and neural bases of higher cognitive functions.* New York: New York Academy of Sciences.

Fagan, J. F., & McGrath, S. (1981). Infant recognition memory and later intelligence. *Intelligence, 5,* 121–130.

Fantuzzo, J., King, J., & Heller, L. R. (1992). Effects of reciprocal peer tutoring on mathematics and school adjustment: A component analysis. *Journal of Educational Psychology, 84,* 331–339.

Fantuzzo, J. W., Riggio, R. E., Connelly, S., & Dimeff, L. A. (1989). Effects of reciprocal peer tutoring on academic achievement and psychological adjustment: A component analysis. *Journal of Educational Psychology, 81,* 173–177.

Fantz, R. L., & Nevis, S. (1967). Pattern preferences and perceptual-cognitive development in early infancy. *Merrill-Palmer Quarterly, 13,* 77–108.

Farah, M. J. (1988). Is visual imagery really visual? Overlooked evidence from neuropsychology. *Psychological Review, 95,* 307–317.

Farkas, G., Sheehan, D., & Grobe, R. P. (1990). Coursework mastery and school success: Gender, ethnicity, and poverty groups within an urban school district. *American Educational Research Journal, 27,* 807–827.

Farnham-Diggory, S. (1992). *The learning-disabled child.* Cambridge, MA: Harvard University Press.

Farr, R., & Beck, M. D. (1991). Formal methods of evaluation. In J. Flood, J. M. Jensen, D. Lapp, & J. R. Squire (Eds.), *Handbook of research on teaching the English language arts* (pp. 489–501). New York: Macmillan.

Farrar, M. J., & Goodman, G. S. (1992). Developmental changes in event memory. *Child Development, 63,* 173–187.

Farrell, E., Peguero, G., Lindsey, R., & White, R. (1988). Giving voice to high school students: Pressure and boredom, ya know what I'm sayin'? *American Educational Research Association, 25,* 489–502.

Faryniarz, J. V., & Lockwood, L. G. (1992). Effectiveness of microcomputer simulations in stimulating environmental problem solving by community college students. *Journal of Research in Science Teaching, 29,* 454–470.

Fass, P. S. (1989). *Outside in: Minorities and the transformation of American education.* New York: Oxford University Press.

Faw, H. W., & Waller, T. G. (1976). Mathemagenic behaviors and efficiency in learning from prose. *Review of Educational Research, 46,* 691–720.

Fayol, M., Abdi, H., & Gombert, J-E. (1987). Arithmetic problems formulation and working memory load. *Cognition and Instruction, 4,* 187–202.

Feingold, A. (1992). Sex differences in variability in intellectual abilities: A new look at an old controversy. *Review of Educational Research, 62,* 61–84.

Feitelson, D. (1988). *Facts and fads in beginning reading.* Norwood, NJ: Ablex.

Feldhusen, J. F. (1986). A conception of giftedness. In R. J. Sternberg & J. E. Davidson (Eds.), *Conceptions of giftedness* (pp. 112–127). Cambridge, UK: Cambridge University Press.

Feldhusen, J. F., & Kolloff, M. B. (1981). Me: A self-concept scale for gifted students. *Perceptual and Motor Skills, 53,* 319–323.

Feldman, D. H. (1979). The mysterious case of extreme giftedness. In A. H. Passow (Ed.), *The gifted and the talented: Their education and development.* The Seventy-Eighth Yearbook of the National Society for the Study of Education. Chicago: University of Chicago Press.

Feldman, D. H. (1982). *Developmental approaches to giftedness and creativity.* San Francisco: Jossey-Bass.

Feldman, D. H. (with the assistance of A. C. Benjamin) (1986). Giftedness as a developmentalist sees it. In R. J. Sternberg & J. E. Davidson (Eds.), *Conceptions of giftedness* (pp. 285–305). Cambridge, UK: Cambridge University Press.

Feldman, D. H. (1988). *Nature's gambit: Child prodigies and the development of human potential.* New York: Basic Books.

Feltovich, P. J., Johnson, P. E., Moller, J. H., & Swanson, D. B. (1984). LCS: The role and development of medical knowledge in diagnostic expertise. In W. J. Clancey & E. H. Shortliffe (Eds.), *Readings in medical artificial intelligence: The first decade.* Reading, MA: Addison-Wesley.

Feltz, D. L., Landers, D. M., & Becker, B. J. (1988). A revised meta-analysis of the mental practice literature on motor skill performance. In D. Druckman & J. A. Swets (Eds.), *Enhancing human performance: Issues, theories and techniques: Background papers* (pp. 1–65). Washington, DC: National Research Council.

Fenaigle, G. von (1813). *The new art of memory.* London: Sherwood, Neely, & Jones.

Fennema, E. (1974). Sex differences in mathematics learning: Why??? *The Elementary School Journal, 75,* 183–190.

Fennema, E., Carpenter, T. P., & Peterson, P. L. (1989). Teachers' decision making and cognitively guided instruction: A new paradigm for curriculum development. In K. Clements & N. F. Ellerton (Eds.), *Facilitating change in mathematics education.* Geelong, Victoria, Australia: Deakin University Press.

Fennema, E., & Franke, M. L. (1992). Teachers' knowledge and its impact. In D. A. Grouws (Ed.), *Handbook of research on mathematics teaching and learning* (pp. 147–164). New York: Macmillan.

Fernandez, R. J., & Samuels, M. A. (1986). Intellectual dysfunction: Mental retardation and dementia. In M. A. Samuels (Ed.), *Manual of neurologic therapeutics* (pp. 30–50). Boston: Little, Brown & Co.

Ferreiro, E. (1985). Literacy development: A psychogenetic approach. In D. R. Olsen, N. Torrance, & A. Hildyard (Eds.), *Literacy, language, and learning: The nature and consequences of reading and writing.* Cambridge, UK: Cambridge University Press.

Feshbach, S., Adelman, H., & Fuller, W. (1977). Prediction of reading and related academic problems. *Journal of Educational Psychology, 69,* 299–308.

Feurstein, R. (1979). *The dynamic assessment of retarded performers: The Learning Potential*

Assessment Device, theory, instrument, and techniques. Baltimore: University Park Press.

Feurstein, R. (1980). *Instrumental enrichment: An intervention program for cognitive modifiability.* Baltimore: University Park Press.

Feurstein, R., Rand, Y., Hoffman, M., & Miller, R. (1979). Cognitive modifiability in retarded adolescents: Effects of instrumental enrichment. *American Journal of Mental Deficiency, 83,* 539–550.

Fey, J. T. (1990). Quantity. In L. A. Steen (Ed.), *On the shoulders of giants: New approaches to numeracy* (pp. 61–94). Washington, DC: National Academy Press.

Field, D. (1987). A review of preschool conservation training: An analysis of analyses. *Developmental Review, 7,* 210–251.

Field, T. (1991). Quality infant day-care and grade school behavior and performance. *Child Development, 62,* 863–870.

Fillmore, L. W. (1992). Against our best interest: The attempt to sabotage bilingual education. In J. Crawford (Ed.), *Language loyalties: A source book on the official English controversy* (pp. 367–376). Chicago: University of Chicago Press.

Finch, A., Wilkinson, M., Nelson, W., & Montgomery, L. (1975). Modification of an impulsive cognitive tempo in emotionally disturbed boys. *Journal of Abnormal Child Psychology, 3,* 45–52.

Fincham, F. D., Hokoda, A., & Sanders, R., Jr. (1989). Learned helplessness, text anxiety, and academic achievement: A longitudinal analysis. *Child Development, 60,* 138–145.

Fingeret, A. (1985). *North Carolina adult basic education instructional program evaluation.* North Carolina ABE Evaluation Project. Raleigh, NC: North Carolina State University.

Finke, R. A. (1989). *Principles of mental imagery.* Cambridge MA: MIT Press.

Finn, C. E., Jr. (1991). *We must take charge: Our schools and our future.* New York: Free Press.

Finn, J. D. (1989). Withdrawing from school. *Review of Educational Research, 59,* 117–142.

Finn, J. D., & Achilles, C. M. (1990). Answers and questions about class size: A statewide experiment. *American Educational Research Journal, 27,* 557–577.

Firestone, W. A. (1991). Educators, researchers, and the effective schools movement. In J. R. Bliss, W. A. Firestone, & C. E. Richards (Eds.), *Rethinking effective schools research and practice* (pp. 12–27). Englewood Cliffs, NJ: Prentice-Hall.

Fischer, F. E. (1990). A part-part-whole curriculum for teaching number in the kindergarten. *Journal for Research in Mathematics Education, 21,* 207–215.

Fishbein, H. D., Eckart, T., Lauver, E., Van Leeuwen, R., & Langmeyer, D. (1990). Learners' questions and comprehension in a tutoring setting. *Journal of Educational Psychology, 82,* 163–170.

Fitzgerald, J. (1987). Research on revision in writing. *Review of Educational Research, 57,* 481–506.

Fitzgerald, J. (1992). Variant views about good thinking during composing: Focus on revision. In M. Pressley, K. R. Harris, J. T. Guthrie (Eds.), *Promoting academic competence and literacy in school* (pp. 337–358). San Diego: Academic Press.

Fitzgerald, J., & Markham, L. (1987). Teaching children about revision in writing. *Cognition and Instruction, 4,* 3–24.

Fivush, R. (1987). Scripts and categories: Interrelationships in development. In U. Neisser (Ed.), *Concepts and conceptual development: Ecological and intellectual factors in categorization* (pp. 234–254). Cambridge, UK: Cambridge University Press.

Fivush, R., Hudson, J., & Nelson, K. (1984). Children's long-term memory for a novel event: An exploratory study. *Merrill-Palmer Quarterly, 30,* 303–316.

Fivush, R., Kuebli, J., & Clubb, P. A. (1992). The structure of events and event representations: A developmental analysis. *Child Development, 63,* 188–201.

Fixsen, D. L., Phillips, E. L., & Wolf, M. M. (1973). Achievement Place: Experiments in self-government with pre-delinquents. *Journal of Applied Behavior Analysis, 6,* 31–47.

Fjellstrom, G. G., Born, D., & Baer, D. M. (1988). Some effects of telling preschool children to self-question in a matching task. *Journal of Experimental Child Psychology, 46,* 419–437.

Flavell, J. H. (1963). *The developmental psychology of Jean Piaget.* Princeton, NJ: van Nostrand.

Flavell, J. H. (1971). Stage-related properties of cognitive development. *Cognitive Psychology, 2,* 421–453.

Flavell, J. H. (1972). An analysis of cognitive-developmental sequences. *Genetic Psychology Monographs, 86,* 279–350.

Flavell, J. H. (1985). *Cognitive development.* Englewood Cliffs, NJ: Prentice-Hall.

Flavell, J. H., Beach, D. H., & Chinsky, J. M. (1966). Spontaneous verbal rehearsal in a memory task as a function of age. *Child Development, 37,* 283–299.

Flavell, J. H., Friedrichs, A. G., & Hoyt, J. D. (1970). Developmental changes in memorization processes. *Cognitive Psychology, 1,* 324–340.

Fleisher, L. S., Jenkins, J. R., & Pany, D. (1979). Effects on poor readers comprehension of training in rapid decoding. *Reading Research Quarterly, 15,* 30–48.

Fletcher, J. D., Hawley, D. E., & Piele, P. K. (1990). Costs, effects, and utility of microcomputer assisted instruction in the classroom. *American Educational Research Journal, 27,* 783–806.

Fletcher, R. (1991). Intelligence, equality, character, and education. *Intelligence, 15,* 139–149.

Flood, J. (1977). Parental styles in reading episodes with young children. *Reading Teacher, 30,* 864–867.

Flower, L. (1987). *Interpretive acts: Cognition and construction of discourse* (Occasional Paper No. 1). Berkeley: University of California, Center for the Study of Writing.

Flower, L. (1989). *Problem-solving strategies for writing,* 3rd ed. San Diego: Harcourt, Brace, Jovanovich.

Flower, L., & Hayes, J. (1980). The dynamics of composing: Making plans and juggling constraints. In L. Gregg and E. Steinberg (Eds.), *Cognitive processes in writing* (pp. 31–50). Hillsdale, NJ: Erlbaum & Associates.

Flower, L. S., & Hayes, J. R. (1981). A cognitive process theory of writing. *College Composition and Communication, 32,* 365–387.

Flower, L., Stein, V., Ackerman, J., Kantz, M. J., McCormick, K., & Peck, W. C. (1990). *Reading to write: Exploring a cognitive and social process.* New York: Oxford University Press.

Flowers, D. L., Wood, F. B., & Naylor, C. E. (1991). Regional cerebral bloodflow correlates of language processes in reading disability. *Archives of Neurology, 48,* 637–643.

Fodor, J. A. (1983). *The modularity of mind.* Cambridge, MA: MIT Press.

Fodor, J. A., & Pylyshen, Z. W. (1988). Connectionism and cognitive architecture: A critical analysis. In S. Pinker & J. Mehler (Eds.), *Connections and symbols* (pp. 3–71). Cambridge, MA: MIT Press. (Reprinted from *Cognition, 28.*)

Fodor, J. D., Fodor, J. A., & Garrett, M. (1975). The psychological unreality of semantic representation. *Linguistic Inquiry, 6,* 515–531.

Foos, P. W., & Fisher, R. P. (1988). Using tests as learning opportunities. *Journal of Educational Psychology, 80,* 179–183.

Ford, D. H. (1987). *Humans as self-constructing living systems: A developmental perspective on behavior and personality.* Hillsdale, NJ: Erlbaum & Associates.

Foree, D. D., & LoLordo, V. M. (1973). Attention in the pigeon: Differential effects of food-getting versus shock-avoidance procedures. *Journal of Comparative and Physiological Psychology, 85,* 551–558.

Forrest-Pressley, D. L., & Gilles, L. A. (1983). Children's flexible use of strategies during reading. In M. Pressley & J. R. Levin (Eds.), *Cognitive strategy research: Educational applications.* New York: Springer-Verlag.

Forrest-Pressley, D. L., & Waller, T. G. (1984). *Cognition, metacognition, and reading.* New York: Springer-Verlag.

Fowler, A. (1988). Determinants of rate of language growth in children with Down Syndrome. In L. Nadel (Ed.), *The psychobiology of Down syndrome* (pp. 217–246). Cambridge, MA: MIT Press.

Fox, N. A., & Bell, M. A. (1990). Electrophysiological indices of frontal lobe development: Relations to cognitive and affective behavior in human infants over the first year of life. In A. Diamond (Ed.), *The development and neural bases of higher cognitive functions* (pp. 677–704). New York: New York Academy of Sciences.

Francis, P. L., Self, P. A., & Horowitz, F. D. (1987). The behavioral assessment of the neonate: An overview. In J. D. Osofsky (Ed.), *Handbook of infant development* (pp. 723–779). New York: John Wiley & Sons.

Franklin, M. E. (1992). Culturally sensitive instructional practices for African-American learners with disabilities. *Exceptional Children, 59*, 115–122.

Fraser, K., & Edwards, J. (1985). The effects of training in concept mapping on student achievement in traditional tests. *Research in Science Teaching, 15*, 158–165.

Frearson, W. M., & Eysenck, H. J. (1986). Intelligence, reaction time (RT), and a new "odd-man-out" RT paradigm. *Personality and Individual Differences, 7*, 807–817.

Fredericksen, N. (1984). The real test bias: Influences of testing on teaching and learning. *American Psychologist, 39*, 193–202.

Freebody, P., & Anderson, R. C. (1983). Effects of vocabulary difficulty, text cohesion, and schema availability on reading comprehension. *Reading Research Quarterly, 18*, 277–294.

Freebody, P., & Byrne, B. (1988). Word-reading strategies in elementary school children: Relations to comprehension, reading time, and phonemic awareness. *Reading Research Quarterly, 23*, 441–453.

Freeman, D. J., & Porter, A. C. (1989). Do textbooks dictate the content of mathematics instruction in elementary schools? *American Educational Research Journal, 26*, 403–421.

Freund, L. S. (1990). Maternal regulation of children's problem-solving behavior and its impact on children's performance. *Child Development, 61*, 113–126.

Frey, K. S., & Ruble, D. N. (1987). What children say about classroom performance: Sex and grade differences in perceived competence. *Child Development, 58*, 1066–1078.

Frick, T. W. (1990). Analysis of patterns in time: A method of recording and quantifying temporal relations in education. *American Educational Research Journal, 27*, 180–204.

Friedman, L. (1989). Mathematics and the gender gap: A meta-analysis of recent studies on sex differences in mathematical tasks. *Review of Educational Research, 59*, 185–213.

Frith, U. (1979). Reading by eye and writing by ear. In P. A. Kolers, M. Wrolstad, & H. Bouma (Eds.), *Processing of visible language*, Vol. 1 (pp. 379–390). New York: Plenum Press.

Fuchs, D., & Fuchs, L. S. (1986). Test procedure bias: A meta-analysis of examiner familiarity effects. *Review of Educational Research, 56*, 243–262.

Fuchs, D., Fuchs, L. S., & Fernstrom, P. (1993). A conservative approach to special education reform: Mainstreaming through transenvironmental programming and curriculum-based measurement. *American Educational Research Journal, 30*, 149–177.

Fuchs, L. S., & Fuchs, D. (1990). Curriculum-based assessment. In C. R. Reynolds & R. W. Kamphaus (Eds.), *Handbook of psychological and educational assessment of children: Intelligence and achievement* (pp. 435–455). New York: Guilford.

Fuchs, L. S., Fuchs, D., Hamlett, C. L., & Stecker, P. M. (1990). The role of skills analysis in curriculum-based measurement in math. *School Psychology Review, 19*, 6–22.

Fuchs, L. S., Fuchs, D., Hamlett, C. L., & Stecker, P. M. (1991). Effects of curriculum-based measurement and consultation on teacher planning and student achievement in mathematics operations. *American Educational Research Journal, 28*, 617–641.

Fuchs, L. S., Fuchs, D., & Maxwell, L. (1988). The validity of informal measures of reading comprehension. *Remedial and Special Education, 9* (2), 20–29.

Fuson, K. (1988). *Children's counting and concept of numbers.* New York: Springer-Verlag.

Fuson, K. C. (1992). Research on learning and teaching addition and subtraction of whole numbers. In G. Leinhardt, R. Putnam, & R. A. Hattrup (Eds.), *Analysis of arithmetic for mathematics teaching* (pp. 53–187). Hillsdale, NJ: Erlbaum & Associates.

Fuson, K. C., & Fuson, A. M. (1991). Instruction supporting children's counting on for addition and counting up for subtraction. *Journal for Research in Mathematics Education, 22*, 72–78.

Fuson, K., & Willis, G. (1988). Subtraction by counting up: More evidence. *Journal for Research in Mathematics Education, 19*, 402–420.

Gaddes, W. H. (1985). *Learning disabilities and brain function*, 2nd ed. New York: Springer-Verlag.

Gagné, R. M. (1965). *The conditions of learning.* New York: Holt.

Gagné, R. M., & Brown, L. T. (1961). Some factors in the programming of conceptual learning. *Journal of Experimental Psychology, 62*, 313–321.

Gagné, R. M., & Dick, W. (1983). Instructional psychology. *Annual Review of Psychology, 34*, 261–295.

Gajar, A. H. (1980). Characteristics across exceptional categories: EMR, LD, and ED. *Journal of Special Education, 14*, 165–173.

Galaburda, A. (1983). Developmental dyslexia: Current anatomical research. *Annals of Dyslexia, 33*, 41–53.

Galaburda, A. M., Sherman, G. F., Rosen, G. D., Aboitz, F., & Geschwind, N. (1985). Developmental dyslexia: Four consecutive patients with cortical anomalies. *Archives of Neurology, 35*, 812–817.

Galbraith, R., & Jones, T. (1976). *Moral reasoning: A teaching handbook for adapting Kohlberg to the classroom.* Minneapolis: Greenhaven Press.

Galef, B. G., Jr. (1988). Imitation in animals: History, definition, and interpretation of data from the psychological laboratory. In T. R. Zentall & B. G. Galef, Jr. (eds.), *Social learning: Psychological and biological perspectives* (pp. 3–28). Hillsdale, NJ: Erlbaum.

Galin, D. (1989). EEG studies in dyslexia. In D. J. Bakker & H. van der Vlugt (Eds.), *Learning disabilities*, Vol. 1, *Neuropsychological correlates and treatment.* Amsterdam: Swets Publishing.

Galotti, K. M. (1989). Gender differences in self-reported moral reasoning: A review and new evidence. *Journal of Youth and Adolescence, 18*, 475–488.

Galotti, K. M., Kozberg, S. F., & Farmer, M. C. (1991). Gender and developmental differences in adolescents' conceptions of moral reasoning. *Journal of Youth and Adolescence, 20*, 13–30.

Gal'perin, P. (1969). Stages in the development of mental acts. In M. Cole & I. Maltzman (Eds.), *A handbook of contemporary Soviet psychology* (pp. 249–273). New York: Basic Books.

Galton, F. (1869). *Hereditary genius: An inquiry into its laws and consequences.* London: Macmillan.

Gambrell, L. B., & Bales, R. J. (1986). Mental imagery and the comprehension-monitoring performance of fourth- and fifth-grade poor readers. *Reading Research Quarterly, 21*, 454–464.

Garber, H. L., Hodge, J. D., Rynders, J., Dever, R., & Velu, R. (1991). The Milwaukee Project: Setting the record straight. *American Journal of Mental Deficiency, 95*, 493–525.

Garcia, G. E. (1991). Factors influencing the English reading test performance of Spanish-speaking Hispanic children. *Reading Research Quarterly, 26*, 371–392.

Garcia, J. (1981). The logic and limits of mental ability testing. *American Psychologist, 36*, 1172–1180.

Garcia, J., & Garcia y Robertson, R. (1985). Evolution of learning mechanisms. In B. L. Hammonds (Ed.), *Psychology and learning* (pp. 191–243). Washington, DC: American Psychological Association.

Garcia, J., & Koelling, R. A. (1966). Relation of cue to consequence in avoidance learning. *Psychonomic Science, 4*, 123–124.

Gardner, E. (1975). *Fundamentals of neurology*, 6th ed. Philadelphia: W.B. Saunders Co.

Gardner, H. (1983). *Frame of mind: The theory of multiple intelligences.* New York: Basic Books.

Gardner, H. (1991). The tensions between education and development. *Journal of Moral Education, 20*, 113–125.

Gardner, H. (1993). *Multiple intelligences: The theory in practice: A reader.* New York: Basic Books.

Gardner, R. C. (1980). On the validity of affective variables in second language acquisition: Conceptual, contextual, and statistical considerations. *Language Learning, 30*, 255–270.

Gardner, R. C. (1983). Learning another language: A true social psychological experiment. *Journal of Language and Social Psychology, 2*, 219–239.

Gardner, R., & Lambert, W. (1972). *Attitudes and motivation in second language learning.* Rowley, MA: Newbury House.

Gardner, W., & Rogoff, B. (1982). The role of instruction in memory development: Some methodological choices. *Quarterly Newsletter of the Laboratory of Comparative Human Cognition, 4*, 6–12.

Garner, R. (1992). Learning from school texts. *Educational Psychologist, 27*, 53–63.

Garner, R., Alexander, P. A., Gillingham, M. G., Kulikowich, J. M., & Brown, R. (1991). Interest and learning from text. *American Educational Research Journal, 28*, 643–660.

Garner, R., Gillingham, M. G., & White, C. S. (1989). Effects of "seductive details" on macroprocessing and microprocessing in adults and children. *Cognition and Instruction, 6,* 41–57.

Garnett, P. J. (1987). Exemplary practice in secondary chemistry education. In K. Tobin & B. J. Fraser (Eds.), *Exemplary practice in science and mathematics education.* Perth, Western Australia: Western Australian Institute of Technology. (Cited in Garnett, P. J., & Tobin, K. [1988]. Teaching for understanding: Exemplary practice in high school chemistry. *Journal of Research in Science Teaching, 26,* 1–14.)

Garskof, B. E., & Houston, J. P. (1963). Measurement of verbal relatedness: An idiographic approach. *Psychological Review, 70,* 277–288.

Garth, T. R. (1923). A comparison of the intelligence of Mexican and mixed and full blood Indian children. *Psychological Review, 30,* 388–401.

Gaskins, I. W., Anderson, R. C., Pressley, M., Cunicelli, E. A., & Satlow, E. (1992). The moves strategy instruction teachers make. *Elementary School Journal, 93,* 277–304.

Gaskins, I. W., & Elliot, T. T. (1991). *Implementing cognitive strategy instruction across the school: The Benchmark manual for teachers.* Cambridge, MA: Brookline Books.

Gates, B. (Guest Ed.) (1990). Special Issue: Perspectives on morality and moral education east and west. *Journal of Moral Education, 19* (3).

Gauvain, M., & Rogoff, B. (1989). Collaborative problem solving and children's planning skills. *Developmental Psychology, 25,* 139–151.

Gayford, C. (1989). A contribution to a methodology for teaching and assessment of group problem-solving in biology among 15 year old pupils. *Journal of Biological Education, 23,* 193–198.

Gayford, C. (1992). Patterns of group behavior in open–ended problem solving in science classes of 15-year-old students in England. *International Journal of Science Education, 14,* 41–49.

Geary, D. C. (1990). A componential analysis of an early learning deficit in mathematics. *Journal of Experimental Child Psychology, 49,* 363–383.

Geary, D. C., Bow-Thomas, C., & Yao, Y. (1992). Counting knowledge and skill in cognitive addition: A comparison of normal and mathematically disabled children. *Journal of Experimental Child Psychology, 54,* 372–391.

Geary, D. C., & Brown, S. C. (1991). Cognitive addition: Strategy choice and speed-of-processing differences in gifted, normal, and mathematically disabled children. *Developmental Psychology, 27,* 398–406.

Geary, D. C., Brown, S. C., & Samaranayake, V. A. (1991). Cognitive addition: A short longitudinal study of strategy choice and speed-of-processing differences in normal and mathematically disabled children. *Developmental Psychology, 27,* 787–797.

Geary, D. C., & Burlingham-Dubree, M. (1989). External validation of the strategy choice for addition. *Journal of Experimental Child Psychology, 47,* 175–192.

Geary, D. C., Widaman, K. F., & Little, T. D. (1986). Cognitive addition and multiplication: Evidence for a single memory network. *Memory and Cognition, 14,* 478–487.

Geisenger, K. F. (1992a). Fairness and selected psychometric issues in the psychological testing of Hispanics. In K. F. Geisinger (Ed.), *Psychological testing of Hispanics* (pp. 17–42). Washington, DC: American Psychological Association.

Geisenger, K. F. (1992b). The metamorphosis of test validation. *Educational Psychologist, 27,* 197–222.

Geisler, C. (1991). Toward a sociocognitive model of literacy: Constructing mental models in a philosophical conversation. In C. Bazerman & J. Paradis (Eds.), *Textual dynamics of the professions: Historical and contemporary studies of writing in professional communities* (pp. 171–190). Madison: University of Wisconsin Press.

Gelman, R., & Baillargeon, R. (1983). A review of some Piagetian concepts. In J. H. Flavell & E. M. Markman (Eds.), *Handbook of child psychology,* Vol. 3: *Cognitive development.* New York: Wiley.

Gelman, R., & Cohen, M. (1988). Qualitative differences in the way Down Syndrome and normal children solve a novel counting problem. In L. Nadel (Ed.), *The psychobiology of Down Syndrome* (pp. 51–100). Cambridge, MA: MIT Press.

Gelman, R., & Gallistel, C. R. (1978). *The child's understanding of number.* Cambridge, MA: Harvard University Press.

Gelman, R., Massey, C. M., & McManus, M. (1991). Characterizing supporting environments for cognitive development: Lessons from children in a museum. In L. Resnick, J. M. Levine, & S. D. Teasley (Eds.), *Perspectives on socially shared cognition* (pp. 226–256). Washington, DC: American Psychological Association.

General Accounting Office (1989). *Effective schools programs: Their extent and characteristics.* Washington, DC: General Accounting Office.

Genesee, F. (1985). Second language learning through immersion: A review of U.S. programs. *Review of Educational Research, 55,* 541–562.

Gentile, C. (1992). *Exploring new methods for collecting students' school-based writing.* Washington, DC: U.S. Department of Education.

Gentner, D. (1989). The mechanisms of analogical learning. In S. Vosniadou & A. Ortony (Eds.), *Similarity and analogical reasoning* (pp. 199–241). Cambridge, UK: Cambridge University Press.

Gentner, D., & Gentner, D. (1983). Flowing waters or teeming crowds: Mental models of electricity. In D. Gentner & A. Stevens (Eds.), *Mental models* (pp. 101–129). Hillsdale, NJ: Erlbaum & Associates.

Gentner, D., & Stevens, A. (Eds.) (1983). *Mental models.* Hillsdale, NJ: Erlbaum & Associates.

Gerst, M. S. (1971). Symbolic coding processes in observational learning. *Journal of Personality and Social Psychology, 19,* 7–17.

Geschwind, N., & Galaburda, A. M. (1987). *Cerebral lateralization: Biological mechanisms, associations, and psychology.* Cambridge, MA: MIT Press.

Gettinger, M. (1989). Effects of maximizing time spent and minimizing time needed for learning on pupil achievement. *American Educational Research Journal, 26,* 73–91.

Ghatala, E. S. (1986). Strategy-monitoring training enables young learners to select effective strategies. *Educational Psychologist, 21,* 43–54.

Ghatala, E. S., Levin, J. R., Pressley, M., & Goodwin, D. (1986). A componential analysis of the effects of derived and supplied strategy-utility information on children's strategy selections. *Journal of Experimental Child Psychology, 41,* 76–92.

Ghiselin, B. (Ed.) (1952). *The creative process.* New York: Mentor.

Ghiselli, E. E. (1966). *The validity of occupational aptitude tests.* New York: Wiley.

Ghiselli, E. E. (1973). The validity of aptitude tests in personnel selection. *Personnel Psychology, 26,* 461–477.

Gibbs, J. C., Arnold, K. D., & Burkart, J. E. (1984). Sex differences in the expression of moral judgment. *Child Development, 55,* 1040–1043.

Gibbs, J. C., Arnold, K. D., Morgan, R. L., Schwartz, E. S., Gavaghan, M. P., & Tappan, M. B. (1984). Construction and validation of a multiple-choice measure of moral reasoning. *Child Development, 55,* 527–536.

Gibbs, J. C., Basinger, K. S., & Fuller, D. (1992). *Moral maturity: Measuring the development of sociomoral reflection.* Hillsdale, NJ: Erlbaum & Associates.

Gibbs, J. C., & Widaman, K. F. (1982). *Social intelligence: Measuring the development of sociomoral reflection.* Englewood Cliffs, NJ: Prentice-Hall.

Gibbs, J. C., Widaman, K. F., & Colby, A. (1982). Construction and validation of a simplified, group-administrable equivalent to the Moral Judgment Interview. *Child Development, 53,* 895–910.

Gibson, E. J. (1969). *Principles of perceptual learning and development.* New York: Appleton-Century-Crofts.

Gibson, E. J. (1982). The concept of affordances in development: The renascence of functionalism. In W. A. Collins (Ed.), *The concept of development: The Minnesota symposium on child psychology,* Vol. 15 (pp. 55–81). Hillsdale, NJ: Erlbaum & Associates.

Gibson, E. J. (1991). *The odyssey in learning and perception.* Cambridge, MA: MIT Press.

Gibson, J. J. (1979). *The ecological approach to visual perception.* Boston: Houghton-Mifflin.

Gibson, K. R. (1991a). Basic neuroanatomy for the nonspecialist. In K. R. Gibson & A. C. Petersen (Eds.), *Brain maturation and cognitive development: Comparative and cross-cultural perspectives* (pp. 13–25). New York: Aldine de Gruyter.

Gibson, K. R. (1991b). Myelination and behavioral development: A comparative perspective on questions of neoteny, altriciality and intelligence. In K. R. Gibson & A. C. Petersen (Eds.), *Brain maturation and cognitive development: Comparative and cross-cultural perspectives* (pp. 29–63). New York: Aldine de Gruyter.

Gibson, K. R., & Petersen, A. C. (1991). Introduction. In K. R. Gibson & A. C. Petersen (Eds.), *Brain maturation and cognitive development: Comparative and cross-cultural perspectives* (pp. 3–12). New York: Aldine de Gruyter.

Gick, M. L., & Holyoak, K. J. (1980). Analogical problem solving. *Cognitive Psychology, 12,* 306–355.

Gick, M. L., & Holyoak, K. J. (1983). Schema induction and analogical transfer. *Cognitive Psychology, 15,* 1–38.

Gickling, E. E., & Armstrong, D. L. (1978). Levels of instructional difficulty as related to on-task behavior, task completion, and comprehension. *Journal of Learning Disabilities, 11,* 559–566.

Gickling, E. E., Shane, R. L., & Croskery, K. M. (1989). Developing mathematical skills in low-achieving high school students through curriculum-based assessment. *School Psychology Review, 18,* 344–355.

Gilbert, N., Spring, C., & Sassenrath, J. (1977). Effects of overlearning and similarity on transfer in word recognition. *Perceptual and Motor Skills, 44,* 591–598.

Gilewski, M. J., & Zelinski, E. M. (1986). Questionnaire assessment of memory complaints. In L. W. Poon (Ed.), *Handbook for clinical memory assessment of older adults* (pp. 93–107). Washington, DC: American Psychological Association.

Gilger, J. W. (1991). Differential assortative mating found for academic and demographic variables as a function of time and assessment. *Behavior Genetics, 21,* 131–150.

Gilligan, C. (1982). *In a different voice: Psychological theory and women's development.* Cambridge, MA: Harvard University Press.

Gilligan, C., & Attanucci, J. (1988). Two moral orientations. In C. Gilligan, J. V. Ward, & J. M. Taylor with B. Bardige (Eds.), *Mapping the moral domain: A contribution of women's thinking to psychological theory and education* (pp. 73–86). Cambridge, MA: Harvard University Press.

Gilligan, C., Kohlberg, L., Lerner, E., & Belensky, M. (1971). Moral reasoning about sexual dilemmas: The development of an interview and scoring system. In *Technical Report of the Commission on Obscenity and Pornography,* Vol. 1 (No. 5256–0010). Washington, DC: Superintendent of Documents: U.S. Government Printing Office.

Gilligan, C., Lyons, N. P., & Hanmer, T. J. (1990). *Making connections: The relational worlds of adolescent girls at Emma Willard School.* Cambridge, MA: Harvard University Press.

Gipson, M. H., Abraham, M. R., & Renner, J. W. (1989). Relationships between formal-operational thought and conceptual difficulties in genetics problem solving. *Journal of Research in Science Teaching, 26,* 811–821.

Glaser, R., & Chi, M. T. H. (1988). Introduction: What is it to be an expert? In M. T. H. Chi, R. Glaser, & M. J. Farr (Eds.), *The nature of expertise* (pp. xv–xxiix). Hillsdale, NJ: Erlbaum & Associates.

Glaser, B., & Strauss, A. (1967). *The discovery of grounded theory.* Chicago: Aldine.

Glass, A. L., Holyoak, K. J., & O'Dell, C. (1974). Production frequency and the verification of quantified statements. *Journal of Verbal Learning and Verbal Behavior, 13,* 237–254.

Glass, G. V., McGaw, B., & Smith, M. L. (1981). *Meta-analysis in social research.* Newbury Park, CA: Sage.

Glass, G. V., & Smith, M. L. (1979). Meta-analysis of the research on class size and achievement. *Educational Evaluation and Policy Analysis, 1,* 2–16.

Glasson, G. E. (1989). The effects of hands-on and teacher demonstration laboratory methods on science achievement in relation to reasoning ability and prior knowledge. *Journal of Research in Science Teaching, 26,* 121–131.

Gleitman, L. R. (1986). Biological preprogramming for language learning. In S. L. Friedman, K. A. Klivington, & R. W. Peterson (Eds.), *The brain, cognition, and education* (pp. 120–151). Orlando, FL: Academic Press.

Glenberg, A. M., & Epstein, W. (1987). Inexpert calibration of comprehension. *Memory and Cognition, 15,* 84–93.

Glenberg, A. M., Wilkinson, A. C., & Epstein, W. (1982). The illusion of knowing: Failure in the self-assessment of comprehension. *Memory and Cognition, 10,* 597–602.

Glenberg, A. M., Sanocki, T., Epstein, W., & Morris, C. (1987). Enhancing calibration of comprehension. *Journal of Experimental Psychology: General, 116,* 119–136.

Glenwick, D. S. (1976). Training impulsive children in verbal self-regulation by use of natural change agents (Doctoral dissertation, University of Rochester, 1976). *Dissertation Abstracts International 459-B.* (University Microfilms No. 76–14,758.)

Gliessman, D. H., Pugh, R. C., Dowden, D. E., & Hutchins, T. F. (1988). Variables influencing the acquisition of a generic teaching skill. *Review of Educational Research, 58,* 25–46.

Glover, J. A. (1989). The "testing" phenomenon: Not gone but nearly forgotten. *Journal of Educational Psychology, 81,* 392–399.

Glover, J. A., & Corkill, A. J. (1987). Influence of paraphrased repetitions on the spacing effect. *Journal of Educational Psychology, 87,* 198–199.

Glover, J. A., Dinnel, D. L., Halpain, D. R., McKee, T. K., Corkill, A. J., & Wise, S. L. (1988). Effects of across-chapter signals on recall of text. *Journal of Educational Psychology, 80,* 3–15.

Glynn, S. M. (1991). Explaining science concepts: A teaching-with-analogies model. In S. M. Glynn, R. H. Yeany, & B. K. Britton (Eds.), *The psychology of learning science* (pp. 219–240). Hillsdale, NJ: Erlbaum & Associates.

Glynn, S. M., Andre, T., & Britton, B. K. (1986). *Design of instructional text. Educational Psychologist* (Special issue), *21* (4).

Glynn, S. M., Muth, K. D., & Britton, B. K. (1990). Thinking aloud about concepts in science text: How instructional objectives work. In H. Mandl, E. De Corte, S. N. Bennett, & H. F. Friedrich (Eds.), *Learning and instruction: European research in an international context,* Vol. 2 (pp. 215–223). Oxford, UK: Pergamon Press.

Glynn, S. M., Yeany, R. H., & Britton, B. K. (1991). A constructive view of learning science. In S. M. Glynn, R. H. Yeany, & B. K. Britton (Eds.), *The psychology of learning science* (pp. 3–19). Hillsdale, NJ: Erlbaum & Associates.

Goetz, E. T., Anderson, R. C., & Schallert, D. L. (1981). The representation of sentences in memory. *Journal of Verbal Learning and Verbal Behavior, 20,* 369–385.

Goetz, E. T., Sadoski, M., Olivarez, A., Jr., Calero-Breckheimer, A., Garner, P., & Fatemi, Z. (1992). The structure of emotional response in reading a literary text: Quantitative and qualitative analyses. *Reading Research Quarterly, 27,* 360–372.

Goetz, E. T., Schallert, D. L., Reynolds, R. E., & Radin, D. I. (1983). Reading in perspective: What real cops and pretend burglars look for in a story. *Journal of Educational Psychology, 75,* 500–510.

Goldberg, R. A., Schwartz, S., & Stewart, M. (1977). Individual differences in cognitive processes. *Journal of Educational Psychology, 69,* 9–14.

Goldberg, S., & DeVitto, B. A. (1983). *Born too soon: Preterm birth and early development.* San Francisco: W.H. Freeman & Co.

Goldberger, A. S. (1977). Twin methods: A skeptical view. In P. Taubman (Ed.), *Kinometrics: Determinants of socioeconomic success between and within families.* Amsterdam: North-Holland.

Golden, C. J., Zillmer, E., & Spiers, M. (1992). *Neuropsychological assessment and intervention.* Springfield, IL: Charles C Thomas.

Goldenberg, C. (1989). Parents' effects on academic grouping for reading: Three case studies. *American Educational Research Journal, 26,* 329–352.

Goldenberg, C. (1992). The limits of expectations: A case for case knowledge about teacher expectancy effects. *American Educational Research Journal, 29,* 517–544.

Goldman, J., & Coté, L. (1991). Aging of the brain: Dementia of the Alzheimer's type. In E. R. Kandel, J. H. Schwartz, & T. M. Jessell (Eds.), *Principles of neural science,* 3rd ed. (pp. 974–983). New York: Elsevier.

Goldman, S. R., Mertz, D. L., & Pellegrino, J. W. (1989). Individual differences in extended practice functions and solution strategies for basic addition facts. *Journal of Educational Psychology, 81,* 481–496.

Goldman, S. R., Pellegrino, J. W., & Mertz, D. L. (1988). Extended practice of basic addition facts: Strategy changes in learning-disabled students. *Cognition and Instruction, 5,* 223–265.

Goldman-Rakic, P. S. (1987). Development of

cortical circuitry and cognitive function. *Child Development, 58,* 601–622.

Goldman-Rakic, P. S., Isseroff, A., Schwartz, M. L., & Bugbee, N. M. (1983). The neurobiology of cognitive development. In M. M. Haith & J. J. Campos (Volume Eds.) and P. H. Mussen (General Ed.), *Handbook of child psychology*, Vol. II, *Infancy and developmental psychobiology* (pp. 281–344). New York: John Wiley & Sons.

Goldsmith-Phillips, J. (1989). Word and context in reading development: A test of the interactive-compensatory hypothesis. *Journal of Educational Psychology, 81,* 299–305.

Goldstein, H., & Mousetis, L. (1989). Generalized language learning by children with severe mental retardation: Effects of peers' expressive modeling. *Journal of Applied Behavioral Analysis, 22,* 245–259.

Good, T. L., & Brophy, J. E. (1986). School effects. In *Handbook of research on teaching,* 3rd ed. (pp. 570–602). New York: Macmillan.

Good, T. L., Grouws, D. A., Mason, D. A., Slavings, R. L., & Cramer, K. (1990). An observational study of small-group mathematics instruction in elementary school. *American Educational Research Journal, 27,* 755–782.

Gooden, W. E. (1989). Development of black men in early adulthood. In R. L. Jones (Ed.), *Black adult development and aging* (pp. 63–89). Berkeley, CA: Cobb & Henry.

Goodlad, J. I. (1984). *A place called school: Prospects for the future.* New York: McGraw-Hill.

Goodlad, J. I., & P. Keating (Eds.), (1990). *Access to knowledge: An agenda for our nation's schools.* New York: College Entrance Examination Board.

Goodman, J. F. (1990). Infant intelligence: Do we, can we, should we assess it? In C. R. Reynolds & R. W. Kamphaus (Eds.), *Handbook of psychological and educational assessment of children: Intelligence and achievement* (pp. 183–208). New York: Guilford Press.

Goodman, K. S. (1965). A linguistic study of cues and miscues in reading. *Elementary English, 42,* 639–642.

Goodman, K. S. (1967). Reading: A psycholinguistic guessing game. *Journal of the Reading Specialist, 6,* 126–135.

Goodman, K. S. (1989). Whole-language research: Foundations and development. *Elementary School Journal, 90,* 207–221.

Goodman, K. S., & Goodman, Y. M. (1979). Learning to read is natural. In L. B. Resnick & P. A. Weaver, *Theory and practice of early reading,* Vol. 1 (pp. 137–154). Hillsdale, NJ: Erlbaum & Associates.

Goodman, R. (1987). The developmental neurobiology of language. In W. Yule & M. Rutter (Eds.), *Language development and disorders* (pp. 129–145). Oxford, UK: Blackwell.

Goodman, Y. M. (1991). Informal methods of evaluation. In J. Flood, J. M. Jensen, D. Lapp, & J. R. Squire (Eds.), *Handbook of research on teaching the English language arts* (pp. 502–509). New York: Macmillan.

Goss, A. M. (1968). Estimated versus actual physical strength in three ethnic groups. *Child Development, 39,* 283–290.

Goswami, U. (1986). Children's use of analogy in learning to read: A developmental study. *Journal of Experimental Child Psychology, 42,* 73–83.

Goswami, U. (1988). Orthographic analogies and reading development. *Quarterly Journal of Experimental Psychology, 40,* 239–268.

Goswami, U. (1991). Analogical reasoning: What develops? A review of research and theory. *Child Development, 62,* 1–22.

Goswami, U. (1992). *Analogical reasoning in children.* Hillsdale, NJ: Erlbaum & Associates.

Goswami, U., & Bryant, P. E. (1990). *Phonological skills and learning to read.* Hillsdale, NJ: Erlbaum & Associates.

Goswami, U., & Bryant, P. (1992). Rhyme, analogy, and children's reading. In P. B. Gough, L. C. Ehri, & R. Treiman (Eds.), *Reading acquisition* (pp. 49–63). Hillsdale, NJ: Erlbaum & Associates.

Gottesman, I. I. (1963). Genetic aspects of intelligent behavior. In N. Ellis (Ed.), *Handbook of mental deficiency.* New York: McGraw-Hill.

Gottfredson, D. C., Gottfredson, G. D., & Hybl, L. G. (1993). Managing adolescent behavior: A multiyear, multischool study. *American Educational Research Journal, 30,* 179–215.

Gottfried, A. W. (1984). Home environment and early cognitive development: Integration, meta-analyses, and conclusions. In A. W. Gottfried (Ed.), *Home environment and early cognitive development: Longitudinal research* (pp. 329–342). Orlando, FL: Academic Press.

Gough, P. B., Juel, C., & Griffith, P. L. (1992). Reading, spelling, and the orthographic cipher. In P. B. Gough, L. C. Ehri, & R. Treiman (Eds.), *Reading acquisition* (pp. 35–48). Hillsdale, NJ: Erlbaum & Associates.

Gould, S. J. (1981). *The mismeasure of man.* New York: W.W. Norton Co.

Grabe, M. (1989). Evaluation of purposeful reading skills in elementary-age students. *Journal of Educational Psychology, 81,* 628–630.

Graeber, A. O., Tirosh, D., & Glover, R. (1989). Preservice teachers' misconceptions in solving verbal problems in multiplication and division. *Journal for Research in Mathematics Education, 20,* 95–102.

Graesser, A. C. (1981). *Prose comprehension beyond the word.* New York: Springer-Verlag.

Graesser, A. C., Hoffman, N. L., & Clark, L. F. (1980). Structural components of reading time. *Journal of Verbal Learning and Verbal Behavior, 19,* 135–151.

Graesser, A. C., & McMahen, C. L. (1993). Anomalous information triggers questions when adults solve quantitative problems and comprehend stories. *Journal of Educational Psychology, 85,* 136–151.

Graham, S. (1990). The role of production factors in learning disabled students' compositions. *Journal of Educational Psychology, 82,* 781–791.

Graham, S., & Barker, G. P. (1990). The down side of help: An attributional-developmental analysis of helping behaviors as a low-ability cue. *Journal of Educational Psychology, 82,* 7–14.

Graham, S., & Golan, S. (1991). Motivational influences on cognition: Task involvement, ego involvement, and depth of information processing. *Journal of Educational Psychology, 83,* 187–194.

Graham, S., & Harris, K. R. (1987). Improving composition skills of inefficient learners with self-instructional strategy training. *Topics in Language Disorders, 7,* 66–77.

Graham, S., & Harris, K. R. (1988). Instructional recommendations for teaching writing to exceptional children. *Exceptional Children, 54,* 506–512.

Graham, S., & Harris, K. R. (1989a). A components analysis of cognitive strategy instruction: Effects on learning disabled students' composition and self-efficacy. *Journal of Educational Psychology, 81,* 353–361.

Graham, S., & Harris, K. R. (1989b). Cognitive training: Implications for written language. In J. N. Hughes & R. J. Hall (Eds.), *Cognitive-behavioral psychology in the schools* (pp. 247–279). New York: Guilford Press.

Graham, S., & Harris, K. R. (1992). Self-regulated strategy development: Programmatic research in writing. In B. Y. L. Wong (Ed.), *Contemporary intervention research in learning disabilities: An international perspective* (pp. 47–64). New York: Springer-Verlag.

Graham, S., Harris, K. R., MacArthur, C., & Schwartz, S. (1991). Writing instruction. In B. Wong (Ed.), *Learning about learning disabilities* (pp. 309–343). New York: Academic Press.

Graham, S., & MacArthur, C. (1988). Improving learning disabled students' skill at revising essays produced on a word processor: Self-instructional strategy training. *Journal of Special Education, 22,* 133–152.

Graham, S., Schwartz, S., & MacArthur, C. (1991). *Learning disabled and normally achieving students' knowledge of the writing process: Attitudes toward writing and self-efficacy.* College Park, MD: University of Maryland, Department of Special Education.

Graham, T., & Perry, M. (1993). Indexing transitional knowledge. *Developmental Psychology, 29,* 779–788.

Grant, C. A. (Ed.) (1992). *Research and multi-cultural education: From the margins to the mainstream.* Washington, DC: The Falmer Press.

Graves, M. F., & Slater, W. H. (1991). A response to "Instructional texts rewritten by five expert teams." *Journal of Educational Psychology, 83,* 147–148.

Graves, M., Slater, W. H., Roen, D., Redd-Boyd, T., Duin, A. H., Furniss, D. W., and Hazelline, P. (1988). Some characteristics of memorable expository writing: Effects of revisions by writers with different backgrounds. *Research in the Teaching of English, 22,* 242–265.

Grayson, D. A. (1989). Twins reared together: Minimizing shared environmental effects. *Behavior Genetics, 19,* 593–603.

Graziano, W. G., Varca, P. E., & Levy, J. C. (1982). Race of examiner effects and the validity of intelligence tests. *Review of Educational Research, 52,* 469–498.

Greenfield, P. M. (1984). A theory of the teacher in the learning activities of everyday life. In B. Rogoff & J. Lave (Eds.), *Everyday cognition: Its development in social context* (pp. 117–138). Cambridge, MA: Harvard University Press.

Greenfield, P. M., & Savage-Rumbaugh, E. S. (1990). Grammatical combination in *Pan paniscus:* Processes of learning and invention in the evolution and development of language. In S. T. Parker & K. R. Gibson (Eds.), *"Language" and intelligence in monkeys and apes* (pp. 540–578). Cambridge, UK: Cambridge University Press.

Greenlee, M. E., Hiebert, E. H., Bridge, C. A., & Winograd, P. N. (1986). The effects of different audiences on young writers' letter writing. In J. Niles & R. Lalik (Eds.) *Solving problems in literacy: Learners, teachers, and researchers* (pp. 281–289). Rochester, NY: National Reading Conference.

Greeno, J. G. (1991). Number sense as situated knowing in a conceptual domain. *Journal for Research in Mathematics Education, 22,* 170–218.

Greeno, J. G. (1992). Mathematical and scientific thinking in classrooms and other situations. In D. F Halpern (Ed.), *Enhancing thinking skills in the sciences and mathematics* (pp. 39–62). Hillsdale, NJ: Erlbaum & Associates.

Greenough, W. T. (1987). Experience and brain development. *Child Development, 58,* 539–559.

Greenough, W. T., Black, J. E., & Wallace, C. S. (1987). Experience and brain development. *Child Development, 58,* 539–559.

Greenough, W. T., & Juraska, J. M. (1986). *Developmental neuropsycho-biology.* Orlando, FL: Academic Press.

Greenwood, C. R., Delquadri, J. C., & Hall, R. V. (1989). Longitudinal effects of classwide peer tutoring. *Journal of Educational Psychology, 81,* 371–383.

Griffith, D. R. (1992). Prenatal exposure to cocaine and other drugs: Developmental and educational prognoses. *Phi Delta Kappan, 74,* 30–34.

Griffith, P. L. (1991). Phonemic awareness helps first graders invent spellings and third graders remember correct spellings. *Journal of Reading Behavior, 23,* 215–233.

Grinder, R. E. (1985). The gifted in our midst: By their divine deeds, neuroses, and mental test scores we have known them. In F. D. Horowitz & M. O'Brien (Eds.), *The gifted and talented: Developmental perspectives* (pp. 5–35). Washington, DC: American Psychological Association.

Groen, G. J., & Parkman, J. M. (1972). A chronometric analysis of simple addition. *Psychological Review, 79,* 329–343.

Groen, G., & Resnick, L. (1977). Can preschool children invent addition algorithms? *Journal of Educational Psychology, 69,* 645–652.

Gross-Glenn, K., Duara, R., Yoshii, F., Barker, W. W., Chen, J. Y., Apicella, A., Boothe, T., & Lubs, H. A. (1988). PET-scan reading studies of familial dyslexics [Abstract]. *Journal of*

Clinical and Experimental Neuropsychology, 10, 34–35.

Grossman, H. J. (Ed.) (1983). *Manual on terminology and classification in mental retardation* (3rd revision). Washington, DC: American Association on Mental Deficiency.

Guba, E. G. (Ed.) (1990). *Paradigm dialog.* Newbury, CA: Sage.

Guba, E. G., Lincoln, Y. S. (1982). Epistemological and methodological bases of naturalistic inquiry. *Educational Communication and Technology Journal, 30,* 233–252.

Guilford, J. P. (1967). *The nature of human intelligence.* New York: McGraw-Hill.

Gunstone, R. F., & White, R. T. (1981). Understanding of gravity. *Science Education, 65,* 291–299.

Guralnick, M. J. (1976). Solving complex perceptual discrimination problems: Techniques for the development of problem-solving strategies. *American Journal of Mental Deficiency, 81,* 18–25.

Guri-Rozenblit, S. (1989). Effects of a tree diagram on students' comprehension of main ideas in an expository text with multiple themes. *Reading Research Quarterly, 24,* 236–247.

Guthke, J., & Wingenfeld, S. (1992). The learning test concept: Origins, state of the art, and trends. In H. C. Haywood & D. Tzuriel (Eds.), *Interactive assessment* (pp. 64–93). New York: Springer-Verlag.

Guthrie, J. T. (1984). Literacy for science and technology. *Journal of Reading, 27,* 478–480.

Guthrie, J. T. (1988). Locating information in documents: Examination of a cognitive model. *Reading Research Quarterly, 23,* 178–199.

Guthrie, J. T., Bennett, S., & Weber, S. (1991). Processing procedural documents: A cognitive model for following written directions. *Educational Psychology Review, 3,* 249–265.

Guthrie, J. T., & Dreher, M. J. (1990). Literacy as search: Explorations via computer. In D. Nix & R. Spiro (Eds.), *Cognition education and multimedia: Exploring ideas in high technology.* Hillsdale, NJ: Erlbaum & Associates.

Guthrie, J. T., & Pressley, M. (1992). Reading as cognition and the mediation of experience. In M. J. Dreher & W. H. Slater (Eds.), *Elementary school literacy: Critical issues* (pp. 241–260). Norwood, MA: Christopher-Gordon Publishers.

Guttentag, R. E. (1984). The mental effort requirement of cumulative rehearsal: A developmental study. *Journal of Experimental Child Psychology, 37,* 92–106.

Guttentag, R. E., Ornstein, P. A., & Siemens, L. (1987). Children's spontaneous rehearsal: Transitions in strategy acquisition. *Cognitive Development, 2,* 307–326.

Guttmann, J., Levin, J. R., & Pressley, M. (1977). Pictures, partial pictures, and young children's oral prose learning. *Journal of Educational Psychology, 69,* 473–480.

Guzzetti, B. J., Snyder, T. E., Glass, G. V., & Gamas, W. S. (1993). Promoting conceptual

change in science: A comparative meta-analysis of instructional interventions from reading education and science education. *Reading Research Quarterly, 28,* 117–159.

Haas, C., & Flower, L. (1988). Rhetorical reading strategies and the construction of meaning. *College Composition and Communication, 39,* 167–183.

Haberlandt, K. (1980). Story grammar and reading time of story constituents. *Poetics, 9,* 99–116.

Haberman, M. (1992). The pedagogy of poverty versus good teaching. *Phi Delta Kappan, 73,* 290–294.

Haensly, P. A., & Torrance, E. P. (1990). Assessment of creativity in children and adolescents. In C. R. Reynolds & R. W. Kamphaus (Eds.), *Handbook of psychological and educational assessment of children: Intelligence and achievement* (pp. 697–722). New York: Guilford Press.

Hagen, J. W., Barclay, C. R., Anderson, B. J., Feeman, D. J., Segal, S. S., Bacon, G., & Goldstein, G. W. (1990). Intellective functioning and strategy use in children with insulin-dependent diabetes mellitus. *Child Development, 61,* 1714–1727.

Haier, R. J., Siegel, B. V., Nuechterlein, K. H., Hazlett, E., Wu, J. C., Paek, J., Browning, H. L., & Buchsbaum, M. S. (1988). Cortical glucose metabolic rate correlates of abstract reasoning and attention studied with positron emission tomography. *Intelligence, 12,* 199–217.

Hakstian, A. R., & Cattell, R. B. (1978). Higher stratum ability structure on a basis of twenty primary abilities. *Journal of Educational Psychology, 70,* 657–659.

Hakuta, K. (1986). *Mirror of language: The debate on bilingualism.* New York: Basic Books.

Hakuta, K. (1987). Degree of bilingualism and cognitive ability in mainland Puerto Rican children. *Child Development, 58,* 1372–1388.

Haladyna, T. M., Nolen, S. B., & Haas, N. S. (1991). Raising standardized achievement test scores and the origins of test score pollution. *Educational Researcher, 20* (5), 2–7.

Hall, E. R., Esty, E. T., & Fisch, S. M. (1990). Television and children's problem-solving behavior: A synopsis of an evaluation of the effects of *Square One* TV. *Journal of Mathematical Behavior, 9,* 161–174.

Hall, J. A. (1984). *Nonverbal sex differences: Accuracy of communication and expressive style.* Baltimore: Johns Hopkins Press.

Hall, V. C., & Edmondson, B. (1992). Relative importance of aptitude and prior domain knowledge on immediate and delayed posttests. *Journal of Educational Psychology, 84,* 219–223.

Hall, V. C., & Merkel, S. P. (1985). Teacher expectancy effects and educational psychology. In J. B. Dusek (Ed.), *Teacher expectancies* (pp. 67–92). Hillsdale, NJ: Erlbaum & Associates.

Haller, E. P., Child, D. A., & Walberg, H. J. (1988). Can comprehension be taught? A quantitative synthesis of "metacognitive" studies. *Educational Researcher, 17* (9), 5–8.

Halpern, D. F. (1992). *Sex differences in cognitive*

abilities, 2nd ed. Hillsdale, NJ: Erlbaum & Associates.

Halpern, D. F., Hansen, C., & Riefer, D. (1990). Analogies as an aid to understanding and memory. *Journal of Educational Psychology, 82,* 298–305.

Halstead, W. C. (1947). *Brain and intelligence.* Chicago: University of Chicago Press.

Hammond, K. J. (1990). Case-based planning: A framework for planning from experience. *Cognitive Science, 14,* 385–443.

Hamond, N. R., & Fivush, R. (1991). Memories of Mickey Mouse: Young children recount their trip to Disneyworld. *Cognitive Development, 6,* 433–448.

Hampson, E. (1990a). Estrogen-related variations in human spatial and articulatory-motor skills. *Psychoendrocrinology.*

Hampson, E. (1990b). Variations in sex-related cognitive abilities across the menstrual cycle. *Brain and Cognition.*

Hampson, E., & Kimura, D. (1988). Reciprocal effects of hormonal fluctuations on human motor and perceptual-spatial skills. *Behavioral Neuroscience, 102,* 456–495.

Hancock, C., Kaput, J. J., & Goldsmith, L. T. (1992). Authentic inquiry with data: Critical barriers to classroom implementation. *Educational Psychologist, 27,* 337–364.

Haney, W. (1991). We must take care: Fitting assessments to functions. In V. Perrone (Ed.). *Expanding student assessment* (pp. 142–163). Alexandria, VA: Association for Supervision and Curriculum Development.

Hanford, G. H. (1991). *Life with the SAT: Assessing our young people and our times.* New York: College Entrance Examination Board.

Hanna, E., & Meltzoff, A. N. (1993). Peer imitation by toddlers in laboratory, home, and daycare contexts: Implications for social learning and memory. *Developmental Psychology, 29,* 701–710.

Hansen, J. S. (1969). The impact of the home literacy environment on reading attitude. *Elementary English, 46,* 17–24.

Hansen, J. (1992). Literacy portfolios: Helping students know themselves. *Educational Leadership, 49* (8), 66–68.

Hansen, J., & Pearson, P. D. (1983). An instructional study: Improving the referential comprehension of good and poor fourth grade readers. *Journal of Educational Psychology, 75,* 821–829.

Hanson, S. L., & Ginsburg, A. L. (1988). Gaining control: Values and high school success. *American Educational Research Journal, 25,* 334–365.

Hardiman, P. T., Pollatsek, A., & Weil, A. D. (1986). Learning to understand the balance beam. *Cognition and Instruction, 3,* 1–30.

Hardy-Brown, K. (1983). Universals and individual differences: Disentangling two approaches to the study of language acquisition. *Developmental Psychology, 19,* 610–624.

Hardy-Brown, K., & Plomin, R. (1985). Infant communicative development: Evidence from adoptive and biological families for genetic and environmental influences on rate differences. *Developmental Psychology, 21,* 378–385.

Hardy-Brown, K., Plomin, R., & DeFries, J. C. (1981). Genetic and environmental influences on rate of communicative development in the first year of life. *Developmental Psychology, 17,* 704–717.

Haroutunian-Gordon, S. (1991). *Turning the soul: Teaching through conversation in the high school.* Chicago: University of Chicago Press.

Harrell, R., Capp, R., Davis, D., Peerless, J., & Ravitz, L. (1981). Can nutritional supplements help mentally retarded children? *Proceedings of the National Academy of Science, 78,* 574–578.

Harrell, T. W., & Harrell, M. S. (1945). Army General Classification Test scores for civilian occupations. *Educational and Psychological Measurement, 5,* 229–239.

Harris, K. R. (1988, April). *What's wrong with strategy intervention research: Intervention integrity.* Presented at the annual meeting of the American Educational Research Association, New Orleans.

Harris, K. R., & Graham, S. (1985). Improving learning disabled students' composition skills: Self-control strategy training. *Learning Disability Quarterly, 8,* 27–36.

Harris, K. R., & Graham, S. (1992). Self-regulated strategy development: A part of the writing process. In M. Pressley, K. R. Harris, & J. T. Guthrie (Eds.), *Promoting academic competence and literacy in school* (pp. 277–309). San Diego: Academic Press.

Harris, K. R., & Pressley, M. (1991). The nature of cognitive strategy instruction: Interactive strategy construction. *Exceptional Children, 57,* 392–404.

Harris, L. J. (1988). Right-brain training: Some reflections on the application of research on cerebral hemispheric specialization to education. In D. L. Molfese & S. J. Segalowitz (Eds.), *Brain lateralization in children* (pp. 207–236). New York: Guilford Press.

Harry, B. (1992). An ethnographic study of cross-cultural communication with Puerto Rican-American families in the special education system. *American Educational Research Journal, 29,* 471–494.

Harshman, R. A., Hampson, E., & Barenboim, S. A. (1983). Individual differences in cognitive abilities and brain organization: Part I: Sex and handedness differences in ability. *Canadian Journal of Psychology, 37,* 144–192.

Harter, M. R. (1991). Event-related potential indices: Learning disabilities and visual processing. In J. E. Obrzut & G. W. Hynd (Eds.), *Neuropsychological foundations of learning disabilities: A handbook of issues, methods, and practice* (pp. 437–473). San Diego: Academic Press.

Harter, S. (1981). A new self-report scale of intrinsic versus extrinsic orientation in the classroom: Motivational and informational components. *Developmental Psychology, 17,* 300–312.

Harter, S., Whitesell, N. R., & Kowalski, P. (1992). Individual differences in the effects of educational transitions on young adolescent's perceptions of competence and motivational orientation. *American Educational Research Journal, 29,* 777–807.

Hartley, J. (1983). Notetaking research: Resetting the scoreboard. *Bulletin of the British Psychological Society, 36,* 13–14.

Hartley, J., & Marshall, S. (1974). On notes and notetaking. *University Quarterly, 28,* 225–235.

Hartman, D. K. (1992). Eight readers reading: The intertextual links of able readers using multiple passages. *Reading Research Quarterly, 27,* 122–123.

Hartsfield, F., Licht, B., Swenson, C., & Thiele, C. (1989, August). *Control beliefs and behavior problems of elementary school children.* Paper presented at the meeting of the American Psychological Association, New Orleans.

Hasher, L., Stoltzfus, E. R., Zacks, R. T., & Rypma, B. (1991). Age and inhibition. *Journal of Experimental Psychology: Learning, Memory, and Cognition, 17,* 163–169.

Hatano, G., Amaiwa, S., & Shimuzu, K. (1987). Formation of a mental abacus for computation and its use as a memory device for digits: A developmental study. *Developmental Psychology, 23,* 832–838.

Hatano, G., & Inagaki, K. (1991). Sharing cognition through collective comprehension activity. In L. Resnick, J. M. Levine, & S. D. Teasley (Eds.), *Perspectives on socially shared cognition* (pp. 331–348). Washington, DC: American Psychological Association.

Hatano, G., Miyake, Y., & Binks, M. G. (1977). Performance of expert abacus operators. *Cognition, 5,* 47–55.

Hativa, N. (1988). Computer-based drill and practice in arithmetic: Widening the gap between high- and low-achieving students. *American Educational Research Journal, 25,* 366–397.

Hatta, T., Hirose, T., Ikeda, K., & Fukuhara, H. (1989). Digit memory of Soroban experts: Evidence of utilization of mental imagery. *Applied Cognitive Psychology, 3,* 23–33.

Hawkins, J. D., Doueck, H. J., & Lishner, D. M. (1988). Changing teaching practices in mainstream classrooms to improve bonding and behavior of low achievers. *American Educational Research Journal, 25,* 31–50.

Hawkins, J. D., & Lam, T. (1987). Teacher practices, social development and delinquency. In J. D. Burchard & S. N. Burchard (Eds.), *Prevention of delinquent behavior* (pp. 241–274). Beverly Hills, CA: Sage.

Hayes, J. R. (1985). Three problems in teaching general skills. In S. F. Chipman, J. W. Segal, & R. Glaser (Eds.), *Thinking and learning skills,* Vol. 2, *Research and open questions* (pp. 391–405). Hillsdale, NJ: Erlbaum & Associates.

Hayes, J. R., Flower, L., Schriver, K., Stratman, J., & Carey, L. (1987). Cognitive processes in revision. In S. Rosenberg (Ed.), *Advances in applied psycholinguistics: Reading, writing, and language processing.* Cambridge, UK: Cambridge University Press.

Hayes, J. R., Waterman, D. A., & Robinson, C. S. (1977). Identifying relevant aspects of a problem text. *Cognitive Science, 1,* 297–313.

Hayes-Roth, B., & Thorndyke, P. W. (1979). Integration of knowledge from text. *Journal of Verbal Learning and Verbal Behavior, 18,* 91–108.

Haywood, H. C., & Tzuriel, D. (1992a). Epilogue: The status and future of interactive assessment. In H. C. Haywood & D. Tzuriel (Eds.), *Interactive assessment* (pp. 504–508). New York: Springer-Verlag.

Haywood, H. C., & Tzuriel, D. (1992b). *Interactive assessment.* New York: Springer-Verlag.

Haywood, H. C., Tzuriel, D., & Vaught, S. (1992). Psychoeducational assessment from a transactional perspective. In H. C. Haywood & D. Tzuriel (Eds.), *Interactive assessment* (pp. 38–63). New York: Springer-Verlag.

Healy, V. C. (1989). The effects of advance organizer and prerequisite knowledge passages on the learning and retention of science concepts. *Journal of Research in Science Teaching, 26,* 627–642.

Hearnshaw, L. (1979). *Cyril Burt: Psychologist.* Ithaca, NY: Cornell University Press.

Heath, S. B. (1982). What no bedtime story means: Narrative skills at home and school. *Language in Society, 11,* 49–76.

Hebb, D. O. (1949). *The organization of behavior.* New York: Wiley.

Heckhausen, J. (1987). Balancing for weaknesses and challenging developmental potential: A longitudinal study of mother-infant dyads in apprenticeship interactions. *Developmental Psychology, 23,* 762–770.

Hedges, L. V., & Olkin, I. (1985). *Statistical methods for meta-analysis.* New York: Academic Press.

Hedges, L. V., & Stock, W. (1983). The effect of class size: An examination of rival hypotheses. *American Educational Research Journal, 20,* 63–85.

Heese, J. J. III, & Anderson, C. W. (1992). Students' conceptions of chemical change. *Journal of Research in Science Teaching, 29,* 277–299.

Heindel, P., & Kose, G. (1990). The effects of motoric action and organization on children's memory. *Journal of Experimental Child Psychology, 50,* 416–428.

Heinze-Fry, J. A., & Novak, J. D. (1990). Concept mapping brings long-term movement toward meaningful learning. *Science Education, 74,* 461–472.

Hembree, R. (1988). Correlates, causes, effects, and treatment of test anxiety. *Review of Educational Research, 58,* 47–77.

Hembree, R. (1992). Experiments and relational studies in problem solving: A meta-analysis. *Journal for Research in Mathematics Education, 23,* 242–273.

Hembree, R., & Dessart, D. (1986). Effects of hand-held calculators in precollege mathematics education: A meta-analysis. *Journal for Research in Mathematics Education, 17,* 83–99.

Henderson, V. L., & Dweck, C. S. (1990). Motivation and achievement. In S. S. Feldman & G. R. Elliott (Eds.), *At the threshold: The developing adolescent* (pp. 308–329). Cambridge, MA: Harvard University Press.

Hendrickson, D. E., & Hendrickson, A. E. (1980). The biological basis of individual differences in intelligence. *Personality and Individual Differences, 1,* 3–33.

Henry, M., & Renaud, H. (1972). Examined and unexamined lives. *The Research Reporter, 7,* 5–8.

Hernstein, R. (1971). I.Q. *The Atlantic Monthly, 228,* 43–64.

Hershenson, M., Munsinger, H., & Kessen, W. (1965). Preferences for shapes of intermediate variability in the newborn human. *Science, 147,* 630–631.

Hertzog, C. (1989). Influences of cognitive slowing on age differences in intelligence. *Developmental Psychology, 25,* 636–651.

Hertzog, C., Hultsch, D. F., & Dixon, R. A. (1989). Evidence for convergent validity of two self-report metamemory questionnaires. *Developmental Psychology, 25,* 687–700.

Hess, R. D., Chih-Mei, C., & McDevitt, T. M. (1987). Cultural variations in family beliefs about children's performance in mathematics: Comparisons among People's Republic of China, Chinese-American, and Caucasian-American families. *Journal of Educational Psychology, 79,* 179–188.

Hess, R. D., & Shipman, V. C. (1965). Early experience and the specialization of cognitive modes in children. *Child Development, 36,* 869–886.

Hess, R. D., Shipman, V., & Jackson, D. (1965). Early experience and the socialization cognitive models in children. *Child Development, 36,* 869–886.

Hess, T. M. (1992). Adult age differences in script content and structure. In R. L. West & J. D. Sinnott (Eds.), *Everyday memory and aging: Current research and methodology* (pp. 87–100). New York: Springer-Verlag.

Hess, T. M., & Slaughter, S. J. (1990). Schematic influences on scene memory. *Developmental Psychology, 26,* 855–865.

Hewitt, P. G. (1987). *Conceptual physics.* Menlo Park, CA: Addison-Wesley.

Hewson, P. W., & Thorley, R. (1989). The conditions of conceptual change in the classroom. *International Journal of Science Education, 11,* 541–553.

Heyns, B. (1978). *Summer learning and the effects of schooling.* New York: Academic Press.

Heyns, B. (1987). Schooling and cognitive development: Is there a season for learning? *Child Development, 58,* 1151–1160.

Hidi, S. (1990). Interest and its contribution as a mental resource for learning. *Review of Educational Research, 60,* 549–571.

Hidi, S., & Baird, W. (1988). Strategies for increasing text-based interest and students' recall of expository text. *Reading Research Quarterly, 23,* 465–483.

Hidi, S., & Klaiman, R. (1983). Notetaking by experts and novices: An attempt to identify teachable strategies. *Curriculum Inquiry, 13,* 377–395.

Hiebert, J., & Carpenter, T. P. (1992). Learning and teaching with understanding. In D. A. Grouws (Ed.), *Handbook of research on mathematics teaching and learning* (pp. 65–97). New York: Macmillan.

Hiebert, J., & Wearne, D. (1992). Links between teaching and learning place value with understanding in first grade. *Journal for Research in Mathematics Education, 23,* 98–122.

Hier, D. B., LeMay, M., Rosenberger, P. B., & Perlo, V. P. (1978). Developmental dyslexia: Evidence for a subgroup with a reversal of cerebral asymmetry. *Archives of Neurology, 35,* 90–92.

Higgins, A. (1987). A feminist perspective on moral education. *Journal of Moral Education, 16,* 240–247.

Hill, D. (1991). Tasting failure: Thoughts of an at-risk learner. *Phi Delta Kappan, 73,* 308–310.

Hill, R. D., Evankovich, K. D., Sheikh, J. H., & Yesavage, J. A. (1987). Imagery mnemonic training in a patient with primary degenerative dementia. *Psychology and Aging, 2,* 204–205.

Hinsley, D., Hayes, J. R., & Simon, H. A. (1977). From words to equations. In P. Carpenter & M. Just (Eds.), *Cognitive processes in comprehension.* Hillsdale, NJ: Erlbaum & Associates.

Hintzman, D. L. (1974). Theoretical implications of the spacing effect. In R. L. Solso (Ed.), *Theories in cognitive psychology: The Loyola symposium.* Hillsdale, NJ: Erlbaum & Associates.

Hird, J. S., Landers, D. M., Thomas, J. R., & Horan, J. J. (1991). Physical practice is superior to mental practice in enhancing cognitive and motor performance. *Journal of Sports & Exercise Psychology, 13,* 281–293.

Hirsch, E. D., Jr. (1987). *Cultural literacy: What every American needs to know.* Boston: Houghton Mifflin Co.

Hirsch, E. D., Kett, J. F., & Trefil, J. (1988). *The dictionary of cultural literacy.* Boston: Houghton Mifflin Co.

Hishitani, S. (1990). Imagery experts: How do expert abacus operators process imagery? *Applied Cognitive Psychology, 4,* 33–46.

Hitchcock, G., & Hughes, D. (1989). *Research and the teacher: A qualitative introduction to school-based research.* New York: Routledge.

Ho, H-Z., Baker, L. A., & Decker, S. N. (1988). Covariation between intelligence and speed of cognitive processing: Genetic and environmental influences. *Behavior Genetics, 18,* 247–261.

Hobbs, S. A., & Lahey, B. B. (1983). Behavioral treatment. In T. H. Ollendick & M. Hersen (Eds.), *Handbook of child psychopathology* (pp. 427–460). New York: Plenum.

Hobbs, S. A., & Sexson, S. B. (1993). Cognitive development and learning in the pediatric organ transplant recipient. *Journal of Learning Disabilities, 26,* 104–114.

Hock, M., Deshler, D. D., & Schumaker, J. B. (1991). *Annual report on the GOALS program.* Lawrence, KS: University of Kansas, Institute for Research in Learning Disabilities.

Hoffman, H. S. (1969). Stimulus factors in conditioned suppression. In B. A. Campbell & R. M. Church (Eds.), *Punishment and aversive behavior* (pp. 185–234). New York: Appleton-Century-Crofts.

Hoffman, M. L. (1970). Moral development. In P. H. Mussen (Ed.), *Carmichael's manual of child psychology*, 3rd ed., Vol. 2 (pp. 261–360). New York: John Wiley & Sons.

Hofmeister, A. M., Engelmann, S., & Carnine, D. (1989). Developing and validating science education videodiscs. *Journal of Research in Science Teaching, 26*, 665–677.

Hoge, R. D. (1988). Issues in the definition and measurement of the giftedness construct. *Educational Researcher, 17* (7), 12–16.

Holland, A., & Andre, T. (1987). Participation in extracurricular activities in secondary school: What is known, what needs to be known? *Review of Educational Research, 57*, 437–466.

Holland, A., & Andre, T. (1988). Beauty is in the eye of the reviewer. *Review of Educational Research, 58*, 113–118.

Holland, J. G., & Skinner, B. F. (1961). *The analysis of behavior*. New York: McGraw-Hill.

Holland, J. H., Holyoak, K. J., Nisbett, R. E., & Thagard, P. R. (1986). *Induction: Processes of inference, learning, and discovery*. Cambridge, MA: MIT Press.

Hollander, B. (1920). *In search of the soul*. New York: E. P. Dutton.

Holliday, W. G. (1990, June). *Two of the leading problems facing researchers in science teaching*. Presidential address. Atlanta: National Association for Research in Science Teaching.

Holliday, W. G., & Benson, G. (1991). Enhancing learning using questions adjunct to science charts. *Journal of Research in Science Teaching, 28*, 97–108.

Holliday, W. G., & McGuire, B. (1992). How can comprehension adjunct questions focus students' attention and enhance concept learning of a computer-animated science lesson? *Journal of Research in Science Teaching, 29*, 3–15.

Holloway, S. D. (1988). Concepts of ability and effort in Japan and the United States. *Review of Educational Research, 58*, 327–345.

Holmes, B. C. (1987). Children's inferences with print and pictures. *Journal of Educational Psychology, 79*, 14–18.

Holmes, C. T., & Matthews, K. M. (1984). The effects of nonpromotion on elementary and junior high school pupils: A meta-analysis. *Review of Educational Research, 54*, 225–236.

Holstein, C. (1976). Development of moral judgment: A longitudinal study of males and females. *Child Development, 47*, 51–61.

Homme, L. E. (1965). Perspectives on psychology: XXIV. Control of coverants, the operants of the mind. *Psychological Record, 15*, 501–511.

Hong, E., & O'Neil, H. F. (1992). Instructional strategies to help learners build relevant mental models in inferential statistics. *Journal of Educational Psychology, 84*, 150–159.

Hooper, S. R., & Willis, W. G. (1989). *Learning disability subtyping: Neuropsychological foundations, conceptual models, and issues in clinical differentiation*. New York: Springer-Verlag.

Hoover, S. M., & Feldhusen, J. F. (1990). The scientific hypothesis formulation ability of gifted ninth-grade students. *Journal of Educational Psychology, 82*, 838–848.

Horgan, D. D., & Morgan, D. (1990). Chess expertise in children. *Applied Cognitive psychology, 4*, 109–128.

Horn, C. C., & Manis, F. R. (1987). Development of automatic and speeded reading of printed words. *Journal of Experimental Child Psychology, 44*, 92–108.

Horn, J. L. (1968). Organization of abilities and the development of intelligence. *Psychological Review, 75*, 242–259.

Horn, J. L. (1985). Remodeling old models of intelligence. In B. Wolman (Ed.), *Handbook of intelligence* (pp. 267–300). New York: Wiley.

Horn, J. L., & Cattell, R. B. (1967). Age differences in fluid and crystallized intelligence. *Acta Psychologica, 26*, 107–129.

Horn, J. L., & Hofer, S. M. (1992). Major abilities and development in the adult period. In R. J. Sternberg & C. A. Berg (Eds.), *Intellectual development* (pp. 44–99). Cambridge, UK: Cambridge University Press.

Horn, J. L., & Stankov, L. (1982). Auditory and visual factors of intelligence. *Intelligence, 6*, 165–185.

Horton, M. S. (1982). *Category familiarity and taxonomic organization in young children*. Unpublished doctoral dissertation. Stanford University, Stanford, CA.

Howe, K. R. (1988). Against the quantitative-qualitative incompatibility thesis. *Educational Researcher, 17* (8), 10–16.

Howe, M. J. A. (1990). *The origins of exceptional abilities*. Oxford, UK: Basil Blackwell.

Howell, K. W., & Morehead, M. K. (1987). *Curriculum-based evaluation for special and remedial education: A handbook for deciding what to teach*. Columbus, OH: Merrill Publishing Co.

Howlin, P., & Rutter, M. (1987). The consequences of language delay for other aspects of development. In W. Yule & M. Rutter (Eds.), *Language development and disorders* (pp. 271–294). Philadelphia: J.B. Lippincott Co.

Hoyles, C., & Noss, R. (Eds.) (1992). *Learning mathematics and LOGO*. Cambridge, MA: MIT Press.

Huba, M. E. (1984). The relationship between linguistic awareness in prereaders and two types of experimental instruction. *Reading World, 23*, 347–363.

Hubel, D. H., & Wiesel, T. N. (1970). The period of susceptibility to the physiological effects of unilateral eye closure in kittens. *Journal of Physiology, 206*, 419–436.

Huberman, M. (1987). How well does educational research really travel? *Educational Researcher, 16* (1), 5–13.

Hudson Institute (1987). *Workforce 2000*. Indianapolis, IN: Hudson Institute.

Hudson, J. A. (1988). Children's memory for atypical actions in script based stories: Evidence for a disruption effect. *Journal of Experimental Child Psychology, 46*, 159–173.

Hudson, J. A. (1990). Constructive processes in children's event memory. *Developmental Psychology, 26*, 180–187.

Hudson, J. A., & Fivush, R. (1991a). As time goes by: Sixth graders remember a kindergarten experience. *Applied Cognitive Psychology, 5*, 347–360.

Hudson, J. A., & Fivush, R. (1991b). Planning in the preschool years: The emergence of plans from general event knowledge. *Cognitive Development, 6*, 393–415.

Hudson, J. A., Fivush, R., & Kuebli, J. (1992). Scripts and episodes: the development of event memory. *Applied Cognitive Psychology, 6*, 483–505.

Hudson, J., & Nelson, K. (1983). Effects of script structure on children's story recall. *Developmental Psychology, 19*, 625–635.

Hudson, J. A., & Shapiro, L. R. (1991). From knowing to telling: The development of children's scripts, stories, and personal narratives. In A. McCabe & C. Peterson (Eds.), *Developing narrative structure* (pp. 89–136). Hillsdale, NJ: Erlbaum & Associates.

Hudson, J. A., & Slackman, E. A. (1990). Children's use of scripts in inferential text processing. *Discourse Processes, 13*, 375–385.

Hull, D. L. (1988). *Science as a process*. Chicago: University of Chicago Press.

Hull, G. A. (1987). The editing process in writing: A performance study of more skilled and less skilled writers. *Research in the Teaching of English, 21*, 8–29.

Hulme, C., & MacKenzie, S. (1992). *Working memory and severe learning difficulties*. Hillsdale, NJ: Erlbaum & Associates.

Humes, A. (1983). Putting writing research into practice. *Elementary School Journal, 81*, 3–17.

Hunt, E., Frost, N., & Lunneborg, C. (1973). Individual differences in cognition. In G. Bower (Ed.), *The psychology of learning and motivation: Advances in research and theory*, Vol. 7 (pp. 127–139). New York: Academic Press.

Hunt, E., Lunneborg, C., & Lewis, J. (1975). What does it mean to be high verbal? *Cognitive Psychology, 7*, 194–227.

Hunter, C. S. J., & Harman, D. (1979). *Adult illiteracy in the United States: A report to the Ford Foundation*. New York: McGraw-Hill.

Hunter, J. E., & Hunter, R. F. (1984). Validity and utility of alternative predictors of a job performance. *Psychological Bulletin, 96*, 72–98.

Hunter-Blanks, P., Ghatala, E. S., Pressley, M., & Levin, J. R. (1988). Comparison of monitoring during study and during testing on a sentence-learning task. *Journal of Educational Psychology, 80*, 279–283.

Husén, T. (1959). *Psychological twin research*. Stockholm: Almqvist & Wiksell.

Husik, F. T., Linn, M. C., & Sloane, K. D. (1989). Adapting instruction to the cognitive demands of learning to program. *Journal of Educational Psychology, 81*, 570–583.

Huston, A. C., & Carpenter, C. J. (1985). Gender differences in preschool classrooms: The effects of sex-typed activity choices. In L. C. Wilkinson & C. B. Marrett (Eds.), *Gender influences on classroom interaction* (pp.143–165). Orlando, FL: Academic Press.

Hutchins, E. (1991). The social organization of distributed cognition. In L. Resnick, J. M. Levine, & S. D. Teasley (Eds.), *Perspectives on socially shared cognition* (pp. 283–307).

Washington, DC: American Psychological Association.

Huttenlocher, J., Haight, W., Bryk, A., Seltzer, M., & Lyons, T. (1991). Early vocabulary growth: Relation to language input and gender. *Developmental Psychology, 27*, 236–248.

Huttenlocher, P. R. (1979). Synaptic density in human frontal cortex-developmental changes and effects of aging. *Brain Research, 163*, 195–205.

Hyde, J. S., Fennema, E., & Lamon, S. J. (1990). Gender differences in mathematics performance: A meta-analysis. *Psychological Bulletin, 107*, 139–155.

Hyde, J. S., & Jenkins, J. J. (1973). Recall for words as a function of semantic, graphic, and syntactic orienting tasks. *Journal of Verbal Learning and Verbal Behavior, 12*, 471–480.

Hyde, J. S., & Linn M. C. (1988). Gender differences in verbal ability: A meta-analysis. *Psychological Bulletin, 104*, 53–69.

Hyman, H., Wright, C., & Reed, J. (1975). *The enduring effects of education.* Chicago: University of Chicago Press.

Hyman, I. A. (1990). *Reading, writing, and the hickory stick: The appalling story of physical and psychological abuse in American schools.* San Diego: Lexington Books.

Hyman, I. A., & Wise, J. H. (Eds.) (1977). *Corporal punishment in American education.* Philadelphia: Temple University Press.

Hynd, C. R., & Alvermann, D. E. (1986). The role of refutation text in overcoming difficulty with science concepts. *Journal of Reading, 29*, 440–446.

Hynd, G. W., & Semrud-Clikeman, M. (1989). Dyslexia and brain morphology. *Psychological Bulletin, 106*, 447–482.

Idol, L. (1987). Group story mapping: A comprehension strategy for both skilled and unskilled readers. *Journal of Learning Disabilities, 20*, 196–205.

Idol, L., & Croll, V. J. (1987). Story-mapping training as a means of improving reading comprehension. *Learning Disability Quarterly, 10*, 214–229.

Idol, L., & Jones, B. F. (Eds.) (1990). *Educational values and cognitive reform: Implications for reform.* Hillsdale, NJ: Erlbaum & Associates.

Inagaki, K. (1981). Facilitation of knowledge integration through classroom discussion. *The Quarterly Newsletter of the Laboratory of Comparative Human Cognition, 3*, 26–28.

Inagaki, K., & Hatano, G. (1989). *Learning histories of vocal and silent participants in group discussion.* Paper presented at the annual meeting of the Japanese Psychological Association, Tsukuba Japan.

Infant Health and Development Program (1990). Enhancing the outcomes of low-birth-weight premature infants. *Journal of the American Medical Association, 263*, 3035–3042.

Inhelder, B., & Piaget, J. (1958). *The growth of logical thinking from childhood to adolescence.* New York: Basic Books.

Inhelder, B., & Piaget, J. (1964). *The early growth of logic in the child.* New York: W.W. Norton Co.

Inhelder, B., Sinclair, H., & Bovet, M. (1974). *Learning and the development of cognition.* Cambridge, MA: Harvard University Press.

Iran-Nejad, A. (1990). Active and dynamic self-regulation of learning processes. *Review of Educational Research, 60*, 573–602.

Iser, W. (1978). *The act of reading: A theory of aesthetic response.* Baltimore: Johns Hopkins University Press.

Itakura, K. (1967). Instruction and learning of concept "force" in static based on Hypothesis-Experiment-Instruction: A new method of science teaching. *Bulletin of the National Institute for Educational Research, 52*, 1–121.

Itard, J. (1801). The wild boy of Aveyron. In L. Malson (Ed.) (E. Fawcett & J. White, translators), *Wolf children.* London: New Left Books.

Iversen, S., & Tumner, W. E. (1993). Phonological processing skills and the reading recovery program. *Journal of Educational Psychology, 85*, 112–120.

Iwasa, N. (1992). Postconventional reasoning and moral education in Japan. *Journal of Moral Education, 21*, 3–16.

Iwawaki, S., & Vernon, P. E. (1988). Japanese abilities and achievement. In S. H. Irvine & J. W. Berry (Eds.), *Human abilities in cultural context* (pp. 358–382). Cambridge, MA: Cambridge University Press.

Jackson, N. E., & Butterfield, E. C. (1986). A conception of giftedness designed to promote research. In R. J. Sternberg & J. E. Davidson (Eds.), *Conceptions of giftedness* (pp. 151–181). Cambridge, UK: Cambridge University Press.

Jackson, N. E., & Myers, M. G. (1982). Letter naming time, digit span, and precocious reading achievement. *Intelligence, 6*, 311–329.

Jacobi, M. (1991). Mentoring and undergraduate academic success: A literature review. *Review of Educational Research, 61*, 505–532.

Jacobs, J. E. (1991). Influence of gender stereotypes on parent and child mathematics attitudes. *Journal of Educational Psychology, 83*, 518–527.

Jacobs, J. E., & Wigfield, A. (1989). Sex equity in mathematics and science education: Research-policy links. *Educational Psychology Review, 1*, 39–56.

Jacobsen, B., Lowery, B., & DuCette, J. (1986). Attributions of learning disabled children. *Journal of Educational Psychology, 78*, 59–64.

Jacobson, J. L., Jacobson, S. W., Padgett, R.J., Brumitt, G. A., & Billings, R. L. (1992). Effects of prenatal PCB exposure on cognitive processing efficiency and sustained attention. *Developmental Psychology, 28*, 297–306.

Jacobvitz, D., & Sroufe, L. A. (1987). The early caregiver-child relationship and attention-deficit disorder with hyperactivity in kindergarten: A prospective study. *Child Development, 58*, 1488–1495.

James, W. (1983). *The principles of psychology.* Cambridge, MA: Harvard University Press.

Jamieson, D. W., Lydon, J. E., Stewart, G., & Zanna, M. P. (1987). Pygmalion revisited: New evidence for student expectancy effects in the classroom. *Journal of Educational Psychology, 79*, 461–466.

Jaynes, G. D., & Williams, R. M. Jr. (1989). *A common destiny: Blacks and American society.* Washington, DC: National Academy Press.

Jencks, C., Smith, M., Acland, H., Bane, M. J., Cohen, D., Gintis, H., Heyns, B., & Mitchelson, S. (1972). *Inequality: A reassessment of the effects of family and schooling in America.* New York: Basic Books.

Jenkins, J. J. (1974). Remember that old theory of memory? Well, forget it! *American Psychologists, 29*, 785–795.

Jensen, A. R. (1968). Patterns of mental ability and socioeconomic status. *Proceedings of the National Academy of Science, 60*, 1330–1337.

Jensen, A. R. (1969). How much can we boost IQ and scholastic achievement? *Harvard Educational Review, 39*, 1–123.

Jensen, A. R. (1972). *Genetics and education.* New York: Harper & Row.

Jensen, A. R. (1973). *Educability and group differences.* New York: Harper & Row.

Jensen, A. R. (1976). Test bias and construct validity. *Phi Delta Kappan,* December, 340–346.

Jensen, A. R. (1980). *Bias in mental testing.* New York: Free Press.

Jensen, A. R. (1981). *Straight talk about mental tests.* New York: Free Press.

Jensen, A. R. (1982). Reaction time and psychometric g. In H. J. Eysenck (Ed.), *A model for intelligence.* Berlin: Springer-Verlag.

Jensen, A. R. (1992). Understanding g in terms of information processing. *Educational Psychology Review, 4*, 271–308.

Jensen, A. R., Schafer, E. W. P., & Crinella, F. M. (1981). Reaction time, evoked brain potentials, and psychometric *g* in the severely retarded. *Intelligence, 5*, 179–197.

Jepson, K. L., & Labouvie-Vief, G. (1992). Symbolic processing of youth and elders. In R. L. West & J. D. Sinnott (Eds.), *Everyday memory and aging: Current research and methodology* (pp. 124–137). New York: Springer-Verlag.

Jernigan, T. L., Hesselink, J. R., Sowell, E., & Tallal, P. A. (1991). Cerebral structure on magnetic resonance imaging in language- and learning-impaired children. *Archives of Neurology, 48*, 539–545.

John-Steiner, V. (1985). *Notebooks of the mind: Explorations of thinking.* Albuquerque: University of New Mexico Press.

Johnson, D. K. (1988). Adolescents' solutions to dilemmas in fables: Two moral orientations—two problem-solving strategies. In C. Gilligan, J. V. Ward, & J. M. Taylor with B. Bardige (Eds.), *Mapping the moral domain: A contribution of women's thinking to psychological theory and education* (pp. 49–72). Cambridge, MA: Harvard University Press.

Johnson, D. K., Brown, L. M., & Christopherson, S. B. (1990). Adolscents' moral dilemmas: The context. *Journal of Youth and Adolescence, 19*, 615–622.

Johnson, D., & Johnson, R. (1974). Instructional goal structure: Cooperative versus competitive or individualistic. *Review of Educational Research, 44,* 213–240.

Johnson, D. W., & Johnson, R. (1975). *Learning together and alone: Cooperation, competition, and individualization.* Englewood Cliffs, NJ: Prentice-Hall.

Johnson, D. W., & Johnson, R. (1979). Conflict in the classroom: Controversy and learning. *Review of Educational Research, 49,* 51–70.

Johnson, D. W., & Johnson, R. (1985). Classroom conflict: Controversy over debate in learning groups. *American Educational Research Journal, 22,* 237–256.

Johnson, D., Maruyama, G., Johnson, R., Nelson, D., & Skon, L. (1981). Effects of cooperative, competitive, and individualistic goal structures on achievement: A meta-analysis. *Psychological Bulletin, 89,* 47–62.

Johnson, D., & Myklebust, H. R. (1967). *Learning disabilities: Educational principles and practice.* New York: Grune & Stratton.

Johnson, J. S., & Newport, E. L. (1989). Critical period effects in second language learning: The influence of maturational state on the acquisition of English as a second language. *Cognitive Psychology, 21,* 60–99.

Johnson, M. H. (Ed.) (1993). *Brain development and cognition.* Cambridge, MA: Blackwell.

Johnson, W. B., Packer, A. E., et al. (1987). *Workforce 2000: Work and workers for the twenty-first century.* Indianapolis, IN: Hudson Institute.

Johnson-Laird, P. N. (1983). *Mental models.* Cambridge, MA: Harvard University Press.

Johnson-Laird, P. N. (1989). Mental models. In M. I. Posner (Ed.), *Foundations of Cognitive Science* (pp. 469–499). Cambridge, MA: MIT Press.

Johnston, P., & Allington, R. (1991). Remediation. In R. Barr, M. L. Kamil, P. Mosenthal, & P. D. Pearson (Eds.), *Handbook of reading research,* Vol. II (pp. 984–1012). New York: Longman.

Jones, B. F., & Idol, L. (Ed.) (1990). *Dimensions of thinking: Review of research.* Hillsdale, NJ: Erlbaum & Associates.

Jones, L. V. (1984). White–black achievement differences: The narrowing gap. *American Psychologist, 39,* 1207–1213.

Jones, M. G., & Wheatley, J. (1988). Factors influencing the entry of women into science and related fields. *Science Education, 72,* 127–142.

Jones, M. G., & Wheatley, J. (1990). Gender differences in teacher-student interactions in science classrooms. *Journal of Research in Science Teaching, 27,* 861–874.

Jordan, B. (1989). Cosmopolitical obstetrics: Some insights from the training of traditional midwives. *Social Science and Medicine, 28,* 925–944.

Jordan, N. C., Huttenlocher, J., & Levine, S. C. (1992). Differential calculation abilities in young children from middle- and low-income families. *Developmental Psychology, 28,* 644–653.

Jose, P., & Brewer, W. F. (1984). The development of story liking: Character identification, suspense, and outcome resolution. *Developmental Psychology, 20,* 911–924.

Joshua, S., & Dupin, J. J. (1987). Taking into account student conceptions in instructional strategy: An example in physics. *Cognition and Instruction, 4,* 117–135.

Joynson, R. B. (1989). *The Burt affair.* London: Routledge Chapman-Hall.

Juel, C. (1988). Learning to read and write: A longitudinal study of 54 children from first through fourth grades. *Journal of Educational Psychology, 80,* 417–447.

Juel, C. (1990). Effects of reading group assignment on reading development in first and second grade. *Journal of Reading Behavior, 22,* 233–254.

Juel, C., Griffith, P. L., & Gough, P. B. (1986). Acquisition of literacy: A longitudinal study of children in first and second grade. *Journal of Educational Psychology, 78,* 243–255.

Just, M. A., & Carpenter, P. A. (1987). *The psychology of reading and language comprehension.* Needham Heights, MA: Allyn and Bacon.

Just, M. A., & Carpenter, P. A. (1992). A capacity theory of comprehension: Individual differences in working memory. *Psychological Review, 99,* 122–149.

Juvonen, J. (1988). Outcome and attributional disagreements between students and their teachers. *Journal of Educational Psychology, 80,* 330–336.

Kagan, D. M. (1990). How schools alienate students at risk: A model for examining proximal classroom variables. *Educational Psychologist, 25,* 105–125.

Kagan, J., Moss, H., & Sigel, I. (1963). Psychological significance of types of conceptualization. *Monographs of the Society for Research in Child Development, 28* (2, Serial No. 86).

Kagen, R. M. (1977). Generalization of verbal self-instructional training in cognitively impulsive children. Doctoral dissertation, University of Texas at Austin, 1976. *Dissertation Abstracts International, 37,* 4148B.

Kahle, J. (1984). *Girl-friendly science.* Presented at the annual meeting of the American Association for the Advancement of Science, New York. (Cited in Eccles, 1989.)

Kahle, J. B., & Lakes, M. K. (1983). The myth of equality in science classrooms. *Journal of Research in Science Teaching, 20,* 131–140.

Kahle, J. B., Matyas, M. L., & Cho, H. (1985). An assessment of the impact of science experiences on the career choices of male and female biology students. *Journal of Research in Science Teaching, 22,* 385–394.

Kail, R. (1986). Sources of age difference in speed of processing. *Child Development, 57,* 969–987.

Kail, R. (1991). Processing time declines exponentially during childhood and adolescence. *Developmental Psychology, 27,* 259–266.

Kail, R. (1992). Processing speed, speech rate, and memory. *Developmental Psychology, 28,* 899–904.

Kamii, C. K. (1985). *Young children reinvent arith-*

metic. New York: Teachers College, Columbia University.

Kamin, L. J. (1974). *The science and politics of IQ.* New York: Wiley.

Kamphaus, R. W., Kaufman, A. S., & Harrison, P. L. (1990). Clinical assessment practice with the Kaufman Assessment Battery for Children (K-ABC). In C. R. Reynolds & R. W. Kamphaus (Eds.), *Handbook of psychological and educational assessment of children: Intelligence & achievement* (pp. 259–276). New York: Guilford Press.

Kandel, E. R. (1991). Brain and behavior. In E. R. Kandel, J. H. Schwartz, & T. M. Jessel (Eds.), *Principles of neural science* (pp. 5–17). New York: Elsevier.

Kanfer, F., & Zich, J. (1974). Self-control training: The effect of external control on children's resistance to temptation. *Developmental Psychology, 10,* 108–115.

Kaniel, S., & Tzuriel, D. (1992). Mediated learning experience approach in the assessment and treatment of borderline psychotic adolescents. In H. C. Haywood & D. Tzuriel (Eds.), *Interactive assessment* (pp. 399–418). New York: Springer-Verlag.

Kardash, C. A. M., Royer, J. M., & Greene, B. A. (1988). Effects of schemata on both encoding and retrieval of information from prose. *Journal of Educational Psychology, 80,* 324–329.

Kasik, M. M., Sabatino, D. A., & Spoentgen, P. (1987). In S. J. Ceci (Ed.), *Handbook of cognitive, social, and neuropsychological aspects of learning disabilities,* Vol. 2 (pp. 251–272). Hillsdale, NJ: Erlbaum & Associates.

Kastner, S. B., & Rickards, C. (1974). Mediated memory with novel and familiar stimuli in good and poor readers. *Journal of Genetic Psychology, 124,* 105–113.

Katz, I. (1967). Some motivational determinants of racial differences in intellectual achievement. *International Journal of Psychology, 2,* 1–12.

Kaufman, A. S. (1990). *Assessing adolescent and adult intelligence.* Boston: Allyn & Bacon.

Kaufman, A. S., Reynolds, C. R., & McLean, J. E. (1989). Age and WAIS-R intelligence in a national sample of adults in the 20- to 74-year-old age range: A cross-sectional analysis with education level controlled. *Intelligence, 13,* 235–253.

Kausler, D. H. (1990). *Motivation, human aging, and cognitive performance* (pp. 172–182). San Diego: Academic Press.

Kausler, D. H. (1991). *Experimental psychology, cognition, and human aging.* New York: Springer-Verlag.

Kavale, K. A. (1982). Meta-analysis of the relationship between visual perceptual skills and reading achievement. *Journal of Learning Disabilities, 15,* 42–51.

Kavale, K. A., & Forness, S. R. (1992). History, definition, and diagnosis. In N. N. Singh & I. L. Beale (Eds.), *Learning disabilities: Nature, theory, and treatment* (pp. 3–43). New York: Springer-Verlag.

Kavathatzopoulos, I. (1991). Kohlberg & Piaget:

Differences and similarities. *Journal of Moral Education, 20,* 47–54.

Kaye, D. B., deWinstanley, P., Chen, Q., & Bonnefil, V. (1989). Development of efficient arithmetic computation. *Journal of Educational Psychology, 81,* 467–480.

Keating, D. P., & Bobbitt, B. (1978). Individual and developmental differences in cognitive processing components of mental ability. *Child Development, 49,* 155–169.

Kee, D. W. (in press). Developmental differences in associative memory: Strategy use, mental effort and knowledge-access interactions. In H. W. Reese (Ed.), *Advances in child development and behavior,* Vol. 25. New York: Academic Press.

Kee, D. W., Gottfried, A. W., Bathurst, K., & Brown, K. (1987). Left-hemisphere language specialization: Consistency in hand preference and sex differences. *Child Development, 58,* 718–724.

Keeney, F. J., Cannizzo, S. R., & Flavell, J. H. (1967). Spontaneous and induced verbal rehearsal in a recall task. *Child Development, 38,* 953–966.

Keller, C. E., & Lloyd, J. W. (1989). Cognitive training: Implications for written language. In J. N. Hughes & R. J. Hall (Eds.), *Cognitive-behavioral psychology in the schools* (pp. 280–304). New York: Guilford Press.

Keller, C. E., & Sutton, J. P. (1991). Specific mathematics disorders. In J. E. Obrzut & G. W. Hynd (Eds.), *Neuropsychological foundations of learning disabilities* (pp. 549–571). San Diego: Academic Press.

Keller, F. S. (1968). "Good-bye teacher . . ." *Journal of Applied Behavior Analysis, 1,* 79–89.

Kemper, T. L. (1988). Neuropathology of Down syndrome. In L. Nadel (Ed.), *The psychobiology of Down syndrome* (pp. 269–289). Cambridge, MA: MIT Press.

Kendall, P. C. (1990). Challenges for cognitive strategy training. *American Journal of Mental Deficiency, 94,* 365–367.

Kendall, P. C., & Braswell, L. (1985). *Cognitive-behavioral therapy for impulsive children.* New York: Guilford.

Kennedy, B. A., & Miller, D. J. (1976). Persistent use of verbal rehearsal as a function of information about its value. *Child Development, 47,* 566–569.

Kersh, B. Y. (1958). The adequacy of "meaning" as an explanation of superiority of learning by independent discovery. *Journal of Educational Psychology, 49,* 282–292.

Kerwin, M. L. E., & Day, J. D. (1985). Peer influences on cognitive development. In J. B. Pryor & J. D. Day (Eds.), *The development of social cognition* (pp. 211–228). New York: Springer-Verlag.

Ketcham, R., & Snyder, R. T. (1977). Self-attitudes of the intellectually and socially advantaged student: Normative study of the Piers-Harris' children's self-concept scale. *Psychological Reports, 40,* 111–116.

Kevles, D. J. (1985). *In the name of eugenics: Genetics and the uses of human heredity.* Berkeley: University of California Press.

Kiernan, C. (1985). Behaviour modification. In A. M. Clarke, A. D. B. Clarke, & J. M. Berg (Eds.), *Mental deficiency: The changing outlook* (pp. 465–511). New York: Free Press.

Kiewra, K. A. (1985). Investigating notetaking and review: A depth of processing alternative. *Educational Psychologist, 20,* 23–32.

Kiewra, K. A. (1989a). A review of note-taking: The encoding-storage paradigm and beyond. *Educational Psychology Review, 1,* 147–172.

Kiewra, K. A. (1989b). Cognitive aspects of autonomous note taking: Control processes, learning strategies, and prior knowledge. *Educational Psychologist, 23,* 39–56.

Kiewra, K. A., DuBois, N. F., Christian, D., & McShane, A. (1988). Providing study notes: Comparison of three types of notes for review. *Journal of Educational Psychology, 80,* 595–597.

Kiewra, K. A., & Fletcher, H. J. (1984). The relationship between notetaking variables and achievement measures. *Human Learning, 3,* 273–280.

Kiewra, K. A., Mayer, R. E., Christenen, M., Kim, S., & Risch, N. (1991). Effects of repetition on recall and notetaking: Strategies for learning from lectures. *Journal of Educational Psychology, 83,* 120–123.

Kimball, M. M. (1989). A new perspective on women's math achievement. *Psychological Bulletin, 105,* 198–214.

Kimura, D. (1987). Are men's and women's brains really different? *Canadian Psychology, 28,* 133–147.

King, A. (1989). Effects of self-questioning training on college students' comprehension of lectures. *Contemporary Educational Psychology, 14,* 366–381.

King, A. (1990). Enhancing peer interaction and learning in the classroom through reciprocal questioning. *American Educational Research Journal, 27,* 664–687.

King, A. (1991). Effects of training in strategic questioning on children's problem-solving performance. *Journal of Educational Psychology, 83,* 307–317.

King, A. (1992). Comparison of self-questioning, summarizing, and notetaking-review as strategies for learning from lectures. *American Educational Research Journal, 29,* 303–323.

King, E. M., & Friesen, D. T. (1972). Children who read in kindergarten. *Alberta Journal of Educational Research, 18,* 147–161.

King-Sears, M. E., Richardson, M., & Ray, R. M. (1992). Generalizing curriculum-based measurement from university coursework to school-based practice: Train and hope? *LD Forum, 17* (3), 25–28.

Kinsbourne, M., & Hiscock, M. (1983). The normal and deviant development of functional lateralization of the brain. In M. M. Haith & J. J. Campos (Eds.; P. H. Mussen, General Ed.), *Handbook of child psychology,* Vol. II, *Infancy and developmental psychobiology* (pp. 157–280). New York: Wiley.

Kintsch, W. (1974). *The representation of meaning in memory.* Hillsdale, NJ: Erlbaum & Associates.

Kintsch, W. (1980). Semantic memory: A tutorial. In R. S. Nickerson (Ed.), *Attention and performance 8.* Hillsdale, NJ: Erlbaum & Associates.

Kintsch, W. (1982). Text representations. In W. Otto & S. White (Eds.), *Reading expository material* (pp. 87–102). New York: Academic Press.

Kintsch, W. (1983). Memory for text. In A. Flammer & W. Kintsch (Eds.), *Discourse processing* (pp. 186–204). Amsterdam: North-Holland.

Kintsch, W. (1988). The role of knowledge in discourse comprehension: A construction-integration model. *Psychological Review, 95,* 163–182.

Kintsch, W. (1989). Learning from text. In L. B. Resnick (Ed.), *Knowing, learning, and instruction: Essays in honor of Robert Glaser* (pp. 25–46). Hillsdale, NJ: Erlbaum & Associates.

Kintsch, W., & Greene, E. (1978). The role of culture-specific schemata in the comprehension and recall of stories. *Discourse Processes, 1,* 1–13.

Kintsch, W., & Keenan, J. M. (1973). Reading rate and retention as a function of the number of propositions in the base structure of sentences. *Cognitive Psychology, 5,* 257–279.

Kintsch, W., Kozminsky, E., Streby, W. J., McKoon, G., & Keenan, J. M. (1975). Comprehension and recall as a function of content variables. *Journal of Verbal Learning and Verbal Behavior, 14,* 196–214.

Kintsch, W., Mandel, T. S., & Kozminsky, E. (1977). Summarizing scrambled stories. *Memory and Cognition, 5,* 547–552.

Kintsch, W., & van Dijk, T. A. (1978). Toward a model of discourse comprehension and production. *Psychological Review, 85,* 363–394.

Kintsch, W. E., & Vipond, D. (1979). Reading comprehension and readability in educational practice and psychological theory. In L. G. Nilsson (Ed.), *Perspectives on memory research* (pp. 329–365). Hillsdale, NJ: Erlbaum & Associates.

Kintsch, W., & Yarbrough, C. J. (1982). Role of rhetorical structure in text comprehension. *Journal of Educational Psychology, 74,* 828–834.

Kirsch, I. S., & Jungeblut, A. (1986). *Literacy: Profile of America's young adults.* Princeton, NJ: Educational Testing Service.

Kistner, J. A., Osborne, M., & LeVerrier, L. (1988). Causal attributions of learning-disabled children: Developmental patterns and relation to academic progress. *Journal of Educational Psychology, 80,* 82–89.

Klainen, S., & Fensham, P. J. (1987). Learning achievement in upper secondary school chemistry in Thailand: Some remarkable sex reversals. *International Journal of Science Education, 9,* 217–227.

Klainen, S., Fensham, P. J., & West, L. H. T. (1989). Successful achievements by girls in physics learning. *International Journal of Science Education, 11,* 101–112.

Klausmeier, H. J. (1990). Conceptualizing. In B. F. Jones & L. Idol (Eds.), *Dimensions of thinking and cognitive instruction* (pp. 93–138). Hillsdale, NJ: Erlbaum & Associates.

Klibanoff, L. S., & Haggart, S. A. (1981). *Report No. 8: Summer growth and the effectiveness of summer school.* Technical Report prepared for the Office of Program Evaluation, U.S. Department of Education, Mountain View, CA: RMC Research Corporation.

Kliegl, R., Smith, J., & Baltes, P. B. (1989). Testing-the-limits and the study of adult age differences in cognitive plasticity of a mnemonic skill. *Developmental Psychology, 25,* 247–256.

Kliegl, R., Smith, J., & Baltes, P. B. (1990). On the locus and process of magnification of age differences during mnemonic training. *Developmental Psychology, 26,* 894–904.

Kloosterman, P. (1988). Self-confidence and motivation in mathematics. *Journal of Educational Psychology, 80,* 345–351.

Kloster, A. M., & Winne, P. H. (1989). The effects of different types of organizers on students' learning from text. *Journal of Educational Psychology, 81,* 9–15.

Knapczyk, D. R. (1989). Generalization of student question asking from special class to regular class settings. *Journal of Applied Behavior Analysis, 22,* 77–83.

Knight, P. (1992). How I use portfolios in mathematics. *Educational Leadership, 49 (8),* 71–72.

Knopf, M., & Neidhardt, E. (1989). Aging and memory for action events: The role of familiarity. *Developmental Psychology, 25,* 780–786.

Koballa, T. R. (1988). Persuading girls to take elective physical science courses in high school: Who are the credible communicators? *Journal of Research in Science Teaching, 25,* 465–478.

Kohlberg, L. (1969). Stage and sequence: The cognitive-developmental approach to socialization. In D. Goslin (Ed.), *Handbook of socialization theory and research.* New York: Rand McNally.

Kohlberg, L. (1981). *The philosophy of moral development: Moral stages and the idea of justice: Essays on moral development, 1.* San Francisco: Harper & Row.

Kohlberg, L. (1984). *The psychology of moral development: Essays on moral development, 2.* San Francisco: Harper & Row.

Kohlberg, L., & Candee, D. (1984). The relationship of moral judgement to moral action. In W. Kurtines & J. Gewirtz (Eds.), *Morality, moral behavior, and moral development.* New York: Wiley.

Kohlberg, L., & Elfenbein, D. (1976). Capital punishment, moral development, and the constitution. In H. A. Bedau & C. M. Pierce (Eds.), *Capital punishment in the United States* (pp. 247–296). New York: AMS Press.

Kohlberg, L., Kauffman, K., Sharf, P., & Hickey, J. (1974). *The just community approach to corrections.* Cambridge, MA: Moral Education Research Foundation.

Kohlberg, L., Levine, C., & Hewer, A. (1983). Moral stages: A current formulation and a response to critics. *Contributions to Human Development, 10.* Basel: S. Karger.

Kohlberg, L., & Mayer, R. (1972). Development as the aim of education: The Dewey view. *Harvard Educational Review, 42,* 449–496.

Kohlberg, L., & Power, C. (1981). Moral development, religious thinking, and the question of a seventh stage. *Zygon, 16,* 203–260.

Kohlberg, L., Yaeger, J., & Hjertholm, E. (1968). Private speech: Four studies and a review of theories. *Child Development, 39,* 691–736.

Kohs S. C. (1923). *Intelligence measurement.* New York: Macmillan.

Kolb, B. (1989). Brain development, plasticity, and behavior. *American Psychologist, 44,* 1203–1212.

Kolers, P. A. (1975). Specificity of operations in sentence recognition. *Cognitive Psychology, 7,* 289–306.

Komarovsky, M. (1985). *Women in college: Shaping new feminine identities.* New York: Basic Books.

Konner, M. (1991). Universals of behavioral development in relation to brain myelination. In K. R. Gibson & A. C. Petersen (Eds.), *Brain maturation and cognitive development: Comparative and cross-cultural perspectives* (pp. 181–223). New York: Aldine de Gruyter.

Koocher, G. P., & Keith-Spiegel, P. C. (1990). *Children, ethics, & the law.* Lincoln: University of Nebraska Press.

Körkel, J. (1987). *Die Entwicklung von Gedächtnis und Metagedächtnisleistung in Abhängigkeit von bereichsspezifischen Vorkenntnissen.* Frankfurt/Main: Lang.

Kornhaber, M., Krechevsky, M., & Gardner, H. (1990). Engaging intelligence. *Educational Psychologist, 25,* 177–199.

Kos, R. (1991). Persistence of reading disabilities: The voices of four middle school students. *American Educational Research Journal, 28,* 875–895.

Koshmider, J. W., & Ashcraft, M. H. (1991). The development of children's mental multiplication skills. *Journal of Experimental Child Psychology, 51,* 53–89.

Kosslyn, S. M. (1975). Information representation in visual images. *Cognitive Psychology, 7,* 341–370.

Kosslyn, S. M. (1976). Can imagery be distinguished from other forms of internal representation? Evidence from studies of information retrieval times. *Memory and Cognition, 4,* 291–297.

Kosslyn, S. M., & Koenig, O. (1992). *Wet mind: The new cognitive neuroscience.* New York: Free Press.

Kosslyn, S. M., Margolis, J. A., Barrett, A. M., Goldknopf, E. J., & Daly, P. F. (1990). Age differences in imagery abilities. *Child Development, 61,* 995–1010.

Kovacs, M., Goldston, D., & Ivengar, S. (1992). Intellectual development and academic performance of children with insulin-dependent diabetes mellitus: A longitudinal study. *Developmental Psychology, 28,* 676–684.

Kozma, R. B. (1991). Learning with media. *Review of Educational Research, 61,* 179–212.

Kozol, J. (1985). *Illiterate America.* Garden City, NY: Anchor Press/Doubleday.

Kozol, J. (1991). *Savage inequalities: Children in America's schools.* New York: Crown.

Krajcik, J. S. (1991). Developing students' understanding of chemical concepts. In S. M. Glynn, R. H. Yeany, & B. K. Britton (Eds.), *The psychology of learning science* (pp. 117–147). Hillsdale, NJ: Erlbaum & Associates.

Krajcik, J. S., & Peters, H. (1989). *Molecular velocities* [microcomputer program]. Oakdale, IA: Conduit, University of Iowa.

Krasner, S. M. (1985). *Developmental aspects of communication in children with Down's syndrome.* Unpublished Ph.D. thesis. University of St. Andrews, Scotland.

Kreitler, S., & Kreitler, H. (1990). Cognitive antecedents of imitativeness and persistence in children with mental retardation. *American Journal of Mental Deficiency, 94,* 342–343.

Krug, D., Davis, T. B., & Glover, J. A. (1990). Massed versus distributed repeated reading: A case of forgetting helping recall? *Journal of Educational Psychology, 82,* 366–371.

Kruglanski, A. W., Friedman, I., & Zeevi, G. (1971). The effects of extrinsic incentives on some qualitative aspects of task performance. *Journal of Personality, 39,* 606–617.

Kuczynski, L., Zahn-Waxler, C., & Radke-Yarrow, M. (1987). Development and content of imitation in the second and third years of life: A socialization perspective. *Developmental Psychology, 23,* 276–282.

Kuder, G. F., & Richardson, M. W. (1937). The theory of estimation of test reliability. *Psychometrica, 2,* 151–160.

Kuhara-Kojima, K., & Hatano, G. (1991). Contribution of content knowledge and learning ability to the learning of facts. *Journal of Educational Psychology, 83,* 253–263.

Kuhl, J. (1985). Volitional mediators of cognition-behavior consistency: Self-regulatory processes and action versus state orientation. In J. Kuhl & J. Beckmann (Eds.), *Action control: From cognition to behavior.* West Berlin: Springer-Verlag.

Kuhn, D. (1989). Children and adults as intuitive scientists. *Psychological Review, 96,* 674–689.

Kuhn, D. (1991). *The skills of argument.* Cambridge: Cambridge University Press.

Kuhn, D., Amsel, E., & O'Loughlin, M. (1988). *The development of scientific thinking skills.* San Diego: Academic Press.

Kuhn, D., Kohlberg, L., Langer, J., & Haan, N. (1977). The development of formal operations in logical and moral judgment. *Genetic Psychology Monographs, 95,* 97–188.

Kuhn, D., & Phelps, E. (1982). The development of problem-solving strategies. In H. Reese (Ed.), *Advances in child development and behavior,* Vol. 17 (pp. 1–44). New York: Academic Press.

Kulik, C-l. C., Kulik, J. A., & Bangert-Drowns, R. L. (1990). Effectiveness of mastery learning programs: A meta-analysis. *Review of Educational Research, 60,* 265–299.

Kulik, J. A., & Kulik, C-L. C. (1988). Timing of feedback and verbal learning. *Review of Educational Research, 58,* 79–97.

Kulm, G. (Ed.) (1990). *Assessing higher order thinking in mathematics*. Washington, DC: American Association for the Advancement of Science.

Kurtines, W., & Grief, E. B. (1974). The development of moral thought: Review and evaluation of Kohlberg's approach. *Psychological Bulletin, 81*, 453–470.

Kurtz, B. E. (1990). Cultural influences on children's cognitive and metacognitive development. In W. Schneider & F. E. Weinert (Eds.), *Interactions among aptitudes, strategies, and knowledge in cognitive performance* (pp. 177–199). New York: Springer-Verlag.

Kutas, M., & Van Petten, C. (1988). Event-related brain potential studies of language. In P. Ackles, J. R. Jennings, & M. Coles (Eds.), *Advances in psychophysiology*. Greenwich, CT: JAI Press.

Kutnick, P. (1988). "I'll teach you!" Primary school teachers' attitudes to and use of moral education in the curriculum. *Journal of Moral Education, 17*, 40–51.

Kutnick, P. (1990). A survey of primary school teachers' understanding and implementation of moral education in Trinidad and Tobago. *Journal of Moral Education, 19*, 48–57.

LaBerge, D., & Samuels, S. J. (1974). Toward a theory of automatic information processing in reading. *Cognitive Psychology, 6*, 293–323.

Labouvie-Vief, G. (1985). Intelligence and cognition. In J. E. Birren & K. W. Schaie (Eds.). *Handbook of the psychology of aging*, 2nd ed. (pp. 500–530). New York: Van Nostrand Reinhold.

Labouvie-Vief, G., Schell, D. A., & Weaverdyck, S. E. (1981). *Recall deficit in the aged: A fable recalled*. Unpublished manuscript. Detroit: Wayne State University, Department of Psychology.

Ladas, H. S. (1980). Note taking on lectures: An information-processing approach. *Educational Psychologist, 15*, 44–53.

Laffal, J. (1965). *Pathological and normal language*. New York: Atherton Press.

Lam, T. C. M. (1992). Review of practices and problems in the evaluation of bilingual education. *Review of Educational Research, 62*, 181–204.

Lambiotte, J. G., Dansereau, D. F., Cross, D. R., & Reynolds, S. B. (1989). Multirelational semantic maps. *Educational Psychology Review, 1*, 331–367.

Lampert, M. (1990). When the problem is not the question and the solution is not the answer: Mathematical knowing and teaching. *American Educational Research Journal, 27*, 29–64.

Lane, M. K., & Hodkin, B. (1985). Role of atypical exemplars of social and nonsocial superordinate categories within the class inclusion paradigm. *Developmental Psychology, 21*, 909–915.

Lange, G. (1973). The development of conceptual and rote recall skills among school age children. *Journal of Experimental Child Psychology, 15*, 394–406.

Lange, G. (1978). Organization-related processes in children's recall. In P. A. Ornstein (Ed.), *Memory development in children* (pp. 101–128). Hillsdale, NJ: Erlbaum & Associates.

Lange, G., MacKinnon, G. E., & Nida, R. E. (1989). Knowledge, strategy, and motivational contributions to preschool children's object recall. *Developmental Psychology, 25*, 772–779.

Langer, E. J. (1989). *Mindfulness*. Reading, MA: Addison-Wesley.

Langer, J. A. (1986). *Children reading and writing: Structures and strategies*. Norwood, NJ: Ablex.

Langer, J. A. (1990). The process of understanding: Reasons for literary and instructional purposes. *Research in Teaching of English, 24*, 229–258.

Langer, J. A., & Applebee, A. N. (1984). Language, learning, and interaction: A framework for improving the teaching of writing. In A. N. Applebee (Ed.), *Contexts for learning to write: Studies of secondary school instruction* (pp. 169–181). Norwood, NJ: Ablex.

Langer, J. A., & Applebee, A. N. (1987). *How writing shapes thinking: A study of teaching and learning*. Champaign, IL: National Council of Teachers of English.

Langer, J. A., Bartolome, L., Vasquez, O., & Lucas, T. (1990). Meaning construction in school literacy tasks: A study of bilingual students. *American Educational Research Journal, 27*, 427–471.

Laosa, L. M. (1978). Maternal teaching strategies in Chicano families of varied educational and socioeconomic levels. *Child Development, 49*, 1129–1135.

Laosa, L. M. (1980). Maternal teaching strategies in Chicano and Anglo-American families: The influence of culture and education on maternal behavior. *Child Development, 51*, 759–765.

Laosa, L. M. (1982). School, occupation, culture, and family: The impact of parental schooling on the parent-child relationship. *Journal of Educational Psychology, 74*, 791–827.

Lapp, D., Flood, J., & Farnan, N. (Eds.) (1989). *Content area reading and learning*. Englewood Cliffs, NJ: Prentice-Hall.

Larroche, J. C. (1966). The development of the central nervous system during intrauterine life. In S. Faulkner (Ed.), *Human development* (pp. 257–276). Philadelphia: W.B. Saunders Co.

Larry P. v. Riles 343 F. Supp. 1306 (N. D. Cal. 1979), aff'd 502 F. 2d (9th Cir. 1974); 495 F. Supp. 926 (N. D. Cal. 1979), aff'd. in part and rev'd in part, 793 F. 2d 969 (9th Cir. 1984).

Larsen, J. P., Hoien, T., Lundberg, I., & Ødegaard, S. (1990). MRI evaluation of the size and symmetry of the planum temporale in adolescents with developmental dyslexia. *Brain and Language, 39*, 289–301.

Larson, K. A., & Gerber, M. M. (1992). Metacognition. In N. N. Singh & I. L. Beale (Eds.), *Learning disabilities: Nature, theory, and treatment* (pp. 126–169). New York: Springer-Verlag.

Lasch, C. (1979). *The culture of narcissism: American life in an age of diminishing expectations*. New York: Norton.

Lasky, R. E. (1974). The ability of six-year-olds, eight-year-olds, and adults to abstract visual patterns. *Child Development, 45*, 626–632.

Lau v. Nichols (1974). 414 U. S. 563.

Laughon, P. (1990). The dynamic assessment of intelligence: A review of three approaches. *School Psychology Review, 19*, 459–470.

Lave, J., & Wenger, E. (1991). *Situated learning: Legitimate peripheral participation*. Cambridge: Cambridge University Press.

LaVoie, J. C. (1973). Punishment and adolescent self-control. *Developmental Psychology, 8*, 16–24.

LaVoie, J. C. (1974). Cognitive determinants of resistance to deviation in seven-, nine-, and eleven-year-old children of low and high maturity of moral judgment. *Developmental Psychology, 10*, 393–403.

Lawrence, J. A., & Helm, A. (1987). Consistencies and inconsistencies in nurses' ethical reasoning. *Journal of Moral Education, 16*, 167–176.

Lawson, A. E. (1983). Predicting science achievement: The role of developmental level, disembedding ability, mental capacity, prior knowledge, and beliefs. *Journal of Research in Science Teaching, 20*, 117–129.

Lawson, A. E., & Renner, J. W. (1975). Piagetian theory and biology teaching. *American Biology Teacher, 37*, 336–343.

Lawson, A. E., & Snitgen, D. A. (1982). Teaching formal reasoning in a college biology course for preservice teachers. *Journal of Research in Science Teaching, 19*, 233–248.

Lawson, A. E., & Thompson, L. D. (1988). Formal reasoning ability and misconceptions concerning genetics and natural selection. *Journal of Research in Science Teaching, 25*, 733–746.

Lawson, A. E., & Wollman, W. T. (1976). Encouraging the transition from concrete to formal cognitive functioning: An experiment. *Journal of Research in Science Teaching, 13*, 413–430.

Lawson, M. J. (1990). The case for instruction in the use of general problem-solving strategies in mathematics teaching: A comment on Owen and Sweller. *Journal for Research in Mathematics Education, 21*, 403–415.

Lawson, M. J., & Fuelop, S. (1980). Understanding the purpose of strategy training. *British Journal of Educational Psychology, 50*, 175–180.

Lazar, I., Darlington, R., Murray, H., Royce, J., & Sipper, A. (1982). Lasting effects of early childhood education: A report from the consortium for longitudinal studies. *Monographs of the Society for Research in Child Development, 47* (2–3, Whole No. 195).

Leal, L. (1987). Investigation of the relation between metamemory and university students' examination performance. *Journal of Educational Psychology, 79*, 35–40.

Lee, T. D., & Genovese, E. D. (1988). Distribution of practice in motor skill acquisition: Learning and performance effects reconsidered. *Research Quarterly for Exercise and Sport, 59*, 277–287.

Lee, V. E., & Bryk, A. S. (1986). Effects of single-sex secondary schools on student achievement and attitudes. *Journal of Educational Psychology, 78,* 381–395.

Lee, V. E., & Bryk, A. S. (1989). Effects of single-sex schools: Response to Marsh. *Journal of Educational Psychology, 81,* 647–650.

LeFevre, J., & Dixon, P. (1986). Do written instructions need examples? *Cognition and Instruction, 3,* 1–30.

LeFevre, J-A., Kulak, A. G., & Bisanz, J. (1991). Individual differences and developmental change in the associative relations among numbers. *Journal of Experimental Child Psychology, 52,* 256–274.

Lehman, D. R., & Nisbett, R. E. (1990). A longitudinal study of the effects of undergraduate training on reasoning. *Developmental Psychology, 26,* 952–960.

Lehman, J. D., Carter, C., & Kahle, J. B. (1985). Concept mapping, Vee mapping and achievement: Results of a field study with black high school students. *Journal of Research in Science Teaching, 27,* 663–674.

Lehr, S. (1988). The child's developing sense of theme as a response to literature. *Reading Research Quarterly, 23,* 337–357.

Lehrer, R. (1989). Computer-assisted strategic instruction. In C. B. McCormick, G. Miller, & M. Pressley (Eds.), *Cognitive strategy research: From basic research to educational applications* (pp. 303–320). New York: Springer-Verlag.

Lehrer, R., Guckenberg, T., & Lee, O. (1988). Comparative study of the cognitive consequences of inquiry-based Logo instruction. *Journal of Educational Psychology, 80,* 543–553.

Lehrer, R., & Littlefield, J. (1991). Misconceptions and errors in LOGO: The role of instruction. *Journal of Educational Psychology, 83,* 124–133.

Lehrer, R., Randle, L., & Sancilio, L. (1989). Learning preproof geometry with LOGO. *Cognition and Instruction, 6,* 159–184.

Leichter, H. P. (1984). Families as environments for literacy. In H. Goelman, A. Oberg, & F. Smith (Eds.), *Awakening to literacy.* Exeter, NH: Heinemann.

Leinhardt, G., & Greeno, J. G. (1986). The cognitive skill of teaching. *Journal of Educational Psychology, 78,* 75–95.

Lemoine, H. E., Levy, B. A., & Hutchinson, A. (1993). Increasing the naming speed of poor readers: Representations formed across repetitions. *Journal of Experimental Child Psychology, 55,* 297–328.

Lenneberg, E. (1967). *Biological foundations of language.* New York: Wiley.

Leonard, L. H. (1989). A comparison of student reactions to biology instruction by interactive videodisc or conventional laboratory. *Journal of Research in Science Teaching, 26,* 95–104.

Leonard, W. H. (1992). A comparison of student performance following instruction by interactive videodisc versus conventional laboratory. *Journal of Research in Science Teaching, 29,* 93–102.

Lepper, M. R. (1983). Extrinsic reward and intrinsic motivation: Implications for the classroom. In J. M. Levine & M. C. Wang (Eds.), *Teacher and student perceptions: Implications for learning.* Hillsdale, NJ: Erlbaum & Associates.

Lepper, M. R., Aspinwall, L. G., Mumme, D. L., & Chabey, R. W. (1990). Self-perception and social-perception processes in tutoring: Subtle social control strategies of expert tutors. In J. M. Olson & M. P. Zanna (Eds.), *Self-inference processes: The Ontario symposium* (pp. 217–237). Hillsdale, NJ: Erlbaum & Associates.

Lepper, M. R., Greene, D., & Nisbett, R. E. (1973). Undermining children's intrinsic interest with extrinsic rewards: A test of the "overjustification" hypothesis. *Journal of Personality and Social Psychology, 28,* 129–137.

Lepper, M. R., & Hodell, M. (1989). Intrinsic motivation in the classroom. In C. Ames & R. Ames (Eds.), *Research on motivation in education,* Vol. 3, *Goals and cognitions* (pp. 73–105). San Diego: Academic Press.

Lepper, M. R., & Malone, T. W. (1987). Intrinsic motivation and instructional effectiveness in computer-based education. In R. E. Snow & M. J. Farr (Eds.), *Aptitude, learning, and instruction,* Vol. 3, *Conative and affective process analyses* (pp. 255–286). Hillsdale, NJ: Erlbaum & Associates.

Lerner, R. M. (1986). *The nature of human plasticity.* New York: Cambridge University Press.

Lerner, R. M. (1990). Plasticity, person-context relations, and cognitive training in the aged years: A developmental contextual perspective. *Developmental Psychology, 26,* 911–915.

Lerner, R. M., & Busch-Rossnagel, N. (Eds.) (1981). *Individuals as producers of their own development: A life-span perspective.* New York: Academic Press.

Lesgold, A. M. (1972). Pronominalizations: A device for unifying sentences in memory. *Journal of Verbal Learning and Verbal Behavior, 11,* 316–323.

Lesgold, A. M. (1984). Acquiring expertise. In J. R. Anderson & S. M. Kosslyn (Eds.), *Tutorials in learning and memory* (pp. 31–60). San Francisco: W.H. Freeman.

Lesgold, A., Glaser, R., Rubinson, H., Klopfer, D., Feltovich, P., & Wang, Y. (1988). Expertise in a complex skill: Diagnosing x-ray pictures. In M. T. H. Chi, R. Glaser, & M. J. Farr (Eds.), *The nature of expertise* (pp. 311–342). Hillsdale, NJ: Erlbaum & Associates.

Lester, B. M., Corwin, M. J., Sepkoski, C., Seifer, R., Peucker, M., McLaughlin, S., & Golub, H. L. (1991). Neurobehavioral syndromes in cocaine-exposed newborn infants. *Child Development, 62,* 694–705.

Lester, B. M., & Dreher, M. (1989). Effects of marijuana use during pregnancy on newborn cry. *Child Development, 60,* 765–771.

Levin, J. R. (1976). What have we learned about maximizing what children can learn? In J. R. Levin & V. L. Allen (Eds.), *Cognitive learning in children.* New York: Academic Press.

Levin, J. R. (1982). Pictures as prose-learning devices. In A. Flammer & W. Kintsch (Eds.), *Discourse processing* (pp. 412–444). Amsterdam: North-Holland.

Levin, J. R. (1983). Pictorial strategies for school learning: Practical illustrations. In M. Pressley & J. R. Levin (Eds.), *Cognitive strategy research: Educational applications* (pp. 213–237). New York: Springer-Verlag.

Levin, J. R. (1985). Educational applications of mnemonic pictures: Possibilities beyond your wildest imagination. In A. A. Sheikh (Ed.), *Imagery in education: Imagery in the educational process* (pp. 63–87). Farmingdale, NY: Baywood.

Levin, J. R. (1986). Four cognitive principles of learning strategy research. *Educational Psychologist, 21,* 3–17.

Levin, J. R., & Lesgold, A. M. (1978). On pictures in prose. *Educational Communication and Technology, 26,* 233–243.

Levin, J. R., McCabe, A. E., & Bender, B. G. (1975). A note on imagery-inducing motor activity in young children. *Child Development, 46,* 263–266.

Levin, J. R., & Pressley, M. (1981). Improving children's prose comprehension: Selected strategies that seem to succeed. In C. M. Santa & B. L. Hayes (Eds.), *Children's prose comprehension* (pp. 44–71). Newark, DE: International Reading Association.

Levin, J. R., Yussen, S. R., DeRose, T. M., & Pressley, M. (1977). Developmental changes in assessing recall and recognition memory. *Developmental Psychology, 13,* 608–615.

Levin, M. E., & Levin, J. R. (1990). Scientific mnemonics: Methods for maximizing more than memory. *American Educational Research Journal, 27,* 301–321.

Levin, T., Sabar, N., & Libman, Z. (1991). Achievements and attitudinal patterns of boys and girls in science. *Journal of Research in Science Teaching, 28,* 315–328.

Levine, J. M. (1983). Social comparison and education. In J. M. Levine & M. C. Wang (Eds.), *Teacher and student perceptions: Implications for learning* (pp. 29–55). Hillsdale, NJ: Erlbaum & Associates.

Levine, J. M., & Moreland, R. L. (1991). Culture and socialization in work groups. In L. Resnick, J. M. Levine, & S. D. Teasley (Eds.), *Perspectives on socially shared cognition* (pp. 257–279). Washington, DC: American Psychological Association.

Levine, S. C., Jordan, N. C., & Huttenlocher, J. (1992). Development of calculation abilities in young children. *Journal of Experimental Child Psychology, 53,* 72–103.

Levinson, D. F., Darrow, C. N., Klien, E. B., Levinson, M. H., & McKee, B. (1978). *The seasons of a man's life.* New York: Ballantine Books.

Levy, G. D., & Fivush, R. (1993). Scripts and gender: A new approach for examining gender-role development. *Developmental Review, 13,* 126–146.

Levy, J. (1976). Cerebral lateralization and spatial ability. *Behavior Genetics, 6,* 171–188.

Lewandowski, L. (1992). Neuropsychological assessment: Case studies. In J. E. Obrzut & G. W. Hynd (Eds.), *Neuropsychological foundations of learning disabilities* (pp. 685–710). San Diego: Academic Press.

Lewis, A. B. (1989). Training students to represent arithmetic word problems. *Journal of Educational Psychology, 81,* 521–531.

Lewis, A. B., & Mayer, R. E. (1987). Students' miscomprehension of relational statements in arithmetic word problems. *Journal of Educational Psychology, 79,* 363–371.

Lewis, L. (1989). New educational techologies for the future. In S. B. Merriam & P. M. Cunningham (Eds.), *Handbook of adult and continuing education* (pp. 613–627). San Francisco: Jossey-Bass.

Lewontin, R. C. (1974). *The genetic basis of evolutionary change.* New York: Columbia University Press.

Lewontin, R. C., Rose, S., & Kamin, L. J. (1984). *Not in our genes: Biology, ideology, and human nature.* New York: Pantheon Books.

Lezotte, L. (1986). *Reflections and future directions.* Paper presented at the Annual Meeting of the American Educational Research Association, San Francisco.

Lhyle, K. G., & Kulhavy, R. W. (1987). Feedback processing and error correction. *Journal of Educational Psychology, 79,* 320–322.

Liberman, I. Y., & Liberman, A. M. (1990). Whole language versus code emphasis: Underlying assumptions and their implications for reading instruction. *Annals of Dyslexia, 40,* 51–76.

Licht, B. (1983). Cognitive-motivational factors that contribute to the achievement of learning-disabled children. *Journal of Learning Disabilities, 16,* 483–490.

Licht, B. (1992). Achievement-related beliefs in children with learning disabilities. In L. J. Meltzer (Ed.), *Strategy assessment and instruction for students with learning disabilities: From theory to practice* (pp. 195–220). Austin, TX: PRO-ED.

Licht, B. G., & Dweck, C. S. (1984). Determinants of academic achievement: The interaction of children's achievement orientation with skill area. *Developmental Psychology, 20,* 628–636.

Licht, B. G., Kistner, J. A., Ozkaragoz, T., Shapiro, S., & Clausen, L. (1985). Causal attributions of learning disabled children: Individual differences and their implications for persistence. *Journal of Educational Psychology, 77,* 208–216.

Lickona, T. (Ed.) (1976). *Moral development and behavior.* New York: Holt, Rinehart, & Winston.

Lickona, T. (1991). *Educating for character: How our schools can teach respect and responsibility.* New York: Bantam Books.

Lidz, C. S. (1987). *Dynamic assessment.* New York: Guilford.

Lie, A. (1991). Effects of a training program for stimulating skills in word analysis in first-grade children. *Reading Research Quarterly, 26,* 234–250.

Lieberman, P. (1984). *The biology and evolution of language.* Cambridge, MA: Harvard University Press.

Lieberman, P. (1989). Some biological constraints on universal grammar and learnability. In M. L. Rice & R. L. Schiefelbusch (Eds.),

The teachability of language (pp. 199–225). Baltimore: Paul H. Brookes.

Light, L. L. (1992). The organization of memory in old age. In F. I. M. Craik & T. A. Salthouse (Eds.), *The handbook of aging and cognition* (pp. 111–165). Hillsdale, NJ: Erlbaum & Associates.

Light, L. L., & Capps, J. L. (1986). Comprehension of pronouns in younger and older adults. *Developmental Psychology, 22,* 580–585.

Lincoln, Y. S., & Guba, E. G. (1985). *Naturalistic inquiry.* Newbury Park, CA: Sage.

Lindow, J., Marrett, C. B., & Wilkinson, L. C. (1985). Overview. In L. C. Wilkinson & C. B. Marrett (Eds.), *Gender influences on classroom interaction* (pp. 1–15). Orlando, FL: Academic Press.

Linn, M. C., Clement, C., Pulos, S., & Sullivan, P. (1989). Scientific reasoning during adolescence: The influence of instruction in science knowledge and reasoning strategies. *Journal of Research in Science Teaching, 26,* 171–187.

Linn, M. C., & Pulos, S. M. (1983). Male-female differences in predicting displaced volume: Strategy usage, aptitude relationships, and experience influences. *Journal of Educational Psychology, 14,* 30–46.

Linn, M. C., & Songer, N. B. (1991). Teaching thermodynamics to middle school students: What are appropriate cognitive demands? *Journal of Research in Science Teaching, 28,* 885–918.

Linn, R. L., Graue, M. E., & Sanders, N. M. (1990). *Comparing state and district test results to national norms: Interpretations of "Scoring above the national average"* (Technical Report No. 308). Los Angeles: UCLA, Center for Research on Evaluation, Standards, and Student Testing.

Lipman, M. (1974). *Harry Stottlemeier's Discovery.* Upper Montclair, NJ: International Association of Philosophy for Children.

Lipman, M. (1985). Thinking skills fostered by philosophy for children. In J. W. Segal, S. F. Chipman, & R. Glaser (Eds.), *Thinking and learning skills,* Vol. 1, *Relating instruction to research* (pp. 83–108). Hillsdale, NJ: Erlbaum & Associates.

Lipman, M. (1991). *Thinking in education.* Cambridge, UK: Cambridge University Press.

Lipman, M., Sharp, A. M., & Oscanyan, F. S. (1980). *Philosophy in the classroom.* Philadelphia: Temple University Press.

Lipsitt, L. P. (1990). Learning processes in the human newborn: Sensitization, habituation, and classical condition. In A. Diamond (Ed.), *The development and neural bases of higher cognitive functions* (pp. 113–127). New York: New York Academy of Sciences.

Lockheed, M. E. (1985). Some determinants and consequences of sex segregation in the classroom. In L. C. Wilkinson & C. B. Marrett (Eds.), *Gender influences on classroom interaction* (pp. 167–184). Orlando, FL: Academic Press.

Locurto, C. (1988). On the malleability of IQ. *The Psychologist, 11,* 431–435.

Locurto, C. (1990). The malleability of IQ as

judged from adoption studies. *Intelligence, 14,* 275–292.

Locurto, C. (1991a). Beyond IQ in preschool programs? *Intelligence, 15,* 295–312.

Locurto, C. (1991b). Hands on the elephant: IQ, preschool programs, and the rhetoric of innoculation—A reply to commentaries. *Intelligence, 15,* 335–349.

Locurto, C. (1991c). *Sense and nonsense about IQ: The case for uniqueness.* New York: Praeger.

Loehlin, J. C., Horn, J. M., & Willerman, L. (1989). Modeling IQ change: Evidence from the Texas adoption project. *Child Development, 60,* 993–1004.

Loehlin, J. C., & Nichols, R. C. (1976). *Heredity, environment, and personality.* Austin: University of Texas Press.

Loman, N. L., & Mayer, R. E. (1983). Signaling techniques that increase the understandability of expository prose. *Journal of Educational Psychology, 75,* 402–412.

Lonky, E., Roodin, P. A., & Rybash, J. M. (1988). Moral judgment and sex role orientation as a function of self and other presentation mode. *Journal of Youth and Adolescence, 17,* 189–195.

Lorch, R. F. Jr. (1989). Text-signaling devices and their effects on reading and memory processes. *Educational Psychology Review, 1,* 209–234.

Lorch, R. F. Jr., Lorch, E. P., & Inman, W. E. (1993). Effects of signaling topic structure on text recall. *Journal of Educational Psychology, 85,* 281–290.

Lorch, R. F. Jr., Lorch, E. P., & Klusewitz, M. A. (1993). College students' conditional knowledge about reading. *Journal of Educational Psychology, 85,* 239–252.

Lord, C. G., Umezaki, K., & Darley, J. M. (1990). Developmental differences in decoding the meanings of the appraisal actions of teachers. *Child Development, 61,* 191–200.

Lou, H. C., Henriksen, L., & Bruhn, P. (1984). Focal cerebral hypoperfusion in children with dysphasia and/or attention deficit disorder. *Archives of Neurology, 41,* 825–829.

Lovaas, O. I., Schaeffer, B., & Simmons, J. Q. (1965). Building social behavior in autistic children by use of electric shock. *Journal of Experimental Research in Personality, 1,* 99–109.

Loveland, K. K., & Olley, J. G. (1979). The effect of external reward on interest and quality of task performance in children of high and low intrinsic motivation. *Child Development, 50,* 1207–1210.

Lovett, M. W., Warren-Chaplin, P. M., Ransby, M. J., & Borden, S. L. (1990). Training the word recognition skills of reading disabled children: Treatment and transfer effects. *Journal of Educational Psychology, 82,* 769–780.

Ludeke, R. J., & Hartup, W. W. (1983). Teaching behaviors of 9- and 11-year-old girls in mixed-age and same-age dyads. *Journal of Educational Psychology, 75,* 909–914.

Luhmer, K. (1990). Moral education in Japan. *Journal of Moral Education, 19,* 172–181.

Lundberg, I. (1991). Phonemic awareness can be developed without reading instruction. In S. A. Brady & D. P. Shankweiler (Eds.),

Phonological processes in literacy: A tribute to Isabelle Y. Liberman (pp. 47–53). Hillsdale, NJ: Erlbaum & Associates.

Lundberg, I., Frost, J., & Peterson, O. (1988). Effects of an extensive program for stimulating phonological awareness in preschool children. *Reading Research Quarterly, 23,* 263–284.

Lundeberg, M. A. (1987). Metacognitive aspects of reading comprehension: Studying understanding in legal case analysis. *Reading Research Quarterly, 22,* 407–432.

Lundeberg, M. A. (1990). Supplemental instruction in chemistry. *Journal of Research in Science Teaching, 27,* 145–155.

Lundeberg, M. A., & Fox, P. W. (1991). Do laboratory findings on test expectancy generalize to classroom outcomes? *Review of Educational Research, 61,* 94–106.

Luria, A. R. (1961). An objective approach to the study of the abnormal child. *American Journal of Orthopsychiatry, 31,* 1–14.

Luria, A. R. (1966). *Higher cortical functions in man.* New York: Basic.

Luria, A. R. (1973). *The working brain.* New York: Basic.

Luria, A. R. (1982). *Language and cognition.* New York: Wiley.

Luther, M., & Wyatt, F. (1989). A comparison of Feuerstein's method of LPAD assessment with conventional IQ testing on disadvantaged North York high school students. *International Journal of Dynamic Assessment and Instruction, 1,* 49–64.

Lyman, F. Jr. (1992). Think-pair-share, thinktrix, thinklinks, and weird facts: An interactive system for cooperative learning. In N. Davidson & T. Worsham, *Enhancing thinking through cooperative learning* (pp. 169–181). New York: Teachers College Press, Columbia University.

Lyon, G. R., Newby, R. E, Recht, D., & Caldwell, J. (1991). Neuropsychology and learning disabilities. In B. Y. L. Wong (Ed.), *Learning about learning disabilities* (pp. 376–406). San Diego: Academic Press.

Lyons, N. (1987). Ways of knowing, learning, and making choices. *Journal of Moral Education, 16,* 226–239.

Lyons, N. P. (1988). Two perspectives: On self, relationships, and morality. In C. Gilligan, J. V. Ward, & J. M. Taylor with B. Bardige (Eds.), *Mapping the moral domain: A contribution of women's thinking to psychological theory and education* (pp. 21–48). Cambridge, MA: Harvard University Press.

Macario, J. F., Shipley, E. F., & Billman, D. O. (1990). Induction from a single instance: Formation of a novel category. *Journal of Experimental Child Psychology, 50,* 179–199.

MacArthur, C., & Graham, S. (1987). Learning disabled students' composing with three methods: Handwriting, dictation, and word processing. *Journal of Special Education, 21,* 22–42.

MacArthur, C., Graham, S., & Schwartz, S. (1991). Knowledge of revision and rising be-

havior among learning disabled students. *Learning Disability Quarterly, 14,* 61–73.

MacArthur, C. Schwartz, S., & Graham, S. (1991). Effects of a reciprocal peer revision strategy in special education classrooms. *Learning Disabilities Research and Practice, 6,* 201–210.

MacKay, D. G. (1981). The problem of rehearsal or mental practice. *Journal of Motor Behavior, 13,* 274–285.

MacKay, D. G. (1982). The problem of flexibility, fluency, and speed-accuracy trade-off in skilled behavior. *Psychological Review, 89,* 483–506.

MacKinnon, D. W. (1978). *In search of human effectiveness.* Buffalo: Creative Education Foundation.

MacMillan, D. L., & Knopf, E. D. (1971). Effects of instructional set on perceptions of event outcomes by EMR and nonretarded children. *American Journal of Mental Deficiency, 76,* 185–189.

MacPherson, E. M., Candee, B. L., & Hohman, R. J. (1974). A comparison of three methods for eliminating disruptive classroom behavior. *Journal of Applied Behavior Analysis, 7,* 287–297.

Madden, N. A., Slavin, R. E., Karweit, N. L., Dolan, L. J., & Wasik, B. A. (1993). Success for all: Longitudinal effects of a restructuring program for inner-city elementary schools. *American Educational Research Journal, 30,* 123–148.

Madigan, S. A. (1969). Intraserial repetition and coding processes in free recall. *Journal of Verbal Learning and Verbal Behavior, 8,* 828–835.

Madison, P. (1969). *Personality development in college.* Reading, MA: Addison-Wesley.

Maehr, M. L., & Midgley, C. (1991). Enhancing student motivation: A schoolwide approach. *Educational Psychologist, 26,* 399–428.

Mahoney, M. J. (1974). *Cognition and behavior modification.* Cambridge, MA: Ballinger.

Maki, R. H., & Berry, S. L. (1984). Metacomprehension and text material. *Journal of Experimental Psychology: Learning, Memory, and Cognition, 10,* 663–679.

Maki, R. H., Foley, J. M., Kajer, W. K., Thompson, R. C., & Willert, M. G. (1990). Increased processing enhances calibration of comprehension. *Journal of Experimental Psychology: Learning, Memory, and Cognition, 16,* 609–616.

Maki, R. H., & Serra, M. (1992). The basis of test predictions for text material. *Journal of Experimental Psychology: Learning, Memory, and Cognition, 18,* 116–126.

Malcolm, S. (1984). *Equity and excellence: Compatible goals.* Washington, DC: AAAS Publications.

Malik, A. A. (1990). A psycholinguistic analysis of the reading behavior of EFL-proficient readers using culturally familiar and culturally nonfamiliar expository texts. *American Educational Research Journal, 27,* 205–223.

Mallory, M. E. (1989). Q-sort definition of ego identity status. *Journal of Youth and Adolescence, 18,* 399–412.

Malone, T. W., & Lepper, M. R. (1987). Making

learning fun: A taxonomy of intrinsic motivation for learning. In R. E. Snow & M. J. Farr (Eds.), *Aptitude, learning, and instruction,* Vol. 3, *Conative and affective process analyses* (pp. 223–253). Hillsdale, NJ: Erlbaum & Associates.

Maltzman, I. (1968). Theoretical conceptions of semantic conditioning and generalization. In T. R. Dixon & D. L. Horton (Eds.), *Verbal behavior and general behavior theory* (pp. 291–339). Englewood Cliffs, NJ: Prentice-Hall.

Mandler, J. M. (1978). A code in the node: The use of a story schema in retrieval. *Discourse Processes, 1,* 14–35.

Mandler, J. M. (1984). *Stories, scripts, and scenes: Aspects of schema theory.* Hillsdale, NJ: Erlbaum & Associates.

Mandler, J. M. (1987). On the psychological reality of story structure. *Discourse Processes, 10,* 1–29.

Mandler, J. M. (1992a). How to build a baby: II. Conceptual primitives. *Psychological Review, 99,* 587–604.

Mandler, J. M. (1992b). The foundations of conceptual thought in infancy. *Cognitive Development, 7,* 273–285.

Mandler, J. M., & DeForest, M. (1979). Is there more than one way to recall a story? *Child Development, 50,* 886–889.

Mandler, J. M., & Goodman, M. S. (1982). On the psychological validity of story structure. *Journal of Verbal Learning and Verbal Behavior, 21,* 507–523.

Mandler, J. M., & Johnson, N. S. (1977). Remembrance of things parsed: Story structure and recall. *Cognitive Psychology, 9,* 111–151.

Mani, K., & Johnson-Laird, P. N. (1982). The mental representation of spatial descriptions. *Memory and Cognition, 10,* 181–187.

Mannes, S. M., & Kintsch, W. (1987). Knowledge organization and text organization. *Cognition and Instruction, 4,* 91–116.

Manning, B. H. (1988). Application of cognitive behavior modification: First and third graders self-management of classroom behaviors. *American Educational Research Journal, 25,* 193–212.

Manning, B. H. (1990). Cognitive self-instruction for an off-task fourth grader during independent academic tasks: A case study. *Contemporary Educational Psychology, 15,* 36–46.

Manning, B. H. (1991). *Cognitive self-instruction for classroom processes.* Albany: State University of New York Press.

Mansfield, R. S., Busse, T. V., & Krepelka, E. J. (1978). The effectiveness of creativity training. *Review of Educational Research, 48,* 517–536.

Mantzicopoulos, P., & Morrison, D. (1992). Kindergarten retention: Academic and behavioral outcomes through the end of second grade. *American Educational Research Journal, 29,* 182–198.

Mantzicopoulos, P., Morrison, D. C., Hinshaw, S. P., & Carte, E. T. (1992). Nonpromotion in kindergarten: The role of cognitive, perceptual, visual-motor, behavioral, achievement, socioeconomic, and demographic characteristics. *American Educational Research Journal, 26,* 107–121.

Maosen, Li (1990). Moral education in the People's Republic of China. *Journal of Moral Education, 19,* 159–171.

Maple, S. A., & Stage, F. K. (1991). Influence on the choice of math/science major by gender and ethnicity. *American Educational Research Journal, 28,* 37–60.

Marantz, M. (1988). Fostering prosocial behaviour in the early childhood classroom: Review of the research. *Journal of Moral Education, 17,* 27–39.

Maratsos, M. P. (1989). Innateness and plasticity in language acquisition. In M. L. Rice & R. L. Schiefelbusch (Eds.), *The teachability of language* (pp. 105–125). Baltimore: Paul H. Brookes.

Marcia, J. E. (1966). Development and validation of ego-identity status. *Journal of Personality and Social Psychology, 3,* 551–558.

Marín, G. (1992). Issues in the measurement of acculturation among Hispanics. In K. F. Geisinger (Ed.), *Psychological testing of Hispanics* (pp. 235–252). Washington, DC: American Psychological Association.

Markman, E. M. (1989). *Categorization and naming in children.* Cambridge, MA: MIT Press.

Markman, E. M., & Callanan, M. A. (1983). An analysis of hierarchical classification. In R. Sternberg (Ed.), *Advances in the psychology of human intelligence,* Vol. 2. (pp. 325–365). Hillsdale, NJ: Erlbaum & Associates.

Markman, E. M., & Siebert, J. (1976). Classes and collections: Internal organization and resulting holistic properties. *Cognitive Psychology, 8,* 561–577.

Markovà, I. (1990). Introduction. In I. Markovà & K. Foppa (Eds.), *The dynamics of dialogue* (pp. 1–22). New York: Springer-Verlag.

Marks, M., Pressley, M., Coley, J. D., Craig, S., Gardner, R., Rose, W., & DePinto, T. (1993). Teachers' adaptations of reciprocal teaching: Progress toward a classroom compatible version of reciprocal teaching. *Elementary School Journal, 94,* 267–283.

Markus, H., & Nurius, P. (1986). Possible selves. *American Psychologist, 41,* 954-969.

Marlowe, J., & Culler, K. (1987). How we're adding racial balance to the math equation. *Executive Educator.*

Marmor, G. S. (1975). Development of kinetic images: When does the child first represent movement in mental images? *Cognitive Psychology, 7,* 548–559.

Marsh, G., Desberg, P., & Cooper, J. (1977). Developmental strategies in reading. *Journal of Reading Behavior, 9,* 391–394.

Marsh, G., Friedman, M., Desberg, P., & Saterdahl, K. (1981). Comparison of reading and spelling strategies in normal and reading-disabled children. In M. P. Friedman, J. P. Das, & N. O'Connor (Eds.), *Intelligence and learning* (pp. 363–367). New York: Plenum.

Marsh, G., Friedman, M., Welch, V., & Desberg, P. (1981). A cognitive-developmental theory of reading acquisition. In G. E. MacKinnon & T. G. Waller (Eds.), *Reading research: Advances in theory and practice,* Vol. 3 (pp. 199–221). New York: Academic Press.

Marsh, H. W. (1987). The big-fish-little-pond effect on academic self-concept. *Journal of Educational Psychology, 79,* 280–295.

Marsh, H. W. (1989a). Effects of attending single-sex and coeducational high schools on achievement, attitudes, behaviors, and sex differences. *Journal of Educational Psychology, 81,* 70–85.

Marsh, H. W. (1989b). Effects of single-sex and coeducational schools: A response to Lee and Bryk. *Journal of Educational Psychology, 81,* 652–653.

Marsh, H. W. (1990a). Causal ordering of academic self-concept and academic achievement: A multiwave, longitudinal panel analysis. *Journal of Educational Psychology, 82,* 646–656.

Marsh, H. W. (1990b). The structure of academic self-concept: The Marsh/Shavelson model. *Journal of Educational Psychology, 82,* 623–636.

Marsh, H. W. (1992a). Content specificity of relations between academic achievement and academic self-concept. *Journal of Educational Psychology, 84,* 35–42.

Marsh, H. W. (1992b). Extracurricular activities: Beneficial extension of the traditional curriculum or subversion of academic goals? *Journal of Educational Psychology, 84,* 553–562.

Marsh, H. W., & Craven, R. G. (1991). Self-other agreement on multiple dimensions of preadolescent self-concept: Inferences by teachers, mothers, and fathers. *Journal of Educational Psychology, 83,* 393–404.

Marsh, H. W., Craven, R. G., & Debus, R. (1991). Self-concepts of young children 5 to 8 years of age: Measurement and multidimensional structure. *Journal of Educational Psychology, 83,* 377–392.

Marshall, J. D. (1984a). Process and product: Case studies of writing in two content areas. In A. N. Applebee (Ed.), *Contexts for learning to write: Studies of secondary school instruction* (pp. 149–168). Norwood, NJ: Ablex.

Marshall, J. D. (1984b). Schooling and the composing process. In A. N. Applebee (Ed.), *Contexts for learning to write: Studies of secondary school instruction* (pp. 103–119). Norwood, NJ: Ablex.

Marshall, J. (1987). The effects of writing on students' understanding of literary text. *Research in the Teaching of English, 21,* 31–63.

Marshall-Goodell, B. S., Tassinary, L. G., & Cacioppo, J. T. (1990). Principles of bioelectrical measurement. In J. T. Cacioppo & L. G. Tassinary (Eds.), *Principles of psychophysiology* (pp. 113–148). Cambridge, UK: Cambridge University Press.

Marston, D., & Magnusson, D. (1985). Implementing curriculum-based measurement in special and regular education settings. *Exceptional Children, 52,* 266–276.

Martin, J., & Martin, W. (1983). *Personal development: Self-instruction for personal agency.* Calgary, Alberta, Canada: Detselig Enterprises.

Martin, J. H., Brust, J. C. M., & Hilal, S. (1991). Imaging the living brain. In E. R. Kandel, J. H. Schwartz, & T. M. Jessel (Eds.), *Principles of neural science* (pp. 309–324). New York: Elsevier.

Martin, J. R. (1987). Transforming moral education. *Journal of Moral Education, 16,* 204–213.

Martin, J. R. (1992). *The schoolhome: Rethinking schools for changing families.* Cambridge, MA: Harvard University Press.

Martin, V. L., & Pressley, M. (1991). Elaborative-interrogation effects depend on the nature of the question. *Journal of Educational Psychology, 83,* 113–119.

Martin, W. G., & Harel, G. (1989). Proof frames of preservice elementary teachers. *Journal for Research in Mathematics Education, 20,* 41–51.

Martindale, C. (1991). *Cognitive psychology: A neural-network approach.* Pacific Grove, CA: Brooks/Cole.

Martinez, J. L. Jr., & Kesner, R. P. (1991). *Learning and memory: A biological view,* 2nd ed. San Diego: Academic Press.

Martinez, M. E. (1992). Interest enhancements to science experiments: Interactions with student gender. *Journal of Research in Science Teaching, 29,* 167–177.

Marton, F., & Säljö, R. (1976). On qualitative differences in learning: I: Outcome and process. *British Journal of Educational Psychology, 46,* 4–11.

Marzano, R. J. (1992). *A different kind of classroom: Teaching with dimensions of learning.* Alexandria, VA: Association for Supervision and Curriculum Development.

Marzano, R. J., Brandt, R. S., Highes, C. S., Jones, B. F., Presseisen, B. Z., Rankin, S. C., & Suhor, C. (1988). *Dimensions of thinking: A framework for curriculum and instruction.* Alexandria, VA: Association for Curriculum and Supervision.

Mason, C. L. (1992). Concept mapping: A tool to develop reflective science instruction. *Science Education, 76,* 51–63.

Mason, C. L., & Kahle, J. B. (1988). Student attitudes toward science and science-related careers: A program designed to promote a stimulating gender-free learning environment. *Journal of Research in Science Teaching, 26,* 25–39.

Mason, D. A., & Good, T. L. (1990). *The effects of two small-group models of active teaching and active learning on elementary school mathematics achievement* (Technical Report No. 478). Columbia, MO: Center for Research in Social Behavior, University of Missouri.

Mastropieri, M. A., & Scruggs, T. E. (1989). Constructing more meaningful relationships: Mnemonic instruction for special populations. *Educational Psychology Review, 1,* 83–111.

Mastropieri, M. A., & Scruggs, T. E. (1991). *Teaching students ways to remember: Strategies for learning mnemonically.* Cambridge, MA: Brookline Books.

Mathews, J. (1993). Psst, kid, wanna buy a...used math book? *Newsweek,* March 1, 62–63.

Mathews, M. M. (1966). *Teaching to read: Historically considered.* Chicago: University of Chicago Press.

Mathison, S. (1988). Why triangulate? *Educational Researcher, 17 (2)*, 13–17.

Matsuzawa, T. (1990). Spontaneous sorting in human and chimpanzee. In S. T. Parker & K. R. Gibson (Eds.), *"Language" and intelligence in monkeys and apes* (pp. 451–468). Cambridge, UK: Cambridge University Press.

Mattarazzo, J. D. (1972). *Wechsler's measurement and appraisal of adult intelligence*, 5th ed. Baltimore: Williams & Wilkins.

Maxwell, M. (1979). *Improving student learning skills*. San Francisco: Jossey-Bass.

Mayer, R. E. (1975). Forward transfer of different reading strategies evoked by testlike events in mathematics text. *Journal of Educational Psychology, 67*, 165–169.

Mayer, R. E. (1977). The sequencing of instruction and the concept of assimilation-to-schema. *Instructional Science, 6*, 369–388.

Mayer, R. E. (1979). Can advance organizers influence meaningful learning. *Review of Educational Research, 49*, 371–383.

Mayer, R. E. (1980). Elaboration techniques that increase the meaningfulness of technical text: An experimental test of the learning strategy hypothesis. *Journal of Educational Psychology, 72*, 770–784.

Mayer, R. E. (1981). Frequency norms and structural analysis of algebra story problems into families, categories, and templates. *Instructional Science, 10*, 135–175.

Mayer, R. E. (1982). Memory for algebra story problems. *Journal of Educational Psychology, 74*, 199–216.

Mayer, R. E. (1985). Structural analysis of science prose: Can we increase problem-solving performance? In B. K. Britton & J. B. Black (Eds.), *Understanding expository prose: A theoretical and practical handbook for analyzing explanatory text* (pp. 65–87). Hillsdale, NJ: Erlbaum & Associates.

Mayer, R. E. (1989a). Models for understanding. *Review of Educational Research, 59*, 43–64.

Mayer, R. E. (1989b). Systematic thinking fostered by illustrations in scientific text. *Journal of Educational Psychology, 81*, 240–246.

Mayer, R. E., & Anderson, R. B. (1991). Animations need narrations: An experimental test of a dual-coding hypothesis. *Journal of Educational Psychology, 83*, 484–490.

Mayer, R. E., & Anderson, R. B. (1992). The instructive animation: Helping students build connections between words and pictures in multimedia learning. *Journal of Educational Psychology, 84*, 444–452.

Mayer, R. E., & Bromage, B. K. (1980). Different recall protocols for technical texts due to advance organizers. *Journal of Educational Psychology, 72*, 209–225.

Mayer, R. E., & Cook, L. K. (1981). Effects of shadowing on prose comprehension and problem solving. *Memory and Cognition, 9*, 101–109.

Mayer, R. E., & Gallini, J. K. (1990). When is an illustration worth ten thousand words? *Journal of Educational Psychology, 82*, 715–726.

Mayer, R. E., Larkin, J. H., & Kadane, J. (1984). A cognitive analysis of mathematical problem solving ability. In R. Sternberg (Ed.), *Advances in the psychology of human intelligence* (pp. 231–273). Hillsdale, NJ: Erlbaum & Associates.

McArthur, D., Stasz, C., & Zmuidzinas, M. (1990). Tutoring techniques in algebra. *Cognition and Instruction, 7*, 197–244.

McCall, R. B., & Carriger, M. S. (1993). A meta-analysis of infant habituation and recognition memory performance as predictors of later IQ. *Child Development, 64*, 57–79.

McCarthy, K. A., & Nelson, K. (1981). Children's use of scripts in story recall. *Discourse Processes, 4*, 59–70.

McCarthy, L. P. (1987). A stranger in strange lands: A college student writing across the curriculum. *Research in the Teaching of English, 21*, 233–265.

McCarthy, R. A., & Warrington, E. K. (1990). *Cognitive neuropsychology: A clinical introduction*. San Diego: Academic Press.

McCauley, C., Kellas, G., Dugas, J., & DeVillis, R. F. (1976). Effects of serial rehearsal training of memory search. *Journal of Educational Psychology, 68*, 474–481.

McClelland, J. L., & Rumelhart, D. E. (1981). An interactive activation model of context effects in letter perception: Part 1. An account of basic findings. *Psychological Review, 88*, 375–407.

McClelland, J. L., & Rumelhart, D. E. (1986). *Parallel distributed processing*, Vol. 2. Cambridge, MA: MIT Press.

McClelland, J. L., & Rumelhart, D. E. (1988). *Explorations in parallel distributed processing: A handbook of models, programs, and exercises*. Cambridge, MA: MIT Press.

McCloskey, M. (1983). Naive theories of motion. In D. Gentner & A. Stevens (Eds.), *Mental models* (pp. 299–324). Hillsdale, NJ: Erlbaum & Associates.

McCloskey, M. (1992). Cognitive mechanisms in numerical processing: Evidence from acquired dyscalculia. *Cognition, 44*, 107–157.

McConkie, G. W., Rayner, K., & Wilson, S. J. (1973). Experimental manipulation of reading strategies. *Journal of Educational Psychology, 65*, 1–8.

McConkie, G. W., Zola, D., Blanchard, H. E., & Wolverton, G. S. (1982). Perceiving words during reading: Lack of facilitation from prior peripheral exposure. *Perception and Psychophysics, 32*, 271–281.

McCormick, C. B., Busching, B. A., & Potter, E. F. (1992). Children's knowledge about writing: The development and use of evaluative criteria. In M. Pressley, K. R. Harris, & J. T. Guthrie (Eds.), *Promoting academic competence and literacy in school* (pp. 311–336). San Diego: Academic Press.

McCormick, C. B., & Levin, J. R. (1987). Mnemonic prose-learning strategies. In M. A. McDaniel & M. Pressley (Eds.), *Imagery and related mnemonic processes: Theories, individual differences, and applications* (pp. 407–427). New York: Springer-Verlag.

McCutchen, D., & Perfetti, C. A. (1983). Local coherence: Helping young writers manage a complex task. *Elementary School Journal, 84*, 71–75.

McDaniel, M. A., & Einstein, G. O. (1989). Material-appropriate processing: A contextualist approach to reading and studying strategies. *Educational Psychology Review, 1*, 113–145.

McDaniel, M. A., & Schlager, M. S. (1990). Discovery learning and transfer of problem-solving skills. *Cognition and Instruction, 7*, 129–159.

McDonnell, J., & Ferguson, B. (1989). A comparison of time delay and decreasing prompt hierarchy strategies in teaching banking skills to students with moderate handicaps. *Journal of Applied Behavior Analysis, 22*, 85–91.

McFie, J. (1961). The effects of hemispherectomy on intellectual functioning in cases of infantile hemiplegia. *Journal of Neurology, Neurosurgery Psychiatry, 24*, 20.

McGaw, B., & Grotelueshen, A. (1972). Direction of the effect of questions in prose material. *Journal of Educational Psychology, 63*, 580–588.

McGill-Franzen, A. M. (1987). Failure to learn to read: Formulating a policy problem. *Reading Research Quarterly, 22*, 475–90.

McGilly, K., & Siegler, R. S. (1989). How children choose among serial recall strategies. *Child Development, 60*, 172–182.

McGinley, W. (1992). The role of reading and writing while composing from sources. *Reading Research Quarterly, 27*, 226–248.

McKeown, M. G., Beck, I. L., Sinatra, G. M., & Loxterman, J. A. (1992). The contribution of prior knowledge and coherent text to comprehension. *Reading Research Quarterly, 27*, 78–93.

McKinney, J. D., & Speece, D. L. (1986). Longitudinal stability and academic consequences of behavioral subtypes of learning disabled children. *Journal of Educational Psychology, 78*, 365–372.

McKoon, G., & Ratcliff, R. (1979). Priming in episodic and semantic memory. *Journal of Verbal Learning and Verbal Behavior, 18*, 463–480.

McLaughlin, B. (1984). *Second-language acquisition in childhood*. Hillsdale, NJ: Erlbaum & Associates.

McLoyd, V. C. (1979). The effects of extrinsic rewards of differential value on high and low intrinsic interest. *Child Development, 50*, 1010–1019.

McNamee, G. D. (1979). The social interaction origins of narrative skills. *Quarterly Newsletter of the Laboratory of Comparative Human Cognition, 1*, 63–68.

Means, B., & Knapp, M. S. (1992). Cognitive approaches to teaching advanced skills to educationally disadvantaged students. *Phi Delta Kappan, 73*, 282–289.

Means, M., & Voss, J. (1985). Star Wars: A developmental study of expert and novice knowledge structures. *Journal of Memory and Language, 24*, 746–757.

Meece, J. L., Blumenfeld, P. C., & Hoyle, R. H. (1988). Students' goal orientations and cognitive engagement in classroom activities. *Journal of Educational Psychology, 80*, 514–523.

Mehan, H. (1979). *Social organization in the class-*

room. Cambridge, MA: Harvard University Press.

Meichenbaum, D. (1977) *Cognitive behavior modification.* New York: Plenum.

Meichenbaum, D. (1990). Cognitive perspective on teaching self-regulation. *American Journal of Mental Deficiency, 94,* 367–369.

Meichenbaum, D., & Asarnow, J. (1979). Cognitive-behavioral modification and metacognitive development: Implications for the classroom. In P. C. Kendall & S. D. Hollon (Eds.), *Cognitive-behavioral interventions* (pp. 11–35). New York: Academic Press.

Meichenbaum, D., & Goodman, J. (1969). Reflection-impulsivity and verbal control of motor behavior. *Child Development, 40,* 785–797.

Meichenbaum, D., & Goodman, J. (1971). Training impulsive children to talk to themselves: A means of developing self-control. *Journal of Abnormal Child Psychology, 77,* 115–126.

Meisels, S. J., & Plunkett, J. W. (1988). Developmental consequences of preterm birth: Are there long-term effects? In P. B. Baltes, D. L. Featherman, & R. M. Lerner (Eds.), *Life-span development and behavior,* Vol. 9 (pp. 87–128). Hillsdale, NJ: Erlbaum & Associates.

Mellor, S. (1989). Gender differences in identity formation as a function of self-other relationships. *Journal of Youth and Adolescence, 18,* 361–375.

Meloth, M. S. (1990). Changes in poor readers' knowledge of cognition and the association of knowledge of cognition with regulation of cognition and reading comprehension. *Journal of Educational Psychology, 82,* 792–798.

Meltzer, L. J. (1987). *The surveys of problem-solving and educational skills (SPES).* Cambridge, MA: Educator's Publishing Service.

Meltzer, L. J. (1991). Problem-solving strategies and academic performance in learning disabled students: Do subtypes exist? In L. V. Feagans, E. J. Short, & L. J. Meltzer (Eds.), *Subtypes of learning disabilities* (pp. 163–188). Hillsdale, NJ: Erlbaum & Associates.

Meltzer, L. J. (1992). Strategy use in students with learning disabilities: The challenge of assessment. In L. J. Meltzer (Ed.), *Strategy assessment and instruction for students with learning disabilities: From theory to practice* (pp. 93–136). Austin, TX: PRO-ED.

Meltzer, L. J., Solomon, B., Fenton, T., & Levine, M. D. (1989). A developmental study of problem-solving strategies in children with and without learning difficulties. *Journal of Applied Developmental Psychology, 10,* 171–193.

Meltzoff, A. N. (1985). Immediate and deferred imitation in fourteen- and twenty-four-month-old infants. *Child Development, 56,* 62–72.

Meltzoff, A. N., & Gopnik, A. (1989). On linking nonverbal imitation, representation, and language learning in the first two years of life. In G. E. Speidel & K. E. Nelson (Eds.), *The many faces of imitation in language learning* (pp. 23–51). New York: Springer-Verlag.

Meltzoff, A. N., & Moore, M. K. (1977).

Imitation of facial and manual gestures by human neonates. *Sciences, 198,* 75–78.

Meltzoff, A. N., & Moore, M. K. (1983). Newborn infants imitate adult facial gestures. *Child Development, 54,* 702–709.

Mensh, E., & Mensh, H. (1991). *The IQ mythology.* Carbondale, IL: Southern Illinois University Press.

Mentkowski, M., & Strait, M. (1983). *A longitudinal study of student change in cognitive development, learning styles, and generic abilities in an outcome-centered liberal arts curriculum* (Final Report to the National Institute of Education, Research Report No. 6). Milwaukee, WI: Alverno College, Office of Research and Evaluation.

Merbaum, M. (1973). The modification of self-destructive behavior by mother-therapist using aversive stimulation. *Behavior Therapy, 4,* 442–447.

Mercer, J. R. (1979). *System of multicultural pluralistic assessment (SOMPA): Technical manual.* San Antonio, TX: Psychological Corporation.

Merighi, J., Edison, M., & Zigler, E. (1990). The role of motivational factors in the functioning of mentally retarded individuals. In R. M. Hodapp, J. A. Burack, & E. Zigler (Eds.), *Issues in the developmental approach to retardation* (pp. 114–134). Cambridge, England: Cambridge University Press.

Merriam, S. B., & Cunningham, P. M. (1989). *Handbook of adult and continuing education.* San Francisco: Jossey-Bass.

Messer, S. B. (1976). Reflection-impulsivity: A review. *Psychological Bulletin, 83,* 1026–1052.

Messick, S., & Jungeblut, A. (1981). Time and method in coaching for the SAT. *Psychological Bulletin, 89,* 191–216.

Meyer, B. J. F. (1975). *The organization of prose and its effects on memory.* Amsterdam: North Holland.

Meyer, B. J. F., Brandt, D. H., & Bluth, G. J. (1980). Use of top-level structure in text: Key for reading comprehension of ninth-grade students. *Reading Research Quarterly, 16,* 72–103.

Meyer, B. J. F., Young, C. J., & Bartlett, B. J. (1989). *Memory improved: Reading and memory enhancement across the life span through strategic text structures.* Hillsdale, NJ: Erlbaum & Associates.

Meyer, D., Schvaneveldt, R. W., & Ruddy, M. G. (1975). Loci of contextual effects on word recognition. In P. M. A. Rabbitt & S. Dornic (Eds.), *Attention and performance V* (pp. 98–118). London: Academic Press.

Meyer, M., & Booker, J. (1991). *Eliciting and analyzing expert judgement: A practical guide.* London: Academic Press.

Meyer, W., Bachmann, M., Biermann, U., Hempelmann, M., Ploger, F., & Spiller, H. (1979). The informational value of evaluative behavior: Influence of praise and blame on perceptions of ability. *Journal of Educational Psychology, 71,* 259–268.

Meyers, J., Gelzheiser, L., Yelich, G., & Gallagher, M. (1990). Classroom, remedial, and resource teachers' views of pullout programs. *Elementary School Journal, 90,* 533–545.

Meyers, L. F. (1988). Using computers to teach children with Down Syndrome spoken and written language skills. In L. Nadel (Ed.), *The psychobiology of Down Syndrome* (pp. 247–265). Cambridge, MA: MIT Press.

Mezirow, J., Darkenwald, G. C., & Knox, A. B. (1975). *Last gamble on education: Dynamics of adult basic education.* Washington, DC: Adult Education Association of the United States.

Michael, A. L., Klee, T., Bransford, J. D., & Warren, S. F. (1993). The transition from theory to therapy: Test of two instructional methods. *Applied Cognitive Psychology, 7,* 139–153.

Michael, B. (Ed.) (1990). *Volunteers in public schools.* Washington, DC: National Academy Press.

Michael, J. L. (1985). Behavioral analysis: A radical perspective. In B. L. Hammonds (Ed.), *Psychology and learning: Master lectures.* Washington, DC: American Psychological Association.

Michael, J., & Meyerson, L. (1962). A behavioral approach to human control. *Harvard Educational Review, 32,* 382–402.

Mikulecky, L. (1987). The status of literacy in our society. *Research in literacy: Thirty-seventh yearbook of the National Reading Conference* (pp. 24–34). Chicago: National Reading Conference.

Miles, H. L. W. (1990). The cognitive foundations for reference in a signing orangutan. In S. T. Parker & K. R. Gibson (Eds.), *"Language" and intelligence in monkeys and apes* (pp. 511–539). Cambridge, UK: Cambridge University Press.

Miller, A. I. (1984). *Imagery in scientific thought: Creating 20th-century physics.* Boston: Birkhäuser.

Miller, G. A. (1956). The magical number seven, plus-or-minus two: Some limits on our capacity for processing information. *Psychological Review, 63,* 81–97.

Miller, G. A., Gallanter, E., & Pribram, K. H. (1960). *Plans and the structure of behavior.* New York: Holt, Rinehart, & Winston.

Miller, G. E., & Pressley, M. (1989). Pictures versus question elaboration on young children's learning of sentences containing high- and low-probability content. *Journal of Experimental Child Psychology, 48,* 431–450.

Miller, J. F. (1988). The developmental asynchrony of language development in children with Down syndrome. In L. Nadel (Ed.), *The psychobiology of Down syndrome* (pp. 167–198). Cambridge, MA: MIT Press.

Miller, P. H., Woody-Ramsey, J., & Aloise, P. A. (1991). The role of strategy effortfulness in strategy effectiveness. *Developmental Psychology, 27,* 738–745.

Miller, S. E., Leinhardt, G., & Zigmond, N. (1988). Influencing engagement through accommodation: An ethnographic study of at-risk students. *American Educational Research Journal, 25,* 465–487.

Miltenberger, R. G., & Thiesse-Duffy, E. (1988). Evaluation of home-based programs for teaching personal safety skills to children. *Journal of Applied Behavior Analysis, 21,* 81–87.

Minsky, M. (1975). A framework for representing knowledge. In P. H. Winston (Ed.), *The psychology of computer vision* (pp. 211–277). New York: McGraw-Hill.

Minsky, M. (1986). *The society of mind.* New York: Simon & Schuster.

Minstrell, J. (1982, January). Explaining the "at rest" condition of an object. *The Physics Teacher, 20*, 10–14.

Mischel, W. (1968). *Personality and assessment.* New York: Wiley.

Mitchell, J. V., Jr. (Ed.) (1985). *The ninth mental measurements yearbook* (Vol. 1–2). Lincoln: The Buros Institute of Mental Measurements of the University of Nebraska–Lincoln.

Mitchell, R. (1992). *Testing for learning: How new approaches to evaluation can improve American schools.* New York: Free Press.

Mitman, A. L., Mergendoller, J. R., Marchman, V. A., & Packer, M. J. (1987). Instruction addressing the components of scientific literacy and its relation to student outcomes. *American Educational Research Journal, 24*, 611–633.

Moccia, R. E., McKnight, P., Deshler, D. D., & Schumaker, J. B. (1990). *The 1990 INROADS Program Report.* Lawrence KS: University of Kansas, Institute for Research on Learning Disabilities.

Moely, B. E. (1977). Organizational factors in the development of memory. In R. V. Kail & J. W. Hagen (Eds.), *Perspectives on the development of memory and cognition* (pp. 203–236). Hillsdale, NJ: Erlbaum & Associates.

Moely, B. E., Hart, S. S., Leal, L., Santulli, K. A., Rao, N., Johnson, T., & Hamilton, L. B. (1992). The teacher's role in facilitating memory and study strategy development in the elementary school classroom. *Child Development, 63*, 653–672.

Moely, B. E., Olson, F. A., Halwes, T. G., & Flavell, J. H. (1969). Production deficiency in young children's clustered recall. *Developmental Psychology, 1*, 26–34.

Moffitt, T. E. (1990). Juvenile delinquency and attention deficit disorder: Boys' developmental trajectories from age 3 to age 15. *Child Development, 61*, 893–910.

Mokros, J. R., & Tinker, R. F. (1987). The impact of microcomputer-based labs on children's abilities to interpret graphs. *Journal of Research in Science Teaching, 24*, 369–383.

Molfese, D. L., & Segalowitz, S. J. (1988). *Brain lateralization in children: Developmental implications.* New York: Guilford.

Montague, M., & Bos, C. S. (1990). Cognitive and metacognitive characteristics of eighth grade students' mathematical problem solving. *Learning and Individual Differences, 2*, 371–388.

Mooney, R. J. (1990). Learning plan schemata from observation: Explanation-based learning for plan recognition. *Cognitive Science, 14*, 483–509.

Morales v. Shannon, 516 F. 2d 411 (1975).

Morales, R. V., Shute, V. J., & Pellegrino, J. W. (1985). Developmental differences in understanding and solving simple word problems. *Cognition and Instruction, 2*, 41–57.

Morgan, B., & Gibson, K. R. (1991). Nutritional and environmental interactions in brain development. In K. R. Gibson & A. C. Petersen (Eds.), *Brain maturation and cognitive development: Comparative and cross-cultural perspectives* (pp. 91–106). New York: Aldine de Gruyter.

Morine-Dershimer, G. (1979). *Teacher plan and classroom reality: The S. Bay study, part 4.* Research Monograph, Institute for Research on Teaching, University of Michigan.

Morocco, C., & Neuman, S. (1986). Word processors and the acquisition of writing strategies. *Journal of Learning Disabilities, 19*, 243–247.

Morris, R. D., Krawiecki, N. S., Wright, J. A., & Walter, L. W. (1993). Neuropsychological, academic, and adaptive functioning in children who survive in-hospital cardiac arrest and resuscitation. *Journal of Learning Disabilities, 26*, 46–51.

Morrissett, I. (Ed.) (1980). *Social studies in the 1980s: A report of project SPAN.* Alexandria, VA: Association for Supervision and Curriculum Development.

Morrow, L. M. (1989). *Literacy development in the early years: Helping children read and write.* Boston: Allyn & Bacon.

Morrow, L. M. (1983). (1983). Home and school correlates of early interest in literature. *Journal of Education Research, 76*, 221–230.

Morrow, L. M. (1990). Preparing the classroom environment to promote literacy during play. *Early Childhood Research Quarterly, 5*, 537–554.

Morrow, L. M., & Smith, J. K. (1990). The effects of group size on interactive storybook reading. *Reading Research Quarterly, 25*, 213–231.

Morrow, L. M., & Weinstein, C. S. (1986). Encouraging voluntary reading: The impact of a literacy program on children's use of library corners. *Reading Research Quarterly, 21*, 330–346.

Morse, L. W., & Handley, H. M. (1985). Listening to adolescents: Gender differences in science classroom interactions. In L. C. Wilkinson & C. B. Marrett (Eds.), *Gender influences on classroom interaction* (pp. 37–56). Orlando, FL: Academic Press.

Morson, G. S., & Emerson, C. (1990). *Mikhail Bakhtin: Creation of a prosaics.* Stanford, CA: Stanford University Press.

Mortimore, P. (1991). Effective schools from a British perspective: Research and practice. In J. R. Bliss, W. A. Firestone, & C. E. Richards (Eds.), *Rethinking effective schools research and practice* (pp. 76–90). Englewood Cliffs, NJ: Prentice-Hall.

Morton, J. (1979). Facilitation in word recognition: Experiments causing change in the logogen model. In P. A. Kolers, M. E. Wrolstad, & H. Bouma (Eds.), *Processing of visible language* (pp. 259–268). New York: Plenum.

Moshman, D. (1982). Exogenous, endogenous, and dialectical constructivism. *Developmental Review, 2*, 371–384.

Mudre, L. H., & McCormick, S. (1989). Effects of meaning-focused cues on underachieving readers' context use, self-corrections, and literal comprehension. *Reading Research Quarterly, 24*, 89–113.

Mulick, J, A. (1990). The ideology and science of punishment in mental retardation. *American Journal of Mental Deficiency, 94*, 142–156.

Mullen, B., & Rosenthal, R. (1985). *BASIC meta-analysis: Procedures and programs.* Hillsdale, NJ: Erlbaum & Associates.

Mullis, I. V. S. (1989). What high-school juniors know about biology: Perspectives from NAEP, the nation's report card. In W. R. Rosen (Ed.), *High-School Biology, Today and Tomorrow* (pp. 91–98). Washington, DC: National Academy Press.

Mullis, J. V. S., Owen, E. H., & Phillips, G. W. (1990). *Accelerating academic achievement.* Princeton, NJ: National Assessment of Educational Progress, Educational Testing Service.

Munsinger, H., & Weir, M. W. (1967). Infants' and young children's preference for complexity. *Journal of Experimental Child Psychology, 5*, 69–73.

Murnane, R. J., & Raizen, S. A. (1988). *Improving indicators of the quality of science and mathematics education in grades K–12.* Washington, DC: National Academy Press.

Mussen, P. H. (ed.) (1983). *Handbook of child psychology,* 4th ed. New York: John Wiley & Sons.

Muth, K D., Glynn, S. M., Britton, B. K., & Graves, M. F. (1988). Thinking out loud while studying text: Rehearsing key ideas. *Journal of Educational Psychology, 80*, 315–318.

Nadel, L. (Ed.) (1988). *The psychobiology of Down Syndrome.* Cambridge, MA: MIT Press.

NAEP (1985). *National Assessment of Educational Progress.* Princeton, NJ: Educational Testing Service.

Naglieri, J. A., & Prewett, P. N. (1990). Nonverbal intelligence measures: A selected review of instruments and their use. In C. R. Reynolds & R. W. Kamphaus (Eds.), *Handbook of psychological and educational assessment of children: Intelligence and achievement* (pp. 348–370). New York: Guilford Press.

Nagy, W., & Anderson, R. (1984). How many words are there in printed school English? *Reading Research Quarterly, 19*, 304–330.

Nagy, W., Anderson, R. C., Schommer, M., Scott, J. A., & Stallman, A. C. (1989). Morphological families in the internal lexicon. *Reading Research Quarterly, 24*, 262–282.

Nash, J. G., Schumacher, G. M., & Carlson, B. W. (1993). Writing from sources: A structure-mapping model. *Journal of Educational Psychology, 85*, 159–170.

National Center for Education Statistics (1992). *Digest of education statistics.* Washington, DC: U.S. Department of Education.

National Commission on Testing and Public Policy (1989). *From gatekeeper to gateway: Transforming testing in America.* Chestnut Hill, MA: National Commission on Testing and Public Policy, Boston College.

National Council of Teachers of Mathematics (1989). *Curriculum and evaluation standards for* school mathematics. Reston, VA: National Council of Teachers of Mathematics.

National Council of Teachers of Mathematics (1991). *Professional standards for teaching mathematics.* Reston, VA: National Council of Teachers of Mathematics.

National Research Council (1991). *In the mind's eye: Enhancing human performance.* Washington, DC: National Academy Press.

National Science Foundation (1978). *Report of the 1977 national survey of science.* Washington, DC: Natural Science Foundation.

Neale, M. C., & McArdle, J. J. (1990). The analysis of assortative mating: A LISREL model. *Behavior Genetics, 20,* 287–297.

Nebes, R. D. (1992). Cognitive dysfunction in Alzheimer's disease. In F. I. M. Craik & T. A. Salthouse (Eds.), *The handbook of aging and cognition* (pp. 373–446). Hillsdale, NJ: Erlbaum & Associates.

Necka, E. (1992). Cognitive analysis of intelligence: The significance of working memory processes. *Personality and Individual Differences, 13,* 1031–1046.

Needleman, H. L. (1992). Childhood exposure to lead: A common cause of school failure. *Phi Delta Kappan, 74,* 35–37.

Needleman, H. L., & Bellinger, D. (1991). The health effects of low level exposure to lead. *Annual Review of Public Health, 12,* 111–140.

Neely, J. H. (1976). Semantic priming and retrieval from lexical memory: Evidence for facilitatory and inhibitory processes. *Memory and Cognition, 4,* 648–654.

Neely, J. H. (1977). Semantic priming and retrieval from lexical memory: Roles of inhibitionless spreading activation and limited capacity attention. *Journal of Experimental Psychology, 106,* 226–254.

Neisser, U. (1967). *Cognitive psychology.* New York: Appleton-Century-Crofts.

Nelson, D. G. K. (1990). When experimental findings conflict with everyday observations: Reflections on children's category learning. *Child Development, 61,* 606–610.

Nelson, J., & Hayes, J. R. (1988). *How the writing context shapes college students' strategies for writing from sources.* (Technical Report No. 16.) Berkeley: University of California and Carnegie-Mellon University, Center for Study of Writing at University of California and Carnegie-Mellon.

Nelson, K. (1974). Concept, word, and sentence: Interrelations in acquisition and development. *Psychological Review, 81,* 267–285.

Nelson, K. (1978). How children represent their world in and out of language. In R. S. Siegler (Ed.), *Children's thinking: What develops?* (pp. 255–273). Hillsdale, NJ: Erlbaum & Associates.

Nelson, K., & Gruendel, J. (1981). Generalized event representations: Basic building blocks of cognitive development. In A. Brown & M. Lamb (Eds.), *Advances in developmental psychology,* Vol. 1 (pp. 231–247). Hillsdale, NJ: Erlbaum & Associates.

Nelson, K. E., Heimann, M., Lutfi, A. A., & Wroblewski, R. (1989). Implications for language acquisition models of childrens' and

parents' variations in imitation. In G. E. Speidel & K. E. Nelson (Eds.), *The many faces of imitation in language learning* (pp. 305–323). New York: Springer-Verlag.

Nelson-Le Gall, S., Kratzer, L., Jones, E., & DeCooke, P. (1990). Children's self-assessment of performance and task-related help seeking. *Journal of Experimental Child Psychology, 49,* 245–263.

Neman, R., Roos, P., McCann, B. M., Menolascino, F., & Heal, L. W. (1974). Experimental evaluation of sensorimotor patterning with mentally retarded children. *American Journal of Mental Deficiency, 79,* 372–384.

Nesher, P., & Kilpatrick, J. (Eds.) (1990). *Mathematics and cognition: A research synthesis by the international group for the psychology of mathematics education.* Cambridge, UK: Cambridge University Press.

Nettelbeck, T., & Brewer, N. (1981). Studies of mild mental retardation and timed performance. In N. R. Ellis (Ed.), *International review of research in mental retardation,* Vol. 10 (pp. 61–106). New York: Academic Press.

Neuman, S. B. (1988). The displacement effect: Assessing the relation between television viewing and reading performance. *Reading Research Quarterly, 23,* 414–440.

Neuman, S. B., & Koskinen, P. (1992). Captioned television as comprehensible input: Effects of incidental word learning from context for language minority students. *Reading Research Quarterly, 27,* 94–106.

Neuman, S. B., & Roskos, K. (1992). Literacy objects as cultural tools: Effects on children's literacy behaviors in play. *Reading Research Quarterly, 27,* 202–225.

Neves, D. M., & Anderson, J. R. (1981). Knowledge compilation: Mechanisms for the automatization of cognitive skills. In J. R. Anderson (Ed.), *Cognitive skills and their acquisition* (pp. 251–272). Hillsdale, NJ: Erlbaum & Associates.

Newby, T. J. (1991). Classroom motivation: Strategies of first-year teachers. *Journal of Educational Psychology, 83,* 195–200.

Newcombe, N., & Dubas, J. S. (1992). A longitudinal study of predictors of spatial ability in adolescent females. *Child Development, 63,* 37–46.

Newelle, A. (1990). *Unified theories of cognition.* Cambridge, MA: Harvard University Press.

Newell, A., & Rosenbloom, P. S. (1981). Mechanisms of skill acquisition and the law of practice. In J. R. Anderson (Ed.), *Cognitive skills and their acquisition.* Hillsdale, NJ: Erlbaum & Associates.

Newell, A., & Simon, H. A. (1972). *Human problem solving.* Englewood Cliffs, NJ: Prentice-Hall.

Newell, G. (1984). Learning from writing in two content areas: A case study/protocol analysis. *Research in the Teaching of English, 18,* 205–287.

Newell, G., Suszynski, K., & Weingart, R. (1989). The effects of writing in a reader-based and text-based mode on students' understanding

of two short stories. *Journal of Reading Behavior, 21,* 37–58.

Newkirk, T. (1991). The high school years. In J. Flood, J. M. Jensen, D. Lapp, & J. R. Squire (Eds.), *Handbook of research on teaching the English language arts* (pp. 3–17). New York: Macmillan.

Newman, A. P., & Beverstock, C. (1990). *Adult literacy: Contexts and challenges.* Newark, DE: International Reading Association.

Newman, D., Griffin, P., & Cole, M. (1989). *The construction zone: Working for cognitive change in school.* Cambridge, UK: Cambridge University Press.

Newman, L. S. (1990). Intentional and unintentional memory in young children: Remembering versus playing. *Journal of Experimental Child Psychology, 50,* 243–258.

Newman, P., & Newman, B. (1978). Identity formation and the college experience. *Adolescence, 13,* 311–326.

Newman, R. S. (1990). Children's help-seeking in the classroom: The role of motivational factors and attitudes. *Journal of Educational Psychology, 82,* 71–80.

Newman, R. S., & Goldin, L. (1990). Children's reluctance to seek help with schoolwork. *Journal of Educational Psychology, 82,* 92–100.

Newmann, F. (1988). Can depth replace coverage in the high school curriculum? *Phi Delta Kappan, 68* (5), 345–348.

Newmann, F. (1990a). Higher-order thinking in social studies: A rationale for the assessment of classroom thoughtfulness. *Journal of Curriculum Studies, 22,* 41–56.

Newmann, F. (1990b). Qualities of thoughtful social studies classes: An empirical profile. *Journal of Curriculum Studies, 22,* 253–275.

Newmann, F. (1991a). Higher-order thinking in the teaching of social studies: Connections between theory and practice. In J. F. Voss, D. N. Perkins, & J. W. Segal (Eds.), *Informal reasoning and education* (pp. 381–400). Hillsdale, NJ: Erlbaum & Associates.

Newmann, F. M. (1991b). Promoting higher order thinking in social studies: Overview of a study of 16 high school departments. *Theory and Research in Social Education, 19,* 324–340.

Newmann, F. M. (1991c). Student engagement in academic work: Expanding the perspective on secondary school effectiveness. In J. R. Bliss, W. A. Firestone, & C. E. Richards (Eds.), *Rethinking effective schools research and practice* (pp. 58–75). Englewood Cliffs, NJ: Prentice-Hall.

Newmann, F. (1991d). The prospects for classroom thoughtfulness in high school social studies. In C. Collins (Ed.), *Building the quality of thinking in and out of our schools in the twenty-first century.* Hillsdale, NJ: Erlbaum & Associates.

Newmann, F., Onosko, J., & Stevenson, R. (1990). Staff development for higher-order thinking: A synthesis of practical wisdom. *Journal of Staff Development, 11* (3), 48–55.

Niaz, M. (1988). Manipulation of M demand of chemistry problems and its effect on student performance: A neo-Piagetian study. *Journal of Research in Science Teaching, 25,* 643–657.

Niaz, M. (1989). Relation between Pascual-Leone's structural and functional M-space and its effect on problem solving in chemistry. *International Journal of Science Education, 11,* 93–99.

Nicholls, J. G. (1989). *The competitive ethos and democratic education.* Cambridge, MA: Harvard University Press.

Nicholls, J. G., & Nelson, J. R. (1992). Students' conceptions of controversial knowledge. *Journal of Educational Psychology, 84,* 224–230.

Nicholls, J. G., & Thorkildsen, T. A. (1987, October). *Achievement goals and beliefs: Individual and classroom differences.* Presented at the meeting of the Society for Experimental Social Psychology, Charlottesville, VA.

Nicholson, T. (1991). Do children read words better in context or in lists? A classic study revisited. *Journal of Educational Psychology, 83,* 444–450.

Nicholson, T., Bailey, J., & McArthur, J. (1991). Context cues in reading: The gap between research and popular opinion. *Journal of Reading: Writing and Learning Disabilities, 7,* 33–41.

Nicholson, T., Lillas, C., & Rzoska, A. (1988). Have we been misled by miscues? *The Reading Teacher, 42,* 6–10.

Nickerson, R. S. (1988). On improving thinking through instruction. In E. Z. Rothkopf (Ed.), *Review of Research in Education,* Vol. 15 (pp. 3–57). Washington, DC: American Educational Research Association.

Nickerson, R. S., Perkins, D. N., & Smith, E. E. (1985). *The teaching of thinking.* Hillsdale, NJ: Erlbaum & Associates.

Ninio, A. (1980). Picture-book reading in mother-infant dyads belonging to two subgroups in Israel. *Child Development, 51,* 587–590.

Nist, S. L., Simpson, M. L., Olejnik, S., & Mealey, D. L. (1991). The relation between self-selected study processes and test performance. *American Educational Research Journal, 28,* 849–874.

Noddings, N. (1984). *Caring: A femine approach to ethics and moral education.* Berkeley: University of California Press.

Noddings, N. (1987). Do we really want to produce good people? *Journal of Moral Education, 16,* 177–188.

Nolen, S. B. (1988). Reasons for studying: Motivational orientations and study strategies. *Cognition and Instruction, 5,* 269–287.

Nolte, R. Y., & Singer, H. (1985). Active comprehension: Teaching a process of reading comprehension and its effects on reading achievement. *Reading Teacher, 39,* 24–31.

Northcutt, N. (1975). *Adult functional competency: A summary.* Austin, TX: Adult Performance Level Project.

Noss, R., & Hoyles, C. (1992). In C. Hoyles & R. Noss (Eds.), *Learning mathematics and LOGO* (pp. 431–468). Cambridge, MA: MIT Press.

Novak, J. D., & Gowin, D. B. (1984). *Learning how to learn.* New York: Cambridge University Press.

Novak, J. D., & Musonda, D. (1991). A twelve-year longitudinal study of science concept learning. *American Educational Research Journal, 28,* 117–153.

Nunnally, J. C. (1978). *Psychometric theory,* 2nd ed. New York: McGraw-Hill.

Nussbaum, J., & Novick, S. (1982). Alternative frameworks, conceptual conflict and accommodation: Toward a principled teaching strategy. *Instructional Science, 11,* 183–200.

Nye, P. A., Crooks, T. J., Powley, M., & Tripp, G. (1984). Student note-taking related to university examination performance. *Higher Education, 13,* 85–97.

Nystrand, M. (1986). *The structure of written communication: Studies in reciprocity between writers and readers.* New York: Academic Press.

Oakes, J. (1985). *Keeping track: How schools structure inequality.* New Haven, CT: Yale University Press.

Oakes, J. (1987). Tracking in secondary schools: A contextual perspective. *Educational Psychologist, 22,* 129–154.

Oakes, J. (1990). Opportunities, achievement, and choice: Women and minority students in science and mathematics. In C. B. Cazden (Ed.), *Review of Research in Education,* Vol. 16 (pp. 153–222). Washington, DC: American Educational Research Association.

Oakhill, J., & Garnham, A. (1988). *Becoming a skilled reader.* London: Basil Blackwell.

Oakland, T., & Parmelee, R. (1985). Mental measurement of minority-group children. In B. B. Wolman (Ed.), *Handbook of intelligence: Theories, measurements, and applications* (pp. 699–736). New York: John Wiley & Sons.

Oden, G. C. (1987). Concept, knowledge, and thought. *Annual Review of Psychology, 38,* 203–227.

O'Donnell, R. C. (1991). Theory, research, and practice in teaching English language arts. In J. Flood, J. M. Jensen, D. Lapp, & J. R. Squire (Eds.), *Handbook of research on teaching the English language arts* (pp. 132–142). New York: Macmillan.

Okebukola, P. A. (1990). Attaining meaningful learning of concepts in genetics and ecology: An examination of the potency of the concept-mapping technique. *Journal of Research in Science Teaching, 27,* 493–504.

Olive, J. (1991). LOGO programming and geometric understanding: An in-depth study. *Journal for Research in Mathematics Education, 22,* 90–111.

O'Malley, C., & Draper, S. (1992). Representation and interaction: Are mental models all in the mind? In Y. Rogers, A. Rutherford, & P. A. Bibby (Eds.), *Models in the mind: Theory, perspective, and application* (pp. 73–99). London: Academic Press.

O'Malley, M., & Chamot, A. U. (1990). *Learning strategies in second language acquisition.* Cambridge, UK: Cambridge University Press.

O'Neil, J. (1992). Putting performance assessment to the test. *Educational Leadership, 49 (8),* 14–19.

Onosko, J. (1989). Comparing teachers' thinking about promoting students' thinking. *Theory and Research in Social Education, 17,* 174–195.

Onosko, J. (1991). Barriers to the promotion of higher-order thinking in social studies. *Theory and Research in Social Education, 19,* 340–365.

Onosko, J. (1992). Exploring the thinking of thoughtful teachers. *Educational Leadership, 49 (7),* 40–43.

Onosko, J. J., & Newmann, F. M. (1994). Creating more thoughtful learning environments. In J. Mangieri & C. C. Block (Eds.), *Advanced educational psychology: Enhancing mindfulness.* Fort Worth, TX: Harcourt, Brace, Jovanovich.

Oppenheim, R. W. (1981). Neuronal cell death and some related phenomena during neurogenesis: A selective historical review and progress report. In W. M. Cowman (Ed.), *Studies in developmental neurobiology* (pp. 74–133). Oxford University Press: New York.

Oprea, J. M. (1988). Computer programming and mathematical thinking. *Journal of Mathematical Behavior, 7,* 175–190.

Ornstein, P. A., Naus, M. J., & Liberty, C. (1975). Rehearsal and organizational processes in children's memory. *Child Development, 46,* 818–830.

Ornstein, R. (1977). *The psychology of consciousness.* New York: Harcourt, Brace, Jovanovich.

Ornstein, R. (1978). The split and whole brain. *Human Nature, 1,* 76–83.

Orr, J. (in press). Sharing knowledge, celebrating identity: War stories and community memory among service technicians. In D. S. Middleton & D. Edwards (Eds.), *Collective remembering: Memory in society.* Beverly Hills, CA: Sage Publications.

Orton, S. T. (1925). "Word-blindness" in school children. *Archives of Neurology and Psychiatry, 14,* 581–615.

Orton, S. T. (1926). Reading disability. *Genetic Psychology Monographs, 14,* 335–453.

Orton, S. T. (1928). Specific reading disability—strephosymbolia. *Journal of the American Medical Association, 90,* 1095–1099.

Orton, S. T. (1937). *Reading, writing, and speech problems in children.* New York: W.W. Norton.

Osborne, R., & Freyberg, P. (1985). *Learning in science: The implications of children's science.* London: Heinemann.

O'Shea, L. J., Sindelar, P. T., & O'Shea, D. J. (1985). The effects of repeated readings and attentional cues on reading fluency and comprehension. *Journal of Reading Behavior, 17,* 129–142.

O'Sullivan, J. T. (1993). Preschoolers' beliefs about effort, incentive, and recall. *Journal of Experimental Child Psychology, 55,* 396–414.

O'Sullivan, J. T., & Pressley, M. (1984). Completeness of instruction and strategy transfer. *Journal of Experimental Child Psychology, 38,* 275–288.

O'Sullivan, P. J., Ysseldyke, J. E., Christenson, S. L., & Thurlow, M. L. (1990). Mildly handicapped elementary students' opportunity to learn during reading instruction in mainstream and special education settings. *Reading Research Quarterly, 25,* 131–146.

O'Tuel, F. S., & Darby, D. (1993, April). Instrumental enrichment for 4–6 grades: Can it raise achievement scores? Is three years too few? Presented at the annual meeting of the American Educational Research Association, Atlanta.

Ovander, C. J., & Collier, V. P. (1985). *Bilingual and ESL classrooms*. New York: McGraw-Hill.

Owen, E., & Sweller, J. (1985). What do students learn while solving mathematics problems? *Journal of Educational Psychology, 77*, 272–284.

Owen, E., & Sweller, J. (1989). Should problem solving be used as a learning device in mathematics? *Journal for Research in Mathematics Education, 20*, 322–328.

Paas, F. G. W. C. (1992). Training strategies for attaining transfer of problem-solving skill in statistics: A cognitive-load approach. *Journal of Educational Psychology, 84*, 429–434.

Paivio, A. (1971). *Imagery and verbal processes*. New York: Holt, Rinehart, & Winston.

Paivio, A. (1983). The empirical case for dual coding theory. In J. C. Yuille (Ed.), *Imagery, memory, and cognition: Essays in honor of Allan Paivio* (pp. 307–332). Hillsdale, NJ: Erlbaum & Associates.

Paivio, A. (1986). *Mental representations: A dual-coding approach*. New York: Oxford University Press.

Paivio, A., & Begg, I. (1981). *Psychology of language*. Englewood Cliffs, NJ: Prentice-Hall.

Palincsar, A. S., & Brown, A. L. (1984). Reciprocal teaching of comprehension-fostering and monitoring activities. *Cognition and Instruction, 1*, 117–175.

Palmatier, R. A., & Bennett, J. M. (1974). Notetaking habits of college students. *Journal of Reading, 18*, 215–218.

Palmer, E. L. (1984). Providing quality television for America's children. In J. P. Murray & G. Salomon (Eds.), *The future of children's television* (pp. 103–124). Boys Town, NE: Boys Town Center.

Palumbo, D. B. (1990). Programming language/problem-solving research: A review of relevant issues. *Review of Educational Research, 60*, 65–89.

Panksepp, J. (1986). The neurochemistry of behavior. *Annual Review of Psychology, 7*, 77–108.

Pappas, C. C. (1987). Exploring the textual properties of "protoreading." In R. Steele & T. Threadgold (Eds.), *Language topics: Essays in honour of Michael Halliday*, Vol. 1 (pp. 137–162). Amsterdam: John Benjamins.

Parents in Action on Special Education v. Hannon et al. (1980, July). No. 74 C 3586, United States District of Illinois, Eastern Division, slip opinion.

Paris, S. G., Lawton, T. A., Turner, J. C., & Roth, J. L. (1991). A developmental perspective on standardized achievement testing. *Educational Researcher, 20* (5), 12–20.

Paris, S. G., Lipson, M. Y., & Wixson, K. K. (1983). Becoming a strategic reader. *Contemporary Educational Psychology, 8*, 293–316.

Paris, S. G., & Oka, E. R. (1986). Children's reading strategies, metacognition, and motivation. *Developmental Review, 6*, 25–56.

Park, H-S., & Gaylord-Ross, R. (1989). A problem-solving approach to social skills training in employment settings with mentally retarded youth. *Journal of Applied Behavior Analysis, 22*, 373–380.

Parke, R. D. (1969). Effectiveness of punishment as an interaction of intensity, timing, agent nurturance and cognitive structuring. *Child Development, 40*, 213–236.

Parke, R. D. (1974). Rules, roles, and resistance to deviation in children: Explorations in punishment, discipline and self-control. In A. D. Pick (Ed.), *Minnesota symposium on child psychology*, Vol. 8. (pp. 111–144). Minneapolis: University of Minnesota Press.

Parker, S. T., & Gibson, K. R. (Eds.) (1990). *"Language" and intelligence in monkeys and apes*. Cambridge, UK: Cambridge University Press.

Parks, R. W., Loewenstein, D. A., Dodrill, K. L., Barker, W. W., Yoshii, F., Chang, J. Y., Emran, A., Apicella, A., Sheramata, W. A., & Duara, R. (1988). Cerebral metabolic effects of a verbal fluency test: A PET scan study. *Journal of Clinical and Experimental Neuropsychology, 10*, 565–575.

Parmelee, A. H., Jr., & Sigman, M. D. (1983). Perinatal brain development and behavior. In M. M. Haith & J. J. Campos (Volume Ed.) and P. H. Mussen (General Ed.), *Handbook of child psychology*, Vol. II, *Infancy and developmental psychobiology* (pp. 95–155). New York: John Wiley & Sons.

Parsons, J., & Ruble, D. (1977). The development of achievement-related expectancies. *Child Development, 48*, 1075–1079.

Pascarella, E. T., Smart, J. C., Ethington, C. A., & Nettles, M. T. (1987). The influence of college on self-concept: A consideration of race and gender differences. *American Educational Research Journal, 24*, 49–77.

Pascarella. E. T., & Terenzini, P. T. (1991). *How college affects students*. San Francisco: Jossey-Bass.

Pasch, M., & Oakley, N. (1985, April). *An evaluation study of project LEARN: Students and tutors 1982–84*. Paper presented at the 69th annual meeting of the American Educational Research Association, Chicago.

Pascual-Leone, J. (1970). A mathematical model for the transition rule in Piaget's developmental stages. *Acta Psychologica, 32*, 301–345.

Patterson, C. J., & Mischel, W. (1976). Effects of temptation-inhibiting and task-facilitating plans on self-control. *Journal of Personality and Social Psychology, 33*, 209–217.

Pauker, S. G., Gorry, G. A., Kassirer, J. P., & Schwartz, W. B. (1976). Towards the simulation of clinical cognition: Taking the present illness by computer. *The American Journal of Medicine, 60*, 981–996.

Pea, R. D., & Kurland, D. M. (1984). On the cognitive effects of learning computer programming. *New Ideas in Psychology, 2*, 137–168.

Pearl, R. (1982). LD children's attributions for success and failure: A replication with a labeled LD sample. *Learning Disability Quarterly, 5*, 173–176.

Pearl, R., Bryan, T., & Herzog, A. (1990). Resisting or acquiescing to peer pressure to engage in misconduct: Adolescents' expectations of probable consequences. *Journal of Youth and Adolescence, 19*, 43–55.

Pearson, D. A., & Lane, D. M. (1991). Auditory attention switching: A developmental study. *Journal of Experimental Child Psychology, 51*, 320–334.

Pearson, J. A. (1991). Testing the ecological validity of teacher-provided versus student-generated postquestions in reading college science text. *Journal of Research in Science Teaching, 28*, 485–504.

Pearson, P. D., & Dole, J. A. (1987). Explicit comprehension instruction: A review of research and a new conceptualization of instruction. *Elementary School Journal, 88*, 151–165.

Pearson, P. D., Hansen, J., & Gordon, C. (1979). The effect of background knowledge on young children's comprehension of explicit and implicit information. *Journal of Reading Behavior, 11*, 201–209.

Pellegrini, A. D., Perlmutter, J. C., Galda, L., & Brody, G. H. (1990). Joint reading between black Head Start children and their mothers. *Child Development, 61*, 443–453.

Penn, W. Y. Jr. (1990). Teaching ethics—a direct approach. *Journal of Moral Education, 19*, 124–138.

Pennington, B. F., Groisser, D., & Welsh, M. C. (1993). Contrasting cognitive deficits in attention deficit hyperactivity disorder versus reading disability. *Developmental Psychology, 29*, 511–523.

Pennington, B. F., Van Orden, G. C., Smith, S. D., Green, P. A., & Haith, M. M. (1990). Phological processing skills and deficits in adult dyslexics. *Child Development, 61*, 1753–1778.

Pennock-Román, M. (1992). Interpreting test performance in selective admissions for Hispanic students. In K. F. Geisinger (Ed.), *Psychological testing of Hispanics* (pp. 99–136). Washington, DC: American Psychological Association.

Perfetti, C. A. (1992). The representation problem in reading acquisition. In P. B. Gough, L. C. Ehri, & R. Treiman (Eds.), *Reading acquisition* (pp. 145–174). Hillsdale, NJ: Erlbaum & Associates.

Perfetti, C. A., & Lesgold, A. M. (1977). Discourse comprehension and sources of individual differences. In M. A. Just & P. A. Carpenter (Eds.), *Cognitive processes in comprehension*. Hillsdale, NJ: Erlbaum & Associates.

Perkins, D. F. (1981). *The mind's best work*. Cambridge, MA: Harvard University Press.

Perkins, D. F., & Simmons, R. (1988). Patterns of misunderstanding: An integrative model for science, math, and programming. *Review of Educational Research, 58*, 303–326.

Perlmutter, B. F. (1987). Personality variables and peer relations of children and adolescents with learning disabilities. In S. J. Ceci (Ed.), *Handbook of cognitive, social, and neuropsychological aspects of learning disabilities*, Vol. 1. (pp. 339–359). Hillsdale, NJ: Erlbaum & Associates.

Perlmutter, M., Behrend, S. D., Kuo, F., &

Muller, A. (1989). Social influences on children's problem solving. *Developmental Psychology, 25,* 744–754.

Perrig, W., & Kintsch, W. (1985). Propositional and situational representations of text. *Journal of Memory and Language, 24,* 503–518.

Perrone, V. (1991a). *Expanding student assessment.* Alexandria, VA: Association for Supervision and Curriculum Development.

Perrone, V. (1991b). On standardized testing. *Childhood Education, 67,* 132–142.

Perrone, V., et al. (1985). *Portraits of high schools: A supplement to high school: A report on secondary education in America.* Princeton, NJ: Carnegie Foundation for the Advancement of Teaching.

Perry, M. (1991). Learning and transfer: Instructional conditions and conceptual change. *Cognitive Development, 6,* 449–468.

Perry, M., VanderStoep, S. W., & Yu, S. L. (1993). Asking questions in first-grade mathematics classes: Potential influences on mathematical thought. *Journal of Educational Psychology, 85,* 31–40.

Perry, R. P., & Penner, K. S. (1990). Enhancing academic achievement in college students through attributional retraining and instruction. *Journal of Educational Psychology, 82,* 263–271.

Perry, W. (1970). *Forms of ethical and intellectual development in the college years.* New York: Holt.

Perry, W. (1981). Cognitive and ethical growth. In A. Chickering, et al. (Eds.), *The modern American college: Responding to the new realities of diverse students and a changing society.* San Francisco: Jossey-Bass.

Petersen, S. E., Fox, P. T., Posner, M. I., Mintun, M., & Raichle, M. E. (1988). Positron emission tomographic studies of the cortical anatomy of single-word processing. *Nature, 331,* 585–589.

Petersen, S. E., Fox, P. T., Snyder, A. Z., & Raichle, M. E. (1990). Activation of extrastriate and frontal cortical areas by visual words and word-like stimuli. *Science, 249,* 1041–1044.

Peterson, M. E., & Haines, L. P. (1992). Orthographic analogy training with kindergarten children: Effects of analogy use, phonemic segmentation, and letter-sound knowledge. *Journal of Reading Behavior, 24,* 109–127.

Peterson, M. J., Meagher, R. B., Jr., Chait, H., & Gillie, S. (1973). The abstraction and generalization of dot patterns. *Cognitive Psychology, 4,* 378–398.

Peterson, P. L. (1979). Direct instruction reconsidered. In P. L. Peterson & H. J. Walberg (Eds.), *Research on teaching: Concepts, findings, and implications* (pp. 57–69). Berkeley, CA: McCutchan.

Peterson, P. L. (1988). Selecting students and services for compensatory education: Lessons from aptitude-treatment interaction research. *Educational Psychologist, 23,* 313–352.

Peterson, P. L., Carpenter, T., & Fennema, E. (1989). Teachers' knowledge of students' knowledge in mathematics problem solving: Correlational and case analyses. *Journal of Educational Psychology, 81,* 558–569.

Peterson, P. L., & Comeaux, M. A. (1987). Teachers' schemata for classroom events: The mental scaffolding of teachers' thinking during classroom instruction. *Teaching & Teacher Education, 3,* 319–331.

Peterson, P., & Janicki, T. (1979). Individual characteristics and children's learning in large-group and small-group approaches. *Journal of Educational Psychology, 71,* 677–687.

Peterson, P., Janicki, T., & Swing, S. (1981). Ability X treatment interaction effects on children's learning in large-group and small-group approaches. *American Educational Research Journal, 18,* 452–474.

Peterson, P., & Swing, S. R. (1985). Students' cognition as mediators in effectiveness of small-group learning. *Journal of Educational Psychology, 77,* 299–312.

Peterson, S. E., DeGracie, J. S., & Ayabe, C. R. (1987). A longitudinal study of the effects of retention/promotion on academic achievement. *American Educational Research Journal, 24,* 107–118.

Petitto, A. L. (1985). Division of labor: Procedural learning in teacher-led small groups. *Cognition and Instruction, 2,* 233–270.

Pfundt, H., & Duit, R. (1991). *Bibliography: Students' alternative frameworks and science education,* 3rd ed. Kiel, Germany: IPN.

Phelps, M. E., Mazziotta, J. C., & Huang, S-C. (1982). Study of cerebral function with positron computed tomography. *Journal of Cerebral Blood Flow Metabolism, 2,* 113–162.

Phillips, B. N. (1963). Age changes in accuracy of self-perceptions. *Child Development, 34,* 1041–1046.

Phillips, D. A. (1987). Socialization of perceived academic competence among highly competent children. *Child Development, 58,* 1308–1320.

Phillips, E. L. (1968). Achievement Place: Token reinforcement procedures in a home-style rehabilitation setting for "pre-delinquent" boys. *Journal of Applied Behavior Analysis, 1,* 213–223.

Phillips, E. L., Phillips, E. A., Fixsen, D. L., & Wolf, M. M. (1971). Achievement Place: Modification of the behaviors of pre-delinquent boys within a token economy. *Journal of Applied Behavior Analysis, 4,* 45–59.

Piaget, J. (1929). *The child's conception of the world.* London: Routledge & Kegan Paul.

Piaget, J. (1932). *The moral judgment of the child.* New York: Harcourt, Brace.

Piaget, J. (1954 [1937]). *The construction of reality in the child.* New York: Basic Books.

Piaget, J. (1965). *The moral judgment of the child.* New York: Free Press.

Piaget, J. (1967). *Biologie et connaissance.* Paris: Gallimard.

Piaget, J. (1970). Piaget's theory. In P. H. Mussen (Ed.), *Carmichael's manual of child psychology,* 3rd ed., Vol. 1 (pp. 703–732). New York: John Wiley & Sons.

Piaget, J. (1972). Intellectual evolution from adolescence to adulthood. *Human Development, 15,* 1–12.

Piaget, J. (1983). Piaget's theory. In W. Kesson (Ed.) & P. H. Mussen (General Ed.), *History, theory, and methods,* Vol. 1, *Handbook of child psychology* (pp. 103–128). New York: John Wiley & Sons.

Piaget, J., & Inhelder, B. (1971). *Mental imagery in the child.* New York: Basic Books.

Pichert, J. W., & Anderson, R. C. (1977). Taking different perspectives on a story. *Journal of Educational Psychology, 69,* 309–315.

Pikulski, J. J. (1991). The transition years: Middle school. In J. Flood, J. M. Jensen, D. Lapp, & J. R. Squire (Eds.), *Handbook of research on teaching the English language arts* (pp. 303–319). New York: Macmillan.

Pinnell, G. S. (1989). Reading recovery: Helping at-risk children learn to read. *Elementary School Journal, 90,* 161–183.

Pintrich, P. R., & De Groot, E. V. (1990). Motivational and self-regulated learning components of classroom academic performance. *Journal of Educational Psychology, 82,* 33–40.

Pirolli, P. L., & Anderson, J. R. (1985). The role of learning from examples in the acquisition of recursive programming skills. *Canadian Journal of Psychology, 39,* 240–272.

Pirolli, P., & Bielaczyc, K. (1989). Empirical analyses of self-explanation and transfer in learning to program. *Proceedings of the Ninth Annual Conference of the Cognitive Science Society* (pp. 450–457). Hillsdale, NJ: Erlbaum & Associates.

Pirozzolo, F. J. (1979). *The neuropsychology of developmental reading disorders.* New York: Praeger.

Pitts, C. E. (Ed.) (1971). *Operant conditioning in the classroom.* New York: Crowell.

Pizzini, E. L., & Shepardson, D. P. (1992). A comparison of the classroom dynamics of a problem-solving and traditional laboratory model of instruction using path analysis. *Journal of Research in Science Teaching, 29,* 243–258.

Plessas, G. P., & Oakes, C. R. (1964). Prereading experiences of selected early readers. *Reading Teacher, 17,* 241–245.

Plomin, R., DeFries, J. C., & Fulker, D. W. (1988). *Nature and nurture during infancy and early childhood.* New York: Cambridge University Press.

Plomin, R., DeFries, J. C., & McClearn, G. E. (1990). *Behavioral genetics: A primer,* 2nd ed. New York: W.H. Freeman & Co.

Plummer, D. L., & Graziano, W. G. (1987). Impact of grade retention on the social development of elementary school children. *Developmental Psychology, 23,* 267–275.

Poche, C., Yoder, P., & Miltenberger, R. (1988). Teaching self-protection to children using television techniques. *Journal of Applied Behavior Analysis, 21,* 253–261.

Pogrow, S. (1992). What to do about Chapter 1: An alternative view from the street. *Phi Delta Kappan, 73,* 624–630.

Polya, G. (1954a). *Mathematics and plausible reasoning: (a) Induction and analogy in mathematics.* Princeton, NJ: Princeton University Press.

Polya, G., (1954b). *Patterns of plausible inference*. Princeton, NJ: Princeton, University Press.

Polya, G. (1957). *How to solve it*. New York: Doubleday.

Polya, G. (1981). *Mathematical discovery* (combined paperback edition). New York: Wiley.

Pontecorvo, C., & Zucchermaglio, C. (1990). A passage to literacy: Learning in social context. In Y. M. Goodman (Ed.), *How children construct literacy: Piagetian perspectives* (pp. 59–98). Newark, DE: International Reading Association.

Poon, L. W. (1985). Differences in human memory with aging: Nature, causes, and clinical implications. In J. E. Birren & K. W. Schaie (Eds.), *Handbook of the psychology of aging* (pp. 427–462). New York: van Nostrand.

Poon, L. W. (1986). *Handbook for clinical memory assessment of older adults*. Washington, DC: American Psychological Association.

Popham, W. J. (1987). The merits of measurement-driven instruction. *Phi Delta Kappan, 68,* 679–682.

Poplin, M. S. (1988a). Holistic/constructivist principles of the teaching/learning process: Implications for the field of learning disabilities. *Journal of Learning Disabilities, 21,* 401–416.

Poplin, M. S. (1988b). The reductionistic fallacy in learning disabilities: Replicating the past by reducing the present. *Journal of Learning Disabilities, 21,* 389–400.

Popper, K. (1961). *The logic of scientific discovery*. New York: Harper & Row.

Porter, A. C. (1991). Good teaching of worthwhile mathematics to disadvantaged students. In M. S. Knapp & P. M. Shields (Eds.), *Better schooling for the children of poverty: Alternatives to conventional wisdom* (pp. 125–148). Berkeley, CA: McCutchan Publishing Co.

Posner, M. L. (1969). Abstraction and the process of recognition. In G. H. Bower & J. T. Spence (Eds.), *The psychology of learning and motivation*, Vol. 3 (pp. 43–100). New York: Academic Press.

Posner, G. J., Strike, K. A., Hewson, P. W., & Gertzog, W. A. (1982). Accommodation of a scientific conception: Toward a theory of conceptual change. *Science Education, 66,* 211–227.

Posner, M. I., & Keele, S. W. (1968). On the genesis of abstract ideas. *Journal of Experimental Psychology, 77,* 353–363.

Posner, M. I., & Keele, S. W. (1970). Retention of abstract ideas. *Journal of Experimental Psychology, 83,* 304–308.

Posner, M. I., Petersen, S. E., Fox, P. T., & Raichle, M. E. (1988). Localization of cognitive operations in the human brain. *Science, 240,* 1627–1631.

Powell, A. G., Farrar, E., & Cohen, D. K. (1985). *The shopping mall high school*. Boston: Houghton Mifflin.

Powell, R. E., Locke, D. C., & Sprinthall, N. A. (1991). Female offenders and their guards: A programme to promote moral and ego development of both groups. *Journal of Moral Education, 20,* 191–203.

Power, F. C., Higgins, A., & Kohlberg, L. (1989). *Lawrence Kohlberg's approach to moral education*. New York: Columbia University Press.

Power, F. C., & Power, M. R. (1992). A raft of hope: Democratic education and the challenge of pluralism. *Journal of Moral Education, 21,* 193–205.

Powers, S. I. (1988). Moral judgement development within the family. *Journal of Moral Education, 17,* 209–219.

Pratt, A. C., & Brady, S. (1988). Relation of phonological awareness to reading disability in children and adults. *Journal of Educational Psychology, 80,* 319–323.

Pratt, M. W., Boyes, C., Robins, S., & Manchester, J. (1989). Telling tales: Working memory, and the narrative cohesion of story retellings. *Developmental Psychology, 25,* 628–635.

Pratt, M. W., Kerig, P., Cowan, P. A., & Cowan, C. P. (1988). Mothers and fathers teaching 3-year-olds: Authoritative parenting and adult scaffolding of young children's learning. *Developmental Psychology, 24,* 832–839.

Prawat, R. S. (1989). Promoting access to knowledge, strategy, and disposition in students: A research synthesis. *Review of Educational Research, 59,* 1–42.

Prechtl, H. F. R. (1986). New perspectives in early human development. *European Journal of Obstetrics, Gynecology, and Reproductive Biology, 21,* 347–354.

Pressey, S. L. (1926). A simple apparatus which gives tests and scores—and teaches. *School and Society, 23,* 373–376.

Pressey, S. L. (1963). Teaching machine (and learning theory) crisis. *Journal of Applied Psychology, 47,* 1–6.

Pressley, G. M. (1976). Mental imagery helps eight-year-olds remember what they read. *Journal of Educational Psychology, 68,* 355–359.

Pressley, M. (1977). Imagery and children's learning: Putting the picture in developmental perspective. *Review of Educational Research, 47,* 586–622.

Pressley, M. (1979). Increasing children's self-control through cognitive interventions. *Review of Educational Research, 49,* 319–370.

Pressley, M. (1982). Elaboration and memory development. *Child Development, 53,* 296–309.

Pressley, M. (1983). Making meaningful materials easier to learn. In M. Pressley & J. R. Levin (Eds.), *Cognitive strategy research: Educational applications* (pp. 239–266). New York: Springer-Verlag.

Pressley, M. (1986). The relevance of the good strategy user model to the teaching of mathematics. *Educational Psychologist, 21,* 139–161.

Pressley, M. (1987). Are keyword methods limited to slow presentation rates? An empirically-based reply to Hall and Fuson (1986). *Journal of Educational Psychology, 79,* 333–335.

Pressley, M. (1990). Four more considerations about self-regulation among mentally retarded persons. *American Journal of Mental Deficiency, 94,* 369–371.

Pressley, M. (1992). Comments on interpretation of results in Beck, McKeown, Sinatra, & Loxterman (1991). *Reading Research Quarterly, 27,* 108.

Pressley, M. (1993). Teaching cognitive strategies to brain-injured clients: The good information processing perspective. *Seminars in Speech and Language.*

Pressley, M., Borkowski, J. G., & Johnson, C. J. (1987). The development of good strategy use: Imagery and related mnemonic strategies. In M. A. McDaniel & M. Pressley (Eds.), *Imagery and related mnemonic processes: Theories, individual differences, and applications* (pp. 274–301). New York: Springer.

Pressley, M., Borkowski, J. G., & O'Sullivan, J. T. (1984). Memory strategy instruction is made of this: Metamemory and durable strategy use. *Educational Psychologist, 19,* 94–107.

Pressley, M., Borkowski, J. G., & O'Sullivan, J. T. (1985). Children's metamemory and the teaching of memory strategies. In D. L. Forrest-Pressley, G. E. MacKinnon, & T. G. Waller (Eds.), *Metacognition, cognition, and human performance* (pp. 111–153). New York: Academic Press.

Pressley, M., Borkowski, J. G., & Schneider, W. (1987). Cognitive strategies: Good strategy users coordinate metacognition and knowledge. In R. Vasta & G. Whitehurst (Eds.), *Annals of child development*, Vol. 5. (pp. 89–129). Greenwich, CT: JAI Press.

Pressley, M., Borkowski, J. G., & Schneider, W. (1989). Good information processing: What it is and what education can do to promote it. *International Journal of Educational Research, 13,* 857–867.

Pressley, M., & Brewster, M. E. (1990). Imaginal elaboration of illustrations to facilitate fact learning: Creating memories of Prince Edward Island. *Applied Cognitive Psychology, 4,* 359–370.

Pressley, M., Cariglia-Bull, T., Deane, S., & Schneider, W. (1987). Short-term memory, verbal competence, and age as predictors of imagery instructional effectiveness. *Journal of Experimental Child Psychology, 43,* 194–211.

Pressley, M., El-Dinary, P. B., & Brown, R. (1992). Skilled and not-so-skilled reading: Good information processing and not-so-good information processing. In M. Pressley, K. R. Harris, & J. T. Guthrie (Eds.), *Promoting academic competence and literacy: Cognitive research and instructional innovation* (pp. 91–127). San Diego: Academic Press.

Pressley, M., El-Dinary, P. B., & Brown, R. (in press). A transactional strategies instruction Christmas carol. In A. McKeough, J. Lupart, & A. Marini (Eds.), *Teaching for transfer: Fostering gernalization in learning*. Hillsdale, NJ: Erlbaum & Associates.

Pressley, M., El-Dinary, P. B., & Brown, R. (1994b). Transactional instruction of reading comprehension strategies. In J. Mangieri & C. Collins (Ed.), *Creating powerful thinking in teachers and students: Diverse perspectives.* (pp. 112–139). Fort Worth, TX: Harcourt, Brace.

Pressley, M., El-Dinary, P. B., Gaskins, I., Schuder, T., & Bergman, J. L., Almasi, J., & Brown, R. (1992). Beyond direct explanation:

Transactional instruction of reading comprehension strategies. *Elementary School Journal, 92,* 513–556.

Pressley, M., El-Dinary, P. B., Marks, M. B., Brown, R., & Stein, S. (1992). Good strategy instruction is motivating and interesting. In K. A. Renninger, S. Hidi, & A. Krapp (Eds.), *The role of interest in learning and development* (pp. 333–358). Hillsdale, NJ: Erlbaum & Associates.

Pressley, M., & Forrest-Pressley, D. L. (1985). Questions and children's cognitive processing. In A. Graesser & J. Black (Eds.), *Psychology of questions* (pp. 277–296). Hillsdale, NJ: Erlbaum & Associates.

Pressley, M., Forrest-Pressley, D., Elliott-Faust, D. L., & Miller, G. E. (1985). Children's use of cognitive strategies, how to teach strategies, and what to do if they can't be taught. In M. Pressley & C. J. Brainerd (Eds.), *Cognitive learning and memory in children* (pp. 1–47). New York: Springer-Verlag.

Pressley, M., Gaskins, I. W., Cunicelli, E. A., Burdick, N. J., Schaub-Matt, M., Lee, D. S., & Powell, N. (1991). Strategy instruction at Benchmark School: A faculty interview study. *Learning Disability Quarterly, 14,* 19–48.

Pressley, M., Gaskins, I. W., Wile, D., Cunicelli, B., & Sheridan, J. (1991). Teaching literacy strategies across the curriculum: A case study at Benchmark School. In J. Zutell & S. McCormick (Eds.), *Learner factors/teacher factors: Issues in literacy research and instruction: Fortieth yearbook of the National Reading Conference* (pp. 219–228). Chicago: National Reading Conference.

Pressley, M., & Ghatala, E. S. (1989). Metacognitive benefits of taking a test for children and young adolescents. *Journal of Experimental Child Psychology, 47,* 430–450.

Pressley, M., & Ghatala, E. S. (1990). Self-regulated learning: Monitoring learning from text. *Educational Psychologist, 25,* 19–34.

Pressley, M., Harris, K. R., & Marks, M. B. (1992). But good strategy instructors are constructivists! *Educational Psychology Review, 4,* 3–31.

Pressley, M., Heisel, B. E., McCormick, C. G., & Nakamura, G. V. (1982). Memory strategy instruction with children. In C. J. Brainerd & M. Pressley (Eds.), *Progress in cognitive development research,* Vol. 2, *Verbal processes in children* (pp. 125–159). New York: Springer-Verlag.

Pressley, M., Johnson, C. J., Symons, S., McGoldrick, J. A., & Kurita, J. A. (1989). Strategies that improve children's memory and comprehension of text. *Elementary School Journal, 90,* 3–32.

Pressley, M., & Levin, J. R. (1977a). Developmental differences in subjects' associative learning strategies and performance: Assessing a hypothesis. *Journal of Experimental Child Psychology, 24,* 431–439.

Pressley, M., & Levin, J. R. (1977b). Task parameters affecting the efficacy of a visual imagery learning strategy in younger and older children. *Journal of Experimental Child Psychology, 24,* 53–59.

Pressley, M., & Levin, J. R. (1978).

Developmental constraints associated with children's use of the keyword method for foreign language vocabulary learning. *Journal of Experimental Child Psychology, 26,* 359–372.

Pressley, M., Levin, J. R., & Delaney, H. D. (1982). The mnemonic keyword method. *Review of Educational Research, 52,* 61–92.

Pressley, M., Levin, J. R., & Ghatala, E. S. (1984). Memory strategy monitoring in adults and children. *Journal of Verbal Learning and Verbal Behavior, 23,* 270–288.

Pressley, M., Levin, J. R., & Ghatala, E. S. (1988). Strategy-comparison opportunities promote long-term strategy use. *Contemporary Educational Psychology, 13,* 157–168.

Pressley, M., Levin, J. R., Ghatala, E. S., & Ahmad, M. (1987). Test monitoring in young grade-school children. *Journal of Experimental Child Psychology, 43,* 96–111.

Pressley, M., Levin, J. R., & McDaniel, M. A. (1987). Remembering versus inferring what a word means: Mnemonic and contextual approaches. In M. G. McKeown & M. E. Curtis (Eds.), *The nature of vocabulary acquisition* (pp. 107–127). Hillsdale, NJ: Erlbaum & Associates.

Pressley, M., & MacFadyen, J. (1983). Mnemonic mediator retrieval at testing by preschool and kindergarten children. *Child Development, 54,* 474–479.

Pressley, M., McDaniel, M. A., Turnure, J. E., Wood, E., & Ahmad, M. (1987). Generation and precision of elaboration: Effects on intentional and incidental learning. *Journal of Experimental Psychology: Learning, Memory, and Cognition, 13,* 291–300.

Pressley, M., Ross, K. A., Levin, J. R., & Ghatala, E. S. (1984). The role of strategy utility knowledge in children's strategy decision making. *Journal of Experimental Child Psychology, 38,* 491–504.

Pressley, M., Samuel, J. Hershey, M. M., Bishop, S. L., & Dickinson, D. (1981). Use of a mnemonic technique to teach young children foreign language vocabulary. *Contemporary Educational Psychology, 6,* 110–116.

Pressley, M., Schuder, T., SAIL Faculty and Administration, Bergman, J. L., & El-Dinary, P. B. (1992). A researcher-educator collaborative interview study of transactional comprehension strategies instruction. *Journal of Educational Psychology, 84,* 231–246.

Pressley, M., Snyder, B. L., & Cariglia-Bull, T. (1987). How can good strategy use be taught to children? Evaluation of six approaches. In S. M. Cormier & J. D. Hagman (Eds.), *Transfer of learning: Contemporary research and applications* (pp. 81–120). San Diego: Academic Press.

Pressley, M., Snyder, B. L., Levin, J. R., Murray, H. G., & Ghatala, E. S. (1987). Perceived readiness for examination performance (PREP) produced by initial reading of text and text containing adjunct questions. *Reading Research Quarterly, 22,* 219–236.

Pressley, M., Symons, S., McDaniel, M. A., Snyder, B. L., & Turnure, J. E. (1988). Elaborative interrogation facilitates acquisition of confusing facts. *Journal of Educational Psychology, 80,* 268–278.

Pressley, M., Wood, E., Woloshyn, V. E., Martin, V., King, A., & Menke, D. (1992). Encouraging mindful use of prior knowledge: Attempting to construct explanatory answers facilitates learning. *Educational Psychologist, 27,* 91–110.

Previc, F. H. (1991). A general theory concerning the prenatal origins of cerebral lateralization in humans. *Psychological Review, 98,* 299–334.

Price, D. W. W., & Goodman, G. S. (1990). Visiting the wizard: Children's memory for a recurring event. *Child Development, 61,* 664–680.

Price, J. H., Desmond, S., & Kukulka, G. (1985). *Journal of School Health, 55,* 107–109.

Prince, G. (1978). Putting the other half of the brain to work. *Training: The Magazine of Human Resources Development, 15,* 57–61.

Pritchard, R. (1990). The effects of cultural schemata on reading processing strategies. *Reading Research Quarterly, 25,* 273–295.

Puckering, C., & Rutter, M. (1987). Environmental influences on language development. In W. Yule & M. Rutter (Eds.), *Language development and disorders* (pp. 103–128). Philadelphia: J. B. Lippincott Co.

Pueschel, S. M. (1988). Visual and auditory processing in children with Down syndrome. In L. Nadel (Ed.), *The psychobiology of Down syndrome* (pp. 199–216). Cambridge, MA: MIT Press.

Purcell-Gates, V. (1991). On the outside looking in: A study of remedial readers' meaning-making while reading literature. *Journal of Reading Behavior, 23,* 235–253.

Purpel, D. E. (1989). *The moral and spiritual crisis in education: A curriculum for justice and compassion in education.* New York: Bergin & Garvey.

Purpel, D., & Ryan, K. (1976). *Moral education . . . it comes with the territory.* Berkeley, CA: McCutchan.

Putnam, R. (1987). Structuring and adjusting content for students: A study of live and simulated tutoring of addition. *American Educational Research Journal, 24,* 13–48.

Putnam, R., Lampert, M., & Peterson, P. L. (1990). Alternative perspectives on knowing mathematics in elementary schools. In C. B. Cazden (Ed.), *Review of Research in Education,* Vol. 16 (pp. 57–150). Washington, DC: American Educational Research Association.

Pylyshen, Z. (1973). What the mind's eye tells the mind's brain: A critique of mental imagery. *Psychological Bulletin, 80,* 1–24.

Rabinowitz, M., Freeman, K., & Cohen, S. (1992). Use and maintenance of strategies: The influence of accessibility on knowledge. *Journal of Educational Psychology, 84,* 211–218.

Rabinowitz, M., & Glaser, R. (1985). Cognitive structure and process in high competent performance. In F. D. Horowitz & M. O'Brien (Eds.), *The gifted and talented: Developmental perspectives* (pp. 75–98). Washington, DC: American Psychological Association.

Rabinowitz, M., & McAuley, R. (1990). Conceptual knowledge processing: An oxymoron? In W. Schneider & F. E. Weinert

(Eds.), *Interactions among aptitudes, strategies, and knowledge in cognitive performance* (pp. 117–133). New York: Springer-Verlag.

Rack, J. P., Snowling, M. J., & Olson, R. K. (1992). The nonword reading deficit in developmental dyslexia: A review. *Reading Research Quarterly, 27,* 28–53.

Radford, J. (1990). *Child prodigies and exceptional early achievers.* New York: Free Press.

Radziszewska, B., & Rogoff, B. (1988). Influence of adult and peer collaborators on children's planning skills. *Developmental Psychology, 24,* 840–848.

Ramey, C. T. (1992). High-risk children and IQ: Altering intergenerational patterns. *Intelligence, 16,* 239–256.

Ramey, C. T., & Campbell, F. A. (1987). The Carolina Abecedarian Project: An educational experiment concerning human malleability. In J. J. Gallagher & C. T. Ramey (Eds.), *The malleability of children.* Baltimore: Brooks.

Rand, Y., & Kaniel, S. (1987). Group administration of the LPAD. In C. Lidz (Ed.), *Dynamic assessment* (pp. 196–214). New York: Guilford.

Rand, Y., Tannenbaum, A. J., & Feurstein, R. (1979). Effects of Instrumental Enrichment on the psychoeducational development of low-functioning adolescents. *Journal of Educational Psychology, 71,* 751–763.

Randhawa, B. S., Beamer, J. E., & Lundberg, I. (1993). Role of mathematics self-efficacy in the structural model of mathematics achievement. *Journal of Educational Psychology, 85,* 41–48.

Rao, N., & Moely, B. E. (1989). Producing memory strategy maintenance and generalization by explicit or implicit training of memory knowledge. *Journal of Experimental Child Psychology, 48,* 335–352.

Rashotte, C. A., & Torgeson, J. K. (1985). Repeated reading and reading fluency in learning disabled children. *Reading Research Quarterly, 20,* 180–188.

Rauh, V. A., Achenbach, T. M., Nurcombe, B., Howell, C. T., & Teti, D. M. (1988). Minimizing adverse effects of low birthweight: Four-year results of an early intervention program. *Child Development, 59,* 544–553.

Ravitch, D. (1989). *The schools we deserve.* New York: Basic Books.

Ravitch, D., & Finn. C. (1987). *What do our 17-year-olds know?* New York: Harper & Row.

Rawls, J. (1971). *A theory of justice.* Cambridge, MA: Harvard University Press.

Raymond, C. (1992). Sex differences in gifted math students' achievement. *APS Observer 5,* (4), 5.

Rayner, K. (1988). Word recognition cues in children: The relative use of graphemic cues, orthographic cues, and grapheme-phoneme correspondence rules. *Journal of Educational Psychology, 80,* 473–479.

Rayner, K., Inhoff, A. W., Morrison, R. E., Slowiaczek, M. L., & Bertera, J. H. (1981). Masking of foveal and parafoveal vision during eye fixations in reading. *Journal of Experimental Psychology: Human Perception and Performance, 7,* 167–179.

Rayner, K., & Pollatsek, A. (1989). *The psychology of reading.* Englewood Cliffs, NJ: Prentice-Hall.

Recht, D. R., & Leslie, L. (1988). Effect of prior knowledge on good and poor readers' memory of text. *Journal of Educational Psychology, 80,* 16–20.

Reder, G., McCormick, C. B., & Esselman, E. (1987). Self-referent processing and recall of prose. *Journal of Educational Psychology, 79,* 343–348.

Reder, L. M., Charney, D. H., & Morgan, K. I. (1986). The role of elaborations in learning a skill from instructional text. *Memory and Cognition, 14,* 64–78.

Redfield, D. L., & Rousseau, E. W. (1981). A meta-analysis of experimental research on teacher questioning behavior. *Review of Educational Research, 51,* 237–246.

Reed, J. H., & Schallert, D. L. (1993). The nature of involvement in academic discourse tasks. *Journal of Educational Psychology, 85,* 253–266.

Reed, S. K. (1972). Pattern recognition and categorization. *Cognitive Psychology, 3,* 382–407.

Reed, S. K. (1989). Constraints on the abstraction of solutions. *Journal of Educational Psychology, 81,* 532–540.

Reed, S. K., Dempster, A., & Ettinger, M. (1985). Usefulness of analogous solutions for solving algebra word problems. *Journal of Experimental Psychology: Learning, Memory, and Cognition, 11,* 106–125.

Reese, H. W., & Overton, W. F. (1970). Models of development and theories of development. In L. R. Goulet & P. B. Baltes (Eds.), *Life-span developmental psychology: Research and theory.* New York: Academic Press.

Reid, M. K., & Borkowski, J. G. (1987). Causal attributions of hyperactive children: Implications for teaching strategies and self-control. *Journal of Educational Psychology, 79,* 296–307.

Reif, F., & Allen, S. (1992). Cognition for interpreting scientific concepts: A study of acceleration. *Cognition and Instruction, 9,* 1–44.

Reisner, E. R., Petry, C. A., & Armitage, M. (1989). *A review of programs involving college students as tutors or mentors in grades K–12.* Washington, DC: Policy Study Associates, Inc.

Reitman, J. S. (1976). Skilled perception in GO: Deducing memory structures from interresponse times. *Cognitive Psychology, 8,* 336–356.

Renick, M. J., & Harter, S. (1989). Impact of social comparisons on the developing self-perceptions of learning disabled students. *Journal of Educational Psychology, 81,* 631–638.

Renninger, K. A. (1990). Children's play interests, representation, and activity. In R. Fivush & J. Hudson (Eds.), *Knowing and remembering in young children* (pp. 127–165). Cambridge, MA: Cambridge University Press.

Renninger, K. A., & Wozniak, R. H. (1985). Effect of interest on attentional shift, recognition, and recall in young children. *Developmental Psychology, 21,* 624–632.

Renzulli, J. S. (1986). The three-ring conception of giftedness: A developmental model for creative productivity. In R. J. Sternberg & J. E. Davidson (Eds.), *Conceptions of giftedness* (pp.

53–92). Cambridge, UK: Cambridge University Press.

Research Advisory Committee (1989). The mathematics education of underserved and underrepresented groups: A continuing challenge. *Journal for Research in Mathematics Education, 20,* 371–375.

Resnick, D. P. (1991). Historical perspectives on literacy and schooling. In S. R. Graubard (Ed.), *Literacy: An overview by fourteen experts* (pp. 15–32). New York: Noonday Press.

Resnick, L. B. (1983). A developmental theory of number understanding. In H. P. Ginsburg (Ed.), *The development of mathematical thinking* (pp. 109–151). New York: Academic.

Resnick, L. B. (1987). Constructing knowledge in school. In L. S. Liben (Ed.), *Development and learning: Conflict or congruence* (pp. 19–50). Hillsdale, NJ: Erlbaum & Associates.

Resnick, L. B., Levine, J. M., & Teasley, S. D. (Eds.) (1991). *Perspectives on socially shared cognition.* Washington, DC: American Psychological Association.

Rest, J. (1968). *Developmental hierarchy in preference and comprehension of moral judgment.* Unpublished Ph.D. dissertation. University of Chicago, 1968.

Rest, J. (1979). *Development in judging moral issues.* Minneapolis: University of Minnesota Press.

Rest, J. R. (1988). Why does college promote development in moral judgement? *Journal of Moral Education, 17,* 183–194.

Rest, J. R., in collaboration with Barnett, R., Bebeau, M., Deemer, D., Getz, I., Moon, Y., Schlaefli, A., Spickelmier, J., Thoma, S., & Volker, J. (1986). *Moral development: Advances in research and theory.* New York: Praeger.

Reuman, D. A. (1989). How social comparison mediates the relation between ability-grouping practices and students' achievement expectancies in mathematics. *Journal of Educational Psychology, 81,* 178–189.

Reyes, L. H., & Stanic, G. M. A. (1988). Race, sex, socioeconomic status, and mathematics. *Journal for Research in Mathematics Education, 19,* 26–43.

Reynolds, A. J. (1989). Early schooling of children at risk. *American Educational Research Journal, 28,* 392–422.

Reynolds, A. R., & Walberg, H. J. (1991). A structural model of science achievement. *Journal of Educational Psychology, 83,* 97–107.

Reynolds, C. R., Chastain, R. L., Kaufman, A. S., & McLean, J. E. (1987). Demographic characteristics and IQ among adults: Analysis of the WISC-R standardization sample as a function of the stratification variables. *Journal of School Psychology, 25,* 323–342.

Reynolds, C. R., & Kaiser, S. M. (1990a). Bias in assessment of aptitude. In C. R. Reynolds & R. W. Kamphaus (Eds.), *Handbook of psychological and educational assessment of children: Intelligence & achievement* (pp. 611–653). New York: Guilford Press.

Reynolds, C. R., & Kaiser, S. M. (1990b). Test bias in psychological assessment. In T. B. Gutkin & C. R. Reynolds (Eds.), *The handbook of school psychology* (pp. 487–525). New York: John Wiley & Sons.

Reynolds, M. C. (Ed.) (1989). *Knowledge base for the beginning teacher.* New York: Pergamon Press.

Reynolds, R. E. (1992). Selective attention and prose learning: Theoretical and empirical research. *Educational Psychology Review, 4,* 345–391.

Reynolds, R. E., Shepard, C., Lapan, R., Kreek, C., & Goetz, E. T. (1990). Differences in the use of selective attention by more successful and less successful tenth-grade readers. *Journal of Educational Psychology, 82,* 749–759.

Reys, B. J. (1989). The calculator as a tool for instruction and learning. In P. R. Trafton & A. P. Schulte (Eds.), *New directions for elementary school mathematics: 1989 yearbook of the National Council of Teachers of Mathematics* (pp. 168–173). Reston, VA: National Council of Teachers of Mathematics.

Reys, R. E. (1984). Mental computation and estimation: Past, present, and future. *Elementary School Journal, 84,* 547–557.

Rice, M. L., Huston, A. C., Truglio, R., & Wright, J. (1990). Words from "Sesame Street": Learning vocabulary from viewing. *Developmental Psychology, 26,* 421–428.

Richardson, A. (1967). Mental practice: A review and discussion. *Research Quarterly, 38,* 95–107, 263–273.

Richardson, S. A., & Koller, H. (1985). Epidemiology. In A. M. Clarke, A. D. B. Clarke, & J. M. Berg (Eds.), *Mental deficiency: The changing outlook,* 4th ed. (pp. 356–400). New York: Free Press.

Richardson, T. M., & Benbow, C. P. (1990). Long-term effects of acceleration on the social-emotional adjustment of mathematically precocious youths. *Journal of Educational Psychology, 82,* 464–470.

Richert, E. S. (1991). Rampant problems and promising practices in identification. In N. Colangelo & G. A. Davis (Eds.), *Handbook of gifted education* (pp. 81–96). Boston: Allyn & Bacon.

Rickards, J. P., & McCormick, C. B. (1988). Effects of interspersed conceptual prequestions on note-taking in listening comprehension. *Journal of Educational Psychology, 80,* 592–594.

Rieber, L. P. (1990). Using computer animated graphics in science instruction with children. *Journal of Educational Psychology, 82,* 135–140.

Rieber, L. P. (1991). Animation, incidental learning, and continuing motivation. *Journal of Educational Psychology, 83,* 318–328.

Riege, W. H., Harker, J. O., & Metter, E. J. (1986). Clinical validators: Brain lesions and brain imaging. In L. W. Poon (Ed.), *Handbook for clinical memory assessment of older adults* (pp. 314–336). Washington, DC: American Psychological Association.

Riesbeck, C. K., & Schank, R. C. (1989). *Inside case-based reasoning.* Hillsdale, NJ: Erlbaum & Associates.

Riley, M. S., & Greeno, J. G. (1988). Developmental analysis of understanding language

about quantities and of solving problems. *Cognition and Instruction, 5,* 49–101.

Riley, M. S., Greeno, J. G., & Heller, J. I. (1983). Development of children's problem-solving ability in arithmetic. In H. P. Ginsburg (Ed.), *The development of mathematical thinking* (pp. 153–196). New York: Academic Press.

Rinehart, S. D., Stahl, S. A., & Erickson, L. G. (1986). Some effects of summarization training on reading and studying. *Reading Research Quarterly, 21,* 422–438.

Ringel, B. A., & Springer, C. J. (1980). On knowing how well one is remembering: The persistence of strategy use during transfer. *Journal of Experimental Child Psychology, 29,* 322–333.

Ringness, T. A. (1961). Self concept of children of low, average, and high intelligence. *American Journal of Mental Deficiency, 65,* 453–461.

Rips, L. J., Shoben, E. J., & Smith, E. E. (1973). Semantic distance and the verification of semantic relations. *Journal of Verbal Learning and Verbal Behavior, 12,* 1–20.

Risberg, J. (1986). Regional cerebral blood flow in neuropsychology. *Neuropsychologia, 24,* 135–140.

Ritter, K. (1978). The development of knowledge of an external retrieval cue strategy. *Child Development 49,* 1227–1230.

Rivera v. City of Wichita Falls, 665 F. 2d 531 (1982).

Rizzo, T. A., Corsaro, W. A., & Bates, J. E. (1992). Ethnographic methods and interpretive analysis: Expanding the methodological options of psychologists. *Developmental Review, 12,* 101–123.

Roberts, B. (1992). The evolution of the young child's concept of *word* as a unit of spoken language. *Reading Research Quarterly, 27,* 124–138.

Roberts, P. (1983). Memory strategy instruction with the elderly: What should memory training be the training of? In M. Pressley & J. R. Levin (Eds.), *Cognitive strategy research: Psychological foundations* (pp. 75–100). New York: Springer-Verlag.

Robertson, E. (1992). Is Dewey's educational vision still viable? In G. Grant (Ed.), *Review of Research in Education,* Vol. 18 (pp. 335–381). Washington, DC: American Educational Research Association.

Robinson, C. S., & Hayes, J. R. (1978). Making inferences about relevance in understanding problems. In R. Revlin & R. E. Mayer (Eds.), *Human reasoning.* Washington, DC: Winston.

Robinson, F. P. (1961). *Effective study* (Rev. ed.). New York: Harper & Row.

Robinson, J. A., & Kingsley, M. E. (1977). Memory and intelligence: Age and ability differences in strategies and organization of recall. *Intelligence, 1,* 318–330.

Rodriguez, O. (1992). Introduction to technical and societal issues in the psychological testing of Hispanics. In K. F. Geisinger (Ed.), *Psychological testing of Hispanics* (pp. 11–16). Washington, DC: American Psychological Association.

Roehler, L. R., & Duffy, G. G. (1984). Direct explanation of comprehension processes. In G.

Duffy, L. R. Roehler, & J. Mason (Eds.), *Comprehension instruction: Perspectives and suggestions* (pp. 265–280). New York: Longmans.

Rogers, H., & Saklofske, D. H. (1985). Self-concept, locus of control and performance expectations of learning disabled children. *Journal of Learning Disabilities, 18,* 273–278.

Rogoff, B. (1990). *Apprenticeship in thinking: Cognitive development in social context.* New York: Oxford University Press.

Rohman, D. G. (1965). Pre-writing: The stage of discovery in the writing process. *College Composition and Communication, 16,* 106–112.

Rohwer, W. D., Jr. (1973). Elaboration and learning in childhood and adolescence. In H. W. Reese (Ed.), *Advances in child development and behavior,* Vol. 8 (pp. 1–57). New York: Academic Press.

Rohwer, W. D., Jr. (1980a). An elaborative conception of learner differences. In R. E. Snow, P. A. Federico, & W. E. Montague (Eds.), *Aptitude, learning, and instruction,* Vol. 2, *Cognitive process analysis of learning and problem solving* (pp. 23–46). Hillsdale, NJ: Erlbaum & Associates.

Rohwer, W. D., Jr. (1980b). How the smart get smarter. *Educational Psychologist, 15,* 34–43.

Rohwer, W. D., Jr., & Litrownik, J. (1983). Age and individual differences in the learning of a memorization procedure. *Journal of Educational Psychology, 75,* 799–810.

Rohwer, W. D., Jr., Raines, J. M., Eoff, J., & Wagner, M. (1977). The development of elaborative propensity during adolescence. *Journal of Experimental Child Psychology, 23,* 472–492.

Rohwer, W. D., Jr., & Thomas, J. W. (1989). The role of autonomous problem-solving activities in learning to program. *Journal of Educational Psychology, 81,* 584–593.

Roller, C. M. (1990). The interaction of knowledge and structure variables in the processing of expository prose. *Reading Research Quarterly, 25,* 79–89.

Romberg, T. A., & Carpenter, T. C. (1986). Research on teaching and learning mathematics: Two disciplines of scientific inquiry. In M. C. Wittrock (Ed.), *Handbook of research on teaching,* 3rd ed. (pp. 850–873). New York: Macmillan.

Rosch, E. (1973). On the internal structure of perceptual and semantic categories. In T. Moore (Ed.), *Cognitive development and the acquisition of language* (pp. 111–144). New York: Academic Press.

Rosch, E. (1975). Cognitive representations of semantic categories. *Journal of Experimental Psychology: General, 104,* 192–233.

Rosch, E. (1978). Principles of categorization. In E. Rosch & B. Lloyd (Eds.), *Cognition and categorization* (pp. 9–31). Hillsdale, NJ: Lawrence Erlbaum Associates.

Rosch, E., & Mervis, C. (1975). Family resemblance studies in the internal structure of categories. *Cognitive Psychology, 7,* 575–605.

Rose, M. (1985). The language of exclusion: Writing instruction in the university. *College English 47,* 341–359.

Rose, M. (1989). *Lives on the boundary: The strug-*

gle and achievements of America's underprepared. New York: Free Press.

Rose, S. A. (1989). Measuring infant intelligence: New perspectives. In M. H. Bornstein & N. A. Krasnegor (Eds.), *Stability and continuity in mental development* (pp. 171–188). Hillsdale, NJ: Erlbaum & Associates.

Rose, S. A., Feldman, J. F., Wallace, I. F., & McCarton, C. (1991). Information processing at 1 year: Relation to birth status and development outcome during the first 5 years. *Developmental Psychology, 27,* 723–737.

Rosen, M. G. (1985). Factors during labor and delivery that influence brain disorders. In J. Freeman (Ed.), *Prenatal and perinatal factors associated with brain disorders* (NIH Publication No. 85–1149). (pp. 237–262). Washington, DC: U.S. Department of Health and Human Services.

Rosenblatt, L. M. (1978). *The reader, the text, the poem: The transactional theory of the literary work.* Carbondale: Southern Illinois University Press.

Rosenblatt, L. M. (1991). Literary theory. In J. Flood, J. M. Jensen, D. Lapp, & J. R. Squire (Eds.), *Handbook of research on teaching the English language arts* (pp. 57–62). New York: Macmillan.

Rosenshine, B. V. (1979). Content, time, and direct instruction. In P. L. Peterson & H. J. Walberg (Eds.), *Research on teaching: Concepts, findings, and implications* (pp. 28–56). Berkeley, CA: McCutchan.

Rosenshine, B., & Chapman, S. (1992, April). *Instructional elements in studies which taught students to generate questions.* Presented at the annual meeting of the American Educational Research Association, San Francisco.

Rosenshine, B., & Meister, C. (1992). *Reciprocal teaching: A review of nineteen experimental studies.* Manuscript submitted for publication consideration. Champaign-Urbana, IL: University of Illinois, Department of Educational Psychology.

Rosenshine, B., & Trapman, S. (1992, April). *Teaching students to generate questions: A review of research.* Presented at the annual meeting of the American Educational Research Association, San Francisco.

Rosenshine, B. V., & Stevens, R. (1984). Classroom instruction in reading. In P. D. Pearson, R. Barr, M. L. Kamil, & P. Mosenthal (Eds.), *Handbook of reading research* (pp. 745–798). New York: Longman.

Rosenthal, R. (1985). From unconscious experimenter bias to teacher expectancy effects. In J. B. Dusek (Ed.), *Teacher expectancies* (pp. 37–65). Hillsdale, NJ: Erlbaum & Associates.

Rosenthal, R., & Jacobson, L. (1968). *Pygmalion in the classroom: Teacher expectation and pupils' intellectual development.* New York: Holt, Rinehart, & Winston.

Rosenthal, T. L., & Zimmerman, B. J. (1978). *Social learning and cognition.* New York: Academic Press.

Roser, N., & Martinez, M. (1985). Roles adults play in prschool responses to literature. *Language Arts, 62,* 485–490.

Ross, A. O. (1981). *Child behavior therapy.* New York: John Wiley & Sons.

Ross, B. H. (1984). Reminders and their effects in learning a cognitive skill. *Cognitive Psychology, 16,* 371–416.

Ross, B. H. (1987). This is like that: The use of earlier problems and the separation of similarity effects. *Journal of Experimental Psychology: Learning, Memory, and Cognition, 13,* 629–639.

Ross, B. H. (1989). Reminders in learning and instruction. In S. Vosniadou & A. Ortony (Eds.), *Similarity and analogical reasoning* (pp. 438–469). Cambridge, UK: Cambridge University Press.

Ross, B. L., & Berg, C. A. (1992). Examining idiosyncracies in script reports across the lifespan: Distortions or derivations of experience? In R. L. West & J. D. Sinnott (Eds.), *Everyday memory and aging: Current research and methodology* (pp. 39–53). New York: Springer-Verlag.

Ross, H. S., & Balzer, R. H. (1975). Determinants and consequences of children's questions. *Child Development, 46,* 536–539.

Ross, H. S., & Killey, J. C. (1977). The effect of questioning on retention. *Child Development, 48,* 312–314.

Ross, J. A. (1988). Controlling variables: A meta-analysis of training studies. *Review of Educational Research, 58,* 405–437.

Ross, L. E., & Ross, S. M. (1984). Oculomotor functioning and the learning and cognitive processes of the intellectually handicapped. In P. H. Brooks, R. Sperber, & C. McCauley (Eds.), *Learning and cognition in the mentally retarded* (pp. 217–235). Hillsdale, NJ: Erlbaum & Associates.

Ross, S. M., & Ross, L. E. (1976). The conditioning of skeletal and autonomic responses: Normal-retardate stimulus trace differences. In N. R. Ellis (Ed.), *International review of research in mental retardation,* Vol. 8. New York: Academic Press.

Rossi, A. (1965). Women in science: Why so few? *Science, 148,* 1196–1201.

Roth, K. J. (1990). Developing meaningful conceptual understanding in science. In B. F. Jones & L. Idol (Eds.), *Dimensions of thinking and cognitive instruction* (pp. 139–175). Hillsdale, NJ: Erlbaum & Associates.

Roth, K. J. (1991). Reading science texts for conceptual change. In C. M. Santa & D. E. Alvermann (Eds.), *Science learning: Processes and applications* (pp. 48–63). Newark, DE: International Reading Association.

Roth, W-M. (1990). Neo-Piagetian predictors of achievement in physical science. *Journal of Research in Science Teaching, 27,* 509–521.

Rothkopf, E. Z. (1966). Learning from written materials: An exploration of the control of inspection of test-like events. *American Educational Research Journal, 3,* 241–249.

Rotter, J. B. (1954). *Social learning and clinical psychology.* Englewood, Cliffs, NJ: Prentice-Hall.

Rovee-Collier, C. (1990). The "memory system" of prelinguistic infants. In A. Diamond (Ed.), *The development and neural bases of higher cognitive functions* (pp. 517–542). New York: New York Academy of Science.

Rovet, J. F., Ehrlich, R. M., Czuchta, D., & Akler, M. (1993). Psychoeducational characteristics of children and adolescents with insulin-dependent diabetes mellitus. *Journal of Learning Disabilities, 26,* 7–22.

Rovet, J. F., Ehrlich, R. M., & Hoppe, M. (1988). Specific intellectual deficits in children with early onset diabetes mellitus. *Child Development, 59,* 226–234.

Rowan, B., & Guthrie, L. F. (1989). The quality of Chapter 1 instruction: Results from a study of twenty-four schools. In R. E. Slavin, N. L. Karweit, & N. A. Madden (Eds.), *Effective programs for students at risk.* Boston: Allyn & Bacon.

Royer, J. M., Abranovic, W. A., & Sinatra, G. M. (1987). Using entering reading comprehension performance as a predictor of performance in college classes. *Journal of Educational Psychology, 79,* 19–26.

Royer, J. M., & Cable, G. W. (1975). Facilitated learning in connected discourse. *Journal of Educational Psychology, 67,* 116–123.

Royer, J. M., & Cable, G. W. (1976). Illustrations, analogies, and facilitative transfer in prose learning. *Journal of Educational Psychology, 68,* 205–209.

Royer, J. M., Marchant, H. G. III, Sinatra, G. M., & Lovejoy, D. A. (1990). The prediction of college course performance from reading comprehension performance: Evidence for general and specific prediction factors. *American Educational Research Journal, 27,* 158–179.

Ruff, H. A., Lawson, K. R., Parrinello, R., & Weissberg, R. (1990). Long-term stability of individual differences in sustained attention in the early years. *Child Development, 61,* 60–75.

Rulon, D. (1992). The just community: A method for staff development. *Journal of Moral Education, 21,* 217–224.

Rumelhart, D. E., & McClelland, J. L. (1986). *Parallel distributed processing,* Vol. 1. Cambridge, MA: MIT Press.

Rumelhart, D. E., & Siple, P. (1974). Process of recognizing tachistoscopically presented words. *Psychological Review, 81,* 99–118.

Rundus, D. (1971). Analysis of rehearsal processes in free recall. *Journal of Experimental Psychology, 89,* 63–77.

Rushton, J. P. (1992). Life-history comparisons between Orientals and whites at a Canadian university. *Personality and individual differences, 13,* 439–442.

Rushton, J. P., Brainerd, C. J., & Pressley, M. (1983). Behavioral development and construct validity: The principle of aggregation. *Psychological Bulletin, 94,* 18–38.

Russell, T., & Johnston, P. (1988, March). *Teachers learning from experiences of teaching: Analysis based on metaphor and reflection.* Presented at the annual meeting of the American Educational Research Association, New Orleans.

Russow, R. A., & Pressley, M. (1993). *Use of graphing calculators increases students' conceptual understanding of graphing: A quasi-experimental and true experimental evaluation.* Technical Report. College Park, MD:

University of Maryland, Department of Human Development (Educational Psychology).

Ruth, L. P. (1991). Who determines policy? Power and politics in English language arts education. In J. Flood, J. M. Jensen, D. Lapp, & J. R. Squire (Eds.), *Handbook of research on teaching the English language arts* (pp. 3–17). New York: Macmillan.

Rutter, M. (1983). School effects of pupil progress: Research findings and policy implications. In L. Shulman & G. Sykes (Eds.), *Handbook of teaching and policy* (pp. 3–41). New York: Longman.

Ryle, G. (1949). *The concept of mind.* New York: Barnes & Noble.

Rynders, J. E., & Horrobin, J. M. (1990). Always trainable? Never educable? Updating educational expectations concerning children with Down Syndrome. *American Journal of Mental Retardation, 95,* 77–83.

Sabar, N., & Levin, T. (1989). Still waters run deep. *Journal of Research in Science Teaching, 26,* 727–735.

Sabers, D. S., Cushing, K. S., & Berliner, D. C. (1991). Differences among teachers in a task characterized by simultaneity, multidimensionality, and immediacy. *American Educational Research Journal, 28,* 63–88.

Sadoski, M. (1983). An exploratory study of the relationship between reported imagery and the comprehension and recall of a story. *Reading Research Quarterly, 19,* 110–123.

Sadoski, M. (1985). The natural use of imagery in story comprehension and recall: Replication and extension. *Reading Research Quarterly, 20,* 658–667.

Sadoski, M., Goetz, E. T., & Fritz, J. B. (1993a). A causal model of sentence recall: Effects of familiarity, concreteness, comprehensibility, and interestingness. *Journal of Reading Behavior, 25,* 5–16.

Sadoski, M., Goetz, E. T., & Fritz, J. B. (1993b). Impact of concreteness on comprehensibility. *Journal of Educational Psychology, 85,* 291–204.

Sadoski, M., Goetz, E. T., & Kangiser, S. (1988). Imagination in story response: Relationship between imagery, affect, and structural importance. *Reading Research Quarterly, 23,* 320–336.

Sadoski, M., Paivio, A., Goetz, E. T. (1991). A critique of schema theory in reading and a dual coding alternative. *Reading Research Quarterly, 26,* 463–486.

Sadoski, M., & Quast, Z. (1990). Reader response and long-term recall for journalistic text: The roles of imagery, affect, and importance. *Reading Research Quarterly, 25,* 256–272.

Sagerman, N., & Mayer, R. E. (1987). Forward transfer of different reading strategies evoked by adjunct questions in science text. *Journal of Educational Psychology, 79,* 189–191.

Salomon, G., & Perkins, D. N. (1989). Rocky roads to transfer: Rethinking mechanisms of a neglected phenomenon. *Educational Psychologist, 24,* 113–142.

Salthouse, T. A. (1982). *Adult cognition: An experimental psychology of human aging.* New York: Springer-Verlag.

Salthouse, T. A. (1985). Speed of behavior and its implications for cognition. In J. E. Birren & K. W. Schaie (Eds.), *Handbook of the psychology of aging,* 2nd ed. (pp. 400–426). New York: Van Nostrand Reinhold.

Salthouse, T. A. (1988). The role of processing resources in cognitive aging. In M. I. Howe & C. J. Brainerd (Eds.), *Cognitive development in adulthood* (pp. 185–139). New York: Springer-Verlag.

Salthouse, T. A. (1992). The information-processing perspective on cognitive aging. In R. J. Sternberg & C. A. Berg (Eds.), *Intellectual development* (pp. 261–277). Cambridge, UK: Cambridge University Press.

Salthouse, T. A., & Babcock, R. L. (1991). Decomposing adult age differences in working memory. *Developmental Psychology, 27,* 763–776.

Salthouse, T. A., Kausler, D. H., & Saults, J. S. (1988). Investigation of student status, background variables, and the feasibility of standard tasks in cognitive aging research. *Psychology and Aging, 3,* 29–37.

Saltz, E., Soller, E., & Sigel, I. (1972). The development of natural language concepts. *Child Development, 43,* 1191–1202.

Salvia, J., & Hughes, C. (1990). *Curriculum-based assessment: Testing what is taught.* New York: Macmillan.

Sameroff, A. J. (1975). Early influences on development: Fact or fancy? *Merrill-Palmer Quarterly, 21,* 267–294.

Sameroff, A. J., & Chandler, M. J. (1975). Reproductive risk and the continuum of caretaking casualty. In F. D. Horowitz, M. Hetherington, S. Scarr-Salapatek, & G. Siegel (Eds.), *Review of child development research,* Vol. 4. (pp. 187–244). Chicago: University of Chicago Press.

Sameroff, A. J., & Fiese, B. H. (1990). Transactional regulation and early intervention. In S. J. Meisels & J. P. Shonkoff (Eds.), *Handbook of early childhood intervention* (pp. 119–149). Cambridge, UK: Cambridge University Press.

Samuels, M. T., Killip, S. M., MacKenzie, H., & Fagan, J. (1992). Evaluating preschool programs: The role of dynamic assessment. In H. C. Haywood & D. Tzuriel (Eds.), *Interactive assessment* (pp. 251–271). New York: Springer-Verlag.

Samuels, M. T., Lamb, C. H., & Oberholtzer, L. (1992). Dynamic assessment of adults with learning difficulties. In H. C. Haywood & D. Tzuriel (Eds.), *Interactive assessment* (pp. 275–299). New York: Springer-Verlag.

Samuels, M., Tzuriel, D., & Malloy-Miller, T. (1989). Dynamic assessment of children with learning disabilities. In R. T. Brown & M. Chazan (Eds.), *Learning difficulties and emotional problems* (pp. 145–165). Calgary: Detselig Enterprises.

Samuels, S. J. (1970). Effects of pictures on learning to read, comprehension, and attitudes. *Review of Educational Research, 40,* 397–407.

Samuels, S. J. (1979). The method of repeated readings. *The Reading Teacher, 32,* 403–408.

Samuels, S. J., Miller, N., & Eisenberg, P. (1979). Practice effects on the unit of word recognition. *Journal of Educational Psychology, 71,* 514–520.

Samuels, S. J., Schermer, N., & Reinking, D. (1992). Reading fluency: Techniques for making decoding automatic. In S. J. Samuels & A. E. Farstrup (Eds.), *What research has to say about reading instruction* (pp. 124–144). Newark, DE: International Reading Association.

Sandoval, J. H., & Mille, M. P. W. (1980). Accuracy judgments of WISC-R items difficulty for minority groups. *Journal of Consulting and Clinical Psychology, 48,* 249–253.

Santa, C. M., & Havens, L. T. (1991). Learning through writing. In C. M. Santa & D. E. Alvermann (Eds.), *Science learning: Processes and applications* (pp. 122–133). Newark, DE: International Reading Association.

Sattler, J. M. (1992). *Assessment of children,* Revised and updated 3rd ed. San Diego: J. M. Sattler.

Sawyer, M. H. (1991). A review of research in revising instructional text. *Journal of Reading Behavior, 23,* 307–333.

Sawyer, R. J., Graham, S., & Harris, K. R. (1992). Direct teaching, strategy instruction, and strategy instruction with explicit self-regulation: Effects on composition skills and self-efficacy of students with learning disabilities. *Journal of Educational Psychology, 84,* 340–352.

Saxe, G. B. (1988). The mathematics of child street vendors. *Child Development, 59,* 1415–1425.

Scarborough, H. S. (1989). Prediction of reading disability from familial and individual differences. *Journal of Educational Psychology, 81,* 101–108.

Scarborough, H. S. (1990). Very early language deficits in dyslexic children. *Child Development, 61,* 1728–1743.

Scardamalia, M., & Bereiter, C. (1986). Research on written composition. In M. C. Wittrock (Ed.), *Handbook of research on teaching,* 3rd ed. (pp. 778–803). New York: Macmillan.

Scarr, S. (1992). Developmental theories for the 1990s: Development and individual differences. *Child Development, 63,* 1–19.

Scarr, S., & Kidd, K. K. (1983). Developmental behavior genetics. In M. M. Haith & J. J. Campos (Eds.) & P. H. Mussen (Gen. Ed.), *Handbook of child psychology,* Vol. II, *Infancy and developmental psychobiology* (pp. 345–433). New York: John Wiley & Sons.

Scarr, S., & McCartney, K. (1983). How people make their own environments: A theory of genotype-environment effects. *Child Development, 54,* 424–435.

Scarr, S., & Weinberg, R. A. (1976). IQ test performance of black children adopted by white families. *American Psychologist, 31,* 726–739.

Scarr, S., & Weinberg, R. A. (1983). The Minnesota adoption studies: Genetic differences and malleability. *Child Development, 54,* 260–268.

Schade, J. P., & van Groeningen, W. B. (1961). Structural organization of the human cerebral cortex. I. Maturation of the middle frontal gyrus. *Acta Anatomica, 47,* 74–85.

Schaie, K. W. (1980). Age changes in intelligence. In R. L. Sprott (Ed.), *Age, learning ability, & intelligence* (pp. 41–77). New York: Van Nostrand.

Schaie, K. W. (1990). Intellectual development in adulthood. In J. E. Birren & K. W. Schaie (Eds.), *Handbook of the psychology of aging,* 3rd ed. (pp. 291–309). San Diego: Academic Press.

Schaie, K. W., & Labouvie-Vief, G. V. (1974). Generational versus ontogenetic components of change in adult cognitive behavior: A fourteen-year cross-sequential study. *Developmental Psychology, 10,* 305–320.

Schank, R. C., & Abelson, R. P. (1977). *Scripts, plans, goals, and understanding.* Hillsdale, NJ: Erlbaum & Associates.

Schauble, L. (1990). Belief revision in children: The role of prior knowledge and strategies for generating evidence. *Journal of Experimental Child Psychology, 49,* 31–57.

Schauble, L., Glaser, R., Raghavan, K., & Reiner, M. (1992). The integration of knowledge and experimentation strategies in understanding the physical system. *Applied Cognitive Psychology, 6,* 321–343.

Schaughnessy, M. (1977). Some needed research in writing. *College Composition and Communication, 28,* 317–321.

Scheffler, I. (1965). *Conditions of knowledge.* Glenview, IL: Scott, Foresman.

Scheid, K. (1993). *Helping students become strategic learners: Guidelines for teaching and choosing instructional materials.* Cambridge, MA: Brookline Books.

Schiefele, U. (1991). Interest, learning, and motivation. *Educational Psychologist, 26,* 299–324.

Schloss, P. J. (1992). Special issue: Integrating learners with disabilities in regular education programs. *Elementary School Journal, 92 (3).*

Schlossberg, N. K., Lynch, A. Q., & Phickering, A. W. (1989). *Improving higher education environments for adults.* San Francisco: Jossey-Bass.

Schmeiser, C. B. (1992). Reactions to technical and societal issues in testing Hispanics. In K. F. Geisinger (Ed.), *Psychological testing of Hispanics* (pp. 79–88). Washington, DC: American Psychological Association.

Schmidt, C. R., Ollendick, T. H., & Stanowicz, L. B. (1988). Developmental changes in the influence of assigned goals on cooperative and competition. *Developmental Psychology, 24,* 574–579.

Schmidt, H. G., De Volder, M. L., De Grave, W. S., Moust, J. H. C., & Patel, V. L. (1989). Explanatory models in the processing of science text: The role of prior knowledge activation through small-group discussion. *Journal of Educational Psychology, 81,* 610–619.

Schmuck, R. A., & Schmuck, P. A. (1992). *Small districts, big problems.* Newbury Park, CA: Corwin.

Schneider, B. H., Clegg, M. R., Byrne, B. M., Ledingham, J. E., & Crombie, G. (1989). Social relations of gifted children as a function of age

and school program. *Journal of Educational Psychology, 81,* 48–56.

Schneider, Wa., Dumais, S. T., & Shiffrin, R. M. (1984). Automatic and controlled processing and attention. In R. Parasuraman & D. R. Davies (Eds.), *Varieties of attention* (pp. 1–27). Orlando, FL: Academic Press.

Schneider, Wa., & Graham, D. J. (1992). Introduction to connections models in education. *Educational Psychologist, 27,* 513–530.

Schneider, Wa., & Shiffrin, R. M. (1977). Controlled and automatic processing: Detection, search, and attention. *Psychological Review, 84,* 1–66.

Schneider, W., & Bjorklund, D. F. (1992). Expertise, aptitude, and strategic remembering. *Child Development, 63,* 461–473.

Schneider, Wo., Borkowski, J. G., Kurtz, B. E., & Kerwin, K. (1986). Metamemory and motivation: A comparison of strategy use and performance in German and American children. *Journal of Cross-Cultural Psychology, 17,* 315–336.

Schneider, W., & Körkel, J. (1989). The knowledge base and text recall: Evidence from a short-term longitudinal study. *Contemporary Educational Psychology, 14,* 382–393.

Schneider, W., Körkel, J., & Weinert, F. E. (1989). Domain-specific knowledge and memory performance: A comparison of high- and low-aptitude children. *Journal of Educational Psychology, 81,* 306–312.

Schneider, W., Körkel, J., & Weinert, F. E. (1990). Expert knowledge, general abilities, and text processing. In W. Schneider & F. E. Weinert (Eds.), *Interactions among aptitudes, strategies, and knowledge in cognitive performance* (pp. 235–251). New York: Springer-Verlag.

Schneider, W., & Pressley, M. (1989). *Memory development between 2 and 20.* New York: Springer-Verlag.

Schoenfeld, A. (1979). Explicit heuristic training as a variable in problem-solving performance. *Journal for Research in Mathematics Education, 10,* 173–187.

Schoenfeld, A. (1985). *Mathematical problem solving.* New York: Academic Press.

Schoenfeld, A. (1987). *Cognitive science and mathematics education.* Hillsdale, NJ: Erlbaum & Associates.

Schoenfeld, A. (1989a). Exploration of students' mathematical beliefs and behavior. *Journal for Research in Mathematics Education, 20,* 338–355.

Schoenfeld, A. (1989b). Teaching mathematical thinking and problem solving. In L. B. Resnick & B. L. Klopfer (Eds.), *Toward the thinking curriculum* (pp. 83–103). (*1989 Yearbook of the Association for Supervision and Curriculum Development*). Washington, DC: ASCD.

Schoenfeld, A. (1992). Learning to think mathematically: Problem solving, metacognition, and sense making in mathematics. In D. A. Grouws (Ed.), *Handbook of research on mathematics teaching and learning* (pp. 334–370). New York: Macmillan.

Schoenfeld, A., & Hermann, D. J. (1982). Problem perception and knowledge structure in expert and novice mathematics problem

solvers. *Journal of Experimental Psychology: Learning, Memory, and Cognition, 5,* 484–494.

Schommer, M. (1990). Effects of beliefs about the nature of knowledge on comprehension. *Journal of Educational Psychology, 82,* 498–504.

Schommer, M., Crouse, A., & Rhodes, N. (1992). Epistemological beliefs and mathematical text comprehension: Believing it is simple does not make it so. *Journal of Educational Psychology, 84,* 435–443.

Schön, D. A. (1983). *The reflective practitioner: How professionals think in action.* London: Temple Smith.

Schön, D. A. (1987). *Educating the reflective practitioner.* San Francisco: Jossey-Bass.

Schön, D. A. (1988). Coaching reflective teaching. In P. P. Grimmett & G. L. Erickson (Eds.), *Reflection in teacher education* (pp. 17–29). New York: Teacher's College Press.

Schrage, M. (1990). *Shared minds: The new technologies of collaboration.* New York: Random House.

Schriver, K. A. (1986, April). *Teaching writers to predict readers' comprehension problems with text.* Paper presented at the annual meeting of the American Educational Research Association, San Francisco.

Schroeder, T. L., & Lester, F. K. Jr. (1989). Developing understanding in mathematics via problem solving. In P. R. Trafton & A. P. Schulte (Eds.), *New directions for elementary school mathematics: 1989 yearbook of the National Council of Teachers of Mathematics* (pp. 31–42). Reston, VA: National Council of Teachers of Mathematics.

Schumaker, J. B., & Deshler, D. D. (1992). Validation of learning strategy interventions for students with learning disabilities: Results of a programmatic research effort. In B. Y. L. Wong (Ed.), *Contemporary intervention research in learning disabilities: An international perspective* (pp. 22–46). New York: Springer-Verlag.

Schumaker, J. B., & Lyerla, K. (1991). *The paragraph writing strategy: Instructor's manual.* Lawrence, KS: University of Kansas, Institute for Research in Learning Disabilities.

Schunk, D. H. (1989). Social cognitive theory and self-regulated learning. In B. J. Zimmerman & D. H. Schunk (Eds.), *Self-regulated learning and academic achievement* (pp. 83–110). New York: Springer-Verlag.

Schunk, D. H. (1990). Goal setting and self-efficacy during self-regulated learning. *Educational Psychologist, 25,* 71–86.

Schunk, D. H. (1991). Self-efficacy and academic motivation. *Educational Psychologist, 26,* 207–232.

Schunk, D. H., & Cox, P. D. (1986). Strategy training and attributional feedback with learning disabled students. *Journal of Educational Psychology, 78,* 201–209.

Schunk, D. H., Hanson, A. R., & Cox, P. D. (1987). Peer-model attributes and children's achievement behaviors. *Journal of Educational Psychology, 79,* 54–61.

Schuster, D. T. (1990). Fulfillment of potential, life satisfaction, and competence: Comparing four cohorts of gifted women at midlife. *Journal of Educational Psychology, 82,* 471–478.

Schwantes, F. M. (1991). Children's use of semantic and syntactic information for word recognition and determination of sentence meaningfulness. *Journal of Reading Behavior, 23,* 335–350.

Schwegler, R. A., & Shamoon, L. K. (1991). Meaning attribution in ambiguous text. In C. Bazerman & J. Paradis (Eds.), *Textual dynamics of the professions: Historical and contemporary studies of writing in professional communities* (pp. 216–233). Madison: University of Wisconsin Press.

Scott, A. C., Clayton, J. E., & Gibson, E. L. (1991). *A practical guide to knowledge acquisition.* Reading, MA: Addison-Wesley Publishing Co.

Scott, D. T. (1987). Premature infants in later childhood: Some recent followup results. *Seminary Perinatology, 11,* 191–199.

Scott, J. A., & Ehri, L. C. (in press). Sight word reading in prereaders: Use of logographic vs. alphabetic access routes. *Journal of Reading Behavior.*

Scott, T., Cole, M., & Engel, M. (1992). Computers and education: A cultural constructivist perspective. In G. Grant (Ed.), *Review of Research in Education,* Vol. 18 (pp. 191–251). Washington, DC: American Educational Research Association.

Scruggs, T. E., & Mastropieri, M. A. (1989). Reconstructive elaborations: A model for content area learning. *American Educational Research Journal, 26,* 311–327.

Secada, W. G. (1991). Selected conceptual and methodological issues for studying the mathematics education of the disadvantaged. In M. S. Knapp & P. M. Shields (Eds.), *Better schooling for the children of poverty: Alternatives to conventional wisdom* (pp. 149–168). Berkeley, CA: McCutchan Publishing Co.

Secada, W. G. (1992). Race, ethnicity, social class, language, and achievement in mathematics. In D. A. Grouws (Ed.), *Handbook of research on mathematics teaching and learning* (pp. 623–660). New York: Macmillan.

Secan, K. E., Egel, A. L., & Tilley, C. S. (1989). Acquisition, generalization, and maintenance of question-answering skills in autistic children. *Journal of Applied Behavior Analysis, 22,* 181–196.

Segal, J. W., Chipman, S. F., & Glaser, R. (1985). *Thinking and learning skills,* Vol. 1, *Relating instruction to research.* Hillsdale, NJ: Erlbaum & Associates.

Segel, E. (1986). "As the twig is bent . . . ": Gender and childhood reading. In E. A. Flynn & P. P. Schweickart (Eds.), *Gender and reading: Essays on readers, texts, and contexts* (pp. 165–186). Baltimore: Johns Hopkins Press.

Seidel, J. F. (1992). Children with HIV-related developmental difficulties. *Phi Delta Kappan, 74,* 38–40, 56.

Seidenberg, M. S. (1989). Visual word recognition and pronunciation: A computational model and its implications. In W. Marslen-Wilson (Ed.), *Lexical representation and process* (pp. 25–74). Cambridge, MA: MIT Press.

Seidenberg, M. S., & McClelland, J. L. (1989). A distributed, developmental model of word recognition and naming. *Psychological Review, 96,* 523–568.

Selfridge, O. G. (1959). Pandemonium: A paradigm for learning. In D. V. Blake & A. M. Uttley (Eds.), *Proceeding of the symposium on the mechanization of thought processes.* London: H.M. Stationery Office.

Seligman, M. E. P., & Hager, J. L. (1972). *Biological boundaries of learning.* New York: Appleton-Century-Crofts.

Semb, G. B., Ellis, J. A., & Araujo, J. (1993). Long-term memory for knowledge learned in school. *Journal of Educational Psychology, 85,* 305–316.

Sendak, M. (1963). *Where the Wild Things Are.* New York: Harper & Row.

Service, V., Lock, A., & Chandler, P. (1989). Individual differences in early communicative development: A social constructivist perspective. In S. von Tetzchner, L. S. Siegel, & L. Smith (Eds.), *The social and cognitive aspects of normal and atypical language development* (pp. 23–49). New York: Springer-Verlag.

Sexson, S. B., & Madan-Swain, A. (1993). School reentry for the child with chronic illness. *Journal of Learning Disabilities, 26,* 115–126.

Seymour, P. H. K., & Elder, L. (1986). Beginning reading without phonology. *Cognitive Neuropsychology, 3,* 1–36.

Shade, B. J. (1982). Afro-American cognitive style: A variable in school success. *Review of Educational Research, 52,* 219–244.

Shanahan, T., & Tierney, R. J. (1990). Reading-writing connections: The relations among three perspectives. In J. Zutell & S. McCormick (Eds.), *Literacy theory and research: Analyses from multiple paradigms, Thirty-ninth yearbook of the National Reading Conference* (pp. 13–34). Chicago: National Reading Conference.

Shapiro, E. S. (1990). An integrated model for curriculum-based assessment. *School Psychology Review, 19,* 331–349.

Sharp, A. M. (1987). What is a 'community of inquiry'? *Journal of Moral Education, 16,* 37–45.

Sharp, A. M., & Reed, R. F. (1992). *Studies in philosophy for children: Harry Stottlemeier's discovery.* Philadelphia: Temple University Press.

Sharp, D., Cole, M., & Lave, C. (1979). Education and cognitive development: The evidence from experimental research. *Monographs of the Society for Research in Child Development, 44* (Serial No. 178).

Shaughnesy, M. P. (1977). *Errors and expectations: A guide for the teacher of basic writing.* New York: Oxford University Press.

Shavelson, R. J., Baxter, G. P., & Pine, J. (1992). Performance assessments: Political rhetoric and measurement reality. *Educational Researcher, 21 (4),* 22–27.

Shavelson, R. J., & Webb, N. M. (1991). *Generalizability theory: A primer.* Newbury Park, CA: Sage.

Shaywitz, S. E., & Shaywitz, B. A. (1992). Learning disabilities and attention deficits in the school setting. In L. J. Meltzer (Ed.), *Strategy assessment and instruction for students with learning disabilities: From theory to practice* (pp. 221–241). Austin, TX: PRO-ED.

Shaywitz, S. E., Shaywitz, B. A., Fletcher, J. M., & Escobar, M. D. (1990). Prevalence of reading disability in boys and girls. *Journal of the American Medical Association, 264,* 998–1002.

Shea, J. B., & Morgan, R. L. (1979). Contextual interference effects on the acquisition, retention, and transfer of a motor skill. *Journal of Experimental Psychology: Human Learning and Memory, 5,* 179–187.

Shell, D. F., Murphy, C. C., & Bruning, R. H. (1989). Self-efficacy and outcome expectancy mechanisms in reading and writing achievement. *Journal of Educational Psychology, 81,* 91–100.

Shepard, L. A. (1989). A review of research on kindergarten retention. In L. A. Shepard & M. L. Smith (Eds.), *Flunking grades: Research and policies on retention* (pp. 64–78). Philadelphia: Falmer Press.

Shephard, L. A. (1993). Evaluating test validity. In L. Darling-Hammond (Ed.), *Review of Research in Education,* Vol. 19 (pp. 405–450). Washington, DC: American Educational Research Association.

Shepard, R. N., & Metzler, J. (1971). Mental rotation of three-dimensional objects. *Science, 171,* 701–703.

Sherris, J. (1984). The effects of concept relatedness of instruction and locus of control orientation on the meaningful learning achievements of high school biology students. *Journal of Research in Science Teaching, 41,* 83–89.

Sherman, L. W. (1988). A comparative study of cooperative and competitive achievement in two secondary biology classrooms: The group investigative model versus an individually competitive goal structure. *Journal of Research in Science Teaching, 26,* 55–64.

Sherman, M., & Key, C. B. (1932). The intelligence of isolated mountain children. *Child Development, 3,* 279–290.

Shiffrin, R. M., & Schneider, Wa. (1977). Controlled and automatic human information processing: perceptual learning, automatic attending, and a general theory. *Psychological Review, 84,* 127–190.

Shimron, J. (1975). Imagery and the comprehension of prose by elementary school children. (Doctoral dissertation, University of Pittsburgh, 1974). *Dissertation Abstracts International, 36,* 795-A (University Microfilms No. 75-18, 254).

Shinn, M. R., Rosenfeld, S., & Knutson, N. (1989). Curriculum-based assessment: A comparison of models. *School Psychology Review, 18,* 299–316.

Shirey, L. L., & Reynolds, R. E. (1988). Effect of interest on attention and learning. *Journal of Educational Psychology, 80,* 159–166.

Shochet, I. M. (1992). A dynamic assessment for undergraduate admission: The inverse relationship between modifiability and predictability. In H. C. Haywood & D. Tzuriel

(Eds.), *Interactive assessment* (pp. 332–355). New York: Springer-Verlag.

Shonkoff, J. P., & Marshall, P. C. (1990). Biological bases of developmental dysfunction. In S. J. Meisels & J. P. Shonkoff (Eds.), *Handbook of early childhood intervention* (pp. 35–52). Cambridge, UK: Cambridge University Press.

Shor, I. (1987). *Freire for the classroom: A sourcebook for liberatory education.* Portsmouth, NH: Heinemann.

Short, E. J., & Ryan, E. B. (1984). Metacognitive differences between skilled and less skilled readers: Remediating deficits through story grammar and attribution training. *Journal of Educational Psychology, 76,* 225–235.

Shulman, L. (1986). Paradigms and research programs in the study of teaching: A contemporary perspective. In M. C. Wittorck (Ed.), *Handbook of research on teaching,* 3rd ed. (pp. 3–36). New York: Macmillan.

Shulman, L. S., & Keislar, E. R. (Eds.) (1966). *Learning by discovery: A critical appraisal.* Chicago: Rand McNally.

Shurkin, J. N. (1992). *Terman's kids: The groundbreaking study of how the gifted grow up.* Boston: Little, Brown & Co.

Shymansky, J. A., Yore, L. D., & Good, R. (1991). Elementary school teachers' beliefs about and perceptions of elementary school science, science reading, science textbooks, and supportive instructional factors. *Journal of Research in Science Teaching, 28,* 437–454.

Siegel, L. S., & Ryan, E. B. (1988). Development of grammatical-sensitivity, phonological, and short-term memory skills in normally achieving and learning disabled children. *Developmental Psychology, 24,* 28–37.

Siegel, L. S., & Ryan, E. B. (1989). The development of working memory in normally achieving and subtypes of learning disabled children. *Child Development, 60,* 973–980.

Siegler, R. S. (1987). The perils of averaging data over strategies: An example from children's addition. *Journal of Experimental Psychology: General, 116,* 1–15.

Siegler, R. S. (1988). Individual differences in strategy choices: Good students, not-so-good students, and perfectionists. *Child Development, 59,* 833–851.

Siegler, R. S. (1989). Hazards of mental chronometry: An example from children's subtraction. *Journal of Educational Psychology, 81,* 497–506.

Siegler, R. S., & Crowley, K. (1991). The microgenetic method: A direct means for studying cognitive development. *American Psychologist, 46,* 606–620.

Siegler, R. S., & Jenkins, E. (1989). *How children discover new strategies.* Hillsdale, NJ: Erlbaum & Associates.

Siegler, R. S., & Shrager, J. (1984). Strategy choices in addition and subtraction: How do children know what to do? In C. Sophian (Ed.), *Origins of cognitive skills* (pp. 229–293). Hillsdale, NJ: Erlbaum & Associates.

Sigman, M., Neumann, C., Jansen, A. A. J., & Bwibo, N. (1989). Cognitive abilities of Kenyan children in relation to nutrition, family characteristics, and education. *Child Development, 60,* 1463–1474.

Silver, E. (Ed.) (1985). *Teaching and learning mathematical problem solving.* Hillsdale, NJ: Erlbaum & Associates.

Silver, E. A. (1987). Foundations of cognitive theory and research for mathematics problem solving instruction. In A. Schoenfeld (Ed.), *Cognitive science and mathematics education* (pp. 33–60). Hillsdale, NJ: Erlbaum & Associates.

Simmons, P. E. (1991). Learning science in software microworlds. In S. M. Glynn, R. H. Yeany, & B. K. Britton (Eds.), *The psychology of learning science* (pp. 241–256). Hillsdale, NJ: Erlbaum & Associates.

Simon, H. A. (1980). Problem solving and education. In D. Tuma & F. Reif (Eds.), *Problem solving and education* (pp. 81–96). Hillsdale, NJ: Erlbaum & Associates.

Simon, H. A., & Chase, W. G. (1973). Skill in chess. *American Scientist, 61,* 394–403.

Simonson, R., & Walker, S. (Eds.) (1988). *The Greywolf annual five: Multicultural literacy.* St. Paul, MN: Greywolf Press.

Simonton, D. K. (1988). *Scientific genius: A psychology of science.* Cambridge, UK: Cambridge University Press.

Simonton, D. K. (1990). Creativity and wisdom in aging. In J. E. Birren & K. W. Schaie (Eds.), *Handbook of the psychology of aging,* 3rd ed. (pp. 320–329). San Diego: Academic Press.

Simpson, M. L., Hayes, C. G., Stahl, N., Connor, R. T., & Weaver, D. (1988). An initial validation of a study strategy system. *Journal of Reading Behavior, 20,* 149–180.

Sinclair, R. L., & Ghory, W. J. (1987). *Reaching marginal students.* Berkeley, CA: McCutchan.

Singer, J. D., Palfrey, J. S., Butler, J. A., & Walker, D. K. (1989). Variation in special education classification across school districts: How does where you live affect what you are labeled? *American Educational Research Journal, 26,* 261–281.

Singer, R. S. (1972). *The psychomotor domain: Movement behavior.* Philadelphia: Lea & Febiger.

Singh, J., Singh, N. N., & Blampied, N. M. (1985). Reading programmes for adult illiterates: A review of instructional methods and materials. *Human Learning, 4,* 143–155.

Singley, M. K., & Anderson, J. R. (1989). *Transfer of cognitive skill.* Cambridge, MA: Harvard University Press.

Sizer, T. R. (1984). *Horace's compromise: The dilemma of the American high school.* Boston: Houghton Mifflin.

Skaalvik, E. M. (1990). Gender differences in general academic self-esteem and in success expectations on defined academic problems. *Journal of Educational Psychology, 82,* 593–598.

Skemp, R. R. (1989). *Mathematics in the primary school.* London: Routledge.

Skinner, B. F. (1953). *Science and human behavior.* New York: Free Press.

Skinner, B. F. (1961). Why we need teaching machines. *Harvard Educational Review, 31,* 377–398.

Skinner, B. F. (1977). Corporal punishment. In I. A. Hyman & J. H. Wise (Eds.), *Corporal punishment in American education* (pp. 335–336). Philadelphia: Temple University Press.

Skinner, B. F. (1987). *Upon further reflection.* Englewood Cliffs, NJ: Prentice-Hall.

Skinner, B. F. (1990). Can psychology be a science of mind? *American Psychologist, 45,* 1206–1210.

Skinner, E. A., Wellborn, J. G., & Connell, J. P. (1990). What it takes to do well in school and whether I've got it: A process model of perceived control and children's engagement and achievement in school. *Journal of Educational Psychology, 82,* 22–32.

Slavin, R. E. (1984). Meta–analysis in education: How has it been used? *Educational Researcher, 13,* 6–15.

Slavin, R. (1985a). An introduction to cooperative learning research. In R. Slavin, S. Sharan, S. Kagan, R. H. Lazarowitz, C. Webb, & R. Schmuck (Eds.), *Learning to cooperate, cooperating to learn* (pp. 5–15). New York: Plenum.

Slavin, R. (1985b). Team–assisted individualization: Combining cooperative learning and individualized instruction in mathematics. In R. Slavin, S. Sharan, S. Kagan, R. H. Lazarowitz, C. Webb, & R. Schmuck (Eds.), *Learning to cooperate, cooperating to learn* (pp. 177–209). New York: Plenum.

Slavin, R. E. (1987a). Grouping for instruction in the elementary school. *Educational Psychologist, 22,* 109–128.

Slavin, R. E. (1987b). Mastery learning reconsidered. *Review of Educational Research, 57,* 175–214.

Slavin, R. E. (1989). Class size and student achievement: Small effects of small classes. *Educational Psychologist, 24,* 99–110.

Slavin, R. E. (1990a). Achievement effects of ability grouping in secondary schools: A best-evidence synthesis. *Review of Educational Research, 60,* 471–499.

Slavin, R. E. (1990b). Mastery learning re-reconsidered. *Review of Educational Research, 60,* 300–302.

Slavin, R. E., Madden, N. A., Karweit, N. L., Dolan, L., Wasik, B. A., Shaw, A., Mainzer, K. L., & Haxby, B. (1991). Neverstreaming: Prevention and early intervention as an alternative to special education. *Journal of Learning Disabilities, 24,* 373–378.

Slavin, R. E., Madden, N. A., Karweit, N. L., Livermon, B. J., & Dolan, L. (1990). Success for all: First-year outcomes of a comprehensive plan for reforming urban education. *American Educational Research Journal, 27,* 255–278.

Slife, B. D., Weiss, J., & Bell, T. (1985). Separability of metacognition and cognition: Problem solving in learning disabled and regular students. *Journal of Educational Psychology, 77,* 437–445.

Smirnov, A. A. (1973). *Problems of the psychology of memory.* New York: Plenum.

Smith, A., & Sugar, O. (1975). Development of above normal language and intelligence: 21 years after left hemispherectomy. *Neurology, 25,* 813–818.

Smith, C. L. (1979). Children's understanding of natural language categories. *Journal of Experimental Child Psychology, 30*, 191–205.

Smith, E. E., & Medin, D. L. (1981). *Categories and concepts.* Cambridge, MA: Harvard University Press.

Smith, F. (1971). *Understanding reading: A psycholinguistic analysis of reading and learning to read.* New York: Holt, Rinehart, & Winston.

Smith, F. (1986). *Insult to intelligence: The bureaucratic invasion of classrooms.* New York: Arbor House.

Smith, G., Spiker, D., Peterson, C., Cicchetti, D., & Justice, P. (1984). Use of megadoses of vitamins with minerals in Down syndrome. *Journal of Pediatrics, 105*, 228–234.

Smith, J., & Baltes, P. B. (1990). A life-span perspective on thinking and problem-solving. In M. Schwebel, C. A. Maher, & N. S. Fagley (Eds.), *Promoting cognitive growth over the life span* (pp. 47–69). Hillsdale, NJ: Erlbaum & Associates.

Smith, M. L. (1991a). Meanings of test preparation. *American Educational Research Journal, 28*, 521–542.

Smith, M. L. (1991b). Put to the test: The effects of external testing on teachers. *Educational Researcher, 20* (5), 8–11.

Smith, M. L., & Glass, G. V. (1987). *Research and evaluation in education and the social sciences.* Englewood Cliffs, NJ: Prentice-Hall.

Smith, M. L., & Shepard, L. A. (1988). Kindergarten readiness and retention: A qualitative study of teachers' beliefs and practices. *American Educational Research Journal, 25*, 307–333.

Smith, S. B. (1983). *The great mental calculators.* New York: Columbia University Press.

Smith, S. D., Kimberling, W. J., Pennington, B. F., & Lubs, H. A. (1983). Specific reading disability: Identification of an inherited form through linkage analysis. *Science, 219*, 1345–1347.

Smith, S. D., Pennington, B. F., Kimberling, W. J., & Ing, P. S. (1990). Familial dyslexia: Use of genetic linkage to identify subtypes. *Journal of the American Academy of Child and Adolescent Psychiatry, 29*, 204–213.

Smith, S. G., & Jones, L. L. (1988). Images, imagination, and chemical reality. *Journal of Chemical Education, 66*, 8–11.

Snow, C. E., Barnes, W. S., Chandler, J., Goodman, I. F., & Hemphill, L. (1991). *Unfulfilled expectations: Home and school influences on literacy.* Cambridge, MA: Harvard University Press.

Sodian, B., & Schneider, W. (1990). Children's understanding of cognitive cuing: How to manipulate cues to fool a competitor. *Child Development, 61*, 697–704.

Sokolov, A. N. (1975). *Inner speech and thought.* New York: Plenum.

Solomon, D., Watson, M. S., Delucchi, K. L., Schaps, E., & Battistich, V. (1988). Enhancing children's prosocial behavior in the classroom. *American Educational Research Journal, 25*, 527–554.

Sommerfeld, M. (1992). "Micro-society" schools tackle real-world woes. *Education Week, 12*, 1, 14.

Song, M-J., Ginsburg, H. P. (1987). The development of informal and formal mathematical thinking in Korean and U.S. children. *Child Development, 58*, 1286–1296.

Soodak, L. C. (1990). Social behavior and knowledge of social "scripts" among mentally retarded adults. *American Journal of Mental Deficiency, 94*, 515–521.

Sophian, C. (1987). Early developments in children's use of counting to solve quantitative problems. *Cognition and Instruction, 4*, 61–90.

Sostek, A. M., Smith, Y. F., Katz, K. S., & Grant, E. G. (1987). Developmental outcome of preterm infants with intraventricular hemorrhage at one and two years of age. *Child Development, 58*, 779–786.

Sowell, E. J. (1989). Effects of manipulative materials in mathematics instruction. *Journal for Research in Mathematics Education, 20*, 498–505.

Spearman, C. (1904). "General intelligence" objectively determined and measured. *American Journal of Psychology, 15*, 201–293.

Spector, B. S., & Gibson, C. W. (1991). A qualitative study of middle school students' perceptions of factors facilitating the learning of science: Grounded theory and existing theory. *Journal of Research in Science Teaching, 28*, 467–484.

Spector, J. E. (1992). Predicting progress in beginning reading: Dynamic assessment of phonemic awareness. *Journal of Educational Psychology, 84*, 353–363.

Speidel, G. E. & Nelson, K. E. (eds.) (1989). *The many faces of imitation in language learning.* New York: Springer-Verlag.

Spielberger, C. D., & DeNike, l. D. (1966). Descriptive behaviorism versus cognitive theory in verbal operant conditioning. *Psychological Review, 73*, 306–326.

Spilich, G. J., Vesonder, G. T., Chiesi, H. L., & Voss, J. F. (1979). Text processing of domain-related information for individuals with high and low domain knowledge. *Journal of Verbal Learning and Verbal Behavior, 18*, 275–290.

Spiro, R. J., Feltovich, P. J., Coulson, R. L., & Anderson, D. K. (1989). Multiple analogies for complex concepts: Antidotes for analogy-induced misconception in advanced knowledge acquisition. In S. Vosniadou & A. Ortony (Eds.), *Similarity and analogical reasoning* (pp. 498–531). Cambridge, UK: Cambridge University Press.

Spitz, H. H. (1986a). *The raising of intelligence: A selected history of attempts to raise retarded intelligence.* Hillsdale, NJ: Erlbaum & Associates.

Spitz, H. H. (1986b). Preventing and curing mental retardation by behavioral intervention: An evaluation of some claims. *Intelligence, 10*, 197–207.

Spitz, H. H. (1991a). Commentary on Locurto's "Beyond IQ in preschool programs?" *Intelligence, 15*, 327–334.

Spitz, H. H. (1991b). Review of *The Milwaukee Project: Preventing mental retardation in children at risk. American Journal on Mental Retardation, 95*, 482–490.

Spitz, H. H. (1992). Does the Carolina Abecedarian Early Intervention Project prevent sociocultural mental retardation? *Intelligence, 16*, 225–237.

Spivey, N. N., & King, J. R. (1989). Readers as writers composing from sources. *Reading Research Quarterly, 24*, 7–26.

Spreen, O., & Strauss, E. (1991). *A compendium of neuropsychological tests: Administration, norms, and commentary.* New York: Oxford University Press.

Springer, S. P., & Deutsch, G. (1989). *Left brain, right brain,* 3rd ed. New York: W.H. Freeman & Co.

Spyridakis, J. H., & Standal, T. C. (1987). Signals in expository prose: Effects on reading comprehension. *Reading Research Quarterly, 22*, 285–298.

Squire, J. R. (1991). The history of the profession. In J. Flood, J. M. Jensen, D. Lapp, & J. R. Squire (Eds.), *Handbook of research on teaching the English language arts* (pp. 3–17). New York: Macmillan.

Stacey, K. (1992). Mathematical problem solving in groups: Are two heads better than one? *Journal of Mathematical Behavior, 11*, 261–275.

Stage, E. K., & Karplus, R. (1981). Mathematical ability: Is sex a factor? *Science, 212*, 114.

Stahl, S. A., & Miller, P. D. (1989). Whole language and language experience approaches for beginning reading: A quantitative research synthesis. *Review of Educational Research, 59*, 87–116.

Stallings, J. (1985). School, classroom, and home influences on women's decisions to enroll in advanced mathematics courses. In S. F. Chipman, L. R. Brush, & D. M. Wilson (Eds.), *Women and mathematics: Balancing the equation* (pp. 199–224). Hillsdale, NJ: Erlbaum & Associates.

Stallings, J., & Kaskowitz, D. (1974). *Follow through classroom observation evaluation 1972–73* (SRI Project URU-7370). Stanford, CA: Stanford Research Institute.

Stanhope, N., Cohen, G., & Conway, M. (1993). Very long-term retention of a novel. *Applied Cognitive Psychology, 7*, 239–256.

Stanley, J. C., Benbow, C. P. (1986). Youth who reason exceptionally well mathematically. In R. J. Sternberg & J. E. Davidson (Eds.), *Conceptions of giftedness* (pp. 361–387). Cambridge, England: Cambridge University Press.

Stanovich, K. E. (1980). Toward an interactive compensatory model of individual differences in the development of reading fluency. *Reading Research Quarterly, 16*, 32–71.

Stanovich, K. (1986). Matthew effects in reading: Some consequences of individual differences in the acquisition of literacy. *Reading Research Quarterly, 21*, 360–407.

Stanovich, K. E. (1990). A call for an end to the paradigm wars in reading research. *Journal of Reading Behavior, 22*, 221–231.

Stanovich, K. E. (1991). Discrepancy definitions of reading disability: Has intelligence led us astray? *Reading Research Quarterly, 26*, 7–29.

Stanovich, K. E., & Cunningham, A. E. (1993).

Where does knowledge come from? Specific associations between print exposure and information acquisition. *Journal of Educational Psychology, 85,* 211–229.

Stanovich, K. E., & West, R. F. (1989). Exposure to print and orthographic processing. *Reading Research Quarterly, 24,* 402–433.

Staszewski, J. J. (1988). The psychological reality of retrieval structures: An investigation of expert knowledge (Doctoral dissertation, Cornell University, 1987). *Dissertation Abstracts International, 48,* 2126B.

Staszewski, J. J. (1990). Exceptional memory: The influence of practice and knowledge on the development of elaborative encoding strategies. In W. Schneider & F. E. Weinert (Eds.), *Interactions among aptitudes, strategies, and knowledge in cognitive performance* (pp. 252–285). New York: Springer-Verlag.

Staver, J. R., & Bay, M. (1989). Analysis of the conceptual structure and reasoning demands of elementary science texts at the primary (K–3) level. *Journal of Research in Science Teaching, 26,* 329–349.

Staver, J. R., & Jacks, T. (1988). The influence of cognitive reasoning level, cognitive restructuring ability, disembedding ability, working memory capacity, and prior knowledge on students' performance on balancing equations by inspection. *Journal of Research in Science Teaching, 25,* 763–775.

Stavy, R. (1991). Using analogy to overcome misconceptions about conservation of matter. *Journal of Research in Science Teaching, 28,* 305–313.

Stedman, L. (1988). The effective schools formula still needs changing: A reply to Brookover. *Phi Delta Kappan, 69* (6), 439–442.

Stein, B. S., & Bransford, J. D. (1979). Constraints of effective elaboration: Effects on precision and subject generation. *Journal of Verbal Learning and Verbal Behavior, 18,* 769–777.

Stein, B. S., Littlefield, J., Bransford, J. D., & Persampieri, M. (1984). Elaboration and knowledge acquisition. *Memory & Cognition, 12,* 522–529.

Stein, M. K., Baxter, J. A., & Leinhardt, G. (1990). Subject-matter knowledge and elementary instruction: A case from functions and graphing. *American Educational Research Journal, 27,* 639–663.

Stein, N. L., & Glenn, C. G. (1979). An analysis of story comprehension in elementary school children. In R. O. Freedle (Eds.), *New directions in discourse processing,* Vol. 2. Norwood, NJ: Ablex.

Stein, N. L., & Nezworski, G. (1978). The effects of organization and instructional set on story memory. *Discourse Processes, 1,* 177–193.

Steinberg, E. R., & Anderson, R. C. (1975). Hierarchical semantic organization in 6-year-olds. *Journal of Experimental Child Psychology, 19,* 544–553.

Steinberg, L., & Dornbusch, S. M. (1991). Negative correlates of part-time employment during adolescence: Replication and elaboration. *Developmental Psychology, 27,* 304–313.

Steinberg, L., Fegley, S., & Dornbusch, S. M.

(1993). Negative impact of part-time work on adolescent adjustment. *Developmental Psychology, 29,* 171–180.

Stensvold, M. S., & Wilson, J. T. (1990). The interaction of verbal ability with concept mapping in learning from a chemistry laboratory activity. *Science Education, 74,* 473–480.

Stern, J. (1985). Biochemical aspects. In A. M. Clarke, A. D. B. Clarke, & J. M. Berg (Eds.), *Mental deficiency: The changing outlook* (pp. 135–212). New York: The Free Press.

Sternberg, R. J. (1977). *Intelligence, information processing, and analogical reasoning: The componential analysis of human abilities.* Hillsdale, NJ: Erlbaum & Associates.

Sternberg, R. J. (1980). Sketch of a componential subtheory of human intelligence. *Behavioral and Brain Sciences, 3,* 573–584.

Sternberg, R. J. (1981). A componential theory of intellectual giftedness. *Gifted Child Quarterly, 25,* 86–93.

Sternberg, R. J. (1983). Components of human intelligence. *Cognition 15,* 1–48.

Sternberg, R. J. (1985). *Beyond IQ: A triarchic theory of human intelligence.* Cambridge, UK: Cambridge University Press.

Sternberg, R. J. (1986). A triarchic theory of intellectual giftedness. In R. J. Sternberg & J. E. Davidson (Eds.), *Conceptions of giftedness* (pp. 223–243). Cambridge, UK: Cambridge University Press.

Sternberg, R. J. (1990). *Metaphors of mind: Conceptions of the nature of intelligence.* Cambridge, UK: Cambridge University Press.

Sternberg, R. J. (1991). Death, taxes, and bad intelligence tests. *Intelligence, 15,* 257–269.

Sternberg, R. J. (1991). Giftedness according to the triarchic theory of human intelligence. In N. Colangelo & G. A. Davis (Eds.), *Handbook of gifted education* (pp. 45–54). Boston: Allyn & Bacon.

Sternberg, R. J., & Davidson, J. E. (1983). Insight in the gifted. *Educational Psychologist, 18,* 51–57.

Sternberg, R. J., & Wagner, R. K. (1985). *Practical intelligence: Origins of competence in the everyday world.* Cambridge, UK: Cambridge University Press.

Sternberg, S. (1966). High-speed scanning in human memory. *Science, 153,* 652–654.

Sternberg, S. (1969). Memory-scanning: Mental processes revealed by reaction-time experiments. *American Scientist, 57,* 421–457.

Stevens, L. J., & Price, M. (1992). Meeting the challenges of educating children at risk. *Phi Delta Kappan, 74,* 18–23.

Stevens, R. J., Madden, N. A., Slavin, R. E., & Farnish, A. M. (1987). Cooperative Integrated Reading and Composition: Two field experiments. *Reading Research Quarterly, 22,* 433–454.

Stevenson, D. L., & Baker, D. P. (1987). The family-school relation and the child's school performance. *Child Development, 58,* 1348–1357.

Stevenson, H. W. (1990). The Asian advantage: The case of mathematics. In J. J. Shields (Ed.), *Japanese schooling: Patterns of socialization, equality, and political control* (pp. 85–95).

University Park, PA: Pennsylvania State University Press.

Stevenson, H. W. (1992). Learning from Asian schools. *Scientific American, 267* (6), 70–76.

Stevenson, H. W., Lee, S. Y., Chen, C., Lummis, M., Stigler, J., Fan, L., & Ge, F. (1990a). Mathematics achievement of children in China and the United States. *Child Development, 61,* 1053–1066.

Stevenson, H. W., Lee, S. Y., Chen, C., Stigler, J. W., Hsu, C., & Kitamura, S. (1990b). Contexts of achievement. *Monographs of the Society for Research in Child Development, 55* (1–2, Serial No. 211).

Stevenson, H. W., Lee, S., & Stigler, J. (1986). Mathematics achievement of Chinese, Japanese, and American children. *Science, 231,* 693–699.

Stevenson, H. W., Lummis, M., Lee, S., & Stigler, J. (1990). *Making the grade in mathematics: Chinese, Japanese, and American children.* Reston, VA: National Council of Teachers of Mathematics.

Stevenson, H. W., Parker, T., Wilkinson, A., Bonnevaux, B., & Gonzalez, M. (1978). Schooling, environment, and cognitive development: A cross-cultural study. *Monographs of the Society for Research in Child Development, 43* (Serial No. 175).

Stevenson, J. (1992). Genetics. In N. N. Singh & I. L. Beale (Eds.), *Learning disabilities: Nature, theory, and treatment* (pp. 327–351). New York: Springer-Verlag.

Stewart, L., & Pascual-Leone, J. (1992). Mental capacity constraints and the development of moral reasoning. *Journal of Experimental Child Psychology, 54,* 251–287.

Sticht, T. G. (1988). Adult literacy education. In E. Z. Rothkopf (Ed.), *Review of Research in Education,* Vol. 15 (pp. 59–96). Washington, DC: American Educational Research Association.

Stigler, J. W. (1984). "Mental abacus": The effect of abacus training on Chinese children's mental calculation. *Cognitive Psychology, 16,* 145–176.

Stigler, J. W., Lee, S., Lucker, G. W., & Stevenson, H. W. (1982). Curriculum and achievement in mathematics: A study of elementary school children in Japan, Taiwan, and the United States. *Journal of Educational Psychology, 74,* 315–322.

Stigler, J. W., Lee, S., & Stevenson, H. W. (1987). Mathematics classrooms in Japan, Taiwan, and the United States. *Child Development, 58,* 1272–1285.

Stigler, J., Lee, S., & Stevenson, H. W. (1990). *Mathematical knowledge of Japanese, Chinese, and American children.* Reston, VA: National Council of Teachers of Mathematics.

Stillings, N. A., Feinstein, M. H., Garfield, J. L., Rissland, E. L., Rosenbaum, D. A., Weisler, S. E., & Baker-Ward, L. (1987). *Cognitive science: An introduction.* Cambridge, MA: MIT Press.

Stipek, D. J., & Daniels, D. H. (1988). Declining perceptions of competence: A consequence of changes in the child or in the educational environment? *Journal of Educational Psychology, 80*, 352–356.

Stipek, D. J., & Hoffman, J. M. (1980). Children's achievement-related expectancies as a function of academic performance histories and sex. *Journal of Educational Psychology, 72*, 861–865.

Stipek, D. J., & Gralinski, J. H. (1991). Gender differences in children's achievement-related beliefs and emotional responses to success and failure in mathematics. *Journal of Educational Psychology, 83*, 361–371.

Stipek, D. J., & Kowalski, P. S. (1989). Learned helplessness in task-orienting versus performance-orienting testing conditions. *Journal of Educational Psychology, 81*, 384–391.

Stipek, D., & MacIver, D. (1989). Developmental change in children's assessment of intellectual competence. *Child Development, 60*, 521–538.

Stodolsky, S. S. (1985). Telling math: Origins of math aversion and anxiety. *Educational Psychologist, 93*, 409–428.

Stodolsky, S. S. (1988). *The subject matters: Classroom activity in math and social studies.* Chicago: University of Chicago Press.

Stodolsky, S. S., Salk, S., & Glaessner, B. (1991). Student views about learning math and social studies. *American Educational Research Journal, 28*, 89–116.

Stokes, T. F., & Baer, D. M. (1977). An implicit technology of generalization. *Journal of Applied Behavior Analysis, 10*, 349–367.

Storfer, M. D. (1990). *Intelligence and giftedness: The contributions of heredity and early environment.* San Francisco: Jossey-Bass.

Strage, A., Tyler, A. B., Rohwer, W. D. Jr., & Thomas, J. W. (1987). An analytic framework for assessing distinctive course features and across grade levels. *Contemporary Educational Psychology, 12*, 280–302.

Strahan, D. B. (1989). How experienced and novice teachers frame their views of instruction: An analysis of semantic ordered trees. *Teaching and Teacher Education, 5*, 53–67.

Strauss, A., & Corbin, J. (1990). *Basics of qualitative research: Grounded theory procedures and techniques.* Newbury Park, CA: Sage.

Strauss, M. S. (1979). Abstraction of prototypical information by adults and 10-month-olds. *Journal of Experimental Psychology: Human Learning and Memory, 5*, 618–632.

Streissguth, A. P., Barr, H. M., Sampson, P. D., Darby, B. L., & Martin, D. C. (1989). IQ at age 4 in relation to maternal alcohol use and smoking during pregnancy. *Developmental Psychology, 25*, 3–11.

Strike, K. A. (1991). The moral role of schooling in a liberal democratic society. In G. Grant (Ed.), *Review of Research in Education,* Vol. 17 (pp. 413–483). Washington, DC: American Educational Research Association.

Stuart, M., & Masterson, J. (1992). Patterns of reading and spelling in 10-year-old children related to prereading phonological abilities. *Journal of Experimental Child Psychology, 54*, 168–187.

Suchman, J. R. (1960). Inquiring training in the elementary school. *Science Teacher, 27*, 42–47.

Sugarman, S. (1983). *Children's early thought.* Cambridge, MA: Cambridge University Press.

Suinn, R. (1993). Imagery. In R. N. Singer, M. Murphy, & L. K. Tennant (Eds.), *Handbook of research on sport psychology* (pp. 492–510). New York: Macmillan.

Sulzby, E. (1985). Children's emergent reading of favorite storybooks: A developmental study. *Reading Research Quarterly, 20*, 458–481.

Sulzby, E. (1988). A study of children's early reading development. In A. D. Pelligrini (Ed.), *Psychological bases for early education* (pp. 39–75). Chichester, UK: John Wiley & Sons.

Sulzby, E., & Teale, W. (1991). Emergent literacy. In R. Barr, M. L. Kamil, P. B. Mosenthal, & P. D. Pearson (Eds.), *Handbook of reading research,* Vol. II (pp. 727–758). New York: Longman.

Summers, M. (1992). Improving primary school teachers' understanding of science concepts—theory into practice. *International Journal of Science Education, 14*, 25–40.

Suppes, P., & Groen, G. J. (1967). Some counting models for first grade performance data on simple addition facts. In J. M. Scandura (Ed.), *Research in mathematics education* (pp. 34–43). Washington, DC: National Council of Teachers of Mathematics.

Sutman, F. (1992). Science content errors: An issue of immediate concern. *Journal of Research in Science Teaching, 29*, 437–439.

Sutton, R. E. (1991). Equity and computers in schools: A decade of research. *Review of Educational Research, 61*, 475–504.

Svenson, O., & Hedonborg, M-L. (1979). Strategies used by children when solving simple subtractions. *Acta Psychologica, 43*, 477–489.

Swanson, H. L. (1989). Verbal coding deficits in learning-disabled readers. A multiple stage model. *Educational Psychology Review, 1*, 235–277.

Swanson, H. L. (1990). Influence of metacognitive knowledge and aptitude on problem solving. *Journal of Educational Psychology, 82*, 306–314.

Swanson, H. L. (1992). Generality and modifiability of working memory among skilled and less skilled readers. *Journal of Educational Psychology, 84*, 473–488.

Swanson, H. L., & Cooney, J. B. (1991). Learning disabilities and memory. In B. Y. L. Wong (Ed.), *Learning about learning disabilities* (pp. 104–127). San Diego: Academic Press.

Swanson, H. L., O'Connor, J. E., & Cooney, J. B. (1990). An information processing analysis of expert and novice teachers' problem solving. *American Educational Research Journal, 27*, 533–556.

Sweller, J. (1988). Cognitive load during problem solving: Effects on learning. *Cognitive Science, 12*, 257–285.

Sweller, J. (1989). Cognitive technology: Some procedures for facilitating learning and problem solving in mathematics and science. *Journal of Educational Psychology, 81*, 457–466.

Sweller, J., & Cooper, G. A. (1985). The use of worked examples as a substitute for problem solving in learning algebra. *Cognition and Instruction, 2*, 59–89.

Sweller, J., & Levine, M. (1982). Effects of goal specificity on means-ends analysis and learning. *Journal of Experimental Psychology: Learning, Memory, and Cognition, 8*, 463–474.

Sweller, J., Mawer, R., & Ward, M. (1983). Development of expertise in mathematical problem solving. *Journal of Experimental Psychology: General, 112*, 639–661.

Swiatek, M. A., & Benbow, C. P. (1991). A 10-year longitudinal follow-up of participants in a fast-paced mathematics course. *Journal for Research in Mathematics Education, 22*, 138–150.

Swing, S. R., Stoiber, K. C., & Peterson, P. L. (1988). Thinking skills versus learning time: Effects of alternative classroom-based interventions on students' mathematics problem solving. *Cognition and Instruction, 5*, 123–191.

Symons, S., & Pressley, M. (1992). *Evaluation of Guthrie's model of search in a text domain.* Manuscript submitted for publication consideration. Wolfville, NS: Acadia University, Department of Psychology.

Symons, S., & Pressly, M. (1993). Prior knowledge affects text search success and extraction of information. *Reading Research Quarterly, 28*, 250–261.

Szetala, W., & Nicol, C. (1992). Evaluating problem solving in mathematics. *Educational Leadership, 49* (8), 42–45.

Taber, K. S. (1992). Girls' interactions with teachers in mixed physics classes: Results of classroom observation. *International Journal of Science Education, 14*, 163–180.

Tang, S-H., & Hall, V. C. (1993, August). *Meta-analytic review of overjustification.* Presented at the annual convention of the American Psychological Association, Toronto.

Tangel, D. M., & Blachman, B. A. (1992). Effect of phoneme awareness instruction on kindergarten children's invented spellings. *Journal of Reading Behavior, 24*, 233–261.

Tannen, D. (1990). *You just don't understand: Women and men in conversation.* New York: Morrow.

Tannenbaum, A. J. (1983). *Gifted children: Psychological and educational perspectives.* New York: Macmillan.

Tannenbaum, A. J. (1986). Giftedness: A psychosocial approach. In R. J. Sternberg & J. E. Davidson (Eds.), *Conceptions of giftedness* (pp. 21–52). Cambridge, UK: Cambridge University Press.

Tarmizi, R. A., & Sweller, J. (1988). Guidance during mathematical problem solving. *Journal of Educational Psychology, 80*, 424–436.

Tarver, S. G., Hallahan, D. P., Cohen, S. B., & Kauffman, J. M. (1977). The development of visual selective attention and verbal rehearsal in learning disabled boys. *Journal of Learning Disabilities, 10*, 26–52.

Tarver, S. G., Hallahan, D. P., Kauffman, J. M., & Ball, D. W. (1976). Verbal rehearsal and selective attention in children with learning disabilities: A developmental lag. *Journal of Experimental Child Psychology, 22*, 375–385.

Task Force on Women, Minorities, and the Handicapped in Science and Technology (1989). *Changing America: The new face of science and engineering*. Washington, DC: Task Force on Women, Minorities, and the Handicapped in Science and Technology.

Tatarsky, J. H. (1974). The influence of dimensional manipulations on class-inclusion performance. *Child Development, 45,* 1173–1175.

Tate, B. G. (1972). Case study: Control of chronic self-injurious behavior by conditioning procedures. *Behavior Therapy, 3,* 72–83.

Taub, H. A. (1974). Coding for short-term memory as a function of age. *Journal of Genetic Psychology, 125,* 309–314.

Taylor, A. M., & Turnure, J. E. (1979). Imagery and verbal elaboration with retarded children: Effects on learning and memory. In N. R. Ellis (Ed.), *Handbook of mental deficiency: Psychological theory and research* (pp. 659–697). Hillsdale, NJ: Erlbaum & Associates.

Taylor, B. M. (1982). Text structure and children's comprehension and memory for expository material. *Journal of Educational Psychology, 74,* 323–340.

Taylor, B. M., & Beach, R. W. (1984). The effects of text structure instruction on middle-grade students' comprehension and production of expository text. *Reading Research Quarterly, 19,* 134–146.

Taylor, B. M., Frye, B. J., & Maruyama, G. M. (1990). Time spent reading and reading growth. *American Educational Research Journal, 27,* 351–362.

Taylor, D., & Strickland, D. (1986). *Family storybook reading*. Exeter, NH: Heinemann Educational Books.

Taylor, J. L., & Chiogioji, E. N. (1988). The Holland and Andre study on extracurricular activities: Imbalanced and incomplete. *Review of Educational Research, 58,* 99–105.

Taylor, M. C. (1989). Adult basic education. In S. B. Merriam & P. M. Cunningham (Eds.), *Handbook of adult and continuing education* (pp. 465–477). San Francisco: Jossey-Bass.

Teale, W. (1978). Positive environments for learning to read: What studies of early readers tell us. *Language Arts, 55,* 922–932.

Terman, L. M. (1925). *Genetic studies of genius, mental and physical traits of a thousand gifted children*. Stanford, CA: Stanford University Press.

Terman, L. M., & Childs, H. G. (1912). A tentative revision and extension of the Binet-Simon Measuring Scale of Intelligence. *Journal of Educational Psychology, 3,* 61–74, 133–143, 198–208, 277–289.

Terman, L. M., & Oden, M. H. (1947). *The gifted child grows up: Twenty-five years' followup of a superior group*. Stanford, CA: Stanford University Press.

Terman, L. M., & Oden, M. H. (1959). *The gifted group in midlife: Thirty years followup of the superior child*. Stanford, CA: Stanford University Press.

Thase, M. E. (1988). The relationship between Down Syndrome and Alzheimer's disease. In L. Nadel (Ed.), *The psychobiology of Down syndrome* (pp. 345–368). Cambridge, MA: MIT Press.

Thimmesch, N. (1984). *Aliteracy: People who can read but won't*. Washington, DC: American Institute for Public Policy Research.

Thoman, E. B., & Ingersoll, E. W. (1993). Learning in premature infants. *Developmental Psychology, 29,* 692–700.

Thomas, E. (1990). Filial piety, social change and Singapore youth. *Journal of Moral Education, 19,* 192–206.

Thomas, M. H., & Dieter, J. N. (1987). The positive effect of writing practice on integration of foreign words in memory. *Journal of Educational Psychology, 79,* 249–253.

Thompson, L. A., Fagan, J. F., & Fulker, D. W. (1991). Longitudinal prediction of specific cognitive abilities from infant novelty preference. *Child Development, 62,* 530–538.

Thoreson, C. E. (Ed.) (1972). *Behavior modification in education: The seventy-second yearbook of the National Society for the Study of Education*, Part 1. Chicago: University of Chicago Press.

Thorkildsen, T. A. (1989). Justice in the classroom: The student's view. *Child Development, 60,* 323–334.

Thorkildsen, T. A. (1991). Defining social goods and distributing them fairly: The development of conceptions of fair testing practices. *Child Development, 62,* 852–863.

Thorkildsen, T. A. (1993). Those who can, tutor: High-ability students' conceptions of fair ways to organize learning. *Journal of Educational Psychology, 85,* 182–190.

Thorndike, R. L., Hagen, E. P., & Sattler, J. M. (1986). *Stanford-Binet intelligence scale: Technical manual,* 4th ed. Chicago: Riverside Press.

Thurstone, L. L. (1938). Primary mental abilities. *Psychometric Monographs,* No. 1. Chicago: University of Chicago Press.

Thurstone, L. L. (1947). *Multiple factor analysis*. Chicago: University of Chicago Press.

Tierney, R. J., LaZansky, J., Raphael, T., & Cohen, P. (1987). Author's intentions and readers' interpretation. In R. J. Tierney, P. L. Anders, & J. N. Mitchell (Eds.), *Understanding readers' understanding* (pp. 205–224). Hillsdale, NJ: Erlbaum & Associates.

Tierney, R. J., Soter, A., O'Flahaven, J. F., & McGinley, W. (1989). The effects of reading and writing upon thinking critically. *Reading Research Quarterly, 24,* 134–173.

Tikhomirov, O. K., & Klochko, V. E. (1981). The detections of contradiction as the initial stage of problem formation. In J. V. Wertsch (Ed.), *The concept of activity in Soviet psychology* (pp. 341–382). Armonk, NY: M. E. Sharpe.

Tingle, J. B., & Good, R. (1990). Effects of cooperative grouping on stoichiometric problem solving in high school chemistry. *Journal of Research in Science Teaching, 27,* 671–683.

Tipper, S. P., Bourque, T. A., Anderson, S. H., & Brehaut, J. C. (1989). Mechanisms of attention: A developmental study. *Journal of Experimental Child Psychology, 48,* 353–378.

Tippett, L. J. (1992). The generation of visual images: A review of neuropsychological research and theory. *Psychological Bulletin, 112,* 415–432.

Tirosh, D., & Graeber, A. O. (1990). Evoking cognitive conflict to explore preservice teachers' thinking about division. *Journal for Research in Mathematics Education, 21,* 98–108.

Titmus, C. J. (Ed.) (1989). *Lifelong education for adults: An international handbook*. Oxford, UK: Pergamon Press.

Tobias, S. (1979). Anxiety research in educational psychology. *Journal of Educational Psychology, 71,* 573–582.

Tobias, S. (1985). Test anxiety: Interference, defective skills, and cognitive capacity. *Educational Psychologist, 20,* 135–142.

Tobias, S. (1987). Mandatory text review and interaction with student characteristics. *Journal of Educational Psychology, 79,* 154–161.

Tobin, K. (1987). The role of wait time in higher cognitive level learning. *Review of Educational Research, 57,* 69–95.

Tobin, K., & Fraser, B. J. (1990). What does it mean to be an exemplary science teacher? *Journal of Research in Science Teaching, 27,* 3–25.

Todorov, T. (1984). *Mikhail Bakhtin: The dialogical principle*. Minneapolis: University of Minnesota Press.

Tomchin, E. M., & Impara, J. C. (1992). Unraveling teachers' beliefs about grade retention. *American Educational Research Journal, 29,* 199–223.

Tomlinson-Keasey, C. (1990). Developing our intellectual resources for the 21st century: Educating the gifted. *Journal of Educational Psychology, 82,* 399–403.

Tomlinson-Keasey, C., & Little, T. D. (1990). Predicting educational attainment, occupational achievement, intellectual skill, and personal adjustment among gifted men and women. *Journal of Educational Psychology, 82,* 442–455.

Tomporowski, P. D., & Simpson, R. G. (1990). Sustained attention and intelligence. *Intelligence, 14,* 31–42.

Toppino, T. C., Kasserman, J. E., & Mracek, W. A. (1991). The effect of spacing repetitions on the recognition memory of young children and adults. *Journal of Experimental Child Psychology, 51,* 123–138.

Torgesen, J. K. (1975). Problems and prospects in the study of learning disabilities. In M. Hetherington & J. Hagen (Eds.), *Review of research in child development,* Vol. 5. Chicago: University of Chicago Press.

Torgesen, J. K. (1977). Memorization processes in reading-disabled children. *Journal of Educational Psychology, 69,* 571–578.

Torgesen, J. K. (1979). What shall we do with psychological processes? *Journal of Learning Disabilities, 12,* 16–23.

Torgesen, J. K. (1980). Conceptual and educational implications of the use of efficient task strategies by learning disabled children. *Journal of Learning Disabilities, 13,* 364–371.

Torgesen, J. K. (1986). Computers and cognition in reading: A focus on decoding fluency. *Exceptional Children, 53,* 157–162.

Torgesen, J. K. (1991). Learning disabilities:

Historical and conceptual issues. In B. Y. L. Wong (Ed.), *Learning about learning disabilities* (pp. 3–37). San Diego: Academic Press.

Torgesen, J. K., Foster, D. F., & Foster, K. C. (1992, April). *Computer-based instruction in phonological awareness: Evaluation of the Daisy Quest program.* Presented at the annual meeting of the American Educational Research Association, San Francisco.

Torgesen, J. K., & Goldman, T. (1977). Verbal rehearsal and short-term memory in reading disabled children. *Child Development, 48,* 56–60.

Torgesen, J. K., & Houck, D. O. (1980). Processing deficiencies of learning disabled children who perform poorly on the digit span test. *Journal of Educational Psychology, 72,* 141–160.

Torgesen, J. K., Kistner, J. A., & Morgan, S. (1987). Component processes in working memory. In J. G. Borkowski & J. D. Day (Eds.), *Cognition in special children: Comparative approaches to retardation, learning disabilities, and giftedness* (pp. 49–85). Norwood, NJ: Ablex.

Torgesen, J. K., & Morgan, S. (1992, April). *Effects of two types of phonological awareness training on word learning in kindergarten children.* Presented at the annual meeting of the American Educational Research Association, San Francisco.

Torgesen, J. K., Morgan, S. T., & Davis, C. (1992). Effects of two types of phonological awareness training on word learning in kindergarten children. *Journal of Educational Psychology, 84,* 364–370.

Townsend, M. A. R. (1989). Facilitating children's comprehension through the use of advance organizers. *Journal of Reading Behavior, 21,* 15–35.

Treagust, D. F. (1991). A case study of two exemplary biology teachers. *Journal of Research in Science Teaching, 28,* 329–342.

Treiman, R. A., & Baron, J. (1981). Segmental analysis ability: Development and relation to reading ability. In G. E. MacKinnon & R. G. Walker (Eds.), *Reading research: Advances in theory and practice,* Vol. 3. San Diego: Academic Press.

Treiman, R., & Baron, J. (1983). Phonemic-analysis training helps children benefit from spelling-sound rules. *Memory and Cognition, 11,* 382–389.

Tryon, R. M. (1927). Standard and new type tests in the social studies. *The Historical Outlook, 18,* 172–178.

Tudge, J. R. H. (1992). Processes and consequences of peer collaboration: A Vygotskian analysis. *Child Development, 63,* 1364–1379.

Tulving, E. (1972). Episodic and semantic memory. In E. Tulving & W. Donaldson (Eds.), *Organization of memory* (pp. 381–403). New York: Academic Press.

Tulving, E. (1983). *Elements of episodic memory.* Oxford, UK: Oxford University Press.

Tunmer, W. E., Herriman, M. L., Nesdale, A. R. (1988). Metalinguistic abilities and beginning reading. *Reading Research Quarterly, 23,* 134–158.

Turnbull, W. W. (1985). *Student change, program change: Why the SAT scores kept falling.* New York: College Entrance Examination Board.

Tyler, R., & Smith, E. (1942). *Appraising and recording student progress.* New York: Harper & Brothers.

Tzuriel, D. (1992). The development of ego identity at adolescence among Israeli Jews and Arabs. *Journal of Youth and Adolescence, 21,* 551–571.

Tzuriel, D., & Feurstein, R. (1992). Dynamic group assessment for prescriptive teaching: Differential effects of treatment. In H. C. Haywood & D. Tzuriel (Eds.), *Interactive assessment* (pp. 187–206). New York: Springer-Verlag.

Tzuriel, D., & Haywood, H. C. (1992). The development of interactive-dynamic approaches to assessment of learning potential. In H. C. Haywood & D. Tzuriel (Eds.), *Interactive assessment* (pp. 3–37). New York: Springer-Verlag.

Ulrich, R., Wolfe, M., & Bluhm, M. (1970). Operant conditioning in the public schools. In R. Ulrich, T. Stachnik, & J. Mabry (Eds.), *Control of human behavior: From cure to prevention* (pp. 334–343). Glenview, IL: Scott, Foresman and Company.

Underwood, B. J. (1966). *Experimental psychology.* New York: Appleton-Century-Crofts.

Underwood, B. J. (1969). Attributes of memory. *Psychological Review, 76,* 559–573.

Underwood, B. J. (1975). Individual differences as a crucible in theory construction. *American Psychologist, 30,* 128–134.

United States of America v. State of South Carolina, 434 U.S. 1026 (1978).

U.S. Department of Education, National Commission on Excellence in Education (1983). *A nation at risk: The imperative for education reform.* Washington, DC: Government Printing Office.

Utley, C. A., Haywood, H. C., & Masters, J. C. (1992). Policy implications of psychological assessment of minority children. In H. C. Haywood & D. Tzuriel (Eds.), *Interactive assessment* (pp. 445–469). New York: Springer-Verlag.

Valdez-Menchaca, M. C., & Whitehurst, G. J. (1992). Accelerating language development through picture book reading: A systematic extension to Mexican day care. *Developmental Psychology, 28,* 1106–1114.

Van der Meer, R., & Valsiner, J. (1988). Lev Vygotsky and Pierre Janet: On the origin of the concept of sociogenesis. *Developmental Review, 8,* 52–65.

van der Meij, H. (1988). Constraints on question asking in classrooms. *Journal of Educational Psychology, 80,* 401–405.

van Dijk, T. A., & Kintsch, W. (1983). *Strategies of discourse comprehension.* New York: Academic Press.

Van Haneghan, J. P. (1990). Third and fifth graders' use of multiple standards of evalua-

tion to detect errors in word problems. *Journal of Educational Psychology, 82,* 352–358.

Van Haneghan, J. P., & Baker, L. (1989). Cognitive monitoring in mathematics. In C. B. McCormick, G. Miller, & M. Pressley (Eds.), *Cognitive strategy research: From basic research to educational applications* (pp. 215–238). New York: Springer-Verlag.

Van Haneghan, J., Barron, L., Young, M., Williams, S., Vye, N., & Bransford, J. (1992). The Jasper series: An experiment with new ways to enhance mathematical thinking. In D. F. Halpern (Ed.), *Enhancing thinking skills in the sciences and mathematics* (pp. 15–38). Hillsdale, NJ: Erlbaum & Associates.

Van Houten, R., & Rolider, A. (1989). An analysis of several variables influencing the efficacy of flash card instruction. *Journal of Applied Behavior Analysis, 22,* 111–118.

van Lehn, K. (1990). *Mind bugs: The origins of procedural misconceptions.* Cambridge, MA: MIT Press.

Van Meter, P., Yokoi, L., & Pressley, M. (1994). College students' (theory of notetaking from their perceptions of notetaking). *Journal of Educational Psychology, 86,* 323–338.

Vasu, E. S., & Howe, A. C. (1989). The effect of visual and verbal modes of presentation on children's retention of images and words. *Journal of Research in Science Teaching, 26,* 401–407.

Vellutino, F. R. (1979). *Dyslexia: Theory and research.* Cambridge, MA: MIT Press.

Venezky, R. L., & Johnson, D. (1973). The development of two letter-sound patterns in grade 1–3. *Journal of Educational Psychology, 64,* 109–115.

Verhoeven, L. T. (1990). Acquisition of reading in a second language. *Reading Research Quarterly, 25,* 90–114.

Vernon, P. A. (1983). Speed of information processing and intelligence. *Intelligence, 7,* 53–70.

Vernon, P. A. (1985). Individual differences in general cognitive ability. In L. C. Hartlage & C. F. Telzrow (Eds.), *The neuropsychology of individual differences.* New York: Plenum.

Vernon, P. A. (1987). New developments in reaction time research. In P. A. Vernon (Ed.), *Speed of information processing and intelligence* (pp. 1–20). Norwood, NJ: Ablex.

Vernon, P. A. (1990a). An overview of chronometric measures of intelligence. *School Psychology Review, 19,* 309–410.

Vernon, P. A. (1990b). The use of biological measures to estimate behavioral intelligence. *Educational Psychologist, 25,* 293–304.

Vernon, P. A. (1991). Studying intelligence the hard way. *Intelligence, 15,* 389–395.

Visalberghi, E., & Fragaszy, D. M. (1990). Do monkeys ape? In S. T. Parker & K. R. Gibson (Eds.), *"Language" and intelligence in monkeys and apes: Comparative developmental perspectives* (pp. 247–273). Cambridge, England: Cambridge University Press.

Vosniadou, S., & Schommer, M. (1988). Explanatory analogies can help children acquire information from expository text. *Journal of Educational Psychology, 80*, 524–536.

Voss, J. F. (1991). Informal reasoning and international relations. In J. F. Voss, D. N. Perkins, & J. W. Segal (Eds.), *Informal reasoning and education* (pp. 37–58). Hillsdale, NJ: Erlbaum & Associates.

Voss, J. F., Blais, J. Menas, M. L., Greene, T. R., & Ahwesh, E. (1989). Informal reasoning and subject matter knowledge in the solving of economics problems by naive and novice individuals. In L. B. Resnick (Ed.), *Knowing, learning, and instruction: Essays in honor of Robert Glaser* (pp. 217–249). Hillsdale, NJ: Erlbaum & Associates.

Voss, J. F., Greene, T. R., Post, T. A., & Penner, B. C. (1983). Problem-solving skill in the social sciences. In G. H. Bower (Ed.), *The psychology of learning and motivation: Advances in research and theory*, Vol. 17 (pp. 165–213). New York: Academic Press.

Voss, J. F., Vesonder, G. T., & Spilich, G. J. (1980). Generation and recall by high-knowledge and low-knowledge individuals. *Journal of Verbal Learning and Verbal Behavior, 19*, 651–667.

Vurpillot, E. (1968). The development of scanning strategies and their relations to visual differentiation. *Journal of Experimental Child Psychology, 6*, 632–650.

Vygotsky, L. S. (1962). *Thought and language.* Cambridge, MA: MIT Press.

Vygotsky, L. S. (1978). *Mind in society: The development of higher psychological processes.* Cambridge, MA: Harvard University Press.

Vygotsky, L. S. (1981). The genesis of higher mental functions. In J. V. Wertsch (Ed.), *The concept of activity in Soviet psychology* (pp. 144–188). Armonk, NY: M.E. Sharpe.

Vygotsky, L. S. (1987). *Thinking and speech* (Edited & Translated by N. Minick). New York: Plenum.

Waddill, P. J., McDaniel, M. A., & Einstein, G. O. (1988). Illustrations as adjuncts to prose: A text-appropriate processing approach. *Journal of Educational Psychology, 80*, 457–464.

Wade, S. E., & Adams, R. B. (1990). Effects of importance and interest on recall of biographic text. *Journal of Reading Behavior, 22*, 331–353.

Wade, S. E., Schraw, G., Buxton, W. M., & Hayes, M. T. (1993). Seduction of the strategic reader: Effects of interest on strategies and recall. *Reading Research Quarterly, 28*, 93–114.

Wade, S. E., Trathen, W., & Schraw, G. (1990). An analysis of spontaneous study strategies. *Reading Research Quarterly, 25*, 147–166.

Wagenaar, W. A. (1986). My memory: A study of autobiographic memory over six years. *Cognitive Psychology, 18*, 225–252.

Wagner, D. A. (1974). The development of short-term and incidental memory: A cross-cultural study. *Child Development, 45*, 389–396.

Wagner, D. A. (1978). Memories of Morocco: The influence of age, schooling, and environment on memory. *Cognitive Psychology, 10*, 1–28.

Wagner, D. A., & Spratt, J. E. (1987). Cognitive consequences of contrasting pedagogies: The effects of Quranic preschooling in Morocco. *Child Development, 58*, 1207–1219.

Walberg, H. J. (1991). Improving school science in advanced and developing countries. *Review of Educational Research, 61*, 25–69.

Walberg, H. J., Harnisch, D., & Tsai, S. L. (1986). Elementary school mathematics productivity in twelve countries. *British Educational Research Journal, 12*, 237–248.

Walczyk, J. J. (1990). Relation among error detection, sentence verification, and low-level reading skills of fourth graders. *Journal of Educational Psychology, 82*, 491–497.

Walczyk, J. J. (1993). Are general resource notions still viable in reading research? *Journal of Educational Psychology, 85*, 127–135.

Walczyk, J. J., & Hall, V. C. (1989). Is the failure to monitor comprehension an instance of cognitive impulsivity? *Journal of Educational Psychology, 81*, 294–298.

Walford, G. (1983). Science education and sexism in the Soviet Union. *School Science Review, 65*, 213–224.

Walk, R. D., & Gibson, E. J. (1961). A comparative and analytical study of visual depth perception. *Psychological Monographs*, No. 519, *75*, No. 15.

Walker, B. J., & Wilson, P. T. (1991). Using guided imagery to teach science concepts. In C. M. Santa & D. E. Alvermann (Eds.), *Science learning: Processes and applications* (pp. 147–155). Newark, DE: International Reading Association.

Walker, C. H. (1987). Relative importance of domain knowledge and overall aptitude on acquisition of domain-related information. *Cognition and Instruction, 4*, 25–42.

Walker, L. (1984). Sex differences in the development of moral reasoning: A critical review. *Child Development, 55*, 677–691.

Walker, L. J. (1989). A longitudinal study of moral reasoning. *Child Development, 60*, 157–166.

Walker, L. J., & Moran, T. J. (1991). Moral reasoning in a communist Chinese society. *Journal of Moral Education, 20*, 139–155.

Walmsley, S. A., & Walp, T. P. (1990). Integrating literature and composing into the language arts curriculum: Philosophy and practice. *Elementary School Journal, 90*, 251–274.

Walters, G. C., & Grusec, J. E. (1977). *Punishment.* San Francisco: W.H. Freeman & Co.

Wandersee, J. H. (1988). Ways students read texts. *Journal of Research in Science Teaching, 25*, 69–84.

Wanner, E. (1975). *On remembering, forgetting, and understanding sentences.* The Hague: Mouton.

Ward, M., & Sweller, J. (1990). Structuring effective worked examples. *Cognition and Instruction, 7*, 1–39.

Ward, T. B., Vela, E., & Hass, S. D. (1990). Children and adults learn family-resemblance categories analytically. *Child Development, 61*, 593–605.

Washington v. Davis, 426 U. S. 229 (1976).

Wasik, B. H., Ramey, C. T., Bryant, D. M., & Sparling, J. J. (1990). A longitudinal study of two early intervention strategies: Project CARE. *Child Development, 61*, 1682–1696.

Wasik, B. A., & Slavin, R. E. (1993). Preventing early reading failure with one-to-one tutoring: A review of five programs. *Reading Research Quarterly, 28*, 178–200.

Waterman, A., & Goldman, J. (1976). A longitudinal study of ego identity development in a liberal arts college. *Journal of Youth and Adolescence, 5*, 361–369.

Watson, B. (1991). Tom Swift, Nancy Drew and pals all had the same dad. *Smithsonian, 22* (7), 50–61.

Watson, D. J. (1989). Defining and describing whole language. *Elementary School Journal, 90*, 129–141.

Watson, J. F. (1830). *Annals of Philadelphia, being a collection of memoirs, anecdotes, and incidents of the city and its inhabitants from the days of the Pilgrim founders.* Philadelphia: E.L. Carey & A. Hart. (Also, New York: G. & C.H. Carvill.)

Weaver, C. (1990). *Understanding whole language: From principles to practice.* Portsmouth, NH: Heinemann.

Weaver, C. A., III, & Kintsch, W. (1991). Expository text. In R. Barr, M. L. Kamil, P. B. Mosenthal, & P. D. Pearson (Eds.), *Handbook of reading research*, Vol. II (pp. 230–245). New York: Longmans.

Weaver, C. A., III, & Kintsch, W. (1992). Enhancing students' comprehension of the conceptual structure of algebra word problems. *Journal of Educational Psychology, 84*, 419–428.

Webb, N. L. (1992). Assessment of students' knowledge of mathematics: Steps toward a theory. In D. A. Grouws (Ed.), *Handbook of research on mathematics teaching and learning* (pp. 661–683). New York: Macmillan.

Webb, N. M. (1984). Sex differences in interaction and achievement in cooperative small groups. *Journal of Educational Psychology, 76*, 33–34.

Webb, N. M. (1989). Peer interaction and learning in small groups. *International Journal of Educational Research, 13*, 21–39.

Webb, N. M. (1991). Task-related verbal interaction and mathematics learning in small groups. *Journal for Research in Mathematics Education, 22*, 366–389.

Webb, N. M., & Kenderski, C. M. (1985). Gender differences in small-group interaction and achievement in high- and low-achieving classes. In L. C. Wilkinson & C. B. Marrett (Eds.), *Gender influences on classroom interaction* (pp. 209–236). Orlando, FL: Academic Press.

Wechsler, D. (1939). *The measurement of adult intelligence.* Baltimore: Williams & Wilkins.

Wechsler, D. (1949). *Manual for the Wechsler intelligence scale for children.* San Antonio, TX: Psychological Corporation.

Wechsler, D. (1955). *Manual for the Wechsler Adult Intelligence Scale.* New York: Psychological Corporation.

Wechsler, D. (1967). *A manual for the preschool*

and primary scale of intelligence. San Antonio, TX: Psychological Corporation.

Wechsler, D. (1981). *WAIS-R: Wechsler Adult Intelligence Scale–Revised.* New York: Psychological Corporation.

Weed, K., Ryan, E. B., & Day, J. (1990). Metamemory and attributions as mediators of strategy use and recall. *Journal of Educational Psychology, 82,* 849–855.

Wegner, D. M. (1987). Transactive memory: A contemporary analysis of the group mind. In B. Mullen & G. Goethals (Eds.), *Theories of group behavior* (pp. 185–208). New York: Springer-Verlag.

Wehlage, G. G. (1986). At-risk students and the need for high school reform. *Education, 107,* 18–28.

Weiderholt, J. L. (1974). Historical perspectives on the education of the learning disabled. In L. Mann & D. Sabatino (Eds.), *The second review of special education* (pp. 103–152). Philadelphia: JSE Press.

Weinberg, R. A., Scarr, S., & Waldman, I. D. (1992). The Minnesota transracial adoption study: A followup of IQ test performance at adolescence. *Intelligence, 16,* 117–135.

Weinberg, R. S. (1982). The relationship between mental preparation strategies and motor performance: A review and critique. *Quest, 33* (2), 195–213.

Weiner, B. (1979). A theory of motivation for some classroom experiences. *Journal of Educational Psychology, 71,* 3–25.

Weiner, B. (1990). History of motivational research in education. *Journal of Educational Psychology, 82,* 616–622.

Weinert, F. E., Knopf, M., Körkel, J., Schneider, W., Vogel, K., & Wetzel, M. (1984). Die Entwicklung einiger Gedächtnisleistungen bei kindern und älternen Erwach senen in Abhängigkeit von kognitiven, meta kognitiven und motivationalen Einflussfaktoren. In K. E. Grossman & P. Lütkenhavs (Eds.), *Bericht über die sechste Tagung Entwicklungpsychologie* (pp. 313–326). Regensburg FRG: Universitäts-Druckerei.

Weinert, F. E., Schneider, W., & Knopf, M. (1988). Individual differences in memory development across the life-span. In P. B. Baltes, D. L. Featherman, & R. M. Lerner (Eds.), *Life-span development and behavior,* Vol. 9 (pp. 39–85). Hillsdale, NJ: Erlbaum & Associates.

Weinstein, C. F., & Mayer, R. F. (1986). The teaching of learning strategies. In M. C. Wittrock (Ed.), *Handbook of research on teaching,* 3rd ed. (pp. 315–327). New York: Macmillan.

Weinstein, R. S. (1976). Reading group membership in first grade: Teacher behaviors and pupil experience over time. *Journal of Educational Psychology, 68,* 103–116.

Weizenbaum, J. (1976). *Computer power and human reason: From judgment to calculation.* San Francisco: Freeman.

Welsh, M. C., Pennington, B. F., Ozonoff, S., Rouse, B., & McCabe, E. R. B. (1990). Neuropsychology of early-treated phenylketonuria: Specific executive function deficits. *Child Development, 61,* 1697–1713.

Wentzel, K. R. (1991a). Relations between social competence and academic achievement in early adolescence. *Child Development, 62,* 1966–1078.

Wentzel, K. R. (1991b). Social competence at school: Relation between social responsibility and academic achievement. *Review of Educational Research, 61,* 1–24.

Wentzel, K. R. (1993). Does being good make the grade? Social behavior and academic competence in middle school. *Journal of Educational Psychology, 85,* 357–364.

Werner, E. E. (1990). Protective factors and individual resilience. In S. J. Meisels & J. P. Shonkoff (Eds.), *Handbook of early childhood interventions* (pp. 97–116). Cambridge, UK: Cambridge University Press.

Werner, E. E., Bierman, J. M., & French, F. E. (1971). *The children of Kauai.* Honolulu: University of Hawaii Press.

Werner, E. E., & Smith, R. S. (1982). *Vulnerable but invincible: A longitudinal study of resilient children and youth.* New York: McGraw-Hill.

Wertsch, J. V. (1979). From social interaction to higher psychological processes: A clarification and application of Vygotsky's theory. *Human Development, 22,* 1–22.

Wertsch, J. V. (Ed.) (1981). *The concept of activity in Soviet psychology.* Armonk, NY: M. E. Sharpe.

Wertsch, J. V. (1985). *Vygotsky and the social formation of mind.* Cambridge, MA: Harvard University Press.

Wertsch, J. V. (1991). *Voices of the mind.* Cambridge, MA: Harvard University Press.

Wertsch, J. V., & Minick, N. J. (1990). Negotiating sense in the zone of proximal development. In M. Schwebel, C. A. Maher, & N. S. Fagley (Eds.), *Promoting cognitive growth over the life span* (pp. 71–88). Hillsdale, NJ: Erlbaum & Associates.

Wheelock, A. (1992). *Crossing the tracks: How "untracking" can save America's schools.* New York: New Press, Norton.

White, B. Y. (1984). Designing computer games to help physics students understand Newton's laws of motion. *Cognition and Instruction, 1,* 69–108.

White, M. (1987). *The Japanese educational challenge: A commitment to children.* New York: Free Press.

White, R. W. (1959). Motivation reconsidered: The concept of competence. *Psychological Review, 66,* 297–333.

Whitehead, A. (1929). *The aims of education.* New York: Macmillan.

Whitehurst, G. J., Falco, F. L., Lonigan, C. J., Fischel, J. E., DeBaryshe, B. D., Valdez-Menchaca, M. C., & Caulfield, M. (1988). Accelerating language development through picturebook reading. *Developmental Psychology, 24,* 552–559.

Whitehurst, G. J., & Valdez-Menchaca, M. C. (1988). What is the role of reinforcement in early language acquisition? *Child Development, 59,* 430–440.

Whitehurst, G. J., & Vasta, R. (1975). Is language acquired through imitation? *Journal of Psycholinguistic Research, 4,* 37–59.

Whitehurst, G. J., & Zimmerman, B. J. (Eds.). (1979). *The function of language and cognition.* New York: Academic Press.

Whitley, B. E. Jr., McHugh, M. C., & Frieze, I. H. (1986). Assessing the theoretical models for sex differences in causal attributions of success and failure. In J. S. Hyde & M. C. Linn (Eds.), *The psychology of gender: Advances through meta-analysis* (pp. 67–101). Baltimore: Johns Hopkins Press.

Whitman, T. L. (1990). Self-regulation and mental retardation. *American Journal on Mental Retardation, 94,* 347–362.

Whittington, D. (1991). What have 17-year-olds known in the past? *American Educational Research Journal, 28,* 759–780.

Widaman, K. F., Geary, D. C., Cormier, P., & Little, T. D. (1989). A componential model for mental addition. *Journal of Experimental Psychology: Learning, Memory, and Cognition, 15,* 898–919.

Widaman, K. F., Little, T. D., Geary, D. C., & Cormier, P. (1992). Individual differences in the development of skill in mental addition: Internal and external validation of chronometric methods. *Learning and Individual Differences, 4,* 167–214.

Wierda, M., & Brookhuis, K. A. (1991). Analysis of cycling skill: A cognitive approach. *Applied Cognitive Psychology, 5,* 113–122.

Wigfield, A. (1988). Children's attributions for success and failure: Effects of age and attentional focus. *Journal of Educational Psychology, 80,* 76–81.

Wigfield, A., Eccles, J. S., MacIver, D., Reuman, D. A., & Midgley, C. (1991). Transitions during early adolescence: Changes in children's domain-specific self-perceptions and general self-esteem across the transition to junior high school. *Developmental Psychology, 27,* 552–565.

Wigfield, A., & Karpathian, M. (1991). Who am I and what can I do? Children's self-concepts and motivation in achievement situations. *Educational Psychologist 26,* 233–262.

Wilhite, S. C. (1989). Headings as memory facilitators: The importance of prior knowledge. *Journal of Educational Psychology, 81,* 115–117.

Wilkinson, L. C., & Marrett, C. B. (Eds.). *Gender influences on classroom interaction.* Orlando: Academic Press.

Willerman, L., Schultz, R., Rutledge, J. N., & Bigler, E. D. (1991). *In vivo* brain size and intelligence. *Intelligence, 15,* 223–228.

Willerman, M., & MacHarg, R. A. (1991). The concept map as an advance organizer. *Journal of Research in Science Teaching, 28,* 705–711.

Williams, J. P. (1980). Teaching decoding with an emphasis on phoneme analysis and phoneme blending. *Journal of Educational Psychology, 72,* 1–15.

Williams, J. P. (1991, November). *Comprehension of learning disabled and nondisabled students: Identification of narrative themes and idiosyncratic text representation.* Presented at the annual meeting of the National Reading Conference, Austin, TX.

Williams, R. L. (1972, September). *The BITCH-100: A culture-specific test.* Paper presented at the meeting of the American Psychological Association, Honolulu.

Williams, T. M. (Ed.) (1986). *The impact of television: A natural experiment in three communities.* New York: Academic Press.

Willis, S. L. (1985). Towards an educational psychology of the older adult learner: Intellectual and cognitive bases. In J. E. Birren & K. W. Schaie (Eds.), *Handbook of the psychology of aging* (pp. 818–847). New York: Van Nostrand Reinhold Company.

Willis, S., & Kenway, J. (1986). On overcoming sexism in schooling to marginalize or mainstream. *Australian Journal of Education, 30,* 132–149.

Willis, W. G., Hooper, S. R., & Stone, B. H. (1992). Neuropsychological theories of learning disabilities. In N. H. Singh & I. L. Beale (Eds.), *Learning disabilities: Nature, theory, and treatment* (pp. 201–245). New York: Springer-Verlag.

Wilson, B. A. (1987). *Rehabilitation of memory.* New York: Guilford.

Wilson, S. (1982). Heritability. *Journal of Applied Problems 19,* 71–85.

Wimmer, H., Landerl, K., Linortner, R., & Hummer, P. (1991). The relationship of phonemic awareness to reading acquisition: More consequence than precondition but still important. *Cognition, 40,* 219–249.

Wineberg, S. S. (1991a). Historical problem solving: A study of the cognitive processes used in the evaluation of documentary and pictorial evidence. *Journal of Educational Psychology, 83,* 73–87.

Wineberg, S. S. (1991b). On the reading of historical texts: Notes on the breach between school and academy. *American Educational Research Journal, 28,* 495–520.

Winer, G. A. (1974). An analysis of verbal facilitation of class-inclusion reasoning. *Child Development, 45,* 224–227.

Winer, G. A. (1980). Class-inclusion reasoning in children: A review of the empirical literature. *Child Development, 51,* 309–328.

Wingfield, L., & Haste, H. (1987). Connectedness and separateness: Cognitive style or moral orientation? *Journal of Moral Education, 16,* 214–225.

Winne, P. H., Woodlands, M. H., & Wong, B. Y. L. (1982). Comparability of self-concept among learning disabled, normal, and gifted students. *Journal of Learning Disabilities, 15,* 470–475.

Winter, D., McClelland, D., & Stewart, A. (1981). *A new case for the liberal arts: Assessing institutional goals and student development.* San Francisco: Jossey-Bass.

Wirtz, W. (Chair) (1977). *On further examination: Report of the advisory panel on the Scholastic Aptitude Test score decline.* New York: College Entrance Examination Board.

Wishart, J. G. (1988). Early learning in infants and young children with Down syndrome. In L. Nadel (Ed.), *The psychobiology of Down syndrome* (pp. 7–50). Cambridge, MA: MIT Press.

Wisniewski, K. E., Miezejeski, C. M., & Hill, A. L. (1988). Neurological and psychological sta-

tus of individuals with Down syndrome. In L. Nadel (Ed.), *The psychobiology of Down Syndrome* (pp. 291–343). Cambridge, MA: MIT Press.

Wissler, C. (1901). The correlation of mental and physical tests. *Psychological Review, 3* (Monograph Supplement 16).

Witherell, C. S. (Guest Ed.) (1991). Special issue: Narrative and the moral realm: Tales of caring and justice. *Journal of Moral Education, 20, (3).*

Wittrock, M. C. (1966). The learning by discovery hypothesis. In L. S. Shulman & E. R. Keislar (Eds.), *Learning by discovery: A critical appraisal* (pp. 33–75). Chicago: Rand-McNally.

Wittrock, M. C. (1990). Generative processes of comprehension. *Educational Psychologist, 24,* 345–376.

Wittrock, M. C. (1992). Generative learning processes of the brain. *Educational Psychologist, 27,* 531–542.

Wittrock, M. C., & Alesandrini, K. (1990). Generation of summaries and analogies and analytic and holistic abilities. *American Educational Research Journal, 27,* 489–502.

Wolf, D., Bixby, J., Glenn, J. III, & Gardner, H. (1991). To use their minds well: Investigating new forms of student assessment. In G. Grant (Ed.), *Review of research in education* (pp. 31–74). Washington, DC: American Educational Research Association.

Wolff, P., & Levin, J. R. (1972). The role of overt activity in children's imagery production. *Child Development, 43,* 537–547.

Wolff, P., Levin, J. R., & Longobardi, E. T. (1972). Motoric mediation in children's paired-associate learning: Effects of visual and tactile contact. *Journal of Experimental Child Psychology, 14,* 176–183.

Woloshyn, V. E., Paivio, A. U., & Pressley, M. (1992). Manuscript in preparation. Ste. Catharine's Canada: Brock University, Faculty of Education.

Woloshyn, V. E., Pressley, M., & Schneider, W. (1992). Elaborative interrogation and prior knowledge effects on learning of facts. *Journal of Educational Psychology, 84,* 115–124.

Woloshyn, V. E., Willoughby, T., Wood, E., & Pressley, M. (1990). Elaborative interrogation facilitates adult learning of factual paragraphs. *Journal of Educational Psychology, 82,* 513–524.

Woloshyn, V. E., Wood, E., & Willoughby, T. (1994). Considering prior knowledge when using elaborative interrogation. *Applied Cognitive Psychology, 8,* 25–36.

Wolpe, J. (1958). *Psychotherapy by reciprocal inhibition.* Stanford, CA: Stanford University Press.

Wolpe, J. (1969). *The practice of behavior therapy.* New York: Pergamon.

Wolters, G., Beishuizen, M., Broers, G., & Knoppert, W. (1990). Mental arithmetic: Effects of calculation procedure and problem difficulty on solution latency. *Journal of Experimental Child Psychology, 49,* 20–30.

Wong, E. D. (1991). Beyond the question/non-question alternative in classroom discussion. *Journal of Educational Psychology, 83,* 159–162.

Wood, E., Pressley, M., & Winne, P. H. (1990). Elaborative interrogation effects on children's learning of factual content. *Journal of Educational Psychology, 82,* 741–748.

Wood, R., & Bandura, A. (1989). Impact of conceptions of ability on self-regulatory mechanisms and complex decision-making. *Journal of Personality and Social Psychology, 56,* 407–415.

Wood, S. S., Bruner, J. S., & Ross, G. (1976). The role of tutoring in problem solving. *Journal of Child Psychology and Psychiatry, 17,* 89–100.

Wood, T. (1988). State-mandated accountability as a constraint on teaching and learning science. *Journal of Research in Science Teaching, 25,* 631–641.

Wood, T., Cobb, P., & Yackel, E. (1991). Change in teaching mathematics: A case study. *American Educational Research Journal, 28,* 587–616.

Wood, T. L., & Wood, W. L. (1988). Assessing potential difficulties in comprehending fourth grade science textbooks. *Science Education, 72,* 561–574.

Woodruff-Pak, D. S., Logan, C. G., & Thompson, R. F. (1990). Neurobiological substrates of classical conditioning across the life span. In A. Diamond (Ed.), *The developmental and neural bases of higher cognitive functions* (pp. 150–178). New York: New York Academy of Sciences.

Woods, B. T. (1980). The restricted effects of right hemisphere lesions after age one; Wechsler test data. *Neuropsychologia, 18,* 65–70.

Woods, S. S., Resnick, L. B., & Groen, G. J. (1975). Experimental test of five process models for subtraction. *Journal of Educational Psychology, 67,* 17–21.

Woodward, J., Carnine, D., & Gersten, R. (1988). Teaching problem solving through computer simulations. *American Educational Research Journal, 25,* 72–86.

Worden, P. E. (1983). Memory strategy instruction with the learning disabled. In M. Pressley & J. R. Levin (Eds.), *Cognitive strategy research: Psychological foundations* (pp. 129–153). New York: Springer-Verlag.

Wozniak, R. (1972). Verbal regulation of motor behavior: Soviet research and non-Soviet replications. *Human Development, 15,* 13–57.

Wright, R. E., & Rosenberg, S. (1993). Knowledge of text coherence and expository writing: A developmental study. *Journal of Educational Psychology, 85,* 152–158.

Wyatt, D., Pressley, M., El-Dinary, P. B., Stein, S., Evans, P., & Brown, R. (1992). *Comprehension strategies, worth and credibility monitoring, and evaluations: Cold and hot cognition when experts read professional articles that are important to them.* Technical Report. College Park, MD: University of Maryland, Department of Human Development.

Wyatt, D., Pressley, M., El-Dinary, P. B., Stein, S., Evans, P., & Brown, R. (1993). Comprehension strategies, worth and credibility monitoring, and evaluations: Cold and hot cognition when experts read professional articles that are important to them. *Learning and Individual Differences, 5,* 49–72.

Wyatt, M. (1992). The past, present, and future need for college reading courses in the U.S. *Journal of Reading, 36,* 10–20.

Yackel, E., Cobb, P., & Wood, T. (1991). Small group interactions as a source of learning opportunities in second grade mathematics. *Journal for Research in Mathematics Education, 22,* 390–408.

Yakovlev, P. I., & Lecours, A.-R. (1967). The myelogenetic cycles of regional maturation of the brain. In A. Minkowski (Ed.), *Regional development of the brain in early life* (pp. 3–70). Oxford, UK: Blackwell.

Yarroch, W. L. (1985). Student understanding of chemical equation balancing. *Journal of Research in Science Teaching, 22,* 449–459.

Yates, F. A. (1966). *The art of memory.* London: Routledge & Kegan Paul.

Yekovich, F. R., Thompson, M. A., & Walker, C. H. (1991). Generation and verification of inferences by experts and trained nonexperts. *American Educational Research Journal, 28,* 189–209.

Ylvisaker, M., Szekeres, S., Hartwick, P., Tworek, P., & Wingate, S. (1991). Cognitive intervention. In G. Wolcott & R. Savage (Eds.), *Educational intervention for children and young adults with acquired brain injury* (pp. 34–71). Austin, TX: Pro-Ed.

Yoakum, C. S., & Yerkes, R. M. (1920). *Army mental tests.* New York: Holt.

Yuill, N., & Joscelyne, T. (1988). Effect of organizational cues and strategies on good and poor comprehenders' story understanding. *Journal of Educational Psychology, 80,* 152–158.

Yuill, N., & Oakhill, J. (1988). Effects of inference awareness training on poor reading comprehension. *Applied Cognitive Psychology, 2,* 33–45.

Yule, W., Gold, R. D., & Busch, C. (1982). Long-term predictive validity of the WPSSI: An 11-year follow-up study. *Personality and Individual Differences, 3,* 65–71.

Yussen, S. R. (1974). Deerminants of visual attention and recall in observational learning by preschoolers and second graders. *Developmental Psychology, 10,* 93–100.

Zahler, D., & Zahler, K. A. (1988). *Test your cultural literacy.* New York: ARCO.

Zeamon, D., & House, B. J. (1979). A review of attention theory. In N. R. Ellis (Ed.), *Handbook of mental deficiency: Psychological theory and research* (pp. 63–120). Hillsdale, NJ: Erlbaum & Associates.

Zellermayer, M., Salomon, G., Globerson, T., & Givon, H. (1991). Enhancing writing-related metacognitions through a computerized writing partner. *American Educational Research Journal, 28,* 373–391.

Zelniker, T., & Jeffrey, W. E. (1976). Reflective and impulsive children: Strategies of information processing underlying differences in problem solving. *Monographs of the Society for Research in Child Development, 41,* 1–46.

Zentall, S. S. (1988). Production deficiencies in elicited language but not in the spontaneous verbalizations of hyperactive children. *Journal of Abnormal Child Psychology 16,* 657–673.

Zentall, S. S. (1989). Self-control training with hyperactive and impulsive children. In J. N. Hughes & R. J. Hall (Eds.), *Cognitive-behavioral psychology in the schools* (pp. 305–346). New York: Guilford Press.

Zentall, S. S. (1990). Fact-retrieval automatization and math problem solving by learning disabled, attention-deficit, and normal adolescents. *Journal of Educational Psychology, 82,* 856–865.

Zentall, S. S., & Gohs, D. E. (1984). Hyperactive and comparison children's response to detailed vs. global cues in communication tasks. *Learning Disability Quarterly, 7,* 77–87.

Zentall, S. S., Gohs, D. E., & Culatta, B. (1983). Language and activity of hyperactive and comparison children in a listening task. *Exceptional Children, 50,* 255–266.

Zentall, T. R., & Galef, B. G., J. (eds.) (1988). *Social learning: Psychological and biological perspectives.* Hillsdale, NJ: Erlbaum & Associates.

Zetlin, A., & Murtaugh, M. (1990). Whatever happened to those with borderline IQs? *American Journal of Mental Deficiency, 94,* 463–469.

Zhu, X., & Simon, H. A. (1987). Learning mathematics from examples and by doing. *Cognition and Instruction, 4,* 137–166.

Zigler, E., & Balla, D. (Eds.) (1982). *Mental retardation: The developmental-difference controversy.* Hillsdale, NJ: Erlbaum & Associates.

Zigler, E., Balla, D., & Hodapp, R. (1984). On the definition and classification of mental retardation. *American Journal of Mental Deficiency, 89,* 215–230.

Zigler, E., & Hodapp, R. M. (1986). *Understanding mental retardation.* Cambridge, UK: Cambridge University Press.

Zigler, E., & Seitz, V. (1975). "An experimental evaluation of sensorimotor patterning": A critique. *American Journal of Mental Deficiency, 79,* 483–492.

Zimmerman, B. J. (1989a). A social cognitive view of self-regulated academic learning. *Journal of Educational Psychology, 81,* 329–339.

Zimmerman, B. J. (1989b). Models of self-regulated learning and academic achievement. In B. J. Zimmerman & D. H. Schunk (Eds.), *Self-regulated learning and academic achievement* (pp. 1–25). New York: Springer-Verlag.

Zimmerman, B. J. (1990a). Self-regulated learning and academic achievement: An overview. *Educational Psychologist, 25,* 3–18.

Zimmerman, B. J. (1990b). Self-regulating academic learning and achievement: The emergence of a social-cognitive perspective. *Educational Psychology Review, 2,* 173–201.

Zimmerman, B. J., Bandura, A., & Martinez-Pons, M. (1992). Self-motivation for academic attainment: The role of self-efficacy beliefs and personal goal setting. *American Educational Research Journal, 29,* 663–676.

Zimmerman, B. J., & Martinez-Pons, M. (1986). Development of a structured interview for assessing student use of self-regulated learning strategies. *American Educational Research Journal, 23,* 614–628.

Zimmerman, B. J., & Martinez-Pons, M. (1988). Construct validation of a strategy model of student self-regulated learning. *Journal of Educational Psychology, 80,* 284–290.

Zimmerman, B. J., & Martinez-Pons, M. (1990). Student differences in self-regulated learning: Relating grade, sex, and giftedness to self-efficacy and strategy use. *Journal of Educational Psychology, 82,* 51–59.

Zinchenko, P. I. (1981). Involuntary memory and the goal-directed nature of activity. In J. V. Wertsch (Ed.), *The concept of activity in Soviet psychology* (pp. 300–340). Armonk, NY: M.E. Sharpe, Inc.

Zook, K. B. (1991). Effects of analogical processes on learning and misrepresentation. *Educational Psychology Review, 3,* 41–72.

Zook, K. B., & DiVesta, F. J. (1991). Instructional analogies and conceptual misrepresentations. *Journal of Educational Psychology, 83,* 246–252.

Name Index

Subject Index